**Less managing. More teaching. Greater learning.**

 **INSTRUCTORS...**

Would you like your **students** to show up for class more **prepared**? *(Let's face it, class is much more fun if everyone is engaged and prepared...)*

Want ready-made application-level **interactive assignments,** student progress reporting, and auto-assignment grading? *(Less time grading means more time teaching...)*

Want an **instant view of student or class performance** relative to learning objectives? *(No more wondering if students understand...)*

Need to **collect data and generate reports** required for administration or accreditation? *(Say goodbye to manually tracking student learning outcomes...)*

Want to **record and post your lectures** for students to view online?

 With **McGraw-Hill's *Connect*™ Marketing,**

**INSTRUCTORS GET:**

- Interactive Applications – **book-specific interactive assignments** that require students to APPLY what they've learned.

- Simple **assignment management,** allowing you to spend more time teaching.

- **Auto-graded** assignments, quizzes, and tests.

- **Detailed Visual Reporting** where student and section results can be viewed and analyzed.

- Sophisticated **online testing** capability.

- A **filtering and reporting** function that allows you to easily assign and report on materials that are correlated to accreditation standards, learning outcomes, and Bloom's taxonomy.

- An easy-to-use **lecture capture** tool.

# STUDENTS...

Want an online, **searchable version** of your textbook?

Wish your textbook could be **available online** while you're doing your assignments?

### *Connect™ Plus Marketing* **eBook**

If you choose to use *Connect™ Plus Marketing*, you have an affordable and searchable online version of your book integrated with your other online tools.

### *Connect™ Plus Marketing* **eBook offers features like:**

- Topic search
- Direct links from assignments
- Adjustable text size
- Jump to page number
- Print by section

# STUDENTS...

Want to get more **value** from your textbook purchase?

Think learning marketing should be a bit more **interesting**?

### **Check out the STUDENT RESOURCES section under the** *Connect™* **Library tab.**

Here you'll find a wealth of resources designed to help you achieve your goals in the course. You'll find things like **quizzes, PowerPoints, and Internet activities** to help you study. Every student has different needs, so explore the STUDENT RESOURCES to find the materials best suited to you.

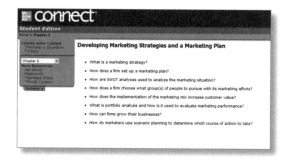

# Marketing

Marketing is the activity, set of institutions, and processes for creating, capturing, communicating, delivering, and exchanging offerings that have value for customers, clients, partners, and society at large.

*The definition of marketing, established by the American Marketing Association, October 2007.*

mhhe.com/grewal3e

# Marketing

## Third Edition

**Dhruv Grewal, Ph.D.**
*Babson College*

**Michael Levy, Ph.D.**
*Babson College*

Mc Graw Hill

*Connect*
*Learn*
*Succeed*™

MARKETING

Published by McGraw-Hill/Irwin, a business unit of The McGraw-Hill Companies, Inc., 1221 Avenue of the Americas, New York, NY, 10020. Copyright © 2012, 2010, 2008 by The McGraw-Hill Companies, Inc. All rights reserved. No part of this publication may be reproduced or distributed in any form or by any means, or stored in a database or retrieval system, without the prior written consent of The McGraw-Hill Companies, Inc., including, but not limited to, in any network or other electronic storage or transmission, or broadcast for distance learning.

Some ancillaries, including electronic and print components, may not be available to customers outside the United States.

This book is printed on acid-free paper.

4 5 6 7 8 9 0 DOW/DOW 1 0 9 8 7 6 5 4 3 2

ISBN      978-0-07-802883-0

MHID      0-07-802883-3

Vice president and editor-in-chief: *Brent Gordon*
Editorial director: *Paul Ducham*
Publisher: *Doug Hughes*
Executive Editor: *Sankha Basu*
Executive director of development: *Ann Torbert*
Development editor II: *Kelly Delso*
Vice president and director of marketing: *Robin J. Zwettler*
Marketing director: *Amee Mosley*
Marketing manager: *Katie Mergen*
Vice president of editing, design, and production: *Sesha Bolisetty*
Lead project manager: *Christine A. Vaughan*
Senior buyer: *Carol A. Bielski*
Senior designer: *Mary Kazak Sander*
Senior photo research coordinator: *Jeremy Cheshareck*
Photo researcher: *Michael Hruby*
Senior media project manager : *Susan Lombardi*
Media project manager: *Joyce J. Chappetto*
Interior design: *Pam Verros*
Cover image: *Anna Reed*
Typeface: *10/12 Palatino*
Compositor: *Lachina Publishing Services*
Printer: *R. R. Donnelley*

Library of Congress Cataloging-in-Publication Data

Grewal, Dhruv.
    Marketing / Dhruv Grewal, Michael Levy. — 3rd ed.
        p. cm.
    Includes bibliographical references and index.
    ISBN-13: 978-0-07-802883-0 (alk. paper)
    ISBN-10: 0-07-802883-3 (alk. paper)
    1. Marketing. I. Levy, Michael, 1950– II. Title.
HF5415.G675 2012
658—dc22
                                        2010042318

*We dedicate this book to the memory of our fathers,*
*Inder Grewal (1933 to 2007)*
*and*
*Norman Levy (1926 to 2010),*
*for encouraging us to pursue our goals*
*and follow our own paths.*

# about the authors

*Authors Michael Levy (left) and Dhruv Grewal (right).*

## Dhruv Grewal

**Dhruv Grewal Ph.D.** (Virginia Tech) is the Toyota Chair in Commerce and Electronic Business and a Professor of Marketing at Babson College. He was awarded the 2010 AMS Cutco/Vector Distinguished Educator Award, the 2010 Lifetime Achievement Award in Retailing (AMA Retailing SIG), and in 2005 the Lifetime Achievement in Behavioral Pricing Award (Fordham University, November 2005). He is a Distinguished Fellow of the Academy of Marketing Science. He was ranked 1st in the marketing field in terms of publications in the top-six marketing journals during the 1991–1998 period and again for the 2000–2007 period. He has served as VP Research and Conferences, American Marketing Association Academic Council (1999–2001), and as VP Development for the Academy of Marketing Science (2000–2002). He was co-editor of *Journal of Retailing* from 2001 to 2007. He co-chaired the 1993 Academy of Marketing Science Conference, the 1998 Winter American Marketing Association Conference, the 2001 AMA doctoral consortium, and the American Marketing Association 2006 Summer Educators Conference.

He has published over 95 articles in journals such as the *Journal of Retailing, Journal of Marketing, Journal of Consumer Research, Journal of Marketing Research,* and *Journal of the Academy of Marketing Science,* as well as other journals. He currently serves on numerous editorial review boards, such as the *Journal of Retailing, Journal of Marketing, Journal of the Academy of Marketing Science, Journal of Interactive Marketing, Journal of Business Research,* and *Journal of Public Policy & Marketing.*

He has won a number of awards for his teaching: 2005 Sherwin-Williams Distinguished Teaching Award, Society for Marketing Advances, 2003 American Marketing Association, Award for Innovative Excellence in Marketing Education, 1999 Academy of Marketing Science Great Teachers in Marketing Award, Executive MBA Teaching Excellence Award (1998), School of Business Teaching Excellence Awards (1993, 1999), and Virginia Tech Certificate of Recognition for Outstanding Teaching (1989).

He has taught executive seminars/courses and/or worked on research projects with numerous firms, such as IRI, TJX, Radio Shack, Telcordia, Khimetriks, Profit-Logic, Monsanto, McKinsey, Ericsson, Council of Insurance Agents & Brokers (CIAB), Met-Life, AT&T, Motorola, Nextel, FP&L, Lucent, Sabre, Goodyear Tire & Rubber Company, Sherwin Williams, Esso International, Asahi, and numerous law firms. He has taught seminars in the United States, Europe, and Asia.

## Michael Levy

**Michael Levy Ph.D.** (Ohio State University) is the Charles Clarke Reynolds Professor of Marketing and Director of the Retail Supply Chain Institute at Babson College. He received his Ph.D. in business administration from The Ohio State University and his undergraduate and M.S. degrees in business administration from the University of Colorado at Boulder. He taught at Southern Methodist University before joining the faculty as professor and chair of the marketing department at the University of Miami.

Professor Levy received the 2009 Lifetime Achievement Award from the American Marketing Association Retailing Special Interest Group. He was rated one of the Best Researchers in Marketing in a survey published in *Marketing Educator* in Summer 1997. He has developed a strong stream of research in retailing, business logistics, financial retailing strategy, pricing, and sales management. He has published over 50 articles in leading marketing and logistics journals, including the *Journal of Retailing, Journal of Marketing, Journal of the Academy of Marketing Science,* and *Journal of Marketing Research.* He currently serves on the editorial review board of the *Journal of Retailing, International Journal of Logistics Management, International Journal of Logistics and Materials Management,* and *European Business Review.* He is co-author of *Retailing Management,* eighth edition (2012), the best-selling college-level retailing text in the world. Professor Levy was co-editor of the *Journal of Retailing* from 2001 to 2007. He co-chaired the 1993 Academy of Marketing Science conference and the 2006 Summer AMA conference.

Professor Levy has worked in retailing and related disciplines throughout his professional life. Prior to his academic career, he worked for several retailers and a housewares distributor in Colorado. He has performed research projects with many retailers and retail technology firms, including Accenture, Federated Department Stores, Khimetrics (SAP), Mervyn's, Neiman Marcus, ProfitLogic (Oracle), Zale Corporation, and numerous law firms.

# Building From Experience

*Marketing*, **Third Edition,** builds from Dhruv Grewal's and Michael Levy's experiences in the classroom and in the marketplace and interacting with marketing instructors and students. Six essential features that the Third Edition is built upon are highlighted below:

**Learning Orientation:** Each chapter features Learning Objectives at the outset (icons that relate the learning objectives to the chapter content); Check Yourself questions at the end of each section; and a Summing Up review of the learning objectives, Marketing Application questions, and Quiz Yourself questions at the end of the chapter.

**Student Focused:** The text content is engaging and provides illustrations that are highly relevant to students. The content is presented in a visual fashion to facilitate learning.

**State of the Art Instructor's Resources:** Our monthly newsletter continues to gain rave reviews. Each newsletter highlights 10–12 current marketing applications and provides appropriate discussion questions and answers and links to interesting ads and videos. Additionally, we provide PowerPoint® slides on this content. This will enable instructors to deliver state-of-the-art marketing content on a daily basis.

**Applying Concepts:** Comprehensive frameworks that organize key concepts are presented in each chapter. These frameworks integrate essential marketing concepts and content with emerging concepts and content.

**Interactive Technology:** Interactive Toolkits, Interactive Presentations, Applications, and LearnSmart, all based in *Connect* make *Marketing*, Third Edition the most comprehensive and usable marketing book (augmented by its ancillaries) in the marketplace.

**Assessment:** To aid in self-assessment of how they are doing, students can use Check Yourself questions at the end of each section, Quiz Yourself questions at chapter end, Practice Quizzes on the book's student Web site, instructor-created quizzes on Connect, or the continuous learning and assessment provided by LearnSmart.

# New to the Third Edition

## Some exciting new additions in the Third Edition include:

The authors continue to incorporate appropriate context that reflects the new American Marketing Association definition of marketing. The American Marketing Association states that "**Marketing** is the activity, set of institutions, and processes for creating, capturing, communicating, delivering, and exchanging offerings that have value for customers, clients, partners, and society at large."

- Given the strategic thrust of the definition of marketing as creating value, this concept permeates the book from the Jeans cover to the Adding Value illustrations incorporated in every chapter.

  Each chapter begins with key learning objectives; these learning objectives with numbered icons are placed adjacent to the appropriate material in the chapter; and are reviewed at the end of each chapter.

- In today's marketplace, there is a growing emphasis on the use of social media by marketers. These examples have been integrated throughout the book. A number of the Power of the Internet examples pertain to use of social media (e.g., Power of the Internet 1.1: Facebook Networks the Web).

- Given the emphasis of the role of marketing on society at large, the authors have enhanced their discussion on the role of corporate social responsibility in Chapter 3. They continue to emphasize the importance of ethics and societal issues through the text with Ethical and Societal Dilemma illustrations throughout the text. These illustrations end with questions that are posed from the marketer's point of view to encourage readers to think about these issues and how to address them.

- All of the chapter opener examples are new. The illustrations have been carefully chosen to be sure to resonate with college students and increase their engagement with the marketing content.

- The majority of the end-of-chapter case studies are new and the others have been updated. For example, the Chapter 1 case pertains to the launch of the iPad, a product that has captured the attention of the world.

- Chapter 2, "Developing Marketing Strategies and a Marketing Plan," begins with a detailed illustration of how the war between Starbucks, McDonald's, and Dunkin' Donuts has heated up. This illustration is woven through many of the key concepts introduced in the chapter.

- In Chapter 3, "Marketing Ethics," the authors illustrate the difference between ethics and corporate social responsibility. They integrate the detailed material on corporate social responsibility (previously in Chapter 4) at the end of this chapter.

- A new framework has been added to Chapter 10, "Product, Branding, and Packaging Decisions," to communicate the level of complexity of products in the marketplace.

- Chapter 17, "Integrated Marketing Communications," offers a revised Integrated Marketing Media framework to reflect the increase in both mobile marketing and marketing using social media.

When the authors sat down to write this book, it seemed imperative that the evolution of the field and practice of marketing be at the forefront. They wanted to be sure that they were fully educating today's students about current marketing trends and practices, so they integrated newer concepts such as value creation, globalization, technology, ethics, and services marketing into the traditional marketing instruction. In this book, they examine how firms analyze, create, deliver, communicate, and capture value. The authors explore both the fundamentals in marketing and new influences, such as how social media are shaping the way businesses communicate with their customers in today's marketing environment.

*Marketing*, Third Edition, reflects not only the current trends in the marketplace, but also the needs of instructors and students. During the writing and revising of this book and earlier editions, the authors have sought the advice and expertise of hundreds of marketing and educational professionals and have taken all of their guidance to heart. They are grateful to the hundreds of individuals who participated in the focus groups, surveys, and personal conversations that helped mold this book, and hope that you will enjoy the results.

# More Teaching

## McGraw-Hill *Connect Marketing*

## Less Managing. More Teaching. Greater Learning.

*McGraw-Hill Connect Marketing* is an online assignment and assessment solution that connects students with the tools and resources they need to achieve success.

*McGraw-Hill Connect Marketing* helps prepare students for their future by prompting them to complete homework in preparation for class, master concepts, and review for exams.

Sales Promotion: Getting a Good Deal

Business-to-business sales promotion techniques

Consumer sales promotion techniques

1 of 1    1 - Sales Promotion: Getting a Good

Product Placements

Product placements show products in television shows and movies.

3 of 6    3 - Product Placements

## Interactive Presentations

Specific to this textbook, the interactive presentations in *Connect* are engaging, online, professional presentations covering the same learning objectives and concepts directly from the chapters. Interactive Presentations teach students the core learning objectives in a multimedia format, bringing the content of the course to life. Instructors can assign this content for a grade, meaning students come to class with better knowledge of chapter material. Interactive presentations are a great prep tool for students—and when students are better prepared, they are more engaged and more participative in class.

# Greater Learning

## Adapt

LearnSmart, a study tool also within *Connect*, offers inteligent flashcards that identify the relationships between concepts and serve new concepts to each student only when he or she is ready. It adapts automatically, so students spend less time on the topics they understand and practice more those they have yet to master.

## Empower

LearnSmart provides continual reinforcement and remediation, but gives only as much guidance as students need.

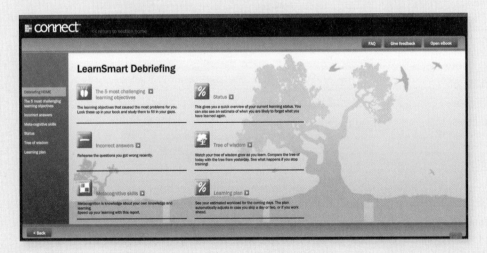

## Enable

LearnSmart integrates diagnostics as part of the learning experience. This enables instructors to assess which concepts students have efficiently learned on their own, thus freeing class time for more applications and discussion.

# Interactive Learning

## Connect Interactive Applications

Engaging students beyond simply reading and recall, students practice key concepts by *applying* them with these textbook specific interactive exercises in every chapter.

Critical thinking makes for a higher level of learning. Each interactive application is followed up by a series of *concept checks* to reinforce key topics and further increase student understanding. Students walk away from interactive applications with more practice and better understanding than simply reading the chapter. All interactive applications are automatically scored and entered into the instructor gradebook.

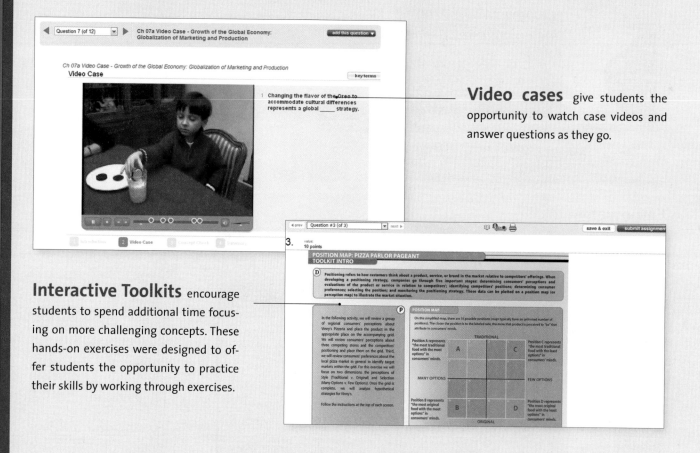

**Video cases** give students the opportunity to watch case videos and answer questions as they go.

**Interactive Toolkits** encourage students to spend additional time focusing on more challenging concepts. These hands-on exercises were designed to offer students the opportunity to practice their skills by working through exercises.

**Decision generators** require students to make real business decisions based on specific real world scenarios and cases.

**Self-assessments** allow students to evaluate skills and assess personal progress.

**Comprehensive cases** encourage students to read a case and answer open-ended discussion questions to demonstrate writing and critical-thinking skills.

# Applying Concepts

## Online Learning Center (www.mhhe.com/grewal3e)

The Online Learning Center helps students use *Marketing*, third edition, effectively.

*Some features on the website are:*

- **The Interactive Student Toolkits** – available for specific chapters offer students interactive, gradeable assignment focusing on challenging, but pertinent concepts such as SWOT Analysis, Compensatory vs. Noncompensatory Consumer Decision Making, Vendor Evaluation Analysis, marketing Positioning Map, Service Quality, Breakeven Analysis, Customer Lifetime Value, and Return on Investment.

- **Self-Quizzes** – quizzes focusing on key concepts and providing immediate feedback offer students the opportunity to determine their level of understanding.

- **Marketer's Showdown** – nine cases focusing on up-to-the-minute issues in the music, automotive, and soft drink industries. These cases are designed to allow students to analyze the marketing problem, choose a proposed solution, and then watch their proposal debated by marketing professionals. After the debate, students have the opportunity to change their plan or stick to their guns, then see the outcome of their decisions.

- **iPod Content** – narrated PowerPoint® Presentations, quizzes, and audio lectures.

# Student-Focused Features

## Developing Marketing Strategies and a Marketing Plan

People can grab a cup of coffee virtually anywhere. Yet somehow Starbucks, Dunkin' Donuts, and McDonald's have turned this common beverage into a market offering worth pursuing. To accomplish this transformation, the three java giants have distinguished themselves using varied marketing strategies aimed at slightly different audiences. And thus the humble cup of coffee has become something much, much more.

**McDonald's.** Known better for its Big Macs, McNuggets, and low prices, McDonald's Corp. is the most recent entrant into the coffee war. The company initiated its attack by improving its drip coffee and adding espresso drinks. More recently, it has challenged Starbucks supremacy in the iced coffee drink market by introducing its own blended coffee drinks and fruit smoothies. This move came in response to the growing popularity of cold coffee drinks, which deliver a healthy profit margin to vendors.

By offering its drinks below competitors' prices and in the more family-oriented atmosphere of its 32,000 stores in 117 countries, McDonald's hopes to lure customers away from Starbucks and Dunkin' Donuts, as well as upsell some of its existing coffee-drinking clientele. It increased visibility for its new blended drinks by offering large fountain drinks for a dollar in the weeks around the introduction of the new beverages. But McDonald's target audience in general is less educated and affluent than a typical Starbucks shopper, so the company has been careful not to appear too upscale, even as it offers drinks previously viewed as luxuries. In its advertising, McDonald's mainly portrays its McCafé drinks as a way to add fun to everyday life at an affordable price.

**Dunkin' Donuts.** Dunkin' Donuts sells 52 varieties of donuts and other baked goods. But the majority of the company's profits now come from its coffee drinks, of which it sells approximately 1 billion each year. With its nearly 9,000 stores in 31 countries, Dunkin'

### LEARNING OBJECTIVES

- **L01** Define a marketing strategy.
- **L02** Describe the elements of a marketing plan.
- **L03** Analyze a marketing situation using SWOT analyses.
- **L04** Describe how a firm chooses which consumer group(s) to pursue with its marketing efforts.
- **L05** Outline the implementation of the marketing mix as a means to increase customer value.
- **L06** Summarize portfolio analysis and its use to evaluate marketing performance.
- **L07** Describe how firms grow their business.

**Chapter Opening Vignettes** focusing on well-known companies like McDonalds, Apple, and Domino's draw students into a discussion about some of the challenges these companies face.

## Check Yourself

Questions positioned throughout the chapter after key points allow students to stop and think about what they have learned.

areas, Southwest has built a very high wall around its position as the value player in the airline industry.

### CHECK YOURSELF

1. What are the various components of a marketing strategy?
2. List the four macro strategies that can help a firm develop a sustainable competitive advantage.

scribe the elements marketing plan.

## THE MARKETING PLAN

Effective marketing doesn't just happen. By creating a *marketing plan*, firms like Starbucks, McDonald's, and Dunkin' Donuts carefully plan their marketing strategies to react to changes in the environment, the competition, and their customers.

**Real-World Examples** are used to illustrate concepts throughout the text. The authors give students the opportunity to think about how concepts are used in their everyday life. This is shown through various boxed elements:

- **Adding Value** – illustrate how companies add value not only in providing products and services, but in making contributions to society.

- **Ethical & Societal Dilemmas** – emphasize the role of marketing in society.

- **Power of the Internet** – discuss how Internet applications and social media are used in marketing products.

- **Superior Service** – highlight the emerging role of the service industry.

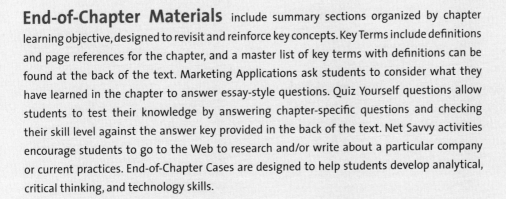

**Ethical and Societal Dilemma 2.1**

**Starbucks Working to Make the Earth a Better Place**

To ensure it adds value to the broader society that makes up its macroenvironment, Starbucks rates its own corporate social responsibility performance in five categories: ethical sourcing, environment, community, wellness, and diversity. Its brand equity improves in response to its proactive efforts along these socially responsible dimensions; customers feel good about their buying experience, and Starbucks develops stronger relationships with suppliers, both locally and globally.

With regard to its focus on ethical sourcing and sustainable coffee production, Starbucks maintains its C.A.F.E. (Coffee and Farmer Equity) program. The C.A.F.E. guidelines include a scorecard that rates coffee farmers according to their product quality, economic accountability, social responsibility, and environmental leadership. Third parties evaluate whether suppliers meet Starbucks' standards under the C.A.F.E. program. In just a few years, suppliers from 13 different countries gained C.A.F.E. approval. In turn, Starbucks increased the amount of coffee that it purchased from verified suppliers, from 77 percent to 81 percent, on its way to its goal of having "100% of our coffee certified or verified by an independent third party."

On a more local level, Starbucks sometimes experiences opposition from local communities that believe its stores will ruin the historical ambiance of an area. To take the needs of local communities into consideration, Starbucks attempts to address historic preservation, environmental, infrastructure, job, and urban revitalization concerns. For example, in La Mesa, California, Starbucks overcame opposition by supporting local events and businesses. In addition, it formed a joint venture with Johnson Development Corporation (JDC) to develop urban coffee opportunities. By opening in diverse urban areas, Starbucks helps stimulate economic growth in the areas by creating jobs, using local suppliers, and attracting other retailers to the area.

**Superior Service 2.1**

As most U.S.-based airlines race for the bottom, in terms of both cost and customer service, Singapore Airlines continues to maintain its industry-leading levels of customer satisfaction on its international flights. The airline's commitment to excellence has been an important part of its brand strategy since the company's inception.

In its early days, Singapore Airlines faced stiff competition. So the airline elected to position itself as a leader in technology, innovation, quality, and customer service. Over the ensuing decades, it has remained committed to that strategy, introducing such customer-friendly services as hot meals, free alcoholic and nonalcoholic drinks, scented hot towels, video-on-demand for all travelers, and personal entertainment systems. When other airlines imitate its ideas, Singapore Airlines develops new ones, such as a centralized, all-in-one business panel with in-seat power supply and USB ports; a 15.4-inch LCD screen in its video systems; and a seat that folds out fully to a flat bed for business class.

Although the airline's cabin crew consists of both men and women, they are referred to as Singapore Girls. The women dress in a signature sarong, created by a French haute-couture designer. All crew members receive rigorous training to ensure they maintain a peaceful and elegant cabin ambiance and caring service.

Staying ahead of the competition requires continual investment in innovation; a price Singapore Airlines is willing to pay to earn the significant rewards it seeks in the form of a loyal and motivated staff and return customers. To remain competitive, the airline's financial structure accommodates innovation without passing any exorbitant costs on to consumers. With that kind of business sense, it's no wonder Singapore Airlines remains profitable even as other airlines struggle to survive.

SINGAPORE AIRLINES
**NEW BUSINESS CLASS**
*the most spacious the world has ever seen*

*Caption needed*

**End-of-Chapter Materials** include summary sections organized by chapter learning objective, designed to revisit and reinforce key concepts. Key Terms include definitions and page references for the chapter, and a master list of key terms with definitions can be found at the back of the text. Marketing Applications ask students to consider what they have learned in the chapter to answer essay-style questions. Quiz Yourself questions allow students to test their knowledge by answering chapter-specific questions and checking their skill level against the answer key provided in the back of the text. Net Savvy activities encourage students to go to the Web to research and/or write about a particular company or current practices. End-of-Chapter Cases are designed to help students develop analytical, critical thinking, and technology skills.

**Marketing Applications** Each chapter concludes with eight to eleven Marketing Applications. These essay-style questions determine whether students have grasped the concepts covered in each chapter by asking them to apply what they have learned to marketing scenarios that are relevant to their lives.

# Innovative Instructor Resources

## McGraw-Hill Higher Education and Blackboard have teamed up. What does this mean for you?

1. **Your life, simplified.** Now you and your students can access McGraw-Hill's *Connect* right from within your Blackboard course—all with one single sign-on. Say goodbye to the days of logging in to multiple applications.

2. **Deep integration of content and tools.** Not only do you get single sign-on with *Connect*, but you also get deep integration of McGraw-Hill content and content engines right in Blackboard. Whether you're choosing a book for your course or building *Connect* assignments, all the tools you need are right where you want them—inside of Blackboard.

3. **Seamless gradebooks.** Are you tired of keeping multiple gradebooks and manually synchronizing grades into Blackboard? We thought so. When a student completes an integrated *Connect* assignment, the grade for that assignment automatically (and instantly) feeds your Blackboard grade center.

4. **A solution for everyone.** Whether your institution is already using Blackboard or you just want to try Blackboard on your own, we have a solution for you. McGraw-Hill and Blackboard can now offer you easy access to industry leading technology and content, whether your campus hosts it, or we do. Be sure to ask your local McGraw-Hill representative for details.

## Student progress tracking

*Connect* keeps instructors informed about how each student, section, and class is performing, allowing for more productive use of lecture and office hours. The progress-tracking function enables instructors to:

- view scored work immediately and track individual or group performance with assignment and grade reports.

- access an instant view of student or class performance relative to learning objectives.

- collect data and generate reports required by many accreditation organizations, such as AACSB.

Click a subcategory to view **section** details

expand all | collapse all                                                                                          export to excel ☒

| AACSB | # questions | # times submitted | # students submitted | category score |
|---|---|---|---|---|
| ▼ AACSB: Analytic | 15 | 2727 | 25/25 | 46.11% |
| Cumulative Quiz-Chapters 1,2,3 (Graded) | 6 | 450 | 25/25 | 14.27% |
| Homework-Chapter 3 Part 2 (Graded) | 6 | 1512 | 25/25 | 63.17% |
| Homework-Chapter 3 Part 1 (Graded) | 3 | 765 | 25/25 | 59.2% |
| ▶ AACSB: Reflective Thinking | 26 | 4995 | 25/25 | 39.65% |

| Bloom's | # questions | # times submitted | # students submitted | category score |
|---|---|---|---|---|
| ▼ Bloom's: Analysis | 21 | 4074 | 25/25 | 28.42% |
| Cumulative Quiz-Chapters 1,2,3 (Graded) | 7 | 525 | 25/25 | 13.96% |
| Homework-Chapter 3 Part 2 (Graded) | 7 | 1764 | 25/25 | 41.74% |
| Homework-Chapter 3 Part 1 (Graded) | 7 | 1785 | 25/25 | 24.99% |
| ▶ Bloom's: Application | 1 | 255 | 25/25 | 58.43% |
| ▶ Bloom's: Comprehension | 7 | 1239 | 25/25 | 58.0% |
| ▶ Bloom's: Knowledge | 12 | 2154 | 25/25 | 43.39% |

## McGraw-Hill *Connect Plus Marketing*

McGraw-Hill reinvents the textbook learning experience for the modern student with *Connect Plus Marketing*. A seamless integration of an eBook and *Connect*, *Connect Plus Marketing* provides all of the *Connect* features plus the following:

- An integrated eBook, allowing for anytime, anywhere online access to the textbook.
- Dynamic links between the problems or questions assigned to students and the location in the eBook where that problem or question is covered.
- Powerful search function to pinpoint and connect key concepts in a snap.

In short, *Connect Marketing* offers instructors and students powerful tools and features that optimize time and energy, enabling instructors to focus on course content, teaching, and student learning. Offering a wealth of content resources for instructors and students, this state-of-the-art interactive system supports instructors in preparing students for the world that awaits with adaptive engaging textbook specific online content.

For more information about Connect, go to **connect.mcgraw-hill.com**, or contact your local McGraw-Hill sales representative.

## CourseSmart LearnSmart. Choose Smart.

CourseSmart is a new way for faculty to find and review eTextbooks. It's also a great option for students who are interested in accessing their course materials digitally and saving money.

CourseSmart offers thousands of the most commonly adopted textbooks across hundreds of courses from a wide variety of higher education publishers. It is the only place for faculty to review and compare the full text of a textbook online, providing immediate access without the environmental impact of requesting a print exam copy.

With the CourseSmart eTextbook, students can save up to 45 percent off the cost of a print book, reduce their impact on the environment, and access powerful Web tools for learning. CourseSmart is an online eTextbook, which means users access and view their textbook online when connected to the Internet. Students can also print sections of the book for maximum portability. CourseSmart eTextbooks are available in one standard online reader with full text search, notes, and highlighting, and e-mail tools for sharing notes between classmates. For more information on CourseSmart, go to **http://www .coursesmart.com.**

# Traditional Instructor Resources

## Online Learning Center for Instructors
## www.mhhe.com/grewal3e

The Online Learning Center offers instructors a one-stop, secure site for essential course materials, allowing instructors to save prep time before class. The instructor's site offers:

- Instructor's Manual
- PowerPoint® Presentations
- Testbank/EZ Test
- Newsletters
- Videos
- Marketer's Showdown

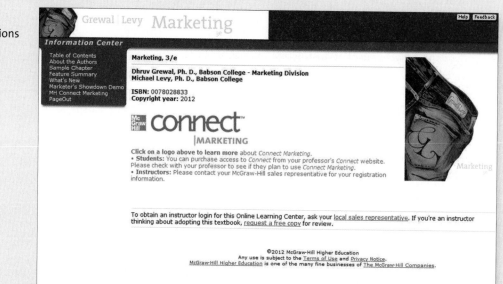

## Instructor's Resource CD (IRCD):

This CD contains the Instructor's Manual containing everything an instructor needs to prepare a lecture, including lecture outlines, discussion questions and links to each chapter's PowerPoint® slides, Test Bank and Computerized Test Bank (including multiple choice, short answer, essay, and application questions), and PowerPoint® slides (including exhibits and images from the text as well as additional lecture support materials). The Online Learning Center contains a basic version of the media-enhanced PowerPoint® Presentations® that are found on the IRCD. The media-enhanced version has video and commercials embedded into the presentations and makes for an engaging and interesting classroom lecture. There is also a basic version of the PowerPoint® slides for easier online delivery and customization, as well as auto-narrated slides. ISBN: 007450922

## Video DVD:

A selection of 18 case videos, including 6 brand new videos for this edition, that tie directly to the material covered in the text. The first one drives home the image on the cover and describes how Mars Inc., the maker of M&M's, has added value by allowing consumers to customize their own M&M's with personalized greetings. Based on feedback received from contact with over 100 instructors, these videos are five to six minutes in length each, instead of the usual 12- to 15-minute videos in many other supplement packages. The shorter videos are much easier for instructors to implement in their courses. ISBN: 007450965

## Monthly Newsletter

Each month instructors using *Marketing*, Third Edition will receive a newsletter which includes many of the hottest topics in marketing today. Each newsletter contains 8–10 articles, videos, and podcasts on the latest happenings in the Marketing discipline, with abstracts and a guide that explains where the information can be implemented in an instructor's course.

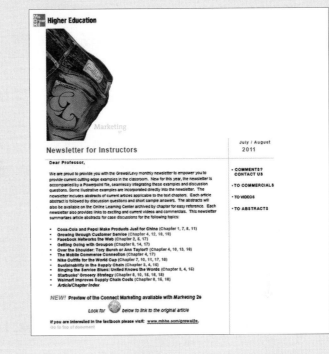

## Marketing Plan Pro

Marketing Plan Pro is the most widely used marketing plan software program in the industry, and it includes everything students need to create professional, complete, and accurate marketing plans. Marketing Plan Pro can be packaged with *Marketing*, Third Edition for a nominal fee.

# Responding to Learning Needs

## CREATE

Instructors can now tailor their teaching resources to match the way they teach! With McGraw-Hill Create, www.mcgrawhillcreate.com, instructors can easily rearrange chapters, combine material from other content sources, and quickly upload and integrate their own content, like course syllabus or teaching notes. Find the right content in Create by searching through thousands of leading McGraw-Hill textbooks. Arrange the material to fit your teaching style. Order a Create book and receive a complimentary print review copy in 3–5 business days or a complimentary electronic review copy (eComp) via e-mail within an one hour. Go to www.mcgrawhillcreate. com today and register.

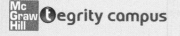

## Tegrity Campus: Lectures 24/7

Tegrity Campus is a service that makes class time available 24/7 by automatically capturing every lecture in a searchable format for students to review when they study and complete assignments. With a simple one-click start-and-stop process, you capture all computer screens and corresponding audio. Students can replay any part of any class with easy-to-use browser-based viewing on a PC or Mac.

Educators know that the more students can see, hear, and experience class resources, the better they learn. In fact, studies prove it. With patented Tegrity "search anything" technology, students instantly recall key class moments for replay online, or on iPods and mobile devices. Instructors can help turn all their students' study time into learning moments immediately supported by their lecture.

To learn more about Tegrity watch a 2-minute Flash demo at **http://tegritycampus .mhhe.com.**

## Assurance of Learning Ready

Many educational institutions today are focused on the notion of assurance of learning, an important element of some accreditation standards. *Marketing* is designed specifically to support instructors' assurance of learning initiatives with a simple, yet powerful solution.

Each test bank question for *Marketing* maps to a specific chapter learning outcome/objective listed in the text. Instructors can use our test bank software, EZ Test and EZ Test Online, or *Connect Marketing* to easily query for learning outcomes/objectives that directly relate to the learning objectives for their course. Instructors can then use the reporting features of EZ Test to aggregate student results in similar fashion, making the collection and presentation of assurance of learning data simple and easy.

## AACSB Statement

The McGraw-Hill Companies is a proud corporate member of AACSB International. Understanding the importance and value of AACSB accreditation, *Marketing*, Third Edition, recognizes the curricula guidelines detailed in the AACSB standards for business accreditation by connecting selected questions in the text and the test bank to the six general knowledge and skill guidelines in the AACSB standards.

The statements contained in *Marketing*, Third Edition, are provided only as a guide for the users of this textbook. The AACSB leaves content coverage and assessment within the purview of individual schools, the mission of the school, and the faculty. While *Marketing*, Third Edition, and the teaching package make no claim of any specific AACSB qualification or evaluation, we have within *Marketing*, Third Edition, labeled selected questions found throughout the supplementary materials according to the six general knowledge and skills areas.

## McGraw-Hill Customer Care Contact Information

At McGraw-Hill, we understand that getting the most from new technology can be challenging. That's why our services don't stop after you purchase our products. You can e-mail our Product Specialists 24 hours a day to get product-training online. Or you can search our knowledge bank of Frequently Asked Questions on our support website. For Customer Support, call **800-331-5094**, e-mail **hmsupport@mcgraw-hill.com**, or visit **www.mhhe.com/support**. One of our Technical Support Analysts will be able to assist you in a timely fashion.

# acknowledgments

We'd like to acknowledge the considerable contributions of Britt Hackmann (Babson College), Kate Woodworth, and Elisabeth Nevins Caswell for their help throughout the development of this edition of *Marketing*.

We wish to express our sincere appreciation to Leroy Robinson of University of Houston–Clear Lake for preparing the Instructor's Manual and the PowerPoint slides, Melissa Martin of George Mason Community College and Barbara Black, University of Miami for the test bank, and Kelly Luchtman for the video production. The support, expertise, and occasional coercion from our publisher Doug Hughes, executive editor Sankha Basu, editorial coordinator Gabriela Gonzalez, and development editor Kelly Delso are greatly appreciated. The book would also never have come together without the editorial and production staff at McGraw-Hill/Irwin: Katie Mergen, marketing manager; Christine Vaughan, lead project manager; Mary Kazak Sander, senior designer; Jeremy Cheshareck, senior photo research coordinator; Mike Hruby, photo researcher; Sue Lombardi and Joyce Chappetto, media project managers; and Carol Bielski, senior buyer.

Our colleagues in industry have been invaluable in providing us with case, video, advertising, and photo materials. They include Andrea Gallagher (IRI); Marty Ordman and Betta Gallego (Dole); Michael Buckley, Mark Bauer, and Max Ward (Staples); Peter Meehan and Nell Newman (Newman's Own Organics); Steve Swasey (NetFlicks); Will Bortz (Taco-Bell); Dan Sullivan (New Balance); Ryan Bowling (Mars North America); Ann Mukherjee (Frito Lay); Molly Starmann (McDonald's); and Carol Sagers (McDonald's).

Over the years, we have had the opportunity to work with many talented and insightful colleagues. We have benefited from our research and discussions with them. Some of these colleagues are: Ross Petty, Danna Greenberg, Kate McKone-Sweet, Nancy Dlott and Anne Roggeveen (Babson College); Larry D. Compeau (Clarkson University); Rajesh Chandrashekaran (Fairleigh Dickinson University); Jeanne S. Munger (University of Southern Maine); Arun Sharma, A. Parasuraman, R. Krishnan, Howard Marmorstein, Anuj Mehrotra, and Michael Tsiros (all from University of Miami); Glenn Voss and Mitzi Montoya-Weiss (North Carolina State University); Kathleen Seiders (Boston College); Rob Palmatier (University of Cincinnati); Praveen Kopalle, Scott Neslin, and Kusum Ailawadi (Dartmouth); Robert Peterson and Andrea Godfrey (University of California at Riverside); Don Lehmann (Columbia); Ruth Bolton, Steve Brown, and Terry Bristol (Arizona State University); Julie Baker and William Cron (Texas Christian University); Venkatesh Shankar, Len Berry, and Manjit Yadav (Texas A&M); Jerry Gotlieb (University of Western Kentucky); Hooman Estelami (Fordham University); Rajiv Dant and Ken Evans (University of Oklahoma); Monika Kukar Kinney (University of Richmond); Ronnie Goodstein (Georgetown); Anthony Miyazaki and Walfried Lassar (Florida International University); Gopal Iyer and Tamara Mangleburg (Florida Atlantic University); David Hardesty (University of Kentucky); Greg Marshall (Rollins College); M. Joseph Sirgy, Julie Ozanne, and Ed Fern (Virginia Tech); Merrie Brucks and Ajith Kumar (University of Arizona); Valerie Folkes (University of Southern California); Carolyn Costley (University of Waikato); William Dodds (Ft. Lewis College); Ramon Avila (Ball State University); Douglas M. Lambert and Walter

Zinn (The Ohio State University); Eugene Stone-Romeo (University of Central Florida); Joan Lindsey-Mullikin and Norm Borin (Cal Poly San Luis Obispo); Abhijit Biswas and Sujay Dutta (Wayne State University); Wagner Kamakura (Duke); Raj Srivastava (Emory); Cheryl Nikata (University of Illinois, Chicago); K. Sivakumar (Lehigh University); Namwoon Kim (Hong Kong Polytechnic University); Raj Suri (Drexel); Jean-Charles Chebat (HEC Montreal); Thomas Rudolph (St. Gallen University); and Zhen Zhu (Suffolk University).

For their contributions to the first edition of *Marketing*, we gratefully acknowledge:

Dennis Arnett
*Texas Tech University*

Laurie Babin
*University of Louisiana at Monroe*

Ainsworth Bailey
*University of Toledo*

Joyce Banjac
*Myers University*

Harvey Bauman
*Lees McRae College*

Oleta Beard
*University of Washington*

Sandy Becker
*Rutgers Business School*

Ellen Benowitz
*Mercer County Community College*

Gary Benton
*Western Kentucky University*

Joseph Ben-Ur
*University of Houston at Victoria*

Patricia Bernson
*County College of Morris*

Harriette Bettis-Outland
*University of West Florida*

Parimal Bhagat
*Indiana University of Pennsylvania*

Jan Bingen
*Little Priest Tribal College*

John Bishop
*University of South Alabama–Mobile*

Nancy Bloom
*Nassau Community College*

Claire Bolfing
*James Madison University*

Karen Bowman
*University of California*

Tom Boyd
*California State University–Fullerton*

Nancy Boykin
*Tarleton State University*

Cathy Brenan
*Northland Community and Technical College*

Martin Bressler
*Houston Baptist University*

Claudia Bridges
*California State University*

Greg Broekemier
*University of Nebraska Kearney*

Gary Brunswick
*Northern Michigan University*

John Buzza
*Monmouth University*

Rae Caloura
*Johnson & Wales University*

Michaelle Cameron
*St. Edwards University*

Lindell Chew
*Linn University of Missouri*

Dorene Ciletti
*Duquesne University*

Terry Clark
*Southern Illinois University–Carbondale*

Joyce Claterbos
*University of Kansas*

Gloria Cockerell
*Collin County College*

Paul Cohen
*Florida Atlantic University*

Mark E Collins
*University of Tennessee*

Clare Comm
*University of Massachusetts, Lowell*

Sherry Cook
*Southwest Missouri State University*

Stan Cort
*Case Western Reserve University*

Keith Cox
*University of Houston*

Ian Cross
*Bentley College*

Geoffrey Crosslin
*Kalamazoo Valley Community College*

Joseph DeFilippe
*Suffolk County Community College*

George Deitz
*University of Memphis*

Kathleen DeNisco
*Erie Community College*

Tilokie Depoo
*Monroe College*

Monique Doll
*Macomb Community College*

Kim Donahue
*Indiana University*

Kimberly Donahue
*Indiana University–Purdue University at Indianapolis*

Jim D'Orazio
*Cleveland State University*

James Downing
*University of Illinois–Chicago*

Michael Drafke
*College of DuPage*

Leon Dube
*Texas A & M University*

Colleen Dunn
*Bucks County Community College*

John Eaton
*Arizona State University–Tempe*

Nancy Evans
*New River Community College*

Keith Fabes
*Berkeley College*

Tina Facca
*John Carroll University*

Joyce Fairchild
*Northern Virginia Community College*

David J. Faulds
*University of Louisville*

Larry Feick
*University of Pittsburg*

Karen Flaherty
*Oklahoma State University–Stillwater*

Leisa Flynn
*Florida State University*

William Foxx
*Auburn University*

Douglas Friedman
*Penn State University*

Stan Garfunkel
*Queensborough Community College*

Stanley Garfunkel
*Queensborough Community College*

S. J. Garner
*Eastern Kentucky University*

David Gerth
*Nashville State Community College*

Peggy Gilbert
*Missouri State University*

Kelly Gillerlain
*Tidewater Community College*

Jana Goodrich
*Penn State Behrend*

Robin Grambling
*University of Texas at El Paso*

Kimberly D. Grantham
*University of Georgia*

James I. Gray
*Florida Atlantic University*

Kelly Gredone
*Bucks County Community College*

Michael Greenwood
*Mount Wachusett Community College*

Barbara Gross
*California State University–Northridge*

David Grossman
*Florida Southern College*

Hugh Guffey
*Auburn University*

Reetika Gupta
*Lehigh University*

John Hafer
*University of Nebraska at Omaha*

Allan Hall
*Western Kentucky University*

Joan Hall
*Macomb Community College*

Clark Hallpike
*Elgin Community College*

James E. Hansen
*University of Akron*

Dorothy Harpool
*Wichita State University*

Lynn Harris
*Shippensburg University*

Linda Hefferin
*Elgin Community College*

Lewis Hershey
*Fayetteville State University*

Tom Hickman
*Loyola University*

Robbie Hillsman
*University of Tennessee–Martin*

Nathan Himelstein
*Essex County College*

Adrienne Hinds
*Northern Virginia Community College at Annandale*

John Hobbs
*University of Oklahoma*

Don Hoffer
*Miami University*

Ronald Hoverstad
*University of the Pacific*

Kris Hovespian
*Ashland University*

James Hunt
*University of North Carolina Wilmington*

Shane Hunt
*Arkansas State University*

Julie Huntley
*Oral Roberts University*

Sean Jasso
*University of California–Riverside*

Doug Johansen
*University of North Florida*

Candy Johnson
*Holyoke Community College*

Keith Jones
*North Carolina A&T University*

Janice Karlen
*CUNY - Laguardia Community College*

Eric J. Karson
*Villanova University*

Imran Khan
*University of South Alabama–Mobile*

Todd Korol
*Monroe Community College*

Dennis Lee Kovach
*Community College of Allegheny County*

Dmitri Kuksov
*Washington University–St Louis*

Jeff Kulick
*George Mason University*

Michelle Kunz
*Morehead State University*

John Kuzma
*Minnesota State University at Mankato*

Sandie Lakin
*Hesser College*

Timothy Landry
*University of Oklahoma*

Don Larson
*Ohio State University*

Felicia Lassk
*Northeastern University*

J. Ford Laumer
*Auburn University*

Kenneth Lawrence
*New Jersey IT*

Rebecca Legleiter
*Tulsa CC Southeast Campus*

Hillary Leonard
*University of Rhode Island*

Natasha Lindsey
*University of North Alabama*

Paul Londrigan
*Mott Community College*

Terry Lowe
*Heartland Community College*

Dolly Loyd
*University of Southern Mississippi*

Harold Lucius
*Rowan University*

Alicia Lupinacci
*Tarrant Community College*

Stanley Madden
*Baylor University*

Lynda Maddox
*George Washington University*

Cesar Maloles
*California State University, East Bay*

Karl Mann
*Tennessee Tech University*

Cathy Martin
*University of Akron*

Carolyn Massiah
*University of Central Florida*

Tamara Masters
*Brigham Young University*

Erika Matulich
*University of Tampa*

Bob Mayer
*Mesa State College*

Nancy McClure
*University of Central Oklahoma*

Mohan Menon
*University of South Alabama*

Michelle Meyer
*Joliet Junior College*

Ivor Mitchell
*University of Nevada Reno*

Mark Mitchell
*University of South Carolina*

Steven Moff
*Pennsylvania College of Technology*

Rex Moody
*University of Colorado*

Rex Moody
*Central Washington University at Ellensburg*

Farrokh Moshiri
*University of California–Riverside*

Dorothy Mulcahy
*Bridgewater State College*

James Munch
*Wright State University–Dayton*

Suzanne Murray
*Piedmont Technical College*

James E. Murrow
*Drury University*

Noreen Nackenson
*Nassau Community College*

Sandra Blake Neis
*Borough of Manhattan Community College*

John Newbold
*Sam Houston State University*

Keith Niedermeier
*University of Pennsylvania*

Martin Nunlee
*Syracuse University*

Hudson Nwakanma
*Florida A & M University*

Lois Olson
*San Diego State University*

Karen Overton
*Houston Community College*

Deborah L. Owens
*University of Akron*

Esther Page-Wood
*Western Michigan University*

Richard Pascarelli
*Adelphi University*

Michael Pearson
*Loyola University*

Jerry Peerbolte
*University of Arkansas–Fort Smith*

Glenn Perser
*Houston Community College*

Diane Persky
*Yeshiva University*

Susan Peters
*California State Polytechnic University at Pomona*

Renee Pfeifer-Luckett
*University of Wisconsin at Whitewater*

Gary Pieske
*Minnesota State Community and Technical College*

Jeff Podoshen
*Temple University*

Carmen Powers
*Monroe Community College*

Mike Preis
*University of Illinois–Champaign*

Rosemary Ramsey
*Wright State University*

Srikumar Rao
*Long Island University*

Kristen Regine
*Johnston & Wales University*

Joseph Reihing
*Nassau Community College*

William Rice
*California State University–Fresno*

Patricia Richards
*Westchester Community College*

Eric Rios
*Eastern University*

Janet Robinson
*Mount St. Mary's College*

Heidi Rottier
*Bradley University*

Juanita Roxas
*California State Polytechnic University*

Donald Roy
*Middle Tennessee State University*

Shikhar Sarin
*Boise State University*

Carl Saxby
*University of Southern Indiana*

Diana Scales
*Tennessee State University*

James Schindler
*Columbia Southern University*

Jeffrey Schmidt
*University of Oklahoma–Norman*

Laura Shallow
*St. Xavier University*

Rob Simon
*University of Nebraska–Lincoln*

Erin Sims
*Devry University at Pomona*

Lois J. Smith
*University of Wisconsin*

Brent Sorenson
*University of Minnesota–Crookston*

James Spiers
*Arizona State University–Tempe*

Geoffrey Stewart
*University of Louisiana*

John Striebich
*Monroe Community College*

Randy Stuart
*Kennesaw State University*

James Swanson
*Kishwaukee College*

James Swartz
*California State Polytechnic University*

Robert R. Tangsrud, Jr.
*University of North Dakota*

Steve Taylor
*Illinois State University*

Sharon Thach
*Tennessee State University*

Mary Tharp
*University of Texas at San Antonio*

Frank Tobolski
*Lake in the Hills*

Louis A. Tucci
*College of New Jersey*

Ven Venkatesan
*University of Rhode Island at Kingston*

Deirdre Verne
*Westchester Community College*

Steve Vitucci
*Tarleton University Central Texas*

Keith Wade
*Webber International University*

Wakiuru Wamwara-Mbugua
*Wright State University–Dayton*

Bryan Watkins
*Dominican University, Priory Campus*

Ron Weir
*East Tennessee State University*

Ludmilla Wells
*Florida Gulf Coast University*

Thomas Whipple
*Cleveland State University*

Tom Whitman
*Mary Washington College*

Kathleen Williamson
*University of Houston–Clear Lake*

Phillip Wilson
*Midwestern State University*

Doug Witt
*Brigham Young University*

Kim Wong
*Albuquerque Tech Institute*

Brent Wren
*University of Alabama–Huntsville*

Alex Wu
*California State University–Long Beach*

Poh-Lin Yeoh
*Bentley College*

*Marketing*, Second Edition benefited from the reviews, focus groups, and individual discussions with several leading scholars and teachers of marketing. Together, these reviewers spent hundreds of hours reading, discussing, and critiquing the manuscript.

We gratefully acknowledge:

Maria Aria
*Camden County College*

Dennis Arnett
*Texas Tech University*

Gerard Athaide
*Loyola College of Maryland*

Aysen Bakir
*Illinois State University*

Hannah Bell-Lombardo
*Bryant University*

Amit Bhatnagar
*University of Wisconsin, Milwaukee*

Linda Calderone
*SUNY, Farmingdale*

Nathaniel Calloway
*University of Maryland, University College*

Carlos Castillo
*University of Minnesota, Duluth*

Eve Caudill
*Winona State University*

Carmina Cavazos
*University of Saint Thomas*

Melissa Clark
*University of North Alabama*

Brent Cunningham
*Jacksonville State University*

Charlene Davis
*Trinity University*

Joseph Defilippe
*Suffolk County Community College, Brentwood*

Alan Friedenthal
*Kingsborough Community College*

George Goerner
*Mohawk Valley Community College*

Tom Greene
*Eastern Washington University*

Don Hanson
*Bryant University*

Jeffrey Harper
*Texas Tech University*

Charlane Held
*Onondaga Community College*

Jonathan Hibbard
*Boston University*

Craig Hollingshead
*Texas A&M University, Kingsville*

Donna Hope
*Nassau Community College*

Carol Johanek
*Washington University, St. Louis*

Maria Johnson
*Macomb Commity College, Clinton Township*

Rajiv Kashyap
*William Paterson University*

Josette Katz
*Atlantic Cape Community College*

Garland Keesling
*Towson University*

Marilyn Lavin
*University of Wisconsin, Whitewater*

Freddy Lee
*California State University, Los Angeles*

Guy Lochiatto
*Massachusetts Bay Community College*

Paul Londrigan
*Mott Community College*

Moutusi Maity
*University of Wisconsin, Whitewater*

Dennis Menezes
*University of Louisville, Louisville*

Linda Morable
*Richland College*

Brian Murray
*Jefferson Community College*

John Newbold
*Sam Houston State University*

Daniel Onyeagba
*Argosy University, Atlanta*

Terry Paul
*Ohio State University, Columbus*

Renee Pfeifer-Luckett
*University of Wisconsin, Whitewater*

Frank Alan Philpot
*George Mason University*

Susan Price
*California Polytechnic State University*

Lori Radulovich
*Baldwin-Wallace College*

Bruce Ramsey
*Franklin University*

Tom Rossi
*Broome Community College*

Linda Salisbury
*Boston College*

Nick Sarantakes
*Austin Community College*

Dwight Scherban
*Central Connecticut State University*

Dan Sherrell
*University of Memphis*

Karen Smith
*Columbia Southern University*

Randy Stuart
*Kennesaw State University*

Sue Taylor
*Southwestern Illinois College*

Sue Umashankar
*University of Arizona*

Deborah Utter
*Boston University*

Bronis Verhage
*Georgia State University*

Suzanne Walchli
*University of the Pacific*

Ludmilla Wells
*Florida Gulf Coast University*

Douglas Witt
*Brigham Young University, Provo*

Courtney Worsham
*University of South Carolina*

Joseph Yasaian
*McIntosh College*

Paschalina Ziamou
*Bernard M. Baruch College*

In our continuous efforts to offer a market-driven text, we have developed this new edition based on recommendations from extensive reviews. We would like to thank the following reviewers for their thoughtful consideration and helpful contributions to the Third Edition.

We gratefully acknowledge:

Beng Ong
*California State University, Fresno*

Farrokh Moshiri
*University of California, Riverside*

Lisa Simon
*California Polytechnic State University,
San Luis Obispo*

Kimberly Ann Donahue
*Indiana University*

John Striebich
*Monroe Community College*

Maria McConnnell
*Lorain County Community College*

Todd Korol
*Monroe Community College*

Melissa Martin
*George Mason University*

Monique Doll
*Macomb Community College*

Carolyn A. Massiah
*University of Central Florida*

Kellie Emrich
*Cuyahoga Community College*

Catherine Campbell
*University of Maryland*

Timothy W. Aurand
*Northern Illinois University*

Praveen Aggarwal
*University of Minnesota Duluth*

Julie Z. Sneath
*University of South Alabama*

Ann T. Kuzma
*Minnesota State University, Mankato*

Rob Simon
*University of Nebraska, Lincoln*

Wendi Achey
*Northampton Community College*

Lauren Ruth Skinner
*University of Alabama at Birmingham*

Philip Shum
*William Paterson University*

Suzy Murray
*Piedmont Technical College*

Clayton L. Daughtrey
*Metropolitan State College of Denver*

Alan J. Bush
*University of Memphis*

Glen H. Brodowsky
*California State University, San Marcos*

Jeffrey B. Schmidt
*University of Oklahoma*

Ann Renee Root
*Florida Atlantic University*

Letty Workman
*Utah Valley University*

Deirdre Verne
*Westchester Community College*

Claudia Mendelson Bridges
*California State University, Sacramento*

Michael Dore
*University of Oregon*

Melissa Moore
*Mississippi State University*

We express our thanks to all faculty who have contributed to the development of digital learning content:

Barbara Black
*University of Miami*

Jerri Buiting
*Baker College of Flint*

Monique Doll
*Macomb Community College*

Kim Donahue
*Indiana University – Purdue University, Indianapolis*

Lisa Hadley
*Southwest Tennessee Community College*

John Hafer
*University of Nebraska, Omaha*

Shane Hunt
*Arkansas State University*

Todd Korol
*Monroe Community College*

Terry Lowe
*Illinois State University*

Melissa Martin
*George Mason University*

Carolyn Messiah
*University of Central Florida*

Michelle Meyer
*Joliet Junior College*

Jeanne Munger
*University of Southern Maine*

Leroy Robinson
*University of Houston, Clear Lake*

Lauren Spinner Beitelspacher
*University of Alabama, Birmingham*

John Striebech
*Monroe Community College*

Lois Olson
*San Diego State University*

Mark Zarycki
*Hillsborough Community College*

We'd also like to thank Beck and Patrick of We Write Good, and Ginny Monroe of Deadline Driven, as well as the team at Hurix: Sumesh Yoganath, Namrata Gunjal, and Ashwin Srivastav for their contributions.

# brief contents

Choices for a Sustainable Future
Kimberly-Clark

**SECTION 3**   Targeting the Marketplace   227

# Marketing

**Third Edition**

# Assessing the Marketplace

Section 1, Assessing the Marketplace, starts out with an introduction to marketing in Chapter 1. Chapter 2 describes how a firm develops its marketing strategy and decides on a marketing plan. A central theme of Chapter 2 is how firms effectively create, capture, deliver, and communicate value to their customers. Chapter 3 discusses marketing ethics and presents an ethical decision framework in which the key ethical concepts are linked back to the marketing plan introduced in Chapter 2. Finally, Chapter 4, Analyzing the Marketing Environment, focuses on how marketers can systematically uncover and evaluate opportunities.

# Overview of Marketing

Think of all the people you know who own—or wish they owned—an iPod or an iPad. What makes these such hot items? After all, iPods are just one of the many portable media players on the market, and Apple's mobile tablet offers essentially the same functions as a smartphone.[1]

The difference is in Apple's award-winning commitment to innovation.[2] Innovation isn't just about building a better mousetrap. As Apple knows, it's about combining technology and design into an end result that quickly and reliably meets customers' needs.[3] Apple's products integrate well with one another, which makes it easy for customers to obtain music, photos, and content on all their different devices, which they can do at ever increasing speed in more and more mobile environments.

The various iPod models are designed to appeal to different types of users, ranging from those who want music while they exercise and need only a small device and limited features, to game players and movie buffs who need a larger display, more storage capacity, Internet connectivity, and a video camera. To offer value to another group of customers, namely, advertisers, Apple launched an advertising platform that will make interactive ads available on the iPod touch.[4] These solutions all constitute great value, because users want them and are willing to pay for them. They also have helped keep iPod at the top of the MP3 market ever since its introduction.[5]

The latest introduction from Apple, iPads provide easy touch-screen access to the Web, e-mail, music, videos, and photos on a high-resolution, 9.7-inch display. These devices can be personalized for work or play (or both), because owners can turn to the nearly 150,000 apps available through the company's App Store. They also can purchase thousands of books, television episodes, and movies through iTunes and iBookstore. Again, Apple is not so shortsighted that it forgot its advertisers: The iPad provides a far more interesting and interactive way for advertisers to reach potential customers on a nicer, larger, clearer screen than any smartphone currently achieves.

## LEARNING OBJECTIVES

**LO1** Define the role of marketing in organizations.

**LO2** List the elements of the marketing mix.

**LO3** Describe how marketers create value for a product or service.

**LO4** Understand why marketing is important both inside and outside the firm.

While these products are new, the actual technology is not what earns Apple its position as an innovator. As a former CEO noted years ago, "People talk about the technology, but Apple was a marketing company. It was the marketing company of the decade."[6] Apple succeeds because the revolutionary products it releases to the market provide the best value to customers.

● ● ●

Define the role of marketing in organizations.

# WHAT IS MARKETING?

Unlike other subjects you may have studied, marketing already is very familiar to you. You start your day by agreeing to do the dishes in exchange for a freshly made cup of coffee. Then you fill up your car with gas. You attend a class that you have chosen and paid for. After class, you pick up lunch at the cafeteria, which you eat while reading a book on your iPad. Then you leave campus to have your hair cut and take in a movie. On your bus ride back to school, you pass the time by buying a few songs from Apple's iTunes. In each case, you have acted as the buyer and made a decision about whether you should part with your time and/or money to receive a particular service or merchandise. If, after you return home, you decide to sell some clothes you don't wear much anymore on eBay, you have become a seller. And in each of these transactions, you were engaged in marketing.

The American Marketing Association states that "marketing is the activity, set of institutions, and processes for creating, *capturing,* communicating, delivering, and exchanging offerings that have value for customers, clients, partners, and society at large."[7] What does this definition really mean? Good marketing is not a random activity; it requires thoughtful planning with an emphasis on the ethical implications of any of those decisions on society in general. Firms develop a marketing plan (Chapter 2) that specifies the marketing activities for a specific period of time. The marketing plan is broken down into various components—how the product or service will be conceived or designed, how much it should cost, where and how it will be promoted, and how it will get to the consumer. In any exchange, the parties to the transaction should be satisfied. In our previous example, you should be satisfied or even delighted with the song you downloaded, and Apple should be satisfied with the amount of money it received from you. The core aspects of marketing are shown in Exhibit 1.1. Let's see how these core aspects look in practice.

## Marketing Is about Satisfying Customer Needs and Wants

Understanding the marketplace, and especially consumer needs and wants, is fundamental to marketing success. In the broadest terms, the marketplace refers to the world of trade. More narrowly, however, the *marketplace* can be segmented into groups of people who are pertinent to an organization for particular reasons. For example, the marketplace for toothpaste users may include most of the people in the world, but the makers of Crest could also divide them into adolescent, adult, and senior users or perhaps into smokers, coffee drinkers, and wine drinkers. If you manufacture a toothpaste that removes coffee stains, you want to know for which marketplace segments your product is most relevant, and then make sure that you build a marketing strategy that targets those

*Crest developed Whitestrips to satisfy its customers who want white teeth.*

**EXHIBIT 1.1**   Core Aspects of Marketing

groups. Certain coffee-drinking customers may prefer Crest Whitestrips, whereas others, who also drink coffee, may opt for GoSmile to obtain a more high-end at-home whitening procedure, and still others choose to purchase professional whitening treatments from a licensed dentist.

Although marketers would prefer to sell their products and services to everyone, it is not practical to do so. Because marketing costs money, good marketers carefully seek out potential customers who have both an interest in the product and an ability to buy it. For example, most people need some form of transportation, and many people would probably like to own the new hybrid from Lexus. At over $100,000, the Lexus LS 600h L is one of the most sophisticated hybrid cars on the market. But Lexus is not actually interested in everyone who wants an LS 600h L, because not everyone can afford to spend that much on a car. Instead, Lexus defines its viable target market as those consumers who want and *can afford* such a product.[8] Although not all companies focus on such a specific, and wealthy, target, all marketers are interested in finding the buyers who are most likely to be interested in their offers.

## Marketing Entails an Exchange

Marketing is about an exchange—the trade of things of value between the buyer and the seller so that each is better off as a result. As depicted in Exhibit 1.2, sellers provide products or services, then communicate and facilitate the delivery of their offering to consumers. Buyers complete the exchange by giving money and information to the seller. Suppose you learn about a new Taylor Swift album by hearing one of her songs on XM Satellite radio. The same day, a friend tweets that

**EXHIBIT 1.2**   Exchange: Underpinning of Seller-Buyer Relationships

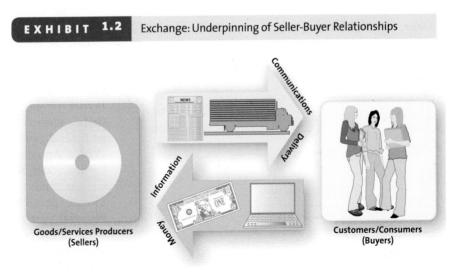

*Purchasing a Taylor Swift song from the iTunes store entails an exchange. The customer gets the song, and Apple gets money and information.*

she loves the new album on her Twitter account, and you visit the Taylor Swift Facebook fan page, which is full of recommendations. From there, you click into the iTunes Store, where you can purchase the song you heard, multiple songs, or the entire new album. You begin with the song you heard, which you continue to love after hearing it several times, and go back to iTunes and take advantage of its offer to complete the album by downloading the rest of the songs to your iTunes library. Your billing information is already in the company's system, so you do not have to enter your credit card number or other information. Furthermore, iTunes creates a record of your purchase, which it uses, together with your other purchase trends, to create personalized recommendations of other albums or songs that you might like. Thus, Apple uses the valuable information you provide to facilitate future exchanges and solidify its relationship with you.

**LO2** List the elements of the marketing mix.

## Marketing Requires Product, Price, Place, and Promotion Decisions

Marketing traditionally has been divided into a set of four interrelated decisions known as the marketing mix, or four Ps: product, price, place, and promotion (as defined in Exhibit 1.3).[9] The four Ps, or marketing mix, are the controllable set of activities that the firm uses to respond to the wants of its target markets. But what does each of the Ps mean?

**Product: Creating Value** Although marketing is a multifaceted function, its fundamental purpose is to create value by developing a variety of offerings, including goods, services, and ideas, to satisfy customer needs. Take water, for example. Not too long ago, consumers perceived this basic commodity as, well, simply water. Water came out of a faucet and was consumed for drinking and washing. But taking a cue from European firms like Perrier (France) and San Pellegrino (Italy), several U.S.-based firms such as Poland Springs, Smartwater, and Pepsi's Aquafina created a product, bottled water, with benefits that consumers find valuable. In addition to easy, portable access to water, an essential part of this newly created value is the product's brand image, which lets users say to the world, "I'm healthy," "I'm smart," and "I'm chic."[10]

| EXHIBIT 1.3 | The Marketing Mix | |
|---|---|---|
| **Marketing Mix: 4 Ps** | **Value** | |
| Product | Creating | |
| Price | Capturing | |
| Place | Delivering | |
| Promotion | Communicating | |

Nike primarily makes shoes but adds value to its products by offering custom designs under its Nike ID brand and enlisting popular celebrities such as Rafael Nadal to add their names to the designs that increase their fashionable appeal.

Products are typically goods of some kind, but products can also be services. Goods are items that you can physically touch. Nike shoes, Poland Springs water, Pepsi-Cola, Budweiser, Kraft cheese, Tide, the iPad, and countless other familiar products are examples of goods.

Unlike goods, services are intangible customer benefits that are produced by people or machines and cannot be separated from the producer. When people buy tickets—whether for airline travel, a sporting event, or the theater—they are paying not for the physical stub but for the experience they gain. Hotels, insurance agencies, and spas provide services. Getting money from your bank, whether through an ATM or from a teller, is receiving a service. The cash machines add value to the banking experience because they are conveniently located, fast, and easy to use. As described in Superior Service 1.1, the Ritz-Carlton Hotel Company adds value to its offering by providing over-the-top customer service.

Many offerings in the market combine goods and services. When you go to an optical center, you get your eyes examined (a service) and purchase new contact lenses (a good). If you enjoy Sting, you can attend a concert (a service that can be provided only at one particular time and place on a given night). At the concert you might have the chance to purchase a Sting concert T-shirt (a good that derives extra value from the associated concert service). You might even manage to get your shirt signed by Sting himself. You would have obtained a tangible good that caps and extends a satisfying service experience.

Ideas also can be marketed—opinions, programs, and philosophies. For instance, groups promoting bicycle safety go to schools, give talks, and sponsor bike helmet poster contests for the members of their primary market—children. Then their secondary target market segment, parents and siblings, gets involved

*Rafael Nadal adds value to the Nike brand*

*A Sting concert is a service, but a Sting T-shirt purchased at the concert is a product.*

## Superior Service 1.1

### Ritz-Carlton Hotel Makes Customer Service an Art[11]

The Ritz-Carlton Hotel Company, a winner of the Malcolm Baldrige National Quality Award, enjoys a great reputation as a top luxury hotel because it provides excellent customer service.

To provide this excellent service, Ritz-Carlton trains its employees in the company's 12 service values and how to execute them. Ritz-Carlton employees are prepared to go above and beyond ordinarily expected service levels for each customer.

Employees attend daily 15-minute "lineup" meetings to hear a "wow" story about exemplary service provided by an employee somewhere in the world. For example, when a guest at The Ritz-Carlton Resorts of Naples was about to miss an international flight because he had left some precious belongings in his hotel room, a hotel staff member personally collected and delivered the misplaced items to the airport. On another occasion, a Ritz-Carlton concierge booked a last-minute helicopter ride to whisk a frantic guest to his son's baseball game. The same stories are told in hotels in 21 countries, so a waiter in Naples, Florida, will hear the same story as a concierge in Naples, Italy. These "wow" stories recognize employees for outstanding performance, motivate employees who hear them to embrace the 12 service values of the hotel, and reinforce each service value. Ritz-Carlton understands the power of storytelling as a tactic to train employees. (This training method is productively applied to industries other than hotel chains.)

To remind employees of the Ritz-Carlton values, they all carry the chain's "Gold Standards" printed on a wallet-size card. The card displays the hotel's motto ("We Are Ladies and Gentlemen Serving Ladies and Gentlemen"), the three steps for high-quality service (warm and sincere greeting, anticipation of and compliance with guests' needs, and fond farewell), and the 12 service values of the hotel, including "I build strong relationships and create Ritz-Carlton guests for life" (No. 1) and "I am proud of my professional appearance, language, and behavior" (No. 10).

The result of such training and reinforcement is highly motivated employees who not only know the company's

*The Ritz-Carlton Hotel Chain is an award-winning firm because it provides excellent customer service.*

mission to deliver exceptional customer service but also understand how to apply the mission with its service values to everyday situations.

Products can be duplicated, but excellent customer service makes consumers emotionally attached and loyal to the experience and the associated brand.

---

through their interactions with the young contest participants. The exchange of value occurs when the children listen to the sponsors' presentation and wear their helmets while bicycling, which means they have adopted, or become "purchasers," of the safety idea that the group marketed.

**Price: Capturing Value**  Everything has a price, though it doesn't always have to be monetary. Price is everything the buyer gives up—money, time, energy—in exchange for the product. Marketers must determine the price of a product carefully on the basis of the potential buyer's belief about its value. For example, United Airlines can take you from New York to Denver. The price you pay for that service depends on how far in advance you book the ticket, the time of year, and whether you want to fly coach or business class. If you value the convenience of buying your ticket at the last minute for a ski trip between Christmas and New Year's Day and you want to fly business class, you can expect to pay four or five times as much as you would for the cheapest available ticket. That is, you have traded off a lower price for convenience. For marketers, the key to determining prices is figuring out how much customers are willing to pay so that they are satisfied with the purchase and the seller achieves a reasonable profit.

**Place: Delivering the Value Proposition**  The third P, place, represents all the activities necessary to get the product to the right customer when that customer wants it. Specifically, supply chain management is the set of approaches and techniques that firms employ to efficiently and effectively integrate their suppliers, manufacturers, warehouses, stores, and other firms involved in the transaction (e.g., transportation companies) into a seamless value chain in which merchandise is produced and distributed in the right quantities, to the right locations, and at the right time, while minimizing systemwide costs and satisfying the service levels required by the customers. Many marketing students initially overlook the importance of supply chain management because a lot of the activities are behind the scenes. But without a strong and efficient supply chain system, merchandise isn't available when customers want it. Then customers are disappointed, and sales and profits suffer.

But if the supply chain works, no one is disappointed. Imagine a seafood lover, landlocked in Idaho. She cannot manage to fly to Miami Beach regularly to visit Joe's Stone Crab; that just would not be practical. But Joe's wants to make sure it can provide her with the product she wants, so it has established a supply chain in which consumers can place orders through its Internet site (http://www.joes stonecrab.com). Joe's packages the orders and works with its supply chain partner, FedEx, to ensure the crabs get delivered to any location in the continental United States, including Idaho, by the end of the next business day. This service adds so much value that Joe's Stone Crabs can command a price premium—a medium-sized stone crab dinner for two is $112.95.[12] But for the seafood lover in Idaho, the ease with which she receives her seafood fix makes the price worthwhile.

**Promotion: Communicating the Value Proposition**  Even the best products, whether goods or services, will go unsold if marketers cannot communicate, or promote, their value to customers. Promotion thus is communication by a

*If you want Stone Crabs and you live in Wyoming, order online from Joe's Stone Crabs and you will have them the next day.*

*Calvin Klein is known for selling youth, fun, and sex appeal in its fragrance promotions. In this photo, ck one models dance to the sounds of DJ Ruckus as they live in a billboard shaped like a giant ck one bottle overlooking the streets of Times Square in New York City.*

marketer that informs, persuades, and reminds potential buyers about a product to influence their opinions and elicit a response. Promotion generally can enhance a product's value, as happened for Calvin Klein fragrances. The company's provocative advertising helped create an image that says far more than "use this product and you will smell good." Rather, the promotion sells youth, style, and sex appeal. Power of the Internet 1.1 considers how Facebook communicates its value by encouraging networks of users and businesses outside its site.

## Marketing Can Be Performed by Both Individuals and Organizations

Imagine how complicated the world would be if you had to buy everything you consumed directly from producers or manufacturers. You would have to go from farm to farm buying your food and then from manufacturer to manufacturer to purchase the table, plates, and utensils you need to eat that food. Fortunately, marketing intermediaries, such as retailers, accumulate merchandise from producers in large amounts and then sell it to you in smaller amounts. The process by which businesses sell to consumers is known as B2C (business-to-consumer) marketing, whereas the process of selling merchandise or services from one business to another is called B2B (business-to-business) marketing. With the advent of various Internet auction sites (e.g., eBay) and social media, consumers have started marketing their products and services to other consumers. This third category, in which consumers sell to other consumers, is C2C marketing. These marketing transactions are illustrated in Exhibit 1.4.

Individuals can also undertake activities to market themselves. When you apply for a job, for instance, the research you do about the firm, the resume and cover letter you submit with your application, and the way you dress for an interview and conduct yourself during it are all forms of marketing activities. Accountants, lawyers, financial planners, physicians, and other professional service providers also constantly market their services one way or another.

## Marketing Impacts Various Stakeholders

Most people think of marketing as a way to facilitate the sale of products or services to customers or clients. But marketing can also impact several other stakeholders, such as partners in the supply chain, employees, and society at large.

## Power of the Internet 1.1 — Facebook Networks the Web[13]

Facebook would prefer it if you checked your account daily (or even hourly). Its 400 million users spend an average of 6.5 hours a month on the site, and Facebook is the fourth most frequently visited site in the United States. But to encourage users to show up even more often, Facebook is working to become better integrated with other Web sites they are likely to use. For example, if you visit a particular online game each day, Facebook wants to make sure you think of visiting your Facebook account too, so it adds its icon to the bottom of the opening page.

The benefits to Facebook seem evident, but such increased networking also aids advertisers and users. Its Open Graph program helps businesses find promising customers by combining information across various sites. For example, after you use Yelp to look for Asian food restaurants in the downtown area of your city, Yelp can also access songs that you like on Pandora and recommend concert venues in the same area that will be hosting shows of potential interest to you. Your Facebook preferences also might provide your favorite music, restaurants, and movies. IMDB, the comprehensive site for movie lovers, is partnering with Facebook. The company's annual advertising revenues of more than $1 billion continue to grow as advertising on the site becomes more and more useful and relevant.

For users, Facebook works to enable interactions. For example, if you watch the funniest video you have ever seen on YouTube, you can rely on Facebook's social plug-ins technology to share the content with all your Facebook friends immediately and with great ease. While reading an article on CNN.com, you can watch a Facebook newsfeed that shows how many of your friends also shared or liked that article. Because Facebook (and Twitter, for that matter), has

*Facebook's founder, Mark Zuckerberg, is the youngest billionaire in the world due to his 24 percent share in Facebook.*

made it very easy for companies to place "Share" buttons on their Web pages, more and more traffic joins Facebook.

In one more step on its journey to become ubiquitous in users' lives, Facebook is developing an online, credit-based payment system. To earn credits, users might respond to offers, such as watching a video, or transfer reward points earned on their Chase credit cards to their Facebook credit accounts. This virtual currency makes it easier for users to purchase Facebook's and its partners' applications, instead of requiring separate credits for each application. In this sense, Facebook aims to be your one-stop shop for virtually anything that interests you online.

Supply chain partners, whether they are manufacturers, wholesalers, retailers, or other intermediaries like transportation or warehousing companies, are involved in marketing to one another. Manufacturers sell merchandise to retailers, but the retailers often have to convince manufacturers to sell to them. After many years of not carrying Ralph Lauren products, JCPenney has co-introduced with Ralph Lauren a line of clothing and home furnishings called American Living, sold exclusively at JCPenney, that does not bear the Ralph Lauren name.[14]

**EXHIBIT 1.4** Marketing Can Be Performed by Both Individuals and Organizations

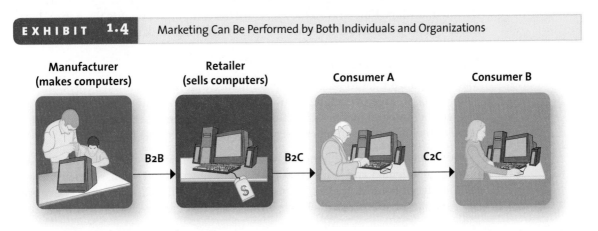

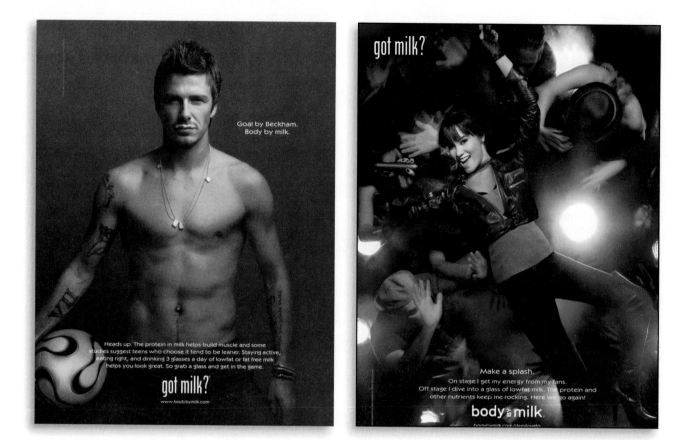

*The dairy industry's "Got Milk" ad campaign has created high levels of awareness about the benefits of drinking milk and has increased milk consumption by using celebrities like soccer star David Beckham and singer/songwriter/actress Demi Lovato.*

More and more firms develop marketing programs to attract the "best and brightest" employees. According to a recent poll, more than 25 percent of *Fortune* 200 companies devote some resources to programs that will improve their image among potential employees.[15] These programs, called employment marketing, involve undertaking marketing research to understand what potential employees are seeking, as well as what they think about the firm; developing a value proposition and an employment brand image; communicating that brand image to potential employees; and then fulfilling the brand promise by ensuring the employee experience matches that which was advertised.[16] Marriott, Nike, Starbucks, Southwest Airlines, and SAS are some companies that focus on employment marketing. The U.S. military also has stepped up its efforts to encourage people to join.

Marketing often is designed to benefit an entire industry or society at large. The dairy industry has used a very successful, award-winning campaign with its slogan "Got Milk" aimed at different target segments. This campaign has not only created high levels of awareness about the benefits of drinking milk but also increased milk consumption in various target segments, perhaps in response to the use of various celebrities, from David Beckham and Alex Rodriguez to Mischa Barton and Mary Kate and Ashley Olsen. This campaign benefits the entire dairy industry and promotes the health benefits of drinking milk to society at large.

## Marketing Helps Create Value

Marketing didn't get to its current prominence among individuals, corporations, and society at large overnight. To understand how marketing has evolved into its present-day integral business function of creating value, let's look for a moment at some of the milestones in marketing's short history (Exhibit 1.5).

**Production-Oriented Era**  Around the turn of the twentieth century, most firms were production oriented and believed that a good product would sell itself. Henry Ford, the founder of Ford Motor Co., once famously remarked, "Customers can have any color they want so long as it's black." Manufacturers were concerned with product

| EXHIBIT 1.5 | Marketing Evolution: Production, Sales, Marketing, and Value |

**Turn of the century** | **1920** | **1950** | **1990**

Production ▷ Sales ▷ Marketing ▷ Value-based marketing ▷

innovation, not with satisfying the needs of individual consumers, and retail stores typically were considered places to hold the merchandise until a consumer wanted it.

**Sales-Oriented Era** Between 1920 and 1950, production and distribution techniques became more sophisticated, and the Great Depression and World War II conditioned customers to consume less or manufacture items themselves, so they planted Victory Gardens instead of buying produce. As a result, manufacturers had the capacity to produce more than customers really wanted or were able to buy. Firms found an answer to their overproduction in becoming sales oriented; they depended on heavy doses of personal selling and advertising.

**Market-Oriented Era** After World War II, soldiers returned home, got new jobs, and started families. At the same time, manufacturers turned from focusing on the war effort toward making consumer products. Suburban communities, featuring cars in every garage, sprouted up around the country, and the new suburban fixture, the shopping center, began to replace cities' central business districts as the hub of retail activity and a place to just hang out. Some products, once in limited supply because of World War II, became plentiful. And the United States entered a buyers' market—the customer became king! When consumers again had choices, they were able to make purchasing decisions on the basis of factors such as quality, convenience, and price. Manufacturers and retailers thus began to focus on what consumers wanted and needed before they designed, made, or attempted to sell their products and services. It was during this period that firms discovered marketing.

**Value-Based Marketing Era** Most successful firms today are market oriented.[17] That means they generally have transcended a production or selling orientation and attempt to discover and satisfy their customers' needs and wants. Before the turn of the twenty-first century, better marketing firms recognized that there was more to good marketing than simply discovering and providing what consumers wanted and needed; to compete successfully, they would have to give their customers greater value than their competitors did.

Value reflects the relationship of benefits to costs, or what you *get* for what you *give*.[18] In a marketing context, customers seek a fair return in goods and/or services for their hard-earned money and scarce time. They want products or services that meet their specific needs or wants and that are offered at competitive prices. The challenge for firms is to find out what consumers are looking for and attempt to provide those very goods and services and still make a profit.

Every value-based marketing firm must implement its strategy according to what its customers value. Sometimes providing greater value means providing a

## Adding Value 1.1   Jeans—From Bronco to Boardroom

When blue jeans first hit the market in 1873,[19] they were working-man's wear: Rugged cotton pants with metal rivets at stress points to help prevent rips. The pants, created by tailor Jacob Davis and a dry goods businessman named Loeb "Levi" Strauss, were an instant success, flying off the shelves at the then-exorbitant cost of $1 per pair. Today, blue jeans still fly off the shelves, but at substantially higher prices and with so many different styles and details that they are appropriate casual and businesswear for both men and women. In fact, blue jeans show up at formal occasions without raising eyebrows. The evolution of jeans—and how they have managed to remain a wardrobe staple for over a century despite changes in fashion—illustrates how customer perception can increase or undermine the value of a product.

In the 1930s, movie cowboys popularized jeans, creating a market among urban "cowboys" who aspired to a rugged look but wanted comfortable clothing. In the 50s, jeans-clad movie idol James Dean became the symbol of adolescent rebellion,[20] and teenagers donned jeans to symbolize the departure from their parents' values. Throughout the 60s and early 70s, jeans acquired embroidery, flared bottoms, beads, and paint and began appearing in tie-dye to match the fashions of the day. They also acquired rips and frays, signs of wear that would soon evolve into fashionable styling on new jeans. Late in the 1970s, designers caught denim fever, and costly versions appeared with tags bearing names such as Jordache, Sasson, Gloria Vanderbilt, Gucci, and Calvin Klein.[21]

Using new styles and finishes, these designers revitalized the jeans market throughout the 80s, turning the $1 working-man's pant into a garment that retailed from $200 to $2000. Even the originals had a new value: A pair of 1850 Levis 501s sold on eBay for $60,000. Designer jeans for men became popular, and consumers began paying more attention to the tops, shoes, and accessories they wore with their jeans. This interest led to a new value for garments such as jeweled shirts, denim vests and jackets, and shoes from designer heels to basic ballet flats. Meanwhile, the old standby—basic blue jeans from Levi's, Lee's, or Wrangler's—continued to find a solid customer base with a price point in the comfortable double digits for most.

But then the fashion pendulum swung back. Whereas jeans in the 50s signaled youth and rebellion, they were viewed as pants for parents by teenagers coming of age in the 90s. Jeans were only acceptable to teens if they looked vintage or second-hand. Levi Strauss & Company, which had remained the preeminent jeans producer despite their patent having expired in the late nineteenth century, began closing factories.

The industry has reacted in a variety of ways to rekindle a sense of consumer value for jeans. Specialty brands such as 7 for All Mankind, Citizens of Humanity, Lucky Jeans, and True Religion have entered the market, positioning themselves as hip or edgy. Some brands, like True Religion, have maintained prices as demand has waned, hoping to perpetuate an aura of prestige for their Western-inspired jeans; others have dropped prices, seeking to attract more budget-conscious consumers who want fashionable jeans. Levi Strauss, for instance, has

*Everyone wears jeans everywhere and for every occasion, including Drew Barrymore.*

developed the Signature line that is available exclusively at Walmart for less than $20. Designers who had been in the jeans business for decades have brought back retro styles or hired supermodels to generate renewed interest in their products. Some stores offer organic and green products for environmentally conscious consumers, which are more expensive than their traditionally made counterparts.

Efforts to keep denim king are successful, thanks in part to political and business leaders who, by virtue of appearing in certain venues wearing blue jeans, impart an updated image to the garment. Apple founder Steve Jobs pioneered the business jeans look in the 90s with a pair of Levi's 501s and a black turtleneck. Russia's president Dmitry Medvedev matched jeans with a blazer and buttoned shirt for dinner with President Obama.[22] These trends build on some of the traditional associations with jeans to project an image of a "new" executive: someone who is confident, creative, and willing to dig in and get the job done. The badge of rebellion has transformed into a symbol of power. Today, the uniform of the laborer is even making inroads in some of the last bastions of conservative dress: Country clubs.[23]

Jeans are still jeans—cotton twill pants that are most commonly dyed indigo blue. But now they are worn by men, women, and children. They appear at the White House, the coffee shop, and in the fields. They may sport platinum rivets or strategically placed holes, be purchased ready to wear or tailored for an individual fit. Brands and styles sell for various prices, reflecting the value that each offering provides.

lot of merchandise for relatively little money, such as a Whopper for 99¢ at Burger King or a diamond for 40 percent off the suggested retail price at Costco. But value is in the eye of the beholder and doesn't always come cheap. Satisfied BMW buyers believe their car is a good value because they have gotten a lot of benefits for a reasonable price. People are willing to pay a premium for a BMW because of its extraordinary design and technology, even though cheaper substitutes are available.

To provide additional value to customers, some companies engage in value cocreation.[24] That is, customers can act as collaborators to create the product or service. When clients work with their investment advisors, they cocreate their investment portfolios; when Nike allows customers to submit designs, they cocreate their sneakers. M&M's value cocreation offer lets customers specify their orders online (mymms.com) with customized, personalized messages printed on the candies to celebrate a holiday, a sense of romance, a birthday, or even a business deal. On the site, consumers choose from a menu of products that are not available in stores. In addition to sporting a personalized message, instead of the signature M, the cocreated candy is available in 17 different color choices. And if the customized candy isn't enough, the customer cocreators can order them in embroidered bags.

In the next section, we explore the notion of value-based marketing further. Specifically, we look at various options for attracting customers by providing them with better value than the competition does. Then we discuss how firms compete on the basis of value. Finally, we examine how firms transform the value concept into their value-driven activities.

---

### CHECK YOURSELF

1. What is the definition of marketing?
2. Marketing is about satisfying _____ and _____.
3. What are the four components of the marketing mix?
4. Who can perform marketing?
5. What have been the various eras of marketing?

---

# WHAT IS VALUE-BASED MARKETING?

**L03** Describe how marketers create value for a product or service.

Consumers make explicit and/or implicit trade-offs between the perceived benefits of a product or service and its cost. (See Exhibit 1.6.) Customers naturally seek options that provide the greatest benefits at the lowest costs. On the other side, marketing firms attempt to find the most desirable balance between providing benefits to customers and keeping their own costs down.

To better understand value and develop a value-based marketing orientation, a business must understand what customers view as the key benefits of a given product or service and how to improve on them. For example, some benefits of staying at a Sheraton hotel might include the high level of service quality provided by the personnel, the convenience of booking the room at Sheraton.com, and the overall quality of the rooms and meals offered. In broader terms,

**EXHIBIT 1.6** Benefits and Costs Associated with Value

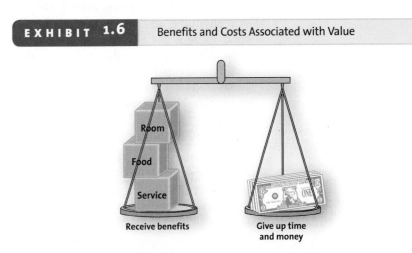

Receive benefits

Give up time and money

In deciding whether to stay at a Sheraton, potential customers trade off the benefits they receive with the money it costs them.

some critical benefits may be service quality, convenience, and merchandise quality. The customer's potential cost elements (for this example in the terms of a value-based marketing strategy) would include the price of the room and meals, the time it takes to book a room or check in at the hotel, and the risk of arriving at the hotel and finding it overbooked.

## How Firms Compete on the Basis of Value

With such a simple formula, marketers should be able to deliver value consistently, right? Well, not exactly. In today's quickly changing world, consistently creating and delivering value is quite difficult. Consumer perceptions change quickly, competitors constantly enter markets, and global pressures continually reshape opportunities. Thus, marketers must keep a vigilant eye on the marketplace so they can adjust their offerings to meet customer needs and keep ahead of their competition.[25]

Value-based marketing isn't just about creating strong products and services; it involves deciding which products/services to provide for whom. For example, Walmart does not serve customers who are looking to impress their friends with conspicuous consumption. Rather, Walmart serves those who want convenient one-stop shopping and low prices—and on those values, it consistently delivers. But good value is not always limited to low prices. Walmart carries low-priced pots, pans, and coffee pots. But cooking enthusiasts may prefer the product selection, quality, and expert sales assistance at Williams-Sonoma. That is, the prices might not be as low as Walmart's, but Williams-Sonoma customers believe they are receiving a good value because they can enjoy that extra selection, quality, and service.

## How Do Firms Become Value Driven?

Firms become value driven by focusing on three activities. First, they share information about their customers and competitors across their own organization and with other firms, such as manufacturers and transportation companies, that help them get the product or service to the marketplace. Second, they strive to balance their customers' benefits and costs. Third, they concentrate on building relationships with customers.

**Sharing Information** In a value-based, marketing oriented firm, marketers share information about customers and competitors and integrate it across the firm's various departments. The fashion designers for J.Crew, for instance, collect purchase information and research customer trends to determine what their customers will want to wear in the next few weeks; simultaneously, the logisticians—those persons in charge of getting the merchandise to the stores— use the same purchase history to forecast sales and allocate appropriate merchandise to individual stores. Sharing and coordinating such information represents a critical success factor for any firm. Imagine what might happen if J.Crew's advertising department were to plan a special promotion but not share its sales projections with those people in charge of creating the merchandise or getting it to stores.

**Balancing Benefits with Costs** Value-oriented marketers constantly measure the benefits that customers perceive against the cost of their offerings. They use available customer data to find opportunities to better satisfy their customers' needs, keep costs down, and develop long-term loyalties. Such a value-based orientation has helped Target and Walmart outperform Standard & Poor's retail index, Kohl's beat other department stores, and Southwest Airlines succeed where mainstream carriers could not.

Southwest Airlines has become the largest U.S. carrier, flying approximately 101 million customers around the country for an average ticket price of $119.16 (compared with JetBlue's average ticket price of $139.40). Southwest makes frequent and short trips, such as Las Vegas to Los Angeles.[26] The company cuts costs through its famous "cattle call" seating methods, in which customers get to choose their seats on a first come, first served basis. For those flyers who value being first on the plane though, the airline also provides an "Early Bird" check-in service for $10 per flight.[27] Some low-frills, low-cost carriers, such as Ryanair and easyJet,[28] have adopted Southwest's model to offer customers cheap intra-Europe airfares too. Ryanair and easyJet generally fly to and from out-of-the-way airports like Stansted, which is 34 miles northeast of London. But many customers balance such inconvenience against the price to determine the value: Consider, for example, the London to Zurich, Switzerland, route for $50 or London to Athens, Greece, for $100. Around the world, conventional airlines have started their own low-frills, low-cost airlines, such as Singapore Airlines' Tiger and the Australian Jetstar, run by Quantas.

Many companies have been able to lower costs and still deliver excellent overall value by focusing on what the customer values. For example, IKEA does not have highly paid salespeople to sell its furniture, but its simple designs mean customers can easily choose a product and assemble it themselves.

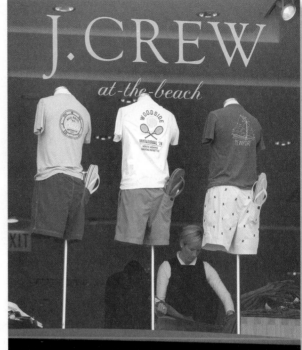

*Collecting and sharing information among departments at J.Crew is important for its success.*

*Southwest Airlines keeps costs low so its customers receive low prices.*

*Furniture retailer IKEA focuses on what its customers value—low prices and great design.*

*UPS works with its corporate shippers to develop efficient transportation solutions.*

**Building Relationships with Customers**
During the past decade or so, marketers have begun to realize that they need to think about their customer orientation in terms of relationships rather than transactions.[29] A transactional orientation regards the buyer–seller relationship as a series of individual transactions, so anything that happened before or after any transaction is of little importance. For example, used car sales typically are based on a transactional approach; the seller wants to get the highest price for the car, the buyer wants to get the lowest, and neither expects to do business with the other again.

A relational orientation, in contrast, is based on the philosophy that buyers and sellers should develop a long-term relationship. According to this idea, the lifetime profitability of the relationship is what matters, not how much money is made during each transaction. Thus, Apple makes its new innovations compatible with existing products to encourage consumers to maintain a long-term relationship with the company across all their electronic needs. In a more service-oriented setting, UPS works with its corporate shippers to develop efficient transportation solutions. Over time, UPS then becomes part of the fabric of the shippers' organizations, and their operations become intertwined. In this scenario, they have developed a valuable long-term relationship.

Firms that practice value-based marketing use a process known as customer relationship management (CRM), a business philosophy and set of strategies, programs, and systems that focus on identifying and building loyalty among the firm's most valued customers.[30] Firms that employ CRM systematically collect information about their customers' needs and then use that information to target their best customers with the products, services, and special promotions that appear most important to them.

Now that we've examined what marketing is and how it creates value, let's consider how it fits into the world of commerce, as well as into society in general.

**CHECK YOURSELF**

1. Does providing a good value mean selling at a low price?
2. What type of relationship is best for providing value to customers?

**EXHIBIT  1.7**      Importance of Marketing

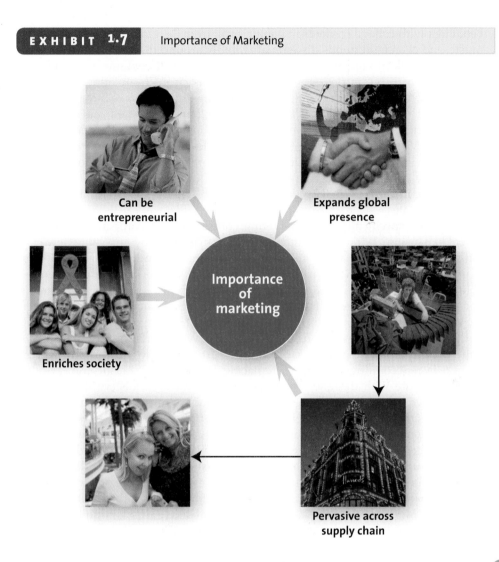

Can be
entrepreneurial

Expands global
presence

Enriches society

**Importance
of
marketing**

Pervasive across
supply chain

# WHY IS MARKETING IMPORTANT?

**L04**  Understand why marketing is important both within and outside the firm

Marketing once was only an afterthought to production. Early marketing philosophy went something like this: "We've made it; now how do we get rid of it?" However, marketing not only has shifted its focus dramatically, but also has evolved into a major business function that crosses all areas of a firm or organization, as illustrated in Exhibit 1.7. Marketing advises production about how much of the company's product to make and then tells logistics when to ship it. It creates long-lasting, mutually valuable relationships between the company and the firms from which it buys. It identifies those elements that local customers value and makes it possible for the firm to expand globally. Marketing has had a significant impact on consumers as well. Without marketing, it would be difficult for any of us to learn about new products and services. Understanding marketing can even help you find a job after you finish school.

## Marketing Expands Firms' Global Presence

A generation ago, Coca-Cola was available in many nations, but Levi's and most other U.S. brands weren't. Blue jeans were primarily an American product—made in the United States for the U.S. market. But today most jeans, including those of Levi Strauss & Co., are made in places other than the United States and are available nearly everywhere. Thanks to MTV and other global entertainment venues, cheap foreign travel, and the Internet, you share many of your consumption behaviors with college students in countries all over the globe. The best fashions, music, and even food trends disseminate rapidly around the world.

Take a look at your next shopping bag. Whatever it contains, you will find goods from many countries—produce from Mexico, jeans from Japan, electronics from Korea. Global manufacturers and retailers continue to make inroads into the U.S. market. Companies such as Honda, Swatch, Sony, Heineken, and Nestlé sell as well in the United States as they do in their home countries. Sweden's fashion retailer H&M operates in 37 countries;[31] its upscale competitor, Spain's Zara, operates in over 70 countries.[32] The Dutch grocery store giant Ahold is among the top five grocery store chains in the United States, though you may never have heard of it because it operates under names such as Stop & Shop, GIANT, and Peapod in the United States.[33]

But how specifically does marketing contribute to a company's successful global expansion? Without the knowledge that firms gain by analyzing new customers' needs and wants on a segment-by-segment, region-by-region basis—one of marketing's main tasks—virtually no firm would succeed internationally or be able to expand globally. To appeal to its European customer base, McDonald's had to remodel its stores to the extent that most U.S. customers might not even recognize them as their familiar fast-food restaurant.[34] European consumers, who tend to view meals as occasions to be savored, have less interest in McDonald's American value offering—that is, consistent fast food at low prices. So the restaurant is redecorating in Europe, replacing bolted-down, plastic, yellow-and-white furniture with designer chairs and dark leather upholstery that create a more relaxed, sophisticated atmosphere. The chain is implementing nine different designs, depending on which one is most appropriate for the specific location and clientele. The designs range from "purely simple," with minimalist décor in neutral colors, to "Qualité," featuring large pictures of lettuces and tomatoes and gleaming stainless-steel kitchen utensils. The key to any successful makeover, whether it be global or local, is the same as the key to any strategy change: Make sure the change upgrade doesn't go so far that the firm loses the equity it has in its identity. McDonald's uniform quality control achieves this continuity—even if seated in upholstered leather chairs, customers know they are in a McDonald's.

## Marketing Is Pervasive across the Supply Chain

Firms do not work in isolation. Manufacturers buy raw materials and components from suppliers, which they sell to retailers or other businesses after they have turned the materials into products (see Exhibit 1.8). Every time materials or products are bought or sold, they are transported to a different location, which sometimes requires that they be stored in a warehouse operated by yet another organization. Such a group of firms that make and deliver a given set of goods and services is known as a supply chain.

**EXHIBIT 1.8**     Supply Chain

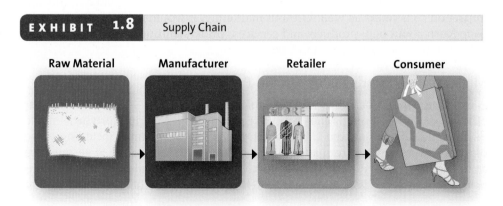

| Raw Material | Manufacturer | Retailer | Consumer |

As we discussed earlier, some supply chain participants have a transactional orientation in which the participating parties don't care much about their trading partners as the merchandise passes among them. Each link in the chain is out for its own best interest. Manufacturers, for example, want the highest price, whereas retailers want to buy the product at the lowest. As participants in transactions supply chain members do not enjoy any cooperation or coordination. But for the supply chain to provide significant value to the ultimate customer, the parties must establish long-term relationships with one

*Levi Strauss & Co. helps retailers manage their inventory so they don't run out of stock.*

another and cooperate to share data, make joint forecasts, and coordinate shipments. Effectively managing supply chain relationships often has a marked impact on a firm's ability to satisfy the consumer, which results in increased profitability for all parties.

Consider Levi Strauss & Co. and its close relationship with its major retailers. Not too many years ago, only about 40 percent of orders from the jeans manufacturer to its retailers arrived on time, which made it very difficult for retailers to keep all sizes in stock and therefore keep customers, who are generally not satisfied with anything less than the correct size, happy. Today, Levi's uses an automatic inventory replenishment system through which it manages the retailers' inventory itself. When a customer buys a pair of jeans, the information is transferred directly from the retailer to Levi's, which then determines which items the retailer needs to reorder and automatically ships the merchandise. The relationship benefits all parties: Retailers don't have to worry about keeping their stores stocked in jeans and save money because they don't have to invest as much money in inventory. Because Levi's has control of the jeans inventory, it can be assured that it won't lose sales because its retailers have let their inventory run down. Finally, customers benefit by having the merchandise when they want it—a good value.

A supply chain comprises more than buyers and sellers, however. Firms build strategic alliances with consulting firms, marketing research firms, computer firms, and transportation firms, to name just a few. For example, UPS provides much more than a package delivery service; it also offers insurance services, supply chain management, and e-commerce support to small- and medium-sized customers. Through UPS Capital, firms can even obtain funds to finance their inventory or ease their cash flow.[35]

## Marketing Enriches Society

Should marketing focus on factors other than financial profitability, like good corporate citizenship? Many of America's best known corporations seem to think so; they encourage their employees to participate in activities that benefit their communities and they invest heavily in socially responsible activities and charities. For example, from the very start, when Kellogg functioned primarily as a purveyor of Corn Flakes, it maintained a strong commitment to enhancing the welfare of its many stakeholders—not just customers, but also employees, shareholders, and the

| **EXHIBIT 1.9** | Ben & Jerry's Mission |
| --- | --- |

■ **Product Mission**
  To make, distribute and sell the finest quality all natural ice cream and euphoric concoctions with a continued commitment to incorporating wholesome, natural ingredients and promoting business practices that respect the Earth and the Environment.

■ **Economic Mission**
  To operate the company on a sustainable financial basis of profitable growth, increasing value for our stockholders and expanding opportunities for development and career growth for our employees.

■ **Social Mission**
  To operate the company in a way that actively recognizes the central role that business plays in society by initiating innovative ways to improve the quality of life locally, nationally and internationally.

community at large. Its "Vision and Mission statements" thus include ideas about social responsibility, sustainable growth, and strategic and operating principles.[36] Furthermore, it commits itself as follows:

■ Our people: Committed to excellence, passionate about achieving our goals, eagerly embracing new challenges.

■ Our strategy: Focused and consistent, delivers sustainable and dependable performance.

■ Our business model: Resilient and proven, relevant in all economies, drives long-term health of the company.

■ Our brands: Recognized and loved around the world, in strong categories, responsive to advertising and brand building.[37]

*Kellogg helps enrich society. If it puts too many yellow Froot Loops in a box, for instance, it donates it to charity instead of throwing the box away.*

The firm's commitment to a broader civic responsibility, regardless of where it does business, stems from its corporate mission statement, which promises its "commitment to provide and maintain environmentally responsible practices for the communities in which we are located." Although initially a U.S. firm, Kellogg runs facilities in Australia, Germany, India, and Korea as well, and in all these communities, it engages in recycling campaigns and implements water management systems. Thus, the employees, its investors, and, perhaps most important, its customers are reassured, knowing that Kellogg aims to make all of its cartons out of 100 percent recycled fiber. When products suffer minor quality defects, such as too many yellow Froot Loops in a box, the company does not just waste them but instead donates them to charitable organizations and thus benefits the community as well.

Similar sentiments are echoed by Colgate-Palmolive, which clearly states that "our three fundamental values—Caring, Global Teamwork and Continuous Improvement—are part of everything we do."[38] Management at Ben & Jerry's, the Vermont-based ice cream producer, actively embraces social responsibility by focusing the company around three key types of missions: product, economic, and social (see Exhibit 1.9).[39]

These firms, and hundreds more like them, recognize that including a strong social orientation in business is a sound strategy that is in both its own and its customers' best interest. It shows the consumer marketplace that the firm will be around for the long run and can be trusted with their business. In a volatile market, investors view firms that operate with high levels of corporate responsibility and ethics as safe investments. Similarly, firms have come to realize that good corporate citizenship through socially responsible actions should be a priority because it will help their bottom line in the long run. In a world in which consumers constantly hear about examples of corporate malfeasance and ethical lapses, the need for companies to live up to their ethical promises becomes ever more important, as Ethical and Societal Dilemma 1.1 outlines.

---

## Ethical and Societal Dilemma 1.1　✋　Firms Swing the Ethical Pendulum Both Ways

Consumers and media watchers at the end of the 2000s could hardly avoid feeling as if a lot of corporate executives might have skipped the chapter on ethics in their marketing courses. From the near failure of Bear Stearns, to the actual collapse of Lehman Brothers, to concerns about the profits earned by Goldman Sachs, the financial industry seemed mired in ethically questionable practices.

What led to these ethical lapses? It was not a lack of direction; all these companies had published Codes of Ethics in place.[40] For example, Lehman Brothers' Code read, in part:

> It is crucial that all books of account, financial statements and records of the Firm reflect the underlying transactions and any disposition of assets in a full, fair, accurate and timely manner.... Additionally, each individual involved in the preparation of the Firm's financial statements must prepare those statements in accordance with Generally Accepted Accounting Principles ... so that the financial statements present fairly, in all material respects, the financial position, results of operations and cash flows of the Firm.[41]

And yet a more than 2,200-page report submitted during Lehman's bankruptcy proceedings concluded that several of the firm's top executives were "grossly negligent" and

*(continued)*

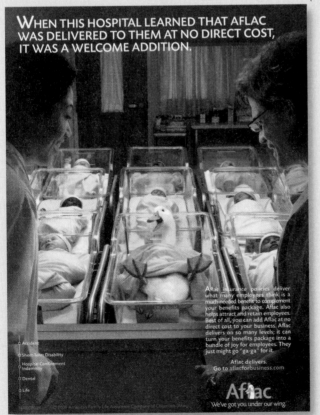

*Insurance company, Aflac, is consistently on lists produced by industry observers of respected and ethical companies.*

## Marketing Can Be Entrepreneurial

*Entrepreneurs Steve Jobs and Ed Catmull founded Pixar Studios, producers of* Toy Story; A Bug's Life; Monsters, Inc; *and* Wall-E.

Marketing plays a major role in the successes of numerous ventures initiated by entrepreneurs, people who organize, operate, and assume the risk of a new business venture.[45] Key to the success of many such entrepreneurs is that they identify and aim to satisfy unfilled needs. Some examples of successful ventures (and their founders) that understood their customers' unmet needs include:

- Ben & Jerry's (Ben Cohen and Jerry Greenfield).
- Amazon (Jeff Bezos).
- Netflix (Reed Hastings)
- Pixar Studios (Steve Jobs and Ed Catmull).
- *The Oprah Winfrey Show* and other ventures (Oprah Winfrey).

Steve Jobs is the cofounder, along with Ed Catmull, of Pixar Studios, a movie studio focused on cutting-edge, computer-animated films. The studio has been incredibly successful, most famously for *Toy Story* (all three of them); *A Bug's Life; Monsters, Inc.; Finding Nemo; Ratatouille;* the Best Picture Academy Award nominee *Up;* and *Wall-E.* The company has earned 24 Academy Awards in 24 years. But when a chasm opened between Pixar and its distributor Disney after a long and fruitful relationship, Disney executives learned just what kind of monetary value Pixar represented to their bottom line and acquired Pixar for $7.4 billion.[46]

Another extraordinary entrepreneur and marketer is Oprah Winfrey. A self-made billionaire before she turned 50, Oprah went from being the youngest person and first African-American woman to anchor news at WTVF-TV in Nashville, Tennessee, to being only the third woman in history to head her own production studio. Under the Oprah banner are a variety of successful endeavors including Harpo Films, Oprah's Book Club, Oprah.com, and the Oxygen television network. In addition to producing the two highest rated talk shows on TV, *The Oprah Winfrey Show* and *Dr. Phil*, Oprah's Harpo studio has produced acclaimed films such as *Beloved*. Oprah's philanthropic contributions are vast and varied. Through the Oprah Winfrey Foundation and Oprah's Angel Network, women around the world have raised over $50 million for scholarships, schools, women's shelters, and youth centers.[47]

These distinguished entrepreneurs had a vision of how certain combinations of products and services could satisfy unfilled needs. All understood the marketing opportunity (i.e., the unfilled need), conducted a thorough examination of the marketplace, and developed and communicated the value of their products and services to potential consumers.

*When you think of Oprah Winfrey, think big: Harpo Productions, Inc.; O, The Oprah Magazine; O at Home magazine; Harpo Films; the Oxygen television network; not to mention her philanthropic work with the Oprah Winfrey Foundation.*

## CHECK YOURSELF

1. List five functions that illustrate the importance of marketing.
2. A firm doing the right thing emphasizes the importance of marketing to _____.

## Summing Up

**L01**  **Define the role of marketing in organizations.**

Marketing is the activity, set of institutions, and processes for creating, capturing, communicating, delivering, and exchanging offerings that have value for customers, clients, partners, and society at large. Marketing strives to *create value* in many ways. If marketers are to succeed, their customers must believe that the firm's products and services are valuable; that is, they are worth more to the customers than they cost. Another important and closely related marketing role is to *capture value* of a product or service based on potential buyers' beliefs about its value. Marketers also enhance the value of products and services through various forms of *communication*, such as advertising and personal selling. Through communications, marketers educate and inform customers about the benefits of their products and services and thereby increase their perceived value. Marketers facilitate the *delivery of value* by making sure the right products and services are available when, where, and in the quanti-

ties their customers want. Better marketers are not concerned about just one transaction with their customers. They recognize the value of loyal customers and strive to develop *long-term relationships* with them.

**L02**  **List the elements of the marketing mix.**

The marketing mix commonly refers to the four Ps: product, price, place, and promotion. These marketing mix elements are the crucial controllable activities that a firm can use to influence their customers and/or respond to marketing opportunities.

**L03**  **Describe how marketers create value for a product or service.**

Value represents the relationship of benefits to costs. Firms can improve their offerings' value by increasing benefits, reducing costs, or both. The best firms integrate a value orientation into everything they do. If an activity doesn't increase benefits or reduce costs, it probably shouldn't occur. Firms become value driven by finding out as much as they can about their customers and those customers' needs and wants. They share this information with their partners, both up and down the supply chain, so the entire chain collectively can focus on the customer. The key to true value-based marketing is the ability to design products and services that achieve precisely the right balance between benefits and costs. Value-based marketers aren't necessarily worried about how much money they will make on the next sale. Instead, they are concerned with developing a lasting relationship with their customers so those customers return again and again.

**LO4**  **Understand why marketing is important both within and outside the firm.**

Successful firms integrate marketing throughout their organizations so that marketing activities coordinate with other functional areas such as product design, production, logistics, and human resources, enabling them to get the right product to the right customers at the right time. Marketing helps facilitate the smooth flow of goods through the supply chain, all the way from raw materials to the consumer. From a personal perspective, the marketing function facilitates your buying process and can support your career goals. Marketing also can be important for society through its embrace of solid, ethical business practices. Firms "do the right thing" when they sponsor charitable events, seek to reduce environmental impacts, and avoid unethical practices; such efforts endear the firm to customers. Finally, marketing is a cornerstone of entrepreneurship. Not only have many great companies been founded by outstanding marketers, but an entrepreneurial spirit pervades the marketing decisions of great firms of all sizes.

## Key Terms

- B2C (business-to-consumer), 12
- B2B (business-to-business), 12
- C2C (consumer-to-consumer), 12
- customer relationship management (CRM), 20
- employment marketing, 14
- entrepreneur, 26
- exchange, 7
- goods, 9
- ideas, 9
- marketing, 6
- marketing mix (four Ps), 8
- marketing plan, 6
- relational orientation, 20
- services, 9
- supply chain, 22
- transactional orientation, 20
- value, 15
- value cocreation, 17

## Marketing Applications

1. Do you know the difference between needs and wants? When firms wishing to sell mobile devices (e.g., iPad) develop their marketing strategy, do they concentrate on satisfying their customers' needs or wants? What about a utilities company, such as the local power company? A humanitarian agency, such as Doctors without Borders?

2. People can apply marketing principles to finding a job. If the person looking for a job is the product, describe the other three Ps.

3. One of your friends was recently watching TV and saw an advertisement that she liked. She said, "Wow, that was great marketing!" Was the ad in fact marketing?

4. Mercedes-Benz manufactures the Smart Car, which sells for around $16,000, and the SL 65 AMG 2-door

Roadster for over $100,000. Is Mercedes providing the target markets for these cars with a good value? Explain.

5. Assume you have been hired into the marketing department of a major consumer products manufacturer, such as Nike. You are having lunch with some new colleagues in other departments—finance, manufacturing, and logistics. They are arguing that the company could save millions of dollars if it just got rid of the marketing department. Develop an argument that would persuade them otherwise.

6. Why do marketers find it important to embrace societal needs and ethical business practices? Provide an example of a societal need or ethical business practice that a specific marketer is addressing.

## Quiz Yourself

1. The "Got Milk" advertising campaign was designed to help market a(n):
   a. individual.
   b. firm.
   c. industry.
   d. organization.

2. The evolution of marketing progressed along the continuum:
   a. sales, marketing, value-based marketing, production.
   b. marketing, value-based marketing, production, sales.
   c. value-based marketing, production, sales, marketing.
   d. production, sales, marketing, value-based marketing.

(Answers to these two questions can be found on page 607.)

Go to www.mhhe.com/grewal3e to practice by answering an additional 11 questions.

## Net Savvy

1. Visit Pandora (http://www.pandora.com/corporate/mgp), whose music database and customer knowledge are incomparable. Find out what the Music Genome Project is. What value does Pandora provide customers? What are the advantages and disadvantages to using Pandora versus listening to music through another channel?

2. Go to Facebook.com, and click on "About" at the bottom of the page, then click on the Info tab. What is Facebook's mission? How could a marketer use Facebook, and what other social media tools could they use? What are the drawbacks a marketer might face when using Facebook?

## Chapter Case Study

### IPAD LAUNCH

When Apple launched its new mobile tablet in April 2010, customers lined the sidewalks waiting for their chance to purchase the company's newest product. But this remarkable scene was nothing new for Apple's sales staff: The introductions of iPhone models have generated the same, if not more, excitement.

The mobile tablet is a totally new breed of electronic device though.[48] Combining many of the advantages of smartphones and laptop computers, Apple's version packs in the abilities to browse the Web, read and send e-mail, listen to music, watch HD movies and television shows, read ebooks, play games, and view photos, all into a machine that weighs less than any laptop but has a screen larger than any smartphone. And the screen is more than just big. With a wide viewing angle, high resolution, and advanced technology, it brings images to life, delivers crisp text, and takes gaming to a new level. The screen also replaces the need for mouse navigation and clicks. The user interacts directly with images through iPad's touch technology, literally bringing the power and resources of the Web to the user's fingertips. This touch technology also enables the tablet's on-screen keyboard, which is nearly full size.

To make its new product even more appealing to consumers, Apple loaded the iPad with a dozen applications that make it possible to run the more than 140,000 apps actually available at the App Store, including those purchased previously for an iPhone or iPod touch. Among the offerings are apps convenient for business travelers or students who need to produce formatted documents, presentations, and spreadsheets. Online Apple stores supply content, including more than 11 million songs, 50,000 television episodes, and 8,000 movies available through the iTunes Store, as well as electronic books to be found in the iBookstore. Any material downloaded to an iPad from these sites automatically syncs with the user's iTunes library and can also be synced with a desktop or laptop computer. The iPad even has a speaker and a microphone.[49]

Apple's new product thus poses a serious threat to the future of laptop computers, especially among users who are primarily interested in surfing the Web, e-mailing, gaming, listening to music, watching videos, viewing pictures, social networking, or creating and editing small spreadsheets or written documents. Also threatened are Amazon's Kindle and Barnes and Noble's Nook.

What's interesting about this threat though is that tablet computers have been launched before with little success, and the iPad lacks some popular features available on laptops, such as a WebCam and USB ports. Nevertheless, financial analysts have predicted robust sales,[50] and the company's shares hit an all-time high in the days before iPads hit the shelves.[51]

The new product created similar excitement for advertisers, who saw opportunities to reach consumers in more interesting and interactive ways. Ads operate within an application, so users can view or interact with an ad or even make a purchase without leaving the site they had been visiting.[52] Current ads use a variety of tactics, including copy, images, games, and videos, to increase the emotional appeal of the advertised products. For example, Nike's "Nike Football + Coach Edition" helps soccer coaches train athletes through training videos and virtual skirmishes with professional players. Some of the more adventuresome advertisers take advantage of the tablet's special features, such as an interactive function that allows users to mimic pouring a cup of coffee into a mug by turning the iPad.

Mobile advertising got off to a slow start, and the iPad, although promising, isn't a miracle cure any more than it is a guaranteed replacement for laptop computers and smartphones. Advertisers need to adapt their mobile advertising approach to make it suitable for the iPad.[53] The tablet lacks Flash video technology, so customers trying to access Web sites or ads built with Flash will run into difficulties, and the format and capabilities of the device are still new to advertisers. Rather than risk alienating potential customers with unattractive, distorted, or problem-laden advertising, companies are moving slowly to take advantage of all the possible features. Nor can marketers measure the success of a campaign using iPad, which has caused some companies to rely on more traditional advertising channels until a measurement method is available. Apple is expected to address these shortcomings, as well as add still more apps, over time.

Apple's earlier launches for the iPhone and iPod Touch revolutionized the way consumers connect to the Web via portable devices.[54] And then, just as competitors believed they were catching up, Apple upped the ante again with the iPad.[55] This level of innovation is key to Apple's success. Unlike its competitors, the company has retained its commitment to innovation despite growth, a commitment that makes a difference to its customers, its advertisers, and its shareholders.

## Questions

1.  With regard to the assertion (in the chapter's opening vignette) that Apple is a marketing company rather than a technology company, assess the launch of the iPad. Use both the information included in the case study and your own experience with Apple's marketing tactics to illustrate your discussion.

2.  Which features of the iPad create the most value for users? Which create the most value for Apple's partners (e.g., advertisers)?

3.  List the specific product and service elements contained within an iPad.

# Developing Marketing Strategies and a Marketing Plan

**P**eople can grab a cup of coffee virtually anywhere. Yet somehow Starbucks, Dunkin' Donuts, and McDonald's have turned this common beverage into a market offering worth pursuing. To accomplish this transformation, the three java giants have distinguished themselves using varied marketing strategies aimed at slightly different audiences. And thus the humble cup of coffee has become something much, much more.

**Starbucks.** The international empire of more than 16,500 stores in 49 countries that is Starbucks Coffee Company was based on the idea that enjoying a cup of coffee should be a social experience. Many stores have overstuffed chairs or patio seating, as well as Wi-Fi access and multiple electrical outlets for customers working on computers. Over time, in addition to its brewed coffee and espresso drinks, the company added premade breakfast sandwiches, lunch items, coffee-related merchandise and accessories, branded beverages (e.g., Tazo, Ethos Water),[1] and books, music, and films.

But the company has shifted away from its European café ethos, increasingly catering to coffee drinkers on the run. Fewer Starbucks customers linger over coffee in the store;[2] many take advantage of the store's drive-up windows. When the economy plunged, Starbucks customers found it harder to justify expensive coffee, which helped create the opening for Dunkin' Donuts and McDonald's. When these competitors rolled out their iced beverages, Starbucks was in the midst of a massive restructuring, designed to return it to its earlier, more successful business model.[3] To retain cold coffee customers, Starbucks improved its blended frappucino drinks by offering them with soy milk, decaffeinated, and with low-calorie syrups.

Starbucks elected not to slash its prices to compete with McDonald's and Dunkin' Donuts though; instead, it plans to create value for customers by reinventing its founding success formula that emulated a European café—great cup-at-a-time made coffee and a comfortable atmosphere. The company has also mounted a social

## LEARNING OBJECTIVES

**LO1** Define a marketing strategy.

**LO2** Describe the elements of a marketing plan.

**LO3** Analyze a marketing situation using SWOT analyses.

**LO4** Describe how a firm chooses which consumer group(s) to pursue with its marketing efforts.

**LO5** Outline the implementation of the marketing mix as a means to increase customer value.

**LO6** Summarize portfolio analysis and its use to evaluate marketing performance.

**LO7** Describe how firms grow their business.

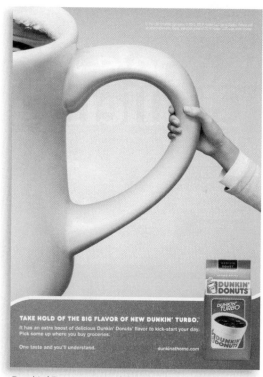

*Dunkin' Donuts appeals to the "average joe" who demands a variety of coffee options at conveniently located stores.*

*McDonald's is on the attack against both Dunkin' Donuts and Starbucks for their share of the coffee market.*

responsibility advertising campaign that reminds consumers of its humanitarian and outreach programs, asking them to consider not just the price of their coffee but also its global impact and cost.[4] In addition, the company constantly stresses that all coffee is not the same and that it uses the best beans.

**Dunkin' Donuts.** Dunkin' Donuts sells 52 varieties of donuts and other baked goods. But the majority of the company's profits now come from its coffee drinks, of which it sells approximately 1 billion each year. With its nearly 9,000 stores in 31 countries,[5] Dunkin' Donuts positions itself as the coffee spot for the "average Joe," those customers who need breakfast and a caffeine hit on their way to work rather than Wi-Fi and a sunny place to sit for hours. The chain further distinguishes itself by promoting its double-brewed coffee, which helps maintain the coffee flavor even when customers add milk, sugar, and ice.

Straddling this middle position between upscale coffee drinkers and those content to grab a cup at a convenience store, Dunkin' Donuts sells more than a dozen different coffee drinks, including flavored, iced, and blended beverages, but it also keeps its prices low. The company recently rolled out an iced dark roast that is bolder than other inexpensive coffees. The new blend is designed to appeal to men and attract the growing segment of coffee drinkers who want their coffee to taste like coffee, not like ice cream.

**McDonald's.** Known better for its Big Macs, McNuggets, and low prices, McDonald's Corp. is the most recent entrant into the coffee war. The company initiated its attack by improving its drip coffee and adding espresso drinks.[6] More recently, it has challenged Starbucks supremacy in the iced coffee drink market by introducing its own blended coffee drinks and fruit smoothies. This move came in response to the growing popularity of cold coffee drinks,[7] which deliver a healthy profit margin to vendors.

By offering its drinks below competitors' prices and in the more family-oriented atmosphere of its 32,000 stores in 117 countries,[8] McDonald's hopes to lure customers away from Starbucks and Dunkin' Donuts, as well as upsell some of its existing coffee-drinking clientele. It increased visibility for its new blended drinks by offering large fountain drinks for a dollar in the weeks around the introduction of the new beverages.[9] But McDonald's target audience in general is less educated and affluent than a typical Starbucks shopper, so the company has been careful not to appear too upscale, even as it offers drinks previously viewed as luxuries. In its advertising, McDonald's mainly portrays its McCafé drinks as a way to add fun to everyday life at an affordable price.[10]

In this chapter, we start by discussing a *marketing strategy*, which outlines the specific actions a firm intends to implement to appeal to potential customers. Then we discuss how to do a *marketing plan*, which provides a blueprint for implementing the marketing strategy. The chapter concludes with a discussion of strategies firms use to grow.

# WHAT IS A MARKETING STRATEGY?

**L01** Define a marketing strategy.

A marketing strategy identifies (1) a firm's target market(s), (2) a related marketing mix—its four Ps—and (3) the bases on which the firm plans to build a sustainable competitive advantage. A sustainable competitive advantage is an advantage over the competition that is not easily copied and thus can be maintained over a long period of time. A competitive advantage acts like a wall that the firm has built around its position in a market. This wall makes it hard for outside competitors to contact customers inside—otherwise known as the marketer's target market. Of course, if the marketer has built a wall around an attractive market, competitors will attempt to break down the wall. Over time, advantages will erode because of these competitive forces, but by building high, thick walls, marketers can sustain their advantage, minimize competitive pressure, and boost profits for a longer time. Thus, establishing a sustainable competitive advantage is key to long-term financial performance.

Starbucks, Dunkin' Donuts, and McDonald's appeal to different target markets, and they implement their marketing mixes (their four Ps) in very different ways. In essence, they have different marketing strategies. Although the chains' customers all seek a good cup of coffee and a pastry, Starbucks attempts to reach those who also want a coffee-drinking experience that includes a nice, warm, social atmosphere and personal "baristas" willing to make their esoteric drinks. For these benefits, people are willing to pay relatively high prices. Dunkin' Donuts' customers, in contrast, are not particularly interested in the experience. They want a good-tasting cup of coffee at a fair price, and they want to get in and out of the store quickly. Finally, McDonald's offers a fine quality cup of coffee at a relatively low price, but it adds the benefit of being available across the chain's massive retail network and providing a more extensive food menu from which to choose.

## Building a Sustainable Competitive Advantage

What about these different sellers' respective marketing mixes provides sustainable competitive advantages? After all, there are stores and restaurants that sell coffee and pastries in every neighborhood (not to mention coffeemakers in virtually every home) in which there is a Starbucks, McDonald's, or Dunkin' Donuts. Many of the alternatives offer great coffee and pastries. If one of the competitors lowered its prices, the others, as well as the additional competition in the area, would likely match the reduction. If one company introduced a peppermint swirl cappuccino for the holiday season, other stores in the area could do the same. Thus, just because a firm implements an element of the marketing mix better than the competition, it does not necessarily mean that the advantage is sustainable.

Establishing a competitive advantage means that the firm, in effect, builds a wall around its position in the market. When the wall is high, it will be hard for competitors outside the wall to enter the market and compete for the firm's target customers.

Over time, all advantages get eroded by competitive forces, but by building high, thick walls, firms can sustain their advantage, minimize competitive pressure, and boost profits for a longer time. Thus, establishing a sustainable competitive advantage is the key to positive long-term financial performance.

| **EXHIBIT 2.1** | Macro Strategies for Developing Customer Value |

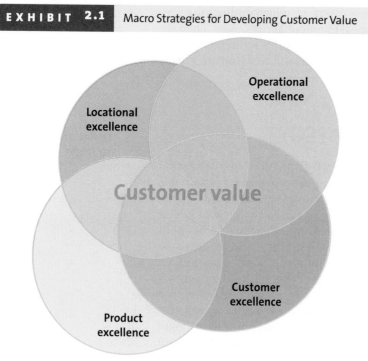

There are four macro, or overarching, strategies that focus on aspects of the marketing mix to create and deliver value and to develop sustainable competitive advantages, as we depict in Exhibit 2.1:[11]

- **Customer excellence:** Focuses on retaining loyal customers and excellent customer service.

- **Operational excellence:** Achieved through efficient operations and excellent supply chain and human resource management.

- **Product excellence:** Having products with high perceived value and effective branding and positioning.

- **Locational excellence:** Having a good physical location and Internet presence.

## Customer Excellence

**Customer excellence** is achieved when a firm develops value-based strategies for retaining loyal customers and provides outstanding customer service.

**Retaining Loyal Customers** Sometimes, the methods a firm uses to maintain a sustainable competitive advantage help attract and maintain loyal customers. For instance, having a strong brand, unique merchandise, and superior customer service all help solidify a loyal customer base. In addition, having loyal customers is, in and of itself, an important method of sustaining an advantage over competitors.

Loyalty is more than simply preferring to purchase from one firm instead of another.[12] It means that customers are reluctant to patronize competitive firms. For example, loyal customers continue to shop at Dunkin' Donuts even if Starbucks opens more convenient locations or provides a slightly superior assortment or slightly lower prices.

More and more firms realize the value of achieving customer excellence through focusing their strategy on retaining their loyal customers. Starbucks doesn't think in terms of selling a single cup of coffee for $2; instead, it focuses on satisfying the customer who spends $25 per week, 50 weeks a year, for 10 years or more. This customer isn't a $2 customer; he's a $12,500 customer. Viewing customers with a lifetime value perspective, rather than on a transaction-by-transaction basis, is key to modern customer retention programs.[13] We will examine how the lifetime value of a customer is calculated in Chapter 9, Appendix 9A.

Marketers use several methods to build customer loyalty. One such way involves developing a clear and precise positioning strategy. For instance, loyal Dunkin' Donuts patrons have such a strong attachment to its products that they would rather go without than go to McDonald's.

Another method of achieving customer loyalty creates an emotional attachment through loyalty programs.[14] These loyalty programs, which constitute part of an overall customer relationship management (CRM) program, prevail in many industries, from airlines to hotels to movie theaters to retail stores. With such programs, firms can identify members through the loyalty card or membership information the consumer provides when he or she makes a purchase. Using that purchase information, analysts determine which types of merchandise certain groups of customers are buying and thereby tailor their offerings to meet the needs of their loyal customers better. For instance, by analyzing their databases, banks develop profiles of customers who have defected in the past and use that information to identify customers who may defect in the future. Once it identifies these customers, the firm can implement special retention programs to keep them.

**Customer Service** Marketers also may build sustainable competitive advantage by offering excellent customer service,[15] though consistency in this area can prove difficult. Customer service is provided by employees, and invariably, humans are less consistent than machines. On every visit, for example, Starbucks must attempt to ensure that every single barista greets customers in a friendly way and makes drinks consistently. But what happens when a barista comes to work in a bad mood or simply forgets to add nutmeg to a drink? Firms that offer good customer service must instill its importance in their employees over a long period of time so that it becomes part of the organizational culture.

Although it may take considerable time and effort to build a reputation for customer service, once a marketer has earned a good service reputation, it can sustain this advantage for a long time, because a competitor is hard pressed to develop a comparable reputation. Superior Service 2.1 describes the superb customer service at Singapore Airlines.

## Superior Service 2.1 — Singapore Airlines Leads in Customer Satisfaction

As most U.S.-based airlines race for the bottom, in terms of both cost and customer service, Singapore Airlines continues to maintain its industry-leading levels of customer satisfaction on its international flights.[16] The airline's commitment to excellence has been an important part of its brand strategy since the company's inception.

In its early days, Singapore Airlines faced stiff competition. So the airline elected to position itself as a leader in technology, innovation, quality, and customer service. Over the ensuing decades, it has remained committed to that strategy, introducing such customer-friendly services as hot meals, free alcoholic and nonalcoholic drinks, scented hot towels, video-on-demand for all travelers, and personal entertainment systems. When other airlines imitate its ideas, Singapore Airlines develops new ones, such as a centralized, all-in-one business panel with in-seat power supply and USB ports; a 15.4-inch LCD screen in its video systems; and a seat that folds out fully to a flat bed for business class.[17]

Although the airline's cabin crew consists of both men and women, they are referred to as Singapore Girls.[18] The women dress in a signature sarong, created by a French haute-couture designer. All crew members receive rigorous training to ensure they maintain a peaceful and elegant cabin ambiance and caring service.

Staying ahead of the competition requires continual investment in innovation, a price Singapore Airlines is willing to pay to earn the significant rewards it seeks in the form of a loyal and motivated staff[19] and return customers. To remain competitive, the airline's financial structure accommodates innovation without passing any exorbitant costs on to consumers. With that kind of business sense, it's no wonder Singapore Airlines remains profitable even as other airlines struggle to survive.

*Singapore Airlines continues to provide new and innovative customer service offerings to stay ahead of its competition.*

*Some firms develop a sustainable competitive advantage through operational excellence with efficient operations and excellent supply chain management.*

*When Netflix receives DVDs from customers, they are immediately sorted and shipped to the next customer.*

## Operational Excellence

Firms achieve **operational excellence**, the second way to achieve a sustainable competitive advantage, through their efficient operations, excellent supply chain management, strong relationships with their suppliers, and excellent human resource management (which yields productive employees).

**Efficient Operations** All marketers strive for efficient operations to get their customers the merchandise they want, when they want it, in the required quantities, and at a lower delivered cost than that of their competitors. By so doing, they ensure good value to their customers, earn profitability for themselves, and satisfy their customers' needs. In addition, efficient operations enable firms either to provide their consumers with lower-priced merchandise or, even if their prices are not lower than those of the competition, to use the additional margin they earn to attract customers away from competitors by offering even better service, merchandise assortments, or visual presentations.

**Excellent Supply Chain Management and Strong Supplier Relations** Firms achieve efficiencies by developing sophisticated distribution and information systems as well as strong relationships with vendors. Like customer relationships, vendor relations must be developed over the long term and generally cannot be easily offset by a competitor.[20] Furthermore, firms with strong relationships may gain exclusive rights to (1) sell merchandise in a particular region, (2) obtain special terms of purchase that are not available to competitors, or (3) receive popular merchandise that may be in short supply.

The supply chain for Netflix represented a remarkable innovation when the company first started: With its 50 high-tech distribution centers, it can get movies to 97 percent of its subscribers overnight.[21] When the DVDs arrive back at its facilities, Netflix immediately sorts them for distribution to the next customer, and it sorts its mailed bundles by zip code so the U.S. Post Office doesn't have to do so—

which in turn earns Netflix a better shipping rate. The Case Study at the end of this chapter provides additional information about the methods Netflix has used to become a dominant player in the movie rental industry.

**Human Resource Management** Employees play a major role in the success of all firms. Those who interact with customers in providing services for customers are particularly important for building customer loyalty. Knowledgeable and skilled employees committed to the firm's objectives are critical assets that support the success of companies such as Southwest Airlines, Whole Foods, and The Container Store.[22]

JCPenney chairman and CEO Mike Ullman believes in the power of the employee for building a sustainable competitive advantage.[23] He has said, "The associates are the first customers we sell. If it doesn't ring true to them, it's impossible to communicate and inspire the customer." To build involvement and commitment among its employees, Penney's has dropped many of the traditional pretenses that defined an old-style hierarchical organization. For instance, at the Plano, Texas, corporate headquarters, all employees are on a first-name basis, have a flexible workweek, and may attend leadership workshops intended to build an executive team for the future.

## Product Excellence

**Product excellence**, the third way to achieve a sustainable competitive advantage, occurs by providing products with high perceived value and effective branding and positioning. Some firms have difficulty developing a competitive advantage through their merchandise and service offerings, especially if competitors can deliver similar products or services easily. However, others have been able to maintain their sustainable competitive advantage by investing in their brand itself; positioning their product or service using a clear, distinctive brand image; and constantly reinforcing that image through their merchandise, service, and promotion. For instance, *Business Week*'s top global brands—Coca-Cola, Microsoft, IBM, GE, Nokia, Toyota, Intel, McDonald's, Disney, and Mercedes—are all leaders in their respective industries, at least in part because they have strong brands and a clear position in the marketplace.[24]

For 3M, innovation is the central rule of its corporate culture; it spends approximately 6 percent of its sales on research and development.[25] Therefore, the company is well known for developing the first audio tapes, Scotchgard, Post-It Notes, and so on, and customers know they can turn to 3M to solve their needs. For example, for all those people who store their digital photographs on their computer and never print them, 3M offers Post-It Photo Paper that can be stuck to any surface for others to see.

*3M has always provided customer value through, among other things, product excellence by developing innovative products like Post-It Notes.*

## Locational Excellence

**Locational Excellence** is particularly important for retailers and service providers. Many say "The three most important things in retailing are location, location, location." For example, most people will not walk or drive very far when looking to buy a cup of coffee. A competitive advantage based on location is sustainable because it is not easily duplicated. Dunkin' Donuts and Starbucks have developed a strong competitive advantage with their location selection. They have such a high density of stores in some markets that it makes it very difficult for a competitor to enter a market and find good locations. But McDonald's did not need to worry about finding new locations when it entered the coffee battle; its stores already appear nearly everywhere!

## Multiple Sources of Advantage

Southwest consistently has positioned itself as a carrier that provides good service at a good value—customers get to their destination on time for a reasonable price without having to pay extra for checked luggage. At the same time, its customers know not to have extraordinary expectations. They don't expect food service or seat assignments. But they do expect—and even more important, get—on-time flights that are reasonably priced. By developing its unique capabilities in several areas, Southwest has built a very high wall around its position as the value player in the airline industry.

### CHECK YOURSELF

1. What are the various components of a marketing strategy?
2. List the four macro strategies that can help a firm develop a sustainable competitive advantage.

**LO2** Describe the elements of a marketing plan.

# THE MARKETING PLAN

Effective marketing doesn't just happen. By creating a *marketing plan,* firms like Starbucks, McDonald's, and Dunkin' Donuts carefully plan their marketing strategies to react to changes in the environment, the competition, and their customers. A marketing plan is a written document composed of an analysis of the current marketing situation, opportunities and threats for the firm, marketing objectives and strategy specified in terms of the four Ps, action programs, and projected or proforma income (and other financial) statements.[26] The three major phases of the marketing plan are planning, implementation, and control.[27]

Although most people do not have a written plan that outlines what they are planning to accomplish in the next year, and how they expect to do it, firms do need such a document. It is important that everyone involved in implementing the plan knows what the overall objectives for the firm are and how they are going to be met. Other stakeholders, such as investors and potential investors, also want to know what the firm plans to do. A written marketing plan also provides a reference point for evaluating whether or not the firm has met its objectives.

A marketing plan entails five steps, depicted in Exhibit 2.2. In Step 1 of the planning phase, marketing executives, in conjunction with other top managers, define the mission and/or vision of the business. For the second step, they evaluate the situation by assessing how various players, both in and outside the organization, affect the firm's potential for success (Step 2). In the implementation phase, marketing managers identify and evaluate different opportunities by engaging in a process known as segmentation, targeting, and positioning (STP) (Step 3). They then are responsible for implementing the marketing mix using the four Ps (Step 4). Finally, the control phase entails evaluating the performance of the marketing strategy using marketing metrics and taking any necessary corrective actions (Step 5).

As indicated in Exhibit 2.2, it is not always necessary to go through the entire process for every evaluation (Step 5). For instance, a firm could evaluate its performance in Step 5, then go directly to Step 2 to conduct a situation audit without redefining its overall mission.

We will first discuss each step involved in developing a marketing plan. Then we consider ways of analyzing a marketing situation, as well as identifying and evaluating marketing opportunities. We also examine some specific strategies marketers use to grow a business. Finally, we consider how the implementation of the marketing mix increases customer value. A sample marketing plan is provided in Appendix 2A, following this chapter.

**EXHIBIT 2.2**　The Marketing Plan

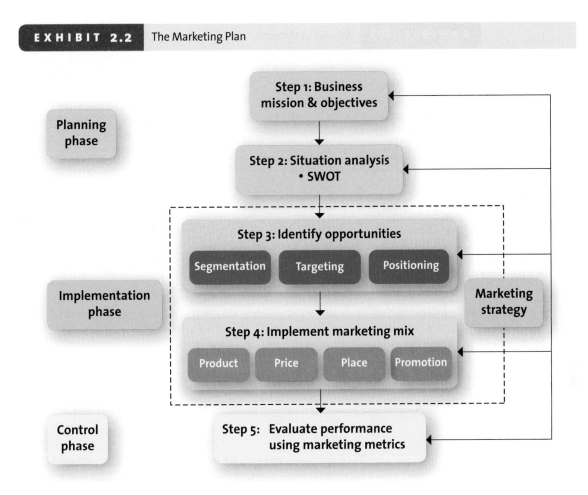

## Step 1: Define the Business Mission

The mission statement, a broad description of a firm's objectives and the scope of activities it plans to undertake,[28] attempts to answer two main questions: What type of business are we? What do we need to do to accomplish our goals and objectives? These fundamental business questions must be answered at the highest corporate levels before marketing executives can get involved. Most firms want to maximize stockholders' wealth by increasing the value of the firms' stock and paying dividends.[29] However, owners of small, privately held firms frequently have other objectives, such as achieving a specific level of income and avoiding risks. (See Exhibit 2.3 for several mission statement examples.) Nonprofit organizations instead have nonmonetary objectives, like eliminating drunk driving, encouraging research, or redressing educational inequities. In its mission statement, Starbucks explicitly recognizes that its quality coffee is as important as its impact on society.[30] Dunkin' Brands' mission statement is broader, to encompass both its Dunkin' Donuts and Baskin Robbins businesses. McDonald's has the most global mission, because its footprint is worldwide. For all these firms, marketing is primarily responsible for enhancing the value of the company's offering for its customers and other constituents, whether in pursuit of a profit or not. Another key goal or objective often embedded in a mission statement is how the firm is building a sustainable competitive advantage.

## Step 2: Conduct a Situation Analysis

After developing its mission, a firm should perform a situation analysis, using a SWOT analysis that assesses both the internal environment with regard to its

**LO3** Analyze a marketing situation using SWOT analysis.

> ### EXHIBIT 2.3    Mission Statements
>
> **MADD's** mission is to stop drunk driving, support the victims of this violent crime, and prevent underage drinking.
>
> **The Hudson Institute** is a nonpartisan policy research organization dedicated to innovative research and analysis that promotes global security, prosperity, and freedom.
>
> **Teach for America's** mission is to build the movement to eliminate educational inequity by enlisting our nation's most promising future leaders in the effort.
>
> **Starbucks** aims to inspire and nurture the human spirit—one person, one cup and one neighborhood at a time.
>
> **Dunkin' Brands'** mission is to lead and build great brands. For more than 50 years, we've been doing just that by leading the "Quick Quality" segment of the food and beverage industry. Dunkin' Brands goes beyond what people expect from a traditional quick service experience to deliver best-in-class menu items to eat, drink, and enjoy.
>
> **McDonald's** wants to "be our customers' favorite place and way to eat." Our worldwide operations have been aligned around a global strategy called the Plan to Win centering on the five basics of an exceptional customer experience—People, Products, Place, Price and Promotion. We are committed to improving our operations and enhancing our customers' experience.

Sources: http://www.madd.org/About-us/About-us/Mission-Statement.aspx; http://www.hudson.org/learn/index.cfm?fuseaction=mission statement; http://www.teachforamerica.org/mission/mission_and_approach.htm; http://www.starbucks.com/about-us/company-information/mission-statement;http://www.dunkinbrands.com/aboutus/; http://www.aboutmcdonalds.com/mcd/our_company/mcd_faq/student_research.html.

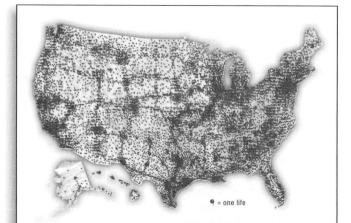

## If 17,000 people died tomorrow, would you notice?

Of course you would. There would be 24-hour news coverage. Dramatic headlines. And a devastating effect on our country forever. But last year, drinking and driving did kill about 17,000 people. It injured half a million more. But because it happened over a year rather than in a single day, most of us hardly noticed. It's a growing problem, with a simple answer. If you drink, find a safe way home. And help remove the marks that drunk driving leaves on our country.

*What is the mission for a non-profit organization like Mothers Against Drunk Driving (MADD)?*

Strengths and Weaknesses and the external environment in terms of its Opportunities and Threats. Additionally, it should assess the opportunities and uncertainties of the marketplace due to changes in Cultural, Demographic, Social, Technological, Economic, and Political forces (CDSTEP). These factors are discussed in more detail in Chapter 4. With this information, firms can anticipate and interpret change, so they can allocate appropriate resources.

Consider how a corporation like Starbucks might conduct a SWOT analysis, as outlined in Exhibit 2.4. Although our discussion focuses on Starbucks, marketing managers find it helpful to perform SWOT analyses for competing firms, like McDonald's and Dunkin' Donuts. Because a company's strengths (Exhibit 2.4, upper left) refer to the positive internal attributes of the firm, in this example we might include Starbucks' international reputation as a quality coffee purveyor. Furthermore, to sell its varied products, Starbucks can rely on its massive retail store network of 16,000 locations worldwide in 50 countries; five million customers per day visit Starbucks worldwide, and the average customer visits 12–15 times per month.[31] Beyond the stores, Starbucks licenses its brands to business partners that produce ready-to-drink products, such as Frappuccino® and Starbucks DoubleShot® drinks, and gourmet ice creams, which sell in grocery and convenience stores. These varied and plentiful retail locations represent a significant strength that the company can leverage to bring other products to market.

**EXHIBIT  2.4**  **SWOT Analysis for Starbucks, McDonald's, and Dunkin' Donuts**

|  |  | Environment | Evaluation |
|---|---|---|---|
|  |  | *Positive* | *Negative* |
| **Starbucks** | **Internal** | **Stengths** | **Weaknesses** |
|  |  | Strong brand identity | Reliance on joint ventures and licensed stores |
|  |  | Retail & grocery store network | Rapid growth erodes customer experience |
|  | **External** | **Opportunities** | **Threats** |
|  |  | Expansion in China | Potential saturation of the U.S. market |
| **McDonald's** | **Internal** | **Strengths** | **Weaknesses** |
|  |  | Strong brand identity | Sensitive to changing global markets |
|  |  | Global retail store network | Price elastic target market |
|  | **External** | **Opportunities** | **Threats** |
|  |  | New product categories | Future sourcing sustainability |
|  |  | Ronald McDonald house | Customers nonacceptance of McCafe |
| **Dunkin' Donuts** | **Internal** | **Strengths** | **Weaknesses** |
|  |  | Strong regional brand identity | Mass-market focused |
|  |  | Loyalty program | Franchise inconsistency |
|  | **External** | **Opportunities** | **Threats** |
|  |  | Retail store growth in the U.S. | Intense competition in the specialty and overall coffee market |
|  |  | Global retail expansion | Economic instability for franchisees |

Yet every firm has its weaknesses, and Starbucks is no exception. The weaknesses (Exhibit 2.4, upper right) are negative attributes of the firm. Starbucks' precipitous growth has called into question one of its original and primary benefits to consumers—the experience of watching their drinks being made by hand by a professional barista. Starbucks started grinding its espresso beans in advance and using automatic espresso machines, which adversely affected the store's ambiance and the coffee's flavor. It also added breakfast sandwiches, which many customers didn't like. Starbucks took decisive action to deal with these weaknesses by concentrating its training efforts on providing a more personal experience in the stores and tweaking some of its recipes.[32]

Opportunities (Exhibit 2.4, lower left) pertain to positive aspects of the external environment. Among Starbucks' many opportunities, the most significant may be its ability to build its current brand and businesses. In 2009, $110 million of Starbucks' $562 million in profits came from international business, and the huge, mostly untapped Chinese market offers a remarkable opportunity for enormous

*Starbucks' strengths include a strong brand identity and a retail store and grocery network.*

*Threats to Starbucks' marketing strategy and plan may include further downturns in the U.S. economy, potential adverse health effects of coffee, and increased competition.*

future growth.[33] Starbucks already has grown into an international brand but also has significant opportunities for much greater international expansion. In addition to such traditional growth, Starbucks continues to emphasize its social responsibility, including its support of fair-trade coffee and clean production conditions for coffee growers and beans. As the consumer environment appears poised to become even more "green," Starbucks' existing socially responsible practices may provide it an opportunity to appeal even more to environmentally conscious or green consumers.

Threats (Exhibit 2.4, lower right) represent the negative aspects of the company's external environment. For example, despite its expansion internationally, most Starbucks retail locations are in the United States, a market that some observers suggest may be close to saturation. If U.S. demand were to drop, whether because of economic conditions or shifts in the coffee market, Starbucks would be in real trouble. Starbucks also must keep abreast of any new research that suggests negative health effects from caffeine. Perhaps even more pressing, competitors such as Peet's Coffee and Caribou Coffee continue to pursue Starbucks' position as the market leader, while other outlets like Dunkin' Donuts and McDonald's offer similar products at lower prices.

 Describe how a firm chooses which consumer group(s) to pursue with its marketing efforts.

## Step 3: Identifying and Evaluating Opportunities Using STP (Segmentation, Targeting, and Positioning)

After completing the situation audit, the next step is to identify and evaluate opportunities for increasing sales and profits using STP (segmentation, targeting, and positioning). With STP, the firm first divides the marketplace into subgroups or segments, determines which of those segments it should pursue or target, and finally decides how it should position its products and services to best meet the needs of those chosen targets.

**Segmentation**  Many types of customers appear in any market, and most firms cannot satisfy everyone's needs. For instance, among Internet users, some do research online, some shop, some look for entertainment, and many may do all three. Each of these groups might be a market segment consisting of consumers who respond similarly to a firm's marketing efforts. The process of dividing the market into groups of customers with different needs, wants, or characteristics—who therefore might appreciate products or services geared especially for them—is called market segmentation.

Let's look at Hertz, the car rental company (see Exhibit 2.5). Some of the segments that Hertz targets include single people and couples wanting to have a bit of fun (Hertz's Fun Collection, including the Corvette ZHZ and Chevrolet Camaro); business customers and families who prefer a luxurious ride (its Prestige Collection, which features the Cadillac Escalade and Infiniti QX56); environmentally conscious customers (Green collection of cars such as the Toyota Prius and Ford Fusion); and families (SUV/Minivan collection). The company also offers commercial vans for service customers.[34] Thus, Hertz uses a variety of demographics—gender, age, income, interests—to identify customers who might want the Fun, Prestige, Green, and SUV/Minivan collections, but it also applies psychological or behavioral factors, such as a preference for style or a need to move possessions across town, to identify likely consumers of the Fun Collection and its commercial vans.

**Targeting**  After a firm has identified the various market segments it might pursue, it evaluates each segment's attractiveness and decides which to pursue using a process known as target marketing or targeting. From our previous example, Hertz realizes that its primary appeal for the SUV/Minivan collection centers on young families, so the bulk of its marketing efforts for this business is directed toward that group.

**EXHIBIT 2.5**  Hertz Market Segmentation

|  | **Segment 1** | **Segment 2** | **Segment 3** | **Segment 4** | **Segment 5** |
|---|---|---|---|---|---|
| **Segments** | single people and couples wanting to have a bit of fun | business customers and families who prefer a luxurious side | Environmentally conscious customers | Families | Commercial customers |
|  | Fun Collection | Prestige Collection | Green Collection | SUV/minivan & crossover | Commercial Van/Truck |
| **Cars Offered** | Corvette ZHZ | Infiniti QX56 | Toyota Prius | Toyota Rav 4 | Commercial Van/Truck |
|  | Chevrolet Camaro | Cadillac Escalade | Ford Fusion | Ford Explorer | Ford Cargo Van |

Soft drink manufacturers also divide their massive markets into submarkets or segments. Coca-Cola, for instance, makes several different types of Coke, including regular, Coke II, and Cherry Coke. Among its diet colas, it targets Coke Zero to men and Diet Coke to women, because men prefer not to be associated with diets. It also markets Sprite to those who don't like dark colas, Fruitopia and Minute Maid for more health-conscious consumers, and Dasani bottled water for purists.

**Positioning**  Finally, when the firm decides which segments to pursue, it must determine how it wants to be positioned within those segments.

**Market positioning** involves the process of defining the marketing mix variables so that target customers have a clear, distinctive, desirable understanding

*Hertz targets several markets. Its "Fun Collection" (left) appeals to single people and couples wanting to have fun; while its "Prestige Collection" (right) appeals to its business customers and families who prefer a luxurious ride.*

of what the product does or represents in comparison with competing products. Hertz positions itself as a quality car (and truck) rental company that is the first choice for each of its target segments. In its marketing communications, it stresses that customers will get peace of mind when they rent from Hertz, the market leader in the car rental business, and be able to enjoy their journey (e.g., leisure consumers) and reduce travel time (e.g., business consumers).[35]

To segment the coffee drinker market, Starbucks uses a variety of methods, including geography (e.g., college campuses versus shopping/business districts) and benefits (e.g., drinkers of caffeinated versus decaffeinated products). After determining which of those segments represent effective targets, Starbucks positions itself as a firm that develops a variety of products that match the wants and needs of the different market segments—espresso drinks, coffees, teas, bottled drinks, pastries, and cooler foods.

After identifying its target segments, a firm must evaluate each of its strategic opportunities. A method of examining which segments to pursue is described in the Growth Strategies section later in the chapter. Firms typically are most successful when they focus on opportunities that build on their strengths relative to those of their competition. In Step 4 of the marketing plan, the firm implements its marketing mix and allocates resources to different products and services.

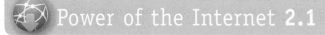

## Power of the Internet 2.1    Spreading Positive Self-Esteem Online

In its efforts to build "brand evangelists" for its products, Dove has attempted to harness the immense power of the Internet by engaging online customers deeply. Dove's mission statement reads "to make more women feel beautiful every day by widening stereotypical views of beauty," and its campaigns fit that ideal by spanning a broad spectrum of target markets. Let's consider a timeline of its efforts.

In 2003, the DOVE Campaign for Real Beauty began, developed in response to "The Real Truth About Beauty: A Global Report." This report demonstrated that popular beauty images in the United States were unattainable for most women. They prioritized thinness, youth, and blond hair, leaving little room for anyone who fell outside these borders.[36]

In 2006, Dove kicked off its online Real Beauty campaign by posting its "Evolution" video on YouTube. The campaign was one of the most successful viral marketing campaigns ever; the first day, it prompted 40,000 views, and then reached 1.7 million views in the first month.[37] The video demonstrated the distorted perception of beauty that resulted from advertising. In the online video, a model transforms from a normal-looking woman to a billboard pin-up after undergoing hours of makeup. Even then, the image on the billboard gets altered by Photoshop. The video ends with a tagline: "No wonder our perception of beauty is distorted."

In 2007, "Evolution" won one of the most prestigious advertising awards, the Grand Prix for viral marketing at Cannes.[38] According to Dove, it chose the Internet as its release platform for "Evolution" because it freed the advertising team from time constraints. The marketers wanted to run a spot that was 74 seconds long, and U.S. television sold advertising spots only in 30 or 60 second increments. Furthermore, through the Internet, Dove could connect directly with its customers.

In its ongoing marketing efforts, Dove attempts to keep customers engaged with its brand by updating the campaign

*Dove uses the Internet to promote the notion that beauty should not be defined by self-limiting stereotypes.*

but following the same mission. Online, Dove invites consumers to interact with the brand by making a "Self-Esteem bubble" that contains words and images that make them happy, take quizzes about their body image, upload videos, use online editing tools, and vote on one another's submissions. By talking about how to build self-esteem and recognizing the fallacies that exist in advertising images, Dove hopes to improve the self-esteem and lives of everyone.[39]

However, in one break from its mission statement, in 2010, Dove has added men to its target market. Its Dove Men+Care line pursues the segment of men who have not previously identified with male grooming products and its advertising in the past.[40]

Thus, Dove has figured out several ways to use the power of the Internet to connect with its core customers and create high-impact marketing events—and at a reasonable price.

With the growth of the Internet and the younger demographics of its core customer base, Unilever's Dove line of soaps and lotions has positioned itself to appeal to younger, more Internet-savvy, and more masculine target markets using innovative marketing campaigns. (See Power of the Internet 2.1.)

## Step 4: Implement Marketing Mix and Allocate Resources

When the firm has identified and evaluated different growth opportunities by performing an STP analysis, the real action begins. It has decided what to do, how to do it, and how many resources should be allocated to it. In the fourth step of the planning process, marketers implement the actual marketing mix—product, price, promotion, and place—for each product and service on the basis of what they believe their target markets will value. At the same time, they make important decisions about how they will allocate their scarce resources to their various products and services.

**L05** Outline the implementation of the marketing mix as a means to increase customer value.

*Amazon.com developed the first e-book reader, the Kindle, a product that has helped change the traditional book business and the way people read books forever.*

**Product and Value Creation** Products, which include services, constitute the first of the four Ps. Because the key to the success of any marketing program is the creation of value, firms attempt to develop products and services that customers perceive as valuable enough to buy. Amazon. com, for example, developed the first e-book reader, the Kindle, to enable customers to read anything they wanted to by downloading it onto this new mobile reading device.

We have alluded to 3M and its well-known research and development efforts. Adding Value 2.1 discusses how 3M creates value for its customers by creating new products for them.

**Price and Value Capture** Recall that the second element of the marketing mix is price. As part of the exchange process, a firm provides a product or a service, or some

---

### Adding Value 2.1  |  Innovation at 3M

When a company pours billions of dollars into research and development, a struggling economy is a serious problem. If profits fall, who has money for innovation, right? Not so for 3M. This longtime innovator cites a multipronged mission that includes satisfying customers with "innovative technology and superior quality, value, and service," as well as earning "the admiration of all those associated with 3M worldwide" (among other goals).[41] Its product offering spans an incredible range of categories, from health care and highway safety to office and pet care products.[42]

Because it remains constantly committed to providing useful, new solutions to its customers, 3M continues to reinvest a significant percentage of its revenues in research.[43] Furthermore, in line with 3M's commitment to "value and develop our employees' diverse talents, initiative, and leadership," it allows its researchers to spend time pursuing their own interests—some of science's most important discoveries occur during unrelated research, after all.

But these creative researchers cannot do it all on their own. An obvious but still rather uncommon approach to matching product development with customer needs is to involve customers in the process of innovation.[44] Corporate clients in particular are experts in their businesses; they know their demands better than anyone. By interacting with these expert customers and combining their needs with its own broad range of technical expertise and infrastructure, 3M produces novel solutions to difficult challenges.

Many of these interactions take place at the company's customer innovation centers, where visitors outline their business goals for 3M experts and tour the manufacturer's core technologies. Exposure to these technologies, 3M has learned, helps stimulate creative ideas about ways to combine or adapt existing science in one sector to provide solutions in another. A new technology in aerospace, for example, could lead to a breakthrough in health care. These innovation centers are so successful that 3M has opened nearly two dozen, and companies like Hershey and Pitney Bowes are following suit.

*Amazon's Kindle e-books provide its customers with a good value—what they get for what they have to pay for it.*

combination thereof, and in return, it gets money. Value-based marketing requires that firms charge a price that customers perceive as giving them a good value for the product they receive. Clearly, it is important for a firm to have a clear focus in terms of what products to sell, where to buy them, and what methods to use in selling them. But pricing is the only activity that actually brings in money by influencing revenues. If a price is set too high, it will not generate much volume. If a price is set too low, it may result in lower-than-necessary margins and profits. Therefore, price should be based on the value that the customer perceives. Amazon's Kindle comes in two sizes, the 6-inch display and the 9.7-inch display priced at $259 and $489, respectively. The larger Kindle has substantial more storage capacity.

**Place and Value Delivery**   For the third P, place, the firm must be able, after it has created value through a product and/or service, to make the product or service readily accessible when and where the customer wants it. Amazon.com sells its Kindle through its website and is now also selling it in Target so that customers can try it out before buying it.[45] As the e-reader market expands with many competitors including Barnes & Noble's Nook, Sony's e-reader, and Apple's iPad, all are available in bricks and mortar stores. All of the e-readers have their own e-bookstores where books, magazines, and newspapers are available for sale and then instantly downloadable.[46]

*Amazon promotes its Kindle e-book reader in advertisements like this to communicate its attributes and value to its customers.*

**Promotion and Value Communication**   The fourth and last P of the marketing mix is promotion. Marketers communicate the value of their offering, or the value proposition, to their customers through a variety of media including television, radio, magazines, sales forces, and the Internet.

Amazon currently has the largest e-bookstore (The Kindle Store), with over 500,000 titles for customers to choose from, a significant advantage worthy of promotion giving them a greater advantage from a pure reading point of view. Apple's iPad is the only e-reader that is also a multifunctional device with Internet browsing, application usability, e-mail, and the like. Each of the e-readers is marketing its advantages. Some are partnering with media companies to gain exclusive or early access to certain content.

Let's look at Starbucks' four Ps. It provides high quality coffee-based drinks and foods with good service to its customers. The drinks are priced from $2 to $5, and the pastries and sandwiches are $2 to $6. Starbucks stores are conveniently located near other retail stores and pedestrian traffic. Starbucks communicates its commitment to social responsibility and to providing customers high quality and excellent service via advertising and social media.

## Step 5: Evaluate Performance Using Marketing Metrics

The final step in the planning process includes evaluating the results of the strategy and implementation program using marketing metrics. A metric is a measuring system that quantifies a trend, dynamic, or characteristic. Metrics are used to explain why things happened, and to project the future. They make it possible to compare results across regions, strategic business units (SBUs), product lines, and time periods. The firm can determine why it achieved or did not achieve its performance goals with the help of these metrics. Understanding the causes of the performance, regardless of whether that performance exceeded, met, or fell below the firm's goals, enables firms to make appropriate adjustments.

Typically, managers begin by reviewing the implementation programs, and their analysis may indicate that the strategy (or even the mission statement) needs to be reconsidered. Problems can arise both when firms successfully implement poor strategies and when they poorly implement good strategies.

**Who Is Accountable for Performance?**  At each level of an organization, the business unit and its manager should be held accountable only for the revenues, expenses, and profits that they can control. Thus, expenses that affect several levels of the organization (such as the labor and capital expenses associated with operating a corporate headquarters) shouldn't be arbitrarily assigned to lower levels. In the case of a store, for example, it may be appropriate to evaluate performance objectives based on sales, sales associate productivity, and energy costs. If the corporate office lowers prices to get rid of merchandise and therefore profits suffer, then it's not fair to assess a store manager's performance based on the resulting decline in store profit.

Performance evaluations are used to pinpoint problem areas. Reasons performance may be above or below planned levels must be examined. Perhaps the managers involved in setting the objectives aren't very good at making estimates. If so, they may need to be trained in forecasting.

Actual performance may be different than the plan predicts because of circumstances beyond the manager's control—like a global recession. Assuming the recession wasn't predicted, or was more severe or lasted longer than anticipated, there are several relevant questions: How quickly were plans adjusted? How rapidly and appropriately were pricing and promotional policies modified? In short, did the manager react to salvage an adverse situation, or did those reactions worsen the situation?

**Performance Objectives and Metrics**  Many factors contribute to a firm's overall performance, which makes it hard to find a single metric to evaluate performance. One approach is to compare a firm's performance over time or to competing firms, using common financial metrics such as sales and profits. Another method of assessing performance is to view the firm's products or services as a portfolio. Depending on the firm's relative performance, the profits from some products or services are used to fuel growth for others.

**Financial Performance Metrics**  Some commonly used metrics to assess performance include revenues, or sales, and profits. For instance, sales are a global measure of a firm's activity level. However, a manager could easily increase sales by lowering prices, but the profit realized on that merchandise (gross margin) would suffer as a result. Clearly, an attempt to maximize one metric may lower another. Managers must therefore understand how their actions affect multiple performance metrics. It's usually unwise to use only one metric because it rarely tells the whole story.

| EXHIBIT 2.6 | Performance Metrics: Starbucks versus McDonald's | | | |
|---|---|---|---|---|
| | | **2008** | **2009** | **% Change** |
| **Starbucks**[47] | Net Sales | $10.4B | $9.8B | −9% |
| | Net Profit | $843M | $894M | 6% |
| | Net Profit/Net Sales | **8.1%** | **9%** | **0.9%** |
| **McDonald's**[48] | Net Sales | $23.5B | $22.7B | −3.5 |
| | Net Profit | $4.3B | $4.5B | 4.5% |
| | Net Profit/Net Sales | **18.2%** | **19.8%** | **1.6%** |

Note: Dunkin' Donuts is a private company so the sales and profits are unavailable.

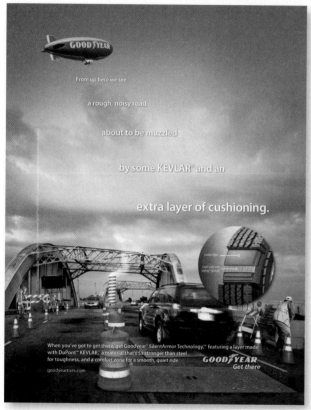

*Goodyear, one of the largest tire firms in the world, organizes its strategic business units by geography.*

In addition to assessing the absolute level of sales and profits, a firm may wish to measure the relative level of sales and profits. For example, a relative metric of sales or profits is their increase or decrease over the prior year. In addition, a firm may compare its growth in sales or profits relative to other benchmark companies (e.g., Coke may compare itself to Pepsi).

The metrics used to evaluate a firm vary depending on (1) the level of the organization at which the decision is made and (2) the resources the manager controls. For example, while the top executives of a firm have control over all of the firm's resources and resulting expenses, a regional sales manager has control only over the sales and expenses generated by his or her salespeople.

Let's look at Starbucks' sales revenue and profits (after taxes) and compare them with those of McDonald's (Exhibit 2.6). Clearly on the profits side, Starbucks is growing at the fastest pace (6 percent versus 4.5 percent for McDonald's). However, McDonald's profit as a percentage of sales is much higher (19.8 percent versus 9 percent). As this exhibit demonstrates, it is important to look simultaneously at multiple performance metrics.

Furthermore, as the collective corporate consciousness of the importance of social responsibility grows, firms are starting to report corporate social responsibility metrics in major areas, such as their impact on the environment, their ability to diversify their workforce, energy conservation initiatives, and their policies on protecting the human rights of their employees and the employees of their suppliers. Ethical and Societal Dilemma 2.1 examines how Starbucks is working to tackle important societal issues.

 **L06** Summarize portfolio analysis and its use to evaluate marketing performance.

**Portfolio Analysis** In portfolio analysis, management evaluates the firm's various products and businesses—its "portfolio"—and allocates resources according to which products are expected to be the most profitable for the firm in the future. Portfolio analysis is typically performed at the strategic business unit (SBU) or product line level of the firm, though managers also can use it to analyze brands or even individual items. An SBU is a division of the firm itself that can be managed and operated somewhat independently from other divisions and may have a different mission or objectives. For example, Goodyear is one of the largest tire firms in the world, selling its products on six continents in over 180 countries and with sales of over $16 billion. It has four SBUs that are organized by geography: North American Tire; Europe, Middle East, and African Tire; Latin American Tire; and Asia Pacific Tire.[49]

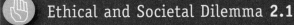

## Ethical and Societal Dilemma **2.1**

### Starbucks Working to Make the Earth a Better Place

To ensure it adds value to the broader society that makes up its macroenvironment, Starbucks rates its own corporate social responsibility performance in five categories: ethical sourcing, environment, community, wellness, and diversity.[50] Its brand equity improves in response to its proactive efforts along these socially responsible dimensions; customers feel good about their buying experience, and Starbucks develops stronger relationships with suppliers, both locally and globally.

With regard to its focus on ethical sourcing and sustainable coffee production, Starbucks maintains its C.A.F.E. (Coffee and Farmer Equity) program. The C.A.F.E. guidelines include a scorecard that rates coffee farmers according to their product quality, economic accountability, social responsibility, and environmental leadership. Third parties evaluate whether suppliers meet Starbucks' standards under the C.A.F.E. program. In just a few years, suppliers from 13 different countries gained C.A.F.E. approval. In turn, Starbucks increased the amount of coffee that it purchased from verified suppliers, from 77 percent to 81 percent, on its way to its goal of having "100% of our coffee certified or verified by an independent third party."

On a more local level, Starbucks sometimes experiences opposition from local communities that believe its stores will ruin the historical ambiance of an area. To take the needs of local communities into consideration, Starbucks attempts to address historic preservation, environmental, infrastructure, job, and urban revitalization concerns. For example, in La Mesa, California, Starbucks overcame opposition by supporting local events and businesses. In addition, it formed a joint venture with Johnson Development Corporation (JDC) to develop urban coffee opportunities. By opening in diverse urban areas, Starbucks helps stimulate economic growth in the areas by creating jobs, using local suppliers, and attracting other retailers to the area.

Starbucks has also launched a program that focuses on the needs of the more than 1 billion people globally who lack access to safe drinking water. On World Water Day, Starbucks sponsors three-mile walks in many cities, as well as a virtual online walk, to symbolize and raise awareness about the average distance that women and children walk to get drinking water each day. Starbucks' Ethos Water brand contributes 5 cents for each bottle of water sold in Starbucks stores to humanitarian water programs around the world, in countries such as Bangladesh, Ethiopia, and Kenya. Thus far, it has contributed $6 million to help solve the world's water crisis, thereby aiding approximately 420,000 people who lack consistent access.[51]

*(continued)*

*On World Water Day, Starbucks sponsored walks to symbolize and raise awareness about the average length that women and children walk to get drinking water each day.*

*(continued)*

Lack of water is not the only health worry facing people across the world. By posting nutrition information in its stores, Starbucks attempts to aid in the effort to reduce the prevalence of obesity and diabetes among it consumers. According to one report, communicating this information has prompted Starbucks customers to lower their calorie intake, but not their purchase amounts. In contrast, Dunkin' Donuts stores that post their nutrition information suffer significant losses in market share.[52]

To address the health and welfare of its own employees (whom the company calls "partners"), Starbucks not only offers generous health benefits packages but also has undertaken a Thrive Wellness Initiative (TWI) for its 145,000 partners.[53] The stated purpose of TWI is to care for the well-being of employees. For example, the newest portion of the TWI is Kinetix, a program that offers classes on nutrition and exercise, as well as eight weeks of sessions with a personal trainer.

Finally, just as it expects its coffee producers to engage in environmentally friendly practices, Starbucks itself attempts to use renewable energy and reduce its negative impact on the environment. Furniture and fixtures in stores are made of sustainable building materials. As a member of the Sustainable Packaging Coalition, Starbucks also works to replace conventional packaging with green alternatives.

A product line, in contrast, is a group of products that consumers may use together or perceive as similar in some way. One line of product for Goodyear could be car, van, SUV, and light truck while another line could be racing tires or aviation tires.

One of the most popular portfolio analysis methods, developed by the Boston Consulting Group (BCG), requires that firms classify all their products or services into a two-by-two matrix, as depicted in Exhibit 2.7.[54] The circles represent brands, and their sizes are in direct proportion to the brands' annual sales. The horizontal axis represents the relative market share.

**EXHIBIT 2.7**    Boston Consulting Group Product Portfolio Analysis

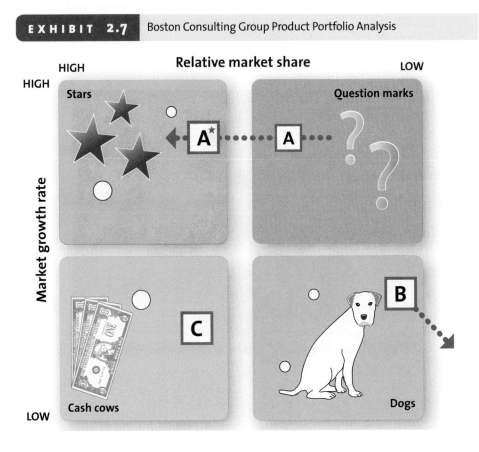

In general, market share is the percentage of a market accounted for by a specific entity[55] and is used to establish the product's strength in a particular market. It is usually discussed in units, revenue, or sales. A special type of market share metric, relative market share, is used in this application because it provides managers with a product's relative strength, compared to that of the largest firm in the industry.[56]

The vertical axis in the matrix in Exhibit 2.7 is the market growth rate, or the annual rate of growth of the specific market in which the product competes. Market growth rate thus measures how attractive a particular market is. Each quadrant has been named on the basis of the amount of resources it generates for and requires from the firm.

**Stars** Stars (upper left quadrant) occur in high-growth markets and are high market share products. That is, stars often require a heavy resource investment in such things as promotions and new production facilities to fuel their rapid growth. As their market growth slows, stars will migrate from heavy users of resources to heavy generators of resources and become cash cows.

**Cash Cows** Cash cows (lower left quadrant) are in low-growth markets but are high market share products. Because these products have already received heavy investments to develop their high market share, they have excess resources that can be spun off to those products that need it. For example, the firm may decide to use the excess resources generated by Brand C to fund products in the question mark quadrant.

**Question Marks** Question marks (upper right quadrant) appear in high-growth markets but have relatively low market shares; thus, they are often the most managerially intensive products in that they require significant resources to maintain and potentially increase their market share. Managers must decide whether to infuse question marks with resources generated by the cash cows, so that they can become stars, or withdraw resources and eventually phase out the products. Brand A, for instance, is currently a question mark, but by infusing it with resources, the firm hopes to turn it into a star.

**Dogs** Dogs (lower right quadrant) are in low-growth markets and have relatively low market shares. Although they may generate enough resources to sustain themselves, dogs are not destined for "stardom" and should be phased out unless they are needed to complement or boost the sales of another product or for competitive purposes. In the case depicted in Exhibit 2.7, the company has decided to stop making Brand B.

Although quite useful for conceptualizing the relative performance of products or services and using this information to allocate resources, the BCG approach, and others like it, is often difficult to implement in practice. In particular, it is difficult to measure both relative market share and industry growth. Furthermore, other measures easily could serve as substitutes to represent a product's competitive position and the market's relative attractiveness. Another issue for marketers is the potential self-fulfilling prophecy of placing a product or service into a quadrant. That is, suppose a product is classified as a dog though it has the potential of being a question mark. The firm might reduce support for the product and lose sales to the point that it abandons the product, which might have become profitable if provided with sufficient resources.

Because of these limitations, many firms have tempered their use of matrix approaches to achieve a more balanced approach to evaluating products and services and allocating their resources. Instead of assigning allocation decisions to the top levels of the organization, many firms start at lower management levels and employ checks and balances to force managers at each level of the organizational hierarchy to negotiate with those above and below them to reach their final decisions.

## Strategic Planning Is Not Sequential

The planning process as we have discussed it (refer again to Exhibit 2.2) suggests that managers follow a set sequence when they make strategic decisions. That is, after they've defined the business mission, they perform the situation analysis, identify strategic opportunities, evaluate alternatives, set objectives, allocate resources, develop the implementation plan, and, finally, evaluate their performance and make adjustments. But in practice, actual planning processes can move back and forth among these steps. For example, a situation analysis may uncover a logical alternative, even though this alternative might not be included in the mission statement, which would mean that the mission statement would need to be revised. The development of the implementation plan might reveal that insufficient resources have been allocated to a particular product for it to achieve its objective. In that case, the firm would need to either change the objective or increase the resources; alternatively, the marketer might consider not investing in the product at all.

Now that we have gone through the steps of the marketing plan, let's look at some growth strategies that have been responsible for making many marketing firms successful.

> ### CHECK YOURSELF
> 1. What are the five steps in creating a marketing plan?
> 2. What tool helps a marketer conduct a situation analysis?
> 3. What is STP?

**LO7** Describe how firms grow their business.

# GROWTH STRATEGIES

Firms consider pursuing various market segments as part of their overall growth strategies, which may include the four major strategies shown in Exhibit 2.8.[57] The rows in the exhibit distinguish those opportunities a firm possesses in its current markets from those it has in new markets, whereas the columns distinguish between the firm's current marketing offering and that of a new opportunity. Let's consider each of the strategies in detail.

**EXHIBIT 2.8**  Market/Product and Services Strategies

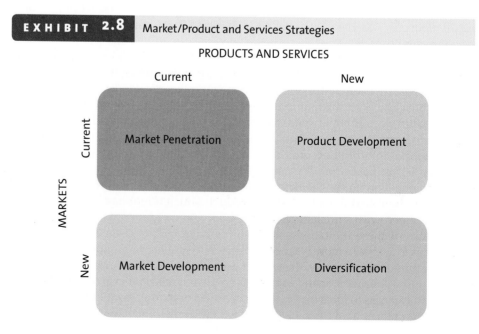

## Market Penetration

A market penetration strategy employs the existing marketing mix and focuses the firm's efforts on existing customers. Such a growth strategy might be achieved by attracting new consumers to the firm's current target market or encouraging current customers to patronize the firm more often or buy more merchandise on each visit. A market penetration strategy generally requires greater marketing efforts, such as increased advertising and additional sales and promotions, or intensified distribution efforts in geographic areas in which the product or service already is sold.

To penetrate its target market, TV network MTV found that it needed new ways to engage its viewers. The young audience to which MTV traditionally appeals now consists of text-messaging, video-gaming multitaskers who no longer accept plain video programming on their televisions. Thus, the network is working hard to develop additional strategies and outlets to retain viewers, as well as to encourage them to spend more time interacting with its content. MTV discovered that interactions with the audience through alternative channels increase ratings for the show. Therefore, in addition to producing and airing reality shows such as *The Hills*, MTV has a virtual community (virtual.mtv.com), in which fans of the show may create an avatar, shop to outfit that avatar, and design a "crib" in "Lauren Conrad's Design studio." By providing *The Hills* fans with a dedicated forum, blog, and activities, MTV encourages them to connect and debate about the drama between Heidi and Spencer, Kristin Cavallari and Brodie, and Audrina and Justin. Not only can viewers talk about the characters as if they were friends, but they can buy the products they wear and download the music played during the show.[58]

*MTV provides a dedicated forum and blog so fans can discuss* The Hills' *stars Kristin Cavallari and Lauren Bosworth.*

## Market Development

A market development strategy employs the existing marketing offering to reach new market segments, whether domestic or international. International expansion generally is riskier than domestic expansion because firms must deal with differences in government regulations, cultural traditions, supply chains, and language. However, many U.S. firms, including MTV, enjoy a competitive advantage in global markets—such as Mexico, Latin America, Europe, China, and Japan— because, especially among young people, American culture is widely emulated for consumer products.

For example, because of rising prosperity worldwide and rapidly increasing access to cable television that offers U.S. programming, fashion trends from the United States have spread to young people in emerging countries. Since its founding in 1981, MTV has expanded well beyond the United States, with niche sites in more than 20 countries, including the United Kingdom, Japan, Brazil, and India. It is available in 440 million households in 150 countries and 28 languages.[59] And thus, the global MTV generation prefers soft drinks to tea, athletic shoes to sandals, French fries to rice, and credit cards to cash. To achieve such growth, MTV leveraged its existing media content but also delivers culturally relevant content using local DJs and show formats.

*Using a product development growth strategy, MTV's The Hills' target market is attracted to new MTV programming and online blogs.*

## Product Development

The third growth strategy option, a product development strategy, offers a new product or service to a firm's current target market. Consider MTV's dynamic lineup: The network constantly develops new pilots and show concepts to increase the amount of time viewers can spend watching MTV. For example, each version of *The Real World* reality series, and new series such as *Jersey Shore* and *I'm Hustling the Hamptons*, represent new programs designed to attract and retain existing viewers. Along with its new TV series, MTV develops new online products to engage consumers through more than 25 niche blogs, as well as websites that it uses to dominate a greater share of viewers' minds and time. These various MTV-branded niche sites pertain to social, political, and environmental issues that appeal to different segments in its target market. The sites further encourage viewers to get involved in real-world issues (not *The Real World* issues), such as digital disrespect through mobile technologies. By visiting the sites, MTV promises that consumers can share mobile content, educate themselves, and take action on important issues.[60]

## Diversification

A diversification strategy, the last of the growth strategies from Exhibit 2.8, introduces a new product or service to a market segment that currently is not served. Diversification opportunities may be either related or unrelated. In a related diversification opportunity, the current target market and/or marketing mix shares something in common with the new opportunity.[61] In other words, the firm might be able to purchase from existing vendors, use the same distribution and/or management information system, or advertise in the same newspapers to target markets that are similar to their current consumers. MTV has pursued a related diversification by introducing TV series that focus, instead of on wealth, celebrities, and excessive youth culture (e.g., *The Hills, My Super Sweet 16*), on more positive social messages. Its new series, *The Buried Life*, still should appeal to viewers of *The Hills*, because it stars popular television celebrities. However, the plotlines of the show revolve around how these stars help underprivileged groups. Nick Lachey, formerly the lead character in *Newlyweds*, now appears on *Taking the Stage*, a reality series that considers the efforts and struggles of students in a performing arts school in Cincinnati.[62]

*MTV creates new shows by pursuing a related diversification strategy. The stars of* The Buried Life, *Ben Nemtim, Dave Lingwood, Duncan Penn, and Jonnie Penn, are already popular MTV celebrities.*

In contrast, in an unrelated diversification, the new business lacks any common elements with the present business. Unrelated diversifications do not capitalize on core strengths associated either with markets or with products. Thus, they would be viewed as being very risky. Revisiting our example of the technology innovation company 3M, we find an excellent and successful example of unrelated diversification strategies: what began as a sandpaper products company now markets its products in six major business segments, from consumer office supplies to orthodontic technologies.[63]

## CHECK YOURSELF

1. What are the four growth strategies?
2. What type of strategy is growing the business from existing customers?
3. Which strategy is the riskiest?

## Summing Up

**LO1** **Define a marketing strategy.**

A marketing strategy identifies (1) a firm's target markets(s), (2) a related marketing mix (four Ps), and (3) the bases on which the firm plans to build a sustainable competitive advantage. Firms use four macro strategies to build their sustainable competitive advantage. Customer excellence focuses on retaining loyal customers and excellent customer service. Operational excellence is achieved through efficient operations and excellent supply chain and human resource management. Product excellence entails having products with high perceived value and effective branding and positioning. Finally, locational excellence entails having a good physical location and Internet presence.

**LO2** **Describe the elements of a marketing plan.**

A marketing plan is composed of an analysis of the current marketing situation, its objectives, the strategy for the four Ps, and appropriate financial statements. A marketing plan represents the output of a three-phase process: planning, implementation, and control. The planning phase requires that managers define the firm's mission and vision and assess the firm's current situation. It helps answer the questions, "What business are we in now, and what do we intend to be in the future?" In the second phase, implementation, the firm specifies, in more operational terms, how it plans to implement its mission and vision. Specifically, to which customer groups does it wish to direct its marketing efforts, and how does it use its marketing mix to provide good value? Finally, in the control phase, the firm must evaluate its performance using appropriate metrics to determine what worked, what didn't, and how performance can be improved in the future.

**LO3** **Analyze a marketing situation using SWOT analyses.**

SWOT stands for strengths, weaknesses, opportunities, and threats. A SWOT analysis occurs during the second step in the strategic planning process, the situation analysis. By analyzing what the firm is good at (its strengths), where it could improve (its weaknesses), where in the marketplace it might excel (its opportunities), and what is happening in the marketplace that could harm the firm (its threats), managers can assess their firm's situation accurately and plan its strategy accordingly.

**LO4** **Describe how a firm chooses which consumer group(s) to pursue with its marketing efforts.**

Once a firm identifies different marketing opportunities, it must determine which are the best to pursue. To accomplish this task, marketers go through a segmentation, targeting, and positioning (STP) process. Firms segment various markets by dividing the total market into those groups of customers with different needs, wants, or characteristics who therefore might appreciate products or services geared especially toward them. After identifying the different segments, the firm goes after, or targets, certain groups on the basis of the firm's perceived ability to satisfy the needs of those groups better than competitors and profitably. To complete the STP process, firms position their products or services according to the marketing mix variables so that target customers have a clear, distinct, and desirable understanding of what the product or service does or represents relative to competing products or services.

**L05  Outline the implementation of the marketing mix as a means to increase customer value.**

The marketing mix consists of the four Ps—product, price, place, and promotion—and each P contributes to customer value. To provide value, the firm must offer a mix of products and services at prices their target markets will view as indicating good value. Thus, firms make trade-offs between the first two Ps, product and price, to give customers the best value. The third P, place, adds value by getting the appropriate products and services to customers when they want them and in the quantities they need. The last P, promotion, informs customers and helps them form a positive image about the firm and its products and services.

**L06  Summarize portfolio analysis and its use to evaluate marketing performance.**

Portfolio analysis is a management tool used to evaluate the firm's various products and businesses—its "portfolio"—and allocate resources according to which products are expected to be the most profitable for the firm in the future.

A popular portfolio analysis tool developed by the Boston Consulting Group classifies all products into four categories. The first, stars, are in high growth markets and have high market shares. The second, cash cows, are in low-growth markets, but have high market share. These products generate excess resources that can be spun off to products that need them. The third category, question marks, are in high-growth markets, but have relatively low market shares. These products often utilize the excess resources generated by the cash cows. The final category, dogs, are in low-growth markets and have relatively low market shares. These products are often phased out.

**L07  Describe how firms grow their business.**

Firms use four basic growth strategies: market penetration, market development, product development, and diversification. A market penetration strategy directs the firm's efforts toward existing customers and uses the present marketing mix. In other words, it attempts to get current customers to buy more. In a market development strategy, the firm uses its current marketing mix to appeal to new market segments, as might occur in international expansion. A product development growth strategy involves offering a new product or service to the firm's current target market. Finally, a diversification strategy takes place when a firm introduces a new product or service to a new customer segment. Sometimes a diversification strategy relates to the firm's current business, such as when a women's clothing manufacturer starts making and selling men's clothes, but a more risky strategy is when a firm diversifies into a completely unrelated business.

## Key Terms

- control phase, 40
- customer excellence, 36
- diversification strategy, 56
- implementation phase, 40
- locational excellence, 39
- market development strategy, 55
- market growth rate, 53
- market penetration strategy, 55
- market positioning, 45
- market segment, 44
- market segmentation, 44

- market share, 53
- marketing plan, 40
- marketing strategy, 35
- metric, 49
- mission statement, 41
- operational excellence, 38
- planning phase, 40
- product development strategy, 56
- product excellence, 39
- product line, 50
- products, 47

- related diversification, 56
- relative market share, 53
- situation analysis, 41
- STP, 44
- strategic business unit (SBU), 50
- sustainable competitive advantage, 35
- target marketing/targeting, 44
- unrelated diversification, 57

## Marketing Applications

1. How has MTV created a sustainable competitive advantage?

2. Perform a SWOT analysis for your college or university.

3. How does McDonald's segment its market? Describe the primary target markets for McDonald's. How does it position its various products and services so that they appeal to these different target markets?

4. Pick your favorite product, service provider, or retailer. How does it add value through the implementation of the four Ps?

5. Of the four growth strategies described in the chapter, which is the most risky? Which is the easiest to implement? Why?

6. Choose three companies. You believe the first builds customer value through product excellence, the second through operational excellence, and the third through customer excellence. Justify your answer.

7. You are on the job market and have received offers from three very different firms. Develop a marketing plan to help market yourself to prospective employers.

## Quiz Yourself

www.mhhe.com/grewal3e

1. In 2006, Ford Motor Company announced it would severely cut back automobile production. For parts companies supplying Ford Motor this represented a:
   a. weakness.
   b. opportunity.
   c. situational selling problem.
   d. threat.
   e. strategic business promotion efficiency.

2. Carla, a manager of a local coffee shop, in response to increased competition from Starbucks, has been directed by her regional marketing manager to cut prices on seasonal items, run an ad in the local paper, and tell distributors to reduce deliveries for the next month. Which stage of the strategic marketing planning process is Carla engaged in?
   a. Evaluate performance.
   b. Define the business mission.
   c. Situation analysis.
   d. Implement marketing mix and resources.
   e. Identify and evaluate opportunities.

(Answers to these two questions can be found on page 607.)

Go to www.mhhe.com/grewal3e to practice by answering an additional 11 questions.

## Toolkit

### SWOT ANALYSIS

Assume you are a marketing analyst for a major company and are trying to conduct a situation analysis using a SWOT analysis. Use the toolkit provided at www.mhhe.com/grewal3e to complete the SWOT grids for each company using the appropriate items.

## Net Savvy

1. The lines of food products produced under the Newman's Own and Newman's Own Organic labels align with the company's claims to engage in "Shameless Exploitation in Pursuit of the Common Good" (www.newmansown.com) and produce "Great Tasting Food That Happens to Be Organic" (www.newmansownorganics.com). Visit both sites and review the descriptions of the company, its mission, and its values. Discuss which aspects of its mission and values might be considered progressive. Does this progressive attitude create a special position for Newman's Own products in the market that contributes to a sustainable competitive advantage?

2. More and more firms seem to be entering the dating service industry. Visit www.eharmony.com and tour its website to find the types of activities and methods such companies use to help match compatible couples. Then visit www.match.com and do the same. What are the similarities and differences of these two online dating services? Pick one and perform a SWOT analysis for it.

## Chapter Case Study

### NETFLIX VERSUS BLOCKBUSTER AND THE VIDEO RENTAL INDUSTRY

Every evening, millions of Americans settle in to watch a video. Whether it's catching up on a missed episode of *The Wire*, checking out the Sundance Film Festival winners, viewing the latest blockbuster movie, or screening *Shrek* one more time for the kids, videos are our favorite form of entertainment. This pastime represents a multimillion-dollar industry for video rental agencies, which must find and retain their own customer base in the changing world of technology innovation and Internet commerce. These companies are in the same market, but they pursue different strategies.

**Blockbuster:** Blockbuster, Inc., initially followed the traditional video rental model and retains those roots. Brick-and-mortar stores, located in accessible and busy areas, stock between 1,000 and 3,000 titles in different genres and formats.[64] Members check out their selections in person and return the videos by the end of the rental period. Constrained by size, Blockbuster was unable to compete with online competitors offering over 100,000 titles,[65] so the company launched Blockbuster by Mail. For a monthly fee, members rent as many movies as they like, with up to three videos out at any given time. Movies are delivered and returned by mail, although membership options include the ability to exchange videos at store locations, which allows customers to peruse physical inventory and make last-minute decisions.[66] With this model, Blockbuster now matches Netflix's title offerings, and mail delivery time for both companies is the same.

To keep pace with technology advancements, Blockbuster moved into on-demand digital delivery of films. However, the company's pay-per-view price structure and limited number of supported devices (Blu-ray players and HDTVs) don't have the same customer appeal as Netflix's model, which includes unlimited streaming in its membership costs. An advantage for Blockbuster, however, is its first-run movie offerings.

Despite these efforts, Blockbuster has lost both earnings and market share. One difficulty the company faces is its late fees, which are not charged by competitors. Blockbuster eliminated these fees but later reinstated them, a move that has confused and irritated customers[67] but, perhaps, necessary for Blockbuster since these fees account for approximately 20 percent of revenues for traditional video rental stores. The company also suffers from publicity about its financial difficulties, including stories of store closings, disastrous earnings, and rumors of bankruptcy.[68]

**Netflix:** With no brick-and-mortar stores, Netflix relies on the Internet for customer orders and the mail system for disk delivery. The company's roughly 14 million subscribers[69] choose from flat-rate monthly subscription options that allow up to eight movies out at a time. No rental periods or late fees exist, and customers return videos using a pre-paid and pre-addressed envelope. Netflix automatically mails the next video on the customer's video queue according to the subscription terms. Queues can be updated whenever a customer chooses; underlying software makes recommendations based on customer choices and rankings. Netflix charges extra for Blu-Ray, which is included in Blockbuster plans.

The company's decision to let customers view unlimited streaming of movies and TV shows for a monthly fee is an important part of its marketing strategy. Although this service does not include recently aired television shows, the com-

| EXHIBIT 2.9 | Comparing Netflix, Blockbuster, and Comcast Cable Movie Rental Services |

| Monthly Plan | Netflix | Blockbuster by Mail | Netflix Blue-Ray DVDs ADD-on | Blockbuster Blue-Ray DVDs ADD-on | Blockbuster Total Access ADD-on | Comcast Cable |
|---|---|---|---|---|---|---|
| 1 DVD at a time (limit 2) | 4.99 | N/A | $1 | N/A | N/A | |
| 1 DVD out at a time | 8.99 | 8.99 | $2 | FREE | $3 | Starting at $29.99 per month for cable service |
| 2 DVDs out at a time | 13.99 | 13.99 | $3 | FREE | $3 | |
| 3 DVDs out at a time | 16.99 | 16.99 | $4 | FREE | $3 | |
| Unlimited streaming DVD | FREE | $2.99+ per download | FREE | | $2.99+ per download | $4.99–$9.99 per download |

pany's instant downloadable option is used by over 55 percent of its members.[70] To grow this delivery option, which Blockbuster was slow to tap, Netflix has developed platforms to deliver its titles to the Nintendo Wii, Xbox 360, PlayStation 3, and TiVo. The Wii alone expands Netflix's potential members by 30 million users. Netflix also supports decks from Panasonic, Insignia, and Seagate, and a number of Android and Apple mobile devices including the iPad.[71]

**Cable, Satellite, Telcos:** While streaming represents an area of potential growth for Netflix, it's also an arena where they face tough competition from satellite, cable, and telephone companies that deliver digital media. Unlike video rental competitors, these companies don't deal with physical media at all, which reduces their delivery costs and simplifies their supply chain.

With 16 million customers, DirecTV is the largest satellite television provider in the United States.[72] Customers rent one video at a time, making their selections from the Internet or a set-top box. Choices are beamed to the customer's home digital-video recorder via satellite and are available for viewing for up to two days. Rental fees are charged per movie rather than on a subscription basis. The company's most significant advantage is that it has negotiated contracts with major movie studios that will allow it to offer new movies without the 28-day black-out period required of Netflix. Additionally its streaming quality is better than that currently offered by Netflix.

Cable companies like Comcast Corp. are also targeting Netflix subscribers by increasing the number of offered titles and advertising how easy it is to rent a movie using a remote control rather than waiting for a mail delivery or driving to a video rental store. These companies may be well-positioned for the future, as physical media may go the way of VCRs. See Exhibit 2.9 to compare the different DVD rental options.

## Questions

1. Explain Netflix's marketing strategy. Can it sustain its competitive advantage? Why or why not?

2. Perform a SWOT analysis for Netflix. What are its biggest threats? Which opportunities should it pursue?

3. What is the best way for Netflix to grow its business? Justify your answer.

# 2A

# Writing a Marketing Plan

*Have a plan. Follow the plan, and you'll be surprised how successful you can be. Most people don't have a plan. That's why it's easy to beat most folks.*

—Paul "Bear" Bryant, football coach, University of Alabama

## WHY WRITE A MARKETING PLAN?[1]

As a student, you likely plan out much in your life—where to meet for dinner, how much time to spend studying for exams, which courses to take next semester, how to get home for winter break, and so on. Plans enable us to figure out where we want to go and how we might get there.

For a firm, the goal is not much different. Any company that wants to succeed (which means any firm whatsoever) needs to plan for a variety of contingencies, and marketing represents one of the most significant. A marketing plan—which we defined in Chapter 2 as a written document composed of an analysis of the current marketing situation, opportunities and threats for the firm, marketing objectives and strategy specified in terms of the four Ps, action programs, and projected or proforma income (and other financial) statements—enables marketing personnel and the firm as a whole to understand their own actions, the market in which they operate, their future direction, and the means to obtain support for new initiatives.[2]

Because these elements—internal activities, external environments, goals, and forms of support—differ for every firm, the marketing plan is different for each firm as well. However, several guidelines apply to marketing plans in general; this Appendix summarizes those points and offers an annotated example.

# MARKETING PLAN VERSUS BUSINESS PLAN

Of course, firms consider more than marketing when they make plans and therefore commonly develop business plans as well. Yet as this book highlights, marketing constitutes such an important element of business that business plans and marketing plans coincide in many ways.[3] Both marketing and business plans generally encompass

1. Executive summary.
2. Company overview.
3. Objectives or goals, usually according to strategic plan and focus.
4. Situation analysis.
5. Market/product/customer analysis.
6. Marketing strategy.
7. Financial projections.
8. Implementation plan.
9. Evaluation and control metrics.

However, a business plan also includes details about R&D and operations, and both may feature details about other key topics, depending on the focus of the company and the plan.

# STRUCTURE OF A MARKETING PLAN

This section briefly describes each of the elements of a marketing plan.[4]

## Executive Summary

The executive summary essentially tells the reader why he or she is reading this marketing plan—what changes require consideration, what new products need discussion, and so forth—and suggests possible actions to take in response to the information the plan contains.

## Company Overview

In this section, the plan provides a brief description of the company, including perhaps its mission statement, background, and competitive advantages.

## Objectives/Goals

This section offers more specifics about why readers are reading the marketing plan. What does the company want to achieve, both overall and with this particular marketing plan?

## Situation Analysis

Recall from Chapter 2 that a situation analysis generally relies on SWOT considerations; therefore, this section describes the strengths, weaknesses, opportunities, and threats facing the company.

## STP Analysis

The analysis proceeds by assessing the market in which the company functions, the products it currently offers or plans to offer in the future, and the characteristics of current or potential customers.

## Marketing Strategy

The marketing strategy may be very specific, especially if the plan pertains to, for example, a stable product in a familiar market, or it may be somewhat open to varied possibilities, such as when the firm plans to enter a new market with an innovative product.

## Financial Projections

On the basis of the knowledge already obtained, the marketing plan should provide possible developments and returns on the marketing investments outlined in the marketing strategy.

## Implementation Plan

This portion of the marketing plan includes the timing of promotional activities, when monitoring will take place, and how expansions likely will proceed.

## Evaluation Metrics and Control

The firm must have a means of assessing the marketing plan's recommendations; the marketing plan therefore must indicate the methods for undertaking this assessment, whether quantitatively or qualitatively.

## Appendix

The final section(s) offers additional information that might be of benefit, such as a list of key personnel, data limitations that may influence the findings, and suggestions of the plan, relevant legislation, and so forth.

# INFORMATION SOURCES[5]

When writing a marketing plan, you likely can turn to a variety of your firm's in-house information sources, including annual reports, previous marketing plans, published mission statements, and so on. In addition, various sources offer suggestions and examples that may provide you with direction and ideas. A reference librarian can help you find many of these sources, which likely are available through your university's library system.

- Knowthis.com—"a knowledge source for marketing"
  http://www.knowthis.com/tutorials/principles-of-marketing/how-to-write-a-marketing-plan/21.htm.
- Encyclopedia of American Industries—introduces industry structure; arranged by SIC and NAICS codes.
- Standard & Poor's NetAdvantage—surveys of more than 50 different industries, with financial data about companies in each industry.
- Investext Plus—brokerage house reports.
- IBISWorld—market research on thousands of industries; classified by NAICS code.
- Statistical Abstract of the United States—a vast variety of statistics on a wealth of topics.
- U.S. Bureau of the Census—detailed statistical data gathered every 10 years on all aspects of the U.S. population.
- County Business Patterns: U.S. Bureau of the Census—payroll and employee numbers for most NAICS codes.

- Consumer Expenditure Study: U.S. Bureau of Labor Statistics—income and expenditures by household, classified by various demographics.
- LifeStyle Market Analyst—lifestyle information about geographic areas, lifestyle interest groups, and age and income groups.
- Mediamark Reporter—information about demographics, lifestyles, product and brand usage, and advertising media preferences.
- Scarborough Arbitron—local market consumer information for various media in 75 local markets for consumer retail shopping behavior, product consumption, media usage, lifestyle behavior, and demographics.
- Simmons Study of Media and Markets—products and consumer characteristics; various media audiences and their characteristics.
- Sourcebook America—demographic data, including population, spending potential index, income, race, and *Tapestry* data, presented by state, county, DMA, and zip code, as well as business data by county and zip code.
- Rand McNally Commercial Atlas and Marketing Guide—maps and tables showing demographic, industrial, transportation, railroad, airline, and hospital data.
- "Survey of Buying Power," Sales and Marketing Management—current state, county, city, and town estimates of population by age, retail sales by store group, effective buying income, and buying power index.
- Annual & 10-K reports from *Thomson One Banker, Edgar,* and *LexisNexis*— business descriptions, product listings, distribution channels, possible impact of regulations and lawsuits, and discussions of strategic issues.
- MarketResearch.com Academic—market research reports on a variety of consumer products.
- Mintel Reports Database—market research reports focusing on consumer products, lifestyles, retailing, and international travel industry.

## LINGUISTIC AND VISUAL SUGGESTIONS

Again, recall that all marketing plans differ, because all firms differ. However, just as rules exist that dictate what makes for good writing, some rules or guidelines apply to all well-written marketing plans.

- Maintain a professional attitude in the writing and presentation.
- Keep descriptions and summaries concise. Get to the point.
- Use standard, edited English.
- Proofread the entire plan multiple times to catch grammatical, spelling, or other such errors that could dampen the professionalism of the writing.
- Adopt a businesslike tone; avoid flowery or jargon-filled writing.
- Employ direct, rather than passive, and present, rather than past, tense whenever possible (e.g., "We plan to achieve 30 percent growth in two years" rather than "The plan was that 30 percent growth would be achieved by the firm within two years").
- Be positive.
- Yet avoid meaningless superlatives (e.g., "Our goal is tremendous growth").
- Be specific; use quantitative information whenever possible.
- Insert graphics to convey important concepts succinctly, including photos, graphs, illustrations, and charts.
- However, avoid using so many visual elements that they clutter the plan.

- Lay out the plan clearly and logically.
- Organize sections logically, using multiple levels of headings, distinguished clearly by font differences (e.g., bold for first-level heads, italics for second-level heads).
- Consider the use of bullet points or numbered lists to emphasize important points.
- Exploit modern technology (e.g., graphics software, page layout software, laser printers) to ensure the plan looks professional.
- Adopt an appropriate font to make the text easy to read and visually appealing—avoid using anything smaller than 10-point font at a minimum.
- Avoid unusual or decorative fonts; stick with a common serif type to make the text easy to read.
- Consider binding the report with an attractive cover and clear title page.
- Generally aim for a plan that consists of 15–30 pages.

# PEOPLEAHEAD MARKETING PLAN ILLUSTRATION[6]

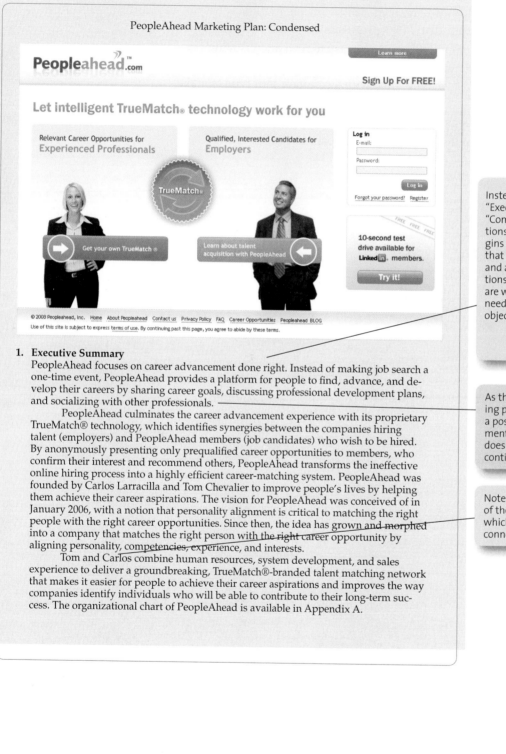

PeopleAhead Marketing Plan: Condensed

Instead of using separate "Executive Summary" and "Company Overview" sections, this marketing plan begins with a general overview that includes both aspects and answers the key questions: "What type of business are we?" and "What do we need to do to accomplish our objectives?" (see Chapter 2).

## 1. Executive Summary

PeopleAhead focuses on career advancement done right. Instead of making job search a one-time event, PeopleAhead provides a platform for people to find, advance, and develop their careers by sharing career goals, discussing professional development plans, and socializing with other professionals.

As this plan does, a marketing plan should start with a positive, upbeat assessment of what the company does and what it hopes to continue doing.

PeopleAhead culminates the career advancement experience with its proprietary TrueMatch® technology, which identifies synergies between the companies hiring talent (employers) and PeopleAhead members (job candidates) who wish to be hired. By anonymously presenting only prequalified career opportunities to members, who confirm their interest and recommend others, PeopleAhead transforms the ineffective online hiring process into a highly efficient career-matching system. PeopleAhead was founded by Carlos Larracilla and Tom Chevalier to improve people's lives by helping them achieve their career aspirations. The vision for PeopleAhead was conceived of in January 2006, with a notion that personality alignment is critical to matching the right people with the right career opportunities. Since then, the idea has grown and morphed into a company that matches the right person with the right career opportunity by aligning personality, competencies, experience, and interests.

Note the personalization of the company founders, which may help readers feel connected to the company.

Tom and Carlos combine human resources, system development, and sales experience to deliver a groundbreaking, TrueMatch®-branded talent matching network that makes it easier for people to achieve their career aspirations and improves the way companies identify individuals who will be able to contribute to their long-term success. The organizational chart of PeopleAhead is available in Appendix A.

## 2. Strategic Objectives

### 2.1. Mission

PeopleAhead's mission is to help individuals with career advancement and improve the human capital in companies. The site will act as a networking platform for professionals and career matching as opposed to job and resume-posting searches.

> The paragraph provides a general outline of the firm's objectives; the bulleted list offers more specific goals, and the subsequent sections go into more detail about the various factors that may influence these objectives.

### 2.2. Goals:

- Use brand matching technology: TrueMatch®
- Build critical mass of users.
- Drive traffic to the Web site through marketing blitzes.
- Utilize word-of-mouth advertising from satisfied users.

### 2.3. Business Summary

- *Business Customers:* This group provides PeopleAhead's revenues. Customers purchase contact information about the Top Ten PROfiles gleaned from the individual member base that have been sorted and ranked by the TrueMatch® technology. PeopleAhead will focus on small and medium businesses (see Market Segmentation section), because these entities are underserved by large competitors in the online recruitment market, and because research shows that this demographic has a less efficient recruitment process that would benefit most readily from PeopleAhead's services. Within this segment, customers include HR managers who are responsible for the sourcing of candidates, functional area managers who require new talent for their team, and executives whose business objectives rely on human capital and efficiency of operations.

> By referring to another section, the plan makes clear where it is heading and enables readers to cross-reference the information.

- *Individual Members:* This group does not pay for services but is the main source of data points for PeopleAhead's TrueMatch® system. PeopleAhead will focus on building a base of individual members who range from recent graduates to individuals with 5–7 years of continuous employment. Ideal members are those who are currently employed or will be graduating within nine months and are "poised" to make a career change. These individuals can utilize the services to the fullest extent and are valuable candidates for business customers.

> The plan acknowledges both a general, potential target market and the ideal targets.

### 2.4. Competitive Advantage

- *TrueMatch® offers a branded technology,* marketed to both business customers and individual candidates for its "black box" value proposition, which establishes PeopleAhead as the category leader for recruitment-matching software. This technology provides a point of differentiation from competitors, which may have technically similar matching software but constantly need to reinforce their marketing messages with explanations of their value proposition.

> As Chapter 2 suggests, the plan notes PeopleAhead's sustainable competitive advantage as part of its overall mission statement.

- *For individual candidates,* PeopleAhead will be the favored career advancement platform online, where individuals enthusiastically create a history and have connections (invited friends, coworkers, and mentors) in place that will make PeopleAhead a staple among their favorite Web sites. PeopleAhead delivers TrueMatch® career opportunities, professional development plans that let people establish a professional record, and valuable career advancement tools, including automatic position feedback, "recommend-a-friend," and team-based career networking.
- *For business customers,* PeopleAhead makes online sourcing and qualification of candidates quick and efficient by prequalifying potential candidates, seeking recommendations for hard-to-find individuals, and delivering only the Top 10 most highly

qualified candidates who have preconfirmed interest in the available position. PeopleAhead will be the most effective candidate-company matching platform available in the market, delivering prequalified, preconfirmed candidates.

3. Situation Analysis—Online Recruitment

Online recruitment is the system whereby companies use the Web to locate and qualify prospective candidates for available positions. The methods employed by online recruitment service providers to serve this market range from resume aggregation to assessment test application to linking strategies. However, the common underlying objective is to locate candidates who would not be found by traditional recruitment methods and use computing power to qualify candidates quickly and with more accuracy than would be possible manually.

**3.1. Industry Analysis**

Large online recruitment Web sites make this a tedious process by requiring companies to search through many resumes manually to find the "right" candidate. Other sites solicit recommendations for positions. However, resumes are often "enhanced," such that almost all candidates appear qualified, and information found in the resume or provided through a recommendation is simply not sufficient to make an educated hiring decision. Companies need more information and intelligent tools that make this screening process more accurate.

*3.1.1. Market Size:*

The market size for both member segments in 2005 was as follows:

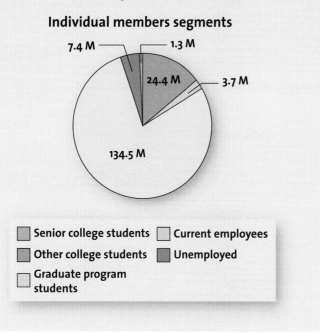

### Individual members segments

7.4 M — 1.3 M

24.4 M — 3.7 M

134.5 M

◼ Senior college students ◻ Current employees

◼ Other college students ◼ Unemployed

◻ Graduate program
students

In discussing both the external market and the internal advantages of PeopleAhead, the plan carefully distinguishes between individual job candidates and businesses, thus differentiating the focus and objectives according to this segmentation.

Figures provide a visually attractive break in the text and summarize a lot of information in an easy-to-read format.

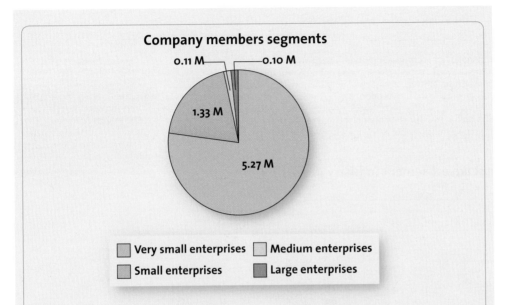

**Company members segments**

The most critical issue in examining market size is the relationship between the number of companies and the number of workers employed, because sales are based on the number of positions (profiles purchased), not the number of companies that use the service.

The following figure shows the number of people employed by each enterprise market segment as of January 2006, according to the U.S. Department of Labor. This segment information will be useful in defining PeopleAhead's target market.

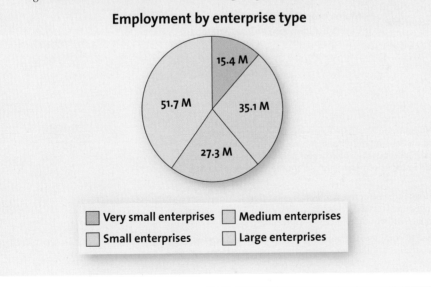

**Employment by enterprise type**

### 3.1.2. Market Growth

PeopleAhead will operate in the online recruitment market. The growth of this industry is subject to two primary constraints: U.S. economic health and online recruitment advertisement adoption rates. Understanding these constraints will help identify PeopleAhead's opportunity. General indicators suggest the U.S. economy (GDP) will grow at an average annual rate of 4% for the next decade.[7] Online recruitment advertising is expected to grow by 35% per year to reach $7.6 billion by 2010.[8] Not only is the market expanding, but it is exhibiting rapid adoption by new entities, as the following graph shows.[9]

**Recruitment advertisement industry growth**

Another visually attractive graph summarizes complicated information easily. The use of high-quality color can add a professional feel to a marketing plan.

### 3.1.3. Market Needs

- **The right person for the right position:** The right employee for one company or position is not the same for all others. Not only must companies locate intelligent individuals with relevant experience, but they also prefer people who are aligned with the position requirements in terms of personality, competencies, and fit with the company culture.

- **Prescreening qualification tools:** Increasing the number of candidates through online recruitment can be advantageous, but it can also be a hindrance. When sourcing candidates, recruiters need tools that help them qualify applicants.

- **Time savings:** Companies need to complete the online sourcing and qualification of candidates quickly. Leaving positions unfilled can cause critical performance gaps to emerge within the company.

### 3.1.4. Market Trends

The methods by which online recruitment service providers deliver candidates has been undergoing a migration from resume aggregation and search services like Monster and CareerBuilder to new Web 2.0 methodologies that include passive recruitment, "meta tagging," and social networking.

The underlying objective of these Web 2.0 services is to allow individuals to remain on a few, trusted Web sites while enabling companies to access those individuals for financial purposes. In parallel, the focus is moving from aggregation of unique visitors toward engaging existing users more intensively. Internet users are growing familiar with sites that encourage socializing, collaborating, and distributing private information online to help improve network benefits and need to be engaged to maintain contact.

Before engaging in a firm-specific SWOT analysis (see Chapter 2), this marketing plan assesses the external market environment further and thus establishes a basis for the subsequent SWOT analysis.

### 3.2. SWOT Analysis

Using a table and bullet points, the plan summarizes a lot of information succinctly and clearly.

|  | Positive | Negative |
|---|---|---|
| **Internal** | **STRENGTHS** | **WEAKNESSES** |
|  | • Industry best practices: The networking model used by PeopleAhead draws on the industry accepted "best practices" contact protocols drawn from multiple industries, including online feedback, recruitment, and social networking and offline professional networking. TrueMatch® software aligns business objectives with appropriate candidates.<br>• Team expertise: The combined talents of the founders include human resources, system development, sales, and marketing.<br>• Web development expertise: PeopleAhead has partnered with an award-winning European software development provider. This company provides quality usually reserved for high-budget projects, at terms that are favorable for a start-up company. | • Absence of industry "influentials": As a start-up, PeopleAhead does not currently have resources to attract influential industry managers.<br>• Inability to guarantee critical mass: As is true of many Internet companies, the business must solve the "chicken and egg" puzzle to build critical mass.<br>• Verifying efficiency of matching capabilities: In theory, the system has an absolute guarantee of effectivity; computations make decisions rather than humans. However, the matching capabilities must be verified as accurate to gain widespread acceptance.<br>• Broad target market: Because PeopleAhead is targeting a wide range of businesses, the product being developed has not been "customized" ideally for each segment. |
| **External** | **OPPORTUNITIES** | **THREATS** |
|  | • Service gap: Recruiters are not pleased with current online recruitment vendors.<br>• Industry gap: Job turnover is every 3.5 years per person.<br>• Demand for productive candidates.<br>• Online recruitment advertising: Growing by 35% per year, to reach $7.6 billion by 2010.[10] | • Convergence: existing competitors may form strategic alliances and establish powerful positions before PeopleAhead can establish itself.<br>• Inability to protect model: Very little intellectual property created by online Web sites is protected by law. Although PeopleAhead will |

Note that the analysis uses outside sources to support its claims.

*(continued)*

**External OPPORTUNITIES**

- Fragmented business models: Online recruitment is fragmented by recruitment methodology: active (people who need jobs), passive (people who are not looking but would move if enticed), poised (people unsatisfied with jobs they have), and network (finding people of interest based on who or what they know).

**THREATS**

pursue aggressive IP protection strategies, the model could be copied or mimicked by competitors.
- Inadequate differentiation: Inability to explain our differentiation would relegate PeopleAhead to (unfair) comparisons with competitors. Without differentiation, PeopleAhead will not be able to create scale through network effects.

### 3.3. Competition

Most online recruitment Web sites compete in the active recruitment market, including Monster, CareerBuilder, and Yahoo/HotJobs. The pervasive segment includes job seekers who actively look for jobs, post their resumes, and search for jobs on company Web sites. Most active recruiters offer free services to users and charge companies on a fee basis. Companies can post jobs and search for candidate resumes in the database (average fee for local searches is $500 and nationwide is $1,000). In this first-generation online recruitment business model, competitors face the challenge to make the process more user friendly and reduce the effort required to make these sites deliver results.

- **Monster:** Monster.com is the sixteenth most visited Web site in the United States, with more than 43 million professionals in its viewer base. Monster earns revenue from job postings, access to its resume database, and advertisements on Web sites of partner companies.
- **Careerbuilder:** Careerbuilder.com has experienced 75% growth for the past five years. This job post/resume search company uses its media ownership to attract "passive" candidates from partner Web sites. It achieves growth through affiliate partnerships that host job searches on affiliated Web pages, such as Google, MSN, AOL, USA Today, Earthlink, BellSouth, and CNN. Job posting is the primary activity, sold together with or separately from resume searches.
- **Passive Recruitment:** The second generation of online recruitment locates candidates who are not necessarily looking for jobs but who could be convinced to move to a new position if the right opportunity was presented. The most recognized competitors in this category include Jobster, LinkedIn, and H3 (Appendix B).

### 3.4. Company Analysis

PeopleAhead's mission is simple: improve people's lives through career advancement. PeopleAhead recognizes that career advancement means many things to many people and provides a fresh perspective on career networking that is flexible yet powerful:

- **Users are not alone:** Finding a job is not easy. Why search solo? PeopleAhead unites groups of friends, coworkers, and mentors to create natural, team-based career discovery.
- **Job posting is not natural:** People spend countless hours searching job listings and posting resumes, only to be overlooked because their writing style or resume format does not match an overburdened recruiter's preference. Good people make great companies, not resumes. PeopleAhead's TrueMatch® technology matches the right people with the right position. No posting, no applying—just good, quality matches.

---

If PeopleAhead chooses to adopt a competitor-based pricing strategy (see Chapter 13), detailed information about how other recruitment firms work will be mandatory.

Information about competitors' revenues, customers, growth, and so forth often is available publicly through a variety of sources.

For information that may not belong in the main text, an appendix offers an effective means to provide detail without distracting readers.

This section offers the "product" component of the market/product/customer analysis. Because PeopleAhead's product is mostly a service (see Chapter 12), it focuses on some intangible features of its offering.

- **Professionals being professionals:** There is a place online for social networking, pet networking, and music networking. So why is there no outlet for career networking online—the activity that consumes the majority of our professional lives? PeopleAhead is a place where professionals share their experiences, achievements and objectives with other professionals that care and can be found by employers who value their professionalism.

The last—and some would say most important—piece of the analysis puzzle: customers.

### 3.5. Customer Analysis

PeopleAhead's R&D efforts show that the impetus to improve recruitment effectivity is pervasive and that unmet needs revolve around a few core issues: the ability to find qualified talent, establishing a fit between the candidate and the company culture, verifying the candidate's career progression, and working quickly and cost effectively. The following customer characteristics represent ideal attributes that align with PeopleAhead's service offering. This information might be used in conjunction with the Marketing Strategy.

#### 3.5.1. Business Customer

- **Industry:** Because companies that value human capital are more likely to take a chance on a start-up that promotes professional development, the broadly defined professional services industry, including insurance, banking, and consulting, is the primary focus.
- **Functional area:** PeopleAhead's system identifies "people" people, so positions that require human interaction are more aligned with system capabilities than those with stringent skill requirements, sets such as programming or accounting.
- **Size:** Large businesses (>1000 employees) have high volume requirements and demand vendors with proven track records; small businesses (<25 employees) hire fewer people and may not justify acquisition costs. PeopleAhead aligns best with medium-sized customers.
- **Hiring need:** PeopleAhead serves two types of searches very well: those with too many applicants and those with too few applicants. By drawing applicants that most systems overlook and delivering only the most qualified applicants, the system assures the right candidate is identified quickly.

Although the introduction to this appendix and the plan's organization suggest that analyses of competitors, products, and customers are separate, as this plan shows, a firm usually cannot address one without considering the other. Here, in the "customer" section, the plan notes what its competitors fail to do and therefore why it offers a more valuable service.

#### 3.5.2. Individual Member

- **Background:** People who value professional development and are familiar with computer networking technologies; most are likely college educated, motivated by career success, and aware of their professional competencies/deficiencies.
- **Situation:** Members should have a professional development plan to share with others who can help them achieve their objectives—likely people who are inquisitive about their professional future and not content with their current situation. The common industry terminology for this group of people is "poised candidates."

  **Outlook:** Proactive people who research, plan, self-educate, and talk about their career. Probably the clearest example of proactivity is a student who devotes time, effort, and financial resources toward career advancement.

Understanding a target customer is not just about numbers. PeopleAhead tries to consider what customers think and feel when searching for jobs too.

4. Marketing Strategy

### 4.1. Market Segmentation

*4.1.1. Business Customers*

- **Small enterprises.** Businesses with 10–99 employees. Companies with less than 10 employees are categorized as "Very Small Enterprises" and will not be a primary target market.
- **Medium enterprises.** Businesses with 100–1,000 employees.

*4.1.2. Individual Members*

- **Senior college students.** Students in the process of searching for a first career.
- **Graduate program students.** Mid-career candidates searching for new career opportunities, such as internships, part-time during enrollment, or full-time after graduation.
- **Current employees.** Persons who are currently employed but are poised to locate better career opportunities.
- **Unemployed.** Persons searching for job not included in previous segments.

### 4.2. Target Market

PeopleAhead plans to focus resources on small to medium enterprises (SMEs) in the New England Metro market, including Boston, Providence, Hartford, Stamford, Norwalk, Worcester, and Springfield. Online recruitment companies compete for national recruitment spending, but most job seekers are locally based, so market penetration is possible by covering a single geographical location. By maintaining this focus, PeopleAhead will be better equipped to build a critical mass of users that represent the job-seeking population and thus improve both users' and customers' experience, customer service, and the use of financial resources.

### 4.3. User Positioning

To the proactive professional, PeopleAhead is career advancement done right—providing a platform to discover, plan, and advance careers by uniting friends, coworkers, and mentors with companies searching for the right talent.

5. Marketing Mix

### 5.1. Products/Services Offered

The first planned offering is **group profiling;** users self-associate with groups to share development plans. Access to groupings is permission based and similar to social networking. Members will be able to share professional experiences with people they know. Group profiling may prompt "voyeur" networking, such that members join to view the profiles of the people they know.

PeopleAhead will then open **group profiling to business customers,** who will be granted access to groups of members to target people they want to hire.

The next added feature will be **user feedback** on professional development plans. PeopleAhead will track data from successful member profile matches to provide feedback for members who have not been matched successfully.

---

*The plan continues with the same segmentation throughout. Here the plan discusses targeting and what makes each segment attractive.*

*By already identifying key markets in the previous section, the plan provides a foundation for a more specific targeting statement in this section.*

*The final step in the STP process: Positioning for the segmented, targeted market.*

*PeopleAhead's mission*

*Given its own section in this plan, a discussion of the marketing mix constitutes a key element of the strategic planning process (see Chapter 2).*

*According to well-known marketing concepts, the marketing mix consists of the four Ps: product (service here), price, place (distribution here), and promotion.*

*The product (service) offering must establish the value for consumers: Why should they expend effort or resources to obtain the offering?*

### 5.2. Price

In addition to a basic pricing schedule, PeopleAhead will offer bulk pricing and contract pricing to business customers to satisfy unique customer needs. The pricing model is expected to remain constant, but customer feedback will be analyzed to ensure alignment with their requirements.

Continuing the new customer acquisition plan, PeopleAhead will encourage new trials by offering promotional pricing to new customers.

### 5.3. Distribution

- **PeopleAhead Challenge:** The PeopleAhead Challenge will act as a primary user acquisition strategy. Selection will be focused on successful target segments demanded by customers.
- **Direct Sales:** Direct customer contact is the preferred method of communication during the first six months. Telesales is the anticipated eventual sales model, due to reduced costs and quicker customer sales cycle, but it limits intimacy between the customer and PeopleAhead. During the initial stages, intimacy and excellent customer service are more highly desired than reduced cost, and direct sales achieves that objective.
- **Industry Events:** Attendance at HR industry and recruitment events will supplement direct sales efforts.
- **Challenge Groups:** Word-of-mouth distribution by PeopleAhead members.

### 5.4. Promotion

- **Public Profiling:** When the product is ready, with proper precautions for protecting competitive advantages, PeopleAhead can increase its Web presence. Strategies include contributing articles to recruitment publishers, writing op/ed pieces, public profiling of the founders on Web sites like LinkedIn, Ziggs, and zoominfo, and blogging.
- **Blogger Community Testimonials:** Influential users of blogs will be invited to try the system and be granted "exclusive" access to the inner workings of the site. A subsequent linking blitz will put opinion pieces in front of recruiters, job seekers, and the investment community.
- **Strategic Alliances:** PeopleAhead offers a product that complements the services offered by many large organizations. Partner opportunities exist with
    a. Universities, colleges, academic institutions
    b. Professional associations, clubs, industry affiliation groups
    c. Online associations, groups, blogs
    d. Professional services firms, outplacement firms, and executive search firms

Strategic alliances serve multiple purposes: They can help PeopleAhead increase public exposure, increase the user base, expand product offerings, and increase revenue opportunities. These benefits will be considered and partnerships proposed prior to the official launch. For strategic purposes, PeopleAhead prefers to focus on product development in the near term (3 months) and then reassess potential alliances after system efficacy has been proven.

> Making the product (service) available where and when consumers want it may seem somewhat easier for PeopleAhead because of the vast development of the Internet; however, the firm still needs to consider how it can ensure people know where and how to access its offering.

> The plan offers a specific time frame, which recognizes the potential need to make changes in the future, as the market dictates.

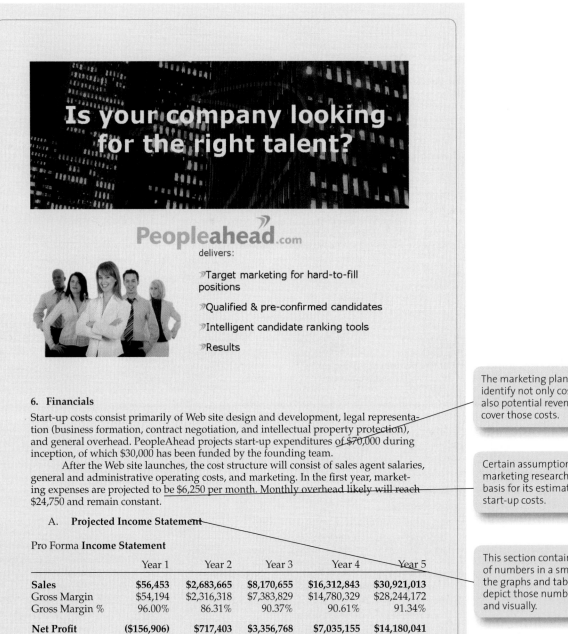

### 6. Financials

Start-up costs consist primarily of Web site design and development, legal representation (business formation, contract negotiation, and intellectual property protection), and general overhead. PeopleAhead projects start-up expenditures of $70,000 during inception, of which $30,000 has been funded by the founding team.

After the Web site launches, the cost structure will consist of sales agent salaries, general and administrative operating costs, and marketing. In the first year, marketing expenses are projected to be $6,250 per month. Monthly overhead likely will reach $24,750 and remain constant.

### A.  Projected Income Statement

Pro Forma **Income Statement**

|  | Year 1 | Year 2 | Year 3 | Year 4 | Year 5 |
|---|---|---|---|---|---|
| **Sales** | **$56,453** | **$2,683,665** | **$8,170,655** | **$16,312,843** | **$30,921,013** |
| Gross Margin | $54,194 | $2,316,318 | $7,383,829 | $14,780,329 | $28,244,172 |
| Gross Margin % | 96.00% | 86.31% | 90.37% | 90.61% | 91.34% |
| **Net Profit** | **($156,906)** | **$717,403** | **$3,356,768** | **$7,035,155** | **$14,180,041** |

The marketing plan needs to identify not only costs but also potential revenues to cover those costs.

Certain assumptions or marketing research form the basis for its estimation of start-up costs.

This section contains a lot of numbers in a small space; the graphs and tables help depict those numbers clearly and visually.

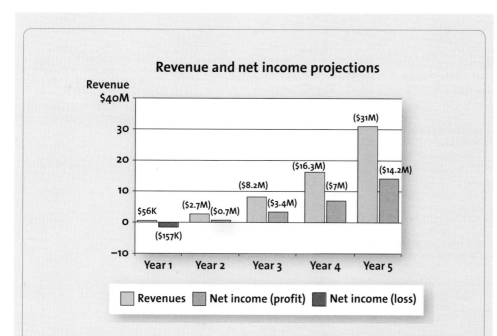

**Revenue and net income projections**

Revenue $40M

Legend: Revenues | Net income (profit) | Net income (loss)

Year 1: $56K, ($157K)
Year 2: ($2.7M), ($0.7M)
Year 3: ($8.2M), ($3.4M)
Year 4: ($16.3M), ($7M)
Year 5: ($31M), ($14.2M)

### 7. Implementation Plan

The launch of PeopleAhead will use a phased approach, beginning with building brand awareness. Brand awareness should be developed through the founders' visible presence at professional events, online searches, membership in professional associations, networking, and strategic alliances. This visibility will help gain investment capital.

#### 7.1. Objective—Growth

- During the first six months of commercial availability , the primary objective is to expand both the user and customer base to maintain a 100:1 user to customer ratio.

    - **Business Customers:** Sign 24 regular customers and 72 occasional customers. Execute 117 position matches.

    - **Individual Members:** Convert 10,000 people to PeopleAhead members.

#### 7.2. Marketing Objectives—Growth

- **PeopleAhead Challenge:** Pursue groups that were effective during Beta trial and represent a cohesive set of profiles. Expand and refine the Challenge to reflect lessons learned.

- **Increase member networking activity:** Increase user numbers through networking initiated by existing members. Improve user experience to promote networking.

- **Increase profile completeness:** Increase user engagement with platform.

- **Generate traffic.**

- **Public relations campaign (PR):** Increase awareness of PeopleAhead brand through concentrated PR efforts directed at the target market of customers and users.

> This plan divides the objectives into three categories: overall objective, marketing, and financial. Although this is a marketing plan, it must also include other aspects that influence marketing, such as financial status.

### 7.3. Financial Objectives

- **Efficient marketing expenditures:** 9,000 target users (10,000 year-end total – 1,000 during beta) × $5.00 target acquisition cost = $45,000 budget.
- **Revenue:** $482.50 per position × 117 positions = $56,452.50 revenue.

> By offering quantitative, direct goals, PeopleAhead ensures that it can measure its progress toward those goals.

### 7.4. Key Success Factors:

- **Economical marketing to relevant constituents:** PeopleAhead needs to establish communication (distribution) channels that pinpoint relevant constituents in a manner consistent with mission values. Limited by resources, chosen channels must aggregate many relevant eyes with free, minimal, or deferred costs involved.

- **Crafting of brand identity:** The contrast between PeopleAhead and competitors lies not only in product differentiation but also in the company's mission statement and delivery. One-time job search is available from thousands of online recruitment sources. Social networking has been covered from diverse angles, attracting many different audiences. The challenge is to associate www.PeopleAhead.com and True-Match® technology with "career advancement done right." The goal is to become the only company that a person thinks of for long-term career discovery, advancement, and development.

- **Efficient value delivery:** The base of customers (both individual and business) needs to receive the proposed value in a timely manner, with consideration given to quality versus quantity of results, alignment with existing objectives, and overall experience with the PeopleAhead brand.

- **Critical mass of business customers and individual users:** The matching process requires that both customers and users exist in the system from the outset of commercialization. This need brings to the forefront the "chicken and egg" scenario; establishing either customers or users requires the other constituent to exist already. The exact number that constitutes "critical mass" ranges from 100 users per position to 10 users per position, depending on compatibility between each constituency.

- **System effectivity:** The ability of PeopleAhead's TrueMatch® software to provide relevant candidate recommendations is critical. The effectiveness of the software depends on the algorithms that match users with positions and the networking protocol that initiates recommendations between users and the people they know. Proposing an inappropriate match could jeopardize the credibility of the system.

- **Intellectual property (IP) strategy:** PeopleAhead is engaged in two primary segments of online enterprise: online recruitment and social networking. Existing competitors have made many efforts to protect their methodologies through U.S. patents. However, precedent has not been established for the legal assertions made by these companies. As a result, PeopleAhead will assume an offensive IP strategy, consisting of diligent IP infringement review, patent application where appropriate, and aggressive trade secret protection of best practices.

- **Financial support:** The founders' investment is sufficient to form the business core and take delivery of PeopleAhead's Web site and software. Financial support will be required to fund operations, execute the IP strategy, and secure customers and users to meet financial targets. Without funding, PeopleAhead will not be able to proceed beyond the product development stage.

- **Sales process:** PeopleAhead's business model requires the acquisition of both business customers who have available positions and users who will be matched with those positions. These two constituents may be reached through different sales processes without overlap.

8.  **Evaluation & Control**

PeopleAhead will evaluate user profiles to identify sets of profiles that are valuable to new business customers, which will aid in the selection of subsequent target market customers.

*8.1. Business Customer*

Face-to-face meetings, phone conversations, and e-mail survey contacts with people from a range of industries, company sizes, and functional areas provide a means to (1) build relationships with prospective customers, (2) understand customer needs, and (3) ensure alignment between PeopleAhead's product and customers' recruitment preferences. A summary of the key findings is listed here:

- **Employee fit:** Will the applicant fit our corporate culture? Will the applicant fit with the team we're considering? Will the applicants' competencies fit with the position requirements?
- **Pay for performance:** Objections to recruitment services focus not on price (though it is a consideration) but rather on lack of performance.
- **Unqualified applicants:** Many people who want a job apply, whether they are qualified or not. Recruiters then must scan resumes and weed out unqualified applicants instead of getting to know the qualified applicants.
- **Hard costs vs. soft costs:** Most companies track the recruitment costs of hiring providers, but few measure the time costs of hiring, opportunity costs of hiring the wrong employee, or productivity costs of leaving a position unfilled. Recruitment performance must be easy to measure. Value selling is difficult in the human resources departments.
- **Valuable recommendations:** Most recruiters use online recruitment as a necessary but ineffective means of candidate sourcing, secondary to recommendations. Recommendations include the recommender's judgment of the candidate's fit with the available position.

*8.2. Individual Members*

Periodic surveys of various prospective users of online recruitment services indicate (1) current services, (2) methods that work well, and (3) biggest problems with online recruitment providers. The following is a qualitative summary of the key findings:

- **Willingness to try:** Careers are important to people; they are averse to spending time uploading resume information to online recruitment Web sites only because of the lack of perceived value. They will spend time when the career opportunities are perceived as valuable.
- **Frustration:** Job seekers are frustrated with available online recruitment providers. Networking is the favored method for career advancement.
- **Lack of differentiation:** Regardless of the qualifications a job seeker possesses, it is difficult to make them evident in a traditional resume.
- **Motivation shift over time:** Early professionals are motivated by financial rewards. Mid-career professionals recommend people because it helps the people they know. Late career professionals hope to improve their own job search opportunities.

**Appendix A. Organizational Chart of PeopleAhead**

**Appendix B. Competition: Passive Recruiters**

> The evaluation section retains the segmentation scheme established previously between business customers and individual members.

> Additional useful information that might clutter the plan should appear in an appendix, but is not included in this illustration.

# Marketing Ethics

**A**s heart disease and obesity increase in this country, consumers and advocacy groups lobby for healthier foods. In response, many states have banned trans fats, and fast-food and other chain restaurants with 20 or more locations are required to post calorie counts on menus, menu boards, and drive-throughs.[1] Fats, calories, sugars, and sugar substitutes have all come under attack. Now it's salt's turn as the Institute of Medicine challenges the Food and Drug Administration to regulate added salts.[2]

Legislation like this casts a negative light on food manufacturers, who are accused of lining their own pockets at the expense of the nation's health. The larger and more successful the company, the more likely it is to draw scrutiny and to make headlines if its practices are faulty. This situation creates challenges for marketers, who must offset negative publicity to protect the company's reputation.

Kellogg's, the world leader for cereal production and a major producer of snack foods, was singled out by the UK's food regulatory body and health groups for the amount of salt in its cereals.[3] Britons consume 43 percent more than the recommended salt limit; the country also has over 14,000 deaths annually attributable to high blood pressure, heart attacks, and strokes—diseases associated with high sodium intake. In response, the company, which posted over $1.2 billion in net income in 2009,[4] announced it is reducing salt in some of its cereals by up to one-third, eliminating an annual total of about 300 tons of salt from the country's diet.

As the story spread, Kellogg's sought to position itself as an industry leader rather than a scapegoat. In addition to agreeing to reduce salt, the company pointed out it has been gradually decreasing levels of the substance in its cereals for more than a decade.[5] Then Kellogg's took its message one step further, asking all breakfast cereal manufacturers in Europe to follow suit.

The request that competition join efforts to limit salt is more than a health initiative. With consumer taste buds accustomed to salty foods, Kellogg's fears they may lose customers if they are alone

## LEARNING OBJECTIVES

**LO1** Identify the ethical values marketers should embrace.

**LO2** Distinguish between ethics and social responsibility.

**LO3** Identify the four steps in ethical decision making.

**LO4** Describe how ethics can be integrated into a firm's marketing strategy.

**LO5** Describe the ways in which corporate social responsibility programs help various stakeholders.

in their sodium reduction efforts. Marketers, however, had found a way to transform a negative scenario into a positive one. Rather than trying to hide problems, they had recast them and embraced the media attention.

This approach is inherent in Kellogg's corporate messaging as well. As the company searches for tasty new formulations that, hopefully, don't involve increased sugar or sugar substitutes, it has joined the legions of companies that publish corporate responsibility reports. Kellogg's report lays out its efforts and its challenges, which include taste differences in different countries, consumer belief that "reduced salt" equals "reduced taste," and a lack of promising alternatives to salt. While some critics argue that a corporate responsibility report isn't a solution, these documents provide public acknowledgment of problems and document the steps the company is taking to address them.

● ● ●

Which is the more important corporate objective: making a profit or obtaining and keeping customers?[6] Although firms cannot stay in business without earning a profit, using profit as the sole guiding light for corporate action can lead to short-term decisions that cause the firm to lose customers in the long run. The balancing act may turn out to be the quest to place the company on the firmest footing possible.

This question leads into the primary ethical dilemma facing managers, that is, how to balance shareholder interests with the needs of society. In the Kellogg's example, managers resolved their balancing act by choosing to focus on the long-term societal benefits, potentially at the cost of short-term revenues.

In another well-known example, Mattel chose to export the production of more than 800 million of its most popular toys, including Barbie dolls, Matchbox cars, and Laughing Elmo, to China and apparently skimped on safety controls and design assurances.[7] Toys reported produced by one of Mattel's contractors had been subcontracted out to another factory that used lead paint, which can cause blood and brain disorders, especially in children. Although its initial choice appears to have been for short-term profits, Mattel also began a recall to pull all the harmful toys from the market, which implied a shift in its priorities.

*In one month, Mattel recalled more than 20 million potentially dangerous products.*

When customers believe they can no longer trust a company or that the company is not acting responsibly, they will no longer support that company by purchasing its products or services or investing in its stock. For marketers, the firm's ability to build and maintain consumer trust by conducting ethical transactions must be of paramount importance.

In this chapter, we start by examining what marketing ethics is and why behaving ethically is so important to successful marketing and to long-term profits. We then discuss how firms can create an ethical climate among employees, whose individual behavior can affect the ability of the firm to act ethically. To help you make ethical marketing decisions, we provide a framework for ethical decision making and then examine some ethical issues within the context of the marketing plan (from Chapter 2). Finally, we present some scenarios that highlight typical ethical challenges marketing managers often must face.

## THE SCOPE OF MARKETING ETHICS

Business ethics refers to the moral or ethical dilemmas that might arise in a business setting. Marketing ethics, in contrast, examines those ethical problems that are specific to the domain of marketing. Firms' attempts

to apply sound ethical principles must be a continuous and dynamic process.[8] The nearby cartoon illustrates the importance of making good ethical decisions. Because the marketing profession is often singled out among business disciplines as the root cause of a host of ethical lapses (e.g., unethical advertising, the promotion of shoddy products), anyone involved in marketing must recognize the ethical implications of their actions. These can involve societal issues, such as the sale of products or services that may damage the environment; global issues, such as the use of child labor (see Chapter 7 as well); and individual consumer issues, such as deceptive advertising[9] or the marketing of dangerous products.[10]

# ETHICAL ISSUES ASSOCIATED WITH MARKETING DECISIONS

Unlike other business functions such as accounting or finance, people in marketing interact directly with the public. Because they are in the public eye, it should not be surprising that marketing and sales professionals sometimes rank poorly in ratings of the most trusted professions. In a recent Gallup survey, most professions were rated much higher than marketing or advertising professions—though car salespeople came in last, advertising practitioners, insurance salespeople, and stockbrokers fared only slightly better, about the same as congresspeople[11] (see Exhibit 3.1). For marketers, who depend on the long-term trust of their customers, this low ranking is very disappointing.

Yet there is some good news too.[12] Although many consumers remain highly skeptical of business, and especially of marketing, the marketing function interacts with a vast number of entities outside the firm on a regular basis. Therefore, it has a tremendous opportunity to build public trust. Creating an ethical climate that establishes the health and well-being of consumers as the firm's number one priority just makes good business sense.

## Creating an Ethical Climate in the Workplace

The process of creating a strong ethical climate within a marketing firm (or in the marketing division of any firm) includes having a set of values that guides decision making and behavior, like Johnson & Johnson's Credo. General Robert Wood Johnson wrote and published the first "Credo" for Johnson & Johnson (J&J) in 1943[13]—a one-page document outlining the firm's commitments and responsibilities to its various stakeholders. The J&J Credo can be summarized as follows:

> We believe our first responsibility is to doctors, nurses, patients, mothers, fathers, and all others who use our products and services. We are responsible to our employees. We must respect their dignity and recognize their merit. Compensation must be fair and adequate and working conditions

| EXHIBIT 3.1 | Attitudes about Ethical Standards of Various Professions |

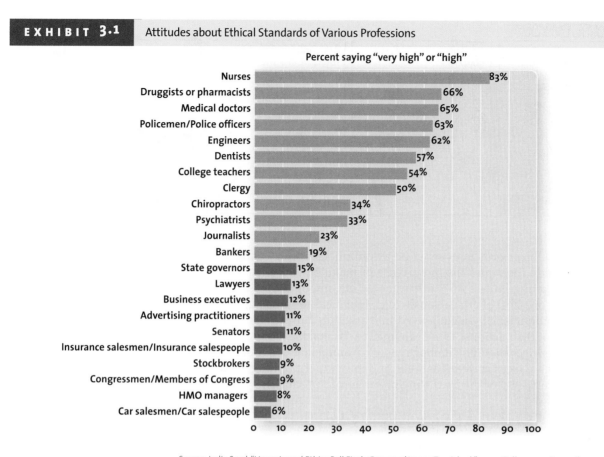

Percent saying "very high" or "high"

| Profession | Percent |
| --- | --- |
| Nurses | 83% |
| Druggists or pharmacists | 66% |
| Medical doctors | 65% |
| Policemen/Police officers | 63% |
| Engineers | 62% |
| Dentists | 57% |
| College teachers | 54% |
| Clergy | 50% |
| Chiropractors | 34% |
| Psychiatrists | 33% |
| Journalists | 23% |
| Bankers | 19% |
| State governors | 15% |
| Lawyers | 13% |
| Business executives | 12% |
| Advertising practitioners | 11% |
| Senators | 11% |
| Insurance salesmen/Insurance salespeople | 10% |
| Stockbrokers | 9% |
| Congressmen/Members of Congress | 9% |
| HMO managers | 8% |
| Car salesmen/Car salespeople | 6% |

Source: Lydia Saad, "Honesty and Ethics Poll Finds Congress' Image Tarnished," www.Gallup.com, December 9, 2009.

*Nurses and doctors are among the most trusted professionals.*

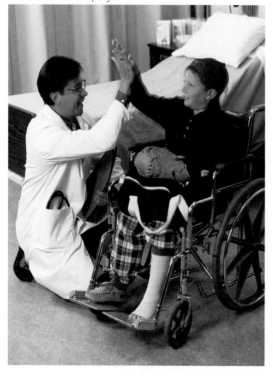

clean, orderly, and safe. We are responsible to the communities in which we live and work and to the world community as well. Our final responsibility is to our stockholders. When we operate according to these principles, the stockholders should realize a fair return.

Today, J&J continues to follow this credo in its daily business practices, as was evidenced by the infamous Tylenol recall. In the 1980s, seven people taking Tylenol died of cyanide poisoning. Without worrying initially about whether the poison got into the products during production or on the shelf, J&J immediately and voluntarily withdrew all Tylenol from the market until it could ensure its products' safety.

Even more recently, J&J responded to new limits on acetaminophen dosages (the active ingredient in Tylenol) by reassuring consumers that they were safe—as long as they followed the dosage instructions on the packaging.[14] In advertising communications that touted Tylenol as "the safest brand of pain reliever you can choose," J&J also was careful to remind people that taking more than the recommended dosage could cause them serious liver damage.

But not all firms operate according to the principles in J&J's Credo. For instance, Merck & Co. withdrew its highly successful drug Vioxx from the marketplace in 2004 because of evidence that it increased the chance of heart attacks and strokes in patients taking the drug.[15] The move came at least four years after studies showed that patients taking Vioxx had an increased incidence of cardiovascular problems compared to an older drug. Although

Merck continued to monitor these ongoing studies, it did not act nor did it initiate new studies. In another pharmaceutical example, AstraZeneca, the maker of the schizophrenia drug Seroquel, faced sanctions and fines for misrepresenting the appropriate uses of the drug to medical practitioners. Eventually, AstraZeneca agreed to pay $520 million to settle the claims of its unethical, "off-label" marketing efforts.[16] Would Merck and AstraZeneca have performed more ethically had they been working with J&J's Credo for ethical behavior?

Everyone within a firm must share the same understanding of its ethical values and how they translate into the business activities of the firm and must share a consistent language to discuss them. Once the values are understood, the firm must develop explicit rules and implicit understandings that govern all the firm's transactions. Top management must commit to establishing an ethical climate, and employees throughout the firm must be dedicated to that climate, because the roots of ethical conflict often are the competing values of individuals. Each individual holds his or her own set of values, and sometimes those values result in inner turmoil or even conflicts between employees. For instance, a salesperson may believe that it is important to make a sale because her family depends on her for support, but at the same time, she may feel that the product she is selling is not appropriate for a particular customer. Once the rules are in place, there must be a system of controls that helps resolve such dilemmas and rewards appropriate behavior—that is, behavior consistent with the firm's values—and punishes inappropriate behavior.

Many professions, including marketing, have their own codes of ethics that firms and individuals in the profession agree to abide by. The generally accepted code in marketing, developed by the American Marketing Association (see Exhibit 3.2), flows from universal norms of conduct to the specific values to which marketers should aspire.[17] Each subarea within marketing, such as marketing research, advertising, pricing, and so forth, has its own code of ethics that deals with the specific issues that arise when conducting business in those areas.

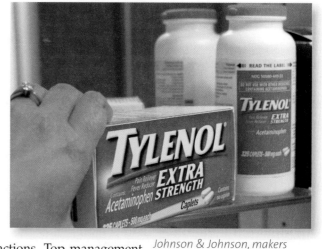

*Johnson & Johnson, makers of Tylenol, continues to live up to its credo that outlines its commitments and responsibilities to its shareholders. It recently responded to new limits on Tylenol's active ingredient by reassuring customers that they were safe as long as they followed dosage instructions.*

**LO1**　Identify the ethical values marketers should embrace.

*It is not always clear why people act unethically and sometimes illegally, but when they do, many people may be harmed. Here, file boxes are hauled to the federal courthouse for the fraud and conspiracy trial of former Enron executives.*

**Ethical Norms and Values for Marketers**

**PREAMBLE**

The American Marketing Association commits itself to promoting the highest standard of professional ethical norms and values for its members (practitioners, academics and students). Norms are established standards of conduct that are expected and maintained by society and/or professional organizations. Values represent the collective conception of what communities find desirable, important and morally proper. Values also serve as the criteria for evaluating our own personal actions and the actions of others. As marketers, we recognize that we not only serve our organizations but also act as stewards of society in creating, facilitating and executing the transactions that are part of the greater economy. In this role, marketers are expected to embrace the highest professional ethical norms and the ethical values implied by our responsibility toward multiple stakeholders (e.g., customers, employees, investors, peers, channel members, regulators and the host community).

**ETHICAL NORMS**

As Marketers, we must:

- **Do no harm.** This means consciously avoiding harmful actions or omissions by embodying high ethical standards and adhering to all applicable laws and regulations in the choices we make.
- **Foster trust in the marketing system.** This means striving for good faith and fair dealing so as to contribute toward the efficacy of the exchange process as well as avoiding deception in product design, pricing, communication, and delivery of distribution.
- **Embrace ethical values.** This means building relationships and enhancing consumer confidence in the integrity of marketing by affirming these core values: honesty, responsibility, fairness, respect, transparency and citizenship.

**ETHICAL VALUES**

**Honesty**—to be forthright in dealings with customers and stakeholders. To this end, we will:

- Strive to be truthful in all situations and at all times.
- Offer products of value that do what we claim in our communications.
- Stand behind our products if they fail to deliver their claimed benefits.
- Honor our explicit and implicit commitments and promises.

**Responsibility**—to accept the consequences of our marketing decisions and strategies. To this end, we will:

- Strive to serve the needs of customers.
- Avoid using coercion with all stakeholders.
- Acknowledge the social obligations to stakeholders that come with increased marketing and economic power.
- Recognize our special commitments to vulnerable market segments such as children, seniors, the economically impoverished, market illiterates and others who may be substantially disadvantaged.
- Consider environmental stewardship in our decision-making.

*(continued)*

Now let's examine the ethical role of the individuals within the firm and how individuals contribute to the firm's ethical climate.

## The Influence of Personal Ethics

Every firm is made up of individuals, each with his or her own needs and desires. Let's start by looking at why people may make *un*ethical decisions and how firms can establish a process for decision making that ensures they choose ethical alternatives instead.

**Why People Act Unethically** Every individual is a product of his or her culture, upbringing, genes, and various other influences. In spite of these factors, however, people do continue to grow emotionally in their understanding of what is and is not ethical behavior. As a six-year-old child, you might have thought nothing of taking your brother's toy and bonking him on the head with it. As an adult, you probably have outgrown this behavior. But all of us vary in the way we view more complex situations, depending on our ethical understandings.

Think again of Mattel's and others' product recalls we discussed at the beginning of the chapter. How can certain manufacturers engage in such egregious behavior as using lead paint on toys marketed toward young children? What makes people take actions that create so much harm? Are all the individuals who contributed to that behavior just plain immoral? These simple questions have complex answers, which often suggest decisions made on the basis of expediency.

**EXHIBIT 3.2**

*(continued)*

**Fairness**—to balance justly the needs of the buyer with the interests of the seller. To this end, we will:
- Represent products in a clear way in selling, advertising and other forms of communication; this includes the avoidance of false, misleading and deceptive promotion.
- Reject manipulations and sales tactics that harm customer trust.
- Refuse to engage in price fixing, predatory pricing, price gouging or "bait-and-switch" tactics.
- Avoid knowing participation in conflicts of interest. Seek to protect the private information of customers, employees and partners.

**Respect**—to acknowledge the basic human dignity of all stakeholders. To this end, we will:
- Value individual differences and avoid stereotyping customers or depicting demographic groups (e.g., gender, race, sexual orientation) in a negative or dehumanizing way.
- Listen to the needs of customers and make all reasonable efforts to monitor and improve their satisfaction on an ongoing basis.
- Make every effort to understand and respectfully treat buyers, suppliers, intermediaries and distributors from all cultures.
- Acknowledge the contributions of others, such as consultants, employees and coworkers, to marketing endeavors.
- Treat everyone, including our competitors, as we would wish to be treated.

**Transparency**—to create a spirit of openness in marketing operations. To this end, we will:
- Strive to communicate clearly with all constituencies.
- Accept constructive criticism from customers and other stakeholders.
- Explain and take appropriate action regarding significant product or service risks, component substitutions or other foreseeable eventualities that could affect customers or their perception of the purchase decision.
- Disclose list prices and terms of financing as well as available price deals and adjustments.

**Citizenship**—to fulfill the economic, legal, philanthropic and societal responsibilities that serve stakeholders. To this end, we will:
- Strive to protect the ecological environment in the execution of marketing campaigns.
- Give back to the community through volunteerism and charitable donations.
- Contribute to the overall betterment of marketing and its reputation.
- Urge supply chain members to ensure that trade is fair for all participants, including producers in developing countries.

**Implementation**

We expect AMA members to be courageous and proactive in leading and/or aiding their organizations in the fulfillment of the explicit and implicit promises made to those stakeholders. We recognize that every industry sector and marketing sub-discipline (e.g., marketing research, e-commerce, internet selling, direct marketing, and advertising) has its own specific ethical issues that require policies and commentary. An array of such codes can be accessed through links on the AMA Web site. Consistent with the principle of subsidiarity (solving issues at the level where the expertise resides), we encourage all such groups to develop and/or refine their industry and discipline-specific codes of ethics to supplement these guiding ethical norms and values.

For example, a brand manager for a car company discovers from conversations with a member of the development team that the hot new energy-efficient hybrid model that is set to go into full production shortly has a potentially dangerous design flaw. There are two options for the brand manager: delay production and remedy the design flaw, which pushes production off schedule, delays revenue, and may result in layoffs and loss of the manager's bonus; or stay on schedule, put the flawed design into production, achieve planned revenues and bonus, and hope it does not result in injuries to consumers and loss of revenue for the firm due to recalls later on. This type of dilemma occurs nearly every day in thousands of different business environments.

When asked in a survey whether they had seen any unethical behavior among their colleagues, chief marketing officers responded that they had observed employees participating in high pressure, misleading, or deceptive sales tactics (45 percent); misrepresenting company earnings, sales, and/or revenues (35 percent); withholding or destroying information that could hurt company sales or image (32 percent); and conducting false or misleading advertising (31 percent).[18] Did all the marketers in these situations view their actions as unethical? Probably not. There may have been extenuating circumstances. In marketing, managers often face the choice of doing what is beneficial for them and possibly the firm in the short run and doing what is right and beneficial for the firm and society in the long run.

For instance, a manager might feel confident that earnings will increase in the next few months and therefore believe it benefits himself, his branch, and his

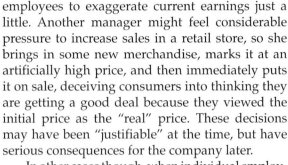

*What is the "real" price? Did the manager bring the T-shirts in at an artificially high level and then immediately mark them down?*

employees to exaggerate current earnings just a little. Another manager might feel considerable pressure to increase sales in a retail store, so she brings in some new merchandise, marks it at an artificially high price, and then immediately puts it on sale, deceiving consumers into thinking they are getting a good deal because they viewed the initial price as the "real" price. These decisions may have been "justifiable" at the time, but have serious consequences for the company later.

In other cases though, when individual employees act unethically, the company must address their actions decisively. For example, when Avon recently found some evidence that top executives in one of its national branches were taking bribes, it immediately suspended the president, chief financial officer, top government affairs officer, and head of the internal audit division. The suspensions will remain in place until the company can prove the charges and determine whether the illegal tactics involve more than these four members.[19]

To avoid dire consequences, the short-term goals of each employee must be aligned with the long-term goals of the firm. In our hybrid car example, the brand manager's short-term drive to receive a bonus conflicted with the firm's long-term aim of providing consumers with safe, reliable cars. To align personal and corporate goals, firms need to have a strong ethical climate, explicit rules for governing transactions including a code of ethics, and a system for rewarding and punishing inappropriate behavior.

In the next section, we add the concept of corporate social responsibility to our discussion of ethics.

**L02** Distinguish between ethics and social responsibility.

*Dannon is both ethical and socially responsible. It has an ethical commitment to make healthy food. It is socially responsible since it is involved in many activities and charities that help people.*

## Ethics and Corporate Social Responsibility

Although no single, established definition of the concept exists,[20] corporate social responsibility generally entails voluntary actions taken by a company to address the ethical, social, and environmental impacts of its business operations and the concerns of its stakeholders. The AMA's definition refers to it as the serious consideration of "the impact of the company's actions and operating in a way that balances short-term profit needs with society's long-term needs, thus ensuring the company's survival in a healthy environment."[21] This notion goes beyond the individual ethics that we've discussed so far, but for a company to act in a socially responsible manner, the employees of the company must also first maintain high ethical standards and recognize how their individual decisions lead to optimal collective actions of the firm. Firms with strong ethical climates tend to be more socially responsible.

However, it is important to distinguish between ethical business practices and corporate social responsibility programs. Ideally, firms should implement programs that are socially responsible, AND its employees should act in an ethically responsible manner. (See Exhibit 3.3, upper left quadrant.) Dannon yogurt, for example, has long supported internal research into healthy eating, which supports its ethical

Nothing *stirs you* like The Original

SINCE 1942
**DANNON**
Fruit on the Bottom
Strawberry

Try these and other great flavors!

commitment to bring "health food to as many people as possible."[22] It is also socially responsible since it donates food and money to the hunger-relief charity Feeding America, encourages employees to volunteer in their communities, holds annual "Children's Day" outreach programs, and reduces its environmental footprints.

Being socially responsible is generally considered to be above and beyond the norms of corporate ethical behavior. For example, a firm's employees may conduct their activities in an ethically acceptable manner but the firm may still not be considered socially responsible because their activities have little or no impact on anyone other than their closest stakeholders: their customers, employees, and stockholders (Exhibit 3.3, upper right quadrant).

Employees at some firms that are perceived as socially responsible can nevertheless take actions that are viewed as unethical (Exhibit 3.3, lower left quadrant). For instance, a firm might be considered socially responsible because it makes generous donations to charities but is simultaneously involved in questionable sales practices. Ethically, how do we characterize a firm that obtains its profits through illicit actions but then donates a large percentage of those profits to charity? The worst situation, of course, is when firms behave both unethically AND in a socially unacceptable manner (Exhibit 3.3, lower right quadrant).

Consumers and investors increasingly appear to want to purchase products and services from and invest in companies that act in socially responsible ways. They also may be willing to pay more if they can be assured the companies truly are ethical.[23] According to a recent poll conducted by *Time Magazine*, even in economically constrained settings, 38 percent of U.S. consumers actively tried to purchase from companies they considered responsible. The magazine thus cites the rise of the "ethical consumer" and the evolution of the social contract "between many Americans and businesses about what goes into making the products we buy."[24]

With such ethical consumers making up more and more of the market, many large companies have recognized that they must be perceived as socially responsible by their stakeholders to earn their business. Other companies began their operations with such a commitment, as Adding Value 3.1 describes.

We cannot expect every member of a firm to always act ethically. However, a framework for ethical decision making can help move people to work toward common ethical goals.

| **EXHIBIT 3·3** | Ethics versus Social Responsibility |

|  | Socially Responsible | Socially Irresponsible |
|---|---|---|
| **Ethical** | Both ethical and socially responsible | Ethical firm not involved with the larger community |
| **Unethical** | Questionable firm practices, yet donates a lot to the community | Neither ethical nor socially responsible |

## The Barefoot Entrepreneur[25]

Blake Mycoskie doesn't just want his customers to buy his shoes; he wants to turn them into benefactors. In this innovative approach to marketing, his company, TOMS Shoes, does not just engage in charitable acts; the charitable acts are the company. There is no separating TOMS from the social responsibility it embraces.

In 2006, Mycoskie started manufacturing a revised version of a traditional Argentinean shoe called *alpargatas* and selling them to consumers outside their generally impoverished source nation. The combination of the comfortable shoes and the extreme poverty he observed led to a simple code: "You buy a pair of TOMS, and I give a pair to a child on your behalf. One for One."

The campaign called "His Shoe Drops," during which Mycoskie brings thousands of pairs of shoes to poorer children in underdeveloped nations, has led to the distribution of approximately 600,000 pairs of shoes, as of April 2010. As the company has grown, it also has added lines of vegan and recycled shoes.

Each year, TOMS also hosts "One Day Without Shoes," a campaign to raise awareness in developed nations about how difficult it can be to function without shoes. In the 2010 iteration, one-quarter of a million people participated, leaving their shoes at home for the entire day. The company also partners with groups such as Insight Argentina, an organization offering volunteer activities in Argentina to help address its most pressing social issues.

If TOMS has given away 600,000 shoes, that means consumers have bought just as many—at an average price of $55 per pair. Clearly, the value they find in these cloth shoes goes well beyond the simple linen and canvas parts that go into making them.

*When you buy a pair of TOMS shoes, it gives a pair to a child in need.*

## A Framework for Ethical Decision Making

**L03**  Identify the four steps in ethical decision making.

Exhibit 3.4 outlines a simple framework for ethical decision making. Let's consider each of the steps.

**Step 1: Identify Issues**  The first step is to identify the issue. For illustrative purposes, we'll investigate the use (or misuse) of data collected from consumers by

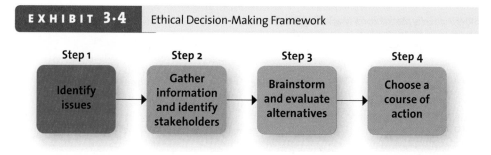

**EXHIBIT 3·4**    Ethical Decision-Making Framework

| **Step 1** | **Step 2** | **Step 3** | **Step 4** |
|---|---|---|---|
| Identify issues | Gather information and identify stakeholders | Brainstorm and evaluate alternatives | Choose a course of action |

a marketing research firm. One of the issues that might arise is the way the data are collected. For instance, are the respondents told about the real purpose of the study? Another issue might be whether the results are going to be used in a way that might mislead or even harm the public, such as selling the information to a firm to use in soliciting the respondents.

### Step 2: Gather Information and Identify Stakeholders
In this step, the firm focuses on gathering facts that are important to the ethical issue, including all relevant legal information. To get a complete picture, the firm must identify all the individuals and groups that have a stake in how the issue is resolved.

Stakeholders typically include the firm's employees and retired employees, suppliers, the government, customer groups, stockholders, and members of the community in which the firm operates. Beyond these, many firms now also analyze the needs of the industry and the global community, as well as "one off" stakeholders, such as future generations and the natural environment itself. In describing its sustainability and transparency efforts for example, the electronics firm Philips notes that it tries to communicate with and consider "anyone with an interest in Philips."[26]

Exhibit 3.5 illustrates a stakeholder analysis matrix for our example.[27] Notice that each stakeholder has responsibilities to the others. In this case, the marketing researcher has ethical responsibilities to the public, the research subjects, and the client company, while the client has ethical responsibilities to the researcher, the subjects, and the public. Acknowledging the interdependence of responsibilities ensures that everyone's perspective is considered in the firm's decision making.

### Step 3: Brainstorm and Evaluate Alternatives
After the marketing firm has identified the stakeholders and their issues and gathered the available data, all parties relevant to the decision should come together to brainstorm any alternative courses of action. In our example, these might include halting the market research project, making responses anonymous, instituting training on the AMA Code of Ethics for all researchers, and so forth. Management then reviews and refines these alternatives, leading to the final step.

### Step 4: Choose a Course of Action
The objective of this last step is to weigh the various alternatives and choose a course of action that generates the best solution for the stakeholders using ethical practices. Management will rank the alternatives in order of preference, clearly establishing the advantages and disadvantages of each. It is also crucial to investigate any potential legal issues associated with each alternative. Of course, any illegal activity should immediately be rejected.

To choose the appropriate course of action, marketing managers will evaluate each alternative using a process something like the sample ethical decision-making

*An employee is acting in a socially responsible manner if he coaches the community's youth baseball team.*

| EXHIBIT 3·5 | Stakeholder Analysis Matrix for a Marketing Research Firm | | |
|---|---|---|---|
| **Stakeholder** | **Stakeholders' Concerns** | **Result or Impact on the Stakeholder** | **Potential Strategies for Obtaining Support and Diminishing Impact** |
| **The Public** | ■ Get inaccurate and biased results.<br>■ Publish false, misleading, or out of context results. | ■ Lose trust in marketing research professionals.<br>■ Lose trust in the marketing research process. | ■ Report accurate results.<br>■ Report study context and methodology.<br>■ Comply with American Marketing Association's (AMA) Code of Ethics. |
| **The Subjects/ Respondents** | ■ Invade privacy. Privacy will be compromised if they answer the survey.<br>■ Use marketing research as a guise to sell consumers goods or services. | ■ Lose trust in the marketing research process.<br>■ Refuse to participate in future marketing research projects.<br>■ Provide incorrect information. | ■ Comply with American Marketing Association's (AMA) Code of Ethics.<br>■ Protect respondents' confidential data.<br>■ Report aggregate rather than individuals' results. |
| **The Client** | ■ Conduct research that was not needed.<br>■ Use an inadequate sample to generalize to their target market.<br>■ Disclose sensitive data to others. | ■ Reduce their spending and reliance on marketing research.<br>■ Make marketing decisions without doing research or doing inadequate research. | ■ Ensure that the marketing research vendor signs a confidentiality agreement.<br>■ Comply with American Marketing Association's (AMA) Code of Ethics. |

*Source:* http://www.marketingpower.com (accessed September 1, 2008).

| EXHIBIT 3.6 | Ethical Decision-Making Metric I |
|---|---|

| | **Confidence in Decision** | | | | | | |
|---|---|---|---|---|---|---|---|
| | **Confident** | | | | | **Not Very Confident** | |
| **Criteria** | **1** | **2** | **3** | **4** | **5** | **6** | **7** |
| 1. Have I/we thought broadly about any ethical issues associated with the decision that must be made? | | | | | | | |
| 2. Have I/we involved as many people as possible who have a right to offer input or have actual involvement in making this decision and action plan? | | | | | | | |
| 3. Does this decision respect the rights and dignity of the stakeholders? | | | | | | | |
| 4. Does this decision produce the most good and the least harm to the relevant stakeholders? | | | | | | | |
| 5. Does this decision uphold relevant conventional moral rules? | | | | | | | |
| 6. Can I/we live with this decision alternative? | | | | | | | |

*Source:* Adapted from Kate McKone-Sweet, Danna Greenberg, and Lydia Moland, "Approaches to Ethical Decision Making," Babson College Case Development Center, 2003.

metric in Exhibit 3.6. The marketer's task here is to ensure that he or she has applied all relevant decision-making criteria and to assess his or her level of confidence that the decision being made meets those stated criteria. If the marketer isn't confident about the decision, he or she should reexamine the other alternatives.

By using such an ethical metric or framework, decision makers will include the relevant ethical issues, evaluate the alternatives, and choose a course of action that will help them avoid serious ethical lapses. Ethical and Societal Dilemma 3.1 illustrates how the ethical decision-making metric in Exhibit 3.6 can be used to make ethical business decisions.

---

### Ethical and Societal Dilemma 3.1 · A Questionable Promotion

Steve Jansen, the marketing manager for a retail store in a small town in the Midwest, received a notice about an upcoming promotion from the national chain to which his store belongs. The promotion is for a diet product called LeanBlast, which targets women between the ages of 20 and 30. Jenna Jones, the celebrity who will be featured in the promotion, is a young actress who recently lost weight and transitioned from child star to adult actor. Jenna is very popular with younger girls, who still watch her early television series in reruns. The promotion is expected to generate a 30–40 percent increase in sales, and because LeanBlast has a high margin, the company looks for a sharp increase in revenue for this category. On the financial side, the promotion looks like a great opportunity for the store.

Recently, however, a local girl died from complications associated with an eating disorder. Her death at the age of 16 triggered a wide range of responses in the community to address eating disorders, as well as efforts to establish a healthier environment for young women.

Not only is Steve extremely nervous about the community's response to this campaign, but he also is personally disturbed by the campaign because he knew the family of the girl who died. In addition, he has been thinking about his own adolescent daughters, who idolize Jenna, the celebrity endorsing the product. He wonders what his daughters' response will be to this campaign.

Using his training in ethical decision making, Steve sat down to evaluate his alternatives, beginning with identifying the various stakeholders that might be impacted by his decision. He came up with the following list: the employees, the shareholders, the customers, and the broader community. Each set of stakeholders has a different interest in the campaign and its outcome.

Steve then arrived at three possible alternatives:

1. Run the campaign as instructed.
2. Modify the campaign by stressing that products such as LeanBlast are to be used only by adult women who are overweight and only with the supervision of a medical professional.
3. Refuse to run this promotion in the local area.

Steve's next step was to evaluate each alternative through a series of questions similar to those in Exhibit 3.6:

*Question 1: Have I thought about the ethical issues involved in my decision?*

Steve feels confident that he has identified all the relevant ethical issues associated with this decision, so he gives this question a score of one.

*Question 2: Do I need to include anyone else in the decision process?*

Because this decision ultimately belongs to him, Steve feels the responsibility to make it, and he believes he has an adequate understanding of all affected parties' positions on the issue. He does not believe that additional input would assist his decision making. Again, he gives this question a score of one.

*(continued)*

*(continued)*

*Question 3: Which of my alternatives respects the rights and dignity of the stakeholders and can be universally applied?*[28]

In this case, Steve already has identified the relevant stakeholders as the local community, the customers, the employees, and the stockholders. The first alternative seems to violate the tenet of respect for persons, because many in the community will find the promotion offensive and contrary to the community's stated goals. The second alternative is an improvement over the first but still potentially offensive. Steve believes the third alternative—not running the promotion—is the right choice according to this criterion. Given this choice, he gives this question a score of one.

*Question 4: Which alternative will produce the most good and the least harm?*[29]

Using this criterion, the first alternative benefits those adult women who need and want LeanBlast. If the promotion achieves its projected revenues, it also benefits the employees and Steve, in that they will post above-average revenues in the category. The promotion also will draw traffic into the store and thereby increase storewide sales figures. However, the promotion harms those who have been affected by the recent tragedy, as well as those teenagers and young girls who would be drawn to the product in an attempt to emulate Jenna Jones's lean body image. Steve scores this alternative a six.

The second alternative requires that Steve supplement the promotion by spending extra funds to stress the proper use of products like LeanBlast, though it is not clear how effective the extra spending will be. Steve scores this alternative a four.

The third alternative costs the store the sales revenue it will lose by not participating in the promotion, and the national chain may assess Steve's store a penalty for failing to participate. The benefits of the third alternative are harder to quantify because most of them are social benefits. The costs, however, are very real in terms of lost revenue. Despite the potential loss, Steve scores this alternative a two.

*Question 5: Do any of the alternatives violate a conventional moral rule?*[30]

Here Steve has an even more difficult time. None of the alternatives violates a conventional moral rule; all fall within legitimate business practices. So, he gives this question a neutral four.

*Question 6: Which alternatives can I personally live with?*[31]

The first alternative is not one that Steve feels he can accept. He finds the choice of a young celebrity somewhat disturbing because her appeal is to a younger audience than the stated target market. Steve is forced to wonder whether the firm is trying to get younger women interested in its products. So, he gives this alternative a seven.

The second alternative is more acceptable to Steve, but he is still concerned about the impact of the promotion, regardless of any modifications he might make. He scores this alternative a neutral four.

Steve can most easily live with the third alternative of choosing not to run the promotion. This alternative is the one he can most easily justify and discuss with his family and friends. So, he gives this alternative a one.

On the basis of this exercise, Steve decides to call the national office to inform the parent company of his decision not to run the promotion in his store. Although Steve is extremely nervous while making this call, he is pleasantly surprised to hear that the national office also has been having some reservations about LeanBlast's choice of celebrity. Management clearly understands Steve's concerns about his community and in fact even offers to help Steve finance an educational session about eating disorders for his employees and the community. Steve decides that doing the right thing feels pretty good.

# INTEGRATING ETHICS INTO MARKETING STRATEGY

**LO4** Describe how ethics can be integrated into a firm's marketing strategy.

Ethical decision making is not a simple process, though it can get easier as decision makers within the firm become accustomed to thinking about the ethical implications of their actions from a strategic perspective. In this section, we examine how ethical decision making can be integrated into the marketing plan introduced in Chapter 2.

The questions vary at each stage of the strategic marketing planning process. For instance, in the planning stage, the firm will decide what level of commitment to its ethical policies and standards it is willing to declare publicly. In the implementation stage, the tone of the questions switches from "can we?" serve the market with the firm's products or services in an ethically responsible manner to "should we?" be engaging in particular marketing practices. The key task in the control phase is to ensure that all potential ethical issues raised during the planning process have been addressed and that all employees of the firm have acted ethically. Let's take a closer look at how ethics can be integrated at each stage of the strategic marketing planning process.

## Planning Phase

Marketers can introduce ethics at the beginning of the planning process simply by including ethical statements in the firm's mission or vision statements. Johnson & Johnson has its Credo; other firms use mission statements that include both ethical and social responsibility precepts for shaping the organization. For instance, the mission statement for natural skin care company Burt's Bees is to "create natural, Earth-friendly personal care products formulated to help you maximize your well-being and that of the world around you,"[32] which reflects what is good not only for its customers, but for society in general. General Mills provides a Code of Conduct that defines the ethical priorities of the organization and its commitment to implanting those values in all that the firm does. For example, it encourages employees to set an example of strong ethical behavior by maintaining employee and consumer privacy, advertising responsibly, and refraining from giving and taking gifts or bribes from its B2B partners. The firm's commitment to such ideals is set at the very top. See the letter from General Mills' CEO in Exhibit 3.7.[33]

In addition, General Mills has announced it will be switching to whole grains in all its breakfast cereal lines, making it the first of the mass-marketed cereal manufacturers to do so. This switch has been applauded by nutritionists who claim it dramatically improves the dietary benefits of the cereals. General Mills made the switch not necessarily to increase consumer demand; rather, in keeping with its stated values, it improved its cereal products to improve the health of its consumers.[34]

*General Mills is switching to whole grains in all of its breakfast cereal lines, which should improve the dietary benefits.*

**EXHIBIT 3·7**     Introduction to General Mills' "A Champion's Code of Conduct" by its CEO

Dear Colleague,

We hold ourselves to a very high standard at General Mills. Nowhere is that more true than in our expectations for ethical conduct in every aspect of our business.

For General Mills, high ethical standards are not something new. It is who we are.

We are proud of our brands and proud of what we do. We believe in ourselves, we believe in each other, and we believe in General Mills.

If you ever encounter an ethical dilemma in your job or role here at General Mills, you may be momentarily surprised. But it can happen. There are times in the conduct of any large and intricate business when ethical dilemmas can arise. At those moments, you must step back to decide whether a decision or action is right – right for our shareholders and consistent with our ethical standards.

If you ever face such a moment, you must do the right thing. We expect you to do the right thing. And we expect you to ask for help if you are in doubt as to the right course of action.

Our Code of Conduct is designed to help you better understand the policies and principles that drive our business and make this a great place to work and ultimately, to help you make decisions consistent with those policies and principles. I encourage you to read it, keep it and refer to it to help make certain that your day-to-day actions and decisions proudly reflect the values of General Mills – the Company of Champions.

Sincerely,

*KJPowell*

Ken Powell
Chief Executive Officer

Source: http://www.generalmills.com/corporate/commitment/corp.aspx (accessed January 18, 2010).

During the planning stage, ethical mission statements can take on another role as a means to guide a firm's SWOT analysis. Newman's Own (see Adding Value 3.2), for example, has what most of us would consider a simple but powerful mission statement.

## Implementation Phase

In the implementation phase of the marketing strategy, when firms are identifying potential markets and how to successfully deliver the 4Ps to them, firms must consider several ethical issues. Sometimes a firm's choice of a target market and how the firm pursues it can lead to charges of unethical behavior. For instance, Molson Brewery launched a Facebook campaign targeted toward college students in which it asked them to post party pictures, which it would use to identify the "top party school." This effort not only encouraged underage, illegal drinking but also deeply irritated university communities across both Canada and the United States, who

## Adding Value 3.2    Newman's Own: Making a Difference[35]

Newman's Own began as a simple concept: The company would sell salad dressing in antique wine bottles with parchment labels and use the proceeds to benefit charities. In 1982, the founders of Newman's Own, actor Paul Newman and A. E. Hotchner, produced their first batch of salad dressing in Newman's basement to give as holiday gifts. When they also decided to check with a local grocer to see if it would be interested in the product, they found they could sell 10,000 bottles in two weeks. The rapid growth of Newman's Own surprised the founders, and the nonprofit organization quickly grew to include dozens of products, as well as a line of organic foods that Paul Newman's daughter, Nell Newman, would spin off on her own. Today, Newman's Own and Newman's Own Organic products are sold in 15 countries and include dozens of lines, from coffee to popcorn to dog food. Profits from Newman's Own—over $280 million since 1982—have been donated to thousands of charities, especially Newman's Hole in the Wall Gang camps for children with life-threatening diseases.

What about how Newman's Own adds value? First, Newman's Own is made of good, natural ingredients, and of course, Newman's Own Organics are organic. Second, it gives all its profits to charity—the ultimate gesture of social responsibility. Third, it treats its stakeholders well, with an eye toward strong ethical practices. It pays its employees well and lets them, at times, select charities for them to support. It also keeps an eye toward purchasing fair trade merchandise—a practice that requires producers to pay workers a living wage, well more than the prevailing minimum wage, and offer other benefits, like onsite medical treatment. For instance, after Nell Newman visited and met the people that harvested its coffee, she insisted that the firm purchase only fair trade coffee.[36] Finally, and totally unique to Newman's Own, is its association with the beloved actor, who passed away in 2008.

But not all of Newman's Own's success can be attributed to image or even to consumers who want something that reminds them of the man who played Butch Cassidy and Fast Eddie Felson. Some of Newman's Own's most popular items have resulted from partnerships with established companies, which allowed their well-known products to receive the "Newman's Own" touch. For example, Fig Newmans™ exists because a license from Kraft grants the company the right to use a name similar to Fig Newtons. In turn, Newman's Own licenses its brand for use on coffee and salad dressings at McDonald's. The partners don't even have to be food companies: In a tie-in with Netflix, the company recommends that consumers try Newman's Own frozen pizzas while watching a movie at home. Associations with a firm with such a high profile mission as Newman's are beneficial to all.

The unique mission of the company and the entrepreneurial flair of the founders made this nonprofit a smashing, ongoing success. Employees of Newman's Own have the great satisfaction of giving back to society, various charities benefit from the donations, and customers enjoy good food with a clear conscience.

*Since 1982, Newman's Own has given over $280 million to charities like Newman's Hole in the Wall Gang camps for children with life-threatening diseases.*

had little interest in being thus identified. Although the student groups might be responsive to the firm's efforts, they did not represent an appropriate target market.

Power of the Internet 3.1 examines an example of the ethical conflicts companies can encounter when doing business globally, in this case Google's experience in China.

An issue related to the ethical implementation of a marketing strategy is the problem of policing potential violations of human rights and child-labor laws. Many firms have had to publicly defend themselves against allegations of human rights, child-labor, or other abuses involving the factories and countries in which

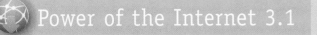

### Power of the Internet 3.1

**For the Heavyweight Championship of the World: Google versus China**

Google, the most used Internet search engine on the Web, brings a world of information into people's lives. Built on the principle that freedom of information is a fundamental right of individuals as well as good for business,[37] it plays a strong role in shifting perceptions from an "us versus them" mentality to a sense of global community. But doing business in a global environment means running up against different values and laws, as Google recently found out in its China operations.[38]

Since 2005, Google has had a presence on Chinese soil and has complied with the country's laws requiring self-censorship for its search results while it has tried to establish itself in the world's largest Internet market. But in the aftermath of a 2010 attack by Chinese hackers that included breaking into e-mail accounts of some of the country's human rights advocates, Google began directing Chinese users to its search engine in Hong Kong. The Hong Kong site is uncensored.[39]

Google's position, backed by the White House, is that the move was triggered by China's restrictive attitudes toward human rights activists and free speech.[40] The Chinese government sees the matter differently. Maintaining that companies operating in China need to abide by Chinese laws, the government insists that its actions are the same as those of other countries limiting public exposure to content that is pornographic or violent or that encourages subversive, extremist, or racist behaviors. Furthermore China reprimanded Google for turning a commercial issue into a political one.

Other American Internet companies have struggled with Chinese laws as they have tried to do business in this growing market. The repercussions of Google's move may impact the future of foreign companies in China, as well as China's ability to grow and integrate with the rest of the world.

Conflicting ethical standards make global business challenging. As a company based in the United States, should Google maintain its "freedom of information" credo, or should it adopt the ethical standards of each of the other countries in which it operates?

their goods are made.[41] Due to the efforts of some U.S. firms, and nonprofit organizations, fewer imported goods are produced in sweatshop conditions today. Some firms are quite proactive in enforcing the labor practices of their suppliers. Limited Brands, for instance, was one of the first U.S. apparel manufacturers to develop and implement policies requiring observance by vendors and their subcontractors and suppliers of core labor standards as a condition of doing business. Among other things, this requirement ensures that each supplier pays minimum wages and benefits; limits overtime to local industry standards; does not use prisoners, forced labor, or child labor; and provides a healthy and safe environment.[42] Many other companies that produce or sell goods made in low-wage countries conduct similar self-policing. Self-policing allows companies to avoid painful public revelations. Adding Value 3.3 examines how Walmart is pushing its vendors to be environmentally responsible.

Once the strategy is implemented, controls must be in place to be certain that the firm has actually done what it has set out to do. These activities take place in the next phase of the strategic marketing planning process.

## Control Phase

During the control phase of the strategic marketing planning process, managers must be evaluated on their actions from an ethical perspective. Systems must be in place to check whether each potential ethical issue raised in the planning process was actually successfully addressed. Systems used in the control phase must also react to change. The emergence of new technologies and new markets ensures that new ethical issues continually arise. Many firms have emergency response plans in place just in case they ever encounter a situation similar to the Tylenol tampering emergency or an industrial accident at a manufacturing plant. Ethics thus remains an ongoing crucial component of the strategic marketing planning process and should be incorporated into all the firm's decision making down the road.

## Adding Value 3.3　　　It Isn't Easy to Sell to Walmart[43]

Walmart is known for its low prices, and for driving its vendors to tears to get them. Now it is pressuring its vendors to also supply it with environmentally friendly merchandise with labels to prove it. In the future, merchandise sold at Walmart will have the environmental equivalent of nutritional labels, providing information on the product's carbon footprint, the amount of water and air pollution used to produce it, and other environmental issues. To measure how a vendor's products are doing, it has developed a sustainability index that simultaneously takes several issues into consideration.

Walmart is also requiring its top 200 factories to become 20 percent more energy-efficient by 2012, a feat that many experts believe may be impossible, even with Walmart's help. Initial results are promising, however. For example, Jiangsu Redbud Dyeing Technology in China has cut coal consumption by one-tenth and is attempting to cut its toxic emissions to zero.

Walmart hasn't always been touted as a good corporate citizen. In the 1990s, it came to light that workers at some factories producing clothing for Walmart were subjected to inhumane conditions. More recently, two governmental organizations accused Walmart of buying from 15 factories that engage in abuse and labor violations, including child labor use, 19-hour shifts, and below subsistence wages. It and other companies have also been accused of dumping hazardous waste in Oklahoma City.

Some wonder why Walmart is attempting to position itself as the retail industry's sustainability leader. Certainly initiatives that show that it is a good corporate citizen enhance its image. But it expects it to be good for business as well. Its customers, especially those born from 1980 to 2000, are increasingly concerned about how the products they use impact the environment and the people that produce them. Also, Walmart believes that many of these initiatives will help streamline supply chain processes and therefore provide additional financial benefits to its suppliers and customers.

*To encourage the purchase of environmentally friendly products, in the future Walmart will provide customers the environmental equivalent of nutrition labels that provide information on environmental issues such as its carbon footprint.*

---

### CHECK YOURSELF

1. What ethical questions should a marketing manager consider at each stage of the marketing plan?

---

# UNDERSTANDING ETHICS USING SCENARIOS

In the final section of this chapter, we present a series of ethical scenarios designed to assist you in developing your skills at identifying ethical issues. There may be no one right answer to the dilemmas below, just as there may be no one correct answer to many of the ethical situations you will face throughout your career. Instead, these scenarios can help you develop your sensitivity toward ethical issues, as well as your ethical reasoning skills.

Exhibit 3.8 provides an alternative ethical decision-making metric to Exhibit 3.6 to assist you in evaluating these scenarios. By asking yourself these questions, you can gauge your own ethical response. If your scores tend to be in the green area (1 and 2), then the situation is not an ethically troubling situation for you. If, in contrast, your scores tend to be in the red area (6 and 7), it is ethically troubling

| **EXHIBIT 3.8** | Ethical Decision-Making Metric II |
| --- | --- |

| Test | Decision | | | | | | |
| --- | --- | --- | --- | --- | --- | --- | --- |
| | Yes | | Maybe | | | No | |
| | 1 | 2 | 3 | 4 | 5 | 6 | 7 |
| **The Publicity Test**<br>Would I want to see this action that I'm about to take described on the front page of the local paper or in a national magazine? | | | | | | | |
| **The Moral Mentor Test**<br>Would the person I admire the most engage in this activity? | | | | | | | |
| **The Admired Observer Test**<br>Would I want the person I admire most to see me doing this? | | | | | | | |
| **The Transparency Test**<br>Could I give a clear explanation for the action I'm contemplating, including an honest and transparent account of all my motives, that would satisfy a fair and dispassionate moral judge? | | | | | | | |
| **The Person in the Mirror Test**<br>Will I be able to look at myself in the mirror and respect the person I see there? | | | | | | | |
| **The Golden Rule Test**<br>Would I like to be on the receiving end of this action and all its potential consequences? | | | | | | | |

*Source:* Adapted from Tom Morris, *The Art of Achievement: Mastering the 7 Cs of Success in Business and in Life* (Kansas City, MO: Andrew McMeel Publishing, 2002); http://edbrenegar.typepad.com/leading_questions/2005/05/real_life_leade.html (accessed December 29, 2007).

and you know it. If your scores are scattered or in the yellow area, you need to step back and reflect on how you wish to proceed.

## Scenario 1: R.J. Reynolds: Promotions to the Youth Market

Tobacco giant R.J. Reynolds sent a set of coasters featuring its cigarette brands and recipes for mixed drinks with high alcohol content to young adults, via direct mail, on their 21st birthdays (the legal age for alcohol consumption). The alcohol brands in the recipes included Jack Daniels, Southern Comfort, and Finlandia Vodka. The reverse side of the coaster read, "Go 'til Daybreak, and Make Sure You're Sittin'." The campaign, called "Drinks on Us," clearly promoted abusive and excessive drinking. This campaign was eventually stopped because the cigarette company did not have permission to use the alcohol brands.

The FDA (Food and Drug Administration) has recently been given the authority to regulate tobacco, including banning certain products, limiting nicotine, and blocking labels such as "low tar" and "light" that could wrongly imply certain products are less harmful.[44] The law doesn't let the FDA ban nicotine or tobacco entirely. A committee has been formed to study several issues, including dissolvable tobacco products, product changes, and standards, and report back to the FDA. Of particular interest is the increase in the share of smokers using menthol cigarettes from 31 to almost 34 percent in four years, with more pronounced increases among young smokers. It also showed that among black smokers, 82.6 percent used menthol cigarettes, compared with 32.3 percent for Hispanic smokers and 23.8 percent for white smokers.[45] A ban on cigarettes with flavors like clove, chocolate, or fruit took effect in 2009, because they are believed to appeal to youth.

After graduation, you have an offer to work in either marketing or sales at R.J. Reynolds. The pay and benefits are very competitive. The job market is tight, and if you don't get a job right away you will have to live with your parents. Should you take the job?

## Scenario 2: Car Manufacturer Gives Bribes for Contracts

A car and truck manufacturer just found out that two of its overseas business units have been engaging in bribery over a ten-year period of time. The company paid $56 million in bribes to more than 20 countries to gain government contracts for their vehicles.[46] The company is now paying millions in criminal and civil charges because of its violation of the Foreign Corrupt Practices Act (FCPA), and admits to earning more than $50 million in profits based on its corrupt transactions. The car company recorded the bribe payments as "commissions," "special discounts," or "necessary payments." Should the manufacturer discontinue its operations with the countries that were unlawfully bribed to buy its cars? Are financial fines sufficient to repair the problem? How can companies be sure the commissions they earn are true commissions and not a bribe?

## Scenario 3: Retailers Lack Ethical Guidelines

Renata has been working at Peavy's Bridal for less than a year now. Her sales figures have never been competitive with those of her coworkers, and the sales manager has called her in for several meetings to discuss her inability to close the sale. Things look desperate; in the last meeting, the sales manager told her that if she did not meet her quota next month, the company would likely have to fire her.

In considering how she might improve her methods and sales, Renata turned to another salesperson, namely, the one with the most experience in the store. Marilyn has been with Peavy's for nearly 30 years, and she virtually always gets the sale. But how?

"Let me tell you something sweetie," Marilyn tells her. "Every bride-to-be wants one thing: to look beautiful on her wedding day, so everyone gasps when they first see her. And hey, the husband is going to think she looks great. But let's be honest here—not everyone is all that beautiful. So you have to convince them that they look great in one, and only one, dress. And that dress had better be the most expensive one they try, or they won't believe you anyway! And then you have to show them how much better they look with a veil. And some shoes. And a tiara . . . you get the picture! I mean, they need all that stuff anyway, so why shouldn't we make them feel good while they're here and let them buy from us?"

Should she follow Marilyn's advice and save her job?

## Scenario 4: Who Is on the Line?

A California company, Star38, invented a computer program that allowed certain telephone users to avoid caller ID systems. For $19.99 per month and $0.07 per minute, a caller could log on to the company's website and type in the number he or she wanted to call, as well as the number he or she wanted to appear on the caller ID screen of the receiving phone. For an additional fee, the caller could create a name to appear along with the phony phone number. Star38 intended to sell its service to collection agencies, private detectives, and law enforcement agencies.

Is this an ethical business plan? Would your answer be the same if Star38 sold its services to any individual who signed up?

Marvin Smith, who runs a collection agency in Austin, Texas, is considering signing up for Star38. Should he?[47]

## Scenario 5: West Virginia T-Shirts

A popular teen clothing retailer is selling a T-shirt for $22.50 picturing a map of West Virginia and the slogan: "It's All Relative in West Virginia." The governor of West Virginia has requested that the retailer remove the shirt from its stores and destroy all remaining inventory. In a letter to the president of the retail chain, the governor stated that this slogan is extremely offensive and perpetuates a negative stereotype of his state that undermines the state's efforts to portray the true spirit and values of its citizens.

The communications director for the retailer, in response to the governor's request, stated that the retailer had no plans to remove the shirt, a very popular item. He also stated that the retailer means no disrespect and in fact loves West Virginia. The retailer offers shirts depicting most of the 50 states, which it regards as a way of celebrating the states. By means of example, the communications director pointed to another T-shirt currently on sale: "New Hampshire: 40 Million Squirrels Can't Be Wrong."

Do you think the retailer's response to the governor was appropriate? Was the governor's request appropriate? What would you have done if you had been the retailer? Would your response be different if you knew that this retailer had previously been accused of using pornography in the marketing of its clothing?[48]

## Scenario 6: Giving Credit Where Credit Isn't Due

A catalog retailer that carries home and children's items, such as children's furniture, clothing, and toys, was seeking a way to reach a new audience and stop the declining sales and revenue trends it was suffering. A market research firm hired by the cataloger identified a new but potentially risky market: lower-income single parents. The new market seemed attractive because of the large number of single parents, but most of these homes were severely constrained in terms of their monetary resources.

The research firm proposed that the cataloger offer a generous credit policy that would allow consumers to purchase up to $500 worth of merchandise on credit without a credit check, provided they signed up for direct payment of their credit account from a checking account. Because these were high-risk consumers, the credit accounts would carry extremely high interest rates. The research firm believed that even with losses, enough accounts would be paid off to make the venture extremely profitable for the catalog retailer.

Should the cataloger pursue this new strategy?

## Scenario 7: The Jeweler's Tarnished Image

Sparkle Gem Jewelers, a family-owned and -operated costume jewelry manufacturing business, traditionally sold its products only to wholesalers. Recently, however, Sparkle Gem was approached by the charismatic Barb Stephens, who convinced the owners to begin selling through a network of distributors she had organized. The distributors recruited individuals to host "jewelry parties" in their homes. Sparkle Gem's owners, the Billing family, has been thrilled with the revenue generated by these home parties and started making plans for the expansion of the distributor network.

However, Mrs. Billing just received a letter from a jewelry party customer, who expressed sympathy for her loss. Mrs. Billing was concerned and contacted the letter writer, who told her that Barb Stephens had come to the jewelry party at her church and told the story of Sparkle Gem. According to Stephens's story,

Mrs. Billing was a young widow struggling to keep her business together after her husband had died on a missionary trip. The writer had purchased $200 worth of jewelry at the party and told Mrs. Billing that she hoped it helped. Mrs. Billing was stunned. She and her very much alive husband had just celebrated their 50th wedding anniversary.

What should Mrs. Billing do now?

## Scenario 8: No Wonder It's So Good

Enjoy Cola is a new product produced by ABC Beverage and marketed with the slogan "Relax with Enjoy." Unlike other colas on the market, Enjoy does not contain caffeine and therefore is positioned as the perfect beverage to end the day or for a slow-paced weekend, and as a means to help consumers relax and unwind. The market response has been tremendous, and sales of Enjoy have been growing rapidly, especially among women.

ABC Beverage decided not to list on the ingredients label that Enjoy contains a small amount of alcohol because it is not required to do so by the government unless the alcohol content is more than 1 percent.

Mia Rodriguez, the marketing director for Enjoy, only recently learned that Enjoy contains small amounts of alcohol and is troubled about ABC's failure to disclose this information on the ingredients list. She worries about the impact of this omission on consumers who have alcohol sensitivities or those who shouldn't be consuming alcohol, such as pregnant women and recovering alcoholics.

What should Rodriguez do? What would you do in her position?

## Scenario 9: Bright Baby's Bright Idea

Bartok Manufacturing produces a line of infant toys under the "Bright Baby" brand label. The Consumer Product Safety Commission (CPSC) recently issued a recall order for the Bright Baby car seat gym, a very popular product. According to the CPSC, the gym contains small parts that present a choking hazard. The CEO of Bartok Manufacturing, Bill Bartok, called an executive meeting to determine the firm's strategy in response to the recall.

Mike Henderson, Bartok's CFO, stated that the recall could cost as much as $1 million in lost revenue from the Bright Baby line. Noting that there had been no deaths or injuries from the product, just the potential for injury, Henderson proposed that the remaining inventory of car seat gyms be sold where there are no rules such as the CPSC's. Sue Tyler, the marketing director for Bartok, recommended that the product be repackaged and sold under a different brand name so that the Bright Baby name would not be associated with the product. Bartok, though a bit leery of the plan, agreed to go along with it to avoid the monetary losses.

What would you have recommended to the CEO?

### Scenario 10: Money from Mailing Lists[49]

Sports Nostalgia Emporium sells autographed sports memorabilia online. Recently, the Director of Marketing, John Mangold, started using a mailing list he had purchased from Marketing Metrix, a marketing research firm that sells consumer information. Mangold relies on such purchased mailing lists to grow the company and sends printed catalogs to thousands of people each month. The mailing lists he gets from Marketing Metrix are much more effective than other mailing lists and generate almost twice as much revenue.

In a recent conversation with a sales representative from Marketing Metrix, Mangold discovered the reason its lists were so effective: Marketing Metrix tracks the online behavior of consumers and uses that information to create targeted lists. The mailing lists that Mangold has been using consist of consumers who visited the websites of Sports Nostalgia Emporium's competitors. Based on what he can discern, Mangold believes that these consumers are not aware that someone is collecting information about their online behavior, along with their names and addresses, and selling it to other firms.

Should Mangold continue to use the Marketing Metrix mailing list? If so, should he tell his new customers how he got their names and addresses? Do consumers need to give consent before firms can collect information about their behavior?

### Scenario 11: The Blogging CEO[50]

David Burdick is the CEO of ACME Bubblegum, a successful public company. As one of the cofounders of the company, Burdick has enjoyed speaking and writing about the success of ACME Bubblegum for several years. Typically, he speaks at conferences or directly to the press, but recently, he has been blogging about his firm anonymously. Specifically, he defended a recent advertising campaign that was

unpopular among consumers and pointedly attacked one of ACME Bubblegum's competitors. Burdick deeply enjoys his anonymous blogging and believes that none of his readers actually know that he works for ACME Bubblegum.

Should Burdick be allowed to praise his company's performance anonymously online? Should he be allowed to attack his competitors without disclosing his relationship with the company? How would you feel if the CEO of a company at which you shopped was secretly writing criticisms of his or her competition? How would you feel if you knew a writer for your favorite blog was actually closely involved in a company that the blog community discussed?

# CORPORATE SOCIAL RESPONSIBILITY

**L05** Describe the ways in which corporate social responsibility programs help various stakeholders.

In 1906, Upton Sinclair published *The Jungle*, his novel exposing the horrific conditions in U.S. meat-packing plants, which prompted President Theodore Roosevelt and Congress to force meat companies to take responsibility for the safety of their products. The notion of societal marketing and corporate social responsibility has changed significantly since then, and recent decades have seen its prevalence increase rapidly. Today, companies are undertaking a wide range of corporate social responsibility initiatives, such as establishing corporate charitable foundations, supporting and associating with existing nonprofit groups, supporting minority activities, and following responsible marketing, sales, and production practices.

Some economists and social commentators suggest that CSR (corporate social responsibility) is unnecessary, that the goal of any corporation in a capitalist economy is single and simple: Make money.[51] How does it benefit the company or its shareholders if a company worries about such unquantifiable issues as being a good citizen? But the fallout from the recent global economic crisis seems to have pushed economists to repudiate this school of thought.

When companies embrace CSR, they appeal not only to their shareholders, but to their primary *stake*holders, including their own employees, consumers, the marketplace, and society at large. Exhibit 3.9 highlights the critical inputs and outputs involved in a corporate social responsibility program.[52] On the input side, the firm considers its customers, the company, and various causes/issues that it believes are important and which the firm can make a significant difference by supporting.

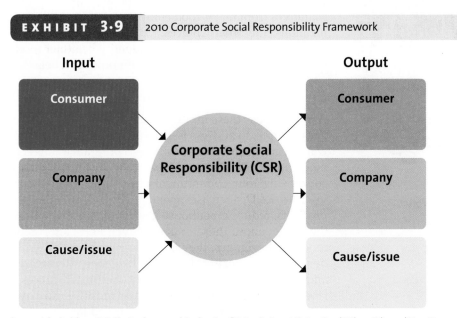

| **EXHIBIT 3·9** | 2010 Corporate Social Responsibility Framework |

*Source:* Adapted from C. B. Bhattacharya and Sankar Sen, "Doing Better at Doing Good: When, Why and How Consumers Respond to Corporate Social Initiatives," *California Management Review*, 47 (Fall 2004), pp. 9–24.

With this information it designs its CSR program, and then in terms of outputs, it measures how well the program satisfies the objectives of the same three stakeholder groups—customers, company, and causes/issues.

## Inputs

The key inputs that a firm needs to understand and appreciate consist of three main categories: consumer, company, and cause/issue. We look at each separately.

**Consumer**  Environmental changes affect firms and the consumers that patronize them. For instance, the growing number of women, senior citizens, and minorities in the workforce has changed the way firms do business and their view of how they interact with society. (See Chapter 4.) Corporate social responsibility programs must take these shifts and trends into account and react to them quickly. A few of the trends that are receiving the most attention include interest in the environment, respecting and protecting privacy in an electronic world, and ensuring healthiness of products, especially those aimed at children.

**Company**  As a firm develops its CSR programs, it needs to think about its overall firm strategy. Programs and causes that fit well with the strategy and the industry in which the firm works likely will lead to better results for all stakeholders. For instance, General Electric, a 128-year-old company that consists of various brands competing in a vast range of industries (e.g., consumer appliances and electronics; network television, film, and media; railway equipment), refers to itself as follows: "GE is a diversified global infrastructure, finance and media company that is built to meet essential world needs. The company is one of the world's leading energy, water, transportation and health technology suppliers."[53]

*To address issues such as global warming, water scarcity, and energy, GE uses a program it calls ecomagination™, which encompasses a business strategy comprised of four commitments: to double investments in clean R&D, increase revenues from ecomagination products, reduce greenhouse gas emissions, and inform the public about these issues.*

**ecomagination**
a GE commitment

**Imagine creating fresh water from seawater.**

Over 1 billion people live without easy access to clean, fresh water. That's why GE's advanced desalination technology turns salt water into fresh where it's needed most – whether it's for drinking, irrigation or industry. Already, we reclaim more than 7 billion litres of water every day. It's just another way GE is transforming imagination into reality.

 GE imagination at work

www.ge.com/ecomagination

**Cause/Issue**  The causes and societal issues that could be adopted by firms are too numerous to mention, ranging from environmental causes to making Americans healthier, for example, America on the Move (AOM). The actual number of nonprofit organizations in the United States from which firms can choose to support exceeds 1.5 million.[54]

AOM has successfully helped launch a variety of initiatives, including the SmartChoices™ label on foods. Developed by nutritionists, food policy experts, representatives from major food companies, and health organizations, the SmartChoices™ program is designed to provide a science-based way to identify healthier foods by placing the Smart Choice logo on product labels.[55]

## Developing a CSR Program

A firm will use these inputs to develop its CSR program. For example, to address issues such as global warming, water scarcity, and energy, GE uses a program it calls ecomagination™, which encompasses a business strategy comprising four commitments: to double investments in clean R&D, increase revenues from ecomagination products, reduce greenhouse gas emissions, and inform the public about these issues.[56] Given Pepsi's focus on food and beverages, they have partnered with AOM to develop more healthy food and beverage alternatives, and are therefore able to display the SmartChoices™ label on many of their products, including Frito-Lay's Ruffles, which now contain less saturated fat.[57]

## Outputs

More firms are realizing that doing good for society can also result in a better bottom line because of increased value for customers, happier employees, and/or greater efficiency. Like the inputs, the outputs of these CSR activities are grouped into three main categories: consumer, company, and cause/issue. We look at each separately.

**Consumer** CSR often increases consumer awareness of the firm in the short run, which in turn leads to better brand equity and sales in the long run. GE's ecoimagination program increases awareness of alternative sources of energy, while Pepsi's support of AOM and use of SmartChoices™ labels increase awareness of the need to eat healthier choices.

**Company** The output of these CSR initiatives can result in significant positive word-of-mouth for the company, as well as increased profits. In addition, if the company provides a CSR message for their employees to deliver that they feel passionately about, they will deliver it with conviction, having an enormous impact on their customers.

**Cause/Issue** Finally, appropriate linkages between firms and their causes/issues benefit the cause and create better awareness of its objectives in the short run and more resources (workers and money) in the long run that it can devote toward its honorable mission. For example, to reduce greenhouse gas emissions (GHG), GE established its 1–30–30 plan. The "1" stands for the percentage that GE will reduce its GHG emissions worldwide by 2012; the first "30" indicates its commitment to reduce its GHG emissions by 30 percent by 2008; and the last "30" refers to the 30 percent improvement in its energy efficiency that it plans to achieve by the end of 2012. In 2008, compared with the 2004 benchmark, its GHG emissions had fallen by 13 percent, though GE asserted that when it took economic indicators into consideration, it could claim to have met its first 30 percent goal.[58]

---

**CHECK YOURSELF**

1. How has corporate social responsibility evolved since the turn of the twentieth century?
2. Identify the inputs and outputs of the corporate social responsibility framework.

---

## Summing Up

**L01** **Identify the ethical values marketers should embrace.**

Being a part of an ethically responsible firm should be important to every employee, but it is particularly important to marketers, because they interact most directly with customers and suppliers, which offers a multitude of ethical questions and opportunities. AMA's Code of Ethics indicates that the basic ethical values marketers should aspire to are honesty, responsibility, fairness, respect, openness, and citizenship.

**L02** **Distinguish between ethics and social responsibility.**

Individuals and firms can (and should) act ethically, but the outcome of their acts may not affect society in general. An ethical act may only affect the firm's immediate stakeholders, such as its employees, customers, and suppliers. To be socially responsible, a firm also must take actions that benefit the community in a larger sense, such as helping people who have been affected by a natural disaster like a hurricane.

**L03** **Identify the four steps in ethical decision making.**

First, firms can include ethics and social responsibility in their corporate mission. Second, they should institute policies and procedures to ensure that everyone working for the firm is acting in an ethically responsible manner. Third, firms can model their ethical policies after a well-established code of ethics like the one provided by the American Marketing Association. Fourth, when making ethically sensitive decisions, firms can utilize a metric such as Ethical Decision-Making Metric I, shown in Exhibit 3.6, or Ethical Decision-Making Metric II, shown in Exhibit 3.8.

**L04** **Describe how ethics can be integrated into a firm's marketing strategy.**

Ethical and socially responsible considerations should be integrated into the firm's mission statement, as long as top management follows through and commits to supporting a strong ethical climate within the organization. When considering their marketing strategy, firms should ask not only "can we implement a certain policy?" but also "should we do it?" Finally, in the control phase, marketers must determine whether they truly have acted in an ethical and socially responsible manner. If not, they should make changes to the marketing strategy.

**L05** **Describe the ways in which corporate social responsibility programs help various stakeholders.**

To answer this question, we first have to identify the various stakeholders of a company, namely, customers, employees, stockholders, and the community. CSR benefits these stakeholders as follows:

- Customers. When companies adopt CSR, customers know that they can trust the firms to provide healthy, ethically acceptable products and services. Many customers also feel better about buying from a company that engages in responsible practices, which provides them with the additional value of feeling good about buying from that company.

- Employees. A firm committed to CSR likely treats its employees with decency and respect. For many employees (especially members of Generation Y), working for an irresponsible firm would be antithetical to their own morals and values.

- Stockholders. When a CSR initiative, such as using more efficient packaging, improves a company's profits by reducing costs, stockholders enjoy an immediate improvement in their investment. Some investors also choose which stocks to buy on the basis of the company's responsible stances.

- Community. This last stakeholder can be a local, national, or global community. The benefits of CSR in all cases are numerous— cleaner air and water, aid to the underprivileged, and healthier product options all can result from CSR by companies.

## Key Terms

- business ethics, 84
- corporate social responsibility, 90
- ethical climate, 85
- marketing ethics, 84

## Marketing Applications

1. Why are marketers likely to be faced with more ethical dilemmas than members of other functional areas, like finance, accounting, or real estate?

2. Develop an argument for why a children's toy manufacturer should build and maintain an ethical climate.

3. A pharmaceutical company gives generously to charities and sponsors cancer awareness programs. It also charges remarkably high prices and receives high margins for life-saving medications, mostly targeted toward elderly consumers. Evaluate this company from an ethical and social responsibility perspective.

4. A large U.S.-based dog food company is negotiating with a company in Korea to make a new line of organic dog food. The manufacturer wants a high-quality product at a reasonable cost but is concerned that the Korean workers will be underpaid and asked to work long hours in unpleasant conditions. Develop a stakeholder analysis matrix similar to that in Exhibit 3.5 to assess the impact of this decision on the relevant stakeholders.

5. Based on the dog food manufacturing scenario you developed for Question 4, provide responses to Ethical Decision-Making Metric I from Exhibit 3.6. Provide a rationale for your confidence score for each question.

6. A company that makes granola and other "healthy" snacks has the following mission statement: "Our goal is to profitably sell good-tasting, healthy products and to better society." Although its products are organic, they also are relatively high in calories. The company gives a small portion of its profits to the United Way. Evaluate the mission statement by using Ethical Decision-Making Metric II from Exhibit 3.8.

7. The granola company described in the previous question is thinking about starting an advertising campaign directed at children that would air on Saturday morning television. Explain why you think it should or should not do so by using the ethical decision-making metrics in both Exhibits 3.6 and 3.8. Which metric do you find more useful?

8. A health inspector found some rodent droppings in one batch of granola made by this same company. What should the company do? Base your decision on either of the ethical decision-making metrics in Exhibits 3.6 and 3.8, whichever you prefer.

9. Choose a company that you believe is particularly socially responsible. Using the Corporate Social Responsibility Framework in Exhibit 3.9, justify your choice.

## Quiz Yourself

www.mhhe.com/ grewal3e

1. Johnson & Johnson's 1943 "Credo" was considered radical at the time because it:
   a. parodied the Communist Manifesto.
   b. proposed socialized medicine.
   c. put customers first.
   d. was issued by a general.
   e. sought to undermine American capitalism.

2. Recognizing that parents, children, teachers, staff, and taxpayers all have a vested interest in the problem of deteriorating school facilities, and then listening to each group's concerns, a school board would most likely next:
   a. identify issues of concern to lawmakers.
   b. assess the impact of their actions beyond the classroom.

   c. engage in brainstorming and evaluate alternatives.
   d. choose a course of action.
   e. all of the above.

   (Answers to these two questions can be found on page 607.)

   Go to www.mhhe.com/grewal3e to practice by answering an additional 11 questions.

## Net Savvy

1. Perhaps no subdiscipline of marketing receives more scrutiny regarding ethical compliance than direct marketing, a form of nonstore retailing in which customers are exposed to and purchase merchandise or services through an impersonal medium such as telephone, mail, or the Internet.[59]

Ethical issues in direct marketing cover a broad spectrum because this means of selling is conducted through all forms of communication. The Direct Marketing Association (DMA) takes ethics very seriously and has numerous programs to ensure its member organizations comply with its Code of Ethics. Go to the website for the Direct Marketing Association (www.the-dma.org/). Click on "Advocacy Issues." List the different ways that the DMA was involved in assisting consumers and the industry to create a more ethical marketplace.

2. An increasing number of firms are stating their strong commitment to corporate social responsibility initiatives. The Corporate Social Responsibility Newswire Service keeps track of these various initiatives and posts stories on its website about what various corporations are doing. Go to http://www.csrwire.com/ and choose one story. Write a description of the corporation and the initiative.

## Chapter Case Study

### WHOSE SIDE ARE YOU ON?[60]

Britt Smith was recently hired by a large architecture and engineering firm as an assistant account manager in the government contracts division. The firm specializes in building hospitals, schools, and other large-scale projects. Britt is excited to learn that she will be part of the marketing team that presents the firm's proposals to the clients. In this case the clients are primarily federal and state governmental agencies. The presentations are elaborate, often costing $50,000 or more to prepare. But the projects can be worth millions to the firm, so the investment is worth it. The firm has a solid record for building quality projects, on time, and the majority of the time within budget. The firm also has an impressive track record, being awarded government contracts an incredible 85 percent of the time. No other firm in the industry comes close to this record.

The first project Britt is assigned to is an enormous project to design a new military hospital complex. The team leader, Brian Jenkins, has stressed how crucial it is for the firm to land this contract. He hints that if the team is successful the members will be well compensated. In fact, Britt heard that the members of the winning team for the last contract this size each received a $10,000 bonus.

Not long after the project commences, Brian invites Britt to have lunch so they can get to know each other better. During lunch, a man approaches Brian and asks if he has received the information. The man says that he knows that with this information the firm is a sure winner. He also reminds Brian that he is due a bonus for getting such crucial information. After he leaves Brian explains that the man is George Miller, who was the former head of the division awarding the hospital contract. George has been helping Brian by talking to the decision team and getting information relevant to the bid. Brian explains that the information George has gathered about the internal discussions among the buying team will be what makes their proposal a clear winner, obviously good news for the team since a winning bid means bonuses are almost assured.

After lunch Britt looks at the firm's ethics manual that she was given just last week at a new employee orientation. Lobbying without disclosure and paying for insider information are clearly discussed as unethical practices in the manual. Yet Brian seemed perfectly comfortable discussing George's role with Britt.

Britt decides she should check with another team member about the use of insider information, so she asks Sue Garcia. Sue tells Britt that this kind of thing happens all the time. She jokes that most of the people in the division have at one time or another worked for the government. They all still know people in the various agencies. As far as Sue is concerned, friends will talk and that is not illegal, so

*Should Britt go to the company's ethics officer and report what she knows about the use of insider information?*

there is no problem. It's a win–win situation: the government will get its building, the firm its funding, and the employees their bonuses.

Britt realizes that with her overdue credit card bill and her needed car repairs, the bonus money would really help out. Besides, she is the most junior member of the team. If all the others are comfortable with this practice, why should she be concerned? After all, it is just friends talking, isn't it?

## Questions

1. Using the framework for ethical decision making presented in the chapter (Exhibit 3.6), analyze Britt's dilemma. Should she go to the company's ethics officer and report what she knows about the use of insider information?

2. Do you feel that Britt, as the most junior member of the team, has less of an ethical duty than more senior members of the team do? Why or why not?

3. If you were the ethics officer for this firm, would you address the belief among employees that it is acceptable to discuss a pending proposal with members of the decision team? If so, how? If you would not discuss this belief, why not?

Choices for a Sustainable Future

Kimberly-Clark

2009 Sustainability Report Summary

# Analyzing the Marketing Environment

Many of Kimberly-Clark's family care and personal care brands, such as Depends, Kleenex, Scott, Huggies, and Pull-Ups, are constructed using wood fiber, such that they pose a potential burden on forestlands. A substantial portion of these daily use, disposable products ultimately is headed for overflowing landfills. But because most consumers prefer greener products, Kimberly-Clark continually seeks to minimize its environmental impact in its overall effort to improve the value of its at-home, professional, and health care product offerings.

Kimberly-Clark regards sustainability as a natural extension of its corporate values, which include quality, service, and fair dealing.[1] It also recognizes that creating greener products begins at the design stage. In 2009, the company began using specialized tools to help product designers analyze the environmental impact of products across their full life cycle. Developers thus can select the most environmentally friendly design.

The next step is procuring source materials in a way that does not deplete or destroy fragile natural resources. For Kimberly-Clark, that means using wood fiber from recycled sources or well-managed forestlands, especially those certified by recognized forestry management systems like the Forest Stewardship Council (FSC). It also means using more environmentally preferred fibers in its products while maintaining the highest standards for quality and performance. In response to consumer and retailer demand, Kimberly-Clark is increasing the percentage of FSC-certified fiber in its consumer tissues and working toward a goal of purchasing 100 percent of wood fiber from suppliers that have been certified as using responsible forestry.

To improve environmental practices in manufacturing and throughout the supply chain, Kimberly-Clark focuses on reducing energy and water use, reducing packaging and materials, cutting carbon emissions, and minimizing waste. Factories strive for more energy-efficient equipment and lighting, increased reliance on renewable energy sources, reduced water use, and protection of

## LEARNING OBJECTIVES

**LO1** Outline how customers, the company, competitors, and corporate partners affect the marketing strategy.

**LO2** Explain why marketers must consider their macroenvironment when they make decisions.

**LO3** Describe the differences among the various generational cohorts.

**LO4** Identify important social trends.

waterways from industrial waste. The company also trains employees in better use of resources. These sustainable practices help decrease production costs, an important benefit in a challenging economy.

Environmental initiatives also lead to new products. Rolls of bath tissue produced by Kimberly-Clark Professional, for example, are now coreless. In response to consumer interest in eco-friendly products, the company launched a line of products made from a blend of recycled and virgin fiber. The wipes included in this line are free of dye and alcohol and break up after being flushed. In Korea, Kimberly-Clark markets a brand of diaper that is 20 percent more biodegradable than conventional premium diapers; in the United States, the company offers Huggies Pure & Natural, touted as "better for baby, with steps toward a better world." The company also works with external firms to turn used product packaging into new products.

To improve its sustainability efforts, Kimberly-Clark collaborates with groups like Greenpeace and the World Wildlife Fund. These organizations assist in setting standards for fiber procurement, helping ensure that business can find ways to prosper without compromising the planet.

Kimberly-Clark's commitment to being a good corporate citizen extends to its involvement in the communities it serves. Employees donate money and time to local charities, and the company's foundation provides support for groups like Boys & Girls Clubs of America, UNICEF, the American Red Cross, and United Way.

These initiatives help Kimberly-Clark improve operational efficiency, develop products that meet customer expectations, and manage the risk of dependence on natural resources or negative public scrutiny. As Kimberly-Clark and many other companies have discovered, working toward social, economic, and environmental sustainability is not only the right thing to do; it's critical to business survival.

**LO1**  Outline how customers, the company, competitors, and corporate partners affect the marketing strategy.

# A MARKETING ENVIRONMENT ANALYSIS FRAMEWORK

As the example of Kimberly-Clark suggests, marketers continue to find changes in what their customers want and adapt their product and service offerings accordingly. By paying close attention to customer needs and continuously monitoring the business environment in which the company operates, a good marketer can identify potential opportunities.

Exhibit 4.1 illustrates factors that affect the marketing environment, whose centerpiece, as always, is consumers. Consumers may be influenced directly by the immediate actions of the focal company, the company's competitors, and corporate partners that work with the firm to make and supply products and services to consumers. The firm and therefore consumers indirectly are influenced by the macroenvironment, which includes various impacts of culture, demographics, and social, technological, economic, and political/legal factors. We discuss each of these factors in the macroenvironment in detail in this chapter and suggest how they might interrelate.

| **EXHIBIT 4.1** | Understanding the Marketing Environment |
|---|---|

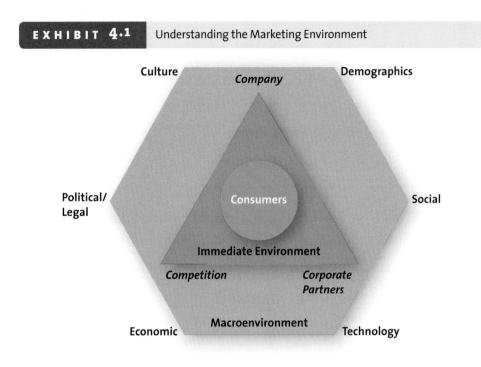

As illustrated in Exhibit 4.1, the consumer is the center of all marketing efforts. One of the goals of value-based marketing is to provide greater value to consumers than competitors offer. Therefore, the marketing firm must consider the entire business process from a consumer's point of view.[2] Consumers' needs and wants, as well as their ability to purchase, depend on a host of factors that change and evolve over time. Firms use various tools to keep track of competitors' activities and communicate with corporate partners. Furthermore, they monitor their macroenvironment to determine how such factors influence consumers and how they should respond to them. Sometimes, a firm can even anticipate trends.

# THE IMMEDIATE ENVIRONMENT

Exhibit 4.2 illustrates the factors that affect consumers' immediate environment: the company's capabilities, competitors, competitive intelligence, and corporate partners.

## Company Capabilities

In the immediate environment, the first factor that affects the consumer is the firm itself. Successful marketing firms focus on satisfying customer needs that match their core competencies. The primary strength of Pepsi is the manufacture, distribution, and promotion of carbonated beverages, but it has also successfully leveraged its core competency in the bottled water arena with its Aquafina brand, after recognizing the marketplace trend toward and consumer desire for bottled water. Marketers can use an analysis of the external environment, like the SWOT analysis described in Chapter 2, to categorize an opportunity as either attractive or unattractive. If it appears attractive, they can assess it in terms of their existing competencies.

## Competitors

Competition also significantly affects consumers in the immediate environment. It is therefore critical that marketers understand their firm's competitors, including

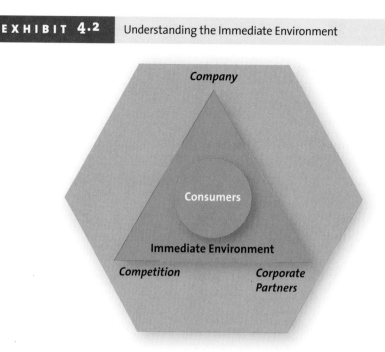

**EXHIBIT 4.2**    Understanding the Immediate Environment

their strengths, weaknesses, and likely reactions to the marketing activities that their own firm undertakes. When Kimberly-Clark introduced Pull-Ups to extend its Huggies line of diapers, Procter & Gamble was quick to respond with Easy-Ups for its Pampers brand to ensure potty-training parents still considered its brand. Similarly, if Brawny claims an innovation in paper towels, Kimberly-Clark's Viva brand will need to respond in kind.

*Proctor & Gamble quickly introduced Easy-Ups diapers as a response to competition.*

## Corporate Partners

Few firms operate in isolation. For example, automobile manufacturers collaborate with suppliers of sheet metal, tire manufacturers, component part makers, unions, transport companies, and dealerships to produce and market their automobiles successfully. Parties that work with the focal firm are its corporate partners. Consider an example that demonstrates the role these partners play and how they work with the firm to create a single, efficient manufacturing system. Unlike most outdoor clothing manufacturers that use synthetic nonrenewable materials, Nau makes outdoor and ski clothing from renewable sources such as corn and recycled plastic bottles. It was founded by a team of entrepreneurs who left companies such as Nike and Patagonia. To develop clothing from sustainable materials that were rugged and beautiful, these founders turned to manufacturing partners around the world to develop new fabrics, such as PLA (polyactic acid),

*Nau works with its corporate partners to develop outdoor and ski clothing from renewable resources such as corn and recycled plastic bottles.*

a fast-wicking biopolymer made from corn. To complement the new fabrics, the company uses only organic cotton and wool from "happy sheep," provided by partners in the ranching industry that embrace animal-friendly practices. Thus, not only does Nau represent the cutting-edge of sustainability and green business, but it also clearly demonstrates how "going green" can prompt companies to work more closely with their partners to innovate.[3]

---

## CHECK YOURSELF

1. What are the components of the immediate environment?

---

# MACROENVIRONMENTAL FACTORS

**L02** Explain why marketers must consider their macroenvironment when they make decisions.

In addition to understanding their customers, the company itself, their competition, and their corporate partners, marketers must understand the macroenvironmental factors that operate in the external environment, namely, the culture, demographics, social issues, technological advances, economic situation, and political/regulatory environment, or CDSTEP, as shown in Exhibit 4.3.

## Culture

We broadly define culture as the shared meanings, beliefs, morals, values, and customs of a group of people.[4] Transmitted by words, literature, and institutions, culture gets passed down from generation to generation and learned over time. You participate in many cultures: Your family has a cultural heritage, so perhaps your mealtime traditions include eating rugelach, a traditional Jewish pastry, or sharing corned beef and cabbage to celebrate your Irish ancestry on St. Patrick's Day. Your school or workplace also shares its own common culture. In a broader sense, you also participate in the cultural aspects of the town and country in which you live. The challenge for marketers is to have products or services identifiable by and relevant to a particular group of people. Our various cultures influence what,

**EXHIBIT 4·3**     The Macroenvironment

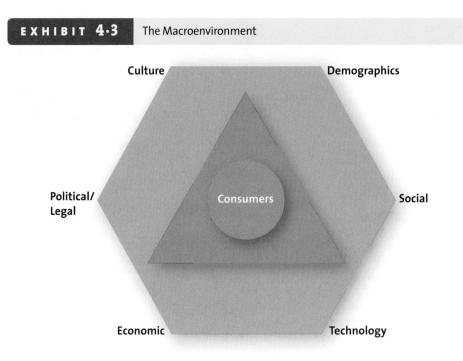

why, how, where, and when we buy. Two dimensions of culture that marketers must take into account as they develop their marketing strategies are the culture of the country and that of a region within a country.

**Country Culture**  The visible nuances of a country culture, such as tools and artifacts, behavior, dress, symbols, physical settings, ceremonies, language differences, colors and tastes, and food preferences, are easy to spot. But the subtle aspects of culture generally are trickier to identify and navigate. Yet some firms manage to do so. BMW's Mini and other global automobile manufacturers have successfully bridged the cultural gap by producing advertising that appeals to the same target market across countries. The pictures and copy are the same. The only thing that changes is the language.

**Regional Culture**  The region in a particular country in which people live affects the way they refer to a particular product category. For instance, 38 percent of Americans refer to carbonated beverages as "soda," whereas another 38 percent call it "pop," and an additional 19 percent call any such beverage a "Coke," even when it is Pepsi. Eat lunch in Indiana, and you'll have the best luck ordering a "pop" from the Midwesterner who owns the restaurant, but if you then head to Atlanta for dinner, you'd better order your "Coke," regardless of the brand you prefer. Head to Massachusetts, and the term is "soda," but if you move to Texas, you might be asked if you'd like a Dr Pepper—a generic term for carbonated beverages in the Lone Star state because it was first formulated there in 1885.[5] Imagine the difficulty these firms have in developing promotional materials that transcend these regional boundaries.

## Demographics

Demographics indicate the characteristics of human populations and segments, especially those used to identify consumer markets. Typical demographics such as age—which includes generational cohorts—gender, race, and income are readily available from market research firms like ACNielsen or the U.S. Census Bureau. Nielsen collects information about television viewership and sells it to TV networks and potential advertisers. The networks then use this information to set their advertising fees, whereas advertisers use it to choose the best shows on which

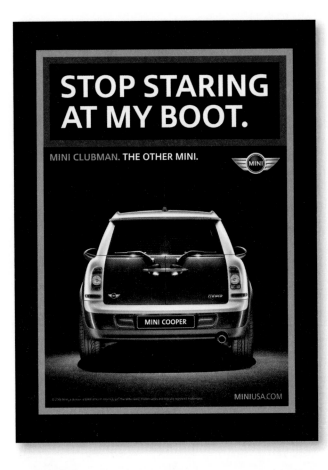

to advertise. For a show popular among the desirable 18- to 35-year-old viewing segment, a network can charge the highest fees. But advertisers also might want to know whether a show is more popular with women than men or with urban or rural viewers. Armed with such information, advertisers ensure that viewers of Monday Night Football likely see more ads for beer and razors—products that speak largely to the game's mostly male demographic—whereas ads during daytime soap operas tend to feature cleaning products and diapers to appeal to the stay-at-home moms who often watch such shows. Demographics thus provide an easily understood "snapshot" of the typical consumer in a specific target market, as the next few sections detail.

*Some firms like BMW's Mini have successfully bridged the cultural gap by producing advertising that appeals to the same target market across countries.*

**Generational Cohorts**  Consumers in a generational cohort—a group of people of the same generation—have similar purchase behaviors because they have shared experiences and are in the same stage of life. For instance, Baby Boomers (people born after World War II, 1946–1964) and Generation Yers (people born between 1977 and 2000) both gravitate toward products and services that foster a casual lifestyle; however, they tend to do so for different reasons. The aging Baby Boomers, who grew up with jeans and khakis and brought casual dressing into the business arena, are often trying to maintain their youth. Yers, in contrast, typically wear jeans for status. There are many ways to cut the generational pie; we discuss four major groups, as shown in Exhibit 4.4.

**LO3** Describe the differences among the various generational cohorts.

**Seniors**  Seniors make up America's fastest growing group, and there are currently 39 million seniors in the United States.[6] Although this group tends to complain, needs special attention, and takes time browsing before purchasing,

| **EXHIBIT 4·4** | Generational Cohorts | | | |
|---|---|---|---|---|
| **Generational Cohort** | **Gen Y** | **Gen X** | **Baby Boomers** | **Seniors** |
| Range of Birth Years | 1977–2000 | 1965–1976 | 1946–1964 | Before 1946 |
| Age in 2012 | 12–35 | 36–47 | 48–66 | 67 and older |

*Seniors often fall prey to unscrupulous marketers.*

they also have time to shop and money to spend. They like items "made in the USA," natural fibers, recognizable brand names (but generally not designer labels), value, quality, and classic styles. They're typically loyal and willing to spend but also are extremely quality conscious and demand hassle-free shopping and convenient locations. Because most mature customers don't need the basics, they prefer to buy a few high-quality items rather than a large number of low-quality items.[7] Can you see how important it is for marketers to understand these facts about seniors?

Furthermore, many seniors prefer to stick with older technologies, yet they also constitute the fastest-growing segment of Internet users; 32 percent of people older than 65 years, or nearly 18 million people, use the Internet.[8] When they are online, seniors e-mail, check the news and weather, and share photos—just like virtually every other Internet user—but they also often investigate big purchases, like leisure travel, investments, and luxury cars. They do not, however, tend to play online games, use instant messaging, or show up on youth-oriented sites.[9]

The Internet, however, can seem threatening to seniors, who often live alone and on fixed incomes—but not just to seniors; other populations also are vulnerable to unscrupulous marketing practices, as Ethical and Societal Dilemma 4.1 notes.

## Ethical and Societal Dilemma 4.1

### Predatory Lenders Target Vulnerable Consumers

The global financial crisis that started in 2008 made terms like "subprime loans" and "derivatives" familiar to people worldwide. The details of how and why the global economy suffered such a massive downturn are incredibly complex, even for many economists. But in the simplest terms, the first domino to fall in the overall global collapse was the prevalence and then failure of questionable lending practices.[10]

To increase the number of sales on their books, mortgage lenders encouraged increasingly risky borrowers to take out loans they could not pay back. As long as housing prices kept increasing though, the borrowers were able to refinance or rely on the equity in their houses to survive. But when things came to a head, many of these homeowners faced foreclosure and the loss of their homes. Some observers suggested that the borrowers themselves were responsible; they should not have taken out loans they could not repay. And there is some merit to that claim.

However, studies also show that many vulnerable populations, including senior citizens and recent immigrants, were targeted by unscrupulous lenders that used aggressive marketing and sales tactics. Many of the seniors surveyed indicated they had never sought out the loan but instead were contacted by the lender, often repeatedly through the mail, online, by phone, and even in person through door-to-door solicitations. Elderly women seemed especially prone to these tactics.[11]

The resulting predatory loans, especially to consumers with poor credit ratings, often contained high fees and hidden costs, in addition to higher-than-market rates of interest.[12] Indeed, two-thirds of the loans reviewed in a study prior to the market collapse were found to be predatory: They contained onerous fees and penalties. As the market continues to shift and banks pull back on their riskier loans, the impact may again be most damaging for the most vulnerable portions of the population. For consumers who have declared bankruptcy or fallen on financial hard times, subprime loans might have been a needed service. Without them, seniors and others often find themselves without what had been their biggest asset.

*No matter how old they get, Baby Boomers will always love rock 'n roll.*

**Baby Boomers** After World War II, the birth rate in the United States rose sharply, resulting in a group known as the Baby Boomers, the 78 million Americans born between 1946 and 1964. Although the Baby Boomer generation spans 18 years, experts agree that its members share several traits that set them apart from those born before World War II. First, they are individualistic. Second, leisure time represents a high priority for them. Third, they believe that they will always be able to take care of themselves, partly evinced by their feeling of economic security, even though they are a little careless about the way they spend their money. Fourth, they have an obsession with maintaining their youth. Fifth and finally, they will always love rock 'n roll.

Although the Baby Boomers' quest for youth has provided a massive market for antiaging products, cosmetics, pharmaceuticals, and biotechnology, as they age, their interests are shifting—especially because they are entering their retirement years during one of the worst economic recessions in recent history. For example, whereas Boomers once devoted significant amounts of their income to luxuries, today their spending on home décor has dropped by 27 percent. Instead, they are focusing on what they consider necessities: adding to their depleted savings accounts and ensuring their access to the best health care and wellness services.[13]

That does not mean that as they grow older, Baby Boomers will automatically start to act like the senior cohort though. Boomers are already accustomed to spending money on themselves, which makes them more likely to acquiesce to hiring health care workers, for example.[14] In addition, many of them prefer to continue working past retirement age, often because they have not saved enough for what may be a 30-year retirement. To respond to this trend, lenders are creating new forms of loans, such as reverse mortgages that convert home equity into a steady stream of income. Typically these loans do not have to be repaid until the homeowner dies, moves permanently, or sells the home.

**Generation X** The next group, Generation X (Xers), includes those born between 1965 and 1976 and represents some 41 million Americans. Very unlike their Baby Boomer parents, Xers are the first generation of latchkey children (those who grew up in homes in which both parents worked), and 50 percent of them have divorced parents. Unlike most previous generations, they are unlikely to enjoy greater economic prosperity than their parents.[15]

*Generation Y are the children of Baby Boomers and constitute more than 60 million members in the United States.*

Although fewer in number than Generation Y or Baby Boomers,[16] Gen Xers possess considerable spending power because they tend to get married later and buy houses later in life. They're much less interested in shopping than their parents and far more cynical, which tends to make them astute consumers. They demand convenience and tend to be less likely to believe advertising claims or what salespeople tell them. Because of their experience as children of working parents, who had little time to shop, Xers developed shopping savvy at an early age and knew how to make shopping decisions by the time they were teenagers. As a result, they grew more knowledgeable about products and more risk averse than other generational cohorts.

**Generation Y** Generation Y, also called millennials, constitutes more than 60 million members in the United States alone and were born between 1977 and 2000. Also children of the Baby Boomers, this group is the biggest cohort since the original postwar boom. It also varies the most in age, ranging from teenagers to young adults who have their own families.[17] Now that Gen Y is entering the workplace, it is becoming apparent that its members have different expectations and requirements than those of other cohorts. Gen Y puts a strong emphasis on balancing work and life—these young adults want a good job, but they also want to live in a location that supports their lifestyle.

The younger edge of this group (often referred to as "tweens") has never lived without the Internet or easy access to cell phones, which makes them technologically savvy. It also makes them expect easy access to virtually everything, prompting one observer to refer to them as the "entitled generation." But they also are incredibly proficient at tasks that overwhelm other generations, such as multitasking to conduct business deals on their laptops while also updating their Facebook status through a mobile application and also chatting on their wireless headset with their friends.

**Income** Income distribution in the United States has grown more polarized—the highest-income groups are growing, whereas many middle- and lower-income groups' real purchasing power keeps declining. Although the trend of wealthy households outpacing both poor and middle classes is worldwide, it is particularly prominent in the United States. The average annual income of the richest 10 percent of the population is $93,000; that of the poorest 10 percent is only $5,800. The total income of the top 3 million Americans equals the income of the 166 million Americans at the bottom of the income pyramid.[18] The increase in wealthy families may be due to the maturing of the general population, the increase in dual-income households, and the higher overall level of education. It also may prompt some ethical concerns about the distribution of wealth. However, the broad range in incomes creates marketing opportunities at both the high and low ends of the market.

Although some marketers choose to target only affluent population segments, others have had great success delivering value to middle- and low-income earners. Consider, for example, the toys presented by the specialty retailer Hammacher Schlemmer versus the mass appeal of Walmart's toy sections. Toy buyers at Walmart are looking for inexpensive products; those at Hammacher Schlemmer go to great lengths to find unusual toys like the Fuel Cell Car and Experiment Kit pictured.[19] Or note the variety of cellular phone plans, from unlimited access to prepaid cards, designed to enable everyone to use a phone.[20]

*The Fuel Cell Car and Experiment Kit appeals to an affluent customer at specialty retailer, Hammacher Schlemmer.*

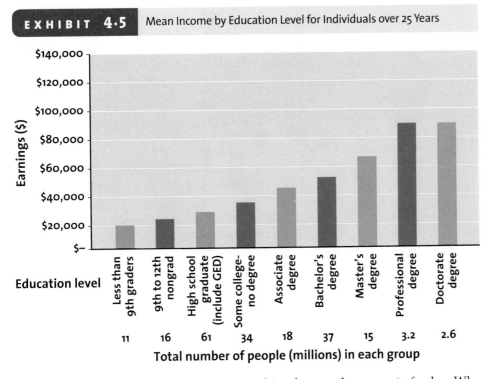

**EXHIBIT 4·5** Mean Income by Education Level for Individuals over 25 Years

Earnings ($)

$140,000
$120,000
$100,000
$80,000
$60,000
$40,000
$20,000
$–

**Education level**

Less than 9th graders
9th to 12th nongrad
High school graduate (include GED)
Some college-no degree
Associate degree
Bachelor's degree
Master's degree
Professional degree
Doctorate degree

| 11 | 16 | 61 | 34 | 18 | 37 | 15 | 3.2 | 2.6 |

**Total number of people (millions) in each group**

Another aspect of the income demographic relates to the concept of value. Why are customers searching for value more today than in recent decades? During the first three decades after World War II, most American families experienced real income growth, but in the late 1970s through early 2000s, that growth began to stagnate. Family incomes have stayed slightly ahead of inflation (the general rate of price increases), but their health care costs, property taxes, and tuition bills have risen much faster than inflation.

**Education** Studies show that higher levels of education lead to better jobs and higher incomes.[21] (See Exhibit 4.5.) According to the U.S. Bureau of Labor Statistics, employment that requires a college or secondary degree accounts for nearly half of all projected job growth in the near future. Moreover, average annual earnings are higher for those with degrees than for those without. Those who did not graduate from high school have an average annual salary of about $24,000; high school grads earn $30,000; those with a bachelor's degree earn $53,000.

For some products, marketers can combine education level with other data like occupation and income and obtain pretty accurate predictions of purchase behavior. For instance, a full-time college student with a part-time job may have relatively little personal income but will spend his or her disposable dollars differently than would a high school graduate who works in a factory and earns a similar income. College students tend to play sports and go to nightclubs, whereas high school graduates are more likely to watch sports and go to bars. Marketers need to be quite cognizant of the interaction among education, income, and occupation.

**Gender** Years ago, gender roles appeared clear, but those male/female roles have been blurred. This shift in attitude and behavior affects the way many firms design and promote their products and services. More firms are careful about gender neutrality in positioning their products and attempt to transcend gender boundaries, especially through increased interactions with their

*Women are no longer the only family members doing the grocery shopping.*

*Thousands of people line up for the start of the 2007 Nike Women's Marathon in San Francisco.*

customers. On the basis of its research with men for example, the children's stroller company Bugaboo International designed a high-tech, black-and-chrome contraption with dirt bike tires.

Rather than rely on stereotypical feminine appeals, Nike also has recognized the increasing numbers of women who engage in physically challenging activities. For the 2010 version of its annual Women's Marathon in San Francisco, Nike registered 20,000 competitors in just three weeks. In addition to encouraging women to take up the challenge, with the tagline "Run to Be," Nike provides special events for women along the course, such as a "chocolate mile," pedicure stations, and free massages—though it also notes that men are welcome to participate. Every participant also receives a "finisher's" necklace from Tiffany & Co.[22]

*The United States is like a salad bowl, made up of people from every corner of the world.*

**Ethnicity**[23] Because of immigration and increasing birth rates among various ethnic and racial groups, the United States continues to grow more diverse. Approximately 80 percent of all population growth in the next 20 years is expected to come from African American, Hispanic, and Asian communities. Minorities now represent approximately one-quarter of the population; by 2050, they will represent about 50 percent, and nearly a quarter of the population will be Hispanic. Most foreign-born Americans and recent immigrants tend to concentrate in a handful of metropolitan areas, such as New York, Los Angeles, San Francisco, and Chicago.

Between 2009 and 2012, Hispanic and Asian consumer groups are predicted to spend nearly $2 trillion,[24] making them incredibly powerful groups in terms of disposable income. Advertisers spend significantly to market products to Hispanic consumers, and they have increased their focus on communication channels that appeal to Hispanic consumers, such as Telemundo, CNNenEspanol.com, and Vanidades. Although African American households tend to be less affluent than other groups, they also represent some retailers' best customers. For instance, African Americans spend proportionally more on women's dress shoes, clothing for teenagers, jewelry, women's athletic wear, and children's shoes than do other ethnic groups. Finally, Asian Americans make up only about 3 percent of the U.S. population, but they also represent the fastest-growing minority population, tend to earn more, have more schooling, and be more likely to be professionally employed or own a business. However, across the board, marketers cannot assume they can use a single strategy to appeal to all minority groups. For example, the Chinese, Japanese, Indian, Korean, and Southeast Asian subgroups, such as the Vietnamese and Cambodian, all speak different languages and come from different regional and country cultures.

 **LO4**     Identify important social trends.

## Social Trends

Various social trends appear to be shaping consumer values in the United States and around the world, including a greater emphasis on thrift, health and wellness concerns, greener consumption, privacy concerns, and time-poor societies.

**Price Sensitivity**  American society is a consumer society, and yet the recent economic impacts of a recession and the housing crash have prompted many people to embrace the idea of spending less as a virtuous pursuit. Bloggers describe their efforts to get by on less, whether their plan involves spending only $1 per day on food or refusing to buy new clothing (other than underwear) for a year.[25] Not everyone is quite so extreme though; consumers across the board appear to be attempting to save more, spend less on luxuries, and manage to get by without dipping into their savings.

In response, marketers offer ways to make spending easier for thrifty customers. For example, Virgin Atlantic hosts a service called Taxi2 to make it easier for passengers to share rides and therefore save money from the airport to their destination, even if they fly other airlines. Imagine you will be arriving into New York's JFK and need to get to a hotel on the West Side of Manhattan. Before getting on the plane, you log on to Taxi2, provide your flight information and specific destination (as well as whether you prefer a same-sex taxi partner), and come away with the name of a "matched traveler" who is arriving around the same time and going to the same general location.[26]

**Health and Wellness Concerns** Recent news stories have made many consumers increasingly aware of the threats of worldwide pandemics or epidemics. From SARS to bird flu to H1N1, consumers worry about their health and that of their children. They increasingly demand products that can help them keep themselves and family safe. And thus was born one of the most recent product trends: hand sanitizer. The recession-proof gel saw 70 percent sales increases in 2009. An all-natural version introduced in a limited distribution market sold 40,000 two-ounce bottles—in one week. The entrepreneurs behind this product even added a luxury component to their offer by including aloe vera, so their product softens hands even as it sanitizes.[27]

*The Hispanic market is so large in some areas of the United States that marketers develop entire marketing programs just to meet Hispanics' needs.*

Health concerns, especially those pertaining to children, extend far beyond short-term crises though. In the past 20 years, child obesity has doubled and teenage obesity tripled in the United States, leading to skyrocketing rates of high blood pressure, high cholesterol, early signs of heart disease, and Type 2 diabetes among children. New guidelines therefore require advertisers to market food in reasonably proportioned sizes. Advertised food items must provide basic nutrients, have less than 30 percent of their total calories from fat, and include no added sweeteners. The advertising also cannot be aired during children's programming, and companies cannot link unhealthy foods with cartoon and celebrity figures. For example, Burger King no longer uses SpongeBob SquarePants to promote burgers and fries.[28]

*Subway appeals to customers wanting healthier quick service food alternatives.*

**Greener Consumers**[29] **Green marketing** involves a strategic effort by firms to supply customers with environmentally friendly merchandise. Many consumers, concerned about everything from the purity of air and water to the safety of beef and salmon, believe that each person can make a difference in the environment. For example, nearly half of U.S. adults now recycle their soda bottles and newspapers, and European consumers are even more green. Germans are required by law to recycle bottles, and the European Union does not allow beef raised on artificial growth hormones to be imported.

Demand for green-oriented products has been a boon to the firms that supply them. Marketers encourage consumers to replace older versions of washing machines and dishwashers with water- and energy-saving models and to invest in phosphate-free laundry powder and mercury-free and rechargeable batteries. New markets emerge for recycled building products, packaging, paper goods, and even sweaters and sneakers, as well as for more efficient appliances, lighting, and heating and cooling systems in

**Get your kids to eat better without ever raising your voice.**

Childhood obesity is a growing issue and a big concern. And we're doing something to combat it. Our SUBWAY FRESH FIT FOR KIDS™ meal fits into the American Heart Association's approach to a healthy lifestyle. And best of all, it's a fast, tasty way to give kids a "better for them" meal. Finally there's fast food you can feel good about.

American Heart Association | Proud sponsor of the American Heart Association's Jump Rope for Heart.

## Adding Value 4.1    Puma Sacks the Box

When is a shoebox not a shoebox? For the running shoe company Puma, the answer is when it becomes a Clever Little Bag.

More than a decade ago, Puma launched a social and environmental sustainability campaign that included several green initiatives. The company's long-term commitment to green business practices has produced several innovations, including its methods of sourcing raw materials from Cotton made in Africa—a project that promotes sustainable cotton farming in Africa—and opening the first carbon-neutral headquarters in the industry. Puma's most recent advance replaces traditional shoeboxes with a reusable bag/box combination that protects shoes, from the factory door to the customer's closet.[30]

Created by industrial designer Yves Béhar, the bag is the solution selected from 2000 ideas and approximately 40 prototypes.[31] PUMA projects the design will cut the company's paper use by 65 percent and reduce the amount of water and energy used during manufacturing by at least 60 percent annually. Because the box and bag constitute one unit, the company also has eliminated the need for a shopping bag for purchased shoes.

The benefits of the Clever Little Bag don't stop there. The new package design weighs less than traditional shoe boxes, which reduces shipping costs and saves hundreds of thousands of gallons of fuel each year. PUMA also switched from polyethylene to greener materials for its apparel shopping bags and gave its T-shirts an extra fold to decreasing packaging size. These efforts keep 29 million plastic bags from becoming postconsumer waste and reduce both fuel consumption and $CO_2$ emissions during transport. PUMA intends to employ 100 percent sustainable materials in its packaging by 2015.

Consumer reaction to the new packaging, however, is mixed. Some detractors point out that it still contains most of a box, albeit without a top, while others wonder why nearly two years were needed to develop a solution already employed by the British Shoe Corporation. "A good example of greenwash," commented one consumer, and another found it "sad . . . that companies don't think of these small things and big consequences before putting products on the market."[32] These comments clearly indicate the challenges corporations face when publicizing their sustainability messages.

---

homes and offices. Some companies simply change their packaging to appeal to green consumers; for example, for its SunChips line, Frito-Lay has introduced a fully compostable bag.[33] Adding Value 4.1 offers another such example.

These green products and initiatives suggest a complicated business model. Are they good for business? Some are more expensive than traditional products and initiatives. Are consumers interested in or willing to pay the higher prices for green products? Are firms really interested in improving the environment, or are they disingenuously practicing marketing products or services as being environmentally friendly with the purpose of gaining public approval and sales, rather than actually improving the environment? Consumers should question whether a firm is spending significantly more money and resources just advertising being green, or truly operating with consideration for the environment and using resources on environmentally sound practices.[34]

**Privacy Concerns**  More and more consumers worldwide sense a loss of privacy. At the same time that the Internet has created an explosion of accessibility to consumer information, and improvements in computer storage facilities and the manipulation of information have led to more and better security and credit check services, privacy concerns mount. When Facebook quietly altered its policies to grant third-party companies access to its users' information, consumers rapidly spread the word—often using Facebook to do so—on how to opt out, and Congress took up the banner to force Facebook to reconsider.[35]

The Federal Trade Commission (FTC), responding to consumer outcries regarding unwanted telephone solicitations, has registered more than 157 million phone numbers in the Do Not Call Registry. This action was designed to protect consumers against intrusions that Congress determined to be particularly invasive.[36] Unfortunately, the Do Not Call Registry may have eliminated many honest telemarketers, leaving the wires open for the crooked groups who often use nontraceable recordings to reach potential customers at home. In the end, most companies are moving resources away from telephone campaigns and refocusing them elsewhere.

## Superior Service 4.1     Grocery Retailers Help Time-Poor Consumers

Traditional methods of shopping for and preparing food have always been time-consuming. Restaurants, and particularly fast-food restaurants, have helped lighten this burdensome task for decades. But as consumers become more time-pressed and as traditional grocery stores are feeling increased competition from superstores like Walmart and Target and warehouse stores like Costco and Sam's Club, some grocery retailers are developing innovative methods of helping consumers put food on their families' tables.[37]

Through its Signature Café line for example, Safeway provides entrees, side dishes, sandwiches, and pizzas—offerings popular enough that it earned $100 million in sales of these items in 2009.[38] Even Walgreens, a chain not traditionally known for fresh food items, plans to jump on the bandwagon with salads, fries, and pizzas in its 7,000 U.S. stores.[39]

Hannaford stores in the northeastern United States offer "Cooking School to Go" meals that have precut and premeasured ingredients for everything needed in a recipe.[40] The meals for two people cost $12, and the meals for 4 people cost $20. The packages are small and the containers are numbered so that cooking is very easy even for those who are "cooking challenged." There are no ingredients left out, not even the quarter teaspoon of cumin, or the teaspoon of canola oil. Hannaford also arranges their stores in a logical manner, facilitating a quick and easy shopping experience. For example, the cream and half-and-half are located next to the coffee, and the packaged granola is next to the bulk granola.

Hannaford has streamlined the checkout process by organizing checkout lines like a bank. One line is formed, and customers are helped at the next available register. Customers who have more than 25 items can choose "Go Cart Curb Service." The customer leaves the cart with a store employee, who scans all of the groceries and then meets the customer at the car in the covered bay. The customer can then use a wireless unit to pay for the groceries with a credit card.

*Self-checkout lanes speed the shopping process, but do they improve customer service?*

**A Time-Poor Society** Reaching a target market has always been a major challenge, but it is made even more complicated by several trends that increase the difficulty of grabbing those markets' attention. First, in the majority of families, both parents work, and the kids are busier than ever. Since 1973, the median number of hours that people say they work has jumped from 41 to 49 a week. During that same period, reported leisure time has dropped from 26 to 19 hours a week.[41] Second, recording devices such as TiVo or DVR systems for cable television subscribers have become more widespread, and many time-strapped consumers simply record their favorite television shows to watch at their convenience. By fast-forwarding through the commercials, they can catch an entire one-hour show in approximately 47 minutes—which means they miss all the messages advertisers are attempting to send them. Third, many consumers attempt to cope with their lack of leisure time by multitasking—watching television or listening to music while talking on the telephone or doing homework. Their divided attention means they simply cannot focus as well on advertisements that appear in the media.

Marketers must adjust to the challenge of getting consumers' attention. Noting that many viewers of cooking shows spend little time cooking themselves, the Bravo television network partnered with an in-home food delivery service to sell *Top Chef*–branded frozen dinners. Consumers can order meals similar to those prepared on the show, like Lee Anne Wong's chicken in red curry sauce; request a bottle of *Top Chef*–branded Quickfire Cabernet Sauvignon to go with it; and even try their hand at cooking themselves, maybe on the weekends, by using the related line of knives and other equipment.[42] Other options include moving advertising expenditures from traditional to innovative venues, such as instant messaging, Internet-based reviews and ads, movie screens, fortune cookies, baggage claim conveyor belts, billboards, airplane boarding passes, and ads in airports and on taxis, buses, and mass transport vehicles—to name just a few.

Retailers are doing their part by making their products available to customers whenever and wherever they want. For instance, many retailers have become full-fledged multichannel retailers that offer stores, catalogs, and Internet shopping options. Others, like Office Depot and Walgreens, have extended their hours of operation so that their customers can shop during hours they aren't working. Automated processes like self-checkout lanes and electronic kiosks speed the shopping process and provide customers with product and ordering information. Grocery stores and home improvement centers have been particularly aggressive in developing strategies to help time-poor customers, as Superior Service 4.1 describes.

To find and develop such methods to make life easier for consumers in the time-poor society, marketers often rely on technology, another macroenvironmental factor and the topic of the next section.

## Technological Advances

Technological advances have accelerated greatly during the past few decades, improving the value of both products and services. Since the birth of the first Generation Y baby in 1977, the world has realized the commercial successes of smartphones, including the iPhone, Blackberry, and Droid; MP3 players; access to the Internet virtually everywhere through WiFi and 3G; and digital and video cameras. Power of the Internet 4.1 describes some of the latest offerings along these lines. Flat-screen and high-definition televisions, as well as video on demand, have changed the way we view television, and their impact is only expected to increase in the next few years. On the retail side, firms are able to track an item from the moment it was manufactured, through the distribution system, to the retail store, and into the hands of the final consumer. Because they are able to determine exactly how much of each product is at a given point in the supply chain, retailers can also communicate with their suppliers—probably over the Internet—and collaboratively plan to meet their inventory needs. Exhibit 4.6 shows when some of these technological advances were introduced and their annual sales.

## Economic Situation

Marketers monitor the general economic situation, both in their home country and abroad, because it affects the way consumers buy merchandise and spend money. Some major factors that influence the state of an economy include the rate of inflation, foreign currency exchange rates, and interest rates.

Inflation refers to the persistent increase in the prices of goods and services. Increasing prices cause the purchasing power of the dollar to decline; in other words, the dollar buys less than it used to.

**EXHIBIT 4.6**   Advances in Technology

|  | Cell Phone | LCD Televisions | MP3 Player | Internet Access | Digital Camera | iPhone |
|---|---|---|---|---|---|---|
| Year Introduced | 1984 | 1988 | 1991 | 1993 | 1998 | 2007 |
| 2006 Sales | $115.5 Million | $924 Million | $719 Million | $582 Million | $828 Million | $360 Million |

*Source:* http://www.infotechtrends.com (accessed May 16, 2010).

On your next ski vacation, you can take most of the guesswork out of your trip just by turning to your mobile phone.

Unsure of the conditions on the mountain? Check out the North Face Snow Report, an application that provides official weather reports and snow conditions. It also enables users to tweet about the conditions they see in real time, so your fellow ski bums can clue you in to deteriorating conditions.

It might be a long drive to get to the mountain with the best snow, so you also might download the SitOrSquat app from Charmin, which gives you a list of bathrooms, categorized by amenities, in your chosen area. For example, if you need handicap access, you can determine which bathrooms offer it. You can also get a rating from other users or add a new facility you might find.

If your traveling companions include species other than humans, download Purina's Petcentric app to find a restaurant that will let you bring Fido for a meal, a park that encourages visitors, and a hotel that permits animals who want to stay the night. And if you can't find an accommodating hotel, Petcentric offers a list of kennels nearby.

Finally, imagine that you've arrived late at the hotel, gotten the dog settled in, and need some food before you turn in early so you can hit the slopes in the morning. If you order from Domino's, the company's website allows you to track exactly where your pizza is, from the moment you place the order to the minute it leaves the store on its way to you.

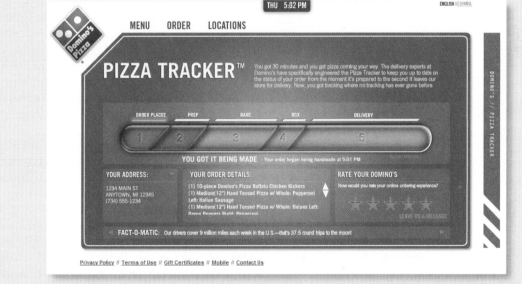

*Domino's Pizza Tracker allows customers to track where your pizza is, from the moment you place an order to the minute it leaves the store on its way to you.*

In a similar fashion, foreign currency fluctuations can influence consumer spending. For instance, in the summer of 2002, the euro was valued at slightly less than U.S. $1. By the middle of 2010, it was worth $1.24, but only after it had risen to an all-time high of $1.60 in 2008.[44] As the euro becomes more expensive compared with the dollar, merchandise made in Europe and other countries tied to the euro becomes more costly to Americans, whereas products made in the United States cost less for European consumers.

Finally, interest rates represent the cost of borrowing money. When customers borrow money from a bank, they agree to pay back the loan, plus the interest that accrues. The interest, in effect, is the cost to the customers or the fee the bank charges those customers for borrowing the money. Likewise, if a customer opens a savings account at a bank, he or she will earn interest on the amount saved, which means the interest becomes the fee the consumer gets for "loaning" the money to the bank. If the interest rate goes up, consumers have an incentive to save more,

*Tourists from other countries flock to the United States to shop because the value of the dollar is low compared to their own currency.*

because they earn more for loaning the bank their money; when interest rates go down, however, consumers generally borrow more.

How do these three important economic factors—inflation, foreign currency fluctuations, and interest rates—affect firms' ability to market goods and services? Shifts in the three economic factors make marketing easier for some and harder for others. For instance, when inflation increases, consumers probably don't buy less food, but they may shift their expenditures from expensive steaks to less expensive hamburgers. Grocery stores and inexpensive restaurants win, but expensive restaurants lose. Consumers also buy less discretionary merchandise, though off-price and discount retailers often gain ground at the expense of their full-price competitors. Similarly, the sales of expensive jewelry, fancy cars, and extravagant vacations decrease, but the sale of low-cost luxuries, such as personal care products and home entertainment, tends to increase.

## Political/Regulatory Environment

The **political/regulatory environment** comprises political parties, government organizations, and legislation and laws. Organizations must fully understand and comply with any legislation regarding fair competition, consumer protection, or industry-specific regulation. Since the turn of the century, the government has enacted laws that promote both fair trade and competition by prohibiting the formation of monopolies or alliances that would damage a competitive marketplace, fostering fair pricing practices for all suppliers and consumers, and promoting free trade agreements among foreign nations.

Legislation has also been enacted to protect consumers in a variety of ways. First, regulations require marketers to abstain from false or misleading advertising practices that might mislead consumers, such as claims that a medication can cure a disease when in fact it causes other health risks. Second, manufacturers are required to refrain from using any harmful or hazardous materials (e.g., lead in toys) that might place a consumer at risk. Third, organizations must adhere to fair and reasonable business practices when they communicate with consumers. For example, they must employ reasonable debt collection methods and disclose any finance charges, and they are limited with regard to their telemarketing and e-mail solicitation activities.

Last but not least, the government enacts laws focused on specific industries. These laws may be geared toward increasing competition, such as the deregulation of the telephone and energy industries, in which massive conglomerates like Ma Bell, the nickname for AT&T, were broken into smaller, competing companies. Or they may come in response to current events, such as the laws passed following the terrorist attacks of September 11, 2001, when the government ushered in the Air Transportation Safety and System Stabilization Act to ensure that airlines could remain in business. A summary of the most significant legislation affecting marketing interests appears in Exhibits 4.7 and 4.8.

### CHECK YOURSELF

1. What are the six key macroenvironmental factors?
2. Differentiate between country culture and regional culture.
3. Identify the different generational cohorts. What key dimension is used to classify an individual into a given cohort?
4. What are some important social trends shaping consumer values these days?

| EXHIBIT **4·7** | Consumer Protection Legislation |
| --- | --- |

| Year | Law | Description |
| --- | --- | --- |
| 1906 | Federal Food and Drug Act | Created the Food and Drug Administration. Prohibited the manufacture or sale of adulterated or fraudulently labeled food and drug products. |
| 1938 | Food, Drug and Cosmetics Act | Strengthens the 1906 Federal Food and Drug Act by requiring that food be safe to eat and be produced under sanitary conditions; drugs and devices are safe and effective for their intended use; and cosmetics are safe and made from appropriate ingredients. |
| 1966 | Fair Packaging and Labeling Act | Regulates packaging and labeling of consumer goods; requires manufacturers to state the contents of the package, who made it, and the amounts contained within. |
| 1966 | Child Protection Act | Prohibits the sale of harmful toys and components to children. Sets the standard for child-resistant packaging. |
| 1967 | Federal Cigarette Labeling and Advertising Act | Requires cigarette packages to display this warning: "Warning: The Surgeon General Has Determined That Cigarette Smoking Is Dangerous To Your Health." |
| 1972 | Consumer Product Safety Act | Created the Consumer Product Safety Commission, which has the authority to regulate safety standards for consumer products. |
| 1990 | Children's Television Act | Limits the number of commercials shown during children's programming. |
| 1990 | Nutrition Labeling and Education Act | Requires food manufacturers to display nutritional contents on product labels. |
| 1995 | Telemarketing Sales Rule | Regulates fraudulent activities conducted over the telephone. Violators are subject to fines and actions enforced by the FTC. |
| 2003 | Controlling the Assault of Non-Solicited Pornography and Marketing Act of 2003 (CAN-SPAM Act) | Prohibits misleading commercial e-mail, particularly misleading subject and from lines. |
| 2003 | Amendment to the Telemarketing Sales Rule | Establishes a National Do Not Call Registry, requiring telemarketers to abstain from calling consumers who opt to be placed on the list. |

| EXHIBIT **4·8** | Competitive Practice and Trade Legislation |
| --- | --- |

| Year | Law | Description |
| --- | --- | --- |
| 1890 | Sherman Antitrust Act | Prohibits monopolies and other activities that would restrain trade or competition. Makes fair trade within a free market a national goal. |
| 1914 | Clayton Act | Supports the Sherman Act by prohibiting the combination of two or more competing corporations through pooling ownership of stock and restricting pricing policies such as price discrimination, exclusive dealing, and tying clauses to different buyers. |
| 1914 | Federal Trade Commission | Established the Federal Trade Commission (FTC) to regulate unfair competitive practices and practices that deceive or are unfair to consumers. |
| 1936 | Robinson-Patman Act | Outlaws price discrimination toward wholesalers, retailers, or other producers. Requires sellers to make ancillary services or allowances available to all buyers on proportionately equal terms. |
| 1993 | North American Free Trade Agreement (NAFTA) | International trade agreement among Canada, Mexico, and the United States removing tariffs and trade barriers to facilitate trade among the three nations. |

## Summing Up

**L01** **Outline how customers, the company, competitors, and corporate partners affect the marketing strategy.**

Everything a firm does should revolve around the customer; without the customer, nothing gets sold. Firms must discover their customers' wants and needs and then be able to provide a valuable product or service that will satisfy those wants or needs. If there were only one firm and many customers, a marketer's life would be a piece of cake. But because this situation rarely occurs, firms must monitor their competitors to discover how they might be appealing to their customers. Without competitive intelligence, a firm's customers might soon belong to its competitors. Though life certainly would be easier without competitors, it would be difficult, if not impossible, without corporate partners. Good marketing firms or departments work closely with suppliers, marketing research firms, consultants, and transportation firms to coordinate the extensive process of discovering what customers want and finally getting it to them when and where they want it. Each of these activities—discovering customer needs, studying competitors' actions, and working with corporate partners—helps add value to firms' products and services.

**L02** **Explain why marketers must consider their macroenvironment when they make decisions.**

What are the chances that a fast-food hamburger restaurant would be successful in a predominantly Hindu neighborhood? Not good. Marketers must be sensitive to such cultural issues to be successful, and they must also consider customer demographics—age, income, market size, education, gender, and ethnicity—to identify specific customer target groups. In any society, major social trends influence the way people live. Understanding these trends—such as green marketing, privacy issues, and the time-poor society—can help marketers serve their customers better. In no other time in history has technology moved so rapidly and had such a pervasive influence on the way we live. Not only do marketers help identify and develop technologies for practical, everyday uses, but technological advances help marketers provide consumers with more products and services more quickly and efficiently. The general state of the economy influences how people spend their discretionary income. When the economy is healthy, marketing success comes relatively easily. But when the economy gets bumpy, only well-honed marketing skills can yield long-term successes. Naturally, all firms must abide by the law, and many legal issues affect marketing directly. These laws pertain to competitive practices and protecting consumers from unfair or dangerous products.

**L03** **Describe the differences among the various generational cohorts.**

Generational cohorts are a group of consumers of the same generation. They are likely to have similar purchase and consumption behaviors due to their shared experiences and stage of life. The four main types include Gen Y (born 1977–2000), Gen X (1965–1976), Baby Boomers (1946–1964), and Seniors (before 1946).

**L04** **Identify important social trends.**

Social trends have a tremendous impact on what consumers purchase and consume. Understanding these trends—such as price sensitivity, health and wellness, green marketing, privacy issues, and the time-poor society—can help marketers serve their customers better.

## Key Terms

- Baby Boomers, 123
- country culture, 120
- culture, 119
- demographics, 120
- economic situation, 130
- foreign currency fluctuations, 131
- Generation X, 123
- Generation Y, 124
- generational cohort, 121
- green marketing, 127
- inflation, 130
- interest rates, 131
- macroenvironmental factors, 119
- millennials, 124
- political/regulatory environment, 132
- seniors, 121
- technological advances, 130

## Marketing Applications

1. Assume you are going to open a new store. Describe it. Who are your competitors? What would you do to monitor your competitors' actions? Who are your customers? What are you going to do to appeal to them? What are your social responsibilities, and how will you meet them?

2. To which generational cohort do you belong? What about your parents? How do you approach buying a computer differently than your parents would? What about buying an outfit to wear to a party? How can firms use their knowledge of generational cohorts to market their products and services better?

3. How can firms use customer demographics like income, market size, education, and ethnicity to market to their customers better?

4. Identify some of the ethnicity changes in the United States. Describe how they might affect the marketing practices of (a) a regional newspaper in Texas, (b) food retailers in cities, and (c) a home furnishing store in New York City.

5. Identify some recent technological innovations in the marketplace and describe how they have affected consumers' everyday activities.

6. Why should a T-shirt shop in the United States care about the value of the Hong Kong dollar?

7. Time-poor consumers have adopted various approaches to "buy" themselves more time, such as (a) voluntarily simplifying their complex lives, (b) using new technologies for greater empowerment and control, (c) using their time productively when traveling or commuting, and (d) multitasking. Identify and describe some products and services that consumers use to implement each of these strategies.

8. Identify a company that you believe does a particularly good job of marketing to different cultural groups. Justify your answer.

## Quiz Yourself

www.mhhe.com/grewal3e

1. When marketers look at advertising media they often begin with viewer or listener profiles such as age, income, gender, and race. They then compare the media profile with their target audience. These marketers are using _____ to see if the media "fits" with their advertising agenda.

   a. country culture
   b. regional culture
   c. demographics
   d. macromarketing measures
   e. scenario planning

2. Many American consumers are purchasing hybrid automobiles even though they are more expensive and sometimes less fuel efficient when compared to compact conventional cars. Automobile marketers recognize that these consumers:

   a. value contributing to a greener environment.
   b. are economically irrational.
   c. are responding to global corporate pressure for social responsibility.
   d. would prefer an SUV.
   e. all of the above.

   (Answers to these two questions are provided on page 607.)

   Go to www.mhhe.com/grewal3e to practice an additional 11 questions.

## Net Savvy

1. Seventh Generation is the leading brand of nontoxic, environmentally safe household products in the United States. Visit its website (http://www.seventhgeneration.com) and review the philosophy behind the business. Next, review the site to identify the products the company offers. Briefly summarize some of the consumer trends you think are reflected. Describe the ways in which Seventh Generation's products address the wants and needs of its customers.

2. The Internet has been a double-edged sword for consumers. On the one hand, it provides easy access to many businesses and sources for information. On the other hand, consumers must give up some of their privacy to access this information. The Electronic Privacy Information Center (http://www.epic.org), founded in 1994, attempts to focus public attention on privacy issues. Browse through the topics on the left on social networking, Facebook, and

Smart Grids. What steps does EPIC suggest consumers take to protect their privacy online? What policy recommendations does it make regarding legal restrictions on companies?

## Chapter Case Study

### NIKE: DELIVERING INNOVATION AND INSPIRATION

Nike fans want to jump higher, land softer, and look cooler. But do they care about saving the planet? Maybe, but that's only one concern for Nike CEO Mark Parker, who is tasked mainly with ensuring the company continues to produce shoes that young athletes want to buy, so the company can generate profits even in a sluggish economy.

### COMPANY HISTORY

The global athletic footwear giant now known as Nike began as Blue Ribbon Sports in 1964 under the leadership of Phil Knight and track coach Bill Bowerman.[45] The idea was to create better shoes for athletes—an idea that grossed about $8,000 that first year. Eight years later, Knight and Bowerman founded Nike, and the company grew from its beginnings in Oregon to a presence that stretches across the globe, operates in more than 160 countries, and reported revenues of $19.2 billion at the close of the 2009 fiscal year. In addition to athletic footwear, Nike sells sports apparel and equipment and owns several subsidiaries, including Cole Haan, Converse Inc., the clothing company Hurley International, and NIKE Golf.

### FACTORS IN THE MACROENVIRONMENT

Like many companies, Nike outsources production to developing countries, where labor costs are more advantageous.[46] The model works well for these countries, which welcome the new jobs, but comes at a cost for both Nike and the communities where shoes are made: Initially, the manufacturing process exposed workers and the environment to toxins. Nike invested heavily in clean-up efforts but faced continuing criticism for the atrocious working conditions in its manufacturing facilities. When it claimed, accurately but perhaps not ethically, that the contract manufacturers are responsible for the poor conditions at their own facilities, communicating the message hurt Nike's image further. The company changed tactics and began insisting that its manufacturing partners improve labor standards. It embraced this new position so completely that Nike's current head of corporate responsibility admits the company's earlier stance was "defensive, aggressive, and isolationist."[47] When the company recognized its ability to influence change, it also committed to improving resource use across its entire supply chain.[48]

But as Nike learned from its own clean-up efforts, going green costs money, and spending capital reduces profits for shareholders and can drive up costs for consumers. Financial outlays are particularly difficult during recessions. However, according to the current CEO Parker and other forward-thinking executives, investment in environmentally and socially friendly initiatives in the present helps reduce waste throughout the supply chain and protect companies from long-term economic challenges, like rising energy costs.

### ENVIRONMENTALLY ORIENTED PRODUCTS: AIR JORDAN XX3 AND TRASH TALK

Although Nike made substantial progress replacing chemical glues with safer water-based adhesives in its shoes and protecting workers from toxicity, the company also challenged itself to create a new shoe design that eliminates the need for toxic adhesives. The first product, the Air Jordan XX3, fits together like puzzle pieces rather than relying on chemical adhesives. Most pieces are joined with a "3-D" sewing machine that stitches the shoe in an upright position, though the shoes also contain water-based glues and small amounts of chemical adhesives.

The shoe accomplishes what it is meant to in terms of reducing greenhouse gases, and the company proclaims its confidence in the shoe's ability to hold up on the court. But success in the market is no slam dunk. When he first saw the design, Michael Jordan—the namesake of the line, who has endorsed Nike shoes for decades—commented, "It better work right." Athletes primarily demand shoes that perform well under pressure, so XX3s will have to match or outperform previous models on measures such as spring, cushioning, and stability. Sustainable environmental practices are unlikely to be an NBA player's first consideration during a playoff game.

Another new basketball shoe, the Nike Trash Talk, is made from leftover shoe leather and reground materials from other shoes. Used occasionally on the court by Phoenix Suns All-Star guard Steve Nash, Trash Talk shoes remain a limited edition, intended to help the company determine the advisability and viability of scaling salvage manufacturing into other shoe lines.

*The Nike Air Jordan XX3 has a suggested retail price of $185.*

## DEMONSTRATING RESPONSIBILITY AT HOME AND ABROAD

Having learned from its past mistakes, Nike now works toward an equitable and empowered workforce and better working conditions for its own workers, as well as for workers throughout the industry.[49] Initially, the company established a Code of Conduct and required its manufacturing partners to abide by those standards for environment, safety, and health. Simply policing conditions did not solve all the problems, so Nike evolved its approach to work with manufacturers and identify the root cause of Code of Conduct violations. To help address excessive overtime, equitable wages, and other employee-related issues, the company is integrating human resources management systems into its facilities and working with other brands and nongovernmental agencies to address community issues that may help the workforce thrive.

The company has adopted "lean manufacturing" from the car industry. In this process, small teams of workers build entire items rather than taking one step before the other as the item moves down an assembly line. This technique saves about 15 cents per shoe; the company also believes the new manufacturing approach will help workers feel more empowered and more equal. Caught in the middle among consumers looking for low prices, shareholders wanting strong returns, workers who want and deserve fair pay, and a global recession, Nike continues to view its challenges as opportunities for innovation.

## Questions

1. List the various macroenvironmental factors that influence Nike's strategy. Which seem most pertinent?

2. The case notes that performance is the most important decision criterion for professional basketball players. What criteria might be most important for regular consumers who also buy these shoes?

3. How does lean manufacturing coordinate or support green marketing?

**SECTION 2**

Assessing the Marketplace

**Understanding the Marketplace**

Targeting the Marketplace

Value Creation

Value Capture

Value Delivery: Designing the Channel and Supply Chain

Value Communication

# Understanding the Marketplace

**CHAPTER 5**
Consumer Behavior

**CHAPTER 6**
Business-to-Business Marketing

**CHAPTER 7**
Global Marketing

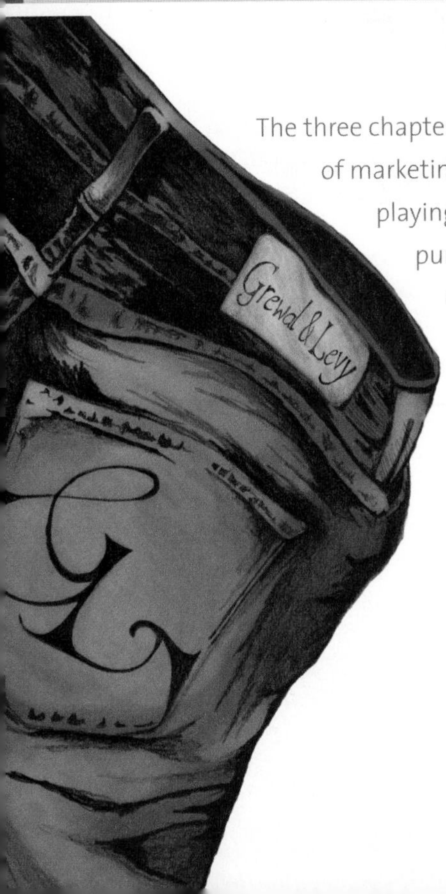

The three chapters in Section Two, Understanding the Marketplace, focus on three levels of marketing: to individual consumers; from business to business; and on the global playing field. Chapter 5, Consumer Behavior, discusses why individual consumers purchase products and services. The consumer decision process is highlighted. Chapter 6, Business-to-Business Marketing, explores the whys and hows of business-to-business buying. Finally, Chapter 7, Global Marketing, focuses on global markets. Thus, the three chapters in Section Two move from creating value for the individual consumer, to creating value for the firm or business, to creating value on the global level.

# Consumer Behavior

The fashion industry has largely ignored plus size consumers. But as the numbers of plus size consumers continue to climb, that means a lot of customers, and significant buying power, that fashion brands need if they hope to survive, especially in tough economic times. Some retailers and fashion designers have realized the importance of catering to this growing segment.

For men, access to larger sizes generally has been greater than it is for women. In any department store, customers are likely to find a "Big and Tall" department with sizes up to 4XXX, for shirts, pants, suits, and undergarments for men. The clothing environment is quite different for women. The plus size market has been served mostly by a few specialty retailers, such as Lane Bryant, Fashion Bug, and Torrid (for teens), as well as hidden, back-of-the-store "Women's" sections in department stores. Today designers are expanding their size ranges. Rickie Freeman's Teri Jon line, for instance, now features size 18 for the first time.

Designers cannot simply increase their sizes and assume larger consumers will buy. They will need to identify, understand, and carefully consider the demands of women with specific and unique fit and style requirements. Therefore, Macy's private-label INC line offers a plus size division that maintains the brand image of trendy fashions for working women. To ensure it can fit anyone who comes into the store, the regular line goes up to a size 16 or XL, and then the plus size versions start at 16W and continue to 3X.[1]

Specialty retailers also find larger women a profitable market segment. For younger plus-size consumers, the Hot Topic chain offers Torrid, which is enjoying significant sales growth. According to the company's president, Chris Daniel, the brand caters to "curvy fashionistas" who live by a "if you've got it, flaunt it mentality."[2]

But if larger is the norm, and retailers are succeeding by catering to larger shoppers, why does much of the fashion world seem to assume that larger women don't care about fashion? The desire to look and feel good is universal. For many societies, outer appearance

**LEARNING OBJECTIVES**

**LO1** Articulate the steps in the consumer buying process.

**LO2** Describe the difference between functional and psychological needs.

**LO3** Describe factors that affect information search.

**LO4** Discuss postpurchase outcomes.

**LO5** List the factors that affect the consumer decision process.

**LO6** Describe how involvement influences the consumer decision process.

defines the inner person, and people use clothing to project an image or tell others who they are. By limiting the sizes it offers, the clothing industry thus has restricted how larger women can present themselves.

Even when designers offer other options, retailers often impose restrictions that eventually harm their bottom line. One designer tells of her success in getting major department stores to purchase her extended line—but then they only ordered one of each of the larger sizes and two of the traditional sizes 8 and 10. Thus, because for many designers larger sizes sell out first, the brand loses sales, and the retailer suffers the negative repercussions of frequent stockouts because they fail to carry enough size 12s, 14s, or 16s.[3]

We are all consumers, and we take this status for granted. But we are also complex and irrational creatures who cannot always explain our own choices and actions, making the vitally important job of marketing managers even more difficult, as they are tasked with explaining consumers' behavior so that marketers have as good an understanding of their customers as possible.

To understand consumer behavior, we must ask *why* people buy products or services. Using principles and theories from sociology and psychology, marketers have been able to decipher many consumer choices and develop basic strategies for dealing with consumers' behavior. Generally, people buy one product or service instead of another because they perceive it to be the better value for them; that is, the ratio of benefits to costs is higher for the product or service than for any other.[4]

However, "benefits" can be subtle and far from rationally conceived, as we shall see. Consider Katie Smith, who is considering a dress purchase for a job interview. She requires something fashionable but professional looking, and doesn't want to spend a lot of money. In making the decision about where she should buy the dress, Katie asks herself:

- Which alternative gives me the best overall value—the most appropriate, yet fashionable dress at the lowest price?
- Which alternative is the best investment—the dress that I can get the most use out of?

Because Katie might have several different reasons to choose a particular store or dress, it is critical for companies like Fashion Bug or Macy's to key in on the specific benefits that are most important to her. Only then can they create a marketing mix that will satisfy Katie.

In this chapter, we explore the process that consumers go through when they buy products and services. Then we discuss the psychological, social, and situational factors that influence this consumer decision process. Throughout the chapter, we emphasize what firms can do to influence consumers to purchase their products and services.

## THE CONSUMER DECISION PROCESS

**LO1** Articulate the steps in the consumer buying process.

The consumer decision process model represents the steps that consumers go through before, during, and after making purchases.[5] Because marketers often find it difficult to determine how consumers make their purchasing decisions, it is useful for us to break down the process into a series of steps and examine each individually, as shown in Exhibit 5.1.

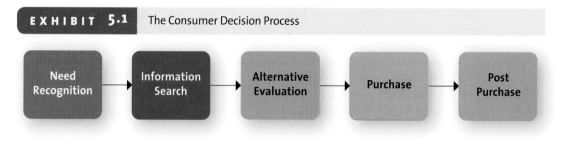

| EXHIBIT 5.1 | The Consumer Decision Process |

Need Recognition → Information Search → Alternative Evaluation → Purchase → Post Purchase

## Need Recognition

The consumer decision process begins when consumers recognize they have an unsatisfied need and they would like to go from their actual, needy state to a different, desired state. The greater the discrepancy between these two states, the greater the need recognition will be. For example, your stomach tells you that you are hungry, and you would rather not have that particular feeling. If you are only a little hungry, you may pass it off and decide to eat later. But if your stomach is growling and you cannot concentrate, the *need*—the difference between your actual (hungry) state and your desired (not hungry) state—is greater, and you'll want to eat immediately to get to your desired state. Furthermore, your hunger conceivably could be satisfied by a nice healthy salad, but what you really *want* is a bowl of ice cream. *Wants* are goods or services that are not necessarily needed but are desired.[6] Regardless of the level of your hunger, your desire for ice cream will never be satisfied by any type of salad. Consumer needs and wants like these can be classified as functional, psychological, or both.[7]

**Functional Needs** Functional needs pertain to the performance of a product or service. For years, materials like GORE-TEX, Polartec, and Thinsulate have been viewed as functionally superior to others that might be used in rugged, high-performance outerwear. Knowing that consumers seek out these materials, high-end outdoor manufacturers such as The North Face prominently display the material content on each piece of clothing and equipment they offer.

*Do Christian Louboutin's shoes satisfy functional or psychological needs?*

**Psychological Needs** Psychological needs pertain to the personal gratification consumers associate with a product and/or service.[8] Shoes, for instance, provide a functional need—to keep feet clean and protect them from the elements. So why would anyone pay more than a thousand dollars for a pair of shoes that may do neither? Because they seek to satisfy psychological needs. Christian Louboutin's shoes with their signature red sole may be the hottest shoe on the market.[9] Sarah Jessica Parker sports several pairs in *Sex and the City* and in real life; BMW even featured the shoe in a commercial. Virtually every modern fashion icon, including Nicole Kidman, Catherine Deneuve, Cameron Diaz, Ashley Olsen, Gwyneth Paltrow, and Angelina Jolie, have been photographed wearing Louboutin shoes. And yet a black python-and-lace shoe with a 14 cm heel is not a particularly practical means of spending $1,500. As a result of all the media attention, though, there is a strong demand for Louboutin shoes by women who just love exciting (and expensive) shoes.

**LO2** Describe the difference between functional and psychological needs.

*Customers satisfy their functional needs with high-performance outerwear made with materials like Polartec.*

These examples highlight the fact that the vast majority of products and services are likely to satisfy both functional and psychological needs, albeit in different degrees. Whereas the functional characteristics of GORE-TEX are its main selling point, it also maintains a fashion appeal for mountain climber wannabes. In contrast, Christian Louboutin shoes satisfy psychological needs that overshadow the functional needs they serve. You can get a $15 haircut at SuperCuts or spend $50 or more to get basically the same thing at an upscale salon. Are the two haircuts objectively different? The answer might vary depending on which

POLARTEC®

you believe represents a good haircut and a good value: One person might value getting a really good deal; another might enjoy the extra attention and amenities associated with a fancy salon.

These needs appear universal as well. As the middle class in India grows, more and more consumers are willing to spend money on a haircut in a salon—a luxury previously considered frivolous in a country where most people cut their own hair or visit roadside barbers. Yet the Jawed Habib chain has expanded to 155 hair salons and 42 training academies across Asia.[10]

A key to successful marketing is determining the correct balance of functional and psychological needs that best appeals to the firm's target markets. Marriott is carefully balancing this fine line, as we discuss in Adding Value 5.1.

## Adding Value 5.1    Enhancing the Customer Experience[11]

If a hotel chain relies on a solid reputation for simple reliability, what's the point of providing luxuries that customers consider unnecessary or even frivolous? The answer, according to the Marriott chain, is that there is no point. In the modern economic environment, Marriott is focusing on what matters most to guests. Many hotel consumers just step on the newspapers delivered to their doors, without ever picking them up to read. The various Marriott brands—including Courtyard, Residence Inn, Fairfield Inn, and the Ritz-Carlton—therefore have discontinued deliveries of approximately 50,000 papers daily. The cost savings enable Marriott to avoid massive layoffs, which supports its core value of taking care of employees and thereby encouraging them to treat customers well.

Facing declines in revenues per available room of 17 percent in the first three months of 2009, the company also turned to creative alternatives, such as serving irregular bacon slices, as opposed to uniform cuts, to save $2 million.

The switch to Edy's brand ice cream, instead of Häagen-Dazs, saves money and facilitates employees' jobs, because the less dense dessert is easier to scoop. Yet even as it cuts costs, Marriott recognizes the need to attract more customers, so it offers free nights and discounted rates, including $85 in Medan, Indonesia, and $120 at a casino and beach resort in Curacao.

To avoid negative repercussions from these cuts, Marriott wants to enhance the customer experience in other ways, such as making lobbies more inviting. Called Great Rooms by the chain, these hotel lobbies provide free Wi-Fi and modular furniture that can be arranged to encourage meetings, socializing, or casual dining. The hotel also hopes that while they chat or meet, guests might purchase a latte or a glass of wine from the hotel's cafe. Marriott is focusing on key customer needs and wants—good deals and necessary amenities—while cutting costs on features that guests probably never even notice.

*Marriott focuses on what is really important to its customers. But they save money by switching from Häagen-Dazs to Edy's brand ice cream.*

## Search for Information

The second step, after a consumer recognizes a need, is to search for information about the various options that exist to satisfy that need. The length and intensity of the search are based on the degree of perceived risk associated with purchasing the product or service. If the way your hair is cut is important to your appearance and self-image, you may engage in an involved search for the right salon and stylist. Alternatively, an athlete looking for a short "buzz" cut might go to the closest, most convenient, and cheapest barber shop. Regardless of the required search level, there are two key types of information search: internal and external.

**Internal Search for Information**  In an internal search for information, the buyer examines his or her own memory and knowledge about the product or service, gathered through past experiences. For example, every time Katie wants to eat salad for lunch, she and her friends go to Applebees. She relies on her memory of past experiences when making this purchase decision.

**External Search for Information**  In an external search for information, the buyer seeks information outside his or her personal knowledge base to help make the buying decision. Consumers might fill in their personal knowledge gaps by talking with friends, family, or a salesperson. They can also scour commercial media for unsponsored and (it is hoped) unbiased information, such as that available through *Consumer Reports*, or peruse sponsored media such as magazines, television, or radio. Sometimes consumers get commercial exposures to products or services without really knowing it.

L03    Describe factors that affect information search.

*If you go to Applebees every time you want a salad for lunch, you are relying on your memory of past experiences.*

One source of information consumers turn to more and more frequently is the Internet.[12] For example, while watching an episode of CW's *Gossip Girl*, Katie saw the character Blair wearing a fantastic outfit consisting of a peasant blouse and leggings. She pulled her laptop over, went to the CW network site (store.cwtv .com), selected *Gossip Girl*, and then clicked on "Shop the Look." A long list of items included both items: the blouse was designed by Joie and available for sale for $248, and the leggings by LnA cost $105.[13] But Katie is also a savvy shopper, so she searched "lna leggings" on Google and found that through the company's site, she could get a cropped version on sale for only $45.[14] Satisfied with that purchase, she began flipping through a magazine and saw Reese Witherspoon wearing a pair of jeans she loved. This time, she navigated her mouse directly to www. MyTrueFit.com, which featured those very jeans, designed by 7 for All Mankind, on its home page.[15] Katie entered her measurements and style preferences, and True Jeans returned recommendations of jeans that would be a good fit for her.

*If you want to buy the dress that CW's* Gossip Girl *character, Blair (on right), is wearing, go to www.store.cwtv.com and click on "Shop the Look."*

All Katie's searches are examples of external searches for information. Katie used the television show's dedicated site to find a style she liked; she referred to a magazine for additional style tips; and she found jeans that will be a perfect fit for her using the Web. All these events took place without Katie leaving her home to go to the store or try on dozens of pairs of pants.

**Factors Affecting Consumers' Search Processes**  It is important for marketers to understand the many factors that affect consumers' search processes. Among them are the following three factors.

**The Perceived Benefits versus Perceived Costs of Search**  Is it worth the time and effort to search for information about a product or service? For instance, most families spend a lot of time researching the housing market in their preferred area before they make a purchase because homes are a very expensive and important purchase with significant safety and enjoyment implications. They likely spend much less time researching which inexpensive dollhouse to buy for the youngest member of the family.

**The Locus of Control**  People who have an internal locus of control believe they have some control over the outcomes of their actions, in which case they generally engage in more search activities. With an external locus of control, consumers believe that fate or other external factors control all outcomes. In that case, they believe it doesn't matter how much information they gather; if they make a wise decision, it isn't to their credit, and if they make a poor one, it isn't their fault. People who do a lot of research before purchasing individual stocks have an internal locus of control; those who purchase mutual funds are more likely to believe that they can't predict the market and probably have an external locus of control.

**Actual or Perceived Risk**  Five types of risk associated with purchase decisions can delay or discourage a purchase: performance, financial, social, physiological, and psychological. The higher the risk, the more likely the consumer is to engage in an extended search.

Performance risk involves the perceived danger inherent in a poorly performing product or service. An example of performance risk is the possibility that Katie Smith's new interview dress is prone to shrinking when dry cleaned.

Financial risk is risk associated with a monetary outlay and includes the initial cost of the purchase, as well as the costs of using the item or service.[16] Katie is concerned not only that her new dress will provide her with the professional appearance she is seeking, but also that the cost of dry cleaning will not be exorbitant. Retailers recognize buying professional apparel can be a financial burden and therefore offer guarantees that the products they sell will perform as expected. Their suppliers are also well aware that dry cleaning is expensive and can limit the life of the garment, so many offer easy-to-care-for washable fabrics.

Social risk involves the fears that consumers suffer when they worry others might not regard their purchases positively. When buying a dress, consumers like Katie consider what her friends would like. Alternatively, since this job interview is so important, Katie might make a conscious effort to assert a distinctive identity or make a statement by buying a unique, more stylish, and possibly more expensive dress than her friends would typically buy.

Physiological risk could also be called safety risk. Whereas performance risk involves what might happen if a product does not perform as expected, physiological (or safety) risk refers to the fear of an actual harm should the product not perform properly. Although physiological risk is typically not an issue with apparel, it can be an important issue when buying other products, such as a car. External agencies and government bodies publish safety ratings for cars to help assuage this risk. Consumers compare the safety records of their various choices because they recognize the real danger to their well-being if the automobile they purchase fails to perform a basic task, such as stopping when the driver steps on the brakes or protecting the passengers in the cabin even if the car flips.

Finally, psychological risks are those risks associated with the way people will feel if the product or service does not convey the right image. Katie Smith,

*Since there is a social risk associated with buying a dress, a woman might consult her friends.*

*The Gap and Ann Taylor are in Katie Smith's retrieval set (the stores she remembers), but not in her evoked set (the stores she considers for purchases of business attire.)*

thinking of her dress purchase, read several fashion magazines and sought her friends' opinions because she wanted people to think she looked great in the dress, and she wanted to get the job!

## Evaluation of Alternatives

Once a consumer has recognized a problem and explored the possible options, he or she must sift through the choices available and evaluate the alternatives. Alternative evaluation often occurs while the consumer is engaged in the process of information search. For example, Katie Smith would rule out various stores because she knows they won't carry the style she needs for the job interview. Once in the store, she would try on lots of dresses and eliminate those that don't fit, don't look good on her, or aren't appropriate attire for the occasion. Consumers forgo alternative evaluations altogether when buying habitual (convenience) products; you'll rarely catch a loyal Pepsi drinker buying Coca-Cola.

**Attribute Sets** Research has shown that a consumer's mind organizes and categorizes alternatives to aid his or her decision process. Universal sets include all possible choices for a product category, but because it would be unwieldy for a person to recall all possible alternatives for every purchase decision, marketers tend to focus on only a subset of choices. One important subset is retrieval sets, which are those brands or stores that can be readily brought forth from memory. Finally, a consumer's evoked set comprises the alternative brands or stores that the consumer states he or she would probably actually consider when making a purchase decision. If a firm can get its brand or store into a consumer's evoked set, it has increased the likelihood of purchase and therefore reduced search time because the consumer will think specifically of that brand when considering choices.

Katie Smith, for example, knows that there are a lot of apparel stores (universal set). However, only some have the style that she is looking for, such as Macy's, Ann Taylor, The Gap, and Banana Republic (retrieval set). She recalls that Ann Taylor is where her mother shops and The Gap is a favorite of her younger sister. But she is sure that Banana Republic and Macy's carry business attire she would like, so only those stores are in her evoked set.

When consumers begin to evaluate different alternatives, they often base their evaluations on a set of important attributes or evaluative criteria. Evaluative criteria consist of salient, or important, attributes about a particular product. For example, when Katie is looking for her dress, she might consider things like the selling price, fit, materials and construction quality, reputation of the brand, and the service support that the retailer offers. At times, however, it becomes difficult to evaluate different brands or stores because there are so many choices,[17] especially when those choices involve aspects of the garment that are difficult to evaluate, such as materials and construction quality.

Consumers utilize several shortcuts to simplify the potentially complicated decision process: determinant attributes and consumer decision rules. Determinant attributes are product or service features that are important to the buyer and on which competing brands or stores are perceived to differ.[18] Because many important and desirable criteria are equal among the various choices, consumers look for something special—a determinant attribute—to differentiate one brand or store from another. Determinant attributes may appear perfectly rational, such as a low price for milk, or they may be more subtle and psychologically based, such as the red soles on a pair of Christian Louboutin heels. Consumer decision rules are the set of criteria that consumers use consciously or subconsciously to quickly and efficiently select from among several alternatives. These rules take several different forms: *compensatory, noncompensatory,* or *decision* heuristics.

**Compensatory** A compensatory decision rule assumes that the consumer, when evaluating alternatives, trades off one characteristic against another, such that good characteristics compensate for bad characteristics.[19] For instance, Morgan Jackson is looking to buy a laptop and is considering several factors such as speed, weight, screen size, price, and accessories. But even if the laptop is priced a little higher than Morgan was planning to spend, a superb overall rating offsets, or compensates for, the higher price.

Although Morgan probably would not go through the formal process of making the purchasing decision based on the multi-attribute model described in Exhibit 5.2, this exhibit illustrates how a compensatory model would work.[20] Morgan assigns weights to the importance of each factor. These weights must add up to 1.0. So, for instance, processing speed is the most important, with a weight of .4, and screen size is least important with a weight of .1. She assigns weights to how well each of the laptops might perform, with 1 being very poor and 10 being very good. Morgan thinks Sony has the best processing speed, so she assigns it a 10. Then she multiplies each performance rating by its importance rating to get an overall score for each computer. The rating for Sony in this example is the highest of the three laptops $[(.4 \times 10) + (.1 \times 8) + (.3 \times 6) + (.2 \times 8) = 8.2]$. The multi-attribute model allows the trade-off between the various factors to be explicitly incorporated into the purchase decision.

**Noncompensatory** Sometimes, however, consumers use a noncompensatory decision rule, in which they choose a product or service on the basis of one characteristic or one subset of a characteristic, regardless of the values of its other attributes.[21] Thus, though Sony received the highest overall score of 8.2, Morgan might still pick Lenovo because she is particularly price sensitive, and it had the highest score on price.

**Decision Heuristics** Not everyone uses compensatory or noncompensatory decision rules. Some use decision heuristics, which are mental shortcuts that help

| **EXHIBIT 5.2** | Compensatory Purchasing Multi-Attribute Model for Buying a Computer | | | | |
|---|---|---|---|---|---|
| | Processing Speed | Weight | Price | Screen Size | Overall Score |
| Importance Weight | 0.4 | 0.1 | 0.3 | 0.2 | |
| Sony | 10 | 8 | 6 | 8 | 8.2 |
| Dell | 8 | 9 | 8 | 3 | 7.1 |
| Lenovo | 6 | 8 | 10 | 5 | 7.2 |

a consumer narrow down choices. Some examples of these decision heuristics include the following:

- *Price.* Consumers can choose the more expensive option, thinking they are getting better quality along with the higher price ("You get what you pay for"), or they might buy the one priced in the middle of the alternatives, neither the most expensive nor the cheapest, thinking that it is a good compromise between the two extremes.[22]

- *Brand.* Always buying brand name goods allows some consumers to feel safe with their choices. Purchasing a national brand, even if it is more expensive, gives many consumers the sense that they are buying a higher quality item.[23]

- *Product presentation.* Many times, the manner in which a product is presented can influence the decision process. For example, two comparable homes that are comparably priced will be perceived quite differently if one is presented in perfectly clean and uncluttered condition, with fresh flowers and the smell of chocolate chip cookies wafting about, whereas the other appears messy, has too much furniture for the rooms, and emits an unappealing smell. Consumers want to see that some effort has been put into the selling process, and just the way the product is presented can make or break a sale.[24]

Once a consumer has considered the possible alternatives and evaluated the pros and cons of each, he or she can move toward a purchase decision. Power of the Internet 5.1 illustrates how social networks help consumers choose among alternatives.

## CHECK YOURSELF

1. What is the difference between a need and a want?
2. Distinguish between functional and psychological needs.
3. What are the various types of perceived risk?
4. What are the differences between compensatory and noncompensatory decision rules?

## Purchase and Consumption

After evaluating the alternatives, customers are ready to buy. However, they don't always patronize the store or purchase the brand or item on which they had originally decided. Their choice may not be available at the retail store or there may be some other stumbling block. Retailers use the conversion rate to measure how well they convert purchase intentions into actual purchases. One method of measuring the conversion rate is the number of real or virtual abandoned carts in the retailer's store or on its website.

Retailers use various tactics to increase the chances that customers will convert their

*Gilt.com encourages customers to buy now by offering a limited number of items for a short time period.*

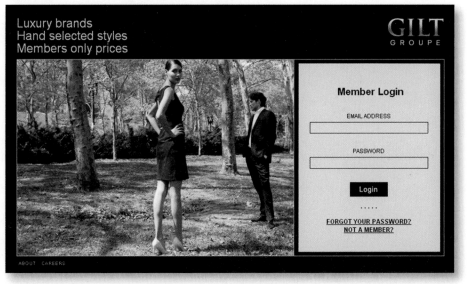

## Power of the Internet 5.1    Friends Make Shopping Easier[25]

At one time, you needed to convince friends to get in the car and go shopping with you to get their opinion on an item you were considering for purchase. Thanks to the Internet though, social shopping has become far easier and more user friendly, because consumers can bring along friends without anyone ever leaving their home. Applications, such as a technology called ShopTogether, allow for collaborations among friends on the retailers' sites.

Friend-based merchandising means that customers bring their friends to the e-retailer so they can shop together. According to the company that produces ShopTogether, retailers using this technology find that shoppers place 25 percent more items in their carts, spend 400 percent more time on the site, and increase their order value by 50 percent. Other estimates indicate retailers also achieve a 15 percent increase in online sales and much higher *conversion rates*—that is, the number of browsing customers who become actual purchasing customers.

On the Charlotte Russe website for example, the teen-oriented apparel retailer allows customer to scan, browse independently, or see what friends are viewing, as well as show friends some items, chat with those friends, and then save the favorite items in a list. Other retailers using the ShopTogether technology include GNC and Lillian Vernon.

The art e-retailer Novica uses Sesh.com, a sophisticated technology shoppers can use to discuss products in a chat window. Friends also can write notes to others in the various sections and use a "pen" to draw on the site. One person controls the navigation at a time, guiding the others through the site as they discuss the products together.

Finally, Facebook applications give friends easy access to many retail sites, because they offer an "e-mail a friend" feature, which sends a link of the product to an e-mail address, as well as a Facebook link to invite friends' comments on a product. In turn, e-retailers place their own Facebook link on their sites to encourage such uses.

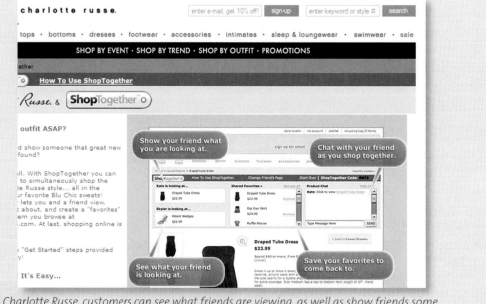

*At Charlotte Russe, customers can see what friends are viewing, as well as show friends some items, chat with those friends, and then save the favorite items in a list.*

positive evaluations into purchases. They can reduce the number of abandoned carts by making it easier to purchase merchandise. Most important, they should have the merchandise in stock that customers want. They can also reduce the actual wait time to buy merchandise by having more checkout lanes open and placing them conveniently inside the store. To reduce perceived wait times, they install digital displays to entertain customers waiting in line.[26]

The conversion rate is particularly low for consumers using an Internet channel because they are able to look at products, throw them in their cart, and delay a purchase decision. To encourage customers to make a purchase decision, Zappos.com and Overstock.com create urgency by alerting customers when an item they have put in their shopping cart is almost sold out. Other sites, such as Gilt, offer

**EXHIBIT 5·3** | Postpurchase Outcomes

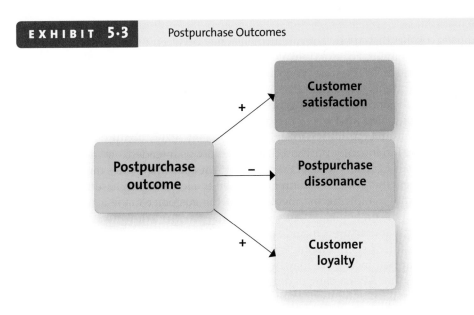

items for a specified 36-hour period or until they run out, and Neiman Marcus runs two-hour, online-only sales. Many retailers send reminder e-mails to visitors about items in carts they have abandoned.[27]

## Postpurchase

**L04** Discuss postpurchase outcomes.

The final step of the consumer decision process is postpurchase behavior. Marketers are particularly interested in postpurchase behavior because it entails actual rather than potential customers. Satisfied customers, whom marketers hope to create, become loyal, purchase again, and spread positive word of mouth, so they are quite important. There are three possible positive postpurchase outcomes, as illustrated in Exhibit 5.3: customer satisfaction, postpurchase cognitive dissonance, and customer loyalty (or disloyalty).

**Customer Satisfaction** Setting unrealistically high consumer expectations of the product through advertising, personal selling, or other types of promotion may lead to higher initial sales, but it eventually will result in dissatisfaction if the product fails to achieve high performance expectations (for a related discussion about communication gaps, see Chapter 12). This failure can lead to dissatisfied customers and the potential for negative word of mouth.[28] Setting customer expectations too low is an equally dangerous strategy. Many retailers don't "put their best foot forward." For instance, no matter how good the merchandise and service may be, if a store is not clean and appealing from the entrance, customers are not likely to enter.

Marketers can take several steps to ensure postpurchase satisfaction, such as:

- Build realistic expectations, not too high and not too low.
- Demonstrate correct product use—improper usage can cause dissatisfaction.
- Stand behind the product or service by providing money-back guarantees and warranties.
- Encourage customer feedback, which cuts down on negative word of mouth and helps marketers adjust their offerings.
- Periodically make contact with customers and thank them for their support. This contact reminds customers that the marketer cares about their business and wants them to be satisfied. It also provides an opportunity to correct any problems. Customers appreciate human contact, though it is more expensive for marketers than e-mail or postal mail contacts.

**Postpurchase Cognitive Dissonance**  Postpurchase cognitive dissonance is an internal conflict that arises from an inconsistency between two beliefs, or between beliefs and behavior. For example, you might have buyer's remorse after purchasing an expensive TV because you question whether a high-priced TV is appreciably better quality than a similar-size TV at a lower price. Thus, postpurchase cognitive dissonance generally occurs when a consumer questions the appropriateness of a purchase after his or her decision has been made.

Postpurchase cognitive dissonance is especially likely for products that are expensive, are infrequently purchased, do not work as intended, and are associated with high levels of risk. Marketers direct efforts at consumers after the purchase is made to address this issue.[29] General Electric sends a letter to purchasers of its appliances, positively reinforcing the message that the customer made a wise decision by mentioning the high quality that went into the product's design and production. Some clothing manufacturers include a tag on their garments to offer the reassurance that because of their special manufacturing process, perhaps designed to provide a soft, vintage appearance, there may be variations in color that have no effect on the quality of the item. After a pang of dissonance, satisfaction may set in.

Let's check back in with our friend Katie to recognize these effects. When Katie purchased her interview dress at Macy's, she tried it on for some of her friends. Her boyfriend said he loved it, but several of her girlfriends seemed less impressed. Katie thought it made her look more mature. Because of these mixed signals, some dissonance resulted and manifested itself as an uncomfortable, unsettled feeling. To reduce the dissonance, Katie could take several actions:

- Take back the dress.
- Pay attention to positive information, such as looking up ads and articles about this particular dress designer.
- Seek more positive feedback from friends.
- Seek negative information about dresses made by designers not selected.

Having rejected the first alternative, after a while satisfaction with her experience probably will have resulted from these postpurchase behaviors and Katie can enjoy her dress.

*Loyal Best Buy, Macy's, and Sears customers will only shop at those stores and will include no other firms in their evoked set.*

**Customer Loyalty**  In the postpurchase stage of the decision-making process, marketers attempt to solidify a loyal relationship with their customers. They want customers to be satisfied with their purchases and to buy from the same company again. Loyal customers will buy only certain brands and shop at certain stores, and they include no other firms in their evoked set. As we explained in Chapter 2, such customers are therefore very valuable to firms, and marketers have designed customer relationship management (CRM) programs specifically to retain them.

**Undesirable Consumer Behavior**  Although firms want satisfied, loyal customers, sometimes they fail to attain them. Passive consumers are those who don't repeat purchase or don't recommend the product to others. More serious and potentially damaging, however, is negative consumer behavior, such as negative word of mouth and rumors.

Negative word of mouth occurs when consumers spread negative information about a product, service, or store to others. When customers' expectations are met or even exceeded, they often don't tell anyone about it. But when consumers believe that they have been treated unfairly in some way, they usually want to complain, often to many people. The Internet has provided an effective method of spreading negative word of mouth to millions of people instantaneously through personal blogs, Twitter, and corporate websites. To lessen the impact of negative word of mouth, firms provide customer service representatives—whether online, on the phone, or in stores—to handle and respond to complaints. If the customer believes that positive action will be taken as a result of the complaint, he or she is less likely to complain to family and friends or through the Internet (a detailed example is presented in Chapter 12).

---

### CHECK YOURSELF

1. Identify the five stages in the consumer decision process.

---

# FACTORS INFLUENCING THE CONSUMER DECISION PROCESS

**L05** List the factors that affect the consumer decision process.

The consumer decision process can be influenced by several factors, as illustrated in Exhibit 5.4. First are the elements of the marketing mix, which we discuss throughout this book. Second are psychological factors, which are influences internal to the customer, such as motives, attitudes, perception, and learning. Third, social factors, such as family, reference groups, and culture, also influence the decision process. Fourth, there are situational factors, such as the specific purchase situation, a particular shopping situation, or temporal state (the time of day), that affect the decision process.

Every decision people make as consumers will take them through some form of the consumer decision process. But, like life itself, this process does not exist in a vacuum.

## Psychological Factors

Although marketers can influence purchase decisions, a host of psychological factors affect the way people receive marketers' messages. Among them are motives, attitudes, perception, learning, and lifestyle. In this section, we examine how such psychological factors can influence the consumer decision process.[30]

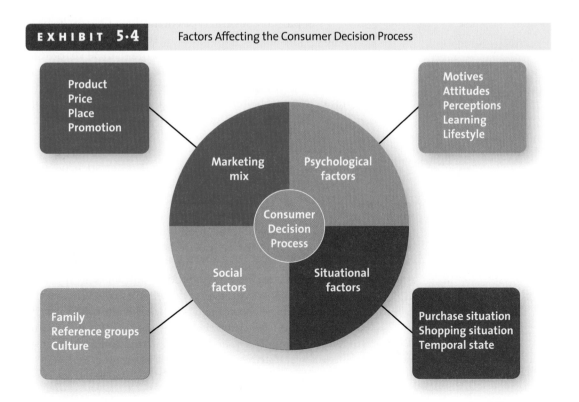

**EXHIBIT 5·4**    Factors Affecting the Consumer Decision Process

Product / Price / Place / Promotion

Motives / Attitudes / Perceptions / Learning / Lifestyle

Marketing mix

Psychological factors

Consumer Decision Process

Social factors

Situational factors

Family / Reference groups / Culture

Purchase situation / Shopping situation / Temporal state

| EXHIBIT  5·5 | Maslow's Hierarchy of Needs |
|---|---|

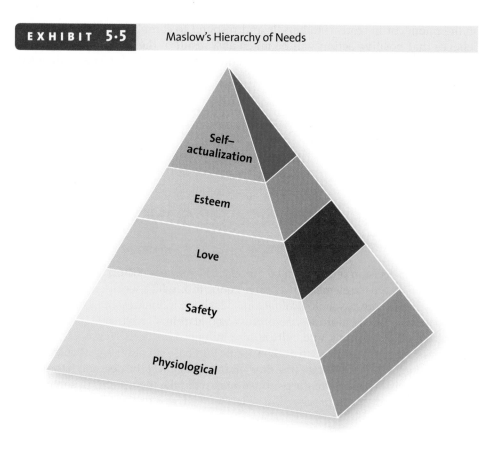

*Taco Bell satisfies physiological needs.*

**Motives**  In Chapter 1, we argued that marketing is all about satisfying customer needs and wants. When a need, such as thirst, or a want, such as a Diet Pepsi, is not satisfied, it motivates us, or drives us, to get satisfaction. So, a **motive** is a need or want that is strong enough to cause the person to seek satisfaction.

People have several types of motives. One of the best known paradigms for explaining these motive types was developed by Abraham Maslow more than 30 years ago, called **Maslow's Hierarchy of Needs**.[31] Maslow categorized five groups of needs, namely, physiological (e.g., food, water, shelter), safety (e.g., secure employment, health), love (e.g., friendship, family), esteem (e.g., confidence, respect), and self-actualization (people engage in personal growth activities and attempt to meet their intellectual, aesthetic, creative, and other such needs). The pyramid in Exhibit 5.5 demonstrates the theoretical progression of those needs.

**Physiological needs** deal with the basic biological necessities of life—food, drink, rest, and shelter. Although for most people in developed countries these basic needs are generally met, there are those in both developed and less-developed countries who are less fortunate. However, everyone remains concerned with meeting these basic needs.[32] Marketers seize every opportunity to convert these needs into wants by reminding us to eat at Taco Bell, drink milk, sleep on a Beautyrest mattress, and stay at a Marriott.

*Ads for crime prevention satisfy safety needs.*

*Yoga satisfies esteem needs by helping people satisfy their inner desires.*

*Which categories of Maslow's Hierarchy of Needs do these magazines fulfill?*

**Safety needs** pertain to protection and physical well-being. The marketplace is full of products and services that are designed to make you safer, such as airbags in cars and burglar alarms in homes, or healthier, such as vitamins and organic meats and vegetables.

**Love needs** relate to our interactions with others. Haircuts and makeup make you look more attractive, and deodorants prevent odor. Greeting cards help you express your feelings toward others.

**Esteem needs** allow people to satisfy their inner desires. Yoga, meditation, health clubs, and many books appeal to people's desires to grow or maintain a happy, satisfied outlook on life.

Finally, **self-actualization** occurs when you feel completely satisfied with your life and how you live. You don't care what others think. You drive a Ford Fusion because it suits the person you are, not because some celebrity endorses it or because you want others to think better of you.

Which of these needs applies when a consumer purchases a magazine? Magazines such as *Weight Watchers*, for instance, help satisfy physiological needs like how to eat healthy but also esteem needs like how to be happy with one's life.[33] Magazines like *Family Circle*, on the other hand, provide tips on how to make the home a safer place to live. Finally, magazines such as *Weddings* help satisfy love and belonging needs, because they provide instructions on topics such as how to prepare gracious invitations for friends and family. Many of these magazines fulfill several needs simultaneously, of course. Good marketers add value to their products or services by nudging people up the needs hierarchy and offering information on as many of the pyramid needs as they can.

**Attitude** We have attitudes about almost everything. For instance, we like this class, but we don't like the instructor. We like where we live, but we don't like the weather. An **attitude** is a person's enduring evaluation of his or her feelings about and behavioral tendencies toward an object or idea. Attitudes are learned and long lasting, and they might develop over a long period of time, though they can also abruptly change. For instance, you might like your instructor for much of the semester—until she returns your first exam. The one thing attitudes have in common for everyone is their ability to influence our decisions and actions.

An attitude consists of three components. The **cognitive component** reflects a person's belief system, or what we believe to be true; the **affective component** involves emotions, or what we feel about the issue at hand, including our like or dislike of something; and the **behavioral component** pertains to the actions we undertake based on what we know and feel. For example, Matt and Lisa Martinez see an advertisement for the latest *Pirates of the Caribbean* movie, showing Johnny Depp dueling with Geoffrey Rush. The ad lists quotes from different movie critics who call it a great and exciting film. Matt and Lisa therefore come to believe that the critics must be correct and that the new *Pirates of the Caribbean* will be a good movie (cognitive component). Later they catch an interview with Johnny Depp, who talks about making the movie and his enjoyment playing Captain Jack Sparrow. Therefore, Matt and Lisa start to believe the movie will be fun and engaging, because they appreciate action adventures and also have enjoyed previous Johnny Depp films (affective component). After weighing their various options—which include various other movies, other entertainment options like attending a concert instead, or just staying home—Matt and Lisa decide to go see the movie (behavioral component).

*Based on positive reviews (cognitive component) and positive feelings toward the actors (affective component), many people went to see Pirates of the Caribbean (behavior component) and came away with a positive attitude toward it.*

Ideally, agreement exists among these three components. But when there is incongruence among the three—if Matt and Lisa read positive reviews and like action films but do not find Johnny Depp an appealing actor—cognitive dissonance might occur. Matt and Lisa might decide their reviews and their liking of action films will outweigh their dislike of Johnny Depp and go see the movie. If they then find the movie unenjoyable, because Johnny Depp is the primary star, they may feel foolish for having "wasted" their money.

Such dissonance is a terrible feeling, which people try to avoid, often by convincing themselves that the decision was a good one in some way.[34] In this example, Matt and Lisa might focus on the special effects and the romantic elements of the movie while mentally glossing over the parts that featured the actor they did not enjoy. In this way, they can convince themselves that the parts they liked were good enough to counterbalance the part they didn't like, and thus, they make their moviegoing experience a positive event overall.

Although attitudes are pervasive and usually slow to change, the important fact from a marketer's point of view is that they can be influenced and perhaps changed through persuasive communications and personal experience. Marketing communication—through salespeople, advertisements, free samples, or other such methods—can attempt to change what people believe to be true about a product or service (cognitive) or how they feel toward it (affective). If the marketer is successful, the cognitive and affective components work in concert to affect behavior. Continuing with our example, suppose that prior to viewing the movie ad, Matt and Lisa thought that *Avatar* would be the next movie they would go see, but they had heard good things about *Pirates of the Caribbean*. The ad positively influenced the cognitive component of their attitude toward *Pirates of the Caribbean*, making it consistent with their affective component.

**Perception** Another psychological factor, perception, is the process by which we select, organize, and interpret information to form a meaningful picture of the world. Perception in marketing influences our acquisition and consumption of goods and services through our tendency to assign meaning to such things as color, symbols, taste, and packaging. Culture, tradition, and our overall upbringing determine our perception of the world. For instance, Lisa Martinez has always wanted an apartment in the Back Bay neighborhood of Boston because her favorite aunt had one, and they had a great time visiting for Thanksgiving one year. However, from his past experiences, Matt has a different perception. Matt thinks Back Bay apartments are small, expensive, and impractical for a couple thinking about having children—though they would be convenient for single people who work in downtown Boston. The city of Boston has worked hard in recent years to overcome the long-standing negative perceptual bias that Matt and many others hold by working with developers to create larger, modern, and more affordable apartments and using promotion to reposition the perception of apartments in the Back Bay for young couples.[35]

**Learning** Learning refers to a change in a person's thought process or behavior that arises from experience and takes place throughout the consumer decision process. For instance, after Katie recognized that she needed a dress for her job interview, she started looking for ads and searching for reviews and articles on the Internet. She learned from each new piece of information, so her thoughts about the look she wanted in a dress were different from those before she had read anything. She liked what she learned about the clothing line from Macy's. She learned from her search, and it became part of her memory to be used in the future, possibly so she could recommend the store to her friends.

Learning affects both attitudes and perceptions. Throughout the buying process, Katie's attitudes shifted. The cognitive component came into play for her when she learned Macy's had one of the most extensive collections of career apparel. Once she was in the store and tried on some dresses, she realized how much she liked the way she looked and felt in them, which involved the affective component. Then she purchased a dress—the behavioral component. Each time she was exposed to information about the store or the dresses, she learned something different that affected her perception. Before she tried them on, Katie hadn't realized how easy it would be to find exactly what she was looking for; thus, her perception of Macy's line of dresses changed through learning.

**Lifestyle** Lifestyle refers to the way consumers spend their time and money to live. For many consumers, the question of whether the product or service fits with their actual lifestyle, which may be fairly sedentary, or their perceived lifestyle, which might be outdoorsy, is an important one. Some of the many consumers sporting North Face jackets certainly need the high-tech, cold weather gear because they are planning their next hike up Mount Rainier and want to be sure they have sufficient protection against the elements. Others, however, simply like the image that the jacket conveys—the image that they might be leaving for their own mountain-climbing expedition any day now—even if the closest they have come has been shoveling their driveway.

A person's perceptions and ability to learn are affected by their social experiences, which we discuss next.

*Children influence parents' purchasing decisions.*

*Famous people, like Sarah Jessica Parker, can be part of your reference group, influencing your purchases.*

## Social Factors

The consumer decision process is influenced from within by psychological factors, but also by the external, social environment, which consists of the customer's family, reference groups, and culture.[36] (See again Exhibit 5.4.)

**Family** Many purchase decisions are made about products or services that the entire family will consume or use. Thus, firms must consider how families make purchase decisions and understand how various family members might influence these decisions.

When families make purchase decisions, they often consider the needs of all the family members. In choosing a restaurant, for example, all the family members may participate in the decision making. In other situations, however, different members of the family may take on the purchasing role. For example, the husband and teenage child may look through car magazines and *Consumer Reports* to search for information about a new car. But once they arrive at the dealership, the husband and wife, not the child, decide which model and color to buy, and the wife negotiates the final deal.[37]

Children and adolescents play an increasingly important role in family buying decisions. Kids in the United States spend over $200 billion a year on personal items such as snacks, soft drinks, entertainment, and apparel. They directly influence the purchase of another $300 billion worth of items such as food, snacks, beverages, toys, health and beauty aids, clothing, accessories, gifts, and school supplies. Their indirect influence on family spending is even higher—$500 billion for items such as recreation, vacations, technology, and even the family car.[38] Even grandparents contribute to the economic impact of children in the United States. It is estimated that grandparents spend $52 billion on purchases for grandchildren.[39]

Influencing a group that holds this much spending power is vitally important. Traditional food retailers are already caught in a squeeze between Walmart, which lures low-end customers, and specialty retailers like Whole Foods, which target the high end. Knowing how children influence food buying decisions is a strategic opportunity for traditional supermarkets and their suppliers to exploit. Currently, the age groups referred to as "Gen X" and "Millennials" (who were born anywhere between 1966 and 1994) tend to shop at Target, Kmart, and Walmart more and spend more at those stores than other generational groups.[40] Getting this group to prefer one store, chain, or product over another can make a difference to the bottom line, as well as in the chances for the firm's survival in a difficult marketplace.[41]

**Reference Groups** A reference group is one or more persons whom an individual uses as a basis for comparison regarding beliefs, feelings, and behaviors. A consumer might have various reference groups, including family, friends, coworkers, or famous people the consumer would like to emulate. These reference groups affect buying decisions by (1) offering information, (2) providing rewards for specific purchasing behaviors, and (3) enhancing a consumer's self-image.

Reference groups provide information to consumers directly through conversation or indirectly through observation. For example, Katie received valuable information from a friend about where she should shop for her interview dress. On another occasion, she heard a favorite cousin who is a fashionista praising the virtues of shopping at Macy's, which solidified her attitude to go there.

Some reference groups also influence behaviors by rewarding behavior that meets with their approval or chastising behavior that doesn't. For example, smokers are often criticized or even ostracized by their friends and made to smoke outside or in restricted areas.

Consumers can identify and affiliate with reference groups to create, enhance, or maintain their self-image. Customers who want to be seen as "earthy" might buy Birkenstock sandals, whereas those wanting to be seen as "high fashion" might buy Christian Louboutin shoes, as we discussed previously in this chapter.

Some stores, like Abercrombie & Fitch, play on these forms of influence and hire sales associates they hope will serve as a reference group for customers who shop there. These "cool," attractive, and somewhat aloof employees are encouraged to wear the latest store apparel—thereby serving as living mannequins to emulate.

**Culture** We defined culture in Chapter 4 as the shared meanings, beliefs, morals, values, and customs of a group of people. As the basis of the social factors that impact your buying decisions, the culture or cultures in which you participate are not markedly different from your reference groups. That is, your cultural group might be as small as your reference group at school or as large as the country in which you live or the religion to which you belong. Like reference groups, cultures influence consumer behavior. For instance, the culture at Katie's college is rather fashion conscious. This influences, to some extent, the way she spends, how she dresses, and where she shops.

## Situational Factors

Psychological and social factors typically influence the consumer decision process the same way each time. For example, your motivation to quench your thirst usually drives you to drink a Coke or a Pepsi, and your reference group at the workplace coerces you to wear appropriate attire. But sometimes, situational factors, or factors specific to the situation, override, or at least influence, psychological and social issues. These situational factors are related to the purchase and shopping situation, as well as to temporal states.[42]

**Purchase Situation** Customers may be predisposed to purchase certain products or services because of some underlying psychological trait or social factor, but these factors may change in certain purchase situations. For instance, Samantha Crumb considers herself a thrifty, cautious shopper—someone who likes to get a good deal. But her best friend is getting married, and she wants to buy the couple a silver tray. If the tray were for herself, she would probably go to Crate & Barrel or possibly even Walmart. But since it is for her best friend, she went to Tiffany & Co. Why? To purchase something fitting for the very special occasion of the wedding.

**Shopping Situation** Consumers might be ready to purchase a product or service but be completely derailed once they arrive in the store. Marketers use several techniques to influence consumers at this choice stage of the decision process. Consider the following techniques.

**Store Atmosphere** Some retailers and service providers have developed unique images that are based at least in part on their internal environment, also known as their *atmospherics*.[43] Research has shown that, if used in concert with other aspects of a retailer's strategy, music, scent, lighting, and even color can positively influence the decision process.[44] Restaurants such as Outback Steakhouse

*The Cheesecake Factory has developed atmospherics that are not only pleasant, but consistent with their image, menu, and service.*

## Superior Service 5.1      Educating Salespeople to Educate Consumers[45]

The traditional image of Starbucks involves baristas brewing gourmet, individually specified cups of coffee. But when Starbucks started to turn its back on its gourmet roots and tried to compete with other fast-food retailers, such as Dunkin' Donuts and McDonald's, the image got pretty blurry. Stores became suffused with the scent of sandwiches rather than roasted coffee, and baristas started hurrying customers through lines instead of treating them like longtime friends. Worried about the effects of these shifting images on its profits, Starbucks closed all of its stores for three hours one day, starting at 5:30 pm, for a session designed to reiterate the coffee house's values, procedures, and ideals, all of which should be focused on the coffee drinking experience. In a video, the company's famous CEO Howard Schultz reminded all his employees that espresso needed to be dispensed into a shot glass, not the actual cup, so that they could inspect the color of each shot before serving it. These and other such details aimed to remind baristas and managers of the passion and commitment the company wants to dedicate to its customers. Personalized attention to each customer was what made Starbucks successful in the first place.

Less well known in the United States, Clarins sells luxury skin care products; it is the leading brand in Europe. To appeal and expand in the United States, Clarins is taking a uniquely hands-on approach by opening treatment rooms inside department stores that offer 45-minute facials for around $50. In Bloomingdale's stores, Clarins' beauty advisors will provide free 20-minute facials to encourage consumers to try products and learn more about their benefits. These introductory offers are designed to get consumers to try the products. But the price premium demanded by this high-end, prestigious brand requires further education for consumers. The best way to provide that education is to ensure that knowledgeable salespeople have been well trained to use the products on others.

In these examples, the salespeople focus primarily on customer education and satisfaction. But what about when salespeople have to focus on the sale, such as when they work on commission? Jordan's Furniture in New England has worked hard to make furniture shopping fun by offering in-store entertainment and food outlets. But after going through all the effort to make the store atmospherics inviting, Jordan's also realized that the quality of its salespeople could mean all the difference between a consumer just visiting the store for fun or making a purchase. It therefore initiated an extensive training program for its entire sales staff to guarantee that salespeople are knowledgeable about anything and everything customers may want to know. The regular training modules take place during workshops at the individual stores, usually before hours over three consecutive days. The sessions focus on various topics, including the differences between solid wood and veneers or the introduction of a new fabric line by a certain manufacturer.

and The Cheesecake Factory has developed internal environments, or atmospherics, that are not only pleasant but also consistent with their image, menu, and service.

**Salespeople** Well-trained sales personnel can influence the sale at the point of purchase by educating consumers about product attributes, pointing out the advantages of one item over another, and encouraging multiple purchases. The salesperson at Tiffany & Co., for instance, explained to Samantha why one silver tray was better than another and suggested some serving pieces to go with it. Superior Service 5.1 examines how some other retailers make sure their salespeople influence the purchase situation positively.

**Crowding** Customers can feel crowded because there are too many people, too much merchandise, or lines that are too long. If there are too many people in a store, some people become distracted and may even leave.[46] Others have difficulty purchasing if the merchandise is packed too closely together. This issue is a particular problem for shoppers with mobility disabilities.

**In-Store Demonstrations** The taste and smell of new food items may attract people to try something they normally wouldn't. Similarly, some fashion retailers offer "trunk shows," during which their vendors show their whole line of merchandise on a certain day. During these well-advertised events, customers are often enticed to purchase that day because they get special assistance from the salespeople and can order merchandise that the retailer otherwise does not carry.

**Promotions** Retailers employ various promotional vehicles to influence customers once they have arrived in the store. An unadvertised price promotion can alter a person's preconceived buying plan. Multi-item discounts, such as "buy 1, get 1 free" sales, are popular means to get people to buy more than they normally would. Because many people regard clipping coupons from the newspaper as too much trouble, some stores make coupons available in the store, on the Internet, or on customers' cell phones. Another form of promotion is offering a "free" gift with the purchase of a good or service. This type of promotion is particularly popular with cosmetics. Ethical and Societal Dilemma 5.1 details some of the concerns that go along with such promotions.

**Packaging** It is difficult to make a product stand out in the crowd when it competes for shelf space with several other brands. This problem is particularly difficult for consumer packaged goods, such as groceries and health and beauty products. Marketers therefore spend millions of dollars designing and updating their packages to be more appealing and eye catching.[47]

*In-store demonstrations entice people to buy.*

**Temporal State** Our state of mind at any particular time can alter our preconceived notions of what we are going to purchase. For instance, some people are "morning people," whereas others function better at night. A purchase situation may thus have different appeal levels depending on the time of day and the type of person the consumer is. Mood swings can alter consumer behavior. Suppose Samantha received a parking ticket just prior to shopping at Tiffany & Co. It is likely that she would be less receptive to the salesperson's influence than if she came into the store in a good mood. Her bad mood might even cause her to have

---

### ✋ Ethical and Societal Dilemma 5.1 · Is a "Free Gift" Really Free?

Some companies seek to short-circuit the consumer decision-making process by offering consumers a free gift as an additional incentive with their purchase. However, these gifts increase the cost of the product or service and therefore mislead consumers about the "real" cost. Are these giveaways a legitimate form of promotion, or do they unnecessarily increase the cost of products or services?

For instance, credit card companies frequently target college students with offers that include free gifts or donations to schools, clubs, or teams. According to the American Bankers Association, 25 percent of all student credit cards are received as part of an on-campus promotion, and there is a growing tendency toward signing up for credit cards on impulse. Although students are not typically seen as good credit risks, credit card companies target them for two reasons: Students represent potential lifetime customers who can develop brand loyalty and eventually use other financial products such as mutual funds, and secondly, credit card companies know that parents frequently help their children pay their debts, even if the parents are under no obligation to assist their children.[48]

One such credit card promotion by Citibank at The Ohio State University offered free sandwiches. The only catch was that a credit card application had to be submitted before any food was served. The Ohio state attorney general found out about the promotion and sued Citibank for violating the state's consumer protection laws. The attorney general accused Citibank of failing to clearly state the offer and tempting students with a prize without disclosing the conditions. Even though Citibank claims that it did not condone the promotion, it is typical of credit card events around the country.

In response to the many credit card promotions targeting college-age students, some colleges and universities are moving to limit the number or type of promotions that can occur on campus. For example, in California, credit card companies cannot give away "free gifts," and in Oklahoma, colleges have been banned by the state legislature from selling student names and e-mail addresses to credit card companies.[49]

Does a free gift deceive a consumer, or is it simply a way to make an offer more attractive?

a less positive postpurchase feeling about the store. Unfortunately, such temporal factors are usually beyond the control of even the most creative marketer.

All the factors that affect the consumer decision process that we have discussed—the marketing mix, psychological factors, social factors, and situational factors—are further impacted by the level of *consumer involvement*, the subject of the next section.

## CHECK YOURSELF

1. What are some examples of needs suggested by Maslow's Hierarchy of Needs?

2. Which social factors likely have the most influence on
   a. The purchase of a new outfit for a job interview?
   b. The choice of a college to attend?

3. List some of the tactics stores can use to influence consumers' decision processes.

**L06** Describe how involvement influences the consumer decision process.

# INVOLVEMENT AND CONSUMER BUYING DECISIONS

Consumers engage in two types of buying processes/decisions depending on their level of involvement: *extended* problem solving for high-priced or risky goods; and *limited* problem solving, which includes impulse buying and habitual decision making. Involvement is the consumer's degree of interest in or concern about the product or service.[50] Consumers may have different levels of involvement for the same type of product. One consumer behavior theory, the *elaboration likelihood model*, illustrated in Exhibit 5.6, proposes that high- and low-involvement consumers process different aspects of a marketing message or advertisement.

If both types of consumers viewed ads for career dresses, the high-involvement consumer (e.g., Katie who is researching buying an important dress for a

**EXHIBIT 5.6**    Elaboration Likelihood Model

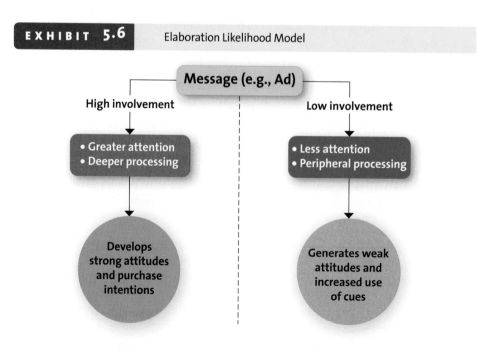

*What type of buying decision does each of these products represent?*

job interview) will scrutinize all the information provided (price, fabric quality, construction) and process the key elements of the message more deeply. As a consequence, Katie, an involved consumer, is likely to either end up judging the ad to be truthful and form a favorable impression of the product or alternatively view the message as superficial and develop negative product impressions (i.e., her research suggests the product is not as good as it is being portrayed).

In contrast, a low-involvement consumer will likely process the same advertisement in a less thorough manner. Such a consumer might pay less attention to the key elements of the message (price, fabric quality, construction) and focus on heuristic elements such as brand name (Macy's I.N.C.), and the presence of a celebrity endorser. The impressions of the low-involvement consumer are likely to be more superficial.

## Extended Problem Solving

The buying process begins when consumers recognize that they have an unsatisfied need. Katie Smith recognized her need to buy a new dress for a job interview. She sought information by asking for advice from her friends, reading fashion magazines, and conducting research online. She visited several stores to determine which had the best options for her. Finally, after considerable time and effort analyzing her alternatives, Katie purchased a dress at Macy's. This process is an example of extended problem solving, which is common when the customer perceives that the purchase decision entails a lot of risk. The potential risks associated with Katie's decision to buy the dress include financial (did I pay too much?) and social (will my potential employer and friends think I look professional?) risks. To reduce her perceived risk, Katie spent a lot of effort searching for information about dresses before she actually made her purchase.

## Limited Problem Solving

Limited problem solving occurs during a purchase decision that calls for, at most, a moderate amount of effort and time. Customers engage in this type of buying process when they have had some prior experience with the product or service and the perceived risk is moderate. Limited problem solving usually relies on past experience more than on external information. For many people an apparel purchase, even a dress for a job interview, could require limited effort.

A common type of limited problem solving is impulse buying, a buying decision made by customers on the spot when they see the merchandise.[51] When Katie went to the grocery store to do her weekly shopping, she saw a display case of popcorn and Dr Pepper near the checkout counter. Knowing that some of her friends were coming over to watch a movie, she stocked up. The popcorn and soda were an impulse purchase. Katie didn't go through the entire decision process; instead, she recognized her need and jumped directly to purchase without spending any time searching for additional information or evaluating alternatives. The grocery store facilitated this impulse purchase by providing easily accessible cues (i.e., by offering the popcorn and soda in a prominent display, at a great location in the store, and at a reasonable price).

Some purchases require even less thought. Habitual decision making characterizes a purchase decision process in which consumers engage in little conscious effort. On her way home from the grocery store, for example, Katie drove past an In-N-Out Burger and swung into the drive-through for a cheeseburger and Diet Coke. She did not ponder the potential benefits of going to Wendy's instead for lunch. Rather, she simply reacted to the cue provided by the sign and engaged in habitual decision making based on past habit. Marketers strive to attract and maintain habitual purchasers by creating strong brands and store loyalty (see Chapters 10 and 11) because these customers don't even consider alternative brands or stores.

*Picking up a hamburger at a drive-through fast-food restaurant like In-N-Out Burger requires little thought. It is a habitual decision.*

### CHECK YOURSELF

1. How do low- versus high-involvement consumers process information in an advertisement?
2. What is the difference between extended versus limited problem solving?

# Summing Up

**L01** **Articulate the steps in the consumer buying process.**

The consumer buying process consists of five main steps: First, during need recognition, consumers simply realize they have an unsatisfied need or want that they want to address. Second, they begin to search for information to determine how to satisfy that need. Third, during the alternative evaluation stage, they assess the various options available to them to determine which is the best for their purposes. Fourth, the purchase stage involves obtaining and using the product. Fifth and finally, consumers enter the postpurchase stage, during which they determine whether they are satisfied or dissatisfied with their choice.

**L02** **Describe the difference between functional and psychological needs.**

Functional needs pertain to the performance of a product or service. Psychological needs pertain to the personal gratification consumers associate with a product and/or service.

**L03** **Describe factors that affect information search.**

The information search that people undertake varies depending on both external and internal factors. Among the former, the type of product or service dictates whether people can make an easy, quick decision or instead must undertake significant research to find the best purchase option. A person's perceptions of the benefits versus the costs of the search also determine how much effort they undertake. These perceptions often relate closely to their perception of the risk involved in their purchase. Finally, people's locus of control, whether external or internal, strongly influences their information search actions.

**L04** **Discuss postpurchase outcomes.**

Marketers hope that after their purchase, consumers are satisfied and pleased with their purchase, which can lead to customer loyalty, another positive postpurchase outcome. However, consumers also may suffer postpurchase dissonance, or buyers' remorse.

**L05** **List the factors that affect the consumer decision process.**

The elements of the marketing mix (product, place, promotion, and price) have significant effects, of course. In addition, social factors, such as family and culture, influence not only what a consumer buys but also how a consumer goes about making a purchase decision. The psychological factors that influence purchase decisions include motives (which can be higher or lower on the hierarchy of needs), attitudes, perceptions, learning, and lifestyle. Finally, the specific factors that mark the purchase situation, like the setting or the time of day, can alter people's decision process.

**L06** **Describe how involvement influences the consumer decision process.**

More involved consumers, who are more interested or invested in the product or service they are considering, tend to engage in extended problem solving. They gather lots of information, scrutinize it carefully, and then make their decisions with caution, to minimize any risk they may perceive. In contrast, less involved consumers often engage in limited problem solving, undertake impulse purchases, or rely on habit to make their purchase decisions.

# Key Terms

- affective component, 156
- attitude, 156
- behavioral component, 156
- cognitive component, 156
- compensatory decision rule, 148
- consumer decision rules, 148
- conversion rate, 149
- culture, 159
- decision heuristics, 148
- determinant attributes, 148
- esteem needs, 155
- evaluative criteria, 147
- evoked set, 147
- extended problem solving, 163
- external locus of control, 146
- external search for information, 145
- financial risk, 146
- functional needs, 143
- habitual decision making, 164
- impulse buying, 164
- internal locus of control, 146
- internal search for information, 145
- involvement, 162
- learning, 157

## Marketing Applications

1. Does buying an Apple iPad satisfy a consumer's functional or psychological need? How might this information help an iPad brand manager better promote the product?

2. When consumers buy new calculators, what sort of information search (internal vs. external) would they conduct? If you were a marketing manager for HP, how would you use this information?

3. Explain the factors that affect the amount of time and effort that a consumer might take when choosing an oral surgeon to get his/her wisdom teeth removed. How would your answer change if the consumer were looking for a dentist to get a cleaning? How should the office manager for a dental practice use this information?

4. When evaluating different alternatives for a Saturday night outing at a fine restaurant, explain the difference between the universal set, the retrieval set, and the evoked set. From which set of alternatives will the consumer most likely choose the restaurant?

5. What can retailers do to make sure they have satisfied customers after the sale is complete?

6. Tazo makes a blend of exotic green teas, spearmint, and rare herbs into a tea called Zen. Using Maslow's Hierarchy of Needs, explain which need(s) are being fulfilled by this tea.

7. Identify and describe the three social factors that influence the consumer decision process. Provide an example of how each of these might influence the purchase of the necessary products and services for a family vacation.

8. Trek has designed a new off-road bicycle designed to stand up to the rugged conditions of trail riding. Develop a theme for an advertising strategy that ensures all three components of attitude are positively covered.

9. What can a marketer do to positively influence a situation in which a consumer is ready to buy but has not yet done so?

10. You were recently hired by a multichannel retailer that promotes itself as an American firm selling only American-made goods. The products featured in advertising and in the catalogs tell the stories of the firms that produced the goods in the United States. The sales response to the firm's Made in America position has been incredible and growth has been impressive. One day while speaking to a vendor, you find out a shipment of merchandise will be delayed since the product is coming from overseas and is late. A few days later you hear a similar story. As it turns out, the firm just barely earns the Made in the USA label. Though technically the products meet a standard to be classified as American made, you worry that the firm is not being entirely truthful to its customers. You decide to write a letter to the VP of Marketing detailing your concerns. What would you put in the letter?

www.mhhe.com/grewal3e

## Quiz Yourself

1. Dawn flies regularly between Atlanta and Los Angeles. She almost always uses Delta and has accumulated a large number of Delta SkyMiles. However, Dawn uses an online fare comparison site each time she looks to book a ticket to see if competitors have a better price or a more convenient schedule. Dawn uses a _____ decision rule.
   a. compensatory
   b. noncompensatory

c. ritual consumption

d. social

e. situational factor

2. Natalie and her fiancé Dow are planning their wedding. She knows her mother wants her to have a traditional church ceremony. She would like to have a ceremony on the beach like many of her friends had. Then there is the problem of who should officiate. Dow is from Thailand and would like to have a monk officiate. Natalie and Dow's wedding decisions are influenced by:

a. impulse, habitual, and limited problem solving process.

b. functional and psychological profit.

c. universal, retrieval, and evoked sets.

d. cognitive, affective, and behavioral environment.

e. family, reference groups, and culture.

(Answers to these two questions are provided on page 607.)

Go to www.mhhe.com/grewal3e to practice an additional 11 questions.

## Toolkit

Jill is trying to decide, once and for all, which soft drink company is her favorite. She has created a chart to help her decide. She has rated Coca-Cola, Pepsi-Cola, and Jones Soda in terms of price, taste, variety, and packaging. She has also assessed how important each of these four attributes is in terms of her evaluations. Please use the toolkit provided at www.mhhe.com/grewal3e to determine which cola Jill will choose using a compensatory model. Which cola would she choose using a noncompensatory model? If you were Jill, which model would you use, the compensatory or the noncompensatory? Why?

## Net Savvy

1. Visit the Harley-Davidson USA website (www.harley-davidson.com) and review the information provided about its Harley Owners Group (H.O.G.), by first going to the "Owners" tab at the top. Describe the efforts the company makes to maintain customer loyalty through its programs. What are the benefits to H.O.G. members? Discuss how these measures might be effective in creating value for members.

2. Customers use a variety of methods to provide feedback to companies about their experiences.

Planetfeedback.com was developed as one such venue. Visit its website (www.planetfeedback.com) and identify the types of feedback that customers can provide. Look over the feedback for Verizon by typing "Verizon" in the company search space. Summarize some of the most recent comments. What is the ratio of positive to negative comments about Verizon during the last year or so? Describe the effect these comments might have on customer perceptions of Verizon.

## Chapter Case Study

### WEIGHT WATCHERS VS. JENNY CRAIG[52]

Ever wanted to lose weight? For about 71 million Americans, the answer is yes.[53] For weight-loss companies, that's the right answer.

The weight-loss industry, worth over $46 billion in 2004, is growing steadily because lifestyles and food choices are working against the desire to lose weight. Most Americans spend their days sitting in front of a computer and their evenings sitting in front of a television. Restaurant meals, prepared foods, and high-fat/high-sugar snacks have replaced home-cooked meals, whole grains, and fresh produce. These habits are fattening profits for the weight-loss industry as well as expanding belt sizes, and by the time you factor in diet pills, specially packaged weight-loss meals and snacks, diet programs, and the whole range of products and services promising bathing-suit bodies, you've got a market projected to be worth $586.3 billion annually.[54] Two recognized diet behemoths, Weight Watchers and Jenny Craig, share a substantial piece of the pie. Both stress flexibility to fit a wide range of lifestyles, and both showcase their success stories. But each approaches dieting differently in their quest for new members.

## THE BIG TWO

Founded in 1963, Weight Watchers International now boasts groups in over 30 countries worldwide. The program encourages members to track their daily food intake, exercise, hunger levels, and emotions related to eating. Dieters record meals and snacks in a paper or electronically based journal. All foods are assigned point values, calculated based on calories, fat, and fiber, and members have a daily point allotment based on individual weight and lifestyle. Although members can follow the Weight Watchers regimen without support, the company notes that the most successful members are those who weigh in at weekly group sessions and attend meetings. During these half-hour meetings, a group leader discusses a particular topic, like holiday eating, measuring and weighing foods for portion control, or eating out. Members are given an opportunity to swap ideas and recipes that have worked for them, admit their mistakes and request support, and be acknowledged for successes. Weight Watcher members can prepare their own food, dine out, or purchase Weight Watcher prepared or endorsed dinners, snacks, and desserts at most grocery stores. Other Weight Watcher products that help with portion control and healthy habits, such as food scales, cookbooks, and water bottles, are sold online and at meetings.

Jenny Craig promises a unique and comprehensive plan for food, body, and mind.[55] Members eat meals and snacks prepared and packaged by Jenny Craig, supplemented by fresh fruits and vegetables. Jenny Craig's foods control portions and accommodate busy schedules by reducing meal prep time. Members meet weekly on a one-on-one basis with a personal counselor and are encouraged to develop an exercise program. Like its major competitor, Jenny Craig offers customized programs for men and teenagers and for those who prefer to lose weight on their own rather than travel to a center.

Other diet programs abound but, while many people lose weight on these regimens, the loss tends to be temporary because the diets are based on unsustainable eating patterns, such as eliminating major food groups. Additionally, the big diet companies offer social reinforcement and flexibility, which appears to help people remain committed to their weight-loss programs.

## DEFINING THE DIFFERENCE

Jenny Craig recently launched an advertising campaign that shows their spokeswoman in a lab coat claiming, "Jenny Craig clients lost twice as much weight, on average, as those on the largest weight-loss program." Inarguably, Weight Watchers is the program referred to, and Weight Watchers sued in response. The claim, they say, is bogus and based on two separate studies that were spaced a decade apart. However the lawsuit indicates the serious nature of the struggle for members. The competition is particularly intense in the early months of the year, when Americans return to the scales after indulging during the holidays.

The two diet giants are locked in another battle as well, this one targeted at men.[56] While a completely different program isn't needed—both sexes need to cut calories and increase exercise—marketing specifically to men has the power to bring in new members. While the Weight Watchers' men's program is the same as the women's program, the men's website is tailored to male interests and concerns, focusing more on working out and less on the eating plan. The men's site also mentions the link between obesity and erectile dysfunction, implying that a man's sex life might improve if he loses weight.

Jenny Craig's men's program is also very similar to its women's program but tweaked to accommodate differences in food cravings and issues with portion control. Men on this program, Jenny Craig promises, can still have a beer and fries once in a while. To further entice men to their program, Jenny Craig uses Jason Alexander, who played George Costanza on the television series *Seinfeld*, as their spokesperson.

## TECHNOLOGY SUPPORT FOR DIETERS

Dieters have a variety of electronic devices to help track food consumption and exercise. Using any Internet-ready device, Weight Watcher members can check point values for foods, including meals at popular restaurants, and add snacks or meals to their daily journal. Similar services and applications for fitness training are available via cell phone applications. Using a camera-equipped cell phone, for example, dieters can photograph a meal and send the picture to a registered dietitian, who replies with recommendations for modifying portions or food choices. Theoretically this approach is more honest than keeping a food diary since dieters may be tempted not to record full amounts. These services require fees.

*Jenny Craig uses Jason Alexander, who played George Costanza on the television series* Seinfield, *as its spokesperson to appeal to men.*

### Questions

1. Trace how you might go through the steps in the consumer decision process if you were thinking of going on a diet and using either of these diet programs.

2. How have Weight Watchers and Jenny Craig created value?

3. Identify the determinant attributes that set the Weight Watchers' and Jenny Craig's programs apart from each other. Use those attributes to develop a compensatory purchasing model like the one found in Exhibit 5.2.

4. How can Weight Watchers and Jenny Craig increase the probability of customer satisfaction?

5. Which factors examined in the chapter do you think would have the most impact on consumers' propensity to go on a diet and choose either of these diet programs?

# Introducing a corporate stimulus package that eliminates the package.

The new Xerox ColorQube™ multifunction printer uses unique cartridge-free Solid Ink technology, which is non-toxic, mess-free and reduces waste by 90%. Better yet, you can also save up to 62% on color prints. The ultimate win-win. What's more, this high-performance line of MFPs can handle the busiest of workloads without compromising image quality. Finally, good news for both business and the environment.

1-800-ASK-XEROX
FinallyColorIsLess.com

Ready For Real Business    **xerox**

# Business-to-Business Marketing

The place of Xerox in the business world was once so dominant that people used "Xerox" as a synonym for "copy." But fewer people apply that terminology anymore, especially after the company foundered in the late 1990s and slid toward bankruptcy.[1]

The CEO Anne Mulcahy adopted several methods to recover: settling an investigation into Xerox's accounting practices by the Securities and Exchange Commission,[2] trimming staff, and cutting costs. Then she began to invest in the development of new products—including faster, less expensive copiers—that could compete with rivals like Canon and Ricoh. She also led the company away from sales of commodities (e.g., desktop printers) toward the development of services and technologies that would run back-office operations for businesses.

This shift in focus meant Xerox moved more into service provision. Its offerings allowed companies to focus on their own growth and innovation, rather than on operational efficiency or technological infrastructure. In turn, Xerox's customer relationships no longer involved one-time sales of massive copiers. Instead, a sales force armed with a range of hardware, software, and service solutions aimed to help clients meet their own business goals.[3] Most of these products and services are sold under bundled lease agreements, which create opportunities for ongoing contacts and future sales.

To expand Xerox's service operations even further, Mulcahy decided to acquire Global Imaging Systems Inc., which provides document management and IT solutions and services for small and mid-size businesses. Then she bought out XMPie, a leading provider of variable information software that could help Xerox help its customers facilitate their personalized marketing campaigns across print, Web, e-mail, and mobile applications.

When Mulcahy retired, observers were nervous; she had exerted a remarkable influence over the company. Ursula M. Burns succeeded her (notably, the first time a woman succeeded another woman as CEO of a major U.S. company; Burns was also the first African-American woman to lead a large-scale U.S. corporation). Despite her

## LEARNING OBJECTIVES

**LO1** Describe the different types of buyers and sellers that participate in business-to-business (B2B) markets.

**LO2** List the steps in the B2B buying process.

**LO3** Identify the different roles within the buying center.

**LO4** Describe the different types of organizational cultures.

**LO5** Detail different buying situations.

predecessor's successes, Burns continued to face significant challenges. For example, the global recession at the end of the 2000s prompted many businesses to cut their spending on office machines and supplies[4]—which are still, despite Mulcahy's efforts, a significant element of Xerox's portfolio. Xerox's expansion to back-office services also puts it into direct competition with powerful rivals such as Dell and Hewlett-Packard.

Burns has gone about acquiring new businesses and launching new products to trigger growth. For example, she negotiated the purchase of Affiliated Computer Services (ACS), which collaborates with business clients to design, develop, and deliver IT effective solutions.[5] She also presided over the introduction of Xerox's new ColorQube color printer, which prints, copies, scans, and faxes at a price up to 62 percent lower than current laser printers.[6] The new product aims to make the price of color printing attractive enough that businesses use it more frequently and therefore replace their current black-and-white printers with the ColorQube.

Xerox's massive sales force, expansive contracts for document handling, innovative new product launches, and aggressive acquisitions are notable especially in terms of their context: They all center on business-to-business relationships among companies.

●  ●  ●

Business-to-business (B2B) marketing refers to the process of buying and selling goods or services to be used in the production of other goods and services, for consumption by the buying organization and/or resale by wholesalers and retailers. Therefore, B2B marketing involves manufacturers (e.g., Xerox, IBM, Ford), wholesalers, and service firms (e.g., UPS, Oracle, Accenture) that market goods and services to other businesses but not to the ultimate consumer. The distinction between a B2B and a business-to-consumer (B2C) transaction is not the product or service itself; rather, it is the ultimate user of that product or service. Another key distinction is that B2B transactions tend to be more complex and involve multiple members of both the buying organization (e.g., buyers, marketing team, product developers) and the selling organization (e.g., sellers, R&D support team); whereas B2C often entails a simple transaction between the retailer and the individual consumer.

The demand for B2B sales is often derived from B2C sales in the same supply chain. More specifically, derived demand reflects the link between consumers' demand for a company's output and the company's purchase of necessary inputs to manufacture or assemble that particular output. For example, if more customers want to purchase staplers (a B2C transaction), a company that produces them must purchase more metal from its supplier to make additional staplers (a B2B transaction).

Similar to organizations that sell directly to final consumers in B2C transactions, B2B firms focus on serving specific types of customer markets by creating value for those customers.[7] For example, Splenda produces a sugar-like component that constitutes a key ingredient in many Betty Crocker products and Coca-Cola's low calorie beverages. Also like B2C firms, many B2B companies find it more productive to focus their efforts on key industries or market segments. Siemens has identified core sectors, including health care, energy, technology, and software, that might benefit from its expertise. Siemens is a leading supplier of automation, transportation, lighting, and building technologies. The company helps cities become more sustainable, helps automate factories for greater productivity and efficiency, and helps buildings become more efficient, safe, and secure.[8]

In this chapter, we look at the different types of B2B markets and examine the B2B buying process, with an eye toward how it differs from the B2C buying process we discussed in Chapter 5. Several factors influence the B2B buying process, and we discuss these as well.

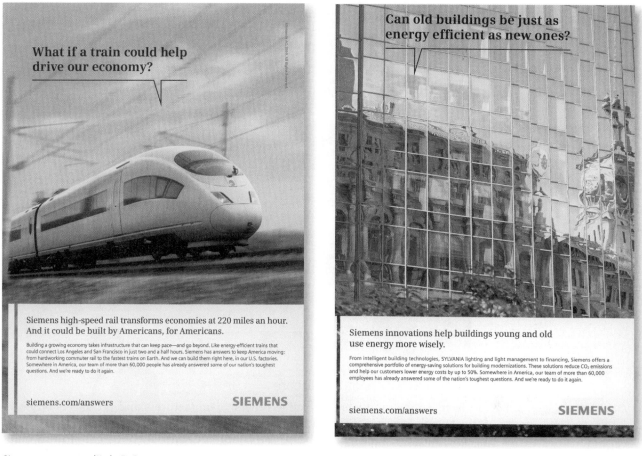

*Siemens serves mulitple B2B target markets.*

## B2B MARKETS

 Describe the different types of buyers and sellers that participate in business-to-business (B2B) markets.

In our opening example of how Xerox markets its products, we described one type of B2B organization, that is, manufacturers or producers. However, resellers, institutions, and governments also may be involved in B2B transactions. Therefore, in the next sections, we describe each of these B2B organizations. (See Exhibit 6.1.)

**EXHIBIT 6.1** B2B Markets

```
                    Resellers
                        │
                        ▼
Manufacturers  ───▶   B2B    ◀───  Institutions
                     Markets
                        ▲
                        │
                    Government
```

*German-based Volkswagen Group communicates directly with suppliers to acquire parts and components for its cars like this Bentley.*

## Manufacturers or Producers

To make the products they sell to others, manufacturers and producers buy raw materials, components, and parts that allow them to manufacture their own goods. For example, the German-based Volkswagen Group, the largest auto manufacturer in Europe, owns and distributes the Audi, Bentley, Bugatti, Lamborghini, Seat, Skoda, VW, and VW Financial Services brands.[9] Whereas formerly, purchasing agents spent 70 percent of their time searching for, analyzing, validating, and forwarding information about parts and components, today they can use VWSupplyGroup.com to communicate with suppliers for all transactions, from procurement to logistics. IBM helped design the group's Internet-based private network that links more than 7,619 suppliers of roughly $77 billion worth of components, automotive parts, and indirect raw materials. Purchasing agents receive product descriptions directly from suppliers online, which means search processes that used to take two hours now require about nine minutes.[10] The more than 111,000 users of the system[11] receive alerts of potential parts shortages before they occur and thus can focus on efficiencies instead of redundant paperwork.

## Resellers

Resellers are marketing intermediaries that resell manufactured products without significantly altering their form. For instance, wholesalers and distributors buy Xerox products and sell them to retailers (B2B transaction), then retailers in turn resell those Xerox products to the ultimate consumer (B2C transaction). Alternatively, these retailers may buy directly from Xerox. Thus, wholesalers, distributors, and retailers are all resellers. Retailers represent resellers and engage in B2B transactions when they buy merchandise for their stores, fixtures, capital investments, leasing locations, and financing operations. Adding Value 6.1 highlights how TJ Maxx buyers work with their partners to buy merchandise for their stores.

## Institutions

Institutions, such as hospitals, educational organizations, and religious organizations, also purchase all kinds of goods and services. A public school system might have a $40 million annual budget for textbooks alone, which gives it significant

*Fashion shows expose retail buyers to new fashions and create media buzz. But the buying takes place during private meetings between vendors and buyers.*

## Adding Value 6.1    Buying for Value

At the pinnacle of the fashion world, designers display their newest creations in runway shows in New York, London, Milan, and Paris. Wholesale buyers thus can inspect new lines of clothing and place orders, build relationships with designers, and spread buzz about new fashions that will be available in their stores. This type of business-to-business interaction also occurs elsewhere in the buying process, but on a different scale. TJ Maxx, for example, uses Internet bloggers to spread the word about its lines.

The parent company of TJ Maxx and Marshalls hosted 13 respected fashion bloggers at its headquarters in Massachusetts,[12] treating them like royalty and putting them up in a luxury hotel. Rather than sponsoring a runway event with size 2 models, TJ Maxx mounted a fashion show game in which the blogger who correctly named the price of a modeled product got to keep it. Some bloggers guessed high, which helped drive home the message that TJ Maxx sells designer merchandise at exceptional prices. Before leaving, bloggers enjoyed a $250 shopping spree at TJ Maxx outlets. As a result they became much more familiar with the store by learning just how far $250 could go.

Not only did this event enhance the company's reputation among influential fashion bloggers, but it also spread the word about another important B2B interaction that differentiates TJ Maxx from both high-end department stores and lower-price competitors. That is, in contrast with widespread assumptions that TJ Maxx purchases whatever other stores couldn't sell,[13] the company buys directly from 10,000 vendors worldwide, the same vendors who sell to department stores. The vast range of upscale products that appear in various categories, including health, beauty, and food items,[14] differs from offerings in other outlets simply in terms of price. These high fashion brands are willing to sell to TJ Maxx because it refuses to advertise specific brand names, thus protecting the high-end image of the brand and avoiding a confrontation with its regular-priced department store customers.

Other of TJ Maxx's offerings do come from department stores. These hand-me-downs may result from poor sales or forecasting errors. By moving these items to TJ Maxx, they benefit vendors, TJ Maxx, and consumers, because the retailer purchases the excess product regularly and sells constantly updated merchandise at a deep discount.[15]

Through this buying process, TJ Maxx works with its partners to ensure end customers are satisfied. Its efforts appear successful; as one blogger announced, "Buy with confidence, ladies."[16]

*TJ Maxx works with its vendors to provide great value to its customers.*

*The U.S. government spends over $5 billion a year on aerospace and defense for everything from nuts and bolts to this F-14 Tomcat jetfighter.*

buying power and enables it to take advantage of bulk discounts. However, if each school makes its own purchasing decisions, the system as a whole cannot leverage its combined buying power. Public institutions also engage in B2B relationships to fulfill their needs for capital construction, equipment, supplies (such as copiers and ink to print all those tests), food, and janitorial services.

## Government

In most countries, the central government is one of the largest purchasers of goods and services. For example, the U.S. federal government spends about $2.8 trillion annually on procuring goods and services.[17] If you add in the amount state and local governments spend, these numbers reach staggering proportions. Specifically, with its estimated outlay of $700 billion for fiscal year 2011, the Pentagon represents a spending force to be reckoned with,[18] especially when it comes to aerospace and defense (A&D) manufacturers, some of the Pentagon's greatest suppliers of products. Policy Studies Inc. (PSI), for instance, offers consulting, technology, and outsourced services to government agencies involved in criminal justice, health care, and human service. One of their most visible services is its child support enforcement programs for state and local government agencies.[19]

**LO2**  List the steps in the B2B buying process.

# THE BUSINESS-TO-BUSINESS BUYING PROCESS

The B2B buying process (Exhibit 6.2) parallels the B2C process, though it differs in many ways. Both start with need recognition, but the information search and alternative evaluation steps are more formal and structured in the B2B process. Typically, B2B buyers specify their needs in writing and ask potential suppliers to submit formal proposals, whereas B2C buying decisions are usually made by individuals or families and do not need formal proposals. Thus, for a family to buy a hammer, all that is required is a trip to the hardware store and perhaps some brief discussion of which hammer will be the best.

For the Pentagon to buy 100,000 hammers, however, it must complete requisition forms, accept bids from manufacturers, and obtain approval for the expenditure. The final decision rests with a committee, as is the case for most B2B buying decisions, which often demand a great deal of consideration. Finally, in B2C buying situations, customers evaluate their purchase decision and sometimes experience postpurchase dissonance. However, formal performance evaluations of the vendor and the products sold generally do not occur, as they do in the B2B setting. Let's examine all six stages in the context of an airport adding concessions to its nonsecurity and security areas.

## Stage 1: Need Recognition

In the first stage of the B2B buying process, the buying organization recognizes, through either internal or external sources, that it has an unfilled need. The Redmond,

**EXHIBIT  6.2**     Business-to-Business Buying Process

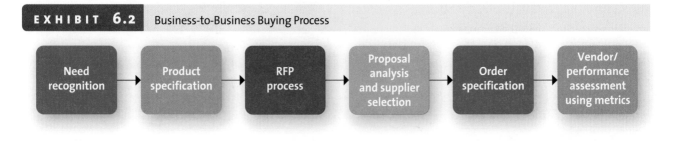

Need recognition → Product specification → RFP process → Proposal analysis and supplier selection → Order specification → Vendor/performance assessment using metrics

Oregon, airport thus wants to offer more concessions and services to its customers as they wait for their flights.[20] In the new environment required by security changes in the past decade, the airport has come to realize that once its 500,000 annual travelers get through the security screening, they have access to a very limited number and variety of vendors.

## Stage 2: Product Specification

After recognizing the need, the organization considers alternative solutions and comes up with potential specifications that vendors might use to develop their proposals. The airport specifications require that the concession stand must be open 365 days a year, with operating hours and staffing levels dependent on the fluctuations in the daily and seasonal passenger traffic. They also must be open one hour before the first morning departure and close no earlier than 30 minutes after the last evening departure. There is limited storage on the premises, and all deliveries must move through the main airport area during nonpeak travel hours. Finally, any products sold by concession stands must be easy for a traveler to carry, pay for, and transport on the plane.

## Stage 3: RFP Process

The **request for proposals (RFP)** is a common process through which organizations invite alternative vendors or suppliers to bid on supplying their required components or specifications. The purchasing company may simply post its RFP needs on its website, as the Redmond airport did,[21] or work through various B2B web portals or contact potential suppliers directly.[22]

*Airports have recognized the need for more concessions and services because travelers have so much time to shop.*

In general, a **web portal** is an Internet site whose purpose is to be a major starting point for users when they connect to the Web. Although there are general portals such as Yahoo or MSN, B2B partners connect to specialized or niche portals to participate in online information exchanges and transactions. These exchanges help streamline procurement or distribution processes. Portals can provide tremendous cost savings because they eliminate periodic negotiations and routine paperwork, and they offer the means to form a supply chain that can respond quickly to the buyer's needs.

Small- to medium-sized companies looking for skilled service workers can use portals like Guru.com, started to help freelance professionals connect with companies that need their services, whether those services entail graphic design and cartooning or finance and accounting advice. Currently, 724,000 professionals list their offerings on this service-oriented professional exchange, and more than 30,000 companies regularly visit the site to post work orders.[23] Guru.com thus provides value to both companies and freelancers by offering not only a site for finding each other but also dispute resolution, escrow for payments, and a means to rate freelancer quality.[24] Businesscoffeeexpress.com is another portal that helps businesses order coffee, condiments, and cups they might need for their offices.

## Stage 4: Proposal Analysis, Vendor Negotiation, and Selection

The buying organization, in conjunction with its critical decision makers, evaluates all the proposals it receives in response to its RFP. Firms are likely to narrow the process to a few suppliers, often those with which they have existing relationships, and discuss key terms of the sale, such as price, quality, delivery, and

| EXHIBIT 6.3 | Evaluating a Vendor's Performance | | |
|---|---|---|---|
| **(1) Key Issues** | **(2) Importance Score** | **(3) Vendor's Performance** | **(4) Importance × Performance (2) × (3)** |
| Customer Service | .30 | 5 | 1.5 |
| Hours Open | .20 | 4 | 0.8 |
| Product Deliveries | .40 | 5 | 2.0 |
| Product Quality | .10 | 3 | 0.3 |
| Total | 1.0 | | 4.6 |

financing. Some firms have a policy that requires them to negotiate with several suppliers, particularly if the product or service represents a critical component or aspect of the business. This policy keeps suppliers on their toes; they know that the buying firm can always shift a greater portion of its business to an alternative supplier if it offers better terms. The airport evaluates proposals on the basis of the amount of experience the vendor has because it wants to ensure each vendor is capable of handling highly stressed airport passengers. The vendor's ability to meet its specifications also is important because if a vendor fails to stay open during the appropriate hours, for example, airport passengers are inconvenienced. The vendor's financial position provides an important indication of whether the vendor will be able to stay in business.

## Stage 5: Order Specification

In the fifth stage, the firm places its order with its preferred supplier (or suppliers). The order includes a detailed description of the goods, prices, delivery dates, and, in some cases, penalties for noncompliance. The supplier then sends an acknowledgment that it has received the order and fills it by the specified date. In the case of the airport concession stands, the terms are clearly laid out regarding when the concession stand will commence its operations, how it will structure its daily deliveries, and the approval process for the construction layout.

## Stage 6: Vendor Performance Assessment Using Metrics

Just as in the consumer buying process, firms analyze their vendors' performance so they can make decisions about their future purchases. The difference is that in a B2B setting, this analysis is typically more formal and objective. Let's consider how the airport might evaluate the concession stand's performance, as in Exhibit 6.3, using the following metrics: customer service, hours of operation, product deliveries, and product quality.

1. The buying team develops a list of issues that it believes are important to consider in the vendor evaluation.

2. To determine the importance of each issue (column 1), the buying team assigns an importance score to each (column 2). The more important the issue, the higher its score, but the importance scores must add up to 1. In this case, the buying team believes that customer service and product deliveries are most important, whereas the hours of operation and product quality are comparatively less important.

3. In the third column, the buying team assigns numbers that reflect its judgments about how well the vendor performs. Using a five-point scale, where 1 equals "poor performance" and 5 equals "excellent performance," the buying team decides that the concession stand has fairly high performance on all issues except product quality.

4. To calculate an overall performance score in the fourth column, the team combines the importance of each issue and the vendor's performance scores by multiplying them. Note that the concession stand performed particularly well on the most important issues. As a result, when we add the importance/performance scores in column 4, we find that the concession stand's overall evaluation is quite high—4.6 on a five-point scale!

**CHECK YOURSELF**

1. Identify the stages in the B2B buying process.
2. How do you perform a vendor analysis?

# THE BUYING CENTER

L03  Identify the different roles within the buying center.

In most large organizations, several people are responsible for buying decisions. These buying center participants can range from employees who have a formal role in purchasing decisions (i.e., the purchasing or procurement department) to members of the design team that is specifying the particular equipment or raw material needed by employees who will be using a new machine that is being ordered. All these employees are likely to play different roles in the buying process, which vendors must understand and adapt to in their marketing and sales efforts.

We can categorize six different buying roles within a typical buying center (Exhibit 6.4). One or more people may take on a certain role, or one person may take on more than one of the following roles: "(1) initiator, the person who first suggests buying the particular product or service; (2) influencer, the person whose views influence other members of the buying center in making the final decision; (3) decider, the person who ultimately determines any part of or the entire buying decision—whether to buy, what to buy, how to buy, or where to buy; (4) buyer, the person who handles the paperwork of the actual purchase; (5) user, the person who consumes or uses the product or service; and (6) gatekeeper, the person who controls information or access, or both, to decision makers and influencers."[25]

To illustrate how a buying center operates, consider purchases made by a hospital. Where do hospitals obtain their x-ray machines, syringes, and bedpans? Why

**EXHIBIT 6.4**   The Buying Center Roles

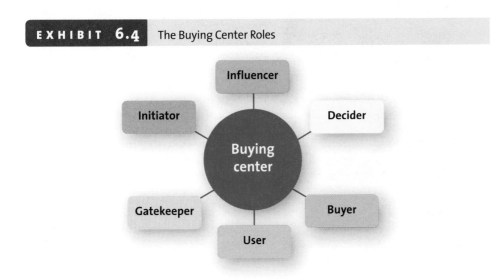

## Ethical and Societal Dilemma 6.1

### But How Does the Doctor Come to Know Best?

Before doctors write a prescription, they must decide which medication is right for their patient from among a variety of drugs from competing pharmaceutical companies. Each medication works in the body in a different way, has a different formulation, and comes with a different price tag. Some are gold standards for treatment, with well-known benefits and side effects. Others are new and reflect researchers' most recent understanding of how our bodies work. But there is also a third, unofficial category: "off-label" uses of drugs approved for one condition that may help with another, such as using anticonvulsants to treat depression.

The thousands of drugs on the market make keeping up with details about safety, results, and usage a difficult task for busy doctors. Therefore, they often rely on a key information source about changes in the pharmaceutical industry, that is, the sales representatives who visit them. According to a recent study, doctors want detailed information about drug safety, pricing, and prescribing, in addition to information about new drugs.[26] The doctors also want to understand the difference between the new drug and the old drug.

Unfortunately, the study also found that sales representatives do not provide these data to the doctors. Instead, they focus on the benefits of their new drugs and avoid volunteering pricing information, side effects data, or comparisons with existing products. Even safety data were skewed toward placing the new drugs in a favorable light. To make matters worse, the study found that when competitors' products were mentioned to doctors, they were generally discussed in unfavorable terms. Even research data about treatments may be biased: Articles in medical journals edited by editors with financial ties to drug or medical device companies downplay the negative effects of products in the interest of making a sale. How can patients be sure, when their doctors face so many conflicts of interest and time pressures, that they are being prescribed the best drug option?

They can't be. New rules regarding relationships among prescribing physicians, pharmaceutical companies, and medical journals may help though. Many medical societies have agreed to restrictions that prohibit gifts from the pharmaceutical or medical device industries.[27] In India, for example, doctors are now prohibited from accepting gifts from drug companies or other suppliers or manufacturers in the health care industry.[28] Most companies also have stringent rules and regulations to ensure that their marketing remains ethical and respects patient privacy,[29] but frequent allegations of misbehavior continue.

In particular, pharmaceutical sales representatives still have a dramatic impact on the doctors' choice in treatment of their patients,[30] though their primary goal is achieving their quarterly sales goals to make a living. Some reps claim they are reporting facts but have received data that hide a dangerous side effect.[31] Yet doctors more frequently visited

by sales representatives often choose to treat patients with drug therapies, rather than alternative, nondrug therapies, even if researchers consider the nondrug therapy superior. These doctors are also less likely to prescribe generic equivalents of costly branded drugs.

Adding to the controversy, drug companies and practicing doctors need a close relationship to support drug development. Doctors provide observations about patient problems that need to be addressed; drug companies manufacture and refine compounds. Will new rules help protect consumers from the losing end of this seemingly necessary conflict of interest?

*From an ethical perspective, what information should pharmaceutical sales representatives provide to doctors?*

are some medical procedures covered in whole or in part by insurance, whereas others are not? Why might your doctor recommend one type of allergy medication instead of another?

**The Initiator—Your Doctor** When you seek treatment from your physician, he or she initiates the buying process by determining the products and services that will best address and treat your illness or injury. For example, say that you fell backward off your snowboard and, in trying to catch yourself, shattered your elbow. You require surgery to mend the affected area, which includes the insertion of several screws to hold the bones in place. Your doctor promptly notifies the hospital to schedule a time for the procedure and specifies the brand of screws she wants on hand for your surgery.

**The Influencer—The Medical Device Supplier, the Pharmacy** For years, your doctor has been using ElbowMed screws, a slightly higher-priced screw. Her first introduction to ElbowMed screws came from the company's sales representative, who visited her office to demonstrate how ElbowMed screws were far superior to those of its competition. Your doctor recognized ElbowMed as a good value. Armed with empirical data and case studies, ElbowMed's sales rep effectively influenced your doctor's decision to use that screw.

**The Decider—The Hospital** Even though your doctor requested ElbowMed screws, the hospital ultimately is responsible for deciding whether to buy ElbowMed screws. The hospital supplies the operating room, instrumentation, and surgical supplies, and therefore, the hospital administrators must weigh a variety of factors to determine if the ElbowMed screw is not only best for the patients but also involves a cost that is reimbursable by various insurance providers.

**The Buyer** The actual buyer of the screw will likely be the hospital's materials manager, who is charged with buying and maintaining inventory for the hospital in the most cost-effective manner. Whereas ElbowMed screws are specific to your type of procedure, other items, such as gauze and sutures, may be purchased through a group purchasing organization (GPO), which obtains better prices through volume buying.

**The User—The Patient** Ultimately, though, the buying process for this procedure will be greatly affected by the user, namely, you and your broken elbow. If you are uncomfortable with the procedure or have read about alternative procedures that you prefer, you may decide that ElbowMed screws are not the best treatment.

**The Gatekeeper—The Insurance Company** Your insurer may believe that ElbowMed screws are too expensive and that other screws deliver equally effective results and therefore refuse to reimburse the hospital in full or in part for the use of the screws.

In the end, the final purchase decision must take into consideration every single buying center participant. Ethical and Societal Dilemma 6.1 examines how the influencer (the pharmaceutical sales representative and pharmaceutical companies) influences the decider (the physician) to suggest purchases ultimately made by the user (the patient).

# ORGANIZATION CULTURE

**L04** Describe the different types of organizational cultures.

A firm's organizational culture reflects the set of values, traditions, and customs that guide its employees' behavior. The firm's culture often comprises a set of unspoken guidelines that employees share with one another through various work situations. For example, Walmart buyers are not allowed to accept even the smallest gift from a vendor, not even a cup of coffee. This rule highlights its overall corporate culture: It is a low-cost operator whose buyers must base their decisions only on the products' and vendors' merits.

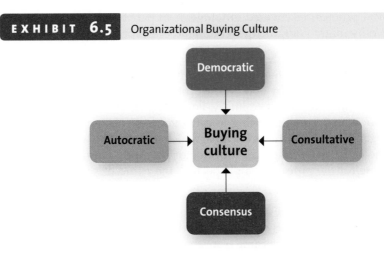

**EXHIBIT 6.5**    Organizational Buying Culture

Organizational culture can have a profound influence on purchasing decisions, and corporate buying center cultures thus might be divided into four general types: autocratic, democratic, consultative, and consensus (as illustrated in Exhibit 6.5). Knowing which buying center culture is prevalent in a given organization helps the seller decide how to approach that particular client, how and to whom to deliver pertinent information, and to whom to make sales presentations.

In an autocratic buying center, though there may be multiple participants, one person makes the decision alone, whereas the majority rules in a democratic buying center. Consultative buying centers use one person to make a decision but solicit input from others before doing so. Finally, in a consensus buying center, all members of the team must reach a collective agreement that they can support a particular purchase.[32]

Cultures act like living, breathing entities that change and grow, just as organizations do. Even within some companies, culture may vary by geography, by division, or by functional department. Whether you are a member of the buying center or a supplier trying to sell to it, it is extremely important to understand its culture and the roles of the key players in the buying process. Not knowing the roles of the key players could waste a lot of time and could even alienate the real decision maker.

## Building B2B Relationships

In B2B contexts, there are a vast variety of ways to enhance relationships, and these methods seem to be advancing and evolving by the minute. For example, blogs and social media can build awareness, provide search engine results, educate potential and existing clients about products or services, and warm up a seemingly cold corporate culture.[33] An expert who offers advice and knowledge about products increases brand awareness, and a blog is a great medium for this information. Web analytics, such as traffic on the website and the number of comments, can offer tangible evaluations, but a better measure is how often the blog gets mentioned elsewhere, the media attention it receives, and the interaction, involvement, intimacy, and influence that it promotes.

The Linkedin.com social network is mainly used for professional networking in the B2B marketplace. Twitter, the microblogging site, is also valuable for B2B marketers, because they can communicate with other businesses as often as they want. Companies like TweetDeck make it easier for companies using Twitter to manage their followers, update their posts, track analytics, and even schedule Tweets, just as they would to manage a traditional marketing campaign.[34] Staples has come up with another means to exploit online technology to improve its B2B relationships, as Power of the Internet 6.1 describes.

The majority of B2B marketers use white papers for their marketing efforts, and 71 percent of B2B buyers regularly read them prior to making a purchase.[35] When executives confront an unfulfilled business need, they normally turn to

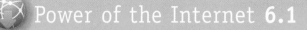

## Power of the Internet 6.1        Staples Businesses stickK to It!

New Year's resolutions are hard to keep, whether for individuals or for companies. To offer some support for small businesses, Staples has launched a new website in partnership with stickK.com. The "stickK to It! Business Challenge" encourages users to set goals and then put up their own money to increase their accountability. If they succeed, they can earn Staples EasyPoints and redeem them for merchandise and services.

Approximately 65,000 users on the site have entered into 42,000 contracts and pledged $4.5 million.[36] Although anyone can enter into a contract, the focus is on small businesses, most of which never measure their performance to determine if they are successful or if they have met their goals. The tough modern economy makes it even more difficult for small businesses to focus on specific goals, especially when they have that next phone call to make, another e-mail to respond to, and one more client to soothe.

For Staples, the initiative may lead to the acquisition of more small business customers. The retailer gains brand recognition due to its nontraditional marketing campaign, and customers will start using Staples products when they reach their goals. If these original small businesses grow into medium or large businesses, Staples likely will continue to enjoy their loyalty, in the form of a much larger business account.

*To improve its relationships with its customers, Staples developed the "stickK to it! Business Challenge," which encourages customers to set goals and put down their own money to increase their accountability.*

white papers. Their B2B partner may have a technologically advanced solution, but buyers have to understand the solution before they can consider a purchase. A good white paper provides information about the industry and its challenges in an educational context, rather than a promotional sense, to avoid seeming like simply propaganda. That is, the goal of white papers is to provide valuable information that a businessperson can easily understand and that will help the company address its problems with new solutions.

## THE BUYING SITUATION

**L05** Detail different buying situations.

The type of buying situation also affects the B2B decision process. Most B2B buying situations can be categorized into three types: new buys, modified rebuys, and straight rebuys. (See Exhibit 6.6.) To illustrate the nuances among these three buying situations, consider how colleges and universities develop relationships with some of their suppliers. Most universities negotiate with sports apparel manufacturers, such as Nike, Reebok, and New Balance, to establish purchasing agreements for their sports teams. Those with successful sports teams have been very

**EXHIBIT 6.6** Buying Situations

successful in managing these relationships. Large universities that win national championships, such as the University of Florida or Duke University, can solicit sponsorships in exchange for free athletic equipment, whereas less popular teams or smaller schools typically must accept an upfront sponsorship and then agree to buy from that vendor for a specified period of time. In exchange for this sponsorship, the vendors gain the right to sell apparel with the university logo and require the school's team to purchase only their equipment. Many apparel companies make a significant portion of their revenue through sponsorship deals that grant them the right to sell apparel with popular university logos.

In a new buy situation, a customer purchases a good or service for the first time,[37] which means the buying decision is likely to be quite involved because the buyer or the buying organization does not have any experience with the item. In the B2B context, the buying center is likely to proceed through all six steps in the buying process and involve many people in the buying decision. Typical new buys might range from capital equipment to components that the firm previously made itself but now has decided to purchase instead. For example, a small college might need to decide which apparel company to approach for a sponsorship. For smaller colleges, finding a company that will sponsor multiple sports teams—such as women's soccer as well as men's basketball—is a priority, though it also must balance other considerations, such as the length of the contract. Some vendors

*Schools like the University of Miami negotiate with sports apparel manufacturers, such as Nike, to get free athletic equipment. The manufacturers, in turn, get to sell apparel with the university logo.*

offer perks to attract new buyers; New Balance offers teams that sign up for long-term contracts custom fittings for their players' shoes. Each season, a sales team from New Balance visits the school and custom fits each player to achieve the best shoe possible.

Another example of a new buy occurs in the fashion industry, as we noted in Adding Value 6.1. That is, runway shows offer wholesale buyers an opportunity to inspect new lines of clothing and place orders. Designer sales often occur during private meetings with buyers, both before and after runway shows. Buyers meet with the designers, discuss the line, and observe a model wearing the clothing. The buyer's challenge then is to determine which items will sell best in the retail stores he or she represents while trying to imagine what the item will look like in regular, as opposed to model, sizes. Buyers must also negotiate purchases for orders that may not be delivered for as much as six months. Buyers can suggest modifications to make the clothing more modest or more comfortable for their customers. Buyers and designers recognize the significant value of this relationship, which occasionally prompts buyers to purchase a few items from a designer, even if those items are not to their taste. Doing so ensures that the buyer will have access to the designer's collection for the next season.[38]

In a modified rebuy, the buyer has purchased a similar product in the past but has decided to change some specifications, such as the desired price, quality level, customer service level, options, or so forth. Current vendors are likely to have an advantage in acquiring the sale in a modified rebuy situation, as long as the reason for the modification is not dissatisfaction with the vendor or its products. The Ohio State University's sports department might compare its contract with University of Michigan's contract with adidas and ask to negotiate a lower price to be comparable with Michigan's.

Straight rebuys occur when the buyer or buying organization simply buys additional units of products that had previously been purchased. A tremendous amount of B2B purchases are likely to fall in the straight rebuy category. For example, sports teams need to repurchase a tremendous amount of equipment that is not covered by apparel sponsorships, such as tape for athletes' ankles or weights for the weight room. The purchase of bottled water also typically involves a straight rebuy from an existing supplier.

These varied types of buying situations call for very different marketing and selling strategies. The most complex and difficult is the new buy, because it requires the buying organization to make changes in its current practices and purchases. As a result, several members of the buying center will likely become involved, and the level of their involvement will be more intense than in the case of modified and straight rebuys. In new buying situations, buying center members also typically spend more time at each stage of the B2B buying process, similar to the extended decision-making process that consumers use in the B2C process. In comparison, in modified rebuys, the buyers spend less time at each stage of the B2B buying process, similar to limited decision making in the B2C process (see Chapter 5).

In straight rebuys, however, the buyer is often the only member of the buying center involved in the process. Like a consumer's habitual purchase, straight rebuys often enable the buyer to recognize the firm's need and go directly to the fifth step in the B2B buying process, skipping the product specification, RFP process, and proposal analysis and supplier selection steps.

Thus, in various ways B2B marketing both differs from and mirrors the consumer behavior (B2C) process we detailed in Chapter 5. The differences, however, in the six stages of the buying process make sense in view of the many unique factors that come into play. The constitution of the buying center (initiator, influencer, decider, buyer, user, and gatekeeper), the culture of the purchasing firm (autocratic, democratic, consultative, or consensus), and the context of the buying situation (new buy, modified rebuy, straight rebuy) all influence the B2B buying process in various ways, which means that sellers must be constantly aware of these factors if they want to be successful in their sales attempts. Finally, just as it has done seemingly everywhere we look, the Internet has radically changed some elements of the B2B world, increasing the frequency of both private electronic exchanges and auctions.

## CHECK YOURSELF

1. What factors affect the B2B buying process?
2. What are the six different buying roles?
3. What is the difference between new buy, straight rebuy, and modified rebuy?

## Summing Up

**L01**  **Describe the different types of buyers and sellers that participate in business-to-business (B2B) markets.**

All firms want to divide the market into groups of customers with different needs, wants, or characteristics who therefore might appreciate products or services geared especially toward them. On a broad level, B2B firms divide the market into four types: manufacturers or producers, resellers, institutions, and government. Manufacturers purchase materials to make their products and components and expertise to help run their businesses, such as computer and telephone systems. Resellers are primarily wholesalers, distributors, or retailers that sell the unchanged products. Institutions include nonprofit organizations such as hospitals, schools, or churches. Finally, governments purchase all types of goods and services, but in the United States, defense is among the largest expenditures.

**L02**  **List the steps in the B2B buying process.**

Similar to the B2C buying process, the B2B process consists of several stages: need recognition; product specification; the RFP process; proposal analysis, vendor negotiation, and selection; order specification; and vendor performance assessment using metrics. The B2B process tends to be more formalized and structured than the customer buying process.

**L03**  **Identify the different roles within the buying center.**

The initiator first suggests the purchase. The influencer affects important people's percep-

tions and final decisions. The decider ultimately determines at least some of the buying decision—whether, what, how, or where to buy. The buyer handles the details of the actual purchase. The user consumes or employs the product or service. The gatekeeper controls information and access to decision makers and influencers.

**L04**  **Describe the different types of organizational cultures.**

Firm culture consists of unspoken guidelines that employees share through various work situations. They generally can be classified as autocratic, such that one person makes most decisions; democratic, where the majority rules; consultative, in which one person makes decisions based on the input of others; or consensus, which requires all members of the team to reach collective agreement.

**L05**  **Detail different buying situations.**

The buying process depends to a great extent on the situation. If a firm is purchasing a product or service for the first time (i.e., new buy), the process is much more involved than if it is engaging in a straight rebuy of the same item again. A modified rebuy falls somewhere in the middle, such that the buyer wants essentially the same thing but with slightly different terms or features.

# Key Terms

- autocratic buying center, 182
- business-to-business (B2B) marketing, 172
- buyer, 179
- buying center, 179
- consensus buying center, 182
- consultative buying center, 182
- decider, 179

- democratic buying center, 182
- derived demand, 172
- distributors, 174
- gatekeeper, 179
- influencer, 179
- initiator, 179
- modified rebuy, 185
- new buy, 184

- organizational culture, 181
- request for proposals (RFP), 177
- resellers, 174
- straight rebuy, 185
- user, 179
- web portal, 177
- wholesalers, 174

# Marketing Applications

1. Provide an example of each of the four key types of B2B organizations.

2. What are the major differences between the consumer buying process discussed in Chapter 5 and the B2B buying process discussed in this chapter?

3. Assume you have written this textbook and are going to attempt to sell it to your school. Identify the six members of the buying center. What role would each play in the decision process? Rank them in terms of how much influence they would have on the decision, with 1 being most influential and 6 being least influential. Will this ranking be different in other situations?

4. Mazda is trying to assess the performance of two manufacturers that could supply music systems for its vehicles. Using the information in the table below, determine which manufacturer Mazda should use.

5. Provide an example of the three types of buying situations that the bookstore at your school might face when buying textbooks.

6. Describe the organizational culture at your school or job. How would knowledge of this particular organization's culture help a B2B salesperson sell products or services to the organization?

7. You have just started to work in the purchasing office of a major pharmaceutical firm. The purchasing manager has asked you to assist in writing an RFP for a major purchase. The manager gives you a sheet detailing the specifications for the RFP. While reading the specifications, you realize that they have been written to be extremely favorable to one bidder. How should you handle this situation?

**Performance Evaluation of Brands**

| Issues | Importance Weights | Manufacturer A's Performance | Manufacturer B's Performance |
|---|---|---|---|
| Sound | 0.4 | 5 | 3 |
| Cost | 0.3 | 2 | 4 |
| Delivery time | 0.1 | 2 | 2 |
| Brand cachet | 0.2 | 5 | 1 |
| Total | 1 | | |

## Quiz Yourself

1. After posting an RFP for telecommunication equipment, the University of Florida received six proposals from qualified vendors. Next, the University of Florida will:

    a. recognize proposal obstacles that the firm must comply with.

    b. revise need recognition through external sources.

    c. invite alternative suppliers to bid on supplying what is requested.

    d. proceed to proposal vendor analysis.

    e. evaluate the proposals and likely narrow the choice to a few suppliers.

2. Raycom Construction needs heavy-duty equipment to install a new pipeline in northern Alaska. Raycom engineers will specify the type and capability requirements for the equipment to be purchased. The Raycom engineers will primarily play the _____ role in the company's buying center.

    a. buyer

    b. initiator

    c. influencer

    d. user

    e. gatekeeper

    (Answers to these two questions are provided on page 607.)

    Go to www.mhhe.com/grewal3e to practice an additional 11 questions.

## Toolkit

### B2B VENDOR ANALYSIS

Help David evaluate two software vendors. He has created a chart to help him decide which one to pick. He has rated the two vendors on brand strength, timeliness of deliveries, product quality, and ease of ordering. His firm is generally most interested in quality and then in timeliness. Reputation is somewhat important. The ease of ordering is least important. Please use the toolkit provided at http://www.mhhe.com/grewal3e to specify the importance weights and help David pick the best software vendor.

## Net Savvy

1. Levi Strauss & Co. maintains a website so that customers can shop online directly with the manufacturer. The website also refers consumers directly to retailers. In comparison, go to http://www.wrangler.com/home, click on the link for where to buy and then on "find it in stores." What do you find when you type in your zip code? How is this type of linking beneficial to both Wrangler and to the various retailers?

2. Siemens worked with the custom motorcycle manufacturer Orange County Chopper to build the Smart Chopper—the first electric motorcycle. Visit http://www.usa.siemens.com/smartchopper/ to learn about the specifications and details of this new form of Chopper. How is Siemens using this innovation to improve its relationships with its business customers? What other outcomes might this services provider expect from its efforts?

# Chapter Case Study

## UPS: FROM SHIPPING TO SUPPLY CHAIN[39]

### OVERVIEW

In 1907, an enterprising teenager borrowed $100 to start a business running errands, delivering packages, carrying notes or bags, and even ferrying food from restaurants to customers. Messengers traveled on foot or, when the trip was longer, by bicycle. More than a century later, that young man's business has morphed into United Parcel Service (UPS), a $45.3 billion company that serves 200 countries and employs more than 408,000 people.[40]

During its 100+ year span, as technology and demands have changed, the company has upgraded its delivery methods by adding trucks, ocean and train delivery, and even its own jet cargo fleet. Although its fleet of trucks might not be quite as environmentally friendly as a bicycle, UPS carefully manages its delivery dispatches in an attempt to minimize both fuel use and emissions. In the air, it adopts a "continuous descent approach" for its carriers, which reportedly reduces pollutants by as much as 34 percent compared with traditional, step-like airplane descents.[41]

UPS also has expanded into international markets and developed systems to help track the more than 15.1 million packages that pass through its corporate hands each day. This expertise prompted UPS's most recent transition: from a global package and information delivery company to a facilitator of global commerce, capable of providing supply chain solutions to customers.

Through acquisitions and restructuring, the company has added logistics and distribution, consulting, mail, e-commerce, financial services, and international trade management to its portfolio of client services. UPS believes that these new services help customers focus on their own core competencies while protecting UPS from competitors. Building a business line based on information technology rather than fuel use also helps improve the company's environmental profile and build a profit stream protected from rising fuel costs.[42]

### COMPETITIVE CHALLENGES

Both FedEx and the United States Postal Service (USPS) are constantly on the lookout for ways to attract business away from UPS. Threatened by drops in regular mail volume, which has largely resulted from increased Internet use, the USPS introduced a flat-rate box, based on size rather than package weight.[43] This move was designed to attract the package shipping business of companies such as Amazon and eBay, which must ship often heavy materials constantly to consumers.

Similar to UPS, FedEx has expanded its service offerings, but its expansion has focused on copying services (FedEx Kinko's), along with virtually real-time tracking of ground, freight, and express shipments. With its $35.5 billion in revenue, more than 275,000 employees, and a daily package total of more than 8 million shipments,[44] FedEx is UPS's greatest competitor.

### ADDING VALUE FOR BUSINESS CUSTOMERS

The expansion of its business offerings enables UPS to handle a vast array of its client company's operations, including storage, assembly, and repair of merchandise. It even provides customer service functions that demand minimal client involvement.[45] For example, for the French pet food company Royal Canin, UPS employees mix, pack, and ship all sold dog and cat food. In addition to cutting the product delivery time, this model eliminates Royal Canin's need for a U.S. warehouse.

For Toshiba, UPS not only transports broken computers but also fixes and ships them back to their original owners, usually within 24 hours! This approach relieves Toshiba of the need to run repair facilities when its core competency is

UPS's "Decision Green" concept appears on all communications including its trucks.

computer production and design. It also gets a repaired machine back to customers more quickly. And when there is a problem, UPS offers perhaps the most valuable service for both Toshiba and its customers, that is, a scapegoat. As CEO Eskew noted, "Customers wanted one throat to choke when the pressure was on to deliver. We offered them UPS's throat."[46]

These supportive relationships entail not just profits but also an element of UPS's approach to environmental sustainability. Its "Decision Green" environmental program comprises three broad elements: practical innovation, supportive relationships, and can-do spirit. The first focuses on the development of "green" solutions for itself and its customers, such as paperless invoicing. The second entails a distinct focus on greening its customers' supply chains through cooperation and supportive relationships. Finally, its "can-do attitude" demands that the company find a balance in the trade-off between environmental concerns and profits.[47]

### SPREADING THE WORD

The "Decision Green" concept is far-reaching; it appears in all communications to customers and employees in an attempt to develop a consistent image of UPS as dedicated, in both its individual efforts and its overall approach, to consideration of the environment.

Furthermore, advertisements directed to its targeted demographic go beyond the conventional methods of television and print media. For example, a recent mobile ad campaign piggybacked on *The New York Times*' BlackBerry application.[48] Using BlackBerries for delivery helped focus messaging on the right audience, because BlackBerry users tend to be businesspeople. If they clicked on a banner that invited users to see how UPS could improve operations for its business customers, the consumers connected to a landing page that featured case studies, videos, and an option to receive additional information.

## Questions

1. Describe how you would expect firms to interact with UPS. Use the steps in the B2B buying process discussed in the chapter to facilitate your discussion.

2. Manufacturers, resellers, government, and autioneers on eBay all have alternative delivery options. Describe some ways that UPS provides greater value to these various types of customers than its competitors can. (It might help to review its website at http://www.UPS.com.)

3. Identify the environmental factors discussed in the case that have influenced the delivery industry during the past decade or so. What additional environmental factors might be important to the delivery industry, and how would they affect UPS's B2B operations?

# Global Marketing

Food: For something so common, well-known, and basic, it certainly has provoked a great deal of controversy, especially of late. Food represents a basic human necessity but also a luxury. It provides fuel for elemental human processes but also an expression of cultural identity. Therefore, when Kraft Foods decided to push the packaged food items that had sold well in the United States around the globe, it had to take all these perspectives, plus some local culinary egos, into careful consideration.

Americans love packaged food and have for decades. In some cases, it even enters national folklore, as in the case of Tang, the powdered, orange-flavored drink that joined the famous astronauts who flew the Mercury and Gemini missions. Advertising at the time exploited the association to encourage kids to dream of space as they drank Tang with their breakfast, but just as the space program appears to be moving to the back burner for the United States, Tang is nearly the last choice in the U.S. powdered drink market, holding only a 2.5 percent market share.[1]

Kraft keeps producing Tang, though, because it provides the company with approximately $750 million in sales every year in various developing markets, including China and Brazil. The company thus ranks Tang among its top 10 brands, along with Oreo, Philadelphia Cream Cheese, and Milka (a German brand of chocolates).[2] Today Kraft is expanding into 10 promising regions that appear to offer great potential for strategic growth (i.e., Brazil, China, southeast Asia, Russia, Australia, Spain, France, Italy, Germany, and the United Kingdom).[3]

Unlike such internationally popular processed food items, Kraft's Macaroni & Cheese dominates the U.S. market but rarely even enters the mindset of Kraft's international marketing team. What makes the difference? Why might a European consumer love Tang but not Easy Mac?

For Italians, food (especially pasta) is a means to show others how much they care, that is, by setting out a huge, home-cooked meal. When food is tied so closely to culture, it becomes difficult for

**LO1** List the factors that aid in the growth of globalization.

**LO2** Describe the components of a country market assessment.

**LO3** Identify the various market entry strategies.

**LO4** Highlight the similarities and differences between a domestic marketing strategy and a global marketing strategy.

foreign brands and alternatives to penetrate the market, whose very identity may be tied to traditional forms of the food. Would a Colombian consumer who roasts and grinds his own coffee beans be interested in a canister of Maxwell House instant coffee?

Food companies have learned that they need to adjust their approaches to potential global markets by recognizing their unique characteristics and consumer demands. There are too many variables involved to assume other countries will act like extensions of the U.S. market. Some of the power brands are unlikely to provoke cultural sensitivity concerns. Who doesn't like Toblerone chocolates?

So what products might an expatriate American in Paris hope to find? The best bet might be to look for a little piece of home in the form of Oreo cookies—as Kraft's latest marketing campaign highlights.[4] Just don't expect the exact same dunkable sandwich cookie that tastes so good with a glass of milk. To gain success internationally, Kraft had to reconfigure the cookie so that it was less expensive and not quite so sweet. The reformulated Oreo's sales have quadrupled in China, making it the top cookie brand in China, and China is the second biggest market for Oreos, just behind the United States.[5]

● ● ●

The increasing globalization of markets affects not only large U.S. corporations like Kraft, which actively search out new markets, but also small- and medium-sized businesses that increasingly depend on goods produced globally to deliver their products and services. Most people may not think about how globalization affects their daily lives, but just take a minute to read the labels on the clothing you are wearing right now. Chances are that most of the items, even if they carry U.S. brand names, were manufactured in another part of the world.

In the United States, the market has evolved from a system of regional marketplaces to national markets to geographically regional markets (e.g., Canada and the United States together) to international markets and finally to global markets. Globalization refers to the processes by which goods, services, capital, people, information, and ideas flow across national borders. Global markets are the result of several fundamental changes, such as reductions or eliminations of trade barriers by country governments, the decreasing concerns of distance and time with regard to moving products and ideas across countries, the standardization of laws across borders, and globally integrated production processes.[6]

Each of these fundamental changes has paved the way for marketing to flourish in other countries. The elimination of trade barriers and other governmental actions, for instance, allows goods and ideas to move quickly and efficiently around the world, which in turn facilitates the quick delivery of goods to better meet the needs of global consumers. When examining countries as potential markets for global products, companies must realize that different countries exist at very different stages of globalization. The World Bank ranks countries according to their degrees of globalization on the basis of a composite metric that examines whether the factors necessary to participate in the global marketplace are present. Countries that score well on the scale represent the best markets for globalized products and services; those lowest on the scale represent the most troublesome markets.[7]

Yet the recent financial meltdown in global markets also has led to suggestions of "de-globalization," especially as flows of capital reverse and global trade shrinks.[8] Fears and risks sparked by the crisis have provoked some increases in protectionism, though research also indicates that the actual impact on global trade has been less stringent than the popular media might suggest. Furthermore,

*How do Legos get from its manufacturer in Denmark to a toy store near your home?*

companies that have already adopted a global strategy come to depend on consistent prices and supplies—and thus on other countries that supply those options.[9] The interdependencies across countries created by several decades of globalization do not simply disappear in the face of a financial crisis, though we also must recognize the significant impact it has had in terms of increasing sensitivity to foreign trade deficits and the sourcing of raw materials worldwide.

Still, most Americans continue to take their easy access to global products and services for granted. When we walk into a toy store, we expect to find Legos from Denmark; in the local sporting goods store, we anticipate finding adidas shoes from Germany; and many consumers choose Havaianas flip-flops from Brazil. But think about the process that enabled these products to arrive in your town. Or consider how a $12 digital camera for your keychain, made in Taiwan, which you purchased at Target, could be produced, transported halfway around the world, and sold for so little money. These are the questions we will be examining in this chapter.

We begin by looking at the growth of the global economy and the forces that led to it. We'll see how firms assess the potential of a given market, make decisions to go global, and—as Kraft did in the opening vignette—choose how and what they will sell globally. Then we explore how to build the marketing mix for global products and consider some of the ethical and legal issues of globalization.

## GROWTH OF THE GLOBAL ECONOMY: GLOBALIZATION OF MARKETING AND PRODUCTION

**L01** List the factors that aid in the growth of globalization

Changes in technology, especially communications technology, have been the driving force for growth in global markets for decades. The telegraph, radio, television, computer, and Internet increasingly connect distant parts of the world. Today, communication is instantaneous. Sounds and images from across the globe are delivered to TV sets, radios, and computers in real time, which enables receivers in all parts of the world to observe how others live, work, and play.

The globalization of production, also known as offshoring, refers to manufacturers' procurement of goods and services from around the globe to take advantage of national differences in the cost and quality of various factors of production (e.g.,

*Many goods and services are provided from other countries, an activity known as offshoring. At this call center in Delhi, India, experts provide information to an Internet service provider in the U.K.*

labor, energy, land, capital).[10] Although it originally focused on relocating manufacturing to lower cost production countries, the practice of offshoring has now grown to include products associated with a knowledge economy: medical services, financial advice, technological support, and consulting. The combined market for offshoring, including IT, call centers, and business processes, is expected to be $605 billion annually.[11] Much of this demand comes from the banking sector; financial services are by far the largest private-sector market for offshoring, accounting for more than 35 percent of all offshoring.[12] Many people believe that a majority of offshoring goes to India or China and the United States is a leader in offshoring. But India represents only 11.5 percent of the offshoring market, and European countries account for 54 percent of all off-shoring contracts.[13] American firms historically have sent work to Canada, where they find a similar business environment but 20 percent lower labor costs and a historically advantageous exchange rate. With the relatively weak dollar though, some of that business is coming back to the United States, because those cost savings no longer exist, and other jobs are going abroad to other key offshoring markets.[14]

Not all offshoring is about inexpensive labor. For some companies such as IBM, offshoring reflects its constant, global hunt for talent as it makes an effort to reduce costs. Krakow, Poland, which receives heavy investments from IBM, may be a low-cost location, especially in comparison with the United States, but it cannot compare to the cost savings available in China or India. However, Krakow also has invested heavily in technical education for its students, and the highly trained group of 150,000 engineers and technicians represents an attractive pool that IBM can tap to support its business.[15]

The growth of global markets also has been facilitated by organizations that are designed to oversee their functioning. Perhaps the most important of these organizations is represented by the General Agreement on Tariffs and Trade (GATT). The purpose of the GATT is to lower trade barriers, such as high tariffs on imported goods and restrictions on the number and types of imported products that inhibited the free flow of goods across borders. Later the GATT was replaced by the World Trade Organization (WTO). The WTO differs from the GATT in that the WTO is an established institution based in Geneva, Switzerland, instead of simply an agreement. Furthermore, the WTO represents the only international organization that deals with the global rules of trade among nations. Its main function is to ensure that trade flows as smoothly, predictably, and freely as possible. The WTO also administers trade agreements, acts as a forum for trade negotiations, settles trade disputes, reviews national trade policies, and assists developing countries in their trade policy issues through technical assistance and training. It has over 150 members.[16] The International Monetary Fund was conceived in 1944, and the initial members signed the agreement in 1945.[17] The primary objective of the IMF is to promote international monetary cooperation and facilitate the expansion and growth of international trade. Along with the IMF, the World Bank Group is dedicated to fighting poverty and improving the living standards of people in the developing world. It is a development bank that provides loans, policy advice, technical assistance, and knowledge-sharing services to low- and middle-income countries in an attempt to reduce poverty.[18] Thus, the key difference between the IMF and the World Bank is that the IMF focuses primarily on maintaining the international monetary system, whereas the World Bank concentrates on poverty reduction through low-interest loans and other programs. For instance, the World Bank Group is the largest external funding source of education and HIV/AIDS programs. Both organizations affect the practice of global marketing in different ways, but together, they enable marketers to participate in the global marketplace by making it easier to buy and sell, financing deserving firms, opening markets to trade, and raising the global standard of living, which allows more people to buy goods and services.

However, these organizations also have been criticized by a diverse group of nongovernmental organizations, religious groups, and advocates for workers and the poor. The primary criticism of the World Bank is that it is merely a puppet of Western industrialized nations that use World Bank loans to assist their globalization efforts. Others argue that the World Bank loans too much money to third-world countries, which makes it almost impossible for these often debt-ridden nations to repay the loans.[19] One of the most persuasive arguments that antiglobalization groups use is that many of the problems related to globalization can be attributed to the seemingly insatiable appetite of countries in North America and Europe, as well as Japan and other industrialized nations, for natural resources, oil, gasoline, timber, food, and so forth.[20] These nations consume 80 percent of the world's resources but are home to only 20 percent of the population. Should firms in industrialized nations be able to utilize these natural resources at a disproportionate rate, regardless of whether their shareholders demand profitable growth?

As the industrialized West has put into place laws that protect workers' rights, workers' safety, and the environment, U.S. firms also have outsourced production to less developed countries that either have no such laws or don't enforce them. Without laws to protect workers and the environment, the factories that produce these goods often exploit both the workers and the environment of these countries. Industrialized nations obtain the goods they crave at low costs, but at what price to the country that provides them? We consider this point in Ethical and Societal Dilemma 7.1.

In many parts of the world, the changes wrought by globalization have moved so fast that cultures have not had time to adapt. Many countries fear that the price for economic success and participation in the global market may be the loss of their individual identities and cultures. The challenge thus becomes whether

## Ethical and Societal Dilemma 7.1 Pity the Poor Behemoth

For international activists, the names Nike and Walmart often provoke strong reactions, and not in the sense that these companies would prefer. Once tarnished with allegations and proven cases of labor violations in their factories in other nations, these companies have continued to struggle to regain their footing and their reputations.

Nike's sweatshop struggles continued for years, as CEO Phil Knight originally dismissed claims that the company was responsible for the treatment of workers in factories with which the company contracted. Yet since the late 1990s, when the scandals dominated news coverage, the company also has instituted codes of conduct and audits for all factories that produce apparel for it.[21] If factories fail to live up to its standards for fair treatment of workers, it drops them from its supply chain—which then means that the local economy falters due to the massive loss of jobs.[22]

Walmart's reputational issues have mostly centered on the destruction it has wrought for mom-and-pop stores, which resulted from its significantly lower prices and greater buying power. These strengths stemmed largely from its supply chain efficiencies—and its reputed willingness to work with international suppliers that enforced inhumane working conditions. For example, in Bangladesh in the 1990s, workers in Walmart factories suffered through 19-hour shifts, making only $20 a month.[23] More recently, Walmart has fought hard to change consumers' and suppliers' perceptions of its image, beginning with public relations campaigns, as well as alterations to its supply chain. Its supplier agreement now mandates all manufacturers must be audited by third parties; the retail giant also is monitoring more than 1,000 suppliers on its own, and by 2012, it will require them to achieve the highest environmental and social ratings if they want to continue supplying the retailer.

*(continued)*

## Ethical and Societal Dilemma 7.1

*(continued)*

Both companies also have signed on to international standards for environmental responsibility. For example, Greenpeace has called Brazilian cattle ranching one of the greatest contributors to Amazon deforestation, which prompted Nike to mandate that by July 1, 2010, its Brazilian leather suppliers must prove their cattle have been raised outside of the Amazon Biome. Walmart similarly has committed to discontinuing contracts with suppliers that contribute to Amazonian deforestation.[24]

For Nike, this commitment implies it must find another source for its leather, one that may compromise the quality of its shoes. Will that make consumers happy? Walmart similarly faces a conflict between the low cost benefits it provides to consumers and the increasing costs associated with responsible business practices. And in both cases, the companies must accept that in some people's minds, they will forever be affiliated with international worker abuses.

*Nike has mandated that its Brazilian leather suppliers prove their cattle have been raised outside the Amazon Biome since Greenpeace has called Brazilian cattle ranching one of the greatest contributors to Amazon deforestation.*

economic needs should be allowed to outweigh cultural preservation. Globalization obviously has its critics, and those critics very well may have a point. But globalization also has been progressing at a steady and increasing pace. With that development in mind, let's look at how firms determine in which countries to expand their operations.

**L02** Describe the components of a country market assessment.

# ASSESSING GLOBAL MARKETS

Because different countries, with their different stages of globalization, offer marketers a variety of opportunities, firms must assess the viability of various potential market entries. As illustrated in Exhibit 7.1, we examine four sets of criteria necessary to assess a country's market: economic analysis, infrastructure and technological analysis, government actions or inactions, and sociocultural analysis. Information about these four areas offers marketers a more complete picture of a country's potential as a market for products and services.

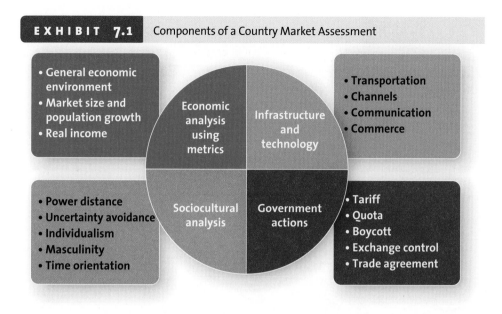

**EXHIBIT 7.1**    Components of a Country Market Assessment

## Economic Analysis Using Metrics

The greater the wealth of people in a country, generally, the better the opportunity a firm will have in that particular country. A firm conducting an economic analysis of a country market must look at three major economic factors using well-established metrics: the general economic environment, the market size and population growth rate, and real income.

**Evaluating the General Economic Environment** In general, healthy economies provide better opportunities for global marketing expansions, and there are several ways a firm can use metrics to measure the relative health of a particular country's economy. Each way offers a slightly different view, and some may be more useful for some products and services than for others.

To determine the market potential for its particular product or service, a firm should use as many metrics as it can obtain. One metric is the relative level of imports and exports. The United States, for example, suffers a trade deficit, which means that the country imports more goods than it exports.[25] For U.S. marketers, this deficit can signal the potential for greater competition at home from foreign producers. Firms would prefer to manufacture in a country that has a trade surplus, or a higher level of exports than imports, because it signals a greater opportunity to export products to more markets.

The most common way to gauge the size and market potential of an economy, and therefore the potential the country has for global marketing, is to use standardized metrics of output. Gross domestic product (GDP), the most widely used of these metrics, is defined as the market value of the goods and services produced by a country in a year. Gross national income (GNI) consists of GDP plus the net income earned from investments abroad (minus any payments made to nonresidents who contribute to the domestic economy). In other words, U.S. firms that invest or maintain operations abroad count their income from those operations in the GNI but not the GDP.[26]

Another frequently used metric of an overall economy is the purchasing power parity (PPP), a theory that states that if the exchange rates of two countries are in equilibrium, a product purchased in one will cost the same in the other, if expressed in the same currency.[27] A novel metric that employs PPP to assess the relative economic buying power among nations is *The Economist*'s Big Mac Index, which suggests that exchange rates should adjust to equalize the cost of a basket of goods and services, wherever it is bought around the world. Using McDonald's Big Mac as the market basket, Exhibit 7.2 shows that the cheapest burger is in

**EXHIBIT 7.2** Big Mac Index: Local Currency Under (–)/Over (+) Valuation against the Dollar

Big Mac index

Local currency under (-)/ over (+) valuation against the dollar, %

Big Mac price*, $

| | 50 | 25 | – | 0 | + | 25 | 50 | 75 | 100 |

6.87 Norway
6.16 Switzerland
4.62† Euro area
4.06 Canada
3.98 Australia
3.75 Hungary
3.71 Turkey
4.58‡ United States
3.54 Japan
3.48 Britain
3.00 South Korea
2.99 United Arab Emirates
2.86 Poland
2.67 Saudi Arabia
2.56 Mexico
2.44 South Africa
2.39 Russia
2.37 Egypt
2.36 Taiwan
2.28 Indonesia
2.16 Thailand
2.12 Malaysia
1.83 China

Sources: McDonald's *The Economist*

*At market exchange rate on March 16th †Weighted average of member countries
‡Average of four cities

China, where it costs $1.83, compared with an average American price of $3.58. In Norway, the same burger costs $6.87. This index thus implies that the Chinese Yuan is 49 percent undervalued, whereas the Norwegian Krone is 94 percent overvalued in comparison with the U.S. dollar.[28]

These various metrics help marketers understand the relative wealth of a particular country, although, as scholars have recently argued, they may not give a full picture of the economic health of a country because they are based solely on material output.[29] As a corollary metric to those described previously, the United Nations has developed the **human development index (HDI)**, a composite metric of three indicators of the quality of life in different countries: life expectancy at birth, educational attainment, and whether the average incomes, according to PPP estimates, are sufficient to meet the basic needs of life in that country. For marketers, these metrics determine the lifestyle elements that ultimately drive consumption (recall that Chapter 5, on consumer behavior, discussed the influence of lifestyle on consumption). The HDI is scaled from 0 to 1; countries that score lower than .5 are classified as nations with low human development, those that score .5–.8 have medium development, and those above .8 are classified as having high human development. Exhibit 7.3 shows a map of the world with the various HDI scores.

These macroeconomic metrics provide a snapshot of a particular country at any one point in time. Because they are standardized metrics, it is possible to compare countries across time and identify those that are experiencing economic growth and increased globalization.

| EXHIBIT 7.3 | Global Human Development Index (HDI) Score |

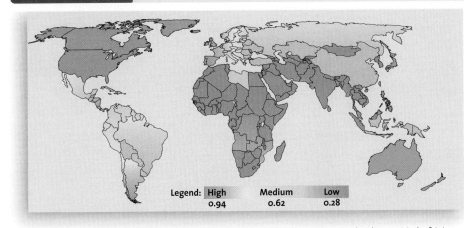

Legend: High 0.94    Medium 0.62    Low 0.28

Source: http://www.nationmaster.com/red/graph/eco_hum_dev_ind-economy-human-development-index&int;=-1&b  map=1#, accessed July 27, 2010.

Although an understanding of the macroeconomic environment is crucial for managers facing a market entry decision, of equal importance is the understanding of economic metrics of individual income and household size.

**Evaluating Market Size and Population Growth Rate**  Global population has been growing dramatically since the turn of the twentieth century (see Exhibit 7.4). The top map represents the world population in 2002. The bottom map is a graphical depiction of what the world population is expected to be in 2050. Note, for instance, how the populations of North and South America are expected to shrink relative to Africa. From a marketing perspective, however, growth has not been equally dispersed. Less developed nations, by and large, are experiencing rapid population growth, while many developed countries are experiencing either zero or negative population growth. The countries with the highest purchasing power today may become less attractive in the future for many products and services because of stagnated growth.

Another aspect of population and growth pertains to the distribution of the population within a particular region; namely, is the population located primarily in rural or urban areas? This distinction determines where and how products and services can be delivered. Long supply chains, in which goods pass through many hands, are necessary to reach rural populations and therefore add costs to products.

*Developed for the Indian market, the Nano is the world's cheapest car—about $2000.*

India's 1.16 billion people live overwhelmingly in rural areas, although the population is moving toward urban areas to meet the demands of the growing industrial and service centers located in major cities such as Bangalore and New Delhi. This population shift, perhaps not surprisingly, is accompanied by rapid growth in the middle class.[30]

Due to relatively careful banking policies and minimal dependence on exports for its growth, India has been comparatively protected from the impact of the global financial crisis. Another major trend in India involves the age of the population; the median age of India's citizens is 25.3 years, whereas that in the United States is 36.7 years.[31] The business impacts of these combined trends of increasing urbanization, a growing middle class, a

**EXHIBIT 7.4** Change in World Population

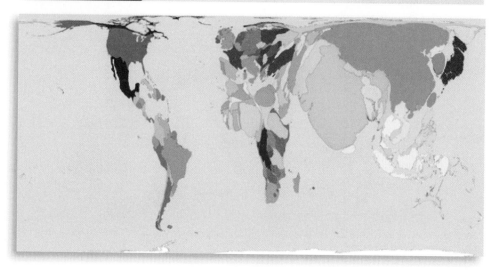

*Source:* www.worldmapper.org (accessed April 21, 2010).

degree of protectionism by the central government, and a youthful populace make India an absolutely enormous market for consumer goods.

In the capital of India, New Delhi, for example, the crowded streets traditionally have been filled with horse-drawn carts, bicycles, scooters, and taxis. Yet the growing Indian middle class is demanding more products previously available only to the wealthy. Therefore, the Nano, the world's cheapest car, has begun to appear, jockeying for position with the multitude of other vehicles. The Nano costs only about 100,000 rupees ($2000). It weighs less than half a Honda Accord; and it gets 56 miles per gallon. It can even achieve a top speed of 60 miles per hour, though it needs 23 seconds to reach that speed from a standstill.[32] During the 16-day prebooking period that the manufacturer initiated on April 9, 2009, it received orders for 203,000 of the tiny car.[33]

Similarly, the prevalence of cell phones has grown with the emerging Indian middle class. Fifteen years ago, the country hosted only 5 million total telecom connections, and that number included ground lines. Today, there are more than 545 million.[34] The rapid growth rates of industries create significant opportunities for global companies to sell products. In the telecommunications industry, for example, sellers of accessories such as ringtones and new batteries are enjoying a greatly expanded market. In general, India's economy is expected to continue to outpace world growth.[35]

But is it in the best interest of a rapidly developing country such as India to welcome foreign retailers? Ethical and Societal Dilemma 7.2 considers this question.

**Evaluating Real Income** Firms can make adjustments to an existing product or change the price to meet the unique needs of a particular country market. Such shifts are particularly common for low priced consumer goods. For instance, Procter & Gamble developed a single-use shampoo packet for consumers in less developed nations that cannot afford an entire bottle at one time. To increase consumption of Coca-Cola in rural India the company lowered its price to the equivalent of about 10 cents per bottle, while Cadbury International introduced the Dairy Milk Shots for the equivalent of about four cents.[36] Textbook publishers sell paperback versions of U.S. books for a fraction of their U.S. price to countries where students would not be able to otherwise afford a text. But pricing adjustments aren't made only for inexpensive products. Fashion and jewelry manufacturers also make downward adjustments to their prices in countries where the incomes of their target markets cannot support higher prices.

## Ethical and Societal Dilemma **7.2** Retail Concerns for India

With over one billion people and an expanding middle and upper class, India is one of the world's fastest-growing retail markets. But retailers seeking opportunity in India face challenges that range from convoluted foreign direct investment rules to cultural differences that affect buyer habits and preferences.[37] Foreign companies, for example, can own up to 51 percent of a "single-brand" retailer like a Nike outlet, but cannot invest in other kinds of direct-to-consumer multi-brand retail outlets. This restriction covers supermarket chains and big-box stores like Walmart.[38]

The restrictions are popular among Indians who are concerned that giant retailers like Walmart will destroy India's small family-owned stores and force Indians to change from their familiar shop-based shopping patterns to a more Westernized experience. These traditional shops account for 95 percent of India's retail commerce[39] and are both popular and familiar. For example, Kishore Biyani's supermarkets in Mumbai, India, were initially designed like most Western-style supermarkets.[40] But customers walked down the wide, well-lit aisles, past neatly stocked shelves, and out the door without buying. Biyani recognized that his target markets did not like the sterile, unfamiliar environment, so he

*(continued)*

*Although family-owned stores (left) currently account for 95 percent of India's retail commerce, the Indian population and government are concerned that big box stores like Walmart (right) will take over if they are not restricted.*

## Ethical and Societal Dilemma 7.2

*(continued)*

redesigned his stores to make them more like a public market. The approach worked: His company, Panaloon Retail (India), Ltd., is now one of the country's largest retailers.

However, traditional approaches have their downsides, including an intricate web of middlemen, which reduce profits and drive up consumer prices. Experienced retailers like Walmart can introduce modernization and efficiency, two factors that can help in important areas like controlling food-price inflation and improving the quality of food.[41]

Each year, retailers in India experience perishable inventory losses, such as grains and produce, due to supply chain inefficiencies. In other countries, supermarket chains and big-box stores reduce those losses through careful supply chain management. Strong relationships with vendors and bulk purchasing help these large retailers keep prices low while helping to ensure that food is fresh when it reaches shelves.

Walmart could provide all those benefits to India, but its interest in the country isn't entirely altruistic. The largest retailer and grocery retailer in the world[42] also sees an opportunity for global growth in the emerging economy. Walmart solved its regulatory problem in India by forming a joint venture with Indian business conglomerate Bharti Enterprises. Under this arrangement, Walmart contributes its supply chain and back-end logistics expertise while Bharti owns and manages the wholesale and retail stores where merchandise is sold.[43] The arrangement isn't ideal for Walmart, which loses control over an important aspect of operations, but it does establish a foothold in the country.

Walmart has backtracked to the beginning of the produce supply chain in India—local farmers—to improve productivity.[44] Initiatives include improved insect control and germination and growing practices and a more informed approach to fertilization. These practices have helped increase crop yields by 25 percent. Benefits don't stop there: Farmers are seeing 5 to 7 percent higher income from Walmart than from local wholesale markets. They are also avoiding transportation costs since Walmart collects its produce from the fields,[45] but this practice cuts out Indian distributors who rely on farm business for their livelihood.

What will be the effect on the economy and culture of India if Walmart and other large global retailers are successful in India? What will become of the small family-owned businesses and wholesalers? Do you think the Indian government should relax its restrictions on foreign retailers or increase them? Do you think Indian consumers will switch to Westernized shopping experiences or continue bringing their business to familiar shops? How would you balance the needs of farmers, distributors, and consumers? How would you balance the need for corporate growth with government restrictions and consumer preferences in a foreign market?

*For a country to be a viable option for a new market entry, firms must assess its transportation, distribution channels, communications, and commercial infrastructure.*

## Analyzing Infrastructure and Technological Capabilities

The next component of any market assessment is an infrastructure and technological analysis. Infrastructure is defined as the basic facilities, services, and installations needed for a community or society to function, such as transportation and communications systems, water and power lines, and public institutions like schools, post offices, and prisons.

Marketers are especially concerned with four key elements of a country's infrastructure: transportation, distribution channels, communications, and commerce. First, there must be a system to transport goods throughout the various markets and to consumers in geographically dispersed marketplaces—trains, roads, refrigeration. Second, distribution channels must exist to deliver products in a timely manner and at a reasonable cost. Third, the com-

**EXHIBIT 7.5** Government Actions

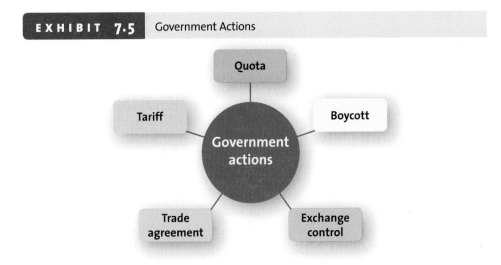

munications system, particularly media access, must be sufficiently developed to allow consumers to find information about the products and services available in the marketplace. Fourth, the commercial infrastructure, which consists of the legal, banking, and regulatory systems, allows markets to function. In the next section, we focus on how issues pertaining to the political and legal structures of a country can affect the risk that marketers face in operating in a given country.

## Analyzing Government Actions

Governmental actions, as well as the actions of nongovernmental political groups, can significantly influence firms' ability to sell goods and services, because they often result in laws or other regulations that either promote the growth of the global market or close off the country and inhibit growth. These issues include tariffs, quotas, boycotts, exchange controls, and trade agreements. (See Exhibit 7.5.)

Tariffs  A tariff (also called a duty) is a tax levied on a good imported into a country. In most cases, tariffs are intended to make imported goods more expensive and thus less competitive with domestic products,[46] which in turn protects domestic industries from foreign competition. In other cases, tariffs might be imposed to penalize another country for trade practices that the home country views as unfair. When China entered the World Trade Organization, it agreed to a "safeguard" provision imposed by the United States, which stated that U.S. companies harmed by Chinese imports could ask for protection from a "surge" of Chinese alternatives. The provision was invoked for the first time in September 2009, when President Barack Obama announced a 35 percent tariff on Chinese tires for automobiles and light trucks, largely in response to pressures from the United Steel Workers Union.[47]

In lieu of tariffs, countries can utilize antidumping laws to protect domestic companies against foreign competition. Dumping occurs when a foreign producer sells its offering in a foreign market at a price less than its production costs to gain market share.[48] When a foreign company is found to have engaged in dumping, U.S. law allows for fines, and those collected fines then get distributed to U.S. companies affected by the dumping practices. Such practices are not, of course, limited to the United States. In early 2010, India imposed heavy antidumping fines on South Korea when it increased exports of phosphorous to India from 772 tons to 15,408 tons in just one year.[49]

Quotas  A quota designates the maximum quantity of a product that may be brought into a country during a specified time period. Many U.S. quotas on foreign-made textiles were eliminated in 2005, which increased the amount of imported apparel products sold in the United States.

Tariffs and quotas also can have a fundamental and potentially devastating impact on a firm's ability to sell products in another country. Tariffs artificially raise prices and therefore lower demand, and quotas reduce the availability of imported merchandise. Conversely, tariffs and quotas benefit domestically made products because they reduce foreign competition.

**Boycott** A boycott pertains to a group's refusal to deal commercially with some organization to protest against its policies. Boycotts might be called by governments or nongovernmental organizations, such as trade unions or environmental groups. Although most are called by nongovernmental organizations, they still can be very political.

**Exchange Control** Exchange control refers to the regulation of a country's currency exchange rate, the measure of how much one currency is worth in relation to another.[50] A designated agency in each country, often the Central Bank, sets the rules for currency exchange, though in the United States, the Federal Reserve sets the currency exchange rates. In recent years, the value of the U.S. dollar has changed significantly compared with other important world currencies. When the dollar falls, it has a twofold effect on U.S. firms' ability to conduct global business. For firms that depend on imports of finished products, raw materials that they fabricate into other products, or services from other countries, the cost of doing business goes up dramatically. At the same time, buyers in other countries find the costs of U.S. goods and services much lower than they were before.

**Trade Agreements** Marketers must consider the trade agreements to which a particular country is a signatory or the trading bloc to which it belongs. A trade agreement is an intergovernmental agreement designed to manage and promote trade activities for a specific region, and a trading bloc consists of those countries that have signed the particular trade agreement.[51]

Some major trade agreements cover two-thirds of the world's international trade: the European Union (EU), the North American Free Trade Agreement (NAFTA), Central America Free Trade Agreement (CAFTA), Mercosur, and the Association of Southeast Asian Nations (ASEAN).[52] These trade agreements are summarized in Exhibit 7.6. The EU represents the highest level of integration across individual nations, whereas the other agreements vary in their integration levels.

**European Union** The EU is an economic and monetary union that currently contains 27 countries, as illustrated in Exhibit 7.7. Croatia, Macedonia, and Turkey head a list of additional petitioners for membership, but they have not yet been granted full membership.[53] The European Union represents a significant restructuring of the global marketplace. By dramatically lowering trade barriers between member nations, the union has changed the complexion of the global marketplace.

| **EXHIBIT 7.6** | Trade Agreements |
|---|---|
| **Name** | **Countries** |
| European Union | There are 27 member countries of the EU: Austria, Belgium, Bulgaria, Cyprus, Czech Republic, Denmark, Estonia, Finland, France, Germany, Greece, Hungary, Ireland, Italy, Latvia, Lithuania, Luxembourg, Malta, Netherlands, Poland, Portugal, Romania, Slovakia, Slovenia, Spain, Sweden, and the United Kingdom.[54] There are three official candidate countries to join the EU: Croatia, Macedonia, and Turkey. |
| NAFTA | United States, Canada, and Mexico. |
| CAFTA | United States, Costa Rica, the Dominican Republic, El Salvador, Guatemala, Honduras, and Nicaragua. |
| Mercosur | Full members: Argentina, Brazil, Paraguay, Uruguay, and Venezuela. |
| ASEAN | Brunei Darussalam, Cambodia, Indonesia, Laos, Malaysia, Myanmar, Philippines, Singapore, Thailand, and Vietnam. |

**EXHIBIT 7.7**　　Map of the European Union[54]

Having one currency, the euro, across Europe has simplified the way many multinational companies market their products. For instance, prior to the conversion to the euro in 1999, firms were unable to predict exchange rates. This barrier made it difficult to set consistent prices across countries. After the euro replaced the traditional European currencies, stable prices resulted. Products could be preticketed for distribution across Europe. In addition, patent requirements were simplified because one patent application could cover multiple countries. Similarly, the rules governing data privacy and transmission, advertising, direct selling, and other marketing issues have been streamlined and simplified, allowing more seamless trade.

**North American Free Trade Agreement (NAFTA)**  NAFTA is limited to trade-related issues, such as tariffs and quotas, among the United States, Canada, and Mexico.

**Central American Free Trade Agreement (CAFTA)**  CAFTA is a trade agreement among the United States, Costa Rica, the Dominican Republic, El Salvador, Guatemala, Honduras, and Nicaragua.[55]

**Mercosur**  Translated from the Spanish, Mercosur means the Southern Common Market. This group covers most of South America. In 1995, Mercosur member nations created the Free Trade Area of the Americas (FTAA), primarily in response to NAFTA.

**Association of Southeast Asian Nations (ASEAN)**  Originally formed to promote security in Southeast Asia during the Vietnam War, ASEAN changed its mission to building economic stability and lowering trade restrictions among the six member nations in the 1980s.

These trading blocs affect how U.S. firms can conduct business in the member countries. Some critics contend that such blocs confer an unfair advantage on their member nations because they offer favorable terms for trade, whereas others believe they stimulate economies by lowering trade barriers and allowing higher levels of foreign investment.

## Analyzing Sociocultural Factors

Understanding another country's *culture* is crucial to the success of any global marketing initiative. Culture, or the shared meanings, beliefs, morals, values, and customs of a group of people, exists on two levels: visible artifacts (e.g., behavior, dress, symbols, physical settings, ceremonies) and underlying values (thought processes, beliefs, and assumptions). Visible artifacts are easy to recognize, but businesses often find it more difficult to understand the underlying values of a culture and appropriately adapt their marketing strategies to them.[56]

For example, IKEA stores across the globe are open seven days a week—except in France. French law prevents retailers from selling on Sundays, and when IKEA tried to challenge the law by keeping one of its stores open, it provoked a lawsuit from a French workers' union. Although IKEA would love to sell over the whole weekend, when it earns approximately one-quarter of its weekly revenues, neither the workers' unions nor French consumers are likely to change their ways any time soon; leaving Sunday as a day of relaxation constitutes a fundamental foundation of French culture.[57] For the Swiss, a similar prohibition against Sunday retailing may soon fall to the wayside though. If stores remain closed, Switzerland will continue to lose tourism revenues, because most foreign visitors, who tend to visit on the weekend, are accustomed to shopping on Sundays. Opening retail stores on Sundays could mean increased consumption and wages for workers who work more hours, as well as employment for more people. But the loss of a day traditionally designated for family time and relaxation might be something the country cannot abide.[58] There may be no completely right answer to this dilemma, but global marketers clearly must be aware of the regulations and cultural norms of the countries they enter.

*The European Union has resulted in lowering trade barriers and strengthening global relationships among member nations.*

One important cultural classification scheme that firms can use is Geert Hofstede's cultural dimensions concept, which sheds more light on these underlying values. Hofstede believes cultures differ on five dimensions:[59]

1. **Power distance:** Willingness to accept social inequality as natural.

2. **Uncertainty avoidance:** The extent to which the society relies on orderliness, consistency, structure, and formalized procedures to address situations that arise in daily life.

3. **Individualism:** Perceived obligation to and dependence on groups.

4. **Masculinity:** The extent to which dominant values are male oriented. A lower masculinity ranking indicates that men and women are treated equally in all aspects of society; a higher masculinity ranking suggests that men dominate in positions of power.

5. **Time orientation:** Short- versus long-term orientation. A country that tends to have a long-term orientation values long-term commitments and is willing to accept a longer time horizon for, say, the success of a new product introduction.

*Ikea in France*

To illustrate two of the five dimensions, consider the data and graph in Exhibit 7.8. Power distance is on the vertical axis and individualism is on the horizontal axis. Several Latin American countries cluster high on power distance but low on individualism; the United States, Australia, Canada, and the United Kingdom, in contrast, cluster high on individualism but low on power distance. Using this information, firms should expect that if they design a marketing campaign that stresses equality and individualism, it will be well accepted in English-speaking countries, all other factors being equal. The same campaign, however, might not be as well received in Latin American countries.

Another means of classifying cultures distinguishes them according to the importance of verbal communication.[60] In the United States and most European countries, business relationships are governed by what is said and written down, often through formal contracts. In countries such as China and South Korea, however, most relationships rely on nonverbal cues, so that the situation or context

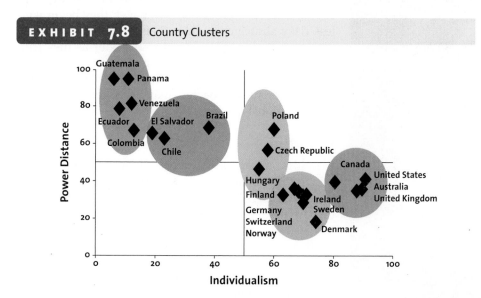

**EXHIBIT 7.8**  Country Clusters

means much more than mere words. For instance, business relationships in China often are formalized by just a handshake, and trust and honor are often more important than legal arrangements.

Overall, culture affects every aspect of consumer behavior: why people buy, who is in charge of buying decisions, and how, when, and where people shop. After marketing managers have completed the four parts of the market assessment, they are better able to make informed decisions about whether a particular country possesses the necessary characteristics to be considered a potential market for the firm's products and services. In the next section, we detail the market entry decision process, beginning with a discussion of the various ways firms might enter a new global market.

### CHECK YOURSELF

1. What are key metrics that can help analyze the economic environment of a country?
2. What types of government actions should we be concerned about as we evaluate a country?
3. What are five important cultural dimensions?

**L03**   Identify the various market entry strategies.

# CHOOSING A GLOBAL ENTRY STRATEGY

*The Rolex brand is such a valuable asset that to protect it, the firm must continually watch for counterfeit merchandise and sales through unauthorized dealers.*

When a firm has concluded its assessment analysis of the most viable markets for its products and services, it must then conduct an internal assessment of its capabilities. As we discussed in Chapter 2, this analysis includes an assessment of the firm's access to capital, the current markets it serves, its manufacturing capacity, its proprietary assets, and the commitment of its management to the proposed strategy. These factors ultimately contribute to the success or failure of a market expansion strategy, whether at home or in a foreign market. After these internal market assessments, it is time for the firm to choose its entry strategy.

A firm can choose from many approaches when it decides to enter a new market, which vary according to the level of risk the firm is willing to take. Many firms actually follow a progression in which they begin with less risky strategies to enter their first foreign markets and move to increasingly risky strategies as they gain confidence in their abilities and more control over their operations, as illustrated in Exhibit 7.9. We examine these different approaches that marketers take when entering global markets, beginning with the least risky.

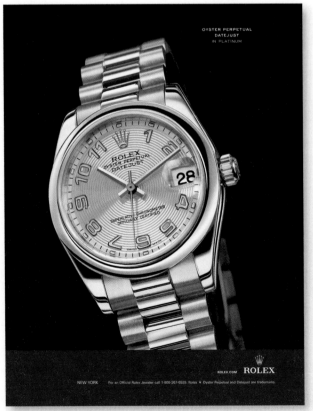

## Exporting

**Exporting** means producing goods in one country and selling them in another. This entry strategy requires the least financial risk but also allows for only a limited return to the exporting firm. Global expansion often begins when a firm receives an order for its product or service from another country, in which case it faces little risk because it has no investment in people, capital equipment, buildings, or infrastructure.[61] By the same token, it is difficult to achieve economies of scale when everything has to be shipped internationally. The Swiss watchmaker Rolex

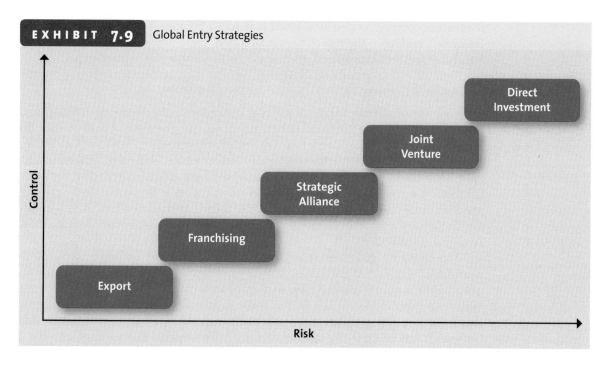

**EXHIBIT 7.9** Global Entry Strategies

sells relatively small numbers of expensive watches all over the world. Because its transportation costs are relatively small compared with the cost of the watches, the best way for it to service any market is to export from Switzerland.

## Franchising

Franchising is a contractual agreement between a firm, the franchisor, and another firm or individual, the franchisee. A franchising contract allows the franchisee to operate a business—a retail product or service firm or a B2B provider—using the name and business format developed and supported by the franchisor. Many of the best-known retailers in the United States are also successful global franchisers, including McDonald's, Pizza Hut, Starbucks, Domino's Pizza, KFC, and Holiday Inn, all of which have found that global franchising entails lower risks and requires less investment than does opening units owned wholly by the firm. However, when it engages in franchising, the firm has limited control over the market operations in

*KFC and Pizza Hut are successful global franchisors.*

the foreign country, its potential profit is reduced because it must be split with the franchisee, and, once the franchise is established, there is always the threat that the franchisee will break away and operate as a competitor under a different name.

## Strategic Alliance

Strategic alliances refer to collaborative relationships between independent firms, though the partnering firms do not create an equity partnership; that is, they do not invest in one another. Therefore, when Cisco Systems Inc., San Jose, California, and Tata Consultancy Services, Mumbai, India, entered into their strategic alliance, they both continued to develop market-ready infrastructure and network solutions for customers, but they relied on each other to provide the training and skills that one or the other might have lacked. At the same time, Cisco maintains alliances with various other companies, including Microsoft, Nokia, IBM, Accenture, and SAP.[62]

The changing global economy also has led European car manufacturers to consider alliances and partnerships as means to address international markets. Confronting a glut of unsold cars, as European consumers put off big purchases, Volkswagen purchased a $2.5 billion stake in Suzuki to access Asian car buyers. Italy's Fiat has gone a different route: It plans to develop cars in a partnership with Chrysler.[63] According to the head of sales for Volkswagen, "Europe appears to be a fairly saturated market," which means carmakers have little choice but to investigate other, global options to sell their products in markets that might still be growing.

## Joint Venture

A joint venture forms when a firm entering a new market pools its resources with those of a local firm to form a new company in which ownership, control, and profits are shared. (Recall the discussion of Walmart's joint venture in India from Ethical and Societal Dilemma 7.2.) In addition to sharing the financial burden, the local partner offers the foreign entrant greater understanding of the market and access to resources such as vendors and real estate. In some cases, joint ventures span several markets, as when the Japanese electronics superstar Sony teamed up

*Volkswagen's Audi division has a joint venture with Chinese manufacturer First Automotive Works (FAW).*

with the Swedish communication firm Ericsson. A truly global venture, its central management is located in London, and it maintains R&D facilities in India, the United States, Sweden, Japan, China, Germany, and the United Kingdom. In 2009, the venture was the fourth-largest mobile phone provider in the world.[64]

China, India, and many other countries usually require joint ownership of firms entering their domestic markets, though many of these restrictions are loosening as a result of WTO negotiations and ever-increasing globalization pressures. However, problems with this entry approach can arise when the partners disagree or if the government places restrictions on the firm's ability to move its profits out of the foreign country and back to its home country.

## Direct Investment

Direct investment requires a firm to maintain 100 percent ownership of its plants, operation facilities, and offices in a foreign country, often through the formation of wholly owned subsidiaries. This entry strategy requires the highest level of investment and exposes the firm to significant risks, including the loss of its operating and/or initial investments. For example, a dramatic economic downturn caused by a natural disaster, war, political instability, or changes in the country's laws can increase a foreign entrant's risk considerably. Many firms believe that in certain markets, these potential risks are outweighed by the high potential returns. With this strategy, none of the potential profits must be shared with other firms. In addition to the high potential returns, direct investment offers the firm complete control over its operations in the foreign country.

ING Group, a financial services firm based in The Netherlands, decided to enter the U.S. market through a wholly owned subsidiary. Attracted by the United States' position as the world's largest financial services market, as well as regulations friendly to ING's desire to provide banking services, insurance, and asset management products (e.g., mortgages, investment accounts), ING began an aggressive entry into the U.S. market. Forgoing traditional bank branches, ING established ING Direct and operates purely online. Currently ING employs over 10,000 people in the United States.[65] Although it began with online savings accounts, ING has expanded into investment accounts and online mortgage services and now has 7.5 million customers and more than $77 billion in assets in the United States.[66]

As we noted, each of these entry strategies entails different levels of risk and rewards for the foreign entrant. But even after a firm has determined how much risk it is willing to take, and therefore how it will enter a new global market, it still must establish its marketing strategy, as we discuss in the next section.

### CHECK YOURSELF

1. Which global entry strategy has the least risk and why?
2. Which global entry strategy has the most risk and why?

# CHOOSING A GLOBAL MARKETING STRATEGY

**LO4** Highlight the similarities and differences between a domestic marketing strategy and a global marketing strategy.

Just like any other marketing strategy, a global marketing strategy includes two components: determining the target markets to pursue and developing a marketing mix that will sustain a competitive advantage over time. In this section, we examine marketing strategy as it relates specifically to global markets.

## Target Market: Segmentation, Targeting, and Positioning

Global segmentation, targeting, and positioning (STP) are more complicated than domestic STP for several reasons. First, firms considering a global expansion have much more difficulty understanding the cultural nuances of other countries. Second, subcultures within each country also must be considered. Third, consumers often view products and their role as consumers differently in different countries.[67] A product, service, or even a retailer often must be positioned differently in different markets. For example, Ford enjoyed success with its F-Series trucks for many years[68] but this vehicle isn't as appealing to the Indian market, where small cars are growing in popularity. So Ford targeted India's small-car market segment with a new model, the Figo. The company focuses on other market segments with models like the Ikon, which is designed to appeal to upwardly mobile urban men looking to purchase an affordable luxury car, and with the Fusion. The Fusion, a model that incorporates the benefits of a sedan and a utility vehicle, targets young families.[69]

The Figo contains technology and architecture proven in other markets as well as features derived from consumer research and testing on India's roads. Since many small-car buyers are first-time automobile owners, the model focuses on value for money[70] through fuel efficiency, low maintenance costs, and technology enhancements that improve ride and handling on India's rough roads and crowded streets.[71] Introducing a model to compete in this segment is critical to Ford, which saw its sales in India decline nearly 9 percent at a time when total passenger vehicle sales gained 12 percent. With nearly three-quarters of cars sold in India being in the small car category, the company saw an opportunity to gain lost ground.[72]

But Ford isn't the only car company aware of the potential in India's small car market. Suzuki and Hyundai, which sell several models of small cars, dominate the market, while other car manufacturers such as Honda and Nissan have either already introduced small car models or plan to do so soon.[73] To define a position for the Figo that sets it apart from competitors, Ford needed to improve upon or include features that appeal to small-car buyers while offering a lower price than similar cars available in India.[74] For example, the measurements of the Figo make it the longest compact hatchback in India as well as the lowest and sleekest, while its base model price specifically targets competitors.

Ford's segmentation, targeting, and positioning strategy for India have been successful, with the Figo setting sales records in the first month of availability. But the company must continually monitor economic and social trends to protect its position within the market and adjust its products and marketing strategies to meet the changing needs of global markets. In this way, global marketing is similar to national marketing.

When it identifies its positioning within the market, the firm then must decide how to implement its marketing strategies using the marketing mix. Just as firms adjust their products and services to meet the needs of national target markets, they must alter their marketing mix to serve the needs of global markets.

## The Global Marketing Mix

During the early stages of globalization, in the 1950s and 1960s, large U.S. firms were uniquely positioned in the global marketplace because they had the skills necessary to develop, promote, and market brand name consumer products. In the 1970s and 1980s however, Japanese firms dominated the global marketplace because they could exploit their skills in production, materials management, and new product development. Today, retailers such as Walmart, financial services firms such as Citicorp, and software firms such as Microsoft are dominating the newest stage of globalization by exploiting their technological skills, while Asian and South and Central American countries dominate the manufacturing of con-

*Ford has introduced the Figo to first-time value-driven automobile owners in India.*

sumer products.[75] In the following section, we explore the four Ps (product, price, promotion, place) from a global perspective.

**Global Product or Service Strategies** There are three potential global product strategies:

■ Sell the same product or service in both the home country market and the host country.

■ Sell a product or service similar to that sold in the home country but include minor adaptations.

■ Sell totally new products or services.

The strategy a firm chooses depends on the needs of the target market. The level of economic development, as well as differences in product and technical standards, helps determine the need for and level of product adaptation. Cultural differences such as food preferences, language, and religion also play a role in product strategy planning.

Russia, one of the largest "new" markets in the world, is notable for its past development, including its long-standing embrace of communism. Consumption was limited, with few foreign options available. However, as it moves toward a market-based economy, consumers are happily learning to spend the money they

*Campbell's research found that Russians eat a lot of soup, and they want time-saving preparation help. So it developed broths and bases to enable cooks to prepare soups with their own flair.*

have, even though average monthly income levels hover at around $300. As the retail market expands rapidly—expectations indicate it will grow by 84 percent by 2011—companies investigate these latest consumers. They have disposable income, because they generally live mortgage free; receive heavily subsidized electricity and gas; have very little debt (because credit was not available under communism); and have little interest in saving, because history has taught them that they were likely to lose any pensions they might have saved. Yet the shift to a market economy also has been marked by terrible levels of corruption, including unnecessary bureaucracy, bribery, and uncertain legislation.[76] (For further discussion of a country moving from a communist to a market economy, see the Case Study at the end of this chapter.)

In such varied cultural settings, bringing even the simplest consumer goods to new markets can be challenging. For example, Campbell discovered that though Russia and China are two of the largest markets for soup in the world, cooks in those countries have unique demands. Chinese consumers drink 320 billion bowls of soup each year, and Russian buyers consume 32 billion servings, compared with only 14 billion bowls of soup served in the United States. However, Chinese cooks generally refuse to resort to canned soup; though the average Chinese consumer eats soup five times each week, he or she also takes great pride in preparing it personally with fresh ingredients. In contrast, Campbell found that Russian consumers, though they demand very high quality in their soups, had grown tired of spending hours preparing their homemade broths. To identify opportunities in these markets, Campbell sent teams of social anthropologists to study how Chinese and Russian cooks prepare and consume soup. Primarily, the soup company found that it would need to change its products to focus more on broths and bases, which would enable local cooks to save preparation time but also add their own flair to the meals and make them seem homemade. Campbell also changed its recipes slightly to reflect local tastes.[77]

The level of economic development also affects the global product strategy because it relates directly to consumer behavior. For instance, consumers in developed countries tend to demand more attributes in their products than do consumers in less developed countries. In the United States, Honda does not offer its line of "urban" motorcycles, available in Mexico and China, because the product line resembles a motor scooter more than a motorcycle, which does not tend to appeal to American consumers. Motorcycles sold in the United States have more horsepower and bigger frames and come with an array of options that are not offered in other countries.

*The level of economic development affects the global product strategy. Consumers in the United States prefer larger motorcycles with more amenities, like the Honda Goldwing on the left with the air bag deploying. Motorcycles in India are generally smaller, like the Pleasure scooter on the right, which is a joint venture between Honda Motor Company of Japan and Hero Group, the world's largest manufacturer.*

## Adding Value **7.1**　　Is One World Car Enough for All of Us?[78]

Gertrude Stein famously wrote, "A rose is a rose is a rose." But in the world of global marketing, that line has never seemed to hold particularly true. Is a car the same as a car the same as a car, the world over?

Previous developments would suggest not. Consider, for example, our discussion of the Nano, the 1300-pound mini-car that enjoyed great success in India. In the United States, where car buyers love huge SUVs, roads have plenty of room for several cars side by side, and the car culture is well developed, such an automobile is unlikely to prompt much excitement.

But Ford CEO Alan Mulally seems determined to find a car that everyone will appreciate, whether they live in New Delhi, New York, or Newfoundland. He chose the name "Fiesta," despite some concerns that the previous iteration of this name was an unpopular, unattractive subcompact in the 1970s. Yet the name also is recognizable, and it does not suffer from any negative translations or connotations in various languages (e.g., Volkswagen's Bora model sounded too much like "boring" in English, so it changed the name to Jetta). Therefore, whatever market it appeared in, the one-world car would be the Fiesta.

This choice offers several benefits for the automaker; in particular, it saves on some of its marketing costs. That is, Ford needs only one logo for the Fiesta, and perhaps even one set of marketing communications in various international markets. In addition, it prevents consumer confusion, which is common in an online world when a company uses the same name for different lines. For example, the Ford Fusion is a sedan in Europe but an SUV in the United States. An online shopper who clicks on the wrong link would be terribly confused.

The universal Fiesta entered the European market in 2008 and soon became the top-selling small car on that continent. Ford plans to roll out the same car in the United States in 2011, after investing heavily in determining which features would appeal across the board. For example, it attempted to make the Fiesta aesthetically pleasing across cultures, without increasing costs.

Some firms also might standardize their products globally but use different promotional campaigns to sell them. The original Pringles potato chip product remains the same globally, as do the images and themes of the promotional campaign, with limited language adaptations for the local markets, though English is used whenever possible. However, the company does change Pringles' flavors in different countries, including paprika-flavored chips sold in Italy and Germany.[79]

Yet again, the firm might just take its existing product and market it "as is" in all foreign markets. Ford Motor Co., for example, envisions a "world car" that will sell everywhere, as we discuss in Adding Value 7.1.

**Global Pricing Strategies** Determining the selling price in the global marketplace is an extremely difficult task.[80] Many countries still have rules governing the competitive marketplace, including those that affect pricing. For example, in parts of Europe, including Belgium, Italy, Spain, Greece, and France, sales are allowed only twice a year, in January and June or July. In most European countries, retailers can't sell below cost, and in others they can't advertise reduced prices in advance of sales or discount items until they have been on the shelves more than a month. For firms such as Walmart and other discounters, these restrictions threaten their core competitive positioning as the lowest-cost provider in the market. Other issues, such as tariffs, quotas, antidumping laws, and currency exchange policies, can also affect pricing decisions.[81]

Competitive factors influence global pricing in the same way they do home country pricing, but because a firm's products or services may not have the same positioning in the global marketplace as they do in their home country, market prices must be adjusted to reflect the local pricing structure. Spain's fashion retailer Zara, for instance, is relatively inexpensive in the EU but is priced about 40 percent higher in the United States, putting it right in the middle of its moderately priced competition.[82] Because it is important for Zara to get its fashions to the United States in a timely manner, it incurs additional transportation expenses, which it passes on to its North American customers. Finally, as we discussed previously in this chapter, currency fluctuations impact global pricing strategies.

*Spain's fashion retailer Zara is priced higher in the United States than in Spain because it ships its merchandise to the United States from Spain by air.*

**Global Distribution Strategies** Global distribution networks form complex value chains that involve middlemen, exporters, importers, and different transportation systems. These additional middlemen typically add cost and ultimately increase the final selling price of a product. As a result of these cost factors, constant pressure exists to shorten distribution channels wherever possible.

The number of firms with which the seller needs to deal to get its merchandise to the consumer determines the complexity of a channel. In most developing countries, manufacturers must go through many different types of distribution channels to get their products to end users, who often lack adequate transportation to shop at central shopping areas or large malls. Therefore, these consumers shop near their homes at small, family-owned retail outlets. To reach these small retail outlets, most of which are located far from major rail stations or roads, marketers have devised a variety of creative solutions. Unilever's strategy in India is a prime example of how a global company can adopt its distribution network to fit local conditions. Unilever trained 25,000 Indian women to serve as distributors, who in turn extended Unilever's reach to 80,000 villages across India. The program generates $250 million each year just in villages that otherwise would be too costly to serve.[83] For examples of other new distribution strategies, consider Superior Service 7.1.

**Global Communication Strategies**  The major challenge in developing a global communication strategy is identifying the elements that need to be adapted to be effective in the global marketplace. For instance, literacy levels vary dramatically across the globe. In Argentina, 2.8 percent of the adult population is illiterate, compared with 7.3 percent in the Philippines and a whopping 53 percent in Mozambique.[84] Media availability also varies widely; some countries offer only state-controlled media. Advertising regulations differ too. In an attempt at standardization, the EU recently recommended common guidelines for its member countries regarding advertising to children and is currently initiating a multiphase ban on "junk food" advertising.[85]

Differences in language, customs, and culture also complicate marketers' ability to communicate with customers in various countries. Language can be particularly vexing for advertisers. For example, in the United Kingdom, a thong is only a sandal, whereas in the United States, it can also be an undergarment. To avoid the potential embarrassment that language confusion can cause, firms spend millions of dollars to develop brand names that have no preexisting meaning in any known language, such as Accenture (a management consulting firm) or Avaya (a subsidiary of Lucent Technologies, formerly Bell Labs).

---

### Superior Service 7.1　　Hey Neighbor, Can You Spare a Battery Pack?[86]

Rising fuel costs are changing the way that companies do business. In the past, U.S. companies would outsource manufacturing, obtain materials from all across the world, and then ship the goods to the final destination.

For example, Tesla Motors used to manufacture 1000-pound automobile battery packs in Thailand, ship them to Britain for installation, and then ship the nearly assembled cars to the United States. This model made sense when fuel prices ranged around $10 per barrel, but now that the price has risen by more than tenfold, transportation costs overwhelm such supply chains. Moving goods is very expensive, and many items, especially those with smaller margins (e.g., food), have simply become too expensive to transport. If they were available and the transportation costs were passed on to consumers, avocados from South Africa would cost a U.S. grocery shopper as much as a rib eye steak.

In the new economy, the neighborhood effect instead is catching on; it tries to put factories close to both the suppliers of components and final consumers to reduce the transportation costs. The result is also a boon for consumers, in that they have ready access to the supply lines from which they gather their purchases. But for many companies, existing supply chains mean that they still rely on massive container ships.

A 40-foot container ship sailing from Shanghai to the United States today costs $8000 compared with $3000 a decade ago, and it moves slower too, in an attempt to save fuel.

Just-in-time (JIT) systems aim to have components arrive at the exact time they are needed, in an effort to minimize warehousing costs. But modern companies may be forced to buy whichever components are available in the vicinity of their place of need, rather than buying the cheapest products in the world. Furthermore, recalls of millions of vehicles by the world's most famous JIT practitioner Toyota have raised some questions about the potential downsides to JIT. If the goal is to meet production deadlines at all costs, is the result an unsafe product?[87]

Finally, due to outsourcing, the United States may have lost significant production skills. However, the advantages of closer production and decreased transportation costs may mean that more companies, especially those specializing in heavy goods (e.g., furniture companies IKEA and La-Z-Boy) will be turning to increased domestic production in the various places they sell products. In all these developments, the question becomes whether the greater service, safety, and satisfaction that neighborhood sourcing might provide can offset the cost benefits of global sourcing.

---

Within many countries there are multiple variants on a language. For example, China hosts three main languages, and firms such as Mercedes-Benz have adapted their names for each language. Thus, Mercedes-Benz is known by three Chinese names in Asia: *peng zee* in Cantonese for Hong Kong, *peng chi* in Mandarin for Taiwan, and *ben chi* in Mandarin for mainland China. Nokia, in contrast, chose to use only one name throughout China and thus is known as *nuo jee ya* in Mandarin.[88] As China continues to develop, having more than one name to represent a product or service likely will become increasingly inefficient.

Even with all these differences, many products and services serve the same needs and wants globally with little or no adaptation in their form or message. Firms with global appeal can run global advertising campaigns and simply translate the wording in the advertisements and product labeling. Nike has taken advantage of the universal nature of its product and combined it with the widespread appeal of pop music to create such an advertising campaign, as we outline in Adding Value 7.2. However, this example also clearly demonstrates the variation that almost invariably marks marketing communications across cultures.

Some products require a more localized approach because of cultural and religious differences. In a classic advertisement for Longines watches, a woman's bare arm and hand appear, with a watch on her wrist. The advertisement was considered too risqué for Muslim countries, where women's bare arms are never displayed in public, but the company simply changed the advertisement to show a gloved arm and hand wearing the same watch.

Even among English speakers there can be significant differences in the effectiveness of advertising campaigns. Take the popular "What Happens in Vegas Stays in Vegas" advertising campaign, which has been very successful and spawned numerous copycat slogans in the United States. Essentially, the U.S. mass market thought the provocative campaign pushed the envelope, but just far enough to be entertaining. However, when the Las Vegas tourism group extended its advertising

## Adding Value 7.2    Cover Art as Cover Ads[89]

The Japanese pop singer Shoko Nakagawa appears on the cover of her album in a "Hug Me" T-shirt with a pink polka-dot bow on top of her head. She also holds a Court Force Nike sneaker. In the United States, such an image would imply the singer had sold out and probably affect marketability. But in Japan, the combination of advertising and an album cover comes across as artistic expression.

Furthermore, Japanese consumers tend to appreciate items with limited availability. Therefore, the album covers with the Nike shoes are positioned as limited editions, with only 3,000 made. Another pop group created two limited edition album covers, one with the five members of the group holding Nike shoes with their eyes open, and another with their eyes closed. Both versions of the albums sold out almost immediately, followed up by extensive blogs with photos and massive amounts of buzz.

The collectibility of these covers ensures that Nike will achieve continuous advertising. Consumers will save the album art as collector's items, meaning the ad not only lives on forever but even becomes an item that should increase in popularity and value. And since the album covers are already valuable, owners likely will tend to maintain them in perfect condition, with the Nike brand name always visible.

In the United States, such an obvious ad on an album cover might make it seem like the artist had violated artistic principles, just to make more money. Yet the taboo against pairing art and brand names only exists when the placement seems too prominent. Because she is singing about "Fashion," Lady Gaga can list a wealth of names,

J'adore Vivienne, habillez-moi

Gucci, Fendi, et Prada, Valentino, Armani too

...love them Jimmy Choos...

J'adore Weitzman, habillez-moi

Louis, Dolce Gabbana, Alexander McQueen, eh ou!

...love those Manolos

and not cause anyone to protest.

*Lady Gaga can mix fashion with her music and get away with it.*

to the United Kingdom, it found that the ad campaign was not nearly as effective. After conducting focus groups, the group found that British consumers did not find the advertisements edgy enough for their more irreverent British tastes. In response, the advertising agency began studying British slang and phrases to find ways to make the campaign even sexier and more provocative.[90]

### CHECK YOURSELF

1. What are the components of a global marketing strategy?
2. What are the three global product strategies?

## Summing Up

**LO1**  **List the factors that aid in the growth of globalization.**

Technology, particularly in the communication field, has facilitated the growth of global markets. Firms can communicate with their suppliers and customers instantaneously, easily take advantage of production efficiencies in other countries, and bring together parts and finished goods from all over the globe. International organizations such as the World

Trade Organization, the International Monetary Fund, and the World Bank Group also have reduced or eliminated tariffs and quotas, worked to help people in less developed countries, and facilitated trade in many areas.

**LO2 Describe the components of a country market assessment.**

First, firms must assess the general economic environment. For instance, countries with a trade surplus, strong domestic and national products, growing populations, and income growth generally are relatively more favorable prospects. Second, firms should assess a country's infrastructure. To be successful in a particular country, the firm must have access to adequate transportation, distribution channels, and communications. Third, firms must determine whether the proposed country has a political and legal environment that favors business. Fourth, firms should be cognizant of the cultural and sociological differences between their home and host countries and adapt to those differences to ensure successful business relationships.

**LO3 Identify the various market entry strategies.**

Firms have several options for entering a new country, each with a different level of risk and involvement. Direct investment is the most risky but potentially the most lucrative. Firms

that engage in a joint venture with other firms already operating in the host country share the risk and obtain knowledge about the market and how to do business there. A strategic alliance is similar to a joint venture, but the relationship is not as formal. A less risky method of entering a new market is franchising, in which, as in domestic franchise agreements, the franchisor allows the franchisee to operate a business using its name and strategy in return for a fee. The least risky method of entering another country is exporting.

**LO4 Highlight the similarities and differences between a domestic marketing strategy and a global marketing strategy.**

The essence of a global marketing strategy is no different from that of a domestic strategy. The firm starts by identifying its target markets, chooses specific markets to pursue, and crafts a strategy to meet the needs of those markets. However, additional issues make global expansion more difficult. For instance, should the product or service be altered to fit the new market better? Does the firm need to change the way it prices its products in different countries? What is the best way to get the product or service to the new customers? How should the firm communicate its product or service offering in other countries?

## Key Terms

- boycott, 206
- direct investment, 213
- dumping, 205
- duty, 205
- exchange control, 206
- exchange rate, 206
- exporting, 210
- franchisee, 211
- franchising, 211
- franchisor, 211
- General Agreement on Tariffs and Trade (GATT), 196
- globalization, 194

- globalization of production, 195
- gross domestic product (GDP), 199
- gross national income (GNI), 199
- human development index (HDI), 200
- infrastructure, 204
- International Monetary Fund (IMF), 196
- joint venture, 212
- offshoring, 195

- purchasing power parity (PPP), 199
- quota, 205
- strategic alliance, 212
- tariff, 205
- trade agreements, 206
- trade deficit, 199
- trade surplus, 199
- trading bloc, 206
- World Bank Group, 196
- World Trade Organization (WTO), 196

## Marketing Applications

1. What is globalization? Why is it important for marketers to understand what globalization entails?

2. The World Trade Organization, World Bank, and International Monetary Fund all work in differ-

ent ways to facilitate globalization. What role (or roles) does each organization play in the global marketplace?

3. Moots is a high-end bicycle manufacturer located in Steamboat Springs, Colorado. Assume the company is considering entering the U.K., Chinese, and Indian markets. When conducting its market assessment, what economic factors should Moots consider to make its decision? Which market do you expect will be more lucrative for Moots? Why?

4. Now consider the political, economic, and legal systems of China, India, and the United Kingdom. Explain why you think one country might be more hospitable to Moots than the others.

5. Volkswagen sells cars in many countries throughout the world, including Mexico and Latin America. How would you expect its market position to differ in those countries compared with that in the United States?

6. CITGO, the petroleum company owned by the Venezuelan government, sells its products throughout the world. Do you anticipate that its

market positioning and advertising differ in different countries? Why or why not?

7. What are the benefits of being able to offer a globally standardized product? What types of products easily lend themselves to global standardization?

8. Compare and contrast Ford's global marketing strategy for Figo and Fiesta.

9. Assume you work for a U.S.-based medical imaging services firm that positions itself as having experts who personally review and diagnose clients' films and tests. Clients are unaware that most of the diagnosis and review work, bookkeeping, and other record keeping are done by a company in India. The local doctor's office simply reviews the recommendations and signs off on the diagnosis. Yet as your manager points out, the American medical practice still supervises each patient's account. After recent news stories about the practice of offshoring sensitive transactions, clients have been commenting about how grateful they are to have a local firm. What, if anything, should you tell your clients about the firm's practice of offshoring?

---

www.mhhe.com/
grewal3e

## Quiz Yourself

1. The Big Mac Index is a novel metric of:
   a. GDP
   b. purchasing power parity
   c. per capita GNI
   d. economic appetite
   e. international trade calories

2. Many of the best-known American retailers, like KFC and McDonald's, have expanded globally using:
   a. franchising
   b. exporting

   c. joint venture
   d. direct investment
   e. strategic alliance

   (Answers to these two questions are provided on page 607.)

   Go to www.mhhe.com/grewal3e to practice an additional 11 questions.

---

## Net Savvy

1. For many small businesses, the idea of entering a foreign market is frightening. The U.S. national government, as well as most state governments, now offers assistance designed specifically for small-business owners. One such organization is the Massachusetts Export Center. Visit its website at www.mass.gov/export/ and examine the types of services it provides for businesses. Now click on

   the Export Statistics link. To what five countries did Massachusetts export the most? Do any of these countries surprise you?

2. Boeing is a global brand, yet in each country, it alters its promotions to meet local tastes. Go to www.boeing.com/worldwide.html and visit the U.K. site. Now click through to three non-Western countries. How are these websites different?

| Chapter Case Study |
| --- |

### P&G TAKES ON THE WORLD, ONE SMILE, ONE DIAPER CHANGE AT A TIME

The People's Republic of China was founded October 1, 1949, with Beijing as its capital. During the remainder of the twentieth century, China, which is roughly the size of the continental United States, experienced civil unrest, major famine, foreign occupation, and a strict one-party Communist regime under Mao Zedong. However, since 1978, China's leadership, while maintaining communist political ideals, also has embraced market-oriented economic development, which has led to startlingly rapid gains. For many Chinese, recent developments have dramatically improved their living standards and their levels of personal freedom, though in a somewhat piecemeal fashion.

The shift from a centrally planned system to increasing liberalization in the economy since that 1978 change prompted a tenfold increase in China's gross domestic product (GDP). Measured in terms of purchasing power parity (PPP), China is the second largest economy in the world, after only the United States, and foreign direct investment in the country reached $108 billion in 2008.[91] With regard to general economic growth, the country suffers from a drastically unequal distribution, in which the coastal areas have developed the most and the most rapidly. Such uneven economic development creates a significant migrant workforce, estimated to number around 150 million people, who subsist on part-time, low paying jobs in villages and cities.[92]

Despite such inequality in development, the economic outlook for China appeared quite good—GDP growth rates reached approximately 10 percent in 2008. However, the 2009 global financial crisis hit China hard, reducing demand for Chinese exports for the first time in a long time. Government forces have vowed to make the country less dependent on exports for its GDP growth, with an economic policy that hinges on creating more jobs; moreover, mounting external pressure suggests revaluing the Chinese currency, the Renminbi.[93]

Actual growth of the 1.3 billion–strong Chinese population slowed as a result of government population controls, which limited each family to only one child. Although China's median age is slightly younger than that of the United States

*Since 1988, when P&G entered the Chinese market, it has developed and distributed many new products to meet the unique needs of this very diverse market.*

currently, at 34.1 years, the one-child policy means that China is one of the most rapidly aging countries in the world. Today, approximately 72 percent of the population falls between the ages of 15 and 65 years. These market conditions make China an excellent target for consumer goods, assuming they can be produced at the right price. With only 10 percent of the population below the poverty line and a market of nearly 1.3 billion consumers,[94] it should be obvious why a wide variety of companies, including the consumer goods giant Procter & Gamble (P&G), are targeting the Chinese market with some of their most popular brands.

For its investments in China, P&G has decided on a slow-growth strategy, which enables it to study the market and adapt popular American products to Chinese tastes. For instance, P&G is positioning its Crest toothpaste as a major consumer brand, which demands that the company employ some of its most sophisticated product development and consumer targeting techniques.[95]

When P&G first entered the market, it assumed it could scrimp on quality to lower the price for this less developed market. Some crashing failures convinced the company to adopt a new strategy for adapting products to the market: "Delight, don't dilute."[96] As it has learned these lessons, it has slowly introduced dozens of other popular American brands, including Oil of Olay, Pampers, and Whisper. These brands now account for $2.5 billion in annual sales for the consumer products goliath, making it the largest consumer products company in China.[97] To support these sales, it employs 6,300 workers in China and has built a sophisticated distribution network.[98]

The well-developed Chinese coastal cities, where P&G currently sells most of its products, are becoming increasingly competitive as more and more global companies join in the hunt for the massive Chinese market. To continue growing and reaching China's untapped rural market, P&G is targeting rural Chinese with what it considers household staples, such as Crest toothpaste.

The first step P&G took before entering the rural market was to examine the distribution network. Most rural Chinese consumers shop in small stores and lack access to the supermarkets that can be found in the cities. To adapt to this distribution challenge, P&G has created an army of sales representatives who visit and service these stores. It even agreed to work with China's Commerce Ministry to train locals in 10,000 villages in the ways and methods of running retail stores.

After building its distribution system, P&G conducted extensive, and expensive, market research to identify toothpaste product attributes that were most important to Chinese consumers. It turns out that their tastes are remarkably heterogeneous. Therefore, P&G created several flavors targeted at different, specific demographics within China—Crest Salt White for certain rural areas, and Morning Lotus Fragrance for city dwellers.

To convince mothers to use Pampers, rather than traditional cloth diapers for their babies, P&G commissioned a scientific study of babies' sleep habits, in collaboration with the Beijing Children's Hospital Sleep Research Center. Data collected from nearly 7,000 home visits in eight Chinese cities revealed that babies who wore disposable diapers fell asleep 30 percent faster than those wearing cloth, and then slept an additional half-hour every night. For sleep-deprived mothers in any culture, these results would seem irresistible. In addition, P&G's study linked the better sleep to improved cognitive development in children, which appealed especially to Chinese parents who widely prize academic achievement.[99]

So far, this multi-pronged approach—that is, building a hard-to-mimic distribution network, adapting global products to local tastes, and appealing to local consumer needs—has made Crest and Pampers success stories in China. But competitors, such as Dutch Unilever and the local Chinese company Nice Group, are doing their best to imitate P&G. At the moment, P&G has the advantage, and it hopes to hold on to it by helping Chinese consumers develop strong brand preferences.

## Questions

1. Consumers' tastes for toothpaste in China typically vary from region to region, as well as across various demographic dimensions, such as age, income, and education. In contrast, tastes for toothpaste are fairly narrow in the United States. Why is there such a pronounced difference between these two markets?

2. Instead of partnering with a local company in a joint venture, P&G is building its own distribution network. What type of entry strategy is this, and are there any other entry strategies that would be appropriate for P&G to use in this situation? Why or why not? If so, which ones?

3. Describe how P&G's distribution and product variation give it an advantage over its competitors. Is there anything you would have done differently to enter this market?

# TARGETING THE MARKETPLACE

**CHAPTER 8**
Segmentation, Targeting, and Positioning

**CHAPTER 9**
Marketing Research

Section Three, Targeting the Marketplace, contains two chapters. Chapter 8 focuses on segmentation, targeting, and positioning. In this chapter, we examine how firms segment the marketplace, then pick a target market, and finally position their goods/services in line with their customers' needs and wants. Chapter 9 on marketing research identifies the various tools, techniques, and metrics that marketers use to uncover customers' needs and wants and to ensure that they create goods and services that provide value to their target markets.

# Segmentation, Targeting, and Positioning

**K**nown for its assortment of sexy intimate apparel and sleepwear, Victoria's Secret recently posted net sales of $5.6 million across its more than 1,000 stores.[1] But when the economy flagged and consumers cut spending, Victoria's Secret's parent company, Limited Brands Inc., turned its attention to specific market segments to offset falling sales.

Many of Victoria's Secret's undergarments attempt to conjure romance and seduction, which places them firmly in the category of discretionary expenses. At the same time though, all women need bras and panties, which makes them necessities. In a struggling economy, the company therefore introduced lower-priced offerings while simultaneously reducing inventory.[2] "Everyday" bras, for example, retail for $29.50, about half the price of other styles. The Seven-Way bra, a previous but discontinued best seller,[3] has returned to store shelves—it gives women the option of owning a single bra that functions well under different silhouettes rather than requiring them to purchase a separate classic bra, strapless bra, and racer-back bra. Victoria's Secret also makes sure it appeals to women who are more concerned with curves than cost by offering the Miraculous push-up bra, which adds two cup sizes.

A similar reduced-price concept in its Pink product line involves the Wear Everywhere bra, which costs $32 for a package of two. The Pink subbrand, launched in 2004, targets women between the ages of 18 and 30 years.[4] Rather than glamorous or sexy, Pink garments and accessories are intended to be comfortable and cute. In addition to underwear, the line includes brightly colored sweatshirts, T-shirts, pajamas, pillows and bedding, sandals, and swimwear. Through co-branding efforts, Pink offers merchandise imprinted with logos and names from 57 different U.S. colleges and universities, as well as the United States Army and Navy. A more recent initiative designed to capture female athletics fans (and their male admirers) features branding by 11 major league baseball teams.[5]

## LEARNING OBJECTIVES

**LO1** Identify the five steps in the segmentation, targeting, and positioning process.

**LO2** Outline the different methods of segmenting a market.

**LO3** Describe how firms determine whether a segment is attractive and therefore worth pursuing.

**LO4** Articulate the difference among targeting strategies: undifferentiated, differentiated, concentrated, or micromarketing.

**LO5** Define positioning, and describe how firms do it.

Using price points to segment its market; customizing color, fabrics, and styles to appeal to various target audiences; associating its brand with supermodels, baseball teams, and colleges; reaching different shoppers through different stores and assortments; and promoting products through multiple selling channels all may help Limited Brands out of the red . . . and feeling in the pink!

● ● ●

In Chapter 1, we learned that marketing is about satisfying consumers' wants and needs. Chapter 2 noted how companies analyze their markets to determine the different kinds of products and services people want. But it is not sufficient just to produce such offerings. Firms must also position their offerings in the minds of their target market in such a way that these consumers understand why they meet their needs better than other, competitive offerings.

This process requires a marketing plan, as we discussed in Chapter 2. As you should recall, the third step of this plan is identifying and evaluating opportunities by performing an STP (segmentation, targeting, and positioning) analysis. This chapter focuses on that analysis.

**L01** Identify the five steps in the segmentation, targeting, and positioning process.

# THE SEGMENTATION, TARGETING, AND POSITIONING PROCESS

In this chapter, we discuss how a firm conducts a market segmentation or STP analysis (see Exhibit 8.1). We'll first discuss a firm's overall strategy and objectives, methods of segmenting the market, and which segments are worth pursuing. Then we discuss how to choose a target market or markets by evaluating each segment's attractiveness and, on the basis of this evaluation, choosing which segment or segments to pursue. Finally, we describe how a firm develops its positioning strategy.

Although the STP process in Exhibit 8.1 makes it appear that the decision making is linear, this need not be the case. For instance, a firm could start with a strategy but then modify it as it gathers information about the segments' attractiveness.

## Step 1: Establish Overall Strategy or Objectives

The first step in the segmentation process is to articulate the vision or objectives of the company's marketing strategy clearly. The segmentation strategy must be consistent with and derived from the firm's mission and objectives, as well as its current situation—its strengths, weaknesses, opportunities, and threats (SWOT). Coca-Cola's objective, for instance, is to increase sales in a mature industry. The company knows its strengths are its brand name and its ability to place new products on retailers' shelves, but its primary weakness is that it has not had a product line for emerging market segments. Identifying this potentially large and profitable market segment

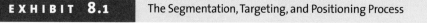

| EXHIBIT 8.1 | The Segmentation, Targeting, and Positioning Process |
| --- | --- |

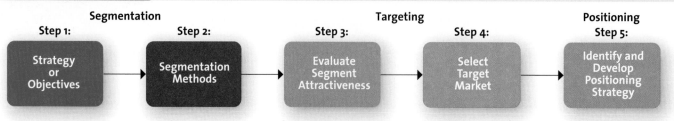

| Segmentation | | Targeting | | Positioning |
| --- | --- | --- | --- | --- |
| Step 1: | Step 2: | Step 3: | Step 4: | Step 5: |
| Strategy or Objectives | Segmentation Methods | Evaluate Segment Attractiveness | Select Target Market | Identify and Develop Positioning Strategy |

before many of its mainstream competitors offers a great opportunity, though following through on that opportunity could lead to a significant threat: competitive retaliation. Coca-Cola's recent choice to pursue health-conscious men with products such as Coke Zero thus is clearly consistent with its overall strategy and objectives. (See the Case Study at the end of this chapter for more discussion of Coke's strategy.)

Now let's take a look at the methods of segmenting the market.

*Coke Zero targets health-conscious men.*

## Step 2: Segmentation Methods

The second step in the segmentation process is to use a particular method or combination of methods to segment the market. This step also develops descriptions of the different segments, which helps firms better understand the customer profiles in each segment. With this information, they can distinguish customer similarities within a segment and dissimilarities across segments. Marketers also use geographic, demographic, psychographic, geodemographic, benefit, behavioral segmentation approaches, as Exhibit 8.2 details.

Soft-drink marketers, for instance, divide the carbonated beverage landscape into caffeinated or decaffeinated, regular (with sugar) or diet, and cola versus something else. This segmentation method is based on the benefits that consumers derive from the products.

**Geographic Segmentation**   Geographic segmentation organizes customers into groups on the basis of where they live. Thus, a market could be grouped by country (as Adding Value 8.1 describes), region (northeast, southeast), or areas within a region (state, city, neighborhoods, zip codes). Not surprisingly, geographic segmentation is most useful for companies whose products satisfy needs that vary by region.

Firms can provide the same basic goods or services to all segments even if they market globally or nationally, but better marketers make adjustments to meet the needs of smaller geographic groups. A national grocery store chain like Safeway or Kroger runs similar stores with similar assortments in various locations across the United States. Within those similar stores though, a significant percentage of the

**LO2** Outline the different methods of segmenting a market.

| EXHIBIT **8.2** | Methods for Describing Market Segments |
| --- | --- |
| **Segmentation Method** | **Sample Segments** |
| Geographic | Continent: North America, Asia, Europe, Africa Within U.S.: Pacific, mountain, central, south, mid-Atlantic, northeast |
| Demographic | Age, gender, income |
| Psychographic | Lifestyle, self-concept, self-values |
| Geodemographic | Urban, exurban, established, sophisticated townhouses, bohemians, affluent retirees |
| Benefits | Convenience, economy, prestige |
| Behavioral | Occasion, loyalty |

## Adding Value 8.1 — Competing for Chinese Drivers[6]

For years, the segmentation of the Chinese auto market has been firmly established: Foreign car makers target wealthy, elite segments; the Chinese manufacturers sell to lower income, frugal buyers. But times change, and therefore so must the market segmentation strategies.

As the Chinese economy continues its transition into a market-based approach, more and more entrepreneurs and consumers are entering what might be called the middle class. With their growing disposable income, this segment is highly attractive as a potential car-buying market—for both the foreign, relatively high-priced Chevy and the domestic, lower quality Chery automakers.

The price point at which a family can comfortably afford a basic car is approximately 60,000 yuan (about US $8,800). And the number of Chinese families who can afford this price point continues to grow; current predictions suggest it will reach more than 65 million by 2015.

Therefore, as Chinese automakers work to improve their quality to appeal to these latest consumers, foreign compa-nies work to lower their prices. For example, the Chevrolet Sail is a subcompact car that uses only one-bulb lamps, instead of the more common, more expensive two-bulb design. With such innovations, the Sail is appearing on the market at a starting price of 57,000 yuan (about US $8,400), 25 percent less than the previous model. Nissan plans to launch a similar subcompact called the March, and Toyota is working on something cheaper than its current low-end offer, the Yaris at 92,000 yuan (about US $13,500).

On the other side of the market, the Chinese car manu-facturer Geely wants people to be surprised when it intro-duces is Englon SC6, amazed that a company with a low cost image could produce something so detailed. It will feature a turbo-enhanced 1-liter engine and a significant redesign, still for the same price as the previous model, or 56,000 yuan (about US $8,200). As the lower end gets bet-ter and the higher end gets cheaper, the result is increasing convergence in a massive, incredibly competitive market segment.

*The Chevrolet Sail is a subcompact car designed for the Chinese market. Prices start at about $8,400.*

assortment of goods will vary by region, city, or even neighborhood, depending on the different needs of the customers who surround each location.

**Demographic Segmentation** Demographic segmentation groups consumers according to easily measured, objective characteristics such as age, gender, income, and education. These variables represent the most common means to define seg-ments because they are easy to identify and because demographically segmented markets are easy to reach. Therefore, in the specific geographic region of China, carmakers also consider market segments defined by their income, as we noted in Adding Value 8.1. Similarly, Kellogg's uses age segmentation for its line of break-fast cereals. Coco Krispies and Froot Loops are for kids, while Special K and All-Bran are for adults.

One important demographic, gender, plays a very important role in how firms market products and services to men versus women.[7] For instance, TV viewing habits vary significantly between men and women. Men tend to channel surf—switching quickly from channel to channel—and watch prime time shows more often if they are action oriented and have physically attractive cast members. Women, in contrast, tend to view shows to which they can personally relate through the situational plot or characters and those recommended by friends. Thus, a company like Gillette, which sells razors for both men and women, will consider the gender appeal of various shows when it buys advertising time on television.

However, demographics may not be useful for defining the target segments for other companies. For example, demographics are poor predictors of the users of activewear, such as jogging suits and athletic shoes. At one time, firms like Nike assumed that activewear would be purchased exclusively by young, active people, but the health and fitness trend has led people of all ages to buy such merchandise. And even relatively inactive consumers of all ages, incomes, and education find activewear more comfortable than traditional street clothes.

**Psychographic Segmentation**   Of the various methods for segmenting, or breaking down the market, psychographics is the one that delves into how consumers actually describe themselves. Usually marketers determine (through demographics, buying patterns, or usage) into which segment an individual consumer falls. Psychographics studies how people self-select, as it were, based on the characteristics of how they choose to occupy their time (behavior) and what underlying psychological reasons determine those choices.[8] For example, a person might have a strong need for inclusion or belonging, which motivates him or her to seek out activities that involve others, which in turn influences the products he or she buys to fit in with the group. Determining psychographics involves knowing and understanding three components: self-values, self-concept, and lifestyles.

Self-values are goals for life, not just the goals one wants to accomplish in a day. They are the overriding desires that drive how a person lives his or her life. Examples might be the need for self-respect, self-fulfillment, or a specific sense of belonging. This motivation causes people to develop self-images of how they want to be and then images of a way of life that will help them arrive at these ultimate goals. From a marketing point of view, self-values help determine the benefits the target mar-

*Marketers like Benetton want their ads to appeal to people's self-concepts: "I'm like them (or I want to be like them), so I should buy their products."*

ket may be looking for from a product. The underlying, fundamental, personal need that pushes a person to seek out certain products or brands stems from his or her desire to fulfill a self-value.

People's self-image, or self-concept, is the image people ideally have of themselves.[9] For instance, a person who has a goal to belong may see, or want to see, himself as a fun-loving, gregarious type whom people wish to be around. Marketers often make use of this particular self-concept through communications that show their products being used by groups of laughing people who are having a good

*Lululemon Athletica stores sell yoga apparel and accessories, are located in or near affluent neighborhoods, and attract those with strong self-values of physical fitness with a dash of spirituality.*

time. The connection emerges between the group fun and the product being shown and connotes a lifestyle that many consumers seek.

**Lifestyles**, the third component of people's psychographic makeup, are the way we live.[10] If values provide an end goal and self-concept is the way one sees oneself in the context of that goal, lifestyles are how we live our lives to achieve goals.

Luluheads are men and women who patronize yoga apparel and accessories retailer, Lululemon Athletica.[11] This chain of over 120 stores (primarily in the United States and Canada and 9 franchise stores in Australia) located in or near affluent neighborhoods attracts those with strong self-values of physical fitness with a dash of spirituality.[12] Although many of its customers may not achieve the quiet consciousness and svelte bodies of yogis, yoga instructors, and most Lululemon employees, this is the self-concept they aspire to. Shopping there, wearing its clothes, and taking advantage of the Lululemon sponsored clinics and events helps them achieve their desired lifestyle. There is only one catch: one has to be able to afford $98 for a Grove Pant that you are going to get on the floor and sweat in.

The most widely used psychographic tool is **VALS**™, owned and operated by Strategic Business Insights (SBI).[13] Consumers are classified into the eight segments shown in Exhibit 8.3 based on their answers to the questionnaire (http://www.strategicbusinessinsights.com/vals/presurvey.shtml). The vertical dimension of the VALS framework indicates level of resources, including income, education, health, energy level, and degree of innovativeness. The upper segments have more resources and are more innovative than those on the bottom.

The horizontal dimension shows the segments' primary psychological motivation for buying. Consumers buy products and services because of their primary motivations—that is, how they see themselves in the world and how that self-image governs their activities. The three primary motivations of U.S. consumers are ideals, achievement, and self-expression. People who are primarily motivated by ideals are guided by knowledge and principles. Those who are motivated by achievement look for products and services that demonstrate success to their peers. Consumers who are primarily motivated by self-expression desire social or physical activity, variety, and risk.

VALS™ enables firms to identify target segments and their underlying motivations. It shows correlations between psychology and lifestyle choices. For instance, a European luxury automobile manufacturer used VALS™ to identify online, mobile applications that would appeal to affluent, early-adopter consumers within the next five years.[14] The VALS™ analysis enabled the company to prioritize the most promising applications to develop. In another case, VALS™ was used to help a medical center identify customers most interested and able to afford cosmetic surgery. Based on the underlying motivations of its target customers, the center and its ad agency developed an ad campaign so successful that it had to be pulled early to avoid overbooking at the surgical center.

Firms are finding that psychographic segmentation schemes like VALS™ are often more useful for predicting consumer behavior than are demographics. This is because people who share demographics often have very different psychological traits. Take, for example, Jack and John, both 30-year-old, married, college graduates. Demographically, they are the same, but Jack is risk-averse and John is a risk taker. Jack is socially conscious and John is focused on himself. Lumping Jack and John together as a target does not make sense because the ways they think and act are totally different from each other.

There are limitations to using psychographic segmentation, however. Psychographics are a more expensive means to identify potential customers. With

| EXHIBIT 8.3 | VALS™ Framework |
|---|---|

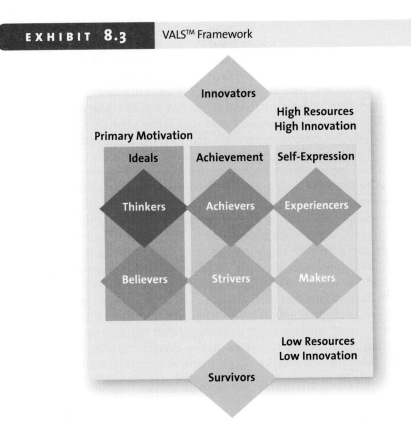

demographics, for example, a firm like Nike can easily identify its customers as, say, men or women and then direct its marketing strategies to each group differently. The problem is that not all men are alike, as we saw with Jack and John. Women are not all alike either! To identify VALS Thinkers or Makers, companies use the VALS questionnaire in surveys or focus groups. VALS provides segment description linkages with consumer product and media data, communication styles, and zip code locations.[15]

*It is just as easy to identify Thinkers (left) as it is Makers (right). A person is given the VALS questionnaire and the VALS program at SRIC-BI runs the answers through the computer for scoring to determine the VALS type.*

Geodemographic Segmentation Because "birds of a feather flock together," geodemographic segmentation uses a combination of geographic, demographic, and lifestyle characteristics to classify consumers. Consumers in the same neighborhoods tend to buy the same types of cars, appliances, and apparel and shop at the same types of retailers. Two of the most widely used tools for geodemographic segmentation are PRIZM (Potential Rating Index by Zip Market), developed by Nielsen Claritas (www.mybestsegments.com), and ESRI's (www.esri.com) Tapestry. Using detailed demographic data and information about the consumption and media habits of people who live in each U.S. block tract (zip code + 4), PRIZM can identify 66 geodemographic segments or neighborhoods. Each block group then can be analyzed and sorted by more than 60 characteristics, including income, home value, occupation, education, household type, age, and several key lifestyle variables. The information in Exhibit 8.4 describes two PRIZM clusters.

Geodemographic segmentation can be particularly useful for retailers because customers typically patronize stores close to their neighborhood. Thus, retailers can use geodemographic segmentation to tailor each store's assortment to the preferences of the local community. If a toy store discovers that one of its stores is surrounded by Big Sky Families, it might adjust its offering to include less expensive toys. This kind of segmentation is also useful for finding new locations; retailers identify their "best" locations and determine what types of people live in the area surrounding those stores, according to the geodemographic clusters. They can then find other potential locations where similar segments reside.

| EXHIBIT 8.4 | PRIZM Clusters | |
|---|---|---|
| **Segment Name** | **Bohemian Mix** | **Big Sky Families** |
| **Segment Number** | 16 | 33 |
| **Demographics traits:** | | |
| **Urbanicity:** | Urban | Rural |
| **Median Household Income:** | $55,665 | $57,074 |
| **Age Ranges:** | <55 | 25–44 |
| **Presence of Kids:** | Family Mix | HH w/ Kids |
| **Homeownership:** | Renters | Mostly Owners |
| **Employment Levels:** | White Collar, Mix | Blue Collar, Service, Mix |
| **Education Levels:** | College Grad | Some College |
| **Ethnic Diversity:** | White, Black, Asian, Hispanic | White |
| **Lifestyle traits:** | | |
| | Shop at Express, 3mo | Own Horse |
| | Own/Lease New Volkswagen | Buy Children's Clothes, 6mos |
| | Go Snowboarding, 1yr | Own Satellite Dish |
| **Food & drink:** | | |
| | Drink Corona Extra Beer, 1wk | Use Baby Foods, 1wk |
| | Buy from Au Bon Pain, 1mo | Buy from Family Restaurant, Child Decides, 6mo |
| | Buy from Dunkin Donuts, 1mo | Buy from Hardee's, 1mo |
| **Media usage:** | | |
| | Read The New Yorker, Last Issue | Read Hunting, Last Issue |
| | Visit Internet Movie Database (imdb.com), 1mo | Visit nascar.com, 1mo |
| | Write a Blog Online, 1mo | Watch The Disney Channel, 1wk |

Source: The Nielsen Company, Nielsen PRIZM 2009.

## Power of the Internet 8.1          How to Attract Women

One easy way to determine what customers want and need is to ask them directly. So when Unilever, the company behind the world's most popular personal care brand for men,[16] wanted to develop a new fragrance to help keep "guys a step ahead in the dating game," they enlisted 25 college-age consumers to help.[17] These men and women, recruited through the Axe fan community on Facebook, met face-to-face with other product stakeholders such as advertising and marketing staff and research and development personnel. Over the course of a week, the group defined an unfulfilled need in the target population, developed a product idea to help fulfill the need, and sketched the basics of an advertising campaign.

The final product represented a surprising change in the company's understanding of the realities of the dating world and a corresponding shift in communication strategies. Previously Axe messaging showed women succumbing instantly to any male bearing a hint of the fragrance. But consumer feedback indicated immediate conquest wasn't enough: Men felt the need to keep changing themselves, even during the course of a single date, to keep women interested. In response, Unilever created Twist, which exploits the natural tendency of fragrances to shift from a strong scent (which masks the smell of the alcohol-based propellants included in any perfume) to a subtler, richer, longer-lasting fragrance. Twist ads show the product's magical benefit as a man transforms again and again, regaining the interest of his gorgeous date each time she catches a whiff of his Twist. Naturally the ads scored well in testing because the most important consumer stakeholders participated in their creation.

The development of the Twist campaign demonstrates how companies tap directly into the needs and ideas of target audiences through a technique known as *crowdsourcing*. The feedback helps speed product development and lower costs; it also gives companies access to low-cost creative talent—their own customers. Uniliver's young male customers benefit from a product that provides them with an important benefit—how to attract women!

**Benefit Segmentation** Benefit segmentation groups consumers on the basis of the benefits they derive from products or services. Because marketing is all about satisfying consumers' needs and wants, dividing the market into segments whose needs and wants are best satisfied by the product benefits can be a very powerful tool.[18] It is effective and also relatively easy to portray a product's or service's benefits in the firm's communication strategies. Power of the Internet 8.1 describes how one company ensured its communications would focus on the benefits most important to its clients by recruiting them from their user community on Facebook.

Starwood, one of the world's largest hotel and leisure companies, is master at benefit segmentation.[19] Many of their brands attract its guests because it has clearly articulated in promotions the benefits of staying at a particular hotel, and then once there, follows through on the promise. For instance, its W® hotels have world class restaurants and trendy bars and lounges. Its relatively sparsely furnished, but ultramodern rooms appeal to a younger, hip clientele. Element℠, another Starwood hotel brand, is very different than W®. With the first Element℠ hotel opening in 2008, it appeals to clients requiring extended stay accommodations. These hotels are modern with an emphasis on nature and energy conservation.

Hollywood is a constant and effective practitioner of benefit segmentation. Although all movies may seem to provide the same service—entertainment for a few hours—film producers know that people visit the theater or rent films to obtain a vast variety of benefits and market them accordingly. Need a laugh? Try the latest comedy from Judd Apatow. Want to cry and then feel warm and fuzzy? Go to a romance movie. By the time you leave the theater you will feel heartwarmed and happy because the lead characters will have overcome their differences to find love.

**Behavioral Segmentation** Behavioral segmentation divides customers into groups based on how they use the product or service. Some common behavioral measures include occasion and loyalty.

*Airlines use a loyalty segmentation strategy to attract frequent fliers. It costs less for frequent flyer members with more miles to have access to airlines' elite lounges.*

**Occasion** Behavioral segmentation based on when a product or service is purchased or consumed is called occasion segmentation. For example, Men's Wearhouse uses this type of segmentation to develop its merchandise selection and its promotions. Sometimes men need a suit for work, while other times it is for a special occasion like a prom or a wedding. Snack food companies like Frito-Lay make and promote their snacks for various occasions—individual servings of potato chips for a snack on the run and 16-ounce bags for parties.

**Loyalty** Firms have long known that it pays to retain loyal customers. Loyal customers are those who feel so strongly that the firm can meet their relevant needs best that any competitors are virtually excluded from their consideration; that is, these customers buy almost exclusively from the firm. These loyal customers are the most profitable in the long term.[20] In light of the high cost of finding new customers and the profitability of loyal customers, today's companies are using loyalty segmentation and investing in retention and loyalty initiatives to retain their most profitable customers.

Airlines, for instance, definitely believe that all customers aren't created equal. At United Airlines, the customers who have flown the most miles with the company, the "Premier Executive 1K," receive guaranteed reservations even on sold-out flights, priority check-in, special seating priorities, dedicated reservation services, and priority waitlist status.[21] According to Hollywood, flying 10 million miles, like George Clooney's character in *Up in the Air*, even gets you a dedicated customer service line.[22] None of these special services are available to the occasional flyer.

**Using Multiple Segmentation Methods** Although all segmentation methods are useful, each has its unique advantages and disadvantages. For example, segmenting by demographics and geography is easy because information about who the customers are and where they are located is readily available, but these characteristics don't help marketers determine their customers' needs. Knowing what benefits

*Nicole Miller works with its retailers by providing preticketed merchandise on hangers. It also exchanges information using an advanced EDI system.*

customers are seeking or how the product or service fits a particular lifestyle is important for designing an overall marketing strategy, but such segmentation schemes present a problem for marketers attempting to identify specifically which customers are seeking these benefits. Thus, firms often employ a combination of segmentation methods, using demographics and geography to identify and target marketing communications to their customers, then using benefits or lifestyles to design the product or service and the substance of the marketing message. Adding Value 8.2 contains an excellent example of this combination.

Consider a new Saks Fifth Avenue department store: The chain has chosen the location for its new store carefully, knowing that each store needs to reflect and support the purchasing needs of the community that it serves. After determining that a new location can, in general, support its overall product mix, the Saks organization closely considers the characteristics of the location and builds a store-specific product mix that reflects the lifestyle of its customers and their demographics. Thus, Saks is using psychographic segmentation and demographic segmentation.

The New York flagship Saks store accounts for one-fifth of the company's annual revenue, and the target market at this location tends to include 46- to 57-year-old women who prefer classic styles for work and slightly more modern looks for the weekend. But such a selection does not resonate with Birmingham, Alabama. Through market research, Saks found that its merchandise was too conservative and expensive for the slightly younger customer base there, who would travel as far as Atlanta, Georgia, to shop.

*Saks Fifth Avenue develops its merchandise assortment strategy based on the customers that patronize its stores. Its New York flagship store has a sizable market of 46- to 57-year-old women who prefer classic styles for work and more modern looks for the weekend.*

## Adding Value 8.2  China Mobile Grows through Segmentation

China Mobile is the world's largest provider of cell phone service with more than 530 million subscribers—more than the entire population of the United States—and it continues to grow at the astounding rate of 5 million customers per month.[23] China Mobile built its early success by marketing in urban China. As cell phone penetration in Chinese cities rose to nearly 100 percent, China Mobile realized that China's interior, home to more than 700 million people, experienced cell phone penetration of only 12 percent.[24] To reach this enormous rural market, China Mobile invested in 230,000 cellular towers, a number that dwarfs the investment of Cingular, the largest U.S. carrier, with its 47,000 towers. With nearly one-quarter of a billion towers throughout China, 97 percent of the Chinese population have access to China Mobile's signal. Thus, whether they're riding inside subway cars in Beijing or climbing to the top of Mount Everest, customers can still use their China Mobile phones.[25]

China Mobile's tremendous success results in part from the company's careful and targeted segmentation of the Chinese cellular market. Segments of Chinese mobile phone users, according to the company, include wealthy businessmen, college students, and rural farmers. To serve these groups, various service plans aim to maximize handset penetration, then increase the use of value-added services that appeal to certain groups, such as ringtones.

### Rural Segment

In the rural segment, China Mobile faces the challenge of winning customers without sacrificing its profit margins. The average income in rural China is only $400 per year, which leaves little discretionary spending room for expensive cell phones.[26] However, by carefully targeting rural populations with the right mix of services, the company has been able to maintain its profit margins. To keep costs low, China Mobile buys little in the way of advertising and instead relies on influential locals to persuade others to purchase handsets and prepaid cards.

The China Mobile service plan for farmers costs $0.25 per month, though placing or receiving individual calls and text messages entails an extra cost. What makes China Mobile's rural plans more attractive than those of its competitors remains the vast array of available value-added products. For example, the basic service plan includes free access

*(continued)*

## Adding Value **8.2**

*(continued)*

to China Mobile's Agricultural Information Service, which delivers information about the production, supply, and sale of agricultural products among other important bits of information for this rural segment.[27]

### Wealthy Businessmen Segment

In a completely different market, China Mobile still must compete in the saturated urban segment. It does so by targeting wealthy businessmen who demand services that will make their lives more enjoyable. To attract this segment, China Mobile offers Go-Tone, which is relatively expensive at $6.40 per month, to provide mobile access to exclusive golf clubs and special VIP waiting rooms in Chinese airports.

### College Segment

Not unlike farmers, college students worry about costs, but their wishes and demands are markedly different. To attract budget-conscious students, China Mobile offers the M-Zone plan for $2 a month. Targeted at customers who are avid music lovers in their 20s, M-Zone keeps them informed and grants them access to recent hits and releases by well-known artists. These consumers are predominately interested in short text messages and music downloads. Therefore, in addition to phone-related features, China Mobile offers this segment exclusive concerts featuring popular performers.[28]

*To target the rural customer segment, China Mobile has a special low cost program with several value-added services.*

*China Mobile targets the college segment with a relatively low cost program and special services like exclusive concerts featuring popular performers.*

To adapt its merchandise to each geographic area, Saks has come up with nine segments to describe the sites where it has stores, classified according to the degree of fashion—"Park Avenue" classic, "uptown" modern, "Soho" trendy, or contemporary—as well as the preferred pricing levels based on demographics—"good," "better," and "best," ranging from moderately priced to expensive—that characterize customers of that particular store. With this combination of demographic and psychographic segmentation, as detailed in Exhibit 8.5, Saks can deliver the appropriate merchandise to each of its stores.[29]

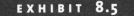

| | | **Level of Fashion** | | |
|---|---|---|---|---|
| | | **LOW** | | **HIGH** |
| | | "Park Avenue" classic | "Uptown" modern | "Soho" trendy |
| **Benefits based on customer demographics** | Good | Birmingham, AL | | Atlanta, GA |
| | Better | New York City | | Atlanta, GA |
| | Best | | New York City | |

**EXHIBIT 8.5** Multiple Segmentation Example Using Saks Fifth Avenue

## CHECK YOURSELF

1. What are the various segmentation methods?

## Step 3: Evaluate Segment Attractiveness

**L03** Describe how firms determine whether a segment is attractive and therefore worth pursuing.

The third step in the segmentation process involves evaluating the attractiveness of the various segments. To undertake this evaluation, marketers first must determine whether the segment is worth pursuing, using several descriptive criteria: Is the segment identifiable, substantial, reachable, responsive, and profitable (see Exhibit 8.6)?

**Identifiable** Firms must be able to identify who is within their market to be able to design products or services to meet their needs. It is equally important to ensure that the segments are distinct from one another, because too much overlap between segments means that distinct marketing strategies aren't necessary to meet segment members' needs. Thus, Conde Nast is able to identify its market for *Modern Bride* magazine by purchasing mailing lists of people that have bridal registries. It also knows that *Modern Bride* customers are somewhat distinct from those who subscribe to *GQ*.

**Substantial** Once the firm has identified its potential target markets, it needs to measure their size. If a market is too small or its buying power insignificant, it won't generate sufficient profits or be able to support the marketing mix activities. As we discussed in Adding Value 8.1, before China's economy started growing, there were not enough middle-class car buyers to push foreign automakers to design an entry-

**EXHIBIT 8.6** Evaluation of Segment Attractiveness

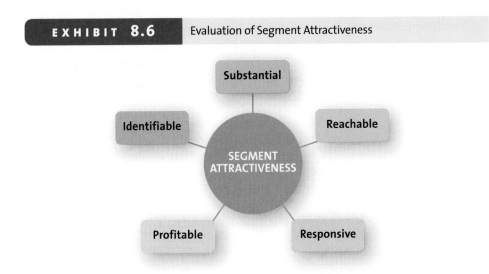

*Can General Motors compete with other luxury car companies for the very lucrative luxury car segment?*

level vehicle. It was only after that number reached substantial numbers that it became worthwhile for them to market to these identified consumers.

**Reachable** The best product or service cannot have any impact, no matter how identifiable or substantial the target market is, if that market cannot be reached (or accessed) through persuasive communications and product distribution. The consumer must know the product or service exists, understand what it can do for him or her, and recognize how to buy it. If Victoria's Secret fails to tell women that it is offering some less luxurious options, shoppers will just walk right past the store and buy basic bras from the Macy's store in the same mall, for example.

**Responsive** For a segmentation strategy to be successful, the customers in the segment must react similarly and positively to the firm's offering. If, through the firm's distinctive competencies, it cannot provide products or services to that segment, it should not target it. For instance, General Motors (GM) has introduced a line of cars to the large and very lucrative luxury car segment. People in this market typically purchase Porsches, BMWs, Audis, and top-of-the-line Lexuses. In contrast, GM has been somewhat successful competing for the middle-priced family-oriented car and light truck segments. Thus, though the luxury car segment meets all the other criteria for a successful segment, GM took a big risk in attempting to pursue this market.

**Profitable** Marketers must also focus their assessments on the potential profitability of each segment, both current and future. Some key factors to keep in mind in this analysis include market growth (current size and expected growth rate), market competitiveness (number of competitors, entry barriers, product substitutes), and market access (ease of developing or accessing distribution channels and brand familiarity). Some straightforward calculations can help illustrate the profitability of a segment:[30]

$$\text{Segment profitability} = (\text{Segment size} \times \text{Segment adoption percentage} \times \\ \text{Purchase behavior} \times \text{Profit margin percentage}) - \text{Fixed costs}$$

where

Segment size = Number of people in the segment

Segment adoption percentage = Percentage of customers in the segment who are likely to adopt the product/service

Purchase behavior = Purchase price × Number of times the customer would buy the product/service in a year

Profit margin percentage = (Selling price – Variable costs) / Selling price

Fixed costs = Advertising expenditure, rent, utilities, insurance, and administrative salaries for managers

To illustrate how a business might determine a segment's profitability, consider Camillo's start-up lawn service. He is trying to determine whether to target homeowners or businesses in a small Midwestern town. Exhibit 8.7 estimates the profitability of the two segments. The homeowner segment is much larger than the business segment, but there are already several lawn services with established customers. There is much less competition in the business segment. So, the segment adoption rate for the homeowner segment is only 1 percent, compared to 20 percent for the business segment. Camillo can charge a much higher price to businesses, and they utilize lawn services more frequently. The profit margin for the

| EXHIBIT 8.7 | Profitability of Two Market Segments for Camillo's Lawn Service |

|  | Homeowners | Businesses |
| --- | --- | --- |
| Segment size | 75,000 | 1,000 |
| Segment adoption percentage | 1% | 20% |
| Purchase behavior<br>    Purchase price<br>    Frequency of purchase | $100<br>12 times | $500<br>20 times |
| Profit margin percentage | 60% | 80% |
| Fixed costs | $400,000 | $1,000,000 |
| Segment profit | $140,000 | $600,000 |

business segment is higher as well because Camillo can utilize large equipment to cut the grass and therefore save on variable labor costs. However, the fixed costs for purchasing and maintaining the large equipment are much higher for the business segment. Further, he needs to spend more money obtaining and maintaining the business customers. He would use less expensive door-to-door flyers to reach the household customers. Finally, on the basis of these assumptions, Camillo decides the business segment is more profitable for his lawn service.

This analysis provides an estimate of the profitability of two segments at one point in time. It is also useful to evaluate the profitability of a segment over the lifetime of one of its typical customers. To address this issue, marketers consider factors such as how long the customer will remain loyal to the firm, the defection rate (percentage of customers who switch on a yearly basis), the costs of replacing lost customers (advertising, promotion), whether customers will buy more or more expensive merchandise in the future, and other such factors. We explicitly address the lifetime value of customers in the Appendix following the next chapter.

Now that we've evaluated each segment's attractiveness (Step 3), we can select the target markets to pursue (Step 4).

## Step 4: Select Target Market

**LO4** Articulate the difference among targeting strategies: undifferentiated, concentrated, or micromarketing.

The fourth step in the STP process is to select a target market. The key factor likely to affect this decision is the marketer's ability to pursue such an opportunity or target segment. Thus, as we mentioned in Chapter 2, a firm assesses both the attractiveness of the target market (opportunities and threats based on the SWOT analysis and the profitability of the segment) and its own competencies (strengths and weaknesses based on SWOT analysis) very carefully.

Determining how to select target markets is not always straightforward. Exhibit 8.8 illustrates several targeting strategies. We discuss each of these basic targeting strategies next.

**Undifferentiated Targeting Strategy, or Mass Marketing**  When everyone might be considered a potential user of its product, a firm uses an undifferentiated targeting strategy. (See Exhibit 8.8.) Clearly, such a targeting strategy focuses on the similarities in needs of the customers as opposed to the differences. If the product or service is perceived to provide similar benefits to most consumers, there simply is little need to develop separate strategies for different groups.

Although not a common strategy in today's complex marketplace, an undifferentiated strategy is used for many basic commodities, such as salt or sugar. However, even those firms that offer salt and sugar now are trying to differentiate their products. Similarly, everyone with a car needs gasoline. Yet gasoline companies have vigorously moved from an undifferentiated strategy to a differentiated one by targeting their market into low-, medium-, and high-octane gasoline users.

**EXHIBIT 8.8**     Targeting Strategies

**Differentiated**

**Undifferentiated or mass marketing**

**Targeting Strategies**

**Concentrated**

**Micromarketing or one-to-one**

*Conde Nast has more than 20 niche magazines focused on different aspects of life.*

**Differentiated Targeting Strategy**  Firms using a differentiated targeting strategy target several market segments with a different offering for each (see Exhibit 8.8). Conde Nast has more than 20 niche magazines focused on different aspects of life—from *Vogue* for fashionistas to *Bon Appetit* for foodies to *GQ* for fashion-conscious men to *The New Yorker* for literature lovers to *Golf Digest* for those who walk the links.

Firms embrace differentiated targeting because it helps them obtain a bigger share of the market and increase the market for their products overall. Readers of *Golf Digest* probably are unlike readers of *Architectural Digest* in their interests, as well as in their demographics, such as gender, age, and income. Providing products or services that appeal to multiple segments helps diversify the business and therefore lowers the company's (in this case, Conde Nast's) overall risk. Even if one magazine suffers a circulation decline, the impact on the firm's profitability can be offset by revenue from another publication that continues to do well. But a differentiated strategy is likely to be more costly for the firm.

**Concentrated Targeting Strategy**  When an organization selects a single, primary target market and focuses all its energies on providing a product to fit that market's needs, it is using a concentrated targeting strategy (Exhibit 8.8). Entrepreneurial start-up ventures often benefit from using a concentrated strategy, which allows them to employ their limited resources more efficiently. Newton Running, for instance, has concentrated its targeting strategy on runners—but not all runners, only those that seek to land on the forefoot. This design is thought to be more natural, efficient, and less injury producing than other, more traditional running shoes. In comparison, although also known for running shoes, Nike uses a differentiated targeting strategy because it makes shoes for several segments including basketball, football, skateboarders, and the more fashion-conscious with its subsidiary brand, Cole-Haan.

**Micromarketing**[31] Take a look at your collection of belts. Have you ever had one made to match your exact specifications? (If you're interested, try www.leathergoodsconnection.com.) When a firm tailors a product or service to suit an individual customer's wants or needs, it is undertaking an extreme form of segmentation called micromarketing or one-to-one marketing (Exhibit 8.8). Small producers and service providers generally can tailor their offering to individual customers more easily, whereas it is far more difficult for larger companies to achieve this degree of segmentation. Nonetheless, companies like Dell (computers) and Lands' End (shirts) have capitalized on Internet technologies to offer custom products. Dell allows the customers to choose the size, color, parts, and the software included in their computer. Lands' End allows the customer to choose from a variety of options in the fabric, type of collar, sleeve, shape, and based on the customer's specific measurements. Another illustration is provided in Superior Service 8.1 on page 247.

The Internet facilitates this segmentation strategy.[32] Companies can cater to very small segments, sometimes as small as one customer at a time, efficiently and inexpensively (e.g., mortgage and insurance sites provide personalized quotes). An Internet-based company can offer one-to-one service more inexpensively in other venues, such as a retail store or phone contact. For example, frequent fliers of American Airlines can check prices and choose special services online at a fraction of the cost that the company would incur for a phone consultation with a ticket agent.

The Internet also simplifies customer identification. Cookies, or small text files a website stores in a visitor's browser, provide a unique identification of each potential customer who visits a site and details how the customer has searched through the site. Marketers also can ask visitors to fill out an online registration form. On the basis of such information, the company can make a variety of recommendations to customers. Amazon.com is renowned for the algorithms it uses to provide recommendations for related products to customers as they browse the site, which match customer profiles to those of other customers. The marketing strategy therefore is customized in real time, using known and accurate data about the customer. Staples offers merchandise at different prices in different parts of the country—simply by asking customers to enter their zip codes.

Customers can even do the work themselves. Mars' M&M's site (www.mymms.com) lets customers customize their own M&M's with personalized greetings, including messages for birthday parties, sporting events, graduations, and weddings—as well as wedding proposals! Both online and in stores, Build-A-Bear lets young (or not so young) customers design their very own stuffed furry friend with unique clothes, accessories, sounds, and the name printed on its birth certificate.

Some consumers appreciate such custom-made goods and services because they are made especially for them, which means they'll meet the person's

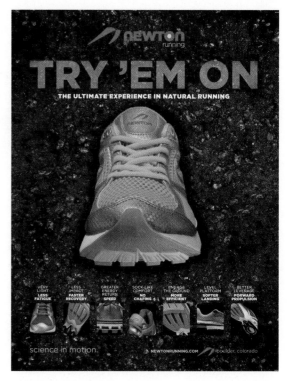

*Newton Running has concentrated its targeting strategy on runners that seek to land on the forefoot.*

*www.mymms.com adds value by allowing customers to customize their candy.*

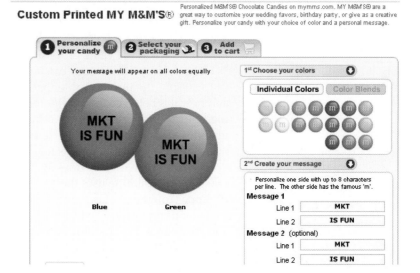

*Build-A-Bear lets customers design their own stuffed furry friend with unique clothes, accessories, sounds, and the name printed on its birth certificate.*

needs exactly. If a tailor measures you first and then sews a suit that fits your shoulders, hips, and leg length exactly, it probably will fit better than an off-the-rack suit that you pick up at a department store. But such products and services are typically more expensive than ready-made offerings and often take longer to obtain. You can purchase a Lands' End shirt at Sears and wear it out of the store. The firm's custom shirts, in contrast, take five to six weeks to make and deliver. And if you visited an old-fashioned tailor, the processes of measuring you, ordering the material, and sewing the pants might take several months.

Ethical and Societal Dilemma 8.1 examines the issue of marketing certain products to teens.

 **LO5**    Define positioning, and describe how firms do it.

## Step 5: Develop Positioning Strategy

The last step in developing a market segmentation strategy is positioning. Market positioning involves a process of defining the marketing mix variables so that target customers have a clear, distinctive, desirable understanding of what the product does or represents in comparison with competing products.

*French retailer Hermes is positioned as a luxury brand, which makes its customers less price-sensitive for its products like this handmade Birkin bag which retails for $9,000.*

**Positioning Methods** Firms position products and services based on different methods such as the value proposition, salient attributes, symbols, and competition.

The positioning strategy can help communicate the firm or the product's **value proposition**, the unique value that a product or service provides to its customers, and how it is better than and different from those of competitors. Firms thus position their products and services according to value and salient attributes. Value is a popular positioning method because the relationship of price to quality is among the most important considerations for consumers when they make a purchase decision.

Remember that value does not necessarily mean low priced though. The watchmaker Patek Philippe uses the advertising tagline, "You never actually own a Patek Philippe. You merely take care of it for the next generation," to encourage buyers to consider its arm candy an investment.[33] The long-running campaign takes on added effectiveness in the modern economic downturn, especially as a way to market a luxury brand in a necessity-focused economy. Other brands that rely on a similar idea of luxury value include Hermes, Chanel, and Mercedes-Benz.

## Superior Service 8.1

### Let's See, for This Trip, I'll Take Soft Jazz, a Firm Pillow, and Jasmine in My Hotel Room, Please

A chef may add or omit specific ingredients to accommodate a diner's needs or preferences. A dressmaker may create a wedding gown based on an oral description of the bride's perfect dress. But what about a vacation designed just for you, right down to the scent in your room and the type of fresh juice available in your private bar? This approach to micromarketing on the ultra-luxury level is the concept behind Conrad Bali, a property of Conrad Hotel & Resorts, where the "luxury is as unique as every guest."[34]

The personalization efforts begin on the property's website (www.myconradbali.com), which organizes visitors' options into each of the five senses: Sight choices refer to available excursions or the newspaper at the front stoop, the sound selections range from jazz to pop, aromatherapies balance emotions and release stress or yield a sense of love; touch options pertain to pillow firmness and robe size, and taste selections enable visitors to reserve particular wines. Using the "My Balance" tool, visitors select spa services and activities in advance.

And then when they arrive at the hotel, each guest receives a personal assistant, available 24 hours a day, ready to cater to his or her every whim. Each room overlooks the ocean, lagoons, gardens, or the resort.[35] Impressive suites average around 1,200 square feet and feature amenities like separate dining rooms with private bars, large plasma televisions, bathrooms with soaking tubs, private terraces, complimentary breakfast and evening cocktails, and even a private pool!

In contrast, the lodging industry as a whole has been moving toward more limited services and joint reservations systems[36] that reduce costs but do little to promote a sense of personalization. Rather than offering afternoon tea, they are offloading their food business to third-party caterers, and reservations options refer to adding a car rental or airline ticket rather than a bottle of cabernet and a flower petal bath with hibiscus and coconut milk.

The challenges associated with a struggling global economy and threats of terrorism make it increasingly difficult for luxury hoteliers to appeal to business and personal travelers.[37] Competition remains fierce in this sector, and standards continue to rise constantly in the struggle to attract and retain discerning clientele. Improved amenities and services mean higher costs for the properties and higher prices for visitors. Is the individual personalization provided by the Conrad Bali enough, or is it targeting a market segment that is insufficient to maintain the hotel's profit margin?

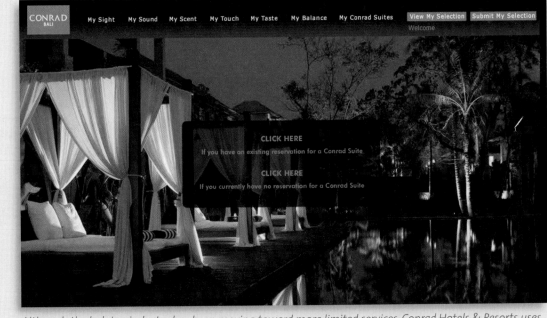

*Although the lodging industry has been moving toward more limited services, Conrad Hotels & Resorts uses a micromarketing approach to provide a unique experience to every guest.*

Another common positioning strategy focuses on the product attributes that are most important to the target market. Volvo, the car company traditionally positioned for the safety-conscious driver, wants to stretch its safety image to one focused on driving performance and excitement. The company expects the positioning adjustment to be a long and concentrated effort, because so many of

## Ethical and Societal Dilemma 8.1 | Designer Labels Target Teens

What happens when marketing to a segment works too well? Take, for example, designer labels targeting teens 13 to 17 years of age. Designer labels account for over 15 percent of teen clothing purchases; just a few years earlier, these labels earned less than 10 percent. Yet among adults older than 18 years old, the 7 percent market share designer labels maintain has remained constant for several years.[38] So what can explain these trends?

High-end designers are taking advantage of teens' desire for fashion and bragging rights to sell apparel to younger consumers by targeting them intensively with advertising and product placements. Luxury brands targeting kids include Dolce & Gabbana and Armani, which have created their own separate teen lines, as well as Michael Kors, Coach, Dooney & Bourke, and Dior, which target these young consumers with accessories. Even retailers are cashing in on the trend; department stores such as Nordstrom have added Burberry and Prada products to their children's departments. As a result, Tweens are showing up for their middle school classes with their $225 Dooney & Bourke gym bags in tow.[39]

The effects of intense advertising to kids also appear in the form of more sophisticated brand opinions among younger and younger consumers. A few years ago, 15 percent of teens claimed to love Armani; today, that level has reached 27 percent. In schools across the country, the effects of increased advertising to kids also results in massive increases in "fashion bullying"—when students are targeted because they do not wear the "right" clothing or designers. More than one-third of all middle school students say that they have been bullied because of what they wear. Although this form of bullying certainly is not new, guidance counselors say that fashion bullying has reached a new level of intensity as more designers launch collections targeted at kids.

In response to these concerns, some companies, including Coach and Tiffany & Co., have taken steps to reduce their exposure to the teen market. Tiffany's increased silver prices because too many teenagers were visiting their stores, which created the risk of alienating its traditional core consumers—those who purchase the high-end retailer's most expensive items. Even though 5 percent of Coach sales are to teenagers, the company has chosen not to market to them directly and limits exposure among the 13- to 18-year-old segment to publicity through secondary sources such as fashion and gossip magazines.[40]

Fashion companies thus face an ethical dilemma: How much should they target teens? Clearly, these companies hope to gain lifetime aficionados by reaching out to consumers at a young age, with the goal of turning them into loyal return customers.

*(continued)*

*Should fashion companies target teens?*

## Ethical and Societal Dilemma 8.1

*(continued)*

However, some advertising appears to be encouraging fashion bullying. Furthermore, luxury purchases such as designer handbags and totes are specifically designed to be artificially exclusive. When teens buy luxury goods at more than twice the rate of the general population, it suggests that parents are funding a fashion habit that they may not engage in themselves and that may not be sustainable for those children when they grow up and have to pay their own way. Should the designers care?

Volvo's boxier vehicles remain on the road today, which reinforces its more conservative image. Volvo's goal is not to abandon the safety notions associated with the brand but rather to expand its image to compete with other top luxury brands.[41]

A well-known symbol can also be used as a positioning tool. What comes to mind when you think of Colonel Sanders, the Jolly Green Giant, the Gerber Baby, or Tony the Tiger? Or consider the Texaco star, the Nike swoosh, or the Ralph Lauren polo player? These symbols are so strong and well known that they create a position for the brand that distinguishes it from its competition. Many such symbols are registered trademarks that are legally protected by the companies that developed them.

Firms can choose to position their products or services against a specific competitor or an entire product/service classification. For instance, 7-Up positioned its product as "the Uncola" to differentiate it from caramel-colored cola beverages like Pepsi and Coke. Goodrich tires were promoted as "the other guys," or the ones without the blimp, to set them apart from Goodyear tires.

Marketers must be careful, however, that they don't position their product too closely to their competition. If, for instance, their package or logo looks too much like a competitor's, they might be opening themselves up to a trademark infringement lawsuit. For example, numerous store brands have been challenged for having packaging confusingly similar to that of national brands. Similarly, McDonald's sues anyone who uses the "Mc" prefix, including McSleep Inns and McDental Services,

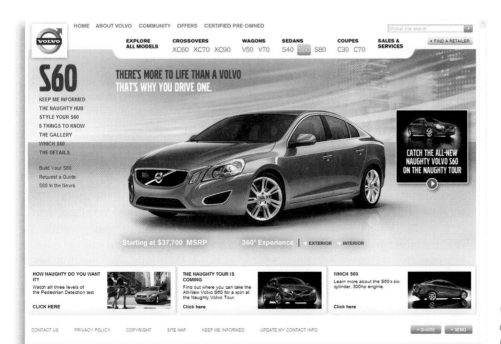

*Volvo is repositioning its cars from safe to safe and performance.*

What if you ate vegetables just because you liked them?

Green Giant™ Broccoli Cheese Sauce

Healthy for dinner, but with its delicious 3 cheese blend, you'll want it all the time. **For the love of vegetables.**

*The Jolly Green Giant is such a well-known symbol that it can be used as a positioning tool.*

even though in the latter case there was little possibility that consumers would believe the fast-food restaurant company would branch out into dental services.

**Positioning Using Perceptual Mapping** Now that we have identified the various methods by which firms position their products and services, we discuss the actual steps they go through to establish that position. When developing a positioning strategy, firms go through five important steps. Before you read about these steps, though, examine Exhibit 8.9, a hypothetical perceptual map of the soft drink industry in the United States. A perceptual map displays, in two or more dimensions, the position of products or brands in the consumer's mind. We have chosen two dimensions for illustrative purposes: strong versus light taste (vertical) and fun versus healthy (horizontal). Also, though this industry is quite complex, we have simplified the diagram to include only a few players in the market. The position of each brand is denoted by a small circle, and the numbered asterisks denote consumers' ideal points—where a particular market segment's ideal product would lie on the map. The larger the asterisk, the larger the market.

To derive a perceptual map such as this, marketers follow five steps.

1. **Determine consumers' perceptions and evaluations of the product or service in relation to competitors'.** Marketers determine their brand's position by asking consumers a series of questions about their and competitors' products. For instance, they might ask how the consumer uses the existing product or services, what items the consumer regards as alternative sources to satisfy his or her needs, what the person likes or dislikes about the brand in relation to competitors, and what might make that person choose one brand over another.

2. **Identify competitors' positions.** When the firm understands how its customers view its brand relative to competitors', it must study how those same competitors position themselves. For instance, POWERade positions itself closely to Gatorade, which means they appear next to each other on the perceptual map and appeal to target market 3. They are also often found next to each other on store shelves, are similarly priced, and are viewed by customers as sports drinks. Gatorade also knows that its sports drink is perceived to be more like POWERade than like its own Propel Fitness Water (located near target market 4), Coke (target market 1), or Sunkist orange soda (target market 2).

3. **Determine consumer preferences**. The firm knows what the consumer thinks of the products or services in the marketplace and their positions relative to one another. Now it must find out what the consumer really wants, that is, determine the "ideal" product or service that appeals to each market. For example, a huge market exists for traditional Gatorade, and that market is shared by POWERade. Gatorade also recognizes a market, depicted as the ideal product for segment 5 on the perceptual map, of consumers who would prefer a less sweet, less calorie-laden drink that offers the same rejuvenating properties as Gatorade. Currently, no product is adequately serving market 5.

| EXHIBIT 8.9 | Perceptual Map for U.S. Soft Drink Industry |

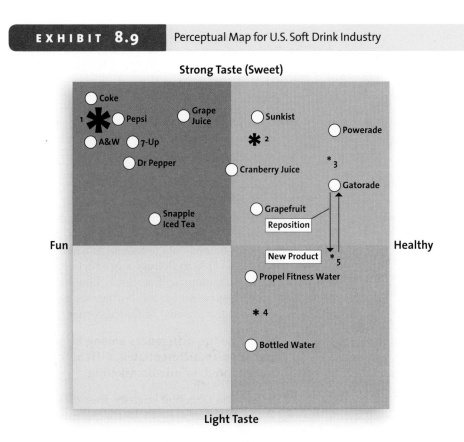

**Strong Taste (Sweet)**

Coke

1 ✳ Pepsi    Grape Juice    Sunkist    Powerade

A&W    7-Up    ✳ 2

Dr Pepper    Cranberry Juice    ✳ 3

Gatorade

Grapefruit
Reposition

**Fun**    **Healthy**

Snapple Iced Tea

New Product    ✳ 5

Propel Fitness Water

✳ 4

Bottled Water

**Light Taste**

4. **Select the position**. Continuing with the Gatorade example, the company has three choices to appeal to the "less sweet sports drink" target market 5. It could develop a new product to meet the needs of market 5. Alternatively, it could adjust or reposition its marketing approach—its product and promotion—to sell original Gatorade to market 5 (arrow pointing down from Gatorade to the ideal point for segment 5). Finally, it could ignore what target market 5 really wants and hope that consumers will be attracted to the original Gatorade because it is closer to their ideal product than anything else on the market (arrow pointing up from the ideal point for segment 5 to Gatorade).

5. **Monitor the positioning strategy**. Markets are not stagnant. Consumers' tastes shift, and competitors react to those shifts. Attempting to maintain the same position year after year can spell disaster for any company. Thus, firms must always view the first three steps of the positioning process as ongoing, with adjustments made in Step 4 as necessary.

*Gatorade with football player Jason Taylor (left) and POWERade with soccer player David Beckham (right) are positioned to compete for target markets in Exhibit 8.9.*

## CHECK YOURSELF

1. What is a perceptual map?
2. Identify the five positioning steps.

## Summing Up

**L01  Identify the five steps in the segmentation, targeting, and positioning process.**

The first step involves clear articulation of a firm's strategy and objectives. The second step is to use a segmentation method to segment the marketplace into different segments based on customer similarities within a segment and dissimilarities across segments. The third step is to evaluate the attractiveness of the various segments. The fourth step is selecting a target market. The fifth step is to identify and develop the position strategy.

**L02  Outline the different methods of segmenting a market.**

There is really no one "best" method to segment a market. Firms choose from various methods on the basis of the type of product/service they offer and their goals for the segmentation strategy. For instance, if the firm wants to identify its customers easily, demographic or geographic segmentation likely will work best. But if it is trying to dig deeper into why customers might buy its offering, then psychographic, geodemographic, benefits, or behavioral segmentation (occasion and loyalty) work best. Typically, a combination of several segmentation methods is most effective.

**L03  Describe how firms determine whether a segment is attractive and therefore worth pursuing.**

Marketers use several criteria to assess a segment's attractiveness. First, the customer should be identifiable—companies must know what types of people are in the market so they can direct their efforts appropriately. Second, the market must be substantial enough to be worth pursuing. If relatively few people appear in a segment, it is probably not cost-effective to direct special marketing mix efforts toward them. Third, the market must be reachable—the firm must be able to reach the seg-

ment through effective communications and distribution. Fourth, the firm must be responsive to the needs of customers in a segment. It must be able to deliver a product or service that the segment will embrace. Finally, the segment must be profitable, both in the near term and over the lifetime of the customer.

**L04  Articulate the differences among targeting strategies: undifferentiated, differentiated, concentrated, or micromarketing.**

Firms use a targeting strategy after they have identified its segments. An undifferentiated strategy uses no targeting at all and works only for products or services that most consumers consider to be commodities. The difference between a differentiated and a concentrated strategy is that the differentiated approach targets multiple segments, whereas the concentrated targets only one. Larger firms with multiple product/service offerings generally use a differentiated strategy; smaller firms or those with a limited product/service offering often use a concentrated strategy. Firms that employ a micromarketing or one-to-one marketing strategy tailor their product/service offering to each customer—that is, it is custom made. In the past, micromarketing was reserved primarily for artisans, tailors, or other craftspeople who would make items exactly as the customer wanted. Recently, however, larger manufacturers and retailers have begun experimenting with custom-made merchandise as well. Service providers, in contrast, are largely accustomed to customizing their offering.

**L05  Define positioning, and describe how firms do it.**

Positioning is the "P" in the STP (segmentation, targeting, and positioning) process. It refers to how customers think about a product, service, or brand in the market relative to competitors' offerings. Firms position their products and services according to several criteria. Some focus on their offering's value—customers get a lot for what the product or service costs. Others determine the most important attributes for customers and position their offering on the basis of those attributes. Symbols can also be used for positioning, though few products or services are associated with symbols that are compelling enough to drive people to buy. Finally, one of the most common positioning methods relies on the favorable comparison of the firm's offering with the products or services marketed by competitors. When developing a positioning strategy and a perceptual map, firms go through five steps. First they determine consumers' perceptions and evaluations of the product or service in relation to competitors. Second, they identify competitors' positions. Third, they determine consumer preferences. Fourth, they select the position. Finally, they monitor the positioning strategy.

## Key Terms

- behavioral segmentation, 237
- benefit segmentation, 237
- concentrated targeting strategy, 244
- demographic segmentation, 232
- differentiated targeting strategy, 244
- geodemographic segmentation, 236
- geographic segmentation, 231
- ideal point, 250
- lifestyles, 234
- loyalty segmentation, 238
- micromarketing, 245
- occasion segmentation 238
- one-to-one marketing, 245
- perceptual map, 250
- psychographics, 233
- psychographic segmentation, 233
- self-concept, 233
- self-values, 233
- undifferentiated targeting strategy (mass marketing), 243
- Value and Lifestyle Survey (VALS™), 234
- value proposition, 246

## Marketing Applications

1. What segmentation methods would you suggest for a small entrepreneur starting his own business selling T-shirts? Justify why you would recommend those methods.

2. You have been asked to identify various segments in the market and then a potential targeting strategy. Describe the segments for your pet supply store, and then justify the best targeting strategy to use.

3. How and why would a retailer use micromarketing?

4. You have been asked to evaluate the attractiveness of a group of identified potential market segments. What criteria will you use to evaluate those segments? Why are these appropriate criteria?

5. A small-business owner is trying to evaluate the profitability of different segments. What are the key factors you would recommend she consider? Over what period of time would you recommend she evaluate?

6. Think about the various nationwide restaurant chain brands that you know (e.g., Burger King, Applebee's, Ruth's Chris Steakhouse). How do those various brands position themselves in the market?

7. Put yourself in the position of an entrepreneur who is developing a new product to introduce into the market. Briefly describe the product. Then, develop the segmentation, targeting, and positioning strategy for marketing the new product. Be sure to discuss (a) the overall strategy, (b) characteristics of the target market, (c) why that target market is attractive, and (d) the positioning strategy. Provide justifications for your decisions.

8. Think of a specific company or organization that uses various types of promotional material to market its offerings. The Web, magazine ads, newspaper ads, catalogs, newspaper inserts, direct mail pieces, and flyers might all be sources for a variety of promotional materials. Locate two or three promotional pieces for the company and use them as a basis to analyze the segments being targeted. Describe the methods used for segmenting the market reflected in these materials, and describe characteristics of the target market according to the materials. Be sure to include a copy of all the materials used in the analysis.

9. You have been hired recently by a large bank in its credit card marketing division. The bank has relationships with a large number of colleges and prints a wide variety of credit cards featuring college logos, images, and the like. You have been asked to oversee the implementation of a new program targeting the freshman class at the schools with which the bank has a relationship. The bank has already purchased the names and home addresses of the incoming freshman class. You have been told that no credit checks will be required for these cards as long as the student is over 18 years of age. The bank plans a first day of school marketing blitz that includes free hats, T-shirts, and book promotions, as well as free pizza, if the students simply fill out an application. Do you think it is a good idea to target this program to these new students?

www.mhhe.com/
grewal3e

## Quiz Yourself

1. Adidas Group owns Reebok, adidas, and Taylor-Made brands. Adidas uses the different brands to pursue a(n) _____ strategy.
   a. concentrated targeting
   b. micromarketing
   c. benefit segmentation
   d. differentiated targeting
   e. undifferentiated targeting

2. Talbots' target customers are college-educated women between 35 and 55 years old with average household income of $75,000 or more. Talbots is describing its market using a _____ segmentation approach.
   a. self-actualization
   b. geodemographic
   c. psychographic
   d. demographic
   e. geographic

(Answers to these two questions are provided on page 607.)

Go to www.mhhe.com/grewal3e to practice an additional 11 questions.

## Toolkit

**MARKET POSITION MAP ANALYSIS**
Assume you are a brand manager for a major manufacturer. You have identified a number of market segments and are trying to understand how your products are positioned relative to those of other manufacturers. Use the toolkit provided at www.mhhe.com/grewal3e to conduct a market position analysis.

## Net Savvy

1. Go to the Nielsen Claritas website (www.mybestsegments.com). Click on the tab that says "ZIP Code Look-Up," then enter your zip code to learn which segments are the top five in your zip code. Follow the links for each of the five most common PRIZM segments to obtain a segment description. Write up a summary of your results. Discuss the extent to which you believe these are accurate descriptions of the main segments of people who reside in your zip code.

2. Go to the VALS website (http://www.strategicbusinessinsights.com/vals/presurvey.shtml), and click on the link to complete the VALS survey. After you submit your responses, a screen will display your primary and secondary VALS types. Click on the colored names of each segment to get additional information about them, and print out your results. Assess the extent to which these results reflect your lifestyle, and identify which characteristics accurately reflect your interests and activities and which do not.

### COCA-COLA

Back in 1886, an Atlanta pharmacist created a caramel-colored liquid and brought it down the street to Jacobs' Pharmacy, where it was mixed with carbonated water and sold for five cents a glass. The beverage caught on, and sales took off from the initial average of nine drinks a day to today's total of 1.6 billion servings of Coke products consumed daily. The success spawned bottling plants, six-pack cartons, international distribution—and imitators. By the early 1930s, Pepsi, created in 1902, had survived two bankruptcies and was expanding as well.[42]

Both companies went decades marketing only one brand, but Coca-Cola added Fanta, Sprite, TAB, and Fresca in the 50s and 60s and Diet Coke in the early 80s, while Pepsi launched Diet Pepsi and Mountain Dew. Since then, both companies have grown and developed new brands designed to attract market segments. Today Coke products are sold in more than 200 countries. Pepsi is available in nearly the same number of countries[43] and other cola products have entered the marketplace. To grow and increase sales in this mature market, Coca-Cola must either take customers away from other beverage companies or encourage existing customers to drink more cola—both challenging tasks. Part of the company's solution pertains to its approach to new product development for different market segments.[44]

### MARKET SEGMENTATION STRATEGY

As the market tightened and consumer values changed, Coke responded by developing more unique products for various specific market segments. Because those unique products appeal to specific groups, Coke can increase its sales without cannibalizing the sales of its other products. In addition to the products mentioned above, the company launched caffeine-free Coke and Diet Coke to appeal to cola drinkers who wanted to cut back their caffeine intake. By introducing decaffeinated versions of its traditional sodas, Coca-Cola could increase the number of sodas it sells each day without hurting sales, because the consumers targeted by these products already had been avoiding or minimizing Coca-Cola consumption to reduce their caffeine intake.

### DIETERS SEGMENT

When Americans became concerned with weight, Coca-Cola introduced Diet Coke, which became the number one selling diet soft drink in America within a year of hitting shelves. In 1986, Diet Cherry Coke joined the brand, followed by Diet Coke with Lemon. Diet Coke with Vanilla and Diet Coke with Lime followed quickly, along with Diet Black Cherry Vanilla Coke. As consumers sought to improve their health, the company introduced Diet Coke Plus, which is the familiar beverage with added vitamins and minerals.

### "REAL MEN" SEGMENT

Women hoping to drop a dress size may turn to diet sodas, but "real men" don't want to be caught with a "girly" diet drink. Coca-Cola had a response for them too: the high-profile launch of Coke Zero, which avoided the dreaded word "diet"[45] and specifically targets men through its packaging, promotions, and image. By targeting men between the ages of 18 and 34 who wanted to drink a low-calorie cola but would not be seen buying or sipping Diet Coke, Coca-Cola increased its sales of Coke-branded products by one-third.[46]

## THE "DIY" SEGMENT

Soda fountain sales have remained an important part of Coke's business since the company's inception. To boost its cola sales in restaurants, Coke combined the soda fountain concept with the "do it yourself" trend to offer customers up to 104 individualized flavor choices.[47] The new machine, called a Freestyle, was created by the designers of Ferrari race cars. Size-controlled shots of concentrated flavors are released into carbonated water mid-stream, so that the drink is mixed in the air; special technology keeps one consumer's beverage from picking up flavors from the last drink poured. The Freestyle allows mom to have a Diet Coke with Lime and dad to have a Coke Zero with Lime while the kids have a Caffeine-Free Vanilla Coke and a Caffeine-Free Diet Cherry Vanilla Coke.

## MARKETING VALUE TO SEGMENTS

A successful new product introduction needs to combine an innovative product with a marketing campaign that communicates the value of that new product to the targeted segment. The Coke Zero launch provides a perfect illustration of this point. Coca-Cola designed a campaign supported by advertisements on television and radio, in print, on outdoor billboards, and online, as well as widespread sampling programs and opportunities.[48] Television commercials for Coke Zero show male athletes like Pittsburgh Steeler Troy Polamalu in a remake of the popular "Mean Joe Greene" commercial[49] or a young man confronted by an ex-girlfriend and her new boyfriend taking a deep swallow of Coke Zero. His guzzling is rewarded with a curvaceous blonde asking if he prefers whipped cream or chocolate.[50] The media strategy tried to expose as many men as possible to the new product, spending a significant bulk of the media budget on outdoor advertising.

## RESULTS OF COCA-COLA'S SEGMENTATION EFFORTS

By using gender to segment the diet cola market, Coca-Cola was able to customize the advertising for Coca-Cola Zero to appeal to men, whereas Diet Coke ads could concentrate on women. In turn, Coke gained closer connections for its different products with each product's targeted market segment, and Coke Zero became one of the most successful launches in the company's long history.[51] While the Freestyle dispenser is only available in test markets, in some stores where it is available the machine has bumped up beverage sales by 10 percent at a time when fountain sales on the whole are slipping.

Through its efforts to identify and target such specific market segments, Coca-Cola has grown its stable of consumer brands to more than 450 products.[52] While Coca-Cola remains the most valuable brand, Diet Coke and Coca-Cola Zero have joined it as billion-dollar products.

### Questions

1. Which types of segmentation strategies does Coca-Cola use to categorize the cola beverage market?
2. Are these types effective in this market? Provide support for your answer.

# Marketing Research

For many years, Domino's primary market offer was cheap pizza delivered fast. Its entire marketing plan revolved around the idea of speed, including its "30 minutes or its free" slogan, its mascot the Noid, and even the layout of its stores. The promise of fast or free pizza put Domino's on the map, and on many customers' speed dials.

But the focus on speed (even after Domino's was forced to rescind its timed promise after being sued by the family of a woman killed by a speeding delivery driver[1]) meant the company had little time to focus on much else, like whether the actual pizzas were any good. Not until Papa John's entered the national U.S. scene, with its promises of better taste and quality ingredients, did Domino's even set out to find what the market thought of its food and what it might want from a fast-food delivery chain.

The research it conducted told the company what customers knew only too well: The crust was tasteless, the sauce boring, and the toppings low quality. Speed was no longer enough, because consumers could get better quality at around the same price and speed from other chains. Domino's thus realized it needed to revamp its menu and come up with new recipes for the items that would remain on offer.

First, it expanded its menu to include items that compete directly with companies that traditionally stress the quality of their offerings. For example, Domino's toasted sandwiches seem to be targeting Quizno's, which emphasizes the taste and high quality of its ingredients. It also added dessert items like Brownie Squares and Oreo Dessert Pizza to encourage consumers to think of it as a source of a complete meal.

Second, it launched a new advertising campaign designed to emphasize the results of its marketing research. Domino's shows focus groups in which customers express their negative opinions—crusts like cardboard, sauce that tastes like ketchup. One participant cuts right to the heart of the matter by saying, "Domino's pies were even worse than microwave and totally void of flavor." Then the new CEO appears, claiming the chain had no choice but to be honest about its old pizza recipe if it were to have any hope of winning back

## LEARNING OBJECTIVES

**LO1** Identify the five steps in the marketing research process

**LO2** Summarize the differences between secondary data and primary data.

**LO3** Describe the various internal and external secondary data sources.

**LO4** Describe the various primary data collection techniques.

**LO5** Examine the circumstances under which collecting information on consumers is ethical.

customers. Other ads highlight chefs employed by Domino's, who flinch and shake their heads as they hear the reviews. But the next step is for them to talk about how the new pizza recipes are so much better than the old and promise that customers will love the changes. The campaign has continued with video shots of Domino's representatives visiting the focus group complainers at their homes, with the new recipe. Universally, the man who hated the crust and the woman who found the sauce tasteless express their conversion and conviction that they will now start buying from Domino's.

With this feedback, Domino's gained the confidence to offer a money-back guarantee. This time, the guarantee focuses not on speed but on quality. The only way for the company to have determined that what customers wanted was taste, rather than speed, was for it to ask. Such questions and asking them are at the heart of marketing research.[2]

As the Domino's example shows, marketing research is a key prerequisite to successful decision making. It consists of a set of techniques and principles for systematically collecting, recording, analyzing, and interpreting data that can aid decision makers involved in marketing goods, services, or ideas.[3] When marketing managers attempt to develop their strategies, marketing research can provide valuable information that will help them make segmentation, positioning, product, place, price, and promotion decisions.

Firms invest billions of dollars in marketing research every year. The largest U.S.-based marketing research firm, the ACNielsen Company, earns annual worldwide revenues of $5 billion.[4] Why do marketers find this research valuable? First, it helps reduce some of the uncertainty under which they currently operate. Successful managers know when research might help their decision making and then take appropriate steps to acquire the information they need. Second, marketing research provides a crucial link between firms and their environments, which enables them to be customer oriented because they build their strategies by using customer input and continual feedback. Third, by constantly monitoring their competitors, firms can anticipate and respond quickly to competitive moves.

If you think market research is applicable only to corporate or retailing ventures, think again. Not-for-profit organizations and governments also use research to serve their constituencies better. The political sector has been slicing and dicing the voting public for decades to determine relevant messages for different demographics. Politicians desperately want to understand who makes up the voting public to determine how to reach them. Not only do they want to know your political views, but they also want to understand your media habits, such as what magazines you subscribe to, so they can target you more effectively.

To do so, they rely on the five-step marketing research process we outline in this chapter. We also will discuss some of the ethical implications of using the information that these databases can collect. In Appendix 9A, we will detail the concept of customer lifetime value (CLV), a popular marketing metric to determine a customer's value to a firm.

# THE MARKETING RESEARCH PROCESS

Managers consider several factors before embarking on a marketing research project. First, will the research be useful? Will it provide insights beyond what the managers already know and reduce uncertainty associated with the project? Second, is top management committed to the project and willing to abide by the results of the research? Related to both of these questions is the value of the research. Marketing

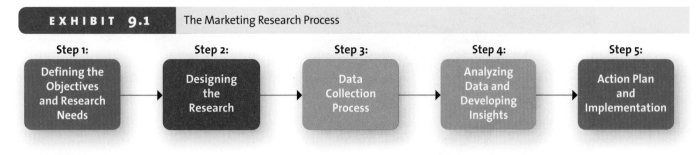

**EXHIBIT 9.1**     The Marketing Research Process

| Step 1: | Step 2: | Step 3: | Step 4: | Step 5: |
|---|---|---|---|---|
| Defining the Objectives and Research Needs | Designing the Research | Data Collection Process | Analyzing Data and Developing Insights | Action Plan and Implementation |

research can be very expensive, and if the results won't be useful or management does not abide by the findings, it represents a waste of money. Third, should the marketing research project be small or large? A project might involve a simple analysis of data that the firm already has, or it could be an in-depth assessment that costs hundreds of thousands of dollars and takes months to complete.

The marketing research process itself consists of five steps (see Exhibit 9.1). Although we present the stages of the marketing research process in a step-by-step progression, of course research does not always, or even usually, happen that way. Researchers go back and forth from one step to another as the need arises. For example, marketers may establish a specific research objective, which they follow with data collection and preliminary analysis. If they uncover new information during the collection step or if the findings of the analysis spotlight new research needs, they might redefine their objectives and begin again from a new starting point. Another important requirement before embarking on a research project is to plan the entire project in advance. By planning the entire research process prior to starting the project, researchers can avoid unnecessary alterations to the research plan as they move through the process.

# MARKETING RESEARCH PROCESS STEP 1: DEFINING THE OBJECTIVES AND RESEARCH NEEDS

**LO1** Identify the five steps in the marketing research process.

Because research is both expensive and time-consuming, it is important to establish in advance exactly what problem needs to be solved. To do so, marketers must clearly define the objectives of their marketing research project.

Consider two scenarios:

**Scenario 1:**   McDonald's wants a better understanding of its customers' experience. It also needs to understand how customers view the experience at Wendy's, a main competitor. Finally, McDonald's hopes to gain some insight into how it should set a price and market its latest combo meal of a hamburger, fries, and drink. Any one of these questions could initiate a research project. The complexity of the project that the company eventually undertakes depends on how much time and resources it has available, as well as the amount of in-depth knowledge it needs.

Researchers assess the value of a project through a careful comparison of the benefits of answering some of their questions and the costs associated with conducting the research.

**Scenario 2:**   A marketer of a national brand of men's cologne sets out to evaluate its position in the marketplace relative to that of its competitors (i.e., a benchmarking project). The specific purpose of the marketing research is twofold: to determine the brand's current relative market share (see Chapter 2) and to assess how that position will change in the next few years.

*If McDonald's were to do research to better understand its customers' experience, it would study both the McDonald's experience and that of its major competitors, like Wendy's.*

Regardless of which specific goals the company has, its marketing research efforts and resources will be wasted if its research objectives are poorly defined. Poor design arises from three major sources:

- Basing research on irrelevant research questions.
- Focusing on research questions that marketing research cannot answer.
- Addressing research questions to which the answers are already known.

For companies with track records of anticipating new technologies, fashions, or gadgets that consumers will demand, as well as the core competencies to deliver them in a timely manner, lengthy marketing research studies likely will not add significantly to the benefits of their own intuition. However, timely and focused marketing research could help them refine their ideas and prototypes.

When researchers have determined what information they need to address a particular problem or issue, the next step is to design a research project to meet those objectives.

## MARKETING RESEARCH PROCESS STEP 2: DESIGNING THE RESEARCH

*McDonald's assesses its customers' market experience by examining available data, and then asks customers about their experience with products like Happy Meals.*

The second step in the marketing research project involves design. In this step, researchers identify the type of data needed and determine the type of research necessary to collect it. Recall that the objectives of the project drive the type of data needed, as outlined in Step 1. Let's look at how this second step works, using our two research scenarios: the McDonald's customer experience and price research and the men's cologne firm's benchmarking study.

In our hypothetical Scenario 1, McDonald's needs to ask its customers about their McDonald's experience. However, because people don't always tell the whole truth in surveys, the company also may want to observe customers to see how they actually enter the stores, interact with employees, and consume the product. The project's design might begin with available data, such as information that shows that people with children often come into the restaurants at lunchtime and order Happy Meals. Then the McDonald's market researchers can start to ask customers specific questions about their McDonald's experience.

In Scenario 2, identifying the marketing metric needed for the first purpose—determining relative market share—is fairly straightforward. It requires finding the company's sales during a particular time frame relative to that of the largest firm in the industry.[5] Identifying the marketing metric needed for the second purpose— assessing the extent to which the firm's market position will improve, stay the same, or deteriorate—is not as easy to obtain. For example, the cologne company's marketers might want to assess customers' brand loyalty, because if the company enjoys high levels of loyalty, the future looks rosier than if loyalty is low. Their relative market share in relation to that of its competitors over time can also shed light on the future of its market position. The firm will want to know which firms have been gaining relative market share and which are losing.

*To determine the relative market share for Tag Cologne for Men, it is necessary to determine its sales and relative market position.*

# MARKETING RESEARCH PROCESS STEP 3: DATA COLLECTION PROCESS

Data collection begins only after the research design process. Based on the design of the project, data can be collected from secondary or primary data sources. Secondary data are pieces of information that have been collected prior to the start of the focal research project. Secondary data include both external and internal data sources. Primary data, in contrast, are those data collected to address specific research needs. Some common primary data collection methods include focus groups, in-depth interviews, and surveys.

## Secondary Data

A marketing research project often begins with a review of the relevant secondary data. Secondary data might come from free or very inexpensive external sources, such as census data, information from trade associations, and reports published in magazines. Although readily accessible, these inexpensive sources may not be specific or timely enough to solve the marketer's research needs and objectives. So firms purchase secondary data from specialized research firms. Additionally, secondary sources can be taken from internal sources, including the company's sales invoices, customer lists, and other reports generated by the company itself. We now examine these external and internal sources of secondary data in more detail.

**LO2** Summarize the differences between secondary data and primary data.

**Inexpensive External Secondary Data** Some sources of external secondary data can be quickly accessed at a relatively low cost. The Census of Retail Trade and County Business Patterns, for example, provides data about sales of different types of retail establishments. If you wanted to open a new location of a business you are already operating, these data may help you determine the size of your potential market.

**LO3** Describe the various internal and external secondary data sources.

Sometimes, however, these inexpensive data sources are not adequate to meet researchers' needs. Because the data initially were acquired for some purpose other than the research question at hand, they may not be completely relevant or timely. The U.S. Census is a great source of demographic data about a particular market area, and it can be easily accessed at a low cost. However, the data are collected only at the beginning of every decade, so they quickly become outdated. Right now, firms are fortunate because the 2010 Census is relatively current and up-to-date. If an entrepreneur wanted to open a retail flooring store in 2014 though, the data would already be four years old, and the housing market might be much stronger than it was in 2010. Researchers must also pay careful attention to how other sources of inexpensive secondary data were collected. Despite the great deal of data available on the Internet, easy access does not ensure that the data are trustworthy.

**Syndicated External Secondary Data** Although the secondary data described above is either free or inexpensively obtained, marketers can purchase external secondary data called syndicated data, which are available for a fee from commercial research firms such as Information Resources Inc. (IRI), the National Purchase Diary Panel, and ACNielsen. Exhibit 9.2 contains information about various firms that provide syndicated data. For our hypothetical cologne marketer in Scenario 2, the pertinent data available from these sources might include the prices of different colognes, sales figures, growth or decline in the category, and advertising and promotional spending. McDonald's is likely to gather pertinent data about sales from its franchisees. However, it would likely get competitor data, overall food consumption data, and other data about the quick service restaurant category from appropriate syndicated data providers.

Consumer packaged goods firms that sell to wholesalers often lack the means to gather pertinent data directly from the retailers that sell their products to consumers, which makes syndicated data a valuable resource for them. Some syndicated data providers also offer information about shifting brand preferences and product usage in households, which they gather from scanner data and consumer panels.

Scanner data is used in quantitative research obtained from scanner readings of UPC codes at check-out counters. Whenever you go into your local grocery

*When designing a marketing research project, a firm like Smellswell Cologne must first specify its objectives—what it really needs to know!*

| **EXHIBIT 9.2** | Syndicated Data Providers and Some of Their Services |
|---|---|
| **ACNielsen**<br>(www.acnielsen.com) | With its *Market Measurement Services*, the company tracks the sales of consumer packaged goods, gathered at the point of sale in retail stores of all types and sizes. |
| **Information Resources Inc.**<br>(www.infores.com) | *InfoScan* store tracking provides detailed information about sales, share, distribution, pricing, and promotion across a wide variety of retail channels and accounts. |
| **J.D. Power and Associates**<br>(www.jdpower.com) | Widely known for its automotive ratings, it produces quality and customer satisfaction research for a variety of industries. |
| **Mediamark Research Inc.**<br>(www.mediamark.com) | Supplies multimedia audience research pertaining to media and marketing planning for advertised brands. |
| **National Purchase Diary Panel**<br>(www.npd.com) | Based on detailed records consumers keep about their purchases (i.e., a diary), it provides information about product movement and consumer behavior in a variety of industries. |
| **NOP World**<br>(www.nopworld.com) | The *mKids US* research study tracks mobile telephone ownership and usage, brand affinities, and entertainment habits of American youth between 12 and 19 years of age. |
| **Research and Markets**<br>(www.researchandmarkets.com) | Promotes itself as a "one-stop shop" for market research and data from most leading publishers, consultants, and analysts. |
| **Roper Center for Public Opinion Research**<br>(www.ropercenter.uconn.edu) | The *General Social Survey* is one of the nation's longest running surveys of social, cultural, and political indicators. |
| **Simmons Market Research Bureau**<br>(www.smrb.com) | Reports on the products American consumers buy, the brands they prefer, and their lifestyles, attitudes, and media preferences. |
| **Yankelovich**<br>(www.yankelovich.com) | The *MONITOR* tracks consumer attitudes, values, and lifestyles shaping the American marketplace. |

*Syndicated external secondary data is obtained from scanner data obtained from scanner readings of UPC codes at check-out counters (left) and from panel data collected from consumers that electronically record their purchases (right).*

## Adding Value **9.1**    SymphonyIRI and the Value of Information

Information Resources Inc., which in 2010 rebranded itself as SymphonyIRI, provides market research and analytical services to the consumer packaged goods, health care, and retail industries. Ninety-five percent of the *Fortune* Global 500 in the consumer packaged goods and retail industries use IRI market research to make their business decisions.[6] For its clients—which include Anheuser-Busch, ConAgra, CVS, Johnson & Johnson, and PepsiCo—SymphonyIRI collects, monitors, and manages a variety of data in some of the most active research markets in the world, including the United States and Europe.

SymphonyIRI tracks a host of data to deliver detailed findings that are designed to grow and enhance clients' operations. To identify trends in private-label sales, for instance, it collects sales data from the scanners at the checkout from almost 95,000 retail stores throughout the United States and Europe,[7] then cross-references these data with data collected from a panel of 70,000 households that SymphonyIRI has armed with personal scanners to track their household purchases.

Recently, IRI published a report tracking the increase in private-label brands (see Chapter 10) in the consumer packaged goods industry. If a grocery store chooses to offer its own brand of detergent, it must engage in competition with various branded detergents, such as Tide, Cheer, and All. In the past, private-label products often were positioned as more affordable versions of popular brands and tended to target and attract price-conscious consumers. However, according to IRI's findings, recent trends indicate private-label sales are growing across consumer segments.[8]

*IRI research on private-label bottled water provides information to bottling companies that enables them to adjust their marketing strategies to react to competitive action.*

Some interesting patterns with regard to consumer reactions to price changes have also emerged from IRI's analysis. As prices for certain staples such as chicken, peanut butter, milk, and pasta increase, consumers opt to switch to less expensive private-label offerings. This trend is especially strong for chicken, for which producers have reduced the number of coupons they offered while simultaneously increasing their prices. On the basis of these findings, the IRI data suggest that producers should identify how brand loyal and price sensitive their customers really are before they make decisions about whether to stop offering coupons or raise prices.[9] As these examples show, IRI's research delivers actionable insights that businesses throughout the world value.

*Symphony IRI provides market research and analytical services to the consumer packaged goods, health care, and retail industries.*

store, your purchases are rung up using scanner systems. The data from these purchases are likely to be acquired by leading marketing research firms, such as SymphonyIRI or ACNielsen, which use this information to help leading consumer packaged good firms (e.g., Kellogg's, Pepsi, Sara Lee) assess what is happening in the marketplace. For example, a firm can use scanner data to determine what would happen to its sales if it reduced the price of its least popular product by 10 percent in a given month by lowering the price in some markets and leaving it the same in others. Do sales increase, decrease, or stay the same?

Panel data is information collected from a group of consumers, that is, the panel, over time. The data collected from the panelists may be a record of their purchases (i.e., secondary data), or responses to a survey that the client has hired the firm to conduct (i.e., primary data). Secondary panel data may show, for example, that when Diet Pepsi is offered at a deep discount, 80 percent of Diet Coke switchers purchased Diet Pepsi. (How marketing researchers use scanner and panel data to answer specific research questions is discussed in the primary data section.) Adding Value 9.1 describes the valuable information that IRI provides to its customers.

*Marketers use data mining techniques to determine what items people buy at the same time so they can be promoted and displayed together.*

Both panel and scanner research provide firms with a comprehensive picture of what consumers are buying or not buying. The key difference between scanner research and panel research is how the data are aggregated. Scanner research typically focuses on weekly consumption of a *particular product* at a given unit of analysis (e.g., individual store, chain, region), whereas panel research focuses on the total weekly consumption by a *particular person or household.*

**Internal Secondary Data** Companies also generate a tremendous amount of internal secondary data from their day-to-day operations. One of the most valuable resources such firms have at their disposal is their rich cache of customer information and purchase history. However, it can be difficult to make sense of the millions and even billions of pieces of individual data, which are stored in large computer files called data warehouses. For this reason, firms find it necessary to use data mining techniques to extract valuable information from their databases.

## Data Mining

Data mining uses a variety of statistical analysis tools to uncover previously unknown patterns in the data or relationships among variables. Some retailers try to customize their product and service offerings to match the needs of their customers.

*U.K. grocer Tesco uses the data it collects from its loyalty card customers to develop products that appeal to different market segments.*

*The information collected from 50 million CVS ExtraCare loyalty card holders helps CVS determine which discounts to offer, where to send direct mail, and how it should alter the product mix that each store carries.*

For instance, the U.K. grocer Tesco uses its loyalty card to collect massive amounts of information about its individual customers. Every time a loyalty card member buys something, the card is scanned, capturing the purchase data. The analyzed data has enabled them to identify three income groups: upscale, middle income, and less affluent. Tesco has created products for each group, according to their preferences, and is able to target promotions to each customer according to his or her income classification. Since 2000, Tesco's market share has grown over 20 percent.[10]

Data mining can also enable a home improvement retailer such as Lowe's to learn that 25 percent of the time its customers buy a garden hose, they also purchase a sprinkler. With such information, the retailer may decide to put the garden hoses next to the sprinklers in the store. Outside the retail realm, an investment firm might use statistical techniques to group clients according to their income, age, type of securities purchased, and prior investment experience. This categorization identifies different segments, to which the firm can offer valuable packages that meet their specific needs. The firm also can tailor separate marketing programs to each of these segments. Data mining thus can be useful for a broad range of situations and organizations.

To be successful, data mining efforts are usually coupled with additional marketing research. Although Tesco's loyalty program has succeeded in helping the firm segment and target its customers, many similar programs are ineffective because the firms fail to gain enough knowledge about their customers to really garner loyalty. Many loyalty program rewards have mass market appeals that simply create short-term sales or offer benefits the customer does not want. Additional marketing research can determine what each customer really values and thus help the company attract truly loyal customers. For example, CVS uses data from its loyalty card program to be able to offer rewards that match the customer's prior purchases. For instance, if a CVS customer buys baby products, she may receive a coupon for diapers.

CVS also uses sales data to study how customers shop. The combination of sales data and loyalty card information lets the retailer identify its high-value customers, as well as the specific kinds of products that the most unprofitable customers purchase. Since CVS first created its ExtraCare loyalty card, more than 50 million customers have signed up for the program.[11] These 50 million informants help the

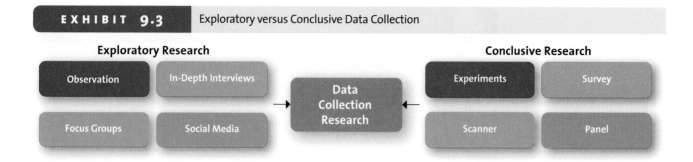

**EXHIBIT 9.3**    Exploratory versus Conclusive Data Collection

drugstore chain determine which discounts to offer, where to send direct mail, and how it should alter the product mix that each store carries. It has learned, for example, that the average cardholder shops at CVS 11 times per year, but the top 30 percent of its shoppers visit a store 27 times per year.[12] By identifying common characteristics of frequent shoppers, CVS can ensure that it meets their needs effectively and target similar consumers with its advertising.

Finally, firms can use secondary data to assess the profitability of their customers by determining the customer lifetime value (CLV). More details about calculating CLV are found in Appendix 9A.

> ## CHECK YOURSELF
> 1.  What is the difference between internal and external secondary research?

## Data Collection Techniques

In many cases, the information researchers need is available only through primary data, or data collected to address specific research needs. Depending on the nature of the research problem, the primary data collection method can employ an exploratory research method or a conclusive research method.

As its name implies, exploratory research attempts to begin to understand the phenomenon of interest; it also provides initial information that helps the researcher more clearly formulate the research objectives. Exploratory research is more informal and qualitative than conclusive research methods and includes observation, following social media sites, in-depth interviews, focus groups, and projective techniques (see Exhibit 9.3, left side).

If the firm is ready to move beyond the preliminary insights gained from exploratory research, it likely is ready to engage in conclusive research, which provides the information needed to confirm those insights and which managers can use to pursue appropriate courses of action. For marketing researchers, because it is often quantitative in nature, conclusive research offers a means to confirm implicit hunches through surveys, formal studies such as specific experiments, scanner and panel data, or some combination of these. (See Exhibit 9.3, right side.) In the case of conclusive research, it also enables the researcher to test his or her predictions.

We now examine each of these primary data collection techniques starting with the exploratory and ending with the conclusive.

**Observation** Observation entails examining purchase and consumption behaviors through personal or video camera scrutiny. For example, researchers might observe customers while they shop or when they go about their daily lives, during which processes they use a variety of products. Observation can last for a very brief period of time (e.g., two hours watching teenagers shop for clothing in the

**LO4** Describe the various primary data collection techniques.

## Ethical and Societal Dilemma 9.1 Watching Consumers

How does sitting in a mall or standing in a store checking out the people in the corner add up to bona fide market research? Well, for Paco Underhill and his company Envirosell, that's just another day on the job.

Envirosell's wide-ranging projects encompass firms in a broad variety of industries. According to its mission statement, Envirosell focuses "on how people, products and spaces interrelate. Our research environments, once rooted in bricks and mortar retail, now span to cover spaces as huge and chaotic as train stations and airports. We've worked in libraries, doctor offices, model homes, showrooms, and every kind of food service imaginable. Our clients are merchants, consumer goods manufacturers, banks, trade associations, not for profits, government agencies and the full spectrum of design, advertising and marketing agencies. Want us to look at something new? Cool, we'd like the challenge."[13]

For Staples, for example, Envirosell observed consumers in 12 stores, videotaping their movements through the stores for eight hours each research day, as a means to better understand how consumers actually shopped around the various departments to gather products, view signs, and interact with sales associates. Envirosell researchers also conduct interviews with shoppers. On the basis of the results of these studies, Staples rolled out a new store format that focuses on solving customer problems by combining service with self-service rather than just selling individual items. Staples associates can now provide a higher level of service in those areas that demand it, and the new store format gives customers the tools to be self-sufficient if they choose to browse on their own.

Using observational research, marketing research can identify information that would not be accessible to them through more traditional marketing research means—a respondent to a simple questionnaire or people involved in an interview probably would not be able to provide insightful information about the patterns they follow when walking through a store or a mall. But the method also extends into people's homes. For example, the Swiss sensory firm Givaudan conducted observational research with Chinese consumers to determine how they cook and consume chicken. The research team followed a volunteer, Mrs. Wu, as she shopped in the local market for the exact chicken she wanted butchered to take home. It then entered her home, observed as she cooked it (until she shooed them out of the kitchen so she could arrange the final dish), and sat with the family as they ate. The researchers noted each ingredient Mrs. Wu used, the exact methods she applied to create the meal, and even how the family disposed of the bones. (For your information, in China, it is considered perfectly acceptable to spit out bones onto the tablecloth.)

*(continued)*

mall), or it may take days or weeks (e.g., researchers live with families to observe their use of products). When consumers are unable to articulate their experiences, observation research becomes particularly useful; how else could researchers determine which educational toys babies choose to play with or confirm details of the buying process that consumers might not be able to recall accurately? Ethical and Societal Dilemma 9.1 describes observational research and raises the question, Should people be informed that they are being watched?

Social Media Social media sites are a booming source of data for marketers. Marketers believe that social media can provide valuable information that could aid them in their marketing research and strategy endeavors. These social media sites can provide insights into what consumers are saying about the firm's own products or its competitor's products. Companies are learning a lot about their customers' likes, dislikes, and preferences not only by monitoring their past purchases, but by monitoring their interactions with social network sites like Facebook. Customers appear keen to submit their opinions about their own and friends' purchases and interests to polls and blogs. Marketers are paying attention to online reviews about everything from restaurants, to running shoes, to jeans.[14]

## Ethical and Societal Dilemma 9.1

*(continued)*

As a summary of their report notes, their research confirmed that "consuming chicken in China involves an array of sensory experiences—visual, olfactory, gustatory and tactile—so profoundly different from Western experience that an understanding of chicken flavor cannot be understood without referencing Chinese culture as its source."[15]

In most cases, researchers obtain consent from the consumers they are watching and videotaping; in other cases though, they do not. The ethical dilemma for marketing researchers then centers around whether using observational techniques in which the subjects are not informed that they are being studied, like viewing customers in a mall or a retail store, violates the rule of fair treatment. Observing uninformed consumers very well may lead to important insights that would not otherwise be discovered. But do the results justify the methodology?

*Do you believe it is ethical for a firm to record the movements and activities of customers as they shop in a store? Would your opinion be different if the customers were informed that they were being watched?*

Some firms are learning to use social media in very creative ways. The market research firm Communispace actually builds branded online communities for companies, such as Kraft. When it considered the launch of its South Beach product line, Kraft hired Communispace to create a virtual community of target consumers: 150 women who wanted to lose weight and 150 "health and wellness" opinion leaders. The participants openly shared their frustrations and difficulties managing their weight, because the community environment prompted them to sense that everyone else on the site struggled with similar issues and concerns. By monitoring the community, Kraft learned that it would need to educate consumers about the South Beach Diet and would need to offer products that could address cravings throughout the day, not just at mealtimes. Six months after the line's introduction, Kraft had earned profits of $100 million.[16]

Many companies, including Ford Motor Co., PepsiCo, Coca-Cola, and Southwest Airlines, have added "heads of social media" to their management teams. These heads of social media take responsibility for scanning the Web for blogs, postings, tweets, or Facebook posts in which customers mention their experience with a brand. By staying abreast of this continuous stream of information, companies can gather the most up-to-date news about their company, products, and services, as well as their competitors. These social media searches allow companies to learn about customers' perceptions and resolve customer complaints they may never have heard about through other channels.[17]

*Although relatively expensive, in-depth interviews can reveal information that would be difficult to obtain with other methods.*

**In-Depth Interview** In an in-depth interview trained researchers ask questions, listen to and record the answers, and then pose additional questions to clarify or expand on a particular issue. For instance, in addition to simply watching teenagers shop for apparel, interviewers might stop them one at a time in the mall to ask them a few questions, such as: "We noticed that you went into and came out of Abercrombie & Fitch very quickly without buying anything. Why was that?" If the subject responds that no one had bothered to wait on her, the interviewer might ask a follow-up question like, "Oh? Has that happened to you before?" or "Do you expect sales assistance there?" The results often provide insights that help managers better understand the nature of their industry, as well as important trends and consumer preferences, which can be invaluable for developing marketing strategies.

In-depth interviews provide quite a few benefits. They can provide a historical context for the phenomenon of interest, particularly when they include industry experts or experienced consumers. They also can communicate how people really feel about a product or service at the individual level, a level that rarely emerges from other methods that use group discussions. Finally, marketers can use the results of in-depth interviews to develop surveys.

In-depth interviews, however, are relatively expensive and time consuming. One interview may cost $200 or more, depending on the length and the characteristics of the people used in the sample. For instance, if the sample requires medical doctors, the costs of getting interviews will be higher than intercepting teenagers in a mall.

*Campbell's Soup learned from focus groups that women want a nutritious soup that contains ingredients they would use if they made it from scratch. This information helped them develop their Select Harvest line.*

**Focus Group Interviews** In focus group interviews, a small group of persons (usually 8 to 12) comes together for an intensive discussion about a particular topic. Using an unstructured method of inquiry, a trained moderator guides the conversation on the basis of a predetermined general outline of the topics of interest. Researchers usually record the interactions by video- or audiotape so they can carefully comb through the interviews later (or feature them in advertisements, as Domino's did in the opening vignette) to catch any patterns of verbal or nonverbal responses. In particular, focus groups gather qualitative data about initial reactions to a new or existing product or service, opinions about different competitive offerings, or reactions to marketing stimuli, like a new ad campaign or point-of-purchase display materials.[18]

To obtain new information to help it continue its innovative success derived from its 2007 introduction of low sodium choices, Campbell's Soup conducted extensive focus groups with female shoppers who indicated they would buy ready-to-eat soups. The groups clearly revealed the women's top priorities: a nutritious soup that contained the ingredients they would use if they made soup. They wanted, for example, white meat chicken, fresh vegetables, and sea salt. In addition, these focus group participants were equally clear about what they did not want, like high fructose corn syrup, MSG, and other stuff whose names they could not even pronounce.[19] The resulting Select Harvest product line showcases the 100 percent natural, flavorful, and healthful ingredients, including vegetables and whole grains. The packaging also reflects the focus groups' preferences, using a simple, clean design that highlights the short list of ingredients. In the first year on the market, the line generated $202 million in sales.[20]

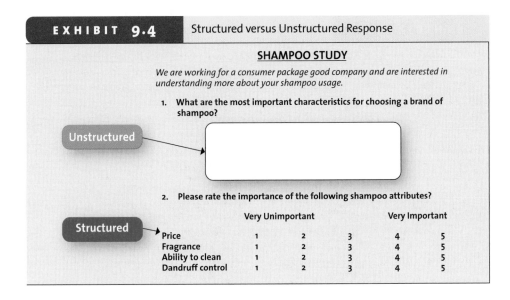

| EXHIBIT 9.4 | Structured versus Unstructured Response |

**SHAMPOO STUDY**

*We are working for a consumer package good company and are interested in understanding more about your shampoo usage.*

1. **What are the most important characteristics for choosing a brand of shampoo?**

Unstructured →

2. **Please rate the importance of the following shampoo attributes?**

|  | Very Unimportant |  |  | Very Important |  |
|---|---|---|---|---|---|
| Structured → Price | 1 | 2 | 3 | 4 | 5 |
| Fragrance | 1 | 2 | 3 | 4 | 5 |
| Ability to clean | 1 | 2 | 3 | 4 | 5 |
| Dandruff control | 1 | 2 | 3 | 4 | 5 |

## CHECK YOURSELF

1. What are the types of exploratory research?

**Survey Research** Arguably the most popular type of conclusive primary collection method, and the first we discuss (see again Exhibit 9.3), is a **survey**, which is a systematic means of collecting information from people using a questionnaire. A **questionnaire** is a form that features a set of questions designed to gather information from respondents and thereby accomplish the researchers' objectives. Individual questions on a questionnaire can be either unstructured or structured. **Unstructured questions** are open ended and allow respondents to answer in their own words. An unstructured question like "What are the most important characteristics for choosing a brand of shampoo?" yields an unstructured response. However, the same question could be posed to respondents in a structured format by providing a fixed set of response categories, like price, fragrance, ability to clean, and dandruff control, and then asking respondents to rate the importance of each. **Structured questions** thus are closed-ended questions for which a discrete set of response alternatives, or specific answers, is provided for respondents to evaluate (see Exhibit 9.4).

Developing a questionnaire is part art and part science. The questions must be carefully designed to address the specific set of research questions. Moreover, for a questionnaire to produce meaningful results, its questions cannot be misleading in any fashion (e.g., open to multiple interpretations), and they must address only one issue at a time. Furthermore, they must be worded in vocabulary that will be familiar and comfortable to those being surveyed. More specifically, the questions should be sequenced appropriately: general questions first, more specific questions next, and demographic questions at the end. Finally, the layout and appearance of the questionnaire must be professional and easy to follow, with appropriate instructions in suitable places. For some tips on what not to do when designing a questionnaire, see Exhibit 9.5.

*Survey research uses questionnaires to collect primary data. Questions can be either unstructured or structured.*

| **EXHIBIT 9.5** | What Not to Do When Designing a Questionnaire | |
|---|---|---|
| **Issue** | **Good Question** | **Bad Question** |
| Avoid questions the respondent cannot easily or accurately answer. | When was the last time you went to the grocery store? | How much money did you spend on groceries last month? |
| Avoid sensitive questions unless they are absolutely necessary. | Do you take vitamins? | Do you dye your gray hair? |
| Avoid double-barreled questions, which refer to more than one issue with only one set of responses. | 1. Do you like to shop for clothing? 2. Do you like to shop for food? | Do you like to shop for clothing and food? |
| Avoid leading questions, which steer respondents to a particular response, irrespective of their true beliefs. | Please rate how safe you believe a BMW is on a scale of 1 to 10, with 1 being not safe and 10 being very safe. | BMW is the safest car on the road, right? |
| Avoid one-sided questions that present only one side of the issue. | To what extent do you believe fast food contributes to adult obesity using a five-point scale? 1: Does not contribute, 5: Main cause | Fast food is responsible for adult obesity: Agree/Disagree |

*Source:* Adapted from A. Parasuraman, Dhruv Grewal, and R. Krishnan, *Marketing Research*, 2nd ed. (Boston: Houghton Mifflin, 2007), ch. 10.

Marketing surveys can be conducted either online or offline, but online marketing surveys offer researchers the chance to develop a database quickly with many responses, whereas offline marketing surveys provide a more direct approach that includes interactions with the target market. Web surveys have steadily grown as a percentage of all quantitative surveys. Online surveys have a lot to offer marketers with tight deadlines and smaller budgets.[21] Response rates are relatively high. Typical response rates run from 1 to 2 percent for mail and 10 to 15 percent for phone surveys. For online surveys, in contrast, the response rate can reach 30 to 35 percent, or even higher in business-to-business research. It is inexpensive. An average 20-minute phone interview can cost $30 to $40, compared with $7 to $10 for an online interview. Costs likely will continue to fall more as users become more familiar with the online survey process. Results are processed and received quickly. Reports and summaries can be developed in real time and delivered directly to managers in simple, easy-to-digest reports, complete with color, graphics, and charts. Traditional phone or mail surveys require laborious data collection, tabulation, summary, and distribution before anyone can grasp their results. The Internet can also be used to collect data other than that available from quantitative surveys. If consumers give a firm permission to market to them, the firm can collect data about their usage of its website and other Internet applications. In addition, open-ended questionnaires can be used to collect more in-depth qualitative data.

Finally, as Sony found, online surveys can be fun for consumers. After suffering sales declines in the face of the changes in the music market induced by iTunes and the like, Sony decided that to conduct effective market research, it needed "surveytainment"—attention-grabbing, hip questions and technology that feature superb graphic capabilities, clips of audio and video, and drag-and-drop rankings, as well as collaborative tools. With whiteboard application for example, panelists can create an attractive album cover for a Sony artist by rearranging and altering provided images. Although this feedback is certainly more complex than a simple survey, it also enables panelists to describe exactly what they want to see and suggest the images they maintain for certain artists or brands.[22]

Going back to our hypothetical McDonald's Scenario 1, no company can ask every customer their opinions or observe every customer, so the researchers involved must choose a group of customers who represent the customers of interest, or a sample, and then generalize their opinions to describe all customers with the same characteristics. They may choose the sample participants at random so as to represent the entire customer market. Or they may choose to select the sample on the basis of some characteristic, such as whether they have children, so they can research the experience associated with buying a Happy Meal.

Marketing researchers use scales to measure certain concepts using different types of questions. In our hypothetical McDonald's scenario, assume the research team has developed a questionnaire (see Exhibit 9.6), using a few different types of measures. Section A measures the customer's experience in McDonald's, Section

| **EXHIBIT 9.6** | A Hypothetical Fast-Food Survey |
|---|---|

Please take a few minutes to tell us about your experience at McDonald's and Wendy's. For each question, please respond by checking the box that applies or writing your response in the space provided.

**Please Evaluate Your Experience at McDonald's**

| A. McDonald's | Strongly Disagree 1 | Disagree 2 | Neither Agree or Disagree 3 | Agree 4 | Strongly Agree 5 |
|---|---|---|---|---|---|
| McDonald's food tastes good | ❑ | ❑ | ❑ | ☑ | ❑ |
| McDonald's is clean | ❑ | ❑ | ❑ | ☑ | ❑ |
| McDonald's has low prices | ❑ | ❑ | ❑ | ☑ | ❑ |

| B. Wendy's | Strongly Disagree 1 | Disagree 2 | Neither Agree or Disagree 3 | Agree 4 | Strongly Agree 5 |
|---|---|---|---|---|---|
| Wendy's food tastes good | ❑ | ❑ | ❑ | ☑ | ❑ |
| Wendy's is clean | ❑ | ❑ | ❑ | ☑ | ❑ |
| Wendy's has low prices | ❑ | ❑ | ❑ | ☑ | ❑ |

**C. McDonald's**

| | Never | 1-2 times | 3-4 times | More than 5 times |
|---|---|---|---|---|
| In the last month, how many times have you been to McDonald's? | ❑ | ❑ | ❑ | ☑ |
| On average, how much do you spend each visit at McDonald's? | $ _____ | | | |
| What is your favorite item at McDonald's? | _____ | | | |

**D. Please Tell Us about Yourself**

| | under 16 | 17-24 | 25-35 | 36+ |
|---|---|---|---|---|
| What is your age? | ❑ | ❑ | ❑ | ❑ |
| What is your Gender? | Male ❑ | Female ❑ | | |

B measures the customer's experience in Wendy's, Section C measures the customer's habits at McDonald's, and Section D measures customer demographics.[23]

Furthermore, suppose the research team administered the survey to 1,000 customers. The results of the first question, "McDonald's food tastes good," were as follows:

| 1 | 2 | 3 | 4 | 5 |
|---|---|---|---|---|
| **Strongly Disagree** | **Disagree** | **Neither Agree nor Disagree** | **Agree** | **Strongly Agree** |
| N = 50 | N = 50 | N = 100 | N = 300 | N = 500 |

Their responses are indicated by "N = ." Marketers could report several metrics. But two common metrics would be that 80 percent [(300 + 500)/1000] of respondents had high satisfaction since they responded to "agree" or "strongly agree." It could also be reported that satisfaction was high because the mean was 4.15 [(50 × 1 + 50 × 2 + 100 × 3 + 300 × 4 + 500 × 5)/1000] on the five-point scale.

### Panel & Scanner-Based Research

As discussed previously, panel and scanner research can be either secondary or primary. Walmart's Asda subsidiary in the United Kingdom uses an 18,000-customer panel they call "Pulse of the Nation" to help them determine the products to carry. Asda sends e-mails to each participant with product images and descriptions of potential new products. The customers' responses indicate whether they think the product should be carried in the stores. As a thank-you for participating, those customers who respond are automatically entered in a drawing for free prizes.[24]

In the next section we discuss an example of how scanner data is used in experimental research.

### Experimental Research

Experimental research (experiment) is a type of conclusive and quantitative research that systematically manipulates one or more variables to determine which variables have a causal effect on another variable. For example, in Scenario 1, the hypothetical McDonald's research team was trying to determine the most profitable price for a new menu combo item (hamburger, fries, and drink). Assume that the fixed cost of developing the item is $300,000 and the variable cost, which is primarily composed of the cost of the food itself, is $2.00. McDonald's puts the item on the menu at four different prices in four different markets. (See Exhibit 9.7.) In general, the more expensive the item, the less it will sell. But by running this experiment, the restaurant chain determines that the most profitable item is the second least expensive item ($5.00). These findings suggest some people may have believed the most expensive item ($7.00) was too expensive, so they refused to buy it. The least expensive item ($4.00) sold fairly well, but

| EXHIBIT 9.7 | | Hypothetical Pricing Experiment for McDonald's | | | |
|---|---|---|---|---|---|
| | **1** | **2** | **3** | **4** | **5** |
| **Market** | **Unit Price** | **Market Demand at Price (in Units)** | **Total Revenue (Col. 1 × Col. 2)** | **Total Cost of Units Sold ($300,000 Fixed Cost 1 $2.00 Variable Cost)** | **Total Profits (Col. 3 / Col. 4)** |
| 1 | $4 | 200,000 | $800,000 | 700,000 | $100,000 |
| 2 | 5 | 150,000 | $750,000 | 600,000 | $150,000 |
| 3 | 6 | 100,000 | $600,000 | 500,000 | $100,000 |
| 4 | 7 | 50,000 | $350,000 | 400,000 | ($50,000) |

*Using an experiment, McDonald's would "test" the price of new menu items to determine which is the most profitable.*

McDonald's did not make as much money on each item sold. In this experiment, the changes in price likely caused the changes in quantities sold and therefore affected the restaurant's profitability.

Regardless of how it gets done though, collecting data can be an expensive process for smaller businesses working on a shoestring budget. Tips for conducting marketing research on a shoestring budget are provided in Adding Value 9.2.

Now that we have discussed the various secondary and primary data collection methods, we can see that both primary data and secondary data have certain inherent advantages and disadvantages. For a summary of the advantages and disadvantages of each type of research, see Exhibit 9.8.

| **EXHIBIT 9.8** | Advantages and Disadvantages of Secondary and Primary Data | | |
|---|---|---|---|
| **Type** | **Examples** | **Advantages** | **Disadvantages** |
| **Secondary Research** | ❏ Census data<br>❏ Sales invoices<br>❏ Internet information<br>❏ Books<br>❏ Journal articles<br>❏ Syndicated data | ❏ Saves time in collecting data because they are readily available<br>❏ Free or inexpensive (except for syndicated data) | ❏ May not be precisely relevant to information needs<br>❏ Information may not be timely<br>❏ Sources may not be original, and therefore usefulness is an issue<br>❏ Methodologies for collecting data may not be appropriate<br>❏ Data sources may be biased |
| **Primary Research** | ❏ Observed consumer behavior<br>❏ Focus group interviews<br>❏ Surveys<br>❏ Experiments | ❏ Specific to the immediate data needs and topic at hand<br>❏ Offers behavioral insights generally not available from secondary research | ❏ Costly<br>❏ Time consuming<br>❏ Requires more sophisticated training and experience to design study and collect data |

## Adding Value 9.2    Marketing Research on a Shoestring Budget

Imagine your company needs some research conducted but has a relatively small budget. Fortunately, marketing research does not have to have a high price tag, though it always takes drive and knowledge. Here are some ways to uncover the information you and your company might need without breaking the bank.

*Objective: What is it that you need to know?*

■ **Network.** Use your phone directory on your cell phone and call friends and professional colleagues. In most cases, researchers probably already know people in the industry who will be able to share their knowledge. They can help marketers determine what their objectives should be in upcoming research projects.

*Customer Analysis: Who are your customers, and what do they want?*

■ **Customers.** Talk with current and prospective customers. Ask them the right questions, and they will provide the necessary answers. This approach is remarkably cheap because it entails only the researcher's labor, though it will require a large time commitment.

■ **Online.** Use a search engine like Google by simply typing in some appropriate keywords.

■ **U.S. Census Bureau.** The U.S. Census Bureau is an important source of information. At www.census.gov, industry, demographic, and economic reports are all accessible for free. Although not known for its ease of use, the Web site offers a wealth of information.

*Competitive Analysis: What are your competitors doing?*

■ **Websites.** Visit competitors' websites, if they have them. Learn about their products and services, pricing, management team, and philosophies. Read their press releases. You can even infer what part of the business is thriving through reading their career pages.

■ **SEC Filings.** If competitors are public, they are required to file 10K forms annually with the Securities Exchange Commission (SEC). These SEC filings often provide sales and expense numbers, in addition to other important information in the footnotes.

■ **Go There.** If competitors are smaller mom-and-pop stores, visit them. Hang out in front of the store armed with a pad and paper and count the number of people who walk in, then the percentage of people that walk out having purchased something. Use logic and judgment. Have the customers purchased items that appear to have higher profit margins? Find out where and what competitors are advertising.

■ **NAICS Codes.** For a wider view of the competitive industry, review the North American Industry Classification System (NAICS) codes. The NAICS identifies companies operating in an industry sector with a six digit code. The government's website at www.census.gov/epcd/www/naics.html helps pinpoint the correct NAICS code and can generate an industry-specific report.

*Focus Groups, Surveys, and Analyst Reports: What detailed information can you gather?*

■ **Be Specific.** Determine precisely what information is required. It is very costly to pay for research that does not assist in a decision or provide strategic direction.

■ **Surveys.** Determine what form will provide the most value. Phone surveys cost about $40 per interview, mailings average from $5,000 to $15,000 for 200 responses, and e-mail or Web-based surveys usually are much cheaper.

■ **Focus Groups.** Although focus groups can be more expensive, there are ways to cut corners. Develop the questions in-house, and don't outsource the moderator or facility. It is important, however, to find the right participants.

■ **Analyst Reports.** Prewritten reports, covering a broad price range and a wide variety of questions, are available for purchase from the hundreds of companies that write and sell reports. Two of the best known are found at www.forrester.com and www.hoovers.com.

---

### CHECK YOURSELF

1. What are the types of conclusive research?
2. What are the advantages and disadvantages of primary and secondary research?

---

## MARKETING RESEARCH PROCESS STEP 4: ANALYZING DATA AND DEVELOPING INSIGHTS

The next step in the marketing research process—analyzing and interpreting the data—should be both thorough and methodical. To generate meaningful information, researchers analyze and make use of the collected data. In this context, data can be defined as raw numbers or other factual information that, on their own, have limited value to marketers. However, when the data are interpreted, they become information, which results from organizing, analyzing, and interpreting data and putting the data into a form that is useful to marketing decision makers. For example, a check-out scanner in the grocery store collects sales data about individual consumer purchases. Not until those data are categorized and examined do they provide information about which products and services were purchased together or how an in-store promotional activity translated into sales.

For example, in our hypothetical cologne benchmarking example, the firm learns from secondary data sources that it is priced lower than its competition, spends more money on traditional advertising in fashion magazines, and is slowly losing market share to a new upstart competitor. Putting these disparate data points together provides information that indicates the need to find out what is so good about the competitor's new cologne. It commissions a series of focus groups, which is useful in developing a survey of users of its cologne and of its competitor. The survey provides conclusive information it uses to change its strategy. In particular, it found out that the scent was a little too strong and wasn't as appealing to its younger target market. It also found out that peers have a tremendous influence on scent preferences. So it decided to tone down the scent and reapportion its promotional budget to include more innovative social media initiatives through Twitter, Facebook, and YouTube. Data analysis might be as simple as calculating the average purchases of different customer segments or as complex as forecasting sales by market segment using elaborate statistical techniques.

Continuing the McDonald's example in scenario 1, the results of the survey found in Exhibit 9.6 are summarized in Exhibit 9.9. They indicate that McDonald's and Wendy's scored the same on the cleanliness of the restaurant, but McDonald's had lower prices, while Wendy's food tasted better. McDonald's may want to improve the taste of their food in order to better compete with Wendy's.

Cablecom, Switzerland's largest cable operator, has begun increasing the sophistication of its marketing research analyses. It serves over a million customers in 10 countries offering them a variety of services.[25] Much of its growth stems from its efforts to satisfy current customers and attract new ones. As the company continued to grow, it quickly learned that it was much easier to retain customers than to try to win them back. Thus, Cablecom turned to rigorous marketing research to understand why and when customers cancel their service. By analyzing the enormous amount of information that it possesses about its customers, Cablecom has developed statistical models that help identify when a customer is dissatisfied with his or her service. Once the company identifies an unhappy customer, it can follow up and proactively address that customer's issues. By mining customer data and information, the company also reduced its churn levels from 19 percent to 2 percent. Churn is the number of participants who discontinue their use of a service divided by the average number of total participants. With these changes, the company can

---

**EXHIBIT 9.9**     Survey Results for McDonald's and Wendy's

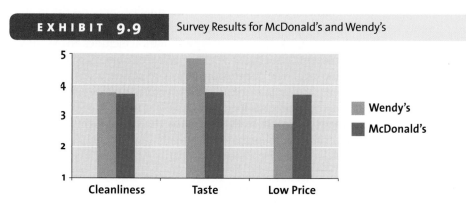

---

As one of the largest casino operators in the world, Harrah's Entertainment runs more than 50 casinos in 13 states and five countries under a variety of brand names, including Caesar's Palace, Horseshoe, and Harrah's. Its facilities typically include hotel and convention space, restaurants, and entertainment facilities.[26] But the company runs another type of facility as well, one that few gamers likely would find as entertaining: It collects a vast amount of data about its millions of customers' preferences and gaming activities. Specifically, Harrah's tracks thousands of details about each visitor, from how much they gamble on each visit to whether they like NASCAR racing.

When Harrah's assigned managers to analyze the data, it found what it considered some surprising information. Conventional wisdom in the gambling industry states that "high rollers" are the most important customers, whereas Harrah's found that the most profitable customers were average, middle-aged working people who gambled only $100–$500 per trip but also visited several times per year.[27]

Next, Harrah's studied these most profitable visitors and found that they were not interested in typical casino incentives, such as free rooms or meals. Instead, what these loyal customers wanted was better service. From this research, Harrah's created their Total Rewards loyalty card program, which classifies four tiers of players—Gold, Platinum, Diamond, and Seven Stars—according to their playing level. Each segment also consists of approximately 90 different groups, based on geography, demographics, psychographics, and usage patterns.

In the Total Rewards program, customers can earn reward credits toward future vacations, sporting events, and merchandise. They also get more of what they want,

namely, better service through shorter waits in line. While competing casino operators are trying to lure customers by adding amenities like luxury spas, upscale shopping centers, and fabulous shows, Harrah's is garnering a very loyal following by catering to those who prefer to drop by for an hour after work to play the slots. Total Gold customers must stand in regular lines at the reception desk and restaurants, whereas Total Platinum customers are directed to shorter lines, and the ultra-privileged Total Diamond customers bypass most lines altogether. The company has also made sure that its entire four-tier promotion remained very conspicuous, which makes customers more interested in rising to the higher tiers. Harrah's use of marketing research thus, in an unavoidable pun, has really paid off big![28]

*Harrah's uses marketing research to provide its distinct customer segments with the services they want.*

---

focus on what it does best, namely, delivering telecommunication service to homes.[29] The purpose of converting data to information is to describe, explain, predict, and/or evaluate a particular situation, as Harrah's does in Superior Service 9.1.

## MARKETING RESEARCH PROCESS STEP 5: ACTION PLAN AND IMPLEMENTATION

In the final phase in the marketing research process, the analyst prepares the results and presents them to the appropriate decision makers, who undertake appropriate marketing strategies. A typical marketing research presentation includes an executive summary, the body of the report (which discusses the research objectives, methodology used, and detailed findings), the conclusions, the limitations, and appropriate supplemental tables, figures, and appendixes. To be effective, a written report must be short, interesting, methodical, precise, lucid, and free of errors.[30] Furthermore, the reports should use a style appropriate to the audience, devoid of technical jargon, and include recommendations that managers can actually implement.

Let's go back to the McDonald's hypothetical scenario. According to the research findings, they are doing fine in terms of cleanliness (as good as their competitors), they are perceived to have lower prices, and the taste of their food could be improved.

*Westin Hotels used research to develop its "Renewal Menu" that includes a smoothie to counteract the effects of jet lag, oatmeal cookies, and warm milk to prevent insomnia.*

Based on the analysis and insights gained, McDonald's could hire gourmet chiefs to work with them to improve their menu and offerings. They would also want to highlight these additional offerings in their advertisements and promotions by pointing out how they were designed by gourmet chiefs. They should also consider doing additional pricing research to determine whether their lower prices are positively impacting sales and profits, or whether they should price more competitively with Wendy's.

Now let's look at an example of research conducted by Loews Hotels. They wanted to update their room service menu to match the quality of its high-class spas, high thread count sheets and towels, and knowledgeable concierges. To make changes to the menu, they needed to discover which customers bought room service, if they liked it, and what they would prefer to find on the menu (or, if they did not order, what might prompt them to). According to a marketing research survey, guests who travel 10–15 days per month are those most likely to order room service. These guests hope to fulfill their cravings but also want healthy, tasty items. Instead, they encountered late-night menus that offer unhealthy choices that few people would ever want to eat after midnight. Based on the analysis and insights gained, Loews Hotels updated its menu and its minibars to eliminate artificial transfats from its offerings. Similarly, Westin Hotels moved to a "Renewal Menu" that includes a smoothie to counteract the effects of jet lag, oatmeal cookies, and warm milk to prevent insomnia. It also offers a "Havana treat plate" with bananas, rice, applesauce, and toast for travelers. But the menu was not the only problem. The marketing research also revealed that their hotel guests were not happy with delivery times, prices, and the associated charges. Many Loews hotels also did not have a legitimate chef on staff during late night hours, but instead relied on less skilled employees to whip up basic food items. Through their research, Loews has come to recognize their failure to meet the needs of their room service customers. As Loews improves its service, travelers that stay in hotels nearly half of every month probably will come to value its room service and continue to select Loews based on these criteria.[31]

## CHECK YOURSELF

1. What are the steps in the marketing research process?
2. What is the difference between data and information?

**L05**   Examine the circumstances under which collecting information on consumers is ethical.

# THE ETHICS OF USING CUSTOMER INFORMATION

As we noted in Chapter 3, upholding strong business ethics requires more than a token nod to ethics in the mission statement. A strong ethical orientation must be an integral part of a firm's marketing strategy and decision making. In Chapter 3, we discussed how marketers have a duty to understand and address the concerns of the various stakeholders in the firm.

It is extremely important for marketers to adhere to ethical practices when conducting marketing research. The American Marketing Association, for example, provides three guidelines for conducting marketing research: (1) It prohibits selling or fundraising under the guise of conducting research; (2) it supports maintaining research integrity by avoiding misrepresentation or the omission of pertinent research data; and (3) it encourages the fair treatment of clients and suppliers.[32] Numerous codes of conduct written by various marketing research societies all reinforce the duty of researchers to respect the rights of the subjects in the course of their research. The bottom line: Marketing research should be used only to produce unbiased, factual information.

As technology continues to advance rapidly, especially in terms of a firm's ability to link data sets and build enormous databases that contain information on millions of customers, marketing researchers must be careful to not abuse their ability to access these data, which can be very sensitive. Recent security breaches at some of the United States' largest retailers, banks, credit-reporting services, and peer-to-peer networks have shown just how easily this stored data can be abused.[33] From charitable giving to medical records to Internet tracking, consumers are more anxious than ever about preserving their fundamental right to privacy.

More and more, consumers want to be assured that they have control over the information that has been collected about them through various means, such as a website or product registration or rebate form. Consumers' anxiety has become so intense that the U.S. government has promulgated various regulations, such as the "junk fax prevention act" and "Do Not Call" and "Do Not Email" lists, to give citizens control over who contacts them.[34] When conducting marketing research, researchers must assure respondents that the information they provide will be treated as confidential and used solely for the purpose of research. Without such assurances, consumers will be reluctant to either provide honest responses to marketing research inquiries or even agree to participate in the first place.

Many firms voluntarily notify their customers that any information provided to them will be kept confidential and not given or sold to any other firm. Several organizations, including the Center for Democracy & Technology (CDT) and the Electronic Privacy Information Center (EPIC), have emerged as watchdogs over data mining of consumer information. In addition, national and state governments in the United States play a big part in protecting privacy. In addition to the "Do Not Call" and "Do Not Email" initiatives, companies now are required to disclose their privacy practices to customers on an annual basis. Therefore, marketers must adhere to legislative and company policies, as well as respect consumers' desires for privacy.[35]

## CHECK YOURSELF

1. Under what circumstances is it ethical to use consumer information in marketing research?

## Summing Up

**L01** **Identify the five steps in the marketing research process.**

The first step is to define objectives and research needs, which sounds so simple that managers often gloss over it. But this step is crucial to the success of any research project because, quite basically, the research must answer those questions that are important for making decisions. In the second step, designing the research project, researchers identify the type of data that is needed, whether primary or secondary, on the basis of the objectives of the project from Step 1, and then determine the type of research that enables them to collect those data. The third step involves deciding on the data collection process and collecting the data. The process usually starts with exploratory research methods such as observation, in-depth interviews, or focus groups. The information gleaned from the exploratory research is then used in conclusive research, which may include a survey, an experiment, or the use of scanner and panel data. The fourth step is to analyze and interpret the data and develop insights. The fifth and final step is to develop an action plan and implementation. Although these steps appear to progress linearly, researchers often work backward and forward throughout the process as they learn at each step.

**L02** **Summarize the differences between secondary data and primary data.**

Compared with primary research, secondary research is quicker, easier, and, except for syndicated data, less expensive. The ability to use secondary data also requires less methodological expertise. However, since secondary research is collected for reasons other than those pertaining to the specific problem at hand, the information may be dated, biased, or simply not specific enough to answer the research questions. Primary research, in contrast, can be designed to answer very specific questions, but it also can be expensive and time-consuming.

**L03** **Describe the various external and internal secondary data sources.**

External secondary data are pieces of information that have been collected from other sources, such as the U.S. Census, the Internet, books, articles, trade associations, or syndicated data services. Internal secondary data are derived from internal company records such as sales, customer lists, and other company reports.

**L04** **Describe the various primary data collection techniques.**

Primary data are collected to address specific research needs. Techniques used for exploratory research include observation, social media, in-depth interviews, and focus groups. Techniques used for conclusive research include surveys (both offline and online), scanner, panel, and experiments.

**L05** **Examine the circumstances under which collecting information on consumers is ethical.**

Marketing researchers should only collect information on consumers for the sole purpose of conducting marketing research endeavors. Information should not be collected under the guise of marketing research when the intent is to sell products or fund-raise.

## Key Terms

- churn, 279
- conclusive research, 269
- data, 279
- data mining, 267
- data warehouses, 267
- experimental research, 276
- experiment, 276
- exploratory research, 269
- external secondary data, 263
- focus group interview, 272
- in-depth interview, 272
- information, 279
- internal secondary data, 267
- marketing research, 260
- observation, 269
- panel data, 267
- primary data, 263
- questionnaire, 273
- sample, 275
- scanner data, 264
- secondary data, 263
- structured questions, 273
- survey, 273
- syndicated data, 264
- unstructured questions, 273

## Marketing Applications

1. A large department store collects data about what its customers buy and stores these data in a data warehouse. If you were the store's buyer for men's shoes, what would you want to know from the data warehouse that would help you be a more successful buyer?

2. Identify a not-for-profit organization that might use marketing research, and describe one example of a meaningful research project that it might conduct. Discuss the steps they might engage in for this project.

3. Marketing researchers do not always go through the steps in the marketing research process in sequential order. Provide an example of a research project that might not follow this sequence.

4. Apple is trying to determine if there is a significant market for its merchandise in a specific mall location where it is considering opening a store. Would it be most likely to use primary or secondary data, or a combination of the two, to answer this question?

5. A consumer package goods company (e.g., Pepsi) has just developed a new beverage. The company needs to estimate the demand for such a new product. What sources of syndicated data could it explore?

6. A bank manager notices that by the time customers get to the teller, they seem irritated and impatient. She wants to investigate the problem further, so she hires you to design a research project to figure out what is bothering the customers. They decide to do two studies:

(1) 4–6 focus groups of their customers; and (2) an online survey of 500 customers. Which study was exploratory and which was conclusive?

7. PomWonderful has developed a coffee-flavored pomegranate beverage, and it wants to determine if it should begin to market it throughout the United States. The company used two separate studies for the advertising campaign:

   - A focus group to identify the appropriate advertising message for the new beverage.

   - A survey to assess the effectiveness of the advertising campaign for the new PomWonderful beverage.

   Which study was exploratory and which was conclusive? What other studies would you recommend PomWonderful undertake?

8. Suppose your university wants to modify its course scheduling procedures to better serve students. What are some secondary sources of information that might be used to conduct research into this topic? Describe how these sources might be used. Describe a method you could use to gather primary research data about the topic. Would you recommend a specific order in obtaining each of these types of data? Explain your answer.

9. Marshall is planning to launch a new sandwich shop and is trying to decide what features and prices would interest consumers. He sends a request for a proposal to four marketing research vendors, and three respond, as described in the table below.

   Which vendor should Marshall use? Explain your rationale for picking this vendor over the others.

| Vendor A | Vendor B | Vendor C |
|---|---|---|
| The vendor that Marshall has used in the past estimates it can get the job done for $200,000 and in two months. The vendor plans to do a telephone-based survey analysis and use secondary data from the U.S. Census. | Marshall's key competitor has used this vendor, which claims that it can get the job done for $150,000 and in one month. This vendor plans to do a telephone-based survey analysis and use secondary data. During a discussion pertaining to its price and time estimates, the vendor indicates it will draw on insights it has learned from a recent report prepared for one of Marshall's competitors. | This well-known vendor has recently started to focus on the restaurant industry. It quotes a price of $180,000 and a time of one month. The vendor plans to conduct a Web-based survey analysis and use secondary data. |

## Quiz Yourself

1. Company sales invoices, Census data, and trade association statistics are examples of:
   a. primary data.
   b. data mines.
   c. secondary data.
   d. simplistic data.
   e. syndicated data.

2. Bianca's discount home furnishings store is in a strip mall. She wants to know what other businesses in the strip mall her customers visit when they come to her store. To collect information for this objective, Bianca will most likely use:
   a. door-to-door surveys.
   b. focus group interviews.
   c. observation.
   d. sales invoices.
   e. Census data.

(Answers to these two questions are provided on page 607.)

Go to www.mhhe.com/grewal3e to practice an additional 11 questions.

## Net Savvy

1. Go to the website for the marketing research company SymphonyIRI (www.symphonyiri.com). Click on "News and Events," and click on one of the recent press releases. What was the question SymphonyIRI was solving? What type of research did SymphonyIRI conduct and what insights did they develop for their clients?

2. Visit the Epinions.com website (www.epinions.com), a clearinghouse for consumer reviews about different products and services. Think of a particular business with which you are familiar, and review the ratings and comments for that business. Discuss the extent to which this site might be useful to a marketer for that company who needs to gather market research about the company and its competitors. Identify the type of research this process involves—is it secondary or primary?

## Chapter Case Study

### HOLLYWOOD: RESEARCHING A BLOCKBUSTER[36]

If you made a $150 million investment in a movie, you likely would do everything you could to make it a success, right? So would movie studios, and that's why they invest in rigorous marketing research before they ever release a new movie. Approximately one-third of the budget for studio films goes to marketing the movies, so it needs to be just right.[37] In addition, the entire moviemaking process—which spans optioning, actor selection, script acceptance, advertising, theatrical releases, home media, television rights, and library sales—can take up to three years or more. Thus, even though the process of making a movie—or at least most movies—is more art than science, some very scientific research techniques have become best practices in the movie industry.[38]

Among the most well-known uses of marketing research in Hollywood is pre-release test screenings. During these early, invitation-only viewings of a movie, audiences react to, comment on, and provide feedback about the initial cuts of a film. In most cases today, the movie studio contracts this process out to one of the firms that specialize in audience feedback, such as Nielsen NRG, a division of the Nielsen Company, which itself focuses on serving the entertainment industry.[39] The marketing research company carefully selects several audiences to reflect diverse demographic segments. That way, the movie studio has sufficient information to estimate both the earning potential of the movie among different target markets and the changes it might make to improve that potential.

Let's use a fictional example to examine the test screening process: Paramount is making a blockbuster movie about an archaeologist who successfully fights off an alien invasion of Earth but dies in the end, heroically saving the love of his life. Depending on its research budget, the marketing research company that Paramount hires might start by surveying potential viewers about their interest in action films, aliens, and the actors who play the main characters.

Conventional wisdom in the movie industry divides audiences into four main segments: men younger than 25 years, older men, women younger than 25 years, and older women. For this movie, this research suggests that the two market segments most likely to enjoy the film are men under 25 years and women under 25 years of age, so these filmgoers should be represented at test screenings. (As a rule of thumb, studios only make films that they expect will succeed with at least two segments.[40]) The research firm then must determine the level of detail it should measure, depending on its mandate from the studio. Some movie studios just want a general sense of the film's popularity so that they can allocate their advertising budgets effectively. But Paramount is betting a lot on this summer blockbuster, so it wants scene-by-scene feedback from the prescreening audiences.

At this point, the research firm has several additional choices about how to collect information during the movie. During the screening, it might engage in human observation and carefully record which scenes make the audience laugh or applaud. Alternatively, with mechanical observation, the research firm plants microphones throughout the theater to record the decibel levels of the laughter the movie provokes.[41] In our hypothetical case, let's assume the research firm opts to hand out keypads to the audience members, on which they record whether they like or dislike each scene in the movie as it appears on the screen. At the end of the screening, the research firm conducts in-depth interviews with all audience members to get a better sense of their overall impressions of the film.

How well do you know movie audiences? What do you think they said in response to our alien movie? Those familiar with the industry would likely predict, as we do in our fictional example, that the research firm will find that approximately 90 percent of the audience, and nearly 100 percent of the women, disliked the ending, in which the main character dies. After the research firm takes these results to Paramount, the movie studio likely will choose to change the ending of the film and ensure a happy ending for both the hero and his true love.

Test screenings are just one of the many methods that movie studios employ to increase the chances that they will make a blockbuster. Another area that necessarily receives a lot of attention is actor selection.

To continue the alien movie example, let's go back in time a bit and suppose that the director has yet to start filming but is trying to choose between Leonardo DiCaprio and Harrison Ford for the lead male role and Kate Winslet and Cameron Diaz for the lead female role. Some directors simply choose the actors that make them feel most comfortable, but another option is to use research from the Hollywood Stock Exchange (http://www.hsx.com). This "exchange" actually is a prediction market that HSX Research runs. Prediction markets try to harness the wisdom of crowds to predict future outcomes. In this case, HSX has created a game that enables consumers to buy and sell shares of movies and actors in a simulated stock market. According to HSX Research, the 1.6 million traders on the HSX website predict the popularity of a movie or actor months in advance with remarkable accuracy. In turn, publications like *Forbes* and *The New York Times* cite the Hollywood Stock Exchange as a key example of how firms can efficiently collect information by making market research participants think they are participating in a game. Some industry experts claim that a movie's HSX stock price is the most accurate predictor of actual box office receipts.[42]

Yet, identifying the most popular actors remains challenging because of the speed with which audiences' preferences shift. In 2009, according to a poll by Harris Interactive, the most popular male star was not Jude Law, Denzel Washington (who had ranked first for the previous three years), or Johnny Depp (though he jumped to the number two spot, up from eighth place in 2008). No, it was an 80-year-old man whose most recent role was as a cranky old Korean War veteran. But popular as he may be, Clint Eastwood probably is not going to pull off a romantic lead in the latest action flick.[43]

The moviemaking process is long and involves large amounts of money. Test screenings and prediction markets are just two of the most common methods to evaluate a movie, but as the value and cost of movies continue to increase, so will the use of marketing research.

## Questions

1. Do you think that marketing research improves movies' quality, improves the chance of making a blockbuster, or both?

2. Does it matter whether you do the research in-house or hire a marketing research firm?

3. Visit the top 15 movie stocks according to HSX (http://www.movies.hsx .com/moviestockindex.htm). Do you agree with the predictions of the Hollywood Stock Exchange? How would you use a tool like this if you were a movie producer?

4. Other than prediction markets, which marketing research techniques would you plan to use if you were investing millions of dollars in a movie?

5. What are some ways that a movie studio can test advertisements for a movie, both before the launch and after the movie appears in theaters?

# Using Secondary Data to Assess Customer Lifetime Value (CLV)

This appendix examines how secondary data from customer transactions can help determine the value of a customer over time. Specifically, **customer lifetime value** (CLV) refers to the expected financial contribution from a particular customer to the firm's profits over the course of their entire relationship.[1]

To estimate CLV, firms use past behaviors to forecast future purchases, the gross margin from these purchases, and the costs associated with servicing the customers. Some costs associated with maintaining customer relationships include communicating with customers through advertising, personal selling, or other promotional vehicles to acquire their business initially and then retain them over time.

Measures of customer lifetime value typically apply to a group or segment of customers and use available secondary data. A basic formula for CLV,[2] with the assumption that revenues and profits arrive at the start of the year, is as follows:

To implement this CLV formula, we must answer the following questions:

1.  How many years (t) can we expect to do business with a customer? The total number of years is denoted by T.

2.  What can we expect the annual profits to be from an individual customer or an average customer? These profits are based on sales minus the costs of merchandise and the costs of serving and retaining the customer.

3.  What is the retention rate, that is, the average percentage of customers who continue to purchase from the firm from one time period to another? A 90 percent retention rate means that if we have 100 customers in the first year, we will have 90 at the beginning of the second year.

4.  What is the discount rate (i)? The discount rate is based on the idea that a dollar is worth less in the future than it is today, so the company can use it to

$$CLV = \frac{\sum_{t=1}^{T}[\text{profit at } t \times \text{retention rate}^{t-1}]}{(1 + i)^{t-1}} - \text{acquisition costs}$$

adjust future profits and determine a customer's value today for the customer's purchases in the future. For example, if the discount rate is 10 percent, $100 in profits at the beginning of year 2 are worth only $90.91 (100/(1 + .1)) at the beginning of year 1.

Consider Gregory Missoni, a fairly new client of Very Clean Cleaners who switched from his other dry cleaner because Very Clean sent him $100 worth of coupons in a direct mailing.

*Very Clean Cleaners should consider a Customer's Lifetime Value to determine its service levels.*

Greg just picked up his $200 shirt from Very Clean and found that the dry cleaner had broken a brown button and replaced it with a white button. When he complained, the clerk acted as if it were no big deal. Greg explained to the clerk that it was a very expensive shirt that deserved more careful handling, then asked to speak with the manager. At this point, how important is it that the manager makes sure Greg is satisfied, so that he will continue to bring his dry cleaning to Very Clean Cleaners? To answer this question, the manager uses the following information:

- It cost Very Clean $100 to acquire Greg as a customer. Thus, the acquisition cost is $100.

- Very Clean expects Greg to remain a client for 5 years (time horizon T = 5 years).

- Very Clean expects to make a $1,000 profit each year from Greg's dry cleaning.

- On average, 10 percent of customers defect to another cleaner each year. Therefore, the expected retention rate is 90 percent.

- The discount rate is 10 percent per year (i in this illustration). For simplicity, Very Clean assumes all profits are accrued at the beginning of the year.

Applying the formula, such that CLV equals the profits from years 1–5, less the acquisition costs, we obtain:

$$\text{CLV} = \underbrace{\frac{\$1,000 \times (.90)^0}{(1 + .1)^0}}_{\textbf{Year 1}} + \underbrace{\frac{\$1,000 \times (.90)^1}{(1 + .1)^1}}_{\textbf{Year 2}} + \underbrace{\frac{\$1,000 \times (.90)^2}{(1 + .1)^2}}_{\textbf{Year 3}}$$

$$\underbrace{\frac{\$1,000 \times (.90)^3}{(1 + .1)^3}}_{\textbf{Year 4}} + \underbrace{\frac{\$1,000 \times (.90)^4}{(1 + .1)^4}}_{\textbf{Year 5}} - \$100$$

Or

$$\text{CLV} = \$1,000 + \$818.2 + \$669.4 + \$547.7 + \$448.1 - \$100 = \$3,383.40$$

Let's see how the formula works. The expected profit from Greg is $1,000 per year. Very Clean assumes profits accrue at the beginning of the year, so the profits for the first year equal $1,000; they are not affected by the retention rate or the discount rate.

However, the retention and discount rates have effects on the profits for the subsequent time periods. In the second year, the retention rate, which Very Clean determined was 90 percent (i.e., 90 percent of customers continue to do business with it) modifies profits, such that expected profits in the second year equal $1,000 × 90% = $900. Moreover, the discount rate is applied such that the profits received in the second year are worth less than if they had been received in the first year. Therefore, the $900 received at the beginning of the second year must be divided by 1.1, which is equivalent to $818.20.

Using similar calculations for the third year, the expected profits adjusted for retention are $1,000 × .9 × .9 = $810. The discount rate then reduces the profit to $810 ÷ $1.1^2$ = $669.40 in today's dollars. (Note that the discount rate is squared because it refers to two years in the future.) After calculating the adjusted and discounted profits for the fourth and fifth years in similar fashion, we realize the sum of estimated discounted profits for five years is $3,483.40. However, we still must subtract the $100 spent to acquire Greg, which provides a CLV of $3,383.40.

According to this analysis, it would be a good idea for the manager to take a long-term perspective when evaluating how to respond to Greg's complaint about his button. Greg cannot be viewed as a $2.50 customer, as he would be if Very Clean determined his value based on the cost of laundering his shirt, nor should he be viewed as a $200 customer, based on the cost of the shirt. He actually is worth a lot more than that.

For illustrative purposes, we have simplified the CLV calculations in this example. We assumed that the average profits remain constant at $1,000. But firms usually expect profits to grow over time, or else grow, level off, and then perhaps decline. Retention costs, such as special promotions used to keep Greg coming back, also do not appear in our illustration, though such additional costs would reduce annual profits and CLV. Finally, we assume a five-year time horizon; the CLV obviously would differ for longer or shorter periods. For an infinite time horizon, with first period payments upfront, the formula becomes fairly simple:[3]

$$CLV = \text{profits} \times \left[ 1 + \frac{\text{retention rate}}{(\$1 + \text{discount rate} + \text{retention rate})} \right]$$

$$- \text{ acquisition costs}$$

$$= \$1,000 \times \left[ 1 + \frac{.9}{(1 + .1 - .9)} \right] - \$100$$

$$= \$1,000 \times (1 + 4.5) - \$100$$

$$= \$5,500 - \$100 = \$5,400$$

This illustration thus explains how firms can use secondary data to calculate CLV; it further demonstrates the importance of knowing a customer's lifetime value when executing marketing tactics and strategies. Several Customer Lifetime Value problems can be accessed at www.mhhe.com/grewal3e.

# VALUE CREATION

Section Four devotes three chapters to how marketing contributes to value creation. Chapter 10 and Chapter 11 explore strategies and tactics in the development and management of successful products and their brands. Although many of the concepts involved in developing and managing services are similar to those of physical brands, Chapter 12 addresses the unique challenges of the marketing of services.

# Product, Branding, and Packaging Decisions

Companies, like popular characters in sitcoms, want everyone to know their name. They spend millions of dollars for 30-second advertising spots during "event" opportunities such as the Super Bowl or the series finale of a popular show. Why exactly? Because the sheer number of views that they can earn in a 30-second spot is far more than they ever could through a series of ads in newspapers, magazines, or regular televised programming.

A popular strategy for sports-oriented apparel is to sponsor popular athletes. However, if a particular sponsored athlete were to be injured or suffer through a controversy, the cost might not have been worth the risk. Every two years, companies also can advertise during the Olympic Games, whether winter or summer. For two weeks at a time, with hundreds of hours of televised events, the Olympics offer a unique chance to get a company's name out to a global audience. With so many hours of coverage on multiple channels though, the odds of placing an ad in a coveted spot, that will be watched by a majority of the audience, can be against advertisers. One company has found a way around these risks.

To get its name and image out to the largest audience possible, Polo by Ralph Lauren dressed all the U.S. teams at the 2010 Winter Olympics and will do so at the 2012 Summer Olympics, which extends the agreement in place for the 2008 Beijing Games.[1] Not only is clothing an entire team less costly than signing one star athlete, but it also may reach a wider range of fans (including those who follow curling or the equestrian events), even while it reduces the risk of negative publicity from a single person's mistakes. Polo is betting that the blend of sports enthusiasm and patriotism will cause consumers— including the millions of international viewers who tune in to the Olympic Games, the "ultimate branding opportunity"[2]—to overcome their fear of spending and associate Olympic athletes with the Polo logo. The designs for the 2010 Winter Games included winter-themed

## LEARNING OBJECTIVES

**LO1** Describe the components of a product.

**LO2** Identify the types of consumer products.

**LO3** Explain the difference between a product mix's breadth and a product line's depth.

**LO4** Identify the advantages that brands provide firms and consumers.

**LO5** Explain the various components of brand equity.

**LO6** Determine the various types of branding strategies used by firms.

**LO7** Distinguish between brand extension and line extension.

**LO8** Indicate the advantages of a product's packaging and labeling strategy.

sweaters, caps, and parkas that the athletes wore during the opening and closing ceremonies. Consumers can purchase the very same items in department stores, online, and through Ralph Lauren boutiques. It anticipates a tenfold increase in Vancouver Olympics–themed merchandise over the rate for its Beijing apparel.[3]

Polo replaced the Canadian apparel company Roots, Ltd., that had outfitted the U.S. team for the three previous Games and was scheduled to continue through 2008. The designs it had submitted for Beijing were deemed "too informal" by the U.S. Olympic Committee (USOC). Polo entered the contest with classic, preppy styles and a well-known image and offered to dress the team for the widely viewed opening and closing ceremonies, as well as the athletes' daily interactions. The new look of the U.S. team aims to change perceptions of both the U.S. athletes and Americans in general, making them seem classier and more formal.

How much did this chance to reach an audience of billions cost the company? Specific numbers were not released, but Polo acknowledged that the Olympic sponsorship cost "less than $10 million," or the equivalent of about 90 seconds of advertising during one Super Bowl halftime.[4]

Although Polo may have gotten lucky, in that it swooped in with a viable solution when the USOC found its previous supplier's offer unsatisfactory, it had not just been sitting around with its fingers crossed. The company had locked in the position of Official Outfitter of the U.S. Open and Wimbledon tennis tournaments, which means it dresses more than just U.S. athletes. The Wimbledon agreement runs through 2010. Therefore, for the first time in Wimbledon's nearly 130-year history, a single designer will design, create, and provide the outfits for all on-court officials, including the chair and line judges and ball persons. These highly visible participants will display Polo's image multiple times during the course of the tournament.

Image, of course, is crucial, and Ian Ritchie, Chief Executive, All England Club Wimbledon, notes "Wimbledon and Polo share the same noncompromising standards and determination to maintain and embrace the values for which our two brands are famous throughout the world. The Polo brand will bring to Wimbledon the look of timeless elegance, drawing on our rich history and traditions."[5] A successful branding relationship thus demands a good match between the sponsor and the sponsee. For people who wish to emulate or be associated with Olympic athletes or Wimbledon participants there are of course plenty of opportunities to buy items in retail stores and online.

● ● ●

As a key element of a firm's marketing mix (the four Ps), product strategies are central to the creation of value for the consumer. A **product** is anything that is of value to a consumer and can be offered through a voluntary marketing exchange. In addition to *goods*, such as soft drinks, or *services*, such as a stay in a hotel, products might be *places* (e.g., Six Flags theme parks), *ideas* (e.g., "stop smoking"), *organizations* (e.g., MADD), *people* (e.g., Arnold Schwarzenegger), or *communities* (e.g.,

Facebook.com) that create value for consumers in their respective competitive marketing arenas.

This chapter begins with a discussion of the complexity and types of products. Next we examine how firms adjust their product lines to meet and respond to changing market conditions. Then we turn our attention to branding—why are brands valuable to the firm, and what are the different branding strategies firms use? We also never want to underestimate the value of a product's package and label. These elements should send a strong message from the shelf: Buy me! The final section of this chapter examines packaging and labeling issues.

# COMPLEXITY OF PRODUCTS AND TYPES OF PRODUCTS

 **L01**   Describe the components of a product.

## Complexity of Products

There is more to a product than its physical characteristics or its basic service function. Marketers involved with the development, design, and sale of products think of them in an interrelated fashion as depicted in Exhibit 10.1. At the center is the core customer value, which defines the basic problem-solving benefits that consumers are seeking. When Mars manufactures M&M's, Snickers, and other confectionary products and when Trek designs its bicycles, their core question is: What are customers looking for? With Mars, is it a sweet, great-tasting snack, or is it an energy boost? With Trek, is the bike being used for basic green transportation (a cruiser), or is it for speed and excitement (a road, hybrid, or mountain bike)?

Marketers convert core customer value into an *actual product*. Attributes such as the brand name, features/design, quality level, and packaging are considered, though the importance of these attributes varies depending on the product. The Trek Madon 6 Series, for instance, is positioned as "the most exquisitely engineered bicycle ever made."[6] It features a carbon frame that is light, stiff, and comfortable; an advanced shifting system; and other high-tech features. Not only is it beautiful to look at, but customers can choose from three different fits—pro, performance, and touring.

The associated services in Exhibit 10.1, also referred to as the augmented product, include the nonphysical aspects of the product, such as product warranties,

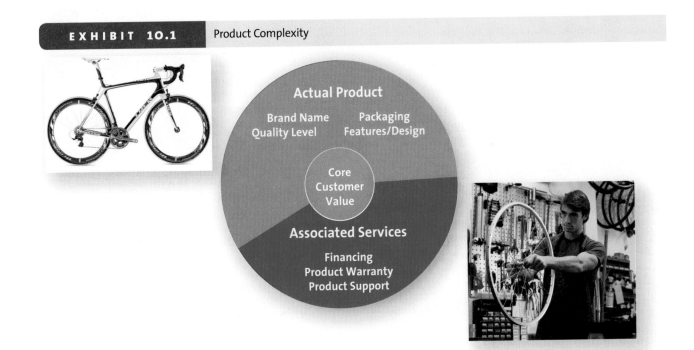

| EXHIBIT 10.1 | Product Complexity |

**Actual Product**

Brand Name          Packaging
Quality Level       Features/Design

Core
Customer
Value

**Associated Services**

Financing
Product Warranty
Product Support

financing, product support, and after-sale service. The amount of associated services varies depending on the product. The associated services for a package of M&M's may include only a customer complaint line, which means they are relatively less important than the associated services for a Trek bicycle. The frame of the Madon 6 Series bicycle is guaranteed for the lifetime of the original owner. Trek sells its bikes only to shops that have the expertise to properly service them. Every possible consumer question is answered on Trek's comprehensive website. Trek even has a financing program that allows customers to purchase a new bike on credit.

When developing or changing a product, marketers start with the core customer value to determine what their potential customers are seeking. Then they make the actual physical product and add associated services to round out the offering.

## Types of Products

Marketers consider the types of products they are designing and selling because it impacts how they promote, price, and distribute their products. There are two primary categories of products and services based on who is buying them: consumers or businesses (Chapter 6 discusses products for businesses).

**LO2**   Identify the types of consumer products.

Consumer products are products and services used by people for their personal use. Marketers further classify these products by the way they are used and purchased.

*A medical professional is a specialty service. Apparel is a shopping product. Soda is a convenience product. Insurance is an unsought service.*

**Specialty Products/Services**   Specialty products/services are products or services toward which customers show such a strong preference that they will expend considerable effort to search for the best suppliers. Road bike enthusiasts, like those interested in the Trek Madone 6 Series, will devote lots of time and effort to selecting just the right one. Other examples might include luxury cars, legal or medical professionals, or designer apparel.

**Shopping Products/Services** Shopping products/services are products or services for which consumers will spend a fair amount of time comparing alternatives, such as furniture, apparel, fragrances, appliances, and travel alternatives. When people need new sneakers, for instance, they will go from store to store shopping— trying shoes on, comparing alternatives, and chatting with salespeople.

**Convenience products/services** Convenience products/services are those products or services for which the consumer is not willing to spend any effort to evaluate prior to purchase. They are frequently purchased commodity items, usually purchased with very little thought, such as common beverages, bread, or soap.

**Unsought products/services** Unsought products/services are products consumers either do not normally think of buying or do not know about. Because of their very nature, these products require lots of marketing effort and various forms of promotion. When new-to-the-world products, like GPS systems, are first introduced, they often represent unsought products. Do you have cold hands and don't know what to do about it? You must not have heard yet of HeatMax HotHands Hand Warmers, air-activated packets that provide warmth for up to 10 hours. Do you have an internship in a less developed country and your regular insurance cannot give you the coverage you may need in the case of an emergency? You now can turn to a Medex insurance policy.

---

**CHECK YOURSELF**

1. Explain the two components of a product.
2. What are the four types of consumer products?

---

# PRODUCT MIX AND PRODUCT LINE DECISIONS

L03 Explain the difference between a product mix's breadth and a product line's depth.

The complete set of all products offered by a firm is called its product mix. For example, an abbreviated version of Kellogg's product mix appears in Exhibit 10.2. The product mix typically consists of various product lines, which are groups of associated items that consumers tend to use together or think of as part of a group of similar products. Kellogg's product lines include ready-to-eat cereal; toaster pastries and wholesome portable breakfast snacks; cookies and crackers; and natural, organic, and frozen items.

| **EXHIBIT 10.2** | Abbreviated List of Kellogg's Product Mix | | |
|---|---|---|---|
| **Product Lines** | | | |
| **Ready-to-Eat Cereal** | **Toaster Pastries and Wholesome Portable Breakfast Snacks** | **Cookies and Crackers** | **Natural, Organic, and Frozen** |
| Kellogg's Corn Flakes<br>All-Bran<br>Apple Jacks<br>Cocoa Krispies<br>Frosted Mini-Wheats<br>Mueslix<br>Kellogg's Raisin Bran<br>Froot Loops<br>Kashi<br>Special K<br>Rice Krispies | Nutri-Grain<br>Special K<br>Kashi<br>Pop-Tarts<br>Bear Naked | Cheez-It<br>Keebler Townhouse<br>Club<br>Famous Amos<br>Fudge Shoppe<br>Murray | Eggo<br>Morningstar Farms<br>Kashi |

Source: Kellogg's 2008 annual report, http://annualreport2008.kelloggcompany.com/brandportfolio.htm (accessed November 23, 2009).

*Kellogg's offers four product lines (breadth), and multiple products within each product line (depth).*

The product mix reflects the breadth and depth of the company's product lines. A firm's product mix breadth represents a count of the number of product lines offered by the firm; Kellogg's has four, as indicated by the four columns in Exhibit 10.2. Product line depth, in contrast, equals the number of products within a product line. Within Kellogg's breakfast snack product line, for example, it offers Nutri-Grain, Special K, and Kashi bars, as well as Pop-Tarts.

The decision to expand or contract product lines depends on several industry-, consumer-, and firm-level factors. Among the industry factors, firms expand the number of their product lines (breadth) when it is relatively easy to enter a specific market (entry barriers are low) and/or when there is a substantial market opportunity.[7] When firms add new lines to their product mix, they often earn significant sales and profits, as was the case with Pepsi's Max line in a number of countries.[8]

However, adding unlimited numbers of new products can have adverse consequences. Too much breadth in the product mix becomes costly to maintain, and too many brands may weaken the firm's reputation.[9] In the past several years, for example, Revlon undertook a significant restructuring. It introduced a new line, Vital Radiance, aimed at women over the age of 45 years. But this line cut into the sales of its other brands and harmed its reputation among younger consumers, so Revlon eliminated the Vital Radiance line, to refocus on those products and markets that were doing well.[10]

Why do firms change their product mix's breadth or depth?

*Pepsi has realized significant growth of sales and profits by its introduction of the Diet Pepsi Max line.*

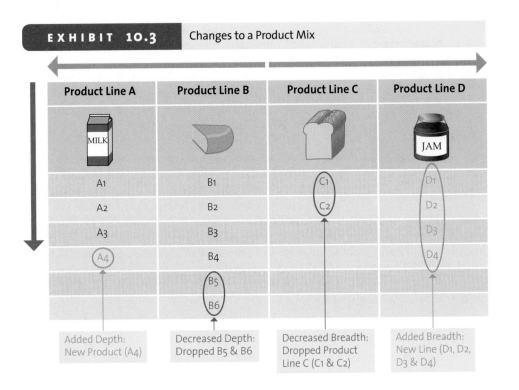

| **EXHIBIT 10.3** | Changes to a Product Mix |

| Product Line A | Product Line B | Product Line C | Product Line D |
| --- | --- | --- | --- |
| MILK | | | JAM |
| A1 | B1 | C1 | D1 |
| A2 | B2 | C2 | D2 |
| A3 | B3 | | D3 |
| A4 | B4 | | D4 |
| | B5 | | |
| | B6 | | |

Added Depth: New Product (A4)

Decreased Depth: Dropped B5 & B6

Decreased Breadth: Dropped Product Line C (C1 & C2)

Added Breadth: New Line (D1, D2, D3 & D4)

## Change Product Mix Breadth

Exhibit 10.3 offers a hypothetical example of a corporation that includes four product lines in its product mix. Firms might change their product mix breadth by either adding to or deleting entire product lines.

**Increase Breadth**  Firms often add new product lines to capture new or evolving markets and increase sales (e.g., Product line D in Exhibit 10.3). Palm, the manufacturer of handheld devices, began with the Pilot line of personal digital assistants (PDAs). The line featured several different versions of the PalmPilot that varied in the features and elements they offered. But as the market advanced, especially with the introduction of Research in Motion's BlackBerry, Palm realized the need for a mobile device that could do more than hold a calendar. It introduced various smartphones and accessories and eliminated its Pilot handheld line.[11]

**Decrease Breadth**  Sometimes it is necessary to delete entire product lines to address changing market conditions or meet internal strategic priorities (e.g., deleting product line C in Exhibit 10.3), as the Palm example shows; newer technology made the Pilot line obsolete.

In the 1980s, frozen yogurt became a low-fat, healthy substitute for ice cream. In the 1990s, the government allowed ice-cream companies to advertise "reduced fat" on their labels, prompting a sharp decline in the sales of frozen yogurt. TCBY, which began as a frozen yogurt shop, sold ice cream from 1996 to 2004 but recently reduced its breadth by eliminating ice cream to concentrate on its original product category, frozen yogurt. The chain renovated its stores and began touting the immune system and weight control benefits of eating frozen yogurt in its promotions.[12]

## Change a Product Line's Depth

As with product mix breadth, firms occasionally either add to or delete from their product line depth (see Exhibit 10.3).

*TCBY has decreased its breadth by eliminating ice cream so it can concentrate on the health benefits of yogurt.*

the Anatomy of
**TCBY Premium Yogurt**

*Johnson & Johnson's Band-Aid Brand has more than 40 SKUs.*

**Increase Depth** Firms might add items to address changing consumer preferences or preempt competitors while boosting sales (see addition of A4 in Exhibit 10.3). Johnson & Johnson's Band-Aid was introduced in 1920 with a one-size-fits-all product. Today it has more than 40 products that help to heal cuts and scrapes. Band-Aid is constantly increasing its depth by introducing new products that solve every possible wound or blister problem. One of its most recent products, called Blister Block, prevents the formation of blisters.[13] Procter & Gamble (P&G), another consumer goods giant, owns Tide detergent, probably the best known detergent brand and a product that enjoys a reputation as an innovative, high-end brand. Yet this market leader faces threats to its dominance, especially from lower priced cleaning agents. To compete P&G increased its product line depth with the introduction of Tide Basic, priced 20 percent cheaper than regular Tide. In this case, the danger of greater depth is that customers will migrate from regular Tide to the cheaper Tide Basic.[14]

**Decrease Depth** From time to time, it is also necessary to delete products within a product line to realign the firm's resources (see deletion of B5 and B6 in Exhibit 10.3). The decision is never taken lightly. Generally, substantial investments have been made to develop and manufacture the products. Yet firms often must prune their product lines to eliminate unprofitable or low margin items and refocus their marketing efforts on their more profitable items. The spice company McCormick eliminates dozens of products each year including some sauces, its Gourmet Collection pepper grinders, Golden Dipt products, and Grill Mates seasonings. The company's growth strategy focuses on introducing new products, increasing overall profit margins, and reducing the complexity of its product lines. Increased commodity costs have also forced lower margin products to be eliminated. McCormick's business-to-business sales to food manufacturers continue to have significant sales gains because these firms are prone to switch to the new, more desirable products.[15]

### CHECK YOURSELF

1. What is the difference between product line breadth and product line depth?
2. Why change product line breadth?
3. Why change product line depth?

## Product Line Decisions for Services

Many of the strategies used to make product line decisions for physical products can also be applied to services. For instance, a service provider like a bank typically offers different product lines for its business and retail (consumer) accounts.

For consumer accounts, banks offer savings and checking accounts to individual consumers. The different types of accounts thus are equivalent to different products within the various product lines (i.e., depth). Bank of America, one of the world's largest financial institutions, which serves more than 59 million customers in the United States and additional customers in 175 other countries,[16] offers a variety of checking account products to meet the needs of its different target markets. For example, with Bank of America Advantage Checking®, customers who maintain higher balances are rewarded with preferred interest and free banking services. For small-business owners who prefer to combine their personal and business accounts, it suggests the Small Business Checking Bundle. Bank of America even offers college accounts, like CampusEdge® Checking, with low opening deposits and low fees.[17]

# BRANDING

A company lives or dies based on brand awareness. Consumers cannot buy products that they don't know exist. Even if the overall brand name is familiar, it won't help sales of individual products unless consumers know what products are available under that name.

Clarins is the top-selling brand of luxury skincare products in Europe. Yet the name Clarins means nothing more than sunscreen and self-tanning products in the United States, with consumers generally unaware that skincare products are available at all. If Clarins wants to grow its market share in the United States, it must raise its brand awareness.

Selling high-end, prestige beauty products often requires a hands-on approach and customer education. Unlike European consumers, who take a long-term approach to skin care regimens, U.S. consumers tend to look for immediate results. To facilitate its name recognition, Clarins is opening treatment rooms inside department stores to offer 45-minute facials for $50, as well as encouraging consumers to partake of free 20-minute facials at cosmetic counters. A shopper that partakes in this service is far more likely to make a purchase, because of their positive experience with the brand and because of a sense of obligation to the retailer for the relatively inexpensive or free facials.[18]

Branding also provides a way for a firm to differentiate its product offerings from those of its competitors. Both Snapple and Tropicana make and sell fruit drinks, yet consumers may choose one over the other because of the associations that the brands evoke. Pioneer televisions use plasma panels manufactured by Panasonic, and yet the brand still enjoys a unique reputation, distinct and perceived by many to be better than Panasonic's.[19] As we discuss in more detail subsequently, brand names, logos, symbols, characters, slogans, jingles, and even distinctive packages constitute the various brand elements firms use,[20] which they usually choose to be easy for consumers to recognize and remember. Most consumers know the Nike swoosh and would recognize it even if the word Nike did not appear on the product or in an advertisement. Exhibit 10.4 summarizes some of these brand elements.

| EXHIBIT 10.4 | What Makes a Brand? |
|---|---|
| **Brand Element** | **Description** |
| Brand name | The spoken component of branding, it can describe the product or service/product characteristics and/or be composed of words invented or derived from colloquial or contemporary language. Examples include Comfort Inn (suggests product characteristics), Apple (no association with the product), or Zillow.com (invented term). |
| URLs (uniform resource locators) or domain names | The location of pages on the Internet, which often substitutes for the firm's name, such as Yahoo! and Amazon. |
| Logos and symbols | Logos are visual branding elements that stand for corporate names or trademarks. Symbols are logos without words. Examples include the Nike swoosh and the Mercedes star. |
| Characters | Brand symbols that could be human, animal, or animated. Examples include the Pillsbury Doughboy and the Keebler Elves. |
| Slogans | Short phrases used to describe the brand or persuade consumers about some characteristics of the brand. Examples include State Farm's "Like A Good Neighbor" and Dunkin Donuts' "America Runs On Dunkin." |
| Jingles/ Sounds | Audio messages about the brand that are composed of words or distinctive music. Examples are Intel's four-note sound signature that accompanies the "Intel Inside" slogan. |

*Source:* Adapted From Kevin Lane Keller, *Strategic Brand Management*, 3rd ed. (Upper Saddle River, NJ: Prentice Hall, 2007).

**L04**    Identify the advantages that brands provide firms and consumers.

## Value of Branding for the Customer and the Marketer

Brands add value to merchandise and services, for both consumers and sellers, beyond physical and functional characteristics or the pure act of performing the service.[21] Let's examine some ways in which brands add value for both customers and the firm.

**Brands Facilitate Purchases** Brands are often easily recognized by consumers, and because they signify a certain quality level and contain familiar attributes, brands help consumers make quick decisions, especially about their purchases.[22] Some people think cola is cola, such that one brand is not too different from another. But branding has made it easy for Pepsi drinkers to find the familiar logo on the store shelf and more likely that they simply buy one of Pepsi's other products, should they decide to switch to a diet soda or a flavored version.

The cola market is a particularly strong example of this benefit. Consumers easily recognize different carbonated beverage brands, such as Pepsi, Coke, Mountain Dew, 7-UP, and Dr Pepper. From promotions, past purchases, or information from friends and family, they recognize the offering before they even read any text on the label, and they likely possess a perception of the brand's level of quality, how it tastes, whether it is a good value, and, most important, whether they like it and want to buy it. Brands enable customers to differentiate one firm or product from another. Without branding, how could we easily tell the difference between Coca-Cola and Pepsi before tasting them?

**Brands Establish Loyalty** Over time and with continued use, consumers learn to trust certain brands. They know, for example, that they wouldn't consider switching brands and, in some cases, feel a strong affinity to certain brands. Pepsi drinkers don't drink Coke, and they would not dream of touching a Dr Pepper. As a result of this loyalty, these companies can maintain great depth in their product lines because their customers will buy other brands within their product mix. All those lines appear together in the same vending machine or in the same section of the supermarket aisle, so a loyal Pepsi drinker who wants a lemon-lime soda should turn first to Sierra Mist, rather than Coca-Cola's version, 7-UP. Companies also apply innovative techniques to strengthen brand loyalty on their Internet sites, as Power of the Internet 10.1 describes.

**Brands Protect from Competition and Price Competition** Strong brands are somewhat protected from competition from other firms and price competition. Because such brands are more established in the market and have a more loyal customer base, neither competitive pressures on price nor retail-level competition is as threatening to the firm. Lacoste is widely known for its golf shirts. Although many similar brands are available and some retailers offer their own brands, Lacoste is perceived to be of superior quality, garners a certain status among its users, and therefore can command a premium price.

**Brands Can Reduce Marketing Costs** Firms with well-known brands can spend relatively less on marketing than firms with little-known brands because the brand sells itself. People have become familiar with the color and design of the Starbucks logo on its products and stores. A loyal Starbucks customer walking down the street need not check out every coffee shop. Rather, he or she can spot the familiar color and design of the store without considering other options. Although firms like Starbucks spend marketing dollars on many types of promotional activities, they can direct their spending to the areas where they gain the most benefit. Starbucks was able to devote most of its marketing budget to introducing its new Via line of instant coffee—which accounted for the company's greatest investment in marketing to date[23]—rather than needing to explain who it is or what its brand represents.

**Brands Are Assets** For firms, brands are also assets that can be legally protected through trademarks and copyrights and thus constitute a unique form

## Power of the Internet 10.1　How Much Is an Amazon.com Customer Worth?[24]

You may be surprised how much an Amazon.com customer is really worth to the company. Apart from having a well-run Internet business, Amazon.com has always focused its strategy around its customers. The Internet retailer began as a book e-tailer and now sells most things under the sun including an array of Web services. It also allows merchants to sell goods on the Internet site.

Jeff Bezos, the company's founder and CEO, has an "obsession" with customers. The customer experience is an important competitive advantage at Amazon.com. Amazon.com figures out what their customers want and how to get it to them quickly. In one instance, a customer ordered a $500 Playstation3, intending it to be a Christmas present. When the package did not arrive, the customer realized upon tracking it that it had already been delivered and signed for, but it was nowhere to be seen. The conclusion was that it was most likely stolen. The customer told Amazon.com about this situation, and with few questions asked, the company sent the customer another Playstation3, and without charging additional shipping charges.

Not only did Amazon.com save a customer's Christmas, but that customer will probably be loyal to Amazon.com

for life. Amazon.com lost $500 plus shipping on a mistake that was not even its fault. In the end, this customer is also going to communicate such an extraordinary experience to everyone because it was truly remarkable.

Maintaining a customer-centric company means the money spent on customer service does not reach the bottom line in the short term. For example, the customer service recovery stated above cost the company a considerable amount of money, but in the long term the company is hoping to have gained a lifetime customer.

Amazon Prime program allows customers to pay an annual fee of $79 to receive unlimited two-day free shipping. The company reckons that in one year, it has over $600 million in forgone shipping revenue. Although some Wall Street analysts may frown on "unnecessary costs," Amazon has 72 million active customers, or those who have spent $184 per year on the site. The average spending per customer the previous year was $150.

What else could Amazon do to acquire and maintain loyal customers? Can you think of any online retailers that outperform Amazon on the service dimension? What do they do?

---

of ownership. Firms sometimes have to fight to keep their brands "pure"—such as the iconic blue box of Tiffany & Co, a revered gift, instantly recognizable as containing high-quality items. To support its premium prices and remain a destination for consumers looking for "the best," Tiffany must work constantly to protect its iconic image. Some of this effort now focuses on yet another iconic name: eBay. In the United States, Tiffany lost a case against eBay in which it was established that the online company does not have legal responsibility to prevent its users from selling counterfeit items. It is up to the trademark holders, like Tiffany, to monitor their sites as long as eBay and others promptly remove material when complaints are filed.[25] In a similar case in France, however, luxury manufacturer and retailer Hermes won against eBay. The Court found that eBay had "committed acts of counterfeit" and "prejudice" against Hermes by failing to monitor the authenticity of goods being sold on its website.[26]

**Brands Impact Market Value** Having well-known brands can have a direct impact on the company's bottom line. The value of a company is its overall monetary worth, comprising a vast number of assets. The value of the brand, just one of these assets, refers to the earning potential of the brand over the next 12 months.[27] The world's 10 most valuable brands for 2009 appear in Exhibit 10.5.

*Firms like Tiffany & Co. work hard to protect its brand, including its famous blue box.*

| EXHIBIT 10.5 | The World's Ten Most Valuable Brands | | |
|---|---|---|---|
| **2009 Rank** | **Brand** | **Country of Ownership** | **2009 Brand Value ($ Billions)** |
| 1 | Coca-Cola | U.S. | 68.7 |
| 2 | IBM | U.S. | 60.2 |
| 3 | Microsoft | U.S. | 56.6 |
| 4 | GE | U.S. | 47.7 |
| 5 | Nokia | Finland | 34.8 |
| 6 | McDonald's | U.S. | 32.2 |
| 7 | Google | U.S. | 31.9 |
| 8 | Toyota | Japan | 31.3 |
| 9 | Intel | U.S. | 30.6 |
| 10 | Disney | U.S. | 28.4 |

*Source:* http://www.interbrand.com/best_global_brands.aspx (accessed April 1, 2010).

**LO5** Explain the various components of brand equity.

## Brand Equity

The value of a brand translates into brand equity, or the set of assets and liabilities linked to a brand that add to or subtract from the value provided by the product or service.[28] Like the physical possessions of a firm, brands are assets a firm can build, manage, and harness over time to increase their revenue, profitability, and overall value. For example, firms spend millions of dollars on promotion, advertising, and other marketing efforts throughout a brand's life cycle. These marketing expenditures, if done carefully, can result in greater brand recognition, awareness, and consumer loyalty for the brand, which all enhance the brand's overall equity.

Ralph Lauren has mastered the art of building brand equity. The name Ralph Lauren, the ubiquitous polo player, and associated brands like Collection Purple Label, Black Label, Blue Label, Lauren, Polo Ralph Lauren, Ralph Lauren, Lauren Home, Big & Tall, RLX, Golf and Pink Pony have engendered a loyal following throughout North America and the rest of the world. Ralph Lauren merchandise can command prices 50 to 100 percent higher than similar quality merchandise from lesser known and appreciated designers and manufacturers. This reputation also encourages interest in brand licensing among other manufacturers. Under the tight control of its parent company, the Ralph Lauren brand has been licensed for bedding and bath, home décor, and home improvement products.[29] A licensed brand is one for which there is a contractual arrangement between firms, whereby one firm allows another to use its brand name, logo, symbols, and/or characters in exchange for a negotiated fee.[30] These licensed products are manufactured and distributed by firms other than Ralph Lauren, but the brand association continues to earn the company great value and brand equity.

How do we know how "good" a brand is, or how much equity it has? Experts look at four aspects of a brand to determine its equity: brand awareness, perceived value, brand associations, and brand loyalty.

**Brand Awareness** Brand awareness measures how many consumers in a market are familiar with the brand and what it stands for and have an opinion about that brand. The more aware or familiar customers are with a brand, the easier their decision-making process will be. Familiarity matters most for products that are bought without much thought, such as soap or chewing gum. However, brand awareness is also important for infrequently purchased items or items the consumer has never purchased before. If the consumer recognizes the brand, it probably has attributes that make it valuable.[31] For those who have never purchased a Toyota, the simple awareness that it exists can help facilitate a purchase.

*These brands are so strong that they have become synonymous with the product itself.*

Certain brands gain such predominance in a particular product market over time that they become synonymous with the product itself; that is, the brand name starts being used as the generic product category. Examples include Kleenex tissue, Clorox bleach, Band-Aid adhesive bandages, and Rollerblade skates. Companies must be vigilant in protecting their brand names, because if they are used so generically, over time, the brand itself can lose its trademark status.

Marketers create brand awareness through repeated exposures of the various brand elements (brand name, logo, symbol, character, packaging, or slogan) in the firm's communications to consumers through advertising, publicity, or other methods (see Chapters 17–19). Because consumer awareness is one of the most important steps in creating a strong brand, firms are willing to spend tremendous amounts of money promoting the brand, especially when they think they can reach a lot of potential consumers.

**Perceived Value** The perceived value of a brand is the relationship between a product or service's benefits and its cost. Customers usually determine the offering's value in relationship to that of its close competitors. If they believe a less expensive brand is about the same quality as a premium brand, the perceived value of that cheaper choice is high. Many private-label brands, which are brands developed by retailers rather than manufacturers, are less expensive than brands developed by manufacturers. These brands, commonly found in supermarkets, drugstores, and apparel stores, have seen a rise in popularity in recent years because of their high perceived value.

In highly competitive markets for finite consumer dollars, the perceived value of a brand also can mean the difference between life and death for a company. Consumers want a reason to buy a particular product or from a particular firm, and they often come up with reasons to support their purchase choices. One way to do so is to believe that a purchase provides benefits for society, as well as themselves. Another is to offer great prices.

Green products are ecologically safer products, such as products that are recyclable, biodegradable, more energy-efficient, and/or have better pollution controls. They may cost slightly higher than conventional products, but some customers are willing to pay more because they perceive a greater value. Tom's of Maine charges around $5.50 for its deodorant (approximately $2 more than mainstream competitors). Consumers know it contains no animal ingredients, artificial preservatives, colors, flavors, scents, or chemicals that may be harsh on not only its customers, but also the environment.[32] By developing a brand reputation that promises natural and organic materials, Tom's can charge more to consumers who prefer to express environmental responsibility in their product choices.

Because good marketing raises customers' quality perceptions relative to price, it also increases perceived value. Many customers tend to associate higher prices with higher quality, but they also have become more informed and perceptive in recent years. Retailers like Target and Kohl's specialize in providing great value. Certainly, merchandise at these stores is not always of the highest quality, and the apparel is not the most fashion-forward. But customers don't necessarily want to buy a paring knife that will last for 50 years or a wastebasket that is suitable for display in a living room, nor do they need to show up at school looking like they came from a fashion show runway. At the same time, these retailers are finding ways to make their offerings even more valuable, such as by hiring high-fashion designers to create reasonably priced lines to feature in their stores. Target pioneered this affordable, well-designed trend with Isaac Mizrahi. H&M has been very successful in hiring Stella McCartney, Karl Lagerfeld, Sonia Rykiel, Roberto Cavalli, and Jimmy Choo. Customers are able to snatch up well-designed pieces for H&M prices.[33]

**Brand Associations** Brand associations reflect the mental links that consumers make between a brand and its key product attributes, such as a logo, slogan, or famous personality. These brand associations often result from a firm's advertising and promotional efforts. For instance, Toyota's hybrid car, the Prius, is known for being economical, a good value, stylish, and good for the environment. BMW and Audi are associated with performance.

Firms also attempt to create specific associations for their brands with positive consumer emotions, such as fun, friendship, good feelings, family gatherings, and parties. State Farm Insurance uses the slogan "like a good neighbor, State Farm is there." Hallmark Cards associates its brand with helping people show they care with quality: "When you care enough to send the very best." Furthermore, the programs on Hallmark television channel are always consistent with the brand's wholesome family image.[34]

Firms sometimes even develop a personality for their brands, as if the brand were human. Brand personality refers to such a set of human characteristics associated with a brand,[35] which has symbolic or self-expressive meanings for consumers.[36] Brand personality elements could include personal issues such as gender, age, or personality and/or physical traits such as fresh, smooth, round, clean, or floral.[37] McDonald's has created a fun-loving, youth-oriented brand personality with its golden arches, brightly lit and colored restaurants, exciting and youthful packaging and advertising, and spokesperson and mascot Ronald McDonald, the clown. But in Europe, where consumers embrace a more "sit-down-to-eat" lifestyle than in the United States, McDonald's restaurants feature cafe lattes, lime-green designer chairs, and dark leather upholstery.[38]

**Brand Loyalty** Brand loyalty occurs when a consumer buys the same brand's product or service repeatedly over time rather than buy from multiple suppliers within the same category.[39] Therefore, brand loyal customers are an important source of value for firms. First, such consumers are often less sensitive to price. In return, firms sometimes reward loyal consumers through loyalty or customer relationship management (CRM) programs, such as points customers can redeem for extra discounts or free services, advance notice of sale items, and invitations to special events sponsored by the company. Second, the marketing costs of reaching loyal consumers are much lower because the firm does not have to spend money on advertising and promotion campaigns to attract these customers. Loyal consumers simply do not need persuasion or an extra push to buy the firm's brands. Third, loyal customers tend to praise the virtues of their favorite products, retailers, or services to others. This positive word of mouth reaches potential customers and reinforces the perceived value of current customers, all at no cost to the firm. Fourth, a high level of brand loyalty insulates the firm from competition because, as we noted in Chapter 2, brand loyal customers do not switch to competitors' brands, even when provided with a variety of incentives.

Millions of people worldwide use Google casually to look up information and check their facts. It is, after all, one of the ten most valuable brands (see Exhibit 10.5). In addition, it is developing a particularly loyal customer base by building a community that has purchased an Android smartphone. The members build and share customized applications and features that they consider to be cool applications. To further strengthen the community, it ran the Android Developer Challenge, offering prizes up to $10 million.[40]

A multitude of other firms, airlines, hotels, long-distance telephone providers, credit card companies, and retailers also have developed frequent buyer/user programs to reward their loyal customers. The better customer relationship management (CRM) programs attempt to maintain continuous contact with loyal customers by sending them birthday cards or having a personal sales associate contact them to inform them of special events and sales. Adding Value 10.1 illustrates just how close a brand can come to a consumer's life—if consumers will let it.

## CHECK YOURSELF

1. How do brands create value for the customer and the firm?
2. What are the components of brand equity?

---

## Adding Value **10.1**  The Brands Singles Choose to Find Them a Friend

In Seattle, natural grocery store chain Whole Foods holds a "singles" night every month, during which it offers wine tastings and snacks, as well as an opportunity for people to mingle and interact.[41] Is Whole Foods trying to turn into Match.com in the produce aisle? In reality, Whole Foods is simply expanding the brand experience for its customers, meaning that the retailer not only sells commodities but also creates communities. Human interactions within the store environment ideally turn into increased sales.

Similarly, REI, the leading outdoor equipment company, offers kayak training; PetSmart and PETCO offer dog training and classes for pet owners; and Cabela's offers classes on trout fishing and gun cleaning in stores that include stuffed game, artificial trout streams, and restaurants.

Numerous Nike stores host running groups that meet every week, after which they stop at a Niketown store for refreshments.[42] Runners can join Nike Plus, which allows them to communicate with a special website that keeps track of their running metrics on their Apple iPods. More than half of the 200,000 runners involved in Nike Plus use this feature more than four times per week. In comparison, even Starbucks' core customers frequent its stores only about 15 times per month.

By extending their brands to match customers' lifestyles and creating and showing support for their communities, companies earn more loyal customers, which turns into higher profits. For customers, in the end, the brand experience is what resonates. If they can find a friend, training partner, or even spouse who shares similar interests,

whether that be natural foods, well-trained dogs, or grueling marathons, they're likely to develop a strong affection for the company. That affection could even get passed down for generations, as couples tell their "how we met" stories to their children and grandchildren: "Well, I was in the cracker aisle, and there was your mother in the cookie aisle . . . ."

How would one of your favorite stores adapt some of these community-building techniques to build its business?

*REI offers kayak training to help build a community and its brand.*

# BRANDING STRATEGIES

Firms institute a variety of brand-related strategies to create and manage key brand assets, such as the decision to own the brands, establishing a branding policy, extending the brand name to other products and markets, cooperatively using the brand name with that of another firm, and licensing the brand to other firms.

## Brand Ownership

Brands can be owned by any firm in the supply chain, whether manufacturers, wholesalers, or retailers. There are two basic brand ownership strategies: manufacturer brands and private-label brands.

**Manufacturer Brands** Manufacturer brands, also known as national brands, are owned and managed by the manufacturer. Some famous manufacturer brands are Nike, Coca-Cola, KitchenAid, and Sony. With these brands, the manufacturer develops the merchandise, produces it to ensure consistent quality, and invests in a marketing program to establish an appealing brand image. The majority of the brands marketed in the United States are manufacturer brands, and manufacturing firms spend millions of dollars each year to promote their brands. For example, in 2009 Procter & Gamble spent $2.2 billion on U.S. advertising, more than any other company, except Verizon.[43] By owning their brands, manufacturers retain more control over their marketing strategy, are able to choose the appropriate market segments and positioning for the brand, and can build the brand and thereby create their own brand equity.

**Private-Label Brands** Private-label brands, also called store brands, house brands, or own brands, are products developed by retailers. Some manufacturers prefer to make only private-label merchandise because the costs of developing and marketing a manufacturer's brand are prohibitive. Other firms manufacture both their own national brand and merchandise for other brands or retailers. In many cases, retailers develop the design and specifications for their private-label products and then contract with manufacturers to produce those products. In other cases, national brand manufacturers work with a retailer to develop a special version of their standard merchandise offering to be sold exclusively by the retailer.

In the past, sales of private-label brands were limited. National brands had the resources to develop loyalty toward their brands through aggressive marketing. It was difficult for smaller local and regional retailers to gain the economies of scale in design, production, and promotion needed to develop well-known brands.

In recent years, as the size of retail firms has increased through growth and consolidation, more retailers have the scale economies to develop private-label merchandise and use this merchandise to establish a distinctive identity. In addition, manufacturers are more willing to accommodate the needs of retailers and develop co-brands for them. Private-label products now account for almost 20 percent of the purchases in North America and close to 30 percent in Europe.[44] Walmart has long positioned itself as a place to save money, and much of its ability to brand itself with this reputation stems from some of its strong private-label brands. Its Great Value store brand is the largest food brand, by both sales and volume, in the United States. Kroger's private label accounts for 27 percent of its sales, and Costco and Trader Joe's both have based their brand identities around their store brands. In the convenience store sector, 7-Eleven is taking the idea of store brands a step further by developing private-label versions of everything it sells, from cooking oil to beef jerky.[45]

There are four categories of private brands: premium, generic, copycat, and exclusive co-brands.

**Premium Brands** Premium brands offer the consumer a private label that is comparable to, or even superior to, a manufacturer's brand quality, sometimes with modest price savings. Examples of premium private labels include Kroger's

Private Selection, Loblaw's President's Choice (Canada), Tesco Finest (U.K.), Woolworth Select (Australia), Pick and Pay (South Africa), and Albert Heijn's AH Select (Netherlands).[46]

President's Choice is Canadian retailer Loblaw's premium private label. It competes on quality, not price. Kellogg has two scoops of raisins in its cereal, but President's Choice cereal has four and is still cheaper. The Decadent chocolate chip cookie under the President's Choice label has 39 percent chocolate chips by weight, compared with 19 percent in Chips Ahoy! In addition, it uses real butter instead of hydrogenated coconut oil and quality chocolate instead of artificial chips. The resulting product is Canada's market leader in chocolate chip cookies, despite being sold only in 20 percent of the market held by Loblaw.[47]

**Generic Brands** Generic brands target a price-sensitive segment by offering a no-frills product at a discount price. These products are used for commodities like milk and eggs in grocery stores and underwear in discount stores. However, even in these markets, the popularity and acceptance of generic products has declined. Consumers question the quality and origin of the products, and retailers have found better profit potential and the ability to build brand equity with manufacturer and store brands. For example, many fruits and vegetables sold through supermarket chains now carry either the manufacturer's brand name (Dole bananas) or the store's.

**Copycat Brands** Copycat brands imitate the manufacturer's brand in appearance and packaging, generally are perceived as lower quality, and are offered at lower prices. Copycat brands abound in drugstores. Many retailers track manufacturer's brands as they introduce new products and then modify them to meet the needs of their target customers. For instance, CVS and Walgreen's brands are placed next to the manufacturer's brands and often look like them. Both the Pepto-Bismol and CVS's generic equivalent are similarly packaged and contain pink liquid.

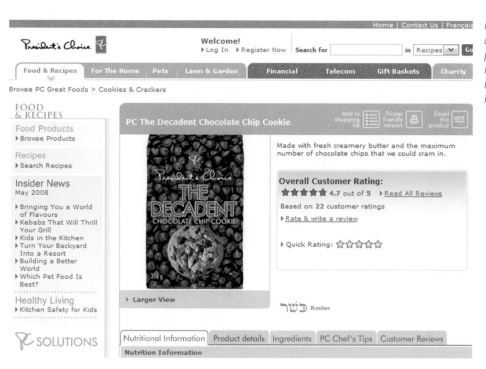

*President's Choice Decadent chocolate chip cookie is a premium private label that is Canada's market leader because of its high-quality ingredients.*

**Exclusive Co-brands** An exclusive co-brand is a brand that is developed by a national brand manufacturer, often in conjunction with a retailer, and is sold exclusively by the retailer. The simplest form of an exclusive co-brand is when a national brand manufacturer assigns different model numbers and has different exterior features for the same basic product sold by different retailers. For example, a Sony TV sold at Best Buy might have a different model number than a Sony TV with similar features available at Walmart. These exclusive models make it difficult for consumers to compare prices for virtually the same television sold by different retailers. Thus, the retailers are less likely to compete on price when selling these exclusive co-brands, their margins for the products are higher, and they are motivated to devote more resources toward selling the exclusive co-brands than they would for similar manufacturer's brands.

A more sophisticated form of exclusive co-branding is when a manufacturer develops an exclusive product or group of related products for a retailer. For example, cosmetics powerhouse Estée Lauder sells three brands of cosmetics and skin care products—American Beauty, Flirt!, and Good Skin—exclusively at Kohl's. The products are priced between mass-market brands such as Cover Girl or Maybelline (sold mainly in drugstores, discount stores, and supermarkets) and Lauder's higher-end brands, sold primarily in more fashion-forward department stores such as Macy's. Macy's is also heavily vested in exclusive co-brands with names like Martha Stewart, Donald Trump, and Tommy Hilfiger. These exclusive co-brands account for more than 16 percent of Macy's sales. Its total private-label sales account for 35 percent of sales—about $25 billion annually.[48]

Whole Foods' very successful 365 Organic brand gives customers an opportunity to buy high-quality products that are less expensive compared to other brands in the store. Examples of these and several other exclusive co-brands you might recognize are found in Exhibit 10.6.

## Naming Brands and Product Lines

Although there is no simple way to decide how to name a brand or a product line, the more the products vary in their usage or performance, the more likely it is that the firm should use individual brands. For example, General Motors utilizes several different individual brands (Cadillac, Chevrolet, GMC), each catering to

| EXHIBIT 10.6 | Exclusive Co-brands | | |
|---|---|---|---|
| **Retailer** | **Manufacturer/Designer** | **Product Category** | **Product Name** |
| **Kohl's** | Estee Lauder | Cosmetics | American Beauty, Flirt, and Good Skin |
| **Walmart** | Mary Kate and Ashley Olsen | Apparel and accessories | Mary Kate and Ashley |
| **Walmart, Best Buy**[49] | Hewlett-Packard | Computers | Hewlett-Packard |
| **Macy's**[50] | Martha Stewart | Soft Home (sheets, towels) | Martha Stewart Collection |
| **Macy's** | Jones Apparel Group (Rachel Roy) | Apparel and accessories | Rachel by Rachel Roy |
| **McDonald's** | Newman's Own Organic | Coffee | Newman's Own Organic |
| **J.C. Penney**[51] | Ralph Lauren | Home goods, apparel, and accessories | American Living |
| **J.C. Penney** | Nicole Miller | Apparel and accessories | Nicole by Nicole Miller |
| **H&M** | Jimmy Choo | Shoes and accessories | Jimmy Choo for H&M |

very different target markets and meeting different needs. Hyundai, on the other hand, utilizes only one brand since usage and level of performance are relatively homogeneous.

**Family Brands**  A firm can use its own corporate name to brand all its product lines and products, so Kellogg's incorporates the company name into the brand names of Kellogg's Rice Krispies. When all products are sold under one family brand, the individual brands benefit from the overall brand awareness associated with the family name. Kellogg's uses its family brand name prominently on its cereal brands (e.g., Kellogg's Special K, Kellogg's Froot Loops, Kellogg's Rice Krispies).

*Kellogg's uses a family branding strategy in which several product lines are sold under one name.*

**Individual Brands**  A firm can use individual brand names for each of its products. For example, while Kellogg's makes good use of the corporate branding strategy, it also allows other products, such as Morningstar Farms, Famous Amos cookies, Keebler cookies, and Cheez-Its, to keep individual identities not readily seen as being under the Kellogg's umbrella.[52]

*Kellogg's also uses an individual branding strategy since Keebler, Cheez-It, Morningstar, and Famous Amos are all marketed using separate names.*

### Brand and Line Extensions[53]

A brand extension refers to the use of the same brand name in a different product line. It is an increase in the product mix's breadth.[54] The dental hygiene market, for instance, is full of brand extensions; Colgate and Crest sell toothpaste, toothbrushes, and other dental hygiene products, even though their original product line was just toothpaste. A line extension is the use of the same brand name

**LO7** Distinguish between brand extension and line extension.

within the same product line, and represents an increase in a product line's depth. Referring back to Exhibit 10.2, Kellogg's Ready-to-Eat Cereal line contains multiple products, some carrying the Kellogg name brand.

There are several advantages to using the same brand name for new products. First, because the brand name is already well established, the firm can spend less in developing consumer brand awareness and brand associations for the new product.[55] Kellogg's has branched out from the cereal company it once was. Its strategy of branding the corporate name into the product name has allowed it to introduce new products quicker and more easily. Kellogg's Eggo Syrup was a natural extension to its product line of breakfast foods.

Second, if either the original brand or the brand extension has strong consumer acceptance, that perception will carry over to the other product. Following its success in the PC market, Dell extended its brand name to monitors, printers, handheld computers, LCD televisions, servers, and network switches, among other related technology products.[56] Similarly, consumers who have not used the Neutrogena brand before trying the brand extension Neutrogena Wave power cleanser might be encouraged to try Neutrogena's core product line of cleansers and moisturizing lotions, especially if their experience with the Wave has been positive.[57]

Third, when brand extensions are used for complementary products, a synergy exists between the two products that can increase overall sales. For example, Frito-Lay markets both chips and dips under its Frito-Lay and Doritos brand names. When people buy the chips, they tend to buy the dips as well.

The Walt Disney Company began as an animation and movie studio and has expanded its brand to include television networks (Disney, ABC, ESPN)[58] and theme parks around the world. Disney's more recent brand extensions have been spurred by market expansion into sophisticated demographic segments. Disney's line of wedding gowns, created in partnership with designer Kirstie Kelly, is inspired by the Disney characters that brides-to-be grew up with: Snow White, Belle, Sleeping Beauty, Jasmine, and Ariel.[59] Other brand Disney extensions include lighting products with the Minka Group, a fashion bath and bedding collection with Dan River, outdoor tabletops and entertaining products with Zak Designs, and furniture with Drexel Heritage.[60]

Not all brand extensions are successful, however. Some can dilute brand equity.[61] **Brand dilution** occurs when the brand extension adversely affects consumer perceptions about the attributes the core brand is believed to hold.[62] Here are some examples of unsuccessful brand extensions:[63]

- Cheetos Lip Balm was based on the idea that if you like Cheetos, you would want to wipe it all over your lips.

- Lifesavers Soda did well in prelaunch taste tests, but didn't in subsequent sales.

- Colgate Kitchen Entrees were microwavable frozen dinner entrees that shared the name with the famous toothpaste.

- Bic thought that since people wanted their disposable lighters and razors, they would also want disposable underwear. They were wrong.

*Lifesavers unsuccessfully attempted a brand extension strategy with its line of soda.*

To prevent the potentially negative consequences of brand extensions, firms consider the following:

- Marketers should evaluate the fit between the product class of the core brand and that of the extension.[64] If the fit between the product categories is high, consumers will consider the extension credible, and the brand association will be stronger for the extension. Thus, when Starbucks introduced its line of instant coffee, VIA, it made sense to its customers.

- Firms should evaluate consumer perceptions of the attributes of the core brand and seek out similar attributes for the extension because brand-specific associations are very important for extensions.[65] For example, if HP printers were associated with reliability, performance, and value, consumers would expect the same brand-specific attributes in other products that carried the HP brand name.

■ Firms should refrain from extending the brand name to too many products and product categories to avoid diluting the brand and damaging brand equity. Donald Trump has been quite successful lending his name to various property, television lines, and Macy's clothing, but was unsuccessful with extending himself to branding steaks.

■ Firms should consider whether the brand extension will be distanced from the core brand, especially if the firm wants to use some but not all of the existing brand associations. Marriott has budget hotels, mid-tier hotels, and luxury hotels. Its luxury hotels, including the Ritz-Carlton, Edition, and Renaissance, do not use the name Marriott at all.[66]

## Co-branding

Co-branding is the practice of marketing two or more brands together, on the same package, promotion, or store. Co-branding can enhance consumers' perceptions of product quality by signaling "unobservable" product quality through links between the firm's brand and a well-known quality brand. For example, Yum Brands, the largest quick service food franchisor, combines two or more of its restaurant chains into one (those being A&W, Kentucky Fried Chicken [KFC], Long John Silver's, Pizza Hut, and Taco Bell). Most typical of the co-branding approach is to pair KFC with Taco Bell or Pizza Hut with Taco Bell.[67] This co-branding strategy is designed to appeal to diverse market segments and to extend the hours in which each restaurant attracts customers. Microsoft has joined with Ford Motors to offer its Sync brand of "in-car communication and entertainment systems" in certain models under the Ford, Lincoln, and Mercury brand names (e.g., Ford Explorer, Lincoln MKZ, Mercury Sable). Commercials name all these brands in touting the new technology, and the Sync website features logos from Microsoft, Mercury, Lincoln, and Ford on the introductory page.[68] Yet co-branding also creates risks, especially when the customers of each of the brands turn out to be vastly different. For example, the Burger King and Häagen-Dazs co-branding strategy failed because the customer profiles for each brand were too different.[69] Co-branding may also fail when there are disputes or conflicts of interest between the co-brands.

## Brand Licensing

Brand licensing is a contractual arrangement between firms, whereby one firm allows another to use its brand name, logo, symbols, and/or characters in exchange for a negotiated fee.[70] Brand licensing is common for toys, apparel, accessories, and entertainment products, such as video games. In the United States and Canada, it generates more than $70 billion in retail sales per year, and $190 billion for the world.[71] The firm that provides the right to use its brand (licensor) obtains revenues through royalty payments from the firm that has obtained the right to use the brand (licensee). These royalty payments sometimes take the form of an up-front, lump-sum licensing fee or may be based on the dollar value of sales of the licensed merchandise.

Giorgio Armani, the well-known fashion designer, not only produces apparel collections, but also has developed a line of high-end electronics in conjunction with Samsung Electronics. As Armani says, "We make as much of a personal statement with mobile phones or the televisions in our living rooms as we do with the shoes and bags we wear." Other products bearing the Armani name include Armani Dolci (chocolate boutique), Armani International (housewares), and Armani Hotels in Milan and Dubai.[72] Other electronics companies have partnered with designers as well, including Prada-designed cell phone for LG Electronics.[73] EA, the video game company, has a licensing agreement with Porsche to market the game *Need for Speed: Porsche Unleashed.* If Porsche isn't luxurious enough, racing game fans can drive a virtual Maserati in *Gran Turismo 5* for the PlayStation.

One very popular form of licensing is the use of characters created in books and other media. Such entertainment licensing has generated tremendous revenues for movie studios. Disney, for instance, flooded retail stores with products based on *The Princess and the Frog* movie. *Star Wars* memorabilia has continued to be successful since the first film was released in the 1970s. A long-standing staple of licensing has been major league sports teams that play in the NBA, NFL, or NHL, as well as various collegiate sports teams.

Licensing is an effective form of attracting visibility for the brand and thereby building brand equity while also generating additional revenue. There are, however, some risks associated with it. For the licensor, the major risk is the dilution of its brand equity through overexposure of the brand, especially if the brand name and characters are used inappropriately.[74]

Consider, for instance, the famous—or possibly infamous—alligator shirt. In 1933, the company founded by Frenchman René Lacoste (the licensor), famous as a tennis player and for his nickname "the alligator," entered into a licensing agreement with André Gillier (the first licensee) to produce a high-quality white knit shirt with a ribbed collar, short sleeves, and a crocodile emblazoned on the right breast. The line expanded to include other casual apparel items, gaining increasing brand equity along the way, such that by 1966, the valuable Lacoste name was licensed to the U.S. manufacturer Izod (the second licensee). Alligator-emblazoned apparel could be found in department stores and country club pro shops into the late 1980s. But Izod also began to sell the alligator apparel in discount stores, and quality and sales suffered, along with its brand equity. Lacoste severed its ties with Izod in 1992 and has since regained its prestige image, appearing in boutiques and exclusive specialty department stores around the world.[75]

Licensing agreements may turn out to be improperly valued if either the licensor or the licensee's market value changes. Suppose a firm has the license to produce sunglasses using a famous sports car brand. If the brand becomes embroiled in a major safety recall, sunglass sales would suffer and the value of the licensing agreement would diminish. In entertainment licensing, both licensors and

*The famous tennis player René "the alligator" Lacoste (left in 1927 photo) cofounded a firm that made a white knit shirt with an alligator emblazoned on the right breast. The brand is still sold today (right) at Lacoste boutiques and stores like Neiman Marcus.*

licensees run the risk that characters based on books and movies will be only a fad. Moreover, the success or failure of merchandise based on movies is directly affected by the success or failure of the movie itself.

## Brand Repositioning

**Brand repositioning** or **rebranding** refers to a strategy in which marketers change a brand's focus to target new markets or realign the brand's core emphasis with changing market preferences.[76] Although repositioning can improve the brand's fit with its target segment or boost the vitality of old brands, it is not without costs and risks. Firms often need to spend tremendous amounts of money to make tangible changes to the product and packages, as well as intangible changes to the brand's image through advertising. These costs may not be recovered if the repositioned brand and messages are not credible to the consumer or if the firm has mistaken a fad for a long-term market trend.

Yet even when they enjoy the benefits of their well-known name and reputations, brands may find it necessary to reposition. For example, Gatorade began solely as a sports drink for professional or collegiate athletes, and then expanded its brand positioning to appeal to a broader swath of serious athletes. The ads focused on active people who gulped down Gatorade to replenish the nutrients they had lost through their strenuous, sweaty activities. Leading up to the 2009 Super Bowl though, a new campaign was initiated, mysteriously at first, asking "What's G?" The promotion, aimed at nonathletes, featured rapper Lil' Wayne, as well as casually dressed (i.e., nonsweaty) sports legends like Serena Williams, Bill Russell, and Muhammad Ali. The Super Bowl ad suggested G was whatever was most important to each athlete. None of these or subsequent ads ever mentioned Gatorade by name. PepsiCo, the corporate owner of Gatorade, hoped to create enough of a tease to force consumers to guess what was being sold or pique their curiosity enough to prompt them to search out the answer to what "G" is on their own. Although the ads designed to reposition Gatorade produced a short-term sales bump, PepsiCo abandoned the idea and has since refocused on their core customer, the sweating masses.[77]

Another example might surprise high school students: Abercrombie & Fitch (A&F), founded in 1892, was a sporting goods and outfitting store for camping, fishing, and hunting gear. Its customers were mainly professional hunters, explorers, trappers, and outdoorsmen, including Theodore Roosevelt, Amelia Earhart, Katharine Hepburn, and Howard Hughes. The 12-story corporate building on Madison Avenue and 45th Street in Manhattan had a log cabin on the roof, a casting pool for fishermen to sample rods and flies, an armored rifle range in the basement, a golf school, and a dog and cat kennel. Although these special features may seem commonplace today at stores like REI and Bass Pro Shops, they were innovative thrills during the company's sporting goods heyday, from 1907 through the early 1960s. The store carried unique exotic items such as hot air balloons, yachting pennants, portable trampolines, treadmills for exercising dogs, and other high-end toys for grownups. But by 1988, it was struggling, facing bankruptcy, and was ultimately purchased by Limited Brands, which repositioned it into a casual luxury lifestyle brand for college students.[78] The hip, controversial image the repositioned brand has achieved seems like the last place Theodore Roosevelt would have spent his time.

## CHECK YOURSELF

1. What are the differences among manufacturer and private-label brands?
2. What is co-branding?
3. What is the difference between brand extension and line extension?
4. What is brand repositioning?

**L08** Indicate the advantages of a product's packaging and labeling strategy.

# PACKAGING

Packaging is an important brand element with more tangible or physical benefits than other brand elements. Packages come in different types and offer a variety of benefits to consumers, manufacturers, and retailers. The primary package is the one the consumer uses, such as the toothpaste tube. From the primary package, consumers typically seek convenience in terms of storage, use, and consumption.

The secondary package is the wrapper or exterior carton that contains the primary package and provides the UPC label used by retail scanners. Consumers can use the secondary package to find additional product information that may not be available on the primary package. Like primary packages, secondary packages add consumer value by facilitating the convenience of carrying, using, and storing the product.

Whether primary or secondary, packaging plays several key roles: It attracts the consumers' attention. It enables products to stand out from their competitors. It offers a promotional tool (e.g., "NEW" and "IMPROVED" promises on labels). Finally, it allows for the same product to appeal to different markets with different sizes, such that convenience stores stock little packages that travelers can buy at the last minute, whereas Costco sells extra large versions of products.

Firms occasionally change or update their packaging as a subtle way of repositioning the product. A change can be used to attract a new target market and/or appear more up to date to its current market. For instance, the Morton Salt umbrella girl has significantly changed since first introduced in 1914, but the slogan "when it rains it pours" endures today. Changes also can make consumers feel that they are receiving something tangible in return for paying higher prices, even when the product itself remains untouched. Whether true or not, consumers see new packaging and tend to think that the "new" product may be worth trying. Dr Pepper Snapple Co. has retooled the packages (with a related ad campaign) for Snapple iced teas to tout its blend of "better stuff"—healthy green and tasty black tea leaves.[79]

Some packaging changes are designed to make the product more ecological, such as PepsiCo's response to concerns about the waste associated with bottled water. To reduce the amount of plastic it uses, PepsiCo has decreased the weight of its water bottles by 20 percent. The "Eco-Fina" bottle is nearly 50 percent lighter than the version introduced in 2002, which means less plastic in landfills. In a

*Snapple changed its packages for Snapple iced teas to tout its blend of "better stuff"– healthy and tasty black tea leaves.*

competitive marketplace, a brand that can associate with less harmful impact on the environment often can gain a significant competitive advantage it can use to induce consumers to purchase in good conscience.[80]

Sometimes packaging changes can backfire though, such as when Tropicana changed its packaging to feature a picture of a glass of juice, rather than the familiar straw in an orange. Customers balked, calling the new image "ugly," "stupid," and reminiscent of "a generic bargain brand."[81] The company poorly misjudged its customers' loyalty to its existing brand position, as exemplified by its packaging. For example, before the change, the president of Tropicana North America claimed, "The straw and orange have been there for a long time, but people have not necessarily had a huge connection to them." After suffering tremendous backlash and deciding to rescind its repackaging decision, the same executive admitted, "What we didn't get was the passion this very loyal small group of consumers have."[82]

Many consumers experience "wrap rage"—a great frustration with packaging that makes it seemingly impossible to get at the actual products. So companies are moving away from traditional clamshells, which are the curved plastic package around many electronics goods, because they are so difficult to open. Costco has replaced the clamshells with packaging made of coated paperboard that still requires scissors to open, but is flat and therefore can be opened easily.

Retailers' and manufacturers' priorities for secondary packaging often differ from those of their customers. They want convenience in terms of displaying and selling the product. In addition, secondary packages often get packed into larger cartons, pallets, or containers to facilitate shipment and storage from the manufacturer to the retailer. These shipping packages benefit the manufacturer and the retailer, in that they protect the shipment during transit; aid in loading, unloading, and storage; and allow cost efficiencies due to the larger order and shipment sizes.

Packaging can also be used in a far more subtle way, namely, to help suppliers save costs. For routine purchases, consumers rarely engage in actual decision making but rather just grab their familiar jar of peanut butter from the shelf. In so doing, they likely never notice that Skippy peanut butter jars have gone from containing 18 ounces to just 16.3 ounces—same appearance, same diameter and height of the jar, same price, but a bigger indent in the bottom.[83] Approximately 30 percent of packaged goods similarly have lost content recently, and most of the changes went unnoticed by consumers.

General Mills even has a department devoted to cost cutting through package redesign or clever content reduction ideas, which it calls the "Holistic Margin Management" department. Because 75 percent of a product's cost may be in the packaging, these savings can represent huge overall savings for the company.[84]

## Product Labeling

Labels on products and packages provide information the consumer needs for his or her purchase decision and consumption of the product. In that they identify the product and brand, labels are also an important element of branding and can be used for promotion. The information required on them must comply with general and industry-specific laws and regulations, including the constituents or ingredients contained in the product, where the product was made, directions for use, and/or safety precautions.

Many labeling requirements stem from various laws, including the Federal Trade Commission Act of 1914, the Fair Packaging and Labeling Act of 1967, and the Nutrition Labeling Act of 1990. Several federal agencies, industry groups, and consumer watchdogs carefully monitor product labels. The Food and Drug Administration is the primary federal agency that reviews food and package labels and ensures that the claims made by the manufacturer are true.

Ethical and Societal Dilemma 10.1 illustrates the problems associated with the different regulations that apply to the bottled water industry, as well as some associated labeling concerns.

---

### Ethical and Societal Dilemma 10.1

#### Calories: zero, Vitamins: zero. How Much Information Can Water Labels Provide?

Water, water everywhere. Especially in developed countries, consumers everywhere can simply turn on the tap, and there it is. And yet firms have been successful in packaging this almost free, natural resource, creating some cachet for it, and selling it.

Bottled water enjoyed double-digit growth, year to year, as U.S. consumers doubled the amount they drank from 1997 to 2007, from 13.4 to 29.3 gallons per year. The popularity and growth of the industry have attracted attention though. Bottled and tap water companies operate under different regulations. Yet many observers and government agencies argue the rules should be the same, with water bottle labeling subject to regulations as detailed as those that the tap water companies experience.

Bottled water, as a food product, currently is regulated by the Food and Drug Administration, so it lists nutrition information and ingredients on the labels (i.e., zero percent of most nutrients; Contents: Water). In contrast, municipal water is controlled by the Environmental Protection Agency, which has more authority to enforce quality standards. The result may be misinformed consumers, many of whom believe bottled water is safer and healthier than tap water. And yet according to the U.S. Government Accounting Office (GAO), the FDA lacks the authority to require that water bottlers use certified water quality tests or report those test results. Also, the existing requirements to ensure safe bottled water, both state and federal, are less comprehensive than the rules about safeguarding tap water.[85]

Even without such regulations though, consumers may be changing their attitudes. In 2008, the bottled water industry experienced flat growth for the first time. The cause may be the economic downturn, which has forced consumers to cut costs wherever possible. Environmental concerns may be another factor since bottled water creates significant waste.

Perhaps better labeling of products will mean even less ambiguity about the value of bottled versus tap water, which could offer opportunities for differentiation among bottled water brands that adopt different bottling and labeling methods.[86]

Would more comprehensive labels on bottled water change your water consumption behavior? Do you believe that bottled water is "better" than tap water? Do you believe that buying bottled water is an ecologically sound purchase decision?

---

A product label is much more than just a sticker on the package; it is a communication tool. Many of the elements on the label are required by laws and regulations (i.e., ingredients, fat content, sodium content, serving size, calories), but other elements remain within the control of the manufacturer. How manufacturers use labels to communicate the benefits of their products to consumers varies by the product. Many products highlight specific ingredients, vitamin content, or nutrient content (e.g., iron). This focus signals to consumers that the product offers these benefits. Although often overlooked, the importance of the label as a communication tool should not be underestimated.

## Summing Up

**L01**  **Describe the components of a product.**

The product itself is important, but so are its associated services, such as support or financing. Other elements combine to produce the core customer value of a product: the brand name, quality level, packaging, and additional features.

**L02**  **Identify the types of consumer products.**

These products tend to be classified into four groups: specialty, shopping, convenience, and unsought products. Each classification involves a different purchase situation and consumer goal.

**L03** **Explain the difference between a product mix's breadth and a product line's depth.**

Breadth, or variety, entails the number of product lines that a company offers. Depth involves the number of categories in one specific product line.

**L04** **Identify the advantages that brands provide firms and consumers.**

Brands play important roles in enabling people to make purchase decisions more easily, encouraging customer loyalty, and reducing costs (e.g., marketing). For firms specifically, they also constitute valuable assets and improve a company's bottom line and help protect against competition.

**L05** **Explain the various components of brand equity.**

Brand equity summarizes the value that a brand adds, or subtracts, from the offering's value. It comprises brand awareness, or how many consumers in the market are familiar with the brand; brand associations, which are the links consumers make between the brand and its image; and brand loyalty, which occurs when a consumer will only buy that brand's offer. Brand equity also encompasses the concept of perceived value, which is a subjective measure that consumers develop to assess the costs of obtaining the brand.

**L06** **Determine the various types of branding strategies used by firms.**

Firms use a variety of strategies to manage their brands. First, they decide whether to offer manufacturer, private-label, or generic brands. Second, they have a choice of using an overall corporate brand or a collection of product line or individual brands. Third, to reach new markets or extend their current market, they can extend their current brands to new products. Fourth, firms can co-brand with another brand to create sales and profit synergies for both. Fifth, firms with strong brands have the opportunity to license their brands to other firms. Sixth and finally, as the marketplace changes, it is often necessary to reposition a brand.

**L07** **Distinguish between brand extension and line extension.**

Whereas a brand extension uses the same brand name for a new product that gets introduced into new or the same markets, a line extension is simply an increase of an existing product line by the brand.

**L08** **Indicate the advantages of a product's packaging and labeling strategy.**

Similar to brands, packaging and labels help sell the product and facilitate its use. The primary package holds the product, and its label provides product information. The secondary package provides additional consumer information on its label and facilitates transportation and storage for both retailers and their customers. Labels have become increasingly important to consumers because they supply important safety, nutritional, and product usage information.

## Key Terms

- associated services, 297
- augmented product, 297
- brand, 303
- brand association, 308
- brand awareness, 306
- brand dilution, 314
- brand equity, 306
- brand extension, 313
- brand licensing, 315
- brand loyalty, 308
- brand personality, 308

- brand repositioning (rebranding), 317
- breadth, 300
- co-branding, 315
- consumer product, 298
- convenience products/ services, 299
- copycat brands, 311
- core customer value, 297
- depth, 300
- exclusive co-brand, 312

- family brands, 313
- generic brands, 311
- green products, 307
- house brands, 310
- individual brands, 313
- licensed brand, 306
- line extension, 313
- manufacturer brands (national brands), 310
- own brands, 310
- perceived value, 307

- premium brands, 310
- primary package, 318
- private-label brands, 310
- product, 296

- product lines, 299
- product mix, 299
- secondary package, 318
- shopping products/services, 299

- specialty products/services, 298
- store brands, 310
- unsought products/services, 299

## Marketing Applications

1. LLBean guarantees that its products will last for-ever. What features of a pair of pants from LLBean would be part of the actual product and which would be part of the associated services?

2. Classify each of the following products into either convenience, shopping, specialty, or unsought goods: toothpaste, life insurance, Sharp TV, Eggo Waffles, lettuce, Coach handbag, adidas soccer cleats, furniture.

3. Suppose you are the home buyer at Blooming-dale's. There is a strong corporate initiative to increase private-label merchandise. Discuss the advantages and disadvantages of making private-label tablecloths.

4. Identify a specific brand that has developed a high level of brand equity. What specific aspects of that brand establish its brand equity?

5. Are you loyal to any brands? If so, pick one and explain why you believe you are loyal, beyond that you simply like the brand. If not, pick a brand that you like and explain how you would feel and act differently toward the brand if you were loyal to it.

6. Sears owns several brands, including DieHard, Kenmore, and Craftsman. Each brand features many models that may appeal to various customer groups. Wouldn't it be easier to just identify them all as Sears? Justify your answer.

7. Identify a specific company that has recently intro-duced a new brand extension to the marketplace. Discuss whether you believe the brand extension example you provided will benefit or harm the firm.

8. Do you think all edible items sold in a grocery store should have an ingredient and nutrition label? Consider the perspectives of consumers, the manu-facturer, and the store.

9. You are the brand manager for a firm that makes herbs, spices, and other food additives. You have had complaints from some of your retail outlets that they are finding empty bottles of pure vanilla extract stashed around the store. Apparently, due to the high (35 percent) alcohol content of pure vanilla extract, people are grabbing the cute little bottles, having a drink, and getting rid of the evidence. Anecdotal evidence from store employees indicates that the majority of the imbibers are teenagers. The cost of placing a tamper proof cap on the extract is a relatively insignificant percentage of the purchase price, but will make it more difficult to open, par-ticularly for older customers. Also, there has been a significant rise in sales to retailers as a result of the vanilla bean "addicts." What should you do?

www.mhhe.com/ grewal3e

## Quiz Yourself

1. Toothpaste, toothbrush, whitening products, kids' oral products, and floss are _____ within Colgate-Palmolive's Oral Care product line.
   a. products
   b. primary packaging parts
   c. product breadth
   d. product extensions
   e. private-label brands

2. It is almost impossible to watch a sporting event on television without seeing Nike's "swoosh" mark, which is Nike's:
   a. name.
   b. symbol.
   c. design.
   d. term.
   e. all of the above.

   (Answers to these two questions are provided on page 607.)

   Go to www.mhhe.com/grewal3e to practice an additional 11 questions.

## Net Savvy

1. Visit the Hershey's website (www.hersheys.com). Click on "Products." Identify and briefly describe Hershey's different *product lines*. What is the depth and the breadth of its product lines?

2. Interbrand Corporation is a leading brand consultancy firm headquartered in New York that conducts research on the monetary value of different brands.

Visit the company's website (www.interbrand.com) and access the most recent "Best Global Brands" survey. Identify the top five brands, their brand values, and their countries of origin. Describe changes in the rankings of these firms from the previous year. Identify the brands with the greatest increase and the greatest decrease in terms of percentage change in brand value from the previous year.

## Chapter Case Study

### COCA-COLA: A HISTORY AND A FUTURE[87]

Visit virtually any restaurant, fast-food joint, or convenience store around the world, and the odds are that you will hear someone ask for a "Coke." Even if the product made by the Coca-Cola Corporation is not readily available, the term "Coke" has become shorthand for virtually any dark-colored carbonated beverage. The consumer may really end up drinking a Pepsi, or a Thums Up, or Parsi Cola, depending on where he or she is ordering, but few servers would correct a patron who asks for Coca-Cola. It takes a special product to get so ingrained in people's minds.

### THE BEGINNING

A potential headache cure invented in 1886 by an Atlanta, Georgia, pharmacist named John Pemberton, Coca-Cola got its name because one of its curative ingredients was an extract of coca leaves, known as cocaine. That ingredient gave the beverage its "kick." By 1929 though, the kick came only from caffeine.[88]

Asa Griggs Candler, who became the first president of the Coca-Cola Company, purchased the small market but popular beverage in 1891. Although he apparently never really appreciated what he had, Candler is credited with getting the Coca-Cola logo into widespread use and acceptance, by embossing it onto items

*Coca-Cola then and now: The price and bottle have changed, but the logo and taste have not.*

such as clocks, scales, and calendars. He then sent the complimentary Coca-Cola emblazoned gifts to pharmacists that were compounding the beverage for customers. He also pioneered the use of coupons that could be redeemed for free drinks. Coca-Cola moved from the pharmacy directly into customers' hands when the company sold the bottling rights, for $1, in 1899.

By mid-century, the influence of World War II moved Coke abroad. The U.S. GIs took bottles of the popular cola with them to Europe, as unofficial brand sponsors who introduced the brand to an entirely new international market. By the end of the war, Coke had earned a market share of more than 60 percent worldwide. [89]

### THE MIDDLE

Coke's success was also partially its undoing though. The Coca-Cola Company introduced new drinks, such as Sprite, Tab, and Fresca, which fragmented its market. Then the increasing popularity of its direct rival Pepsi-Cola—a fellow immigrant from the nineteenth century—brought Coke into yet another war . . . the Cola War. By 1985, Coke had a mere 24 percent market share in the United States. Coca-Cola's response remains fodder for continued debate: With great fanfare, the company announced it had changed the formula for its beverage, and New Coke would soon be appearing on shelves. An uproar, the likes of which had never been seen before, ensued. New Coke did not last long, as customers voiced their complaints over and over again. The company had no choice but to respond; it brought back "Original" Coke with just as much publicity as it had employed to herald its demise. Both products shared shelf space, and they continue to do so in some international markets. [90]

### THE END? NOT REALLY

The never-ending Cola War continues. Coca-Cola spends more money on global sponsorship deals with athletes, sports teams, sports entities (e.g., National Basketball Association), entertainers, and events than does any other company. Its expenditures are in excess of $1 billion a year. These sponsorship efforts publicize a company that globally distributes approximately 300 brands of drinks, including carbonated drinks (e.g., Sprite, various flavors of Coke and Diet Coke), sports drinks (e.g., PowerAde), Dasani bottled water, and Minute Maid fruit juices. The headache cure founded by a Southern pharmacist more than 100 years ago has turned into a multinational conglomerate that offers beverages to slake every type of thirst. [91]

### ONGOING EVOLUTION

No one could accuse Coca-Cola of resting on its laurels. According to the Interbrand agency, it remains the world's most valued brand and continues to increase in value, despite the global recession.[92] And how does Coca-Cola manage this feat? Adapting to an ever-changing environment is key. For example, with mycoke.com, Coca-Cola gives its monthly audience of 58,325 young U.S. users (http://www.quantcast.com/mycoke.com) a forum to discuss and learn about what is happening in the world of the cola. There are links for people to post videos, look up the latest sponsored events, play games, win prizes, and save money. Coca-Cola even maintains a presence on the wildly popular social network Twitter. Coke lovers can chat, see the latest company updates, and check on new product development and upcoming sponsorship events—all in real time (http://twitter.com/cocaCola).

In addition to the technical and online revolution, perhaps the next most significant global trend is an awareness of climate change and the need for individuals, companies, and countries to "go green." Coke therefore is embracing the credo while still maintaining its unique identity and sponsorship strategies.

For example, Coca-Cola is partnering with several entities to spread a green message. With the Westminster City Council in London, England, Coca-Cola has installed 260 recycling bins across the city in an effort to recycle 11,000 tons of waste that would normally be thrown into landfills daily. Of course, London is also the host city for the 2012 Summer Olympics, so its cooperative effort closely ties in with Coca-Cola's long-standing sponsorship (since 1928) of the Olympic Games.[93]

At the 2010 Vancouver Winter Olympics, Coca-Cola conducted a carefully calibrated test of its Commitment 2020 plan, by which it aims to decrease its overall carbon footprint by 15 percent in 10 years.[94] The test determined whether it could achieve a net zero carbon footprint for the two-week period of the Olympics. But the Olympics feature millions of fans from around the world, consuming massive amounts of food and drink, and zero impact is a difficult goal even in normal consumption situations.[95]

However, compared with its relatively simple recycling effort at the 2000 Athens Olympics, Coca-Cola has significantly increased its green efforts to include the production of bottles made from 30 percent plant-based materials, using only hybrid vehicles or electric carts to make deliveries, switching to environmentally friendly coolers, and even sporting company shirts made from recycled plastic bottles.[96]

As one of the first major marketers to commit itself to becoming more environmentally friendly, Coca-Cola remains one of the world's most trusted brands. Its increasing role in responding to and influencing how the world itself is changing and evolving makes Coke a real thing for most of the world.

## Questions

1. Visit the company's website (www.coca-cola.com) and identify and describe the different product lines that it markets.

2. How would you describe its product line breadth?

3. Review the different product categories in each of the company's product lines. Which has the greatest depth? Which has the least?

4. How has the company positioned its brand? How does it go about communicating its position?

# Developing New Products

A company survives changing times not by changing along with them, but by changing before them. The most successful companies are those that can continually develop new products before the consumers even know they want or need them. One of the most innovative companies of all time is Microsoft. After revolutionizing the home computer industry, it set out to be a leader in the information technology home entertainment field. It seems like not a year ever goes by without something new from the brainchild of Bill Gates.

But one area in which Microsoft has been less successful is the search engine market. Life would be very different, and slower, if people lost the ability to find information on virtually any topic immediately through the Internet. And Google, with its nearly 80 percent market share and massive name recognition, is in no real danger from competitors, including Bing.com, the newest Microsoft offering. But Bing is challenging Yahoo.com for the remainder of the market. Perhaps most important, it is distinguishing itself by providing more frequent updates and feature additions than the other search engines. Consumers benefit overall, because Bing is forcing competitors to improve their offering to keep pace with Microsoft or prevent it from stealing market share from them.

In another move to differentiate itself, Bing is promoted as a "decision engine" rather than a search engine.[1] In the words of Bing Group Product Manager Todd Schwartz, "one of the ways we helped customers get to better decisions was by providing a more visual, more intuitive and more organized experience." The newest feature is the integration of Foursquare, a location-based phone application, into Bing Maps results. Users thus can focus in on a particular area, such as South Boston, which means Bing can act like an integrative day planner and list the best things to do in that area. Anyone with questions can move easily into the social forum of Foursquare to get insider scoops, generally not available in "official reviews." Thus, despite Microsoft's problems developing search engines, Bing suggests it intends to stay aggressive in this market.

## LEARNING OBJECTIVES

**LO1** Identify the reasons firms innovate.

**LO2** Describe the different groups of adopters articulated by the diffusion of innovation theory.

**LO3** Identify the factors that determine how fast innovation diffuses.

**LO4** Explain the stages involved in developing a new product or service.

**LO5** Describe the various product life cycle concepts.

Even as Bing attracts a lot of attention for its efforts to infiltrate a market dominated by better known competitors, Microsoft continues to earn high scores in the home gaming system market. It may not be the biggest name in the field (that would arguably be Playstation or Nintendo), but Microsoft has generated buzz by constantly introducing new products such as the Xbox (with its various iterations) and the Game Cube. Never a company to be satisfied with previous successes, Microsoft has extended the Xbox to offer a controller-free gaming system based on Project Natal technology.[2] The need for controllers has heretofore interrupted gamers from achieving total immersion. The Project Natal effort aims to use gamers' bodies as joysticks. For example, if the game requires a user to kick a ball, the user physically kicks his or her leg instead of pushing a button on the controller. By measuring body movements and voice commands with several cameras and a highly specialized microphone, Project Natal allows the gamer to become one with the game.[3]

So where Microsoft may have had a strong hand in turning people into "couch potatoes" by developing products for computers and static game systems, it now has developed a product aimed at getting those very same people up and active, even as they continue to enjoy the video game experience they so appreciate.

● ● ●

Few three-letter words are more exciting than "new." It brings forth an image of freshness, adventure, and excitement. Yet "new" also is a complex term when it comes to market offerings, because it might mean adding something new to an existing product, introducing a flavor never offered before, or relying on different packaging that provides added value. But the most exhilarating type of new product is something never seen before. Thousands of patent applications pursue this elusive prize: a successful and truly innovative new product.

Imagine living 200 years ago: You cook meals on a stove fueled by coal or wood; you write out homework by hand (if you are lucky enough to attend school) and by candlelight. To get to school, you hike along unpaved roads to reach a small, cold, basic classroom with just a few classmates, who listen to a lecture from a teacher writing on a blackboard.

Today, you finish your homework on a laptop computer with word processing software that appears to have a mind of its own and can correct your spelling automatically. Your climate-controlled room has ample electric light. While you work on your laptop, you also talk with a friend using the hands-free headset of your wireless phone. As you drive to school in your car, you pick up fast food from a convenient drive-through window while browsing and listening to your personal selection of songs playing through your car speakers, connected wirelessly to your iPod. Your friend calls to discuss a slight change to the homework, so you pull over to grab your BlackBerry, make the necessary change to your assignment, and e-mail it from your smartphone to your professor. When you arrive at school, you sit in a 200-person classroom, where you can plug in your laptop, take notes on your computer, and digitally record the lecture. The professor adds notes on the day's PowerPoint presentations using her tablet computer. You have already downloaded the PowerPoint presentations and add similar notes through your own laptop. After class, to complete your planning for a last-minute party, you send out a Facebook invitation to your friends and ask for responses to get a headcount. You then instant message your roommate, telling her to get food and drinks for the right number of people, which she orders through an online grocer that will deliver later in the day.

Our lives are defined by the many new products and services developed through scientific and technological advances and by the added features included in products that we have always used. In this second chapter dealing with the first P in the marketing mix (product), we continue our discussion from the preceding chapter and explore how companies add value to product and service offerings through innovation. We also look at how firms develop new products and services on their own. We conclude the chapter with an examination of how new products and services get adopted by the market and how firms can change their marketing mix as the product or service moves through its life cycle.

# WHY DO FIRMS CREATE NEW PRODUCTS?

New market offerings provide value to both firms and customers. But the degree to which they do so depends on how new they really are. When we say a "new product/service," we don't necessarily mean that the market offer has never existed before. Completely new-to-the-market products represent fewer than 10 percent of all new product introductions each year. It is more useful to think of the degree of newness or innovativeness on a continuum from truly "new-to-the-world"—as WiFi was a few years ago—to "slightly repositioned," such as the repositioning of Kraft's Capri Sun brand of ready-to-drink beverages, repackaged in a bigger pouch to appeal more to teens.

Regardless of where on the continuum a new product lies, firms have to innovate. Innovation refers to the process by which ideas get transformed into new offerings, including products, services, processes, and branding concepts that will help firms grow. Without innovation and its resulting new products and services, firms would have only two choices: continue to market current products to current customers or take the same product to another market with similar customers.

Although innovation strategies may not always work in the short run—some estimates indicate that only about 3 percent of new products actually succeed—various overriding and long-term reasons compel firms to continue introducing new products and services, as the following sections describe.

**L01** Identify the reasons firms innovate.

*Dyson has added value by taking a well-known product, the vacuum cleaner, and redesigning it so that it won't lose suction.*

## Changing Customer Needs

When they add products, services, and processes to their offerings, firms can create and deliver value more effectively by satisfying the changing needs of their current and new customers or simply by keeping customers from getting bored with the current product or service offering. Sometimes, companies can identify problems and develop products that customers never knew they needed. For example, a car wash offers a basic wash; a wash and polish; or a wash, polish, and undercarriage wash. Customers may never have thought about washing the undercarriage of their car prior to their exposure to the new service offering. In other cases, the firms take a well-known offering and innovate to make it more interesting, as Dyson has done for the vacuum cleaner. According to the company's mythology, James Dyson caught sight of a local sawmill that used a cyclone to collect sawdust from the air, then decided to apply the concept to a vacuum cleaner so he could establish his company's now familiar promise: a vacuum that won't lose suction.[4] The experience he had developing and

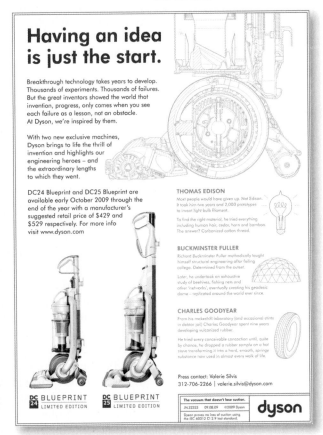

## Adding Value 11.1    Want Beef?[5]

A bad economy, trends toward healthy eating—it all combines to spell trouble for the beef industry. Beef often goes in and out of style, from a healthy must-have food to a heart-clogging cholesterol producer. The National Cancer Institute just issued a new study saying that red meat shortens life spans. And the economy is forcing many consumers to eat out less and conserve on their luxury spending at the grocery store.

The beef industry mostly depends on the restaurant business, which accounts for half its sales. Consumers have not been eating out, and if they do, they are not splurging on steaks. Now, the beef industry is making innovative strides to address changing customer needs by making beef seem like less of a luxury.

There are many pieces of meat on a cow, but some are less desirable because of their toughness or muscle fibers. Recent advances in cutting technology have made more cuts palatable though. Grocery stores stock more of these cuts at lower prices than the premium cuts. For example, "flap meat" is being packaged as "Cordelico Sirloin," and the "ball tip" is being packaged as "Cabrosa Steak." In addition, in-store and online education programs attempt to teach customers how to cook and prepare these different cuts of meats, even revealing how to cut steaks for tender roast or cut beef kabobs from a sirloin steak.

The beef industry now offers approximately $60 million in coupons, each valued at $1, to be used on any beef purchase, six times the amount of coupons given out last year, as well as quantity discounts for customers to purchase large quantities of beef to store in their freezers. The industry also is recommending that retailers put beef on sale to turn inventory quicker.

Even if the industry sells less-than-premium cuts of meat for a lower price, it earns more than it would by turning the meat to hamburger, which fetches an even lower price. By making beef and steaks more accessible and affordable to customers, the market share for beef should improve against its rivals chicken and pork, which are still lower priced.

So what's a pork producer to do? With the beef industry beefing up its brands, how can pork producers maintain or even gain market share given the economy and health concerns?

protecting his innovative technology also formed the company's present innovation process, which relies heavily on secrecy, protection of ideas, and risk taking. Adding Value 11.1 examines how the beef industry adapts to changing consumer needs.

## Market Saturation

The longer a product exists in the marketplace, the more likely it is that the market will become saturated. Without new products or services, the value of the firm will ultimately decline.[6] Imagine, for example, if car companies simply assumed and expected that people would keep their cars until they stopped running. If that were the case, there would be no need to come up with new and innovative models; companies could just stick with the models that sell well. But few consumers actually keep the same car until it stops running. Even those who want to stay with the same make and model often want something new, just to add some variety to their lives. Therefore, car companies revamp their models every year, whether with new features like GPS or a more powerful engine, or by redesigning the entire look of the vehicle. The firms thus sustain their growth by getting consumers excited by the new looks and new features, prompting many car buyers to exchange their old vehicle years before its functional life is over.

Saturated markets can also offer opportunities for a company that is willing to adopt a new process or mentality. At one point in time, mass marketers would not even consider entering a market that they believed would not earn at least $50 million. But Betty Crocker (a General Mills brand) is innovating by looking to niche markets for its future growth. Whereas only 1 percent of the U.S. population suffers from celiac disease—a condition that damages the digestive system when sufferers ingest gluten—approximately 12 percent of U.S. consumers say they want to reduce or eliminate gluten, a wheat protein, from their diet. Therefore, Betty

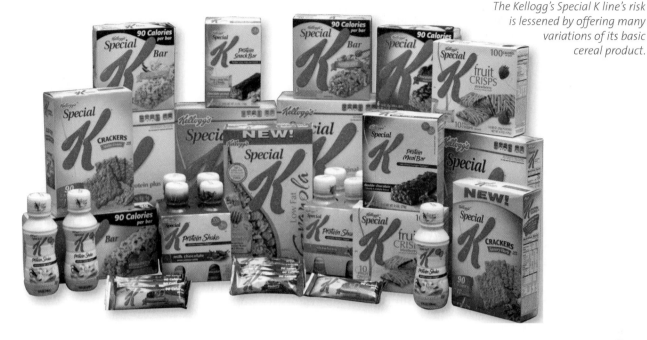

*The Kellogg's Special K line's risk is lessened by offering many variations of its basic cereal product.*

Crocker is innovating its process and products to offer versions of its well-known cake, brownie, and cookie mixes without any gluten at all.[7]

## Managing Risk through Diversity

Through innovation, firms often create a broader portfolio of products, which help them diversify their risk and enhance firm value better than a single product can.[8] If some products in a portfolio perform poorly, others may do well. Firms with multiple products can better withstand external shocks, including changes in consumer preferences or intensive competitive activity. For this reason, firms like 3M demand that a specific percentage of their sales each year must come from new products introduced within the previous few years. In the cereal aisle, Kellogg's Special K offers many variations of its long-standing basic product, including cereal bars, protein shakes, and even protein water. This diversification enables Special K to enjoy more consistent performance than it would with just one kind of Special K cereal.

*Video games, like Madden NFL are "fashionable" because consumers like Lauren Conrad demand new versions. Once they have "beat" the game, they want to be challenged with a new experience.*

## Fashion Cycles

In industries that rely on fashion trends and experience short product life cycles—including apparel, arts, books, and software markets—most sales come from new products. For example, a motion picture generates most of its theater, DVD, and cable TV revenues within a year of its release. If the same selection of books were always for sale, with no new titles, there would be no reason to buy more. Consumers of computer software and video games demand new

*To generate sales, apparel fashion designers produce entirely new product selections a few times per year.*

offers because once they have "beat" the game, they want to be challenged by another game or experience the most recent version, as the remarkable sales of successive versions of the Madden NFL game exemplify.[9] In the case of apparel, fashion designers produce entirely new product selections a few times per year.

## Improving Business Relationships

New products do not always target end consumers; sometimes they function to improve relationships with suppliers. For example, Kraft, the maker of Capri Sun, found that its lemonade flavor was selling poorly. Through a little market research, it realized that the reason was the placement of the packages in pallets. Because it was placed at the bottom of the stack in pallets, lemonade was the last flavor retailers would sell. By changing and innovating its pallet, Kraft offered chimney stacks for each flavor, enabling the retail stockers to reach whichever flavor they needed easily. Sales of Capri Sun's lemonade improved by 162 percent.[10]

Even if they succeed in innovating and creating new products, new-to-the-world products are not adopted by everyone at the same time. Rather, they diffuse or spread through a population in a process known as *diffusion of innovation*.

### ✓ CHECK YOURSELF

1. What are the reasons why firms develop new products?

**L02** Describe the different groups of adopters articulated by the diffusion of innovation theory.

# DIFFUSION OF INNOVATION

The process by which the use of an innovation—whether a product, a service, or a process—spreads throughout a market group, over time and across various categories of adopters, is referred to as **diffusion of innovation**.[11] The theory surrounding diffusion of innovation helps marketers understand the rate at which consumers are likely to adopt a new product or service. It also gives them a means to identify potential markets for their new products or services and predict their potential sales, even before they introduce the innovations.[12]

Truly new product introductions, that is, new-to-the-world products that create new markets, can add tremendous value to firms. These new products, also

*Have you ever heard of any of these products? No wonder. They all failed. Orajel (left) was a "fluoride-free" toothpaste targeted toward young children. Dunk-A-Balls cereal (center) was shaped like basketballs so children could play with them before eating them. The Garlic Cake (right) was supposed to be served as an hors d'oeuvre, but the company forgot to mention potential usage occasions to consumers, so people wondered why they would want to eat one.*

*Apple has introduced several pioneer products in recent years, including the iPhone.*

called pioneers or breakthroughs, establish a completely new market or radically change both the rules of competition and consumer preferences in a market.[13] The Apple iPod is a pioneer product. Not only did it change the way people listen to music, but it also created an entirely new industry devoted to accessories, such as cases, ear buds, docking stations, and speakers. Although Apple offers many of these accessories itself, other companies have jumped on the bandwagon, ensuring that you can strap your iPod to your arm while on the move or insert it into the base of a desk lamp equipped with speakers to get music and light from your desk. And don't forget: The iPod also launched perhaps the most notable other recent pioneer, the iPhone, the innovative iTunes service, and the iPod Touch.[14]

Pioneers have the advantage of being first movers; as the first to create the market or product category, they become readily recognizable to consumers and thus establish a commanding and early market share lead. Studies also have found that market pioneers can command a greater market share over a longer time period than later entrants can.[15]

This finding does not imply, however, that all pioneers succeed.[16] In many cases, imitators capitalize on the weaknesses of pioneers and subsequently gain advantage in the market. Because pioneering products and brands face the uphill task of establishing the market alone, they pave the way for followers, who can spend less marketing effort creating demand for the product line and focus directly on creating demand for their specific brand. Also, because the pioneer is the first product in the market, it often has a less sophisticated design and may be priced relatively higher, leaving room for better and lower-priced competitive products. A majority of new products are failures: As many as 95 percent of all new consumer goods fail, and products across all markets and industries suffer failure rates of 50 to 80 percent.[17]

As the diffusion of innovation curve in Exhibit 11.1 shows, the number of users of an innovative product or service spreads through the population over a period of time and generally follows a bell-shaped curve. A few people buy the product or service at first, then increasingly more buy, and finally fewer people buy as the degree of the diffusion slows. These purchasers can be divided into five groups according to how soon they buy the product after it has been introduced.

| EXHIBIT 11.1 | Diffusion of Innovation Curve |

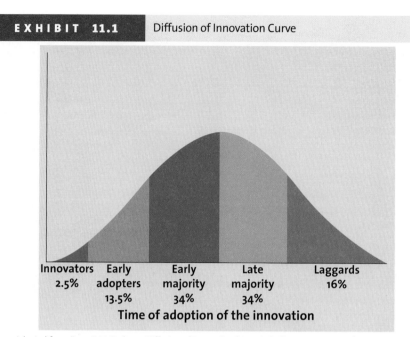

| Innovators 2.5% | Early adopters 13.5% | Early majority 34% | Late majority 34% | Laggards 16% |

**Time of adoption of the innovation**

Source: Adapted from Everett M. Rodgers, *Diffusion of Innovation* (New York: The Free Press, 1983).

## Innovators

**Innovators** are those buyers who want to be the first on the block to have the new product or service. These buyers enjoy taking risks and are regarded as highly knowledgeable. You probably know someone who is an innovator—or perhaps you are one for a particular product or service category. For example, the person who stood in line overnight to be sure to get a ticket for the very first showing of the latest superhero movie is an innovator in that context. Firms that invest in the latest technology, either to use in their products or services or to make the firm more efficient, also are considered innovators. Typically, innovators keep themselves very well informed about the product category by subscribing to trade and specialty magazines, talking to other "experts," engaging in product specific blogs and forums, and attending product-related forums, seminars, and special events. Yet innovators represent only about 2.5 percent of the total market for any new product or service.

*This innovator was the first person to purchase an Apple iPad at this Apple store.*

These innovators are crucial to the success of any new product or service though, because they help the product gain market acceptance. Through talking about and spreading positive word of mouth about the new product, they prove instrumental in bringing in the next adopter category, known as early adopters.[18]

## Early Adopters

The second subgroup that begins to use a product or service innovation is early adopters. They generally don't like to take as much risk as innovators do but instead wait and purchase the product after careful review. Thus, this market waits for the first reviews of the latest Harry Potter movie before purchasing a ticket, though they likely still go a week or two after it opens. They do not stand in line to grab the first PlayStation3 consoles; only after reading the innovators' complaints and praises do they decide whether the new version is worth the cost. Most of them go ahead and purchase though, because early adopters tend to enjoy novelty and often are regarded as the opinion leaders for particular product categories.

This group, which represents about 13.5 percent of all buyers in the market, spreads the word. As a result, early adopters are crucial for bringing the other three buyer categories to the market. If the early adopter group is relatively small, the number of people who ultimately adopt the innovation likely will also be small.

## Early Majority

The early majority, which represents approximately 34 percent of the population, is crucial because few new products and services can be profitable until this large group buys them. If the group never becomes large enough, the product or service typically fails.

The early majority group differs in many ways from buyers in the first two stages. Its members don't like to take as much risk and therefore tend to wait until "the bugs" are worked out of a particular product or service. If we continue our application to movies, this group probably rents the latest Harry Potter movie during the first week it comes out on video. Thus, they experience little risk, because all the reviews are in, and their costs are lower because they're renting the movie instead of going to the theater. When early majority customers enter the market, the number of competitors in the marketplace usually also has reached its peak, so these buyers have many different price and quality choices.

## Late Majority

At 34 percent of the market, the late majority is the last group of buyers to enter a new product market. When they do, the product has achieved its full market potential. Perhaps these movie watchers wait until the newest movie is easy to find at the rental store or put it low on their Netflix queue, to be delivered after the other consumers interested in watching it have already seen it. By the time the late majority enters the market, sales tend to level off or may be in decline.

## Laggards

Laggards make up roughly 16 percent of the market. These consumers like to avoid change and rely on traditional products until they are no longer available. In some cases, laggards may never adopt a certain product or service. When Harry Potter eventually shows up on their regular television networks, they are likely to go ahead and watch it.

## Using the Diffusion of Innovation Theory

 Identify the factors that determine how fast innovations diffuse

Using the diffusion of innovation theory, firms can predict which types of customers will buy their new product or service immediately after its introduction, as well as later as the product gets more and more accepted by the market. With this knowledge, the firm can develop effective promotion, pricing, and other marketing strategies to push acceptance among each customer group. When Amazon first introduced its Kindle e-book reader for around $400, it sold out in less than five hours.[19] The Kindle 2 arrived at an initial price of $359. Within six months, Amazon announced a price level below $300. The price changes likely reflect Amazon's recognition of the market situation. In the time between the first and second editions of the Kindle, competitors including Barnes & Noble, Sony, and Apple threatened to make substantial inroads into e-book territory.[20] Amazon realized "it must push its price down faster in order to establish itself as a leader in the category . . . and remain competitive."[21] However, because different products diffuse at different rates, marketers must work to understand the diffusion curve for each new product and service, as well as the characteristics of the target customers in each stage of the diffusion. The speed with which products or services diffuse depends on several characteristics.

**Relative Advantage** If a product or service is perceived to be better than substitutes, then the diffusion will be relatively quick. For example, the GreenWorks line of natural cleaning products (introduced by Clorox) appeals to consumers because it uses plant- and mineral-based cleaning agents rather than harsh chemicals. The superiority of this product offer earned the line a 2009 "Best New Product Award" from *Good Housekeeping*.[22]

**Compatibility** A diffusion process may be faster or slower, depending on various consumer features, including international cultural differences. For example, the Chinese version of the Web browser Firefox has different features than its Western counterpart because research indicated that Chinese users surf the Internet differently. The Firefox China Edition has more mouse-based controls like a double-click to close a tab on the browser, and a drop-down button on the toolbar for a calculator, screenshot grabber, and image editor.[23]

**Observability** When products are easily observed, their benefits or uses are easily communicated to others, which enhances the diffusion process. Consumers may see their peers using Maybelline Moisture Extreme lipstick, as well as observing commercials for the product featuring Eva Longoria, which convinces them to try it too. Another consumer, observing a lot of Toyota Prius hybrid vehicles on the road, may be curious enough to visit the dealership for a test drive. In contrast, since people may not want to talk about their Botox treatments to reduce wrinkles, the use of this product is less easily observed by others and therefore diffused more slowly.

**Complexity and Trialability** Products that are relatively less complex are also relatively easy to try. These products will generally diffuse more quickly than those that are not so easy to try. For example, a customer who normally buys Simply Orange juice finds a new flavor, Simply Apple, on the shelf and decides to try it because she likes the brand. If she does not like the new flavor, she simply will not purchase it again. But even if the same consumer really likes her Magnavox television, she cannot simply grab a set of Magnavox speakers to install in her home theater. The options available are much more complex, and once she has them installed, she is stuck with these expensive options for a while.

The diffusion of innovation theory thus comes into play in the immediate and long-term aftermath of a new product or service introduction. But before the introduction, firms must actually develop those new offerings. In the next section, we detail the process by which most firms develop new products and services and how they initially introduce them into the market.

## CHECK YOURSELF

1. What are the five groups on the diffusion of innovation curve?
2. What factors enhance the diffusion of a good or service?

# HOW FIRMS DEVELOP NEW PRODUCTS

**L04** Explain the stages involved in developing a new product or service.

The new product development process begins with the generation of new product ideas and culminates in the launch of a new product and the evaluation of its success. The stages of the new product development process, along with the important objectives of each stage, are summarized in Exhibit 11.2.

## Idea Generation

To generate ideas for new products, a firm can use its own internal research and development (R&D) efforts, collaborate with other firms and institutions, license technology from research-intensive firms, brainstorm, research competitors' products and services, and/or conduct consumer research; see Exhibit 11.3. Firms that want to be pioneers rely more extensively on R&D efforts, whereas those that tend to adopt a follower strategy are more likely to scan the market for ideas. Let's look at each of these idea sources.

**Internal Research and Development**  Many firms have their own R&D departments, in which scientists work to solve complex problems and develop new ideas.[24] Historically, firms such as IBM in the computer industry, Black and Decker in the consumer goods industry, 3M in the industrial goods industry, and Merck and Pfizer in the pharmaceuticals industry have relied on R&D development efforts for their new products. In other industries, such as software, music, and motion pictures, product development efforts also tend to come from internal ideas and R&D financial investments.

The product development costs for these firms are quite high, and the resulting new product or service has a good chance of being a technological or market breakthrough. Firms expect such products to generate enough revenue and profits to make the costs of R&D worthwhile. R&D investments, however, generally are considered continuous investments, so firms may lose money on a few new products. In the long run, though, these firms are betting that a few extremely successful new products, often known as blockbusters, can generate enough revenues and profits to cover the losses from other introductions that might not fare so well.

**R&D Consortia**  In recent years, more and more firms have been joining consortia, or groups of other firms and institutions, possibly including government and educational institutions, to explore new ideas or obtain solutions for developing new products. Here, the R&D investments come from the group as a whole, and the participating firms and institutions share the results.

The National Institutes of Health (NIH) is supporting a five-year, $71 million project to conduct clinical trials of treatments for rare diseases and disorders. A clinical trial is a medical study that tests the safety and effectiveness of a drug or treatment in people.[25] To be classified as rare, a disease must affect less than 200,000 people. Pharmaceutical companies are often reluctant to do research and develop products to treat these diseases, because the market is too small to make a profit. Yet approximately 6,000 rare diseases impact 25 million Americans. The NIH therefore sponsors medical foundations to conduct research to treat rare diseases.

---

**EXHIBIT 11.2**  The Product Development Process

| IDEA GENERATION | CONCEPT TESTING | PRODUCT DEVELOPMENT | MARKET TESTING | PRODUCT LAUNCH | EVALUATION OF RESULTS |
|---|---|---|---|---|---|
| Development of viable new product ideas. | Testing the new product idea among a set of potential customers. | Development of prototypes and/or the product. | Testing the actual products in a few test markets. | Full-scale commercialization of the product. | Analysis of the performance of the new product and making appropriate modifications. |

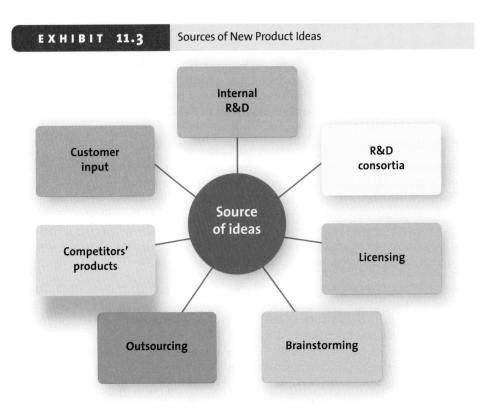

**EXHIBIT 11.3**    Sources of New Product Ideas

The research then gets disseminated to the medical community, thus encouraging the development of drugs and therapies more quickly and at a lower cost than would be possible if the research were privately funded. The NIH currently is working with 10 research consortia and 30 patient advocacy groups in 50 sites in the United States, the United Kingdom, Japan, and Brazil.[26]

**Licensing** For many new scientific and technological products, firms buy the rights to use the technology or ideas from other research-intensive firms through a licensing agreement. This approach saves the high costs of in-house R&D, but it means that the firm is banking on a solution that already exists but has not been marketed. For example, many pharmaceutical firms license products developed by biotechnology firms such as Amgen, Biogen, and Genentech. Because most biotechnology firms are relatively small, tend to be very research focused, and lack the resources and expertise to market their own innovations, they are content to obtain some development financing and royalties on sales of their product from the pharmaceutical firms.[27]

**Brainstorming** Firms often engage in brainstorming sessions during which a group works together to generate ideas. One of the key characteristics of a brainstorming session is that no idea can be immediately accepted or rejected. The moderator of the session may channel participants' attention to specific product features and attributes, performance expectations, or packaging. Only at the end of the session do the members vote on the best ideas or combinations of ideas. Those ideas that receive the most votes are carried forward to the next stage of the product development process.

**Outsourcing** In some cases, companies have trouble moving through these steps alone, which prompts them to turn to outside firms like IDEO, a design firm based in Palo Alto, California. IDEO offers not new products but rather a stellar service that helps clients generate new product and service ideas in industries such as health care, toys, and computers. IDEO employs anthropologists, graphic designers, engineers, and psychologists whose special skills help foster creativity and innovation. For example, Havaianas, a well-known Brazilian manufacturer of flip-flops and originally a shoe manufacturer for coffee farmers, relied on IDEO to develop offerings in a new product category, handbags. For this effort, IDEO interviewed Brazilians and produced hundreds of prototypes to arrive at the perfect bag for the brand.[28] In the case of the American Red Cross, the IDEO project worked to improve the blood donation experience and thereby increase the pool of donors. People who donate blood generally consider it their civic responsibility, whereas nondonors avoid it because they worry about the physical pain or stress. The American Red Cross, with IDEO, therefore developed an environment that celebrated the donor rather than the recipient, using modern décor at donation sites and communicating messages that featured donors' pictures and stories about why they gave blood.[29]

**Competitors' Products**   A new product entry by a competitor may trigger a market opportunity for a firm, which can use reverse engineering to understand the competitor's product and then bring an improved version to market. **Reverse engineering** involves taking apart a product, analyzing it, and creating an improved product that does not infringe on the competitor's patents, if any exist. This copycat approach to new product development is widespread and practiced by even the most research-intensive firms. Copycat consumer goods show up in grocery and drugstore products, as well as in technologically more complex products like automobiles and computers.

**Customer Input**   Listening to the customer in both B2B and B2C markets is essential for successful idea generation.[30] Because customers for B2B products are relatively few, firms can follow their use of products closely and solicit suggestions and ideas to improve those products either by using a formal approach, such as focus groups, interviews, or surveys, or through more informal discussions. The firm's design and development team then works on these suggestions, sometimes in consultation with the customer. This joint effort between the selling firm and the customer significantly increases the probability that the customer eventually will buy the new product.

Customer input in B2C markets comes from a variety of sources. In some cases, consumers may not expressly demand a new product, though their behavior demonstrates their desire for it. After analyzing its sales data, Walmart realized that the majority of its customers always or often buy store brands rather than national brands. So it developed more varied and appealing versions of its Great Value store brand, including all-natural ice cream in innovative flavors like cake batter and mocha mud.[31]

*Staples observed how customers opened their mail in the kitchen when it developed the Mailmate shredder to look like a kitchen appliance.*

Staples was able to observe how people use products in their homes. They observed that people opened their mail in the kitchen and then waited to shred it until they got to their office. Using this information they designed the Mailmate, which is a stainless steel shredder that looks like a kitchen appliance so it could blend in with the kitchen and mail could be shredded instantly after being opened.[32]

Companies realize that their customers are on the Web writing customer reviews on retailers' websites, and talking about their experiences on sites like Yelp.com, or on Twitter. Companies are reaching out to their customers by monitoring their feedback through these online communities in order to develop new products and change existing ones. Many companies are being more proactive by developing their own online communities to focus the conversations around topics in which they are interested. For example, Mzinga creates online communities with companies to engage customers with a brand.

*The bloggers on Myblogspark .com have access to new products and services and participate in exciting giveaways, surveys, and events. The blogs provide ideas for new products or product changes to companies. The site was developed by General Mills and Coyne Public Relations along with hundreds of bloggers.*

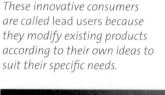

A particularly successful customer input approach is to analyze lead users, those innovative product users who modify existing products according to their own ideas to suit their specific needs.[33] If lead users customize a firm's products, other customers might wish to do so as well. Thus, studying lead users helps the firm understand general market trends that might be just on the horizon. Manufacturers and retailers of fashion products often spot new trends by noticing how innovative trendsetters have altered their clothing and shoes. For example, designers of high-fashion jeans distress their products in different ways depending on signals they pick up "on the street." One season, jeans appear with whiskers, the next season they have holes, the next, paint spots.

At the end of the idea-generation stage, the firm should have several ideas that it can take forward to the next stage: concept testing.

*These innovative consumers are called* lead users *because they modify existing products according to their own ideas to suit their specific needs.*

## Concept Testing

Ideas with potential are developed further into concepts, which in this context refer to brief written descriptions of the product; its technology, working principles, and forms; and what customer needs it would satisfy.[34] A concept might also include visual images of what the product would look like.

Concept testing refers to the process in which a concept statement is presented to potential buyers or users to obtain their reactions. These reactions enable the developer to estimate the sales value of the product or service concept, possibly make changes to enhance its sales value, and determine whether the idea is worth further development.[35] If the concept fails to meet customers' expectations, it is doubtful it would succeed if it were to be produced and marketed. Because concept testing occurs very early in the new product introduction process, even before a real product has been made, it helps the firm avoid the costs of unnecessary product development.

The concept for an electric scooter might be written as follows:

The product is a lightweight electric scooter that can be easily folded and taken with you inside a building or on public transportation. The scooter weighs 25 pounds. It travels at speeds of up to 15 miles per hour and can go about 12 miles on a single charge. The scooter can be recharged in about two hours from a standard electric outlet. The scooter is easy to ride and has simple controls—just an accelerator button and a brake. It sells for $299.[36]

Concept testing progresses along the research techniques described in Chapter 9. The firm likely starts with exploratory research, such as in-depth interviews or focus groups, to test the concept, after which it can undertake conclusive research through Internet or mall-intercept surveys. Video clips on the Internet might show a virtual prototype and the way it works so that potential customers can evaluate the product or service. In a mall-intercept survey, an interviewer would provide a description of the concept to the respondent and then ask several questions to obtain his or her feedback.

The most important question pertains to the respondent's purchase intentions if the product or service were made available. Marketers also should ask whether the product would satisfy a need that other products currently are not meeting. Depending on the type of product or service, researchers might also ask about the expected frequency of purchase, how much customers would buy, whether they would buy it for themselves or as a gift, when they would buy, and whether the price information (if provided) indicates a good value. In addition, marketers usually collect some information about the customers so they can analyze which consumer segments are likely to be most interested in the product. The airline industry is testing a technology that is expected to significantly alleviate the lost baggage problem. (See Superior Service 11.1.)

Some concepts never make it past concept testing stage, particularly if respondents seem uninterested. Those that do receive high evaluations from potential consumers, however, move on to the next step, product development.

## Product Development

Product development or product design entails a process of balancing various engineering, manufacturing, marketing, and economic considerations to develop a product's form and features or a service's features. An engineering team develops a product prototype that is based on research findings from the previous concept testing step, as well as their own knowledge about materials and technology. A prototype is the first physical form or service description of a new product,

---

### Superior Service 11.1 — Airlines Can Improve Luggage Efficiency through RFID[37]

Many problems arise during commercial flights, but the problem of lost luggage might be reduced significantly through the use of radio frequency identification (RFID) tags. These tags replace luggage tags, so that airlines can track each bag as it moves from point A to point B. The RFID system at the Las Vegas airport, for instance, has resulted in less lost baggage, less sorting, and more knowledge about the specific location of bags.

The International Air Transport Association (IATA) may decide to require all airlines to use RFID luggage tags, but airlines have been reluctant to adopt the bagging system because of its additional price. Each tag costs about 15 cents per tag, compared with 4 cents per tag for the existing paper tags that airlines use.

The RFID luggage tags reduce the hassle and money required of airlines and their passengers. U.S. airlines spend about $400 million annually on lost luggage, including reimbursing customers and delivering misplaced bags. With RFID, predictions suggest lost luggage may be reduced by 20 percent, and only 1 percent of bags will have to be manually sorted, compared with the 10–20 percent manually sorted with existing luggage tags. The RFID system is 99 percent accurate in reading tags, a significant improvement over current systems.

The potential mandate from the IATA that all airlines use an RFID tagging system could make flying more enjoyable for customers. The technology offers a huge advantage to customers and could even influence which airlines they choose. Lost or delayed luggage can ruin a traveling experience, so those airlines with a virtually guaranteed luggage arrival system should achieve a strong competitive advantage.

How can marketers use RFID to improve efficiency in other industries?

*Ben & Jerry's Ice Cream uses alpha testing with its own employees to make sure its products have the taste and feel they should.*

still in rough or tentative form, that has the same properties as a new product but is produced through different manufacturing processes—sometimes even crafted individually.[38]

Product prototypes are usually tested through alpha and beta testing. In alpha testing, the firm attempts to determine whether the product will perform according to its design and whether it satisfies the need for which it was intended.[39] Rather than use potential consumers, alpha tests occur in the firm's R&D department. For instance, Ben & Jerry's Ice Cream alpha tests all its proposed new flavors on its own (lucky) employees at its corporate headquarters in Vermont.

Many people, consumer groups, and governmental agencies are concerned when alpha testing involves tests on animals, particularly when it comes to pharmaceuticals and cosmetics. Ethical and Societal Dilemma 11.1 discusses these concerns in the United States and the European Union.

## Ethical and Societal Dilemma 11.1

### Should Firms Test on Animals?

Product testing on animals has been a primary issue for animal rights activists for years.[40] As public opposition to animal testing increases, so do many companies' declarations that they "do not test products on animals." However, such statements can be misleading because even though the whole product may not have been tested on animals, the individual ingredients may have been. To help clarify any confusion, companies can apply to the Coalition for Consumer Information on Cosmetics (CCIC), a national group formed by eight animal welfare group members such as the United States Humane Association and the Doris Day Animal League, and be certified as "cruelty free." They then can purchase the trademarked Leaping Bunny Logo from CCIC for use on their labels.

One of the core values of The Body Shop, and one that has resonated well with its customers, is that its products are free of animal testing. Another major cosmetics manufacturer, Procter & Gamble, has eliminated animal testing on more than 80 percent of its products. It uses a combination of in vitro testing, computer modeling, and historical data to determine the safety of new products and ingredients. These methods are more expensive than more traditional methods, but P&G claims that the results are better. If performed correctly, new chemicals can be either dropped from consideration or pushed forward in as little as three days compared to the six months previously required for animal testing.

In other fields, animal welfare groups continue to push to stop the use of animal testing altogether. The People for the Ethical Treatment of Animals (PETA) publicly cites companies it accuses of engaging in animal testing and other activities considered to be inhumane, and praises those that do not.[41] PETA's efforts have caused firms like Hugo Boss, H&M, and Liz Claiborne to stop buying their wool from Australia because some Australian sheep farmers sheer their sheep's wool in inhumane ways.

The European Union has passed a ban on animal testing altogether. Beginning in 2009, any cosmetic tested on animals, even in other parts of the world, cannot be sold in the European Union. However, the cosmetics industry is worried that this ban will affect not only their companies' sales but also their customers' ability to find the products they want. The EU cosmetics industry successfully lobbied for an extension on certain areas of toxicity testing to provide more time to find alternatives. The cosmetics industry believes it will be difficult to find alternative testing methods in time, and if they cannot, it will have fewer ingredients to make the products consumers want.

*(continued)*

In contrast, beta testing uses potential consumers, who examine the product prototype in a "real use" setting to determine its functionality, performance, potential problems, and other issues specific to its use. The firm might develop several prototype products that it gives to users, then survey those users to determine whether the product worked as intended and identify any issues that need resolution.

Household products manufacturer Kimberly-Clark uses virtual testing in the beta-testing phase of its product development process. The consumer goods company uses a virtual store aisle that mimics a real-life shopping experience by creating a realistic picture of the interior of the store. A retina-tracking device records the movement of a test customer who "shops" the virtual aisle of a store and chooses certain products to investigate further in the virtual simulation. Thus, consumer companies can demonstrate the likely success, or failure, of a product without actually having to produce it for a market and, potentially, expose its secrets to competitors.[42]

## Market Testing

The firm has developed its new product or service and tested the prototypes. Now it must test the market for the new product with a trial batch of products. These tests can take two forms: premarket testing or test marketing.

*Activists of the People for the Ethical Treatment of Animals (PETA) participate in a protest against animal slaughter near a mall where Hermes—the French luxury goods company—has a store in Jakarta, Indonesia. PETA demanded Hermes stop selling exotic animal skin products and released gruesome videos of reptiles being skinned alive in Indonisia.*

(continued)

The issues involved in animal testing are complex. At the broadest level, should firms be allowed to develop products that customers want, even if there is some potential harm to the environment or to those animals that share the environment with humans? More specifically, should firms be allowed to test products on animals, even when those products are not specifically designed to improve the health and well-being of their human users? Does the testing that is performed endanger the lives or health of the animals?

**Premarket Tests**  Firms conduct premarket tests before they actually bring a product or service to market to determine how many customers will try and then continue to use the product or service according to a small group of potential consumers. One popular proprietary premarket test version is called Nielsen BASES. During the test, potential customers are exposed to the marketing mix variables, such as the advertising, then surveyed and given a sample of the product to try.[43] After some period of time, during which the potential customers try the product, they are surveyed about whether they would buy/use the product again. This second survey provides an estimation of the probability of a consumer's repeat purchase. From these data, the firm generates a sales estimate for the new product that enables it to decide whether to introduce the product, abandon it, redesign it before introduction, or revise the marketing plan. An early evaluation of this sort—that is, before the product is introduced to the whole market—saves marketers the costs of a nationwide launch if the product fails.

Sometimes firms simulate a product or service introduction, in which case potential customers view the advertising of various currently available products or services along with advertising for the new product or service. They receive money to buy the product or service from a simulated environment, such as a mock Web page or store, and respond to a survey after they make their purchases. This test thus can determine the effectiveness of a firm's advertising as well as the expected trial rates for the new product.

**Test Marketing**  A method of determining the success potential of a new product, test marketing introduces the offering to a limited geographical area (usually a few cities) prior to a national launch. Test marketing is a strong predictor of product success because the firm can study actual purchase behavior, which is more reliable than a simulated test. A test marketing effort uses all the elements of the marketing mix: It includes promotions like advertising and coupons, just as if the product were being introduced nationally, and the product appears in targeted retail outlets, with appropriate pricing. On the basis of the results of the test marketing, the firm can estimate demand for the entire market.

Procter & Gamble recognized that some consumers, especially college students and young professionals without their own laundry facilities, often just let worn clothes hang next to their shower to freshen them up, rather than hauling them to the Laundromat. It therefore came up with Swash, a line of products that removes wrinkles, eliminate odors, and erases stains quickly and easily. The initial limited tests, which focused on consumers in Lexington, Kentucky, and Columbus, Ohio, confirmed that Swash aligned with their modern, hurried lifestyle. So the company proceeded with its national rollout through online retailers such as Amazon and Drugstore.com.[44]

Test marketing costs more and takes longer than premarket tests, which may provide an advantage to competitors that could get a similar or better product to market first without test marketing. For this reason, some firms might launch new products without extensive consumer testing and rely instead on intuition, instincts, and guts.[45]

*Aimed at college students and young professionals without their own laundry facilities, P&G has introduced Swash, a line of products that removes wrinkles, eliminates odors, and erases stains without washing.*

## Product Launch

If the market testing returns with positive results, the firm is ready to introduce the product to the entire market. This most critical step in the new product introduction requires tremendous financial resources and extensive coordination of all aspects of the marketing

*The new Nano introduced in India costs about $2,000. It weighs less than a Honda Accord, gets 56 miles per gallon, and takes 23 seconds to get to its top speed of 60 miles per hour.*

mix. For example, for Tata Motors to launch its inexpensive (around $2,000) tiny car, the Nano, in India, it had to limit its production to just 500,000 cars per year, though it predicts the market will be larger. The company already suffers from a high debt load after it purchased Jaguar/Land Rover, and it simply cannot afford a bigger rollout.[46] For any firm, if the new product launch is a failure, it may be difficult for the product—and perhaps the firm—to recover.

So what does a product launch involve? First, on the basis of the research it has gathered on consumer perceptions, the tests it has conducted, and competitive considerations, the firm confirms its target market (or markets) and decides how the product will be positioned. Then the firm finalizes the remaining marketing mix variables for the new product, including the marketing budget for the first year.[47]

**Promotion** The test results help the firm determine an appropriate integrated marketing communications strategy.[48] Promotion for new products is required at each link in the supply chain. If the products are not sold and stocked by retailers, no amount of promotion to consumers will sell the products. Trade promotions, which are promotions to wholesalers or retailers to get them to purchase the new products, often combine introductory price promotions, special events, and personal selling. Introductory price promotions are limited-duration, lower-than-normal prices designed to provide retailers with an incentive to try the products. Manufacturers may run a special event in the form of a special display in a grocery aisle, an introductory celebration, or a party in conjunction with an interesting event like the Academy Awards. Another outlet for exposing buyers to new products is a trade show, which is a temporary concentration of manufacturers that provide retailers the opportunity to view what is available and new in the marketplace. The fashion world's equivalent to trade shows are fashion weeks in which fashion manufacturers meet with retailers and have elaborate runway shows to introduce their new products. Finally, as in many B2B sales situations, personal selling may be the most efficient way to get retailers to purchase their products.

Manufacturers also use promotion to generate demand for new products with consumers. If manufacturers can create demand for the products among consumers, they will go to retailers asking for it (*pull* demand; see Chapter 18), thus further inducing retailers to carry the products. These promotions are often coupled with short-term price reductions, coupons, or rebates. Sometimes manufacturers promote new products in advance of the product launch to create excitement with potential customers, as well as to measure the likely demand so they have appropriate supply available. Automobile and motorcycle manufacturers, for instance, advertise their new products months before they are available on the dealers' floors.

For products that are somewhat complex or conceptually new, marketers may need to provide for more consumer education about the product's benefits than they would for simpler and more familiar products. For technical products, technical support staff, like Apple's Geniuses, must be trained to answer customer questions that may arise immediately after the launch. And for other new ideas, the promotion may simply represent an effort to add value to a relatively well-known product, as Adding Value 11.2 describes.

**Place** The manufacturer coordinates the delivery and storage of the new products with its retailers to ensure that they are available for sale when the customer wants them, at the stores the customer is expecting to find them, and in sufficient quantities to meet demand. Manufacturers work with their retailers on decisions such as:

- Should the merchandise be stored at retailers' distribution centers or distributed directly to stores? (See Chapter 15.)
- What initial and fill-in quantities should be shipped?
- Should the manufacturer be involved in reordering decisions?
- Should the merchandise be individually packaged so it is easy to display in the stores?

---

## Adding Value 11.2    Marilyn Monroe Would Love It: Diamonds for Hair Care[49]

In the drive to create the next big thing in hair care products, consumer goods companies search for innovations in a variety of areas—packaging, brand image, and performance benefits, to name a few. But little changes occur in the basics of hair care, which still relies on product lines like shampoo, conditioner, and styling products. To make its latest lines stand out, Nivea has added something new, something that intrinsically has value in financial markets but is being integrated more for its image appeal in this case: diamonds.

With the Diamond Gloss line, Nivea promises that consumers get actual diamonds ground up into their beauty products. But the value doesn't come from inclusion of the dust of the most expensive gemstones in the world. Instead, the company promises added value in the form of a shine like diamonds.

Women who wash and condition their hair with Diamond Gloss products will get "added brilliance" and "light reflection," making their hair seem shinier and healthier. Note that the crushed up diamonds do nothing to improve hair health, and the company is careful to avoid making that claim. Rather, it promotes the idea that the diamonds themselves, when applied to hair, will make it shine like a diamond would.

Under a different brand name, Nivea's parent company, Beiersdorf AG, offers Cellular Radiance Concentrate Pure Gold by la prairie, a liquid skin serum in which 24-carat gold is dissolved. According to the company's promotions, "the

*Does adding crushed diamonds to hair products enhance their value?*

tiny particles melt into the skin to produce an incomparable radiance and a look that speaks of vitality." Again, gold's value in the serum has nothing to do with its trading price or any actual, proven effect on skin. Rather, the value comes from the idea that a consumer can glitter like gold.

The value to the consumer comes from the idea of luxury these products promise. Diamonds in our hair and gold on our faces—the ultimate in precious value. Do you believe these precious materials integrated into beauty products enhance products' value?

- Should price stickers be affixed on the merchandise at the factory or at the store?

- Should the manufacturer be involved in the maintenance of the merchandise once in the store?

Price   Like the promotion of new products, setting prices is a supply chain–wide decision. Manufacturers must decide at what price they would like products to sell to consumers on the basis of the factors to be discussed in Chapters 13 and 14. They often encourage retailers to sell at a specified price known as the manufacturer's suggested retail price (MSRP). Although retailers often don't abide by the MSRP, manufacturers can withhold benefits such as paying for all or part of a promotion or even refusing to deliver merchandise to noncomplying retailers. It is sometimes easier to start with a higher MSRP and then over time lower it than it is to introduce the new product at a low price and then try to raise it.

When setting the MSRP, manufacturers also consider the price at which the new products are sold to the retailers. The retailers not only need to make a profit on each sale, but also may receive a slotting allowance from the manufacturer, which is a fee paid simply to get new products into stores or to gain more or better shelf space for their products.

Timing   The timing of the launch may be important, depending on the product.[50] Hollywood studios typically release movies targeted toward general audiences (i.e., those rated G or PG) during the summer when children are out of school. New automobile models traditionally are released for sale during September, and fashion products are launched just before the season of the year for which they are intended.

## Evaluation of Results

After the product has been launched, marketers must undertake a critical post-launch review to determine whether the product and its launch were a success or failure and what additional resources or changes to the marketing mix are needed, if any. Many firms use panel data to improve the probability of success during the test marketing phase of a new product introduction. The consumer panel data are collected by panelists scanning in their receipts using a home scanning device. This information is used to measure individual household first-time trials and repeat purchases. Through such data the market demand can be estimated and the firm can figure out the best way to adjust their marketing mix. Some products never make it out of the introduction stage, especially those that seem almost laughable in retrospect. Bottled water for pets? Harley-Davidson perfume?[51]

For those products that do move on though, firms can measure the success of a new product by three interrelated factors: (1) its satisfaction of technical requirements, such as performance; (2) customer acceptance; and (3) its satisfaction of the firm's financial requirements, such as sales and profits.[52] If the product is not performing sufficiently well, poor customer acceptance will result, which in turn leads to poor financial performance.

The new product development process, as we have seen, when followed rationally and sequentially, helps avoid such domino-type failures. The *product life cycle*, discussed in the next section, helps marketers manage their products' marketing mix during and after introduction.

## CHECK YOURSELF

1. What are the steps in the new product development process?
2. Identify different sources of new product ideas.

# THE PRODUCT LIFE CYCLE

The product life cycle defines the stages that products move through as they enter, get established in, and ultimately leave the marketplace and thereby offers marketers a starting point for their strategy planning. The stages of the life cycle often reflect marketplace trends, such as the healthy lifestyle trend that places organic and green product categories in their growth stages. Exhibit 11.4 illustrates a typical product life cycle, including the industry sales and profits over time. In their life cycles, products pass through four stages: introduction, growth, maturity, and decline. When the product category first launches, its products initiate the introduction stage. In the growth stage, the product gains acceptance, demand and sales increase, and more competitors emerge in the product category. In the maturity stage, industry sales reach their peak, so firms try to rejuvenate their products by adding new features or repositioning them. If these efforts succeed, the product achieves new life.[53] If not, it goes into decline and eventually exits the market.

Not every product follows the same life cycle curve. Many products, such as home appliances, stay in the maturity stage for a very long time. Manufacturers may add features to dishwashers and washing machines, but the mature product category remains essentially the same and seems unlikely to enter the decline stage unless some innovative, superior solution comes along to replace them.

The product life cycle offers a useful tool for managers to analyze the types of strategies that may be required over the life of their products. Even the strategic emphasis of a firm and its marketing mix (four Ps) strategies can be adapted from insights about the characteristics of each stage of the cycle, as we summarize in Exhibit 11.5.

Let's look at each of these stages in depth.

## Introduction Stage

The introduction stage for a new, innovative product or service usually starts with a single firm, and innovators are the ones to try the new offering. Some new-to-the-world products and services that defined their own product category and industry include the telephone (invented by Alexander Graham Bell in 1876), the transistor

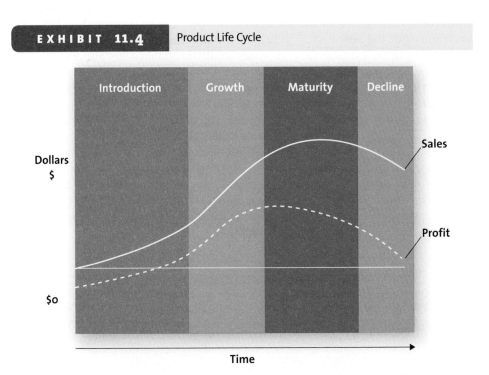

| **EXHIBIT 11.4** | Product Life Cycle |
| --- | --- |

| EXHIBIT 11.5 | Characteristics of Different Stages of the Product Life Cycle | | | |
|---|---|---|---|---|
| | **Introduction** | **Growth** | **Maturity** | **Decline** |
| Sales | Low | Rising | Peak | Declining |
| Profits | Negative or low | Rapidly rising | Peak to declining | Declining |
| Typical consumers | Innovators | Early adopters and early majority | Late majority | Laggards |
| Competitors (number of firms and products) | One or few | Few but increasing | High number of competitors and competitive products | Low number of competitors and products |

semiconductor (Bell Laboratories in 1947), the Walkman portable cassette player (Sony in 1979), the Internet browser (Netscape in 1994), personal digital assistant (Palm in 1996), iTunes (Apple in 2001), and Blu-ray (Sony in 2006). Sensing the viability and commercialization possibilities of a market-creating new product, other firms soon enter the market with similar or improved products at lower prices. The same pattern holds for less innovative products like apparel, music, and even a new soft drink flavor. The introduction stage is characterized by initial losses to the firm due to high start-up costs and low levels of sales revenue as the product begins to take off. If the product is successful, firms may start seeing profits toward the end of this stage.

## Growth Stage

The growth stage of the product life cycle is marked by a growing number of product adopters, rapid growth in industry sales, and increases in both the number of competitors and the number of available product versions.[54] The market becomes more segmented and consumer preferences more varied, which increases the potential for new markets or new uses of the product or service.[55]

Also during the growth stage, firms attempt to reach new consumers by studying their preferences and producing different product variations—varied colors, styles, or features—which enable them to segment the market more precisely. The goal of this segmentation is to ride the rising sales trend and firmly establish the firm's brand, so as not to be outdone by competitors. In recognizing the growing demand for and appeal of organic products, many food manufacturers are working hard to become the first brand that consumers think of when they consider organic products. Del Monte was the first of the major canned vegetable sellers to go organic, releasing organic versions of its tomatoes, green beans, corn, and sweet peas, along with an organic chicken broth product under its College Inn line. The cans feature bold "organic" banners across the front and promise that no pesticides were used to produce the food items. Even though Del Monte products have been around for over 100 years, in this growth category, the company is a newer entrant in the organic market, so it must work to establish its distinctive appeal.[56]

As firms ride the crest of increasing industry sales, profits in the growth stage also rise because of the economies of scale associated with manufacturing and marketing costs, especially promotion and advertising. At the same time, firms that have not yet established a stronghold in the market, even in narrow segments, may decide to exit in what is referred to as an "industry shakeout."

## Maturity Stage

The maturity stage of the product life cycle is characterized by the adoption of the product by the late majority and intense competition for market share among firms. Marketing costs (e.g., promotion, distribution) increase as these firms vigorously defend their market share against competitors. At the same time, they face intense competition on price as the average price of the product falls substantially compared with the shifts during the previous two stages of the life cycle. Lower prices and increased marketing costs begin to erode the profit margins for many firms. In the later phases of the maturity stage, the market has become quite saturated, and practically all potential customers for the product have already adopted the product. Such saturated markets are prevalent in developed countries. In the United States, most consumer packaged goods found in grocery and discount stores are already in the maturity stage.

Firms may pursue several strategies during this stage to increase their customer base and/or defend their market share, such as entry into new markets and market segments and developing new products.

**Entry into New Markets or Market Segments** Because the market is saturated at this point, firms may attempt to enter new geographical markets, including international markets (as we discussed in Chapter 7), that may be less saturated. For example, Whirlpool manufactures washing machines for Brazil, China, and India that it prices lower than those it sells in the United States to attract the large consumer base of lower-income consumers in these countries.[57] In many developing economies, the large and growing proportion of middle-class households is just beginning to buy the home, kitchen, and entertainment appliances that have been fairly standard in U.S. households for several decades. In India alone, the roughly 487 million middle-class consumers spend over $100 billion a year on a variety of consumer products.[58]

However, even in mature markets, firms may be able to find new market segments. Laundry may be a mundane chore that most people dislike, but it is also a huge marketing opportunity. New product development tends to focus on the detergent delivery methods. So in the United States, where laundry tablets have never been very popular (Americans prefer to pour their liquid detergent and thus control the amount they add to the wash basket), Dial has developed a laundry sheet, similar to the dryer sheets used as fabric softeners. This 3-in-1 product includes laundry detergent, fabric softener, and antistatic agents.[59] It is more expensive than buying the three products separately from Dial, but is 20 percent less expensive than purchasing premium brand versions of the three items. Dial hopes to appeal to a new market segment that wants a premium product and save money, without cannibalizing its core customer groups.

*To generate sales in a mature market, Dial Corporation has developed a laundry sheet that includes detergent, fabric softener, and antistatic agents to appeal to a new market segment that wants a premium product while saving money, without cannibalizing its core customer groups.*

**Development of New Products** Despite market saturation, firms continually introduce new products with improved features or find new uses for existing products because they need constant innovation and product proliferation to defend market share from intense competition. Firms such as 3M, P&G, and Hewlett-Packard, for instance, continually introduce new products. Innovations by such firms ensure that they are able to retain or grow their respective market shares. KFC took its expertise with its existing product line consisting of different types of fried chicken and developed Kentucky Grilled Chicken, a relatively innovative product line in an otherwise mature market.[60]

## Decline Stage

Firms with products in the decline stage either position themselves for a niche segment of diehard consumers or those with special needs or completely exit the market. The few laggards that have not yet tried the product or service enter the market at this stage. Take vinyl long-playing records (LPs) for example. In an age of CDs and Internet-downloaded music in MP3 and other formats, it may seem surprising that vinyl records are still made and sold. But though the sales of vinyl LPs have been declining in the past

*KFC used its expertise in chicken preparation to introduce Kentucky Grilled Chicken to stimulate sales in a mature market.*

15 years, about 2 million still are sold in the United States each year. Granted, this is a minuscule number compared with the 800 million CDs sold each year, but diehard music lovers prefer the unique sound of a vinyl record to the digital sound of CDs and music in other formats. Because the grooves in vinyl records create sound waves that are similar to those of a live performance, and therefore provide a more authentic sound, nightclub DJs, discerning music listeners, and collectors prefer them. Even some younger listeners have been buying vinyl records, influenced perhaps by their parents' collections, the sound, or simply the uniqueness of an LP.

Aiding this continued demand is the fact that there are simply too many albums of music from the predigital era that are available only on vinyl. It may take many years, maybe even decades, for all the music from earlier generations to be digitized. Until that time, turntable equipment manufacturers, small record-pressing companies such as Music Connection in Manhattan, and new and emerging record companies, such as Premier Crue Music, continue to have a market that demands their LPs.[61]

## The Shape of the Product Life Cycle Curve

In theory, the product life cycle curve is assumed to be bell shaped with regard to sales and profits. In reality, however, each product or service category has its own individual shape; some move more rapidly through their product life cycles than others, depending on how different the category is from offerings currently in the market and how valuable it is to the consumer. New products and services that consumers accept very quickly have higher consumer adoption rates very early in their product life cycles and move faster across the various stages.

For example, DVD players and DVDs moved much faster than VCRs across the life cycle curve and have already reached the maturity stage, likely because consumers who already owned VCRs were accustomed to recording TV shows and playing prerecorded movies and programs. It also was easy to switch VCR customers to DVD technology because DVDs were more durable and had better resolution than videotapes. Finally, prices for DVDs and DVD players dropped more quickly and drastically than did VCR prices, which made the new technology a better value.

## Strategies Based on Product Life Cycle: Some Caveats

Although the product life cycle concept provides a starting point for managers to think about the strategy they want to implement during each stage of the life cycle of a product, this tool must be used with care. The most challenging part of applying the product life cycle concept is that managers do not know exactly what shape each product's life cycle will take, so there is no way to know precisely what stage a product is in. If, for example, a product experiences several seasons of declining sales, a manager may decide that it has moved from the growth stage to decline and stop promoting the product. As a result, of course, sales decline further. The manager then believes he or she made the right decision because the product continues to follow a predetermined life cycle. But what if the original sales decline was due to a poor strategy or increased competition—issues that could have been addressed with positive marketing support? In this case, the product life cycle decision became a self-fulfilling prophecy, and a growth product was doomed to an unnecessary decline.[62]

Fortunately, new research, based on the history of dozens of consumer products, suggests that the product life cycle concept is indeed a valid idea, and new analytical tools now provide "rules" for detecting the key turning points in the cycle.[63] In the pharmaceutical industry, where breakthrough innovations are few and far between, firms use the product life cycle to identify the consumer promotions needed at each stage to get the most out of their existing brands.[64]

---

### ☑ CHECK YOURSELF

1. What are the stages in the product life cycle?
2. How do sales and profits change during the various stages?

---

## Summing Up

**L01**  **Identify the reasons firms innovate.**

Firms need to innovate to respond to changing customer needs, prevent decline in sales from market saturation, diversify their risk, and respond to short product life cycles, especially in industries such as fashion, apparel, arts, books, and software markets, where most sales come from new products. Finally, innovations can help firms improve their business relationships with suppliers.

**L02**  **Describe the different groups of adopters articulated by the diffusion of innovation theory.**

The diffusion of innovation theory can help firms predict which types of customers will buy their products or services immediately upon introduction, as well as later as they gain more acceptance in the market. Innovators are those buyers who want to be the first to have the new product or service. Early adopters do not take as much risk as innovators but instead wait and

purchase the product after careful review. The members of the early majority really don't like to take risks and therefore tend to wait until "the bugs" have been worked out of a particular product or service. The late majority are buyers who purchase the product after it has achieved its full market potential. Finally, laggards like to avoid change and rely on traditional products until they are no longer available. Laggards may never adopt a certain product or service.

**L03**  **Identify the factors that determine how fast innovations diffuse.**

The factors that determine how fast innovations diffuse are (1) The relative advantage of the new product, i.e., is it perceived to be better than substitutes?; (2) the compatibility of the product, i.e., how easily can it be used with other products or with the way consumers would use the product?; (3) observability, i.e., how easily can the product and its benefits be observed by consumers?; (4) complexity, i.e., how complex is the product?; and, finally, (5) trialability, i.e., how easily can consumers try and use the product?

**L04** **Explain the stages involved in developing a new product or service.**

When firms develop new products, they go through several steps. First, they generate ideas for the product or service using several alternative techniques, such as internal research and development, R&D consortia, licensing, brainstorming, tracking competitors' products or services, or working with customers. Second, firms test their concepts by either describing the idea of the new product or service to potential customers or showing them images of what the product would look like. Third, the design process entails determining what the product or service will actually include and provide. Fourth, firms test-market their designs. Fifth, if everything goes well in the test market, the product is launched. Sixth, firms must evaluate the new product or service to determine its success.

**L05** **Describe the various product life cycle concepts.**

The product life cycle helps firms make marketing mix decisions on the basis of the product's stage in its life cycle. In the introduction stage, companies attempt to gain a strong foothold in the market quickly by appealing to innovators. During the growth stage, the objective is to establish the brand firmly. When the product reaches the maturity stage, firms compete intensely for market share, and many potential customers already own the product or use the service. Eventually, most products enter the decline phase, during which firms withdraw marketing support and eventually phase out the product. Knowing where a product or service is in its life cycle helps managers determine its specific strategy at any given point in time.

## Key Terms

- alpha testing, 342
- beta testing, 343
- breakthrough, 333
- clinical trial, 337
- concept, 340
- concept testing, 340
- decline stage, 348
- diffusion of innovation, 332
- early adopter, 335
- early majority, 335
- first movers, 333
- growth stage, 348

- innovation, 329
- innovator, 334
- introduction stage, 348
- introductory price promotion, 345
- laggards, 335
- late majority, 335
- lead user, 340
- manufacturer's suggested retail price (MSRP), 347
- maturity stage, 348
- pioneer, 333

- premarket test, 344
- product design, 341
- product development, 341
- product life cycle, 348
- prototype, 341
- reverse engineering, 339
- slotting allowance, 347
- test marketing, 344
- trade promotion, 345
- trade show, 345

## Marketing Applications

1. Some people think that a product should be considered "new" only if it is completely new to the market and has never existed before. Describe or give examples of other types of new products.

2. Apple's iPad is smaller than a laptop, but larger than a smartphone. How quickly do you think this product will diffuse among the U.S. population? Describe the types of people who you expect will be in each of the diffusion of innovation stages.

3. Are there any advantages for companies that are the first to introduce products that create new markets? Justify your answer. If you see advantages, explain why some new products still fail.

4. Identify and describe the ways that companies generate new product ideas. Which of these ways involve the customer? How can firms assess the value of the ideas that customers generate?

5. Describe an example of a new product or service that is targeted at the college student market. Using the concept testing discussion in the chapter, describe how you would conduct a concept test for this product or service.

6. How does the Internet help companies gain customer input on their existing and new products?

7. Nature's Path is about to introduce a type of granola and is in the market testing phase of the new product development process. Describe two ways that Nature's Path might conduct initial market testing prior to launching this new product.

8. You are a marketing manager at 3M, responsible for marketing their newest Post-It. How would slotting allowances and trade promotion help promote your product?

9. What type of deodorant do you use? What stage of the product life cycle is it in? Is the deodorant manufacturer's marketing strategy—its four Ps—consistent with the product's stage in its life cycle? Explain.

10. In what stage of the product life cycle is a new model of a PlayStation video game console? Is Sony's marketing strategy—its four Ps—consistent with the product's stage in its life cycle? How is it different from that of the deodorant in the previous question? Explain.

11. You have recently been hired by a cosmetics company in the product development group. The firm's brand is a top-selling, high-end line of cosmetics. The head of the development team has just presented research that shows that "tween" girls, aged 11 to 15, are very interested in cosmetics and have the money to spend. The decision is made to create a line of tween cosmetics based on the existing adult line. As the product moves through development you begin to notice that the team seems to lean toward a very edgy and sexual theme for the line, including naming the various lines "envy," "desire," "prowess," and "fatal attraction." You begin to wonder, is this concept too much for girls in the targeted age group?

www.mhhe.com/
grewal3e

## Quiz Yourself

1. Whenever Donald considers upgrading his personal computer system, he consults with Jeremy, a knowledgeable friend who always has the latest technology. For Donald, Jeremy is a(n) _____ in the diffusion of innovation curve.
   a. innovator
   b. laggard
   c. late majority
   d. early majority
   e. early adopter

2. Zappos.com, an online shoe store, worked to overcome the problem of new product _____ with its easy, no-hassle return procedure.
   a. relative advantage
   b. compatibility
   c. observability
   d. complexity
   e. trialability

(Answers to these two questions are provided on page 608.)

Go to www.mhhe.com/grewal3e to practice an additional 11 questions.

## Net Savvy

1. Go to www.inventables.com. Choose two of the products found at the site. What are some potential applications of these ideas?

2. The automotive industry is constantly adding new and different products and technologies to cars and trucks. Conduct an Internet or library database search for innovative new automotive technologies. Choose products that fit each stage of the product life cycle, and justify your choices.

## Chapter Case Study

### THE SMART(EST) PHONE[65]

In 2007, Apple introduced the iPhone, a purchase comparable to buying three devices in one: an iPod, a wireless phone, and a wireless computer device. On the first day the iPhone was available, consumers lined up in the streets in hopes of getting the opportunity to purchase it. *Time* Magazine then named the iPhone the "Invention of the Year."[66] And today, more than 30 million iPhones have been sold, giving Apple a 100 percent year-over-year rise in sales.[67] Its total share in the U.S. smartphone market of 25 percent runs second to Blackberry's 41 percent share.[68] However, worldwide, Nokia's Symbian owns almost half the smartphone market, followed by Blackberry with 20 percent and the iPhone with 15 percent.[69]

## APPLE INC.

Apple manufactures and sells computer, music, and phone hardware, along with related software. Since its incorporation in 1977[70] under the name Apple Computer Incorporated, Apple has introduced products that challenge conventional approaches in the electronics industry. It pioneered modular design with the Apple II, engineered initial graphical interfaces with the Macintosh, and offered the PowerBook as the first laptop to include a built-in track pad.[71]

In 2001, Apple changed how consumers listen to music when it entered the portable music player market. Since then, it has sold more than 225 million iPods, making it the market leader with a 74 percent market share in the MP3 arena.[72] According to most consumers and technology experts, the success of the iPod resulted from its incredible ease of use. By combining a music store, software, and portable player into one simple system, Apple eliminated the problems consumers faced with other music players and thus created value by simplifying the digital music experience.

Although Apple dominated the dedicated MP3 player market, more and more phone manufacturers were adding music playback to their handsets. Primary phone manufacturers, such as Nokia and Motorola, already had existing relationships with cellular carriers, so they achieved a distinct advantage in the U.S. market, where cellular carriers dominate the distribution market for handsets.

## THE SMARTPHONE MARKET

Apple partnered with AT&T to be the exclusive service provider for the iPhone. The first iPhone entered at $599, and then dropped to $399 shortly after. Since the initial launch, Apple offered newer models, including the 3G and 3GS (16GB or 32GB), priced at $99, $199, or $299, respectively, assuming the customer signs a two-year wireless phone contract. The iPhone's newest features include video capabilities and access to the App store and iTunes store.

The iPhone initiated the growth of the smartphone product life cycle by encouraging many new competitors to enter the market. Now consumers wonder how they ever went anywhere without instant access to their e-mail, music, GPS, Web, games, and various selected applications. In turn, 2010 has been called "the year of the mobile computer," as the smartphone market moves into the mass-market stage.[73] This market has grown considerably as well through new entrants, including Google's Droid, which is selling at a quicker pace than the iPhone.[74] The Droid runs on Google's Android operating system, with integration with Gmail, Google Calendar, and Google Voice, but it currently offers "only" 10,000 applications, compared with the more than 100,000 apps available for the iPhone.[75]

Still, only 21 percent of U.S. wireless subscribers use a smartphone, even as makers add more and more capabilities and prices continue to drop. By the end of 2011, forecasters predict there will be more smartphones than feature cell phones.[76] What makes these devices so powerful is their integration with the customer's surroundings—able to scan prices at a store or look up the nearest coffee shop in an instant.

## THE IPHONE

When Apple entered the market, it was the first to integrate wireless, music, and phone features onto one device, so it needed to market the iPhone's capabilities carefully, including the touchscreen, the GPS maps, e-mail capabilities, and excellent user interface.

To improve the purchasing process, Apple relied on simplification to make the ordeal as painless as possible. Customers who disliked shopping for phones could buy online and register through iTunes or visit an AT&T or an Apple store. Either retail location could help customers with service issues.

For the iPhone's application store, any programmer may build an app and sell it via downloads. In turn, the number of apps has grown so great that users rely completely on their preferred downloads and find themselves lost without the access their iPhone offers. New competitors in the market would have to build off this network, which currently is one of Apple's primary competitive advantages. Each month, approximately $200 million worth of applications sell through Apple's app store; the Android has sold only about $5 million per month.[77]

Although the iPhone is no longer a new product, each year the device will receive improvements, designed to encourage customers to upgrade to a newer version. In the meantime, new applications are constantly launching, supported only on the iPhone. Will the Android network be able to catch up to this vast network of applications?

## Questions

1. At what stage in the product life cycle is the iPhone? What about other smartphones?

2. Given the diffusion of innovation theory, which is the largest and second largest group currently purchasing smartphones? Justify your answer.

3. Will Apple's iPhone maintain its competitive edge, or will Google's Android become the market leader?

4. What would happen to the smartphone market if Android applications were available on the iPhone and vice versa.

# Services: The Intangible Product

Recall from Chapter 11 that the life cycle for some products and services is relatively steep. In that chapter, we talked about how much faster DVDs diffused compared with VCRs. In a similar sense, televisions diffused somewhat slowly, until they eventually reached the maturity stage. Personal computers have moved along this life cycle much more quickly and now appear in approximately as many homes as do televisions. But what do these product life cycles have to do with this chapter on services? Plenty, if you are involved in the manufacture or sale of those personal computers.

As anyone who has ever confronted the "blue screen of death" or an incomprehensible error message—usually on the last page of the paper you were writing—can attest, technical difficulties are terribly frustrating. Perhaps even more frustrating are the hours invested on the telephone, trying to reach a customer service representative, who may or may not be able to help.

Even in this challenging situation, 90 percent of Apple customers report they are very satisfied with its customer service. Part of the reason for this high satisfaction may stem from the product itself; because Apple is less subject to viruses than PCs, consumers may not need customer service as often. More likely though, it results from Apple's efforts to assist Mac, iPod, iPad, and iPhone owners. On purchasing a new Apple, customers may also sign up for "One-to-One" service for $99. In return, they may make appointments for individual assistance with an Apple representative, as many times as they wish, over the course of the following year. Even without buying this upgrade, Apple owners can visit the Apple site and make an appointment with a technician or "Genius" in a local Apple store. If an Apple fan has no store nearby, he or she can look for help online, whether through Apple's own problem solutions or on discussion groups that cover a range of potential problems.

Despite its customer service success, Apple still disappoints about 10 percent of its customers. Its research shows that most customer service failures occur because of confusion about product

## LEARNING OBJECTIVES

**LO1** Describe how the marketing of services differs from the marketing of products.

**LO2** Discuss the four gaps in the Service Gaps Model.

**LO3** Examine the five service quality dimensions.

**LO4** Explain the zone of tolerance concept.

**LO5** Identify three service recovery strategies.

warranties. In the fine print, customers can discover that water damage or abuse voids any product warranty. Not a lot of water, and not an absurd amount of abuse, but any of either. An iPod might stop working because just a drop of water, falling from the headphones, travels down the cord and enters into the jack. This situation infuriates customers, many of whom treat their Apple products with great care. And it is damaging to a company's reputation to sell a product that is considered among the best but not support it with the absolutely best service.

Yet despite these concerns, Apple's customer service remains significantly better than that of virtually any other computer company, for which approximately 25 percent of customers express dissatisfaction. In this prime area, service, Apple can separate itself from the competition without having to make technological advancements. The new iPad may create excitement and media buzz, yet the introduction of a new product is not the only way to attract customers to a company. Services, even as simple as treating the customer as a valued member of the Apple team, can have a remarkable effect too.[1]

● ● ●

Whereas a **service** is any intangible offering that involves a deed, performance, or effort that cannot be physically possessed,[2] **customer service** specifically refers to human or mechanical activities firms undertake to help satisfy their customers' needs and wants. By providing good customer service, firms add value to their products or services.

Exhibit 12.1 illustrates the continuum from a pure service to a pure product. Most offerings, like those of Apple, lie somewhere in the middle and include some service and some product. Even those firms that are engaged primarily in selling a product, like an apparel store, typically view service as a method to maintain a sustainable competitive advantage. This chapter moves on to take an inclusive view of services as anything from pure service businesses to a business that uses service as a differentiating tool to help it sell physical products.

Economies of developed countries like the United States have become increasingly dependent on services. Services account for 76 percent of the U.S. gross domestic product (GDP), a much higher percentage than they did 50, 20, or even 10 years ago. In turn, the current list of *Fortune* 500 companies contains more service companies and fewer manufacturers than in previous decades.[3] This dependence and the growth of service-oriented economies in developed countries have emerged for several reasons.

| EXHIBIT 12.1 | The Service–Product Continuum |
|---|---|

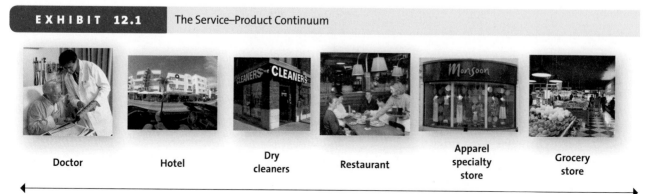

| Doctor | Hotel | Dry cleaners | Restaurant | Apparel specialty store | Grocery store |

◄─────────────────────────────────────────────────────────────►

Service dominant                                                                    Product dominant

First, it is generally less expensive for firms to manufacture their products in less developed countries. Even if the goods are finished in the United States, some of their components likely were produced elsewhere. In turn, the proportion of service production to goods production in the United States, and other similar economies, has steadily increased over time.

Second, people place a high value on convenience and leisure. For instance, household maintenance activities, which many people performed themselves in the past, have become more popular and quite specialized. Food preparation, lawn maintenance, house cleaning, pet grooming, laundry and dry cleaning, hair care, and automobile maintenance are all often performed by specialists.

*As the population ages, the need for health care professionals increases.*

Third, as the world has become more complicated, people are demanding more specialized services—everything from plumbers to personal trainers, from massage therapists to tax preparation specialists, from lawyers to travel and leisure specialists and even health care providers. The aging population in particular has increased the need for health care specialists, including doctors, nurses, and caregivers in assisted living facilities and nursing homes, and many of those consumers want their specialists to provide personalized, dedicated services.

# SERVICES MARKETING DIFFERS FROM PRODUCT MARKETING

**L01** Describe how the marketing of services differs from the marketing of products.

The marketing of services differs from product marketing in respect to four fundamental characteristics of services: Services are intangible, inseparable, variable, and perishable.[4] (See Exhibit 12.2.) This section examines these differences and discusses how they affect marketing strategies.

## Intangible

As the title of this chapter implies, the most fundamental difference between a product and a service is that services are intangible—they cannot be touched, tasted, or seen like a pure product can. When you get a physical examination, you see and hear the doctor, but the service itself is intangible. This intangibility can prove highly challenging to marketers. For instance, it makes it difficult to convey the benefits of services—try describing whether the experience of visiting your dentist was good or bad and why. Service providers (e.g., physicians, dentists) therefore offer cues to help their customers experience and perceive their service more positively, such as a waiting room stocked with television sets, beverages, and comfortable chairs to create an atmosphere that appeals to the target market.

**EXHIBIT 12.2** Core Differences between Services and Goods

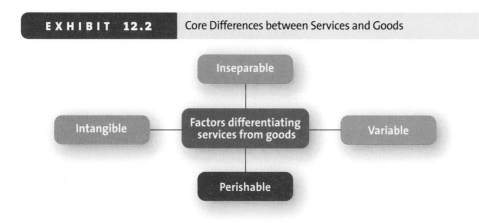

*Since it is difficult to "show" a service, marketers like Six Flags evoke images in its advertising of happy families and friends enjoying a ride at one of its amusement parks.*

A service cannot be shown directly to potential customers and that also makes it difficult to promote. Marketers must therefore creatively employ symbols and images to promote and sell services, like Six Flags does in using its advertising to evoke images of happy families and friends enjoying a roller-coaster ride. Professional medical services provide appropriate images of personnel doing their jobs in white coats surrounded by high-tech equipment. Educational institutions promote the quality of their services by touting their famous faculty and alumni, as well as their accreditations. They also often use images of happy students sitting spellbound in front of a fascinating professor or going on to lucrative careers of their own.

Because of the intangibility of services, the images that marketers use must reinforce the benefit or value that a service provides. Professional service providers, such as doctors, lawyers, accountants, and consultants, depend heavily on consumers' perceptions of their integrity and trustworthiness. Yet the promotional campaigns some of these professionals use have been criticized by their peers and consumer welfare groups. Ethical and Societal Dilemma 12.1 discusses the tensions created when service providers use marketing tactics to attract clients to their service but still attempt to maintain a perception of integrity and trustworthiness.

## Inseparable Production and Consumption

Unlike a pair of jeans that may have been made six months prior to purchase halfway around the world, services are produced and consumed at the same time; that is, the service and its consumption are **inseparable**. When getting a haircut, the customer not only is present but also may participate in the service process. Furthermore, the interaction with the service provider may have an important impact on the customer's perception of the service outcome. If the hair stylist appears to be having fun while cutting hair, it may positively impact the experience.

Because the service is inseparable from its consumption, customers rarely have the opportunity to try the service before they purchase it. And after the service has been performed, it can't be returned. Imagine telling your hair stylist that you want to have the hair around your ears trimmed as a test before doing the entire head. Because the purchase risk in these scenarios can be relatively high, service firms sometimes provide extended warranties and 100 percent satisfaction guarantees.[5] The Choice Hotels chain, for instance, states: "We guarantee total guest satisfaction at Comfort Inn, Comfort Suites, Quality, Sleep Inn, Clarion and MainStay Suites hotels. If you are not satisfied with your accommodations or our service, please advise the front desk of a problem right away."[6]

## Variable

The more humans are needed to provide a service, the more likely there is to be **variability** in the service's quality. A hair stylist may give bad haircuts in the morning because he or she went out the night before. Yet that stylist still may offer a better service than the undertrained stylist working in the next station over. A restaurant, which offers a mixture of services and products, generally can control its food quality but not the variability in food preparation or delivery. If a consumer has a problem with a product, it can be replaced, redone, destroyed, or, if it is already in the supply chain, recalled. In many cases, the problem can even be fixed before the product gets

---

### Ethical and Societal Dilemma 12.1

#### Who Are You Going to Call?

At one time, lawyers in many states were prohibited from advertising their services because many believed that marketing by lawyers would undermine the integrity of the profession. Over time, the laws were repealed. But in the face of the advertising that has ensued, many are questioning whether the marketing tactics of some lawyers have gone too far.

The term "ambulance chaser" usually is used derogatorily to refer to lawyers who solicit clients when they are stressed or their ability to make rational decisions is limited, such as just after a car accident. The term was coined when some personal injury lawyers literally followed ambulances and offered legal services to the injured parties. Critics of lawyers who market their services point to the aggressive advertising and promotional programs these attorneys use, which often prey on potential clients' vulnerabilities after they have been injured or in some way negatively impacted by the actions of others. The lawyers who market themselves this way claim they are providing a valuable service to society.

To respond to the need for ethical guidance, many professional associations offer guidelines and example cases to help members determine which types of advertisements might be considered unethical by peers and other interested parties. For example, the American Bar Association (ABA) has drafted a set of rules that its members must abide by when creating their advertising. It also offers a variety of resources to help lawyers determine what kinds of advertising are appropriate. Among those resources, the ABA offers a website dedicated to "Information on Professionalism and Ethics in Lawyer Advertising," with court rulings about advertising and links to state-specific lawyer association advertising rules.[7] For example, one of the rules that ABA-certified lawyers are expected to follow bans any use of pop-up ads or the use of actors when advertising law services.[8]

For practicing lawyers and other professionals, the ethical dilemma remains: how to balance their need to gain clients through marketing with their need to retain an image of professionalism and integrity. Can marketing be used to communicate the benefits of legal services without preying on the vulnerabilities of consumers?

---

into consumers' hands. But an inferior service can't be recalled; by the time the firm recognizes a problem, the damage has been done.

Marketers also can use the variable nature of services to their advantage. A micromarketing segmentation strategy can customize a service to meet customers' needs exactly (see Chapter 8). Geek Housecalls has a micromarketing segmentation strategy and will come to your home or office to repair or service your PC—setting up a network, cleaning your hard drive, or even tutoring you on the operation of a particular program. Clients are matched with their very own "personal geek" on the basis of their needs, which allows for a fully personalized service offering.

*Computer crashing? Network down? Call Geek Housecalls.*

In an alternative approach, some service providers tackle the variability issue by replacing people with machines. For simple transactions like getting cash, using an ATM is usually quicker and more convenient—and less variable—than waiting in line for a bank teller. Many retailers have installed kiosks with broadband Internet access in their stores. In addition to offering customers the opportunity to order merchandise not available in the store, kiosks can provide routine customer service, freeing employees to deal with more demanding customer requests and problems and reducing service variability. For example, customers can use kiosks to locate merchandise in the store and determine whether specific products, brands, and sizes are available. Kiosks can also be used to automate existing store services, such as gift registry management, rain checks, film drop-off, credit applications, and preordering service for bakeries and delicatessens.

*Since services are perishable, service providers like ski areas offer less expensive tickets at night to stimulate demand.*

### Perishable

Services are perishable in that they cannot be stored for use in the future. You can't stockpile your membership at Gold's Gym like you could a six-pack of V-8 juice, for instance. The perishability of services provides both challenges and opportunities to marketers in terms of the critical task of matching demand and supply. As long as the demand for and the supply of the service match closely, there is no problem, but unfortunately, this perfect matching rarely occurs. A ski area, for instance, can be open as long as there is snow, even at night, but demand peaks on weekends and holidays, so ski areas often offer less expensive tickets during off-peak periods to stimulate demand. Airlines, cruise ships, movie theaters, and restaurants confront similar challenges and attack them in similar ways.

**CHECK YOURSELF**

1. What are the four marketing elements that distinguish services from products?
2. Why can't we separate firms into just service or just product sellers?

**LO2** Discuss the four gaps in the Service Gaps Model.

# PROVIDING GREAT SERVICE: THE GAPS MODEL

Certainly, providing great service is not easy, and it requires a diligent effort to analyze the service process piece by piece in order to improve it. We now examine what is known as the *Gaps Model*, which is designed to highlight those areas where customers believe they are getting less or poorer service than they should (the gaps) and how these gaps can be closed.

Customers have certain expectations about how a service should be delivered. When the delivery of that service fails to meet those expectations, a service gap results. The Gaps Model (Exhibit 12.3) is designed to encourage the systematic examination of all aspects of the service delivery process and prescribe the steps needed to develop an optimal service strategy.[9]

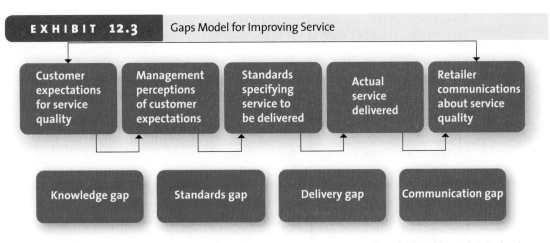

| **EXHIBIT 12.3** | Gaps Model for Improving Service |
| --- | --- |

Customer expectations for service quality

Management perceptions of customer expectations

Standards specifying service to be delivered

Actual service delivered

Retailer communications about service quality

Knowledge gap

Standards gap

Delivery gap

Communication gap

*Sources:* Michael Levy and Barton Weitz, *Retailing Management,* 8th ed. (Burr Ridge, IL: McGraw-Hill, 2012). Adapted from Valarie Zeithaml, A. Parasuraman, and Leonard Berry, *Delivering Quality Customer Service* (New York: The Free Press, 1990) and Valarie Zeithaml, Leonard Berry, and A. Parasuraman, "Communication and Control Processes in the Delivery of Service Quality," *Journal of Marketing* 52, no. 2 (April 1988), pp. 35–48.

As Exhibit 12.3 shows, there are four service gaps:

1.  The knowledge gap reflects the difference between customers' expectations and the firm's perception of those customer expectations. Firms can close this gap by matching customer expectations with actual service through research.

2.  The standards gap pertains to the difference between the firm's perceptions of customers' expectations and the service standards it sets. By setting appropriate service standards and measuring service performance, firms can attempt to close this gap.

3.  The delivery gap is the difference between the firm's service standards and the actual service it provides to customers. This gap can be closed by getting employees to meet or exceed service standards.[10]

4.  The communication gap refers to the difference between the actual service provided to customers and the service that the firm's promotion program promises. If firms are more realistic about the services they can provide and at the same time manage customer expectations effectively, they generally can close this gap.

As we discuss the four gaps subsequently, we will apply them to the experience that Marcia Kessler had with a motel in Maine. She saw an ad for a package weekend that quoted a very reasonable daily rate and listed the free amenities available at Paradise Motel: free babysitting services, a piano bar with a nightly singer, a free Continental breakfast, a heated swimming pool, and newly deco-

*What service gaps did Marcia experience while on vacation at the Paradise Motel in Maine?*

rated rooms. When she booked the room, Marcia discovered that the price advertised was not available during the weekend, and a three-day minimum stay was required. After checking in with a very unpleasant person at the front desk, Marcia and her husband found that their room appeared circa 1950 and had not been cleaned. When she complained, all she got was "attitude" from the assistant manager. Resigned to the fact that they were slated to spend the weekend, she decided to go for a swim. Unfortunately, the water was "heated" by Booth Bay and stood at around 50 degrees. No one was using the babysitting services because there were few young children at the resort. It turned out the piano bar singer was the second cousin of the owner, and he couldn't carry a tune, let alone play the piano very well. The Continental breakfast must

have come all the way from the Continent, because everything was stale and taste-less. Marcia couldn't wait to get home.

## The Knowledge Gap: Understanding Customer Expectations

An important early step in providing good service is knowing what the customer wants. It doesn't pay to invest in services that don't improve customer satisfaction.[11] To reduce the knowledge gap, firms must understand the customers' expectations. To understand those expectations, firms undertake customer research and increase the interaction and communication between managers and employees.

Customers' expectations are based on their knowledge and experiences.[12] Marcia's expectations were that her room at the motel in Maine would be ready when she got there, the swimming pool would be heated, the singer would be able to sing, and the breakfast would be fresh. If the resort never understood her expectations, it is unlikely it would ever be able to meet them.

Expectations vary according to the type of service. Marcia's expectations might have been higher, for instance, if she were staying at a Ritz-Carlton rather than the Paradise Motel. At the Ritz, she might expect employees to know her by name, be aware of her dietary preferences, and have placed fresh fruit of her choice and fresh-cut flowers in her room before she arrived. At the Paradise Motel, she expected easy check-in/check-out, easy access to a major highway, a clean room with a comfortable bed, and a TV, at a bare minimum.

People's expectations also vary depending on the situation. If she had been traveling on business, the Paradise Motel might have been fine (had the room at least been clean and modern), but if she were celebrating her 10th wedding anniversary, she probably would prefer the Ritz. Thus, the service provider needs to not only know and understand the expectations of the customers in its target market but also have some idea of the occasions of service usage.

To help ensure that JetBlue understands customers' expectations, it surveys at least 35 customers from every flight it operates.[13] The airline brings together

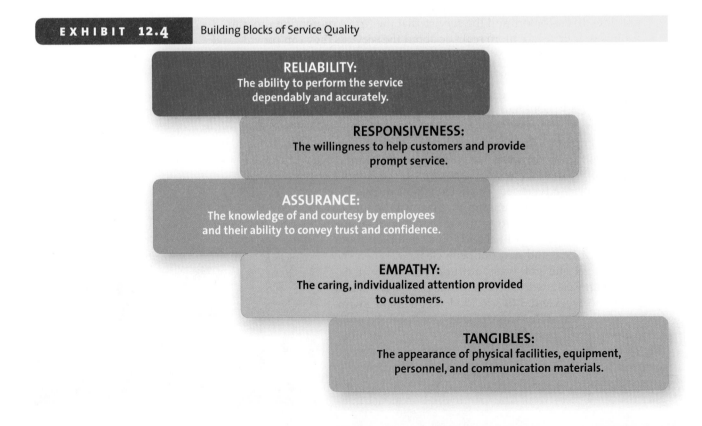

**EXHIBIT 12.4**    Building Blocks of Service Quality

**RELIABILITY:**
The ability to perform the service dependably and accurately.

**RESPONSIVENESS:**
The willingness to help customers and provide prompt service.

**ASSURANCE:**
The knowledge of and courtesy by employees and their ability to convey trust and confidence.

**EMPATHY:**
The caring, individualized attention provided to customers.

**TANGIBLES:**
The appearance of physical facilities, equipment, personnel, and communication materials.

top executives to discuss what customers are saying and how it should respond. Based on customer feedback, it has changed the way it deals with customers faced with delays and cancellations. It also knows which planes have problems with the entertainment system and which airports have the rudest staffs (New York's JFK is first, followed closely by Boston's Logan airport).[14]

**Evaluating Service Quality Using Well-Established Marketing Metrics** To meet or exceed customers' expectations, marketers must determine what those expectations are. Yet because of the intangibility of any service, the service quality, or customers' perceptions of how well a service meets or exceeds their expectations, often is difficult for customers to evaluate let alone express.[15] Customers generally use five distinct service dimensions to determine overall service quality: reliability, responsiveness, assurance, empathy, and tangibles (Exhibit 12.4). Adding Value 12.1 describes how the Broadmoor Hotel maintains its five-star rating by focusing on these five service characteristics.

**LO3** Examine the five service quality dimensions.

If you were to apply the five service dimensions to your own decision-making process when you select a college—which provides the service of education—you might find results like those in Exhibit 12.5.

If your expectations include an individualized experience at a state-of-the-art institution, perhaps University B is a better alternative for you. But if you are relying heavily on academic performance and career placement from your university experience, then University A might be a better choice in terms of the five service dimensions. If a strong culture and tradition are important to you, University A offers this type of environment. What your expectations are has a lot to do with your perception of how your university falls within these service dimensions.

Marketing research (see Chapter 9) provides a means to better understand consumers' service expectations and their perceptions of service quality. This research

| **EXHIBIT 12.5** | Collegiate Service Dimensions | |
|---|---|---|
| | **University A** | **University B** |
| **Reliability** | Offers sound curriculum with extensive placement services and internships. | Curriculum covers all the basics but important courses are not always available. Career placement is haphazard at best. |
| **Responsiveness** | Slow to respond to application. Very structured visitation policy. Rather inflexible with regard to personal inquiries or additional meetings. | Quick response during application process. Open visitation policy. Offers variety of campus resources to help with decision making. |
| **Assurance** | Staff seems very confident in reputation and services. | Informal staff who convey enthusiasm for institution. |
| **Empathy** | Seems to process student body as a whole rather than according to individual needs or concerns. | Very interested in providing a unique experience for each student. |
| **Tangibles** | Very traditional campus with old-world look and feel. Facilities are manicured. Dorm rooms are large, but bathrooms are a little old. | New campus with modern architecture. Campus is less manicured. Dorm rooms are spacious with newer bathrooms. |

## Adding Value **12.1**     The Broadmoor Manages Service Quality for Five-Star Rating

Established in 1891 as a gambling casino and transformed into a "grand resort" in 1918, the Broadmoor, in Colorado Springs, Colorado, is one of the world's premier resorts.[16] It has received a record 50 consecutive years of five-star ratings from the *Forbes Travel Guide*. Perry Goodbar, former vice president of marketing for the Broadmoor, emphasizes, "It's the people who truly make this place special. Exceptional service quality begins with exceptional people." Some aspects of its service quality are as follows:

**Reliability** Every new Broadmoor employee, before ever encountering a customer, attends a two-and-a-half-day orientation session and receives an employee handbook. Making and keeping promises to customers is a central part of this orientation. Employees are trained always to give an estimated time for service, whether it be room service, laundry service, or simply how long it will take to be seated at one of the resort's restaurants. When an employee makes a promise, he or she keeps that promise. Employees are trained to never guess if they don't know the answer to a question. Inaccurate information only frustrates customers. When an employee is unable to answer a question accurately, he or she immediately contacts someone who can.

**Assurance** The Broadmoor conveys trust by empowering its employees. An example of an employee empowerment policy is the service recovery program. If a guest problem arises, employees are given discretionary resources to rectify the problem or present the customer with something special to help mollify them. For example, if a meal is delivered and there's a mistake in the order or how it was prepared, a waiter can offer the guest a free item such as a dessert or, if the service was well below expectations, simply take care of the bill. Managers then review expenses to understand the nature of the problem and help prevent it from occurring again.

**Tangibles** One of the greatest challenges for the Broadmoor in recent years has been updating rooms built in the early part of the twentieth century to meet the needs of twenty-first century visitors. To accomplish this, it spent $200 million between 1992 and 2002 in improvements, renovating rooms, and adding a new outdoor pool complex.

**Empathy** One approach used to demonstrate empathy is personalizing communications. Employees are instructed to always address a guest by name, if possible. To accomplish this, employees are trained to listen and observe carefully to determine a guest's name. Subtle sources for this information include convention name tags, luggage ID tags, credit cards, or checks. In addition, all phones within the Broadmoor display a guest's room number and name on a screen.

**Responsiveness** Every employee is instructed to follow the HEART model of taking care of problems. First, employees must "Hear what a guest has to say." Second, they must "Empathize with them" and then "Apologize for the situation." Third, they must "Respond to the guest's needs" by "Taking action and following up."

*The Broadmoor in Colorado Springs, Colorado is known for exceptional service quality.*

can be extensive and expensive, or it can be integrated into a firm's everyday interactions with customers. Today, most service firms have developed voice-of-customer programs and employ ongoing marketing research to assess how well they are meeting their customers' expectations. A systematic voice-of-customer (VOC) program collects customer inputs and integrates them into managerial decisions.

An important marketing metric to evaluate how well firms perform on the five service quality dimensions (Exhibit 12.4) is the zone of tolerance, which refers to the area between customers' expectations regarding their desired service and the minimum level of acceptable service—that is, the difference between what the customer really wants and what he or she will accept before going elsewhere.[17] To define the zone of tolerance, firms ask a series of questions about each service quality dimension that relates to:

**L04** Explain the zone of tolerance concept.

- The desired and expected level of service for each dimension, from low to high.
- Customers' perceptions of how well the focal service performs and how well a competitive service performs, from low to high.
- The importance of each service quality dimension.

Exhibit 12.6 illustrates the results of such an analysis for Lou's Local Diner, a family-owned restaurant. The rankings on the left are based on a nine-point scale, on which 1 is low and 9 is high. The length of each box illustrates the zone of tolerance for each service quality dimension. For instance, according to the length of the reliability box, customers expect a fairly high level of reliability (top of the box) and will also accept only a fairly high level of reliability (bottom of the box). On the other end of the scale, customers expect a high level of assurance (top of the box) but will accept a fairly low level (bottom of the box). This difference is to be expected, because the customers also were asked to assign an importance score to the five service quality dimensions so that the total equals 100 percent (see bottom of Exhibit 12.6). Looking at the average importance score, we conclude that reliability is relatively important to these customers, but assurance is not. So customers have a fairly narrow zone of tolerance for service dimensions that are fairly important to them and a wider range of tolerance for those service dimensions that are less important. Also note that Lou's Local Diner always rates higher than its primary competitor, Well-Known National Chain, on each dimension.

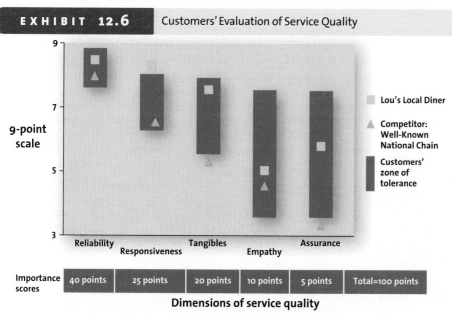

**EXHIBIT 12.6**  Customers' Evaluation of Service Quality

9-point scale

Legend:
- Lou's Local Diner
- Competitor: Well-Known National Chain
- Customers' zone of tolerance

Dimensions: Reliability, Responsiveness, Tangibles, Empathy, Assurance

| Importance scores | 40 points | 25 points | 20 points | 10 points | 5 points | Total=100 points |
|---|---|---|---|---|---|---|

**Dimensions of service quality**

Note: The scale ranges from a 9 indicating very high service quality on a given service quality dimension to a 1 indicating very low service quality.

*Lou's Local Diner always rates higher than its primary competitor, Well-Known National Chain, on each service quality dimension.*

Further note that Well-Known National Chain scores below the zone of tolerance on the tangibles dimension, meaning that customers are not willing to accept the way the restaurant looks and smells. Lou's Local Diner, in contrast, performs above the zone of tolerance on the responsiveness dimension—maybe even too well. Lou's may wish to conduct further research to verify which responsiveness aspects it is performing so well, and then consider toning those aspects down. For example, being responsive to customers' desires to have a diner that serves breakfast 24 hours a day can be expensive and may not add any further value to Lou's Diner, because customers would accept more limited times.

A very straightforward and inexpensive method of collecting consumers' perceptions of service quality is to gather them at the time of the sale. Service providers can ask customers how they liked the service—though customers often are reticent to provide negative feedback directly to the person who provided the service—or distribute a simple questionnaire. Starbucks customers can rate their experience by visiting the Web survey at the bottom of its receipts. Using this method, a complaining customer does not have to make the complaint directly to the barista who may have caused the problem, but Starbucks still gets almost instantaneous feedback. Regardless of how information is collected, companies must take care not to lose it, which can happen if there is no effective mechanism for filtering it up to the key decision makers. Furthermore, in some cases, customers cannot effectively evaluate the service until several days or weeks later. Automobile dealers, for instance, often call their customers a week after they perform a service like an oil change to assess their service quality.[18]

Another excellent method for assessing customers' expectations is making effective use of customer complaint behavior. Even if complaints are handled effectively to solve customers' problems, the essence of the complaint is too often lost on managers. For instance, an airline simply established a policy that said customer service reps could not discuss any issues involving fees to travel agents. So when a customer called to complain about the policy, the representative just shut her down.[19]

Even firms with the best formal research mechanisms in place must put managers on the front lines occasionally to interact directly with the customers. Unless the managers who make the service quality decisions know what their service providers are facing on a day-to-day basis, and unless they can talk directly to the customers with whom those service providers interact, any customer service program they create will not be as good as it could be.

## The Standards Gap: Setting Service Standards

Getting back to the Paradise Motel in Maine, suppose it set out to determine its customers' service expectations and gained a pretty good idea of them. Its work is still far from over; the next step is to set its service standards and develop systems to meet customers' service expectations. How can it make sure that every room is cleaned by 2:00 p.m., or that the breakfast is checked for freshness and quality every day? The employees must be thoroughly trained not only to complete their specific tasks but also to know how to treat guests, and the manager needs to set an example of high service standards, which will permeate throughout the organization.

*Service providers, like this housekeeper at a hotel, generally want to do a good job, but they need to be trained to know exactly what a good job entails.*

**Achieving Service Goals through Training** To consistently deliver service that meets customers' expectations, firms must set specific, measurable goals. To help ensure that quality, the employees should be involved in the goal setting. For instance,

for the Paradise Motel, the most efficient process would be to start cleaning rooms at 8:00 a.m. and finish by 5:00 p.m. But many guests want to sleep late, and new arrivals want to get into their room as soon as they arrive, often before 5:00. So a customer-oriented standard would mandate that the rooms get cleaned between 10:00 a.m. and 2:00 p.m.

Service providers generally want to do a good job, as long as they know what is expected of them.[20] Motel employees should be shown, for instance, exactly how managers expect them to clean a room and what specific tasks they are responsible for performing. In general, more employees will buy into a quality-oriented process if they are involved in setting the goals. For instance, suppose an employee of the motel refuses to clean the glass cups in the rooms because she believes that disposable plastic cups are more ecological and hygienic. If management listens to her and makes the change, it should make the employee all the more committed to the other tasks involved in cleaning rooms.

For frontline service employees, pleasant interactions with customers do not always come naturally. Although people can be taught specific tasks related to their jobs, it is simply not enough to tell employees to "be nice" or "do what customers want." A quality goal should be specific: Greet every customer/guest you encounter with "Good morning/afternoon/evening, Sir or Miss." Try to greet customers by name.

In extreme cases, such training becomes even more crucial. From long ticket lines to cancelled flights to lost baggage to safety concerns, customer service incidents are on the rise in the airline industry. Faced with these mounting complaints, some airlines are attempting to implement better employee training geared toward identifying and defusing potentially explosive situations.

**Commitment to Service Quality** Service providers take their cues from management. If managers strive for excellent service, treat their customers well, and demand the same attitudes from everyone in the organization, it is likely employees will do the same.

The home improvement center Home Depot is working hard to keep up with its rival Lowe's.[21] Top managers, including the CEO, spend time in the stores to understand what its customers want, and it realizes they want professionals and salespeople who actually know how to fix and build things. So the company focuses on hiring people with those skills.

Zappos, the online shoe and apparel retailer now owned by Amazon, achieves high service goals by utilizing training methods considered extreme by other retailers, and by having a strong commitment to service quality by its management team. It is able to deliver high service quality in part because it empowers its employees to satisfy customers no matter what it takes. (See Superior Service 12.1.)

## The Delivery Gap: Delivering Service Quality

The delivery gap is where "the rubber meets the road," where the customer directly interacts with the service provider. Even if there are adequate standards in place, the employees are well-trained, and management is committed to meeting or exceeding customers' service expectations, there can still be a delivery gap. Marcia experienced several delivery gaps at the Paradise Motel: the unclean room, the assistant manager's attitude, the unheated swimming pool, the poor piano bar singer, and the stale food. While some of these issues may have been avoided, it is also possible that the motel had a power outage resulting in the unheated swimming

*Home Depot CEO Frank Blake learned from spending time in stores that his customers want professionals and salespeople that know how to fix and build things.*

## Superior Service 12.1    Zappos Pays $2000 to Quit

Imagine a company where employees are offered $2000 to quit and only 2 or 3 percent accept, where staff is encouraged to tweet during office hours, and where customer service trumps cost-cutting so completely that a call center employee provides contact information for late-night pizza delivery in the caller's hometown even though the company sells shoes. Now imagine a business deal worth $850 million in which the acquirer, online retail giant Amazon, enthusiastically agrees to keep the leadership and staff of its new holding and to protect and maintain the company's corporate culture.[22]

This isn't fantasy; it's Zappos, a Las Vegas–based company that got its start in 1999 selling shoes online. Over time, the company expanded its category offerings but, most significantly, aligned itself with core values that stress extraordinary customer service. When Amazon founder and CEO Jeff Bezos saw Zappos's customer-centric business approach, he extended a partnership opportunity that both organizations feel will generate growth.

Zappos's determination to instill the value of customer satisfaction in employees begins with the interview process. Applicants undergo separate interviews for experience and fit within the company culture. During training, which can last as long as five weeks, all new employees are required to work in the call center. New hires who feel this work is beneath them are paid for their time and shown the door. At no time during training are call center employees given a script, a time limit for calls, or a quota. Rather they are encouraged to make the customer happy, even if satisfaction requires a four-hour phone call or a bouquet of flowers.

Like Amazon, Zappos employs processes that enhance customer loyalty, even if those processes aren't the most cost effective for the company. Customers are encouraged to order multiple products, for example, so they can touch, feel, and try on prospective purchases. Returned items ship free for up to a year. Both the call center and the warehouse

operate 24/7. Items are shipped faster and sooner than the Zappos website indicates, giving customers the sense of speedy service. To add even more value for customers, Zappos also operates a couture site, a discounter site, and outlet stores.

Making one company stand out from the crowd requires legendary customer service and perhaps, according to the Zappos core value list, a little weirdness.

*Zappos employees will do almost anything to satisfy a customer.*

pool, the piano bar singer may have been ill, and the food was stale because of a missed delivery. Even if there are no other gaps, a delivery gap always results in a service failure.

Delivery gaps can be reduced when employees are empowered to act in the customers' and the firm's best interests and supported in their efforts so they can do their jobs effectively.[23] Technology can also be employed to reduce delivery gaps. (See Exhibit 12.7.)

**Empowering Service Providers** In this context, empowerment means allowing employees to make decisions about how service gets provided to customers. When frontline employees are authorized to make decisions to help their customers, service quality generally improves.

Empowerment becomes more important when the service is more individualized. Nordstrom provides an overall objective—satisfy customer needs—and then encourages employees to do whatever is necessary to achieve the objective. For example, a Nordstrom shoe sales associate decided to break up two pairs of shoes,

| EXHIBIT 12.7 | Methods to Reduce Delivery Gaps |

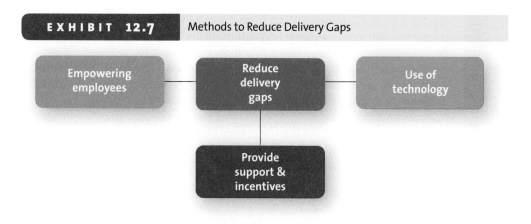

one a size 10 and the other a size 10½, to sell to a hard-to-fit customer. Although the other two shoes were unsalable and therefore made for an unprofitable sale, the customer purchased 5 other pairs that day and became a loyal Nordstrom customer as a result. Empowering service providers with only a rule like "Use your best judgment" (as Nordstrom does) might cause chaos. At Nordstrom, department managers avoid abuses by coaching and training sales people to understand what "Use your best judgment" means.

**Providing Support and Incentives**  A service provider's job can often be difficult, especially when customers are unpleasant or less than reasonable. But the service provider cannot be rude or offensive just because the customer is. The old cliché, "Service with a smile," remains the best approach. To ensure that service is delivered properly, management needs to support the service provider in several ways.

First, managers and coworkers should provide emotional support to service providers by demonstrating a concern for their well-being and standing behind their decisions. Because it can be very disconcerting when a waiter is abused by a customer who believes her food was improperly prepared, for instance, restaurant managers must be supportive and help the employee get through his emotional reaction to the berating experienced.[24] Such support can extend to empowering the waiter to rectify the situation by giving the customer new food and a free dessert, in which case the manager must understand the waiter's decision, not punish him for giving away too much.

Second, service providers require instrumental support—the systems and equipment—to deliver the service properly. Many retailers provide state-of-the-art instrumental support for their service providers. In-store kiosks help sales associates provide more detailed and complete product information and enable them to make sales of merchandise that either is not carried in the store or is temporarily out of stock.

Third, the support that managers provide must be consistent and coherent throughout the organization. Patients expect physicians to provide great patient care using state-of-the-art procedures and medications, but because they are tied to managed-care systems (health maintenance organizations or HMOs), many doctors must squeeze more people into their office hours and prescribe less optimal, less expensive, courses of treatment. These conflicting goals can be so frustrating and emotionally draining on physicians and other health care providers that some have found work outside of medicine.

Fourth, a key part of any customer service program is providing rewards to employees for excellent service. Numerous firms have developed a service reputation by ensuring that their employees recognize the value the firm places on customer service. Travelocity, for example, features employees who champion the customer service experience in a weekly e-mail. Believing that engaged employees

*At Radio Shack, customers can get merchandise information or order products not carried in the store.*

*Which store has better customer service: the one with self-checkout (left), or the store offering a face-to-face interaction with the customer? It depends on who you ask.*

are the key to customer satisfaction, it works to create an atmosphere that reinforces the commitment to customers by encouraging employees to nominate colleagues who exemplify its commitment to customers. Through constant feedback about who is serving the customer best, as well as smaller events such as monthly lunches with the CEO for selected employees, Travelocity creates a business environment that recognizes and rewards customer service.[25] The results for Travelocity include a wealth of awards, such as a top ranking on the Customer Online Respect Survey and a designation as the "World's Leading Travel Internet Site" for ten consecutive years.[26]

**Use of Technology** Technology has become an increasingly important facilitator of the delivery of services. Using technology to facilitate service delivery can provide many benefits, such as access to a wider variety of services, a greater degree of control by the customer over the services, and the ability to obtain information. Management also benefits from the increased efficiency in service processes through reduced servicing costs and, in some cases, can develop a competitive advantage over less service-oriented competitors.[27]

As noted previously, electronic kiosks and other technologies can reduce the variability of providing a service. In addition to kiosks, self-checkout machines can help close the delivery gap. There are more than 100,000 self-checkout machines in use today, and they are multiplying in grocery and discount stores.[28] Walmart, Kroger, Home Depot, Best Buy, Costco, and IKEA already use them. Even libraries nationwide are installing self-checkout machines for books.

Self-checkouts reduce the delivery gap because they appeal to those shoppers who want to move on quickly and believe they can zip through their check-outs faster by using the machines. One reason customers think self-checkout is faster is that they are active when using it, unlike waiting for a cashier, which leaves customers with nothing to do and may make it seem as though time is dragging. In actuality, self-checkout does save between 15 seconds and 15 minutes, depending on the size of an order.

Technological advances that help close the delivery gap are expanding. Salons and cosmetics counters use kiosks to show customers how they would look with different beauty products and various hair colors. Stores enable customers to scan price tags and then have a kiosk recommend complementary items. Touchscreen terminals at tables in Chuck E. Cheese let customers order food and play games, from the comfort of their own table.[29]

The technological delivery of services can cause problems though. Some customers either do not embrace the idea of replacing a human with a machine for business interactions or have problems using the technology. In other cases, the technology may not perform adequately, such as self-checkout scanners that fail to scan all merchandise or ATMs that run out of money or are out of order.

## The Communications Gap: Communicating the Service Promise

Poor communication between marketers and their customers can result in a mismatch between an ad campaign's or a salesperson's promises and the service the firm can actually offer.

Although firms have difficulty controlling service quality because it can vary from day to day and provider to provider, they do have control over how they communicate their service package to their customers. If a firm promises more than it can deliver, customers' expectations won't be met. An advertisement may lure a customer into a service situation once, but if the service doesn't deliver on the promise, the customer will never return. Dissatisfied customers also are likely to tell others about the underperforming service, using word of mouth or, increasingly, the Internet, which has become an important channel for dissatisfied customers to vent their frustrations.

The communications gap can be reduced by managing customer expectations and by promising only what you can deliver, or possibly even a little less.[30] Suppose you need an operation, and the surgeon explains, "You'll be out of the hospital in five days and back to your normal routine in a month." You have the surgery and feel well enough to leave the hospital three days later. Two weeks after that, you're playing tennis again. Clearly, you will tend to think your surgeon is a genius. However, regardless of the operation's success, if you had to stay in the hospital for 10 days and it took you two months to recover, you would undoubtedly be upset.

A relatively easy way to manage customer expectations is to coordinate how the expectation is created and the way the service is provided. Expectations typically are created through promotions, advertising, or personal selling. Delivery is another function altogether. If a salesperson promises a client that an order can be delivered in one day, and that delivery actually takes a week, the client will be disappointed. However, if the salesperson coordinates the order with those responsible for the service delivery, the client's expectations likely will be met.

Customer expectations can be managed when the service is delivered. Recorded messages tell customers who have phoned a company with a query how many minutes they will have to wait before the next operator is available. Business-to-business sellers automatically inform online customers of any items that are out of stock. Whether online or in a store, retailers can warn their customers to shop early during a sale because supplies of the sale item are limited. People are generally reasonable when they are warned that some aspect of the service may be below standard. They just don't like surprises!

## CHECK YOURSELF

1. Explain the four service gaps identified by the Gaps Model.
2. List at least two ways to overcome each of the four service gaps.

**L05**    Identify three service recovery strategies.

# SERVICE RECOVERY

Despite a firm's best efforts, sometimes service providers fail to meet customer expectations. When this happens, the best course of action is to attempt to make amends with the customer and learn from the experience. Of course, it is best to avoid a service failure altogether, but when it does occur, the firm has a unique opportunity to demonstrate its customer commitment.[31] Effective service recovery efforts can significantly increase customer satisfaction, purchase intentions, and positive word of mouth, although customers' postrecovery satisfaction levels usually fall lower than their satisfaction level prior to the service failure.[32]

Power of the Internet 12.1 articulates how the Internet has provided customers with an enormous stage to air their dissatisfaction with a product or service. No longer are dissatisfied customers able to vent their frustrations only to a few friends—now it may be to millions! Service providers beware: if there is a problem, it must be rectified immediately.

The Paradise Motel in Maine could have made amends with Marcia Kessler after its service failures if it had taken some relatively simple, immediate steps: The assistant manager could have apologized for his bad behavior and quickly upgraded her to a suite and/or given her a free night's lodging for a future stay. The motel could also have given her a free lunch or dinner to make up for the

---

### ⬡ Power of the Internet **12.1**    David versus Goliath: Service Providers Beware

Thanks to the Internet, customer service may go viral. According to the old adage, customers having a good experience tell one person, while those having a bad experience tell four, now with blogs, Twitter, YouTube, and similar sites, millions of people learn about service problems in a matter of hours.

United Airlines learned this lesson the hard way. A member of the band Sons of Maxwell watched from a plane window as baggage handlers tossed luggage with little regard for the value or fragility of the instruments in the cargo.[33] Musician Dave Carroll complained immediately to flight attendants, but to no avail. After arriving at his destination, Carroll discovered his $3,500 acoustic guitar was broken. He made it through his performances using alternative guitars and then, on his return flight a week later, complained again about the damaged instrument. Over the next weeks and months, he contacted the airline repeatedly about the problem while also shelling out $1,200 to get his guitar fixed. When Carroll did finally hear from the airline regarding compensation, he was informed that his claim was denied because he hadn't filed it appropriately.

His response was a triad of original songs and videos posted to the Internet. The first tune, called "United Breaks Guitars," suggests that flying a different airline or driving would have been preferable to flying United. The video scored five million hits in a matter of weeks.[34] A month later, the band released another song that poked fun at one of United's customer service employees and the airline's policies for handling baggage complaints. The third tune acknowledges United's attempts to improve and cautions that customers will choose other carriers if improvements aren't forthcoming. Bloggers weren't uniformly impressed by the music, but many responded with their own horror stories of United's customer service, creating a public relations maelstrom for the airline.

United responded with an admission of guilt on Twitter, a $3000 donation to a musical charity, and an ad campaign indicating they took complaints about luggage handling seriously. The company also saw an opportunity to turn a single customer service problem into a training opportunity: With Carroll's permission, they use the video to improve passenger service worldwide.[35]

A well-run company needs a management plan that minimizes the risk of service failures as well as a defined response to customer service problems that go viral. With today's instant communication technology, what could United have done differently to squelch this public relations nightmare?

*United Airlines broke musician Dave Carroll's guitar. So he posted a triad of original songs and videos on the Internet, creating a public relations nightmare for the airline.*

bad breakfast. Alternatively, the assistant manager could have asked Marcia how he could resolve the situation and worked with her to come up with an equitable solution. None of these actions would have cost the motel much money. Yet by using the customer lifetime value approach described in Chapter 9, the motel would have realized that by not taking action, it lost Marcia, who over the next few years could have been responsible for several thousand dollars in sales, as a customer forever. Furthermore, Marcia is likely to spread negative word of mouth about the motel to her friends and family because of its failure to recover. Quite simply, effective service recovery entails (1) listening to the customer, (2) providing a fair solution, and (3) resolving the problem quickly.[36]

## Listening to the Customer

Firms often don't find out about service failures until a customer complains. Whether the firm has a formal complaint department or the complaint is offered directly to the service provider, the customer must have the opportunity to air the complaint completely, and the firm must listen carefully to what he or she is saying.

Customers can become very emotional about a service failure, whether the failure is serious (a botched surgical operation) or minor (the wrong change at a restaurant). In many cases, the customer may just want to be heard, and the service provider should give the customer all the time he or she needs to "get it out." The very process of describing a perceived wrong to a sympathetic listener is therapeutic in and of itself. Service providers therefore should welcome the opportunity to be that sympathetic ear, listen carefully, and appear (and actually be) anxious to rectify the situation to ensure it doesn't happen again.[37]

## Finding a Fair Solution

Most people realize that mistakes happen. But when they happen, customers want to be treated fairly, whether that means *distributive* or *procedural* fairness.[38] Their perception of what "fair" means is based on their previous experience with other firms, how they have seen other customers treated, material they have read, and stories recounted by their friends.

**Distributive Fairness** Distributive fairness pertains to a customer's perception of the benefits he or she received compared with the costs (inconvenience or loss). Customers want to be compensated a fair amount for a perceived loss that resulted from a service failure. If, for instance, a person arrives at the airport gate and finds her flight is overbooked, she may believe that taking the next flight that day and receiving a travel voucher is adequate compensation for the inconvenience. But if no flights are available until the next day, the traveler may require additional compensation, such as overnight accommodations, meals, and a round-trip ticket to be used at a later date.[39]

The key to distributive fairness, of course, is listening carefully to the customer. One customer, traveling on vacation, may be satisfied with a travel voucher, whereas another may need to get to the destination on time because of a business appointment. Regardless of how the problem is solved, customers typically want tangible restitution—in this case, to get to their destination—not just an apology. If providing tangible restitution isn't possible, the next best thing is to assure the customer that steps are being taken to prevent the failure from recurring.

A mother approached Buck Rogers, who was the general manager of the Daytona Cubs minor league baseball team, to inform him that a rowdy patron near her and her young child had been swearing constantly during the game. Rogers immediately offered to change her seat, but the mother did not find this offer sufficient because she believed she could probably hear the swearing fan from anywhere in the ballpark. The woman indicated she would never come back. Trying to find an acceptable solution and not lose the fan, Rogers offered her a free admission to another game and told her that when she returned, her son could throw out the first pitch. The end result of this quick thinking: The woman and her son returned many times.[40]

**Procedural Fairness** With regard to complaints, procedural fairness refers to the perceived fairness of the process used to resolve them. Customers want efficient complaint procedures over whose outcomes they have some influence. Customers tend to believe they have been treated fairly if the service providers follow specific company guidelines. Nevertheless, rigid adherence to rules can have deleterious effects. Have you ever returned an item to a store, even a very inexpensive item, that needed a manager's approval? The process can take several minutes and irritate everyone in the check-out line. Furthermore, most managers' cursory inspection of the item or the situation would not catch a fraudulent return. In a case like this, the procedure the company uses to handle a return probably overshadows any potential positive outcomes. Therefore, as we noted previously, service providers should be empowered with some procedural flexibility to solve customer complaints.

Flexibility entails discretion. Consider the local convenience store that sells both cigarettes and alcohol. The store owner has implemented a policy that everyone who appears to be under 30 years of age who attempts to purchase these items must show valid identification. If the store clerks comply, the customers accept it as part of the purchasing protocol and perceive it as fair for everyone. If a customer looks over 30 years of age, however, but the store clerk asks for identification, this can create a service failure.

A "no questions asked" return policy has been offered as a customer service by many retailers for years. But because of its high cost as a result of customers abusing the policy, many retailers have modified their return policy.[41] Some large retailers, for instance, now limit their returns to 90 days, since this is considered a reasonable amount of time for customers to return an item. Others will only grant a store credit based on the lowest selling price for the item if the customer doesn't have a receipt. In addition, for some consumer electronics products that have been opened, customers must pay a 15 percent restocking fee.

## Resolving Problems Quickly

The longer it takes to resolve a service failure, the more irritated the customer will become and the more people he or she is likely to tell about the problem. To resolve service failures quickly, firms need clear policies, adequate training for their employees, and empowered employees. Health insurance companies, for instance, have made a concerted effort in recent years to avoid service failures that occur because customers' insurance claims have not been handled quickly or to the customers' satisfaction. USAA, a member-owned financial services organization that caters to members of the military and their families, employs telephone representatives who work directly with "action agents" within the organization to resolve customer complaints and identify service failures quickly. Its efforts have paid off; USAA has a high annual customer renewal rate and owns and manages more than $125 billion in assets for 7.2 million members.[42]

**CHECK YOURSELF**

1. Why is service recovery so important to companies?
2. What can companies do to recover from a service failure?

## Summing Up

**LO1** **Describe how the marketing of services differs from the marketing of products.**

Unlike products, services are intangible, inseparable, variable, and perishable. They cannot be seen or touched, which makes it difficult to describe their benefits or promote them. Service providers therefore enhance service delivery with tangible attributes, like a nice atmosphere or price benefits. Services get produced and consumed at the same time, so marketers must work quickly, and they are more variable than products, though service providers attempt to reduce this variability as much as possible. Finally, because consumers cannot stockpile perishable services, marketers often provide incentives to stagger demand.

**LO2** **Discuss the four gaps in the Service Gaps Model.**

The knowledge gap reflects the difference between customers' expectations and the firm's perception of those customer expectations. Firms need to match customer expectations with actual service through research. The standards gap is the difference between the firm's perceptions of customers' expectations and the service standards it sets. Appropriate service standards and measurements of service performance help close this gap. The delivery gap is the difference between the firm's service standards and the actual service it provides to customers. Closing this gap requires adequate training and empowerment of employees. The communication gap refers to the difference between the actual service provided to customers and the service that the firm's promotion program promises. Firms close the communications gap by managing customer expectations and promising only what they can deliver.

**LO3** **Examine the five service quality dimensions.**

First, reliability refers to whether the provider consistently provides an expected level of service. Second, responsiveness means that the provider notes consumers' desires and requests and then addresses them. Third, assurance reflects the service provider's own confidence in its abilities. Fourth, empathy entails the provider's recognition and understanding of consumer needs. Finally, tangibles are the elements that go along with the service, such as the magazines in a doctor's waiting room.

**LO4** **Explain the zone of tolerance concept.**

The area between customers' desired service and the minimum level of service they will accept is the zone of tolerance. It is the difference between what the customer really wants and what he or she will accept before going elsewhere. Firms can assess their customers' zone of tolerance by determining the desired and expected level of service for each service dimension, their perceptions of how well the focal service performs and how well a competitive service performs, and the importance of each service quality dimension.

**LO5** **Identify three service recovery strategies.**

In a best-case scenario, the service never fails. But some failures are inevitable and require the firm to make amends to the customer by (1) listening carefully and letting the customer air his or her complaint, (2) finding a fair solution to the problem that compensates the customer for the failure and follows procedures the customer believes are fair, and (3) resolving the problem quickly.

## Key Terms

- communication gap, 365
- customer service, 360
- delivery gap, 365
- distributive fairness, 377
- emotional support, 373
- empowerment, 372
- inseparable, 362
- instrumental support, 373
- intangible, 361
- knowledge gap, 365
- perishable, 364
- procedural fairness, 378
- service, 360
- service gap, 364
- service quality, 367
- standards gap, 365
- variability, 362
- voice-of-customer (VOC) program, 369
- zone of tolerance, 369

## Marketing Applications

1. Those companies from which you purchase products and services are not pure sellers of services, nor are they pure sellers of products. What services does a pizza restaurant provide? What goods does the Post Office provide?

2. You have been sitting in the waiting room of your mechanic's shop for more than an hour. With the knowledge that products are different from services, develop a list of the things the shop manager could do to improve the overall service delivery. Consider how the shop might overcome problems associated with the tangibility, separability, variability, and perishability of services.

3. You have conducted a zone of tolerance analysis for a local car wash. You find that the length of the reliability and responsiveness boxes are much greater than those of the other three service quality dimensions. You also find that the car wash is positioned above the zone box on reliability but below the box on responsiveness. What should you tell the manager of the car wash to do?

4. Design a simple system for collecting customer information about the services of your car wash client.

5. Think back to your last job. What training did your employer provide regarding how to interact with customers and provide good customer service? What could your employer have done to prepare you better to interact with customers?

6. Provide an example of a specific situation in which a service provider could have avoided a service failure if he or she had been empowered to do so. What should that person have done?

7. What types of support and incentives could your university provide advisors to help make them more attentive to students' needs?

8. What technologies do you use that help facilitate your transactions with a specific retailer or service provider? Would you rather use the technology or engage in a face-to-face relationship with a person? How, if at all, would your parents' answer to these two questions be different?

9. A local health club is running a promotional campaign that promises you can lose an inch a month off your waist if you join the club and follow its program. How might this claim cause a communications gap? What should the club do to avoid a service failure?

10. Suppose the health club didn't listen to your advice and ran the promotional campaign as is. A new member has come in to complain that not only did he not lose inches off his waist, he actually gained weight. How should the health club manager proceed?

11. You are hired by a career consulting firm that promises to market new graduates to high-paying employers. The firm provides potential clients with an impressive list of employers. It charges the clients a fee, and then a separate finder's fee if the client gets a position. The firm aggressively markets its services and has a large client base. You learn that the firm simply takes submitted résumés and posts them to a variety of online job search engines. The firm never actually contacts any firms on its clients' behalf. The CEO, himself a recent college grad, tells you that the firm never promises to actually contact potential employers, only that they have access to employers and will distribute clients' résumés. What do you think of the career consulting firm's practices?

 www.mhhe.com/
grewal3e

## Quiz Yourself

1. A _____ gap reflects the difference between customers' expectations and the firm's perception of those customer expectations.
   a. seniority
   b. knowledge
   c. standards
   d. delivery
   e. communication

2. When approached by a customer, Nordstrom's employees have been trained to drop whatever they are doing, listen carefully, and provide caring, individualized attention to that customer. Nordstrom employees have been trained to emphasize _____ in the five service quality dimensions.
   a. assurance
   b. reliability
   c. tangibles
   d. responsiveness
   e. empathy

(Answers to these two questions are provided on page 608.)

Go to www.mhhe.com/grewal3e to practice an additional 11 questions.

## Toolkit

**SERVICES ZONE OF TOLERANCE**
Use the Toolkit provided at www.mhhe.com/
grewal3e to assess the zone of tolerance for several
service providers.

## Net Savvy

1. What services does JetBlue (www.jetblue.com) offer? Go to JetBlue's website, click on "About JetBlue," then "Why You'll Like Us." Compare the services of JetBlue, American Airlines (www.aa.com), and Virgin America (www.virginamerica.com) to each other. For www.aa.com, go to "Travel Information," then "During Your Flight," for its services. For www .virginamerica.com, go to "Flying with Us," and then "What's on Board."

2. Go to www.consumerist.com. Click on "Topics," then "Above and Beyond." How did these companies close the service gap in these specific examples? Go back to "Topics," then "Other Customer Service." How can the companies described in these examples close the service gap?

## Chapter Case Study

### PUTTIN' ON THE RITZ[43]

Luxury hotels are booming, and hotels are adding more and more expensive rooms to compete for the highest-end customers.[44] Despite the vast number of hotels in the luxury hotel market, though, the undisputed leaders remain Ritz-Carlton hotels. Ritz-Carlton competes by simply offering the best service. So what exactly does this hotel chain do differently than its competitors, and how does it maintain its advantage based on superior service?

Ritz-Carlton, owned by the hotel group Marriott International, consists of 70 hotels in 23 countries around the world. Ritz hotels employ 32,000 people worldwide and train their employees in the efforts necessary to create the perfect service experience.[45] The history of Ritz-Carlton began in 1927 with the opening of the Ritz-Carlton Boston, a hotel renowned for the lengths it would go to for its guests, such as reupholstering the chairs in Winston Churchill's room in red fabric to match his favorite color or redecorating the décor of Joan Crawford's room with a theme of peppermint Lifesavers, her favorite candies.[46]

Ritz-Carlton's superior customer service also is based on highly trained employees who care for their guests, as well as a sophisticated customer relationship management (CRM) system that ensures that Ritz guests receive consistent and superlative service.

### ATTENTION TO EMPLOYEES

Ritz-Carlton combines extensive employee training and careful hiring practices to create an environment that embraces the customer. For example, employees are instructed to never say the word "No" to a guest, and each concierge receives a $2,000 daily fund for each guest that the concierge can use to solve problems for hotel customers. Ritz guests are often surprised by the little things that hotel employees do, but this high-quality service gets eternally reinforced by constant training. For instance, on every shift, on every Ritz property, a 15-minute meeting acts as a refresher to remind employees to act on one of the 12 "Service Values" that constitute the company's "Gold Standard."

Training is only one part of the excellent customer service; before it even gets to that point, the Ritz-Carlton starts by hiring the right kind of employees. It looks for people who are "warm" and "caring" and works to instill the Ritz-Carlton motto: "We are Ladies and Gentlemen serving Ladies and Gentlemen."[47] Before the opening of a Ritz-Carlton, each employee undergoes more than 80 hours of training. Management tries to see that about half are transferred from other Ritz hotels to ensure that a new opening will maintain the customer service and attention to every detail for which the company continues to be so well known.

## SOPHISTICATED IT SYSTEMS

Ritz's CRM system integrates objective customer information with employee observations. The observational data pertains to special requests that customers may make regarding items such as how they like their bed made, to meal preferences. This information is useful to help other employees serve customers in a manner that is likely to exceed their expectations and delight them.

Ritz-Carlton's goal is to encourage guests to engage actively with the Ritz-Carlton brand. Its research shows that customers who connect with the brand spend 23 percent more than other customers. That makes customer service an important driver of company value. After all, a mere 4 percent increase in customer engagement would be worth approximately $40 million in sales to the company! Employees are trained how to engage their customers, realizing, for example, that a rock star and a retired corporate executive probably should be treated differently. Employees are taught to alter their style depending on the situation, because their interactions should differ when greeted by a guest who says, "Good evening, young man; how are you?" versus another who nods, "Hey dude, how's it going?"

*The Ritz-Carlton's motto is "We are Ladies and Gentlemen serving Ladies and Gentlemen."*

## CHALLENGES TO THE MODEL

Yet the modern economic environment makes it difficult to do everything for everyone—even at the Ritz. In an effort to save costs, Marriott has discontinued its deliveries of daily papers in all its hotel chains. The cost savings have enabled Marriott to avoid massive layoffs, which supports its core value of taking care of employees and thereby encouraging them to treat customers well. But it also means that guests who had grown accustomed to finding a paper outside their door each morning are now disappointed.

When it faced additional revenue declines in 2009, Marriott cut costs on items deemed unlikely to affect the customer experience such as replacing Häagen-Dazs with Edy's ice cream, while at the same time improving customers' experience by enhancing the hotel lobbies with free Wi-Fi and modular furniture that can be arranged to encourage meetings, socializing, and casual dining.[48]

## RECOGNITION OF THE BEST

Finally, beyond the impressive loyalty that Ritz-Carlton enjoys from its customers, it has earned some of the most prestigious awards in quality, including the Malcolm Baldrige Award. To share what it has learned with other companies, Ritz-Carlton recently created a customer service training program that costs $1,700 per person. Now banks, hospitals, law firms, and car dealerships—industries often criticized for providing poor service—send their employees to training programs to improve their own level of service. Even employees of Lexus dealerships, Macy's, and Starbucks have been attendees at Ritz training programs.

Students in Ritz's training program learn about how the hotel chain provides the best service to its customers and how they might borrow some of its techniques in their own industry. The people who do the laundry, maintain the landscaping, park guests' cars, and open the doors at the Ritz are all involved in training employees from other companies that turn to the Ritz for help. They offer advice on how to help guests or customers in their own areas of expertise and also how to perform outside of their job description, when called on, even during busy periods, to ensure superb customer service all the time.

## Questions

1. Using the building blocks (five dimensions) of service quality (see again Exhibit 12.4), evaluate the Ritz-Carlton hotel chain.

2. Compare the Ritz-Carlton's service quality performance with that of the most recent hotel in which you stayed.

3. Using the Gaps Model, identify the service gaps you might have noticed during your most recent hotel stay. How might those gaps be closed?

# VALUE CAPTURE

Section Five contains two chapters on pricing dedicated to value capture. Chapter 13 examines the importance of setting the right price, the relationship between price and quantity sold, break-even analysis, the impact of price wars, and how the Internet has changed the way people shop. Chapter 14 looks specifically at how to set prices.

# Pricing Concepts for Establishing Value

P rices constantly change. Few items maintain totally inflexible prices that remain the same, regardless of the changing environment around them. For example, the recent economic meltdown has had worldwide effects, especially in sectors such as real estate and tourism. No region personifies those two industries better than does Las Vegas. Even in the city known for its extravagance, recessions force budget-based thinking.

The story for the city is not all that different than the story for many homeowners: When times were good, they began projects beyond their means, whether that meant a multibillion-dollar hotel complex or a new sunroom added onto the back of a house. When times went bad though, everything stopped, leaving empty lots in Vegas and abandoned foundations on homes. When new hotels cannot pay their mortgages, banks foreclose on them too; the staid Deutsche Bank now owns the ritzy $3.9 million Cosmopolitan Hotel.

Faced with too much supply, including the thousands of hotel rooms added during the boom years, and not enough demand, as travelers turned to more affordable forms of entertainment, businesses in Las Vegas turned to a basic economic response: They lowered their prices. In 2007, a room in one of Steve Wynn's hotels cost around $500 a night; by 2009, consumers could stay for just $109. On a recent check of prices at Hotels.com, the Paris Las Vegas hotel advertised luxury with no resort fees and rooms for around $150, while the Wynn resort promised a $75 credit for stays of at least three nights.[1]

Hotels are not the only ones suffering though; restaurants have largely given up on their high-end stocks of wine and liquor. According to a food and beverage executive with the MGM Grand, visitors to the gambling mecca still have to eat, but "they're just not spending as much money. They might not have that second glass of wine."[2]

The price shifts clearly have had some of their intended effects. For hotels, occupancy rates are a key economic indicator—for every night the room isn't booked, the hotel loses that revenue forever. And occupancy rates have bounced back slightly from a low point of 72 percent to a recent level of 82 percent.

## LEARNING OBJECTIVES

**LO1** List the four pricing orientations.

**LO2** Explain the relationship between price and quantity sold.

**LO3** Explain price elasticity.

**LO4** Describe how to calculate a product's break-even point.

**LO5** Indicate the four types of price competitive levels.

But remember, price is fluid, and another encouraging sign of Las Vegas's economic recovery actually may mean further price cuts. Contradictory? Not quite. The ambitious CityCenter, an 18-million-square-foot resort complex with an estimated cost of $8.5 billion, opened in December 2009, after months of negotiations with bankers that had shied away from loaning the developers so much when their loan business was so tenuous. That's the good news; for hotels citywide though, the bad news is an influx of supply, namely, the 4000 rooms in CityCenter, even as demand remains soft.[3]

Although knowing how consumers arrive at their perceptions of value is critical to developing successful pricing strategies, sellers also must consider other factors—which is why developing a good pricing strategy is such a formidable challenge to all firms. Do it right, and the rewards to the firm will be substantial. Do it wrong, and failure will be swift and severe. But even if a pricing strategy is implemented well, consumers, economic conditions, markets, competitors, government regulations, and even a firm's own products change constantly—and that means that a good pricing strategy today may not remain an effective pricing strategy tomorrow.

So much rides on marketers setting the right price that we take two chapters to explain the role of price in the marketing mix. First, in this chapter, we explain what "price" is as a marketing concept, why it is important, how marketers set pricing objectives, and how various factors influence price setting. In the next chapter, we extend this foundation by focusing on specific pricing strategies that capitalize on capturing value.

Imagine that a consumer realizes that to save money on a particular item, she will have to drive an additional 20 miles. She may determine that her time and travel costs are not worth the savings, so even though the price tag is higher at a nearby store, she judges the overall cost of buying the product there to be lower. To include aspects of price such as this, we may define price as the overall sacrifice a consumer is willing to make to acquire a specific product or service. This sacrifice necessarily includes the money that must be paid to the seller to acquire the item, but it also may involve other sacrifices, whether nonmonetary, like the value of the time necessary to acquire the product or service, or monetary, like travel costs, taxes, shipping costs, and so forth, all of which the buyer must give up to take possession of the product.[4] It's useful to think of overall price like this to see how the narrower sense of purchase price fits in.

Previously, we have defined *value* as the relationship between the product's benefits and the consumer's costs, which is another way of looking at the same thing. Consumers judge the benefits the product delivers against the sacrifice necessary to obtain it, then make a purchase decision based on this overall judgment of value. Thus, a great but overpriced product can be judged as low in value and may not sell as well as an inferior but well-priced item. In turn, we cannot define price without referring specifically to the product or service associated with it. The key to successful pricing is to match the product or service with the consumer's value perceptions.

In this equation, price also provides information about the quality of products and services. If firms can price their products or services too high, can they price them too low as well? Quite simply, yes. Although price represents the sacrifice consumers make to acquire the product or service, looked at the other way around it also provides helpful signals to consumers. A price set too low may signal low quality, poor performance, or other negative attributes about the product or service. Would you trust your looks to a plastic surgeon advertising rhinoplasty surgery (commonly referred to as a nose job) for only $299.99? We discuss this aspect of price in further detail when we talk about specific pricing strategies in the next chapter, but for now, note that consumers don't necessarily want a low price all the time or for all products. Rather, what they want is high value, which may come with a relatively high or low price, depending on the bundle of benefits the product or service delivers. If the firm wants to deliver value and value is judged by the benefits relative to the cost, then pricing decisions are absolutely critical to the effort to deliver value.

Because price is the only element of the marketing mix that does not generate costs, but instead generates revenue, it is important in its own right. Every other element in the marketing mix may be perfect, but with the wrong price, sales and thus revenue will not accrue. Research has consistently shown that consumers usually rank price as one of the most important factors in their purchase decisions.[5]

Knowing that price is so critical to success, why don't managers put greater emphasis on it as a strategic decision variable? Price is the most challenging of the four Ps to manage, partly because it is often the least understood. Historically, managers have treated price as an afterthought to their marketing strategy, setting prices according to what competitors were charging or, worse yet, adding up their costs and tacking a desired profit on to set the sales price. Prices rarely changed except in response to radical shifts in market conditions. Even today pricing decisions are often relegated to standard rules of thumb that fail to reflect our current understanding of the role of price in the marketing mix.

For example, retailers sometimes use a 100 percent markup rule, otherwise known as "keystoning." That is, they simply double what they paid for the item when they price it for resale (price = wholesale cost $\times$ 2). Yet what happens if the store receives a particularly good deal from the manufacturer on an item? If consumers are not sensitive to price changes for the product, should marketers blindly pass this lower price on to consumers? Why lower the price if it will not stimulate more sales? In this case, it might be better for the store not to follow its standard markup practice and instead take the additional profit. Similarly, if the store's cost for an item goes up and consumers are particularly sensitive to price increases for that product, the store might want to take less than 100 percent markup.

As we said, all this is crucial because consumers may use the price of a product or service to judge its quality.[6] Price is a particularly powerful indicator of quality when consumers are less knowledgeable about the product category. For example, researchers at CalTech gave consumers tastes of three "different" bottles of Cabernet Sauvignon—though two of the bottles contained the exact same wine—priced at three different levels. The participants ranked the $90 bottle as much higher quality wine than the $5 bottle, even though they were drinking the same vintage. That is, "people expect expensive wines to taste better, and then their brains literally make it so."[7] Another research team at Stanford conducted a similar study with energy drinks, though their test of value differed. These participants were paid more or less for the same drink, but "the people who paid discounted prices consistently solved fewer puzzles than the people who paid full price for the drinks."[8] Apparently, consumers perceive more expensive products to perform better for them. In summary, marketers should view pricing decisions as a strategic opportunity to create value rather than as an afterthought to the rest of the marketing mix. Let us now turn to the five basic components of pricing strategies.

*Since people use price to judge quality or performance of a product, when a group of people paid less for an energy drink, they were able to solve fewer puzzles than those who paid more.*

# THE FIVE Cs OF PRICING

Successful pricing strategies are built around the five critical components (the five Cs) of pricing found in Exhibit 13.1.

We examine these components in some detail because each makes a significant contribution to formulating good pricing policies.[9] To start, the first step is to develop the company's pricing objectives.

## Company Objectives

**L01**
List the four pricing orientations.

By now, you know that different firms embrace very different goals. These goals should spill down to the pricing strategy, such that the pricing of a company's products and services should support and allow the firm to reach its overall goals. For example, a firm with a primary goal of very high sales growth will likely have a different pricing strategy than a firm with the goal of being a quality leader.

Each firm then embraces objectives that seem to fit with where management thinks the firm needs to go to be successful, in whatever way it defines success. These specific objectives usually reflect how the firm intends to grow. Do managers want it to grow by increasing profits, increasing sales, decreasing competition, or building customer satisfaction?

Company objectives are not as simple as they might first appear. They often can be expressed in slightly different forms that mean very different things. Exhibit 13.2 introduces some common company objectives and corresponding examples of their implications for pricing strategies. These objectives are not always mutually exclusive, because a firm may embrace two or more noncompeting objectives.

**Profit Orientation**  Even though all company methods and objectives may ultimately be oriented toward making a profit, firms implement a profit orientation specifically by focusing on target profit pricing, maximizing profits, or target return pricing.

- Firms usually implement target profit pricing when they have a particular profit goal as their overriding concern. To meet this targeted profit objective, firms use price to stimulate a certain level of sales at a certain profit per unit.

- The maximizing profits strategy relies primarily on economic theory. If a firm can accurately specify a mathematical model that captures all the factors required to explain and predict sales and profits, it should be able to identify the price at which its profits are maximized. Of course, the problem with this approach is that actually gathering the data on all these relevant factors and somehow coming up with an accurate mathematical model is an extremely difficult undertaking.

**EXHIBIT 13.1**     Five Cs of Pricing

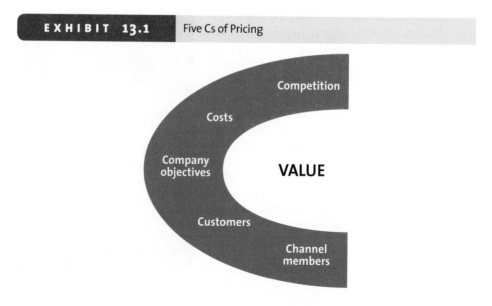

| EXHIBIT 13.2 | Company Objectives and Pricing Strategy Implications |
|---|---|
| **Company Objective** | **Examples of Pricing Strategy Implications** |
| Profit-oriented | Institute a companywide policy that all products must provide for at least an 18 percent profit margin to reach a particular profit goal for the firm. |
| Sales-oriented | Set prices very low to generate new sales and take sales away from competitors, even if profits suffer. |
| Competitor-oriented | To discourage more competitors from entering the market, set prices very low. |
| Customer-oriented | Target a market segment of consumers who highly value a particular product benefit and set prices relatively high (referred to as premium pricing). |

- Other firms are less concerned with the absolute level of profits and more interested in the rate at which their profits are generated relative to their investments. These firms typically turn to target return pricing and employ pricing strategies designed to produce a specific return on their investment, usually expressed as a percentage of sales.

**Sales Orientation** Firms using a sales orientation to set prices believe that increasing sales will help the firm more than will increasing profits. For example, a new health club might focus on unit sales, dollar sales, or market share and therefore be willing to set a lower membership fee and accept less profit at first to focus on and generate more unit sales. In contrast, a high-end jewelry store might focus on dollar sales and maintain higher prices. The jewelry store relies on its prestige image, as well as the image of its suppliers, to provoke sales. Even though it sells fewer units, it can still generate high dollar sales levels.

Finally, some firms may be more concerned about their overall market share than about dollar sales per se (though these often go hand in hand) because they believe that market share better reflects their success relative to the market conditions than do sales alone. A firm may set low prices to discourage new firms from entering the market, encourage current firms to leave the market, and/or take market share away from competitors—all to gain overall market share. For example, though Apple already has sold approximately 6 billion songs since the introduction of its iTunes service, it wants to keep increasing its market share, especially as competitors such as Amazon.com make inroads in this arena. Therefore, instead of 99 cents per song—the fixed pricing structure it previously maintained—Apple sets three price tiers (69 cents, 99 cents, and $1.29) for its songs, according to their popularity and recency. It also offers an option for users to obtain copyright protection: free versions of songs they already own for 30 cents. The songs that are the most popular cost the most, but by charging less for less popular songs, Apple aims to increase its sales per customer.[10]

Yet adopting a market share objective does not always imply setting low prices. Rarely is the lowest-price offering the dominant brand in a given market. Heinz Ketchup, Philadelphia Brand Cream Cheese, Crest toothpaste, and Nike athletic

*Philadelphia Brand Cream Cheese dominates its market AND is a premium-priced brand.*

*Can you tell the difference between the $8,500 and the $320 speakers?*

shoes have all dominated their markets, yet all are premium-priced brands. On the services side, IBM claims market dominance in human resource outsourcing, but again, it is certainly not the lowest price competitor.[11] **Premium pricing** means the firm deliberately prices a product above the prices set for competing products to capture those customers who always shop for the best or for whom price does not matter. Thus, companies can gain market share simply by offering a high-quality product at a fair price as long as they use effective communication and distribution methods to generate high value perceptions among consumers. Although the concept of value is not overtly expressed in sales-oriented strategies, it is at least implicit because, for sales to increase, consumers must see greater value.

**Competitor Orientation** When firms take a **competitor orientation**, they strategize according to the premise that they should measure themselves primarily against their competition. Some firms focus on **competitive parity**, which means they set prices that are similar to those of their major competitors. Another competitor-oriented strategy, **status quo pricing**, changes prices only to meet those of the competition. For example, when Delta increases its average fares, American Airlines and United often follow with similar increases; if Delta rescinds that increase, its competitors tend to drop their fares too.[12] Value is only implicitly considered in competitor-oriented strategies, but in the sense that competitors may be using value as part of their pricing strategies, copying their strategy might provide value.

**Customer Orientation** A **customer orientation** explicitly invokes the concept of value. Sometimes a firm may attempt to increase value by focusing on customer satisfaction and setting prices to match consumer expectations. Or a firm can use a "no-haggle" price structure to make the purchase process simpler and easier for consumers, thereby lowering the overall price and ultimately increasing value. Perhaps the most visible practitioner of no haggle pricing, the Saturn line of GM cars, could not quite weather the storm of economic struggles and is phasing out its operations.

Firms may offer very high-priced, "state-of-the-art" products or services in full anticipation of limited sales. These offerings are designed to enhance the company's reputation and image and thereby increase the company's value in the minds of consumers. Paradigm, a Canadian speaker manufacturer, produces what many audiophiles consider a high-value product, yet offers speakers priced as low as $320 per pair. However, Paradigm also offers a very high-end speaker, for $8,500 per pair. Although few people will spend $8,500 on a pair of speakers, this "statement" speaker communicates what the company is capable of and can increase the image of the firm and the rest of its products—even that $320 pair of speakers. Setting prices with a close eye to how consumers develop their perceptions of value can often be the most effective pricing strategy, especially if it is supported by consistent advertising and distribution strategies.

After a company has a good grasp on its overall objectives, it must implement pricing strategies that enable it to achieve those objectives. As the second step in this process, the firm should look toward consumer demand to lay the foundation for its pricing strategy.

## Customers

When firms have developed their company objectives, they turn to understanding consumers' reactions to different prices. The second C of the five Cs of pricing focuses on the customers. Customers want value, and as you likely recall, price is half of the value equation.

## Adding Value 13.1    How Much Do You Really Value It? Pay What You Want Pricing

When the band Radiohead announced in 2007 that its album *In Rainbows* would sell only online, not in stores, and for as much as fans chose to pay for it, you could practically hear the music industry gasp in surprise. But their generally successful experiment—even though they could have downloaded the music for free, approximately 40 percent of users paid something for it[13]—was neither the first instance of "pay what you want" pricing, nor has it been the last word.

Stephen King is such a popular writer that he pretty well always counts on best-selling releases. In 2000, he tried out a new way to price and sell his latest serial novel. When he published the first installment of *The Plant* on his own website, he vowed that he would keep posting as long as 75 percent of readers, all on the honor system, continued forking over the $1 fee. More than 100,000 people downloaded the initial chapter on the first day it was available, and by the end of that month, 76 percent had paid the requisite fee. He claims he stopped writing not because of the reader contributions—King estimated the online publication would gross $600,000—but because of his other, more traditional publishing commitments.[14]

A more recent example comes from the World of Goo. To celebrate the one-year anniversary of the computer game's release, the publisher, 2D Boy, offered World of Goo on a pay what you want basis and thereby attracted 57,000 new customers, who paid an average of $2.03 for the game. The price paid voluntarily rose over the limited span of time for which the price offer was available, and word of mouth about the game increased its sales by outside vendors by approximately 40 percent.[15]

And if the phenomenon seems limited to the Web, take a trip to Essex, Vermont, where a taxi driver named Eric Hagen allows his passengers to decide how much their trip is worth. He's been so successful that he is even thinking of expanding his business and hiring other drivers.[16] Then go for a meal in Denver at SAME (So All May Eat) Café. It changes its menu daily, and features food that's made from scratch and is largely organic. SAME doesn't have a cash register or credit card machine because it doesn't have set prices. Diners pay what they want.[17]

Do you think a "pay what you want" pricing policy is a sound pricing strategy? Does it make more sense for some products, services, or retailers than for others? How would you determine what is a fair price to pay if faced with "pay what you want"?

---

To determine how firms account for consumers' preferences when they develop pricing strategies, we must first lay a foundation of traditional economic theory that helps explain how prices are related to demand (consumers' desire for products) and how managers can incorporate this knowledge into their pricing strategies.[18] But first read through Adding Value 13.1, which considers how some companies achieve success by allowing customers to decide how much value their products offer.

**Demand Curves and Pricing** A demand curve shows how many units of a product or service consumers will demand during a specific period of time at different prices. Although we call them "curves," demand curves can be either straight or curved, as Exhibit 13.3 shows. Of course, any demand curve relating demand to price assumes that everything else remains unchanged. For the sake of experiment, marketers creating a demand curve assume that the firm will not increase its expenditures on advertising and that the economy will not change in any significant way.

**LO2** Explain the relationship between price and quantity sold.

Exhibit 13.3 illustrates the classic downward-sloping demand curve in which, as price increases, demand for the product or service decreases. In this case, consumers will buy more as the price decreases. In Adding Value 13.1, nearly 17,000 purchasers—the largest group of new buyers—paid only 1 cent for World of Goo, because demand increased as the price fell. We can expect to uncover a demand curve similar to this one for many, if not most, products and services.

The horizontal axis in Exhibit 13.3 measures the quantity demanded for the CDs in units and plots it against the various price possibilities indicated on the vertical axis. Each point on the demand curve then represents the quantity demanded at a specific price. So, in this instance, if the price of a CD is $10 per unit ($P_1$), the demand is 1,000,000 units ($Q_1$), but if the price were set at $15 ($P_2$), the demand would only be 500,000 units ($Q_2$). The firm will sell far more CDs at $10 each than at $15 each. Why? Because of the greater value this price point offers.

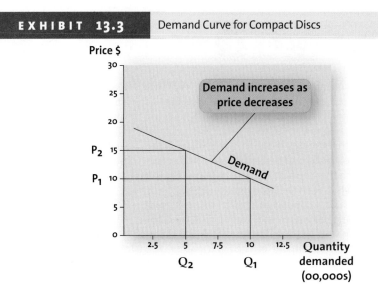

| **EXHIBIT 13.3** | Demand Curve for Compact Discs |

Knowing the demand curve for a product or service enables a firm to examine different prices in terms of the resulting demand and relative to its overall objective. In our preceding example, the music retailer will generate a total of $10,000,000 in sales at the $10 price ($10 × 1,000,000 units) and $7,500,000 in sales at the $15 price ($15 × 500,000 units). In this case, given only the two choices of $10 or $15, the $10 price is preferable as long as the firm wants to maximize its sales in terms of dollars and units. But what about a firm that is more interested in profit? To calculate profit, it must consider its costs, which we cover in the next section.

Interestingly enough, not all products or services follow the downward-sloping demand curve for all levels of price depicted in Exhibit 13.3. Consider **prestige products or services**, which consumers purchase for their status rather than their functionality. The higher the price, the greater the status associated with it and the greater the exclusivity, because fewer people can afford to purchase it. Faberge, the French jeweler known for making jeweled eggs for Russian Tsar Alexander III, among other exotic items, considers itself to be so prestigious that it doesn't even have a physical store. It offers its latest jewelry line on its website (www.faberge.com) for $40,000 to $7 million per item. According to Mark Dunhill, Faberge's CEO, "Our customers won't need to appear outside of a store between 10 in the morning and 6 in the evening. They can log on anytime, while sitting on their yacht, their chalet or their country home."[19] But don't expect to go surfing their site. You need to register, make an appointment, and they will contact you.

With prestige products or services, a higher price may lead to a greater quantity sold, but only up to a certain point. The price demonstrates just how rare, exclusive, and prestigious the product is. When customers value the increase in prestige more than the price differential between the prestige product and other products, the prestige product attains the greater value overall.

However, prestige products can also run into pricing difficulties. The Fender Telecaster and Stratocaster guitars are absolute necessities for any self-respecting guitar hero, but for students just learning or hobbyists, the price of owning a Fender "axe" was simply too much. In response, Fender introduced a separate, budget-priced line of similar guitars under a different brand name, so as not to dilute the prestige of the Fender name. The Squier line, made in Japan with automated manufacturing and less expensive parts, offers a look similar to the famous Fender guitars and performance just a notch below the originals. Today, an American-made Eric Clapton or John Mayer Fender Stratocaster

*With prestige products like this expensive Faberge egg, the higher the price, the higher the status associated with it, and possibly, the more it will sell.*

In a monopoly, one firm provides the product or service in a particular industry, and as such results in less price competition. For example, in the utilities industry, there is only one provider of power in each region of the country—Florida Power and Light Company in most of Florida, and NStar in most of Massachusetts. Power companies operate more efficiently when there is one service provider, so the government regulates the pricing of utility monopolies to prevent them from raising prices uncontrollably. Monopolies have had a long history in the United States, starting with Standard Oil, which the government broke up in 1911. Both professional baseball and football leagues have been involved in monopolistic controversies over the years, as has software giant Microsoft and the diamond supplier De Beers. A monopoly that restricts competition by controlling an industry can be deemed illegal and broken apart by the government.

When a market is characterized by oligopolistic competition, only a few firms dominate. Firms typically change their prices in reaction to competition to avoid upsetting an otherwise stable competitive environment. Examples of oligopolistic markets include the soft drink market and commercial airline travel.

Sometimes reactions to prices in oligopolistic markets can result in a price war, which occurs when two or more firms compete primarily by lowering their prices. Firm A lowers its prices; Firm B responds by meeting or beating Firm A's new price. Firm A then responds with another new price, and so on. In some cases though, these tactics result in predatory pricing, when a firm sets a very low price for one or more of its products with the intent to drive its competition out of business, a possibility exemplified in Ethical and Societal Dilemma 13.1.

## Ethical and Societal Dilemma 13.1     The Battle of the Books

Price wars historically have been commonplace in some industries (e.g., airlines, fast food). But the battle is entering a new arena—the vicious battleground of books.

On one side of the ring sits the American Booksellers Association (ABA), a trade group that represents small, independent bookstores. According to a letter it sent to the U.S. Department of Justice, big retailers such as Amazon, Walmart, and Target actually engage in unfair practices when they price bestselling new releases for as little as $8.98 per book—far below the list prices of around $35.[33]

In the other corner are the big retail companies, and a lot of consumers. Getting Stephen King's *Under the Dome* or John Grisham's *Ford County* for just $9 is deeply appealing to consumers, who are more likely to visit the stores that offer these prices. That consumer behavior is exactly what the retailers are counting on, because if they can get people in stores or to their websites, those buyers are likely to purchase more than just the price-reduced bestseller.[34]

Even as this battle rages, Sony and Google are gunning for Amazon in the e-book realm. Amazon represents the first mover in this competition. Its Kindle book reader is "the most gifted item even in [Amazon's] history,"[35] and predictions estimate the online retailer will sell 2 million units next year. But the profits to Amazon come not from selling the $359 devices but rather from sales of books to read on the Kindle, for which its profit margins are significantly higher than those for traditional books. It can sell e-books for around $10 a pop, without incurring any variable costs for producing more copies.

So how do you compete on price with a company that already prices well below traditional levels? You offer the items for free. If they purchase Sony's Reader for $300, consumers can gain free access to half a million public domain books through Google. Amazon instead offers about one-quarter of a million books, mainly new releases and bestsellers that are not in the public domain yet. In partnering with Google, Sony hopes to penetrate the e-book market; Google hopes to bring even more searchers to its site. The more content available, the more valuable the device is for consumers.[36]

So at what point are price wars problematic? According to the ABA, the precipitous drop in prices represents predatory pricing behavior, designed to drive small sellers out of the market and thus enable the big retailers to do whatever they want, unhindered by compe-

*(continued)*

## Ethical and Societal Dilemma 13.1

*Should large retailers such as Amazon, Walmart, and Target be allowed to sell books by Stephen King for less than the price for which small book sellers can buy his books?*

*(continued)*

tition. And yet the expanded availability of electronic versions of books may mean a market with broader access. For consumers, the price wars mean less expensive access to content today. Will they mean less competition and higher prices in the future though?

Even in the face of declining prices, some consumers continue to pay more, because they value other aspects of the offer. For example, the independent booksellers may not be able to compete on price, but they can offer personalized service, hard-to-find titles, and a cozy atmosphere that the big retailers can never mimic.[37]

Monopolistic competition occurs when there are many firms competing for customers in a given market but their products are differentiated. When so many firms compete, product differentiation rather than strict price competition tends to appeal to consumers. This is the most common form of competition. Hundreds of firms make wristwatches and thus the market is highly differentiated. Timex sells a durable watch that tells time, has a stop watch, and a sporty design. Swatch watches have more style than a Timex, but if you are really looking for a lot of style, fashion designers such as Armani have their own wristwatches. Timepiece aficionados may opt for the high-quality workmanship of a Patek Philippe or a Vacheron Constantin. Depending on the features, style, and quality, companies compete in very different markets for the same product.

With pure competition, there are a large number of sellers of standardized products or commodities that consumers perceive as substitutable, such as grains, gold, meat, spices, or minerals. In such markets, price usually is set according to the laws of supply and demand. For example, wheat is wheat, so it does not matter to a commercial bakery whose wheat it buys. However, the secret to pricing success in a pure competition market is not necessarily to offer the lowest price, because doing so might create a price war and erode profits.

Instead, some firms have brilliantly decommoditized their products. For example, most people feel that all chickens purchased in a grocery are the same. But companies like Tyson's have branded their chickens to move into a monopolistic competitive market.

When a commodity can be differentiated somehow, even if simply by a sticker or logo, there is an opportunity for consumers to identify it as distinct from the rest, and in this case, firms can at least partially extricate their product from a pure competitive market.

## Channel Members

Channel members—manufacturers, wholesalers, and retailers—can have different perspectives when it comes to pricing strategies. Consider a manufacturer that is focused on increasing the image and reputation of its brand but working with a retailer that is primarily concerned with increasing its sales. The manufacturer may desire to keep prices higher to convey a better image, whereas the retailer wants lower prices and will accept lower profits to move the product, regardless of consumers' impressions of the brand. Unless channel members carefully communicate their pricing goals and select channel partners that agree with them, conflict will surely arise.

Channels can be very difficult to manage, and distribution outside normal channels does occur. A gray market, for example, employs irregular but not necessarily illegal methods; generally, it legally circumvents authorized channels of distribution to sell goods at prices lower than those intended by the manufacturer.[38] Many manufacturers of consumer electronics therefore require retailers to sign an agreement that demands certain activities (and prohibits others) before they may become authorized dealers. But if a retailer has too many high-definition TVs in stock, it may sell them at just above its own cost to an unauthorized discount dealer. This move places the merchandise on the street at prices far below what authorized dealers can charge, and in the long term, it may tarnish the image of the manufacturer if the discount dealer fails to provide sufficient return policies, support, service, and so forth.

To discourage this type of gray market distribution, some manufacturers, such as Fujitsu, have resorted to large disclaimers on their websites, packaging, and other communications to warn consumers that the manufacturer's product warranty becomes null and void unless the item has been purchased from an authorized dealer.[39]

---

### CHECK YOURSELF

1. What are the five Cs of pricing?
2. Identify the four types of company objectives.
3. What is the difference between elastic versus inelastic demand?
4. How does one calculate the break-even point in units?

---

# MACRO INFLUENCES ON PRICING

Thus far, we have focused mainly on product- and firm-specific factors—the five Cs—that influence pricing. Now we turn to the broader factors that have a more sweeping effect on pricing in general. In this section, we consider the Internet and various economic factors.

## The Internet

The shift among consumers to acquiring more and more products, services, and information online has made them more price sensitive and opened new categories of products to those who could not access them previously. Gourmet foods, books (and now e-books), music, movies, and electronics are just a few of the product categories that present a significant online presence. Because they have gained access to rare cheeses, breads, meats, spices, and confections, consumers are demanding more from their local grocery stores in terms of selection and variety and have become more sensitive about prices. Furthermore, consumers' ability to buy electronics at highly discounted prices online has pushed bricks-and-mortar stores to attempt to focus consumers' attention on prepurchase advice and expertise, consulting services, and after-sales service—and away from price.

The Internet also has introduced search engines that enable consumers to find the best prices for any product quickly, which again increases their price sensitivity and reduces the costs associated with finding lower-price alternatives.[40] Not only do consumers know more about prices, but they know more about the firms, their products, their competitors, and the markets in which they compete.

Another implication of the Internet for prices has been the growth of online auction sites such as eBay. Gone are the days when sellers had to offer their unwanted items to local buyers at "fire sale" prices. Although there certainly are good deals to be had on eBay, many items can fetch a premium price because bidders tend to get caught up in the bidding process. Also, unique and special-interest items, which previously required professional appraisals before their value could be established, now have millions of potential bidders clearly articulating a value for everything from a 2011 Lexus LX9 for $61,200 to an 18-karat gold Signature S cell phone for $24,100. Many consumers use eBay's prior auction section to determine the prices at which products have sold in the past and establish a value for new offerings.

Power of the Internet 13.1 describes eBay pricing strategies for sellers and buyers.

## Economic Factors

Two interrelated trends that have merged to impact pricing decisions are the increase in consumers' disposable income and status consciousness. Some consumers appear willing to spend money for products that can convey status in some way. Products once considered only for the very rich, such as Rolex watches and Mercedes-Benz cars, are now owned by more working professionals. Although such prestige products are still aimed at the elite, more and more consumers are making the financial leap to attain them.

*Stores like H&M have introduced disposable chic to America.*

At the same time, however, a countervailing trend finds customers attempting to shop cheap. The popularity of everyday low-price retailers like Walmart and Target, extreme value stores such as Dollar General, and wholesale clubs like Costco attract customers who can afford to shop at department and specialty stores, yet find it is cool to save a buck. Retailers like Old Navy and H&M also have introduced disposable chic and cross-shopping into middle America's shopping habits. In this context, **cross-shopping** is the pattern of buying both premium and low-priced merchandise or patronizing both expensive, status-oriented retailers and price-oriented retailers. These stores offer fashionable merchandise at great values—values so good that if items

## Power of the Internet 13.1    Pricing on eBay

Researchers have published dozens of papers using eBay as their data source.[41] One research question often investigated is, "What can sellers do to get the highest price?" Here are a few tips:

1. **Set the starting price relatively low.** It is important to start prices relatively low to stimulate interest among potential bidders. For instance, starting a Nikon camera auction at $0.01 resulted in significantly higher final prices than the average price for all camera auctions. In another case, when the seller started an auction for a kitchen sink at $225, it ended without a single bidder. When reauctioned with a starting price of $75, the sink sold for $275. There is one exception to the start-low rule: If the item is somewhat idiosyncratic and therefore might not have many bids, it is best to set the price closer to the item's actual value.[42]

2. **Use reserve prices with caution, especially for low-priced items.** A reserve price in an auction is secret to potential bidders, and is the minimum amount at which a seller will sell an item. Sellers use reserve prices as protection against selling an item too low. Using a reserve price reduces the probability that the auction will end in a sale. In an experiment using relatively low-value Pokémon trading cards, researchers found that auctions utilizing reserves on average resulted in fewer serious bidders per auction and lower final sale prices. However, other research suggests that for items over $25.00, the reserve might push revenues higher when the auctions end in a successful sale.[43]

3. **Use photos to generate bids.** Listings with photos receive much more traffic than listings without photos. More traffic to the listing results in bids, and the more bids, the higher the sale price.[44]

4. **Don't flood the market.** To sell multiples of an item, don't sell them all at the same time. The market appreciates the illusion of scarcity. Items that are scarce or even unique are perceived to be more valuable. Also, spacing out the listings increases the size of the potential market because people float in and out of the market.

5. **Spell-check.** Misspellings decrease the amount of traffic an auction receives. People search for specific words. If those words are spelled wrong, the item won't pop up. One study found that Michael Jordan shirts listed "Micheal" went unsold almost twice as often as those that were spelled correctly. When sold, the misspelled brand names resulted in lower final sale prices.[45]

6. **Hype it up.** It is good to exaggerate a little. For instance, in selling a handbag, say, "Runway special! A must-have for fall!" Also, if the suggested retail price is relatively high, mention it. One study found that auctions that mention the high retail price in an item description sell for 7 percent more on average.[46]

7. **Hold longer auctions.** Longer auctions tend to fetch higher prices. Research shows that three-day and five-day auctions yield approximately the same prices, seven-day auctions are about 24 percent higher, and 10-day auctions 42 percent higher on average.[47]

8. **Don't end auctions when everyone else does.** A study found that auctions ending during peak hours on eBay are actually 9.6 percent less likely to result in a sale. About 35 percent of auctions end between 5 p.m. and 8:59 p.m., when only 25 percent of bids are placed.[48]

9. **Charge for shipping—but not too much.** Bidders don't pay much attention to shipping costs when placing bids. In one study, CDs listed with a starting price of one cent with $3.99 shipping averaged 21 percent higher final sale prices than CDs set with an opening price of $4 and no shipping charge. When the CDs were listed with a $2 starting price and a $6 shipping cost, five of the 20 CDs went unsold.[49]

10. **Avoid negative feedback.** Sellers who have even a few positive feedback reports are more likely than sellers who have no history to receive bids and to have their auctions result in a sale. Positively rated sellers also receive higher bids.[50]

By implementing these sellers' strategies from a buyer's perspective, one might be able to get some good deals. For instance, if an item has lots of bids, it may sell for an artificially high price. It pays to check out items without pictures or with misspelled words since they get fewer bids and therefore usually end up selling for less. Finally, look for short-duration auctions with items at high starting or reserve prices.

---

last for only a few wearings, it doesn't matter to the customers. The net impact of these contradictory trends on prices has been that some prestige items have become more expensive, whereas many other items have become cheaper.

Finally, the economic environment at local, regional, national, and global levels influences pricing. Starting at the top, the growth of the global economy has changed the nature of competition around the world. Many firms maintain a presence in multiple countries—products get designed in one country, the parts are

*By thinking globally, firms can seek out the most cost-efficient methods of providing goods and services to their customers.*

manufactured in another, the final product assembled in a third, and after-sales service is handled by a call center in a fourth. By thinking globally, firms can seek out the most cost-efficient methods of providing goods and services to their customers.

On a more local level, the economy still can influence pricing. Competition, disposable income, and unemployment all may signal the need for different pricing strategies. For instance, rural areas are often subjected to higher prices because it costs more to get products there and because competition is lower. Similarly, retailers often charge higher prices in areas populated by people who have more disposable income and enjoy low unemployment rates.

## CHECK YOURSELF

1. How have the Internet and economic factors affected the way people react to prices?

## Summing Up

**L01**  **List the four pricing orientations.**

A profit-oriented pricing strategy focuses on maximizing, or at least reaching a target, profit for the company. A sales orientation instead sets prices with the goal of increasing sales levels. With a competitor-oriented pricing strategy, a firm sets its prices according to what its competitors do. Finally, a customer-oriented strategy determines consumers' perceptions of value and prices accordingly.

**L02**  **Explain the relationship between price and quantity sold.**

Generally, when prices go up, quantity sold goes down. Sometimes, however—particularly with prestige products and services—demand actually increases with price.

**L03**  **Explain price elasticity.**

Changes in price generally affect demand; price elasticity measures the extent of this effect. It is based on the percentage change in quantity divided by the percentage change in price. Depending on the resulting value, a market offering can be identified as elastic, such that the market is very price sensitive, or

inelastic, in which case the market cares little about the price.

**L04**  **Describe how to calculate a product's break-even point.**

Because the break-even point occurs when the units sold generate just enough profit to cover the total costs of producing those units, it requires knowledge of the fixed cost, total cost, and total revenue curves. When these curves intersect, the marketer has found the break-even point.

**L05**  **Indicate the four types of price competitive levels.**

In a monopoly setting, either one firm controls the market and sets the price, or many firms compete with differentiated products, rather than on price. Pure competition means that consumers likely regard the products offered by different companies as basic substitutes, so the firms must work hard to achieve the lowest price point, limited by the laws of supply and demand. Finally, in an oligopolistic competitive market, a few firms dominate and tend to set prices according to a competitor-oriented strategy.

## Key Terms

- break-even analysis, 400
- break-even point, 400
- competitive parity, 392
- competitor orientation, 392
- complementary products, 397
- contribution per unit, 401
- cross-price elasticity, 397
- cross-shopping, 406
- customer orientation, 392
- demand curve, 393
- elastic, 396
- fixed costs, 399

- gray market, 405
- income effect, 397
- inelastic, 396
- maximizing profits, 390
- monopoly, 403
- monopolistic competition, 404
- oligopolistic competition, 403
- predatory pricing, 403
- premium pricing, 392
- prestige products or services, 394
- price, 388
- price elasticity of demand, 395

- price war, 403
- profit orientation, 390
- pure competition, 404
- reserve price, 407
- sales orientation, 391
- status quo pricing, 392
- substitute products, 397
- substitution effect, 397
- target profit pricing, 390
- target return pricing, 391
- total cost, 400
- variable costs, 399

## Marketing Applications

1. You and your two roommates are starting a pet grooming service to help put yourselves through college. There are two other well-established pet services in your area. Should you set your price higher or lower than that of the competition? Justify your answer.

2. One roommate believes the most important objective in setting prices for the new pet grooming business is to generate a large profit, while keeping an eye on your competitors' prices; the other roommate believes it is important to maximize sales and set prices according to what your customers expect to pay. Who is right and why?

3. Assume you have decided to buy an advertisement in the local newspaper to publicize your new pet grooming service. The cost of the ad is $1,000. You have decided to charge $40 for a dog grooming, and you want to make $20 for each dog. How many dogs do you have to groom to break even on the cost of the ad? What is your break-even point if you charge $50 per dog?

4. The local newspaper ad isn't helping much; you decide to post your services on an auction site, where customers can bid for your services. What should the starting price of the auction be?

5. Is there a difference between a $5,900 Loro Piana vicuña sweater and a $150 cashmere sweater from L.L. Bean? Have you ever purchased a higher-priced product or service because you thought the quality was better than that of a similar, lower-priced product or service? What was the product or service? Do you believe you made a rational choice?

6. How does the fluctuating value of the euro affect the price of German cars sold in the United States?

7. On your weekly grocery shopping trip, you notice that the price of spaghetti has gone up 50 cents a pound. How will this price increase affect the demand for spaghetti sauce, rice, and Parmesan cheese? Explain your answer in terms of the price elasticity of demand.

8. Zinc Energy Resources Co., a new division of a major battery manufacturing company, recently patented a new battery that uses zinc-air technology. The unit costs for the zinc-air battery are as follows: The battery housing is $8, materials are $6, and direct labor is $6 per unit. Retooling the existing factory facilities to manufacture the zinc-air batteries amounts to an additional $1 million in equipment costs. Annual fixed costs include sales, marketing, and advertising expenses of $1 million; general and administrative expenses of $1 million; and other fixed costs totaling $2 million. Please answer the following questions.

   a. What is the total per-unit variable cost associated with the new battery?

   b. What are the total fixed costs for the new battery?

   c. If the price for the new battery was set at $35, what would the break-even point be?

9. How do pricing strategies vary across markets that are characterized by monopolistic, oligopolistic, and pure competition?

10. Suppose you are in the market for a new Sharp LCD television. You see one advertised at a locally owned

store for $300 less than it costs at HHGregg. The salesperson at the local store tells you that the television came from another retailer in the next state that had too many units of that model. Explain who benefits and who is harmed from such a gray market transaction: you, Sharp, HHGregg, the local store?

11. Has the Internet helped lower the price of some types of merchandise? Justify your answer.

---

www.mhhe.com/
grewal3e

## Quiz Yourself

1. If a shoe company has $1 million in fixed costs, its average shoe sells for $50 a pair, and variable costs are $30 per unit, how many units does the company need to sell to break even?
   a. 5,000
   b. 10,000
   c. 50,000
   d. 100,000
   e. 500,000

2. Ferrari and Lamborghini are manufacturers of very expensive automobiles. Their limited edition cars often sell for $300,000 or more. The cars are considered by most consumers a prestige product, for which demand is likely to be:
   a. cross-price elastic.
   b. price inelastic.
   c. price elastic.
   d. status quo elastic.
   e. derived demand inelastic.

(Answers to these two questions are provided on page 608.)

Go to www.mhhe.com/grewal3e to practice an additional 11 questions.

---

## Toolkit

**BREAK-EVEN ANALYSIS**
A shoe manufacturer has recently opened a new manufacturing plant in Asia. The total fixed costs are $50 million. They plan to sell the shoes to retailers for $50, and their variable costs (material and labor) are $25 per pair. Calculate the break-even volume. Now see what would happen to the break-even point if the fixed costs were increased to $60 million due to the purchase of new equipment, or the variable costs were decreased to $20 due to a new quantity discount provided by the supplier. Please use the toolkit provided at www.mhhe.com/grewal3e to experiment with changes in fixed cost, variable cost, and selling price to see what happens to break-even volume.

---

## Net Savvy

1. Several different pricing models can be found on the Internet. Each model appeals to different customer groups. Go to www.eBay.com and try to buy this book. What pricing options and prices are available? Do you believe that everyone will choose the least expensive option? Why or why not? Now go to www.Amazon.com. Is there more than one price available for this book? If so, what are those prices? Are different versions available? If you had to buy another copy of this book, where would you buy it, and why would you buy it there?

2. Prices can vary, depending on the market being served. Because Dell sells its computers directly to consumers all around the world, the Dell website makes it easy to compare prices for various markets. Go to www.dell.com/home. Choose the "Desktops" drop-down menu, scroll down to "Inspiron" models and determine the price of an Inspiron 580 desktop computer. Next go to http://www.dell.co.uk/, the Dell United Kingdom website, choose the "For Home" drop-down menu and scroll to "Desktops and All-In-Ones." Then choose the "Desktops" drop-down menu and scroll to "Inspiron" models to find the price of the same computer. (If you need to convert currency to U.S. dollars, go to www.xe.com.) How does the price of the desktop computer vary? What would account for these differences in price?

## Chapter Case Study

### PAYING FOR ALL THOSE PINSTRIPES[51]

When the New York Yankees opened their new $1.5 billion stadium at the start of the 2009 baseball season, the team already had sold 85 percent of its premium seating. But a few hundred of the best seats, closest to the action, remained unsold.

At the time, the highest priced seats, those in the first row, were $2500 each. To increase sales, in the spring of 2009, the Yanks cut prices 50 percent to $1250. The $1000 seats also were reduced to $650. Customers who purchased tickets at the full price received a refund. The team needed the brand new stadium to be full all the time to give the impression that it was an exciting place to be. Empty premium seats would be an embarrassment to a marquee team like the Yankees.

And then came October 2009, and the Yankees' 27th World Series victory. Yet even though it had achieved approximately 90 occupancy rates for most of the successful season, the team announced in September that it would lower prices on many season ticket packages, including some of the highest priced ones. For example, the first level of nonpremium seats (one level up, behind home plate) will cost $250 per seat per game, a decrease of almost 25 percent from the previous price of $325. The rationale given for this decrease was that Yankees' general managing partner Hal Steinbrenner was sensitive to the struggling economy and consumer responses, so he would continue to review prices.

This review also included some price increases. The rates for the lowest priced seats, the bleachers, will rise from $12 to $14. After one full season in the stadium, many fans called the bleacher seats the best value in the park, offering a better view than the more expensive upper deck rows.

Part of the Yankees experience is the challenge of getting the tickets. Season ticket subscriptions continue to be high, and people who want individual tickets for a single game may be out of luck. The Yankees' official site shows that seats in Section 201 cost just $14. How much are they really worth? If buyers cannot snatch up the seats quickly enough, StubHub, the official ticket resale site sanctioned by Major League Baseball, offers an alternative: the same seats, with a possible obstructed view, for the season opener, for $135. Want to sit with your feet on the dugout? You can, for just $8000 a seat on StubHub.

And for those who just can't get enough, the Yankees provide other forms of access to the team. In the off-season, fans can purchase behind-the-scenes tours of the Stadium, which includes visits to the dugout, Monument Park (where the Yankees honor their legends, like Ruth and Mantle, as well as 9-11 victims), batting cages, the Yankee Museum, and the clubhouse. For those who want to see their favorite players in the sunshine, tickets to spring training are available for just $17 to $31, though they would have to go to Tampa, Florida, to catch these practice games.

### Questions

1. Which seats in Yankee Stadium does the team management price according to a premium pricing plan? Which seats represent value pricing tactics?

2. What environmental factors influence the prices of Yankee tickets?

3. If Yankee Stadium does not sell out, what are the costs to the company? Consider a broad range of costs, not just the price of the unsold seat.

# Strategic Pricing Methods

**D**eeply discounted products or services cause retailers to lose money. However, if these promotions accomplish other strategic goals, such as bringing in new customers, they can be tremendously valuable. Success depends on reaching a wide audience of interested consumers with a deal that can't be ignored. Finding the model that delivers this one-two punch is the genius behind Groupon.com.

Every day, Groupon alerts its users to a deal.[1] The discounts are based in the hundreds of cities worldwide that Groupon serves and offered to site users in those markets so that a woman living in New York, for example, could find discounts to nail salons nearby. Economically, the deals are attractive: $10 worth of pizza for $5,[2] a 64 percent discount on membership to the Chicago Art Institute, and nearly half off interactive cooking classes that culminate with a four-course gourmet meal.[3] They revolve around social events, like classes or dining out, and are for goods or services that customers may find appealing but have been unwilling to try because of cost.

Although Groupon searches for deals that don't contain fine-print restrictions, the company attaches its own strings to discounts: A minimum number of people must sign up before the promotion takes effect. This caveat motivates users to spread the word via social networking sites. If the minimum isn't reached, the discount does not apply and neither the customer nor the business is charged.

So far, maximums have been more of an issue than minimums. The Chicago Art Institute promotion added 5,000 new members, an impressive addition to the 85,000 members the museum had accumulated in the previous 100 years. The owner of the pizza chain offering 50 percent off coupons had 9,000 responses. Business owners, Groupon warns, need to be ready for this kind of interest. Some small businesses cap their offers to avoid overwhelming staff or frustrating customers who may have to wait months for an appointment.

Groupon itself faces an avalanche of interest from site users and businesses. The down economy creates appeal on the user side, having triggered a 25 percent growth in the company's e-mail base

## LEARNING OBJECTIVES

**LO1** Identify three methods that firms use to set their prices.

**LO2** Describe the difference between an everyday low price strategy (EDLP) and a high/low strategy.

**LO3** Explain the difference between a market penetration and a price skimming pricing strategy.

**LO4** Identify tactics used to reduce prices to consumers.

**LO5** Identify tactics used to reduce prices to businesses.

**LO6** List pricing practices that have the potential to deceive customers.

in one month. Groupon now reaches over 10 million shoppers. Most of these users are young professionals in their 20s and 30s earning more than $100,000 annually, a highly desirable target market.

Businesses see Groupon as a cost-effective way to bring in new customers; 120 were lined up for promotions in Chicago, where Groupon launched in 2008, and Groupon has expanded to other cities and countries. Investors are also excited about Groupon's business model because it doesn't involve inventory or shipping (users print Groupon's voucher and bring it to the vendor). Since most offers are intangibles like services or classes instead of products or goods, Groupon doesn't face problems with stock-outs like other group buying sites.

At a time when retailers are investing their marketing dollars with great care, Groupon's payment structure encourages businesses to sign on. If the promotion is successful, Groupon takes a share of the profits. If it's unsuccessful, neither Groupon nor the company makes money. So far, everyone is a winner.

● ● ●

Coming up with the "right" price is never easy, as the opening example shows. How might a radical shift in prices, both those that consumers are willing to pay and those that auto manufacturers can charge, for instance, affect future sales, whether for sellers of fuel-efficient models or gas guzzlers? What other members of the market would these price changes affect? To answer such questions, we examine various pricing strategies in this chapter.

Chapter 13 was devoted to examining what "price" is, why it is important, how marketers set pricing objectives, and the factors that influence prices. In this chapter, we extend that foundation by focusing on specific considerations for setting pricing strategies and then discuss a number of pricing strategies. We also examine the implications of various pricing tactics for both consumers and businesses and some of the more important legal and ethical issues associated with pricing.

**L01** Identify three methods that firms use to set their prices.

# CONSIDERATIONS FOR SETTING PRICE STRATEGIES

Firms embrace different objectives, face different market conditions, and operate in different manners. Thus, they employ unique pricing strategies that seem best for the particular set of circumstances in which they find themselves. Even a single firm needs different strategies across its products and services and over time as market conditions change. The choice of a pricing strategy thus is specific to the product/service and target market. Although firms tend to rely on similar strategies when they can, each product or service requires its own specific strategy because no two are ever exactly the same in terms of the marketing mix. Three different methods that can help develop pricing strategies—cost-based, competitor-based, and value-based methods—are discussed in this section (see Exhibit 14.1).

## Cost-Based Methods

As their name implies, cost-based pricing methods determine the final price to charge by starting with the cost. Relevant costs (e.g., fixed, variable, and overhead) and a profit are added and this total amount is divided by the total demand

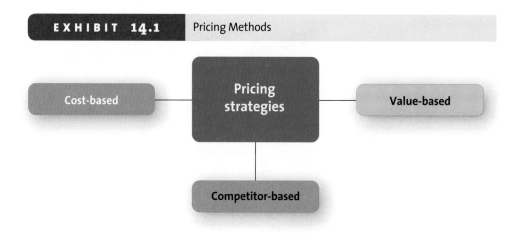

**EXHIBIT  14.1**          Pricing Methods

to arrive at a cost-plus price. For example, the fixed costs to produce an item are $200,000, the variable costs add up to $100,000, and the estimated number of units to be produced is 30,000. Add 100,000 to 200,000, divide by 30,000, and the true unit cost equals $10. If the desired markup is 20 percent, then multiplying $10 by 1.20 results in the cost-plus price for this item of $12. This sales price would be viewed as a cost plus percentage mark-up.

Cost-based methods do not recognize the role that consumers or competitors' prices play in the marketplace. Although relatively simple, compared with other methods used to set prices, cost-based pricing requires that all costs can be identified and calculated on a per-unit basis. Moreover, the process assumes that these costs will not vary much for different levels of production. If they do, the price might need to be raised or lowered according to the production level. Thus, with cost-based pricing, prices are usually set on the basis of estimates of average costs.

## Competitor-Based Methods

Recall from Chapter 13 that some firms set prices according to their competitors' prices. But even if they do not have a strict competition orientation, most firms still know that consumers will compare the prices of their products with the different product/price combinations that competitors offer. Thus, using a competitor-based pricing method, they may set their prices to reflect the way they want consumers to interpret their own prices relative to the competitors' offerings. For example, setting a price very close to a competitor's price signals to consumers that the product is similar, whereas setting the price much higher signals greater features, better quality, or some other valued benefit.

When competitors compete aggressively by setting prices according to what their competitor charges, it can often result in a price war. Airlines often engage in price wars in an attempt to steal customers away from the competition. For example, if Southwest Airlines drops its price of a flight to $30, and in response, United and American Airlines match the low fare, a price war ensues. Price wars can be damaging to companies and may only benefit consumers through overall lower prices. Unless the firm has a real cost advantage and therefore can maintain the lower prices long enough to gain long-lasting customers at the expense of competition, a company may find that the price war leads to an empty victory. That is, it may have earned greater market share at the expense of its competitor, but it may have lost profits by doing so.[4]

## Value-Based Methods

Value-based pricing methods include approaches to setting prices that focus on the overall value of the product offering as perceived by the consumer. Consumers

*Telephone manufacturers use value-based pricing methods like the improvement value method and the cost of ownership method.*

determine value by comparing the benefits they expect the product to deliver with the sacrifice they will need to make to acquire the product. Of course, different consumers perceive value differently. So how does a manager use value-based pricing methods? We consider two key approaches.

**Improvement Value Method** With the first method, the manager must estimate the improvement value of a new product or service. This improvement value represents an estimate of how much more (or less) consumers are willing to pay for a product relative to other comparable products. For example, suppose a major telecommunications company has developed a new cell phone. Using any of a host of research methods—such as consumer surveys—the manager could get customers to assess the new product relative to an existing product and provide an estimate of how much better it is, or its improvement value.

Exhibit 14.2 illustrates how to calculate the improvement value. Consumers evaluate how much better (or worse) the new cell phone is than an existing product on five dimensions: clarity, range, security, battery life, and ease of use. According to the respondents to the survey, the new cell phone has 20 percent more clarity than the comparison phone. These consumers also weight the importance of the five attributes by allocating 100 points among them to indicate their relative importance; for the clarity dimension, this weighting is .40. When the manager multiplies the improvement weight by the relative importance percentage, clarity (20% × 0.40) emerges with a weighted factor of 8 percent. The marketer repeats the process for each benefit and sums the weighted factors to arrive at an approximation of the improvement value of the new product from customers' point of view. In this illustration, the improvement value is equal to 21 percent, so if the other cell phone costs $100, the firm should be able to charge customers a value-based price as high as $121 ($100 × 1.21).

**Cost of Ownership Method** Another value-based method for setting prices determines the total cost of owning the product over its useful life. Using the cost of ownership method, consumers may be willing to pay more for a particular product because, over its entire lifetime, it will eventually cost less to own than a cheaper alternative.[5]

Consider, for example, that an energy-efficient fluorescent lightbulb costs $3.00 and is expected to last 6,000 hours. Alternatively, a conventional lightbulb costs $1.00 but its average life is only 1,500 hours. Even though the fluorescent

| EXHIBIT 14.2 | Improvement Value | | |
|---|---|---|---|
| **Incremental Benefits** | **Improved Value** | **Benefit Weight** | **Weighted Factor** |
| Clarity | 20 | 0.40 | 8% |
| Range | 40% | 0.20 | 8% |
| Security | 10% | 0.10 | 1% |
| Battery life | 5% | 0.20 | 1% |
| Ease of use | 30% | 0.10 | 3% |
| Overall | | 1.00 | 21% |

bulb is expected to last 4 times longer than a conventional bulb, it costs only three times as much. Using the cost of ownership method, and considering the cost per hour, the fluorescent bulb manufacturer could charge $4.00 for each bulb to be equivalent to the cost of the conventional bulb. But since research indicated that many consumers are reluctant to spend $4.00 for a bulb when they are used to getting them for $1.00, the manufacturer chose to charge only $3.00.

**Implementing Value-Based Pricing Methods** Although value-based pricing methods can be quite effective, they also necessitate a great deal of consumer research to be implemented successfully. Sellers must know how consumers in different market segments will attach value to the benefits delivered by their products. They also must account for changes in consumer attitudes because the way customers perceive value today may not be the way they perceive it tomorrow. For example, solid surface countertops, such as those produced by Corian, were "must have" renovations for kitchen remodelers in the early 2000s, because they were priced lower than granite (e.g., around $90 per square foot, compared with around $200 for granite), looked like granite, and offered a wider range of colors than granite. But by 2009, these synthetic materials were far less popular, forcing Corian to drop its prices radically in an attempt to induce builders and homeowners to keep buying. But granite prices fell too, such that both options eventually reached what one kitchen and bath installer called the "market bottom." In the meantime, alternatives such as quartz and recycled glass also had gained consumers' attention, which further drove the prices of Corian and granite down.[6]

Sometimes value-based pricing can go too far, as illustrated in Ethical and Societal Dilemma 14.1.

---

## CHECK YOURSELF

1. What are the three different considerations for setting prices?
2. How can you use value-based methods for setting prices?

---

# PRICING STRATEGIES

**L02** Describe the difference between an everyday low price strategy (EDLP) and a high/low strategy.

In this section, we discuss a number of commonly used price strategies: everyday low pricing, high/low pricing, and new product strategies.[7]

## Everyday Low Pricing (EDLP)

With an **everyday low pricing (EDLP)** strategy, companies stress the continuity of their retail prices at a level somewhere between the regular, nonsale price and the deep-discount sale prices their competitors may offer.[8] By reducing consumers' search costs, EDLP adds value; consumers can spend less of their valuable time comparing prices, including sale prices, at different stores. Utilizing an EDLP strategy, Walmart communicates to consumers that, for any given group of often-purchased items, its prices will tend to be lower than those of any other company in that market. This claim does not necessarily mean that every item that consumers may purchase will be priced lower at Walmart than anywhere else—in fact, some competitive retailers will offer lower prices on some items. However, for an average purchase, Walmart's prices tend to be lower overall. Power of Internet 14.1 reinforces the advantages of offering everyday low prices.

Retailers that utilize EDLP often communicate this strategy by using **odd prices**, or those that end in odd numbers, usually 9. Many sellers believe that consumers mentally truncate the actual price, making the perceived price appear lower than it really is. For example, if the price is $21.99, consumers may focus

## Ethical and Societal Dilemma 14.1

### Do We Have to Pay Twice as Much to See the Boss?

Bruce Springsteen chose to keep prices relatively low for his "Working on a Dream" concert, in homage to his working-man image. Playing at the New Jersey Meadowlands, his home turf, the Boss probably could have sold out a dozen shows, but he scheduled only two, causing demand for the $65–$95 tickets to far exceed supply.[9] When tickets sold out in less than an hour, Ticketmaster directed fans to check TicketsNow, which had tickets available for much higher prices. But the real point of contention for buyers came when they realized that Ticketmaster owns TicketsNow.

When concert tickets go on sale, online ticket brokers like TicketsNow or StubHub often snap up the entire supply. These brokers have software that uses "bots" to buy a large number of tickets at one time. The online brokers that buy the tickets with a face value of, say, $65 can sell them for around $240 on craigslist and as much as $2,000 on other online sites.

Ticketmaster, the initial source for most concert tickets, tries to block resellers from buying up blocks of tickets.[10] Although the technology has improved to prevent these ticket brokers from buying up all tickets at one time, not all tickets are sold through official ticket dealers. The majority of tickets for a concert are reserved for presale through the artist's fan club, the stadium's season ticket holders, and other exclusive agreements. For example, American Express allows its card holders to purchase tickets up to one week in advance on americanexpress.com/entertainment. Thus, the supply of tickets open to the general public is dramatically reduced, making the prices of them on the secondary market much higher.[11]

*Is it ethical to have to pay a significantly higher ticket price to see a Bruce Springsteen concert?*

more on the $21 than on the 99 cents, which may cause them to perceive the price as significantly lower than $22.00, even though that difference is only a penny. Another explanation is that consumers infer that an odd price must have been precisely calculated to wind up with such an odd result. Thus, the price must be fair, because the seller obviously could have rounded it up and taken in a little more money for each item. The main finding from research on the odd pricing

| | |
|---|---|
| Power of the Internet **14.1** | **Price Check on Aisle ... Anywhere**[12] |

Most marketers assume that a Gen X guy and his mom would shop in very different ways. But the latest mobile phone software is blending those shopping methods by helping consumers of all types shop smarter. Eric Olson wanted a Blu-ray version of *Heat*, but at Best Buy, where he was shopping before Christmas, the disc cost $26, which seemed high to the 33-year-old consumer. So he used his Droid smartphone's camera to scan the bar code label, connected to an online application called ShopSavvy, and checked the prices at other stores. Walmart.com was charging only $19.

It is nothing new to check on prices online. It is the mobility of these checks that is really advancing the practice, and making some sellers really nervous. ShopSavvy, by Big In Japan Inc., and Where to Shop, offered by TheFind Inc., locate nearby stores with a desired product but also list which ones are cheapest and closest.

Users need to download these applications and provide basic information—such as their location and the items they want to buy. Some of the applications collect the information automatically by gathering location data from built-in GPS sensors and relying on cameras that can scan bar codes.

Because these technologies rely on the retailers' websites or databases for pricing information, sometimes the details provided are a little out of date, especially if the retailer decides to change the price at the last minute. Some retailers also have tried to withhold the information, though increasing competition with lower-price websites has prompted most of them, including Best Buy, to give the application developers direct access to their product, price, and availability databases. And despite any such accuracy concerns, the applications are proving widely popular, even

among moms. In 2009, downloads of shopping tools for the iPhone increased by 77 percent over the previous year. Eric Olson's mom Carrie Olson regularly uses the RedLaser application to scan the bar codes of books and DVDs, even when she wants "to support the local bookstore, but the price was literally half online. I can't do it then." The question for retailers is "Who can?" If customers can find the best price on their own, how should retailers that cannot necessarily compete on price communicate directly with them?

*It is easy to check prices by scanning a barcode on a mobile phone.*

approach is that odd prices signal to consumers that the price is low.[13]

The bottom line is that if sellers want to imply EDLP, odd prices may be appropriate. However, odd prices also can suggest lower quality.[14] Some consumers may perceive higher value because of the low price (especially if quality is less important to them than price), whereas others may infer lower value on the basis of the low-quality image the odd price suggests (especially if price is less important to them than quality).

## High/Low Pricing

An alternative to EDLP is a high/low pricing strategy, which relies on the promotion of sales, during which prices are temporarily reduced to encourage purchases. A high/low strategy is attractive because it attracts two distinct market segments: those who are not price sensitive and are willing to pay the "high" price and more price-sensitive customers who wait for the "low"

*Odd prices signal to consumers that the price is low.*

*Walmart uses an everyday low pricing (EDLP) strategy.*

*Sears ad with reference price*

sale price. High/low sellers can also create excitement and attract customers through the "get them while they last" atmosphere that occurs during a sale.

Sellers using a high/low pricing strategy often communicate their strategy through the creative use of a reference price, which is the price against which buyers compare the actual selling price of the product and that facilitates their evaluation process. The seller labels the reference price as the "regular price" or an "original price." When consumers view the "sale price" and compare it with the provided reference price, their perceptions of the value of the deal will likely increase.[15]

In the advertisement shown below, Sears has provided a reference price, in smaller print and labeled "Reg.," to indicate that $24.99 is the regular price of Lee jeans. In addition, the advertisement highlights the current "sale" price of $21.99. Thus, the reference price suggests to consumers that they are getting a good deal and will save money. However, as Ethical and Societal Dilemma 14.2 notes, sometimes the veracity of such a reference price is open to challenge.

## EDLP and High/Low Strategies Are Influenced by Price-Quality Relationships

In the end, whether consumers prefer sellers offering EDLP or a high/low strategy depends on how those consumers evaluate prices and quality. Some prefer not to expend the time to find the lowest price and favor EDLP as an efficient way to get low, even if not the very lowest, prices. Other consumers may relish the challenge of getting the lowest price or be so price sensitive that they are willing to expend the time and effort to seek out the lowest price every time.

These decisions get even more complicated, in that customers also infer quality based on whether the seller uses an EDLP or a high/low strategy. Some consumers perceive that sellers that use EDLP carry lower-quality goods, whereas high/low pricing sellers tend to carry better-quality items. In part, this perception forms because consumers view the initial high price at a high/low seller as the reference price. They might assume that the higher the reference price, the higher the merchandise quality. For instance, if a sweater at Macy's originally sold for $150, but is now on sale for $50, many consumers would assume that it is higher quality than a similar regular price $50 sweater at JCPenney.[16]

Let's look at another application of the price-quality relationship. Imagine that you need a new dress shirt because you have an important job interview. You go to brooksbrothers.com and find similar looking shirts for $79.50 (non-iron), $135 (classic cotton), and $295 (luxury). Which are you going to buy? Are you going to risk the success of the interview by purchasing the least expensive shirt? Probably not. Will the interviewee be able to tell the

## Ethical and Societal Dilemma 14.2

### Is It Really 45 Percent Off?[17]

For the truly fashionable—or at least those who consider themselves as members of that group—the trade-off between luxury and affordability can be a tricky one. You want the newest, hottest fashion, but trying to keep up can be exhausting on your wallet. What's a maven to do?

Private sale online sites such as Gilt, RueLaLa, and HauteLook promise a solution. They host limited-time sales of products from high-end fashion brands. A sale starts at a specified time, and lasts for 48 hours or until the sale is sold out. The most popular merchandise will sell out very quickly with only limited quantities available, making customers make decisions on a whim! If you volley back and forth as to whether you should purchase the item, it will already be sold.

So, if you must have the Nova Armored Baby Beaton handbag from Burberry, you can have it for 45 percent off the list price, or $877 instead of $1595, as long as you are on Hautelook .com when the sale starts. But is it really 45 percent off?—45 percent off what? What does the $1595 reference price really mean? Is it the manufacturer's suggested retail price (MSRP) that is placed on the price tag? Did it ever sell at any retail store or online site for $1595?

A reference price like $1595 gives consumers a cue as to what the handbag should be worth. Research shows that the greater the difference between a suggested retail and a sale price, the greater the perceived value. The better the deal, the more consumers will be attracted to buy. Therefore, if the online sites, or any retailer for that matter, inflate the suggested or original price, the percentage discount can seem better than it actually is.

Occasionally these private sale sites have inflated the suggested retail prices to show a greater percentage discount, although they claim that the original prices they list are accurate and come from the manufacturer. Any errors, they argue, are because the manufacturer gave them the wrong price or it is due to employee error. For example if the suggested retail price of the Burberry bag was actually only $1100 instead of $1595, then the bag was only discounted 20 percent. A customer in the heat of the moment may buy the bag because it is reported to be 45 percent off, but if it were 20 percent off, they would not have purchased it.

Should the private sale sites be required to substantiate their reference prices? Which price should they use as the reference price? Is it their responsibility if the manufacturer gives them the wrong pricing information? Do you think they are intentionally misleading their customers?

difference between the $135 classic cotton and the $295 Sea Island cotton shirt? Probably not. You will probably purchase the middle quality shirt because you don't want to look cheap, but you really can't afford the highest priced shirt.[18] When marketers establish a price floor and a price ceiling for an entire line of similar products and then set a few other price points in between to represent distinct differences in quality, the practice is called price lining.

*Some retailers use an everyday low pricing (EDLP) strategy (left), while others use a high-low pricing strategy (right).*

**L03**   Explain the difference between a market penetration and a price skimming pricing strategy.

# NEW PRODUCT PRICING STRATEGIES

Developing pricing strategies for new products is one of the most challenging tasks a manager can undertake. When the new product is similar to what already appears on the market, this job is somewhat easier because the product's approximate value has already been established. But when the new product is truly innovative, or what we call "new to the world," determining consumers' perceptions of its value and pricing it accordingly becomes far more difficult.

The world's cheapest car, for example, is the Nano, which recently began to appear on New Delhi's streets. Most people in this city use scooters, bicycles, or even horse-drawn carts to get around. The Nano tried to convert them into users of safer, enclosed cars, but could not increase the price substantially if it hoped to do so. At 1300 pounds, the Nano weighs less than half a Honda Accord. It also gets 56 miles per gallon, better than the Toyota Prius hybrid, but still can achieve a top speed of 60 miles per hour—though it needs 23 seconds to reach that speed from a standstill.[19] Good marketing research and an obsession with controlling manufacturing costs helped the maker establish a price point that was profitable, yet affordable—100,000 rupees, or about $2000.

Two distinct new product pricing strategies are discussed next. The first, used by the Nano, is called market penetration pricing; while the other is called price skimming.

## Market Penetration Pricing

Firms using a **market penetration strategy** set the initial price low for the introduction of the new product or service. Their objective is to build sales, market share, and profits quickly. The low market penetration price is an incentive to purchase the product immediately. Although it is not always the case, many firms expect the unit cost to drop significantly as the accumulated volume sold increases, an effect known as the **experience curve effect**. With this effect, as sales continue to grow, the costs continue to drop, allowing even further reductions in the price.

In addition to offering the potential to build sales, market share, and profits, penetration pricing discourages competitors from entering the market because the profit margin is relatively low. Furthermore, if the costs to produce the product drop because of the accumulated volume, competitors that enter the market later will face higher unit costs, at least until their volume catches up with the early entrant.

A penetration strategy has its drawbacks. First, the firm must have the capacity to satisfy a rapid rise in demand—or at least be able to add that capacity quickly. Second, low price does not signal high quality. Of course, a price below their expectations decreases the risk for consumers to purchase the product and test its quality for themselves. Third, firms should avoid a penetration pricing strategy if some segments of the market are willing to pay more for the product; otherwise, the firm is just "leaving money on the table."

## Price Skimming

In many markets, and particularly for new and innovative products or services, innovators and early adopters (see Chapter 11) are willing to pay a higher price to obtain the new product or service. This strategy, known

*Made for the Indian market, the Nano is the world's cheapest car—about $2,000.*

as price skimming, appeals to these segments of consumers who are willing to pay the premium price to have the innovation first. This tactic is particularly common in technology markets, where sellers know that fans of the latest game, application, or system are likely to wait in line for hours, desperate to be the first to own the newest version. These innovators are willing to pay the very highest prices to obtain brand-new examples of technology advances, with exciting product enhancements. However, after this high-price market segment becomes saturated and sales begin to slow down, companies generally lower the price to capture (or skim) the next most price sensitive market segment, which is willing to pay a somewhat lower price. For most companies, the price-dropping process can continue until the demand for the product has been satisfied, even at the lowest price points.

The spread of new media for movies illustrates a price skimming strategy. As with VCRs in the 1970s and DVD players in the 1990s, consumers were slow to embrace the new, more expensive Blu-ray discs. But enough early adopters purchased the Blu-ray discs that manufacturers continued to refine Blu-ray players to penetrate wider target markets. Consumers are buying the devices at a faster pace than the earlier movie-playing devices. One obvious reason for this sales growth is that prices for high-quality Blu-ray players have dropped below $150, a steep drop from the $300-plus that retailers charged for debut models.[20]

For price skimming to work though, the product or service must be perceived as breaking new ground in some way, offering consumers new benefits currently unavailable in alternative products. When they believe it will work, though, firms use skimming strategies for a variety of reasons. Some may start by pricing relatively high to signal high quality to the market. Others may decide to price high at first to limit demand, which gives them time to build their production capacities. Similarly, some firms employ a skimming strategy to try to quickly earn back some of the high research and development investments they made for the new product. Finally, firms employ skimming strategies to test consumers' price sensitivity. A firm that prices too high can always lower the price, but if the price is initially set too low, it is almost impossible to raise it without significant consumer resistance.

Furthermore, for a skimming pricing strategy to be successful, competitors cannot be able to enter the market easily; otherwise, price competition will likely force lower prices and undermine the whole strategy. Competitors might be prevented from entering the market through patent protections, their inability to copy the innovation (because it is complex to manufacture, its raw materials are hard to get, or the product relies on proprietary technology), or the high costs of entry.

Skimming strategies also face a significant potential drawback in the relatively high unit costs often associated with producing small volumes of products. Therefore, firms must consider the trade-off between earning a higher price and suffering higher production costs.

Finally, firms using a skimming strategy for new products must face the consequences of ultimately having to lower the price as demand wanes. Margins suffer, and customers who purchased the product or service at the higher initial price may become irritated when the price falls. Adding Value 14.1 illustrates the use of skimming and penetration pricing strategies for technology products.

## CHECK YOURSELF

1. Explain the difference between EDLP and high/low pricing.
2. What pricing strategies should be considered when introducing a new product?

## Adding Value 14.1    Price Skimming in the Cellular Phone Market

When Apple rolled out the latest generation of the iPhone, still exclusively with AT&T, it offered the hot item for just $199. In reality though, AT&T was subsidizing the price of the phone, hoping to sacrifice short-term losses for long-term profits. This decision lowered AT&T's earnings in 2008 and 2009 but might increase overall market share.

At its initial introduction, the iPhone sold for $599, then dropped slightly in price a few months later. The new generation iPhone functions on the 3G network, 10 times faster than the network used for the previous version.

Yet the wireless market continues to be so saturated that the next revenue source through growth must be Internet and entertainment services. Currently, approximately 20 percent of AT&T customers use smart phones, and at the $199 price point, consumers likely will upgrade their current devices or adopt more than one mobile device. The mass

marketing of smart phones in turn should allow more customers to benefit from wireless data, including news, videos, music, and podcasts via mobile services.

The success of the initial version of the iPhone prompted Apple and AT&T to bank on low customer turnover and thus expect profits in the long term from mobile data services. However, Samsung, LG, and BlackBerry now also offer touchscreen phones that will compete with Apple's iPhone, meaning customers, especially those who do not want to switch to AT&T services, have more options.

The next generation smartphone will contain broadband technology, called LTE, which will be much faster than the 3G network and allow streaming video on the wireless network. The networks are only growing faster and better, while also becoming less expensive for consumers.[21]

*Apple used a price skimming strategy when it introduced the iPhone, but quickly lowered the price to attract more customers.*

## PRICING TACTICS

It is important to distinguish clearly between pricing strategies and pricing tactics. A pricing strategy is a long-term approach to setting prices broadly in an integrative effort (across all the firm's products) based on the five Cs (company objectives, costs, customers, competition, and channel members) of pricing discussed in Chapter 13. Pricing tactics, in contrast, offer short-term methods to focus on select components of the five Cs. Generally, a pricing tactic represents either a short-term response to a competitive threat (e.g., lowering price temporarily to meet a competitor's price reduction) or a broadly accepted method of calculating a final price for the customer that is short term in nature. We separate our discussion of pricing tactics into those directed at end consumers and those aimed at intermediaries in a business-to-business (B2B) setting.

## Pricing Tactics Aimed at Consumers

**LO4** Identify tactics used to reduce prices to consumers.

When firms sell their products and services directly to consumers, rather than to other businesses, the pricing tactics they use naturally differ. Some of the tactics aimed directly at consumers include markdowns, quantity discounts, seasonal discounts, coupons, rebates, leasing, price bundling, and leader pricing.

**Markdowns** Markdowns are the reductions retailers take on the initial selling price of the product or service.[22] An integral component of the high/low pricing strategy we described previously, markdowns enable retailers to get rid of slow-moving or obsolete merchandise, sell seasonal items after the appropriate season, and match competitors' prices on specific merchandise. Retailers must get rid of merchandise that isn't selling because holding onto such items hurts the retailer's image and ties up money in inventory that could be used more productively elsewhere.

Retailers also use markdowns to promote merchandise and increase sales. Particularly when used in conjunction with promotions, markdowns can increase traffic into the store, which many retailers view as half the battle. Once customers are in the store, retailers always hope they will purchase other products at regular prices.

**Quantity Discounts for Consumers** The most common implementation of a quantity discount at the consumer level is the size discount. For example, there are three sizes of General Mills' popular cereal Cheerios—10-, 15-, and 20-ounce boxes priced at approximately $3.89, $4.49, and $5.99, respectively. The larger the quantity, the less the cost per ounce, which means the manufacturer is providing a quantity discount. The goal of this tactic is to encourage consumers to purchase larger quantities each time they buy. In turn, these consumers are less likely to switch brands and often tend to consume more of the product, depending on the product usage characteristics. Typically, buying a larger package of toilet tissue does not mean consumers will use it faster, but buying a larger box of cereal may encourage them to eat more of it or eat it more often.[23]

*Customers get a size discount for buying larger sizes. With Cheerios, the larger the box, the less it costs per ounce.*

**Seasonal Discounts** Seasonal discounts are price reductions offered on products and services to stimulate demand during off-peak seasons. You can find hotel rooms, ski lift tickets, snowmobiles, lawn mowers, barbeque grills, vacation packages, flights to certain destinations, and Christmas cards at discounts during their "off" seasons. Some consumers even plan their buying around these discounts, determined to spend the day after Christmas stocking up on discounted wrapping paper and bows for the following year.

**Coupons** Coupons offer a discount on the price of specific items when they're purchased. Coupons are issued by manufacturers and retailers in newspapers, on products, on the shelf, at the cash register, over the Internet, and through the mail.[24] Retailers use coupons because they are thought to induce customers to try products for the first time, convert those first-time users to regular users, encourage large purchases, increase usage, and protect market share against competition. However, the impact of coupons on profitability is questionable.

Coupon promotions, like all temporary promotions, may be stealing sales from a future period without any net increase in sales. For instance, if a supermarket runs a coupon promotion on sugar, households may buy a large quantity of sugar and stockpile it for future use. Thus, unless the coupon is used mostly by new buyers, the net impact on sales is negligible, and there will be a negative

*Coupons offer a discount on the price of specific items when they're purchased.*

impact on profits due to the amount of the redeemed coupons and cost of the coupon redemption procedures.

Coupons may annoy, alienate, and confuse consumers and therefore do little to increase store loyalty. Customers see an ad for a supermarket with a headline reading "Double Coupons" but don't realize there might be conditions, such as a minimum purchase required, or that it may only apply to certain manufacturers.

Recognizing these problems, some retailers have reduced coupon usage and cut the number of days in which customers can redeem coupons. Other retailers, like CVS, are making coupons more attractive to their loyal customers by customizing their content to be in line with their unique needs. For instance, if a customer typically spends a small amount during each shopping trip, the customer will receive coupons that encourage larger purchases, such as "buy one, get one free." If another customer spends a lot each time she shops, but shops sporadically, that customer will get coupons that expire relatively quickly. Unique coupons will also encourage customers to try new brands within categories that they normally purchase, or products that complement their usual purchases, such as shampoo to customers who purchase hair color.[25] Internet sites, such as MyCoupons.com, provide customers with instant coupons. For instance, a customer might go to a Walmart and find a Hot Wheels video game for $29.99. A scan of the bar code on his cell phone to ShopSavvy.com might find the same item at a Target a mile away for $19.99. Another scan to MyCoupons.com provides a coupon for $10, thus saving the customer $20.00 in a matter of minutes.

**Rebates** Rebates provide another form of discounts for consumers off the final selling price. In this case, however, the manufacturer, instead of the retailer, issues the refund as a portion of the purchase price returned to the buyer in the form of cash. Rebates can be even more frustrating than coupons for consumers, but the idea is similar. Whereas a coupon provides instant savings when presented, a rebate promises savings, usually mailed to the consumer at some later date, only if the consumer carefully follows the rules. The "hassle factor" for rebates thus is higher than for coupons. The consumer must first buy the item during a specified time period, then mail in the required documentation—which usually includes the original sales receipt—and finally wait four to six weeks (or more!) for a check to arrive.

Manufacturers generally like rebates because as much as 90 percent of consumers never bother to redeem them. Manufacturers also embrace this form of price reduction because it lets them offer price cuts to consumers directly. With a traditional wholesale price cut from its vendors, retailers can keep the price on the shelf the same and pocket the difference. Rebates can also be rolled out and shut off quickly. That allows manufacturers to fine-tune inventories or respond quickly to competitors without actually cutting prices. Finally, because buyers are required to fill out forms with names, addresses, and other data, rebates become a great way for vendors to build a customer data warehouse. From the retailer's perspective, rebates are more advantageous than coupons since they increase demand in the same way coupons may, but the retailer has no handling costs.

**Leasing** For some products, discounts, coupons, and rebates may not be sufficient to bring the price to within consumers' reach. With a lease, consumers pay a fee to purchase the right to use a product for a specific amount of time. They never own the product; they are just renting it. Leasing products opens up new, less price

## Superior Service 14.1 — Oh, This Old Porsche? I'm Just Leasing It This Month ...

A red Ferrari or a turbo Porsche—or how about a Bentley GTC convertible? Members of the Classic Car Club can drive one each week by paying initiation fees and annual dues of $7,000 to $23,000, plus a daily rental. Customers can drive around in an Audi R8 sports car during a vacation and then show up at a business meeting in a Bentley sedan. It is like Zip Car for the well-to-do. It is not just luxury cars, however. Consumers are leasing everything from fashion to art, putting hard-to-own luxury items within reach of more people.[26] The focus on owning luxury products has become less important than having multiple options, limiting financial exposure, and experiencing products that most people cannot afford to own.

Leasing luxury products involves more than just the product. Those firms that do it well also provide excellent service. For example, the Classic Car Club invites members to weekly happy hour events, offers special activities such as driving a race car around a track, and provides reciprocal privileges for renting in locations where the Club does not exist.

The Wardrobe Company leases designer gowns from Dolce & Gabbana, Carolina Herrera, and Behnaz Sarafpour for 15 percent of the retail price. For frequent event attendees, these prices provide quite a deal! Bag, Borrow, or Steal allows its members to rent premium handbags and jewelry. There are also firms that rent art for a house to make it more appealing to potential buyers.

The flexibility and convenience of leasing ensures customers do not have to make big decisions about big products and yet still get to enjoy the experience.

In this sense, the service of providing the lease goods is just as important as the products themselves. Many customers avoid serious investments and their attendant risk, but they still appreciate the experience of carrying a Louis Vuitton bag for a week or driving a different Ferrari each month. Leasing allows these customers to fulfill their psychological needs and gain the extra perks that go along with the products.

*Want to impress a date? Lease a car from Classic Car Club.*

sensitive, target markets. Some consumers also like leases because they get tired of the product before its useful life is over, and they don't have to worry about selling it, trading it, or throwing it away. Car companies have used leasing options for years to appeal to consumers who plan to keep their cars only for a few years and will want to trade in for a new model sooner rather than later. Other industries are recognizing that what works for Toyotas and Chevy trucks also works for gowns, handbags, art, and luxury cars. As Superior Service 14.1 notes, although consumers lease products, it is the ancillary service that makes it so valuable.

**Price Bundling** When you signed up for your high-speed Internet connection, did you also get cable TV and telephone? If so, you probably pay less than if you were to get the three services separately. This practice of selling more than one product for a single, lower price is called **price bundling**.[27] Firms bundle products or services together to encourage customers to stock up so they won't purchase competing brands, to encourage trial of a new product, or to provide an incentive to purchase a less desirable product or service to obtain a more desirable one in the same bundle.

*Stores like Aldi use a pricing tactic called leader pricing to build store traffic by aggressively pricing and advertising regularly purchased items, often at or just above the store's cost.*

**Leader Pricing**  Leader pricing is a tactic that attempts to build store traffic by aggressively pricing and advertising a regularly purchased item, often priced at or just above the store's cost. The rationale behind this tactic argues that, while in the store to get the great deal on, say, milk, the consumer will also probably pick up other higher margin items that he or she needs. Thus, these higher margin items will more than cover the lower markup on the milk. Imagine the marketing potential of various combinations of products; the store uses leader pricing on cocktail sauce, which gives employees the perfect opportunity to ask, "How about a pound of fresh shrimp to go with the cocktail sauce you're purchasing?" Leader pricing can be illegal under some circumstances, as discussed subsequently in this chapter.

**L05**  Identify tactics used to reduce prices to businesses.

## Business Pricing Tactics and Discounts

The pricing tactics employed in B2B settings differ significantly from those used in consumer markets. Among the most prominent are seasonal and cash discounts, allowances, quantity discounts, and uniform delivered versus zone pricing. (See Exhibit 14.3.)

**Seasonal Discounts**  A seasonal discount is an additional reduction offered as an incentive to retailers to order merchandise in advance of the normal buying season. For instance, Lennox may offer its air conditioner dealers an additional seasonal discount if they place their orders and receive delivery before April 1, prior to the warm months when air conditioner sales are highest. If it can ship earlier in the season, Lennox can plan its production schedules more easily and lessen its finished goods inventory. Its dealers, however, must weigh the benefits of a larger profit because of the discount versus the extra cost of carrying the inventory for a longer period of time.

**Cash Discounts**  A cash discount reduces the invoice cost if the buyer pays the invoice prior to the end of the discount period. Typically, it is expressed in the form of a percentage, such as "3/10, n/30," or "3%, 10 days, net 30," meaning the buyer can take a 3 percent discount on the total amount of the invoice if the bill is paid within 10 days of the invoice date; otherwise the full, or net, amount is due within 30 days. Why do B2B sellers offer cash discounts to customers? By encouraging early payment, they benefit from the time value of money. Getting money earlier rather than later enables the firm to either invest the money to earn a return on it or avoid borrowing money and paying interest on it. In both instances, the firm is better off financially.

| **EXHIBIT 14.3** | Business-to-Business Pricing Tactics |
|---|---|
| **Tactic** | **Description** |
| Seasonal discounts | An additional reduction offered as an incentive to retailers to order merchandise in advance of the normal buying season. |
| Cash discounts | An additional reduction that reduces the invoice cost if the buyer pays the invoice prior to the end of the discount period. |
| Allowances | Advertising or slotting allowances (additional price reductions) offered in return for specific behaviors. Advertising allowances are offered to retailers if they agree to feature the manufacturer's product in their advertising and promotional efforts. Slotting allowances are offered to get new products into stores or to gain more or better shelf space. |
| Quantity discounts | Providing a reduced price according to the amount purchased. |
| Uniform delivered versus zone pricing | Uniform delivered price: shipper charges one rate, no matter where the buyer is located. Zone price: different prices depending on the geographical delivery area. |

**Vendor Allowances** Another pricing tactic that lowers the final cost to channel members is vendor allowances, such as advertising or slotting allowances, offered in return for specific behaviors. An advertising allowance offers a price reduction to channel members if they agree to feature the manufacturer's product in their advertising and promotional efforts. Slotting allowances are fees paid to retailers simply to get new products into stores or to gain more or better shelf space for their products. Some argue that slotting allowances are unethical because they put small manufacturers that cannot readily afford allowances at a competitive disadvantage. Demanding large slotting allowances could be considered a form of bribery—"paying off" the retailer to get preferential treatment.

**Quantity Discounts** A quantity discount provides a reduced price according to the amount purchased. The more the buyer purchases, the higher the discount and, of course, the greater the value.

A cumulative quantity discount uses the amount purchased over a specified time period and usually involves several transactions. This type of discount particularly encourages resellers to maintain their current supplier because the cost to switch must include the loss of the discount. For example, automobile dealers often attempt to meet a quota or a sales goal for a specific time period, such as a quarter or a year. If they meet their quotas, they earn discounts on all the cars they purchased from the manufacturer during that time period in the form of a rebate. For this very reason, you will often find good deals on cars at the end of a quarter or fiscal year. If the dealership can just sell a few more cars to meet its quota, the rebate earned can be substantial, so taking a few hundred dollars less on those last few cars is well worth the opportunity to receive a rebate check worth many times the amount of the losses.

A noncumulative quantity discount, though still a quantity discount, is based only on the amount purchased in a single order. It therefore provides the buyer with an incentive to purchase more merchandise immediately. Such larger, less frequent orders can save manufacturers order processing, sales, and transportation expenses. For example, a retail store might get a 40 percent discount off the manufacturer's suggested retail price for placing a $500 order; a 50 percent discount for an order of $501–$4,999, and a 60 percent discount for an order of greater than $5,000.

**Uniform Delivered versus Zone Pricing** These pricing tactics are specific to shipping, which represents a major cost for many manufacturers. With a uniform delivered pricing tactic, the shipper charges one rate, no matter where the buyer is located, which makes things very simple for both the seller and the buyer. Zone pricing, however, sets different prices depending on a geographical division of the delivery areas. For example, a manufacturer based in New York City might divide the United States into seven different zones and use different shipping rates for each zone to reflect the average shipping cost for customers located therein. This way, each customer in a zone is charged the same cost for shipping. Zone pricing can be advantageous to the shipper because it reflects the actual shipping charges more closely than uniform delivered pricing can.

---

**CHECK YOURSELF**

1. What are some consumer-oriented pricing tactics?
2. What are some business-oriented pricing tactics?

---

# LEGAL AND ETHICAL ASPECTS OF PRICING

 **LO6** List pricing practices that have the potential to deceive customers.

With so many different pricing strategies and tactics, it is no wonder that unscrupulous firms find ample opportunity to engage in pricing practices that can hurt consumers. We now take a look at some of the legal and ethical implications of pricing.

Prices tend to fluctuate naturally and respond to varying market conditions. Thus, though we rarely see firms attempting to control the market in terms of product quality or advertising, they often engage in pricing practices that can unfairly reduce competition or harm consumers directly through fraud and deception. A host of laws and regulations at both the federal and state levels attempt to prevent unfair pricing practices, but some are poorly enforced, and others are difficult to prove.

*The U.K. Advertising Standards Authority forced Tesco to end its "Britain's Biggest Discounter" campaign because it believed it was misleading. Tesco's new slogan, "Helping you spend less every day" is OK, however.*

## Deceptive or Illegal Price Advertising

Although it is always illegal and unethical to lie in advertising, a certain amount of "puffery" is typically allowed (see Chapter 18).[28] But price advertisements should never deceive consumers to the point of causing harm. For example, a local car dealer's advertising that it had the "best deals in town" would likely be considered puffery. In contrast, advertising "the lowest prices, guaranteed" makes a very specific claim and, if not true, can be considered deceptive. The EU takes a more stringent view of puffery than is the case in the United States. For example, when U.K.-based Tesco advertised that it was "Britain's Biggest Discounter," the U.K.'s Advertising Standards Authority forced it to end the campaign, ruling it was misleading, and due to differences in basket items it was difficult to determine if Tesco was less expensive than its competition such as Aldi, Asda.[29]

**Deceptive Reference Prices**  Previously, we introduced reference prices, which create reference points for the buyer against which to compare the selling price. If the reference price is bona fide, the advertisement is informative. If the reference price has been inflated or is just plain fictitious, however, the advertisement is deceptive and may cause harm to consumers. But it is not easy to determine whether a reference price is bona fide. What standard should be used? If an advertisement specifies a "regular price," just what qualifies as regular? How many units must the store sell at this price for it to be a bona fide regular price—half the stock? A few? Just one? Finally, what if the store offers the item for sale at the regular price but customers do not buy any? Can it still be considered a regular price? In general, if a seller is going to label a price as a regular price, the Better Business Bureau suggests that at least 50 percent of the sales have occurred at that price.[30]

*Is this a legitimate sale, or is the retailer using deceptive reference prices?*

**Loss Leader Pricing**  As we discussed previously, leader pricing is a legitimate attempt to build store traffic by pricing a regularly purchased item aggressively but still above the store's cost. Loss leader pricing takes this tactic one step further by lowering the price *below* the store's cost. No doubt you have seen "buy one, get one free" offers at grocery and discount stores. Unless the markup for the item is 100 percent of the cost, these sales obviously do not generate enough revenue from the sale of one unit to cover the store's cost for both units, which means it has essentially priced the total for both items below cost, unless the manufacturer is absorbing the cost of the promotion to generate volume.

**Bait and Switch**  Another form of deceptive price advertising occurs when sellers advertise items for a very low price without the intent to really sell any. This bait-and-switch tactic is a deceptive practice because the store lures customers in with a very low price on an item (the bait), only to aggressively pressure these customers into purchasing a higher-priced model (the switch) by disparaging the low-priced item, comparing it unfavorably with the higher-priced model, or professing an inadequate supply of the lower-priced item. Again, the laws against bait-and-switch practices are difficult to enforce because salespeople, simply as a function of their jobs, are always trying to get customers to trade up to a higher-priced model without necessarily deliberately baiting them. The key to proving deception centers on the intent of the seller, which is also difficult to prove.

## Predatory Pricing

When a firm sets a very low price for one or more of its products with the intent to drive its competition out of business, it is using predatory pricing. Predatory pricing is illegal under both the Sherman Act and the Federal Trade Commission Act because it constrains free trade and represents a form of unfair competition. It also tends to promote a concentrated market with a few dominant firms (an oligopoly).

But again, predation is difficult to prove. First, one must demonstrate intent, that is, that the firm intended to drive out its competition or prevent competitors from entering the market. Second, the complainant must prove that the firm charged prices lower than its average cost, an equally difficult task. The American Booksellers Association, which represents independent booksellers, has asked the U.S. Department of Justice to investigate the practice of selling hardcover best-seller books for approximately $9, about $25 less than the MSRP.[31] It claims that this practice is damaging the book industry by contributing to the demise of independent bookstores which, in turn, harms consumers because it reduces their shopping options. The issue to be resolved by the Justice Department is whether the intent of these large stores is to put the small stores out of business, or whether they are being highly price competitive on books to bring customers into their stores to buy other, more profitable merchandise.

## Price Discrimination

There are many forms of price discrimination, but only some of them are considered illegal under the Clayton Act and the Robinson-Patman Act. When firms sell the same product to different resellers (wholesalers, distributors, or retailers) at different prices, it can be considered price discrimination; usually, larger firms receive lower prices.

We have already discussed the use of quantity discounts, which is a legitimate method of charging different prices to different customers on the basis of the quantity they purchase. The legality of this tactic stems from the assumption that it costs less to sell and service 1,000 units to one customer than 100 units to 10 customers. But quantity discounts must be available to all customers and not be structured in such a way that they consistently and obviously favor one or a few buyers over others. Subtle forms of price discrimination, such as rebates, free delivery, advertising allowances, and other methods used to lower the price without actually changing the invoice, are specifically prohibited by the Robinson-Patman Act. It is, however, perfectly legitimate to charge a different price to a reseller if the firm is attempting to meet a specific competitor's price.

*Is this price discrimination illegal?*

The Robinson-Patman Act does not apply to sales to end consumers, at which point many forms of price discrimination occur. For example, students and seniors often receive discounts on food and movie tickets, which is perfectly acceptable under federal law. Those engaged in online auctions like eBay are also practicing a legal form of price discrimination because sellers are selling the same item to

different buyers at various prices. In addition, to deal ethically with the rising costs of health care, some hospitals offer a "sliding scale" based on income, such that lower-income patients receive discounts or even free medical care, especially for children.[32]

### Price Fixing

Price fixing is the practice of colluding with other firms to control prices. Price fixing might be either horizontal or vertical. Whereas horizontal price fixing is clearly illegal under the Sherman Antitrust Act, vertical price fixing falls into a gray area.[33]

Horizontal price fixing occurs when competitors that produce and sell competing products or services collude, or work together, to control prices, effectively taking price out of the decision process for consumers. This practice clearly reduces competition and is illegal. For instance, six South African airlines have been accused of colluding to hike the price of fares for flights within the country during the World Cup.[34] As a general rule of thumb, competing firms should refrain from discussing prices or terms and conditions of sale with competitors. If firms want to know competitors' prices, they can look at a competitor's advertisements, websites, or stores.

Vertical price fixing occurs when parties at different levels of the same marketing channel (e.g., manufacturers and retailers) agree to control the prices passed on to consumers. Manufacturers often encourage retailers to sell their merchandise at a specific price, known as the manufacturer's suggested retail price (MSRP). Manufacturers set MSRP prices to reduce retail price competition among retailers, stimulate retailers to provide complementary services, and support the manufacturer's merchandise. Manufacturers enforce MSRPs by withholding benefits such as cooperative advertising or even refusing to deliver merchandise to noncomplying retailers. The Supreme Court recently ruled that the ability of a manufacturer to require retailers to sell merchandise at MSRP should be decided on a case-by-case basis, depending on the individual circumstances.[35]

As these legal issues clearly demonstrate, pricing decisions involve many ethical considerations. In determining both their pricing strategies and their pricing tactics, marketers must always balance their goal of inducing customers, through price, to find value and the need to deal honestly and fairly with those same customers. Whether another business or an individual consumer, buyers can be influenced by a variety of pricing methods. It is up to marketers to determine which of these methods works best for the seller, the buyer, and the community.

### CHECK YOURSELF

1. What common pricing practices are considered to be illegal or unethical?

## Summing Up

**LO1** **Identify three methods that firms use to set their prices.**

The various methods of setting prices each have their own set of advantages and disadvantages. The three primary methods are cost-based, competitor-based, and value-based. The cost-based techniques of fixed percentage and mark-up approaches are quick and easy but fail to reflect the competitive environment or consumer demand. Although it is always advisable to be aware of what competitors are doing, using competitor-based pricing should not occur in isolation without considering consumer and competitive reactions. Taking a value-based approach to pricing, whether the improvement value or the total cost of ownership, in conjunction with these other methods provides a nicely balanced method of setting prices.

**L02** **Describe the difference between an everyday low price strategy (EDLP) and a high/low strategy.**

An everyday low pricing strategy is maintained when a product's price stays relatively constant at a level that is slightly lower than the regular price from competitors using a high/low strategy, and is less frequently discounted. Customers enjoy an everyday low pricing strategy because they know that the price will always be about the same and a better price than the competition. Retailers use odd prices to convey this pricing strategy. High/low pricing strategy starts out with a product at one (higher) price, and then discounts the product. This strategy first attracts a less price sensitive customer who pays the regular price, and then a very price sensitive customer who pays the low price.

**L03** **Explain the difference between a market penetration and a price skimming pricing strategy.**

When firms use a price skimming strategy, the product or service must be perceived as breaking new ground or customers will not pay more than what they pay for other products. Firms use price skimming to signal high quality, limit demand, recoup their investment quickly, and/or test people's price sensitivity. Moreover, it is easier to price high initially and then lower the price than vice versa. Market penetration, in contrast, helps firms build sales and market share quickly, which may discourage other firms from entering the market. Building demand quickly also typically results in lowered costs as the firm gains experience making the product or delivering the service.

**L04** **Identify tactics used to reduce prices to consumers.**

Marketers can use price lining to indicate different quality levels to consumers or bundle products to offer lower prices than those charged if the products were purchased separately. To get customers into their stores, retailers also price certain products or services at very low prices, with the hope that these same customers will also buy other, more profitable items. In some methods similar to those used in B2B contexts, sellers offer seasonal and quantity discounts to individual buyers as well. Finally, coupons and rebates offer consumers additional price reductions.

**L05** **Identify tactics used to reduce prices to businesses.**

Seasonal discounts give retailers an incentive to buy prior to the normal selling season, cash discounts prompt them to pay their invoices early, and allowances attempt to get retailers to advertise the manufacturer's product or stock a new product. In addition, quantity discounts can cause retailers to purchase a larger quantity over a specific period of time or with a particular order. Finally, zone pricing bases the cost of shipping the merchandise on the distance between the retailer and the manufacturer—the farther away, the more it costs.

**L06** **List pricing practices that have the potential to deceive customers.**

There are almost as many ways to get into trouble by setting or changing a price as there are pricing strategies and tactics. Three of the most common legal issues pertain to advertising deceptive prices. Specifically, if a firm compares a reduced price with a "regular" or reference price, it must actually have sold that product or service at the regular price. In many states, advertising the sale of products priced below the retailer's cost constitutes an unfair competitive practice, as does bait-and-switch advertising. Charging different prices to different customers is sometimes, but not always, illegal, whereas any collusion among firms to fix prices is always illegal.

## Key Terms

- advertising allowance, 429
- bait-and-switch, 431
- cash discount, 428
- competitor-based pricing method, 415
- cost-based pricing method, 414
- cost of ownership method, 416
- coupon, 425
- cumulative quantity discount, 429
- everyday low pricing (EDLP), 417
- experience curve effect, 422
- high/low pricing, 419
- horizontal price fixing, 432
- improvement value, 416
- leader pricing, 428
- lease, 426
- loss leader pricing, 430
- markdowns, 425
- market penetration strategy, 422
- noncumulative quantity discount, 429

## Marketing Applications

1. Suppose you have been hired as the pricing manager for a drugstore chain that typically adds a fixed percentage onto the cost of each product to arrive at the retail price. Evaluate this technique. What would you do differently?

2. Some high-fashion retailers, notably H&M and Zara, sell what some call "disposable fashion"—apparel priced so reasonably low that it can be disposed of after just a few wearings. Here is your dilemma: You have an important job interview and need a new suit. You can buy the suit at one of these stores for $129 or at Brooks Brothers for $500. Of course, the Brooks Brothers suit is of higher quality and will therefore last longer. How would you use the two value-based approaches described in this chapter to determine which suit to buy?

3. A phone manufacturer is determining a price for its product using a cost-based pricing strategy. The fixed costs are $100,000, and the variable costs are $50,000. If 1,000 units are produced and the company wants to have a 30 percent markup, what is the price of the phone?

4. Identify two stores at which you shop, one of which uses everyday low pricing and another that uses a high/low pricing strategy. Do you believe that each store's chosen strategy is appropriate for the type of merchandise it sells and the market of customers to whom it is appealing? Justify your answer.

5. As the product manager for Whirlpool's line of washing machines, you are in charge of pricing new products. Your product team has developed a revolutionary new washing machine that relies on radically new technology and requires very little water to get clothes clean. This technology will likely be difficult for your competition to copy. Should you adopt a skimming or a penetration pricing strategy? Justify your answer.

6. What is the difference between a cumulative and a noncumulative quantity discount?

7. If you worked for a manufacturing firm located in Oregon and shipped merchandise all over the United States, which would be more advantageous,

a zone or a uniform delivered pricing policy? Why? What if your firm were located in Kansas—would it make a difference?

8. Coupons and rebates benefit different distribution channel members. Which would you prefer if you were a manufacturer, a retailer, and a consumer? Why?

9. Suppose the president of your university got together with the presidents of all the universities in your athletic conference for lunch. They discussed what each university was going to charge for tuition the following year. Are they in violation of federal laws? Explain your answer.

10. Imagine that you are the newly hired brand manager for a restaurant that is about to open. Both the local newspaper and a gourmet food magazine recently ran articles about your new head chef, calling her one of the best young chefs in the country. In response to these positive reviews, the company wants to position its brand as a premium, gourmet restaurant. Your boss asks what price you should charge for the chef's signature filet mignon dish. Other restaurants in the area charge around $40 for their own filet offerings. What steps might you undertake to determine what the new price should be?

11. You have been hired by a regional supermarket chain as the candy and snack buyer. Your shelves are dominated by national firms, like Wrigley's and Nabisco. The chain imposes a substantial slotting fee to allow new items to be added to their stock selection. Management reasons that it costs a lot to add and delete items, and besides, these slotting fees are a good source of revenue. A small, minority-operated, local firm produces several potentially interesting snack crackers and a line of gummy candy, all with natural ingredients, added vitamins, reduced sugar, and a competitive price—and they also happen to taste great. You'd love to give the firm a chance, but its managers claim the slotting fee is too high. Should your firm charge slotting fees? Are slotting fees fair to the relevant shareholders—customers, stockholders, vendors?

## Quiz Yourself

1. In determining the price for his company's new pocket digital camera, Matt is assessing what consumers consider the regular or original price for similar cameras available in the market. Matt is assessing the _____ influence on pricing strategy.
   a. improvement value
   b. odd-even
   c. everyday low pricing
   d. reference-based
   e. cost of ownership

2. When Apple Inc. introduced their iPhone in 2007, they priced it at $599, considerably higher than either their iPod or competing cellular phones. Apple was probably pursuing a _____ pricing strategy.
   a. market penetration
   b. slotting allowance
   c. price fixing
   d. reference
   e. skimming

(Answers to these two questions are provided on page 608.)

Go to www.mhhe.com/grewal3e to practice an additional 11 questions.

## Net Savvy

1. Go to www.coupons.com. In which product categories does this website offer coupons? Choose a product from each category.

   - How effective are coupons for selling these types of products? Why?
   - Do any sellers offer rebates through this site? Why or why not?
   - What are the benefits to the seller of using Coupons.com instead of offering coupons in a newspaper?
   - How do you think Coupons.com makes money? For example, consider what companies are advertising on the site. Do the same companies offer coupons?

2. Visit the website for Bag, Borrow, or Steal (www.bagborroworsteal.com) and select handbags. Click on "Handbags," then choose "Gucci" in the Designer category on the left column, and then "Sort by" price. What is the difference between Gucci's highest and lowest priced bags? Notice that if a product says "Waitlist," it has already been borrowed, but if it says "Borrow," then it is available for you to borrow. Are the bags that are waitlisted the highest priced or the lowest priced? How does Bag, Borrow, or Steal determine the price for different bags if they are made by the same designer?

## Chapter Case Study

### PRICE WARS IN THE WIRELESS MARKET

Cell phone companies may already have all available customers. Cell phone subscriptions have nearly topped 260 million in the United States, and the country's population is 305 million.[36] The remaining 45 million may be too young for a cell phone, or else they've already decided they don't want one. Examining how cell phone companies like Verizon Wireless, AT&T, Sprint, and T-Mobile grow once they've run out of potential customers provides a glimpse into the value of strategic pricing.

### THE PLAYERS

With 98.2 million subscribers,[37] Verizon leads the pack. The company, headquartered in New Jersey, is a joint venture of Verizon Communications and Vodafone. In addition to cell phone service, it offers broadband capability so customers can connect via laptops and smartphones, as well as download and enjoy music, videos, cable television, text and picture messaging, games, and more. Verizon boasts the first wireless consumer 3G multimedia service.

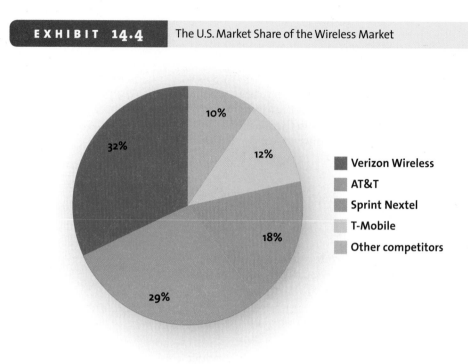

Source: http://www.wikinvest.com/stock/Verizon_Communications_(VZ) (accessed April 18, 2010).

AT&T traces its roots back to 1876 and Alexander Graham Bell's discovery of the telephone. Although it lags behind Verizon in number of subscribers (85.1 million), it bests them at revenue[38] and claims the nation's fastest 3G network and the best worldwide wireless coverage. Exhibit 14.4 shows the U.S. market share of the largest cellular providers. AT&T is the sole U.S. wireless carrier for the iPhone 3GS, a fast, powerful phone that features video recording, a three-megapixel camera, voice control, and plenty of applications. The company also claims to be the nation's largest broadband provider. Consumers committed to their iPhones must use AT&T, but those using a Blackberry can obtain service through Verizon, AT&T, and other carriers.

Sprint Nextel holds third place with 48.1 million customers, although the company has been losing subscribers for the past few years. The company's most recent innovation is that it is the first and only wireless 4G service from a national U.S. carrier.[39] The company brought walkie-talkie service to Blackberries in 2001 and claims to have led the industry in providing access to live streaming video.

T-Mobile, with 33.8 million subscribers, is the leading carrier of smartphones, using Google's Android operating system. Android's open development platform allows developers to build applications that customers download for free, an appealing feature for smartphone users who don't want to be tied to Apple's e-commerce site for purchasing apps. Founded in 1983, the fifth-largest full-service wireless company, U.S. Cellular, claims 6.3 million subscribers.

## MARKET SHARES AND PRICE WARS

For the last decade, the cost of cell service has been going down, and customer bills have remained flat, so increasing prices wasn't an option for building revenue. With no new customers to attract, the major phone companies sought to increase their share of the market. Accomplishing that goal meant attracting customers from competitors, but if the companies tried to lure subscribers with reduced rates, they ran the very real risk of causing harm to their economic bottom line. AT&T and Verizon couldn't afford to do nothing: their consumer landline business was contracting as people gave up their home phones.

So Verizon Wireless cut prices for its unlimited talk and unlimited talk & text plans. The company also lowered costs for its family share plans.[40] AT&T promptly matched Verizon's changes. T-Mobile already had an unlimited talk plan for $60, $10 less than the new prices at AT&T and Verizon. Sprint chimed in that it's "Everything Data" plans are already cheaper than Verizon's, and that its plans can save individuals as much as $240 per year and families almost $600.[41] U.S. Cellular promptly joined in, offering unlimited national individual and unlimited national family plans for the same price as Verizon and AT&T.[42] Companies alerted current customers that they could switch to the new plan without extending their contract.[43]

To avoid shrinking margins from the lower-priced voice plans, the wireless companies compensated with new charges for data. Verizon instigated a mandatory data plan for high-speed 3G customers. While the monthly cost of $9.99 isn't a deal breaker, that charge includes only 25 megabytes of data. Excess usage adds up in a hurry. Both of the big carriers also lowered their price on unlimited voice and data plans for smart phones by $30.[44] But on the flip side, Verizon eliminated a $19.99 monthly data plan.

The goal of cost cuts on voice plans, according to Verizon Wireless CEO Lowell McAdam, is to get customers enrolled in more expensive unlimited plans, especially for data. Capturing market share from competitors is also important, but doesn't hold the same value for generating revenue. Verizon Wireless, for example, may give up $540 million in voice revenue but experience a net gain of $90 million because of changes in data plan sales and because of the healthier margins associated with data plans.[45] In fact, despite the excitement about price cuts, the financial firm JPMorgan estimates that only about 2 percent of wireless subscribers will end up with lower bills.

Networks account for only a piece of a wireless company's revenue stream. Companies also sell handsets, and these handsets are becoming increasingly more sophisticated. Nevertheless, companies are cutting prices on handsets in an effort to attract market share. The reductions negatively impact the companies' bottom line. AT&T, tied to Apple devices, may be selling iPhones for $200 less than it pays for them to lure subscribers to its two-year plans. The company has also reduced the number of handsets it offers from 80 to 50.

The war is far from over. Increased broadband use has challenged overburdened networks, and cell phone companies may be forced to invest in their networks to avoid service failures and customer complaints. If voice plans drop further, revenue from data plans may no longer provide the margins cell phone companies need. Some wireless providers may consolidate; others will fade away.

## Questions

1.  Who are the key players in this industry?
2.  If a price war will reduce margins, as the case suggests, why would any company embrace this strategy?
3.  On what other strategy elements could the wireless companies compete?
4.  Which wireless provider do you use? Why? Given the benefits of each firm's wireless program, did you make the best provider choice? Justify your answer.

# VALUE DELIVERY: DESIGNING THE CHANNEL AND SUPPLY CHAIN

**CHAPTER 15**
Supply Chain and Channel Management

**CHAPTER 16**
Retailing and Multichannel Marketing

Section Six deals with the value delivery system. It is critical that merchandise is delivered in time to stores to meet customer demand. To achieve this, retailers have initiated many innovative programs with their vendors and developed sophisticated transportation and warehousing systems. We devote two chapters to value delivery. Chapter 15 takes a look at the entire supply chain and marketing channel, while Chapter 16 concentrates on retailing and multichannel marketing.

# Supply Chain and Channel Management

G rowth, costs, market demand, and technology advances can cause retail executives to rethink their business processes. The truly savvy managers search for ways to optimize operations even when business is running smoothly, because today's approaches won't necessarily work tomorrow. Perhaps that's what was on the mind of the founder of the fashion retailer group Inditex when he told the company's first deputy chair and CEO, "Once a month, come here thinking that we are near bankruptcy. You will find a lot of things to change."[1]

Room for improvement wasn't obvious with Inditex's major holding, the Zara chain of fashion stores. Zara pioneered the concept of fast fashion, which involves moving trendy styles from concept to store racks in a fraction of the time required by luxury retailers. Zara's advantage over competitors such as The Gap and H&M rises from its highly responsive and tightly organized supply chain. All design, warehousing, distribution, and logistics functions are controlled by the company. Manufacturing outsourcing is confined to more classic styles that are easier to predict and which, therefore, can be made with longer lead times by less expensive vendors.

Contrary to many of its competitors, Zara selects factory locations that are in close geographic proximity to the company's headquarters in Spain. This approach increases labor costs over what they would have been if they had garments made in Asia like most of their competition, but also improves communication, reduces shipping costs and time, and speeds new fashions into the stores. It gives Zara the flexibility to modify operations in one supply chain function to expedite processes in another, such as pricing, tagging, and hanging merchandise on racks in the warehouse so that store employees can move apparel directly from delivery to the sales floor.[2]

Despite the success of this approach—the company boasts an annual growth of approximately 20 percent in sales and number of stores[3]—Zara outgrew it. Fashion trends are, by nature, rapidly changing, and merchandise on Zara's floors changes quickly in response. Sales managers ordered excessive quantities of hot items

## LEARNING OBJECTIVES

**LO1** Define supply chain management.

**LO2** Recognize the value added by the supply chain.

**LO3** Describe the flow of merchandise and the flow of information in the supply chain.

**LO4** Describe how supply chains are managed.

to avoid stockouts, but frequently received fewer units than they had requested because demand exceeded inventory levels. This practice also resulted in inventory sitting in one store when the item could have been sold at another location. The company launches as many as 10,000 new styles into production each year. The need to manufacture these designs in a range of colors and sizes results in approximately 300,000 new SKUs hitting the company's systems each year. Replenishment orders, received twice weekly, exponentially increase that number, resulting in an average shipping total of nearly 2.5 million items per week from the company's distribution center.[4] Zara's legendary supply chain efficiency was in danger of a clogged artery.

In response, Zara adopted mathematical processes that turn human experience and mountains of data into actionable information.[5] The models factor in store manager requests for merchandise replenishments and historical sales of the same item. They also incorporate merchandise display practices, such as removing all sizes of a garment from the sales floor if a popular size is not available. This practice, which is intended to reduce customer frustration over wanting an item that's not available in the correct size, means there is no value to shipping small and large sizes of an item if medium is unavailable since, without the mediums, that garment will remain in the back room. The large and small sizes can be redirected to stores that have all sizes in stock and on the floor.

Taking all individual store information and inventory availability into account, the model calculates replenishment decisions to generate the greatest possible network-wide sales. This method turns replenishment into a proactive process that predicts sales based on a wealth of current and historical objective and subjective information. Zara rolled its new shipping approach out to all stores after a pilot indicated a sales increase of up to 4 percent. In the future, the model may be used to calculate initial allocation of merchandise to stores as well.[6]

● ● ●

In this chapter, we discuss the third P, place, which includes all activities required to get the right product to the right customer when that customer wants it.[7] Students of marketing often overlook or underestimate the importance of place in the marketing mix simply because it happens behind the scenes. Yet place, or supply chain management as it is commonly called, adds value for customers at Zara and other retailers because it gets products to customers efficiently—quickly and at low cost.

As we noted in Chapter 1, **supply chain management** refers to a set of approaches and techniques firms employ to efficiently and effectively integrate their suppliers, manufacturers, warehouses, stores, and transportation intermediaries into a seamless operation in which merchandise is produced and distributed in the right quantities, to the right locations, and at the right time, as well as to minimize systemwide costs while satisfying the service levels their customers require.[8] As we learned in the opening vignette, Zara employs an innovative supply chain that other fashion retailers are trying to emulate. Because the company owns or at least has considerable control over most of its supply chain, it is able to conceive, design, manufacture, transport, and, ultimately sell high-fashion apparel much more quickly and efficiently than many of its major competitors.

| **EXHIBIT 15.1** | Simplified Supply Chain |
|---|---|

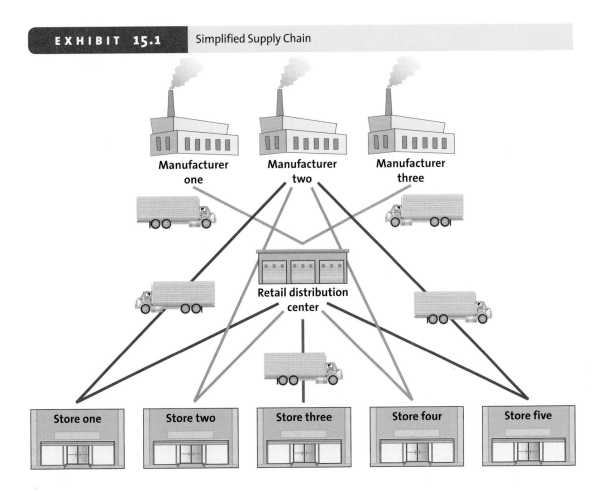

Exhibit 15.1 shows a simplified supply chain, in which manufacturers make products and sell them to retailers or wholesalers. The exhibit would be much more complicated if we had included suppliers of materials to manufacturers and all of the manufacturers, wholesalers, and stores in a typical supply chain. Wholesalers are firms that buy products from manufacturers and resell them to retailers, and retailers sell products directly to consumers. Manufacturers ship to a wholesaler or, in the case of many multistore retailers, to the retailer's distribution center (as is the case for Manufacturer 1 and Manufacturer 3 in Exhibit 15.1) or directly to stores (Manufacturer 2).

Although Exhibit 15.1 shows the typical flow of manufactured goods, many variations to this supply chain exist. Some retail chains, like Home Depot and Costco, function as both retailers and wholesalers. They act as retailers when they sell to consumers directly and as wholesalers when they sell to other businesses, like building contractors or restaurant owners. When manufacturers such as Dell or Avon sell directly to consumers, they are performing both production and retailing activities. When Dell sells directly to a university or business, it becomes a business-to-business (B2B) transaction, but when it sells to students or employees individually, it is a B2C (business-to-consumer) operation.

# SUPPLY CHAIN, MARKETING CHANNELS, AND LOGISTICS ARE RELATED

**L01** Define supply chain management.

People often talk about supply chain management, marketing channel management, and logistics management as if they were the same thing. A marketing channel is the set of institutions that transfer the ownership of and move goods from the point of production to the point of consumption; as such, it consists of all the institutions and marketing activities in the marketing process.[9] Thus, a marketing channel and a supply chain are virtually the same and the terms could be used interchangeably.

Logistics management describes the integration of two or more activities for the purpose of planning, implementing, and controlling the efficient flow of raw materials, in-process inventory, and finished goods from the point of origin to the point of consumption. These activities may include, but are not limited to, customer service, demand forecasting, distribution communications, inventory control, materials handling, order processing, parts and service support, plant and warehouse site selection, procurement, packaging, return goods handling, salvage and scrap disposal, traffic and transportation, and warehousing and storage.[10] Therefore, logistics management is that element of supply chain management that concentrates on the movement and control of physical products; supply chain management as a whole also includes an awareness of the relationships among members of the supply chain or channel and the need to coordinate efforts to provide customers with the best value.

So, are marketing channel management, supply chain management, and logistics management the same or different? To answer this question, we must look at how firms have handled these activities in the past. Marketing channel management traditionally has been the responsibility of marketing departments, under the direction of a marketing vice president. Logistics was traditionally the responsibility of operations, under a vice president of operations. Although their goals were similar, they often saw solutions differently, and sometimes they worked in conflict. For instance, the marketing department's goal might have been to make sales, whereas logistics wanted to keep costs low. Firms have come to realize there is tremendous opportunity in coordinating marketing and logistics activities not only within a firm but also throughout the supply chain. Thus, because supply chain management takes a systemwide approach to coordinating the flow of merchandise, it includes both channel management and logistics and is therefore the term that we use in this chapter.

## SUPPLY CHAINS ADD VALUE

**LO2** Recognize the value added by the supply chain.

Why would a manufacturer want to use a wholesaler or a retailer? Don't these supply chain members just cut into their profits? Wouldn't it be cheaper for consumers to buy directly from manufacturers? In a simple agrarian economy, the best supply chain may in fact follow a direct route from manufacturer to consumer: The consumer goes to the farm and buys food directly from the farmer. Modern "eat local" environmental campaigns suggest just such a process. But before the consumer can eat a fresh steak procured from a local farm, she needs to cook it first. Assuming the consumer doesn't know how to make a stove and lacks the materials to do so, she must rely on a stove maker. The stove maker, who has the necessary knowledge, in turn must buy raw materials and components from various suppliers, make the stove, and then make it available to the consumer. If the stove maker isn't located near the consumer, the stove must be transported to where the consumer has access to it. To make matters even more complicated, the consumer may want to view a choice of stoves, hear about all their features, and have the stove delivered and installed.

Each participant in the supply chain thus adds value.[11] The components manufacturer helps the stove manufacturer by supplying parts and materials. The stove maker then turns the components into the stove. The transportation company gets the stove to the retailer. The retailer stores the stove until the customer wants it, educates the customer about product features, and delivers and installs the stove. At each step, the stove becomes more costly but also more valuable to the consumer.

Even more simple supply chains add value at each step: The farmer who sold the steak to the consumer had to raise and then slaughter the animal, which means that the steak had more value to the consumer than an entire cow would.

Exhibits 15.2A and 15.2B show how using supply chain partners can provide value overall. Exhibit 15.2A shows three manufacturers, each of which sells directly to three consumers in a system that requires nine transactions. Each transaction costs money—for example, the manufacturer must fill the order, package it, write up the paperwork, and ship it—and each cost is passed on to the customer. Exhibit 15.2B shows the same three manufacturers and consumers, but this time they go through a retailer. The number of transactions falls to six, and as transactions are eliminated, the supply chain becomes more efficient, which adds value for customers by making it more convenient and less expensive to purchase merchandise.

*How many companies are involved in making and getting a stove to your kitchen?*

## Supply Chain Management Streamlines Distribution

Supply chain management offers the twenty-first century's answer to a host of distribution problems faced by firms. As recently as the early 1990s, even the most innovative firms needed 15 to 30 days—or even more—to fulfill an order from the warehouse to the customer. The typical order-to-delivery process had several steps: order creation, usually using a telephone, fax, or mail; order processing,

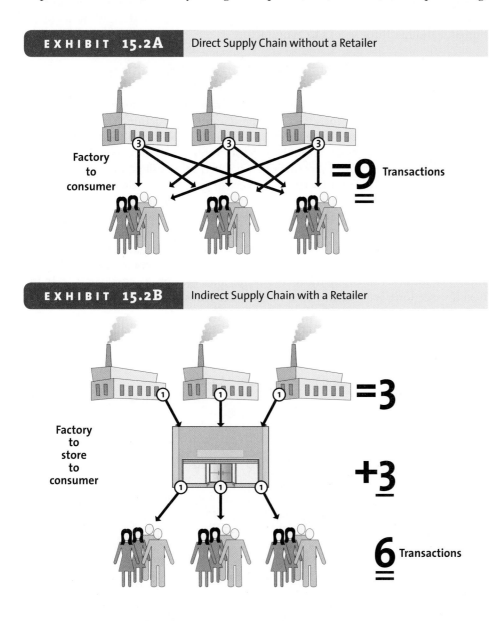

using a manual system for credit authorization and assignment to a warehouse; and physical delivery. Things could, and often did, go wrong. Ordered goods were not available. Orders were lost or misplaced. Shipments were misdirected. These mistakes lengthened the time it took to get merchandise to customers and potentially made the entire process more expensive.

Faced with these predicaments, firms began stockpiling inventory at each level of the supply chain (retailers, wholesalers, and manufacturers), but keeping inventory where it is not needed becomes a huge and wasteful expense. If a manufacturer has a huge stock of items stuck in a warehouse, it not only is not earning profits by selling those items but also must pay to maintain and guard that warehouse.

Therefore, more recently firms have swung in the other direction, as the chapter's opening vignette pointed out. Zara gains its competitive advantage by bringing fashions to the store and the customers much faster than other apparel retailers. It holds minimal inventory, produces new fashions quickly, and rarely gets stuck with old inventory. Deliveries show up at stores twice a week; the newly delivered items rarely remain on retail shelves for more than a week. But this speedy system is not limited to the retail side; Zara also takes only four to five weeks to design a new collection and then about a week to manufacture it, so it continually cycles though its inventory of fabric and materials necessary to make its clothing. Its competitors, in comparison, need an average of six months to design a new collection and another three weeks to manufacture it.

## Supply Chain Management Affects Marketing

Every marketing decision is affected by and has an effect on the supply chain. When products are designed and manufactured, how and when the critical components reach the factory must be coordinated with production. The sales department must coordinate its delivery promises with the factory or distribution centers. A distribution center, a facility for the receipt, storage, and redistribution of goods to company stores or customers, may be operated by retailers, manufacturers, or distribution specialists.[12] Furthermore, advertising and promotion must be coordinated with those departments that control inventory and transportation. There is no faster way to lose credibility with customers than to promise deliveries or run a promotion and then not have the merchandise when the customer expects it.

Five interrelated activities emerge in supply chain management: making information flow, making merchandise flow, managing inventory, designing the supply chain, and managing the relationships among supply chain partners. In the next few sections, we examine each of these activities.

### CHECK YOURSELF

1. How does supply chain management add value?

L03   Describe the flow of merchandise and the flow of information in the supply chain.

# MAKING INFORMATION FLOW

Information flows from the customer to stores, to and from distribution centers, possibly to and from wholesalers, to and from product manufacturers, and then on to the producers of any components and the suppliers of raw materials. To simplify our discussion and because information flows are similar in other supply chain links and B2B channels, we shorten the supply chain in this section to exclude wholesalers, as well as the link from suppliers to manufacturers. Exhibit 15.3 illustrates the

| EXHIBIT 15.3 | Information Flows |
|---|---|

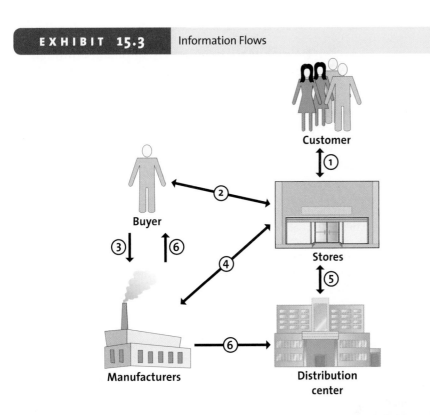

flow of information that starts when a customer buys a Sony HDTV at Best Buy. The flow follows these steps:

**Flow 1 (Customer to Store):** The sales associate at Best Buy scans the Universal Product Code (UPC) tag on the HDTV packaging, and the customer receives a receipt. The UPC tag is the black-and-white bar code found on most merchandise. It contains a 13-digit code that indicates the manufacturer of the item, a description of the item, information about special packaging, and special promotions.[13] In the future, RFID tags, discussed at the end of this chapter, may replace UPC tags.

**Flow 2 (Store to Buyer):** The point-of-sale (POS) terminal records the purchase information and electronically sends it to the buyer at Best Buy's corporate office. The sales information is incorporated into an inventory management system and used to monitor and analyze sales and to decide to reorder more HDTVs, change a price, or plan a promotion. Buyers also send information to stores on overall sales for the chain, how to display the merchandise, upcoming promotions, etc.

**Flow 3 (Buyer to Manufacturer):** The purchase information from each Best Buy store is typically aggregated by the retailer as a whole, which creates an order for new merchandise and sends it to Sony. The buyer at Best Buy may also communicate directly with Sony to get information and negotiate prices, shipping dates, promotional events, or other merchandise-related issues. Power of the Internet 15.1

*The flow of information starts when a sales associate scans the Universal Product Code (UPC) tag on the package.*

## Power of the Internet 15.1     Neiman Marcus Expedites Shipments through Customs

Neiman Marcus receives most of its apparel, accessories, jewelry, and home products from other countries. Because it deals with fashions that have short product life cycles, good communication with its suppliers is essential.[14]

A major impediment to getting deliveries in a timely manner involves the delays caused by the U.S. Customs and Border Protection. These agencies demand comprehensive and complicated paperwork before they will allow shipments into the United States. With so much paperwork, incomplete information and errors are common, which kept Neiman Marcus' shipments from arriving in time. The company therefore instituted an Internet-based system that remains in contact with every business partner that touches a shipment to ensure that the documents are prepared properly for U.S. Customs. Trust is one thing, but this system guarantees that the work gets done correctly. Any missing paperwork prompts an automatic alert to the appropriate business partner, which can then send the required paperwork to U.S. Customs while the shipment is still en route, rather than wait to be notified by Customs after it has arrived. Missing or incorrect documents found by Customs once the shipment has arrived can delay the process even more. This initiative eliminated a full two days from the shipping cycle.

As an added bonus, Neiman Marcus uses the system to comply more closely with import regulations. The duty/tariff laws of different countries vary and can change quickly.

To keep up to date with these changes in the more than 60 countries with which it does business, Neiman Marcus requires vendors to guarantee that they will update any tariff changes on the Internet-based system within 24 hours of the country's rule change. Shipments then receive an HTSUS (harmonized tariff schedule of the United States), making it easier for U.S. Customs to identify the import shipments and move them through the clearance process. As a result, Neiman Marcus shipments have a low risk rating and move through Customs much faster than those of many of its competitors.

Changes like these demonstrate the symbiotic nature of relationships along the supply chain. Retailers with sufficient strength in the marketplace may insist their vendors adhere to a new process that requires investment on the vendor's part. In a recent initiative to address shrinking profits, for example, Neiman Marcus asked its vendors to create designer merchandise at a lower price point.[15] The replicas, produced in the same style and same factory as the more-expensive models, still sport the designer's name but are made from less costly materials. While some suppliers found the request challenging, others embraced it, recognizing an opportunity to protect their futures at a time when high-end consumers are spending less. As news about these lower-cost designer items spreads across the Internet, Neiman will learn whether this approach buoys its flagging sales or sends customers to other stores that have retained their luxury brand image.

*To get merchandise through customs and into stores as quickly as possible, Neiman Marcus has an Internet-based system that remains in contact with every business partner that touches a shipment to ensure that the documents are prepared properly for U.S. customs.*

examines how Neiman Marcus works with its suppliers to expedite a key issue in this flow: U.S. Customs import processes.

**Flow 4 (Store to Manufacturer):** In some situations, the sales transaction data are sent directly from the store to the manufacturer, and the manufacturer decides when to ship more merchandise to the distribution centers and the stores. In other situations, especially when merchandise is reordered frequently, the ordering process is done automatically, bypassing the buyers. By working together, the retailer and manufacturer can better satisfy customer needs.[16]

**Flow 5 (Store to Distribution Center):** Stores also communicate with the Best Buy distribution center to coordinate deliveries and check inventory status. When the store inventory drops to a specified level, more HDTVs are shipped to the store, and the shipment information is sent to the Best Buy computer system.

**Flow 6 (Manufacturer to Distribution Center and Buyer):** When the manufacturer ships the HDTVs to the Best Buy distribution center, it sends an advanced shipping notice to the distribution centers. An advanced shipping notice (ASN) is an electronic document that the supplier sends the retailer in advance of a shipment to tell the retailer exactly what to expect in the shipment. The center then makes appointments for trucks to make the delivery at a specific time, date, and loading dock. When the shipment is received at the distribution center, the buyer is notified and authorizes payment to the vendor.

## Data Warehouse

Purchase data collected at the point of sale (information flow 2 in Exhibit 15.3) goes into a huge database known as a data warehouse. The information stored in the data warehouse is accessible on various dimensions and levels, as depicted in the data cube in Exhibit 15.4.

As shown on the horizontal axis, data can be accessed according to the level of merchandise aggregation—SKU (item), vendor, category (e.g., dresses), or all merchandise. Along the vertical axis, data can be accessed by level of the company—store, divisions, or the total company. Finally, along the third dimension, data can be accessed by point in time—day, season, or year.

**EXHIBIT 15.4**  Retail Data Warehouse

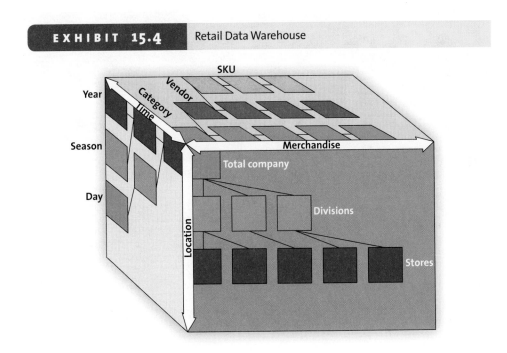

The CEO might be interested in how the corporation is doing generally and could look at the data aggregated by quarter for a merchandise division, a region of the country, or the total corporation. A buyer may be more interested in a particular manufacturer in a certain store on a particular day. Analysts from various levels of the retail operation extract information from the data warehouse to make a plethora of marketing decisions about developing and replenishing merchandise assortments.

In some cases, manufacturers also have access to this data warehouse. They communicate with retailers using electronic data interchange (EDI) and use supply chain systems known as vendor-managed inventory and collaborative planning, forecasting, and replenishment (CPFR), which are all discussed next.

## Electronic Data Interchange

In information flows 3, 4, and 6 in Exhibit 15.3, the retailer and manufacturer exchange business documents through EDI. **Electronic data interchange (EDI)** is the computer-to-computer exchange of business documents from a retailer to a vendor and back. In addition to sales data, purchase orders, invoices, and data about returned merchandise can be transmitted back and forth.

Many retailers now require vendors to provide them with notification of deliveries before they take place using an advanced shipping notice. If the ASN is accurate, the retailer can dispense with opening all the received cartons and checking in merchandise. In addition, EDI enables vendors to transmit information about on-hand inventory status, vendor promotions, and cost changes to the retailer, as well as information about purchase order changes, order status, retail prices, and transportation routings.

Using EDIs, suppliers can describe and show pictures of their products, and buyers can issue requests for proposals. The two parties then can electronically negotiate prices and specify how the product will be made and how it should look.

For example, Cabela's, which has long worked to outfit outdoor enthusiasts and hunters through its catalogs, realized that when it expanded into brick-and-mortar stores as well, it had to update its order management system. If, for instance, a customer in Colorado placed a catalog order, it would be processed in Wheeling, West Virginia. If the item was not in stock there, the old system would

*Cabela's order and fulfillment system links all members of its supply chain to enhance customer service.*

show "out of stock" to the customer, even though it was available at a different distribution center.[17] To address this problem, Cabela's integrated all its distribution channels into its retail order and fulfillment system, which links together all members of the company's supply chain—manufacturers (up to 2,000 of them), distribution centers, stores, individual customers, and the retailer as a whole. With greater knowledge of exactly where products are in the supply chain, Cabela's not only enhances customer service and supplies consumers more efficiently but also achieves much greater inventory visibility and minimizes its supply chain costs.

The use of EDI provides three main benefits to supply chain members. First, EDI reduces the cycle time, or the time between the decision to place an order and the receipt of merchandise. Information flows quicker using EDI, which means that inventory turnover is higher. Second, EDI improves the overall quality of communications through better record keeping; fewer errors in inputting and receiving an order; and less human error in the interpretation of data. Third, the data transmitted by EDI are in a computer-readable format that can be easily analyzed and used for a variety of tasks ranging from evaluating vendor delivery performance to automating reorder processes.

Because of these benefits, many retailers are asking their suppliers to interface with them using EDI. However, small to medium-sized suppliers and retailers face significant barriers, specifically, cost and the lack of information technology (IT) expertise, to becoming EDI enabled. However, EDI remains an important component of any vendor-managed inventory system.

## Vendor-Managed Inventory

Vendor-managed inventory (VMI) is an approach for improving supply chain efficiency in which the manufacturer is responsible for maintaining the retailer's inventory levels in each of its stores.[18] By sharing the data in the retailer's data warehouse and communicating that information via EDI, the manufacturer automatically sends merchandise to the retailer's store or distribution center when the inventory at the store reaches a prespecified level.[19]

In ideal conditions, the manufacturer replenishes inventories in quantities that meet the retailer's immediate demand, reducing stockouts with minimal inventory. In addition to better matching retail demand to supply, VMI can reduce the vendor's and the retailer's costs. Manufacturer salespeople no longer need to spend time generating orders on items that are already in the stores, and their role shifts to selling new items and maintaining relationships. Retail buyers and planners no longer need to monitor inventory levels and place orders.

Frito-Lay and other snack food, candy, and beverage vendors have been involved with VMI in supermarkets for a long time. However, technological advances have increased the sophistication of VMI. The sharing of POS transaction data, for instance, allows manufacturers to sell merchandise on consignment; the manufacturer owns the merchandise until it is sold by the retailer, at which time the retailer pays for the merchandise. Consignment selling provides an incentive for the manufacturer to pick SKUs and inventory levels that will minimize inventory and generate sales. Because the manufacturer is bearing the financial cost of owning the inventory, retailers are more willing to allow the manufacturer to be responsible for determining the inventory plan and appropriate assortment for each store.

Although it is a more advanced level of collaboration than simply using EDI and sharing information, retailers cannot use VMI blindly. Whereas the manufacturer coordinates the supply chain for its specific products, it does not know what other actions the retailer is taking that might affect the sales of its products in the future. For example, Pepsi might not know that a supermarket will be having a big promotion in three weeks for a new beverage introduced by Coca-Cola. The supermarket's buyer must monitor the VMI orders and inform Pepsi to cut back on its usual orders.

### Collaborative Planning, Forecasting, and Replenishment

**Collaborative planning, forecasting, and replenishment (CPFR)** is the sharing of forecast and related business information and collaborative planning between retailers and vendors to improve supply chain efficiency and product replenishment.[20] Although retailers share sales and inventory data when using a VMI approach, the manufacturer remains responsible for managing the inventory. In contrast, CPFR is a more advanced form of retailer–manufacturer collaboration that involves sharing proprietary information, such as business strategies, promotion plans, new product developments and introductions, production schedules, and lead time information.

### Pull and Push Supply Chains

Information flows such as those described previously illustrate a **pull supply chain**—a supply chain in which orders for merchandise are generated at the store level on the basis of sales data captured by POS terminals. Basically, in this type of supply chain, the demand for an item pulls it through the supply chain. An alternative and less sophisticated approach is a **push supply chain**, in which merchandise is allocated to stores on the basis of forecasted demand. Once a forecast is developed, specified quantities of merchandise are shipped (pushed) to distribution centers and stores at predetermined time intervals.

In a pull supply chain, there is less likelihood of being overstocked or out of stock because the store orders merchandise as needed on the basis of consumer demand. A pull approach increases inventory turnover and is more responsive to changes in customer demand. A pull approach becomes even more efficient than a push approach when demand is uncertain and difficult to forecast because the forecast is based on consumer demand.[21]

Although generally more desirable, a pull approach is not the most effective in all situations. First, a pull approach requires a more costly and sophisticated information system to support it. Second, for some merchandise, retailers do not have the flexibility to adjust inventory levels on the basis of demand. For example, commitments must be made months in advance for fashion and private-label apparel. Because these commitments cannot be easily changed, the merchandise has to be preallocated to the stores at the time the orders are formulated. Third, push supply chains are efficient for merchandise that has steady, predictable demand, such as milk and eggs, basic men's underwear, and bath towels. Because both pull and push supply chains have their advantages, most retailers use a combination of these approaches.

### CHECK YOURSELF

1.  What are the supply chain links associated with each information flow?
2.  What is the difference between a push and a pull supply chain?

# MAKING MERCHANDISE FLOW

Exhibit 15.5 illustrates different types of merchandise flows:

1.  Sony to Best Buy's distribution centers, or
2.  Sony directly to stores.
3.  If the merchandise goes through distribution centers, it is then shipped to stores,
4.  and then to the customer.

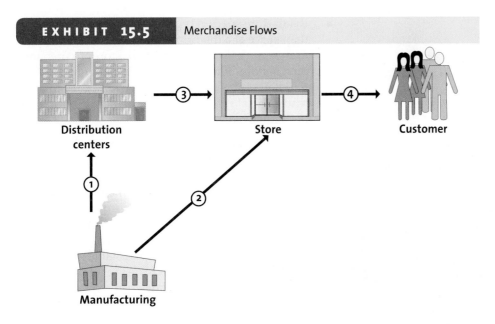

| EXHIBIT 15.5 | Merchandise Flows |

Making merchandise flow involves first deciding if the merchandise is going to go from the manufacturer to a retailer's distribution center or directly on to stores. Once in a distribution center, multiple activities take place before it is shipped on to a store.

## Distribution Centers versus Direct Store Delivery

As indicated in Exhibit 15.5, manufacturers can ship merchandise directly to a retailer's stores—direct store delivery (flow 2)—or to their distribution centers (flow 1). Although manufacturers and retailers may collaborate, the ultimate decision is usually up to the retailer and depends on the characteristics of the merchandise and the nature of demand. To determine which distribution system—distribution centers or direct store delivery—is better, retailers consider the total cost associated with each alternative and the customer service criterion of having the right merchandise at the store when the customer wants to buy it.

There are several advantages to using a distribution center:

■ More accurate sales forecasts are possible when retailers combine forecasts for many stores serviced by one distribution center rather than doing a forecast for each store. Consider a set of 50 Target stores, serviced by a single distribution center, that each carries Michael Graves toasters. Each store normally stocks 5 units for a total of 250 units in the system. By carrying the item at each store, the retailer must develop individual forecasts, each with the possibility of errors that could result in either too much or too little merchandise. Alternatively, by delivering most of the inventory to a distribution center and feeding the stores merchandise as they need it, the effects of forecast errors for the individual stores are minimized, and less backup inventory is needed to prevent stockouts.

■ Distribution centers enable the retailer to carry less merchandise in the individual stores, which results in lower inventory investments systemwide. If the stores get frequent deliveries from the distribution center, they need to carry relatively less extra merchandise as backup stock.

■ It is easier to avoid running out of stock or having too much stock in any particular store because merchandise is ordered from the distribution center as needed.

*The use of distribution centers helps reduce stockouts.*

■ Retail store space is typically much more expensive than space at a distribution center, and distribution centers are better equipped than stores to prepare merchandise for sale. As a result, many retailers find it cost-effective to store merchandise and get it ready for sale at a distribution center rather than in individual stores.

But distribution centers aren't appropriate for all retailers. If a retailer has only a few outlets, the expense of a distribution center is probably unwarranted. Also, if many outlets are concentrated in metropolitan areas, merchandise can be consolidated and delivered by the vendor directly to all the stores in one area economically. Direct store delivery gets merchandise to the stores faster and thus is used for perishable goods (meat and produce), items that help create the retailer's image of being the first to sell the latest product (e.g., video games), or fads. Finally, some manufacturers provide direct store delivery for retailers to ensure that their products are on the store's shelves, properly displayed, and fresh. For example, employees delivering Frito-Lay snacks directly to supermarkets replace products that have been on the shelf too long and are stale, replenish products that have been sold, and arrange products so they are neatly displayed.

Superior Service 15.1 examines how Home Depot improved service to its customers by transitioning from direct store delivery to a more integrated use of distribution centers.

## The Distribution Center

The distribution center performs the following activities: coordinating inbound transportation; receiving, checking, storing, and cross-docking; getting merchandise "floor ready"; and coordinating outbound transportation. To illustrate these activities being undertaken in a distribution center, we'll continue our example of Sony HDTVs being shipped to a Best Buy distribution center.

**Management of Inbound Transportation** Traditionally, buyers focused their efforts, when working with vendors, on developing merchandise assortments, negotiating prices, and arranging joint promotions. Now, buyers and planners are much more involved in coordinating the physical flow of merchandise to the stores. The TV buyer has arranged for a truckload of HDTVs to be delivered to its Houston, Texas, distribution center on Monday between 1:00 and 3:00 p.m. The buyer also specifies how the merchandise should be placed on pallets for easy unloading.

The truck must arrive within the specified time because the distribution center has all of its 100 receiving docks allocated throughout the day, and much of the merchandise on this particular truck is going to be shipped to stores that evening. Unfortunately, the truck was delayed in a snowstorm. The dispatcher—the person who coordinates deliveries to the distribution center—reassigns the truck delivering the HDTVs to a Wednesday morning delivery slot and charges the firm several hundred dollars for missing its delivery time. Although many manufacturers pay transportation expenses, some retailers negotiate with their vendors to absorb this expense. These retailers believe they can lower their net merchandise cost and better control merchandise flow if they negotiate directly with trucking companies and consolidate shipments from many vendors.

## Superior Service 15.1    Home Depot Transitions to Distribution Centers

The ultimate goal of any supply chain is to improve the customer experience. No store manager wants customers leaving empty-handed because the item they wanted wasn't on the shelves. Nor do they want their employees tied up in a back room, hunting missing stock or coping with a delivery overload.

For the first three decades of its existence, Home Depot didn't worry much about its supply chain.[22] It didn't need to: the company was growing, and its warehouse stores doubled as distribution centers. But as the retailer built stores with smaller footprints in secondary markets, fuel costs rose, and competition began nibbling at its profits, Home Depot execs realized supply chain changes were imperative.

Home Depot's original supply chain model involved over three-quarters of its inventory being shipped directly from suppliers to stores, with store managers placing 70 percent of orders. As the business evolved, this approach resulted in a bloated and expensive logistics infrastructure that didn't protect the stores from stockouts.[23] To correct the situation, Home Depot elected to undergo a rapid transformation to a supply chain that relies more heavily on distribution centers. Under the new model, three-quarters of goods ship to stores through flow-through distribution centers that Home Depot calls Rapid Deployment Centers (RDCs). Each RDC serves about 100 stores, and many are highly automated. These RDCs assume responsibility for ordering for stores, which has improved inventory forecasting. Some bulky items, such as lumber and lawn mowers, will continue to ship directly from vendors to stores.

The new model gives Home Depot improved flexibility for getting product into stores, which means stockouts

*Home Depot earmarks as much as $25,000 per quarter to stores that provide the best customer service.*

have decreased. It also increases the speed at which goods move through the supply chain[24] and helps keeps inventory at optimal levels.

**Receiving and Checking Using UPC and Radio Frequency Identification (RFID) Device** Receiving is the process of recording the receipt of merchandise as it arrives at a distribution center. Checking is the process of going through the goods upon receipt to make sure they arrived undamaged and that the merchandise ordered was the merchandise received.

In the past, checking merchandise was a very labor-intensive and time-consuming process. Today, however, many distribution systems using EDI are designed to minimize, if not eliminate, these processes. The advance shipping notice (ASN) tells the distribution center what should be in each carton. A UPC label or radio frequency identification (RFID) tag on the shipping carton that identifies the carton's contents is scanned and automatically counted as it is being received and checked. Radio frequency identification (RFID) tags are tiny computer chips that automatically transmit to a special scanner all the information about a container's contents or individual products. Adding Value 15.1 explains how American Apparel is using RFID tags.

Approximately as large as a pinhead, RFID tags consist of an antenna and a chip that contains an electronic product code that stores far more information about a product than bar (UPC) codes can. The tags also act as passive tracking

## Adding Value 15.1     American Apparel: Now with RFID Chips

American Apparel makes its own rules, a strategy that has helped the clothing retailer grow to over 250 outlets throughout the United States, Europe, and Asia. This trend-setting approach extends from how goods are sourced—the company is vertically integrated in that it owns its sewing, design, and dyeing facilities—to the use of advanced technology to ensure American Apparel's full range of merchandise is available to customers in a timely manner.

One of the first retailers to adopt item-level radio frequency identification (RFID),[25] American Apparel continues to expand its use of this technology to increase efficiency at the retail end of the supply chain.[26] RFID tags are attached to each garment at the company's factories. Stationary tag readers at the Los Angeles distribution center and within individual RFID-enabled stores date and track the merchandise from shipping through purchase, with stops along the way for receiving, reconciling receipt information with advance shipment notification, storing inventory updating, and determining which items will move to the sales floor and which will be stored. A final read before garments are moved to the floor ensures that complete and correct inventory will be displayed. The RFID application used by American Apparel interfaces with the company's software for enterprise resource planning, inventory management, and point-of-sale processes to further streamline all aspects of operation. Once the company installs RFID gates in store doorways, these tags will also act as theft-detection devices.

American Apparel's unique approach to merchandising, which involves displaying only one color, style, and size of each item on the retail floor at a time, places a heavy burden on employees to ensure the floor is properly stocked. Without RFID, replenishing stock involves employees taking point-of-sale information to the back room and hunting for the needed items. This process keeps staff from interactions with customers and results in about 90 percent of its items being on the sales floor at any given time. With the RFID technology, sales information is transmitted electronically to the stock room, and staff can immediately replenish supplies. A doorway antenna scans garment tags as they move from the stock room to the sales floor and updates information for the floor.

In the ten American Apparel stores where RFID technology is in place, the percentage of correct stock on the floor rose to 99 percent, and the availability of merchandise and sales staff to assist customers resulted in a sales increase of 2 to 8 percent in individual stores.[27] The store has realized efficiency gains as well: Restocking now takes two employees instead of six, and weekly inventory is accomplished in one-eighth the staff time.[28] This streamlining may also lead to a reduction in staff turnover because inventory is no longer the frustrating and time-consuming task it once was.

The company's new technology, which is more scalable than the software originally used for the RFID initiative, will allow American Apparel to equip additional stores in a matter of hours. Over time, the retailer intends to deploy RFID in all its outlets so that its customers can find staff assistance and the products they want every time they shop.

If item-level RFID makes sense for American Apparel, what is stopping other retailers, especially apparel retailers, from adopting the technology?

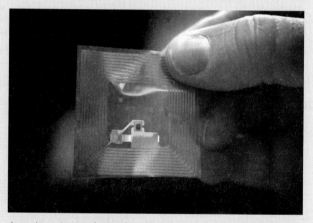

*American Apparel attaches RFID tags to its merchandise to improve product availability and sales.*

devices, signaling their presence over a radio frequency when they pass within a few yards of a special scanner. The tags have long been used in high-cost applications, such as automated highway toll systems and security identification badges.

The prospect of affordable tags is exciting supply chains everywhere. If every item in a store were tagged as described in Adding Value 15.1, RFID technology could be used to locate mislaid products, deter theft, and even offer customers personalized sales pitches through displays mounted in dressing rooms. Ultimately, tags and readers could replace bar codes and checkout labor altogether. Customers could just walk through a door equipped with a sensor, which would read all the tags electronically and charge the purchases directly to the customer's credit card.

One advantage of RFID is that it eliminates the need to handle items individually by enabling distribution centers and stores to receive whole truckloads of merchandise without having to check in each carton. Another advantage is

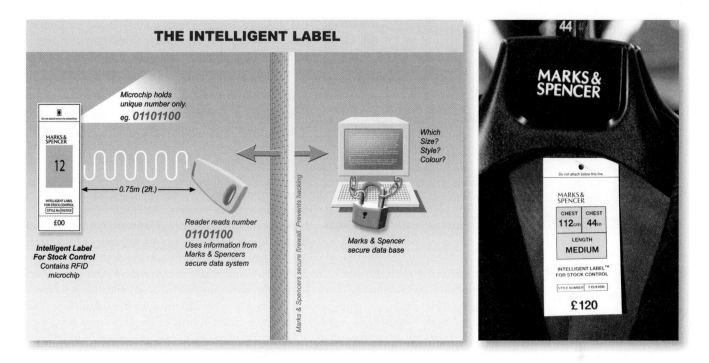

that manufacturers and distributors are able to reduce overall inventory thanks to greater supply chain efficiency. Marks & Spencer (U.K.) is replacing bar codes with an RFID system, including tags for the millions of containers that hold food being shipped from suppliers to its stores. It takes a mere five seconds to receive data from 50 containers, an 85 percent improvement in the time it takes to scan bar codes. The savings of time as well as reduced cost of spoiled food are expected to make the system's $3 million price tag feasible.[29]

*Marks & Spencer (U.K.) is replacing bar codes with an RFID system.*

Other prominent retailers taking advantage of this new technology are Bloomingdale's (a division of Macy's), Walmart, Metro AG(Germany), and Walgreens.[30] To meet these demands, vendors have been forced to make significant investments to acquire the necessary technology and equipment.

Still, the watchword, for both retailers and manufacturers of consumer products, is caution. For most supply chain members, long-term investments in RFID technology are still too risky and expensive. Experts believe it will be 5 to 10 years before RFID tags are prevalent on most consumer products.

**Storing and Cross-Docking** After the merchandise is received and checked, it is either stored or cross-docked. When merchandise is stored, the cartons are transported by a conveyor system and forklift trucks to racks that go from the distribution center's floor to its ceiling. Then, when the merchandise is needed in the stores, a forklift driver goes to the rack, picks up the carton, and places it on a conveyor system that routes the carton to the loading dock of a truck going to the store.

*RFID tags make receiving and checking merchandise accurate, quick, and easy.*

Merchandise cartons that are cross-docked are prepackaged by the vendor for a specific store. The UPC labels on the carton indicate the store to which it is to be sent. The vendor also may affix price tags to each item in the carton. Because the merchandise is ready for sale, it is placed on a conveyor system that routes it from the unloading dock at which it was received to the loading dock for the truck going to the specific store—thus, the name *cross-docked*. The cartons are routed on the conveyor system automatically by sensors that read the UPC label on the cartons. Cross-docked merchandise is in the distribution center only for a few hours before it is shipped to the stores.

Merchandise sales' rate and degree of perishability or fashionability typically determine whether cartons are cross-docked or stored.

*Tesco's Fresh & Easy Neighborhood Markets has its merchandise delivered on roll cages rather than pallets so that employees can easily wheel them onto the retail floor.*

For instance, because Sony's HDTVs sell so quickly, it is in Best Buy's interest not to store them in a distribution center. Similarly, cross-docking is preferable for fashion apparel or perishable meat or produce.

**Getting Merchandise Floor Ready** For some merchandise, additional tasks are undertaken in the distribution center to make the merchandise floor ready. **Floor-ready merchandise** is merchandise that is ready to be placed on the selling floor. Getting merchandise floor ready entails ticketing, marking, and, in the case of some apparel, placing garments on hangers. At Tesco's Fresh & Easy Neighborhood Markets in California, it is essential that products ship in ready-to-sell units so that staff has little manipulation or sorting to do at the distribution center or in the stores. To move the store-ready merchandise it receives from suppliers quickly into the store, Tesco demands that products sit on roll cages rather than pallets. Then, store employees can easily wheel them onto the retail floor. The stores' back rooms have only two or three days' worth of backup inventory, and since the stores are relatively small, about 10,000 square feet, it is important to keep inventory levels low and receive lots of small, accurate deliveries from suppliers.[31]

**Ticketing and marking** refers to affixing price and identification labels to the merchandise. It is more efficient for a retailer to perform these activities at a distribution center than in its stores. In a distribution center, an area can be set aside and a process implemented to efficiently add labels and put apparel on hangers. Conversely, getting merchandise floor ready in stores can block aisles and divert salespeople's attention from their customers. An even better approach from the retailer's perspective is to get vendors to ship floor-ready merchandise, thus totally eliminating the expensive, time-consuming ticketing and marking process.

**Preparing to Ship Merchandise to a Store** At the beginning of the day, the computer system in the distribution center generates a list of items to be shipped to each store on that day. For each item, a pick ticket and shipping label are generated. The **pick ticket** is a document or display on a screen in a forklift truck indicating how much of each item to get from specific storage areas. The forklift driver goes to the storage area, picks up the number of cartons indicated on the pick ticket, places UPC shipping labels on the cartons that indicate the stores to which the items are to be shipped, and puts the cartons on the conveyor system, where they are automatically routed to the loading dock for the truck going to the stores.

**Shipping Merchandise to Stores** Shipping merchandise to stores from a distribution center has become increasingly complex. Most distribution centers run 50–100 outbound truck routes in one day. To handle this complex transportation problem, the centers use sophisticated routing and scheduling computer systems that consider the locations of the stores, road conditions, and transportation operating constraints to develop the most efficient routes. As a result, stores are provided with an accurate estimated time of arrival, and vehicle utilization is maximized.

## Inventory Management through Just-in-Time Systems

Customers demand specific SKUs, and they want to be able to buy them when needed. If, for instance, you want to buy a pair of size 10 Nike Trainer Manny Pacquiao SC 2010 Men's Training Shoe, you probably aren't going to purchase a size 9 Nike Air Max+ 2009 Women's Running Shoe just because the retailer is out of the shoes you want. At the same time, firms can't afford to carry more than they really need of an SKU, because to do so is very expensive. Suppose, for instance, a shoe store carries $1 million worth of inventory at its own expense. Experts estimate that it would cost between 20 and 40 percent of the value of the inventory, or $200,000 to $400,000 per year, to hold that inventory! So firms must balance having enough inventory to satisfy customer demands with not having more than they need.

To help reconcile these seemingly conflicting goals, many firms, including Zara as described in this chapter's opening vignette, have adopted just-in-time (JIT) inventory systems. Just-in-time inventory systems, also known as quick response (QR) systems in retailing, are inventory management systems designed to deliver less merchandise on a more frequent basis than traditional inventory systems. The firm gets the merchandise "just in time" for it to be used in the manufacture of another product, in the case of parts or components, or for sale when the customer wants it, in the case of consumer goods. The JIT systems lower inventory investments, but product availability actually increases.[32]

The benefits of a JIT system include reduced lead time, increased product availability, and lower inventory investment.

Reduced Lead Time  By eliminating the need for paper transactions by mail, overnight deliveries, or even faxes, the EDI in the JIT system reduces lead time, or the amount of time between the recognition that an order needs to be placed and the arrival of the needed merchandise at the seller's store, ready for sale. Because the vendor's computer acquires the data automatically, no manual data entry is required on the recipient's end, which reduces lead time even more and eliminates vendor recording errors. Even better, the shorter lead times further reduce the need for inventory because the shorter the lead time, the easier it is for the retailer to forecast its demand. Zara further reduces lead time by shipping by air all merchandise to stores outside of a few hundred miles of its distribution center.

For example, adidas manufactures sporting goods and distributes them throughout the world to different retailers and wholesalers. Adidas introduces 10,000 new apparel items and 4,000 new footwear items every three months. A high percentage of orders are for priority requests, which must get delivered within one or two days, a very short lead time. Therefore, in addition to providing transportation services, UPS works with adidas by providing it with special labeling, garments on hangers, and advanced shipping notices, services that further reduce the time it takes to get merchandise on the shelves and ready for sale.[33]

Increased Product Availability and Lower Inventory Investment  In general, as a firm's ability to satisfy customer demand by having stock on hand increases, so does its inventory investment; that is, it needs to keep more backup inventory in stock. But with JIT, the ability to satisfy demand can actually increase while

*To reduce lead time, UPS works with adidas by providing it with special labeling, garments on hangers, and advanced shipping notices.*

inventory decreases. Because a firm like Zara can make purchase commitments or produce merchandise closer to the time of sale, its own inventory investment is reduced. Zara needs less inventory because it is getting less merchandise in each order, but receiving those shipments more often. Inventory is even further reduced because firms using JIT like Zara aren't forecasting sales quite as far into the future. For instance, fashion retailers that don't use JIT must make purchase commitments as much as six months in advance and receive merchandise well ahead of actual sales, whereas JIT systems align deliveries more closely with sales.

The ability to satisfy customer demand by keeping merchandise in stock also increases in JIT systems as a result of the more frequent shipments. For instance, if a Zara store runs low on a medium-sized Kelly green sweater, its JIT system ensures a shorter lead time than those of more traditional retailers. As a result, it is less likely that the Zara store will be out of stock for its customers before the next sweater shipment arrives.

**Costs of a JIT System**  Although firms achieve great benefits from a JIT system, it is not without its costs. The logistics function becomes much more complicated with more frequent deliveries. With greater order frequency also come smaller orders, which are more expensive to transport and more difficult to coordinate.

Therefore, JIT systems require a strong commitment by the firm and its vendors to cooperate, share data, and develop systems like EDI and CPFR. Successful JIT systems require not only financial support from top management but also a psychological commitment to partnering with vendors. In some cases, larger firms even pressure their less powerful supply chain partners to absorb many of these expensive logistics costs.

### CHECK YOURSELF

1. How does merchandise flow through a typical supply chain?
2. Why have just-in-time supply chain systems become so popular?

---

LO4

Describe how supply chains are managed.

# MANAGING THE MARKETING CHANNEL AND SUPPLY CHAIN

Supply chains or marketing channels are composed of various entities that are buying, such as retailers or wholesalers; selling, such as manufacturers or wholesalers; or helping facilitate the exchange, such as transportation companies. Like interactions between people, these relationships can range from close working partnerships to one-time arrangements. In almost all cases, though, they occur because the parties want something from one another. For instance, Home Depot wants hammers from Stanley Tool Company, Stanley wants an opportunity to sell its tools to the public, and both companies want UPS to deliver the merchandise.

Each member of the supply chain performs a specialized role. If one member believes that another isn't doing its job correctly or efficiently, it usually can replace that member. So, if Stanley isn't getting good service from UPS, it can switch to FedEx. Likewise, if Home Depot believes its customers don't perceive Stanley tools to be a good value, it may buy from another tool company. Home Depot could even decide to make its own tools or use its own trucks to pick up tools from Stanley. However, even if a supply chain member is replaced, the function it performed remains, so someone needs to complete it.

If a supply chain is to run efficiently, the participating members must cooperate. Often, however, supply chain members have conflicting goals. For instance, Stanley wants Home Depot to carry all its tools but not those of its competitors so that Stanley can maximize its sales. But Home Depot carries a mix of tool brands so it can maximize the sales in its tool category. When supply chain members are

not in agreement about their goals, roles, or rewards, vertical channel conflict or vertical supply chain conflict or discord results.

Horizontal channel conflict or horizontal supply chain conflict can also occur when there is disagreement or discord among members at the same level of marketing channel, such as two competing retailers or two competing manufacturers. For instance, if Home Depot and Lowes engage in a price war on Stanley Tools, all three parties are affected. Home Depot and Lowe's make less money because they are both offering lower prices. Stanley Tools may experience deterioration in its brand image as a result of the lower prices, and increased pressure from Home Depot and Lowe's to recover some of its lost profits. Also, other retailers may stop buying Stanley Tools because they cannot afford to get involved in the price war between Home Depot and Lowe's.

Open, honest communication is a key to supply chain relationships. Buyers and vendors, such as retailers and manufacturers, must understand what drives the other's business, their roles in the relationship, each firm's strategies, and any problems that might arise over the course of the relationship.

For example, Walmart and Procter & Gamble (P&G) recognize that it is in their common interest to remain profitable business partners. Walmart's customers demand and expect to find P&G products in their stores, and P&G needs the sales generated by being in the world's largest retailer. Walmart cannot demand prices so low that P&G cannot make money, and P&G must be flexible enough to accommodate the needs of its biggest customer. With a common goal, both firms have an incentive to cooperate because they know that by doing so, each can boost sales. Common goals also help sustain the relationship when expected benefit flows aren't realized. If one P&G shipment fails to reach a Walmart store on time due to an uncontrollable event like misrouting by a trucking firm, Walmart will not suddenly call off the whole arrangement. Instead, Walmart is likely to view the incident as a simple mistake and remain in the relationship, because Walmart knows that both it and P&G are committed to the same goals in the long run.

There are two non–mutually exclusive ways to manage a marketing channel or supply chain: coordinate the channel using a vertical marketing system or develop strong relationships with supply chain partners.

## Managing the Marketing Channel and Supply Chain through Vertical Marketing Systems

Conflict is likely to occur in any marketing channel or supply chain, but it is more pronounced when members are independent entities. Supply chains that are more closely aligned, whether by contract or ownership, share common goals and therefore are less prone to conflict.

In an independent or conventional supply chain, the several independent members—a manufacturer, a wholesaler, and a retailer—each attempt to satisfy their own objectives and maximize their own profits, often at the expense of the other members, as we portray in Exhibit 15.6.

*The Home Depot and Stanley Tool Company have a mutually beneficial partnership. The Home Depot buys tools from Stanley because their customers find value in Stanley products. Stanley sells tools to Home Depot because they have established an excellent market for its products.*

*Walmart and P&G (makers of Tide laundry detergent) need each other, so they work together to boost sales*

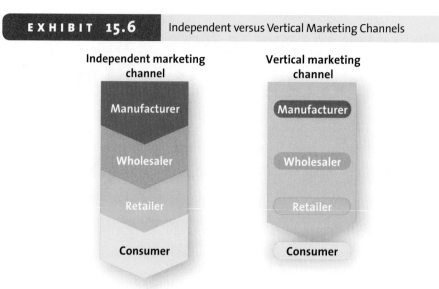

**EXHIBIT 15.6**    Independent versus Vertical Marketing Channels

None of the participants has any control over the others. For instance, the first time Zara purchases cotton fabric from Tessuto e Colore in northern Italy, both parties try to extract as much profit from the deal as possible, and after the deal has been consummated, neither party feels any responsibility to the other. Over time, Zara and Tessuto might develop a relationship in which their transactions become more routinized and automatic, such that Zara depends on Tessuto for fabric, and Tessuto depends on Zara to buy a good portion of its output. This scenario represents the first phase of a vertical marketing system, which is a marketing channel in which the members act as a unified system, as in Exhibit 15.6 (right). There are three types, or phases, of vertical marketing systems, each with increasing levels of formalization and control. The more formal the vertical marketing system, the less likely conflict will ensue.

**Administered Vertical Marketing System**    The Zara/Tessuto supply chain relationship offers an example of an administered vertical marketing system. In an administered vertical marketing system, there is no common ownership and no contractual relationships, but the dominant channel member controls or holds the balance of power in the channel relationship. In our example, because of its size and relative power, Zara imposes some control over Tessuto. Power in a marketing channel is when one firm has the means or ability to have control over the actions of another member in a channel at a different level of distribution, such as if a retailer has power or control over a supplier. A firm like Zara can exercise its power several ways. Reward power is when Zara offers rewards, often a monetary incentive, for getting Tessuto to do what Zara wants. Coercive power is when Zara threatens to punish or punishes another channel member for not undertaking certain tasks, such as delaying payment to Tessuto for a late delivery. Zara may also have referent power over Tessuto if Tessuto wants to be associated with Zara. For instance, by being known as an important Zara supplier, Tessuto may attract other retailers' business. Zara may also exert expertise power over Tessuto because of the expertise Zara has in the manufacturing processes of making apparel. Since Zara has information about fashion trends, it can exert information power over Tessuto. Finally, legitimate power is based on getting a channel member like Tessuto to behave in a certain way because of a contractual agreement between the two firms, a topic that is discussed in the next paragraph. As Zara deals with Tessuto and its other suppliers, it can utilize several of these types of powers to influence the suppliers' behaviors. If either party doesn't like the way the relationship is going, however, it can simply walk away.

**Contractual Vertical Marketing System**    Over time, Zara and Tessuto may formalize their relationship by entering into contracts that dictate various terms, such as how much Zara will buy each month, at what price, and the penalties for late deliveries. In contractual vertical marketing systems like this, independent firms at different levels of the supply chain join together through contracts to obtain economies of scale and coordination and to reduce conflict.[34] Although conflict between the parties might still occur, and Zara may still attempt to exercise its power over Tessuto to influence its behavior, these activities typically become less intense as the marketing channel relationships becomes more formalized through contracts.

Franchising is the most common type of contractual vertical marketing system. Franchising companies and their franchisees account for $2.3 trillion in economic activity and employ 21 million people.[35] Franchising is a contractual agreement between a franchisor and a franchisee that allows the franchisee to operate a retail outlet using a name and format developed and supported by the franchisor. Exhibit 15.7 lists the United States' top franchise opportunities. These rankings, determined by *Entrepreneur* magazine, are created using a number of objective measures, such as financial strength, stability, growth rate, and size of the franchise system.[36]

*Franchises like 7-Eleven allow the owners to own their own business and achieve some of the efficiencies of a vertical marketing system.*

In a franchise contract, the franchisee pays a lump sum plus a royalty on all sales in return for the right to operate a businessin a specific location. The franchisee also agrees to operate the outlet in accordance with the procedures prescribed by the franchisor. The franchisor typically provides assistance in locating and building the business, developing the products or services sold, management training, and advertising. To maintain the franchise's reputation, the franchisor also makes sure that all outlets provide the same quality of services and products.

A franchise system combines the entrepreneurial advantages of owning a business with the efficiencies of vertical marketing systems that function under single ownership (a corporate system, as we discuss next). Franchisees are motivated to make their stores successful because they receive the profits, after they pay the

| EXHIBIT 15.7 | Top Franchise Opportunities | | |
|---|---|---|---|
| **Rank** | **Franchise Name/Description** | **Number of U.S. Outlets** | **Start-Up Cost** |
| 1 | Subway<br>Submarine sandwiches and salads | 22,525 | $84.3–258.3K |
| 2 | McDonald's<br>Hamburgers, chicken, salads | 12,221 | $995.9K–1.8M |
| 3 | 7-Eleven<br>Convenience store | 6,378 | $40.5–775.3K |
| 4 | Hampton Inn/Hampton Inn & Suites<br>Midprice hotels | 1,595 | $3.7M–13.1M |
| 5 | Supercuts<br>Hair salon | 1,027 | $111K–239.7K |
| 6 | H & R Block<br>Tax preparation & electronic filing | 3,999 | $26.4K–$84.1K |
| 7 | Dunkin' Donuts<br>Coffee, doughnuts, baked goods | 6,475 | $537.7K–1.7M |
| 8 | Jani-King<br>Commercial cleaning | 10,663 | $11.4K–35K |
| 9 | Servpro<br>Insurance/disaster restoration and cleaning | 1,478 | $102K–$161K |
| 10 | AMPM Mini Market<br>Convenience store & gas station | 1,055 | $1.8M–7.6M |

*Source:* 2010 Entrepreneur's Franchise 500 Rankings, http://www.entrepreneur.com/franchises/rankings/ franchise500-115608/2010,.html (accessed April 10, 2010).

royalty to the franchisor. The franchisor is motivated to develop new products, services, and systems and to promote the franchise because it receives royalties on all sales. Advertising, product development, and system development are all done efficiently by the franchisor, with costs shared by all franchisees.

**Corporate Vertical Marketing System** Because Zara deals with "fast fashion," it is imperative that it have complete control over the most fashion-sensitive items. So Zara manufactures these items itself and contracts out its less fashionable items to other manufacturers.[37] The portion of its supply chain that Zara owns and controls is called a corporate vertical marketing system. Because Zara's parent company, Inditex, owns the manufacturing plants, warehouse facilities, retail outlets, and design studios, it can dictate the priorities and objectives of that supply chain, and thus conflict is lessened.

## Managing Marketing Channels and Supply Chains through Strategic Relationships

There is more to managing marketing channels and supply chains than simply exercising power over other members in an administered system or establishing a contractual or corporate vertical marketing system. There is also a human side.

In a conventional supply chain, relationships between members often are based on the argument over the split of the profit pie—if one party gets ahead, the other party falls behind. Sometimes this type of transaction is acceptable if the parties have no interest in a long-term relationship. For instance, if Zara sees a fad for a particular fabric, it may only be interested in purchasing from a vendor once. In that case, it might seek to get the best one-time price, even if it means the supplier will make very little money and therefore might not want to sell to Zara again.

More often than not, however, firms seek a strategic relationship, also called a partnering relationship, in which the supply chain members are committed to maintaining the relationship over the long term and investing in opportunities that are mutually beneficial. In a conventional or administered supply chain, there are significant incentives to establishing a strategic relationship, even without contracts or ownership relationships. Both parties benefit because the size of the profit pie has increased, so both the buyer and the seller increase their sales and profits. These strategic relationships are created explicitly to uncover and exploit joint opportunities, so members depend on and trust each other heavily; share goals and agree on how to accomplish those goals; and are willing to take risks, share confidential information, and make significant investments for the sake of the relationship. Successful strategic relationships require mutual trust, open communication, common goals, interdependence, and credible commitments.

**Mutual Trust** Mutual trust holds a strategic relationship together. Trust is the belief that a partner is honest (i.e., reliable, stands by its word, sincere, fulfills obligations) and benevolent (i.e., concerned about the other party's welfare). When vendors and buyers trust each other, they are more willing to share relevant ideas, clarify goals and problems, and communicate efficiently. Information shared between the parties thus becomes increasingly comprehensive, accurate, and timely. For instance, a CPFR system for mutual inventory forecasting would not be possible without mutual trust.

With trust, there's also less need for the supply chain members to constantly monitor and check up on each other's actions because each believes the other won't take advantage, even given the opportunity. Monitoring supply chain members has become particularly important when suppliers are located in less-developed countries, although it is important in all relationships. Issues such as the use of child labor, poor working conditions, and paying below subsistence wages have become a shared responsibility between suppliers and the buying firm. Ethical and Societal Dilemma 15.1 celebrates the great strides that Gap Inc. has made to achieve recognition as one of the World's Most Ethical Companies.

**Open Communication** To share information, develop sales forecasts together, and coordinate deliveries, Zara and its suppliers maintain open and honest communication. This maintenance may sound easy in principle, but most businesses don't tend to share information with their business partners. But open, honest communication is a key to developing successful relationships, because supply chain members need to understand what is driving each other's business, their roles in the relationship, each firm's strategies, and any problems that arise over the course of the relationship.

**Common Goals** Supply chain members must have common goals for a successful relationship to develop. Shared goals give both members of the relationship an incentive to pool their strengths and abilities and exploit potential opportunities together. Such commonality also offers an assurance that the other partner won't do anything to hinder the achievement of those goals within the relationship.

For example, Zara and its local suppliers recognize that it is in their common interest to be strategic partners. Zara needs the quick response local manufacturers afford, and those manufacturers recognize that if they can keep Zara happy, they will have more than enough business for years to come. With common goals, both firms have an incentive to cooperate because they know that by doing so, both

## Ethical and Societal Dilemma 15.1

### Gap Inc. Recognized as One of World's Most Ethical Companies

More companies are realizing that improved conditions for workers means increased productivity and profitability. Competition for recognition as one of the World's Most Ethical Companies[38] now comes from around the world and from a broad range of industries. One of the companies to be repeatedly recognized, Gap Inc. began addressing vendor issues such as child labor, working conditions, and wage standards in the mid 90s.[39] But the specialty retailer discovered that merely drafting standards wasn't enough to guarantee change. Vendors also needed support from personnel close to worksites, and this staff needed to understand local culture and issues as well as be able to communicate with community members in their own language. The company put this support in place, but went even further. They consult with human rights groups working with these communities to prioritize projects likely to provide the most benefit and provide technical support when needed to help factories meet compliance codes.

Focusing on their responsibility to vendors brought new issues to light for Gap officials. For example, in Lesotho, a country in southern Africa, one-third of the workers are HIV-positive. Recognizing the impact this health crisis could have on both productivity and the quality of workers' lives, Gap kicked off an industrywide program that provides AIDS prevention and treatment services. In Sri Lanka, the company partnered with one of its suppliers to bring clean water to workers' villages, thus freeing up time spent by female factory workers responsible for hauling the family's water supply.

These initiatives, says Gap's senior vice president for social responsibility, benefit both company and community. Poor working conditions often go hand-in-hand with poor management and lead to issues with product quality, on-time delivery, and production planning. Management support that improves conditions for workers generally advances overall factory performance, and enhanced employee health and morale mean more vigorous and engaged employees. Gap works to protect the lifestyle of its own employees as well, focusing on a balance between work and life, equitable and fair treatment, and professional development.

Based on input from activist organizations, Gap focuses its social responsibility efforts on the working conditions of its suppliers, but the company has also stepped up environmentally sound practices. Some of these initiatives, such as increasing recycling, have led to corresponding savings in areas like waste disposal. Bottom line, say Gap Inc. managers, social and ethical initiatives benefit individuals, communities, and stockholders, even in a challenging economy.

*(continued)*

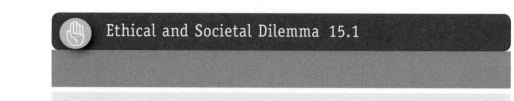

### Ethical and Societal Dilemma 15.1

*(continued)*

   Many other retailers share this belief and are launching their own efforts. The most successful will be those, like Gap, that rely on the expertise of social activists, community programs, and internal teams of social responsibility and compliance staff to find the right set of issues for the company.

   Gap Inc. has come a long way in a relatively short time to be recognized for such high ethical standards. Do you believe that other firms can emulate Gap's actions? What potential impediments stand in their way?

*The Gap contributes half the profits from Gap (Product)$^{RED}$ sales to the Global Fund to help women and children affected by AIDS in Africa.*

can boost sales. For instance, if Zara needs a special production run to make an emergency shipment to New York, the suppliers will work to meet the challenge. If one of Zara's suppliers has difficulty getting a particular fabric or financing its inventory, it is in Zara's best interest to help it because they are committed to the same goals in the long run.

**Interdependence** When supply chain members view their goals and ultimate success to be intricately linked, they develop deeper long-term relationships. Interdependence between the supply chain members that is based on mutual benefits is key to developing and sustaining the relationship.[40] Zara's local suppliers recognize that without Zara, they probably would not have a constant and fairly predictable source of work. Although certainly the more powerful member of the supply chain, Zara also recognizes that they can depend on these suppliers to meet quick deadlines no matter what, thus enabling them to have the most efficient supply chain in the fast fashion space.

**Credible Commitments** Successful relationships develop because both parties make credible commitments to, or tangible investments in, the relationship. These commitments go beyond just making the hollow statement, "I want to be your partner"; they involve spending money to improve the products or services provided to the customer and on information technology to improve supply chain efficiency.[41] For example, if Zara makes a financial commitment to its suppliers to help them develop state-of-the-art manufacturing facilities and computer systems for improved communication, it is making a credible commitment—putting its money where its mouth is.

Just like many other elements of marketing, managing the supply chain can seem like an easy task at first glance: Put the merchandise in the right place at the right time. But the various elements and actors involved in a supply chain create its unique and compelling complexities and require that firms work carefully to ensure they are achieving the most efficient and effective chain possible.

---

## CHECK YOURSELF

1. What are the differences between the three types of vertical marketing systems?
2. How do firms develop strong strategic partnerships with their supply chain partners?

---

## Summing Up

**L01  Define supply chain management.**

Supply chain management refers to the effort to coordinate suppliers, manufacturers, warehouses, stores, and transportation intermediaries so that the merchandise the customer wants is produced in the right quantities and sent to the right locations at the time the customer wants it. Logistics concentrates on the movement and control of the products, whereas supply chain management includes the managerial aspects of the process as well.

**L02  Recognize the value added by the supply chain.**

Without a supply chain, consumers would be forced to find raw materials, manufacture products, and somehow get them to where they could be used, all on their own. Each supply chain member adds value to the product by performing one of these functions. Supply chain management also creates value for each firm in the chain and helps bind together many company functions, including manufacturing, inventory management, transportation, advertising, and marketing.

**L03  Describe the flow of merchandise and the flow of information in the supply chain.**

Information flow involves Flow 1 (customer to store), Flow 2 (store to buyer), Flow 3 (buyer to manufacturer), Flow 4 (store to manufacturer), Flow 5 (store to distribution center), and Flow 6 (manufacturer to distribution center and buyer). Merchandise flow involves Flow 1 (manufacturer to retailer distribution centers), Flow 2 (manufacturer directly to stores), Flow 3 (distribution centers to stores, when shipped first to distribution centers), and Flow 4 (retailer to customer).

**L04  Describe how supply chains are managed.**

The more closely aligned the supply chain members are with each other, the less likely there will be significant conflict. An administered supply chain occurs when a dominant and powerful supply chain member has control over the other members. In a contractual supply chain (e.g., franchising), coordination and control are dictated by contractual relationships between members. Corporate supply chains can operate relatively smoothly because one firm owns the various levels of the chains. Supply chains also can be effectively managed through strong relationships developed with supply chain partners. To create such relationships, the partners must trust each other, communicate openly, have compatible goals, realize there are benefits in being interdependent, and be willing to invest in each other's success.

## Key Terms

- administered vertical marketing system, 462
- advanced shipping notice (ASN), 449
- checking, 455
- coercive power, 462
- collaborative planning, forecasting, and replenishment (CPFR), 452
- consignment, 451
- contractual vertical marketing system, 463
- corporate vertical marketing system, 464
- cross-dock, 457
- cycle time, 451
- dispatcher, 454
- distribution center, 446
- electronic data interchange (EDI), 450

- expertise power, 462
- floor-ready merchandise, 458
- franchising, 463
- horizontal channel conflict (horizontal supply chain conflict), 461
- independent (conventional) supply chain, 461
- information power, 462
- just-in-time inventory systems, 459
- lead time, 459
- legitimate power, 462
- logistics management, 444
- marketing channel, 443
- pick ticket, 458
- power, 462
- pull supply chain, 452
- push supply chain, 452

- quick response, 459
- radio frequency identification (RFID) tag, 455
- receiving, 455
- referent power, 462
- reward power, 462
- strategic relationship (partnering relationship), 464
- supply chain management, 442
- ticketing and marking, 458
- Universal Product Code (UPC), 447
- vendor-managed inventory, 451
- vertical channel conflict (vertical supply chain conflict), 461
- vertical marketing system, 462
- wholesaler, 443

## Marketing Applications

1. Describe supply chain management by identifying the major activities that it involves. Identify several ways that supply chain management adds value to a company's offerings, with regard to both consumers and business partners.

2. Discuss the similarities and differences among the concepts of supply chains, marketing channels, and logistics.

3. In what ways can the flow of information be managed in the supply chain? How can the ready flow of information increase a firm's operating efficiencies?

4. Describe how B2B transactions might employ EDI to process purchase information. Considering the information discussed in Chapter 6 about B2B buying situations, determine which buying situation (new task, modified rebuy, or straight rebuy) would most likely align with the use of EDI technology. Justify your answer.

5. What are the differences between the use of a traditional distribution center and one that relies on cross-docking? Discuss the extent to which one is more efficient than the other, being sure to detail your reasoning.

6. Discuss the advantages to a retailer like Tesco of expending the time and effort to get merchandise floor ready at either the point of manufacture or in the distribution center rather than having retail

store staff members do it in the stores. Provide the logic behind your answer.

7. A JIT inventory system appears to be an important success factor for Zara. Choose a local retailer and examine the advantages and disadvantages of its use of a JIT system. Do you believe it should use JIT? Why?

8. Give an example of a retailer that participates in an independent (conventional) supply chain and one involved in a vertical marketing system. Discuss the advantages and disadvantages of each.

9. For each of the following consumer products, identify the type of vertical marketing system used, and justify your answer: (a) Bertolli pasta sold through grocery stores, (b) Krispy Kreme donuts sold through franchises, and (c) www.polo.com by Ralph Lauren.

10. Why might a big company like Dell want to develop strategic partnerships with locally owned computer stores? Describe what Dell would have to do to maintain such relationships.

11. You are hired as an assistant brand manager for a popular consumer product. One day in an emergency meeting, the brand manager informs the group that there is a problem with one of the suppliers and that he has decided to send you over to the manufacturing facilities to investigate the prob-

lem. When you arrive at the plant, you learn that a key supplier has become increasingly unreliable in terms of quality and delivery. You ask the plant manager why the plant doesn't switch suppliers, because it is becoming a major problem for your brand. He informs you that the troubled supplier is his cousin, whose wife has been very ill, and he just can't switch right now. What course of action should you take?

## Quiz Yourself

www.mhhe.com/ grewal3e

1. Franchising involves a(n) _____ supply chain.
   a. cooperative
   b. corporate
   c. contractual
   d. administered
   e. conventional

2. Flora is frustrated with her company's supply chain management information system. She wants to be able to receive sales data, initiate purchase orders, send and receive invoices, and receive returned merchandise documentation. Flora needs a(n):
   a. cross-docking distribution center.
   b. electronic data interchange.
   c. floor-ready merchandise system.
   d. vertical conflict reduction.
   e. radio frequency identification system.

(Answers to these two questions are provided on page 608.)

Go to www.mhhe.com/grewal3e to practice an additional 11 questions.

## Net Savvy

1. Zappos.com, an online shoe seller, has received praise for its stellar supply chain management. Go to www.zappos.com/warehouse tour.html, look through the warehouse tour, and see how a shoe ultimately reaches the customer. How does its distribution center enable Zappos to adhere to its marketing communications message and provide excellent customer service?

2. Several examples in this chapter highlight ways that Zara International, a division of Inditex, successfully manages its supply chain. Visit Inditex's website (www.inditex.com) and go to "Corporate Responsibility," then review the company's commitment to corporate social responsibility, particularly the section that pertains to its Internal Code of Conduct. Considering the discussion in this chapter about strategic relationships, how does Inditex address the factors necessary for mutually beneficial partnerships, according to its code of conduct?

## Chapter Case Study

### WALMART: PIONEER IN SUPPLY CHAIN MANAGEMENT[42]

Walmart dominates the retailing industry in terms of its sales revenue, its customer base, and its ability to drive down costs and deliver good value to its customers. After all, the world's largest corporation takes pride in having received numerous accolades for its ability to continuously improve efficiency in the supply chain while meeting its corporate mandate of offering customers everyday low prices.

Tight inventory management is legendary at Walmart through its just-in-time techniques that allow the firm to boast one of the best supply chains in the world. Walmart has not only transformed its own supply chain but influenced how vendors throughout the world operate because the company has the economic clout to request changes from its vendor partners and to receive them. Recognized for its ability to obtain merchandise from global sources, Walmart also pioneered the strategy of achieving high levels of growth and profitability through its precision control of manufacturing, inventory, and distribution. Although the company is not unique in this regard, it is by far the most successful and most influential corporation of its kind and has put into practice various innovative techniques.

When Walmart does something, it does it on a massive scale. Walmart's computer system, for example, is second only to that of the Pentagon in storage capacity. Its information systems analyze more than 10 million daily transactions from point-of-sale data and distribute their analysis in real time both internally to its managers and externally via a satellite network to Walmart's many suppliers, who use the information for their production planning and order shipment.

Much of the popularity of supply chain management has been attributed to the success of Walmart's partnership with Procter & Gamble. During the 1980s, the two collaborated in building one of the first CPFR systems, a software system that linked P&G to Walmart's distribution centers, taking advantage of advances in the world's telecommunications infrastructure. When a Walmart store sold a particular P&G item, the information flowed directly to P&G's planning and control systems. When the inventory level of P&G's products at Walmart's distribution center got to the point where it needed to reorder, the system automatically alerted P&G to ship more products. This information helped P&G plan its production. Walmart was also able to track when a P&G shipment arrived at one of its distribution warehouses, which enabled it to coordinate its own outbound shipments to stores. Both Walmart and P&G realized savings from the better inventory management and order processing, savings that in turn were passed on to Walmart's consumers through its everyday low prices.

A history of success doesn't mean Walmart executives can rest. Changes in social values, economic fluctuations, technology advances, and other marketplace factors demand that Walmart continue its search for innovative ways to keep consumer prices down.

## WALMART'S INNOVATIONS

Walmart has pioneered many innovations in the purchase and distribution processes of the products it sells. Over 20 years ago, Walmart drove the adoption of UPC bar codes throughout the retail industry; it also pioneered the use of electronic data interchange (EDI) for computerized ordering from vendors. Its hub-and-spoke distribution network ensures goods are brought to distribution centers around the country and then directed outward to thousands of stores, each of which is within a day's travel. Through the use of cross-docking, one of its best-known innovations, half the goods trucked to a distribution center from suppliers ship to stores within 24 hours. The other half, called "pull stock," is stored at the distribution center until needed at stores.[43] In addition, Walmart uses a dedicated fleet of trucks to ship goods from warehouses to stores in less than 48 hours, as well as to replenish store inventories about twice a week. Thus, with flow-through logistics, the company speeds the movement of goods from its distribution centers to its retail stores around the world.

*Walmart speeds merchandise from its distribution centers to stores.*

Today the retail giant continues to push the supply chain toward greater and greater efficiency, prioritizing customer needs while employing new technologies and greener practices. One of the early adopters of RFID technology to increase efficiency in its supply chain, Walmart discovered the value of balancing vision with technology maturity levels after mandating its suppliers apply RFID tags to crates and pallets bound for its stores.[44] Some companies thrived using the new technology. Others, including Walmart itself, ran into trouble. At the time of the mandate, RFID technology was in its infancy, and costs for planning, hardware, software, and training were prohibitive for many suppliers. Additionally the technology was new enough that the industry lacked best practices for implementation. Indeed, it lacked any examples that might help newcomers avoid pitfalls. Walmart repealed its edict, but continues to probe the usefulness of the technology.

In response to criticism from consumer groups, Walmart tackled environmental sustainability in its supply chain and, as is frequently the case because of the company's size, became a trendsetter for other retailers. After vowing to reduce its greenhouse gas emissions by the equivalent of taking nearly 4 million cars off the roads for a year, Walmart directed its suppliers to think green throughout the full product lifecycle.[45] Suppliers are required to pay for sustainability efforts, a price most accept willingly to retain their rela-

*Walmart has developed a sustainable competitive advantage through efficient supply chain management.*

tionship with Walmart. Many also recognize that reducing energy use will benefit them as energy costs rise. Harnessing energy, increasing recycling, reducing waste, and minimizing packaging and transportation all reduce cost in the supply chain in addition to appealing to today's consumers and preserving global resources.

In a third innovation, Walmart is consolidating its global sourcing.[46] The new model focuses on increasing the percentage of products purchased directly from suppliers and buying from global merchandising centers rather than through individual countries. Third-party procurement providers, who previously enjoyed a substantial business from the retail giant, will find themselves increasingly bypassed in the supply chain. In addition to eliminating the cost of a middleman, this effort may give Walmart increased control over inbound freight. Better control, in turn, can lower inventory costs. Thus Walmart's continuous use of innovations leads to lower inventory and operating costs, which enables Walmart to keep its lean costs.

Walmart continues to hone its management of the flow of products and information among its suppliers, distribution centers, and individual stores through technology to increase its control of logistics and inventory. Thoughtful use of innovation has put Walmart at the top of the retailing game. Not all organizations can pull this approach off so well. Walmart is a unique case in which a single, very powerful firm took primary responsibility for improving performance across its own supply chain. By developing a superior supply chain management system, it has reaped the rewards of higher levels of customer service and satisfaction, lower production and transportation costs, and more productive use of its retail store space. Fundamentally, it boils down to Walmart's ability to link together suppliers, distribution centers, retail outlets, and, ultimately, customers, regardless of their location. Although operational innovation isn't the only ingredient in Walmart's success, it has been a crucial building block for its strong competitive position.

## Questions

1. How does an individual firm like Walmart manage a supply chain, particularly considering that supply chains include multiple firms with potentially conflicting objectives? Describe some of the conflicts that could arise in such a circumstance.

2. What are some of the ways that Walmart's supply chain management system has provided it the benefits of higher levels of product availability and lower merchandise acquisition and transportation costs? Provide specific examples of each benefit.

# Retailing and Multichannel Marketing

**B**arbie already has the enviable advantage of being 50 years old with a perfect figure and no wrinkles, so how could she improve? The answer, for Mattel, lies in taking the brand from a popular doll sold through a variety of channels to a symbol of optimism and possibility for women of all ages.[1]

To launch this expanded view of their iconic female image, Mattel has given her a 37,000-square-foot pink palace in Shanghai—a full-featured megastore with interactive experiences designed to convey that *all* girls just want to have fun . . . and believe that any future is open to them. This location is the only Barbie megastore and indicates a change in Mattel's brand strategy, as well as Barbie's coming of age.

The Barbie experience begins with the building's exterior, which features a lattice pattern on the custom façade. The interior is unmistakably feminine, with soft architectural lines and finishes and plenty of pink. Access to the main floor involves a ride in a pink escalator tube, surrounded by the prerecorded sounds of girls laughing. The retail floors are linked by a spiral staircase that houses 875 hand-made and individually styled Barbies.

In keeping with the goal of expanding the brand into new demographics, the emporium's two lower floors are aimed at the more seasoned end of "girlhood." One floor features wedding gowns and a line of clothing from the designer behind the television show *Sex and the City*. Another floor is home to a café offering food designed by well-known restaurateur/chef David Laris, who also created the Barbie Loves Chocolate brand. Additional appeals to adults include the "Pink Room" bar and the Barbie Spa. Women visiting the spa can enjoy facials, body scrubs, body wraps, manicures, and pedicures, while their junior counterparts can receive face painting, manicures, and haircuts. Exclusive cosmetics and skincare treatments are available for purchase—just some of the more than 1,600 products for sale at the store.

## LEARNING OBJECTIVES

**LO1** Discuss the four factors manufacturers should consider as they develop their strategy for working with retailers.

**LO2** Outline the considerations associated with choosing retail partners.

**LO3** List the three levels of distribution intensity.

**LO4** Describe the various types of retailers.

**LO5** Describe the components of a retail strategy.

**LO6** Identify the benefits of stores.

**LO7** Identify the benefits of multichannel retailing.

**LO8** Detail the challenges of multichannel retailing.

The dolls themselves, and the younger shoppers wanting them, are confined to the fourth floor, but Mattel's devotion to providing these female shoppers with fun is no less complete. In the Barbie Design Center, girls can design their own Barbie look, learn how the doll is created, and take home their custom-designed Barbie and keepsakes. At the Barbie Fashion Stage, girls can select outfits, have their hair and makeup done, and walk the runway in the Barbie Fashion Café. The girls get take-home treasures, including a magazine cover featuring their moment in the spotlight. Younger shoppers can also peruse Barbie fashions and accessories.

Although the Barbie brand is deeply rooted in the idea of looking good, Mattel also touts "aspirational values" through a Career Wall that shows Barbie in more than 100 different careers. Furthermore, the various dolls represent cultures from around the world. Intended to promote the idea that girls and women can accept and embrace who they are while simultaneously improving their lives through career choices, this one-of-a-kind wall stands as a manifestation of Mattel's strategy to understand exactly what the Barbie brand is and how to make it even better.

The pink palace may be the magic ticket for Mattel. Already the store has been awarded the Retail Store of the Year award from *Chain Store Age*, and analysts note that China has provided a fresh start for other brands that seem to have lost their vitality in the United States. The sagging economy has impacted Barbie sales worldwide, but Mattel executives are hopeful that Chinese women, new to the Barbie experience, will bolster sales in the years ahead.

● ● ●

Retailing sits at the end of the supply chain, where marketing meets the consumer. As Mattel realized when it opened its Barbie store, there is more to retailing than just manufacturing a product and making it available to customers. It is primarily the retailer's responsibility to make sure that these customers' expectations are fulfilled.

Retailing is defined as the set of business activities that add value to products and services sold to consumers for their personal or family use. Our definition includes products bought at stores, through catalogs, and over the Internet, as well as services like fast-food restaurants, airlines, and hotels. Some retailers claim they sell at "wholesale" prices, but if they sell to customers for their personal use, they are still retailers, regardless of their prices. Wholesalers (see Chapter 15) buy products from manufacturers and resell them to retailers or industrial or business users.

Retailing today is changing, both in the United States and around the world. Manufacturers no longer rule many supply chains, as they once did. Retailers like Walmart, Carrefour (a French hypermarket), Home Depot, Tesco, Metro (a German retail conglomerate), and Kroger[2]—the largest retailers in the world—dictate to their suppliers what should be made, how it should be configured, when it should be delivered, and, to some extent, what it should cost. These retailers are clearly in the driver's seat.

This chapter extends Chapter 15's discussion of supply chain management by examining why and how manufacturers utilize retailers. The manufacturer's strategy depends on its overall market power and how consistent a new product or product line is with current offerings. Consider the following scenarios:

■ **Scenario 1:** Cosmetics conglomerate Estée Lauder's subsidiary brand M-A-C is introducing a new line of mascara.

- **Scenario 2:** Estée Lauder is introducing a line of scarves, leather goods, and other accessories—products not currently in its assortment.

- **Scenario 3:** Britt, a young entrepreneur, is launching a new line of environmentally friendly (green) cosmetics.

**L01** Discuss the four factors manufacturers should consider as they develop their strategy for working with retailers.

Each of these scenarios is different and requires the manufacturer to consider alternatives for reaching its target markets through retailers.

Exhibit 16.1 illustrates four factors manufacturers consider to establish their strategy for working with retailers.[3] In *choosing retail partners*, the first factor, manufacturers assess how likely it is for certain retailers to carry their products. Manufacturers also consider where their target customers expect to find the products, because those are exactly the stores in which they want to place their products. The overall size and level of sophistication of the manufacturer will determine how many of the supply chain functions it performs and how many it will hand off to other channel members. Finally, the type and availability of the product and the image the manufacturer wishes to portray will determine how many retailers within a geographic region will carry the products.

For the second factor, manufacturers *identify the types of retailers* that would be appropriate to carry their products. Although the choice is often obvious—such as a supermarket for fresh produce—manufacturers may have a choice of retailer types for some products.

As we discussed in Chapter 15, a hallmark of a strong marketing channel is one in which manufacturers and retailers coordinate their efforts. In the third factor, manufacturers and retailers therefore *develop their strategy* by implementing the four Ps.

Finally, many retailers and some manufacturers use a multichannel strategy, which involves selling in more than one channel (e.g., store, catalog, and Internet). The fourth factor therefore consists of examining the circumstances in which sellers may prefer to adopt a particular strategy. Although these four factors are listed consecutively, manufacturers may consider them all simultaneously or in a different order.

*When M-A-C introduces a new line of mascara, it will be carried exclusively in M-A-C stores. Celebrities like Fergie help promote it.*

# CHOOSING RETAILING PARTNERS

Imagine, as a consumer, trying to buy a new leather jacket without being able to visit a retailer or buy online. You would have to figure out exactly what size, color, and style of jacket you wanted. Then you would need to contact various manufacturers, whether in person, by phone, or over the Internet, and order the jacket. If the jacket fit you reasonably well but not perfectly, you still might need to take it to a tailor to have the sleeves shortened. You wouldn't find this approach to shopping very convenient.

**L02** Outline the considerations associated with choosing retail partners.

| **EXHIBIT 16.1** | Factors for Establishing a Relationship with Retailers |
| --- | --- |

| Choosing retailing partners | Identifying types of retailers | Developing a retail strategy | Managing a multichannel strategy |
| --- | --- | --- | --- |

*Revlon might have a difficult time getting CVS to buy a new mascara because its supply chain is not vertically integrated.*

Manufacturers like Estée Lauder use retailers such as Macy's to undertake partnerships that create value by pulling together all these actions necessary for the greatest possible customer convenience and satisfaction. The store offers a broad selection of leather jackets, scarves, and other accessories that its buyers have carefully chosen in advance. Customers can see, touch, feel, and try on any item while in the store. They can buy one scarf or leather jacket at a time or buy an outfit that works together. Finally, the store provides a salesperson to help customers coordinate their outfit and a tailor to make the whole thing fit perfectly.

When choosing retail partners, manufacturers look at the basic channel structure, where their target customers expect to find the products, channel member characteristics, and distribution intensity.

## Channel Structure

The level of difficulty a manufacturer experiences in getting retailers to purchase its products is determined by the degree to which the channel is vertically integrated, as described in Chapter 15; the degree to which the manufacturer has a strong brand or is otherwise desirable in the market; and the relative power of the manufacturer and retailer.

Scenario 1 described above represents a corporate vertical marketing system. Because M-A-C is made by Estée Lauder and operates its own stores, when the new mascara line gets introduced, the stores receive the new line automatically with no decision on the part of the retailer. In contrast, Revlon would have a much more difficult time getting CVS to buy a new mascara line, because these supply chain partners are not vertically integrated.

When an established firm like Estée Lauder enters a new market with scarves, leather goods, and accessories, as is the case in Scenario 2, it cannot place the products with any retailer. It must determine where its customers would expect to find higher-end scarves, leather goods, and accessories and then use its established relationships with cosmetics buyers, the power of its brand, and its overall reputation to leverage its position in this new product area.

Britt (Scenario 3) would have an even more difficult time convincing a retailer to buy and sell her green cosmetics line, because she lacks power in the marketplace—she is small, and her brand is unknown. She would have trouble getting buyers to see her, let alone consider her line. She might face relatively high slotting allowances (Chapter 14) just to get space on retailers' shelves. But like Estée Lauder in Scenario 2, Britt should consider where the end customer expects to find her products, as well as some important retailer characteristics.

## Customer Expectations

Retailers should also know customer preferences regarding manufacturers. Manufacturers, in contrast, need to know where their target market customers expect to find their products and those of their competitors. As we see in the hypothetical example in Exhibit 16.2, Estée Lauder currently sells cosmetics at Dillard's Department Stores, Macy's, and Sears (orange arrows). Its competitor Nars sells at Dillard's and Macy's and also at JCPenney (green arrows). A survey of Estée Lauder customers shows that they would expect to find its clothes at Kohl's, Dillard's, Macy's, and JCPenney (blue box). On the basis of this information, Estée Lauder decides to try selling at Kohl's and JCPenney but to stop selling at Sears to provide greater convenience to customers.

| EXHIBIT 16.2 | Estée Lauder and Nars Distribution |

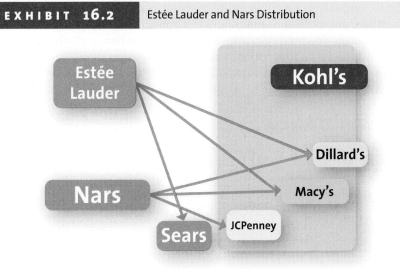

Customers generally expect to find certain products at some stores but not at others. For example, Estée Lauder would not choose to sell to CVS or Dollar General because its customers would not expect to shop at those stores for high-end cosmetics or clothing like Estée Lauder's. Instead, CVS might carry less expensive cosmetic brands, like Revlon and Maybelline, and bargain closeouts probably appear at Dollar General. But Estée Lauder's customers definitely expect to find its clothing offerings at major department stores.

## Channel Member Characteristics

Several factors pertaining to the channel members themselves will help determine the channel structure. Generally, the larger and more sophisticated the channel member, the less likely that it will use supply chain intermediaries. Britt will probably use a group of independent salespeople to help sell her line of green cosmetics, whereas a large manufacturer like Estée Lauder will use its own sales force that already has existing relationships in the industry. In the same way, an independent grocery store might buy merchandise from a wholesaler, but Walmart, the world's largest grocer, only buys directly from the manufacturer. Larger firms often find that by performing the channel functions themselves, they can gain more control, be more efficient, and save money.

**L03** List the three levels of distribution intensity.

## Distribution Intensity

When setting up distribution for the first time, as is the case with Britt's green cosmetics (Scenario 3), or introducing a new product line, as is the case with Estée Lauder's new line of scarves, leather, and accessories (Scenario 2), firms decide the appropriate level of **distribution intensity**—

*Most consumer packaged goods companies, such as Pepsi (top), strive for intensive distribution—they want to be everywhere. But cosmetics firms like Estée Lauder (right) use an exclusive distribution strategy by limiting their distribution to a few select, higher-end retailers in each region.*

the number of channel members to use at each level of the marketing channel. Distribution intensity commonly is divided into three levels: intensive, exclusive, and selective.

**Intensive Distribution**  An *intensive distribution* strategy is designed to place products in as many outlets as possible. Most consumer packaged goods companies, such as Pepsi, Procter & Gamble, Kraft, and other nationally branded products found in grocery and discount stores, strive for and often achieve intensive distribution. Pepsi, for instance, wants its product available everywhere—grocery stores, convenience stores, restaurants, and vending machines. The more exposure the products get, the more they sell.

**Exclusive Distribution**  Manufacturers also might use an *exclusive distribution* policy by granting exclusive geographic territories to one or very few retail customers so no other retailers in the territory can sell a particular brand. Exclusive distribution can benefit manufacturers by assuring them that the most appropriate retailers represent their products. Cosmetics firms such as Estée Lauder, for instance, limit distribution to a few select, higher-end retailers in each region. The company believes that selling its products to drugstores, full-line discount stores, and grocery stores would weaken its image.

When supply is limited or a firm is just starting out, providing an exclusive territory to one retailer or retail chain helps ensure enough inventory to provide the buying public an adequate selection. By granting exclusive territories, Britt guarantees her retailers will have an adequate supply of her green cosmetics. This guarantee gives these retailers a strong incentive to market her products. The retailers that Britt uses know there will be no competing retailers to cut prices, so their profit margins are protected. This knowledge gives them an incentive to carry more inventory and use extra advertising, personal selling, and sales promotions.

**Selective Distribution**  Between the intensive and exclusive distribution strategies lies *selective distribution*, which relies on a few selected retail customers in a territory to sell products. Like exclusive distribution, selective distribution helps a seller maintain a particular image and control the flow of merchandise into an area. These advantages make this approach attractive to many shopping goods manufacturers. Recall that shopping goods are those products for which consumers are willing to spend time comparing alternatives, such as most apparel items, home items like branded pots and pans or sheets and towels, branded hardware and tools, and consumer electronics. Retailers still have a strong incentive to sell the products but not to the same extent as if they had an exclusive territory.

As we noted in Chapter 15, like any large complicated system, a marketing channel is difficult to manage. Whether the balance of power rests with large retailers like Walmart or with large manufacturers like Procter & Gamble, channel members benefit by working together to develop and implement their channel strategy. In the next section, we explore the different types of retailers with an eye toward which would be most appropriate for M-A-C Cosmetics; Estée Lauder's new line of scarves, leather, and accessories; and Britt's new line of environmentally friendly cosmetics.

### CHECK YOURSELF

1. What issues should manufacturers consider when choosing retail partners?
2. What is the difference among intensive, exclusive, and selective levels of distribution intensity?

**L04**  Describe the various types of retailers.

# IDENTIFY TYPES OF RETAILERS

At first glance, identifying which type of retailers Estée Lauder and Britt may wish to pursue when attempting to place their new lines seems straightforward. But the choice is not always easy. Manufacturers need to understand the general char-

**EXHIBIT 16.3** Types of Retailers

| Food | General Merchandise | | Service |
|---|---|---|---|
| Supermarket | Full-Line Discount | Specialty | Auto Rental |
| Supercenter | Category Specialist | Department | Health Spa |
| Convenience | Drug | Off-Price | Vision Center |
| Warehouse Club | | Extreme Value | Bank |

acteristics of different types of retailers to determine the best channels for their product. For instance, the characteristics of a retailer that are important to a food manufacturer may be quite different than those considered valuable by a cosmetics manufacturer. In the next few sections, we examine the various types of retailers, identify some major players, and discuss some of the issues facing each type (Exhibit 16.3).

## Food Retailers

The food retailing landscape is changing dramatically. Twenty years ago, consumers primarily purchased food at conventional supermarkets. Now conventional supermarkets account for slightly more than half of food sales (not including restaurants). The fastest growing sectors of the food retail market are supercenters, warehouse clubs, convenience stores, and extreme value food retailers.[4] While full-line discount stores like Walmart and warehouse clubs like Costco are offering more food items, traditional supermarkets are carrying more nonfood items. Many supermarkets offer pharmacies, health care clinics, photo processing centers, banks, and cafés.

The world's largest food retailer, Walmart, has more than $165 billion in sales of supermarket-type merchandise, followed by Carrefour (France), Tesco (U.K.), Metro Group (Germany), Schwartz Group (Germany), and Kroger (U.S.).[5] The largest supermarket chains in the United States are Kroger, Safeway, Supervalu, Publix, and Ahold US.[6]

**Supermarkets** A conventional supermarket is a self-service retail food store offering groceries, meat, and produce with limited sales of nonfood items, such as health and beauty aids and general merchandise.[7] Perishables including meat, produce, baked goods, and dairy account for 44 percent of supermarket sales and typically have higher margins than packaged goods.[8]

Conventional supermarkets carry about 30,000 individual items or stock keeping units (SKUs). An SKU represents a unique inventory item. Limited assortment supermarkets or extreme value food retailers stock only 2,000 SKUs.[9] The two largest limited assortment supermarket chains in the United States are Save-A-Lot and ALDI. Rather than carry 20 brands of laundry detergent, limited assortment stores offer one or two brands and sizes, one of which is a store brand. These stores are designed to maximize efficiency and reduce costs. For example, merchandise is shipped in cartons or crates that can serve as displays so that no unloading is needed. Some costly services that consumers take for granted, such as free bags and paying with credit cards, are not provided. Stores are typically located in shopping centers with low rents. By trimming costs, limited assortment supermarkets can offer merchandise at 40 percent lower prices than conventional supermarkets.[10]

Although conventional supermarkets still sell a majority of food merchandise, they are under substantial competitive pressure from other types of food retailers, full-line discount chains, supercenters, warehouse clubs, extreme value retailers, convenience stores, and restaurants. Supercenters are attracting an increasing number of conventional supermarket customers with their broader assortments of food and general merchandise at attractive prices. General merchandise discount stores, such as Target and Walmart, and extreme value retailers like Dollar General and Family Dollar stores are increasing the amount of space they devote to consumables. Convenience stores are also selling more fresh merchandise.

To compete successfully against intrusions by other food retailing formats, conventional supermarkets differentiate their offerings by (1) emphasizing fresh perishables, (2) targeting health-conscious and ethnic consumers with new lines of natural, organic, or culture-specific items, (3) providing a better in-store experience with a better overall atmosphere and demonstrations, and (4) offering more private-label brands. Trader Joe's competes successfully against several types of food store formats, partly because it is a hybrid of specialty food stores, conventional grocery stores, and convenience stores. (See Adding Value 16.1.)

## Adding Value 16.1     Trader Joe's Offers the Unexpected[11]

Trader Joe's has created a niche for itself by offering a limited selection of unique and tasty grocery products at reasonable prices and in an environment designed to appeal to busy consumers. When Trader Joe's first opened its doors 50 years ago, it was a chain of convenience stores. But the company's founder saw an opportunity for a more interesting shopping experience and positioned the chain as a hybrid form that combined specialty food stores, conventional grocery stores, and convenience stores. His formula included gourmet foods, neighborhood locations, a moderate store size, and a selection of prepared and packaged food, as well as beverages, snacks, and cleaning products. It also included a friendly, knowledgeable staff and a tropical/nautical theme that evokes a luau rather than a necessary errand to get dinner on the table. But perhaps the most important ingredient in the retailer's success is its private label.

Unlike regular grocery stores, which carry 16 percent private-label products, Trader Joe's 2,000 private-label goods account for up to 70 percent of its inventory. In many instances, consumers prefer Trader Joe's products to national brands, a direct contrast to the conventional view that private-label products are less appealing than their national counterparts. The stores do not stock many popular national brands, nor do they have wide selection in every area. Shoppers looking for hummus have plenty of choices; those shopping for laundry detergent do not. Trader Joe's keeps its assortment varied by purchasing closeout or overstock specialty cheese and wines and by continually searching worldwide for foods that fit their values of taste, innovation, and environmentally friendly practices in production. The company develops small businesses to become its vendors, making the products it sells exclusive to its stores.

*Trader Joe's combines convenience, value, innovative and delicious foods, and a pleasant shopping experience to attract loyal customers.*

Trader Joe's helps its shoppers find value and variety through its *Fearless Flyer* newsletter, which it mails to customers and distributes at the front of the stores. These flyers, described by Trader Joe's as a cross between *Consumer Reports* and *Mad Magazine*, provide product information and list promotions. Employees introduce shoppers to new products by giving out food and drink samples, and they ensure satisfaction by offering a full refund for any product returned by a shopper, no questions asked.

Trader Joe's does lots of things right. But what elements of its strategy give it a distinctive competitive advantage that its rivals can't copy?

**Supercenters** Supercenters are large stores (185,000 square feet) that combine a supermarket with a full-line discount store. Walmart operates 2,700 supercenters in the United States, accounting for 81 percent of total supercenter sales and outpacing its competitors Meijer, SuperTarget (Target), Fred Meyer (Kroger Co.), and Super Kmart Center (Sears Holding). By offering broad assortments of grocery and general merchandise products under one roof, supercenters provide a one-stop shopping convenience to customers.

**Warehouse Clubs** Warehouse clubs are large retailers (100,000–150,000 square feet) that offer a limited and irregular assortment of food and general merchandise, little service, and low prices to the general public and small businesses. The largest warehouse club chains are Costco, Sam's Club (Walmart), and BJ's Wholesale Club (operating only on the East Coast of the United States). Customers are attracted to these stores because they can stock up on large packs of basics like paper towels, mega-sized packaged groceries such as a quart of ketchup, best-selling books and CDs, fresh meat and produce, and an unpredictable assortment of upscale merchandise and services (e.g., jewelry, electronics, home décor) at lower prices than are available at other retail stores. Costco differentiates itself by carrying unique, upscale goods not available elsewhere at low prices. For example, you can buy a five-carat diamond ring for $99,999.99 with an appraised value of $153,450. Sam's Club focuses more on small business customers, providing services such as group health insurance, as well as products that appeal specifically to this market.

*Warehouse clubs like Costco carry an unpredictable assortment of upscale merchandise and services including upscale jewelry at low prices.*

Both Estée Lauder's and Britt's products could be sold in warehouse clubs, but these retailers are probably not the best choices. Both product lines will have an upscale image, which is inconsistent with any warehouse club. If, however, either firm has overstock merchandise as a result of overestimating demand or underestimating returned merchandise from retailers, warehouse clubs are a potential outlet.

**Convenience Stores** Convenience stores provide a limited variety and assortment of merchandise at a convenient location in 3,000- to 5,000-square-foot stores with speedy checkout. They are the modern version of the neighborhood mom-and-pop grocery/general store. Convenience stores enable consumers to make purchases quickly without having to search through a large store and wait in a lengthy checkout line. Convenience store assortments are limited in terms of depth and breadth, and they charge higher prices than supermarkets. Milk, eggs, and bread once represented the majority of their sales, but now most sales come from gasoline and cigarettes.

Convenience stores also face increased competition from other retail formats. Supercenter and supermarket chains are attempting to increase customer store visits by offering gasoline and tying gasoline sales to their frequent shopper programs. Drugstores and full-line discount stores also have easily accessible areas of their stores with convenience store merchandise.

In response to these competitive pressures, convenience stores are taking steps to decrease their dependency on gasoline sales by offering fresh food and healthy fast food, tailoring assortments to local markets, and making their stores even more convenient to shop. Finally, convenience stores are adding new services, such as financial service kiosks that give customers the opportunity to cash checks, pay bills, and buy prepaid telephone minutes, theater tickets, and gift cards.

## General Merchandise Retailers

The major types of general merchandise retailers are department stores, full-line discount stores, specialty stores, category specialists, home improvement centers, off-price retailers, and extreme value retailers.

**Department Stores** Department stores are retailers that carry a broad variety and deep assortment, offer customer services, and organize their stores into distinct departments for displaying merchandise. The largest department store chains in the United States are Macy's, JCPenney, Sears, Kohl's, Nordstrom, Dillard's, and Neiman Marcus.[12] Department stores would be an excellent retail channel for Estée Lauder's and Britt's new lines.

Traditionally, department stores attracted customers by offering a pleasing ambience, attentive service, and a wide variety of merchandise under one roof. They sold both soft goods (apparel and bedding) and hard goods (appliances, furniture, and consumer electronics). But now most department stores focus almost exclusively on soft goods. Each department within the store has a specific selling space allocated to it, as well as salespeople to assist customers. The department store often resembles a collection of specialty shops.

Department store chains can be categorized into three tiers. The first tier includes upscale, high-fashion chains with exclusive designer merchandise and excellent customer service; these stores include Neiman Marcus, Bloomingdale's (Macy's Inc.), Nordstrom, and Saks Fifth Avenue (Saks Inc.). Macy's and Dillard's are in the second tier of upscale traditional department stores, in which retailers sell more modestly priced merchandise with less customer service. The value-oriented third tier, which includes Sears, JCPenney, and Kohl's, caters to more price-conscious consumers. To better compete, department stores are (1) attempting to increase the amount of exclusive and private-label merchandise they sell, (2) strengthening their customer loyalty programs, and (3) expanding their online presence.

**Full-Line Discount Stores** Full-line discount stores are retailers that offer a broad variety of merchandise, limited service, and low prices. The largest full-line discount store chains are Walmart, Target, and Kmart (Sears Holding).[13]

Although full-line discount stores typically carry scarves, leather goods, accessories, and cosmetics, they are not good options for Estée Lauder's or Britt's new lines. Customers do not expect higher-end products in full-line discount stores. Rather, they are looking for value prices on these items and are willing to compromise on quality or cachet.

*Lush cosmetics has its own department within department stores with salespeople dedicated to selling Lush's products.*

Walmart accounts for 67 percent of full-line discount store retail sales in the United States. Full-line discount stores confront intense competition from category specialists that focus on a single category of merchandise, such as Staples, Best Buy, Bed Bath & Beyond, Sports Authority, and Lowe's.[14] In response to this competitive threat, Walmart is converting its discount stores into supercenters. Walmart is expected to reach 3,000 supercenters by 2013, while its discount stores should decrease to around two-thirds of current levels.[15]

Target has experienced considerable growth because its stores offer fashionable merchandise at low prices in a pleasant shopping environment. The retailer has developed an image of "cheap chic" by offering limited-edition exclusive apparel and cosmetic lines secured through its GO International campaign, which has involved teaming with designers such as Zac Posen, Jean Paul Gaultier, Rodarte, and Liberty of London to produce inexpensive, exclusive merchandise. It also has exciting and stylish private-label products under its Up & Up and Bullseye brands.

**Specialty Stores** Specialty stores concentrate on a limited number of complementary merchandise categories and provide a high level of service. Specialty stores tailor their retail strategy toward very specific market segments by offering deep but narrow assortments and sales associate expertise.

*Target has teamed up with Liberty of London to produce limited-edition exclusive apparel at inexpensive prices.*

Estée Lauder's M-A-C line of cosmetics sells in the company's own retail specialty stores, as well as in some department stores. Certain specialty stores would be excellent outlets for the new lines by Estée Lauder and Britt. Customers likely expect to find Estée Lauder lines of scarves, leather, and accessories in women's apparel, gift, or leather stores. Britt's line of green cosmetics would fit nicely in a cosmetics specialty store like Sephora.

Sephora, France's leading perfume and cosmetic chain and a division of the luxury goods conglomerate LVMH (Louis Vuitton–Moët Hennessy), is an example of an innovative specialty-store concept. In the United States, prestigious cosmetics are typically sold in department stores. Each brand has a separate counter with a specially trained salesperson stationed behind the counter to help customers. Sephora is a cosmetic and perfume specialty store offering a deep assortment in a self-service, 6,000- to 9,000-square-foot format. Its stores provide more than 15,000 SKUs and more than 200 brands, including its own private-label brand. Merchandise is grouped by product category, with the brands displayed alphabetically so customers can locate them easily. Customers are free to shop and experiment on their own. Sampling is encouraged. Knowledgeable salespeople are available to assist customers. The low-key, open-sell environment results in customers spending more time shopping.

*Sephora is an innovative specialty store that sells cosmetics.*

**Drugstores**  Drugstores are specialty stores that concentrate on pharmaceuticals and health and personal grooming merchandise. Prescription pharmaceuticals represent almost 70 percent of drugstore sales. The largest drugstore chains in the United States are Walgreens, CVS, and Rite Aid—three chains that account for about 66 percent of U.S. drugstore sales, up from 45 percent in 2002.[16]

Although Estée Lauder's new line would not be consistent with the merchandise found in drugstores, Britt's green cosmetics may be a welcome addition. Some drugstores have recognized consumer demand for green products, even though Britt's cosmetics may be priced higher than its competitors. Britt must decide whether her high-end products will suffer a tarnished image if she sells them in drugstores or if drugstores could be a good channel for increasing her brand awareness.

Drugstores face competition from pharmacies in discount stores and pressure to reduce health care costs. The major drugstore chains are offering a wider assortment of merchandise, including more frequently purchased food items, the convenience of drive-through windows for picking up prescriptions, and in-store medical clinics. To build customer loyalty, the chains are changing the role of their pharmacists from simply dispensing pills (referred to as "count, pour, lick, and stick") to providing health care assistance, such as explaining how to use a nebulizer. Drugstores also are expanding their role as a fill-in trip destination by carrying products typically found in convenience stores, such as beverages, and making them easily accessible at the front of the store.

**Category Specialists**  Category specialists are big box retailers or category killers that offer a narrow but deep assortment of merchandise. Most category specialists use a predominantly self-service approach, but they offer assistance to customers in some areas of the stores. For example, the office supply store Staples has a warehouse atmosphere with cartons of copy paper stacked on pallets plus equipment in boxes on shelves. But in some departments, such as computers or electronics and other high-tech products, salespeople staff the display area to answer questions and make suggestions.

By offering a complete assortment in a category at somewhat lower prices than their competition, category specialists can "kill" a category of merchandise for other retailers, which is why they are frequently called category killers. Using their category dominance, these retailers exploit their buying power to negotiate low prices and are assured of supply when items are scarce. Department stores

*Lowe's is one of the United States' largest home improvement center chains. This category specialist offers equipment and material used by do-it-yourselfers and contractors to make home improvements.*

and full-line discount stores located near category specialists often have to reduce their offerings in the category because consumers are drawn to the deep assortment and low prices at the category killer.

One of the largest and most successful types of category specialists is the home improvement center. A home improvement center is a category specialist offering equipment and material used by do-it-yourselfers and contractors to make home improvements. The largest U.S. home improvement chains are Home Depot and Lowe's. Like warehouse clubs and office supply category specialists, home improvement centers operate as retailers when they sell merchandise to consumers and as wholesalers when they sell to contractors and other businesses. Although merchandise in home improvement centers is displayed in a warehouse atmosphere, salespeople are available to assist customers in selecting merchandise and to tell them how to use it.

**Extreme Value Retailers** Extreme value retailers are small, full-line discount stores that offer a limited merchandise assortment at very low prices. The largest extreme value retailers are Dollar General and Family Dollar Stores.[17]

Like limited assortment food retailers, extreme value retailers reduce costs and maintain low prices by buying opportunistically from manufacturers with excess merchandise, offering a limited assortment, and operating in low-rent locations. They offer a broad but shallow assortment of household goods, health and beauty aids, and groceries. Many value retailers target low-income consumers, whose shopping behavior differs from typical discount store or warehouse club customers. For instance, though these consumers demand well-known national brands, they often cannot afford to buy large-sized packages.

Despite some of these chains' names, few sell merchandise for just a dollar. The two largest—Dollar General and Family Dollar—do not employ a strict dollar limit and sell merchandise for up to $20. The names imply a good value but do not limit customers to the arbitrary dollar price point. Because this segment of the retail industry is growing rapidly, vendors such as Procter & Gamble often create special, smaller packages for extreme value retailers.

Extreme value retailers would not be an obvious consumer choice for Estée Lauder's or Britt's new lines, because these stores are not consistent with the brands' images. But if these manufacturers find themselves in an overstock situation, they could utilize these retailers to reduce inventory. For the same reason, they might use off-price retailers.

*Dollar General is one of the United States' largest extreme value retailers. It has small, full-line discount stores that offer a limited assortment at very low prices.*

**Off-Price Retailers** Off-price retailers, also known as close-out retailers, offer an inconsistent assortment of brand name merchandise at a significant discount from the manufacturer's suggested retail price (MSRP). In today's market, these close-out retailers may be brick-and-mortar stores, online outlets, or a combination of both. America's largest off-price retail chains are TJX Companies (which operates TJMaxx, Marshalls, Winners, HomeGoods, AJWright, and HomeSense), Ross Stores, Burlington Coat Factory, Big Lots Inc., Overstock.com, and Bluefly.com.

Off-price retailers sell brand name and even designer label merchandise at prices 20–60 percent lower than the MSRP, which they can do because of their unique buying and merchandising practices.[18] Most merchandise is bought opportunistically from manufacturers or other retailers with excess inventory at the end of the season. Because of this buying approach, customers cannot be confident that the same merchandise or even type of merchandise will be available each time they visit the store or website. This uncertainty is both a positive and a negative feature for consumers, who might find new bargains on each visit. However, the merchandise might be in odd sizes or unpopular colors and styles, or it may be irregulars (merchandise with minor mistakes in construction). Typically, off-price retailers purchase merchandise at one-fifth to one-fourth of the original wholesale price. Off-price retailers can buy at these low prices because they do not ask suppliers to help them pay for advertising, make them take back unsold merchandise, charge them for markdowns, or ask them to delay payments.

A special type of off-price retailer is outlet stores. Outlet stores are off-price retailers owned by manufacturers or department or specialty store chains. Those owned by manufacturers are also referred to as factory outlets. Manufacturers view outlet stores as an opportunity to improve their revenues from irregulars, production overruns, and merchandise returned by retailers. Outlet stores also allow manufacturers some control over where their branded merchandise may be sold at discount prices. Retailers with strong brand names such as Saks Fifth Avenue (Saks Fifth Avenue OFF 5th) and Brooks Brothers operate outlet stores too. By selling excess merchandise in outlet stores rather than at markdown prices in their primary stores, these department and specialty store chains can maintain an image of offering desirable merchandise at full price. To improve their outlet offerings' consistency, some off-price retailers complement their opportunistically bought merchandise with merchandise purchased at regular wholesale prices. For example, Brooks Brothers' outlet store produces an exclusive line called "346" so that it can always have a consistent product line.

*This outlet mall in San Marco, Texas, has tenants such as Neiman Marcus Last Call, Zegna, Escada, and Salvatore Ferragamo.*

## Services Retailers

The retail firms discussed in the previous sections sell products to consumers.[19] However, services retailers, or firms that primarily sell services rather than merchandise, are a large and growing part of the retail industry. Consider a typical Saturday: After a bagel and cup of coffee at a nearby Peet's Coffee and Tea, you go to the laundromat to wash and dry your clothes, drop a suit off at a dry cleaner, leave film to be developed at a CVS drugstore, and make your way to Jiffy Lube to have your car's oil changed. In a hurry, you drive through a Burger King so you can eat lunch quickly and not be late for your haircut at Supercuts. By midafternoon, you're ready for a workout at your health club. After stopping at home for a change of clothes, you're off to dinner, a movie, and dancing with a

*CVS offers services like photo developing, knowledgeable pharmacists, and drive-through windows.*

friend. Finally, you end your day with a café latte at Starbucks, having interacted with 10 different services retailers during the day.

There are a wide variety of services retailers, along with some national companies that provide these services. These companies are retailers because they sell goods and services to consumers. However, some are not just retailers. For example, airlines, banks, hotels, and insurance and express mail companies sell their services to businesses as well as consumers.

Organizations such as banks, hospitals, health spas, legal clinics, entertainment firms, and universities that offer services to consumers traditionally have not considered themselves retailers. Yet due to increased competition, these organizations are adopting retailing principles to attract customers and satisfy their needs.

Several trends suggest considerable future growth in services retailing. For example, the aging population will increase demand for health care services. Younger people are also spending more time and money on health and fitness. Busy parents in two-income families are willing to pay to have their homes cleaned, lawns maintained, clothes washed and pressed, and meals prepared so they can spend more time with their families.

Now that we've explored the types of stores, we can examine how manufacturers and retailers coordinate their retail strategy using the four Ps.

> ## CHECK YOURSELF
>
> 1. What strategies distinguish the different types of food retailers?
> 2. What strategies distinguish the different types of general merchandise retailers?
> 3. Are organizations that provide services to consumers considered to be retailers?

# DEVELOPING A RETAIL STRATEGY USING THE FOUR Ps

**L05** Describe the components of a retail strategy.

Like other marketers, retailers perform important functions that increase the value of the products and services they sell to consumers. We now examine these functions, classified into the four Ps: product, price, promotion, and place.

*To distinguish itself from competition, Macy's develops private labels like I.N.C. that are produced, marketed, and available only at their stores.*

## Product

A typical grocery store carries 30,000 to 40,000 different items; a regional department store might carry as many as 100,000. Providing the right mix of merchandise and services that satisfies the needs of the target market is one of retailers' most fundamental activities. Offering assortments gives customers a choice. To reduce transportation costs and handling, manufacturers typically ship cases of merchandise, such as cartons of mascara or boxes of leather jackets, to retailers. Because customers generally do not want or need to buy more than one of the same item, retailers break up the cases and sell customers the smaller quantities they desire.

Manufacturers don't like to store inventory because their factories and warehouses are typically not available or attractive shopping venues. Consumers don't want to purchase more than they need because storage consumes space. Neither group likes keeping inventory that isn't being used, because doing so ties up money that could be used for something else. Retailers thus provide, in addition to other values to both manufacturers and customers, a storage function, although many retailers are beginning to push their suppliers to hold the inventory until they need it. (Recall our discussion of JIT inventory systems in Chapter 15.)

It is difficult for retailers to distinguish themselves from their competitors through the merchandise they carry because competitors can purchase and sell many of the same popular brands. Thus, many retailers have developed private-label brands (also called store brands), which are products developed and marketed by a retailer and available only from that retailer. For example, if you want an I.N.C. dress, you have to go to Macy's.

Retailers often work together with their suppliers to develop an exclusive co-brand, which we described in Chapter 10 as a brand that is developed by a national brand vendor, often in conjunction with a retailer, and is sold exclusively by the retailer. So for instance, because Estée Lauder has such a strong brand name and already maintains a strong retail network, it might want to develop an exclusive co-brand with Kohl's. This brand would have a name like Lauder, so that customers would know it was made by Estée Lauder, but it would be available only at Kohl's. Exclusive co-brands have a double benefit: They are available at only one retailer, and they offer name recognition similar to that of a national brand. The disadvantage of exclusive co-brands, from the manufacturer's perspective, is that they can be sold by only one retailer, and therefore, the manufacturer's market is limited. From the retailer's perspective, the disadvantage is that it has to share its profits with the national brand manufacturer, whereas with a private-label brand, it does not.

## Price

Price helps define the value of both the merchandise and the service, and the general price range of a particular store helps define its image. Although both Saks Fifth Avenue and JCPenney are department stores, their images could not be more different. Thus, when Estée Lauder considers which of these firms is most appropriate for its new line of scarves, leather, and accessories, it must keep customers' perceived images of these retailers' price–quality relationship in mind. The company does not, for instance, want to attempt to sell its new line at JCPenney if it is positioning the line with a relatively high price. Price must always be aligned with the other elements of a retailer's strategy: product, promotion, and place. A customer would not expect to pay $20 for a lipstick sold in her local grocery store, but she might question a lipstick's quality if its price is significantly less than $20 at Neiman Marcus. As we discovered in Chapters 13 and 14, there is much more to pricing than simply adding a markup onto a product's cost. Manufacturers must consider at what price they will sell the product to retailers so that both the manufacturer and the retailer can make a reasonable profit. At the same time, both the manufacturer and the retailer are concerned about what the customer is willing and expecting to pay.

*Bass Pro Shops Outdoor World in Lawrenceville, Georgia, uses its 43-foot climbing wall as a way to promote its store.*

## Promotion

Retailers and manufacturers know that good promotion, both within the retail environments and in the media, can mean the difference between flat sales and a growing consumer base. Advertising in traditional media such as newspapers, magazines, and television continues to be important to get customers into stores. Increasingly, electronic communications are being used for promotions as well. Some traditional approaches, such as direct mail, are being reevaluated by retailers, but many are still finding value in sending catalogs to customers and selected mailing lists. Interestingly, catalogs generate online sales, because shoppers can see quality photographs and information about a product in a catalog and then purchase it conveniently via the Web.

*Retailers are investing in M-commerce so their customers can purchase products and services through their mobile devices.*

Companies also offer real-time promotions on their websites. For example, CVS.com contains in-store and online coupons that customers can use immediately on the site or print to use in the store. Coupons.com similarly offers an array of promotions for many grocery store items. Customers can follow this vendor on Twitter @Coupons to find even more savings opportunities.

New technologies thus are expanding the ways in which retailers can reach customers with their advertising message. For example, customers can access a retailer's Internet site using a variety of devices, ranging from a computer to a mobile phone. Due to the rapid growth of domestic and international broadband access through mobile devices, retailers are investing in mobile commerce (M-commerce)—product and service purchases through mobile devices. However, the typical retailer's website is not currently designed to accommodate a mobile device's small screen and slower download speeds. Various firms, including ESPN, therefore have developed special websites for users to access through mobile devices. In addition, retailers have created specialized applications that enable mobile device users to shop or obtain more merchandise information. Technology innovations will continue to provide growing opportunities for new forms of promotion.

Another type of promotion occurs inside the store, where retailers use displays and signs, placed at the point of purchase or in strategic areas such as the end of aisles, to inform customers and stimulate purchases of the featured products.

A coordinated effort between the manufacturer and retailer helps guarantee that the customer receives a cohesive message and that both entities maintain their image. For example, Estée Lauder might work with its most important retailers to develop advertising and point-of-sale signs. It may even help defray the costs of advertising by paying all or a portion of the advertising's production and media costs, an agreement called cooperative (co-op) advertising.

Store credit cards and gift cards are more subtle forms of promotion that also facilitate shopping. Retailers might offer pricing promotions—such as coupons, rebates, in-store or online discounts, or perhaps buy-one-get-one-free offers—to attract consumers and stimulate sales. These promotions play a very important role in driving traffic to retail locations, increasing average purchase size, and creating opportunities for repeat purchases. But retail promotions also are valuable to customers; they inform customers about what is new and available and how much it costs.

In addition to traditional forms of promotion, many retailers are devoting more resources to their overall retail environment as a means to promote and showcase what the store has to offer. These promotions may take the form of recognizable approaches, such as in-store and window displays, or they may be entirely new experiences designed to help retailers draw customers and add value to the shopping experience. Bass Pro Shops Outdoor World in Lawrenceville, Georgia, for instance, offers a 30,000-gallon aquarium stocked with fish for casting demonstrations, an indoor archery range, and a 43-foot climbing wall. These features enhance customers' visual experiences, provide them with educational information, and enhance the store's sales potential by enabling customers to "try before they buy." In addition to adding fun to the shopping experience, these activities help offset the current drop in brick-and-mortar customers engendered by online shopping.

A variety of factors influence whether customers will actually buy once they are in the store. Some of these factors are quite subtle. Consumers' perceptions of value and their subsequent patronage are heavily influenced by their perceptions of the store's "look and feel." Music, color, scent, aisle size, lighting, the availability of seating, and crowding can also significantly affect the overall shopping experience.[20] Therefore, the extent to which stores offer a more pleasant shopping experience fosters a better mood, resulting in greater spending.

Personal selling and customer service representatives are also part of the overall promotional package. Retailers must provide services that make it easier to buy and use products, and retail associates—whether in the store, on the phone, or on the Internet—provide customers with information about product characteristics and availability. These individuals can also facilitate the sale of products or services that consumers perceive as complicated, risky, or expensive, such as an air-conditioning unit, a computer, or a diamond ring. Manufacturers can play an important role in getting retail sales and service associates prepared to sell their products. Britt, for example, could conduct seminars or Webinars about how to use and sell her new line of green cosmetics and supply printed educational materials to sales associates. Last but not least, these individuals handle the transactions that result in a sale. In some retail firms, salesperson and customer service functions are being augmented, or even replaced, by technology in the form of in-store kiosks, the Internet, or self-checkout lanes.

Traditionally, retailers treated all their customers the same. Today, the most successful retailers concentrate on providing more value to their best customers. The knowledge retailers gain from their store personnel, the Internet browsing and buying activities of customers, and the data they collect on customer shopping habits can be used in customer relationship management (CRM). Using this information, retailers may modify product, price, and/or promotion to attempt to increase their **share of wallet**—the percentage of the customer's purchases made from that particular retailer. For instance, multichannel retailers use consumer information collected from the customers' Internet browsing and buying behavior to send dedicated e-mails to customers promoting specific products or services. Retailers also may offer special discounts to good customers to help them become even more loyal.

## Place

Retailers already have realized that convenience is a key ingredient to success, and an important aspect of this success is convenient locations.[21] As the old cliché claims, the three most important things in retailing are "location, location, location." Many customers choose stores on the basis of where they are located, which makes great locations a competitive advantage that few rivals can duplicate. For instance, once Starbucks saturates a market by opening in the best locations, Peet's will have difficulty breaking into that same market—where would it put its stores?

In pursuit of better and better locations, retailers are experimenting with different options to reach their target markets. Walgreens has free-standing stores, unconnected to other retailers, so the stores can offer a drive-up window for customers to pick up their prescriptions. Other stores, like Brookstone, have opened stores where they have a captive market—airports.

*To make their locations more convenient, Walgreens has some free-standing stores, not connected to other retailers, so the stores can offer a drive-up window for customers to pick up their prescriptions.*

# BENEFITS OF STORES FOR CONSUMERS

 Identify the benefits of stores.

In this section, we briefly explore the relative advantages of the most traditional retail channel, the bricks-and-mortar store, from the consumer's perspective. In the following section, we examine how the addition of the Internet channel has added value to retailers' ability to satisfy their customers' needs.

**Browsing** Shoppers often have only a general sense of what they want (e.g., a sweater, something for dinner, a gift) but don't know the specific item they want. They go to a store to see what is available before making their final decision about what to buy. Although some consumers surf the Web and look through catalogs for ideas, many still prefer browsing in stores. Some also employ both approaches, getting a sense of what's available through catalogs or the Internet, and then going to the store to try on apparel or view the actual object.

**Touching and Feeling Products** Perhaps the greatest benefit offered by stores is the opportunity for customers to use all five of their senses—touch, smell, taste, vision, and hearing—to examine products.

**Personal Service** Sales associates have the capability to provide meaningful, personalized information. Salespeople can be particularly helpful when purchasing a complicated product, like consumer electronics, or something the customer doesn't know much about, like raw Japanese selvaged denim jeans.

**Cash and Credit Payment** Stores are the only channel that accepts cash payments. Some customers prefer to pay with cash because it is easy, resolves the transaction immediately, and does not result in potential interest

*At LegoLand in Minneapolis's Mall of America, customers can browse, touch, and feel the product, enjoy personal service, be entertained, and interact with others.*

payments. And, of course, some people don't have a credit card. Some customers also prefer to use their credit card or debit card in person rather than send the payment information electronically via the Internet.

**Entertainment and Social Experience**  In-store shopping can be a stimulating experience for some people, providing a break in their daily routine and enabling them to interact with friends.

**Immediate Gratification**  Stores have the advantage of allowing customers to get the merchandise immediately after paying for it.

**Risk Reduction**  When customers purchase merchandise in stores, the physical presence of the store reduces their perceived risk of buying and increases their confidence that any problems with the merchandise will be corrected.

**L07**  Identify the benefits of multichannel retailing.

# BENEFITS OF THE INTERNET AND MULTICHANNEL RETAILING

In this section, we examine how the addition of the Internet channel to traditional store-based retailers has improved their ability to serve their customers and build a competitive advantage in several ways.

First, the addition of an Internet channel has the potential to offer a greater selection of products. Second, the addition of the Internet channel enables retailers to provide customers with more personalized information about products and services. Third, it offers sellers the unique opportunity to collect information about consumer shopping behavior—information that they can use to improve the shopping experience across all channels. Fourth, providing a multichannel offering increases customer satisfaction and loyalty. Fifth, the Internet channel allows sellers to enter new markets economically.

## Deeper and Broader Selection

One benefit of adding the Internet channel is the vast number of alternatives retailers can make available to consumers without crowding their aisles or increasing their square footage. Stores and catalogs are limited by their size. By shopping on the Internet, consumers can easily "visit" and select merchandise from a broader array of retailers. Individual retailers' websites typically offer deeper assortments of merchandise (more colors, brands, and sizes) than are available in stores or catalogs. This expanded offering enables them to satisfy consumer demand for less popular styles, colors, or sizes. Many retailers also offer a broader assortment (more categories) on their websites. Staples.com, for instance, offers soft drinks and cleaning supplies, which are not available in stores, so that its business customers will view it as a one-stop shop.

Of course not all retailers participating in the Internet channel have broad and deep assortments. Some, like Bag Borrow or Steal, have a very deep assortment but in very few merchandise categories. (See Power of the Internet 16.1.)

## Personalization

Another benefit of adding the Internet channel is the ability to personalize promotions and services economically, including heightened service or individualized offerings.

**Personalized Customer Service**  Traditional Internet channel approaches for responding to customer questions—such as FAQ (frequently asked questions) pages and offering an 800 number or e-mail address to ask questions—often do not provide the timely information customers are seeking. To improve customer service from an electronic channel, many firms offer live, online chats. An online chat provides customers with the opportunity to click a button at any time and

## Power of the Internet 16.1   Renting Luxury[22]

Attracting online customers doesn't rest entirely on service or merchandise available for purchase. For Bag Borrow or Steal, renting upscale handbags, jewelry, watches, and sunglasses online has proved so popular that a typical wholesale buy from a vendor is from $500,000 to $750,000, an amount rare for even the biggest luxury retailers like Bergdorf Goodman.

When the site first started in 2004, 70 percent of its rentals were from its opening price point bags, those under $500, and included many well-known brands such as Kate Spade and Coach. As the company matured, the price point changed, and about 80 percent of Bag Borrow or Steal's rentals are now from designer bags like Gucci and Prada that retail for $1,500 and up.

*Bag Borrow or Steal rents upscale handbags, jewelry, watches, and sunglasses from its online store.*

Part of the site's success is attributable to its hundreds of offerings, which appeal to women who may already own designer accessories but who want more wardrobe options for these highly visible items or to impress their friends. Another reason for success is price. A Chloe Small Paddington Satchel bag that retails for about $1,300 rents for around $100 a week or $250 per month. Customers can save even more by paying a monthly membership fee that allows them to rent for 20 percent off the listed prices as well as some additional perks such as priority access to certain merchandise and reward points. That Chloe bag, for example, costs members $65 per week or $200 per month. If a customer "falls in love" with an item, she has the option to pay a reduced price for it, based on its condition and age. Women clearly love the idea: Bag Borrow or Steal has over a million members. The website also offers an outlet store that sells items at 40–85 percent off the suggested retail price, depending on their condition.

---

have an instant messaging e-mail or voice conversation with a customer service representative. This technology also enables firms to send a proactive chat invitation automatically to customers on the site. The timing of these invitations can be based on the time the visitor has spent on the site, the specific page the customer is viewing, or a product on which the customer has clicked. At Bluefly.com, for example, if a visitor searches for more than three items in five minutes, thereby demonstrating more than a passing interest, Bluefly will display a pop-up window with a friendly face offering help.[23]

Although Amazon.com began as a bookseller, you may now buy just about anything on its site. But the availability of merchandise alone didn't make Amazon the largest Internet-only retailer. Its commitment to customer service garners satisfied, loyal, and profitable customers, as Superior Service 16.1 explains.

*At Bluefly.com, customers can have an instant messaging, e-mail, or voice conversation with a customer service representative.*

**Personalized Offering** The interactive nature of the Internet also provides an opportunity for retailers to personalize their offerings for each of their customers. Just as a well-trained salesperson would make recommendations to customers prior to checkout, an interactive Web page can make suggestions to the shopper about items that he or she might like to see based on previous purchases, what other customers who purchased the same item purchased, or common Web viewing behavior. Amazon serves up personalized home pages with

# Superior Service 16.1

## Amazon Sells Merchandise, but Excels Because of Its Service[24]

Internet shopping provides convenience to shoppers as well as greatly increasing the number and variety of products available for purchase when compared with an actual store. Nevertheless, according to the U.S. Census Bureau, consumers only make 5 percent of their purchases online. The challenge for Internet retailers, analysts agree, is that customers want immediate access, the ability to touch and feel products, and fast returns.

The founder and CEO of the leading online retail site in the United States, Amazon.com, Jeff Bezos is overcoming these deficits by drawing a distinction between customer experience and customer service. The former, in his mind, relates to product cost, availability, and delivery, while the latter involves customer complaints and should occur infrequently. To ensure an optimal customer experience with minimal need for customer service, Amazon is investing billions of dollars in technology research and development.

One promising result is an iPhone application that allows consumers to photograph a product they have found in a brick-and-mortar store and have that product automatically added to their Amazon shopping cart for purchase at the customers' convenience. The application works by sending the image to outsourced laborers, who match it to Amazon's offerings. Currently only available for books, the application gives customers access to Amazon's lower prices as well as customer reviews. If Amazon expands the technology beyond books, consumers may come to view brick-and-mortar stores as a sort of "petting zoo," where they can touch product offerings before buying them elsewhere.

But Amazon isn't stopping there. Previously outside merchants selling on Amazon's site were protected from customer service complaints because problems were directed at the e-tailer giant, no matter who the actual seller was. To improve service across its site, Amazon now insists merchants and buyers correspond through its own e-mail service so it can monitor complaints. The company uses performance metrics relating to stockouts and complaints. Merchants showing problems with more than 1 percent of their orders can be banned from the Amazon site. Reviewing these metrics and monitoring complaints also helps the company identify problems that may need to be solved on a larger scale.

Amazon's fulfillment program further protects the customer experience by allowing merchants to ship boxes of their products to the Amazon warehouse. Amazon handles orders, packing, shipping, complaints, and returns. Merchants pay for the service, but most find it improves their own business because Amazon's customer service representatives are well trained and because Amazon can negotiate lower shipping costs. In some cases, when a popular item runs the risk of selling out on the site, Amazon sends trucks to pick up merchandise rather than waiting for the merchant to ship it.

In addition to usual customer service offerings, such as Amazon Prime's free two-day shipping in return for an annual fee of $79, Amazon periodically employs technology-driven services designed to enhance online shopping for its customers. The Universal Wish List, for example, allows shoppers to click on a product anywhere on the Web, have that product added to a wish list, and then have Amazon retrieve the list. The Gold Box highlights special deals, while Windowshop View gives customers a virtual reality shopping trip by emulating the look of being in a store in 3D graphics.

*Amazon has invested over $10 billion in ten years to improve its customer service. This investment pays off by building customer loyalty and eliminating potential problems before they have a chance to decrease sales.*

information about books and other products of interest based on visitors' past purchases. Amazon.com will also send interested customers customized e-mail messages that notify them that their favorite author or recording artist has published a new book or released a new CD.

Some multichannel retailers are able to personalize promotions and Internet homepages on the basis of several attributes tied to the shopper's current or previous Web sessions, such as the time of day, time zone as determined by a computer's Internet address, and assumed gender.[25] Using this information, a retailer can target promotions for collectibles to those who have previously searched for similar merchandise or deals on down parkas to those living in colder climates. It can also test the effectiveness of different promotions in real time. For instance, if a 5 percent discount works better than $5 off, the retailer will stick with the more successful promotion.

## Gain Insights into Consumer Shopping Behavior

By adding an Internet channel, retailers can obtain valuable insights into how and why customers shop and are dissatisfied or satisfied with their experiences.[26] Cookies can be used proactively as well as reactively to gain consumer behavior insights. For example, a cookie can collect data on how customers navigate through a website, monitoring each mouse click to track characteristics of the products customers considered and what products customers looked at but did not buy.[27] To collect this information from store or catalog shoppers would be difficult; someone would have to follow customers around the store or observe them browsing catalog pages. Accumulated data are useful for determining whether a store, catalog, or website should be laid out according to brands, size, color, or price points to entice shoppers in the future.

Some consumers are concerned, however, about the ability of multichannel sellers to collect information about their purchase history, personal information, and search behavior on the Internet. Consumers may worry about how this information will be used in the future. Will it be sold to other firms, or will the consumer receive unwanted promotional materials online or in the mail? To answer these questions, consider Ethical and Societal Dilemma 16.1.

## Increase Customer Satisfaction and Loyalty

Introducing an Internet channel may lead to some cannibalization. The customers who formerly made purchases at a retailer's store or catalog now make the same purchases through the retailer's Internet channel.[28] However, a growing segment of multichannel shoppers appreciate the variety of purchasing options available to them, repaying retailers by increasing their spending and the share of customers' wallets garnered by the retailer. For example, customers may be introduced to a product in a catalog, get more information on the Internet, and go to the store to buy it. Neiman Marcus has benefited from this approach, discovering that its multichannel customers spend 3.6 times more than single-channel customers do.[29]

## Expand Market Presence

The market for customers that shop in stores is typically limited to consumers living in proximity to those stores. The market for catalogs is limited by the high cost of printing and mailing them and increasing consumer interest in environmentally friendly practices. By adding the Internet channel, retailers can expand their market without having to build new stores or incur the high cost of additional catalogs. Adding an Internet channel is particularly attractive to retailers with strong brand names but limited locations and distribution. For example, retailers such as Nordstrom's, REI, IKEA, and L.L. Bean are widely known for offering unique, high-quality merchandise. If these retailers only had a store or catalog channel, customers would have to travel to major U.S. cities to buy the merchandise they carry.

## Ethical and Societal Dilemma 16.1

### Protecting Customer Privacy

If you knew someone was following you, tracking your footprints in the dirt or peering through your windows, you'd probably feel your privacy had been violated. Yet some Internet retailers are tracking consumer's virtual footprints and observing browsing, shopping, and spending habits. Simultaneously, these retailers are going to great lengths to protect consumer privacy by using advanced security technology to protect personal and financial information for online shoppers. So how do we define privacy in an online environment, and how do we know when privacy has been violated?

This subject comes under extensive debate, because not every individual, culture, or country defines personal privacy the same way. Individuals, for example, may feel that their personal information belongs to them and should not be shared without permission. Alumni associations, in contrast, may feel they have a right to know the whereabouts of their past graduates for fund-raising and networking purposes.

Retailers' gathering and analyzing shoppers' online habits can be profitable to them. One e-commerce marketing company found that consumers are 50 percent more likely to open and click through a targeted e-mail than a generic one and that targeted e-mails generate 50 percent more revenue than generic e-mails.[30] Although some consumers appreciate getting these e-mails, these and similar practices are alarming to privacy and consumer groups and objectionable to many shoppers. The concerns stem more from the possibility of misuse of personal information than from the way information is currently used.

The situation grows more complicated when viewed on a global scale, because privacy laws differ in other countries. The European Union (EU) and other countries have more stringent consumer privacy laws than does the United States. The EU's policy is that consumers must specifically consent to receiving direct marketing e-mail. This consent is referred to as an *opt in*. In contrast, personal information in the United States is generally viewed as being in the public domain, and retailers can direct marketing to consumers unless the consumers explicitly tell retailers not to use their personal information—they must *opt out*. In both the United States and the EU, direct marketing e-mails must contain opt out information.[31]

The Federal Trade Commission (FTC) continues to develop guidelines that protect consumer privacy online. Suggested practices recommend informing consumers of information collection and use, allowing consumers to opt in or opt out and confirm the accuracy of information, and protecting personal information from theft or tampering. The FTC gives special protection to children under the Children's Online Privacy Protection Act (COPPA). It mandates that commercial websites must secure a parent's permission prior to collecting information from a child under 13 years of age.[32]

However, compliance with guidelines for adult sites is voluntary, and is therefore often ignored. Consumer advocacy groups are pushing to make the guidelines mandatory. In response, an increasing number of retailers are disclosing their information-gathering practices and allowing consumers to opt in or out.

**L08** Detail the challenges of multichannel retailing.

# EFFECTIVE MULTICHANNEL RETAILING

Consumers desire a seamless experience when interacting with multichannel retailers. They want to be recognized by a retailer, whether they interact with a sales associate, the retailer's website, or the retailer's call center by telephone. Customers want to buy a product through the retailer's Internet or catalog channels and pick it up or return it to a local store; find out if a product offered on the Internet channel is available at a local store; and, when unable to find a product in a store, determine if it is available for home delivery through the retailer's Internet channel.

However, providing this seamless experience for customers is not easy for retailers. Because each of the channels is somewhat different, a critical decision facing mul-

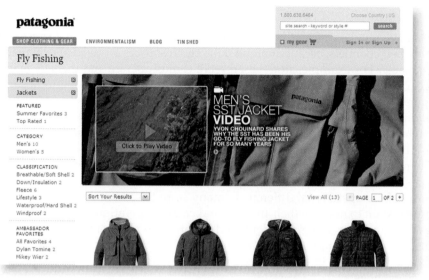

tichannel retailers is the degree to which they should or are able to integrate the operations of the channels. To determine how much integration is best, each retailer must address issues such as integrated CRM, brand image, pricing, and the supply chain.[33]

## Integrated CRM

Effective multichannel operations require an integrated CRM system with a centralized customer data warehouse that houses a complete history of each customer's interaction with the retailer, regardless of whether the sale occurred in a store, on the Internet, or on the telephone.[34] This information storehouse allows retailers to efficiently handle complaints, expedite returns, target future promotions, and provide a seamless experience for customers when they interact with the retailer through multiple channels.

## Brand Image

Retailers need to provide a consistent brand image across all channels. For example, Patagonia reinforces its image of selling high-quality, environmentally friendly sports equipment in its stores, from its catalogs, and on its website. Each of these channels emphasizes function, not fashion, in the descriptions of Patagonia's products. Patagonia's position about taking care of the environment is communicated by carefully lighting its stores and using recycled polyester and organic, rather than pesticide-intensive, cotton in many of its clothes.

*Multichannel retailers like Patagonia sell on the Internet (left), in catalogs (right), and in stores (bottom).*

## Pricing

Pricing represents another difficult decision for a multichannel retailer. Customers expect pricing consistency for the same SKU across channels (excluding shipping charges and sales tax). However, in some cases, retailers need to adjust their pricing strategy because of the competition they face in different channels. For example, Barnes & Noble offers lower prices through its Internet channel (www.bn.com) than within its stores to compete effectively against Amazon.com.

Retailers with stores in multiple markets often set different prices for the same merchandise to compete better with local stores. Customers generally are not aware of these price differences because they are only exposed to the prices in their local markets. However, multichannel retailers may have difficulties sustaining these regional price differences when customers can easily check prices on the Internet.

## Supply Chain

Multichannel retailers struggle to provide an integrated shopping experience across all their channels, because unique skills and resources are needed to manage each channel.[35] For example, store-based retail chains operate and manage many stores, each requiring the management of inventory and people. With Internet and catalog operations, inventory and telephone salespeople instead are typically centralized in one or two locations. Also, retail distribution centers (DCs) supporting a store channel are designed to ship many cartons of merchandise to stores. In contrast, the DCs supporting a catalog and Internet channel are designed to ship a few items to individual customers. The difference in shipping orientation for the two types of operations requires a completely different type of distribution center.

Due to these operational differences, many store-based retailers have a separate organization to manage their Internet and catalog operations. But as the multichannel operation matures, retailers tend to integrate all operations under one organization. For example, both Walmart and JCPenney initially had separate organizations for their Internet channel but subsequently integrated them with stores and catalogs.

## Summing Up

**LO1 Discuss the four factors manufacturers should consider as they develop their strategy for working with retailers.**

When they initiate the decision process for choosing retail partners, manufacturers determine how likely it is that certain retailers would carry their products and whether target customers expect to find their products for sale at those retail locations. Next, manufacturers need to identify types of retailers that would be appropriate locations for their products. After identifying likely and appropriate retailers, manufacturers work with their retailer partners to develop a strategy that comprises the four Ps. Finally, manufacturers, again with their retail partners, must determine which elements of a multichannel strategy will be effective. Manufacturers often make these decisions simultaneously or in varying orders.

**LO2 Outline the considerations for choosing retail partners.**

Manufacturers often start by noting the basic channel structure, which includes the level of vertical integration, the relative strength of the retailer and the manufacturer, and the strength of the brand. They also consider where their target customers expect to find products, which depends largely on the retailer's image. Channel member characteristics also are important inputs, as is the level of distribution intensity.

**LO3 List the three levels of distribution intensity.**

Intensive distribution intensity means the product is available virtually everywhere, in as many places as will agree to carry it. In an exclusive distribution intensity strategy, the manufacturer allows only one retailer (or retail chain) in each area to sell its products. Selective distribution is the middle ground option; several retailers carry the products, but not all of them.

**LO4 Describe the various types of retailers.**

Retailers generally fall into one of three categories: food retailers, general merchandise retailers, or service retailers. Each of the categories consists of various formats, including supermarkets, supercenters, warehouse clubs, convenience stores, department stores, discount stores, specialty retailers, drugstores, category specialists, extreme value retailers, and off-price stores. Although service retailers primarily sell services, if they sell to consumers, they are still retailers. Service retailers include everything from universities to automobile oil change shops.

**LO5 Describe the components of a retail strategy.**

To develop a coordinated strategy—which represents a key goal for an effective channel partnership between retailers and manufacturers—both retailers and manufacturers need to consider all the four Ps in conjunction: product, place, promotion, and price.

**L06**　**Identify the benefits of stores.**

Because consumers often have just a general idea of what they want to purchase, stores' main benefits come from giving shoppers a place to browse. They can touch and feel products, obtain personal services, pay using cash or credit, engage in an entertaining and social experience, receive instant gratification, and reduce their sense of risk.

**L07**　**Identify the benefits of multichannel retailing.**

The various types of retail channels—stores, catalogs, and the Internet—all offer their own benefits but also have their limitations, including benefits and limitations related to availability, convenience, and safety, among others. If a retailer adopts a multichannel strategy, it can exploit the benefits and mitigate the limitations of each channel in order to expand overall market presence. A multichannel strategy offers the chance to gain a greater "share of customers' wallet" and may provide more insight into their buying behaviors.

**L08**　**Detail the challenges of multichannel retailing.**

To function in multiple channels, retailers must organize their operations carefully to ensure an integrated customer experience. In particular, they must have an integrated CRM system and determine how to maintain a consistent brand image across the various channels, whether to charge the same or different prices, and how best to deliver merchandise to multiple channels.

---

## Key Terms

- big box retailers, 484
- cannibalization, 495
- category killers, 484
- category specialists, 484
- close-out retailers, 486
- convenience stores, 481
- conventional supermarket, 479
- cookie, 495
- department stores, 482
- distribution intensity, 477
- drugstores, 484
- exclusive distribution, 478
- extreme value food retailers, 479

- extreme value retailers, 485
- factory outlets, 486
- full-line discount stores, 482
- home improvement center, 485
- intensive distribution, 478
- irregulars, 486
- limited assortment supermarkets, 479
- mobile commerce (M-commerce), 489
- multichannel strategy, 475
- off-price retailers, 486

- online chat, 492
- opt in, 496
- opt out, 496
- outlet stores, 486
- retailing, 474
- selective distribution, 478
- service retailers, 486
- share of wallet, 490
- specialty stores, 483
- stock keeping unit (SKU), 479
- supercenters, 481
- warehouse clubs, 481

---

## Marketing Applications

1. Nike and Puma both make sneakers. Do they pursue an intensive, an exclusive, or a selective distribution intensity strategy? Would you suggest any changes to this strategy?

2. Why don't traditional department stores have the same strong appeal to American consumers that they once enjoyed during their heyday in the last half of the twentieth century? Discuss which types of retailers are now competing with department stores.

3. Assume that adidas, the shoe manufacturer, has decided to sell expensive wristwatches for men and women. What factors should it consider when developing its strategy for choosing retail partners?

4. Some argue that retailers can be eliminated from the distribution channel because they only add costs to the final product without creating any value-added services in the process. Do you agree with this perspective? Are consumers likely to make most purchases directly from manufacturers in the near future? Provide justification for your answers.

5. Assume you have been given some money but told that it must be invested in a retailer's stock. In which type of retailer would you choose to invest? Which specific retailer? Provide a rationale for your answers.

6. Provide examples of how manufacturers work with retailers to jointly plan and implement the four Ps.

7. Why have so many bricks-and-mortar retailers adopted a multichannel strategy?

8. You can purchase apparel at a discount store, specialty store, category specialist, off-price retailer, department store, or Internet-only store. From which of these types of stores do you prefer to buy apparel? Explain why you prefer one type of store over another.

9. Should Britt, a young entrepreneur launching a new line of environmentally friendly (green) cosmetics, sell through a physical store, catalog, or the Internet? Explain two key benefits of each channel for her business.

10. Search the Internet for a product you want to buy. Is there a difference in the prices, shipping charges, or return policies among the different retailers offering the product? From which retailer would you buy? Explain the criteria you would use to make the decision.

11. Name a retailer from which you have received personalized service, product, or promotion offerings online. What form of personalization did you receive? Did the personalization influence your purchase decision? Explain why or why not.

12. Suppose you are the candy buyer for a regional chain of grocery stores. The store policy is to charge a "substantial" slotting fee for the placement of new items. Slotting fees were originally designed to cover the costs of placing new products on the shelves, such as adjustments to computer systems and realignment of warehouse and store space. Over the years, these fees have become larger, and they are now a significant source of revenue for the chain. A local minority-owned manufacturer of a popular brand of specialty candy would like to sell to your chain, but claims that the slotting fee is too high and does not reflect the real cost of adding their candy. Discuss the ethical implications of such a policy. What should the chain do?

---

www.mhhe.com/
grewal3e

## Quiz Yourself

1. The Gap, Lenscrafters, and Foot Locker are all examples of:
   a. department stores.
   b. off-price retailers.
   c. discount stores.
   d. specialty stores.
   e. extreme value retailers.

2. Walmart and Target dominate the _____ industry in the United States.
   a. department store

   b. off-price retailer
   c. discount store
   d. specialty store
   e. category specialist

(Answers to these two questions are provided on page 608.)

Go to www.mhhe.com/grewal3e to practice an additional 11 questions.

---

## Net Savvy

1. How do Jcrew.com and Gap.com provide value to their customers beyond the physical products that they sell? Why would a customer purchase online instead of going to the store? Under what circumstances would the customer prefer a store experience?

2. Select a familiar multichannel retailer. Evaluate its website in terms of how well it provides value to its customers. Do you believe that offering multiple selling channels to customers enhances their shopping experience? How does it help the retailer? Explain your answer.

---

## Chapter Case Study

### STAPLES, INC.[36]

Staples operates in the highly competitive office products market.[37] The office supply category specialists, including Staples, Office Depot, and Office Max (the big three), dramatically changed the landscape of the office supply industry. First, they greatly expanded the use of retail stores and Internet channels as means of distributing office supply products, capitalizing in part on the significant increase in the number of home offices. Prior to the mid-1980s, office supply customers primarily placed their orders through commissioned salespeople or catalogs.

Warehouse clubs, supermarkets, and full-line discount retailers have begun taking market share away from the big three office supply retailers because of their ability to sell the bulk items at lower prices. Retailers such as Walmart and Costco offer low prices on office supplies, which forces the major office supply retailers to offer more than just products, such as extra services and greater customer service. The big three office supply stores have also expanded their business-to-business (B2B) efforts to sell to other companies, such as Wells Fargo or IBM. Staples Advantage, for example, offers a range of products and services to its more than 66,000 B2B customers.[38]

## COMPANY BACKGROUND

Originally opened in 1986 by executive-turned-entrepreneur Tom Stemberg, Staples has reached sales of greater than $23 billion.[39] Staples also has been credited with pioneering the high-volume office products superstore concept. By evolving its original mission of slashing the costs and eliminating the hassles of running an office, to making it easy to buy office products, Staples has become the world's largest office products company.

To distinguish itself in this competitive industry, Staples strives to provide a unique shopping experience to customers in all its market segments. Central to maintaining customer satisfaction is developing strong customer relationship skills and broad knowledge about office products among all associates hired by the company. Therefore, Staples includes formal training as an integral part of the development of its associates.

Another truly important aspect of customer service is the availability of merchandise. In the office supply industry, customers have very specific needs, such as finding an ink cartridge for a particular printer, and if the store is out of stock of a needed item, the customer may never come back.

Staples uses various marketing channels to address the needs of its different segments. Smaller businesses are generally served by a combination of retail stores, the catalog, and the Internet. Retail operations focus on serving the needs of consumers and small businesses, especially through an in-store kiosk that enables customers to order a product that may not be available in the store and receive the product via overnight delivery. In-store kiosks allow them to choose to have the product delivered to their home, business, or local store. If a customer does not want to shop in the store, he or she can visit Staples.com to order required products and select from a much larger assortment. The typical Staples retail store maintains approximately 8,000 stock keeping units (SKUs), but Staples.com offers more than 45,000 SKUs. This multichannel approach allows Staples to increase its productivity by stocking only more popular items in stores but not sacrificing product availability.

## MULTICHANNEL INTEGRATION

Staples' overall goal has been to become the leading office products and service provider by combining its existing experience, extensive distribution infrastructure, and customer service expertise with Web-based information technology. As a result, the integration of different channels of distribution into one seamless customer experience has been of particular interest to the company. Staples, like many other multichannel retailers, has found that many customers use multiple channels to make their Staples purchases and that sales increase when customers use more than one channel (e.g., customers that shop two channels spend twice as much as a single-channel shopper; a tri-channel shopper spends about three times as much as a

*Staples adds value to its customers with services like its Copy and Print centers.*

single-channel shopper). Therefore, the greater the number of channels a particular customer shops, the greater the overall expenditures he or she is likely to make.

Staples faces several challenges in integrating its channels of distribution, however, most of which are related to its Internet channel. First, it must consider the extent to which the Internet may cannibalize its retail store sales. The most attractive aspect of the Internet is its potential to attract new customers and sell more to existing customers. But if overall sales are flat—that is, if online retailing only converts retail store sales to Internet sales—Staples suffers increased overhead costs and poorer overall productivity. Second, Staples must be concerned about the merchandise position of its retail stores compared with that of alternative channels. Because a retail store cannot carry as much merchandise as the Internet channel, the challenge is to keep an appropriate balance between minimizing stockouts and avoiding the proliferation of too many SKUs in retail stores. Finally, Staples has to contend with price competition, both within its own multichannel organization and from competitors.

### STAPLES' ADDED SERVICES[40]

Such competition means that Staples must continue to differentiate itself from other office supply retailers by adding extra value to office supplies, which themselves represent commoditized products. For example, its Copy and Print centers within its big box stores enable customers to order print jobs and receive the help of an in-store print specialist. To increase this business line further, Staples also has opened stand alone Staples Copy and Print centers, which are approximately 2,000 square feet, compared with its typical 30,000-square-foot big box stores. The small size of these stores allows them to be located in metropolitan areas or places where there would not be sufficient space for a large, big box store. Customers can order their copies through the Staples website, then pick them up in the store or have them delivered. The Copy and Print stores also sell basic office supply products that customers may need to pick up at the last minute when they come to collect their print orders.

### Questions

1. Assess the extent to which Staples has developed a successful multichannel strategy. What factors have contributed to its success?

2. What are the advantages and disadvantages of using kiosks as a part of its approach?

3. How should Staples assess which SKUs to keep in its stores versus on the Internet?

4. How do the Staples Copy and Print centers differentiate it from the competition?

# VALUE COMMUNICATION

**CHAPTER 17**
Integrated Marketing Communications

**CHAPTER 18**
Advertising, Public Relations, and Sales Promotions

**CHAPTER 19**
Personal Selling and Sales Management

In Section Seven we explore value communication. Today, value communication methods are more complex because of new technologies that have added e-mail, blogs, Internet, and podcasts to the advertising mix that once utilized only radio, television, newspapers, and magazines to relay messages to consumers. Chapter 17 introduces the breadth of integrated marketing communications. Chapter 18 discusses advertising, public relations, and sales promotions. Chapter 19 covers personal selling.

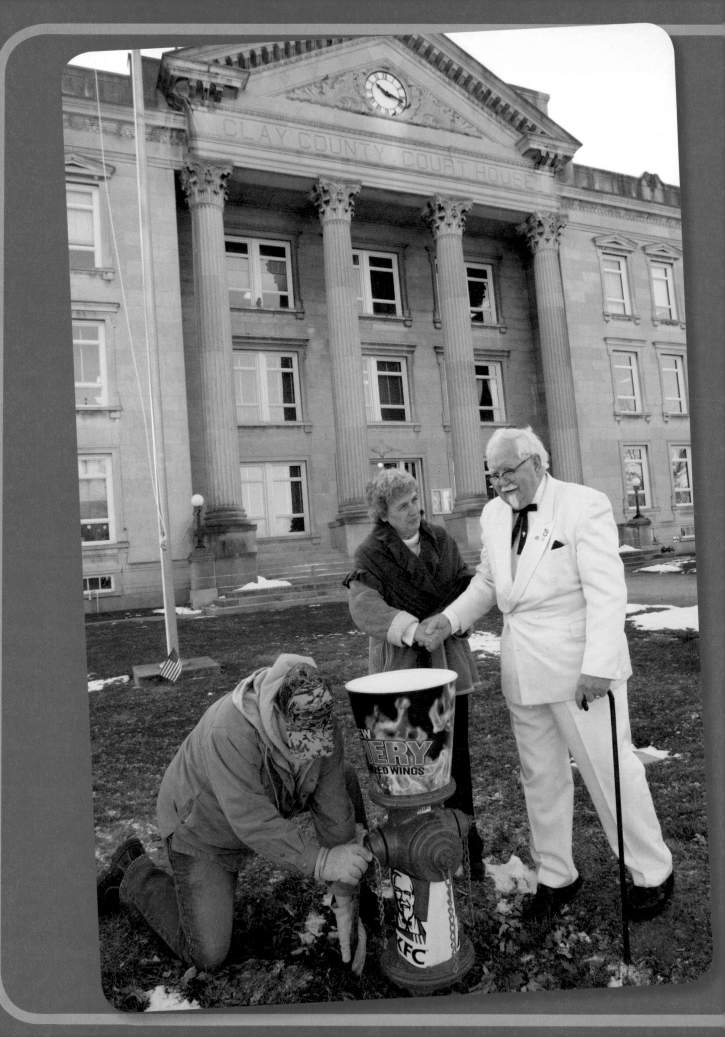

# Integrated Marketing Communications

The incredible expansion of the Internet and online tools have radically changed advertising. More and more, companies spread their messages over all sorts of media—television, print, radio, e-mail, the Internet—and as marketers "think outside the box," the list keeps growing. To really stand out then, a company may need to go ever farther than before.

To achieve success in a market, companies invariably must communicate the value of their offerings in diverse but well-rounded ways. When KFC introduced its "fiery" chicken wings in 2010, it launched television ads, it hung signs in stores, and it touted the new offering on its website. All the communications highlighted the spiciness of the wings and the excitement of the new menu addition.

Then the fast-food giant went a step farther along the line of its new "fiery" theme. Specifically, it paid two cities, Indianapolis and Brazil, Indiana, for the right to paste Colonel Sanders's face on their fire hydrants and city fire extinguishers. Advertisements have appeared for years on other forms of city property, such as benches and mass transit, but this campaign may be the first to appear on emergency equipment.

The campaign maintained a consistent image of KFC as a caring corporation. The money earned from the advertisements on the fire equipment enabled the 8,600-resident Brazil, Indiana, to repair dozens of out-of-service hydrants. In a fiscal situation that the city's Mayor Ann Bradshaw called "not very good," the offer appeared welcome. In Indianapolis, the funds are helping the cash-strapped city "offset some of our budget costs."

As KFC itself noted, "With January being the peak month for residential fires, KFC wanted to raise awareness about this important issue and launch our new KFC Fiery Grilled Wings by supporting local fire departments nationwide.... This unique marketing concept will help pay for new fire extinguishers and fire hydrants in cities in exchange for branding the equipment with Fiery Grilled Wings logos."[1]

Such forms of alternative, but integrated, marketing may become more and more common as people become immune to

## LEARNING OBJECTIVES

**LO1** Identify the components of the communication process.

**LO2** Explain the four steps in the AIDA model.

**LO3** Describe the various integrative communication channels.

**LO4** Explain the various ways used to allocate the IMC budget.

**LO5** Identify marketing metrics used to measure integrated marketing communications (IMC) success.

more traditional forms of marketing communications. In general, "People ignore advertising, they try to get away from it whenever possible," according to Laura Ries, president of the marketing consulting firm Ries & Ries. But KFC wants customers to see its promotions not merely as advertisements but instead as evidence of how it helps communities. Its assistance could also come in the form of fixing potholes and then chalking them with the slogan "Re-Freshed by KFC" or paying for new fire extinguishers or promising a low-calorie meal to customers worried about healthy eating.

In all cases, the message is the same: KFC provides delicious, sometimes spicy food, even as it helps customers and communities.[2]

● ● ●

As the innovative KFC campaign attests, each element of an integrated marketing communication (IMC) strategy must have a well-defined purpose and should support and extend the message delivered by all the other elements. The advertisements in traditional media made consumers aware of the new product. Store signs prompted customers in the franchise's outlets to buy the new offer. The KFC website offered coupons and information. And by adding wraparound signs to a few hydrants and extinguishers in a couple of Midwestern towns, KFC got the nation talking, even as it improved its image as an innovator and caring member of the community. (For a description of how another fast-food chain uses some notably similar elements to create its latest integrated campaign, see the Chapter 18 Case Study, which details the "Whopper Virgins" and "Whopper Sacrifice" campaigns.)

Throughout this book, we have focused our attention on how firms create value by developing products and services. However, consumers are not likely to come flocking to new products and services unless they are aware of them. Therefore, marketers must consider how to communicate the value of a new product and/or service—or more specifically, the value proposition—to the target market. A firm must develop a communication strategy to demonstrate the value of its product. We begin our consideration by examining what IMC is, how it has developed, and how it contributes to value creation.

Integrated marketing communications (IMC) represents the Promotion P of the four Ps. It encompasses a variety of communication disciplines—advertising, personal selling, sales promotion, public relations, direct marketing, and online marketing including social media—in combination to provide clarity, consistency, and maximum communicative impact.[3] Instead of consisting of separated marketing communication elements with no unified control, IMC programs regard each of the firm's marketing communications elements as part of a whole, each of which offers a different means to connect with the target audience. This integration of elements provides the firm with the best means to reach the target audience with the desired message, and it enhances the value story by offering a clear and consistent message.

There are three elements in any IMC strategy: the consumer, the channels through which the message is communicated, and the evaluation of the results of the communication. This chapter is organized around these three elements. In the first section, the focus is on consumers; we examine how consumers receive communications, whether via media or other methods, as well as how the delivery of that communication affects a message's form and contents. The second section examines the various communication channels that make up the components of IMC and how each is used in an overall IMC strategy. The third section considers how the level of complexity in IMC strategies leads marketers to design new ways to measure the results of IMC campaigns.

# COMMUNICATING WITH CONSUMERS

**L01** Identify the components of the communication process.

As the number of communication media has increased, the task of understanding how best to reach target consumers has become far more complex. In this section, we examine a model that describes how communications go from the firm to the consumer and the factors that affect the way the consumer perceives the message. Then we look at how marketing communications influence consumers—from making them aware that a product or service exists to moving them to buy.

## The Communication Process

Exhibit 17.1 illustrates the communication process. Let's first define each component and then discuss how they interact.

**The Sender** The message originates from the sender, who must be clearly identified to the intended audience. For instance, an organization such as Home Depot working with one of its vendors, Stanley Tools, can send a message that it is having a special Father's Day sale.

**The Transmitter** The sender works with the creative department, whether in-house or from a marketing (or advertising) agency, to develop marketing communications. Stanley Tools likely develops ad material with its advertising agency and provides the material to Home Depot. Such an agency or intermediary is the transmitter.

**Encoding** Encoding means converting the sender's ideas into a message, which could be verbal, visual, or both. Home Depot may take out full-page ads in every major newspaper proclaiming: "Amazing Father's Day Deals at 25 Percent Off!" A television commercial showing men examining and testing tools at Home Depot is another way to encode the message that "there are great deals to be had." As the old saying goes, a picture can be worth a thousand words. But the most important facet of encoding is not what is sent but rather what is received. Home Depot shoppers must believe that the sale is substantial enough to warrant a trip to a store.

**The Communication Channel** The communication channel is the medium—print, broadcast, the Internet—that carries the message. Home Depot could transmit through television, radio, and various print advertisements, and it realizes that the media chosen must be appropriate to connect itself (the sender) with its desired recipient. So Home Depot might advertise on HGTV and in *Better Homes and Gardens*.

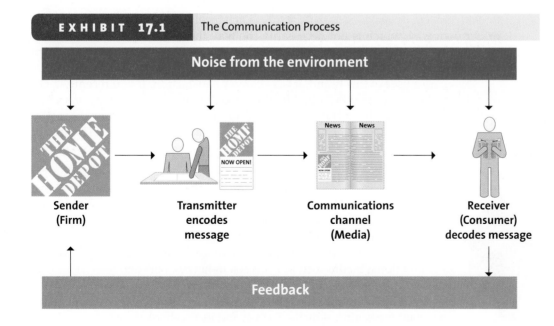

**EXHIBIT 17.1** The Communication Process

Noise from the environment

Sender (Firm) → Transmitter encodes message → Communications channel (Media) → Receiver (Consumer) decodes message

Feedback

CREATE A RECIPE FOR YOUR NEW KITCHEN

THEN SAVOR THE SAVINGS

**NKBA** A beautifully updated kitchen is now more affordable than ever before, with low prices on special-order cabinets and countertops. This includes our exclusive Thomasville Cabinetry, like Blakely Maple shown in Cranberry and River Rock finishes, and Silestone countertop in Sierra Madre. The bigger your kitchen project, the more money you'll save. Get started in-store or online with our free kitchen design services. **That's the power of The Home Depot.**

Get started at homedepot.com/getstarted

More saving. **More doing.**

*Which component of the communication process does this Home Depot ad exemplify?*

**The Receiver** The receiver is the person who reads, hears, or sees and processes the information contained in the message and/or advertisement. The sender, of course, hopes that the person receiving it will be the one for whom it was originally intended. For example, Home Depot wants its message received and decoded properly by the families of fathers who are likely to shop in its stores. Decoding refers to the process by which the receiver interprets the sender's message.

**Noise** Noise is any interference that stems from competing messages, a lack of clarity in the message, or a flaw in the medium, and it poses a problem for all communication channels. Home Depot may choose to advertise in newspapers that its target market doesn't read, which means the rate at which the message is received by those to whom it has relevance has been slowed considerably. As we have already defined, encoding is what the sender intends to say, and decoding is what the receiver hears. If there is a difference between them, it is probably due to noise.

**Feedback Loop** The feedback loop allows the receiver to communicate with the sender and thereby informs the sender whether the message was received and decoded properly. Feedback can take many forms: a customer's purchase of the item, a complaint or compliment, the redemption of a coupon or rebate, and so forth. If Home Depot observes an increase in store traffic and sales, its managers know that their intended audience received the message and understood that there were great Father's Day bargains to be found in the store.

## How Consumers Perceive Communication

The actual communication process is not as simple as the model in Exhibit 17.1 implies. Each receiver may interpret the sender's message differently, and senders often adjust their message according to the medium used and the receivers' level of knowledge about the product or service.

**Receivers Decode Messages Differently** Each receiver decodes a message in his or her own way, which is not necessarily the way the sender intended. Different people shown the same message will often take radically different meanings from it. For example, what does the image on the left convey to you?

If you are a user of this brand, it may convey satisfaction. If you recently went on a diet and gave up your favorite Mexican food, it may convey dismay or a sense of loss. If you have chosen to be a nonuser, it may convey some disgust. If you are a recently terminated employee, it may convey anger. The sender has little, if any, control over what meaning any individual receiver will take from the message.

**Senders Adjust Messages According to the Medium and Receivers' Traits** Different media communicate in very different ways, so marketers make adjustments to their messages and media depending on whether they want to communicate with suppliers, shareholders, customers, or the general public, as well as the specific segments of those groups.[4] For example, Macy's uses traditional media such as print ads in newspapers and television commercials to communicate to its largest customer group, women, ages 25 to 55. But when communicating with the lucrative Generation Y, its efforts center on instant messaging, e-mails, Twitter, and its Facebook page.[5]

*Online grocery retailer, Peapod, adjusted its communication medium and message to attract more customers.*

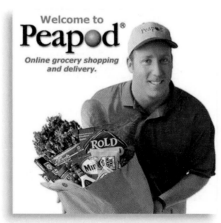

Welcome to **Peapod**®
*Online grocery shopping and delivery.*

*Senders must adjust messages according to the receivers' traits. LG, for instance, uses the ad on the left to target consumers for its Super Blu dual format high-definition player. The LG ad on the right is targeted to the B2B audience. A B2B customer can interact directly with a firm's products using its digital display.*

## The AIDA Model

**L02** Explain the four steps in the AIDA model.

Clearly, IMC is not a straightforward process. After being exposed to a marketing communication, consumers go through several steps before actually buying or taking some other action. There is not always a direct link between a particular marketing communication and a consumer's purchase.

To create effective IMC programs, marketers must understand how marketing communications work. Generally, marketing communications move consumers stepwise through a series of mental stages, for which there are several models. The most common is the AIDA model (Exhibit 17.2),[6] which suggests that Awareness leads to Interest, which leads to Desire, which leads to Action. At each stage, the consumer makes judgments about whether to take the next step in the process. Customers actually have three types of responses, so the AIDA model is also known as the "think, feel, do" model. In making a purchase decision, consumers go through each of the AIDA steps to some degree, but the steps may not always

**EXHIBIT 17.2** The AIDA Model

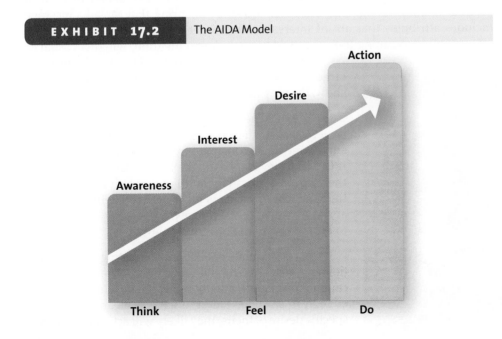

follow the AIDA order. For instance, during an impulse purchase, a consumer may "feel" and "do" before he or she "thinks."

**Awareness** Even the best marketing communication can be wasted if the sender doesn't gain the attention of the consumer first. Brand awareness refers to a potential customer's ability to recognize or recall that the brand name is a particular type of retailer or product/service. Thus, brand awareness is the strength of the link between the brand name and the type of merchandise or service in the minds of customers.

There are a number of awareness metrics, from aided recall to top-of-mind awareness. Aided recall is when consumers indicate they know the brand when the name is presented to them. Top-of-mind awareness, the highest level of awareness, occurs when consumers mention a specific brand name first when they are asked about a product or service. For example, Harley Davidson has top-of-mind awareness if a consumer responds "Harley" when asked about American-made motorcycles. High top-of-mind awareness means that a product or service probably will be carefully considered when customers decide to shop for it. Manufacturers, retailers, and service providers build top-of-mind awareness by having memorable names; repeatedly exposing their name to customers through advertising, locations, and sponsorships; and using memorable symbols.

As an excellent example of the latter method, any time you see two smaller circles sitting atop a larger circle, you likely think of Mickey Mouse ears and Disney. But the company has moved on to images brighter than just some circles and made its name come ever more to the front of young consumers' minds with its stable of teen stars. Starting with Miley Cyrus in 2006, then Selena Gomez in 2007, the Jonas Brothers in 2008, and Demi Lovato in 2009, Disney starts off its stars with Disney Channel shows, records them on the Disney-owned Hollywood Record label, plays the songs in heavy rotation on Radio Disney and Disney movie soundtracks, organizes concert tours with Disney-owned Buena Vista Concerts, and sells tie-in merchandise throughout Disney stores. Each of these marketing elements reminds the various segments of the target market about both the brand (e.g., "Hannah Montana," "Jonas Brothers") and their owner, Disney. With this multichannel approach, Disney gets the same "product" into more markets than would be possible with a more conservative approach—further building top-of-mind awareness for both Disney and its stars.[7]

**Interest** Once the consumer is aware that the company or product exists, communication must work to increase his or her interest level. It isn't enough to let people know that the product exists; consumers must be persuaded that it is a product worth investigating. Marketers do so by ensuring that the ad's message includes attributes that are of interest to the target audience. Disney increases interest in an upcoming tour or record by including a mention, whether casual or not, in the stars' television shows. Because the primary target market for the tour is also probably watching the show, the message gets received by the correct recipient.

**Desire** After the firm has piqued the interest of its target market, the goal of subsequent IMC messages should move the consumer from "I like it" to "I want it." If these Disney stars (e.g., the Jonas Brothers) talk about their upcoming activity and how great it is going to be, the viewing audience is all the more likely to demand access—in this case, probably by begging their parents to buy tickets to the upcoming show.

**Action** The ultimate goal of any marketing communication is to drive the receiver to action. If the message has caught consumers' attention and made them interested enough to consider the product as a means to satisfy a specific desire of theirs, they likely will act on that interest

*If the Jonas Brothers blog about their new album, their fans will want to buy it.*

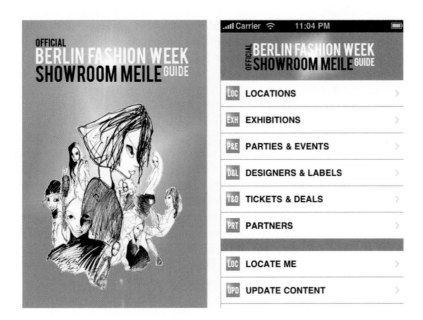

*A lagged effect can occur when, for instance, ads for a new Mercedes-Benz appear in magazines like Berlin's Fashion Week well before it is introduced. As a result, it is difficult to determine which exposure leads to the purchase of a vehicle.*

by either searching for the product or making a purchase. In this case, the young consumers who love the Disney stars prompt their parents to make the actual purchase of a concert ticket or album related to their favorite Disney Channel show.

**The Lagged Effect** Sometimes consumers don't act immediately after receiving a marketing communication because of the lagged effect—a delayed response to a marketing communication campaign. It generally takes several exposures to an ad before a consumer fully processes its message.[8] In turn, measuring the effect of a current campaign becomes more difficult because of the possible lagged response to a previous one.[9] For example, in January 2010, Mercedez-Benz launched its "Is it still a car?" campaign to promote its SLS AMG—a hand-built sports car—with ads in newspapers and television, sponsorship of Berlin's Fashion Week, an online magazine dedicated to the new model, and a new iPhone application. But the car itself would not release until the end of March 2010, so the company would have a hard time determining which exposure actually led consumers to check out or purchase the vehicle.[10]

Now that we've examined various aspects of the communication process, let's look at how specific media are used in an IMC program.

**CHECK YOURSELF**

1.  What are the different steps in the communication process?
2.  What is the AIDA model?

# ELEMENTS OF AN INTEGRATED MARKETING COMMUNICATION STRATEGY

For any communications campaign to succeed, the firm must deliver the right message to the right audience through the right media, with the ultimate goal of profiting from long-term customer relationships rather than just short-term transactions. Reaching the right audience is becoming more difficult, however, as the media environment grows more complicated.[11]

No single channel is necessarily better than another channel; the goal of IMC is to use them in conjunction so that the sum exceeds the total of the individual channels. However, advances in technology have led to a variety of new and traditional media options for consumers, all of which vie for consumers' attention. Print media have also grown and become more specialized. This proliferation of media has led many firms to shift their promotional dollars from advertising to direct marketing, website development, product placements, and other forms of promotion in search of the best way to deliver messages to their target audiences.

 **LO3** Describe the various integrative communication channels.

We now examine the individual elements of IMC and the way each contributes to a successful IMC campaign (see Exhibit 17.3). The elements can be viewed on two axes: passive and interactive (from the consumer's perspective) and offline and online. Some elements (e.g., advertising, sales promotion, public relations, personal selling) are discussed in far more detail in subsequent chapters, so we discuss them only briefly here. Instead, we focus primarily on direct marketing (e-mail, mobile marketing, direct mail, telemarketing) and online marketing (websites, blogs, social media). Note that as the marketer's repertoire of IMC elements has expanded, so too have the ways in which marketers can communicate with their customers. So, for instance, direct marketing appears in all four boxes. Firms have expanded their use of these traditional media (e.g., advertising, public relations, and sales promotions) from pure offline to a combination of offline and online.

## Advertising

Perhaps the most visible of the IMC components, advertising entails the placement of announcements and persuasive messages in time or space purchased in any of the mass media by business firms, nonprofit organizations, government agencies, and individuals who seek to inform and/or persuade members of a particular target market or audience about their products, services, organizations, or ideas.[12] In Chapter 18, we discuss the purpose of advertising and its various types, but for now, we note that advertising is extremely effective for creating awareness of a product or service and generating interest. Mass advertising can entice consumers into a conversation with marketers, though it does not necessarily require much action by consumers, which places it on the passive end of the spectrum. Traditionally, advertising has been passive and offline (e.g., ads on TV, magazines, and newspapers) (see Exhibit 17.3). However, recently there has been a growth in online advertising. However, advertising must break through the clutter of other messages to reach its intended audience. Ethical and Societal Dilemma 17.1 notes the conflict when marketing to children.

**EXHIBIT 17.3** Elements of an IMC Strategy

**Interactive**

- Personal Selling
- Sales Promotions
  (e.g., contests)
- Direct Marketing
  (e.g., telemarketing)

- Direct Marketing
  (e.g., mobile marketing)
- Online Marketing
  (e.g., blogs, social media)

**Offline**    **Online**

- Advertising
- Sales Promotions
  (e.g., coupons)
- Public Relations
- Direct Marketing
  (e.g., catalogs)

- Direct Marketing
  (e.g., e-mail marketing)

**Passive**

# Ethical and Societal Dilemma 17.1

## Who Decides What Is Healthy?

The objective of an integrated marketing communications (IMC) campaign is to build profits by encouraging consumers to purchase more products. But what happens if the campaign leads to harmful behaviors? Companies could claim that shoppers have a choice about the goods they purchase, or assert that marketing influences brand decisions, not eating habits. But marketing directed at children complicates that reasoning, because a fussy child convinced to want certain products by marketing messages that don't tell the whole story can be difficult for parents. Alternatively companies could create healthier products, but in that case, just how is "healthier" defined?

Research shows that childhood and adolescent obesity in the United States is a growing problem.[13] Poor eating habits are clearly a culprit. Even the most well-informed and well-intentioned parent can face a battle in the cereal aisle, where children have been preprogrammed to want the cereals they have seen in television commercials. The advertising is aggressive—before the age of seven, children see an average of 507 cereal ads each year—and these ads affect choices. Research by Yale University's Rudd Center for Food Policy and Obesity and other agencies shows a clear link between the diet and health of young people and food marketing.[14] Exposure is increased through websites like General Mills' Millsberry.com, which offers games centered around Trix, Lucky Charms, and Honey Nut Cheerios, as well as an opportunity to create a virtual buddy and interact with friends in a virtual town. Millsberry promotes healthy living and civic involvement but, ironically, in a world that children access while sitting in front of a computer.[15]

The food industry's SMART CHOICES label is designed for use on foods and beverages that limit "empty calories" such as sugar and fats and include healthy food groups like fruits, whole grains, and vitamins.[16] Yet a healthy choice is a relative term, and most consumers don't know the guidelines for the SMART CHOICE label. The resulting confusion allows some cereal manufacturers to manipulate consumer perceptions about what constitutes a healthy choice. Cinnamon Toast Crunch, for example, meets the criteria for a SMART CHOICE label and has the highest number of ads viewed by children,[17] but do nearly three teaspoons of sugar per three-quarter cup serving translate to healthy? The cereal, which at times has had the highest number of ads viewed by children, is marketed as a good source of calcium and vitamin D and as containing whole grains. Consumers need to read the fine print to discover that it also contains salt and fats and little protein or fiber.

In response to recent public pressure, cereal companies have promised to lower the sugar content in their products, and the largest food manufacturers in the United States have promised to market only "better for you" foods to kids under 12. However, author and teacher Marion Nestle, who has spent her career studying how diet is affected by societal influences,[18] questions whether a minimal reduction in sugar content or a slight bump up in fiber make cereals like Lucky Charms and Froot Loops into health food. Nestle also asks whether a promise to reduce sugar without a deadline attached is a real commitment.[19]

*General Food's Cinnamon Toast Crunch cereal meets the criteria for a SMART CHOICE label, but has nearly three teaspoons of sugar per three-quarter cup serving. Is this cereal really a healthy choice? Should it be advertised to children?*

## Public Relations (PR)

Public relations is the organizational function that manages the firm's communications to achieve a variety of objectives, including building and maintaining a positive image, handling or heading off unfavorable stories or events, and maintaining positive relationships with the media. Like advertising, this tactic is relatively passive, in that customers do not have to take any action to receive it. Public relations activities support the other promotional efforts by the firm by generating "free" media attention, as we discuss further in Chapter 18.

## Sales Promotions

Sales promotions are special incentives or excitement-building programs that encourage the purchase of a product or service, such as coupons, rebates, contests, free samples, and point-of-purchase displays. Marketers typically design these incentives for use in conjunction with other advertising or personal selling programs. Many sales promotions, like free samples or point-of-purchase displays, are designed to build short-term sales, though others, like contests and sweepstakes, have become integral components of firms' CRM programs as means to build customer loyalty. We discuss such sales promotions in more detail in Chapter 18.

## Personal Selling

Personal selling is the two-way flow of communication between a buyer and a seller that is designed to influence the buyer's purchase decision. Personal selling can take place in various settings: face-to-face, video teleconferencing, on the telephone, or over the Internet. Although consumers don't often interact with professional sales people, personal selling represents an important component of many IMC programs, especially in business-to-business (B2B) settings.

The cost of communicating directly with a potential customer is quite high compared with other forms of promotion, but it is simply the best and most efficient way to sell certain products and services. Customers can buy many products and services without the help of a salesperson, but salespeople simplify the buying process by providing information and services that save customers time and effort. In many cases, sales representatives add significant value, which makes the added expense of employing them worthwhile. We devote Chapter 19 to personal selling and sales management.

In the meantime, technology will continue to improve, and other new means of communicating with consumers will be added to the IMC channel mix. Therefore, for now, let's look at how the components of IMC fit together with marketing metrics to achieve the organization's strategic objectives.

## Direct Marketing

The component of IMC that has received the greatest increase in aggregate spending recently is direct marketing, or marketing that communicates directly with target customers to generate a response or transaction.[20] Direct marketing contains a variety of traditional and new forms of marketing communication initiatives. Traditional direct marketing includes mail and catalogs sent through the mail; direct marketing also includes e-mail and mobile marketing.

Internet-based technologies have had a profound effect on direct marketing initiatives. E-mail, for instance, can be directed to a specific consumer. Firms use e-mail to inform customers of new merchandise and special promotions, confirm the receipt of an order, and indicate when an order has been shipped. Currently available technologies also mean handheld devices can function as a payment medium: Just tap your cell phone, and the transaction occurs in much the same way it occurs with a credit card.[21]

The increased use of customer databases has enabled marketers to identify and track consumers over time and across purchase situations, which has contributed to the rapid growth of direct marketing. Marketers have been able to build these databases, thanks to consumers' increased use of credit and debit cards, store-specific credit and loyalty cards, and online shopping, all of which require the buyer to give the seller personal information that becomes part of its database. Because firms understand customers' purchases better when they possess such information, they can more easily focus their direct marketing efforts appropriately. Ethical and Societal Dilemma 17.2 details both the benefits and the concerns associated with how firms use such information to market to customers one at a time.

Direct marketing retailers try to carefully target their customers so they will be more receptive to their messages. Omaha Steaks, for example, sends e-mail coupons for items that customers have purchased previously, mails slick pictures of gourmet steaks and meal packages to addresses that have received orders in the past, and calls customers personally during likely gift-giving occasions, such as the holidays, to offer to repeat a previous gift order. These different forms of direct marketing demonstrate how this IMC format can vary on both the interactivity and online/offline dimensions of the matrix.

Mobile marketing is marketing through wireless handheld devices, such as cellular telephones.[22] Smartphones have become far more than tools to place calls; they offer a kind of mobile computer with the ability to obtain sports scores, weather, music, videos, and text messages, as well as purchase merchandise. Many consumers conceive of their handheld devices as a way to stay in touch with friends, making them largely resistant to the idea of receiving marketing messages on them.[24] Marketing success rests on integrating marketing communications with fun, useful apps that are consistent with these consumer attitudes toward mobile

## Ethical and Societal Dilemma 17.2

### Identifying Web Users

Whereas once companies bought ads on websites related to the product being promoted (e.g., a healthy drink on the GNC website), more targeted advertising now pursues a particular customer rather than all visitors to a particular site.[23] For instance, a behavioral advertising firm like Tacoda can track how a person moves through a Web browser, so that it knows when the user frequents certain sites and thus can determine the particular interests of that consumer. On the basis of the consumer's interests, Tacoda then strategically places advertising on specific sites—but only on that person's browser. Another person who goes to the same website at the same time will receive a different ad, more in line with his or her own interests.

In a nod to privacy concerns, this method of targeted advertising does not provide personal profiles of consumers but rather information about their search activity on the browser. Even when multiple users employ the same computer, advertising firms can distinguish patterns and identify which user is at the computer at certain times. So for instance, if you share your computer with your roommate, advertisers know which of you is using the computer at a particular time, given your browsing habits. Those consumers who do not want their preferences passed on can opt out by changing their browser settings.

As beneficial as this tracking technology may seem for advertisers, it also might enable clever hackers to target computer browsers more easily. If it falls into the wrong hands, information about consumers' browsing and purchasing habits might allow others to impose on users' privacy and security. Furthermore, the technology currently requires consumers to opt out, rather than asking them to opt in, which may leave some consumers unaware of all to which they are agreeing when they employ these sites.

Are consumers' personal privacy rights being unjustly invaded by firms that provide them with targeted advertising based on their browsing habits? Or are the advertising firms engaged in these activities just providing them with helpful information that may make their buying decisions more pleasant and efficient?

*Using the RedLaser shopping comparison application, which lists the prices for that item at various local retailers, consumers take a picture of a product's barcode using their iPhone.*

devices. In response, firms are steadily improving customers' potential experience with their mobile interface.

For example, the RedLaser shopping comparison application for the iPhone takes a picture of a product's bar code and lists the prices for that item available at various local retailers. Google Shopper has the same capability for the Android. NearbyNow and Amazon's mobile applications allow users to buy products and complete their transaction through their cell phones.

Foursquare and WeReward target and send mobile phone users marketing messages based on GPS technology. Started by a video game aficionado,[25] Foursquare awards points to consumers who try local businesses, enabling them to unlock "badges" and earn titles, such as the Mayor of a particular venue.[26] These badges and titles entitle the recipient to discounts or special offers. For example, Starbucks Mayors can unlock their offer to get a $1 discount on a Frappuccino.[27] The application is based on GPS locations, so users can recommend to friends that they visit nearby businesses too. Furthermore, the application's data analytics capabilities allow marketers to track the impact of mobile marketing campaigns. Similarly, WeReward's TechCrunch Disrupt dispenses points for visits to businesses or completed tasks.[28] These points then can be exchanged on the WeReward site for money. The free app requires an iPhone and a Twitter, Facebook, or Foursquare account.

Dozens of other companies are jumping on this mobile phone bandwagon and blasting out messages, for anything from presidential campaigns to pizza specials. Some apps send coupons for nearby businesses, without additional entertainment or requiring the user to participate actively; others give users the means to send themselves desired coupons.

But despite the promise of mobile commerce, it continues to have its drawbacks. One recent study found that 90 percent of U.S. survey respondents had absolutely no interest in receiving mobile ads.[29] Combining geographic location services with social media could increase crime rates;[30] for example, burglars would know how far away from home home owners are, and kidnappers could learn the exact location of young children. Some disreputable companies have hacked into the system and distributed unwanted text messages, harming public

*Foursquare targets and sends mobile phone users marketing messages using GPS technology. It awards points to consumers who check in at local businesses, which entitles them to discounts or special offers.*

*Visitors to theknot.com are part of a community of customers interested in everything having to do with getting married and planning a wedding.*

perceptions of mobile commerce. Understanding and addressing these challenges would help marketers access a worldwide audience, in the form of more than 4.6 billion cell phone users.[31]

## Online Marketing

We now examine in greater depth several electronic media vehicles we mentioned previously: websites, blogs, and social media.

**Websites** Firms are increasing their emphasis on communicating with customers through their websites. They use their websites to build their brand image and educate customers about their products or services and where they can be purchased. Retailers and some manufacturers sell merchandise directly to consumers over the Internet. For example, in addition to selling merchandise, Office Depot's website has a Business Resource Center that provides advice and product knowledge, as well as a source of networks to other businesses. There are forms that businesses use to comply with Occupational Safety and Health Act (OSHA) requirements, check job applicant records, estimate cash flow, and develop a sexual harassment policy; workshops for running a business; and local and national business news. By providing this information on its website, Office Depot reinforces its image as the essential source of products, services, and information for small businesses.

Many firms operate websites devoted to community building. These sites offer an opportunity for customers with similar interests to learn about products and services that support their hobbies and share information with others. Visitors to these websites can also post questions seeking information and/or comments about issues, products, and services. For example, at www.theknot.com, a community site targeting couples planning their weddings, a bride-to-be might ask how to handle an overly zealous bachelor party being planned by the best man. Others who have experienced this problem then can post their advice.

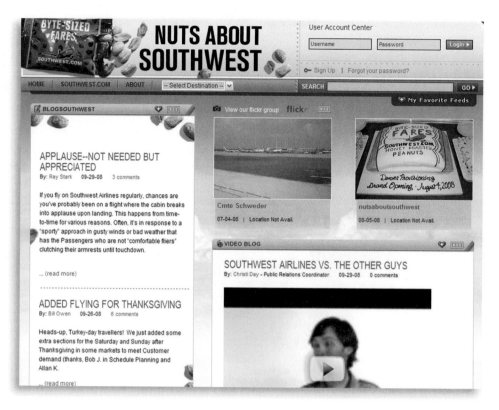

Many firms, especially retailers, encourage customers to post reviews of products they have bought or used and even have visitors to their websites rate the quality of the reviews. Research has shown that these online product reviews increase customer loyalty and provide a competitive advantage for sites that offer them.[32]

**Blogs** A blog (Weblog) contains periodic posts on a common Web page. A well-received blog can communicate trends and special events, create positive word of mouth, connect customers by forming a community, allow the company to respond directly to customers' comments, and develop a long-term relationship with the company. By its very nature, a blog is supposed to be transparent and contain authors' honest observations, which can help customers determine their trust and loyalty levels.

Nowadays, blogs are becoming more interactive as the communication between bloggers and customers has increased. Southwest Airlines' blog, "Nuts about Southwest," is used primarily to connect customers with the company's employees, letting them in on the culture and operations. The corporate contributors include everyone from mechanics to executives to pilots. The blog is also used to announce new product launches and collect information on which to base corporate decisions.[33]

In addition, blogs can be linked to other social media such as Twitter. Consider the situation in which Kevin Smith, the popular director of films such as *Clerks* and *Dogma* and famous for playing Silent Bob in several of his movies, was removed from a Southwest flight because his large size required him to purchase two seats. Smith immediately tweeted about the situation to his more than 1.6 million Twitter followers. Then when he got onto another flight, he followed up with a picture of himself, proclaiming "SouthwestAir! Look how fat I am on your plane! Quick! Throw me off!"[34] Southwest quickly responded on its blog, citing its long-standing rules and concern for other passengers. But the responses have been about equally split in support of the airline and Smith.[35]

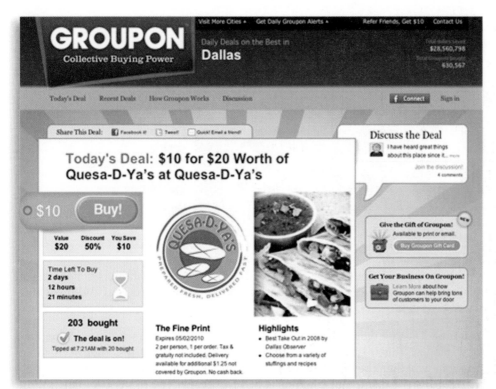

*Groupon alerts its members every day to a deal provided by a retailer or service provider. But the deal doesn't go into effect unless a minimum number of people buy the deal, thus encouraging members to alert their friends through social media sites. If the minimum isn't reached, the deal does not apply.*

**Social Media** Social media is media content distributed through social interactions. Three major online facilitators of social media are YouTube, Facebook, and Twitter. In online social media, consumers review, communicate about, and aggregate information about products, prices, and promotions. This type of social media also allows users to interact among themselves (e.g., form a community). These online communities enable users to provide other like-minded consumers (i.e., members of their community) and marketers their thoughts and evaluations about a firm's products or services. Thus, social media help facilitate the consumer decision process by encouraging need recognition, information search, alternative evaluation, purchase, and postpurchase reviews.

Marketers can use social media to engage their customers in a proactive dialogue with other customers. When a company provides content in a social media website, people often begin sharing and commenting on it. The retailer then must monitor the feedback and respond if necessary—especially if the commentary is negative. When a firm finds an unhappy customer, it should recognize the event as a prime customer service opportunity, engage the consumer, and attempt to remedy the situation. By proactively engaging with its customers, a company can build a stronger brand and customer relationships. Furthermore, companies can develop their brand through social media that depict the company in a certain way, adding a human element that otherwise might not exist. Savvy retailers and manufacturers thus actively leverage the power of online social media and encourage friends to share information. Groupon, for instance, alerts its members to a deal provided by a retailer or service provider every day. For instance, their members in Dallas may wake up to a 50 percent off special for ribs at Sonny Bryan's Barbeque. But the deal doesn't go into effect unless a minimum number of people sign up, thus encouraging members to alert their friends through social media sites. If the minimum isn't reached, the discount does not apply.

Not all social media have positive results though. Social media eliminates boundaries, which often exposes companies to customers' true (and sometimes mean) thoughts and behaviors (e.g., Kevin Smith and Southwest). Furthermore,

The Home Depot has over 6,000 subscribers to its YouTube site with about five million upload views.

a negative posting could elicit a negative response from customers.[36] The largest facilitators of online social media today are YouTube, Facebook, and Twitter, which we discuss next.

**YouTube** On this video-sharing social media platform users upload, share, and view videos. This medium gives companies a chance to express themselves in a different way than they have before. Companies can broadcast their own channel, that is, a YouTube site that contains content relevant only to the company's own products.[37]

YouTube also provides an effective medium for hosting contests and posting instructional videos. The Home Depot has over 6,000 subscribers to its YouTube site with about five million upload views. An array of videos detail new products available in stores, as well as instructional do-it-yourself videos, like "How To Tips for Mowing Your Lawn" or "How To Repair a Toilet."[38] These videos maintain the core identity of the Home Depot brand while also adding value for consumers, who learn useful ways to improve their homes. In this superb example of IMC, Home Depot reinforces its brand image and makes itself more relevant to the consumer's life.

Power of Internet 17.1 highlights how Home Shopping Network (HSN) also uses YouTube to reach shoppers in an exciting new way to maximize the value of its media content.

**Facebook** This social media platform with more than 400 million active users gives companies a forum to interact with fans. Companies have access to the same features that regular users do, including a "wall" where they can post company updates, photos, and videos or participate in a discussion board.

An excellent example of a fan page is that of the value-driven clothing retailer Forever 21:[39] When a fan clicks to indicate that he or she "likes" a certain post, the message gets relayed into a news feed, so every friend of that user sees what he or she likes, creating a huge multiplier effect.[40] Accordingly, marketers must consistently update and maintain their fan pages to exploit them as the tremendous assets they can be.

**Twitter** This microblogging site (users are limited to 140-character messages) is also a platform to facilitate social media. Twitter provides another option for companies and their customers to communicate using social media.

Twitter is actively used by both small and large companies. Small companies with limited marketing budgets love the response they can induce by sending a promotional message immediately. A local bakery tweets, "Two new scones: Lemon Blueberry and Chorizo Cheddar!" and gets responses from 400 Twitter followers—a huge captive audience for a local entity. Even large companies that

## Power of the Internet 17.1 — YouTube and HSN

Begun as a local cable channel in 1982, Home Shopping Network (HSN) offered consumers a central location from which to buy through their televisions.[41] As competition in this field increased, HSN tailored its communication strategy to reach more shoppers. For example, HSN.com was one of the top 10 most visited e-commerce sites in 2009, and its Facebook and MySpace pages fill out HSN's marketing mix. But perhaps the most powerful tool HSN has added to its communications strategy is YouTube.

YouTube videos show up in Google searches, making it an appealing vehicle for retailers,[42] and the site's demographics indicate visitors are affluent, of the age range most appealing to retailers, and racially reflective of the wider U.S. population.[43] By reaching 40–50 percent of the company's target market, YouTube gives HSN a way to interact differently with and further increase its share of wallet with its current customers. The video format humanizes the connection and provides additional information about products.

For example, HSN has a dedicated channel on YouTube that enables it to control the content and look of its page.[44] The site's tracking capabilities also facilitate a deeper understanding of HSN customers,[45] including which other videos and programs attract their attention.

For consumers, YouTube offers a seamless experience. Products promoted on HSN, such as Tori Spelling's jewelry line,[46] are available on YouTube almost immediately after they appear on television. Then HSN marketers can use the information gathered from YouTube to target its direct mail campaigns. For example, it should send jewelry promotions to households that viewed the YouTube video clip for a necklace from the Tori Spelling Collection. Consumer responses get monitored 24/7 and measured against hourly sales goals. There's never a dull moment—it's like the CNN of shopping.

have enough funds to mass market through national campaigns use Twitter as a way to stay in personal touch with their customers.

## CHECK YOURSELF

1. What are the different elements of an IMC program?

When a fan clicks to indicate that he or she "likes" a certain post on Forever21's Facebook page, the message gets relayed into a news feed, so every friend of that user sees what he or she likes, creating a huge multiplier effect.

# PLANNING FOR AND MEASURING IMC SUCCESS

We begin by examining how marketers set strategic goals before implementing any IMC campaign. After they have established those goals, marketers can set the budget for the campaign and choose marketing metrics they will use to evaluate whether it has achieved its strategic objectives.

## Goals

As with any strategic undertaking, firms need to understand the outcome they hope to achieve before they begin. These goals can be short term, such as generating inquiries, increasing awareness, and prompting trial. Or they can be long term in nature, such as increasing sales, market share, and customer loyalty. Selling chicken is always the primary and long-term goal of KFC, but in the short term, its fire hydrant campaign, as described in the chapter's opening vignette, aimed to establish brand awareness and purchase intentions.

These goals, both short and long term, should be explicitly defined and measured. They constitute part of the overall promotional plan, which is usually a subsection of the firm's marketing plan. Another part of the promotional plan is the budget.

**LO4** Explain the various ways used to allocate the IMC budget.

## Setting and Allocating the IMC Budget

Firms use a variety of methods to plan their marketing communications budgets. Because all the methods of setting a promotional budget have both advantages and disadvantages, no one method should be used in isolation.[47]

The objective-and-task method determines the budget required to undertake specific tasks to accomplish communication objectives. To use this method, marketers first establish a set of communication objectives, then determine which media best reach the target market and how much it will cost to run the number and types of communications necessary to achieve the objectives. This process—set objectives, choose media, and determine costs—must be repeated for each product or service. The sum of all the individual communication plan budgets becomes the firm's total marketing communications budget. In addition to the objective-and-task method, various rule-of-thumb methods can be used to set budgets (see Exhibit 17.4).

| **EXHIBIT 17.4** | Rule-of-Thumb Methods | |
|---|---|---|
| **Method** | **Definition** | **Limitations** |
| **Competitive parity** | The communication budget is set so that the firm's share of communication expenses equals its share of the market. | Does not allow firms to exploit the unique opportunities or problems they confront in a market. If all competitors use this method to set communication budgets, their market shares will stay approximately the same over time. |
| **Percentage-of-sales** | The communication budget is a fixed percentage of forecasted sales. | Assumes the same percentage used in the past, or by competitors, is still appropriate for the firm. Does not take into account new plans (e.g., to introduce a new line of products in the current year). |
| **Available budget** | Marketers forecast their sales and expenses, excluding communication, during the budgeting period. The difference between the forecast sales and expenses plus desired profit is reserved for the communication budget. That is, the communication budget is the money available after operating costs and profits have been budgeted. | Assumes communication expenses do not stimulate sales and profit. |

The rule-of-thumb methods shown in Exhibit 17.4 use prior sales and communication activities to determine the present communication budget. Although they are easy to implement, they obviously have various limitations, as noted in the exhibit. Clearly, budgeting is not a simple process. It may take several rounds of negotiations among the various managers, who are each competing for resources for their own areas of responsibility.

## Measuring Success Using Marketing Metrics

Once a firm has decided how to set its budget for marketing communications and its campaigns have been developed and implemented, it reaches the point that it must measure the success of the campaigns, using various marketing metrics.[48] Each step in the IMC process can be measured to determine how effective it has been in motivating consumers to move to the next step in the buying process. However, recall that the lagged effect influences and complicates marketers' evaluations of a promotion's effectiveness, as well as the best way to allocate marketing communications budgets. Because of the cumulative effect of marketing communications, it may take several exposures before consumers are moved to buy, so firms cannot expect too much too soon. They must invest in the marketing communications campaign with the idea that it may not reach its full potential for some time. In the same way, if firms cut marketing communications expenditures, it may take time before they experience a decrease in sales.

**Traditional Media** When measuring IMC success, the firm should examine when and how often consumers have been exposed to various marketing communications. Specifically, they use measures of frequency and reach to gauge consumers' exposure to marketing communications. For most products and situations, a single exposure to a communication is hardly enough to generate the desired response. Therefore, marketers measure the frequency of exposure—how often the audience is exposed to a communication within a specified period of time. The other measure used to measure consumers' exposure to marketing communications is reach, which describes the percentage of the target population exposed to a specific marketing communication, such as an advertisement, at least once.[49] Marketing communications managers usually state their media objectives in terms of gross rating points (GRP), which represents reach multiplied by frequency (GRP = reach × frequency).

GRP can be measured for print, radio, or television, but when they are compared, they must refer to the same medium. Suppose that Kenneth Cole places seven advertisements in *Vogue* magazine, which reaches 50 percent of the "fashion forward" target segment. The total GRP generated by these seven magazine advertisements is 50 reach × 7 advertisements = 350 GRP. Now suppose Kenneth Cole includes 15 television ads as part of the same campaign, run during the program *America's Next Top Model*, which has a rating (reach) of 9.2. The total GRP generated by these 15 advertisements is 138 (9.2 × 15 = 138). However, advertisements

*To calculate the gross rating points for advertising on* America's Next Top Model, *multiply the reach (the percentage of the target population exposed to the ad) times the frequency (how often the audience is exposed to the ad).*

typically appear during more than one television program, so the total GRP actually equals the sum of the GRP generated during *America's Next Top Model* and that which Kenneth Cole gains by advertising during 12 showings of *American Idol*, which earns a rating of 1.8. The total reach then is 138 + (1.8 × 12 = 21.6) = 159.6.

**Web-Based Media** Firms are spending over $24 billion annually on online advertising, which includes paid search, display ads, e-mail, sponsorships, and so forth.[50] Although GRP is an adequate measure for television and radio advertisements, assessing the effectiveness of any Web-based communications efforts in an IMC campaign generally requires Web tracking software to measure how much time viewers spend on particular Web pages, the number of pages they view, how many times users click on banner ads, which website they came from, and so on. All these performance metrics can be easily measured and assessed using a variety of software, including Google analytics.

Facebook also helps companies to see who has been visiting their fan pages, what those people are doing on the fan pages, and who is clicking on their advertisements.[51] By keeping track of who is visiting their fan pages, marketers can better customize the material on their pages by getting to know the people visiting.

## Planning, Implementing, and Evaluating IMC Programs— An Illustration of Google Advertising

Hypothetically, imagine Transit, an upscale sneaker store in New York City modeled after vintage New York City subway trains. Transit's target market is young, well-educated, hip men and women aged 17–34. The owner's experience indicates the importance of personal selling for this market because they (1) make large purchases and (2) seek considerable information before making a decision. Thus, Jay Oliver, the owner, spends part of his communication budget on training his sales associates. Oliver has realized his communication budget is considerably less than that of other sneaker stores in the area. He has therefore decided to concentrate his limited budget on a specific segment and use electronic media exclusively in his IMC program.

The IMC program Oliver has developed emphasizes his store's distinctive image and uses his website, social shopping, and some interesting community building techniques. For instance, he has an extensive customer database (CRM) from which he draws information for matching new merchandise with his customers' past purchase behaviors and little personal nuggets of information that he or other sales associates have collected on the customers. He then e-mails specific customers information about new products that he believes they will be interested in. He also encourages customers to use blogs hosted on his website. Customers chat about the "hot" new sneakers, club events, and races. He does everything with a strong sense of style.

To reach new customers, he is using search engine marketing (SEM). In particular, he is using Google AdWords, a search engine marketing tool offered by Google that allows advertisers to show up in the Sponsored Links section of the search results page based on the keywords potential customers use (see the sponsored link section in the right-hand column of the Google screen grab on page 527).

Oliver must determine the best keywords to use for his sponsored link advertising program. Some potential customers might search using the keywords "sneakers," "sneakers in New York City," "athletic shoes," or other such versions. Using Google AdWords, Oliver can assess the effectiveness of his advertising expenditures by measuring the reach, relevance, and return on investment for each of the keywords that potential customers used during their Internet searches.

To estimate reach, Oliver uses the number of impressions (the number of times the ad appears in front of the user) and the click-through rate (CTR). To calculate CTR, he takes the number of times a user clicks on an ad and divides it by the number of impressions.[52] For example, if a sponsored link was delivered 100 times and 10 people clicked on it, then the number of impressions is 100, the number of clicks is 10, and the CTR would be 10 percent.

The relevance of the ad describes how useful an ad message is to the consumer doing the search. Google provides a measure of relevance through its AdWords system using a Quality Score. This Quality Score looks at a variety of factors to measure how relevant a keyword is to an ad's text and to a user's search query. In general, a high Quality Score means that a keyword will trigger ads in a higher position and at a lower cost per click.[53] In a search for "sneaker store," the Transit ad showed up fourth, suggesting high relevance.

Using the following formula, Oliver also can determine an ad's return on investment (ROI):

$$ROI = \frac{\text{Sales revenue} - \text{Advertising cost}}{\text{Advertising cost}}$$

For the two keyword searches in the table that follows, Oliver finds how much the advertising cost him (Column 3), the sales produced as a result (Column 4), and the ROI (Column 6). For "sneaker store," the Transit website had a lot more clicks than the clicks that were received from "New York City sneakers," 110 versus 40, respectively (Column 2). Even though the sales were lower for the keywords "sneaker store" at \$35/day versus \$40/day for the keywords "New York City sneakers," the ROI was much greater for the "sneaker store" keyword combination. In the future, Oliver should continue this keyword combination in addition to producing others that are similar to it, in the hope that he will attain an even greater return on investment.

| (1) Keyword | (2) Clicks | (3) Cost | (4) Sales | (5) Revenue − Cost (Col. 4 − Col. 3) | (6) ROI (Col. 5 ÷ Col. 3 × 100) |
|---|---|---|---|---|---|
| Sneaker store | 110 | \$10/day | \$35/day | \$25 | 250% |
| New York City sneakers | 40 | \$25/day | \$40/day | \$15 | 60% |

To evaluate his IMC program, Oliver compares the results of the program with his objectives. To measure his program's effectiveness, he conducted an inexpensive online survey using the following questions:

| Communication Objectives | Questions |
|---|---|
| **Awareness** | What stores sell sneakers? |
| **Knowledge** | Which stores would you rate outstanding on the following characteristics? |
| **Attitude** | On your next shopping trip for sneakers, which store would you visit first? |
| **Visit** | Which of the following stores have you been to? |

Here are the survey results for one year:

| Communication Objective | Before Campaign | 6 Months After | One Year After |
|---|---|---|---|
| **Awareness** (% mentioning store) | 38% | 46% | 52% |
| **Knowledge** (% giving outstanding rating for sales assistance) | 9 | 17 | 24 |
| **Attitude** (% first choice) | 13 | 15 | 19 |
| **Visit** (% visited store) | 8 | 15 | 19 |

The results show a steady increase in awareness, knowledge of the store, and choice of the store as a primary source of sneakers. This research provides evidence that the IMC program was conveying the intended message to the target audience.

### CHECK YOURSELF

1. Why is the objective-and-task method of setting an IMC budget better than the rule-of-thumb methods?
2. How would a firm evaluate the effectiveness of its Google advertising?

## Summing Up

**L01** **Identify the components of the communication process.**

The communication process begins with a sender, which provides the message to a transmitter that develops or encodes the message for transmission through a communication channel. When a recipient receives the message, it may have been altered by noise in the environment. To find out, the sender needs to receive some form of feedback from the recipient.

**L02** **Explain the four steps in the AIDA model.**

Awareness is the first "thinking" step, during which the consumer simply recognizes a brand or product. During the interest step, the consumer starts to "feel" and become intrigued enough to explore the product or brand. This interest then leads to another feeling, namely, desire for the marketed item. Finally, to be successful, marketing communication must prompt an action: a purchase, a commitment, a recommendation, or whatever else the company is trying to get consumers to do.

**L03** **Describe the various integrative communication channels.**

Advertising has long been the primary channel for marketing communication and is still a constant presence, but other media channels have become more and more prominent. For example, direct marketing media options, particularly online options, have increased in recent years. Outbound direct marketing telephone calls have declined, but Internet-based technologies like e-mail and M-commerce have increased. Public relations also has become increasingly important as other media forms become more expensive and as consumers grow more skeptical of commercial messages. With regard to new and electronic media, the wealth of recent options include websites, corporate blogs, and social media such as YouTube, Facebook, and Twitter.

**L04** **Explain the various ways used to allocate the IMC budget.**

Various rule-of-thumb methods rely on prior sales and communication activities to determine the best allocation. For example, the competitive parity method sets the budget so that the share of communication expenses equals the firm's share of the market. The percentage-of-sales method, just as it sounds, uses a fixed percentage of sales as the amount of the budget. In contrast, the objective-and-task method establishes specific communication objectives, identifies which media can best attain those objectives, and then determines the related costs to expend.

**L05** **Identify marketing metrics used to measure integrated marketing communications (IMC) success.**

Marketers rely on a mix of traditional and nontraditional measures to determine IMC success. Because potential customers generally need to be exposed to IMC messages several times before they will buy, firms estimate the degree to which customers are exposed to a message by multiplying frequency (the number of times an audience is exposed to a message) by reach (the percentage of the target population exposed to a specific marketing communication). Measuring Internet IMC effectiveness requires different measures, such as click-through tracking that measures how many times users click on banner advertising on websites.

## Key Terms

- advertising, 514
- AIDA model, 511
- aided recall, 512
- blog (Weblog), 520
- brand awareness, 512
- click-through rate (CTR), 527
- communication channel, 509
- decoding, 510
- direct marketing, 516
- encoding, 509
- feedback loop, 510
- frequency, 525

- gross rating points (GRP), 525
- impressions, 527
- integrated marketing communications (IMC), 508
- lagged effect, 513
- mobile marketing, 517
- noise, 510
- objective-and-task method, 524
- personal selling, 516
- public relations, 516
- reach, 525

- receiver, 510
- relevance, 527
- return on investment (ROI), 527
- rule-of-thumb methods, 524
- sales promotions, 516
- search engine marketing (SEM), 526
- sender, 509
- social media 521
- top-of-mind awareness, 512
- transmitter, 509

## Marketing Applications

1. Assume that the contemporary apparel company Juicy Couture has embarked on a new IMC strategy. It has chosen to advertise on TV during the NBC Nightly News and in print in *Time* magazine. The message is designed to announce new styles for the season and uses a 17-year-old woman as the model. Evaluate this strategy.

2. Using the steps in the AIDA model, explain why a potential consumer in question 1 who views Juicy Couture's advertising may not be ready to go out and purchase a new pair of jeans.

3. Suppose a snack company introduces a new product called SumSeeds—sunflower seeds with energy boosters like caffeine, taurine, lysine, and ginseng. How would you expect this product's IMC program to differ from that for regular sunflower seeds sold as snacks?

4. It's holiday time, and you've decided to purchase a jewelry item for the person of your choice at Tiffany & Co. Evaluate how Tiffany's advertising, personal selling, public relations, and electronic media might influence your purchase decision.

How might the relative importance of each of these IMC elements be different if your parents were making the purchase?

5. Suppose you saw your instructor for this course being interviewed on TV about the impact of a big storm on an upcoming holiday's sales. Is this interview part of your college's IMC program? If so, do you believe it benefits the college? How?

6. A retail store places an ad in the local newspaper for yoga wear. The sales of the featured items increase significantly for the next two weeks. Sales in the rest of the sportswear department go up as well. What do you think are the short- and long-term objectives of the ad? Justify your answer.

7. As an intern for Michelin tires, you have been asked to develop an IMC budget. The objective of the IMC strategy is to raise Michelin's market share by 5 percent in the United States in the next 18 months. Your manager explains, "It's real simple; just increase the budget 5 percent over last year's." Evaluate your manager's strategy.

8. You were sitting in the school cafeteria yesterday, and a young man from your marketing class, whom you don't know well, asked if he could sit down. He then started telling you about this very cool new Apple product that allows you to record class lectures and play them back on an MP3 player. Although you recognize the merit in the product, you later find out that he works for Apple. Do you believe his action constitutes an ethical IMC strategy? How will it affect your attitude toward Apple and the potential that you will purchase the product?

## Quiz Yourself

www.mhhe.com/grewal3e

1. Often a(n) _____ accomplishes the task of encoding IMC messages.
   a. advertising agency
   b. consumer interest group
   c. media channel
   d. noise reduction specialist
   e. viral public relations expert

2. Ingrid wants her company to expand its use of public relations. She argues that, as other IMC alternatives become more expensive and _____, public relations should be a larger part of her company's IMC efforts.

   a. online couponing has declined
   b. consumers have become more skeptical of marketing claims
   c. Web tracking software has become more sophisticated
   d. gross rating points have become marginalized
   e. commercial speech has become more effective

(Answers to these two questions are provided on page 608.)

Go to www.mhhe.com/grewal3e to practice an additional 11 questions.

## Net Savvy

1. Visit http://www.thephelpsgroup.com and click on the "Our Work" tab at the top. In the Work Portfolio, compare the IMC for the different companies. What were the goals of the integrated marketing campaign? Which IMC components were used in that particular campaign? How do those components contribute to the success of the IMC campaign in achieving its stated goals?

2. *The Journal of Integrated Marketing Communications*, published annually by graduate students at the Medill School at Northwestern University, attempts to identify best practices and provide "a forum for communications industry professionals and academia to discuss the theory and application of integrated marketing communications." Visit the site at http://jimc.medill.northwestern.edu/JIMCWebsite/site.htm, click on "What Is IMC?" and "IMC Resources." What suggestions does it make? To whom does the site seem targeted?

## Toolkit

### RETURN ON MARKETING EXPENDITURES

Suppose Jay Oliver (marketing manager of Transit sneaker store) is considering two search engine marketing (SEM) options to reach out to new customers to market Transit. In particular, he is using Google AdWords, a search engine marketing tool offered by

Google that allows firms to show up in searches based on the keywords potential customers use. Transit is targeting young adults age 17–28. The sneaker market is about $500,000,000 sales annually, and the target market is about 35% of that. Their gross margins are 20%. Oliver estimates that Transit will capture a 2% market share of the target market with a $500,000 advertising and keyword budget (option 1) and a 3% market share with a $1,000,000 advertising and keyword budget (option 2). Which marketing plan produces the higher ROI for the year? Please use the toolkit provided at www.mhhe.com/grewal3e to assess the ROI of the two options.

| | Chapter Case Study | |
| --- | --- | --- |

## RED BULL GIVES YOU WINGS[54]

**Scene 1:** You're trudging along one day, lost in thought, overwhelmed by all that you have to do this week. The books in your backpack are heavy, your phone keeps beeping to announce new messages from friends and colleagues demanding more from you, and besides all that, the grey weather just has you down. A brightly painted, small SUV with a big can attached to the top screeches to a halt beside you. A young woman, about your age, hops out and hands you a can of Red Bull. "You look like you could use a boost," she says. "Remember, Red Bull gives you wings!"

**Scene 2:** Signs all over town keep promoting an event named with a word you've never heard of: The Flugtag is coming to your town. What in the world is a "Flugtag," and why would anyone attend it? It sounds vaguely German, so you look it up in your German–English dictionary and discover it means "flying day." That sounds intriguing, so you stop by the pier on the advertised date and find the strangest collection of vehicles you've ever seen, all being propelled by people dressed in wild and strange costumes off a 30-foot ramp. Most collapse straight into the water, but a few sort of fly for a few minutes. As you wander closer to a huge silver bus parked near the entrance, a self-described Red Bull roadie hops out to cheer on her favorite team, whom she met during the course of her year traveling the country in this capacity. "Need a Red Bull?" she asks. "Or a pancake? And hey, Red Bull gives you wings."

**Scene 3:** Another long day, and you're vegging out in front of the television. Over the course of the evening, you see a few commercials for Red Bull. One of them shows footage of Shaun White, the Olympic champion, flying through the air on his snowboard (as if he had wings) with a Red Bull helmet over his signature red hair. In another, a man identified as Robbie Maddison rides his dirt bike up a ramp and jumps over the Arc of Paris in Las Vegas, then ends the commercial with a grin and the line, "Welcome to my world. Red Bull gives you wings." Yet another uses animated line drawings to tell a version of the fairy tale about the princess and the frog. In this version, the frog just wants a Red Bull, not a kiss, and after receiving it, flies off, to the frustration of the princess, who mourns, "Red Bull gives you wings."

**Scene 4:** You're out for the night at the local hotspot. The music is loud, the place is crowded, and you'd like to stay all night. In the corner, you spy a neon light surrounding a display case. Inside are rows and rows of shiny Red Bull cans. The bartender, seeing you looking, asks if you'd like one over ice or mixed into an alcoholic beverage. Looking around, you see piles of empty cans on tables, already finished and waiting to be collected. And you note the text on the display case: "Red Bull gives you wings."

In all these scenes, the message remains the same. Can you guess what it is? When Red Bull first launched in 1987, it was limited to Europe. Ten years later, when it spread to the United States for the first time, it already had developed its innovative and unique marketing strategy, which involved opening each market through unique distribution channels, a sense of cool, and widely divergent types of marketing communications that all sent the same message.

Being cool generally means you can't seem like you're trying too hard. So Red Bull has "largely discarded the traditional methods of mass marketing, which many think largely contributes to their mass appeal."[55] For example, rather than getting its name on the mainstream sponsorship opportunities, it supports extreme sports—windsurfing, snowboarding, skateboarding, wakeboarding, cliff-diving, surfing, and Formula-1 racing—as well as art shows, music, and video games.

Thus, when it decided to enter major league, professional sports, it did not follow Jerry Jones into the NFL or Mark Cuban into the NBA. Instead, Red Bull purchased the soccer team New York MetroStars in 2006, along with its stadium, and quickly renamed them both. So the New York Red Bulls play in Red Bull Arena (which opened in 2010). In the same year, it launched Red Bull Racing, a NASCAR team that had expanded to three drivers by 2010.

**Scene 5:**   After all these exposures, you figure you might check out the Red Bull website. It's nearly overwhelming, filled with profiles of sponsored athletes, descriptions of contests, and videos of people enjoying Red Bull. But in among all that you find a link: "Attend Red Bull U." The link takes you to the sister site for Red Bull Student Brand Managers, where you can apply to become an SBM and "bring the Red Bull brand to life in the world of all things college."[56]

As you read further, you find that the gig is not an internship. You would be working for the company, be paid, gain marketing experience, and get a stocked Red Bull mini-fridge to keep in your dorm room—for a minimum commitment of 10 hours per week. You apply, you're accepted, and you're now a Red Bull Student Brand Manager. You're no slacker, and you don't want to go an easy route, just hosting a party or handing out free samples. You want to give people wings. The question is how.

*The Red Bull Chasers driven by Travis Pastrana won and set a new record for the 149-year-old Mt. Washington Auto Race in 2010.*

## Questions

1. As a Student Brand Manager, what event could you sponsor on campus that would resonate with the integrated theme of Red Bull's marketing: "Red Bull gives you wings"?

2. How would you market the event—through what sorts of media?

3. How would you measure the reach of those communications and the success of the event?

   What ethical considerations would you need to address before you invite your fellow students to participate?

Already a Member? Log in Her
eHarmony
Get Matched for Free!
First Name:
I'm a: Woman seeking Men
ZIP Code:
Country: United States
Email:
Note: Your email is used to log back in
Confirm Email:
Password:
Must be at least 5 characters
How did you hear about us? Please select...
Find My Matches
Monica and Josh
MATCHED BY EHARMONY
eHarmony protects your privacy
People cannot "browse" your profile or photos like they can on other dating sites.
Your profile and photos are only seen by a select group - your

# Advertising, Public Relations, and Sales Promotions

I f it ain't broke, don't fix it! This conventional wisdom seems so obvious, and so conventional, that it is the rare company that would go against it. And yet when it comes to their advertising, it seems that more and more companies are going after campaigns that work well in an attempt to make them even more successful.

Consider the eHarmony.com strategy. The company's original advertisements showed a bunch of real couples who described how they fell in love and met through the matchmaking site. The theme was so well disseminated that it received the ultimate compliment: a parody on *Saturday Night Live*. There was no problem with awareness, and the advertising campaign was widely considered a great success.[1]

But eHarmony.com threw it out and started over with ads that aimed to create a more authentic feel by focusing on one couple who talks in depth about their love story and connection. Over time, the company has tinkered with the general formula even further, often combining all the individual couples, whom viewers have come to know and recognize, together in one commercial. Many couples, one couple, or a combination—eHarmony seems unafraid to mix up the plan.

But at least eHarmony kept focus on the same general target market, namely, people looking for love. Another company with widely successful (and parodied) ads for women shook things up during the 2010 Super Bowl by advertising to men instead. A few years ago, Dove made a splash with its "Real Women" campaign that showed actual consumers, rather than rail-thin models, in their underwear. The approach not only generated tremendous buzz for Dove but also prompted a 6 percent increase in sales.[2] Clearly, this campaign worked. So in Super Bowl, Dove changed everything and tried to appeal to men instead. It showed stages in a man's life—birth, childhood, teens, adulthood—and closed with the tagline "Now that you're comfortable with who you are, isn't it time for comfortable skin?"[3]

## LEARNING OBJECTIVES

**LO1** Describe the steps in designing and executing an advertising campaign.

**LO2** Identify three objectives of advertising.

**LO3** Describe the different ways that advertisers appeal to consumers.

**LO4** Identify the various types of media.

**LO5** Identify agencies that regulate advertising.

**LO6** Describe the elements of a public relations toolkit.

**LO7** Identify the various types of sales promotions.

The shift provides another example of continued success; the Dove + Men ad ranked among the top 15 ads shown during the Super Bowl, increased searches for "dove and men" on the Dove website, and earned a 76 percent positive rating among viewers.[4] The buzz is getting further support from Dove's related viral ad campaign—a new tactic on which the company spent more than $153 million in 2009.[5]

Advertising is a paid form of communication, delivered through media from an identifiable source, about an organization, product, service, or idea, designed to persuade the receiver to take some action, now or in the future.[6] This definition provides some important distinctions between advertising and other forms of promotion, which we have discussed in the previous chapter. First, advertising is not free; someone has paid, with money, trade, or other means, to get the message shown. Second, advertising must be carried by some medium—television, radio, print, the Web, T-shirts, sidewalks, and so on. Third, legally, the source of the message must be known or knowable. Fourth, advertising represents a persuasive form of communication, designed to get the consumer to take some action. That desired action can range from "Don't drink and drive" to "Buy a new Mercedes."

Some activities that are called advertising really are not, such as word-of-mouth advertising. Even political advertising technically is not advertising because it is not for commercial purposes and thus is not regulated in the same manner as true advertising.

Advertising encompasses an enormous industry and clearly is the most visible form of marketing communications—so much so that many people think of marketing and advertising as synonymous. Global advertising expenditures are almost $500 billion, and almost half that amount is spent in the United States. Although expenditure has dropped somewhat in the tough economic climate, advertising remains virtually everywhere.[7]

Yet how many of the advertisements you were exposed to yesterday do you remember today? Probably not more than three or four. As you learned in Chapter 5, perception is a highly selective process. Consumers simply screen out messages that are not relevant to them. When you notice an advertisement, you may not react to it. Even if you react to it, you may not remember it later. Even if you do, you still may not remember the brand or sponsor, or, worse yet (from the advertiser's point of view), you may remember it as an advertisement for another product.[8]

To get you to remember their ad and the brand, advertisers must first get your attention. As we discussed in Chapter 17, the increasing number of communication channels and changes in consumers' media usage have made the job of advertisers far more difficult.[9] As our opening examples about eHarmony and Dove demonstrated, advertisers continually endeavor to use creativity and media to reach their target markets.

As a consumer, you are exposed only to the end product—the finished advertisement. But many actions must take place before you actually get to see an ad, as the Toolkit available for this chapter will show you. In this chapter, we examine the ingredients of a successful advertising campaign, from identifying a target audience to creating the actual ad and assessing performance. Although our discussion is generally confined to advertising, much of the process for developing an advertising campaign is applicable to many of the IMC media vehicles discussed in Chapter 17. We conclude our discussion of advertising with regulatory and ethical issues in advertising, then move on to examine public relations and sales promotions and their use.

**EXHIBIT  18.1**    Steps in Planning and Executing an Ad Campaign

| Step 1 | Step 2 | Step 3 | Step 4 | Step 5 | Step 6 | Step 7 |
|--------|--------|--------|--------|--------|--------|--------|
| Identify target audience | Set advertising objectives | Determine the advertising budget | | Evaluate and select media | Create advertisements | Assess impact |

Designing and carrying out a successful advertising program requires much planning and effort. Exhibit 18.1 shows the key steps in the process, each of which helps ensure that the intended message reaches the right audience and has the desired effect. Now let's examine each of these steps.

**LO1**  Describe the steps in designing and executing an advertising campaign.

# STEP 1.  IDENTIFY TARGET AUDIENCE

The success of an advertising program depends on how well the advertiser can identify its target audience. Firms conduct research to identify their target audience, then use the information they gain to set the tone for the advertising program and help them select the media they will use to deliver the message to that audience.

During this research, firms must keep in mind that their target audience may or may not be the same as current users of the product. Think about jewelry. Research shows that in a typical year, some 43 percent of the U.S. adult population—more than 85 million people—purchase jewelry. Although women have a significantly higher purchase incidence (48 percent) than men (36 percent), men spend approximately twice as much on their jewelry purchases than do women. Perhaps it is no surprise that the majority of men's jewelry purchases are gifts for women.[10] So what do these pieces of information tell advertisers? Essentially, if they want to sell jewelry, they need to appeal to either women who will purchase for themselves or men who will purchase for the women in their lives.

Some advertising messages also may be directed at portions of audiences who have not been a traditional part of the marketer's target market but who do have a say in the purchase process. Adding Value 18.1 illustrates Grape Nuts' pursuit of male consumers in particular.

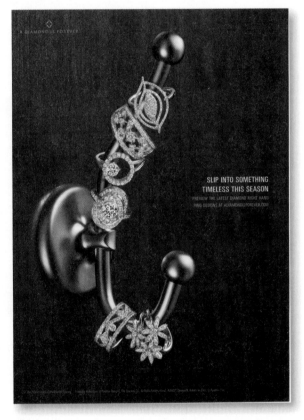

SLIP INTO SOMETHING TIMELESS THIS SEASON

*Who is the target audience for this ad, men or women?*

# STEP 2.  SET ADVERTISING OBJECTIVES

Advertising campaign objectives are derived from the overall objectives of the marketing program and clarify the specific goals that the ads are designed to accomplish. Generally, these objectives appear in the advertising plan, a subsection of the firm's overall marketing plan that explicitly analyzes the marketing and advertising situation, identifies the objectives of the advertising campaign, clarifies a specific strategy for accomplishing those objectives, and indicates how the firm can determine whether the campaign was successful.[11] An advertising plan is crucial because it will later serve as the yardstick against which advertising success or failure is measured.

## Adding Value 18.1    Going Nuts over Men

In the fiercely competitive ready-to-eat breakfast cereal category, Kellogg's and General Mills are the two largest players. Yet Grape Nuts, the Post-owned brand, is initiating a new advertising campaign, with new positioning and a differentiated approach that may alter the cereal category overall. Specifically, Grape Nuts is going after men!

The brand formerly was marketed to women and families who would eat breakfast together. Most cereal brands have followed a similar pattern of domestic positioning. And Grape Nuts marketing executives have kept this strategy, despite market knowledge showing that the product is and always has been eaten mostly by men. Moreover, Grape Nuts has seen a sales decrease of 15 percent in the past year.

The newest advertising devices attempt to entertain and give men a hearty chuckle. Dozens of Webisodes feature ESPN's Kenny Mayne in the voiceover. An MSN site contains

features like "The Guy's Manual," with tips on how to restore vintage cars, as well as how to "look cool driving a minivan." New print ads, running in *Sports Illustrated*, depict men fishing and golfing, with a tongue-in-cheek slogan: "That Takes Grape Nuts." The idea is that Grape Nuts is a masculine cereal—a "power food."

Despite the innovativeness of this advertising campaign though, Grape Nuts executives might have forgotten about the primary household shoppers: women. Will this innovative advertising, aimed appropriately at the target market, ultimately translate into sales in the grocery store? To reinforce its message, Grape Nuts will include in-store marketing in a marketing campaign expected to cost $5 million. This campaign and the increase in advertising may just drive women, who actually buy the product, to choose Grape Nuts for the men in their lives.[12]

*In an attempt to sell Grapenuts cereal to men, Post has developed Webisodes like "The Guy's Manual."*

Generally, in advertising to consumers, the objective is a **pull strategy** in which the goal is to get consumers to pull the product into the supply chain by demanding it. **Push strategies** also exist and are designed to increase demand by focusing on wholesalers, retailers, or salespeople. These campaigns attempt to motivate the seller to highlight the product, rather than the products of competitors, and thereby push the product to consumers. In this chapter, we will focus on pull strategies. Push strategies are examined in Chapters 15, 16, and 19.

All advertising campaigns aim to achieve certain objectives: to inform, persuade, and remind customers. Another way of looking at advertising objectives is to examine an ad's focus. Is the ad designed to stimulate demand for a particular product or service, or more broadly for the institution in general? Also, ads can be used to stimulate demand for a product category or an entire industry, or for a specific brand, firm, or item. First we look at the broad overall objectives of inform, persuade, and remind. Then we examine advertising objectives based on the focus of the ad: product versus institutional.

## Informative Advertising

**Informative advertising** is a communication used to create and build brand awareness, with the ultimate goal of moving the consumer through the buying cycle to a purchase. Such advertising helps determine some important early stages of a product's life cycle (see Chapter 11), particularly when consumers have little information about the specific product or type of product. Retailers often use informative advertising to tell their customers about an upcoming sales event or the arrival of new merchandise, as in the advertisement on the right, designed to inform consumers that Macy's has new merchandise available.

## Persuasive Advertising

When a product has gained a certain level of brand awareness, firms use **persuasive advertising**, which is a communication used to motivate consumers to take action. Persuasive advertising generally occurs in the growth and early maturity stages of the product life cycle, when competition is most intense, and attempts to accelerate the market's acceptance of the product. In later stages of the product life cycle, persuasive advertising may be used to reposition an established brand by persuading consumers to change their existing perceptions of the advertised product. Firms, like Cover Girl in the ad below, often use persuasive advertising to convince consumers to take action—switch brands,[13] try a new product, or even continue to buy the advertised product.

*This ad informs the reader of L.L. Bean's new Signature line and helps build brand awareness.*

*Cover Girl's persuasive ads attempt to motivate consumers to take action: try the product, switch brands, or continue to buy the product.*

*This product-focused advertisement is designed to inform, persuade, or remind consumers about Pepsi Max.*

*The "Got Milk" institutional advertising campaign is used to encourage milk consumption by appealing to consumers' needs to affiliate with milk-mustached celebrities like Rebecca Romijn and her two babies.*

## Reminder Advertising

Finally, reminder advertising is a communication used to remind or prompt repurchases, especially for products that have gained market acceptance and are in the maturity stage of their life cycle. Such advertising certainly appears in traditional media, such as television or print commercials, but it also encompasses other forms of advertising. For example, if you decide to buy toilet paper, do you carefully consider all the options, comparing their sizes, prices, and performance, or do you just grab the first thing you see on the shelf? When your grocery store places a display of Charmin Ultra Soft on the end of the paper products aisle, it relies on your top-of-the-mind awareness of Charmin, which the manufacturer has achieved through advertising. That is, Ultra Soft toilet paper maintains a prominent place in people's memories and triggers their response, without them having to put any thought into it. The advertising and the end cap display thus prompt you, and many other consumers, to respond by buying a package, just the response Charmin hoped to attain.

## Focus of Advertisements

The ad campaign's objectives determine the specific ad's focus. The ad can either be product-focused, institutionally focused, or have a public service focus. Product-focused advertisements inform, persuade, or remind consumers about a *specific product or service*. For instance, the Pepsi Max ad on this page is designed to generate sales for Pepsi Max.

Institutional advertisements inform, persuade, or remind consumers about issues related to places, politics, or an industry. Perhaps the best-known institutional advertising campaign is the long-running "Got Milk?" campaign to encourage milk consumption by appealing to consumers' needs to affiliate with the milk-mustached celebrities shown in the ads.[14] The ads highlight the beneficial properties of milk for building strong bones, which involves a more informative appeal, combined with a mild emotional fear appeal in its assertion that failing to drink milk can lead to medical problems. Its Spanish-language ad campaign, "Toma Leche," similarly touts milk as a "wonder tonic" that fights cavities, sleeplessness, and bone loss. The latest campaign pictures Rebecca Romjin and her two babies, and promises that drinking milk helps families stay together.[15]

A specific category of institutional advertising is public service advertising (PSA). PSA focuses on public welfare and generally is sponsored by nonprofit institutions, civic groups, religious organizations, trade associations, or political groups.[16] Like product and institutionally focused advertising, PSAs also inform, persuade, or remind consumers, but the focus is on the betterment of society. As such, PSAs represent a form of social marketing, which is the application of marketing principles to a social issue to bring about attitudinal and behavioral change among the general public or a specific population segment.

The "Got Milk" campaign is an institutional ad that is ostensibly a PSA designed to stimulate the demand for milk because it is touted to be a healthy food. Another recent PSA campaign is a program sponsored by teen retailer Aeropostale, teen not-for-profit DoSomething.org, and stars Chace Crawford (*Gossip Girl*). It is designed to raise awareness of the growing number of homeless teens in the United States and Canada by encouraging people to collect and donate jeans to homeless youth.[17] PSAs can also be targeted to decrease consumption. For instance, the "Indoor Tanning Is Out" campaign is designed to raise awareness of the increased risk of melanoma, the deadliest form of skin cancer, and decrease usage of tanning salons.[18] Other PSAs have been running for years and have created their own pop culture standards, like Smokey the Bear (wildfire prevention), McGruff the Crime Dog (crime prevention), and Rosie the Riveter (women going to work during World War II).[19]

Because PSAs are a special class of advertising, under Federal Communications Commission (FCC) rules, broadcasters must devote a specific amount of free airtime to them. Also, since they often are designed by top advertising agencies for nonprofit clients, PSAs usually are quite creative and stylistically appealing. For example, what is your reaction to the truth® public service antismoking campaign summarized in Ethical and Societal Dilemma 18.1?

Regardless of whether the advertising campaign's objective is to inform, persuade, or remind, to focus on a particular product or the institution in general, each campaign's objectives must be specific and measurable. For a brand awareness campaign, for example, the objective might be to increase brand awareness among the target market by 50 percent within six months. Another campaign's goal may be to persuade 10 percent of a competitor's customers to switch to the advertised brand. Once the advertising campaign's objectives are set, the firm sets the advertising budget.

*The "Indoor Tanning is Out" public service announcement (PSA) is designed to raise awareness of the increased risk of melanoma, the deadliest form of skin cancer, and decrease usage of tanning salons.*

## STEP 3. DETERMINE THE ADVERTISING BUDGET

The various budgeting methods for marketing communication (Chapter 17) also apply to budgeting for advertising. First, firms must consider the role that advertising plays in their attempt to meet their overall promotional objectives. Second, advertising expenditures vary over the course of the product life cycle. Third, the nature of the market and the product influence the size of advertising budgets. The nature of the market also determines the amount of money spent on advertising. For instance, less money is spent on advertising in B2B (business-to-business) marketing contexts than in B2C (business-to-consumer) markets. Personal selling, as we discuss in Chapter 19, likely is more important in B2B markets.

## STEP 4. CONVEY THE MESSAGE

In this step, marketers determine what they want to convey about the product or service. First, the firm determines the key message it wants to communicate to the target audience. Second, the firm decides what appeal would most effectively convey the message. We present these decisions sequentially, but in reality they must be considered simultaneously.

## Ethical and Societal Dilemma 18.1    Getting to the Truth

Smoking is the single biggest preventable cause of death in the world; someone dies from tobacco use every eight seconds.[20] Smoking causes cancers of the lung, throat, and mouth; it also leads to high blood pressure, heart problems, and lung diseases other than cancer. Yet, in the world, one in five teens between the ages of 13 and 15 smokes, and many of those smokers will reach for their cigarettes for another 15 to 20 years. What can marketers do to help people avoid or quit this hazardous habit?

As part of the historic tobacco settlement between various states attorneys general and the tobacco industry, The American Legacy Foundation donates $300 million each year to educate the public about the dangers of smoking. The Foundation uses this money to fund the truth® campaign, the largest national young anti-smoking campaign and the only campaign not controlled by the tobacco industry. The campaign's goal is to tell the truth about the tobacco industry, including health effects, marketing strategies, and manufacturing practices.[21] Focused primarily on youths between the ages of 12 and 17, the campaign presents facts and allows teens to make their own decisions rather than telling them what they should or should not do.

The campaign had a direct impact on smoking, accelerating the decline in teen smoking during its first two years. Seven years after the truth® was launched, research showed that teens exposed to the campaign had a more accurate perception of the number of their peers who smoke. Since teens want to fit in with their peers, accurate perceptions of the decline in teen smoking can help reduce the number of young people who pick up a cigarette.

To reach teens, truth® uses videos shown online and in cinemas as well as social media, website games, television integration, radio advertising, and live tours. They have employed scare tactics, such as a pile of body bags in front of Philip Morris head-quarters;[22] they have employed humor; and, more recently, they have used animation, sarcasm, and Broadway-style song and dance routines to communicate their message.

But is humor the right way to communicate about a subject that kills millions of people each year? Is a pile of body bags an effective way to reach young smokers, who don't believe nicotine-related diseases will happen to them? Is this kind of messaging, which tobacco companies claim is abusive to them and their employees, appropriate or fair? How would you feel if you worked for a tobacco company? How would you feel about tobacco advertising if someone in your family had emphysema from smoking?

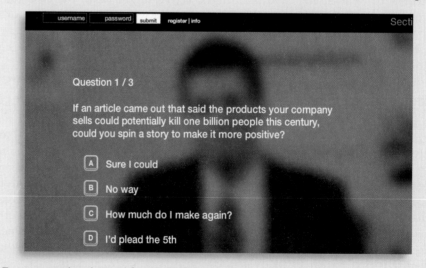

*Teens exposed to the truth® anti-smoking advertising campaign have a more accurate perception of the number of their peers who smoke. Since teens want to fit in with their peers, accurate perceptions can help reduce the number of young people who smoke.*

## The Message

The message provides the target audience with reasons to respond in the desired way. A logical starting point for deciding on the advertising message is to tout the key benefits of the product or service. The message should communicate its problem-solving ability clearly and in a compelling fashion. In this context, advertisers must remember that products and services solve problems, whether real or perceived. That is, people are not looking for 1/4-inch drill bits; they are looking for 1/4-inch holes.[23] Because there are many ways to make a 1/4-inch hole, a firm like Black & Decker must convey to consumers that its drill bit is the best way to get that hole.

Another common strategy differentiates a product by establishing its unique benefits. This distinction forms the basis for the unique selling proposition (USP), which is often the common theme or slogan in an advertising campaign. A good USP communicates the unique attributes of the product and thereby becomes a snapshot of the entire campaign. Some of the most famous USPs include the following:

Red Bull . . . Gives You Wings

United Negro College Fund . . . A mind is a terrible thing to waste.

Nike . . . Just Do It.

State Farm Insurance . . . Like a good neighbor, State Farm is there

TNT . . . We know drama

The selling proposition communicated by the advertising must be not only unique to the brand but also meaningful to the consumer. It furthermore must be sustainable over time, even with repetition.

## The Appeal

**L03** Describe the different ways that advertisers appeal to consumers.

According to early theories of rhetoric (the study of the principles and rules of composition), there are three main types of appeals that an argument may use: logos (logical), ethos (ethical), and pathos (emotional). Advertisers similarly use different appeals to portray their product or service and persuade consumers to purchase them, though advertising tends to combine the types of appeals into two categories: informational and emotional.

**Informational Appeals** Informational appeals help consumers make purchase decisions by offering factual information that encourages consumers to evaluate the brand favorably on the basis of the key benefits it provides.[24] In its advertisements, Exxon Mobil attempts to explain some technical aspects of its products, such as lithium ion batteries, hydrogen technology, biofuels, and $CO_2$ capture technologies, in an attempt to convince consumers that the company is environmentally friendly, efficient, innovative, and responsible.[25] This appeal is well suited to this type of product. By informing consumers about a potential source of its competitive advantage, including tangible features and images of science, the advertising copy directly delivers an informational persuasive message.

**Emotional Appeals** An emotional appeal aims to satisfy consumers' emotional desires rather than their utilitarian needs. These appeals therefore focus on feelings about the self.[26] The key to a successful emotional appeal is the use of emotion to create a bond between the consumer and the brand. The emotions most often invoked in advertising include fear, safety, humor, happiness, love (or sex), comfort, and nostalgia.

Although the term "emotion" often conveys the image of tears, many other effective appeals are used in advertising. People need a sense of self-esteem, so advertisements for Bowflex and Jenny Craig tend to feature celebrities or regular people talking about how much better they feel about themselves after they've joined the program and lost weight. Weight loss ads also tend to play a bit on consumers' fears, showing "before and after" pictures as if the heavier version were a horror to behold. Today political candidates use fear appeals for issues as mundane as garbage removal and as serious as sexual predators. Clearly, fear appeals often work best when the threat appears to be directed toward children or some other innocent victim.

But emotional appeals are not just scary. To market its Fusion Razor, Gillette features Roger Federer and Derek Jeter acting like 1970s disco fanatics, copying

*Chevrolet is providing information to prospective customers by favorably comparing its Equinox FWD to the Toyota Rav4 4X2.*

the famous *Saturday Night Fever* walk to the Bee Gees' "Stayin' Alive." The athletes exude confidence as they admire their clean-shaven faces in a storefront's glass while strutting by. Gillette never mentions the product attributes but rather focuses on the confidence that results from using their product.[27] Similarly, another common appeal is sex and love.[28]

# STEP 5. EVALUATE AND SELECT MEDIA

The content of an advertisement is tied closely to the characteristics of the media that firms select to carry the message, and vice versa. Media planning refers to the process of evaluating and selecting the media mix—the combination of the media used and the frequency of advertising in each medium—that will deliver a clear, consistent, compelling message to the intended audience.[29] For example, Macy's may determine that a heavy dose of television, radio, print, and billboards is appropriate for the holiday selling season between Thanksgiving and the end of the year.

Because the media buy, the actual purchase of airtime or print pages, is generally the largest expense in the advertising budget, marketers must make their decisions carefully. Television advertising is by far the most expensive. Total U.S. advertising expenditures per medium have remained roughly constant for some time, though some shifts are currently taking place. For example, whereas television advertising is consistent at approximately 44 percent, digital advertising is now 17 percent. Spanish-language media also are growing by more than 14 percent per year, whereas newspaper advertising is losing almost an entire percentage point.[30] To characterize these various types of media, we use a dichotomy: mass and niche media.

*A billboard advertising McDonald's on a major highway (top) would target the masses, but a McDonald's billboard in a specific community, like Mt. Horeb (bottom), would target a more focused niche market.*

## Mass and Niche Media

Mass media channels include national newspapers, magazines, radio, and television and are ideal for reaching large numbers of anonymous audience members. Niche media channels are more focused and generally used to reach narrower segments, often with unique demographic characteristics or interests. Specialty television channels (e.g., Home and Garden TV) and specialty magazines such as *Skateboarder* or *Cosmo Girl* all provide examples of niche media. The Internet provides an opportunity to appeal to the masses through ads on the home page of Internet sites like www.comcast.net or www.yahoo.com or more niched opportunities, such as an American Express business card on the *Wall Street Journal* site (www.wsj.com). In a similar fashion, a billboard advertising McDonald's on a

**LO4** Identify the various types of media.

major highway would target the masses, but a McDonald's billboard in a specific community would target a more focused niche market.

## Choosing the Right Medium

For each class of media, each alternative has specific characteristics that make it suitable for meeting specific objectives (see Exhibit 18.2).[31] For example, consumers use different media for different purposes, to which advertisers should match their messages. Television is used primarily for escapism and entertainment, so most television advertising relies on a mix of visual and auditory techniques.

Communication media also vary in their ability to reach the desired audience. For instance, radio is a good medium for products such as grocery purchases or fast food because many consumers decide what to purchase either on the way to the store or while in the store. Because many people listen to the radio in their cars, it becomes a highly effective means to reach consumers at a crucial point in their decision process. As we discussed in Chapter 17, each medium also varies in its reach and frequency. Advertisers can determine how effective their media mix has been in reaching their target audience by calculating the total GRP (reach X frequency) of the advertising schedule, which we discuss next.

## Determining the Advertising Schedule

Another important decision for the media planner is the advertising schedule, which specifies the timing and duration of advertising. There are three types of schedules:[32]

A continuous schedule runs steadily throughout the year and therefore is suited to products and services that are consumed continually at relatively steady rates and that require a steady level of persuasive and/or reminder advertising. For example, Procter & Gamble advertises its Tide brand of laundry detergent continuously.

| EXHIBIT 18.2 | Types of Media Available for Advertising | |
|---|---|---|
| **Medium** | **Advantages** | **Disadvantages** |
| Television | ■ Has wide reach.<br>■ Incorporates sound and video. | ■ Has high cost.<br>■ A lot of channel and program options.<br>■ May increase awareness of competitor's products. |
| Radio | ■ Is relatively inexpensive.<br>■ Can be selectively targeted.<br>■ Has wide reach. | ■ No video limits presentation.<br>■ Consumers give less focused attention than TV.<br>■ Exposure periods are short. |
| Magazines | ■ Are very targeted.<br>■ Subscribers pass along to others. | ■ Are relatively inflexible.<br>■ Takes some time for the magazine to be available. |
| Newspapers | ■ Are flexible.<br>■ Are timely.<br>■ Can localize. | ■ Can be expensive in some markets.<br>■ Advertisements have short life span. |
| Internet | ■ Can be linked to detailed content.<br>■ Is highly flexible and interactive.<br>■ Allows for specific targeting. | ■ Is becoming cluttered.<br>■ The ad may be blocked by software on the computer. |
| Outdoors | ■ Is relatively inexpensive.<br>■ Offers opportunities for repeat exposure.<br>■ Is easy to change. | ■ Is not easily targeted.<br>■ Has placement problems in some markets.<br>■ Exposure time is very short. |
| Direct Mail | ■ Is highly targeted.<br>■ Allows for personalization. | ■ Is relatively expensive.<br>■ Is often considered "junk mail." |

**Flighting** refers to an advertising schedule implemented in spurts, with periods of heavy advertising followed by periods of no advertising. This pattern generally functions for products whose demand fluctuates, such as suntan lotion, which manufacturers may advertise heavily in the months leading up to and during the summer.

**Pulsing** combines the continuous and flighting schedules by maintaining a base level of advertising but increasing advertising intensity during certain periods. For example, the furniture retailer IKEA advertises throughout the year but boosts its advertising expenditures to promote school supplies in August.

# STEP 6. CREATE ADVERTISEMENTS

After the advertiser has decided on the message, type of ad, and appeal, its attention must shift to the actual creation of the advertisement. During this step, the message and appeal are translated creatively into words, pictures, colors, and/or music. Often, the execution style for the ad will dictate the type of medium used to deliver the message. For example, automobile manufacturers and their dealers advertise in many media. To demonstrate an image, they can use television and magazines. To promote price, they can use newspapers and radio. To appeal to specific target markets, they can use some of the electronic media vehicles described in Chapter 17. When using multiple media to deliver the same message, however, they must maintain consistency across the execution styles—that is, integrated marketing—so that the different executions deliver a consistent and compelling message to the target audience.

Although creativity plays a major role in the execution stage, advertisers must remain careful not to let their creativity overshadow the message. Whatever the execution style, the advertisement must be able to attract the audience's attention, provide a reason for the audience to spend its time viewing the advertisement, and accomplish what it set out to do. In the end, the execution style must match the medium and objectives.

Print advertising can be especially difficult because it is a static medium: no sound, no motion, only one dimension. Instead, print relies on several key

*Why is this orangutan smiling? Because the kangaroos have arrived at the Buenos Aires Zoo. This Clio-winning ad delivers a compelling visual, a call to action (visit the zoo), and the advertiser's identification.*

components that appear in most ads: the headline, or large type designed to draw attention and be read first; the body copy, which represents the main text portion of the ad; the background or backdrop for the ad, usually a single color; the foreground, which refers to everything that appears on top of the background; and the branding that identifies the sponsor of the ad. The advertiser must convey its message using these compelling visuals, background colors or images, a logo, and limited text.

The ad on the previous page is an example of a very effective print ad, so effective that it won a Clio, the top advertising award.[33] From the start, this compelling ad makes viewers wonder why the orangutan is smiling, and the answer, that "The kangaroos have arrived," is likely to prompt amused awareness that a new exhibit has opened. The background and foreground match in their coloring, because this advertisement really wants to emphasize the foreground image instead of relying on bright colors to attract readers' attention. Once it has grabbed them with the funky image, the ad ensures that viewers know who is advertising and how to answer the ad's call to action (i.e., visit the zoo) by including the zoo name and logo, even larger than the tagline. In other ads, the advertiser might include a Web address or telephone number to enable the target audience to answer different calls to action. For the Buenos Aires Zoo, though, this ad delivers all the necessary elements: a compelling visual, a call to action, and the advertiser's identification.

## STEP 7. ASSESS IMPACT USING MARKETING METRICS

The effectiveness of an advertising campaign must be assessed before, during, and after the campaign has run. Pretesting refers to assessments performed before an ad campaign is implemented to ensure that the various elements are working in an integrated fashion and doing what they are intended to do.[34] Tracking includes monitoring key indicators, such as daily or weekly sales volume, while the advertisement is running to shed light on any problems with the message or the medium. Posttesting is the evaluation of the campaign's impact after it has been implemented. At this last stage, advertisers assess the sales and/or communication impact of the advertisement or campaign.

Measuring sales impact can be especially challenging because of the many influences other than advertising on consumers' choices, purchase behavior, and attitudes. These influences include the level of competitors' advertising, economic conditions in the target market, sociocultural changes, and even the weather, all of which can influence consumer purchasing behavior. Advertisers must try to identify these influences and isolate those of the particular advertising campaign.

For frequently purchased consumer goods in the maturity stage of the product life cycle such as soda, sales volume offers a good indicator of advertising effectiveness. Because their sales are relatively stable, and if we assume that the other elements of the marketing mix and the environment have not changed, we can attribute changes in sales volume to changes in advertising. Exhibit 18.3 illustrates a hypothetical sales history for Red Bull soda in a grocery store chain. Using a statistical technique called *time-series analysis*, sales data from the past are used to forecast the future. The data in Exhibit 18.3 can be decomposed into its basic trend (green), the seasonal influences (red), and the lift or additional sales caused by the advertising (orange). In this case, the lift caused by the advertising campaign is substantial.

For other types of goods in other stages of the product life cycle, sales data offer but one of the many indicators that marketers need to examine to determine advertising effectiveness. For instance, in high-growth markets, sales growth alone can be misleading because the market as a whole is growing. In such a situation, marketers measure sales relative to those of competitors to determine their relative market share. Firms find cre-

*Sales volume is a good indicator of advertising effectiveness for frequently purchased consumer goods in the maturity stage of the product life cycle, such as Red Bull energy drink.*

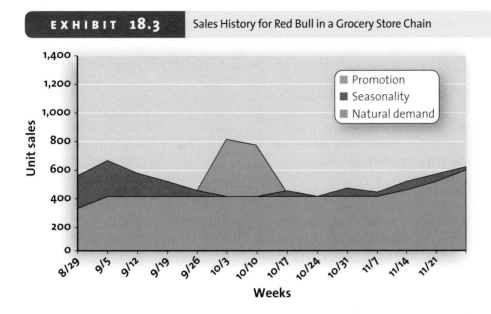

| EXHIBIT 18.3 | Sales History for Red Bull in a Grocery Store Chain |

ative ways to identify advertising effectiveness. For example, digital cable allows them to present a specific advertisement to certain neighborhoods and then track sales by local or regional retailers.

---

**CHECK YOURSELF**

1. What are the steps involved in planning an ad campaign?
2. What are the differences between informational, persuasive, and reminder advertising?
3. What are the pros and cons of the different media types?

---

# REGULATORY AND ETHICAL ISSUES IN ADVERTISING

**L05** Identify agencies that regulate advertising.

In the United States, the regulation of advertising involves a complex mix of formal laws and informal restrictions designed to protect consumers from deceptive practices.[35] Many federal and state laws, as well as a wide range of self-regulatory agencies and agreements, affect advertising (Exhibit 18.4). The primary federal agencies that regulate advertising activities are the Federal Trade Commission (FTC), Federal Communications Commission (FCC), and Food and Drug Administration (FDA). In addition to these agencies, others, such as the Bureau of Alcohol, Tobacco and Firearms and the U.S. Postal Service, regulate advertising to some degree.

The FTC is the primary enforcement agency for most mass media advertising. Occasionally, the FTC and FCC join together to investigate and enforce regulations on particular advertising practices. The Smart Choices program was designed to indicate healthier foods—and yet somehow its logo eventually appeared on boxes of Froot Loops. The confusion and apparent lack of regulation, along with many consumer complaints, led the FDA to issue warning letters that asked manufacturers to review their nutrition labels and claims for accuracy. The program also was suspended while the FDA reviewed the claims the logos were implying.[36]

| EXHIBIT 18.4 | Federal Agencies That Regulate Advertising | |
|---|---|---|
| **Federal Agency** | **General Purpose** | **Specific Jurisdiction** |
| Federal Trade Commission (FTC) (established 1914) | Enforces federal consumer protection laws. | Enforces truth in advertising laws; defines deceptive and unfair advertising practices. |
| Federal Communications Commission (FCC) (1934) | Regulates interstate and international communications by radio, television, wire, satellite, and cable. | Enforces restrictions on broadcasting material that promotes lotteries (with some exceptions); cigarettes, little cigars, or smokeless tobacco products; or that perpetuates a fraud. Also enforces laws that prohibit or limit obscene, indecent, or profane language. |
| Food and Drug Administration (1930) | Regulates food, dietary supplements, drugs, cosmetics, medical devices (including radiation-emitting devices such as cell phones), biologics (biological issues), and blood products. | Regulates package labeling and inserts, definition of terms such as "light" and "organic," and required disclosure statements (warning labels, dosage requirements, etc.). |

*Is this ad an example of puffery or deception?*

Many product categories fall under self-regulatory restrictions or guidelines. For example, advertising to children is regulated primarily through self-regulatory mechanisms designed by the National Association of Broadcasters and the Better Business Bureau's Children's Advertising Review Unit. The only formal regulation of children's advertising appears in the Children's Television Act of 1990, which limits the amount of advertising broadcast during children's viewing hours.[37]

Recently, to make matters even more complicated for advertisers, state attorneys general's offices have begun to inquire into various advertising practices and assert their authority to regulate advertising in their states. The EU also has increased its regulation of advertising for EU member nations. Many of these state and European regulations are more restrictive than existing federal or self-regulatory requirements.

The line between what is legal and illegal is more difficult to discern when it comes to **puffery**, which is the legal exaggeration of praise, stopping just short of deception, lavished on a product.[38] Take, for instance, the following claims found in a classified real estate section: "Lovely Townhome, Feels Like Single Family," "Stunningly Beautiful," "Best Price in Town," "Bargain of the Year." Since all of these claims are highly subjective, and none could be proven true or false, they are considered to be puffery and therefore allowed under the law.

How do the courts determine what makes an ad deceptive, rather than simply puffery? The FTC's position is that it "will not pursue cases involving obviously exaggerated or puffing representations, i.e., those that ordinary consumers do not take seriously."[39] In general, the less specific the claim, the less likely it is considered to be deceptive.

Papa John's Pizza may claim it has "Better ingredients, better pizza," and the courts consider it puffery. But if it claimed to make the top 1 percent of all pizzas, it would be deceptive, unless, of course it could prove that claim. In making the "Better ingredients, better pizza" claim, Papa John's also gave Domino's an effective means to introduce its recent marketing promise. Faced with widespread consumer complaints about its quality, Dominos changed its recipes and began advertising the improvements, including a money-back guarantee for anyone who did not like the new taste. Then it conducted taste tests with its own and Papa John's pizza and trumpeted its victory by contesting the "better" puffery claim.[40]

In the end, puffery is acceptable as long as consumers know that the firm is stretching the truth through exaggeration. But if the consumer knows it's puffery, then why bother?[41]

# PUBLIC RELATIONS

As you may recall from Chapter 17, **public relations (PR)** involves managing communications and relationships to achieve various objectives, such as building and maintaining a positive image of the firm, handling or heading off unfavorable stories or events, and maintaining positive relationships with the media. In many cases, public relations activities support other promotional efforts by generating "free" media attention and general goodwill.

Designers, for example, vie to have celebrities, especially those nominated for awards, wear their fashions on the red carpet. Their brands offer intangible benefits, not just functional benefits. Events such as the Oscars, with its 35 million annual viewers, provide an unparalleled opportunity to showcase the emotional benefits of the brand and make others want to be a part of it. Thus, the celebrities whom designers pursue and offer their items are those who will sell the most or provide the best iconic images. When Fergie wore an Emilio Pucci dress with a Judith Leiber clutch, both brands sent out press releases to make sure everyone knew.[42] The placement of designer apparel at media events benefits both the designer and the celebrity. And neither happens by accident. Public relations people on both sides help orchestrate the events to get the maximum benefit for both parties.

*When Fergie arrived at the 52nd Annual Grammy Awards, she generated positive PR for the designer clothing, shoes, and bag she was wearing.*

Good PR has always been an important success factor. Yet in recent years, the importance of PR has grown as the cost of other forms of marketing communications has increased. At the same time, the influence of PR has become more powerful as consumers have become increasingly skeptical of marketing claims made in other media.[43] In many instances, consumers view media coverage generated through PR as more credible and objective than any other aspects of an IMC program, because the firm does not "buy" the space in print media or time on radio or television.

Certainly the Chili's restaurant chain conducts plenty of media buys in traditional advertising spaces. But it also has partnered, since 2004, with St. Jude's Research Hospital in one of the most successful **cause-related marketing** (i.e., commercial activity in which businesses and charities form a partnership to market an image, product, or service for their mutual benefit)[44] efforts in history. For several years, the restaurant has offered customers the opportunity to purchase a paper icon, in the shape of a chili, natch, that they may color and hang on restaurant walls. The cause marketing campaign runs in September, which is also National Childhood Cancer Awareness Month. On the last Monday of the month, the restaurant puts its money where its mouth is and donates all its profits on sales during the day to St. Jude. In addition to the relatively common Create-a-Chili paper icons, employees of the restaurants make and sell customized T-shirts and wristbands. Chili's also hosts a dedicated website, www.createapepper.com, where civic-minded consumers can purchase or donate more, as well as buy St. Jude–branded Chili's gift cards.[45]

Another very popular PR tool is event sponsorship. **Event sponsorship** occurs when corporations support various activities (financially or otherwise), usually in the cultural or sports and entertainment sectors. Some of them are big name

*Chili's partners with St. Jude's Research Hospital in a cause-related marketing program to raise money for the hospital by donating its profits on the last Monday of September.*

 **LO6**  Describe the elements of a public relations toolkit.

events; the titles of most college football playoff games now include the name of their sponsors (e.g., the Allstate Sugar Bowl). Others are slightly less famous; for example, Rollerblade USA, the maker of Rollerblade in-line skates, sponsors Skate-In-School, a program it developed with the National Association for Sport and Physical Education (NASPE) to promote the inclusion of rollerblading in physical education curricula.

Firms often distribute a PR toolkit to communicate with various audiences. Some toolkit elements are designed to inform specific groups directly, whereas others are created to generate media attention and disseminate information. We depict the various elements of a PR toolkit in Exhibit 18.5.

---

### CHECK YOURSELF

1. Why do companies utilize public relations as part of their IMC strategy?
2. What are the elements of a public relations toolkit?

---

**EXHIBIT 18.5**    Elements of a Public Relations Toolkit

| PR Element | Function |
| --- | --- |
| Publications: Brochures, special-purpose single-issue publications such as books | Inform various constituencies about the activities of the organization and highlight specific areas of expertise. |
| Video and audio: Programs, public service announcements | Highlight the organization or support cause-related marketing efforts. |
| Annual reports | Give required financial performance data and inform investors and others about the unique activities of the organization. |
| Media relations: Press kits, news releases, speeches, event sponsorships | Generate news coverage of the organization's activities or products/services. |
| Electronic media: Websites, e-mail campaigns | Websites can contain all the previously mentioned toolbox elements, while e-mail directs PR efforts to specific target groups. |

# SALES PROMOTION

**L07**  Identify the various types of sales promotions.

Advertising rarely provides the only means to communicate with target customers. As we discussed in Chapter 17, a natural link appears between advertising and sales promotion. Sales promotions are special incentives or excitement-building programs that encourage consumers to purchase a particular product or service, typically used in conjunction with other advertising or personal selling programs. Many sales promotions, like free samples or point-of-purchase (POP) displays, attempt to build short-term sales, whereas others, like loyalty programs, contests, and sweepstakes, have become integral components of firms' long-term customer relationship management (CRM) programs, which they use to build customer loyalty. We present the tools used in sales promotions, along with their advantages and disadvantages, in Exhibit 18.6 and discuss them next. Then, we examine some ways in which integrated marketing communication (IMC) programs make use of sales promotions.

The tools of any sales promotion can be focused on either channel members, such as wholesalers or retailers, or end-user consumers. Just as we delineated for advertising, when sales promotions are targeted at channel members, the marketer is employing a push strategy; when it targets consumers themselves, it is using a pull strategy. Some sales promotion tools can be used with either a push or pull strategy. We now consider each of the tools and how they are used.

## Types of Sales Promotion

**Coupons**  Coupons offer a discount on the price of specific items when they're purchased. Coupons are issued by manufacturers and retailers in newspapers, on

| EXHIBIT 18.6 | Kinds of Sales Promotion | |
| --- | --- | --- |
| **Promotion** | **Advantages** | **Disadvantages** |
| Coupons | ■ Stimulates demand.<br>■ Allows for direct tracing of sales. | ■ Has low redemption rates.<br>■ Has high cost. |
| Deals | ■ Encourages trial.<br>■ Reduces consumer risk. | ■ May reduce perception of value. |
| Premiums (prize or award) | ■ Builds goodwill.<br>■ Increases perception of value. | ■ Consumers buy for premium, not product.<br>■ Has to be carefully managed. |
| Contests | ■ Increases consumer involvement.<br>■ Generates excitement. | ■ Requires creativity.<br>■ Must be monitored. |
| Sweepstakes | ■ Increases involvement with the product. | ■ Sales often decline after the sweepstakes is over. |
| Samples | ■ Encourages trial.<br>■ Offers direct involvement. | ■ Has high cost to the firm. |
| Loyalty Programs | ■ Creates loyalty.<br>■ Encourages repurchase. | ■ Has high cost to the firm. |
| POP Displays | ■ Provides high visibility.<br>■ Encourages brand trial. | ■ Is difficult to get a good location in the store.<br>■ Can be costly to the firm. |
| Rebates | ■ Stimulates demand.<br>■ Increases value perception. | ■ Is easily copied by competitors.<br>■ May just advance future sales. |
| Product Placement | ■ Displays products nontraditionally.<br>■ Demonstrates product uses. | ■ Firm often has little control over display.<br>■ Product can be overshadowed. |

*This sales promotion deal for Payless ShoeSource is a short-term price promotion that encourages consumers to buy a second pair of shoes at one-half off.*

products, on the shelf, at the cash register, over the Internet, and through the mail. Some retailers have linked coupons directly to their loyalty programs. Drugstore giant CVS, for instance, tracks its customers' purchases from its Extra Care loyalty card and gives them coupons that are tailored just for them.[46]

CVS is making its coupons more attractive to its loyal customers by customizing their content to be in line with their unique needs. For instance, if a customer typically spends a small amount during each shopping trip, the customer will receive coupons that encourage larger purchases, such as "buy one, get one free." Internet sites, such as MyCoupons. com, provide customers with instant coupons. For instance, a customer might go to a Walmart and find a Hot Wheels video game for $29.99. A scan of the bar code on his cell phone to ShopSavvy.com might find the same item at a Target a mile away for $19.99. Then he can go to to MyCoupons.com to get a coupon for $10, thus saving the customer $20.00 in a matter of minutes.

A new breed of coupon, printed from the Internet or sent to mobile phones, is packed with information about the customer who uses it.[47] While the coupons look standard, their bar codes can be loaded with a startling amount of data, including identification of the customer, Internet address, Facebook page information, and even the search terms the customer used to find the coupon in the first place. For instance, if a customer came into a store with a coupon for T-shirts, the information on the coupon could reveal if the customer was searching for "underwear" or "muscle shirts."

**Deals**  A **deal** refers generally to a type of short-term price reduction that can take several forms, such as a "featured price," a price lower than the regular price; a "buy one, get one free" offer; or a certain percentage "more free" offer contained in larger packaging. Another form of a deal involves a special financing arrangement, such as reduced percentage interest rates or extended repayment terms. Deals encourage customers to try a product because they lower the risk for consumers by reducing the cost of the good. Deals can also alter perceptions of value—a short-term price reduction may signal a different price/quality relationship than would be ideal from the manufacturer's perspective.

*Customers can obtain instant coupons at MyCoupons.com.*

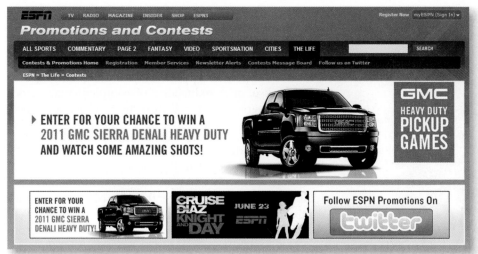

*This contest on the ESPN Web site requires entrants to create and upload a short video demonstrating why they should be the one picked to send to the World Cup.*

**Premiums**  A premium offers an item for free or at a bargain price to reward some type of behavior, such as buying, sampling, or testing. These rewards build good-will among consumers, who often perceive high value in them. Premiums can be distributed in a variety of ways: They can be included in the product packaging, such as the toys inside cereal boxes; placed visibly on the package, such as a coupon for free milk on a box of Cheerios; handed out in the store; or delivered in the mail, such as the free perfume offers Victoria's Secret mails to customers. Furthermore, premiums can be very effective if they are consistent with the brand's message and image and highly desirable to the target market. However, finding a premium that meets these criteria at a reasonable cost can be a serious challenge.

**Contests**  A contest refers to a brand-sponsored competition that requires some form of skill or effort. On ESPN's website, they have a page that has numerous sports-related contests. Some of them include "Get Me to the World Cup spon-sored by Sony" and "Player of the Month presented by Kia."[48] For the Get Me to the World Cup, each contestant is required to create and upload a short video demonstrating why they should be the one picked to send to the World Cup. They also provide a number of sample videos including one by Kobe Bryant.

A form of sales promotion that offers prizes based on a chance drawing of entrants' names, sweepstakes do not require the entrant to complete a task other than buying a ticket or filling out a form. Often the key benefit of sweepstakes is that they encourage current consumers to consume more if the sweepstakes form appears inside the packaging or with the product. Many states, however, specify that no purchase can be required to enter sweepstakes.

**Samples**  Sampling offers potential customers the opportunity to try a product or service before they make a buying decision. Distributing samples is one of the most costly sales promotion tools but also one of the most effective. Quick service restaurants and grocery stores frequently utilize sampling. For instance, Starbucks provides samples of new products to customers. Costco uses so many samples that customers can have an entire meal. Sometimes trial-size samples come in the mail or are distributed in stores.

**Loyalty Programs**  As part of a sales promotion program, loyalty programs are specifically designed to retain customers by offering premiums or other incen-tives to customers who make multiple purchases over time. Such sales promotions are growing increasingly popular and are often tied to long-term CRM systems. (Loyalty programs are examined in Chapters 2 and 16.)

**Point-of-Purchase Displays**  Point-of-purchase (POP) displays are merchan-dise displays located at the point of purchase, such as at the checkout counter in a supermarket. Retailers have long recognized that the most valuable real estate

Point-of-purchase (POP) displays are located at the point of purchase such as a checkout counter in a supermarket. They are very effective for stimulating impulse purchases.

If you think that the Apple computer was accidently placed on NBC's 30 Rock with Kenneth (left) and Jack (right) (Jack McBrayer and Alec Baldwin), think again. It was mostly likely a product placement in which Apple paid to have its product subtly placed on the table.

in the store is at the POP (point of purchase). Customers see products like a magazine or a candy bar while they are waiting to pay for their purchases, and impulsively purchase them. In the Internet version of a point-of-purchase display, shoppers are stimulated by special merchandise, price reductions, or complementary products that Internet retailers feature on the checkout screen.

**Rebates** Rebates are a particular type of price reduction in which a portion of the purchase price is returned by the seller to the buyer in the form of cash. Many products, such as consumer electronics, offer significant mail-in rebates that may lower the price of the item significantly. Some companies enjoy the added exposure when they appear on consumer websites like PriceGrabber.com and Nextag.com where products are sorted by the price and then link the customer to the retailer's website. Firms offer such generous rebates because the likelihood that consumers will actually apply for the rebate is low. The firms garner considerable value from rebates because they attract consumers but they may not have to pay off all the rebates offered. Other firms, like Staples and Apple, have simplified the rebate redemption process with "Easy Rebates" and Apple.com/promo.[49]

**Product Placement** When marketers use product placement, they pay to have their product included in nontraditional situations, such as in a scene in a movie or television program.[50] Product placement has formerly been subtly placed, such as when *American Idol* judges are seen drinking Coca-Cola. In fact, one season of *American Idol* had 580 product placements. Elisa and Jack of *30 Rock* discuss whether McDonald's McFlurry is the best dessert in the world. On CBS's *The Big Bang Theory*, Sheldon says that he "needs access to the Cheesecake Factory walk-in freezer." In *The Biggest Loser*, the contestants have to run from one Subway restaurant to the next.[51]

## Using Sales Promotion Tools

Marketers must be careful in their use of promotions, especially those that focus on lowering prices. Depending on the item, consumers may stock up when items are offered at a lower price, which simply shifts sales from the future to now and thereby leads to short-run benefits at the expense of long-term sales stability. For instance, using sales promotions like coupons to stimulate sales of household cleaning supplies may cause consumers to stockpile the products and decrease demand for those products in the future. But a similar promotion used with a perishable product like Dannon yogurt should increase its demand at the expense of competitors like Yoplait.

Many firms are also realizing the value of cross-promoting, when two or more firms join together to reach a specific target market. To achieve a successful cross-promotion, the two products must appeal to the same target market and together create value for consumers. J. Crew has teamed up with several famous brands, including Belstaff, Levi's Barbour, Timex, and Sperry Top-Sider to offer exclusive products in the J.Crew stores and on its website.[52]

The goal of any sales promotion is to create value for both the consumers and the firm. By understanding the needs of its customers, as well as how best to entice them to purchase or consume a particular product or service, a firm can develop

*J.Crew has teamed up with Sperry Top-Sider to cross-promote and sell exclusive Top-Siders on J.Crew's website.*

promotional messages and events that are of interest to and achieve the desired response from those customers. Traditionally, the role of sales promotion has been to generate short-term results, whereas the goal of advertising was to generate long-term results. As this chapter demonstrates, though, both sales promotion and advertising can generate both long- and short-term effects. The effective combination of both types of activities leads to impressive results for the firm and the consumers.

## Evaluating Sales Promotions Using Marketing Metrics

Many sales promotion opportunities undertaken by retailers are initiated by manufacturers. For example, Sharp might offer the following special promotion to Costco: During a one-week period, Costco can order 46-inch Sharp Aquos LCD HDTVs at $300 below the standard wholesale price. However, if Costco elects to buy these HDTVs at the discounted price, then it must feature them prominently on its Web page for $1199.00 ($350 below the suggested retail price). In addition, Costco must agree to purchase enough of this particular model to have front-of-store displays in each of its stores.

Before Costco decides whether to accept such a trade promotion and then promote the Sharp HDTV to its customers, it needs to assess the promotion's impact on its own profitability. Such a promotion may be effective for Sharp but not for Costco.

To evaluate a trade promotion, the retailer considers:

- The realized margin from the promotion.
- The cost of the additional inventory carried due to buying more than the normal amount.
- The potential increase in sales from the promoted merchandise.
- The long-term impact on sales of the promotion.
- The potential loss suffered when customers switch to the promoted merchandise from more profitable TVs.
- The additional sales made to customers attracted to the store by the promotion.[53]

When the HDTV's price is reduced to $1199.00, Costco will sell more Sharp HDTVs than it normally does. But Costco's margin on the HDTVs will be less because the required retail discount of $350 isn't offset by the normal wholesale discount of $300. In addition, Costco might suffer losses because the promotion encourages customers to buy these special HDTVs, which have a lower margin than Costco makes on its other HDTVs. In contrast, the promotion may attract customers who don't normally shop at Costco but who will visit to buy the Sharp HDTV at the discounted price. These customers might buy additional merchandise, providing a sales gain to the store that it wouldn't have realized if it hadn't promoted this item.

## CHECK YOURSELF

1. What are various forms of sales promotions?
2. What factors should a firm consider when evaluating a sales promotion?

# Summing Up

**LO1  Describe the steps in designing and executing an advertising campaign.**

Firms (1) identify their target market, (2) set advertising objectives, (3) set the advertising budget, (4) depict their product or service, (5) evaluate and select the media, (6) create the ad, and (7) assess the impact of the ad.

**LO2  Identify three objectives of advertising.**

All advertising campaigns are designed to either inform, persuade, or remind customers. Informative advertising is a communication used to create and build brand awareness. Persuasive advertising is a communication used to motivate consumers to take action. Finally, reminder advertising is a communication used to remind or prompt repurchases.

**LO3  Describe the different ways that advertisers appeal to consumers.**

Advertising appeals are either informational or emotional. Informational appeals influence purchase decisions with factual information and strong arguments built around relevant key benefits that encourage consumers to evaluate the brand favorably. Emotional appeals indicate how the product satisfies emotional desires rather than utilitarian needs.

**LO4  Identify the various types of media.**

Firms can use mass media channels like newspapers or television to reach large numbers of anonymous audience members. Niche media, such as cable television and specialty magazines, are generally used to reach narrower segments with unique demographic character-

istics or interests. When choosing the media, firms must match their objectives to the media. Also, certain media are better at reaching a particular target audience than others.

**LO5  Identify agencies that regulate advertising.**

Advertising is regulated by a plethora of federal and state agencies. The most important federal agencies are the FTC, which protects consumers against general deceptive advertising; the FCC, which has jurisdiction over radio, television, wire, satellite, and cable and covers issues regarding the use of tobacco products and objectionable language; and the FDA, which regulates food, dietary supplements, drugs, cosmetics, and medical devices.

**LO6  Describe the elements of a public relations toolkit.**

A variety of elements compose a firm's public relations toolkit. They include publications, video and audio programs, public service announcements, annual reports, media kits (e.g., press kits), news releases, and electronic media (e.g., websites).

**LO7  Identify the various types of sales promotions.**

Sales promotions are special incentives or excitement-building programs that encourage purchase and include coupons, deals, premiums, contests, sweepstakes, samples, POP displays, rebates, and product placement. They either push sales through the channel, as is the case with contests directed toward retail salespeople, or pull sales through the channel, as coupons and rebates do.

## Key Terms

- advertising, 536
- advertising plan, 537
- advertising schedule, 546
- background, 548
- body copy, 548
- branding, 548
- cause-related marketing, 551
- contest, 555
- continuous advertising schedule, 546
- coupon, 553
- cross-promoting, 556
- deal, 554
- emotional appeal, 543
- event sponsorship, 551
- flighting advertising schedule, 547
- foreground, 548
- headline, 548
- informational appeal, 543

- informative advertising, 539
- institutional advertisements, 540
- lift, 548
- loyalty program, 555
- mass media, 545
- media buy, 544
- media mix, 544
- media planning, 544
- niche media, 545
- persuasive advertising, 539
- point-of-purchase (POP) display 555
- posttesting, 548
- premium, 555
- pretesting, 548
- product placement, 556
- product-focused advertisements, 540
- public relations (PR), 551

- public service advertising (PSA), 540
- puffery, 550
- pull strategy, 538
- pulsing advertising schedule, 547
- push strategy, 538
- rebate, 556
- reminder advertising, 540
- sales promotion, 553
- sampling, 555
- social marketing, 540
- sweepstakes, 555
- tracking, 548
- unique selling proposition (USP), 543
- viral marketing campaign, 562

## Marketing Applications

1. Choose one of the ads featured in this book and identify its page number. What are the objectives of this ad? Does the ad have more than one objective? Explain your answer.

2. Using the same ad, explain what kind of appeal it uses. How do you know?

3. Microsoft spends millions of dollars each year on advertising for many different purposes. Provide an example of how they might design an informative ad, a persuasive ad, and a reminder ad.

4. Name a current advertising slogan you believe is particularly effective for developing a unique selling proposition.

5. Bernard's, a local furniture company, target markets to college students with apartments and households of young people purchasing their first furniture items. If you worked for Bernard's, what type of media would you use for your advertising campaign? Justify your answer.

6. Should Bernard's use continuous, pulsing, or flighting for its advertising schedule? Why?

7. Suppose Porsche is introducing a new line of light trucks and has already created the advertising campaign. How would you assess the effectiveness of the campaign?

8. Suppose now that Porsche is planning a sales promotion campaign to augment its advertising campaign for the new line of light trucks. Which push and pull sales promotion tools do you believe would be most effective? Why?

9. Choose an ad that you believe unreasonably overstates what the product or service can do. (If you can't think of a real ad, make one up.) Explain whether the ad is actually deceptive or just puffery. How would your answer change if you lived in France?

10. You are invited to your six-year-old niece's birthday party and bring her the new superhero doll being advertised on television. She's thrilled when she unwraps the gift but is in tears a short time later because her new doll is broken. She explains that on TV, the doll flies and does karate kicks, but when she tried to play with the doll this way, it broke. You decide to call the manufacturer, and a representative tells you he is sorry your niece is so upset but that the ad clearly states the doll does not fly. The next time you see the televised ad, you notice very small print at the bottom that states the doll does not fly. You decide to write a letter to the FTC about this practice. What information should you include in your letter?

## Quiz Yourself

1. The Got Milk (milk moustaches worn by celebrities) ads are examples of successful
   a. persuasive advertising strategies.
   b. public puffery campaigns.
   c. pretracking publicity.
   d. product-focused advertisements.
   e. public service advertising.

2. Campbell Soup Company ran a series of radio ads tied to local weather forecasts. Before an impending storm, the ads said, "Time to stock up on Campbell Soup." During the storm, the ads said, "Stay home and stay warm with Campbell Soup."

The first ad was _____ advertising, while the second ad was _____ advertising.
   a. informative; persuasive
   b. persuasive; reminder
   c. reminder; persuasive
   d. discussive; informative
   e. institutional; persuasive

(Answers to these two questions are provided on page 608.)

Go to www.mhhe.com/grewal3e to practice an additional 11 questions.

## Toolkit

**MAKE AN ADVERTISEMENT**

Suppose you have been hired to develop a new ad for a product or service to target the college student market. The ad will appear in college student newspapers around the world. Please use the toolkit provided at www.mhhe.com/grewal3e to develop the ad.

## Net Savvy

1. Go to the website for the Children's Advertising Review Unit (CARU), one of the major self-regulatory bodies for children's advertising, at www.caru.org. Click on the About Us and examine the activities of CARU. How does this form of regulation complement the more formal regulation of federal and state agencies? Now look under the News and Publications link. Choose one of the press releases and discuss what action CARU took against the identified company or group. What was the main issue in the case?

2. PR Newswire attempts to provide information for "professional communicators." Visit its website at www.prnewswire.com and explore the "Products and Services" it has to offer. What would you consider this organization's primary purpose? To whom does PR Newswire address the advertising appeals on its site?

## Chapter Case Study

### WHAT IS POPULARITY ANYWAY?[54]

When it comes to social networking sites (those Web forums that enable friends to stay in contact, describe themselves and their interests, and measure their popularity by the number of registered friends they maintain), the rules of advertising change radically. Who is advertising to whom, and how can companies—both the networking sites and others that want in on the game—make the best appeal to consumers?

    Consider your own Facebook or MySpace site, assuming you have one. Are all your real-life friends your online friends too? Do you actually know all the friends registered on your online site? In all likelihood, you host online friends you've never met, meaning that your circle of virtual friends is pretty huge compared with the number of people whom you see in person or talk to face to face on a regular basis. That means the audience on social sites also potentially is much bigger than that for other forms of media.

Such huge audiences mean huge interest by advertisers. Advertising on social networking sites actually consists of at least three areas though: Members advertise themselves to gain more friends, the sites advertise to get more members, and outside companies hope to advertise their products to appeal to the vast networks of consumers active on the sites. Let's look at examples of each of these realms in turn.

## MEMBERS ADVERTISING THEMSELVES

Regardless of whether online popularity translated into votes, recent elections at all levels have made the use of Facebook and MySpace pages by political candidates appealing, especially because they saw access to the younger voters who would tend to use social networking sites. Their websites included links to their pages, and in some news releases, they touted the number of friends they had attracted.

Tila Tequila, the model, singer, blogger, and actress, began her career modeling and although featured on the 2006 covers of *Maxim* and *Stuff* magazines, she was relatively unknown.[55] She did not become a celebrity until she joined MySpace in 2003, and became famous because of fans of her site. Tequila mass e-mailed 30,000 to 50,000 people to look at her MySpace page, and they all joined. This was in the early stages of MySpace, when people were only friends with people they were actually friends with, and did not venture out into the online community to make friendships. She appeared on NBC's *Identity* as one of 12 strangers, with her claim to fame being that she had over 1 million MySpace friends. Shortly thereafter, she became the star of *A Shot at Love with Tila Tequila* and many other MTV network shows for people aged 18–34.

Most Facebook users aren't trying to be celebrities or running to become the president of the United States, yet the competition for more and more friends can be fierce, even if the only one who seems to care about it is the member. Some of the most popular fan sites on Facebook, measured in number of fans, include President Barack Obama's and actor Vin Diesel's.[56]

## SITES ADVERTISING THEIR SERVICES

In this area, the advertising tends to be rather untraditional; social networking sites appear to have little use for print, television, or radio and instead rely on advertising within their own sites to spark interest. Facebook not only assures its individual users that it provides a way for them to "connect . . . with the people around you" but also promises advertisers that they can "reach the exact audience [they] want."[57] Thus, Facebook tries to appeal to two different audiences: the users and the advertisers who remain so interested in those users.

## OUTSIDE COMPANIES ADVERTISING ON SITES

Social networks are so popular that marketers yearn for more ways to capitalize quickly on the markets associated with them. Newspapers, television spots, and other traditional advertising media continue to lose ground as consumers spend more time on blogs and online.

Companies can use display advertising with "Facebook Ads," where specific groups of people are targeted based on their profile information, their browsing history, and other factors related to their preferences. If online users on Facebook reveal an interest in ski equipment or Burton snowboards, marketers can target both groups on the basis of these interests.[58]

Companies can also join Facebook by having a Facebook profile page which attracts "fans." This free exposure allows the company to post content and information regarding products, events, news, promotions, and so forth, that they want to tell to their customers. Only the fans of their page will have access to this information, allowing the company to specifically target those Facebook users that opt in to be a fan of the company. The successful companies on Facebook interact with their customers regularly. Some companies even conduct contests using a social network to encourage more people to spread the word.

In 2008, Burger King created the controversial "Whopper Virgins" campaign, offering blind taste tests that compared Burger King and McDonald's hamburgers to people in rural China who had never tasted a hamburger. The resulting viral marketing campaign prompted widespread word-of-mouth advertising. For 2009, Burger King launched a new Facebook campaign in which customers could earn a free Whopper if they delisted 10 friends from their account.[59] The so-called "Whopper Sacrifice" was intended to show what someone would give up for a Whopper, and the campaign attracted the participation of more than 200,000 active users who defriended others.

After a "Whopper Sacrifice," the ex-friends received notification, which was also published on the Facebook "mini-feed" and thus helped spread the word even more quickly. As the campaign caught on, Facebook disabled it. The Facebook page for Burger King now says: "Facebook has disabled Whopper Sacrifice after your love for the Whopper sandwich proved to be stronger than 233,906 friendships." Users can continue to post on the fan page, and many have asked that the campaign come back. By affecting 233,906 people, who were either defriended or actually did the defriending, Burger King considers this viral campaign a success even though it was quickly shut down.

From a market research point of view, companies also can learn a lot about their customers from their interests, their past purchases, and their movement through the social network. Customers appear keen to submit their opinions about their friends' purchases, interests, polls, and blogs. Reviews or votes about BOTOX® treatments, ASICS running sneakers, or the play of an NFL team during the playoffs all constitute new ways that customers communicate with one another—and with marketers who are paying attention. Because modern customers spend a significant amount of time reading reviews and looking at alternative products before actually making a purchase, reviews by other customers have significant impact. People also are likely to trust other users more than an advertising message.

Marketers thus are learning a lot about their customers—everything from how to communicate with them to their likes, dislikes, and preferences. The social atmosphere on the Web should continue to grow, providing an ever-increasing pool of information and marketing opportunities.

## Questions

1. How can social networking sites keep their users on the site and prevent their moving to a different social network?

2. What type of appeal usually gets people to join a social networking site? What type of appeals do members use to get others to become their online friends? What type of appeals do companies advertising on social networking sites use? Explain the differences.

3. How might you measure the value of the advertising by the firms discussed in this case study? What types of analyses might you use?

# Personal Selling and Sales Management

**W**hen IBM salesman Vivek Gupta made a sales call at Vodafone in Mumbai in 2003, he was told there was no chance of a business deal.[1] Four years later, Gupta landed a five-year $600 million contract with the company. His success wasn't a fluke: the 40-year-old's abilities as a salesman have earned him and his family a driver who washes the car on a daily basis, private school for the children, and a 3,100 square-foot home in an apartment complex that has a swimming pool and tennis court. Nor is Gupta simply lucky. His Vodafone sale and similar success with other Indian telecom companies springs from IBM's legendary sales training, hard work, and an understanding of the customer's business and personality.

Gupta has internalized IBM's teaching that the goal of sales is to match an IBM solution to a customer's business need, not just to sell a product and close a deal. Identifying the need may involve in-depth research into a company's business processes and conversations with front-line employees. Gupta, for example, obtained permission to study a telecom business even though his business prospect had expressed no interest in working with IBM. After talking to the telecom's switching center engineers, Gupta learned that the microwave radios used to transmit call signals between towers were failing six or seven times a week. He also built a social relationship with his contact. Once he'd established trust and had a good solution to the microwave radio problem, he approached the prospect a second time about working together. This time, Gupta landed a contract for microwave radios. Over the next 12 months, that deal led to other contracts worth $100 million.

In some cases, the fix Gupta sells involves helping customers position themselves in the market and not simply upgrading a service or improving technical reliability. When Gupta first started with IBM, India was the fastest-growing cell phone market in the world. Wireless telecoms were struggling to find and maintain a toehold; devoting time to marketing and strategizing was nearly impossible. Gupta's solution—offered to a newcomer in the field—was for IBM

## LEARNING OBJECTIVES

**LO1** Describe the value added of personal selling.

**LO2** Define the steps in the personal selling process.

**LO3** Describe the key functions involved in managing a sales force.

**LO4** Describe the ethical and legal issues in personal selling.

to build a flexible, scalable IT infrastructure that connected to the company's key business processes.[2] IBM chose to accept a portion of the company's profits as payment. The company, Bharti Airtel, is now India's largest cell service provider, and the 10-year contract Gupta secured is estimated to be worth $1 billion.

Gupta built business with Vodafone over time as well, simultaneously hinting that letting IBM handle their backroom operations and focusing on strategy might be wise given the impressive growth of competitor Bharti Airtel. A man of patience, he counseled his sales team to move slowly with Vodafone, likening the relationship to a long courtship before approaching the altar. For the first serious date, he sold Vodafone laptops for staff. Next it was IBM servers. Today his presence with Vodafone is so strong that employees joke that they aren't sure if he works for Vodafone or IBM, and his knowledge of the company is so detailed that it outstrips that of most Vodafone employees. The confusion may extend to other IBM salespeople as well, since today's sales staff frequently work onsite with clients.

Gupta's technique is typical of the IBM style. Since its inception, the company has devoted time and energy to training its sales force, reminding trainees "You are not selling machines, you are selling what machines will do."[3] To be successful, salespeople must be able to educate their prospects about the power of IBM's products and services, overcome resistance, and build trust. With the expansion of technology and global business models, salespeople must also understand the capacity of their own companies to meet the evolving needs of prospective clients. Gupta spends time in the research labs and with engineers, learning what technologies are in development and discovering ways emerging and existing tools may help his clients. IBM, which has always had a reputation for knowing how to sell, sends stars like Gupta to an 18-month program that includes classes at foreign business schools, mentoring in how to negotiate complex deals, and online coursework. Other courses help sales staff learn the complexities of emerging markets.

Like its sales strategy, IBM's corporate technology strategy is based on the concept of selling a solution and not a product.[4] With its "edge of network" (EON) systems, IBM is promoting packages of software, hardware, and services designed to run backroom operations. Part of this approach capitalizes on the power of the Internet as a sales tool: Web promotions entice consumers and small businesses to purchase online instead of in brick-and-mortar stores. To counter the effect of losing face-to-face sales contact, the company offers automated services and e-mail updates for customers buying online. Whether angling for the small sale or the large one, IBM's salespeople have the combination of strategy, training, imagination, and vision that their company has the solution to their customers' needs.

● ● ●

Just like advertising, which we discussed in the last chapter, personal selling is so important in integrated marketing communications that it deserves its own chapter. Almost everyone is engaged in some form of selling. On a personal level, you sell your ideas or opinions to your friends, family, employers, and professors. Even if you have no interest in personal selling as a career, a strong grounding in the topic will help you in numerous career choices. Consider, for instance, Harry Turk, a very successful labor attorney. He worked his way through college selling sweaters to fraternities across the country. Although he loved his part-time job, Harry decided to become an attorney. When asked whether he misses selling, he said, "I use my selling skills every day. I have to sell new clients on the idea that I'm the best attorney for the job. I have to sell my partners on my legal point of view. I even use selling skills when I'm talking to a judge or jury." In this chapter, we take a straightforward business perspective on selling.

# THE SCOPE AND NATURE OF PERSONAL SELLING

**L01** Describe the value added of personal selling.

**Personal selling** is the two-way flow of communication between a buyer or buyers and a seller that is designed to influence the buyer's purchase decision. Personal selling can take place in various situations: face-to-face, via video teleconferencing, on the telephone, or over the Internet. Over 14 million people are employed in sales positions in the United States,[5] including those involved in business-to-business (B2B) transactions—like manufacturers' representatives selling to retailers or other businesses—and those completing business-to-consumer (B2C) transactions, such as retail salespeople, real estate agents, and insurance agents. Salespeople are referred to in many ways: sales representatives or reps, account executives, agents. And as Harry Turk found, most professions rely on personal selling to some degree.

Salespeople don't always get the best coverage in popular media. In Arthur Miller's play and the subsequent movie *Death of a Salesman*, the main character, Willie Loman, leads a pathetic existence and suffers from the loneliness inherent in being a traveling salesman.[6] The characters in David Mamet's play *Glengarry Glen Ross* (which was also made into a movie) portray salespeople as crude, ruthless, and of questionable character. Unfortunately, these powerful Pulitzer Prize–winning pieces of literature weigh heavily on our collective consciousness and often overshadow the millions of hardworking professional salespeople who have fulfilling and rewarding careers and who add value to their firm and provide value for their customers.

## Personal Selling as a Career

Personal or professional selling can be a satisfying career for several reasons. First, many people love the lifestyle. Salespeople are typically out on their own. Although they occasionally work with their managers and other colleagues, salespeople are usually responsible for planning their own day. This flexibility translates into an easier balance between work and family than many office-bound jobs can offer. Many salespeople now can rely on virtual offices, which enable them to communicate via the Internet with colleagues and customers. Because salespeople are evaluated primarily on the results they produce, as long as they meet and exceed their goals, they experience little day-to-day supervision.

Second, the variety of the job often attracts people to sales. Every day is different, bringing different clients and customers, often in a variety of places. Their issues and problems and the solutions to those problems all differ and require creativity.[7]

Third, professional selling and sales management can be a very lucrative career. Sales is among the highest-paying careers for college graduates, and compensation often includes perks, such as the use of a company car and bonuses for high performance. A top performer can have a total compensation package of over $150,000; even lower-level salespeople can make well over $50,000. Although the monetary

*Many salespeople now can rely on virtual offices, which enable them to communicate via the Internet with colleagues and customers.*

compensation can be significant, the satisfaction of being involved in interesting, challenging, and creative work is rewarding in and of itself.

Fourth, because salespeople are the frontline emissaries for their firm, they are very visible to management. Furthermore, it is fairly straightforward for management to identify top performers, which means that those high-performing salespeople who aspire to management positions are in a good position to get promoted.

## The Value Added by Personal Selling

Why have salespeople in the supply chain? They are expensive—experts estimate that the average cost of a single B2B sales call is about $400.[8] Some firms have turned to the Internet and technology to lower the cost of personal selling. (See Power of the Internet 19.1.) Other firms, especially certain retailers, have made the decision not to use a sales force and become, for the most part, almost completely self-service. But those that use personal selling as part of their integrated marketing communications program do so because it adds value to their product or service mix—that is, personal selling is worth more than it costs. Personal selling adds value by educating and providing advice, saving the customer time, making things easier for the customer, and helping to build long-term strategic relationships with customers.[9]

**Salespeople Provide Information and Advice** Imagine how difficult it would be to buy a custom suit, a house, or a car without the help of a salesperson. UPS wouldn't dream of investing in a new fleet of airplanes without the benefit of Boeing's selling team. Boeing's sales team can provide UPS with the technical aspects of the aircraft, as well as the economic justification for the purchase. Similarly, retail salespeople can provide valuable information about how a garment fits, new fashions, or directions for operating products. Sure, it could be done, but customers see the value in and are willing to pay indirectly for the education and advice salespeople provide.

**Salespeople Save Time and Simplify Buying** Time is money! Customers perceive value in time and labor savings. In many grocery and drugstore chains, salespeople employed by the vendor supplying merchandise straighten stock, set up displays, assess inventory levels, and write orders. In some cases, such as bakeries or soft drink sales, salespeople and truck drivers even bring in the merchandise and stock the shelves. These are all tasks that retail employees would otherwise have to do.

Sometimes, however, turning over too many tasks to suppliers' salespeople can cause problems. Imagine a grocery store that has turned its inventory management function over to a supplier, like the consumer packaged goods firm Kraft. The supplier might place competitors' products in disadvantageous shelf positions. Unless the relationship involves significant trust or the grocery has precautionary measures in place, the Kraft sales representative might place plenty of Kraft Thousand Island dressing on the shelf but leave little room for its competitors' products, designating a suboptimal amount of shelf space to Wishbone's Thousand Island offering. Although this relationship benefits Kraft, it may not help the grocer, especially if that retailer earns better margins on the competitors' products. Salespeople certainly can help facilitate a buying situation, but they should never be allowed to take it over.

The same might be said of your own personal shopping. When you go to buy a new car, the salesperson likely will work hard to convince you that you should purchase a specific make or model. Although a car salesperson has a significant amount of knowledge about the products and therefore can simplify the car buying process, the final decision must remain up to you, the consumer.

*A good CRM system provides salespeople with the information they need to suggest specific items and services to individual customers.*

## Power of the Internet 19.1    Personal Selling Goes Virtual

Rising fuel costs, increasing staff productivity, cutbacks in airline service, minimizing carbon footprints, reducing corporate expenditure—these are just some of the reasons for meetings to go virtual. Foremost among them is that the technology has matured to where conversing in cyberspace frequently makes more sense than meeting in the same room.[10]

The most advanced of these technologies, *telepresence*, includes three screens that display life-size images of conference attendees, plus an additional screen for shared work. Resolution on the screens exceeds that of high-definition televisions. Images can be magnified, allowing attendees to view minute product details from across the globe. These systems, which also feature custom lighting and acoustics, cost as much as $350,000. For corporations like Cisco, which has more than 200 telepresence rooms, the investment still represents a savings over travel costs. They aren't alone in seeing the value of telepresence: The management consulting and technology service firm Accenture estimates its teleconferencing rooms save millions of dollars each year as well as saving their staff the wear and tear of travel.

Other collaborative technologies involve less financial outlay. Web-meeting services, for example, allow companies to conduct online training, edit documents collaboratively, demonstrate applications, give training or sales presentations, poll attendees, chat online, conduct question and answer sessions, and provide technical support.[11] The only technology required for these and other collaborative tools, like wikis and Internet telephony, is a computer with a Web browser and a

connection to the Internet. For attendees, all that's needed is a URL for the conference site and a registration code.

This technology also helps small companies go global. Lisa Kirschner, president of a Chicago-based marketing and graphic design firm, had a hot lead in Italy.[12] However she lacked the resources to meet in person and felt brainstorming via e-mail would be too cumbersome. Taking the risk of investing in Web conferencing, which was unheard of in her industry, secured her clients in Italy, Japan, and Britain. The technology, she says, has earned her $100,000 worth of business—one-eighth of her annual revenue.

Reduced business travel means a slump in the conference business as well, particularly as the public scrutinizes corporate spending in the wake of government bailouts.[13] Increasingly, companies are relying on technology for virtual conferences. One product, Expos2, digitizes the conference. Attendees begin with a screen showing the convention center layout and follow links to exhibits, programs, and live presentations that have interactive functionality. Digital meeting technology isn't intended to replace face-to-face meetings or travel, but rather to provide an alternative for companies hoping to optimize their travel budgets. Closing a deal, for example, is more likely to occur during an in-person meeting, and business travel to other countries provides important insights into communities and cultures. All transactions benefit from a personal touch. Nevertheless, Web-based and conventional videoconferencing technology will have a profound impact on the way companies do business in the coming years.

*Salespeople no longer have to meet face-to-face with their customers to make the sale.*

*Professional selling can be a very lucrative career and is very visible to management.*

**Salespeople Build Relationships** As we discussed in Chapter 15, building strong marketing channel and supply chain relationships is a critical success factor. Who in the organization is better equipped to manage this relationship than the salesperson, the frontline emissary for the firm? The most successful salespeople are those who build strong relationships with their customers. They don't view themselves as being successful if they make a particular sale or one transaction at a time. Instead, they take a long-term perspective. Thus, building on the relationship concept introduced in Chapter 15, **relationship selling** is a sales philosophy and process that emphasizes a commitment to maintaining the relationship over the long term and investing in opportunities that are mutually beneficial to all parties.[14] Relationship salespeople work with their customers to find mutually beneficial solutions to their wants and needs. A Lenovo sales team, for instance, may be working with your university to provide you with the computer support and security you need for all four years you spend working with the school's network or computer labs.

 Define the steps in the personal selling process.

# THE PERSONAL SELLING PROCESS

Although selling may appear a rather straightforward process, successful salespeople follow several steps. Depending on the sales situation and the buyer's readiness to purchase, the salesperson may not use every step, and the time required for each step will vary depending on the situation. For instance, if a customer goes into The Gap already prepared to purchase some chinos, the selling process will be fairly quick. But if IBM is attempting to sell personal computers for the first time to a university, the process may take several months. With this in mind, let's examine each step of the selling process (Exhibit 19.1).

**EXHIBIT 19.1** The Personal Selling Process

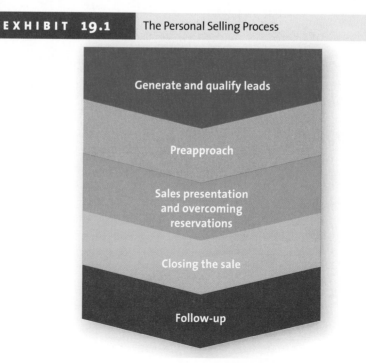

Generate and qualify leads

Preapproach

Sales presentation and overcoming reservations

Closing the sale

Follow-up

## Step 1: Generate and Qualify Leads

The first step in the selling process is to generate a list of potential customers (leads) and assess their potential (qualify leads). Salespeople who already have an established relationship with a customer will skip this step, and it is not used extensively in retail settings. In B2B situations, however, it is important to work continually to find new and potentially profitable customers.

Salespeople can generate and qualify leads in a variety of ways.[15] They can discover potential leads by talking to their current customers, doing research on the Internet, and networking at events such as trade shows and other venues such as industry conferences or chamber of commerce meetings. Salespeople can also generate leads through cold calls.

The Internet has been a boon for generating and qualifying leads. Prior to the Internet's explosion, it was cumbersome to perform research on products, customers, or competitors. Salespeople would rely on a research staff for this information, and it could take weeks for the research to be completed and sent through the mail.

Trade shows also offer an excellent forum for finding leads. These major events are attended by buyers who choose to be exposed to products and services offered by potential suppliers in an industry. Thus, consumer electronics buyers make sure that they attend the annual International Consumer Electronics Show (CES) in Las Vegas, the world's largest trade show for consumer technology (www.cesweb.org). The show is attended by 130,000 people from over 60 countries including vendors, developers, and suppliers of consumer-technology hardware, content, delivery systems, and related products and services. Nearly 2,400 vendor exhibits take up 1.8 million net square feet of exhibit space, showcasing the very latest products and services. Vendors often use the CES to introduce new products, including the first camcorder (1981), high-definition television (HDTV) (1998), and Internet protocol television (IP TV) (2005). In addition to providing an opportunity for retail buyers to see the latest products, the CES conference program features prominent speakers from the technology sector—perhaps most famously, Microsoft's Bill Gates.[16]

Cold calls are a method of prospecting in which salespeople telephone or go to see potential customers without appointments.[17] Telemarketing is similar to a cold call, but it always occurs over the telephone. Sometimes professional tele-

*Trade shows, like the International Consumer Electronics Show in Las Vegas, are an excellent way to generate and qualify leads.*

marketing firms, rather than the firm's salespeople, make such calls. However, cold calls and telemarketing have become less popular than they were in the past. First, the success rate is fairly low because the potential customer's need has not been established ahead of time. As a result, these methods can be very expensive. Second, both federal and state governments have begun to regulate the activities of telemarketers. Federal rules prohibit telemarketing to consumers whose names appear on the national Do-Not-Call list, which is maintained by the Federal Trade Commission. Even for those consumers whose names are not on the list, the rules prohibit calling before 8:00 a.m. or after 9:00 p.m. (in the consumer's time zone) or after the consumer has told the telemarketer not to call. Federal rules also prohibit unsolicited fax messages and unsolicited telephone calls, as well as e-mail messages to cell phones.

After salespeople generate leads, they must qualify those leads by determining whether it is worthwhile to pursue them and attempt to turn them into customers. In B2B settings, where the costs of preparing and making a presentation can be substantial, the seller must assess a lead's potential. Salespeople should consider, for instance, whether the potential customer's needs pertain to a product or a service. They should also assess whether the lead has the financial resources to pay for the product or service.[18] For instance, clients looking to sell multimillion-dollar properties want their real estate agent to qualify potential buyers. Their agent creates a password-protected website that features floor plans and inside views for the shopping convenience of interested buyers. To obtain the password to get into the site, the customer must be prequalified as one that could actually afford to buy the property, saving both the agent and the seller the trouble of showing properties to people who cannot afford to buy.

In a retail setting, qualifying potential customers can be a very dangerous and potentially illegal practice. Retail salespeople should never "judge a book by its cover" and assume that a person in the store doesn't fit the store's image or cannot afford to purchase there. Imagine going to an upscale jewelry store to purchase an engagement ring, only to be snubbed because you are dressed in your everyday, casual school clothes. Adding Value 19.1 examines how retail salespeople have fine-tuned how they approach their customers.

## Step 2: Preapproach and the Use of CRM Systems

The **preapproach** occurs prior to meeting the customer for the first time and extends the qualification of leads procedure described in Step 1. Although the salesperson has learned about the customer during the qualification stage, in this step he or she must conduct additional research and develop plans for meeting with the customer. Suppose, for example, a management consulting firm wants to sell a bank a new system for finding checking account errors. The consulting firm's salesperson should first find out everything possible about the bank: How many checks does it process? What system is the bank using now? What are the benefits of the consultant's proposed system compared with the competition? The answers to these questions provide the basis for establishing value for the customer.

In the past, this customer information, if it was available at all, was typically a manual system that individual salespeople kept in a notebook or on a series of cards. Today, salespeople have all this information available in their firm's CRM system.

Such CRM programs have several components. There is a customer database or data warehouse. Whether the salesperson is working for a retail store or manages a selling team for an aerospace contractor, he or she can record transaction information, customer contact information, customer preferences, and market segment information about the customer. Once the data have been analyzed and CRM programs developed, salespeople can help implement the programs.

*Salespeople input customer information into their PDAs to develop a customer database for CRM systems.*

## Adding Value 19.1    Retail Salespeople Cannot Judge a Book by Its Cover[19]

A woman in workout clothes enters a Madison Avenue jewelry store. Hair bunched in a Scunci, she's sporting a Timex on one wrist, a Nike gym bag over her shoulder, and something that looks suspiciously like dog hair on her sweatshirt. The sales associate, rather than suggesting she's wandered into the wrong store or ignoring her entirely, offers a glass of champagne. The woman, like any customer entering the store, might be a celebrity or a CEO, a serious shopper or a browser. With no way of knowing for sure, successful salespeople treat her and every customer with courtesy and respect.

Up and down Madison Avenue and all the way out to suburban malls, retail managers are recognizing that consumers can no longer be judged by their shoes or accessories, so they are taking measures to improve customer service for everyone. Smart salespeople realize that even wealthy rock stars wear tattered jeans, and everyone wears Nike workout clothes. Since customers can't be judged by their clothing, all customers have to be treated as valuable. The idea is catching on. One enterprising journalist, interested in testing customer service in New York's fashion hub, visited a dozen Madison Avenue stores.[20] Dressed inexpensively and with no intention of purchasing anything, he was greeted and helped immediately at nearly every store. Service went beyond a simple offer of assistance. At one store, a sales clerk kneeled at his feet to help him try on a pair of shoes. At another, an associate produced five sumptuous coats from somewhere beyond the sales floor in response to a request for a gift. Water appeared on a silver tray carried by a uniformed butler, and offers were made to tailor deeply discounted merchandise. Retailers carrying less expensive merchandise, like Gap, Macy's and J. Crew, are trying to improve the shopping experience in their own ways.

Enhancing customer service may take many forms. At Bergdorf Goodman, already known for personalized attention, Saturday morning meetings are devoted to the subject.[21] The luxury goods department store follows up sales as small as $18 with a thank-you note; they even replaced the security company responsible for their doormen to ensure friendly service began at the front door. The Italian fashion house MaxMara conducts employee seminars to provide pointers on sales interactions, and Lord & Taylor sales asso-

*Retail sales people should never "judge a book by its cover" and assume that a person in the store doesn't fit the store's image or cannot afford to purchase there.*

ciates are counseled to comment on the attributes of a product being examined by a customer rather than use the more aggressive sales opener, "Can I help you?" Additional approaches include helping customers track down merchandise at other store locations and having it shipped to a convenient outlet, and asking for customer feedback in person or through follow-up surveys.

Going the extra mile in sales isn't always easy. Salespeople have the difficult job of figuring out what type of a customer they are working with, especially if this is the first time they meet them. Salespeople must rapidly discern customers' personalities and their needs and determine the best selling strategy for meeting those needs. Furthermore, the sales associate has to determine customers' economic comfort level: Underselling the customer can hurt individual salespeople's goals or store sales goals and potentially, even worse, leave customers feeling inadequately served. Overselling, on the other hand, can anger or overwhelm the customer, leading to both a lost sale and a lost customer who may wind up buying nothing at all and maybe never return to the store.

Having done the additional research, the salesperson establishes goals for meeting with the customer. It is important that he or she knows ahead of time exactly what should be accomplished. For instance, the consulting firm's salesperson can't expect to get a commitment from the bank that it will buy on the first visit. But a demonstration of the system and a short presentation about how the system would benefit the customer would be appropriate. It is often a good idea to practice the presentation prior to the meeting using a technique known as role playing, in which the salesperson acts out a simulated buying situation while a colleague or manager acts as the buyer. Afterward, the practice sales presentation can be critiqued and adjustments can be made.

*These salespeople are role playing. The woman standing at the easel is acting out a simulated buying situation while her colleagues act as the buying group. Afterward they will critique her presentation.*

## Step 3: Sales Presentation and Overcoming Reservations

**The Presentation** Once all the background information has been obtained and the objectives for the meeting are set, the salesperson is ready for a person-to-person meeting. Let's continue with our bank example. During the first part of the meeting, the salesperson needs to get to know the customer, get his or her attention, and create interest in the presentation to follow. The beginning of the presentation may be the most important part of the entire selling process, because this is where the salesperson establishes exactly where the customer is in his or her buying process (Exhibit 19.2). (For a refresher on the B2B buying process, see Chapter 6.)

Suppose, for instance, the bank is in the first stage of the buying process, need recognition. It would not be prudent for the salesperson to discuss the pros and cons of different potential suppliers because doing so would assume that the customer already had reached Step 4, proposal analysis and customer selection. By asking a series of questions, however, the salesperson can assess the bank's need for the product or service and adapt or customize the presentation to match the customer's need and stage in the decision process.[22]

Asking questions is only half the battle; carefully listening to the answers is equally important. Some salespeople, particularly inexperienced ones, believe that to be in control, they must do all the talking. Yet it is impossible to really understand where the customer stands without listening carefully. What if the COO says, "It seems kind of expensive"? If the salesperson isn't listening carefully, he or she won't pick up on the subtle nuances of what the customer is really thinking. In this case, it probably means the COO doesn't see the value in the offering.

**EXHIBIT 19.2** Aligning the Personal Selling Process with the B2B Buying Process

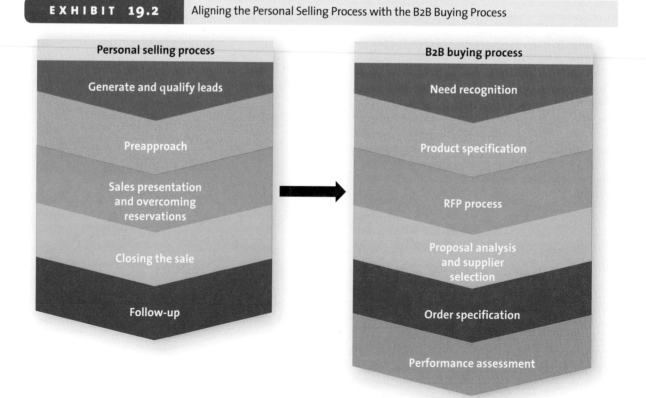

**Personal selling process**

- Generate and qualify leads
- Preapproach
- Sales presentation and overcoming reservations
- Closing the sale
- Follow-up

**B2B buying process**

- Need recognition
- Product specification
- RFP process
- Proposal analysis and supplier selection
- Order specification
- Performance assessment

When the salesperson has gotten a good feel for where the customer stands, he or she can apply that knowledge to help the customer solve the problem or satisfy the need. The salesperson might begin by explaining the features or characteristics of the system that will reduce checking account errors. It may not be obvious, solely on the basis of these features, however, that the system adds value beyond the bank's current practices. Using the answers to some of the questions the salesperson posed earlier in the meeting, he or she can clarify the product's advantages over current or past practices, as well as the overall benefits of adopting the new system. The salesperson might explain, for instance, that the bank can expect a 20 percent improvement in checking account errors and that, because of the size of the bank and number of checks it processes per year, this improvement would represent $2 million in annual savings. Because the system costs $150,000 per year and will take only three weeks to integrate into the current system, it will add significant and almost immediate value.

**Handling Reservations**  An integral part of the sales presentation is handling reservations or objections that the buyer might have about the product or service. Although reservations can arise during each stage of the selling process, they are very likely to occur during the sales presentation. Customers may raise reservations pertaining to a variety of issues, but they usually relate in some way to value, such as that the price is too high for the level of quality or service is doubtful.

Good salespeople know the types of reservations buyers are likely to raise. They may know, for instance, that their service is slower than competitors' or that their selection is limited. Although not all reservations can be forestalled, effective salespeople can anticipate and handle some. For example, when the bank COO said the check service seemed expensive, the salesperson was ready with information about how quickly the investment would be recouped.

As in other aspects of the selling process, the best way to handle reservations is to relax and listen, then ask questions to clarify any reservations.[23] For example, the salesperson could respond to the COO's reservation by asking, "How much do you think the bank is losing through checking account errors?" Her answer might open up a conversation about the positive trends in a cost/benefit analysis. Such questions are usually more effective than trying to prove the customer's reservation is not valid, because the latter approach implies the salesperson isn't really listening and could lead to an argument. In an attempt to handle reservations and start the process of closing the sale, a salesperson may even offer creative deals or incentives that may be unethical.

## Step 4: Closing the Sale

**Closing the sale** means obtaining a commitment from the customer to make a purchase. Without a successful close, the salesperson goes away empty-handed, so many salespeople find this part of the sales process very stressful. Although losing a sale is never pleasant, salespeople who are involved in a relationship with their customers must view any particular sales presentation as part of the progression toward ultimately making the sale. An unsuccessful close on one day may just be a means of laying the groundwork for a successful close the next meeting. Superior Service 19.1 examines the art of *soft-selling*.

Although we have presented the selling process as a series of steps, closing the sale rarely follows the other steps so neatly. However, good salespeople listen carefully to what potential customers say and pay attention to their body language. Reading these signals carefully can help salespeople achieve an early close. Suppose that our hypothetical bank, instead of being in the first step of the buying process, has already explored and bought in to the benefits of a new system and is in fact at the final step of negotiation and selection. An astute salesperson will pick up on these signals and ask for the sale.

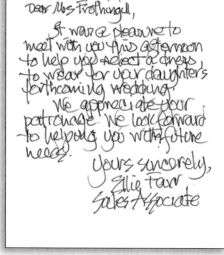

Dear Mrs Frothingall,
It was a pleasure to meet with you this afternoon to help you select a dress to wear for your daughter's forthcoming wedding. We appreciate your patronage. We look forward to helping you with future needs.
Yours sincerely,
Ellie Farr
Sales Associate

*A postsale follow-up letter, call, or e-mail is the first step in initiating a new order and sustaining the relationship.*

## Step 5: Follow-Up

> "It ain't over till it's over."
> —Yogi Berra[24]

With relationship selling, it is never really over, even after the sale has been made. The attitudes customers develop after the sale become the basis for how they will purchase in the future. The follow-up therefore offers a prime opportunity for a salesperson to solidify the customer relationship through great service quality. Let's apply the five service quality dimensions we discussed in Chapter 12 to the follow-up:[25]

- **Reliability.** The salesperson and the supporting organization must deliver the right product or service on time.
- **Responsiveness.** The salesperson and support group must be ready to deal quickly with any issue, question, or problem that may arise.
- **Assurance.** Customers must be assured through adequate guarantees that their purchase will perform as expected.
- **Empathy.** The salesperson and support group must have a good understanding of the problems and issues faced by their customers. Otherwise, they cannot give them what they want.
- **Tangibles.** Because tangibles reflect the physical characteristics of the seller's business, such as its website, marketing communications, and delivery materials, their influence is more subtle than that of the other four service quality dimensions. That doesn't mean they are any less important. For instance, retail customers are generally more pleased with a purchase if it is carefully wrapped in nice paper instead of being haphazardly thrown into a crumpled plastic bag. The tangibles offer a signal that the product is of high quality, even though the packaging has nothing to do with the product's performance.

When customers' expectations are not met, they often complain—about deliveries, the billing amount or process, the product's performance, or after-sale services such as installation or training. Effectively handling complaints is critical to the future of the relationship. As we noted in Chapter 12, the best way to handle complaints is to listen to the customer, provide a fair solution to the problem, and resolve the problem quickly.

The best way to nip a postsale problem in the bud is to check with the customer right after he or she takes possession of the product or immediately after the service has been completed. This speed demonstrates responsiveness and empathy. It also shows the customer that the salesperson and the firm care about customer satisfaction. Finally, a postsale follow-up call, e-mail, or letter takes the salesperson back to the first step in the sales process for initiating a new order and sustaining the relationship.

## CHECK YOURSELF

1. Why is personal selling important to an IMC strategy?
2. What are the steps in the personal selling process?

## Superior Service 19.1          Soft-Selling Works

Ever feel as though a salesperson is trying not to tap his foot or roll his eyes while you decide what flavor ice cream you want? Or have you ever had a sales associate eagerly assure you an outfit looks great on you when the mirror tells you differently? If so, those salespeople are making a significant mistake. By focusing on a single transaction, they could be losing repeat customers. Soft-selling, or acting as a knowledgeable consultant to help customers solve a problem, is far more likely to result in a completed sale in the present and more business in the future.[26]

The soft sell, also known as consultative or customer-centric sales, involves creating and maintaining a pleasant environment, interacting pleasantly with customers, providing useful information about products, helping customers reach a decision, and selling a product or service the sales associate believes in. The concept isn't new: In the days of small neighborhood stores, employees greeted shoppers by name, knew their preferences and personalities, and helped customers track down a product even if it meant calling a competitor. But a focus on profits brought with it the hard sell, characterized by pressure and hype. Over time, hard-selling backfired, driving customers to more pleasant environments for their purchases. Now savvy retailers returning to the original softer approach are building profits, even in the midst of a challenging economy.

Yoforia's frozen yogurt stores in Atlanta provide a good example of soft-selling. Servers greet customers warmly, suggest samples to help with flavor decisions, and describe what makes the yogurt healthy. The result has been a 40 percent increase in sales over the previous year. Soft-selling

has even made it to the Girl Scouts, where parents helping their children hawk Thin Mints and Samoas are making sign-up sheets available in public spaces rather than tracking coworkers to their cubicles.[27]

Consultative selling works well for larger purchases and even in situations when months or years may elapse before a transaction is made. The idea is to provide prospects with quality information that helps them solve business problems.[28] This information may be delivered over lunch or via Webinar, blog, white paper, or e-mail and needn't promote a particular product or service. Rather, the focus should be on reliable content that consumers can use to make a purchase decision. Apple stores, for example, have online screenings about new models and the Genius Bar for free technical help.

Training sales associates in consultative selling requires more subtlety than haranguing staff to close a deal. Sales associates at Container Stores are selected for their ability to solve problems and relate to customers. They work for salary and not for commissions. Servers at Yoforia gain their sales skills through one-on-one interactions with the store's cofounder, Jun Kim, who stresses a good customer experience over making sales. Key to a positive experience, once customers have been welcomed to a pleasant environment, is communicating with customers to determine their needs and using that information to identify appropriate choices and provide advice. Additional products or services should be suggested only if the customer has indicated a potential need. Ultimately, the goal of soft sales is to keep the customer for life and not just for a single transaction.

*The Girl Scouts employ the soft sell approach to sell cookies by encouraging parents to use sign-up sheets in their offices rather than tracking coworkers to their cubicles.*

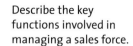

Describe the key functions involved in managing a sales force.

# MANAGING THE SALES FORCE

Like any business activity involving people, the sales force requires management. Sales management involves the planning, direction, and control of personal selling activities, including recruiting, selecting, training, motivating, compensating, and evaluating, as they apply to the sales force.

Managing a sales force is a rewarding yet complicated undertaking. In this section, we examine how sales forces can be structured, some of the most important issues in recruiting and selecting salespeople, sales training issues, ways to compensate salespeople, and finally, how to supervise and evaluate salespeople.

## Sales Force Structure

Imagine the daunting task of putting together a sales force from scratch. Will you hire your own salespeople, or should they be manufacturer's representatives? What will be each salesperson's primary duties: order takers, order getters, sales support? Finally, will they work together in teams? In this section, we examine each of these issues.

**Company Sales Force or Manufacturer's Representative** A company sales force comprises people who are employees of the selling company. Independent agents, also known as manufacturer's representatives, or "reps," are salespeople who sell a manufacturer's products on an extended contract basis but are not employees of the manufacturer. They are compensated by commissions and do not take ownership or physical possession of the merchandise.

Manufacturer's representatives are useful for smaller firms or firms expanding into new markets because such companies can achieve instant and extensive sales coverage without having to pay full-time personnel. Good sales representatives have many established contacts and can sell multiple products from noncompeting manufacturers during the same sales call. Also, the use of manufacturer's representatives facilitates flexibility; it is much easier to replace a rep than an employee and much easier to expand or contract coverage in a market with a sales rep than with a company sales force.

Company sales forces are more typically used for established product lines. Because the salespeople are company employees, the manufacturer has more control over what they do. If, for example, the manufacturer's strategy is to provide extensive customer service, the sales manager can specify exactly what actions a company sales force must take. In contrast, because manufacturer's representatives are paid on a commission basis, it is difficult to persuade them to take any action that doesn't directly lead to sales.

*Order takers process routine orders or reorders or rebuys for products.*

**Salesperson Duties** Although the life of a professional salesperson is highly varied, salespeople generally play three important roles: order getting, order taking, and sales support.

**Order Getting** An order getter is a salesperson whose primary responsibilities are identifying potential customers and engaging those customers in discussions to attempt to make a sale. An order getter is also responsible for following up with the customer to ensure that the customer is satisfied and to build the relationship. In B2B settings, order getters are primarily involved in new buy and modified new buy situations (see Chapter 6). As a result, they require extensive sales and product knowledge training. The Coca-Cola salesperson who goes to Safeway's headquarters to sell a special promotion of Vanilla Coke is an order getter.

**Order Taking** An order taker is a salesperson whose primary responsibility is to process routine orders or reorders or rebuys for products. Colgate employs order takers around the globe who go into stores and

distribution centers that already carry Colgate products to check inventory, set up displays, write new orders, and make sure everything is going smoothly.

**Sales Support** Sales support personnel enhance and help with the overall selling effort. For example, if a Best Buy customer begins to experience computer problems, the company has a Geek Squad door-to-door service as well as support in the store. Those employees who respond to the customer's technical questions and repair the computer serve to support the overall sales process.

**Combination Duties** Although some salespeople's primary function may be order getting, order taking, or sales support, others fill a combination of roles. For instance, a computer salesperson at Staples may spend an hour with a customer educating him or her about the pros and cons of various systems and then make the sale. The next customer might simply need a specific printer cartridge. A third customer might bring in a computer and seek advice about an operating system problem. The salesperson was first an order getter, next an order taker, and finally a sales support person.

Some firms use selling teams that combine sales specialists whose primary duties are order getting, order taking, or sales support but who work together to service important accounts. As companies become larger and products more complicated, it is nearly impossible for one person to perform all the necessary sales functions.

## Recruiting and Selecting Salespeople

When the firm has determined how the sales force will be structured, it must find and hire salespeople. Although superficially this task may sound as easy as posting the job opening on the Internet or running an ad in a newspaper, it must be performed carefully because firms don't want to hire the wrong person—salespeople are very expensive to train.

The most important activity in the recruiting process is to determine exactly what the salesperson will be doing and what personal traits and abilities a person should have to do the job well. For instance, the Coca-Cola order getter who goes to Safeway to pitch a new product will typically need significant sales experience, coupled with great communication and analytical skills. Coke's order takers need to be reliable and able to get along with lots of different types of people in the stores, from managers to customers.

Many firms give candidates personality tests, but stress different personality attributes depending on the requisite traits for the position and the personality characteristics of its most successful salespeople.[29] For instance, impatience is often a positive characteristic of a salesperson because in most sales jobs it creates a sense of urgency to close the sale. But for very large, complicated sales that are made to large institutions, like a bank, an impatient salesperson may irritate the decision makers and kill the deal.

When recruiting salespeople, is it better to look for candidates with innate sales ability, or can a good training program make anyone a successful salesperson? In other words, are good salespeople born or are they made?[30] By a margin of seven to one in a survey of sales and marketing executives, respondents believed that training and supervision are more critical determinants of selling success than the salesperson's inherent personal characteristics.[31] Yet some of those same respondents noted that they knew "born salespeople" and that personal traits are important for successful sales careers. So, it appears that to be a successful salesperson, while it helps to have good training, the first requirement is to possess certain personal traits.

What are those personal traits? Managers and sales experts have identified the following:[32]

- Personality. Good salespeople are friendly, sociable, and, in general, like being around people. Customers won't buy from someone they don't like.
- Optimism. Good salespeople tend to look at the bright side of things. Optimism also may help them be resilient—the third trait.

- Resilience. Good salespeople don't easily take no for an answer. They keep coming back until they get a yes.

- Self-motivation. As we have already mentioned, salespeople have lots of freedom to spend their days the way they believe will be most productive. But if the salespeople are not self-motivated to get the job done, it probably won't get done.

- Empathy. Empathy is one of the five dimensions of service quality discussed previously in this chapter and in Chapter 12. Good salespeople must care about their customers, their issues, and their problems.

## Sales Training

Even people who possess all these personal traits need training. All salespeople benefit from training about selling and negotiation techniques, product and service knowledge, technologies used in the selling process, time and territory management, and company policies and procedures.

Firms use varied delivery methods to train their salespeople, depending on the topic of the training, what type of salesperson is being trained, and the cost versus the value of the training. For instance, an on-the-job training program is excellent for communicating selling and negotiation skills because managers can observe the sales trainees in real selling situations and provide instant feedback. They can also engage in role-playing exercises in which the salesperson acts out a simulated buying situation and the manager critiques the salesperson's performance.

A much less expensive, but for some purposes equally valuable, training method is the Internet. Online training programs have revolutionized the way training happens in many firms. Firms can provide new product and service knowledge, spread the word about changes in company policies and procedures, and share selling tips in a user-friendly environment that salespeople can access anytime and anywhere. Distance learning sales training programs through teleconferencing enable a group of salespeople to participate with their instructor or manager in a virtual classroom. And testing can occur online as well. Online sales training may never replace the one-on-one interaction of on-the-job training for advanced selling skills, but it is quite effective and efficient for many other aspects of the sales training task.

## Motivating and Compensating Salespeople

An important goal for any effective sales manager is to get to know his or her salespeople and determine what motivates them to be effective. Some salespeople prize their freedom and like to be left alone, whereas others want attention and are more productive when they receive accolades for a job well done. Still others are motivated primarily by monetary compensation. Great sales managers determine how best to motivate each of their salespeople according to what is most important to each individual. Although sales managers can emphasize different motivating factors, except in the smallest companies the methods used to compensate salespeople must be fairly standardized and can be divided into two categories: financial and nonfinancial.

**Financial Rewards** Salespeople's compensation usually has several components. Most salespeople receive at least part of their compensation as a salary, a fixed sum of money paid at regular intervals. Another common financial incentive is a commission, which, as we've already mentioned, is money paid as

*Technology has changed the lives of salespeople and sales training. Companies can conduct distance learning and training through videoconferencing.*

a percentage of the sales volume or profitability. A bonus is a payment made at management's discretion when the salesperson attains certain goals. Bonuses usually are given only periodically, such as at the end of the year. A sales contest is a short-term incentive designed to elicit a specific response from the sales force. Prizes might be cash or other types of financial incentives. For instance, Volkswagen may give a free trip to Germany for the salesperson who sells the most Touaregs.

The bulk of any compensation package is made up of salary, commission, or a combination of the two. The advantage of a salary plan is that salespeople know exactly what they will be paid, and sales managers therefore have more control over their salespeople. For instance, salaried salespeople can be directed to spend a certain percentage of their time handling customer service issues. Under a commission system, however, salespeople have only one objective—make the sale! Thus, a commission system provides the most incentive for the sales force to sell.

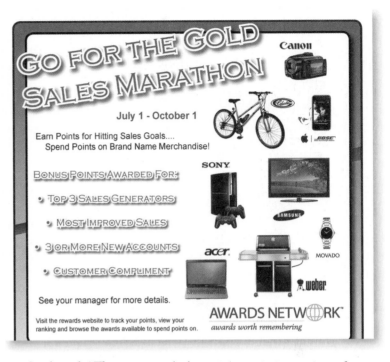

*Sales contests are a type of financial reward that provide prizes like these or other types of financial incentives.*

**Nonfinancial Rewards** As we have noted, good salespeople are self-motivated. They want to do a good job and make the sale because it makes them feel good. But this good feeling also can be accentuated by recognition from peers and management. For instance, the internal monthly magazine at the cosmetics firm Mary Kay provides an outlet for not only selling advice but also companywide recognition of individual salespeople's accomplishments.[33]

Nonfinancial rewards should have high symbolic value, as plaques, pens, or rings do. Free trips or days off are also effective rewards. More important than what the reward is, however, is the way it is operationalized. For instance, an award should be given at a sales meeting and publicized in the company newsletter. It should also be done in good taste, because if the award is perceived as tacky, no one will take it seriously.[34] Mary Kay recognizes salespeople's success with unusually large rewards that have both high symbolic and high material value. More than 100,000 Independent Beauty Consultants and sales directors have earned the use of one of the famous pink Cadillacs, but it is also possible to gain rewards and recognition such as a set of faux pearl earrings within the first week of becoming a consultant.

*Mary Kay gives high-performing salespeople an award that has both high symbolic and material value—a pink Cadillac.*

**Evaluating Salespeople by Using Marketing Metrics**
Salespeople's evaluation process must be tied to their reward structure. If salespeople do well, they should receive their just rewards, in the same way that if you do well on your exams and assignments in a class, you should earn a good grade. However, salespeople should be evaluated and rewarded for only those activities and outcomes that fall under their control. For instance, if Macy's makes a unilateral decision to put Diesel jeans in all its stores after a negotiation with Diesel's corporate headquarters in Italy, the Diesel sales representatives responsible for individual Macy's stores should not receive credit for making the sale, nor should they get all the windfall commission that will ensue from the added sales.

Considering this guiding principle—evaluate and reward salespeople for what they do and not for what they don't do—how should sales managers evaluate their salespeople? The answer is never easy because measures must be tied to performance, and there are many ways to measure performance in a complex job like selling. For example, evaluating performance on the basis of monthly sales alone fails to consider how profitable the sales were, whether any progress was made to build new business that will be realized sometime in the future, or the level of customer service the salesperson provided. Because the sales job is multifaceted with many contributing success factors, sales managers should use multiple measures.[35]

Evaluation measures are either objective or subjective. Sales, profits, and the number of orders represent examples of objective measures. Although each is somewhat useful to managers, such measures do not provide an adequate perspective for a thorough evaluation because there is no means of comparison with other salespeople. For instance, suppose salesperson A generated $1 million last year, but salesperson B generated $1.5 million. Should salesperson B automatically receive a significantly higher evaluation? Now consider that salesperson B's territory has twice as much potential as salesperson A's. Knowing this, we might suppose that salesperson A has actually done a better job. For this reason, firms use ratios like profit per customer, orders per call, sales per hour, or expenses compared to sales as their objective measures.

Whereas objective measures are quantitative, subjective measures seek to assess salespeople's behavior: what they do and how well they do it. By their very nature, subjective measures reflect one person's opinion about another's performance. Thus, subjective evaluations can be biased and should be used cautiously and only in conjunction with multiple objective measures.

---

### CHECK YOURSELF

1. What do sales managers need to do to successfully manage their sales force?
2. What is the difference between monetary and nonmonetary incentives?

---

**LO4** Describe the ethical and legal issues in personal selling.

# ETHICAL AND LEGAL ISSUES IN PERSONAL SELLING

Although ethical and legal issues permeate all aspects of marketing, they are particularly important for personal selling. Unlike advertising and other communications with customers, which are planned and executed on a corporate level, personal selling involves a one-to-one, and often face-to-face, encounter with the customer. Thus, sellers' actions are highly visible not only to customers but also to other stakeholders, such as the communities in which they work.

Ethical and legal issues arise in three areas in personal selling. First, there is the relationship between the sales manager and the sales force. Second, in some situations, an inconsistency might exist between corporate policy and the salesperson's ethical comfort zone. Third, both ethical and legal issues can arise when the salesperson interacts with the customer, especially if that salesperson or the selling firm collects significant information about the customer. To maintain trustworthy customer relationships, companies must take care that they respect customer privacy and respect the information comfort zone—that is, the amount of information a customer feels comfortable providing.[36]

## The Sales Manager and the Sales Force

Like any manager, a sales manager must treat people fairly and equally in everything he or she does. With regard to the sales force, this fairness must include hiring, promotion, supervision, training, assigning duties and quotas, compensation and incentives, and firing.[37] Federal laws cover many of these issues. For instance, equal employment opportunity laws make it unlawful to discriminate against a person in hiring, promotion, or firing because of race, religion, nationality, sex, or age.

## The Sales Force and Corporate Policy

Sometimes salespeople face a conflict between what they believe represents ethical selling and what their company asks them to do to make a sale. Suppose an insurance agent, whose compensation is based on commission, which is a percentage of the agent's sales, sells a homeowner's policy to a family that has just moved to New Orleans, an area prone to flooding as a result of hurricanes. Even though the policy covers hurricane damage, it does not cover water damage from hurricanes. If the salesperson discloses the inadequate coverage, the sale might be lost because additional flood insurance is very expensive. What should the salesperson do? Salespeople must live within their own ethical comfort zone. If this, or any other situation, is morally repugnant to the salesperson, he or she must question whether they want to be associated with the company.[38]

*Salespeople must live within their own ethical comfort zone. Should insurance salespeople disclose inadequate hurricane coverage and risk not making the sale?*

Salespeople also can be held accountable for illegal actions sanctioned by the employer. If the homeowner asks if the home is above the floodplain or whether water damage from flooding is covered by the policy, and it is company policy to intentionally mislead potential customers, both the salesperson and the insurance dealership could be susceptible to legal action.

## The Salesperson and the Customer

As the frontline emissaries for a firm, salespeople have a duty to be ethically and legally correct in all their dealings with their customers. Not only is it the right thing to do, but it simply means good business. Long-term relationships can deteriorate quickly if customers believe that they have not been treated in an ethically proper manner. Unfortunately, salespeople sometimes get mixed signals from their managers or simply do not know when their behaviors might be considered unethical or illegal. Formal guidelines can help, but it is also important to integrate these guidelines into training programs in which salespeople can discuss various issues that arise in the field with their peers and managers. Most important, however, is for sales managers to lead by example. If managers are known to cut ethical corners in their dealings with customers, it shouldn't surprise them when their salespeople do the same. Ethical and Societal Dilemma 19.1 considers the ethical issues that pharmaceutical salespeople face.

---

### CHECK YOURSELF

1. What are three areas of personal selling in which ethical and legal issues are more likely to arise?

## Summing Up

**LO1**   **Describe the value added of personal selling.**

Although the cost of an average B2B sales call is high, many firms believe they couldn't do business without their sales force. Customers can buy many products and services without the help of a salesperson, but in many other cases, it is worth the extra cost built into the price of a product to be educated about the product or get valuable advice. Salespeople can also simplify the buying process and therefore save the customer time and hassle.

**LO2**   **Define the steps in the personal selling process.**

Although we discuss selling in terms of steps, it truly represents a process, and the time spent in each step varies according to the situation. In the first step, the salesperson generates a list of viable customers. During the second step, the preapproach, the salesperson gathers information about the customer and prepares for the presentation. The third step, the sales presentation, consists of a personal meeting between the salesperson and the customer. Through discussion and by asking questions, the salesperson learns where the customer is in the buying process and tailors the discussion around what the firm's product or service can do to meet that customer's needs. During the fourth step, the close, the salesperson asks for the order. Finally, during the follow-up, the salesperson and support staff solidify the long-term relationship by making sure the customer is satisfied with the purchase and addressing any complaints. The follow-up therefore sets the stage for the next purchase.

**L03**  **Describe the key functions involved in managing a sales force.**

The first task of a sales manager, assuming a firm is starting a sales force from scratch, is to determine whether to use a company sales force or manufacturer's representatives. Then sales managers must determine what the primary selling responsibilities will be—order getter, order taker, or sales support. The sales manager recruits and selects salespeople, but because there are all sorts of sales jobs, he or she must determine what it takes to be successful and then go after people with those attributes. In the next step, training, firms can choose between on-the-job and online training. Sales managers are also responsible for motivating and compensating salespeople. Most salespeople appreciate a balance of financial

and nonfinancial rewards for doing a good job. Finally, sales managers are responsible for evaluating their salespeople. Normally, salespeople should be evaluated on a combination of objective measures, such as sales per hour, and subjective measures, such as how friendly they appear to customers.

**L04**  **Describe the ethical and legal issues in personal selling.**

Ethical and legal issues arise in three areas in personal selling. First, ethical and legal issues could arise based on how the sales manager interacts with the sales force. Second, there might be inconsistencies between corporate policy and the salesperson's ethical comfort zone. Finally, ethical and legal issues can arise as the salesperson interacts with customers.

## Key Terms

- bonus, 581
- closing the sale, 575
- cold calls, 571
- commission, 580
- company sales force, 578
- independent agents, 578
- leads, 571
- manufacturer's representative, 578

- order getter, 578
- order taker, 578
- personal selling, 567
- preapproach, 572
- qualify leads, 571
- relationship selling, 570
- reps, 578
- role playing, 573

- salary, 580
- sales contest, 581
- sales management, 578
- sales support personnel, 579
- selling teams, 579
- telemarketing, 571
- trade shows, 571

## Marketing Applications

1. How has your perception of what it would be like to have a career in sales changed since you read this chapter?

2. "Salespeople just make products cost more." Do you agree or disagree with this statement? Discuss why you've taken that position.

3. Choose an industry or a specific company that you would like to work for as a salesperson. How would you generate and qualify leads?

4. Why is it important for salespeople to be good listeners? To be good at asking questions?

5. Suppose you are a salesperson at a high-end jewelry store. What can you do to ensure that your customers are satisfied? Now imagine you are the store manager of the same store; what can you do

in your position to guarantee customers remain happy with the service they receive?

6. Imagine that a time machine has transported you back to 1961. How was a day in the life of a salesperson selling appliances such as washing machines different in 1961 than it is in 2012?

7. What are some of the potentially ethically troubling and illegal situations facing professional salespeople, and how should they deal with them?

8. Why would Gillette use a company sales force, while a small independent manufacturer of organic shaving cream uses manufacturer's representatives?

9. Similar to the way a sales manager evaluates a salesperson, your instructors evaluate your performance to assign you a grade. Choose one of your

classes and analyze the advantages and disadvantages of the objective and subjective bases used to evaluate your performance.

10. A customer has the following reservations. How do you respond?

    a. "I really like all the things this copier does, but I don't think it's going to be very reliable. With all those features, something's got to go wrong."

    b. "Your price for this printer is higher than the price I saw advertised on the Internet."

11. Imagine that you have just been hired by an online start-up company to sell ads on its website. You are asked what you think would be a "fair" compensation package for you. Using the information from the chapter, make a list of all the elements that should be included in your compensation package. What changes, if any, should be made over time?

12. You have taken a summer job in the windows and doors department of a large home improvement store. During sales training, you learn about the products, how to best address customers' needs, and how to sell the customer the best product to fit their needs regardless of price point. One day your manager informs you that you are to recommend Smith Windows to every window customer. Smith Windows are more expensive and don't really provide superior benefit except in limited circumstances. The manager is insistent that you recommend Smith. Not knowing what else to do, you recommend Smith Windows to customers who would have been better served by lower cost windows. The manager rewards you with a sales award. Later the manager tells you that he received an all-expenses-paid cruise for his family from Smith Windows. What, if anything, should you do with this information?

## Quiz Yourself

www.mhhe.com/grewal3e

1. Consumers often ask workers in supermarkets where something is located only to learn the workers are vendors stacking and straightening their companies' products on the store shelves. These manufacturer's sales representatives benefit retailers by _____.

    a. education
    b. advice
    c. saving them time and money
    d. adding product lines
    e. increasing marketing costs to the seller

2. Bridgette went to The Gap ready to buy a new blouse, but was not sure which color or style she wanted. The sales representative, sensing Bridgette's buying mode, began with the _____ stage of the selling process.

    a. generating leads
    b. preapproach
    c. closing the sale
    d. follow-up
    e. sales presentation

    (Answers to these two questions are provided on page 606.)

    Go to www.mhhe.com/grewal3e to practice an additional 11 questions.

## Net Savvy

1. Go to The Salesforce.com's YouTube channel at www.youtube.com/user/salesforce. Watch a few of the short videos and discuss how the tools they are describing would help you as a salesperson.

2. To learn more about careers in sales, go to www.bls.gov/oco/, the website for the Bureau of Labor Statistics. This site contains a wealth of information about careers in all fields. Click on "Sales," then "Sales Occupations." Choose any of the sales fields listed, and explore that career field. What experience is necessary to be hired for that job? What is the median salary? What do earners in the highest 10 percent of performance earn? Is job growth anticipated in that field?

| Chapter Case Study |
| --- |

## ALTA DATA SOLUTIONS: MAKING THE SALE[40]

When Vicki Cambridge reached her office, she had a message from Mike Smith, the regional sales manager, to meet him in his office regarding the Burtell Inc. order. Vicki Cambridge is a senior sales associate for Alta Data Solutions Inc., a firm that markets software and hardware designed for data storage. The Burtell order represents a multimillion-dollar contract for Alta Data Solutions and would help Burtell boost its productivity levels and revenue for the region. To prepare for the meeting, Vicki reviews her sales call report notes on the Burtell account.

### ALTA DATA SOLUTIONS

Alta Data Solutions provides software and hardware solutions to large firms and has an established track record for delivering an exceptional standard of quality and high levels of customer service. This excellent reputation allows Alta Data Solutions to charge a substantial premium, ranging from 10 to 20 percent above the market leader.

The data storage software services market has been dominated for two decades by this market leader. Alta Data Solutions holds the second position in the marketplace, with a considerably lower but growing market share. Only one other competitor, an aggressive, small, low-price player, holds a significant market share; this provider has made inroads into the market in the past several years through its aggressive sales tactics.

Alta Data Solutions has just built a new facility and hired 50 new software programmers. Therefore, the company must generate new business to meet its higher financial goals; even more important in the short run, it must keep the new programmers working on interesting projects to retain them.

### BURTELL INC.

Burtell Inc. is a division of a major U.S.-based consumer products firm. Its purchasing department negotiates contracts for software services and coordinates the interface among a variety of members from different departments. The business environment for consumer products has become highly competitive in recent years, leading to tight budgets and higher levels of scrutiny of the value added by vendors. Competition is fierce, as large numbers of end-user customers are considering vendors that provide the most data analysis with their products.

Burtell Inc. has been consistently buying software development services from the market leader since 1991 and is generally satisfied with its service. A recent change in corporate leadership, however, has increased concerns about its overreliance on one vendor for a particular service. Also, because of the difficult economic climate, the company is concerned about the cost of software services and whether it is necessary to provide such a high service level.

### VICKI'S CALL REPORT

A call report is like a diary of sales calls made to a particular client. The notes in Vicki's Burtell file pertaining to the current negotiations began on June 4:

> June 4  I contacted Bethany O'Meara, Chief Purchasing Officer at Burtell, to introduce myself to her and get a sense of what their future software needs might be. She told me that the slowed business climate had caused Burtell to

*What are the key points Vicki should make in her presentation?*

institute a program for increased efficiency in operations and that they would be looking to negotiate a new contract for software solutions. She gave me some insights into the technological aspects of their needs.

June 18 Met with Jon Aaronson, head of R&D, to explain our productivity-enhancing solutions. Went into considerable depth explaining how Burtell could service their needs and learned what they were looking for in a provider. I went over some specific product specification issues, but Jon did not seem impressed. But he did ask for a price and told me that the final decision rested with Brad Alexander, the Chief Financial Officer.

July 2 Presented to Bethany O'Meara and Jon Aaronson. They first asked about the price. I gave them a quote of $10 million. They suggested that other services were much cheaper. I explained that our price reflected the latest technology and that the price differential was an investment that could pay for itself several times over through faster communication speeds. I also emphasized our reputation for high-quality customer service. While the presentation appeared to meet their software needs, they did not seem impressed with the overall value. I also sent a copy of the presentation in report form to Brad Alexander and attempted to get an appointment to see him.

July 9 Contacted Jon Aaronson by phone. He told me that we were in contention with three other firms and the debate was heated. He stated that the other firms were also touting their state-of-the-art technology. Discussed a lower price of $7 million. Also encouraged him to visit Alta Data Solutions headquarters to meet with the product manager who oversaw the product development efforts and would manage the implementation of the product. He wasn't interested in making the two-day trip even though it would spotlight our core competencies.

July 15 Received a conference call from Brad Alexander and Jon Aaronson to discuss the price. Brad said the price was still too high and that he could not depreciate that amount over the life of the software and meet target levels of efficiency. He wanted a final quote by August 6.

## THE FINAL PITCH

Vicki prepared for her meeting with Mike by going over her notes and market data about the competitors. Mike's voicemail indicated that they would be meeting to put together their best possible proposal.

### Questions

1. Help Vicki prepare her sales presentation. Who should be at the presentation?

2. How should Vicki start the meeting?

3. What are the key points she should make in her presentation?

4. What reservations should she expect? How should she handle them?

# glossary

**actual product** The physical attributes of a product including the brand name, features/design, quality level, and packaging.

**administered vertical marketing system** A *supply chain* system in which there is no common ownership and no contractual relationships, but the dominant channel member controls the channel relationship.

**advanced shipping notice** (ASN) An electronic document that the supplier sends the retailer in advance of a shipment to tell the retailer exactly what to expect in the shipment.

**advertising** A paid form of communication from an identifiable source, delivered through a communication channel, and designed to persuade the receiver to take some action, now or in the future.

**advertising allowance** Tactic of offering a price reduction to channel members if they agree to feature the manufacturer's product in their advertising and promotional efforts.

**advertising plan** A section of the firm's overall marketing plan that explicitly outlines the objectives of the advertising campaign, how the campaign might accomplish those objectives, and how the firm can determine whether the campaign was successful.

**advertising schedule** The specification of the timing and duration of advertising.

**affective component** A component of *attitude* that reflects what a person feels about the issue at hand—his or her like or dislike of something.

**AIDA model** A common model of the series of mental stages through which consumers move as a result of marketing communications: *Awareness* leads to *Interests*, which lead to *Desire*, which leads to *Action*.

**aided recall** Occurs when consumers recognize a name (e.g., of a brand) that has been presented to them.

**alpha testing** An attempt by the firm to determine whether a product will perform according to its design and whether it satisfies the need for which it was intended; occurs in the firm's research and development (R&D) department.

**associated services** (also called augmented product) The non-physical attributes of the product including product warranties, financing, product support, and after-sale service.

**attitude** A person's enduring evaluation of his or her feelings about and behavioral tendencies toward an object or idea; consists of three components: *cognitive*, *affective*, and *behavioral*.

**augmented product** See *associated services*

**autocratic buying center** A buying center in which one person makes the decision alone, though there may be multiple participants.

**B2B (business-to-business)** The process of selling merchandise or services from one business to another.

**B2C (business-to-consumers)** The process in which businesses sell to consumers.

**Baby Boomers** Generational cohort of people born after World War II, between 1946 and 1964.

**background** In an advertisement, the backdrop, which is usually a single color.

**bait and switch** A deceptive practice of luring customers into the store with a very low advertised price on an item (the bait), only to aggressively pressure them into purchasing a higher-priced model (the switch) by disparaging the low-priced item, comparing it unfavorably with the higher-priced model, or professing an inadequate supply of the lower-priced item.

**behavioral component** A component of *attitude* that comprises the actions a person takes with regard to the issue at hand.

**behavioral segmentation** A segmentation method that divides customers into groups based on how they use the product or service. Some common behavioral measures include occasion and loyalty.

**benefit segmentation** The grouping of consumers on the basis of the benefits they derive from products or services.

**beta testing** Having potential consumers examine a product prototype in a real-use setting to determine its functionality, performance, potential problems, and other issues specific to its use.

**big box retailer** Discount stores that offer a narrow but deep assortment of merchandise; see *category killer*.

**blog (Weblog)** A Web page that contains periodic posts; corporate blogs are a new form of marketing communications.

**body copy** The main text portion of an ad.

**bonus** A payment made at management's discretion when the salesperson attains certain goals; usually given only periodically, such as at the end of the year.

**boycott** A group's refusal to deal commercially with some organization to protest against its policies.

**brand** The name, term, design, symbol, or any other features that identify one seller's good or service as distinct from those of other sellers.

**brand association** The mental links that consumers make between a brand and its key product attributes; can involve a logo, slogan, or famous personality.

**brand awareness** Measures how many consumers in a market are familiar with the brand and what it stands for; created through repeated exposures of the various brand elements (brand name, logo, symbol, character, packaging, or slogan) in the firm's communications to consumers.

**brand dilution** Occurs when a brand extension adversely affects consumer perceptions about the attributes the core brand is believed to hold.

**brand equity** The set of assets and liabilities linked to a brand that add to or subtract from the value provided by the product or service.

**brand extension** The use of the same brand name for new products being introduced to the same or new markets.

**branding** In an advertisement, the portion that identifies the sponsor of the ad.

**brand licensing** A contractual arrangement between firms, whereby one firm allows another to use its brand name, logo, symbols, or characters in exchange for a negotiated fee.

**brand loyalty** Occurs when a consumer buys the same brand's product or service repeatedly over time rather than buying from multiple suppliers within the same category.

**brand personality** Refers to a set of human characteristics associated with a brand, which has symbolic or self-expressive meanings for consumers.

**brand repositioning (rebranding)** A strategy in which marketers change a brand's focus to target new markets or realign the brand's core emphasis with changing market preferences.

**breadth** Number of product lines offered by a firm; also known as variety.

**break-even analysis** Technique used to examine the relationships among cost, price, revenue, and profit over different levels of production and sales to determine the *break-even point*.

**break-even point** The point at which the number of units sold generates just enough revenue to equal the total costs; at this point, profits are zero.

**breakthroughs** See *pioneers*.

**bricks-and-mortar retailer** A traditional, physical store.

**business ethics** Refers to a branch of ethical study that examines ethical rules and principles within a commercial context, the various moral or ethical problems that might arise in a business setting, and any special duties or obligations that apply to persons engaged in commerce.

**business-to-business (B2B) marketing** The process of buying and selling goods or services to be used in the production of other goods and services, for consumption by the buying organization, or for resale by wholesalers and retailers.

**buyer** The buying center participant who handles the paperwork of the actual purchase.

**buying center** The group of people typically responsible for the buying decisions in large organizations.

**C2C (consumer-to-consumer)** The process in which consumers sell to other consumers.

**cannibalization** Customers who formerly made purchases through one retail channel switch to a different retail channel without increasing the overall sales to the retailer.

**cash discount** Tactic of offering a reduction in the invoice cost if the buyer pays the invoice prior to the end of the discount period.

**category depth** The number of stock keeping units (SKUs) within a category.

**category killer** A specialist that offers an extensive assortment in a particular category, so overwhelming the category that other retailers have difficulty competing.

**category specialist** A retailer that offers a narrow variety but a deep assortment of merchandise.

**cause-related marketing** Commercial activity in which businesses and charities form a partnership to market an image, a product, or a service for their mutual benefit; a type of promotional campaign.

**channel conflict** When members of a marketing channel are in disagreement or discord. Channel conflict can occur between members of the same marketing channel (see *vertical channel conflict* or *vertical supply chain conflict*) or between members at the same level of a marketing channel (see *horizontal channel conflict* or *horizontal supply chain conflict*).

**checking** The process of going through the goods upon receipt to ensure they arrived undamaged and that the merchandise ordered was the merchandise received.

**churn** The number of consumers who stop using a product or service, divided by the average number of consumers of that product or service.

**click-through rate (CTR)** The number of times a user clicks on an online ad divided by the number of impressions.

**click-through tracking** A way to measure how many times users click on banner advertising on websites.

**clinical trial** Medical test of the safety and efficacy of a new drug or treatment with human subjects.

**close-out retailers** Stores that offer an inconsistent assortment of low priced, brand name merchandise.

**closing the sale** Obtaining a commitment from the customer to make a purchase.

**co-branding** The practice of marketing two or more brands together, on the same package or promotion.

**coercive power** A type of marketing channel power that occurs when the channel member exerting the power threatens to punish or punishes another channel member for not undertaking certain tasks it wants it to do.

**cognitive component** A component of *attitude* that reflects what a person believes to be true.

**cold calls** A method of prospecting in which salespeople telephone or go to see potential customers without appointments.

**collaborative planning, forecasting, and replenishment (CPFR)** An inventory management system that uses an electronic data interchange (EDI) through which a retailer sends sales information to a manufacturer.

**commercial speech** A message with an economic motivation, that is, to promote a product or service, to persuade someone to purchase, and so on.

**commission** Compensation or financial incentive for salespeople based on a fixed percentage of their sales.

**communication channel** The medium—print, broadcast, the Internet—that carries the message.

**communication gap** A type of *service gap*; refers to the difference between the actual service provided to customers and the service that the firm's promotion program promises.

**company sales force** Comprised of people who are employees of the selling company and are engaged in the selling process.

**compensatory decision rule** At work when the consumer is evaluating alternatives and trades off one characteristic against another, such that good characteristics compensate for bad ones.

**competitive intelligence (CI)** Used by firms to collect and synthesize information about their position with respect to their rivals; enables companies to anticipate market developments rather than merely react to them.

**competitive parity** A firm's strategy of setting prices that are similar to those of major competitors.

**competitor orientation** A company objective based on the premise that the firm should measure itself primarily against its competition.

**competitor-based pricing** A strategy that involves pricing below, at, or above competitors' offerings.

**competitor-based pricing method** An approach that attempts to reflect how the firm wants consumers to interpret its products relative to the competitors' offerings; for example, setting a price close to a competitor's price signals to consumers that the product is similar, whereas setting the price much higher signals greater features, better quality, or some other valued benefit.

**complementary products** Products whose demand curves are positively related, such that they rise or fall together; a percentage increase in demand for one results in a percentage increase in demand for the other.

**concentrated targeting strategy** A marketing strategy of selecting a single, primary target market and focusing all energies on providing a product to fit that market's needs.

**concept testing** The process in which a concept statement that describes a product or a service is presented to potential buyers or users to obtain their reactions.

**concepts** Brief written descriptions of a product or service; its technology, working principles, and forms; and what customer needs it would satisfy.

**conclusive research** Provides the information needed to confirm preliminary insights, which managers can use to pursue appropriate courses of action.

**consensus buying center** A buying center in which all members of the team must reach a collective agreement that they can support a particular purchase.

**consignment** Part of a VMI (vendor managed inventory) program whereby the manufacturer owns the merchandise until it is sold by the retailer.

**consultative buying center** A buying center in which one person makes the decision but he or she solicits input from others before doing so.

**consumer decision rules** The set of criteria that consumers use consciously or subconsciously to quickly and efficiently select from among several alternatives.

**consumer product** Products and services used by people for their personal use.

**contest** A brand-sponsored competition that requires some form of skill or effort.

**continuous advertising schedule** Runs steadily throughout the year and therefore is suited to products and services that are consumed continually at relatively steady rates and that require a steady level of persuasive or reminder advertising.

**contractual vertical marketing system** A system in which independent firms at different levels of the supply chain join together through contracts to obtain economies of scale and coordination and to reduce conflict.

**contribution per unit** Equals the price less the variable cost per unit. Variable used to determine the break-even point in units.

**control phase** The part of the strategic marketing planning process when managers evaluate the performance of the marketing strategy and take any necessary corrective actions.

**convenience goods/services** Those for which the consumer is not willing to spend any effort to evaluate prior to purchase.

**convenience store** Type of retailer that provides a limited number of items at a convenient location in a small store with speedy checkout.

**conventional supermarket** Type of retailer that offers groceries, meat, and produce with limited sales of nonfood items,

such as health and beauty aids and general merchandise, in a self-service format.

**conversion rates** Percentage of consumers who buy a product after viewing it.

**cookie** Computer program, installed on hard drives, that provides identifying information.

**cooperative (co-op) advertising** An agreement between a manufacturer and retailer in which the manufacturer agrees to defray some advertising costs.

**copycat brands** Mimic a manufacturer's brand in appearance but generally with lower quality and prices.

**core customer value** The basic problem solving benefits that consumers are seeking.

**corporate brand (family brand)** The use of a firm's own corporate name to brand all of its product lines and products.

**corporate social responsibility** Refers to the voluntary actions taken by a company to address the ethical, social, and environmental impacts of its business operations and the concerns of its stakeholders.

**corporate vertical marketing system** A system in which the parent company has complete control and can dictate the priorities and objectives of the supply chain; it may own facilities such as manufacturing plants, warehouse facilities, retail outlets, and design studios.

**cost of ownership method** A value-based method for setting prices that determines the total cost of owning the product over its useful life.

**cost-based pricing** A pricing strategy that involves first determining the costs of producing or providing a product and then adding a fixed amount above that total to arrive at the selling price.

**cost-based pricing method** An approach that determines the final price to charge by starting with the cost, without recognizing the role that consumers or competitors' prices play in the marketplace.

**countertrade** Trade between two countries where goods are traded for other goods and not for hard currency.

**country culture** Entails easy-to-spot visible nuances that are particular to a country, such as dress, symbols, ceremonies, language, colors, and food preferences, and more subtle aspects, which are trickier to identify.

**coupon** Provides a stated discount to consumers on the final selling price of a specific item; the retailer handles the discount.

**cross-docking distribution center** A distribution center to which vendors ship merchandise prepackaged and ready for sale. So the merchandise goes to a staging area rather than into storage. When all the merchandise going to a particular store has arrived in the staging area, it is loaded onto a truck, and away it goes. Thus, merchandise goes from the receiving dock to the shipping dock—cross dock.

**cross-price elasticity** The percentage change in demand for product A that occurs in response to a percentage change in price of product B; see *complementary products*.

**cross-promoting** Efforts of two or more firms joining together to reach a specific target market.

**cross-shopping** The pattern of buying both premium and low-priced merchandise or patronizing both expensive, status-oriented retailers and price-oriented retailers.

**cultural imperialism** The belief that one's own culture is superior to that of other nations; can take the form of an active, formal policy or a more subtle general attitude.

**culture** The set of values, guiding beliefs, understandings, and ways of doing things shared by members of a society; exists on two levels: visible artifacts (e.g., behavior, dress, symbols, physical settings, ceremonies) and underlying values (thought processes, beliefs, and assumptions).

**cumulative quantity discount** Pricing tactic that offers a discount based on the amount purchased over a specified period and usually involves several transactions; encourages resellers to maintain their current supplier because the cost to switch must include the loss of the discount.

**customer excellence** Involves a focus on retaining loyal customers and excellent customer service.

**customer lifetime value** The expected financial contribution from a particular customer to the firm's profits over the course of their entire relationship.

**customer orientation** A company objective based on the premise that the firm should measure itself primarily according to whether it meets its customers' needs.

**customer relationship management (CRM)** A business philosophy and set of strategies, programs, and systems that focus on identifying and building loyalty among the firm's most valued customers.

**customer service** Specifically refers to human or mechanical activities firms undertake to help satisfy their customers' needs and wants.

**cycle time** The time between the decision to place an order and the receipt of merchandise.

**data** Raw numbers or facts.

**data mining** The use of a variety of statistical analysis tools to uncover previously unknown patterns in the data stored in databases or relationships among variables.

**data warehouses** Large computer files that store millions and even billions of pieces of individual data.

**deal** A type of short-term price reduction that can take several forms, such as a "featured price," a price lower than the regular price; a "buy one, get one free" offer; or a certain percentage "more free" offer contained in larger packaging; can involve a special financing arrangement, such as reduced percentage interest rates or extended repayment terms.

**deceptive advertising** A representation, omission, act, or practice in an advertisement that is likely to mislead consumers acting reasonably under the circumstances.

**decider** The buying center participant who ultimately determines any part of or the entire buying decision—whether to buy, what to buy, how to buy, or where to buy.

**decision heuristics** Mental shortcuts that help consumers narrow down choices; examples include price, brand, and product presentation.

**decline stage** Stage of the product life cycle when sales decline and the product eventually exits the market.

**decoding** The process by which the receiver interprets the sender's message.

**delivery gap** A type of *service gap*; the difference between the firm's service standards and the actual service it provides to customers.

**demand curve** Shows how many units of a product or service consumers will demand during a specific period at different prices.

**democratic buying center** A buying center in which the majority rules in making decisions.

**demographic segmentation** The grouping of consumers according to easily measured, objective characteristics such as age, gender, income, and education.

**demographics** Information about the characteristics of human populations and segments, especially those used to identify consumer markets such as by age, gender, income, and education.

**department store** A retailer that carries many different types of merchandise (broad variety) and lots of items within each type (deep assortment); offers some customer services; and is organized into separate departments to display its merchandise.

**depth** The number of categories within a product line.

**derived demand** The linkage between consumers' demand for a company's output and its purchase of necessary inputs to manufacture or assemble that particular output.

**determinant attributes** Product or service features that are important to the buyer and on which competing brands or stores are perceived to differ.

**differentiated targeting strategy** A strategy through which a firm targets several market segments with a different offering for each.

**diffusion of innovation** The process by which the use of an innovation, whether a product or a service, spreads throughout a market group over time and over various categories of adopters.

**direct investment** When a firm maintains 100 percent ownership of its plants, operation facilities, and offices in a foreign country, often through the formation of wholly owned subsidiaries.

**direct marketing** Sales and promotional techniques that deliver promotional materials individually to potential customers.

**discount store** A type of retailer that offers a broad variety of merchandise, limited service, and low prices.

**disintermediation** A manufacturer sells directly to consumers and bypasses retailers.

**dispatcher** The person who coordinates deliveries to distribution centers.

**distribution center** A facility for the receipt, storage, and redistribution of goods to company stores or customers; may be operated by retailers, manufacturers, or distribution specialists.

**distribution intensity** The number of supply chain members to use at each level of the supply chain.

**distributive fairness** Pertains to a customer's perception of the benefits he or she received compared with the costs (inconvenience or loss) that resulted from a service failure.

**distributor** A type of reseller or marketing intermediary that resells manufactured products without significantly altering their form. Distributors often buy from manufacturers and sell to other businesses like retailers in a B2B transaction.

**diversification strategy** A growth strategy whereby a firm introduces a new product or service to a market segment that it does not currently serve.

**drugstore** A specialty store that concentrates on health and personal grooming merchandise, though pharmaceuticals may represent more than 60 percent of its sales.

**dumping** The practice of selling a good in a foreign market at a price that is lower than its domestic price or below its cost.

**duty** See *tariff*.

**early adopters** The second group of consumers in the diffusion of innovation model, after *innovators,* to use a product or service innovation; generally don't like to take as much risk as innovators but instead wait and purchase the product after careful review.

**early majority** A group of consumers in the diffusion of innovation model that represents approximately 34 percent of the population; members don't like to take much risk and therefore tend to wait until bugs are worked out of a particular product or service; few new products and services can be profitable until this large group buys them.

**economic situation** Macroeconomic factor that affects the way consumers buy merchandise and spend money, both in a marketer's home country and abroad; see *inflation, foreign currency fluctuations,* and *interest rates.*

**elastic** Refers to a market for a product or service that is price sensitive; that is, relatively small changes in price will generate fairly large changes in the quantity demanded.

**electronic data interchange (EDI)** The computer-to-computer exchange of business documents from a retailer to a vendor and back.

**emotional appeal** Aims to satisfy consumers' emotional desires rather than their utilitarian needs.

**emotional support** Concern for others' well-being and support of their decisions in a job setting.

**employment marketing** Marketing programs to attract applicants to the hiring firm.

**empowerment** In context of service delivery, means allowing employees to make decisions about how service is provided to customers.

**encoding** The process of converting the sender's ideas into a message, which could be verbal, visual, or both.

**English auction** Goods and services are simply sold to the highest bidder.

**entrepreneur** A person who organizes, operates, and assumes the risk of a new business venture.

**environmental concerns** Include, but are not limited to, the excessive use of natural resources and energy, refuse from manufacturing processes, excess trash created by consumer goods packages, and hard-to-dispose-of products like tires, cell phones, and computer monitors.

**esteem needs** Needs that enable people to fulfill inner desires.

**ethical climate** The set of values within a marketing firm, or in the marketing division of any firm, that guide decision making and behavior.

**evaluative criteria** Consist of a set of salient, or important, attributes about a particular product.

**event sponsorship** Popular PR tool; occurs when corporations support various activities (financially or otherwise), usually in the cultural or sports and entertainment sectors.

**everyday low pricing (EDLP)** A strategy companies use to emphasize the continuity of their retail prices at a level somewhere between the regular, nonsale price and the deep-discount sale prices their competitors may offer.

**evoked set** Comprises the alternative brands or stores that the consumer states he or she would consider when making a purchase decision.

**exchange** The trade of things of value between the buyer and the seller so that each is better off as a result.

**exchange control** Refers to the regulation of a country's currency *exchange rate.*

**exchange rate** The measure of how much one currency is worth in relation to another.

**exclusive co-brand** Developed by national brand vendor and retailer and sold only by that retailer.

**exclusive distribution** Strategy in which only selected retailers can sell a manufacturer's brand.

**exclusive geographic territories** Territories granted to one or very few retail customers by a manufacturer using an exclusive distribution strategy; no other customers can sell a particular brand in these territories.

**experience curve effect** Refers to the drop in unit cost as the accumulated volume sold increases; as sales continue to grow, the costs continue to drop, allowing even further reductions in the price.

**experiment** See experimental research

**experimental research (experiment)** A type of conclusive and quantitative research that systematically manipulates one or more variables to determine which variables have a causal effect on another variable.

**expertise power** A type of marketing channel power that occurs if the channel member exerting the power has expertise that the other channel member wants or needs and can therefore get them to do what they want.

**exploratory research** Attempts to begin to understand the phenomenon of interest; also provides initial information when the problem lacks any clear definition.

**exporting** Producing goods in one country and selling them in another.

**extended problem solving** A purchase decision process during which the consumer devotes considerable time and effort to analyzing alternatives; often occurs when the consumer perceives that the purchase decision entails a lot of risk.

**external locus of control** Refers to when consumers believe that fate or other external factors control all outcomes.

**external reference price** A higher price to which the consumer can compare the selling price to evaluate the purchase.

**external search for information** Occurs when the buyer seeks information outside his or her personal knowledge base to help make the buying decision.

**external secondary data** Data collected from sources outside of the firm.

**extranet** A collaborative network that uses Internet technology to link businesses with their suppliers, customers, or other businesses.

**extreme value food retailer** See *limited assortment supermarkets.*

**extreme value retailer** A general merchandise discount store found in lower-income urban or rural areas.

**factory outlets** Outlet stores owned by manufacturers.

**family brand** A firm's own corporate name used to brand its product lines and products.

**feedback loop** Allows the receiver to communicate with the sender and thereby informs the sender whether the message was received and decoded properly.

**financial risk** Risk associated with a monetary outlay; includes the initial cost of the purchase, as well as the costs of using the item or service.

**first movers** Product pioneers that are the first to create a market or product category, making them readily recognizable to consumers and thus establishing a commanding and early market share lead.

**fixed costs** Those costs that remain essentially at the same level, regardless of any changes in the volume of production.

**flighting advertising schedule** An advertising schedule implemented in spurts, with periods of heavy advertising followed by periods of no advertising.

**floor-ready merchandise** Merchandise that is ready to be placed on the selling floor immediately.

**focus group interview** A research technique in which a small group of persons (usually 8 to 12) comes together for an intensive discussion about a particular topic, with the conversation guided by a trained moderator using an unstructured method of inquiry.

**foreground** In an advertisement, everything that appears on top of the *background*.

**foreign currency fluctuations** Changes in the value of a country's currency relative to the currency of another country; can influence consumer spending.

**franchisee** See *franchising*.

**franchising** A contractual agreement between a *franchisor* and a *franchisee* that allows the franchisee to operate a business using a name and format developed and supported by the franchisor.

**franchisor** See *franchising*.

**frequency** Measure of how often the audience is exposed to a communication within a specified period of time.

**full-line discount stores** Retailers that offer low prices, limited service, and a broad variety of merchandise.

**functional needs** Pertain to the performance of a product or service.

**gatekeeper** The buying center participant who controls information or access to decision makers and influencers.

**General Agreement on Tariffs and Trade (GATT)** Organization established to lower trade barriers, such as high tariffs on imported goods and restrictions on the number and types of imported products that inhibited the free flow of goods across borders.

**Generation X (Gen X)** Generational cohort of people born between 1965 and 1976.

**Generation Y (Gen Y)** Generational cohort of people born between 1977 and 1995; biggest cohort since the original postwar baby boom.

**generational cohort** A group of people of the same generation—typically have similar purchase behaviors because they have shared experiences and are in the same stage of life.

**generic (house) brand** No-frills products offered at a low price without any branding information.

**geodemographic segmentation** The grouping of consumers on the basis of a combination of geographic, demographic, and lifestyle characteristics.

**geographic segmentation** The grouping of consumers on the basis of where they live.

**global labor issues** Includes concerns about working conditions and wages paid to factory workers in developing countries.

**globalization** Refers to the processes by which goods, services, capital, people, information, and ideas flow across national borders.

**globalization of production** Also known as *offshoring*; refers to manufacturers' procurement of goods and services from around the globe to take advantage of national differences in the cost and quality of various factors of production (e.g., labor, energy, land, capital).

**goods** Items that can be physically touched.

**gray market** Employs irregular but not necessarily illegal methods; generally, it legally circumvents authorized channels of distribution to sell goods at prices lower than those intended by the manufacturer.

**green marketing** Involves a strategic effort by firms to supply customers with environmentally friendly merchandise.

**green product** An ecologically safe product that may be recyclable, biodegradable, more energy-efficient, and/or have better pollution controls.

**gross domestic product (GDP)** Defined as the market value of the goods and services produced by a country in a year; the most widely used standardized measure of output.

**gross national income (GNI)** Consists of GDP plus the net income earned from investments abroad (minus any payments made to nonresidents who contribute to the domestic economy).

**gross rating points (GRP)** Measure used for various media advertising—print, radio, or television; *GRP 5 reach 3 frequency.*

**growth stage** Stage of the product life cycle when the product gains acceptance, demand and sales increase, and competitors emerge in the product category.

**habitual decision making** A purchase decision process in which consumers engage with little conscious effort.

**headline** In an advertisement, large type designed to draw attention.

**high/low pricing** A *pricing* strategy that relies on the promotion of sales, during which prices are temporarily reduced to encourage purchases.

**home improvement center** Category specialist that offers home improvement tools for contractors and do-it-yourselfers.

**horizontal channel conflict** A type of channel conflict in which members at the same level of a marketing channel, for example, two competing retailers or two competing manufacturers, are in disagreement or discord, such as when they are in a price war.

**horizontal price fixing** Occurs when competitors that produce and sell competing products collude, or work together, to control prices, effectively taking price out of the decision process for consumers.

**horizontal supply chain conflict** See *horizontal channel conflict*

**house brand** See *private-label brands*

**human development index (HDI)** A composite measure of three indicators of the quality of life in different countries: life expectancy at birth, educational attainment, and whether the average incomes are sufficient to meet the basic needs of life in that country.

**ideal point** The position at which a particular market segment's ideal product would lie on a *perceptual map*.

**ideas** Intellectual concepts—thoughts, opinions, and philosophies.

**implementation phase** The part of the strategic marketing planning process when marketing managers (1) identify and evaluate different opportunities by engaging in segmentation, targeting, and positioning (see *STP*) and (2) implement the marketing mix using the four Ps.

**impressions** The number of times an advertisement appears in front of the user

**improvement value** Represents an estimate of how much more (or less) consumers are willing to pay for a product relative to other comparable products.

**impulse buying** A buying decision made by customers on the spot when they see the merchandise.

**income effect** Refers to the change in the quantity of a product demanded by consumers due to a change in their income.

**independent agents** Salespeople who sell a manufacturer's products on an extended contract basis but are not employees of the manufacturer; also known as *manufacturer's representatives* or *reps*.

**independent (conventional) supply chain** A loose coalition of several independently owned and operated supply chain members—a manufacturer, a wholesaler, and a retailer—all attempting to satisfy their own objectives and maximize their own profits, often at the expense of the other members.

**in-depth interview** An exploratory research technique in which trained researchers ask questions, listen to and record the answers, and then pose additional questions to clarify or expand on a particular issue.

**individual brands** The use of individual brand names for each of a firm's products.

**inelastic** Refers to a market for a product or service that is price insensitive; that is, relatively small changes in price will not generate large changes in the quantity demanded.

**inflation** Refers to the persistent increase in the prices of goods and services.

**influencer** The buying center participant whose views influence other members of the buying center in making the final decision.

**information** Organized, analyzed, interpreted data that offer value to marketers.

**information power** A type of marketing channel power that occurs if the channel member exerting the power has information that the other channel member wants or needs and can therefore get them to do what they want.

**informational appeal** Used in a promotion to help consumers make purchase decisions by offering factual information and strong arguments built around relevant issues that encourage them to evaluate the brand favorably on the basis of the key benefits it provides.

**informative advertising** Communication used to create and build brand awareness, with the ultimate goal of moving the consumer through the buying cycle to a purchase.

**infrastructure** The basic facilities, services, and installations needed for a community or society to function, such as transportation and communications systems, water and power lines, and public institutions like schools, post offices, and prisons.

**initiator** The buying center participant who first suggests buying the particular product or service.

**innovation** The process by which ideas are transformed into new products and services that will help firms grow.

**innovators** Those buyers who want to be the first to have the new product or service.

**inseparable** A characteristic of a service: it is produced and consumed at the same time; that is, service and consumption are inseparable.

**institutional advertisement** A type of advertisement that informs, persuades, or reminds consumers about issues related to places, politics, or an industry (e.g. Got Milk? ads).

**instrumental support** Providing the equipment or systems needed to perform a task in a job setting.

**intangible** A characteristic of a service; it cannot be touched, tasted, or seen like a pure product can.

**integrated marketing communications (IMC)** Represents the promotion dimension of the four Ps; encompasses a variety of communication disciplines—general advertising, personal selling, sales promotion, public relations, direct marketing, and electronic media—in combination to provide clarity, consistency, and maximum communicative impact.

**intensive distribution** A strategy designed to get products into as many outlets as possible.

**interest rates** These represent the cost of borrowing money.

**internal locus of control** Refers to when consumers believe they have some control over the outcomes of their actions, in which case they generally engage in more search activities.

**internal reference price** Price information stored in the consumer's memory that the person uses to assess a current price offering—perhaps the last price he or she paid or what he or she expects to pay.

**internal search for information** Occurs when the buyer examines his or her own memory and knowledge about the product or service, gathered through past experiences.

**internal secondary data** Data collected from a firm's own data taken from their day-to-day operations.

**International Monetary Fund (IMF)** Established with the original General Agreement on Tariffs and Trade (GATT); primary purpose is to promote international monetary cooperation and facilitate the expansion and growth of international trade.

**intranet** A secure communication system contained within one company, such as between the firm's buyers and distribution centers.

**introduction stage** Stage of the product life cycle when innovators start buying the product.

**introductory price promotion** Short-term price discounts designed to encourage trial.

**involvement** Consumer's interest in a product or service.

**irregulars** Merchandise with minor construction errors.

**joint venture** Formed when a firm entering a new market pools its resources with those of a local firm to form a new company in which ownership, control, and profits are shared.

**just-in-time (JIT) inventory systems** Inventory management systems designed to deliver less merchandise on a more frequent basis than traditional inventory systems; the firm gets the merchandise "just in time" for it to be used in the manufacture of another product, in the case of parts or components, or for sale when the customer wants it, in the case of consumer goods; also known as *quick response (QR) systems* in retailing.

**knowledge gap** A type of *service gap*; reflects the difference between customers' *expectations* and the firm's perception of those expectations.

**laggards** Consumers who like to avoid change and rely on traditional products until they are no longer available.

**lagged effect** A delayed response to a marketing communication campaign.

**late majority** The last group of buyers to enter a new product market; when they do, the product has achieved its full market potential.

**lead time** The amount of time between the recognition that an order needs to be placed and the arrival of the needed merchandise at the seller's store, ready for sale.

**lead users** Innovative product users who modify existing products according to their own ideas to suit their specific needs.

**leader pricing** Consumer pricing tactic that attempts to build store traffic by aggressively pricing and advertising a regularly purchased item, often priced at or just above the store's cost.

**leads** A list of potential customers.

**learning** Refers to a change in a person's thought process or behavior that arises from experience and takes place throughout the consumer decision process.

**lease** A written agreement under which the owner of an item or property allows its use for a specified period of time in exchange for a fee.

**legitimate power** A type of marketing channel power that occurs if the channel member exerting the power has a contractual agreement with the other channel member that requires the other channel member to behave in a certain way. This type of power occurs in an administered vertical marketing system.

**licensed brand** An agreement allows one brand to use another's name, image, and/or logo for a fee.

**lifestyles** A component of *psychographics*; refers to the way a person lives his or her life to achieve goals.

**lift** Additional sales caused by advertising.

**limited assortment supermarkets** Retailers that offer only one or two brands or sizes of most products (usually including a store brand) and attempt to achieve great efficiency to lower costs and prices.

**limited problem solving** Occurs during a purchase decision that calls for, at most, a moderate amount of effort and time.

**line extension** The use of the same brand name within the same product line and represents an increase in a product line's depth.

**locational excellence** A method of achieving excellence by having a strong physical location and/or Internet presence.

**logistics management** The integration of two or more activities for the purpose of planning, implementing, and controlling the efficient flow of raw materials, in-process inventory, and finished goods from the point of origin to the point of consumption.

**loss leader pricing** Loss leader pricing takes the tactic of *leader pricing* one step further by lowering the price below the store's cost.

**love needs** Needs expressed through interactions with others.

**loyalty program** Specifically designed to retain customers by offering premiums or other incentives to customers who make multiple purchases over time.

**loyalty segmentation** Strategy of investing in loyalty initiatives to retain the firm's most profitable customers.

**macroenvironmental factors** Aspects of the external environment that affect a company's business, such as the culture, demographics, social issues, technological advances, economic situation, and political/regulatory environment.

**manufacturer brands (national brands)** Brands owned and managed by the manufacturer.

**manufacturer's representative** See *independent agents*.

**manufacturer's suggested retail price (MSRP)** The price that manufacturers suggest retailers use to sell their merchandise.

**markdowns** Reductions retailers take on the initial selling price of the product or service.

**market development strategy** A growth strategy that employs the existing marketing offering to reach new market segments, whether domestic or international.

**market growth rate** The annual rate of growth of the specific market in which the product competes.

**market penetration strategy** A growth strategy that employs the existing marketing mix and focuses the firm's efforts on existing customers.

**market positioning** Involves the process of defining the marketing mix variables so that target customers have a clear, distinctive, desirable understanding of what the product does or represents in comparison with competing products.

**market segment** A group of consumers who respond similarly to a firm's marketing efforts.

**market segmentation** The process of dividing the market into groups of customers with different needs, wants, or characteristics—who therefore might appreciate products or services geared especially for them.

**market share** Percentage of a market accounted for by a specific entity.

**marketing** An organizational function and a set of processes for creating, *capturing*, communicating, and delivering value to customers and for managing customer relationships in ways that benefit the organization and its stakeholders.

**marketing channel** The set of institutions that transfer the ownership of and move goods from the point of production to the point of consumption; consists of all the institutions and marketing activities in the marketing process.

**marketing ethics** Refers to those ethical problems that are specific to the domain of marketing.

**marketing information system (MkIS)** A set of procedures and methods that apply to the regular, planned collection, analysis, and presentation of information that then may be used in marketing decisions.

**marketing mix (four Ps)** Product, price, place, and promotion—the controllable set of activities that a firm uses to respond to the wants of its target markets.

**marketing plan** A written document composed of an analysis of the current marketing situation, opportunities and threats for the firm, marketing objectives and strategy specified in terms of the four Ps, action programs, and projected or pro forma income (and other financial) statements.

**marketing research** A set of techniques and principles for systematically collecting, recording, analyzing, and interpreting data that can aid decision makers involved in marketing goods, services, or ideas.

**marketing strategy** A firm's target market, marketing mix, and method of obtaining a sustainable competitive advantage.

**Maslow's Hierarchy of Needs** A paradigm for classifying people's motives. It argues that when lower-level, more basic needs (physiological and safety) are fulfilled, people turn to satisfying their higher-level human needs (social and personal); see *physiological, safety, social,* and *personal needs.*

**mass customization** The practice of interacting on a one-to-one basis with many people to create custom-made products or services; providing one-to-one marketing to the masses.

**mass media** Channels that are ideal for reaching large numbers of anonymous audience members; include national newspapers, magazines, radio, and television.

**maturity stage** Stage of the product life cycle when industry sales reach their peak, so firms try to rejuvenate their products by adding new features or repositioning them.

**maximizing profits** A profit strategy that relies primarily on economic theory. If a firm can accurately specify a mathematical model that captures all the factors required to explain and predict sales and profits, it should be able to identify the price at which its profits are maximized.

**M-commerce (mobile commerce)** Communicating with or selling to consumers through wireless handheld devices such as cellular phones.

**media buy** The actual purchase of airtime or print pages.

**media mix** The combination of the media used and the frequency of advertising in each medium.

**media planning** The process of evaluating and selecting the *media mix* that will deliver a clear, consistent, compelling message to the intended audience.

**metric** A measuring system that quantifies a trend, dynamic, or characteristic.

**micromarketing** An extreme form of segmentation that tailors a product or service to suit an individual customer's wants or needs; also called *one-to-one marketing.*

**millennials** Consumers born between 1977 and 2000 and the children of the Baby Boomers.

**mission statement** A broad description of a firm's objectives and the scope of activities it plans to undertake; attempts to answer two main questions: What type of business is it? What does it need to do to accomplish its goals and objectives?

**mobile commerce** See *M-commerce.*

**mobile marketing** Marketing through wireless handheld devices.

**modified rebuy** Refers to when the buyer has purchased a similar product in the past but has decided to change some specifications, such as the desired price, quality level, customer service level, options, or so forth.

**monopolistic competition** Occurs when there are many firms that sell closely related but not homogeneous products; these products may be viewed as substitutes but are not perfect substitutes.

**monopoly** One firm provides the product or service in a particular industry.

**motive** A need or want that is strong enough to cause the person to seek satisfaction.

**multi-attribute model** A compensatory model of customer decision making based on the notion that customers see a product as a collection of attributes or characteristics. The model uses a weighted average score based on the importance of various attributes and performance on those issues.

**multichannel retailers** Retailers that sell merchandise in more than one retail channel (e.g., store, catalog, and Internet).

**multichannel strategy** Selling in more than one channel (e.g., stores, Internet, catalog).

**need recognition** The beginning of the consumer decision process; occurs when consumers recognize they have an unsatisfied need and want to go from their actual, needy state to a different, desired state.

**negative word of mouth** Occurs when consumers spread negative information about a product, service, or store to others.

**new buy** In a B2B setting, a purchase of a good or service for the first time; the buying decision is likely to be quite involved because the buyer or the buying organization does not have any experience with the item.

**niche media** Channels that are focused and generally used to reach narrow segments, often with unique demographic characteristics or interests.

**noise** Any interference that stems from competing messages, a lack of clarity in the message, or a flaw in the medium; a problem for all communication channels.

**noncommercial speech** A message that does not have an economic motivation and therefore is fully protected under the First Amendment.

**noncompensatory decision rule** At work when consumers choose a product or service on the basis of a subset of its characteristics, regardless of the values of its other attributes.

**noncumulative quantity discount** Pricing tactic that offers a discount based on only the amount purchased in a single order; provides the buyer with an incentive to purchase more merchandise immediately.

**North American Industry Classification System (NAICS) codes** U.S. Bureau of Census classification scheme that categorizes all firms into a hierarchical set of six-digit codes.

**objective-and-task method** An IMC budgeting method that determines the cost required to undertake specific tasks to accomplish communication objectives; process entails setting objectives, choosing media, and determining costs.

**observation** An exploratory research method that entails examining purchase and consumption behaviors through personal or video camera scrutiny.

**occasion segmentation** A type of behavioral segmentation based on when a product or service is purchased or consumed.

**odd prices** Prices that end in odd numbers, usually 9, such as $3.99.

**off-price retailer** A type of retailer that offers an inconsistent assortment of merchandise at relatively low prices.

**offshoring** See *globalization of production.*

**oligopolistic competition** Occurs when only a few firms dominate a market.

**one-to-one marketing** See *micromarketing.*

**online chat** Instant messaging or voice conversation with an online sales representative.

**online couponing** A promotional Web technique in which consumers print a coupon directly from a site and then redeem the coupon in a store.

**online referring** A promotional Web technique in which consumers fill out an interest or order form and are referred to an offline dealer or firm that offers the product or service of interest.

**operational excellence** Involves a firm's focus on efficient operations and excellent supply chain management.

**opt in** The option giving consumer complete control over the collection and dissemination of his/her personal information, usually referred to in an Internet setting.

**opt out** The option whereby consumer must actively choose to prevent personal information from being used or shared with third parties, usually referred to in an Internet setting.

**order getter** A salesperson whose primary responsibilities are identifying potential customers and engaging those customers in discussions to attempt to make a sale.

**order taker** A salesperson whose primary responsibility is to process routine orders or reorders or rebuys for products.

**organizational culture** Reflects the set of values, traditions, and customs that guide a firm's employees' behavior.

**outlet stores** Off-price retailers that often stock irregulars, out-of-season merchandise, or overstocks from the parent company.

**own brands** See *private-label brands.*

**panel data** Information collected from a group of consumers.

**panel research** A type of quantitative research that involves collecting information from a group of consumers (the panel) over time; data collected may be from a survey or a record of purchases.

**perceived value** The relationship between a product's or service's benefits and its cost.

**perception** The process by which people select, organize, and interpret information to form a meaningful picture of the world.

**perceptual map** Displays, in two or more dimensions, the position of products or brands in the consumer's mind.

**performance risk** Involves the perceived danger inherent in a poorly performing product or service.

**perishability** A characteristic of a service: it cannot be stored for use in the future.

**personal needs** Relate to ways people satisfy their inner desires.

**personal selling** The two-way flow of communication between a buyer and a seller that is designed to influence the buyer's purchase decision.

**persuasive advertising** Communication used to motivate consumers to take action.

**physiological needs** Those relating to the basic biological necessities of life: food, drink, rest, and shelter.

**physiological risk** The fear of an actual harm should a product not perform properly.

**pick ticket** A document or display on a screen in a forklift truck indicating how much of each item to get from specific storage areas.

**pioneers** New product introductions that establish a completely new market or radically change both the rules of competition and consumer preferences in a market; also called *breakthroughs.*

**planning phase** The part of the strategic marketing planning process when marketing executives, in conjunction with other top managers, (1) define the mission or vision of the business and (2) evaluate the situation by assessing how various players, both in and outside the organization, affect the firm's potential for success.

**point-of-purchase (POP) display** A merchandise display located at the point of purchase, such as at the checkout counter in a grocery store.

**political/regulatory environment** Comprises political parties, government organizations, and legislation and laws.

**pop-up stores** Temporary storefronts that exist for only a limited time and generally focus on a new product or a limited group of products offered by a retailer, manufacturer, or service provider; give consumers a chance to interact with the brand and build brand awareness, but are not designed primarily to sell the product.

**postpurchase dissonance** The psychologically uncomfortable state produced by an inconsistency between beliefs and behaviors that in turn evokes a motivation to reduce the dissonance; buyers' remorse.

**posttesting** The evaluation of an IMC campaign's impact after it is has been implemented.

**power** A situation that occurs in a marketing channel in which one member has the means or ability to have control over the actions of another member in a channel at a different level of distribution, such as if a retailer has power or control over a supplier.

**preapproach** In the personal selling process, occurs prior to meeting the customer for the first time and extends the qualification of leads procedure; in this step, the salesperson conducts additional research and develops plans for meeting with the customer.

**predatory pricing** A firm's practice of setting a very low price for one or more of its products with the intent to drive its competition out of business; illegal under both the Sherman Act and the Federal Trade Commission Act.

**premarket test** Conducted before a product or service is brought to market to determine how many customers will try and then continue to use it.

**premium** An item offered for free or at a bargain price to reward some type of behavior, such as buying, sampling, or testing.

**premium brand** A branding strategy that offers consumers a private label of comparable or superior quality to a manufacturer brand.

**premium pricing** A competitor-based pricing method by which the firm deliberately prices a product above the prices set for competing products to capture those consumers who always shop for the best or for whom price does not matter.

**prestige products or services** Those that consumers purchase for status rather than functionality.

**pretesting** Assessments performed before an ad campaign; is implemented to ensure that the various elements are working in an integrated fashion and doing what they are intended to do.

**price** The overall sacrifice a consumer is willing to make—money, time, energy—to acquire a specific product or service.

**price bundling** Consumer pricing tactic of selling more than one product for a single, lower price than what the items would cost sold separately; can be used to sell slow-moving items, to encourage customers to stock up so they won't purchase competing brands, to encourage trial of a new product, or to provide an incentive to purchase a less desirable product or service to obtain a more desirable one in the same bundle.

**price discrimination** The practice of selling the same product to different resellers (wholesalers, distributors, or retailers) or to the ultimate consumer at different prices; some, but not all, forms of price discrimination are illegal.

**price elasticity of demand** Measures how changes in a price affect the quantity of the product demanded; specifically, the ratio of the percentage change in quantity demanded to the percentage change in price.

**price fixing** The practice of colluding with other firms to control prices.

**price lining** Consumer market pricing tactic of establishing a price floor and a price ceiling for an entire line of similar products and then setting a few other price points in between to represent distinct differences in quality.

**price skimming** A strategy of selling a new product or service at a high price that *innovators* and *early adopters* are willing to pay in order to obtain it; after the high-price market segment becomes saturated and sales begin to slow down, the firm generally lowers the price to capture (or skim) the next most price sensitive segment.

**price war** Occurs when two or more firms compete primarily by lowering their prices.

**pricing tactics** Short-term methods, in contrast to long-term pricing strategies, used to focus on company objectives, costs, customers, competition, or channel members; can be responses to competitive threats (e.g., lowering price temporarily to meet a competitor's price reduction) or broadly accepted methods of calculating a final price for the customer that is short term in nature.

**primary data** Data collected to address specific research needs.

**primary demand advertising** Ads designed to generate demand for the product category or an entire industry.

**primary package** The packaging the consumer uses, such as the toothpaste tube, from which he or she typically seeks convenience in terms of storage, use, and consumption.

**private exchange** Occurs when a specific firm, either buyer or seller, invites others to join to participate in online information exchanges and transactions; can help streamline procurement or distribution processes.

**private-label brands** Brands developed and marketed by a retailer and available only from that retailer; also called *store brands*.

**procedural fairness** Refers to the customer's perception of the fairness of the process used to resolve complaints about service.

**product** Anything that is of value to a consumer and can be offered through a voluntary marketing exchange.

**product assortment** The complete set of all products offered by a firm; also called the *product mix*.

**product category** An assortment of items that the customer sees as reasonable substitutes for one another.

**product design** See *product development*.

**product development** Also called *product design*; entails a process of balancing various engineering, manufacturing, marketing, and economic considerations to develop a product's form and features or a service's features.

**product development strategy** A growth strategy that offers a new product or service to a firm's current target market.

**product excellence** Involves a focus on achieving high-quality products; effective branding and positioning is key.

**product life cycle** Defines the stages that new products move through as they enter, get established in, and ultimately leave the marketplace and thereby offers marketers a starting point for their strategy planning.

**product lines** Groups of associated items, such as those that consumers use together or think of as part of a group of similar products.

**product mix** See *product assortment*. The complete set of all products offered by a firm.

**product placement** Inclusion of a product in nontraditional situations, such as in a scene in a movie or television program.

**product-focused advertisements** Used to inform, persuade, or remind consumers about a specific product or service.

**profit orientation** A company objective that can be implemented by focusing on *target profit pricing, maximizing profits*, or *target return pricing*.

**projective technique** A type of qualitative research in which subjects are provided a scenario and asked to express their thoughts and feelings about it.

**prototype** The first physical form or service description of a new product, still in rough or tentative form, that has the same properties as a new product but is produced through different manufacturing processes, sometimes even crafted individually.

**psychographic segmentation** A method of segmenting customers based on how they spend their time and money, what activities they pursue, and their attitudes and opinions about the world in which they live.

**psychographics** Used in segmentation; delves into how consumers describe themselves; allows people to describe themselves using those characteristics that help them choose how they occupy their time (behavior) and what underlying psychological reasons determine those choices.

**psychological needs** Pertain to the personal gratification consumers associate with a product or service.

**psychological risk** Associated with the way people will feel if the product or service does not convey the right image.

**public relations** The organizational function that manages the firm's communications to achieve a variety of objectives, including building and maintaining a positive image, handling or heading off unfavorable stories or events, and maintaining positive relationships with the media.

**public service advertising (PSA)** Advertising that focuses on public welfare and generally is sponsored by nonprofit institutions, civic groups, religious organizations, trade associations, or political groups; a form of *social marketing*.

**puffery** The legal exaggeration of praise, stopping just short of deception, lavished on a product.

**pull strategy** Designed to get consumers to pull the product into the supply chain by demanding it.

**pull supply chain** Strategy in which orders for merchandise are generated at the store level on the basis of demand data captured by point-of-sales terminals.

**pulsing advertising schedule** Combines the continuous and flighting schedules by maintaining a base level of advertising but increasing advertising intensity during certain periods.

**purchasing power parity (PPP)** A theory that states that if the exchange rates of two countries are in equilibrium, a product purchased in one will cost the same in the other, expressed in the same currency.

**pure competition** Occurs when different companies sell commodity products that consumers perceive as substitutable; price usually is set according to the laws of supply and demand.

**push strategy** Designed to increase demand by motivating sellers—wholesalers, distributors, or salespeople—to highlight the product, rather than the products of competitors, and thereby push the product onto consumers.

**push supply chain** Strategy in which merchandise is allocated to stores on the basis of historical demand, the inventory position at the distribution center, and the stores' needs.

**qualify leads** The process of assessing the potential of sales leads.

**quantity discount** Pricing tactic of offering a reduced price according to the amount purchased; the more the buyer purchases, the higher the discount and, of course, the greater the value.

**questionnaire** A form that features a set of questions designed to gather information from respondents and thereby accomplish the researchers' objectives; questions can be either unstructured or structured.

**quick response** An inventory management system used in retailing; merchandise is received just in time for sale when the customer wants it; see *just-in-time (JIT) systems*.

**quota** Designates the maximum quantity of a product that may be brought into a country during a specified time period.

**radio frequency identification (RFID) tags** Tiny computer chips that automatically transmit to a special scanner all the information about a container's contents or individual products.

**reach** Measure of consumers' exposure to marketing communications; the percentage of the target population exposed to a specific marketing communication, such as an advertisement, at least once.

**rebate** A consumer discount in which a portion of the purchase price is returned to the buyer in cash; the manufacturer, not the retailer, issues the refund.

**receiver** The person who reads, hears, or sees and processes the information contained in the message or advertisement.

**receiving** The process of recording the receipt of merchandise as it arrives at a distribution center or store.

**reference group** One or more persons whom an individual uses as a basis for comparison regarding beliefs, feelings, and behaviors.

**reference price** The price against which buyers compare the actual selling price of the product and that facilitates their evaluation process.

**referent power** A type of marketing channel power that occurs if one channel member wants to be associated with another channel member. The channel member with whom the others wish to be associated has the power and can get them to do what they want.

**regional culture** The influence of the area within a country in which people live.

**related diversification** A growth strategy whereby the current target market and/or marketing mix shares something in common with the new opportunity.

**relational orientation** A method of building a relationship with customers based on the philosophy that buyers and sellers should develop a long-term relationship.

**relationship selling** A sales philosophy and process that emphasizes a commitment to maintaining the relationship over the long term and investing in opportunities that are mutually beneficial to all parties.

**relative market share** A measure of the product's strength in a particular market, defined as the sales of the focal product divided by the sales achieved by the largest firm in the industry.

**relevance** A metric used to determine how useful an advertising message is to the consumer use.

**reminder advertising** Communication used to remind consumers of a product or to prompt repurchases, especially for products that have gained market acceptance and are in the maturity stage of their life cycle.

**reps** See *independent agents*.

**request for proposals (RFP)** A process through which buying organizations invite alternative suppliers to bid on supplying their required components.

**resellers** Marketing intermediaries that resell manufactured products without significantly altering their form.

**reserve price** The price in an auction that is the minimum amount at which a seller will sell an item.

**retailing** The set of business activities that add value to products and services sold to consumers for their personal or family use; includes products bought at stores, through catalogs, and over the Internet, as well as services like fast-food restaurants, airlines, and hotels.

**retrieval set** Includes those brands or stores that the consumer can readily bring forth from memory.

**return on investment (ROI)** The amount of profit divided by the value of the investment. In the case of an advertisement, the ROI is (the sales revenue generated by the ad − the ad's cost) ÷ the ad's cost.

**reverse auction** The buyer provides specifications to a group of sellers, who then bid down the price until the buyer accepts a specific bid.

**reverse engineering** Involves taking apart a competitor's product, analyzing it, and creating an improved product that does not infringe on the competitor's patents, if any exist.

**reward power** A type of marketing channel power that occurs when the channel member exerting the power offers rewards to gain power, often a monetary incentive, for getting another channel member to do what it wants it to do.

**ritual consumption** Refers to a pattern of behaviors tied to life events that affect what and how people consume.

**role playing** A good technique for practicing the sales presentation prior to meeting with a customer; the salesperson acts out a simulated buying situation while a colleague or manager acts as the buyer.

**rule-of-thumb methods** Budgeting methods that base the IMC budget on either the firm's share of the market in relation to competition, a fixed percentage of forecasted sales, or what is left after other operating costs and forecasted sales have been budgeted.

**safety needs** One of the needs in the PSSP hierarchy of needs; pertain to protection and physical well-being.

**safety risk** See *psychological risk*

**salary** Compensation in the form of a fixed sum of money paid at regular intervals.

**sales contest** A short-term incentive designed to elicit a specific response from the sales force.

**sales management** Involves the planning, direction, and control of personal selling activities, including recruiting, selecting, training, motivating, compensating, and evaluating, as they apply to the sales force.

**sales orientation** A company objective based on the belief that increasing sales will help the firm more than will increasing profits.

**sales promotions** Special incentives or excitement-building programs that encourage the purchase of a product or service, such as coupons, rebates, contests, free samples, and point-of-purchase displays.

**sales support personnel** Employees who enhance and help with a firm's overall selling effort, such as by responding to the customer's technical questions or facilitating repairs.

**sample** A group of customers who represent the customers of interest in a research study.

**sampling** Offers potential customers the opportunity to try a product or service before they make a buying decision.

**scanner data** A type of syndicated external secondary data used in quantitative research that is obtained from scanner readings of UPC codes at check-out counters.

**scanner research** A type of quantitative research that uses data obtained from scanner readings of Universal Product Codes (UPCs) at checkout counters.

**scenario planning** A process that integrates macroenvironmental information in an attempt to understand the potential outcomes of different applications of a firm's marketing mix; enables a firm to predict, monitor, and adapt to the ever-changing future.

**search engine marketing (SEM)** A type of Web advertising whereby companies pay for keywords that are used to catch consumers' attention while browsing a search engine.

**seasonal discount** Pricing tactic of offering an additional reduction as an incentive to retailers to order merchandise in advance of the normal buying season.

**secondary data** Pieces of information that have already been collected from other sources and usually are readily available.

**secondary package** The wrapper or exterior carton that contains the primary package and provides the UPC label used by retail scanners; can contain additional product information that may not be available on the primary package.

**selective demand** Demand for a specific brand.

**selective demand advertising** Ads designed to generate demand for a specific brand, firm, or item.

**selective distribution** Lies between the intensive and exclusive distribution strategies; uses a few selected customers in a territory.

**self-actualization** When a person is completely satisfied with his or her life.

**self-concept** The image a person has of him- or herself; a component of *psychographics*.

**self-values** Goals for life, not just the goals one wants to accomplish in a day; a component of *psychographics* that refers to overriding desires that drive how a person lives his or her life.

**selling teams** Combinations of sales specialists whose primary duties are order getting, order taking, or sales support but who work together to service important accounts.

**sender** The firm from which an IMC message originates; the sender must be clearly identified to the intended audience.

**Seniors** America's fastest-growing generational cohort; people aged 55 to 64 years.

**service** Any intangible offering that involves a deed, performance, or effort that cannot be physically possessed; intangible customer benefits that are produced by people or machines and cannot be separated from the producer.

**service gap** Results when a service fails to meet the expectations that customers have about how it should be delivered.

**service quality** Customers' perceptions of how well a service meets or exceeds their expectations.

**service retailer** A firm that primarily sells services rather than merchandise.

**share of wallet** The percentage of the customer's purchases made from a particular retailer.

**shopping products/services** Those for which consumers will spend time comparing alternatives, such as apparel, fragrances, and appliances.

**situation analysis** Second step in a marketing plan; uses a SWOT analysis that assesses both the internal environment with regard to its **S**trengths and **W**eaknesses and the external environment in terms of its **O**pportunities and **T**hreats.

**situational factors** Factor affecting the consumer decision process; those that are specific to the situation that may override, or at least influence, psychological and social issues.

**size discount** The most common implementation of a quantity discount at the consumer level; the larger the quantity bought, the less the cost per unit (e.g., per ounce).

**slotting allowances** Fees firms pay to retailers simply to get new products into stores or to gain more or better shelf space for their products.

**social marketing** The application of marketing principles to a social issue to bring about attitudinal and behavioral change among the general public or a specific population segment.

**social media** Media content used for social interactions such as YouTube, Facebook, and Twitter.

**social risk** The fears that consumers suffer when they worry others might not regard their purchases positively.

**social shoppers** Consumers who seek emotional connections through shopping.

**social shopping** The use of the Internet to communicate about product preferences with other shoppers.

**specialty products/services** Products or services toward which the customer shows a strong preference and for which he or she will expend considerable effort to search for the best suppliers.

**specialty store** A type of retailer that concentrates on a limited number of complementary merchandise categories in a relatively small store.

**standards gap** A type of *service gap*; pertains to the difference between the firm's perceptions of customers' expectations and the service standards it sets.

**status quo pricing** A competitor-oriented strategy in which a firm changes prices only to meet those of competition.

**stock keeping units (SKUs)** Individual items within each product category; the smallest unit available for inventory control.

**store brands** See *private-label brands*.

**STP** The processes of segmentation, targeting, and positioning that firms use to identify and evaluate opportunities for increasing sales and profits.

**straight rebuy** Refers to when the buyer or buying organization simply buys additional units of products that have previously been purchased.

**strategic alliance** A collaborative relationship between independent firms, though the partnering firms do not create an equity partnership; that is, they do not invest in one another.

**strategic business unit (SBU)** A division of the firm itself that can be managed and operated somewhat independently from other divisions and may have a different mission or objectives.

**strategic relationship (partnering relationship)** A supply chain relationship that the members are committed to maintaining long term, investing in opportunities that are mutually beneficial; requires mutual trust, open communication, common goals, and credible commitments.

**structured questions** Closed-ended questions for which a discrete set of response alternatives, or specific answers, is provided for respondents to evaluate.

**substitute products** Products for which changes in demand are negatively related; that is, a percentage increase in the quantity demanded for product A results in a percentage decrease in the quantity demanded for product B.

**substitution effect** Refers to consumers' ability to substitute other products for the focal brand, thus increasing the price elasticity of demand for the focal brand.

**supercenter** Large stores combining full-line discount stores with supermarkets in one place.

**supply chain** The group of firms that make and deliver a given set of goods and services.

**supply chain conflict** See *channel conflict*.

**supply chain management** Refers to a set of approaches and techniques firms employ to efficiently and effectively integrate their suppliers, manufacturers, warehouses, stores, and transportation intermediaries into a seamless value chain in which merchandise is produced and distributed in the right quantities, to the right locations, and at the right time, as well as to minimize systemwide costs while satisfying the service levels their customers require.

**survey** A systematic means of collecting information from people that generally uses a *questionnaire*.

**sustainable competitive advantage** Something the firm can persistently do better than its competitors.

**sweepstakes** A form of sales promotion that offers prizes based on a chance drawing of entrants' names.

**syndicated data** Data available for a fee from commercial research firms such as Information Resources Inc. (IRI), National Purchase Diary Panel, and ACNielsen.

**target marketing/targeting** The process of evaluating the attractiveness of various segments and then deciding which to pursue as a market.

**target profit pricing** A pricing strategy implemented by firms when they have a particular profit goal as their overriding concern; uses price to stimulate a certain level of sales at a certain profit per unit.

**target return pricing** A pricing strategy implemented by firms less concerned with the absolute level of profits and more interested in the rate at which their profits are generated relative to their investments; designed to produce a specific return on investment, usually expressed as a percentage of sales.

**tariff** A tax levied on a good imported into a country; also called a *duty*.

**technological advances** Macroenvironmental factor that has greatly contributed to the improvement of the value of both products and services in the past few decades.

**telemarketing** A method of prospecting in which salespeople telephone potential customers.

**test marketing** Introduces a new product or service to a limited geographical area (usually a few cities) prior to a national launch.

**ticketing and marking** Creating price and identification labels and placing them on the merchandise.

**top-of-mind awareness** A prominent place in people's memories that triggers a response without them having to put any thought into it.

**total cost** The sum of the *variable* and *fixed costs*.

**tracking** Includes monitoring key indicators, such as daily or weekly sales volume, while the advertisement is running to shed light on any problems with the message or the medium.

**trade agreements** Intergovernmental agreements designed to manage and promote trade activities for specific regions.

**trade area** The geographical area that contains the potential customers of a particular retailer or shopping center.

**trade deficit** Results when a country imports more goods than it exports.

**trade shows** Major events attended by buyers who choose to be exposed to products and services offered by potential suppliers in an industry.

**trade surplus** Occurs when a country has a higher level of exports than imports.

**trading bloc** Consists of those countries that have signed a particular trade agreement.

**traditional distribution center** A warehouse in which merchandise is unloaded from trucks and placed on racks or shelves for storage.

**transactional orientation** Regards the buyer-seller relationship as a series of individual transactions, so anything that happened before or after the transaction is of little importance.

**transmitter** An agent or intermediary with which the sender works to develop the marketing communications; for example, a firm's creative department or an advertising agency.

**undifferentiated targeting strategy (mass marketing)** A marketing strategy a firm can use if the product or service is perceived to provide the same benefits to everyone, with no need to develop separate strategies for different groups.

**uniform delivered pricing** The shipper charges one rate, no matter where the buyer is located.

**unique selling proposition (USP)** A strategy of differentiating a product by communicating its unique attributes; often becomes the common theme or slogan in the entire advertising campaign.

**Universal Product Code (UPC)** The black-and-white bar code found on most merchandise.

**universal set** Includes all possible choices for a product-category.

**unrelated diversification** A growth strategy whereby a new business lacks any common elements with the present business.

**unsought product/services** Products or services consumers either do not normally think of buying or do not know about.

**unstructured questions** Open-ended questions that allow respondents to answer in their own words.

**user** The person who consumes or uses the product or service purchased by the buying center.

**value** Reflects the relationship of benefits to costs, or what the consumer *gets* for what he or she *gives*.

**Value and Lifestyle Survey (VALS™)** A psychographic tool developed by SRI Consulting Business Intelligence; classifies consumers into eight segments: innovators, thinkers, believers, achievers, strivers, experiencers, makers, or survivors.

**value-based pricing** A pricing strategy that involves first determining the perceived value of the product from the customer's point of view and then pricing accordingly.

**value-based pricing method** An approach that focuses on the overall value of the product offering as perceived by consumers, who determine value by comparing the benefits they expect the product to deliver with the sacrifice they will need to make to acquire the product.

**value cocreation** Customers act as collaborators with a manufacturer or retailer to create the product or service.

**value proposition** The unique value that a product or service provides to its customers and how it is better than and different from those of competitors.

**variability** A characteristic of a service: its quality may vary because it is provided by humans.

**variable costs** Those costs, primarily labor and materials, that vary with production volume.

**vendor-managed inventory** An approach for improving supply chain efficiency in which the manufacturer is responsible for maintaining the retailer's inventory levels in each of its stores.

**vertical channel conflict** A type of channel conflict in which members of the same marketing channel, for example, manufacturers, wholesalers, and retailers, are in disagreement or discord.

**vertical marketing system** A supply chain in which the members act as a unified system; there are three types: *administrated, contractual,* and *corporate.*

**vertical price fixing** Occurs when parties at different levels of the same marketing channel (e.g., manufacturers and retailers) collude to control the prices passed on to consumers.

**vertical supply chain conflict** See *vertical channel conflict*

**viral marketing** A marketing phenomenon that encourages people to pass along a marketing message to other potential consumers.

**viral marketing campaign** See *viral marketing*.

**virtual community** Online networks of people who communicate about specific topics.

**voice-of-customer (VOC) program** An ongoing marketing research system that collects customer inputs and integrates them into managerial decisions.

**warehouse clubs** Large retailers with an irregular assortment, low service levels, and low prices that often require membership for shoppers.

**Web portal** An Internet site whose purpose is to be a major starting point for users when they connect to the Web.

**Web tracking software** Used to assess how much time viewers spend on particular Web pages and the number of pages they view.

**wholesalers** Those firms engaged in buying, taking title to, often storing, and physically handling goods in large quantities, then reselling the goods (usually in smaller quantities) to retailers or industrial or business users.

**World Bank Group** A development bank that provides loans, policy advice, technical assistance, and knowledge-sharing services to low- and middle-income countries in an attempt to reduce poverty in the developing world.

**World Trade Organization (WTO)** Replaced the GATT in 1994; differs from the GATT in that the WTO is an established institution based in Geneva, Switzerland, instead of simply an agreement; represents the only international organization that deals with the global rules of trade among nations.

**zone of tolerance** The area between customers' expectations regarding their desired service and the minimum level of acceptable service—that is, the difference between what the customer really wants and what he or she will accept before going elsewhere.

**zone pricing** The shipper sets different prices depending on a geographical division of the delivery areas.

# *Quiz Yourself* answer key

## Chapter 1

1. The "Got Milk" advertising campaign was designed to help market an:

   Answer: (c) industry

2. The evolution of marketing progressed along the continuum:

   Answer: (d) production, sales, marketing, value-based marketing

## Chapter 2

1. In 2006, Ford Motor Company announced it would severely cut back automobile production. For parts companies supplying Ford Motor this represented a:

   Answer: (d) threat

2. Carla a manager of a local coffee shop, in response to increased competition from Starbucks, has been directed by her regional marketing manager to cut prices on seasonal items, run an ad in the local paper, and tell distributors to reduce deliveries for the next month. In which stage of the strategic marketing planning process is Carla engaged?

   Answer: (d) implement marketing mix and resources

## Chapter 3

1. Johnson & Johnson's 1943 "Credo" was considered radical at the time because it:

   Answer: (c) put customers first

2. Recognizing that parents, children, teachers, staff, and tax-payers all have a vested interest in the problem of deteriorating school facilities, and then listening to each group's concerns, a school board would most likely next:

   Answer: (c) engage in brainstorming and evaluate alternatives

## Chapter 4

1. When marketers look at advertising media they often begin with viewer or listener profiles such as, age, income, gender, and race. They then compare the media profile with their target audience. These marketers are using _____ to see if the media "fits" with their advertising agenda.

   Answer: (c) demographics

2. Many American consumers are purchasing hybrid automobiles even though they are more expensive and sometimes less fuel efficient when compared to compact conventional autos. Automobile marketers recognize these consumers:

   Answer: (a) value contributing to a greener environment

## Chapter 5

1. Dawn flies regularly between Atlanta and Los Angeles. She almost always uses Delta and has a large amount of Delta Sky miles but she uses an online fare comparison site each time to see if competitors have a better price or more convenient schedule. Dawn uses a _____ decision rule.

   Answer: (a) compensatory

2. Natalie and her fiancé Dow are planning their wedding. She knows her mother wants her to have a traditional church ceremony. She would like to have a ceremony on the beach like many of her friends had. Then there is the problem of who should officiate. Dow is from Thailand and would like to

have a monk officiate. Natalie and Dow's wedding decisions are influenced by:

   Answer: (e) family, reference groups, and culture

## Chapter 6

1. After posting an RFP for telecommunication equipment, USF received six proposals from qualified vendors. Next, USF will:

   Answer: (e) evaluate the proposals and likely narrow the choice to a few suppliers

2. Raycom Construction needs heavy duty equipment to install a new pipeline in northern Alaska. Raycom engineers will specify the type and capability requirements for the equipment to be purchased. The Raycom engineers will primarily play the _____ role in the company's buying center.

   Answer: (c) influencer

## Chapter 7

1. The Big Mac Index is a novel metric of:

   Answer: (b) purchasing power parity

2. Many of the best-known American retailers, like KFC and McDonald's, have expanded globally using:

   Answer: (a) franchising

## Chapter 8

1. Adidas Group owns Reebok, adidas, and TaylorMade brands. Adidas uses the different brands to pursue a(n) _____ strategy.

   Answer: (d) differentiated targeting

2. Talbots' target customers are college-educated women between 35 and 55 years old with average household income of $75,000 or more. Talbots is describing its market using a _____ segmentation approach.

   Answer: (d) demographic

## Chapter 9

1. Company sales invoices, Census data, and trade association statistics are examples of:

   Answer: (c) secondary data

2. Bianca's discount home furnishings store is in a strip mall. She wants to know what other businesses in the strip mall her customers visit when they come to her store. To collect information for this objective, Bianca will most likely use:

   Answer: (c) observation

## Chapter 10

1. Toothpaste, toothbrush, whitening products, kids' oral products, and floss are all _____ within Colgate-Palmolive's Oral Care product line.

   Answer: (a) products

2. It is almost impossible to watch a sporting event on television without seeing Nike's "swoosh" mark, which is Nike's:

   Answer: (b) symbol

## Chapter 11

1. Whenever Donald considers upgrading his personal computer system, he consults with Jeremy, a knowledgeable friend who always has the latest technology. For Donald, Jeremy is an _____ in the diffusion of innovation curve.

   Answer: (a) innovator

2. Zappos.com, an online shoe store, worked to overcome the problem of new product _____ with its easy, no-hassle return procedure.

   Answer: (e) trialability

## Chapter 12

1. A _____ gap reflects the difference between customers' expectations and the firm's perception of those customer expectations.

   Answer: (b) knowledge

2. When approached by a customer, Nordstrom's employees have been trained to drop whatever they are doing, listen carefully, and provide caring, individualized attention to that customer. Nordstrom employees have been trained to emphasize _____ in the five service quality dimensions.

   Answer: (e) empathy

## Chapter 13

1. If a shoe company has $1 million in fixed costs, its average shoe sells for $50 a pair, and variable costs are $30 per unit, how many units does the company need to sell to break even?

   Answer: (c) 50,000

2. Ferrari and Lamborghini are manufacturers of very expensive automobiles. Their limited edition cars often sell for $300,000 or more. The cars are considered by most consumers a prestige product, for which demand is likely to be:

   Answer: (b) price inelastic

## Chapter 14

1. In determining the price for his company's new pocket digital camera, Matt is assessing what consumers consider the regular or original price for similar cameras available in the market. Matt is assessing the _____ influence on pricing strategy.

   Answer: (a) improvement value

2. When Apple Inc. introduced their iPhone in 2007, they priced it at $599, considerably higher than either their iPod or competing cellular phones. Apple Computer was probably pursuing a _____ pricing strategy.

   Answer: (e) skimming

## Chapter 15

1. Franchising involves a _____ supply chain.

   Answer: (c) contractual

2. Flora is frustrated with her company's supply chain management information system. She wants to be able to receive sales data, initiate purchase orders, send and receive invoices, and receive returned merchandise documentation. Flora needs an:

   Answer: (b) electronic data interchange

## Chapter 16

1. The Gap, Lenscrafters, and Foot Locker are all examples of:

   Answer: (d) specialty stores

2. Walmart and Target dominate the _____ industry in the United States.

   Answer: (c) discount store

## Chapter 17

1. Often a(n) _____ accomplishes the task of encoding IMC messages.

   Answer: (a) advertising agency

2. Ingrid wants her company to expand its use of public relations. She argues that as other IMC alternatives become more expensive and _____, public relations should be a larger part of her company's IMC efforts.

   Answer: (b) consumers have become more skeptical of marketing claims

## Chapter 18

1. The Got Milk ads (milk moustaches worn by celebrities) are examples of successful:

   Answer: (e) public service announcements

2. Campbell Soup Company ran a series of radio ads tied to local weather forecasts. Before an impending storm, the ads said, "Time to stock up on Campbell Soup." During the storm, the ads said, "Stay home and stay warm with Campbell Soup." The first ad was _____ advertising, while the second ad was _____ advertising.

   Answer: (b) persuasive; reminder

## Chapter 19

1. Consumers often ask workers in supermarkets where something is located only to learn the workers are vendors stacking and straightening their companies' products on the store shelves. These manufacturer's sales representatives benefit retailers by _____.

   Answer: (c) saving them time and money

2. Bridgette went to the Gap ready to buy a new blouse, but was not sure which color or style she wanted. The sales representative, sensing Bridgette's buying mode, began with the _____ stage of the selling process.

   Answer: (e) sales presentation

# endnotes

## Chapter 1

1. Dan Hope, "The Year of the Tablet: The iPad's Competition," *TechNews Daily*, January 27, 2010.

2. *Bloomberg BusinessWeek*, "Apple Tops *Bloomberg BusinessWeek* Sixth Annual Ranking of the 50 Most Innovative Companies," *Trading Markets.com*, April 15, 2010.

3. Scott Morrison, "Apple Closes in on $50B Mark, a Hurdle That Often Humbles," *WallStreetJournal.com*, January 27, 2010.

4. Samuel Axon, "Five Ways Apple's iAd Will Change the Way You Advertise," *openforum.com*, April 20, 2010.

5. Ginny Mies, "iPods Still Reign Supreme, but Competition Closes In," *Macworld*, September 14, 2009.

6. http://en.wikipedia.org/wiki/Apple_Inc. (accessed April 27, 2010).

7. The American Marketing Association, http://www.marketing power.com/content4620.php (accessed April 22, 2010). Word in italic was added by the authors. Discussions of the latest revision of the AMA's marketing definition are widespread. See Gregory T. Gundlach and William L. Wilkie, "AMA's New Definition of Marketing: Perspective and Commentary on the 2007 Revision," *Journal of Public Policy & Marketing* 28, no. 2 (2008), pp. 259–64; see also the Fall 2007 issue of the *Journal of Public Policy & Marketing* (26, no. 2), which contains eight different perspectives on the new definition.

8. http://www.leftlanenews.com/lexus-ls-600h-l.html.

9. The idea of the four Ps was conceptualized by E. Jerome McCarthy, *Basic Marketing: A Managerial Approach* (Homewood, IL: Richard D. Irwin, 1960). Also see Walter van Watershoot and Christophe Van den Bulte, "The 4P Classification of the Marketing Mix Revisited," *Journal of Marketing* 56 (October 1992), pp. 83–93.

10. Beverage Marketing Corporation, a New York–based research and consulting firm, http://www.bottledwaterweb.com (accessed May 1, 2010).

11. http://corporate.ritzcarlton.com/en/About/Default.htm (accessed April 20, 2010); Carmine Gallo, "How Ritz-Carlton Maintains Its Mystique," *BusinessWeek*, February 13, 2007, accessed electronically; Peter Sanders, "Takin' Off the Ritz—a Tad," *The Wall Street Journal*, June 23, 2006.

12. http://www.joesstonecrab.com/yourdoor/package.html?pi d=alacarte&action=order&viewprices=1 (accessed April 22, 2010).

13. David Goldman, "Get Ready for Some Big Facebook Changes," *CNNMoney.com*, April 21, 2010; Venture Capital Dispatch, "Giving Credits Where Credits Are Due: Facebook to Aid Developers," *The Wall Street Journal*, April 22, 2010; Liz Gannes, "Facebook: The Entire Web Will Be Social," *Gigaom.com*, April 21, 2010; Jessica Vascellaro, "Facebook Wants to Know More Than Just Who Your Friends Are," *The Wall Street Journal*, April 22, 2010; Samuel Axon, "Facebook's Open Graph Personalizes the Web," *Mashable.com*, April 21, 2010; Harry McCracken, "Microsoft Melds Office with Facebook," *Technologizer.com*, April 21, 2010.

14. Stuart Elliot, "No Polo Pony, but Penney's New Label Is Pure Ralph Lauren Americana," *The New York Times*, February 19, 2008.

15. Sharon Sutker McGowan, "Employment Branding: Defining and Delivering Your Employment Promise," *Careerbuilder.com*, http://img.icbdr.com/images/jp/content/whitepapers/WPR -0026_Branding2.pdf (accessed April 27, 2010).

16. http://img.icbdr.com/images/jp/content/whitepapers/WPR -0026_Branding2.pdf (accessed April 22, 2010); http://www .gallup.com/consulting/122909/employment-branding.aspx (accessed April 22, 2010); Stewart Black, "The Employee Value Proposition: How to Be the Employer of Choice," Knowledge @ INSEAD, accessed electronically October 9, 2007; Dina Berta, "Chains Build Employment Brands to Compete for Workers," *Nation's Restaurant News*, December 18, 2006, pp. 10–8; and "'Brand' Your Company to Get—and Keep—Top Employees," *HR Focus*, October 2006, pp. 7–10.

17. George S. Day, "Aligning the Organization with the Market," *Marketing Science Institute* 5, no. 3 (2005), pp. 3–20.

18. Kimmy Wa Chan, Chi Kin (Bennett) Yim, and Simon S.K. Lam, "Is Customer Participation in Value Creation a Double-Edged Sword? Evidence from Professional Financial Services Across Cultures," *Journal of Marketing* 74, no. 3 (May 2010); Dhruv Grewal, Kent B. Monroe, and R. Krishnan, "The Effects of Price Comparison Advertising on Buyers' Perceptions of Acquisition Value and Transaction Value," *Journal of Marketing* 62 (April 1998), pp. 46–60; Kent B. Monroe, *Pricing: Making Profitable Decisions*, 3rd ed. (New York: McGraw-Hill, 2004); Dhruv Grewal and Larry Compeau, "Consumer Responses to Price and Its Contextual Information Cues: A Synthesis of Past Research, a Conceptual Framework, and Avenues for Further Research," *Review of Marketing Research* 3 (2005), Naresh Malhotra (ed.); M. E. Sharpe, Dhruv Grewal, Michael Levy, R. Krishnan, and Jeanne Munger, "Retail Success and Key Drivers," *Retailing in the 21st Century: Current and Future Trends*, Manfred Krafft and Murali Mantrala (eds.) (New York: Springer, 2006), pp. 13–26.

19. http://www.ideafinder.com/history/inventions/bluejeans.htm (accessed July 20, 2010).

20. Lorna, "The History of the Wonderful Fabric, Denim!," DenimBlog .com, February 1, 2010, http://www.denimblog.com/denimblog/ the-history-of-the-wonderful-fabric-denim/ (accessed July 20, 2010).

21. http://en.wikipedia.org/wiki/Designer_jeans (accessed July 20, 2010).

22. Christina Binkley, "The Relentless Rise of Power Jeans," *The Wall Street Journal*, November 6, 2009., http://online.wsj.com/article/ SB10001424052748703574604574501463104873016.html (accessed July 21, 2010).

23. Christina Binkley, "Admitting Jeans to the Club," *The Wall Street Journal*, May 27, 2010, http://online.wsj.com/article/SB10001424 052748704717004575268520888246294.html (accessed July 21, 2010).

24. Neeli Bendapudi and Robert P. Leone, "Psychological Implications of Customer Participation in Co-Production," *Journal of Marketing* 67 (January 2003), pp. 14–28; Beibei Dong, Kenneth R. Evans, and Shaoming Zou, "The Effects of Customer Participation in Co-created Service Recovery," working paper (2007); C. K. Prahalad and Venkatram Ramaswamy, "Co-opting Customer Competence," *Harvard Business Review* 78 (January–February 2000), pp. 79–87; C. K. Prahalad and Venkatram Ramaswamy, *The Future of Competition: Co-Creating Unique Value with Customers* (Cambridge, MA: Harvard Business School Press, 2004); Stephen L. Vargo and Robert F. Lusch, "Evolving to a New Dominant Logic for Marketing," *Journal of Marketing* 68 (January 2004), pp. 1–17; Stephen L. Vargo, Robert F. Lusch, and

Matthew O'Brien, "Competing through Service: Insights from Service-Dominant Logic," *Journal of Retailing* 83, no. 1 (2007), pp. 5–18; Jerry Wind and Arvind Rangaswamy, "Customerization: The Next Revolution in Mass Customization," Marketing Science Institute Working Paper No. 00-108 (Cambridge, MA: Marketing Science Institute, 2000).

25. Raquel Sánchez-Fernández and M. Ángeles Iniesta-Bonillo, "The Concept of Perceived Value: A Systematic Review of the Research," *Marketing Theory* 7 (2007), pp. 427–51; O. Turel, A. Serenko, and N. Bontis, "User Acceptance of Wireless Short Messaging Services: Deconstructing Perceived Value," *Information & Management* 44, no. 1 (2007), pp. 63–73.

26. http://www.wikinvest.com/wiki/JetBlue_Airways_(JBLU) (accessed April 21, 2010); http://www.wikinvest.com/wiki/Southwest_Airlines_Company (accessed April 21, 2010).

27. "Introducing Early Bird Check-In: A More Convenient Way to Travel," http://www.southwest.com/flight/early-bird-faq.html (accessed April 27, 2010).

28. http://www.easyjet.com (accessed April 21, 2010); http://www.ryanair.com (accessed April 21, 2010).

29. Alexander Krasnikov, Satish Jayachandran, and V. Kumar, "The Impact of CRM Implementation on Cost and Profit Efficiencies: Evidence from US Commercial Banking Industry," *Journal of Marketing* 73, no. 6 (November 2009), pp. 61–76; Robert W. Palmatier, Rajiv Dant and Dhruv Grewal, "A Longitudinal Analysis of Theoretical Perspectives of Interorganizational Relationship Performance," *Journal of Marketing* 71 (October 2007). In 2005, the *Journal of Marketing* ran a special section entirely devoted to relationship marketing. The section included these articles: William Boulding, Richard Staelin, Michael Ehret, and Wesley J. Johnston, "A Customer Relationship Management Roadmap: What Is Known, Potential Pitfalls, and Where to Go," *Journal of Marketing* 69, no. 4 (2005), pp. 155–66; Jacquelyn S. Thomas and Ursula Y. Sullivan, "Managing Marketing Communications with Multichannel Customers," *Journal of Marketing* 69, no. 4 (2005), pp. 239–51; Lynette Ryals, "Making Customer Relationship Management Work: The Measurement and Profitable Management of Customer Relationships," *Journal of Marketing* 69, no. 4 (2005), pp. 252–61; and Martha Rogers "Customer Strategy: Observations from the Trenches," *Journal of Marketing* 69, no. 4 (2005), pp. 262–63.

30. V. Kumar, Denish Shah, and Rajkumar Venkatesan, "Managing Retailer Profitability—One Customer at a Time!" *Journal of Retailing* 82, no. 4 (2006), pp. 277–94; R. Venkatesan and V. Kumar, "A Customer Lifetime Value Framework for Customer Selections and Resource Allocation Strategy," *Journal of Marketing* 68, no. 4 (2004), pp. 106–25; V. Kumar, G. Ramani and T. Bohling, "Customer Lifetime Value Approaches and Best Practice Applications," *Journal of Interactive Marketing* 18, no. 3 (2004), pp. 60–72; and J. Thomas, W. Reinartz, and V. Kumar, "Getting the Most Out of All Your Customers," *Harvard Business Review*, July–August 2004, pp. 116–23.

31. http://www.hm.com/us/abouthm_abouthm.nhtml (accessed April 21, 2010).

32. http://www.zara.com (accessed April 21, 2010).

33. http://www.ahold.com (accessed April 21, 2010).

34. Parmy Olson, "McDonalds Goes McChic," *Forbes*, February 16, 2010; http://www.burgerbusiness.com/?p=4559 (accessed April 21, 2010); Julia Werdigier, "To Woo Europeans, McDonald's Goes Upscale, *The New York Times*, August 25, 2007, accessed electronically.

35. http://www.pressroom.ups.com/Site+Guide (accessed April 21, 2010).

36. http://www.kelloggcompany.com/company.aspx?id=888 (accessed April 27, 2010).

37. http://www.kelloggcompany.com/commitments.aspx (accessed April 21, 2010).

38. http://www.colgate.com/app/Colgate/US/Corp/Living OurValues/CoreValues.cvsp (accessed April 21, 2010).

39. http://www.benjerry.com/activism/mission-statement/ (accessed April 21, 2010).

40. Goldman Sachs, "Code of Business Conduct and Ethics," May 2009, http://www2.goldmansachs.com/our-firm/investors/corporate-governance/corporate-governance-documents/code-of-business-conduct-ethics.pdf (accessed April 27, 2010); Securities and Exchange Commission, "Bear Stearns Companies Inc.," 10-K Report, Ex. 14, November 30, 2004, available at http://www.secinfo.com/d13Wqv.zTs.7.htm#1stPage (accessed April 27, 2010).

41. "The Lehman Whistleblower's Letter," *The Wall Street Journal*, March 19, 2010, http://blogs.wsj.com/deals/2010/03/19/breaking-news-here-is-the-letter-at-the-center-of-the-lehman-report/ (accessed April 27, 2010).

42. United States Bankruptcy Court, Southern District of New York, "In re: Lehman Brothers Holdings Inc. et al.," Chapter 11 Case No.: 08_13555 (JMP), March 11, 2010. Available at http://lehmanreport.jenner.com/VOLUME%201.pdf (accessed April 27, 2010).

43. http://www.deloitte.com/view/en_US/us/About/index.htm (accessed April 27, 2010); Michael Price, "Take It from the Top: When Deloitte Execs Made Ethics a Priority, It Filtered Down," *Ethisphere*, November 3, 2009, http://ethisphere.com/take-it-from-the-top-when-deloitte-execs-made-ethics-a-priority-it-filtered-on-down/ (accessed April 27, 2010).

44. Dan Amos, "Aflac's Ethics in Action: Pay for Performance Keep Stakeholders Informed," *Ethisphere*, January 12, 2009, http://ethisphere.com/aflacs-ethics-in-action-pay-for-performance-keep-stakeholders-informed/ (accessed April 27, 2010).

45. http://dictionary.reference.com/search?q=Entrepreneurship (accessed April 21, 2010).

46. www.pixar.com (accessed April 21, 2010).

47. http://www.oprah.com/ (accessed April 21, 2010).

48. "Apple Launches iPad; Magical and Revolutionary Device at an Unbeatable Price," Apple press release, January 27, 2010, http://www.apple.com/pr/library/2010/01/27ipad.html.

49. Walt Mossberg, "Laptop Killer? Pretty Close," *The Wall Street Journal*, April 1, 2010, http://online.wsj.com/article/SB200014240527023042527045751559827114106 78.html (accessed April 26, 2010).

50. Matt Phillips, "Apple iPad Launch: Here Are Wall Street's Expectations," *Marketbeat*, April 2, 2010, http://blogs.wsj.com/marketbeat/2010/04/02/apple-ipad-launch-here-are-wall-streets-expectations/tab/article/ (accessed April 26, 2010).

51. Dan Gallagher, "Interest Builds in Apple Ahead of iPad's Launch," *The Wall Street Journal*, March 30, 2010, http://online.wsj.com/article/SB10001424052702304370304575151991588900032.html (accessed April 26, 2010).

52. Samuel Axon, "Five Ways Apple's iAd Will Change the Way You Advertise," http://www.openforum.com/idea-hub/topics/technology/article/5-ways-apples-iad-will-change-the-way-you-advertise-samuel-axon (accessed April 20, 2010).

53. Suzanne Vranica and Emily Steele, "Marketers Get Ready to Release iPad Ad Campaigns," *The Wall Street Journal*, April 1, 2010, http://online.wsj.com/article/SB10001424052702303338304575156073394630854.html (accessed April 26, 2010).

54. Yukair Iwatani Kane, "Apple Takes Big Gamble on new iPad," *The Wall Street Journal*, January 25, 2010, http://online.wsj.com/article/SB10001424052748704094304575029230041284668.html (accessed April 25, 2010).

55. Scott Morrison, "Apple Closes In on $50B Mark, a Hurdle That Often Humbles," *The Wall Street Journal*, January 27, 2010, http://online.wsj.com/article/BT-CO-20100127-720060.html (accessed April 26, 2010).

## Chapter 2

1. http://www.starbucks.com/aboutus/Company_Factsheet.pdf (accessed November 23, 2007); Joe Nocera, "Give Me a Double Shot of Starbucks Nostalgia," *The New York Times*, March 3, 2007, http://select.nytimes.come/2007/03/03/business/oznocera.html (accessed October 6, 2008).

2. Janet Adamy, "McDonald's Takes on a Weakened Starbucks," *The Wall Street Journal*, January 7, 2008, http://www3.babson.edu/Centers/retail_intelligence/upload/McDonalds_Starbucks_Dunkin'_Donuts_Compete.pdf.

3. Greg Farrell, "Return of the Barista-in-Chief," *The Financial Times*, March 21, 2010, http://uk.buzz.yahoo.com/article/1:financial_tim933:42ad14cdd19f3a6a55d93795e233e372/Return-of-the-barista-in-chief.

4. Emily Bryson York, "All That Advertising Brings Buzz for Coffee Marketers," *Advertising Age*, June 11, 2009.

5. https://www.Dunkin'donuts.com/downloads/pdf/DD_Press_Kit.pdf (accessed April 28, 2010); https://www.Dunkin'donuts.com/aboutus/company/ (accessed April 26, 2010); Julie Bosman, "This Joe's for You?" *The New York Times*, June 8, 2006.

6. Angela Moore, ed., "A New Star Is Emerging at McDonald's Corp.," *Market Watch*, April 21, 2010, http://www.marketwatch.com/story/mcdonalds-and-starbucks-in-coffee-clash-2010-04-21.

7. Gal Tziperman Lotan, "Cold Competition: Chains Roll Out New Iced Coffee Creations," *The Boston Globe*, April 6, 2010, http://www.boston.com/business/articles/2010/04/06/chains_roll_out_new_iced_coffee_creations/#end.

8. McDonald's website, http://www.aboutmcdonalds.com/mcd/our_company.html (accessed April 26, 2010).

9. Paul Ziobro, "McDonald's Bets Pricing Drinks at a $1 Will Heat Up Summer Sales," *The Wall Street Journal*, March 18, 2010, http://online.wsj.com/article/SB10001424052748704743404575127551110770616.html.

10. Julie Jargon, "New Ads Will Stir Up Coffee Ware," *The Wall Street Journal*, May 4, 2009, http://online.wsj.com/article/SB124139141624581429.html.

11. Michael Treacy and Fred Wiersema, *The Disciplines of Market Leaders* (Reading, MA: Addison Wesley, 1995). Treacy and Wiersema suggest the first three strategies. We suggest the fourth—locational excellence.

12. J. Andrew Petersen, Leigh McAlister, David J. Reibstein, Russell S. Winer, V. Kumar, and Geoff Atkinson, "Choosing the Right Metrics to Maximize Profitability and Shareholder Value," *Journal of Retailing* 85, no. 1 (2009), pp. 95–111; Lars Meyer-Waarden, "The Influence of Loyalty Programme Membership on Customer Purchase Behavior," *European Journal of Marketing* 42, no. 1/2 (2008), pp. 87–114; Lars Meyer-Waarden, "The Effects of Loyalty Programs on Customer Lifetime Duration and Share of Wallet," *Journal of Retailing* 83, no. 2 (2007), pp. 223–36; Seigyoung Auh, Simon J. Bell, Colin S. McLeod, and Eric Shih, "Co-production and Customer Loyalty in Financial Services," *Journal of Retailing* 83, no. 3 (2007), pp. 359–70; Ruth N. Bolton, Dhruv Grewal, and Michael Levy, "Six Strategies for Competing through Service: An Agenda for Future Research," *Journal of Retailing* 83, no. 1 (2007), pp. 1–4.

13. Petersen et al., "Choosing the Right Metrics to Maximize Profitability and Shareholder Value"; V. Kumar, "Tough Times Call for CLV," *The Economist*, March 29, 2009; V. Kumar, *Managing Customers for Profit: Strategies to Increase Profits and Build Loyalty* (Philadelphia: Wharton School Publishing, 2008); Meyer-Waarden, "The Effects of Loyalty Programs"; Mert Tokman, Lenita M. Davis, and Katherine N. Lemon, "The WOW Factor: Creating Value through Win-Back Offers to Reacquire Lost Customers," *Journal of Retailing* 83, no. 1 (2007), pp. 47–64; Hean Tat Keh, Yih Hwai Lee, V. Kumar, Denish Shah, and Rajkumar Venkatasan, "Managing Retailer Profitability—One Customer at a Time!" *Journal of Retailing* 82, no. 4 (2006), pp. 277–94.

14. "Do Reward Programs Build Loyalty for Services? The Moderating Effect of Satisfaction on Type and Timing of Rewards," *Journal of Retailing* 82, no. 2 (2006), pp. 127–36.

15. Valarie A. Zeithaml, Mary Jo Bitner, and Dwayne D. Gremler, *Services Marketing: Integrating Customer Focus across the Firm*, 5th ed. (Burr Ridge, IL: McGraw-Irwin, 2009); Mary Jo Bitner, "Self Service Technologies: What Do Customers Expect?" *Marketing Management*, Spring 2001, pp. 10–34; Mary Jo Bitner, Stephen W. Brown, and Matthew L. Meuter, "Technology Infusion in Service Encounters," *Journal of Academy of Marketing Science* 28, no. 1 (2000), pp. 138–49; Matthew L. Meuter, Amy L. Ostrom, Robert I. Roundtree, and Mary Jo Bitner, "Self-Service Technologies: Understanding Customer Satisfaction with Technology-Based Service Encounters," *Journal of Marketing* 64, no. 3 (2000), pp. 50–64; A. Parasuraman and Dhruv Grewal, "The Impact of Technology on the Quality-Value-Loyalty Chain: A Research Agenda," *Journal of the Academy of Marketing Science* 28, no. 1 (2000), pp. 168–74.

16. "Singapore Airlines Tops Survey for Best Service," *The New York Times*, http://community.nytimes.com/comments/intransit.blogs.nytimes.com/2010/03/31/singapore-airlines-tops-survey-for-best-international-service/ (accessed April 27, 2010).

17. Singapore Airlines website, http://www.singaporeair.com/saa/en_UK/content/exp/new/businessclass/seatfeatures.jsp (accessed April 27, 2010).

18. Martin Roll, "Singapore Airlines—An Excellent Asian Brand," *Venture Republic*, http://www.venturerepublic.com/resources/Singapore_Airlines_-_An_Excellent_Asian_Brand.asp (accessed April 27, 2010).

19. Frederik Balfour, "Singapore Airlines Flies Higher," *Bloomberg Business Week*, July 6, 2007, http://www.businessweek.com/globalbiz/content/jul2007/gb2007076_820944.htm.

20. James R. Stock, Stefanie L. Boyer, and Tracy Harmon, "Research Opportunities in Supply Chain Management," *Journal of the Academy of Marketing Science* 38, no. 1 (2010), pp. 32–41. Also see articles in special issue edited by John T. Mentzer and Greg Gundlach, "Exploring the Relationship between Marketing and Supply Chain Management: Introduction to the Special Issue," *Journal of the Academy of Marketing Science* 38, no. 1 (2010), pp. 1–4; S. A. Shaw and J. Gibbs, "Procurement Strategies of Small Marketers Faced with Uncertainty: An Analysis of

Channel Choice and Behavior," *International Review of Market, Distribution and Consumer Research* 9, no. 1 (1999), pp. 61–75.

21. http://www.gallaugher.com/Netflix%20Case.pdf (accessed April 27, 2010); http://www.netflix.com/MediaCenter?id=5206 (accessed April 28, 2010); http://www.hd-report.com/2010/03/04/netflix-vs-blockbuster-why-is-netflix-winning/ (accessed April 28, 2010).

22. David Lei and John Slocum Jr., "Strategic and Organizational Requirements for Competitive Advantage," *Academy of Management Executive*, February 2005, pp. 31–46.

23. Maria Halkias, "Penney Remakes Culture to Remake Image," *The Dallas Morning News*, February 12, 2007.

24. *BusinessWeek*, "The Top 100 Brands," http://bwnt.businessweek.com/brand/2006/ (accessed December 17, 2007).

25. Michael Arndt, "3M's Seven Pillars of Innovation," *BusinessWeek*, May 10, 2006.

26. http://www.marketingpower.com/_layouts/Dictionary.aspx?dLetter=M (accessed April 27, 2010).

27. Donald Lehman and Russell Winer, *Analysis for Marketing Planning*, 6th ed. (Burr Ridge, IL: McGraw-Hill/Irwin, 2004); David Aaker, *Strategic Market Management*, 6th ed. (New York: John Wiley, 2001).

28. Andrew Campbell, "Mission Statements," *Long Range Planning* 30 (1997), pp. 931–33.

29. Alfred Rappaport, *Creating Shareholder Value: The New Standard for Business Performance* (New York: Wiley, 1988); Robert C. Higgins and Roger A. Kerin, "Managing the Growth-Financial Policy Nexus in Marketing," *Journal of Marketing* 59, no. 3 (1983), pp. 19–47; and Roger Kerin, Vijay Mahajan, and P. Rajan Varadarajan, *Contemporary Perspectives on Strategic Market Planning* (Boston: Allyn & Bacon, 1991), chapter 6.

30. http://www.starbucks.com/about-us/company-information/mission-statement (accessed April 26, 2010).

31. http://assets.starbucks.com/assets/company-profile-feb10.pdf (accessed April 26, 2010).

32. Janet Adamy, "Starbucks Keeps Sandwiches, Tweaks Recipe," *The Wall Street Journal*, July 26, 2008; http://www.savethebreakfastsandwich.com/ (accessed May 10, 2010).

33. 2009 Starbucks annual report, http://investor.starbucks.com/phoenix.zhtml?c=99518&p=irol-reportsAnnual.

34. https://www.hertz.com/rentacar/byr/index.jsp?targetPage=vehicleGuideHomeView.jsp (accessed April 26, 2010).

35. https://images.hertz.com/pdfs/VMVWeb.pdf (accessed April 26, 2010); http://www.adweek.com/aw/content_display/creative/new-campaigns/e3i21cea1586dd4edf5d50f9a17e7f18bf3.

36. http://www.dove.us/#/cfrb/about_cfrb.aspx (accessed April 27, 2010); http:www.campaignforrealbeauty.com (accessed April 27, 2010).

37. Rosaura Lezama, Sarah Henry, and Heidi Dangelmaier, "Dove (D)evolution," *BusinessWeek*, November 12, 2007.

38. Raju Mudhar, "Dove's 'Evolution' Ad Wins at Cannes," *The Star*, June 22, 2007.

39. Stacey Cosens, "Is Airbrushing Creating Unachievable Beauty?" *Thelinc.co.uk*, April 6, 2010; Chelsea Twietmeyer, "Media Demand Flawless Image," *Thebakerorange.com*, April 22, 2010; Nicole Sciotti, "Dove Campaign Redefines Beauty," *CardinalCourier.com*, March 31, 2010.

40. David Graham, "Dove's Idea of Real Beauty to Include Average Joes," *Toronto Star*, January 15, 2010; Talking Retail, "Dove Reveals Its Masculine Side—Dove Men+Care," *TalkingRetail.com*, January 15, 2010.

41. http://solutions.3m.com/wps/portal/3M/en_US/about-3M/information/about/us/ (accessed April 28, 2010).

42. Michael Arndt, "3M's Seven Pillars of Innovation," *Business Week*, May 10, 2006, http://www.businessweek.com/innovate/content/may2006/id20060510_682823.htm.

43. Dana Mattioli, Kris Maher, "At 3M, Innovation Comes in Tweaks and Snips," *The Wall Street Journal*, March 2, 2010.

44. Mary Tripsas, "Seeing Customers as Partners in Invention," *The New York Times*, December 26, 2009.

45. Geoffrey A. Fowler and Lauren Pollock, "Target to Sell Amazon's Kindle," *The Wall Street Journal*, April 21, 2010; "IPad vs. Kindle; Who Wins?" *The Wall Street Journal*, January 28, 2010.

46. http://www.barnesandnoble.com/nook/compare/?cds2Pid=30195 (accessed May 4, 2010); http://www.amazon.com/dp/B0015T963C/?tag=googhydr-20&hvadid=5262626577&ref=pd_sl_a6eh7sgtv_e (accessed May 4, 2010).

47. 2009 Starbucks Annual Report; Paul W. Farris, Neil T. Bendle, Phillip E. Pfeifer, and David J. Reibstein, *Marketing Metrics: 50+ Metrics Every Executive Should Master* (Philadelphia: Wharton School Publishing, 2006), p. 1.

48. 2009 McDonalds Annual Report.

49. "Starbucks Shared Plan: Goals and Progress 2009," http://www.starbucks.com/responsibility/learn-more/goals-and-progress (accessed April 28, 2010); http://www.starbucks.com/responsibility/sourcing/coffee (accessed April 28, 2010); "2010 World's Most Ethical Companies," *Ethisphere*, http://ethisphere.com/wme2010/ (accessed April 28, 2010).

50. http://www.ethoswater.com/ (accessed April 28, 2010); http://www.starbucks.com/responsibility/community/ethos-water-fund (accessed April 28, 2010); http://www.starbucks.com/responsibility/sourcing/coffee (accessed April 28, 2010); http://www.marketwatch.com/story/starbucks-releases-2009-global-responsibility-report-2010-04-19?reflink=MW_news_stmp (accessed April 28, 2010); http://www.starbucks.com/assets/ssp-g-p-full-report.pdf (accessed April 28, 2010).

51. Michael Santo, "Starbucks Sales Unchanged Despite Calorie Counting," January 8, 2010, http://www.huliq.com/3257/90244/starbucks-sales-unchanged-despite-calorie-counting (accessed April 28, 2010).

52. https://www.webmdhealth.com/starbucks/default.aspx?secure=1 (accessed April 28, 2010).

53. http://www.goodyear.com/investor/pdf/ar/2009ar.pdf (accessed April 27, 2010).

54. This discussion is adapted from Roger A. Kerin, Eric N. Berkowitz, Steven W. Hartley, and William Rudelius, *Marketing*, 10th ed. (Burr Ridge, IL: McGraw-Hill/Irwin, 2011).

55. Farris et al., *Marketing Metrics: 50+ Metrics Every Executive Should Master*, p. 17.

56. Relative market share = brand's market share ÷ largest competitor's market share. If, for instance, there are only two products in a market, A and B, and product B has 90 percent market share, then A's relative market share is 10 ÷ 90 = 11.1 percent. If, on the other hand, B only has 50 percent market share, then A's relative market share is 10 ÷ 50 = 20 percent. Farris et al., *Marketing Metrics: 50+ Metrics Every Executive Should Master*, p. 19.

57. Roger Kerin, Vijay Mahajan, and P. Rajan Varadarajan, *Contemporary Perspectives on Strategic Market Planning*

(Boston: Allyn & Bacon, 1991), chapter 6; Susan Mudambi, "A Topology of Strategic Choice in Marketing," *International Journal of Market & Distribution Management* (1994), pp. 22–25.

58. David Carr, "Do They Still Want Their MTV?" *The New York Times,* February 19, 2007; Chrissy Le Nguyen, "The Hills: Then and Now," April 27, 2010, http://tv.yahoo.com/slideshow/551/photos/1 (accessed April 28, 2010).

59. http://www.mtvnetworkscareers.com/ (accessed April 26, 2010).

60. http://www.athinline.org (accessed April 28, 2010); http://think.mtv.com (accessed April 28, 2010).

61. A. A. Thompson, A. J. Strickland, and J. E. Gamble, *Crafting and Executing Strategy* (New York: McGraw-Hill Irwin, 2009).

62. Tim Arango, "Make Room, Cynics; MTV Wants to Do Some Good," *The New York Times,* April 18, 2009; Robert Seidman, *tvbythenumbers.com,* January 15, 2010.

63. http://solutions.3m.com/wps/portal/3M/en_US/about-3M/information/about/businesses/ (accessed April 28, 2010).

64. Julie Niederhoff, "Video Rental Developments and the Supply Chain: Netflix, Inc.," http://apps.olin.wustl.edu/workingpapers/pdf/2004-03-225.pdf (accessed April 28, 2010).

65. John M. Gallaugher, PhD, "Netflix Case Study: David Becomes Goliath," http://www.gallaugher.com/Netflix%20Case.pdf (accessed April 28, 2010).

66. "Finding the Cheapest TV-Watching Experience," *The Chicago Tribune,* http://newsblogs.chicagotribune.com/the-problem-solver/2010/04/finding-the-cheapest-tvwatching-experience.html (accessed April 28, 2010).

67. Jeff Chabot, "Netflix vs. Blockbuster—Why Is Netflix Winning?" *HD Report,* March 4, 2010, http://www.hd-report.com/2010/03/04/netflix-vs-blockbuster-why-is-netflix-winning/.

68. Mike Schuster, "How Netflix Succeeded Where Blockbuster Failed," *Minyanville,* April 22, 2010, http://www.minyanville.com/businessmarkets/articles/netflix-blockbuster-movie-rentals-on-demand/4/22/2010/id/27926.

69. Larry Dignan, "Netflix: More Than Half of Subscribers Tap Streaming Video," *CNET News,* April 22, 2010, http://news.cnet.com/8301-1023_3-20003137-93.html.

70. "Netflix: Streaming Drives Q1 Growth," *Media & Entertainment Services Alliance,* April 22, 2010.

71. Scott Stein, "Netflix on iPad, More to Follow?" *CNET Reviews,* April 1, 2010; The Official Netflix Blog, April 2, 2010.

72. Kelly Riddell, "DirecTV Targets Netflix, Offering More Movies Faster," *Bloomberg Businessweek,* April 19, 2010.

## Appendix 2A

1. This Appendix was written by Tom Chevalier, Britt Hackmann, and Elisabeth Nevins Caswell, in conjunction with the textbook authors (Dhruv Grewal and Michael Levy) as the basis of class discussion rather than to illustrate either effective or ineffective marketing practice.

2. http://www.knowthis.com/tutorials/principles-of-marketing/how-to-write-a-marketing-plan.htm (accessed May 16, 2008); see also "Marketing Plan Online," http://www.quickmba.com/marketing/plan/ (accessed May 16, 2008); "Marketing Plan," http://www.businessplans.org/Market.html (accessed May 18, 2008).

3. Roger Kerin, Steven Hartley, and William Rudelius, Marketing (New York: McGraw-Hill/Irwin, 2008), p. 53.

4. Ibid., p. 54; http://www.knowthis.com/tutorials/principles-of-marketing/how-to-write-a-marketing-plan.htm (accessed May 16, 2008).

5. This listing of sources largely comes from the Babson College Library Guide, http://www3.babson.edu/Library/research/marketingplan.cfm, May 12, 2008 (accessed May 15, 2008). Special thanks to Nancy Dlott.

6. This marketing plan presents an abbreviated version of the actual plan for PeopleAhead. Some information has been changed to maintain confidentiality.

7. Publishers' and Advertising Directors' Conference, September, 21, 2005.

8. Mintel International Group, "Online Recruitment–US," January 1, 2005, http://www.marketresearch.com (accessed September 1, 2005).

9. Corzen Inc., May 1, 2004, http://www.wantedtech.com/ (accessed May 17, 2004).

10. Mintel International Group, "Online Recruitment–US."

## Chapter 3

1. Mary Clare Jalonick, "Health Law Will Make Calorie Counts Hard to Ignore," *Heraldnewsonline.com,* March 24, 2010.

2. Deborah Kotz, "Should the Food Industry Ban Added Salt and Sugar?" *USNews.com,* April 21, 2010.

3. Jason Ramsey, "Kellogg's to Reduce Salt in its Cereals by One-Third," *Dipity.com,* February 1, 2010.

4. Michael Connor, "Kellogg's Corporate Responsibility Report: 'Watch the Salt!'" *Business-Ethics.com,* April 7, 2010.

5. Jane Byrne, "Kellogg Calls for Industrywide Engagement on Salt Reduction," *FoodNavigator.com,* January 29, 2010.

6. Theodore Levitt, *Marketing Imagination* (Detroit, MI: The Free Press, 1983).

7. "Mattel Apologizes to China for Recall," *The New York Times,* September 21, 2007, http://www.nytimes.com/2007/09/21/business/worldbusiness/21iht-mattel.3.7597386.html (accessed April 21, 2010); "Plenty of Blame to Go Around," *The Economist,* September 29, 2007.

8. For a detailed compilation of articles that are involved with ethical and societal issues, see: Gregory T. Gundlach, Lauren G. Block, and William W. Wilkie, *Explorations of Marketing in Society* (Mason, OH: Thompson Higher Education, 2007); G. Svensson and G. Wood, "A Model of Business Ethics," *Journal of Business Ethics* 77, no. 3 (2007), pp. 303–22.

9. Christy Ashley and Hillary A. Leonard, "Betrayed by the Buzz? Covert Content and Consumer–Brand Relationships," *Journal of Public Policy & Marketing* 28, no. 2 (2009), pp. 212–20.

10. Elizabeth S. Moore and Victoria J. Rideout, "The Online Marketing of Food to Children: Is it Just Fun and Games?" *Journal of Public Policy & Marketing* 26, no. 2 (2007), pp. 202–20; Elizabeth S. Moore, "Perspectives on Food Marketing and Childhood Obesity: Introduction to the Special Section," *Journal of Public Policy & Marketing* 26, no. 2 (2007), pp. 157–61; Elizabeth S. Moore, "Food Marketing Goes Online: A Content Analysis of Websites for Children," in *Obesity in America: Development and Prevention,* Vol. 2, Hiram E. Fitzgerald and Vasiliki Mousouli, eds. (Westport, CT: Praeger, 2007), pp. 93–115; and William L. Wilkie and Elizabeth S. Moore, "Marketing's

Contributions to Society," *Journal of Marketing* 63 (Special Issue, 1999), pp. 198–219.

11. Lydia Saad, "Honesty and Ethics Poll Finds Congress' Image Tarnished," *www.Gallup.com*, December 9, 2009.

12. http://www.workingvalues.com/Dec06WorkingValues WhtPpr.pdf (accessed January 18, 2010).

13. http://www.jnj.com/our_company/our_credo/index.htm (accessed January 18, 2010).

14. Vanessa O'Connell and Shirley Wang, "J&J Acts Fast on Tylenol," *The Wall Street Journal*, July 9, 2009.

15. Erin Cavusgil, "Merck and Vioxx: An Examination of an Ethical Decision-Making Model," *Journal of Business Ethics* 76 (2007), pp. 451–61.

16. Jeanne Whalen, "AstraZeneca Sharpens Focus on Ethics," *The Wall Street Journal*, December 3, 2009, http://online.wsj.com/article/SB10001424052748704157304574611724066010600.html (accessed April 21, 2010); "AstraZeneca Weighs Response to UK Body on Ethics Code Breach," *The Wall Street Journal*, March 9, 2010, http://online.wsj.com/article/BT-CO-20100309-706314.html (accessed April 21, 2010).

17. http://www.marketingpower.com/AboutAMA/Pages/Statement%20of%20Ethics.aspx (accessed April 21, 2010).

18. http://www.cmomagazine.com/info/release/090104_ethics.html (accessed September 1, 2006).

19. Ellen Byron, "Avon Suspends Four Executives Amid Bribery Probe," The Wall Street Journal, April 13, 2010, http://online.wsj.com/article/SB100014240527023045069045751805010750998806.html?mod=googlenews_wsj (accessed April 21, 2010).

20. In a recent article, Alexander Dahlsrud lists 37 different definitions of the concept! See "How Corporate Social Responsibility Is Defined," *Corporate Social Responsibility and Environmental Management* 15, no. 1 (January/February 2208), pp. 1–13.

21. "Social Responsibility," AMA Dictionary of Marketing Terms, http://www.marketingpower.com/_layouts/Dictionary.aspx?dLetter=S (accessed April 21, 2010).

22. Christopher Marquis, Pooja Shah, Amanda Tolleson, and Bobbi Thomason, "The Dannon Company: Marketing and Corporate Social Responsibility," *Harvard Business School Case 9-410-121*, April 1, 2010.

23. Michael Connor, "Survey: U.S. Consumers Willing to Pay for Corporate Responsibility," *Business Ethics*, March 29, 2010, http://business-ethics.com/2010/03/29/1146-survey-u-s-consumers-willing-to-pay-for-corporate-responsibility/ (accessed April 21, 2010).

24. Richard Stengel, "Doing Well by Doing Good," *Time Magazine*, September 10, 2009, http://www.time.com/time/magazine/article/0,9171,1921591,00.html (accessed April 21, 2010).

25. http://www.toms.com/our-movement; http://www.toms.com/corporate-info/; http://www.insightargentina.org (accessed April 21, 2010); Christina Binkley, "Charity Gives Shoe Brand Extra Shine," *The Wall Street Journal*, April 1, 2010, http://online.wsj.com/article/SB10001424052702304252704575155903198032336.html (accessed April 21, 2010).

26. "2009 World's Most Ethical Companies," *Ethisphere*, http://ethisphere.com/wme2009/ (accessed April 21, 2010).

27. A. Parasuraman, Dhruv Grewal, and R. Krishnan, *Marketing Research*, 2nd ed. (Boston, MA: Houghton Mifflin Company, 2007), pp. 44–49; Allan J. Kimmel and N. Craig Smith, "Deception in Marketing Research: Ethical, Methodological and Disciplinary Implications," *Psychology & Marketing* 18,

no. 7 (2001) p. 663; Ralph W. Giacobbe and Madhav N. Segal, "A Comparative Analysis of Ethical Perceptions in Marketing Research: U.S.A. vs. Canada," *Journal of Business Ethics* 27 (October 2000), pp. 229–46; Naresh K. Malhotra and Gina L. Miller, "An Integrated Model for Ethical Decisions in Marketing Research," *Journal of Business Ethics* 17 (February 1988), pp. 263–80; J. R. Sparks and S. D. Hunt, "Marketing Researcher Ethical Sensitivity: Conceptualization, Measurement, and Exploratory Investigation," *Journal of Marketing*, April 1988, pp. 92–109.

28. This question is based on deontological theory, an ethical theory concerned with duties and rights. Deontological ethical theories are based on the existence of a universal principle—such as respect for others, honesty, fairness, or justice—that forms the basis for determining what is right. See E. Cavusgil, "Merck and Vioxx: An Examination of an Ethical Decision-Making Model," *Journal of Business Ethics* 76, no. 4 (2007), pp. 451–61; Kate McKone-Sweet, Danna Greenberg, and Lydia Moland, "Approaches to Ethical Decision Making," Babson College Case Development Center, 2003.

29. This question is based on the theory of act utilitarianism, which requires that a person act so that his or her actions result in more good than harm to his or her society. In essence, act utilitarianism involves a cost/benefit analysis in which the decision maker accounts for all the possible costs and benefits and arrives at the solution that is optimal for the greatest number of interested parties. In other words, the best decision is the one by which everyone benefits without incurring loss. See McKone-Sweet, Greenberg, and Moland, "Approaches to Ethical Decision Making."

30. This question is based on the theory of rule utilitarianism, which requires that a person act in such a way that the rule on which his or her action is based produces more benefit than harm. For example, the rule "I will do whatever it takes to get ahead" may not always produce the most benefit if getting ahead requires that the person ignore the consequences of his or her actions to others; in this case, the rule is immoral. See McKone-Sweet, Greenberg, and Moland, "Approaches to Ethical Decision Making."

31. This question is based on the theory of personal virtue, which requires a person to act only in such a way that cultivates character traits that enable that person to live peacefully with himself or herself and with others. According to theories promoted by Aristotle, individuals should develop the virtues of honesty, bravery, generosity, and justice for others. See McKone-Sweet, Greenberg, and Moland, "Approaches to Ethical Decision Making."

32. http://www.burtsbees.com/c/story/mission-vision/ (accessed April 21, 2010).

33. http://www.generalmills.com/corporate/commitment/corp.aspx (accessed January 18, 2010).

34. http://www.eatbetteramerica.com/wholegrainnation/ (accessed January 18, 2010).

35. This is excerpted from the Newman's Own Organics video script developed by Jennifer Locke; www.newmansown.com, accessed July 13, 2010; www.newmansownorganics.com, accessed July 13, 2010.

36. Interviews with Nell Newman and Peter Meehan, cofounders of Newman's Own Organic, 2007.

37. Michael Connor, "Clinton Urges 'Principled Stand' on Internet Censorship," *business-ethics.com*, January 21, 2010.

38. Jessica E. Vascellaro and Loretta Chao, "Google Defies China on Web: Search Giant Stops Censoring Its Results; A Toehold Is in Place in Hong Kong," *WallStreetJournal.com,* March 23, 2010.

39. Miguel Helft and David Barboza, "Google Shuts China Site in Dispute over Censorship," *The New York Times,* March 22, 2010.

40. James Hyatt, "Google Halts Censorship on Chinese Search," *business-ethics.com,* March 23, 2010.

41. "In Brief: Retailers Sever Ties over Child Labor," *The Spokesman-Review,* October 31, 2009; George Anderson, "Walmart Says 'No' to Uzbek Cotton over Child Labor," *Retail Wire,* October 1, 2008; Dan McDougall, "Child Sweatshop Shame Threatens Gap's Ethical Image," *The Observer,* October 28, 2007.

42. http://www.limitedbrands.com/social_responsibility/labor/labor.jsp (accessed January 25, 2010); http://www.greenamericatoday.org/ (accessed January 25, 2010).

43. Stephanie Rosenbloom, "At Walmart, Labeling to Reflect Green Intent," *The New York Times,* July 16, 2009; Stephanie Rosenbloom, "Walmart to Toughen Standards," *The New York Times,* October 22, 2008; Adam Aston, "Walmart: Making Its Suppliers Go Green," *Business Week,* May 18, 2009.

44. Michael Felberbaum, "Panel to Examine Menthol Cigarettes' Impact," *Associated Press,* March 29, 2010.

45. Ibid.; based on a study by the Substance Abuse and Mental Health Services Administration in November 2009.

46. Department of Justice, Office of Public Affairs, "Daimler AG and Three Subsidiaries Resolve Foreign Corrupt Practices Act Investigation and Agree to Pay $93.6 Million in Criminal Penalties," press release, April 1, 2010; Michael Connor, "Daimler Agrees to Pay $185 Million to Settle Bribery Charges," Business Ethics, March 26, 2010, http://business-ethics.com/2010/03/26/1354-daimler-to-pay_185-million-to-settle-bribery-charges/ (accessed April 21, 2010).

47. Carolyn Hotchkiss, "Business Ethics: One Slide Cases," Babson College, Wellesley, MA, 2004; Star38 is no longer in business.

48. "West Virginia Governor Seeks Halt of Abercrombie T-Shirts," *USA Today,* March 23, 2003, accessed electronically.

49. Emily Steel, "How Marketers Hone Their Aim Online," *The Wall Street Journal,* June 19, 2007, p. B6.

50. "Mr. Mackey's Offense," *The Wall Street Journal,* July 16, 2007, p. A12.

51. The most famous proponent of this view was Milton Friedman. See for example *Capitalism and Freedom* (Chicago: University of Chicago Press, 2002) or *Free to Choose: A Personal Statement* (Orlando, FL: Harcourt, 1990).

52. Andrew Crane, Abagail McWilliams, Dirk Matten, Jeremy Moon, and Donald S. Siegel, eds., *The Oxford Handbooks of Corporate Social Responsibility* (New York: Oxford University Press, 2008); Donald R. Lichtenstein, Minette E. Drumwright, and Bridgette M. Braig, "The Effect of Corporate Social Responsibility on Customer Donations to Corporate-Supported Nonprofits," *Journal of Marketing* 68, no. 4 (2004), pp. 16–32; Sankar Sen and C. B. Bhattcharya, "Does Doing Good Always Lead to Doing Better? Consumer Reactions to Corporate Social Responsibility," *Journal of Marketing Research* 38 (May 2001), pp. 225–43.

53. http://www.ge.com/news/our_viewpoints/energy_and_climate.html (accessed May 4, 2010); "GE Launches New Ecomagination Healthcare Products, Opens Renewable Energy HQ," February 2, 2010, http://www.greenbiz.com/news/2010/02/02/ge-launches-new-ecomagination-healthcare-products-opens-renewable-energy-hq#ixzzolsaVqopP (accessed May 4, 2010).

54. http://nccsdataweb.urban.org/PubApps/profile1.php (accessed May 4, 2010).

55. James Townsend, "Smart Choice Program Set to Begin, *Functional Ingredients*, June 23, 2009.

56. http://www.ge.com/news/our_viewpoints/energy_and_climate.html (accessed May 4, 2010); "GE Launches New Ecomagination Healthcare Products, Opens Renewable Energy HQ," February 2, 2010, http://www.greenbiz.com/news/2010/02/02/ge-launches-new-ecomagination-healthcare-products-opens-renewable-energy-hq#ixzzolsaVqopP (accessed May 4, 2010).

57. "Frito-Lay Expands Portfolio with New & Lower Sodium Varieties of Top Selling Snacks," Fritolay.com, June 28, 2010.

58. http://ge.ecomagination.com/our-commitments/reduce-emissions.html (accessed May 4, 2010).

59. http://www.marketingpower.com/_layouts/Dictionary.aspx?dLetter=D (accessed January 18, 2010).

60. This case was written by Catharine Curran-Kelly (University of Massachusetts at Dartmouth) in conjunction with the textbook authors (Dhruv Grewal and Michael Levy) as the basis of class discussion rather than to illustrate either effective or ineffective marketing practice.

## Chapter 4

1. Kimberly-Clark website, http://www.kimberly-clark.com/aboutus/company_profile.aspx (accessed May 4, 2010).

2. Peter F. Drucker, *The Essential Drucker* (New York: Harper Collins, 2001).

3. http://www.nau.com (accessed April 29, 2010); Polly Labarre, "Leap of Faith," *Fast Company*, June 2007.

4. Del I. Hawkins and David L. Mothersbaugh, *Consumer Behavior: Building Marketing Strategy*, 11e (Chicago: McGraw-Hill/Irwin, 2009); Philip Cateora and John Graham, *International Marketing*, 13e (Chicago: McGraw-Hill/Irwin, 2006).

5. www.drpepper.com (accessed May 3, 2010).

6. Joanne Fritz, "How One Social Entrepreneur Is Tackling the Online Generation Gap," http://nonprofit.about.com/od/socialentrepreneurs/a/GenerationGap.htm (accessed May 4, 2010); Sharon O'Brien, "Senior Americans Month: This Year, Make It Personal," May 3, 2010, http://seniorliving.about.com/b/2010/05/03/older-americans-month-this-year-make-it-personal.htm (accessed May 4, 2010).

7. Kristin Davis, "Oldies but Goodies; Marketers, Take Note: Baby Boomers Have Lots of Money to Spend," *U.S. News & World Report,* Washington edition, March 14, 2005, p. 45.

8. "Six Million More Consumers Using the Web Than Five Years Ago," December 10, 2009, http://www.idahostatesman.com/103/story/103077.html (accessed December 1, 2006); http://blog.nielsen.com/nielsenwire/online_mobile/six-million-more-seniors-using-the-web-than-five-years-ago/ (accessed May 4, 2010); Sydney Jones and Susannah Fox, "Generations Online in 2009," Pew Internet & American Life Project, January 28, 2009, http://pewresearch.org/pubs/1093/generations-online (accessed May 4, 2010).

9. Ibid.

10. Richard A. Posner, *A Failure of Capitalism* (Boston: Harvard University Press, 2009).

11. Peter J. Boyer, "Eviction: The Day They Came for Addie Polk's House," *The New Yorker*, November 24, 2008.

12. http://www.calreinvest.org/predatory-lending/predatory-mortgage-lending (accessed April 29, 2010).

13. Jessica Rao, "Bust of the Baby Boomer Economy: 'Generation Spend' Tightens Belt," *CNBC.com*, January 21, 2010, http://www.cnbc.com/id/34941331/Bust_of_the_Baby_Boomer_Economy_Generation_Spend_Tightens_Belt (accessed May 4, 2010).

14. Paula Span, "Will Boomers Be Any Different?" *The New York Times*, March 4, 2010, http://newoldage.blogs.nytimes.com/2010/03/04/will-boomers-be-any-different/ (accessed May 4, 2010).

15. Julia B. Issacs, Isabelle V. Sawhill, and Ron Haskins, eds. *Getting Ahead or Losing Ground: Economic Mobility in the United States* (February 2008), http://www.economicmobility.org/assets/pdfs/Economic_Mobility_in_America_Full.pdf (accessed May 4, 2010).

16. "Baby Boomers, Gen X and Gen Y (Consumer Patterns, Behaviors, Lifestyles and Demographics): How Generations Are Changing the Face of Consumer Goods Market," March 10, 2009, http://www.smartbrief.com/news/aaaa/industryBW-detail.jsp?id=98D8B421-C1B2-4ADF-BB75-5041373C3BB1 (accessed May 4, 2010).

17. Suzy Menkes, "Marketing to the Millennials," *The New York Times,* March 2, 2010; Pamela Paul, "Getting Inside Gen Y," *American Demographics* 23, no. 9; Sharon Jayson, "A Detailed Look at the Millenials," *USA Today*, February 23, 2010.

18. OECD, "Growing Unequal? Income Distribution and Poverty in OECD Countries," 2008, http://www.oecd.org/dataoecd/47/2/41528678.pdf (accessed May 4, 2010).

19. http://www.Hammacher.com (accessed May 3, 2010).

20. http://europe.nokia.com/ovi-services-and-apps/nokia-money (accessed May 4, 2010).

21. http://www.census.gov/population/www/socdemo/education/cps2009.html (accessed May 3, 2010); http://www.infoplease.com/ipa/A0883617.html (accessed May 18, 2010).

22. http://inside.nike.com/blogs/nikerunning_events-en_US/?tags=nike_womens_marathon_2010 (accessed May 4, 2010).

23. Tom Pirovano, "U.S. Demographics Are Changing . . . Are Your Marketing Plans Ready?" *NielsenWire*, March 10, 2010, http://blog.nielsen.com/nielsenwire/consumer/u-s-demographics-are-changing-are-your-marketing-plans-ready/ (accessed May 4, 2010); "Cents and Sensibility: Why Marketing to Multicultural Consumers Requires a Subtle Touch," *Knowledge@Wharton*, March 10, 2010, http://www.wharton.universia.net/index.cfm?fa=viewArticle&id=1855&language=english (accessed May 4, 2010); "Ethnic Consumers Hold $282 Billion in Purchasing Power," February 24, 2009, http://news.newamericamedia.org/news/view_article.html?article_id=d4fb122372537fa407312301f85e5446 (accessed May 4, 2010).

24. Ibid.

25. Brad Tuttle, "Cash Crunch: Why Extreme Thriftiness Stunts Are the Rage," *Time*, April 5, 2010, http://www.time.com/time/magazine/article/0,9171,1975323-2,00.html (accessed May 4, 2010).

26. http://www.virgin-atlantic.com/en/us/bookflightsandmore/innovationzone/vjam/taxi2.jsp (accessed May 4, 2010).

27. Katie Johnston, "Flu and Fears Create One Feverish Market," *Boston Globe*, November 13, 2009.

28. "Guidelines for Marketing Food to Kids Proposed," CSPI Press Release, January 5, 2005.

29. This definition of green marketing draws on work by Jacquelyn A. Ottman, *Green Marketing: Opportunity for Innovation* (Chicago: NTC Publishing, 1997).

30. "Sustainable Packaging: PUMA's Launches New Green Packaging and Distribution," *Packaging Digest*, April 13, 2010.

31. "PUMA.safe Launches New Sustainable Packaging Designed by Yves Behar," http://vision.puma.com/us/en/2010/04/puma-launches-new-sustainable-packaging-designed-by-yves-behar/ (accessed May 6, 2010).

32. "The New Puma Fusesafe Packaging," *YouTube.com*, http://www.youtube.com/watch?v=vwRulz8hPKI (accessed May 7, 2010).

33. http://www.sunchips.com/healthier_planet.shtml (accessed May 4, 2010).

34. Michelle Moran, "Green Is the New Black," *Gourmet Retailer*, August 2007.

35. Marshall Kirkpatrick, "Facebook's Zuckerberg Says the Age of Privacy Is Over," January 9, 2010, http://www.readwriteweb.com/archives/facebooks_zuckerberg_says_the_age_of_privacy_is_ov.php (accessed May 4, 2010); Benny Evangelista and Ryan Kim, "Senators Turn Up the Heat on Facebook Privacy Issues," *San Francisco Chronicle*, April 28, 2010, http://articles.sfgate.com/2010-04-28/business/20877750_1_facebook-privacy-issues-users-privacy-zuckerberg (accessed May 4, 2010).

36. http://www.ftc.gov/opa/2008/04/dncfyi.shtm (accessed May 18, 2010).

37. Kevin Coupe, "Fresh Takes on Food," *Chain Store Age*, January 2007.

38. "Safeway CEO Steve Burd Says Fresh, Prepared Food Sales at $100 Million Annually," February 25, 2010, http://freshneasybuzz.blogspot.com/2010/02/safeway-ceo-burd-says-fresh-prepared.html (accessed May 4, 2010).

39. "Walgreen Prepares to Offer Fresh Food, Prepared Meals," *Bloomburg News*, January 15, 2010, http://www.businessweek.com/news/2010-01-15/walgreen-plans-to-offer-fresh-and-prepared-food-to-boost-sales.html (accessed May 4, 2010).

40. www.hannaford.com (accessed January 21, 2008).

41. Bureau of Labor Statistics, "American Time Use Survey Summary," http://www.bls.gov/news.release/atus.nro.htm (accessed May 4, 2010); Martin Peers, "Buddy, Can You Spare Some Time?" *The Wall Street Journal*, January 26, 2004, pp. B1, B3; additional statistics from Harris Interactive.

42. Joel Stein, "TV Dinners Get Literal," *Time*, November 30, 2009.

43. http://www.thenorthface.com/webapp/wcs/stores/servlet/TNFAttachmentDisplay?langId=-1&storeId=207&attachment=/corporate/about_us/company_news/articles/

44. William L. Watts and Lisa Twaronite, "Dollar Sags as Bernanke Cites Growth Risks," *MarketWatch*, July 15, 2008.

45. Nike Web site, http://www.nikebiz.com/company_overview/ (accessed May 7, 2010).

46. Scott Hebert, "Nike's Environmental Record," http://www.heberts.net/nike%E2%80%99s-environmental-record/ (accessed September 11, 2008).

47. Nicholas Casey, "New Nike Sneaker Targets Jocks, Greens, and Wall Street," *WallStreetJournal.com*, http://online.wsj.com/article/SB120303911940170393.html (accessed February 15, 2008).

48. Leora Broydo Vestel, "Nike Makes Environmental Strides and Abandons Carbon Offsets," http://green.blogs.nytimes

.com/2010/02/02/nike-makes-environmental-strides-and -abandons-carbon-offsets/ (accessed February 2, 2010).

49. Nike Corporate Responsibility Report 2007-2009, http://www .nikebiz.com/crreport/ (accessed May 7, 2010).

# Chapter 5

1. "Big Girl in a Skinny World," http://www.marieclaire.com/ fashion/fashionista-blog/ (accessed April 13, 2010).

2. Jayne O'Donnell, "More Retailers Offer Fashionable Clothing for Plus-Size Women," *USA Today*, January 22, 2010, http:// www.usatoday.com/money/industries/retail/2010-01-21-plus -size-fashion_N.htm (accessed April 13, 2010); "About Torrid," https://community.torrid.com/torrid/customer_service/ about_us.asp (accessed April 13, 2010).

3. O'Donnell, "More Retailers Offer Fashionable Clothing."

4. J. Jeffrey Inman, Russell S. Winer, and Rosella Ferraro, "The Interplay among Category Characteristics, Customer Characteristics, and Customer Activities on In-Store Decision Making," *Journal of Marketing* 73, no. 5 (September 2009), pp. 19–29; Rajesh Chandrashekaran and Dhruv Grewal, "Anchoring Effects of Advertised Reference Price and Sale Price: The Moderating Role of Saving Presentation Format," *Journal of Business Research* 59 (October 2006), pp. 1063–71; Dhruv Grewal, Gopalkrishnan R. Iyer, R. Krishnan, and Arun Sharma, "The Internet and the Price-Value-Loyalty Chain," *Journal of Business Research* 56 (May 2003), p. 391.

5. For a detailed discussion of customer behavior, see J. Paul Peter and Jerry C. Olson, *Consumer Behavior and Marketing Strategy*, 9th ed. (New York: McGraw-Hill, 2009); and Michael R. Solomon, *Consumer Behavior: Buying, Having, and Being*, 8th ed. (Upper Saddle River, NJ: Prentice Hall, 2009).

6. Martin R Lautman and Koen Pauwels , "Metrics That Matter: Identifying the Importance of Consumer Wants and Needs," *Journal of Advertising Research* 39, no. 3, pp. 339–59.

7. Liz C. Wang, Julie Baker, Judy A. Wagner, and Kirk Wakefield, "Can a Retail Web Site Be Social?" *Journal of Marketing* 71, no. 3 (2007), pp. 143–57; Guido Gianluigi, Mauro Capestro, and Alessandro M. Peluso, "Experimental Analysis of Consumer Stimulation and Motivational States in Shopping Experiences," *International Journal of Market Research* 49, no. 3 (2007), pp. 365–86; Woonbong Na, Youngseok Son, and Roger Marshall, "Why Buy Second-Best? The Behavioral Dynamics of Market Leadership," *Journal of Product & Brand Management* 15, no. 1 (2007), pp. 16–22; Min-Young Lee, Kelly Green Atkins, Youn-Kyung Kim, and Soo-Hee Park, "Competitive Analyses between Regional Malls and Big-Box Retailers: A Correspondence Analysis for Segmentation and Positioning," *Journal of Shopping Center Research*, April 2006, pp. 81–98; Pamela Sebastian, "'Aspirational Wants' Form the Basis of a Modern Retailing Strategy," *The Wall Street Journal*, October 15, 1998, p. A1; Barry Babin, William Darden, and Mitch Griffin, "Work and/or Fun: Measuring Hedonic and Utilitarian Shopping Value," *Journal of Consumer Research* 20 (March 1994), pp. 644–56.

8. Jing Xu and Norbert Schwarz, "Do We Really Need a Reason to Indulge?" *Journal of Marketing Research* 46, no. 1 (February 2009), pp. 25–36.

9. "Christian Louboutin Styles for the Uptown Girl," http://www .newshoefashion.com/ (accessed April 13, 2010); Cindy Clark, "Christian Louboutin's Red-Soled Shoes Are Red-Hot," *USA Today*, http://www.usatoday.com/life/lifestyle/fashion/2007 -12-25-louboutin-shoes_N.htm (accessed January 2, 2008).

10. Carla Power, "Postcard: New Delhi," *Time*, February 22, 2010.

11. Marc Gunther, "Marriott Gets a Wake-Up Call," *Fortune*, July 6, 2009; Michael S. Rosenwald, "Marriott Profit Tops Wall Street Forecasts: Cost Cutting Boosts Firm in Slowdown," *The Washington Post*, April 24, 2009.

12. Peng Huang, Nicholas H. Lurie, and Sabyasachi Mitra, "Searching for Experience on the Web: An Empirical Examination of Consumer Behavior for Search and Experience Goods," *Journal of Marketing* 73, no. 2 (March 2009), pp. 55–69; Brian T. Ratchford, Debabrata Talukdar, and Myung-Soo Lee, "The Impact of the Internet on Consumers' Use of Information Sources for Automobiles: A Re-Inquiry," *Journal of Consumer Research* 34, no. 1 (2007), pp. 111–19; Glenn J. Browne, Mitzi G. Pitts, and James C. Wetherbe, "Cognitive Shopping Rules for Terminating Information Search in Online Tasks," *MIS Quarterly* 31, no.1 (2007), pp. 89–104.

13. http://store.cwtv.com/detail.php?p=146017&v=cwtv_shows _gossip-girl_character_vanessa&pagemax=all (accessed April 26, 2010).

14. http://www.lnaclothing.com/WOMENatLNAClothing-CID235 .aspx (accessed April 14, 2010).

15. http://www.mytruefit.com (accessed July 20, 2010).

16. Debabrata Talukdar, "Cost of Being Poor: Retail Price and Consumer Price Search Differences across Inner-City and Suburban Neighborhoods," *Journal of Consumer Research* 35, no. 3 (October 2008), pp. 457–71.

17. Benjamin Scheibehenne, Rainer Greifeneder, and Peter M. Todd. "Can There Ever Be Too Many Options? A Meta-Analytic Review of Choice Overload," *Journal of Consumer Research* 37, no. 2 (August 2010), preprint available at http://journals .uchicago.edu/jcr (accessed April 14, 2010).

18. The term *determinance* was first coined by James Myers and Mark Alpert nearly three decades ago; http://www .sawtoothsoftware.com/productforms/ssolutions/ss12.shtml (accessed September 4, 2006).

19. http://www.sawtoothsoftware.com/productforms/ssolutions/ ss12.shtml (accessed September 4, 2006).

20. Julie R. Irwin and Rebecca Walker Naylor, "Ethical Decisions and Response Mode Compatibility: Weighting of Ethical Attributes in Consideration Sets Formed by Excluding versus Including Product Alternatives," *Journal of Marketing Research* 46, no. 2 (April 2009), pp. 234–46; Chris T. Allen, Karen A. Machleit, Susan Schultz Kleine, and Arti Sahni Notani, "A Place for Emotion in Attitude Models," *Journal of Business Research* 58, no. 4 (2005), pp. 494–99; Armin Scholl, Laura Manthey, Roland Helm, and Michael Steiner, "Solving Multiattribute Design Problems with Analytic Hierarchy Process and Conjoint Analysis: An Empirical Comparison," *European Journal of Operational Research* 164, no. 3 (2005), pp. 760–77; Richard Lutz, "Changing Brand Attitudes through Modification of Cognitive Structure," *Journal of Consumer Research* 1, no. 1 (1975), pp. 125–36.

21. Caroline Goukens, Siegfried Dewitte, and Luk Warlop, "Me, Myself, and My Choices: The Influence of Private Self-Awareness on Choice," *Journal of Marketing Research* 46, no. 5 (October 2009), pp. 682–92; Jim Oliver, "Finding Decision Rules with Genetic Algorithms," http://www.umsanet.edu.bo/docentes/ gchoque/MAT420L07.htm (accessed June 2004).

22. Jonathan Levav and A. Peter McGraw, "Emotional Accounting: How Feelings about Money Influence Consumer Choice," *Journal of Marketing Research* 46, no. 1 (February 2009), pp. 66–80; Anne Roggeveen, Dhruv Grewal, and Jerry Gotlieb, "Does the Frame of a Comparative Ad Moderate the Effectiveness of Extrinsic Information Cues?" *Journal of Consumer Research* 33 (June 2006), pp. 115–22; Anthony Miyazaki,

Dhruv Grewal, and Ronald C. Goodstein, "The Effect of Multiple Extrinsic Cues on Quality Perceptions: A Matter of Consistency," *Journal of Consumer Research* 32 (June 2005), pp. 146–53; Paul S. Richardson, Alan S. Dick, and Arun K. Jain, "Extrinsic and Intrinsic Cue Effects on Perceptions of Store Brand Quality," *Journal of Marketing* 58 (October 1994), pp. 28–36; and Rajneesh Suri and Kent B. Monroe, "The Effects of Time Constraints on Consumers' Judgments of Prices and Products," *Journal of Consumer Research* 30 (June 2003), pp. 92–104.

23. J. Josko Brakus, Bernd H. Schmitt, and Lia Zarantonello, "Brand Experience: What Is It? How Is It Measured? Does It Affect Loyalty?" *Journal of Marketing* 73, no. 3 (May 2009), pp. 52–68; Merrie Brucks, Valerie A. Zeithaml, and Gillian Naylor, "Price and Brand Name as Indicators of Quality Dimensions for Consumer Durables," *Journal of the Academy of Marketing Science* 28, no. 3 (2000), pp. 359–74; Niraj Dawar and Philip Parker, "Marketing Universals: Consumers' Use of Brand Name, Price, Physical Appearance, and Retailer Reputation as Signals of Product Quality," *Journal of Marketing* 58 (April 1994), pp. 81–95; and William B. Dodds, Kent B. Monroe, and Dhruv Grewal, "Effects of Price, Brand, and Store Information on Buyers' Product Evaluations," *Journal of Marketing Research* 28 (August 1991), pp. 307–19.

24. Leonard Lee, On Amir, and Dan Ariely, "In Search of Homo Economicus: Cognitive Noise and the Role of Emotion in Preference Consistency," *Journal of Consumer Research* 36, no. 2 (August 2009), pp. 173–87; Mary Jo Bitner, "Servicescapes: The Impact of Physical Surroundings on Customers and Employees," *Journal of Marketing* 56 (April 1992), pp. 57–71; Dhruv Grewal and Julie Baker, "Do Retail Store Environmental Factors Affect Consumers' Price Acceptability? An Empirical Examination," *International Journal of Research in Marketing* 11 (1994), pp. 107–15; Eric R. Spangenberg, Ayn E. Crowley, and Pamela W. Henderson, "Improving the Store Environment: Do Olfactory Cues Affect Evaluations and Behaviors?" *Journal of Marketing* 60 (April 1996), pp. 67–80; and Kirk L. Wakefield and Jeffrey G. Blodgett, "Customer Response to Intangible and Tangible Service Factors," *Psychology and Marketing* 16 (January 1999), pp. 51–68.

25. Amanda Ferrante, "Charlotte Russe Takes Social Shopping a Step Further with ShopTogether App," *The Wall Street Journal,* May 7, 2009; Decision Step, "Social Shopping," http://www.decisionstep .com/solutions/solutions/social-shopping/shoptogether-friends/ (accessed April 13, 2010); http://www.novi=ca.com/ (accessed April 13, 2010); http://www.charlotterusse.com/home/index .jsp?clickid=topnav_logo_img (accessed April 13, 2010).

26. Ruby Roy Dholakia and Miao Zhao, "Retail Web Site Interactivity: How Does It Influence Customer Satisfaction and Behavioral Intentions?" *International Journal of Retail & Distribution Management* 37 (2009), pp. 821–38.

27. Claire Cain Miller, "Closing the Deal at the Virtual Checkout Counter," *The New York Times,* October 12, 2009 (accessed electronically December 13, 2009).

28. "Beware of Dissatisfied Consumers: They Like to Blab," *Knowledge@Wharton,* March, 8, 2006, based on the "Retail Customer Dissatisfaction Study 2006," conducted by the Jay H. Baker Retailing Initiative at Wharton and The Verde Group (accessed electronically); "The Lowdown on Customer Loyalty Programs: Which Are the Most Effective and Why," *Knowledge@Wharton,* September 6, 2006; Sandra Kennedy, "Keeping Customers Happy," *Chain Store Age,* February 2005, p. 24; Heiner Evanschitzky, Gopalkrishnan Iyer, Josef Hesse, and Dieter Ahlert, "E-satisfaction: A Re-examination," *Journal of Retailing* 80, no. 3 (2004), pp. 239–52; Emin Babakus, Carol Bienstock, and James Van Scotter, "Linking Perceived Quality

and Customer Satisfaction to Store Traffic and Revenue Growth," *Decision Sciences* 35 (Fall 2004), pp. 713–38; Jarrad Dunning, Anthony Pecotich, and Aron O'Cass, "What Happens When Things Go Wrong? Retail Sales Explanations and Their Effects," *Psychology & Marketing* (July 2004), pp. 553–68; Richard Oliver, Roland Rust, and Sajeev Varki, "Customer Delight: Foundations, Findings, and Managerial Insights," *Journal of Retailing* 73 (Fall 1997), pp. 311–36; Chezy Ofir and Itamar Simonson, "The Effect of Stating Expectations on Customer Satisfaction and Shopping Experience," *Journal of Marketing Research* 44, no.1 (2007), pp. 164–74.

29. Goutam Challagalla, R. Venkatesh, and Ajay K. Kohli, "Proactive Postsales Service: When and Why Does It Pay Off?" *Journal of Marketing* 73, no. 2 (March 2009), pp. 70–87.

30. For a more extensive discussion on these factors, see Banwari Mittal, *Consumer Behavior* (Cincinnati, OH: Open Mentis, 2008); Peter and Olson, *Consumer Behavior and Marketing Strategy*; Solomon, *Consumer Behavior: Buying, Having, and Being.*

31. A. H. Maslow, *Motivation and Personality* (New York: Harper & Row, 1970).

32. Hazel Rose Markus and Barry Schwartz, "Does Choice Mean Freedom and Well-Being?" *Journal of Consumer Research,* 2010, 37, no. 2, pp. 344–355.

33. Stacy Wood, "The Comfort Food Fallacy: Avoiding Old Favorites in Times of Change," *Journal of Consumer Research* 36, no. 6 (April 2010), pp. 950–63; Stacey Finkelstein and Ayelet Fishbach, "When Healthy Food Makes You Hungry," *Journal of Consumer Research* 36, no. 3 (October 2010), published online, March 10, 2010.

34. Lee, Amir, and Ariely, "In Search of Homo Economicus"; Anish Nagpal and Parthasarathy Krishnamurthy, "Attribute Conflict in Consumer Decision Making: The Role of Task Compatibility," *Journal of Consumer Research* 34, no. 5 (February 2008), pp. 696–705.

35. http://www.bostonbackbay.com/ (accessed April 14, 2010).

36. For more discussion on these factors, see: Mittal, *Consumer Behavior;* Peter and Olson, *Consumer Behavior and Marketing Strategy*; Solomon, *Consumer Behavior: Buying, Having, and Being;* Michael Levy and Barton A. Weitz, *Retailing Management,* 7th ed. (Burr Ridge IL: Irwin/McGraw-Hill, 2009), chapter 4.

37. Juliano Laran, "Goal Management in Sequential Choices: Consumer Choices for Others Are More Indulgent Than Personal Choices," *Journal of Consumer Research,* 2010, 37, no. 2, pp. 304–314.

38. http://www.entrepreneur.com/startingabusiness/ businessideas/startupkits/article190444.html (accessed April 28, 2010); http://www.americanfamilylife.com/factSheet .html (accessed April 28, 2010).

39. Peter Francese, "The Grandparent Economy," *Grandparents .com,* April 20, 2009.

40. Todd Hale, "Mining the U.S. Generation Gaps," *Nielsen Wire,* March 4, 2010, http://blog.nielsen.com/nielsenwire/consumer/ mining-the-u-s-generation-gaps/ (accessed April 14, 2010).

41. Sandra Yin, "Kids' Hot Spots," *American Demographics,* December 1, 2003; Peter Francese, "Trend Ticker: Trouble in Store," *American Demographics,* December 1, 2003.

42. For a greater discussion on these factors, see Mittal, *Consumer Behavior;* Peter and Olson, *Consumer Behavior and Marketing Strategy*; Solomon, *Consumer Behavior: Buying, Having, and Being.*

43. The concept of atmospherics was introduced by Philip Kotler, "Atmosphere as a Marketing Tool," *Journal of Retailing* 49 (Winter 1973), pp. 48–64.

44. Sylvie Morin, Laurette Dubé and Jean-Charles Chebat, "The Role of Pleasant Music in Servicescapes: A Test of the Dual Model of Environmental Perception," *Journal of Retailing* 83, no. 1 (2007), pp. 115–30; Nicole Bailey and Charles S. Areni, "When a Few Minutes Sound Like a Lifetime: Does Atmospheric Music Expand or Contract Perceived Time?" *Journal of Retailing* 82, no. 3 (2006), pp. 189–202; Dhruv Grewal, Julie Baker, Michael Levy, and Glenn B. Voss, "The Effects of Wait Expectations and Store Atmosphere Evaluations on Patronage Intentions in Service-intensive Retail Stores," *Journal of Retailing* 79, no. 4 (2003), pp. 259–68; Anna S. Mattila and Jochen Wirtz, "Congruency of Scent and Music as a Driver of In-Store Evaluations and Behavior," *Journal of Retailing* 77, no. 2 (Summer 2001), pp. 273–89; Teresa A. Summers and Paulette R. Hebert, "Shedding Some Light on Store Atmospherics; Influence of Illumination on Consumer Behavior," *Journal of Business Research* 54, no. 2 (November 2001), pp. 145–50; for a review of this research, see Joseph A. Bellizzi and Robert E. Hite, "Environmental Color, Consumer Feelings, and Purchase Likelihood," *Psychology and Marketing* 9, no. 5 (September–October 1992), pp. 347–63; J. Duncan Herrington and Louis Capella, "Effects of Music in Service Environments: A Field Study," *Journal of Services Marketing* 10, no. 2 (1996), pp. 26–41; Richard F. Yalch and Eric R. Spangenberg, "The Effects of Music in a Retail Setting on Real and Perceived Shopping Times," *Journal of Business Research* 49, no. 2 (August 2000), pp. 139–48; Michael Hui, Laurette Dube, and Jean-Charles Chebat, "The Impact of Music on Consumers' Reactions to Waiting for Services," *Journal of Retailing* 73, no. 1 (1997), pp. 87–104; Julie Baker, Dhruv Grewal, and Michael Levy, "An Experimental Approach to Making Retail Store Environmental Decisions," *Journal of Retailing* 68 (Winter 1992), pp. 445–60; Maxine Wilkie, "Scent of a Market," *American Demographics,* August 1995, pp. 40–49; Spangenberg, Crowley, Henderson, "Improving the Store Environment: Do Olfactory Cues Affect Evaluations and Behaviors?"; Paula Fitzgerald Bone and Pam Scholder Ellen, "Scents in the Marketplace: Explaining a Fraction of Olfaction," *Journal of Retailing* 75, no. 2 (Summer 1999), pp. 243–63.

45. Michael M. Grynbaum, "Starbucks Takes a 3-Hour Coffee Break," *The New York Times,* February 27, 2008; Ellen Byron, "Clarins Puts On Its Best Face in U.S.," *The Wall Street Journal,* March 23, 2009; http://www.questionmark.com/us/casestudies/jordans_furniture.aspx (accessed April 13, 2010).

46. Alexander Chernev and Ryan Hamilton, "Assortment Size and Option Attractiveness in Consumer Choice among Retailers," *Journal of Marketing Research* 46, no. 3 (June 2009), pp. 410–20; Julie Baker, Dhruv Grewal, Michael Levy, and Glenn Voss, "Wait Expectations, Store Atmosphere and Store Patronage Intentions."

47. Pierre Chandon, J. Wesley Hutchinson, Eric T. Bradlow, and Scott H. Young, "Does In-Store Marketing Work? Effects of the Number and Position of Shelf Facings on Brand Attention and Evaluation at the Point of Purchase," *Journal of Marketing* 73, no. 6 (November 2009), pp. 1–17.

48. Charles Delafuente, "Pushing Colleges to Limit Credit Offers to Students," *The New York Times,* October 17, 2007 (accessed electronically December 26, 2007).

49. Better Business Bureau, "Government Regulations to Protect Credit Card Holders," February 18, 2010, http://ct.bbb.org/article/government-regulations-to-protect-credit-card-holders-15354 (accessed April 14, 2010); Jessica Silver-Greenberg, "Selling Students into Credit-Card Debt," *BusinessWeek Online,* October 3, 2007 (accessed December 26, 2007).

50. Mittal, *Consumer Behavior;* Peter and Olson, *Consumer Behavior and Marketing Strategy;* Solomon, *Consumer Behavior: Buying, Having, and Being.*

51. Karen M. Stilley, J. Jeffrey Inman, and Kirk L. Wakefield, "Planning to Make Unplanned Purchases? The Role of In-Store Slack in Budget Deviation," *Journal of Consumer Research,* DOI: 10.1086/651567; R. Puri, "Measuring and Modifying Consumer Impulsiveness: A Cost-Benefit Accessibility Framework," *Journal of Consumer Psychology* 5 (1996), pp. 87–113.

52. This case was written by Kate Woodworth in conjunction with Dhruv Grewal and Michael Levy as the basis of class discussion rather than to illustrate either effective or ineffective marketing practices.

53. Vauhini Vara, "New Gadets Aim to Help Users Watch Their Weight," *The Wall Street Journal Online,* May 12, 2005.

54. Geoff Williams, "Weight Watchers Sues Jenny Craig for Misleading Ads: Let the Mudslinging Begin," *walletpop.com,* January 20, 2010.

55. Jenny Craig official website, http://jennycraig.com/programs/ (accessed April 19, 2010).

56. Jennifer LaRue Huget, "Weight Watchers and Jenny Craig Offer Programs for Men Who Want to Shed Pounds," *The Washington Post,* March 25, 2010.

## Chapter 6

1. Adam Bryant, "Xerox's New Chief Tries to Redefine its Culture," *The New York Times,* February 20, 2010, http://www.nytimes.com/2010/02/21/business/21xerox.html (accessed May 10, 2010).

2. Ashlee Vance, "At Xerox, a Transition for the Record Books," *The New York Times,* May 21, 2009, http://www.nytimes.com/2009/05/22/technology/companies/22xerox.html?_r=1 (accessed May 10, 2010).

3. Xerox 2009 Annual Report, http://www.xerox.com/annual-report-2009/our_business_8.html (accessed May 10, 2010).

4. "Xerox Turnaround Leader to Retire," March 31, 2010, http://www.boston.com/business/technology/articles/2010/03/31/xerox_turnaround_leader_to_retire/ (accessed May 10, 2010).

5. ACS, http://www.acs-inc.com/it_infrastructure_outsourcing_and_services.aspx (accessed May 10, 2010).

6. William M. Bukeley, "Xerox Launches Solid-Ink Color Printer," May 6, 2009, http://blogs.wsj.com/digits/2009/05/06/xerox-launches-revolutionary-color-printer/tab/article/ (accessed May 10, 2010).

7. Arun Sharma, R. Krishnan, and Dhruv Grewal, "Value Creation in Markets: A Critical Area of Focus for Business-to-Business Markets," *Industrial Marketing Management* 30, no. 4 (2001), pp. 391–402; Ajay K. Kohli and Bernard J. Jaworski, "Market Orientation: The Construct, Research Propositions, and Managerial Implications," *Journal of Marketing* 54, no. 2 (1990), pp. 1–13; John C. Narver and Stanly F. Slater, "The Effect of Market Orientation on Business Profitability," *Journal of Marketing* 54, no. 4 (1990), pp. 20–33.

8. http://www.usa.siemens.com/en/about_us/us_business_groups.htm (accessed May 5, 2010).

9. http://www.volkswagenag.com/vwag/vwcorp/content/en/brands_and_companies/automotive_and_financial.html (accessed May 6, 2010); Martin Hofmann, Emily-Sue Sloane, and Elena Malykhina, "VW Revs Its B2B Engine," *Optimize,* March 2004, pp. 22–26.

10. http://www.t-systems.com/tsi/en/34272/Home/Success-Stories/By-Industry/Automotive/Details/ILA-VW-iPAD-L (accessed May 6, 2010); http://www.redbooks.ibm.com/additional_materials/SG247466/Volkswagen_World-class_procurement_strategy.pdf (accessed May 6, 2010).

11. http://www.vwgroupsupply.com/b2b/vwb2b_folder/supply2public/en/die_plattform/daten_und_fakten.html (accessed May 6, 2010).

12. Ikechukwu Onyewuenyi, "TJ Maxx: The World of Off-Price Retailing," myfashionablelife.com, November 30, 2008.

13. "The Truth about TJ Maxx," http://www.thebudgetbabe.com/archives/916-The-Truth-about-TJ-Maxx.html (accessed May 5, 2010).

14. Lydia Dishman, "Is TJ Maxx Poised to Scoop Loehmann's Slice of Designer Pie?" February 2, 2010.

15. "TJ Maxx: The Right Clothes for the Right Price," http://www.thefashionablehousewife.com/08/2009/tj-maxx-the-right-clothes-for-the-right-price/ (accessed May 5, 2010).

16. Ibid.; "The Truth about TJ Maxx."

17. *Budget of the United States Government: Fiscal Year 2010*, Executive Office of the United States: Office of Management and Budget (accessed electronically May 5, 2010).

18. Ibid.

19. http://www.hoovers.com/company/Policy_Studies_Inc/rrjyjxi-1.html (accessed May 21, 2010).

20. Request for Proposal for Retail/Coffee/Snack Food Concession at Roberts Field (RDM), Redmond, Oregon, April 2009, http://doc.ci.redmond.or.us/Airport/Retail-Coffee-Snack-Concession-RFP/RFP-R-C-S-Concession.pdf; www.flyrdm.com (accessed May 6, 2010).

21. Ibid.

22. "The Social Media RFP: How to Get the Best Results," January 18, 2010, http://hashtagsocialmedia.com/blog/tag/request-for-proposal (accessed May 12, 2010).

23. Barry A. Rappaport and Tamara A. Cole, *1997 Economic Census—Construction Sector Special Study, Housing Starts Statistics: A Profile of the Homebuilding Industry* (July 2000).

24. David Whitford, "Hired Guns on the Cheap," *Fortune Small Business*, January 3, 2008.

25. These definitions are provided by www.marketingpower.com (the American Marketing Association's website). We have bolded our key terms.

26. "Study: U.S. Drug Industry Spends Almost Double on Marketing Over R&D," *BrandWeek*, January 3, 2007.

27. Katherine Hobson, "Medical Groups Sign on to Tough Ethics Rules," *The Wall Street Journal*, April 21, 2010, http://blogs.wsj.com/health/2010/04/21/medical-groups-sign-on-to-tough-ethics-rules/tab/article/ (accessed May 12, 2010).

28. Jacob Goldstein, "Scrutiny of Drug-Industry Gifts to Docs Goes Global," *The Wall Street Journal*, January 4, 2010, http://blogs.wsj.com/health/2010/01/04/scrutiny-of-drug-industry-gifts-to-docs-goes-global/tab/article/ (accessed May 12, 2010).

29. http://blogs.wsj.com/health/2010/04/21/medical-groups-sign-on-to-tough-ethics-rules/tab/article/ (accessed May 12, 2010); http://blogs.wsj.com/health/2010/01/04/scrutiny-of-drug-industry-gifts-to-docs-goes-global/tab/article/ (accessed May 12, 2010).

30. http://www.pulsus.com/clin-pha/08_02/lexc_ed.htm (accessed September 6, 2006).

31. Steve Woodruff, "Drug Company Ethics and the Pharmaceutical Industry's Pursuit of Profit," http://www.kevinmd.com/blog/2009/08/drug-company-ethics-and-the-pharmaceutical-industrys-pursuit-of-profit.html (accessed May 12, 2010).

32. http://www.goer.state.ny.us/train/onlinelearning/FTMS/500s1.html (accessed January 22, 2008).

33. Kimberly Maul, "More B-to-B companies Find That Social Media Is an Essential Business Platform," *PRweekus.com*, June 2009; Ellis Booker, "B-to-B Marketers Apply Analytics to Social Media," *BtoB*, April 12, 2010; Elisabeth A. Sullivan, "A Long Slog," *Marketing News*, February 28, 2009.

34. www.tweetdeck.com (accessed July 20, 2010).

35. Daniel B. Honigman, "Make a Statement," *Marketing News*, May 1, 2008.

36. Sarah Mahoney, "Staples Launches Small-Biz Incentive Plan," *Marketing Daily*, January 5, 2010.

37. Barton A. Weitz, Stephen B. Castleberry, and John F. Tanner, *Selling Building Partnerships*, 6th ed. (Burr Ridge, IL: McGraw-Hill/Irwin, 2005), p. 93.

38. Maggie Hira, "How Does a Fashion Buyer Spend a Workday?" http://www.ehow.com/how-does_4601086_fashion-buyer-spend-workday.html (accessed May 12, 2010); U.S. Department of Labor, http://www.bls.gov/oco/ocos023.htm (accessed May 12, 2010); Amanda Fortini, "How the Runway Took Off: A Brief History of the Fashion Show," *Slate Magazine*, February 8, 2006.

39. This case was written by Kate Woodworth in conjunction with Dhruv Grewal and Michael Levy as the basis of class discussion rather than to illustrate either effective or ineffective marketing practices.

40. UPS, http://www.ups.com/content/corp/about/history/1929.html (accessed May 13, 2010).

41. UPS, http://www.community.ups.com/Environment/Innovative+Fleets+and+Facilities (accessed May 18, 2010).

42. Thomas Friedman agrees with this assessment in his best-selling book *The World Is Flat* (New York: Farrar, Straus and Giroux, 2006), in which he cites UPS's supply chain as a prime example of a global "flattener."

43. Sheldon Liber, "FedEx & UPS Challenged by USPS Flat Rates," August 31, 2009, http://www.bloggingstocks.com/2009/08/31/fedex-and-ups-challenged-by-usps-flat-rates/ (accessed May 13, 2010).

44. FedEx, http://about.fedex.designcdt.com/our_company/company_information/fedex_corporation (accessed May 13, 2010).

45. Ibid.

46. Ibid.; http://www.geekpreneur.com/is-insourcing-the-new-in-thing (accessed May 13, 2010).

47. "Decision Green," November 5, 2008, http://www.supplymanagement.ubc.ca/Sustainability/sustainability_partners/sp_ups.htm (accessed May 18, 2010).

48. Gail Tsirulnik, "UPS Debuts B2B Mobile Campaign Targeting Business Decision Makers," *MobileMarketer.com*, November 26, 2009, http://www.mobilemarketer.com/cms/news/advertising/4730.html (accessed May 13, 2010).

## Chapter 7

1. http://www.adclassix.com/ads2/66tangoj.htm (accessed April 20, 2010); Mike Hughlett, "U.S. Food Giants Tailor Products, Marketing to International Palates," *Chicago Tribune*,

March 25, 2010, http://www.chicagotribune.com/business/la-fi-packaged-foods25-2010mar25,0,3956410.story (accessed April 20, 2010).

2. Hughlett, "U.S. Food Giants"; http://www.kraftfoodscompany.com/Brands/largest-brands/Pages/index.aspx (accessed April 20, 2010).

3. Brad Dorfman, "Kraft to Focus on 10 Power Brands, 10 Countries," *Reuters News Service*, September 3, 2008.

4. http://adsoftheworld.com/media/tv/oreo_internet (accessed April 20, 2010).

5. David Tiltman, "Kraft's Asia-Pacific VP Shawn Warren Shares His Recipe for Success," *Media*, January 22, 2010.

6. Pierre-Richard Agenor, *Does Globalization Hurt the Poor?* (Washington, DC: World Bank, 2002); "Globalization: Threat or Opportunity," International Monetary Fund, http://www.imf.org/external/np/exr/ib/2000/041200.htm#II (accessed September 18, 2006).

7. See "World Development Indicators 2009," http://web.worldbank.org/WBSITE/EXTERNAL/DATASTATISTICS/0,,contentMDK:21725423~pagePK:64133150~piPK:64133175~theSitePK:239419,00.html (accessed April 20, 2010).

8. International Monetary Fund, "Crisis Jolts Globalization Process," http://www.imf.org/external/np/exr/Key/global.htm (accessed April 20, 2010); Larry Rohter, "Shipping Costs Start to Crimp Globalization," *The New York Times*, August 3, 2008.

9. Alun Thomas, "Financial Crises and Emerging Market Trade," *IMF Staff Position Note*, March 11, 2009, http://www.imf.org/external/pubs/ft/spn/2009/spn0904.pdf (accessed April 20, 2010); Thomas P.M. Barnett, "The New Rules: Globalization's Next Wave of Integration," *World Politics Review*, January 11, 2010, http://www.globalpolicy.org/globalization/globalization-of-the-economy-2-1/general-analysis-on-globalization-of-the-economy/48617.html (accessed April 20, 2010).

10. Charles W. L. Hill, *Global Business Today*, 5th ed. (New York: McGraw-Hill/Irwin, 2008).

11. Tim Lohman, "Financial Crisis to Drive Offshoring Market: Survey," *Computerworld*, March 31, 2009, http://www.computerworld.com.au/article/297489/financial_crisis_drive_offshoring_market_survey/ (accessed April 20, 2010); Joel D. Pinaroc, "China, India Hold Offshoring Ground," *ZDnet Asia*, October 31, 2007 (accessed January 7, 2008).

12. Andy McCue, "More Firms Setting Up Own Offshoring," *Silicon*, July 13, 2007 (accessed January 7, 2008).

13. Ibid.; Pinaroc, "China, India Hold Offshoring Ground."

14. Ajay Goel, Nazgol Moussavi, and Vats N. Srivatsan, "Time to Rethink Offshoring?" *McKinsey Quarterly*, September 2008; Rachael King, "The Outsourcing Upstarts," *BusinessWeek*, July 31, 2007 (accessed January 7, 2007).

15. Jack Ewing, "Why Krakow Still Works for IBM," *BusinessWeek*, September 25, 2007 (accessed January 7, 2008).

16. http://www.wto.org/english/theWTO_e/whatis_e/tif_e/org6_e.htm (accessed April 17, 2010).

17. http://www.imf.org/external/about/histcoop.htm (accessed April 17, 2010).

18. http://web.worldbank.org/WBSITE/EXTERNAL/EXTABOUTUS/0,,pagePK:50004410~piPK:36602~theSitePK:29708,00.html (accessed April 17, 2010).

19. See http://web.worldbank.org/WBSITE/EXTERNAL/EXTSITETOOLS/0,,contentMDK:20147466~menuPK:344189~pagePK:984

00~piPK:98424~theSitePK:95474,00.html#15 (accessed April 20, 2010); William Easterly, *The White Man's Burden: Why the West's Efforts to Aid the Rest Have Done So Much Ill and So Little Good* (New York: Penguin, 2006).

20. Social Science Research Council, http://www.ssrc.org/sept11/essays/teaching_resource/tr_globalization.htm (accessed April 17, 2010).

21. Nike, "Workers and Factories," http://www.nikebiz.com/responsibility/workers_and_factories.html (accessed April 20, 2010).

22. Eugenia Levenson, "Citizen Nike," *Fortune*, November 17, 2008, http://money.cnn.com/2008/11/17/news/companies/levenson_nike.fortune/index.htm (accessed April 20, 2010).

23. Stephanie Rosenbloom, "Wal-Mart to Toughen Standards," *The New York Times*, October 22, 2008.

24. Stan Lehman, "Nike Won't Use Leather from Amazon-Bred Cattle," *BusinessWeek Online*, July 22, 2009.

25. For example, the deficit for the month of February 2010 was $39.7 billion. See http://www.census.gov/indicator/www/ustrade.html (accessed April 21, 2010).

26. http://www.acdi-cida.gc.ca/CIDAWEB/webcountry.nsf/VLUDocEn/Cameroon-Factsataglance#def (accessed January 3, 2008).

27. http://siteresources.worldbank.org/DATASTATISTICS/Resources/GNIPC.pdf (accessed April 20, 2010); Arthur O'Sullivan, Steven Sheffrin, and Steve Perez, *Macroeconomics: Principles and Tools Activebook*, 5th ed. (Upper Saddle River, NJ: Prentice Hall, 2007).

28. *The Economist*, "The Big Mac Index," March 17, 2010, http://www.economist.com/daily/chartgallery/displaystory.cfm?story_id=15715184 (accessed April 20, 2010).

29. http://hdr.undp.org/reports/global/2001/en/; Nobel Prize–winning economist Amartya Sen has proposed that developing countries also should be measured according to the capabilities and opportunities that people within that particular country possess.

30. T. N. Ninan, "Six Mega-Trends That Define India's Future," *Rediff.com*, January 6, 2007 (accessed January 7, 2007).

31. "India," *The CIA World Factbook*, April 7, 2010, https://www.cia.gov/library/publications/the-world-factbook/geos/in.html (accessed April 20, 2010); "United States," *The CIA World Factbook*, April 7, 2010, https://www.cia.gov/library/publications/the-world-factbook/geos/us.html (accessed April 20, 2010).

32. Jyoti Thottam and Niljanjana Bhowmick, "Nano Power," *Time*, April 13, 2009.

33. Nandini Lakshman, "Indian Car Buyers Snap Up the Nano," May 6, 2009, http://www.time.com/time/world/article/0,8599,1896414,00.html?iid=sphere-inline-sidebar (accessed April 20, 2010).

34. "India," *The CIA World Factbook*.

35. "What's Ahead for the Global Economy in 2008?" Reports from the Knowledge@Wharton Network, *Knowledge@Wharton*, January 9, 2008 (accessed January 10, 2008).

36. "Metro's Business Plan for India Right on Track: Official," March 23, 2010, http://www.livemint.com/2010/03/23162626/Metro8217s-business-plan-fo.html.

37. Arvind R. Singhal, "India's Retail Ties That Bind," *The Wall Street Journal*, February 4, 2010, http://online.wsj.com/article/SB10001424052748704022804575040612838703640.html.

38. Vikas Bijaj, "In India, Wal-Mart Goes to the Farm," *The New York Times*, April 12, 2010, http://www.nytimes.com/2010/04/13/business/global/13walmart.html.

39. Eric Bellman, "In India, a Retailer Finds Key to Success Is Clutter," *The Wall Street Journal*, August 8, 2007, p. A1

40. Ibid.; Singhal, "India's Retail Ties."

41. Dan Mitchell, "Wal-Mart Inches to India," *ABCnews.com*, April 17, 2010, http://abcnews.go.com/Business/TheBigMoney/wal-mart-inches-india/story?id=10363987.

42. Walmart Press Release, "Bharti Enterprises and Wal-Mart Join Hands in Wholesale Cash-and-Carry to Serve Small Retailers, Manufacturers and Farmers," August 6, 2007, http://walmartstores.com/pressroom/news/6638.aspx.

43. Ibid.; Bijaj, "In India, Wal-Mart Goes to the Farm."

44. Ibid.

45. "Coca-Cola Tackles Rural Indian Market," (video) *The Wall Street Journal*, May 3, 2010.

46. David L. Scott, *Wall Street Words: An A to Z Guide to Investment Terms for Today's Investor* (Boston: Houghton Mifflin, 2003).

47. Edmund L. Andrews, "U.S. Adds Tariffs on Chinese Tires," *The New York Times*, September 11, 2009, http://www.nytimes.com/2009/09/12/business/global/12tires.html (accessed April 20, 2010).

48. http://economics.about.com/library/glossary/bldef-dumping.htm (accessed February 5, 2008); Scott, *Wall Street Words*.

49. Government of India, Ministry of Commerce and Industry, "Anti Dumping Cases in India," http://commerce.nic.in/ad_cases.htm (accessed April 20, 2010).

50. "Exchange Rate," http://en.wikipedia.org/wiki/Exchange_rate (accessed January 3, 2008).

51. http://ucatlas.ucsc.edu/trade/subtheme_trade_blocs.php (accessed February 5, 2008).

52. http://www.unescap.org/tid/mtg/postcancun_rterta.pps#1 (accessed January 3, 2008).

53. http://europa.eu/abc/european_countries/candidate_countries/index_en.htm (accessed April 20, 2010).

54. http://en.wikipedia.org/wiki/European_Union (accessed May 19, 2010); http://www.nationsonline.org/oneworld/europe_map.htm (accessed May 19, 2010).

55. http://www.fas.usda.gov/itp/CAFTA/cafta.asp (accessed April 20, 2010).

56. Philip R. Cateora, Mary C. Gilly, and John L. Graham, *International Marketing*, 14th ed. (New York: McGraw-Hill, 2009); Danielle Medina Walker and Thomas Walker, *Doing Business Internationally: The Guide to Cross-Cultural Success*, 2nd ed. (Princeton, NJ: Trade Management Corporation, 2002).

57. Devorah Lauter, "IKEA Fined for Sunday Opening in France," *Forbes*, April 6, 2008.

58. Stefania Summermatter, "Can Sunday Shopping Help Beat the Crisis," *Swissinfo.ch*, August 1, 2009.

59. For a website dedicated to Hofstede's research, see http://www.geert-hofstede.com/. Some of his more influential publications include Geert Hofstede and Gert Jan Hofstede, *Cultures and Organizations: Software of the Mind* (New York: McGraw-Hill/Irwin, 2004); Geert Hofstede, "Management Scientists Are Human," *Management Science*, 40 (January 1994), pp. 4–13; Geert Hofstede and Michael H. Bond, "The Confucius Connection from Cultural Roots to Economic Growth," *Organizational Dynamics*, 16 (Spring 1988),

pp. 4–21. See also Masaaki Kotabe and Kristiaan Helsen, *Global Marketing Management*, 3rd ed. (Hoboken, NJ: John Wiley & Sons, 2004).

60. James W. Carey, *Communication as Culture*, rev. ed. (New York: Routledge, 2009); Tian Feng and Julian Lowe, "The Influence of National and Organizational Culture on Absorptive Capacity of Chinese Companies," *International Journal of Knowledge, Culture, and Change Management* 7, no. 10 (2007), pp. 9–16.

61. Lance Eliot Brouthers, George Nakos, John Hadjimarcou, and Keith D. Brouthers, "Key Factors for Successful Export Performance for Small Firms," *Journal of International Marketing* 17, no. 3 (2009), pp. 21–38; "Selling Overseas," November 12, 2009, http://www.entrepreneur.com/growyourbusiness/internationalexpansion/article204028.html (accessed April 20, 2010).

62. https://www.cisco.com/web/partners/pr67/tcs/index.html (accessed April 20, 2010).

63. Chris Reiter and Andres Cremer, "Fiat, VW Accelerate Carmaking Push beyond Europe," *BusinessWeek*, January 13, 2010, http://www.businessweek.com/news/2010-01-13/fiat-vw-accelerate-overseas-push-to-combat-european-car-glut.html (accessed April 20, 2010); Laurence Frost and Makiko Kitamura, "Peugeot CEO Cites Debt for Failed Mitsubishi Talks," *BusinessWeek*, March 3, 2010, http://www.businessweek.com/news/2010-03-03/peugeot-scraps-mitsubishi-alliance-plan-to-protect-debt-ratings.html (accessed April 20, 2010).

64. http://www.sonyericsson.com/cws/companyandpress/aboutus/mission?cc=us&lc=en (accessed April 20, 2010).

65. "ING Overview," http://home.ingdirect.com/about/about.asp (accessed April 20, 2010).

66. Arkadi Kuhlmann, "First State Boasts First-Class Thinkers," *News Journal*, January 1, 2008 (accessed electronically January 8, 2008).

67. Cateora, Gilly, and Graham, *International Marketing*; Bruce D. Keillor, Michael D'Amico, and Veronica Horton, "Global Consumer Tendencies," *Psychology and Marketing* 18, no. 1 (2001), pp. 1–20.

68. "Top Ten Best-Selling Cars," http://blogs.cars.com/kickingtires/2009/05/top-10-bestselling-cars-april-2009.html (accessed May 24, 2010).

69. Michael J. Ureel, "Ford Looks to Improve Market Share, Sales in Emerging Indian Economy," http://media.ford.com/article_display.cfm?article_id=21882&make_id=trust (accessed May 24, 2010).

70. "Figo Drives New Sales Records for Ford in India," http://media.ford.com/article_display.cfm?article_id=32342 (accessed April 1, 2010).

71. "Figo Chassis Designed for the Global Market—Tailored for Indian Roads," http://www.india.ford.com/servlet/ContentServer?pageid=1178851252772&cid=1248869037192&pagename=FIPL%2FDFYArticle%2FWeb-Standalone&theme=default&direction=ltr&c=DFYArticle&site=FIPL (accessed March 9, 2010).

72. Nikhil Gulati and Santanu Choudhury, "Ford Targets India Market with First Small Car," *The Wall Street Journal*, http://online.wsj.com/article/SB125369081200333397.html, September 23, 2009.

73. Ibid.

74. Ford Figo Review, http://www.cardekho.com/carmodels/Ford/Ford_Figo (accessed May 24, 2010).

75. Hill, *Global Business Today*.

76. "Russia's Retail Revolution,"*Managementtoday.com*, June 3, 2008, http://www.managementtoday.co.uk/search/article/812968/russias-retail-revolution/ (accessed April 20, 2010); Transparency International, "Global Corruption Barometer 2009," http://www.transparency.org/news_room/in_focus/2009/gcb2009 (accessed April 20, 2010).

77. Julie Jargon, "Can M'm, M'm Good Translate?" *The Wall Street Journal*, July 9, 2007, p. A16; "Campbell Outlines Entry Strategy and Product Plans for Russia and China," July 9, 2007, http://investor.shareholder.com/campbell/releasedetail.cfm?releaseid=252914 (accessed January 16, 2008).

78. http://www.pringles.it/ (accessed May 19, 2010).

79. David Kiley, "One World, One Car, One Name," *BusinessWeek*, March 13, 2008, http://www.businessweek.com/magazine/content/08_12/b4076063825013.htm (accessed April 20, 2010); http://www.fordvehicles.com/ (accessed April 20, 2010).

80. Silvia Fabiana, Claire Loupias, Fernando Martins, and Roberto Sabbatini (eds.), *Pricing Decisions in the Euro Era: How Firms Set Prices and Why* (Oxford: Oxford University Press, 2007); Gilly et al., *International Marketing*; Mary Anne Raymond, John F. Tanner Jr., and Jonghoon Kim, "Cost Complexity of Pricing Decisions for Exporters in Developing and Emerging Markets," *Journal of International Marketing* 9, no. 3 (2001), pp. 19–40.

81. Fabiana et al., *Pricing Decisions*; Amanda J. Broderick, Gordon E. Greenley, and Rene Dentiste Mueller, "The Behavioural Homogeneity Evaluation Framework: Multi-level Evaluations of Consumer Involvement in International Segmentation," *Journal of International Business Studies* 38 (2007), pp. 746–63; Terry Clark, Masaaki Kotabe, and Dan Rajaratnam, "Exchange Rate Pass-Through and International Pricing Strategy: A Conceptual Framework and Research Propositions," *Journal of International Business Studies* 30, no. 2 (1999), pp. 249–68.

82. "Fashion Conquistador," *BusinessWeek*, September 4, 2006 (accessed electronically May 19, 2010); http://www.koreatimes.co.kr/www/news/biz/2010/04/123_65160.html (accessed May 19, 2010).

83. Satish Shankar, Charles Ormiston, Nicolas Bloch, Robert Schaus, and Vijay Vishwanath, "How to Win in Emerging Markets," *Bain Briefs*, November 29, 2007.

84. https://www.cia.gov/library/publications/the-world-factbook/fields/2103.html (accessed April 20, 2010).

85. Jess Halliday, "Industry Prepares to Fight Junk Food Ad Watershed," *Food and Drink Europe.com*, January 3, 2008, http://www.foodanddrinkeurope.com/Products-Marketing/Industry-prepares-to-fight-junk-food-ad-watershed (accessed April 20, 2010).

86. Larry Rohter, "Shipping Costs Start to Crimp Globalization," *The New York Times*, August 3, 2008, http://www.nytimes.com/2008/08/03/business/worldbusiness/03global.html (accessed April 20, 2010).

87. William J. Holstein, "How Toyota Manufactured Its Own Fall from Grace," *bnet.com*, February 9, 2010, http://www.bnet.com/2403-13056_23-391889.html (accessed April 21, 2010).

88. http://www.brandchannel.com/features_effect.asp?pf_id=274 (accessed September 6, 2007).

89. Hiroko Tabuchi, "Limited Edition! Limited Edition! Lim...," *The Wall Street Journal*, February 22, 2008; http://www.lyricsmode.com/lyrics/l/lady_gaga/fashion.html.

90. Joan Voight, "How to Customize Your U.S. Branding Effort to Work around the World," *Adweek*, September 3, 2008 (accessed electronically January 9, 2008).

91. "China," *The World Factbook*, April 7, 2010, https://www.cia.gov/library/publications/the-world-factbook/geos/ch.html (accessed April 20, 2010).

92. Ibid.

93. Ibid.; "Country Report: China," *The Economist Intelligence Unit*, January 2008 (accessed electronically January 10, 2008).

94. "China," *The World Factbook*.

95. "Scrambling to Bring Crest to the Masses in China," *BusinessWeek*, June 25, 2007 (accessed electronically January 10, 2008).

96. Mya Frazier, "How P&G Brought the Diaper Revolution to China," *bnet.com*, http://www.bnet.com/2403-13239_23-379838.html (accessed April 20, 2010).

97. http://www.pg.com.cn/job/Overview/Introduction.aspx (accessed May 19, 2010).

98. http://www.pg.com.cn/job/faq.asp (accessed April 20, 2010).

99. Frazier, "How P&G Brought the Diaper Revolution to China."

## Chapter 8

1. LimitedBrands, http://limited.com/brands/vs/vss/index.jsp (accessed May 17, 2010).

2. Elizabeth Holmes, "Victoria's Secret Shifts Focus to Lower-Price Items," *The Wall Street Journal*, August 20, 2009, http://online.wsj.com/article/SB125078611265846741.html (accessed May 17, 2010).

3. Krystina Gustafson, "Victoria's Secret Hopes to Rekindle Desire for Lingerie," *CNBC.com*, November 20, 2009, http://www.cnbc.com/id/34019052/Victoria_s_Secret_Hopes_to_Rekindle_Desire_for_Lingerie (accessed May 17, 2010).

4. http://www.buec.udel.edu/antil/BUAD%20301/BUAD%20301%20Fall%20%2708/Victoria%27s%20Secret%20Pink.pdf (accessed May 17, 2010).

5. "Victoria's Secret PINK and Major League Baseball Properties Announce New Co-Branded Collection," *Forbes.com*, March 15, 2010, http://www.forbes.com/feeds/prnewswire/2010/03/15/prnewswire201003151254PR_NEWS_USPR____NY70507.html (accessed May 17, 2010).

6. Norihiko Shirouzu, "Chinese, Foreign Car Makers Target Same Customers," *The Wall Street Journal*, May 10, 2010, http://online.wsj.com/article/SB10001424052748703686304575227831233334168.html?KEYWORDS=NORIHIKO+SHIROUZU+ (accessed May 18, 2010).

7. Natalie Y. Moore, "Boutiques Aim to Let Men Enjoy Shopping," *Chicago Tribune*, October 16, 2006 (accessed electronically January 1, 2008); Blanca Torres, "More and More, Men Like Shopping," *Contra Costa Times*, October 12, 2006 (accessed electronically January 1, 2008); Nanette Byrnes, "Secrets of the Male Shopper," *BusinessWeek*, September 4, 2006 (accessed electronically January 1, 2008); Melanie Shortman, "Gender Wars," *American Demographics*, April 2002, p. 22.

8. Banwari Mittal, *Consumer Bahavior* (Cincinnati, OH: Open Mentis, 2008); J. Paul Peter and Jerry C. Olson, *Consumer Behavior and Marketing Strategy*, 8th ed. (New York: McGraw-Hill, 2008); Michael R. Solomon, *Consumer Behavior: Buying, Having, and Being*, 7th ed. (Upper Saddle River, NJ: Prentice Hall, 2006); Jagdish Sheth, Banwari Mittal, and Bruce I. Newman, *Customer Behavior: Consumer Behavior and Beyond* (Fort Worth, TX: The Dryden Press, 1999).

9. Chi Kin (Bennett) Yim, Kimmy Wa Chan, and Kineta Hung, "Multiple Reference Effects in Service Evaluations: Role of Alternative Attractiveness and Self-Image Congruity," *Journal of Retailing,* 83 no. 1 (2007), pp.147–157; Tamara Mangleburg, M. Joseph Sirgy, Dhruv Grewal, Danny Axsom, Maria Hatzios, C. B. Claiborne, and Trina Bogle, "The Moderating Effect of Prior Experience in Consumers' Use of User-Image Based versus Utilitarian Cues in Brand Attitude," *Journal of Business & Psychology,* 13 (Fall 1998), pp. 101–113; M. Joseph Sirgy et al., "Direct versus Indirect Measures of Self-Image Congruence," *Journal of the Academy of Marketing Science,* 25, no. 3 (1997), pp. 229–241.

10. Mittal, *Consumer Behavior;* Peter and Olson, *Consumer Behavior and Marketing Strategy;* Solomon, *Consumer Behavior: Buying, Having, and Being;* Sheth, Mittal, and Newman, *Customer Behavior: Consumer Behavior and Beyond.*

11. Bryant Urstadt, "Lust for Lulu," *New York Magazine,* July 26, 2009.

12. http://investor.lululemon.com/secfiling.cfm?filingID=950123 -10-28033 (accessed May 27, 2010).

13. http://www.strategicbusinessinsights.com/vals/store/ USconsumers/intro.shtml, accessed May 18, 2010.

14. http://www.strategicbusinessinsights.com/vals/applications/ apps-pos.shtml, accessed June 1, 2010.

15. "Segmentation and Targeting," http://www.kellogg .northwestern.edu/faculty/sterntha/htm/module2/1.html (accessed January 24, 2008); Michael D. Lam, "Psychographic Demonstration: Segmentation Studies Prepare to Prove Their Worth," *Pharmaceutical Executive,* January 2004.

16. Unilever Web site, http://www.unilever.com/brands/personal carebrands/axe/index.aspx (accessed May 18, 2010).

17. Jack Neff, "Unilever Develops Ambitious Campaign for New Fragrance with the Help of College-Age Fans," *Advertising Age,* February 24, 2010, http://adage.com/article?article_id=142270 (accessed May 15, 2010).

18. For an interesting take on this issue, see Joseph Jaffe, *Flip the Funnel* (Hoboken, NJ: John Wiley & Sons, 2010).

19. http://www.starwoodhotels.com/corporate/company_info .html (accessed May 27, 2010).

20. Yuping Liu, "The Long-Term Impact of Loyalty Programs on Consumer Purchase Behavior and Loyalty," *Journal of Marketing* 71, no. 4 (October 2007), pp. 19–35; V. Kumar and Denish Shah, "Building and Sustaining Profitable Customer Loyalty for the 21st Century," *Journal of Retailing* 80, no. 4 (2004), pp. 317–30.

21. http://www.united.com/page/article/0,6722,1171,00.html (accessed May 27, 2010).

22. Bryan Alexander, "*Up in the Air* Fantasies: What Does 10 Million Miles Get You?" *Time,* December 22, 2009.

23. Janet Ong, "China Mobile Profit Surges 29%," *China Daily,* August 17, 2007 (accessed electronically January 17, 2008).

24. Frederik Balfour, "China Mobile Is Growing Rural," *BusinessWeek,* December 20, 2006 (accessed electronically January 18, 2008).

25. Ibid.

26. Dexter Roberts, "China Mobile's Hot Signal," *BusinessWeek,* February 5, 2007 (accessed electronically Jaunry 18, 2008).

27. www.chinamobileltd.com (accessed July 27, 2010).

28. "China Mobile's CEO Talks Expansion," *BusinessWeek Online,* February 5, 2007 (accessed January 18, 2008).

29. Vanessa O'Connell, "Park Avenue Classic or Soho Trendy?" *The Wall Street Journal,* April 20, 2007.

30. Dhruv Grewal, "Marketing Is All about Creating Value: 8 Key Rules," in *Inside the Mind of Textbook Marketing* (Boston, MA: Aspatore Inc., 2003), pp. 79–96.

31. Thorsten Blecker, *Mass Customization: Challenges and Solutions* (New York: Springer, 2006); B. Joseph Pine, *Mass Customization: The New Frontier in Business Competition* (Cambridge, MA: Harvard Business School Publishing, 1999); James H. Gilmore and B. Joseph Pine, eds., *Markets of One: Creating Customer-Unique Value through Mass Customization* (Cambridge, MA: Harvard Business School Publishing, 2000).

32. G. R. Iyer, A. D. Miyazaki, D. Grewal, and M. Giordano, "Linking Web-Based Segmentation to Pricing Tactics," *Journal of Product & Brand Management* 11, no. 5 (2002), pp. 288–302; B. Jaworski and K. Jocz, "Rediscovering the Consumer," *Marketing Management,* September/October 2002, pp. 22–27; L. Rosencrance, "Customers Balk at Variable DVD Pricing," *Computer World,* September 11, 2000, p. 4; M. Stephanek, "None of Your Business: Customer Data Were Once Gold to E-Commerce; Now, Companies Are Paying a Price for Privacy Jitters," *BusinessWeek,* June 26, 2000, p. 78; D. Wessel, "How Technology Tailors Price Tags," *The Wall Street Journal,* June 23, 2001, p. A1.

33. Allen Adamson, "Pitch Your Luxury Offering as an 'Investment Brand,'" *Forbes,* May 4, 2010, http://www.forbes .com/2010/05/04/luxury-branding-platinum-brands-bmw -hermes-investment-branding-cmo-network-allen-adamson .html (accessed May 18, 2010).

34. Conrad Hotels & Resorts, http://conradhotels1.hilton.com/en/ ch/brand/index.do?it=TNav,About (accessed May 18, 2010).

35. Conrad Bali Fact Sheet, http://conradhotels1.hilton.com/ts/en/ hotels/BPNCICI/docs/Conrad_Bali_Factsheet.pdf (accessed May 15, 2010).

36. Bureau of Labor Statistics, "Career Guide to Industries, 2010-2011 Edition," http://www.bls.gov/oco/cg/cgs036.htm (accessed May 18, 2010).

37. Michael B. Baker, "2010 U.S. Hotel Chain Survey: Ritz-Carlton Knocks Off Four Seasons in Punch-Drunk Luxury Tier," *BTN.com,* March 8, 2010, http://www.btnonline.com/ businesstravelnews/headlines/frontpage_display.jsp?vnu _content_id=1004073141 (accessed May 15, 2010).

38. Vanessa O'Connell, "Fashion Journal: Bubble Gum at Bergdorf's," *The Wall Street Journal,* February 15, 2008 (accessed electronically January 15, 2008).

39. Vanessa O'Connell, "Fashion Bullies Attack—In Middle School," *The Wall Street Journal,* October 25, 2007 (accessed electronically January 15, 2008).

40. Jeanine Poggie, "Designer Brands a High-End Teen Attraction," *Women's Wear Daily,* June 11, 2008 (accessed electronically January 15, 2008).

41. Stuart Schwartzapfel, "Volvo S80: Playing It Too Safe?" *BusinessWeek,* July 23, 2007; Jean Halliday, "Maloney Wants Volvo Viewed as Both Safe and Luxurious," *Advertising Age* 75, no. 12 (2004), p. 22.

42. Coca-Cola website, http://heritage.coca-cola.com/ (accessed May 19, 2010). "Heritage," http://www.thecoca-colacompa-ny.com/heritage/ourheritage.html (accessed May 19, 2010). Pepsi website, http://www.pepsi.com/PepsiLegacy_Book.pdf (accessed May 19, 2010).

43. Gary Benne's Information Site, http://www.garybeene.com/ pepsi/pep-now.htm (accessed May 19, 2010).

44. Betsy McKay, "Zero Is Coke's New Hero," *The Wall Street Journal,* April 17, 2007.

45. Kate Fitzgerald, "Coke Zero," *Advertising Age,* November 12, 2007.

46. "Products," http://www.thecoca-colacompany.com/brands/index.html (accessed May 19, 2010).

47. Valerie Bauerlein, "Coke Goes High-Tech to Mix Its Sodas," *The Wall Street Journal,* http://online.wsj.com/article/SB100014240527487036128045752223500086054976.html (accessed May 10, 2010).

48. "Coca-Cola Announces Plans to Launch Coca-Cola Zero," Coca-Cola Company, News Release, March 21, 2005.

49. "Coke Zero and Coca-Cola to Debut New Ads during Telecast of Super Bowl XLIII," Coca-Cola press release, January 26, 2009.

50. Based on a You Tube search conducted May 20, 2010.

51. Kate MacArthur, "Coke Bets on Zero to Save Cola Category," *Advertising Age,* January 1, 2007.

52. "The Chronicle of Coca-Cola," http://www.thecoca-colacompany.com/heritage/chronicle_global_business.html (accessed May 19, 2010).

## Chapter 9

1. Janet Adamy, "Will a Twist on an Old Vow Deliver for Domino's Pizza?" *The Wall Street Journal,* December 17, 2007.

2. Ashley Heher, "Our Pizza Didn't Taste Good, Domino's Says in New Ads," *Boston Globe,* January 12, 2010; Bruce Horovitz, "Domino's Pizza Delivers Change in its Core Pizza Recipe," *The New York Times,* December 16, 2009.

3. A. Parasuraman, Dhruv Grewal, and R. Krishnan, *Marketing Research,* 2nd ed. (Boston: Houghton Mifflin, 2007), p. 9.

4. Andrew McMains and Noreen O'Leary, "How GM's Woes Will Impact Global Marketing," *Adweek,* June 1, 2009.

5. Relative market share = brand's market share ÷ largest competitor's market share. If, for instance, there are only two products in a market, A and B, and product B has 90 percent market share, then A's relative market share is 10 ÷ 90 = 11.1 percent. If, on the other hand, B only has 50 percent market share, then A's relative market share is 10 ÷ 50 = 20 percent. Paul W. Farris, Neil T. Bendle, Phillip E. Pfeifer, and David J. Reibstein, *Marketing Metrics: 50+ Metrics Every Executive Should Master* (Philadelphia: Wharton School Publishing, 2006), p. 19.

6. "About," http://symphonyiri.com/About/tabid/59/Default.aspx (accessed April 7, 2010).

7. "Who We Are," http://iridev.blueboltlive.com/About/WhoWeAre/tabid/62/Default.aspx (accessed April 7, 2010).

8. "New IRI Private Label Report Uncovers Emerging Trends and Key Success Factors in Challenging Economy," April 21, 2009, http://iridev.blueboltlive.com/Insights/ArticleDetail/tabid/117/ItemID/793/View/Details/Default.aspx (accessed April 7, 2010).

9. "Private Label 2008: U.S. & Europe," *Times and Trends,* IRI, November 2008.

10. Marc-Andre Kamel, Nick Greenspan, and Rudolf Pritzl, "Standardization Is Efficient but Localization Helps Shops to Stand Out," *The Wall Street Journal,* January 21, 2009.

11. "CVS Press Kit—ExtraCare," http://phx.corporate-ir.net/phoenix.zhtml?c=183405&p=irol-cvsextracare (accessed April 9, 2010).

12. Bill Brohaugh, "Three Women," *Colloquy,* Summer 2007.

13. "History: The Science of Shopping," http://www.envirosell.com/index.php?option=com_content&task=view&id=40&Itemid=45 (accessed April 6, 2010).

14. Elisabeth A. Sullivan, "Be Sociable," *Marketing News,* January 15, 2008.

15. Michael P. Cook and Hy Mariampolski, "How Culture Helps Marketers Understand Sensory Experiences," *Quirk's Marketing Research Review,* November 2009, p. 26.

16. "Client Story: Kraft," http://www.communispace.com/assets/pdf/C_Cli_casestudy_kraft_final.pdf (accessed April 6, 2010).

17. Sarah Needleman, "For Companies, a Tweet in Time Can Avert PR Mess," *The Wall Street Journal,* August 3, 2009.

18. Richard A. Krueger and Mary Anne Casey, *Focus Groups: A Practical Guide for Applied Research* (Thousand Oaks, CA: Sage Publications, 2009).

19. "Campbell's Select Harvest Soups Top 2009 IRI New Product Pacesetters List: Second Time in Three Years That Campbell's Soups Top List," *MarketWatch,* March 23, 2010, http://www.marketwatch.com/story/campbells-select-harvest-soups-top-2009-iri-new-product-pacesetters-list-2010-03-23?reflink=MW_news_stmp (accessed April 7, 2010).

20. http://www.campbellsoup.com/select.aspx (accessed April 7, 2010).

21. Floyd J. Fowler, *Survey Research Methods* (Thousand Oaks, CA: Sage Publications, 2009); Don A. Dillman, Glenn Phelps, Robert Tortora, Karen Swift, Julie Kohrell, Jodi Berck, and Benjamin L. Messer, "Response Rate and Measurement Differences in Mixed-Mode Surveys Using Mail, Telephone, Interactive Voice Response (IVR) and the Internet," *Social Science Research* 38 (March 2009), pp. 1–18.

22. Emily Goon, "Friends or Foes? The Internet vs. the Music Industry," *Quirk's Marketing Research Review,* April 2010, p. 22.

23. Detailed illustrations of scales are provided in two books: Gordon C. Bruner, *Marketing Scales Handbook, Volume V: A Compilation of Multi-Item Measures* (Carbondale, IL: GCBII Productions, 2009); William O. Bearden and Richard G. Netemeyer, *Handbook of Marketing Scales: Multi-Item Measures for Marketing and Consumer Behavior Research* (Thousand Oaks, CA: Sage Publications, 1999). Sources for the scales used in the exhibit are Dhruv Grewal, Gopalkrishnan Iyer, Jerry Gotlieb, and Michael Levy, "Developing a Deeper Understanding of Post-Purchase Perceived Risk and Repeat Purchase Behavioral Intentions in a Service Setting," *Journal of the Academy of Marketing Science* 35, no. 2 (2007), pp. 250–58; Anthony Miyazaki, Dhruv Grewal, and Ronald C. Goodstein, "The Effect of Multiple Extrinsic Cues on Quality Perceptions: A Matter of Consistency," *Journal of Consumer Research* 32 (June 2005), pp. 146–53.

24. https://pulse.asda.com (accessed April 15, 2010); Joel Warady, "Asda Takes the 'Pulse of the Nation,'" *Retail Wire,* July 16, 2009.

25. "About Cablecom," http://www.cablecom.ch/en/about (accessed March 30, 2010).

26. http://www.harrahs.com (accessed March 30, 2010).

27. Sudhir H. Kale and Peter Klugsberger, "Reaping Rewards," *Marketing Management,* July/August 2007.

28. Charles Higgins, "Harrah's Total Rewards Players Club Initiates at Planet Hollywood on April 1st," *Las Vegas Examiner,* March 28, 2010; Gary Loveman, "Diamonds in the Data Mine," *Harvard Business Review* 81, no. 5 (May 2003), pp. 109–13; http://www.harrahs.com (accessed April 15, 2010); Thomas Hoffman, "Harrah's Bets on Loyalty Program in Caesars Deal," *computerworld.com,* June 27, 2005 (accessed February 22, 2006).

29. "Cablecom," http://www.spss.com/success/template_view.cfm?Story_ID=208 (accessed March 30, 2010).

30. For a more thorough discussion of effective written reports, see Parasuraman, Grewal, and Krishnan, *Marketing Research*, chapter 16.

31. Susan Stellin, "Rewriting the Room Service Menu," *The New York Times*, January 30, 2007.

32. http://www.marketingpower.com/AboutAMA/Pages/Statement%20of%20Ethics.aspx, accessed April 16, 2010; http://www.helleniccomserve.com/marketingcodeofethics.html (accessed March 25, 2010).

33. Federal Trade Commission, "Widespread Data Breaches Uncovered by FTC Probe: FTC Warns of Improper Release of Sensitive Consumer Data on P2P File-Sharing Networks," February 22, 2010, http://www.ftc.gov/opa/2010/02/p2palert.shtm (accessed April 7, 2010).

34. http://www.copia.com/tcpa/ (accessed March 24, 2010).

35. Cecilia Kang, "Library of Congress Plan for Twitter: A Big, Permanent Retweet," *Washington Post*, April 16, 2010; www.cdt.org (accessed April 16, 2010); Mark Penn, "Did Google Violate Privacy Laws?" www.politicallyillustrated.com (accessed April 2, 2010); https://www.donotcall.gov/ (accessed April 16, 2010); Lona M. Farr, "Whose Files Are They Anyway? Privacy Issues for the Fundraising Profession," *International Journal of Nonprofit and Voluntary Sector Marketing* 7, no. 4 (November 2002), p. 361.

36. This case was written by Colin Fox in conjunction with the textbook authors Dhruv Grewal and Michael Levy as the basis of class discussion rather than to illustrate either effective or ineffective marketing practices.

37. Tad Friend, "The Cobra: Inside a Movie Marketer's Playbook," *The New Yorker*, January 19, 2009.

38. Maureen Nevin Duffy, "Cantor Fitzgerald's Virtual Trading Platform Helps Film Producers Project Their Grosses," *Securities Industry News*, September 3, 2007 (accessed electronically February 5, 2008).

39. "Nielsen NRG," http://www.nielsen.com/solutions/nrg.html (accessed February 5, 2008).

40. Friend, "The Cobra."

41. Parasuraman, Grewal, and Krishnan, *Marketing Research*.

42. Anita Elberse and Bharat Anand, "The Effectiveness of Pre-Release Advertising for Motion Pictures: An Empirical Investigation Using a Simulated Market," *Information Economics and Policy*, July 10, 2007 (accessed electronically February 5, 2008).

43. "2009 Shakes Up America's Favorite Movie Stars," *Quirk's Marketing Research Review*, February 2010, p. 1.

## Appendix 9A

1. V. Kumar, A. Petersen and R. P. Leone, "How Valuable Is the Word of Mouth?" *Harvard Business Review*, October 2007, pp. 139–146; V. Kumar and Morris George, "Measuring and Maximizing Customer Equity: A Critical Analysis," *Journal of the Academy of Marketing Science*, 35, no. 2 (June 2007), pp. 157–171; V. Kumar, Denish Shah, and Rajkumar Venkatesan, "Managing Retailer Profitability: One Customer at a Time!" *Journal of Retailing*, 82, no. 4 (October 2006), pp. 277–294; V. Kumar, "Profitable Relationships," *Marketing Research: A Magazine of Management and Applications*, 18, no. 3 (Fall 2006), pp. 41–46; V. Kumar, "Customer Lifetime Value: A Databased Approach," *Journal of Relationship Marketing*, 5, no. 2/3 (2006), pp. 7–35; Sunil Gupta, Dominique Hanssens, Bruce Hardie, William Kahn, V. Kumar, Nathaniel Lin, Nalini Ravishanker, and S. Sriram, "Modeling Customer Lifetime Value," *Journal of Service Research*, 9 (November 2006), pp. 139–155; V. Kumar, R. Venkatesan, and Werner Reinartz, "Knowing What to Sell, When and to Whom," *Harvard Business Review*, March, 2006, pp. 131–137; Werner Reinartz, J. Thomas, and V. Kumar, "Balancing Acquisition and Retention Resources to Maximize Profitability," *Journal of Marketing*, 69 (January 2005), pp. 63–79; R. Venkatesan and V. Kumar, "A Customer Lifetime Value Framework for Customer Selection and Resource Allocation Strategy," *Journal of Marketing*, 68 (October 2004), pp. 106–125; V. Kumar and J. Andrew Petersen, "Maximizing ROI or Profitability: Is One Better Than the Other," *Marketing Research: A Magazine of Management and Applications*, 16, no. 3 (Fall 2004), pp. 28–34; V. Kumar, G. Ramani, and T. Bohling, "Customer Lifetime Value Approaches and Best Practice Applications," *Journal of Interactive Marketing* 18, no. 3 (Summer 2004), pp. 60–72; J. Thomas, Werner Reinartz, and V. Kumar, "Getting the Most out of All Your Customers," *Harvard Business Review* (July–August 2004), pp. 116–123; Werner Reinartz and V. Kumar, "The Impact of Customer Relationship Characteristics on Profitable Lifetime Duration," *Journal of Marketing*, 67 (January 2003), pp. 77–99; Werner Reinartz and V. Kumar, "The Mismanagement of Customer Loyalty," *Harvard Business Review* (July 2002), pp. 86–97; W. Reinartz and V. Kumar, "On the Profitability of Long Lifetime Customers: An Empirical Investigation and Implications for Marketing," *Journal of Marketing*, 64 (October 2000), pp. 17–32.

2. We have made some minor adjustments to the formula suggested by Gupta et al., "Modeling Customer Lifetime Value."

3. Sunil Gupta and Donald R. Lehmann, *Managing Customers as Investments* (Philadelphia, PA: Wharton School Publishing, 2005); Gupta et al., "Modeling Customer Lifetime Value."

## Chapter 10

1. http://blog.girvin.com/?p=1850 (accessed March 30, 2010); Rachel Dodes and Stephanie Kang, "Polo to Outfit U.S. Team For the Beijing Olympics," *The Wall Street Journal*, April 7, 2008; Cheryl Lu-Lien Tan, "Fashion Makes Few Waves at Olympic Opening Ceremony," *The Wall Street Journal*, August 16, 2008; Polo Ralph Lauren Press Release, "Polo Ralph Lauren Signs 5-Year Global Partnership with the All England Club, Wimbledon," April 25, 2006.

2. David Lauren, senior vice president of advertising, marketing, and communications for Ralph Lauren, quoted in Samantha Critchell, "Ralph Lauren Winter Olympics Designs Revealed," November 4, 2009 (Video), *Huffington Post*, November 4, 2009.

3. Rachel Dodes, "Polo Ralph Lauren Lengthens Its Olympic Run," *The Wall Street Journal*, July 2, 2009.

4. Ibid.

5. Ian Ritchie, Chief Executive, All England Club Wimbledon, quoted in "Designer to Become the Tournament's First Ever Outfitter–Will Dress All On-Court Officials and Ball Persons," *PR Newswire*, April 25, 2009.

6. http://www.trekbikes.com/us/en/bikes/road/madone/6_series/meet_madone/ (accessed February 9, 2010).

7. Kostas Axarloglou, "Product Line Extensions: Causes and Effects," *Managerial & Decision Economics* 29, no. 1 (2008), pp. 9–21; Michaela Draganska and Dipak C. Jain, "Product-Line Length as a Competitive Tool," *Journal of Economics & Management Strategy* 14, no. 1 (2005), pp. 1–28; William P. Putsis Jr. and Barry L. Bayus, "An Empirical Analysis of Firms' Product Line Decisions," *Journal of Marketing Research* 38, no. 1 (February 2001), pp. 110–18.

8. Bruce G. S. Hardie and Leonard M. Lodish, "Perspectives: The Logic of Product-Line Extensions," *Harvard Business Review,* November–December 1994, p. 54; Kate MacArthur, "Pepsi Goes on $55 Mil Binge for Diet Max," *Advertising Age,* June 25, 2007.

9. Paraskevas C. Argouslidis and George Baltas, "Structure in Product Line Management: The Role of Formalization in Service Elimination Decisions," *Journal of the Academy of Marketing Science* 35, no. 4 (2007), pp. 475–91; John A. Quelch and David Kenny, "Extend Profits, Not Product Lines," *Harvard Business Review,* September–October 1994, pp. 153–60.

10. Simon Pittman, "Revlon Switches CEO as Pressure Mounts over Performance," *Cosmeticsdesign.com,* September 19, 2006.

11. Philip Lam, "Palm Hints at New Touchstone Product Line," www.techmeme.com, April 12, 2009.

12. Molly Knight, "Cold Competition," *Shopping Centers Today,* February 2008.

13. http://www.band-aid.com (accessed December 10, 2009).

14. Ellen Byron, "Tide Turns 'Basic' for P&G in Slump," *The Wall Street Journal,* August 6, 2009.

15. "Discontinued Products List," http://www.mccormick.com/ DiscontinuedProducts.aspx (accessed January 14, 2010).

16. http://newsroom.bankofamerica.com/index.php?s=press _releases&item=7964 (accessed January 29, 2008).

17. http://www.bankofamerica.com/deposits/checksave/ (accessed December 10, 2009).

18. Ellen Byron, "Clarins Puts On Its Best Face in U.S.," *The Wall Street Journal,* March 23, 2009; Michelle F. Guthrie, and Hye-Shin Kim, "The Relationship between Consumer Involvement and Brand Perceptions of Female Cosmetic Consumers," *Journal of Brand Management* 17 (2009), pp. 114–33.

19. *Consumer Reports,* "TV Buying Guide: Brands," http://www .consumerreports.org/cro/electronics-computers/tvs-services/ tvs/tv-buying-advice/tv-brands/tvs-brands.htm (accessed December 9, 2009).

20. Kevin Lane Keller, *Strategic Brand Management: Building, Measuring, and Managing Brand Equity,* 3rd ed. (Upper Saddle River, NJ: Prentice Hall, 2007).

21. This discussion of the advantages of strong brands is adapted from Keller, *Strategic Brand Management,* pp. 104–12; and Elizabeth S. Moore, William L. Wilkie, and Richard J. Lutz, "Passing the Torch: Intergenerational Influences as a Source of Brand Equity," *Journal of Marketing* 66, no. 2 (2002), p. 17. See also Kevin Lane Keller and Donald R. Lehmann, "Brands and Branding: Research Findings and Future Priorities," *Marketing Science* 25 (November 2006), pp. 740–59.

22. Kevin Lane Keller and Donald R Lehmann, "Assessing Long-Term Brand Potential," *Journal of Brand Management* 17 (2009), pp. 6–17.

23. Lisa Jennings, "Starbucks Puts Spotlight on Instant Coffee Rollout," *Nation's Restaurant News,* September 29, 2009.

24. Evan Carmichael, "Obsess Over Your Customers—Jeff Bezos," *www.youngentrepreneur.com,* April 7, 2009; Joe Nocera, "Put Buyers First? What a Concept," *The New York Times,* January 5, 2008

25. Brad Stone, "Court Clears eBay in Suit over Sale of Counterfeit Goods," *The New York Times,* July 15, 2008.

26. Katya Foreman, "Court Rules for Hermes in eBay Counterfeit Suit," *WWD,* June 5, 2008.

27. http://www.interbrand.com/best_global_brands.aspx (accessed January 14, 2010). The net present value of the earnings over the next 12 months is used to calculate the value.

28. David Aaker, *Brand Portfolio Strategy: Creating Relevance, Differentiation, Energy, Leverage, and Clarity* (New York: Free Press, 2004); David A. Aaker, *Managing Brand Equity* (New York: Free Press, 1991).

29. Polo Ralph Lauren Corporate Annual Report 2008, available at http://library.corporate-ir.net/library/65/659/65933/ items/299215/RL_AR_Final.pdf (accessed January 14, 2010).

30. Keller, *Strategic Brand Management: Building, Measuring, and Managing Brand Equity.*

31. Lopo L. Rego, Matthew T. Billett, and Neil A. Morgan, "Consumer-Based Brand Equity and Firm Risk," *Harvard Business Review* 73, no. 6, November 2009, p. 47–60; Natalie Mizik, and Robert Jacobson, "Valuing Branded Businesses," *Harvard Business Review* 73, no. 6 (November 2009), p. 137–53; Shuba Srinivasan, and Seenu Srinivasan, *Brand Equity: Measuring, Analyzing, and Predicting* (Boston: Harvard Business Press, May 8, 2006); David Aaker, *Building Strong Brands* (New York: Simon & Schuster, 2002); David A. Aaker, "Measuring Brand Equity across Products and Markets," *California Management Review* 38 (1996), pp. 102–20.

32. Tom's of Maine, "What's Not in Our Products," http://www .tomsofmaine.com/products/ingredients-not-in-our-products .aspx (accessed December 9, 2009).

33. Kara G. Morrison, "Chic on the Cheap," *The Detroit News,* February 15, 2008; http://www.fxmagazine.co.uk/story .asp?storyCode51632 (accessed March 15, 2008).

34. www.hallmarkchannel.com (accessed January 14, 2010).

35. Rohir Bhargava, *Personality Not Included: Why Companies Lose Their Authenticity and How Great Brands Get It Back* (New York: McGraw Hill, 2008); Jennifer L. Aaker, "Dimensions of Brand Personality," *Journal of Marketing Research* 34, no. 3 (1997), pp. 347–56.

36. Kevin Lane Keller, "Conceptualizing, Measuring, and Managing Customer-Based Brand Equity," *Journal of Marketing,* 57, no. 1 (1993), pp. 1–22.

37. Yuksel Ekinci and Sameer Hosany, "Destination Personality: An Application of Brand Personality to Tourism Destinations," *Journal of Travel Research* 45, no. 2 (2006), pp. 127–39; T. H. Freling and Forbes, "An Empirical Analysis of the Brand Personality Effect," *Journal of Product & Brand Management* 14, no.7 (2005), pp. 404–13.

38. Julia Werdigier, "To Woo Europeans, McDonald's Goes Upscale," *The New York Times,* August 25, 2007.

39. http://www.marketingpower.com/_layouts/Dictionary .aspx?dLetter=B (accessed December 14, 2009).

40. Google, "Android Developer Challenge," http://code.google .com/android/adc/ (accessed December 9, 2009).

41. Daniel Barbarisi, "Singles Night at the Supermarket," *Providence Journal,* August 22, 2008; Jonathan Birchall, "Just Do It, Marketers Say," *Financial Times,* April 30, 2007 (accessed electronically January 11, 2008).

42. http://inside.nike.com/blogs/nikerunning_training-en_US/ 2009/06/04/start-your-summer-with-run-club (accessed December 16, 2009).

43. http://www.tns-mi.com/news/09162009.htm (accessed January 11, 2010).

44. Lien Lamey, Barbara Deleersnyder, Marnik G. Dekimpe, and Jan-Benedict E.M. Steenkamp, "How Business Cycles Contribute to Private-Label Success: Evidence from the United States and Europe," *Journal of Marketing* 71 (January 2007), pp. 1–15;

PLMA (2009), http://www.plmainternational.com/es/private_label_es2.htm.

45. Elliot Zwiebach, "Private Label Sales Pressure CPGs: Costco," *Supermarket News*, May 29, 2009; Associated Press, "Wal-Mart Adds Products as Store Brands Boom," March 17, 2009; Matthew Boyle, Timothy Martin, "Kroger's Net Rises 8.1%, Aided by Private-Label Gains," *The Wall Street Journal*, March 10, 2009.

46. Tom Robbins, "Pick n Pay Revamps Convenience," *Fastmoving.co.za*, June 25, 2008; Nirmalya Kumar and Jan-Benedict E. M. Steenkamp, "Premium Store Brands: The Hottest Trend in Retailing," in *Private Label Strategy: How to Meet the Store Brand Challenge* (Cambridge, MA: Harvard Business School Press, February 2007).

47. Ibid.

48. Lisa Biank Fasig, "Celebrities, Designers Court Macy's for Exclusive Lines," *Business Courier of Cincinnati*, August 31, 2009.

49. Christopher Lawton, "Tweaking the Standard-Issue PC," *The Wall Street Journal*, June 14, 2007, p. D1.

50. Ibid.

51. Ibid.; Stuart Elliott, "No Polo Pony, but Penney's New Label Is Pure Ralph Lauren Americana," *The New York Times*, February 19, 2009.

52. 2008 Kellogg's Annual report, http://annualreport2008.kelloggcompany.com/brandportfolio.htm (accessed November 25, 2009).

53. The distinction between brand and line extensions is clarified in Barry Silverstein, "Brand Extensions: Risks and Rewards," *Brandchannel.com*, January 5, 2009.

54. For recent research on brand extensions, see Thorsen Hennig-Thurau, Mark B. Houson, and Torsten Heitjans, "Conceptualizing and Measuring the Monetary Value of Brand Extensions: The Case of Motion Pictures," *Journal of Marketing* 73, no. 6 (November 2009), pp. 167–83; Rohini Ahluwalia, "How Far Can a Brand Stretch? Understanding the Role of Self-Construal," *Journal of Marketing Research* 45, no. 3 (2008); Byung Chul Shine, Jongwon Park, and Robert S. Wyer, "Brand Synergy Effects in Multiple Brand Extensions," *Journal of Marketing Research* 44, no. 4 (2007), pp. 663–70; Gochen Wu and Yung-Ghien Yen, "How the Strength of Parent Brand Associations Influences the Interaction Effects of Brand Breadth and Product Similarity with Brand Extension Evaluations," *Journal of Product & Brand Management* 16, no. 4–5 (2007), pp. 334–41; Franziska Volckner and Henrik Sattler, "Drivers of Brand Extension Success," *Journal of Marketing* 70, no. 2 (2006), pp. 18–34; Subramanian Balachander and Sanjoy Ghose, "Reciprocal Spillover Effects: A Strategic Benefit of Brand Extensions," *Journal of Marketing* 67, no. 1 (2003), pp. 4–13; Kalpesh Kaushik Desai and Kevin Lane Keller, "The Effects of Ingredient Branding Strategies on Host Brand Extendibility," *Journal of Marketing* 66, no. 1 (2002), pp. 73–93; Tom Meyvis and Chris Janiszewski, "When Are Broader Brands Stronger Brands? An Accessibility Perspective on the Success of Brand Extensions," *Journal of Consumer Research* 31, no. 2 (2004), pp. 346–57.

55. David Aaker, "Brand Extensions: The Good, the Bad, and the Ugly," *Sloan Management Review* 31 (Summer 1990), pp. 47–56.

56. http://www.dell.com (accessed December 19, 2007).

57. www.neutrogena.com (accessed January 13, 2010); Vanitha Swaminathan, Richard J. Fox, and Srinivas K. Reddy, "The Impact of Brand Extension Introduction on Choice," *Journal of Marketing* 65, no. 3 (2001), pp. 1–15.

58. http://amedia.disney.go.com/investorrelations/factbook_2008.pdf (accessed December 16, 2009).

59. http://www.disneybridal.com/ (accessed December 16, 2009); Merissa Marr, "Fairy-Tale Wedding? Disney Can Supply the Gown," *The Wall Street Journal*, February 22, 2007.

60. https://enterpriseportal.disney.com/gopublish/sitemedia/dcp/Home/Press%20Room/Press%20Kits/WDS_General%20Release1_FINAL.pdf, accessed August 3, 2010; http://www.drexelheritage.com/c-51-walt-disney-signature.aspx, accessed August 3, 2010; http://www.minkagroup.net/SearchAdvanceProducts.aspx?a=327&f=7&licensed=1 (accessed December 16, 2009); Susan Gunelius, "Disney Extends Its Brand Presence Everywhere," www.brandcurve.com (accessed July 1, 2007); Susan Gunelius, "Disney Co. Chooses ESPN Brand over Disney Brand," May 16, 2008, http://www.corporate-eye.com/blog/2008/05/disney-co-chooses-espn-brand-over-disney-brand/ (accessed December 9, 2009).

61. Devon DelVecchio and Daniel C. Smith, "Brand-Extension Price Premiums: The Effects of Perceived Fit and Extension Product Category Risk," *Journal of the Academy of Marketing Science* 33, no. 2 (2005), pp. 184–96; Jennifer Aaker, Susan Fournier, and S. Adam Brasel, "When Good Brands Do Bad," *Journal of Consumer Research* 31, no. 1 (2004), pp. 1–16.

62. Costas Hadjicharalambous, "A Typology of Brand Extensions: Positioning Cobranding as a Sub-Case of Brand Extensions," *Journal of American Academy of Business* 10, no. 1 (2006), pp. 372–77; H. Sjodin and F. Torn, "When Communication Challenges Brand Associations: A Framework for Understanding Consumer Responses to Brand Image Incongruity," *Journal of Consumer Behaviour* 5, no. 1 (2006), pp. 32–42; C. H. Chen and S. K. Chen, "Brand Dilution Effect of Extension Failure—A Taiwan Study," *Journal of Product and Brand Management* 9, no. 4 (2000), pp. 243–54.

63. Mario Marsicano, "Cheetos Lip Balm & More Bizarre Brand Extensions," *The Wall Street Journal*, July 15, 2009.

64. David A. Aaker and Kevin Lane Keller, "Consumer Evaluations of Brand Extensions," *Journal of Marketing* 54, no. 1 (1990), pp. 27–41.

65. Guoqun Fu, Jiali Ding, and Riliang Qu "Ownership Effects in Consumers' Brand Extension Evaluations," *Journal of Brand Management* 16 (2009), pp. 221–33; Christoph Burmann, Sabrina Zeplin and Nicola Riley, "Key Determinants of Internal Brand Management Success: An Exploratory Empirical Analysis," *Journal of Brand Management* 16 (2009), pp. 264–84; Raisa Yakimova and Michael Beverland, "The Brand-Supportive Firm: An Exploration of Organisational Drivers of Brand Updating," *Journal of Brand Management* 12, no. 6 (2005), pp. 445–60.

66. http://www.marriott.com/corporateinfo/glance.mi (accessed December 17, 2009).

67. Cathy Enz, "Multibranding Strategy: the Case of Yum! Brands," *Cornell Hotel & Restaurant Administration Quarterly*, February 2005.

68. http://www.fordvehicles.com/innovation/sync/?brand=flm (accessed December 17, 2009).

69. T. Kippenberger, "Co-Branding as a Competitive Weapon," *Strategic Direction* 18, no. 10 (2002), pp. 31–33.

70. Keller, *Strategic Brand Management: Building, Measuring, and Managing Brand Equity.*

71. PRLog.org Press Release: "'License India' to Hold Mumbai's First Ever Brand Licensing Conference," January 28, 2009; www.licensingexpo.com (accessed February 23, 2010).

72. Florence Flabricant, "Caution: Your Armani Suite May Require Alterations," *The New York Times*, April 7, 2009; Samsung press release, "Giorgio Armani, Samsung, and Microsoft Present the New Giorgio Armani—Samsung Smartphone," October 12, 2009; Stacy Meichtry, "Armani Links with Samsung for Electronics Line," *The Wall Street Journal*, September 24, 2007.

73. http://www.pradaphonebylg.com/, accessed August 1, 2010; http://us.gran-turismo.com/us/, accessed August 1, 2010.

74. Keller, *Strategic Brand Management: Building, Measuring, and Managing Brand Equity*.

75. http://www.lacoste.com/usa/, accessed August 1, 2010.

76. Laurent Muzellec and Mary Lambkin, "Corporate Rebranding and the Implications for Brand Architecture Management: The Case of Guinness (Diageo) Ireland," *Journal of Strategic Marketing* 16, no. 4. (2008), pp. 283–99; W. Lomax and M. Mador, "Corporate Re-Branding: from Normative Models to Knowledge Management," *Journal of Brand Management* 14, no.1/2 (2006), pp. 82–95; B. Merrilees and D. Miller, "Principles of Corporate Rebranding," *European Journal of Marketing* 42, no. 5/6 (2008), pp. 537–52; L. Muzellec and M. Lambkin, "Corporate Rebranding: Destroying, Transferring or Creating Brand Equity?" *European Journal of Marketing* 40, no. 7/8 (2006), pp. 803–24;Yakimova and Beverland, "The Brand-Supportive Firm"; Stephen Brown, Robert V. Kozinets, and John F. Sherry Jr., "Teaching Old Brands New Tricks: Retro Branding and the Revival of Brand Meaning," *Journal of Marketing* 67, no. 2 (2003), p. 19.

77. Suzanne Vranica and Betsy McKay, "Gatorade Quietly Aims to Revive Brand," *The Wall Street Journal*, January 7, 2009; Gatorade, http://www.gatorade.com/Products/g.aspx#/products/g (accessed December 10, 2009).

78. www.fragrancex.com/products/_bid_Abercrombie—-am—-Fitch-am-cid_perfume-am-lid_A__brand_history.html (accessed March 17, 2008).

79. Brian Steinberg, "Recognition Factor," *Boston Globe*, March 25, 2009.

80. Valerie Bauerlein, "Pepsi to Pare Plastic for Bottled Water," *The Wall Street Journal*, March 25, 2009.

81. Steve Inskeep, "Consumers Reject New Tropicana Carton," *Morning Edition*, February 23, 2009.

82. Stuart Elliot, "Tropicana Discovers Some Buyers Are Passionate about Packaging," *The New York Times*, February 22, 2009.

83. Chris Serres, "It's True: Food Packages Shrunk Last Year," *Minneapolis Star Tribune*, December 31, 2008.

84. Ibid.

85. U.S. Government Accounting Office, "Bottled Water: FDA Safety and Consumer Protections Are Often Less Stringent Than Comparable EPA Protections for Tap Water," July 8, 2009.

86. Associated Press, "Stricter Labeling Urged for Bottled Water," *The Wall Street Journal*, July 8, 2008.

87. This case was written by Kate Woodworth in conjunction with the textbook authors (Dhruv Grewal and Michael Levy) as a basis for class discussion rather than to illustrate either effective or ineffective marketing practice.

88. http://heritage.coca-cola.com/ (accessed April 1, 2010); Brad Cook, "Coca-Cola a Classic," *Brandweek.com*, December 2, 2002.

89. Ibid.

90. Ibid.

91. Ibid.

92. http://www.interbrand.com/best_global_brands.aspx (accessed January 12, 2010); Emily Fredrix, "Coca-Cola Still Viewed as Most Valuable Brand," *USA Today*, September 18, 2009.

93. Richard Ameyaw, "Coca-Cola Puts Recycling Bins around London," *Peagle.co.uk*, March 26, 2010.

94. Anne Marie Mohan, "Coca-Cola Details 'Commitment 2020': 15% Reduction in Carbon Footprint by 2020," *GreenerPackage.com*, July 27, 2009 (accessed April 2, 2010).

95. Ariel Schwartz, "The Coke Challenge: Zero Waste at the Olympics," *Fast Company*, February 3, 2010.

96. Natalie Zmuda, "Coca-Cola Goes Completely Green at Olympics," *Advertising Age*, February 01, 2010.

## Chapter 11

1. Renay San Miguel, "Bing's New Bells and Whistles Could Leave Searchers' Heads Ringing," *TechNewsWorld*, March 29, 2010; Nicholas Kolakowski, "Bing versus Google, Windows Phone 7 Dominated Microsoft's Week," *Eweek.com*, March 28, 2010; http://www.youtube.com/xboxprojectnatal (accessed March 30, 2010); Clayton Morris, "The Death of the Couch-Potato Gamer," *FoxNews.com*, March 26, 2010.

2. http://www.xbox.com/en-US/live/projectnatal/ (accessed March 1, 2010).

3. *Time Magazine*, "The 50 Best Inventions of 2009," November 12, 2009.

4. "A New Idea," http://www.dyson.com/insidedyson/article.asp?aID=newidea&disType=&dir=&cp=&hf=1&js=1 (accessed December 14, 2009).

5. Lauren Etter, "Beef Industry Fights for Room at the Table," *The Wall Street Journal*, March 26, 2009.

6. Koen Pauwels, Jorge Silva-Risso, Shuba Srinivasan, and Dominique M. Hanssens, "New Products, Sales Promotions, and Firm Value: The Case of the Automobile Industry," *Journal of Marketing* 68, no. 4 (2008), p. 142.

7. Ilan Brat, "For General Mills, Wheat-Free Items and Tricky to Make, Cheap to Market," *The Wall Street Journal*, July 2, 2009.

8. Kalpesh Kaushik Desai and Kevin Lane Keller, "The Effects of Ingredient Branding Strategies on Host Brand Extendibility," *Journal of Marketing* 66, no. 1 (2002), pp. 73–93.

9. Tom Ivan, "EA CFO: Madden NFL 10 Sales 'Discouraging,'" *Edge*, September 11, 2009.

10. http://www.ideo.com/work/featured/kraft (accessed January 18, 2010).

11. http://www.marketingpower.com/_layouts/Dictionary.aspx?dLetter=D (accessed December 17, 2009).

12. Barak Libai, Eitan Muller, and Renana Peres, "The Diffusion of Services," *Journal of Marketing Research* 46 (April 2009), pp. 163–75; Yvonne van Everdingen, Dennis Fok, and Stefan Stemersch, "Modeling Global Spillover of New Product Takeoff," *Journal of Marketing Research* 46 (October 2009), pp. 637–52.

13. Rosabeth Moss Kanter, *SuperCorp: How Vanguard Companies Create Innovation, Profits, Growth, and Social Good* (New York: Crown Business, 2009); Rajesh K. Chandy, Jaideep C. Prabhu,

and Kersi D. Antia, "What Will the Future Bring? Dominance, Technology Expectations, and Radical Innovation," *Journal of Marketing* 67, no. 3 (2003), pp. 1–18; Harald J. van Heerde, Carl F. Mela, and Puneet Manchanda, "The Dynamic Effect of Innovation on Market Structure," *Journal of Marketing Research* 41, no. 2 (2004), pp. 166–83.

14. Apple, http://www.apple.com/ipodtouch/ (accessed December 14, 2009); Ethan Smith and Yukari Iwatani Kane, "Apple Plots Reboot of iTunes for Web," *The Wall Street Journal*, December 11, 2009; Angus Loten, "The iPhone Economy Emerges," *Inc.com*, June 1, 2007 (accessed January 30, 3008); Clayton M. Christensen and Michael E. Raynor, *The Innovator's Solution* (Boston: Harvard Business School Press, 2003).

15. James L. Oakley, Adam Duhachek, Subramanian Balachander, and S. Sriram, "Order of Entry and the Moderating Role of Comparison Brands in Brand Extension Evaluation," *Journal of Consumer Research* 34, no. 5 (2008), pp. 706–12; Fernando F. Suarez and Gianvito Lanzolla, "Considerations for a Stronger First Mover Advantage Theory," *Academy of Management Review* 33, no. 1 (2008), pp. 269–70; Ralitza Nikolaeva, "The Dynamic Nature of Survival Determinants in E-commerce," *Journal of the Academy of Marketing Science* 35, no. 4 (2007), pp. 560–71; Philip Kotler, *Marketing Management*, 11th ed. (Upper Saddle River, NJ: Prentice-Hall, 2003), pp. 330–31; G. S. Carpenter and Kent Nakamoto, "Consumer Preference Formation and Pioneering Advantage," *Journal of Marketing Research* 26, no. 3 (1989), pp. 285–98; Glen L. Urban, T. Carter, S. Gaskin, and Z. Mucha, "Market Share Rewards to Pioneering Brands: An Empirical Analysis and Strategic Implications," *Management Science* 32 (1986), pp. 645–59. Kotler's work was based on the following research: William T. Robinson and Claes Fornell, "Sources of Market Pioneer Advantages in Consumer Goods Industries," *Journal of Marketing Research* 22, no. 3 (1985), pp. 305–17.

16. Matt Haig, *Brand Failures* (London: Kogan Page, 2005); Raji Srinivasan, Gary L. Lilien, and Arvind Rangaswamy, "First in, First out? The Effects of Network Externalities on Pioneer Survival," *Journal of Marketing* 68, no. 1 (2004), p. 41.

17. K. Tyagi, "New Product Introductions and Failures under Uncertainty," *International Journal of Research in Marketing* 23, no. 2 (2006), pp. 199–213; Lori Dahm, "Secrets of Success: The Strategies Driving New Product Development at Kraft," *Stagnito's New Products Magazine* 2 (January 2002), p. 18ff; Cyndee Miller, "Little Relief Seen for New Product Failure Rate," *Marketing News*, June 21, 1993, pp. 1, 10; *BusinessWeek*, "Flops," August 16, 1993, p. 76ff.

18. Jacob Goldenberg, Sangman Han, Donald R. Lehmann, and Jae Weon Hong, "The Role of Hubs in the Adoption Process," *Journal of Marketing* 73 (March 2009), pp. 1–13.

19. Erica Ogg, "ZOMG: Amazon.com Drops Kindle Price 10 Percent," *CNET News*, May 27, 2008.

20. Dylan F. Tweney, "Large-Screen Kindle Won't Mean Squat if Apple Tablet Arrives," *Wired*, May 4, 2009.

21. Melissa J. Perenson, "Kindle 2 Price Plunge Signals E-Book Reader Market Competition," *PC World*, July 8, 2009.

22. http://www.greenworkscleaners.com/our_story/ (accessed December 15, 2009); http://www.bestnewproductawards .com/press_release.html, December 30, 2008 (accessed December 15, 2009).

23. Sarah Perez, "Firefox China Edition: Everything a Local Browser Should Be," *ReadWriteWeb.com*, November 24, 2008.

24. L. M. De Luca and K. Atuahene-Gima, "Market Knowledge Dimensions and Cross-Functional Collaboration: Examining the Different Routes to Product Innovation Performance," *Journal of Marketing* 71 (2007), pp. 95–112; Subin Im and John P. Workman Jr., "Market Orientation, Creativity, and New Product Performance in High-Technology Firms," *Journal of Marketing* 68, no. 2 (2004), p. 114.

25. http://www.arimidex.com/glossary/index.asp (accessed April 9, 2008).

26. Ted Agres, "Support for Orphan Diseases," *Drug Discovery & Development* 9, no. 7 (2006), pp. 6–8.

27. Stefan Stremersch and Walter Van Dyck, "Marketing of the Life Sciences: A New Framework and Research Agenda for a Nascent Field," *Journal of Marketing* 73 (July 2009), pp. 4–30; Standard & Poor's, *Industry Surveys: Healthcare: Pharmaceuticals*, June 24, 2004.

28. "Brand Strategy for Havianas," IDEO Case study, 2009.

29. "American Red Cross Donor Experience," IDEO Case Study, 2007.

30. Pilar Carbonell, Ana I. Rodríguez-Escudero, and Devashish Pujari, "Customer Involvement in New Service Development: An Examination of Antecedents and Outcomes," *Journal of Product Innovation Management* 26 (September 2009), pp. 536–50; Glen L. Urban and John R. Hauser, "'Listening In' to Find and Explore New Combinations of Customer Needs," *Journal of Marketing* 68, no. 2 (2004), p. 72.

31. Associated Press, "Wal-Mart Adds Products as Store Brands Boom," *Boston Globe*, March 17, 2009; Matthew Boyle, "Wal-Mart Gives Its Store Brand a Makeover," *BusinessWeek*, March 16, 2009.

32. Interview with Jevin Eagle, Executive Vice President of Merchandising and Marketing at Staples, on June 18, 2009.

33. Jim Highsmith, *Agile Product Management: Creating Innovative Products* (Boston: Addison-Wesley, 2009); http://www .betterproductdesign.net/tools/user/leaduser.htm (accessed November 12, 2004); Eric von Hippel, *The Sources of Innovation* (New York: Oxford University Press, 1988); Glen L. Urban and Eric von Hippel, "Lead User Analysis for the Development of Industrial Products," *Management Science* 34 (May 1988), pp. 569–82; Eric von Hippel, "Lead Users: A Source of Novel Product Concepts," *Management Science* 32 (1986), pp. 791–805; Eric von Hippel, "Successful Industrial Products from Consumers' Ideas," *Journal of Marketing* 42, no. 1 (1978), pp. 39–49.

34. Karl T. Ulrich and Steven D. Eppinger, *Product Design and Development*, 4th ed. (Boston: Irwin-McGraw-Hill, 2008).

35. http://www.marketingpower.com (accessed December 17, 2009).

36. Ulrich and Eppinger, *Product Design and Development*.

37. Daniel Michaels, "Carriers, Airports Use Scanners, Radio Tags and Software to Improve Tracking of Luggage," *Tech Journal*, September 30, 2009; "A New Way to Prevent Lost Luggage," *The Wall Street Journal*, February 27, 2007.

38. Min Zhao, Steven Hoeffler, and Darren W. Dahl, "The Role of Imagination-Focused Visualization on New Product Evaluation," *Journal of Marketing Research* 46 (February 2009), pp. 46–55; http://www.marketingpower.com (accessed December 17, 2009).

39. Ulrich and Eppinger, *Product Design and Development*.

40. "EU to Ban Animal Tested Cosmetics," www.cnn.com (accessed March 31, 2006); Tonya Vinas, "P&G Seeks Alternatives to Animal Tests," *Industry Week* 253, no. 7 (2004), p. 60; Guy Montague-Jones, "Search for Alternatives to Animal Testing Remains Slow," January 11, 2008; Gary Anthes, "P&G Uses

Data Mining to Cut Animal Testing," *Computerworld.com*, December 6, 1999.

41. http://www.peta.org; "Mars Candy Kills," http://www.marscandykills.com (accessed January 17, 2010); http://www.peta.org//actioncenter/index.asp (accessed January 17, 2010); www.mccruelty.com (accessed January 17, 2010); https://secure.peta.org/site/Advocacy?cmd=display&page=UserAction&id=2305 (accessed January 17, 2010).

42. Ellen Byron, "A Virtual View of the Store Aisle," *The Wall Street Journal*, October 3, 2007.

43. http://en-us.nielsen.com/tab/product_families/nielsen_bases (accessed December 9, 2009).

44. http://www.swashitout.com/ (accessed December 16, 2009); Elaine Wong, "P&G's Swash Targets GenYers," *Brandweek*, December 5, 2009.

45. Gernot H. Gessinger, *Materials and Innovative Product Development: From Concept to Market* (Oxford: Elsevier, 2009); Patricia Sellers, "P&G: Teaching an Old Dog New Tricks," *Fortune*, May 31, 2004, pp. 166–80.

46. Jyoti Thottam Pune and Niljanjana Bhowmick, "Nano Power," *Time*, April 13, 2009.

47. Product Development Management Association, *The PDMA Handbook of New Product Development*, 2nd ed., Kenneth K. Kahn, ed. (New York: John Wiley & Sons, 2004).

48. Christian Homburg, Jan Wieske, and Torsten Bornemann, "Implementing the Marketing Concept at the Employee–Customer Interface: The Role of Customer Need Knowledge," *Journal of Marketing* 73 (July 2009), pp. 64–81; Ashwin W. Joshi and Sanjay Sharma, "Customer Knowledge Development: Antecedents and Impact on New Product Success," *Journal of Marketing* 68, no. 4 (2004), p. 47.

49. http://www.beiersdorf.com/Brands_Innovations/Innovations.html?TG=Brands_Sustainability (accessed December 16, 2009); http://www.nivea.com/highlights/int_product/show/nhc_diamond_gloss/ (accessed December 16, 2009).

50. Yuhong Wu, Sridhar Balasubramanian, and Vijay Mahajan, "When Is a Preannounced New Product Likely to Be Delayed?" *Journal of Marketing* 68, no. 2 (2004), p. 101.

51. http://www.walletpop.com/specials/top-25-biggest-product-flops-of-all-time (accessed December 16, 2009).

52. http://www.pdma.org/ (accessed January 18, 2010).

53. Theodore Levitt, *Marketing Imagination* (New York: The Free Press, 1986).

54. Donald R. Lehmann and Russell S. Winer, *Analysis for Marketing Planning*, 7th ed. (Burr Ridge IL: McGraw-Hill/Irwin, 2008).

55. Ibid.; Glen L. Urban and John R. Hauser, *Design and Marketing of New Products*, 2nd ed. (Upper Saddle River, NJ: Prentice Hall, 1993), pp. 120–21.

56. http://www.organicearthday.org/DelMonteFoods.htm (accessed January 18, 2010); http://www.delmonte.com/Products/ (accessed January 18, 2010).

57. "Whirlpool Washing Machines," March 25, 2009, http://www.scribd.com/doc/13643826/Whirlpool-Washing-Machines (accessed December 29, 2009); Miriam Jordan and Jonathan Karp, "Machines for the Masses; Whirlpool Aims Cheap Washer at Brazil, India and China; Making Do with Slower Spin," *The Wall Street Journal*, December 9, 2003, p. A19.

58. "The New Global Middle Class: Potentially Profitable—But also Unpredictable," *Knowledge@Wharton*, July 9, 2008; Eric D. Beinhocker, Diana Farrell, and Adil S. Zainulbhai, "Tracking the Growth of India's Middle Class," *McKinsey Quarterly*, August

2007; Om Malik, "The New Land of Opportunity," *Business 2.0*, July 2004, pp. 72–79.

59. Ellen Byron, "Purex Tackles Tough Market, Using New Spin," *The Wall Street Journal*, April 28, 2009.

60. Noreen O'Leary, "KFC's Grilled Chicken Tops Most-Recalled '09 Launches," *Brandweek*, December 12, 2009; Natalie Zmuda, "Big Spenders Get the Most Buzz," *Advertising Age*, July 27, 2009; Lisa Respers France, "Oprah Coupon Craze Leaves KFC Customers Hungry for More," CNN.com, May 8, 2009.

61. Steven Levenstein, "Sony's New USB Turntable Sparks Vinyl Revival," www.inventospot.com, March 14, 2008; http://www.electronichouse.com/article/vinyl_the_classic_format/C155 (accessed March 16, 2008); Roy Bragg, "LP Vinyl Records Are Making a Comeback in Audiophile Circles," Knight Ridder Tribune Business News, January 3, 2004 (ProQuest Document ID: 521358371); Susan Adams, "You, the Record Mogul," *Forbes*, October 27, 2003, p. 256ff.

62. Goutam Challagalla, R. Venkatesh, and Ajay Kohli, "Proactive Postsales Service: When and Why Does It Pay Off?" *Journal of Marketing* 73 (March 2009), pp. 70–87; Kevin J. Clancy and Peter C. Krieg, "Product Life Cycle: A Dangerous Idea," *Brandweek*, March 1, 2004, p. 26; Nariman K. Dhalla and Sonia Yuseph, "Forget the Product Life-Cycle Concept," *Harvard Business Review* (January–February 1976), p. 102ff.

63. Peter Golder and Gerard Tellis, "Cascades, Diffusion, and Turning Points in the Product Life Cycle," MSI Report No. 03-120, 2003.

64. Jay Bolling, "DTC: A Strategy for Every Stage," *Pharmaceutical Executive*, November 2003, pp. 110–17.

65. This case was written by Colin Fox and Britt Hackmann in conjunction with the textbook authors (Dhruv Grewal and Michael Levy) as a basis for class discussion rather than to illustrate either effective or ineffective marketing practice.

66. Lev Grossman, "Invention of the Year: The iPhone," *Time*, November 1, 2007.

67. David Goldman, "Apple Doubles iPhone Sales in Record Quarter," *CNN Money*, January 25, 2010.

68. Ali Sarmad, "iPhone, Android Gain Market Share at Microsoft and Palm's Expense," *CNN Money*, February 9, 2010.

69. Philip Elmer-DeWitt, "Apple, Android, RIM Gain Market Share," *CNN Money*, February 23, 2010.

70. www.apple.com/investor/ (accessed March 31, 2010).

71. Tom Hormby, "Birth of the PowerBook: How Apple Took Over the Portable Market in 1991," *Low End Mac*, November 23, 2005.

72. James Delahunty, "iPod Market Share at 73.8 Percent, 225 Million iPods Sold, More Games for Touch Than PSP & NDS: Apple," *Afterdawn.com*, September 9, 2009; Nick Wingfield, "A New Wireless Player Hopes to Challenge iPod," *The Wall Street Journal*, April 9, 2007; John Markoff, "Apple Cuts iPhone Price Ahead of Holidays," *The New York Times*, September 6, 2007.

73. Dan Gallagher, "Analyst: RIMM, Nokia Tops in 'Year of the Mobile Computer,'" *MarketWatch*, March 26, 2010.

74. http://blog.seattlepi.com/microsoft/archives/198339.asp (accessed March 31, 2010).

75. Jerry Rocha, "The Droid: Is this the Smartphone Consumers Are Looking For?" *Nielsen Wire*, November 11, 2009.

76. Roger Entner, "Smartphones to Overtake Feature Phones in U.S. by 2011," *Nielsen Wire*, March 26, 2010.

77. Om Malik, "How Big Is the Apple iPhone App Economy? The Answer Might Surprise You," *GigaOm.com*, August 27, 2009.

# Chapter 12

1. http://www.apple.com/support (accessed January 20, 2010); Erika Morphy, "The Bright Spots and Sore Spots of Apple Customer Service," *Dallas Morning News*, July 28, 2009.

2. Valarie A. Zeithaml, Mary Jo Bitner, and Dwayne D. Gremler, *Services Marketing: Integrating Customer Focus across the Firm*, 5th ed. (Burr Ridge, IL: McGraw-Irwin, 2009); Leonard L. Berry and A. Parasuraman, *Marketing Services: Competing through Quality* (New York: The Free Press, 1991), p. 5.

3. http://earthtrends.wri.org/searchable_db/results.php ?years=20052005&variable_ID=216&theme=5&cID=190&ccID (accessed February 25, 2010).

4. Zeithaml, Bitner, and Gremler, *Services Marketing*; Valarie A. Zeithaml, A. Parasuraman, and Leonard L. Berry, *Delivering Quality Service: Balancing Customer Perceptions and Expectations* (New York: The Free Press, 1990).

5. Dhruv Grewal, Michael Levy, Gopal Iyer, and Jerry Gotlieb, "Developing a Deeper Understanding of Post-Purchase Perceived Risk and Repeat Purchase Behavioral Intentions in a Service Setting," *Journal of the Academy of Marketing Science* 35, no. 2 (2007), pp. 250–58; Mary Jo Bitner, Stephen W. Brown, and Matthew L. Mueter, "Technology Infusion in Service Encounters," *Journal of the Academy of Marketing Science* 28, no. 1 (2000), pp. 138–49; Jerry Gotlieb, Dhruv Grewal, Michael Levy, and Joan Lindsey-Mullikin, "An Examination of Moderators of the Effects of Customers' Evaluation of Employee Courtesy on Attitude toward the Service Firm," *Journal of Applied Social Psychology* 34 (April 2004), pp. 825–47.

6. Choice Hotels, "Special Guest Policies," http://www.choicehotels .com/ires/en-US/html/GuestPolicies (accessed February 2, 2010).

7. Peter H. Geraghty, "New New York Rules on Lawyer Advertising," *ABA EthicSearch* (accessed February 20, 2008).

8. Center for Professional Responsibility, http://www.abanet .org/cpr/professionalism/lawyerAd.html (accessed February 20, 2008).

9. The discussion of the Gaps Model and its implications draws heavily from Michael Levy and Barton A. Weitz, *Retailing Management*, 7th ed. (Burr Ridge, IL: Irwin/McGraw-Hill, 2009) and also is based on Deon Nel and Leyland Pitt, "Service Quality in a Retail Environment: Closing the Gaps," *Journal of General Management* 18 (Spring 1993), pp. 37–57; Zeithaml, Parasuraman, and Berry, *Delivering Quality Service*; Valerie Zeithaml, Leonard Berry, and A. Parasuraman, "Communication and Control Processes in the Delivery of Service Quality," *Journal of Marketing* 52, no. 2 (April 1988), pp. 35–48.

10. Zhen Zhu, Cheryl Nakata, K. Sivakumar and Dhruv Grewal, "Self-Service Technology Effectiveness: The Roles of Interactivity, Comparative Information, and Individual Differences on Perceived Control and Interface Evaluation," *Journal of the Academy of Marketing Science* 35, no. 4 (2007), pp. 492–506; Zhen Zhu, Cheryl Nakata, K. Sivakumar, and Dhruv Grewal, "Fix It or Leave It? Customer Recovery from Self-Service Technology Failures," working paper, 2010, Babson College; Peter C. Verhoef, Katherine N. Lemon, A. Parasuraman, Anne Roggeveen, Michael Tsiros, and Leonard A. Schlesinger, "Customer Experience Creation: Determinants, Dynamics and Management Strategies," *Journal of Retailing* 85, no. 1 (2009), pp. 31–41; Mary Jo Bitner, "Self-Service Technologies: What Do Customers Expect? In This High-Tech World, Customers Haven't Changed —They Still Want Good Service," *Marketing Management*, Spring 2001, pp. 10–15; Chezy Ofir and Itamar Simonson, "The Effect of Stating Expectations on Customer Satisfaction and Shopping Experience." *Journal of Marketing Research* 44 (February 2007), p. 37; Jackie L M Tam, "Managing Customer Expectations in Financial Services: Opportunities and Challenges," *Journal of Financial Services Marketing* 11 (May 2007), pp. 281–89.

11. Adam Braff and John C. DeVine, "Maintaining the Customer Experience," *The McKinsey Quarterly*, December 2008.

12. J. Aspara and H. Tikkanen, "Interactions of Individuals' Company-Related Attitudes and Their Buying of Companies' Stocks and Products," *Journal of Behavioral Finance* 9 (2008), pp. 85–94; Caroline Goukens, Siegfried Dewitte, and Luk Warlop, "Me, Myself, and My Choices: The Influence of Private Self-Awareness on Choice," *Journal of Marketing Research* 46 (October 2009), pp. 703–14.

13. Kemba J. Dunham, "Beyond Satisfaction," *The Wall Street Journal*, October 30, 2006, p. R4.

14. Barney Beal, "Text Analytics Software, Net Promoter Score Helps JetBlue Take Off with Customer Service," *SearchCRM .com*, June 4, 2009.

15. Zeithaml, Bitner, and Gremler, *Services Marketing*; Zhen Zhu, K. Sivakumar, and A. Parasuraman, "A Mathematical Model of Service Failure and Recovery Strategies," *Decision Science* 35 (Summer 2004), pp. 493–525; Roland T. Rust and Tuck Siong Chung, "Marketing Models of Service and Relationships," *Marketing Science* 25 (November 2006), pp. 560–80; A. Parasuraman, "Modeling Opportunities in Service Recovery and Customer-Managed Interactions," *Marketing Science* 25 (November 2006), pp. 590–93; Zeithaml, Parasuraman, and Berry, *Delivering Quality Service*.

16. Personal communication, Allison Scott, Director of Communications, The Broadmoor; Czaplewski, Andrew, Olson, Eric M., and Slater, Stanley F. "Applying the RATER Model for Service Success: Five Service Attributes Can Help Maintain Five-Star Ratings," *Marketing Management*, January/ February 2002, pp. 14–20. Reprinted by permission. http:// www.forbestravelguide.com/five-star-spas.htm (accessed March 19, 2010); Allison Scott, "New Renovations Add to the Guest and Meeting Experience," www.release-news.com (accessed March 9, 2010); http://www.broadmoor.com/luxury -resort-services.php (accessed March 19, 2010); Bill Radford, "Broadmoor's Penrose Room Dons a 5th Gem," *The Colorado Springs Gazette*, November 7, 2007; "Grand Plans for a Grande Dame," Lodging Hospitality, September 1, 2007, pp. 17–18.

17. Stephen L. Vargo, Kaori Nagao, Yi He, and Fred W. Morgan, "Satisfiers, Dissatisfiers, Criticals, and Neutrals: A Review of Their Relative Effects on Customer (Dis)Satisfaction," *Academy of Marketing Science Review* (January 2007), p. 1; Chezy Ofir and Itamar Simonson, "The Effect of Stating Expectations on Customer Satisfaction and Shopping Experience," *Journal of Marketing Research* 44 (February 2007), p. 37; Torsten Ringberg, Gaby Odekerken-Schröder, and Glenn L. Christensen, "A Cultural Models Approach to Service Recovery," *Journal of Marketing* 71 (July 2007), p. 194; Leonard Berry and A. Parasuraman, "Listening to the Customer—The Concept of a Service-Quality Information System," *Sloan Management Review* 38, no. 3 (1997), pp. 65–77.

18. Goutam Challagalla, R. Venkatesh, and Ajay K. Kohli, "Proactive Postsales Service: When and Why Does It Pay Off?" *Journal of Marketing* 73 (March 2009), pp. 70–87.

19. Janelle Barlow, "A Complaint Is a Gift Corner," http://www .tmius.com/2cigcorn.HTML (accessed January 29, 2010).

20. Hazel-Anne Johnson and Paul Spector, "Service with a Smile: Do Emotional Intelligence, Gender, and Autonomy Moderate

the Emotional Labor Process?" *Journal of Occupational Health Psychology*, October 2007, pp. 319–33; Merran Toerien and Celia Kitzinger, "Emotional Labour in Action: Navigating Multiple Involvements in the Beauty Salon," *Sociology*, August 2007, pp. 645–62.

21. Jennifer Reingold, "Home Depot's Total Rehab," *CNNMoney .com*, September 19, 2008.

22. Ellen Davis, "Building a Brand That Matters, One Employee at a Time: The Zappos Story," *Shop.org*, February 3, 2009; Ellen Davis, "How Zappos.com Streamlines Its Channels," *NRFtech*, August 11, 2008; Matt Mickiewicz, "How Zappos Does Customer Service and Company Culture," *Sitepoint.com*, March 30, 2009, http://www.sitepoint.com/blogs/2009/03/30/how-zappos -does-customer-service-and-company-culture/ (accessed March 22, 2010); Benn Parr, "Here's Why Amazon Bought Zappos," *Masahable.com*, July 22, 2009, http://mashable .com/2009/07/22/amazon-bought-zappos/ (accessed March 22, 2010).

23. Michael T. Manion and Joseph Cherian, "Do Services Marketers' Success Measures Match Their Strategies?" *Journal of Services Marketing* 23, no. 7 (2009), pp. 476–86; Alison M. Dean and Al Rainnie, "Frontline Employees' Views on Organizational Factors That Affect the Delivery of Service Quality in Call Centers," *Journal of Services Marketing* 23, no. 5 (2009), pp. 326–37; James R. Detert and Ethan R. Burris, "Leadership Behavior and Employee Voice: Is the Door Really Open?" *Academy of Management Journal* 50 (August 2007), pp. 869–84; Gilad Chen, Bradley L. Kirkman, Ruth Kanfer, Don Allen, and Benson Rosen, "A Multilevel Study of Leadership, Empowerment, and Performance in Teams," *Journal of Applied Psychology* 92 (March 2007), p. 331; Adam Rapp, Michael Ahearne, John Mathieu, and Niels Schillewaert, "The Impact of Knowledge and Empowerment on Working Smart and Working Hard: The Moderating Role of Experience," *International Journal of Research in Marketing* 23 (September 2006), pp. 279–93; Jim Poisant, *Creating and Sustaining a Superior Customer Service Organization: A Book about Taking Care of the People Who Take Care of the Customers* (Westport, CT: Quorum Books, 2002); "People-Focused HR Policies Seen as Vital to Customer Service Improvement," *Store*, January 2001, p. 60; Michael Brady and J. Joseph Cronin, "Customer Orientation: Effects on Customer Service Perceptions and Outcome Behaviors," *Journal of Service Research*, February 2001, pp. 241–51; Michael Hartline, James Maxham III, and Daryl McKee, "Corridors of Influence in the Dissemination of Customer-Oriented Strategy to Customer Contact Service Employees," *Journal of Marketing* 64, no. 2 (April 2000), pp. 25–41.

24. Jason Colquitt, Jeffery LePine, and Michael Wesson, *Organizational Behavior: Improving Performance and Commitment in the Workplace*, 2nd ed. (Burr Ridge, IL: McGraw-Hill, 2010); Felicitas M. Morhart, Walter Herzog, and Torsten Tomczak, "Brand-Specific Leadership: Turning Employees into Brand Champions," *Journal of Marketing* 73 (September 2009), pp. 122–42; Julie Holliday Wayne, Amy E. Randel, and Jaclyn Stevens, "The Role of Identity and Work–Family Support in Work–Family Enrichment and Its Work-Related Consequences," *Journal of Vocational Behavior* 69 (December 2006), p. 445; Alicia Grandey and Analea Brauburger, "The Emotion Regulation behind the Customer Service Smile," in *Emotions in the Workplace: Understanding the Structure and Role of Emotions in Organizational Behavior*, eds. R. Lord, R. Klimoski, and R. Kanfer (San Francisco: Jossey-Bass, 2002); Mara Adelman and Aaron Ahuvia, "Social Support in the Service Sector: The Antecedents, Processes, and Consequences of Social Support

in an Introductory Service," *Journal of Business Research* 32 (March 1995), pp. 273–82.

25. Carmine Gallo, "Bringing Passion to Starbucks, Travelocity," *BusinessWeek*, January 9, 2008 (accessed April 1, 2008).

26. "Travelocity," http://www.sabre-holdings.com/ourBrands/ travelocity.html (accessed February 2, 2010); "Awards," http:// svc.travelocity.com/about/newsroom/awards_main/1,5711,,00 .html (accessed February 2, 2010).

27. Suzanne C. Makarem, Susan M. Mudambi, and Jeffrey S. Podoshen, "Satisfaction in Technology-Enabled Service Encounters," *Journal of Services Marketing* 23, no. 1 (2009), pp. 134–44; Lawrence F. Cunningham, Clifford E. Young, and James Gerlach, "A Comparison of Consumer Views of Traditional Services and Self-Service Technologies," *Journal of Services Marketing* 23, no. 1 (2003), pp. 11–23; Rhett H. Walker, Margaret Craig-Lees, Robert Hecker, and Heather Francis, "Technology-Enabled Service Delivery: An Investigation of Reasons Affecting Customer Adoption and Rejection," *International Journal of Service Industry Management* 13, no. 1 (2002), pp. 91–107.

28. Retail Banking Research, "New Study Says Self-Checkout Terminals to Quadruple by 2014," *Kiosk Marketplace*, July 21, 2009.

29. Anne Eisenberg, "Thinking of Going Blond? Consult the Kiosk First," *The New York Times*, March 29, 2009; Marianne Wilson, "Digital Dining," *Chain Store Age*, September 2008.

30. Anita Whiting and Noveen Donthu, "Closing the Gap between Perceived and Actual Waiting Times in a Call Center: Results from a Field Study," *Journal of Services Marketing* 23, no. 5 (2009), pp. 279–328; Subimal Chatterjee, Susan A. Slotnick, and Matthew J. Sobel, "Delivery Guarantees and the Interdependence of Marketing and Operations," *Production and Operations Management* 11, no. 3 (Fall 2002), pp. 393–411; Piyush Kumar, Manohar Kalawani, and Makbool Dada, "The Impact of Waiting Time Guarantees on Customers' Waiting Experiences," *Marketing Science* 16, no. 4 (1999), pp. 676–785.

31. Dhruv Grewal, Anne Roggeveen and Michael Tsiros, "Compensation as a Service Recovery Strategy: When Does It Work?" *Journal of Retailing* 84, no. 4 (2008), pp. 424–34; Michelle L. Roehm and Michael K. Brady, "Consumer Responses to Performance Failures by High-Equity Brands," *Journal of Consumer Research* 34 (December 2007), pp. 537–45; Hui Liao, "Do It Right This Time: The Role of Employee Service Recovery Performance in Customer-Perceived Justice and Customer Loyalty after Service Failures," *Journal of Applied Psychology* 92 (March 2007), p. 475; K. Douglas Hoffman, Scott W. Kelley, and H. M. Rotalsky, "Tracking Service Failures and Employee Recovery Efforts," *Journal of Services Marketing* 9, no. 2 (1995), pp. 49–61; Scott W. Kelley and Mark A. Davis, "Antecedents to Customer Expectations for Service Recovery," *Journal of the Academy of Marketing Science* 22 (Winter 1994), pp. 52–61; Terrence J. Levesque and Gordon H. G. McDougall, "Service Problems and Recovery Strategies: An Experiment," *Canadian Journal of Administrative Sciences* 17, no. 1 (2000), pp. 20–37; James G. Maxham III and Richard G. Netemeyer, "A Longitudinal Study of Complaining Customers' Evaluations of Multiple Service Failures and Recovery Efforts," *Journal of Marketing* 66, no. 3 (October 2002), pp. 57–71; Amy K. Smith, Ruth N. Bolton, and Janet Wagner, "A Model of Customer Satisfaction with Service Encounters Involving Failure and Recovery," *Journal of Marketing Research* 36, no. 3 (August 1999), pp. 356–372; Scott R. Swanson and Scott W. Kelley, "Attributions and Outcomes of the Service Recovery Process," *Journal of Marketing Theory and Practice* 9 (Fall 2001), pp. 50–65; Stephen S. Tax and Stephen W. Brown, "Recovering and Learning from Service Failure,"

*Sloan Management Review* 40, no. 1 (1998), pp. 75–88; Stephen S. Tax, Stephen W. Brown, and Murali Chandrashekaran, "Consumer Evaluations of Service Complaint Experiences: Implications for Relationship Marketing," *Journal of Marketing* 62, no. 2 (April 1998), pp. 60–76; Scott Widmier and Donald W. Jackson Jr., "Examining the Effects of Service Failure, Customer Compensation, and Fault on Customer Satisfaction with Salespeople," *Journal of Marketing Theory and Practice* 10 (Winter 2002), pp. 63–74; Valarie A. Zeithaml and Mary Jo Bitner, *Services Marketing: Integrating Customer Focus across the Firm* (New York: McGraw-Hill, 2003).

32. Peter C. Verhoef, Katherine N. Lemon, A. Parasuraman, Anne Roggeveen, Michael Tsiros, and Leonard A. Schlesinger, "Customer Experience Creation: Determinants, Dynamics and Management Strategies," *Journal of Retailing* 85, no. 1 (2009), pp. 31-41; Beibei Dong, Kenneth R. Evans, and Shaoming Zou, "The Effects of Customer Participation in Co-created Service Recovery," *Journal of the Academy of Marketing Science* 36 (Spring 2008), pp. 123–37; Grewal, Roggeveen, and Tsiros, "Compensation as a Service Recovery Strategy; Michelle L. Roehm and Michael K. Brady, "Consumer Responses to Performance Failures by High-Equity Brands," *Journal of Consumer Research* 34 (December 2007), pp. 537–45; James Maxham III, "Service Recovery's Influence on Consumer Satisfaction, Positive Word-of-Mouth, and Purchase Intentions," *Journal of Business Research*, October 2001, pp. 11–24; Michael McCollough, Leonard Berry, and Manjit Yadav, "An Empirical Investigation of Customer Satisfaction after Service Failure and Recovery," *Journal of Service Research*, November 2000, pp. 121–37.

33. Christopher Reynolds, "Smashed Guitar, YouTube Song—United Is Listening Now," *Los Angeles Times*, July 7, 2009.

34. Steve Keenan, "United Broke My Guitar: Song 2," *Times Online*, August 19, 2009.

35. Alison Bonaquro, "United Broke His Guitar and Learned a Lesson," http://blog.cmt.com/2009-07-10/united-broke-his-guitar-and-learned-a-lesson/, July 10, 2009.

36. Dhruv Grewal, Anne L. Roggeveen, and Michael Tsiros, "The Effect of Compensation on Repurchase Intentions in Service Recovery," *Journal of Retailing* 84, no. 4 (2008), pp. 424–34; "Correcting Store Blunders Seen as Key Customer Service Opportunity," *Stores*, January 2001, pp. 60–64; Stephen W. Brown, "Practicing Best-in-Class Service Recovery: Forward-Thinking Firms Leverage Service Recovery to Increase Loyalty and Profits," *Marketing Management*, Summer 2000, pp. 8–10; Tax, Brown, and Chandrashekaran, "Customer Evaluations"; Amy Smith and Ruth Bolton, "An Experimental Investigation of Customer Reactions to Service Failures and Recovery Encounters: Paradox or Peril?" *Journal of Service Research* 1 (August 1998), pp. 23–36; Cynthia Webster and D. S. Sundaram, "Service Consumption Criticality in Failure Recovery," *Journal of Business Research* 41 (February 1998), pp. 153–59.

37. Grewal, Roggeveen, and Tsiros, "The Effect of Compensation on Repurchase Intentions."

38. Yany Grégoire, Thomas M. Tripp, and Renaud Legoux, "When Customer Love Turns into Lasting Hate: The Effects of Relationship Strength and Time on Customer Revenge and Avoidance," *Journal of Marketing* 73 (November 2009), pp. 18–32.

39. Grewal, Roggeveen, and Tsiros, "The Effect of Compensation on Repurchase Intentions"; Amy K. Smith, Ruth N. Bolton, and Janet Wagner, "A Model of Customer Satisfaction with Service Encounters Involving Failure and Recovery," *Journal of Marketing Research* 36 (August 1999), pp. 356–72; Scott R. Swanson and Scott W. Kelley, "Attributions and Outcomes of the Service Recovery Process," *Journal of Marketing: Theory and Practice* 9 (Fall 2001), pp. 50–65.

40. David Carter and Darren Rovell, "It's a Homerun: Customer Service Greatness in the Minor Leagues," *Financial Times*, June 27, 2003.

41. Jayne O'Donnell, "Some Retailers Tighten Return Policies," *USA Today*, February 1, 2008.

42. https://my.usaa.com/inet/ent_utils/McStaticPages?key=my_usaa_what_is_usaa (accessed March 19, 2010).

43. This case was written by Colin Fox and Britt Hackmann in conjunction with the textbook authors (Dhruv Grewal and Michael Levy) as the basis of class discussion rather than to illustrate either effective or ineffective marketing practice. See Suzanne Marta, "As Ritz Opening Nears, Every Detail Counts," *Knight Ridder Tribune Business News*, August 6, 2007; Jack Gordon, "Redefining Elegance," *Training* 44, no. 2 (2007), pp. 14–20; Jennifer Saranow, "Turning to Luxury Hotels for Service Ideas; Companies Lacking in Customer Savvy Try the Special Touch," *The Wall Street Journal*, July 19, 2006.

44. "Luxury Hotels—Business Is Up and Hotels Are Upgrading," *BusinessWeek*, January 20, 2008 (accessed electronically February 26, 2008).

45. "Fact Sheet," http://corporate.ritzcarlton.com/en/Press/FactSheet.htm (accessed February 26, 2008).

46. "Our History," http://corporate.ritzcarlton.com/en/About/OurHistory.htm (accessed February 26, 2008).

47. "Working at the Ritz Carlton," http://corporate.ritzcarlton.com/en/Careers/WorkingAt.htm (accessed February 26, 2008).

48. Marc Gunther, "Marriott Gets a Wake-Up Call," *Fortune*, July 6, 2009.

## Chapter 13

1. http://www.hotels.com (accessed January 6, 2010); http://www.visitlasvegas.com/vegas/special-offers (accessed January 6, 2010).

2. T. R. Witcher, "The Good Times Stop Rolling: Vegas Meets the Recession," *Time*, December 29, 2008.

3. Joel Stein, "Less Vegas: The Casino Town Bets on a Comeback," *Time*, August 14, 2009; T. R. Witcher, "How Las Vegas' Opulent CityCenter Survived Dubai," *Time*, December 19, 2009.

4. Hooman Estelami, Dhruv Grewal, and Anne L. Roggeveen, "The Effect of Policy Restrictions on Consumer Reactions to Price-Matching Guarantees," *Journal of the Academy of Marketing Science* 35, no. 2 (2007), pp. 208–19; Monika Kukar-Kinney and Dhruv Grewal, "Comparison of Consumer Reactions to Price-Matching Guarantees in Internet and Bricks-and-Mortar Retail Environments," *Journal of the Academy of Marketing Science* 35, no. 2 (2007), pp. 197–207; Sujay Dutta, Abhijit Biswas, and Dhruv Grewal, "Low Price Signal Default: An Empirical Investigation with Low-Price Guarantees," *Journal of the Academy of Marketing Science* 35, no. 1 (2007), pp. 76–88; Kent B. Monroe, *Pricing: Making Profitable Decisions*, 3rd ed. (New York: McGraw-Hill, 2003); Dhruv Grewal, Kent B. Monroe, and R. Krishnan, "The Effects of Price Comparison Advertising on Buyers' Perceptions of Acquisition Value and Transaction Value," *Journal of Marketing* 62 (April 1998), pp. 46–60.

5. Jennifer Frighetto, "U.S. Consumers Place More Importance on Price and Value," *ACNielsen*, October 28, 2008; Laura Wood, "It's Not Easy Being Green, Part 2," *Research and Markets*, October 6, 2009; Food Marketing Institute, "American Shoppers

Economize, Show Greater Interest in Nutrition and Awareness of Food Safety Issues, According to Trends in the United States," *Consumer Attitudes and the Supermarket*, 2003; "The New Value Equation," *Supermarket News* 50 (June 10, 2002), p. 12.

6. Anthony Miyazaki, Dhruv Grewal, and Ronnie Goodstein, "The Effects of Multiple Extrinsic Cues on Quality Perceptions: A Matter of Consistency," *Journal of Consumer Research* 32 (June 2005), pp. 146–53; William B. Dodds, Kent B. Monroe, and Dhruv Grewal, "The Effects of Price, Brand, and Store Information on Buyers' Product Evaluations," *Journal of Marketing Research* 28 (August 1991), pp. 307–19.

7. Johan Lehrer, "Grape Expectations: What Wine Can Tell Us about the Nature of Reality," *Boston Globe*, February 24, 2008.

8. Ibid.

9. Bang-Ning Hwang, Jack Tsai, Hsiao-Cheng Yu, and Shih-Chi Chang, "An Effective Pricing Framework in a Competitive Industry: Management Processes and Implementation Guidelines," *Journal of Revenue and Pricing Management*, November 13, 2009; Oliver Roll, "Pricing Trends from a Management Perspective," *Journal of Revenue and Pricing Management* 8 (July 3, 2009), pp. 396–98; Robert J. Dolan, "Note on Marketing Strategy," *Harvard Business School* (November 2000), pp. 1–17; Dhruv Grewal and Larry D. Compeau, "Pricing and Public Policy: An Overview and a Research Agenda," *Journal of Public Policy & Marketing* 18 (Spring 1999), pp. 3–11.

10. Ethan Smith and Yukari Iwatani Kane, "Apples Changes Tune on Music Pricing," *The Wall Street Journal*, January 7, 2009.

11. "IBM Market Share Leader in Human Resources (HR) Business Transformation Outsourcing, Enterprise Sector," press release.

12. Rebecca Heslin, "Virgin America Joins Airline Fare Sale Stampede," *USA Today*, January 6, 2010; "Delta Rescinds Fare Increase on Some of Its U.S. Routes," *Salt Lake City News*, September 11, 2007 (accessed electronically January 3, 2010).

13. "For Radiohead Fans, Does 'Free' + 'Download' = 'Freeload'?" ComScore press release, November 5, 2007.

14. Stephen King, "Messages from Stephen," http://www.stephenking.com/stephens_messages.html (accessed January 6, 2010). See especially his entries from December 4, 2000.

15. Barb Dybwald, "World of Goo's Pay What You Want Pricing: 'Huge Success,'" www.mashable.com, November 2009.

16. Katie Hammel, "Vermont Cab Driver Offers 'Pay What You Want' Fares," www.gadling.com August 5, 2009. For an academic perspective on this phenomenon, see Ju-Young Kim, Martin Natter, and Martin Spann, "Pay What You Want: A New Participative Pricing Mechanism," *Journal of Marketing* 73 (January 2009), pp. 44–58.

17. Jared Jacang Maher, "SAME Cafe: The Restaurant Where You Pay What You Can, *Westword.com*, February 25, 2009.

18. Monroe, *Pricing: Making Profitable Decisions*.

19. William Lee Adams, "Would You Buy this $320,000 Brooch Online?" *Time*, November 9, 2009.

20. Fender U.S. Price Lists, http://www.fender.com/resources/price_lists.php (accessed January 6, 2010).

21. Monroe, *Pricing: Making Profitable Decisions*. See also Richard B. McKenzie, *Why Popcorn Costs So Much at the Movies: And Other Pricing Puzzles* (New York: Springer, 2008).

22. http://www.marketingpower.com/_layouts/Dictionary.aspx?dLetter=C (accessed January 8, 2010).

23. http://www.marketingpower.com/_layouts/Dictionary.aspx?dLetter=S (accessed January 8, 2010).

24. Joan Lindsey-Mullikin and Dhruv Grewal, "Market Price Variation: The Availability of Internet Market Information," *Journal of the Academy of Marketing Science* 34, no. 2 (2006), pp. 236–43.

25. Suzanne Marta, "As Ritz Opening Nears, Every Detail Counts," *Knight Ridder Tribune Business News*, August 6, 2007.

26. Jack Gordon, "Redefining Elegance, *Training* 44, no. 2 (2007), pp. 14–20.

27. Ibid.

28. Kevin Sack, "Despite Recession, Personalized Health Care Remains in Demand," *The New York Times*, May 11, 2009; Lori Calabro, "At Your Beck and Call," *CFO Magazine*, September 1, 2007 (accessed electronically February 4, 2008).

29. Vanessa O'Connell, "Posh Retailers Pile on Perks for Top Customers," *The Wall Street Journal*, April 26, 2007 (accessed electronically February 4, 2008); "InCircle," http://www.incircle.com/store/catalog/templates/Entry.jhtml?itemId=cat103411&parentId=cat103410&parentId=cat000001&icid=points1 (accessed January 6, 2010).

30. Julie Jargon and Lauren Etter, "Food Makers Struggle to Pass on High Costs," *The Wall Street Journal*, October 3, 2007, p. A2.

31. Andrew Adam Newman, "If You're Nervous, Deodorant Makers Have a Product for You," *The New York Times*, February 17, 2009.

32. Cenk Koça and Jonathan D. Bohlmann, "Segmented Switchers and Retailer Pricing Strategies," *Journal of Marketing* 72, no. 3 (2008), pp. 124–42; Ruth N. Bolton and Venkatesh Shankar, "An Empirically Derived Taxonomy of Retailer Pricing and Promotion Strategies," *Journal of Retailing* 79, no. 4 (2003), pp. 213–24; Rajiv Lal and Ram Rao, "Supermarket Competition: The Case of Every Day Low Pricing," *Marketing Science* 16, no. 1 (1997), pp. 60–80.

33. American Booksellers Association, "ABA Asks Department of Justice to Investigate Bestseller Price Wars," October 22, 2009.

34. Jeff Jacoby, "Latest Battle in Book Price Wars," *Boston Globe*, October 28, 2009.

35. Michelle Meyers, "Kindle Is Most Gifted Amazon Item, Ever," *Cnet News*, December 29, 2009.

36. Geoffrey Fowler and Jessica Vascellaro, "Sony, Google Challenge Amazon," *The Wall Street Journal*, March 17, 2009; Brad Stone, "Sony Reaches Deal to Share in Google's E-Book Library," *The New York Times*, March 19, 2009; Canadian Writers, "Publishers Gather to Consider Google Book Digitization," *CBC News*, March 23, 2009.

37. Jacoby, "Latest Battle"; Michael Bungert, *Termination of Price Wars: A Signaling Approach* (Frankfurt Mm Main: Springer Verlag, 2003); A. R. Rao, M. E. Bergen, and S. Davis, "How to Fight a Price War," *Harvard Business Review* 78 (March–April 2000), pp. 107–16.

38. *Merriam-Webster's Dictionary of Law*, 1996.

39. http://www.plasmavision.com/warranty.htm (accessed January 7, 2010).

40. Uptal Dholakia, Barbara Kahn, Randy Reeves, Aric Rindfleish, David Stewart, and Earl Taylor, "Consumer Behavior in a Multichannel, Multimedia Retailing Environment," *Journal of Interactive Marketing*, forthcoming; P. K. Kannan, Barbara K. Pope, and Sanjay Jain, "Pricing Digital Content Product Lines: A Model and Application for the National Academies Press," *Marketing Science*, forthcoming; Brian Ratchford, "Online Pricing: Review and Directions for Research," *Journal of Interactive Marketing* 23, no. 1 (2009), pp. 82–90; Koen Pauwels and Allen Weiss, "Moving from Free to Fee: How Online Firms Market to Successfully

Change Their Business Model," *Journal of Marketing Perspectives* 19, no. 2 (2008), pp. 139–58; Dhruv Grewal, Gopalkrishnan R. Iyer, R. Krishnan, and Arun Sharma, "The Internet and the Price-Value-Loyalty Chain," *Journal of Business Research* 56 (May 2003), pp. 391–98; Gopalkrishnan R. Iyer, Anthony D. Miyazaki, Dhruv Grewal, and Maria Giordano, "Linking Web-Based Segmentation to Pricing Tactics," *Journal of Product & Brand Management* 11, no. 4–5 (2002), pp. 288–302; Xing Pan, Brian T. Ratchford, and Venkatesh Shankar, "Can Price Dispersion in Online Markets Be Explained by Differences in E-Tailer Service Quality?" *Journal of the Academy of Marketing Science* 30, no. 4 (2002), pp. 433–45; Michael D. Smith, "The Impact of Shopbots on Electronic Markets," *Journal of the Academy of Marketing Sciences* 30, no. 4 (2002), pp. 446–54; Michael D. Smith and Erik Brynjolfsson, "Consumer Decision-Making at an Internet Shopbot: Brand Still Matters," *The Journal of Industrial Economics* 49 (December 2001), pp. 541–58; Fang-Fang Tang and Xiaolin Xing, "Will the Growth of Multi-Channel Retailing Diminish the Pricing Efficiency of the Web?" *Journal of Retailing* 77, no. 3 (2001), pp. 319–33; Erik Brynjolfsson and Michael D. Smith, "Frictionless Commerce? A Comparison of Internet and Conventional Retailers," *Management Science* 46, no. 4 (2000), pp. 563–85; Florian Zettlemeyer, "Expanding to the Internet: Pricing and Communications Strategies When Firms Compete on Multiple Channels," *Journal of Marketing Research* 37 (August 2000), pp. 292–308; Rajiv Lal and Miklos Sarvary, "When and How Is the Internet Likely to Decrease Price Competition?" *Marketing Science* 18, no. 4 (1999), pp. 485–503; Joseph P. Bailey, "Electronic Commerce: Prices and Consumer Issues for Three Products: Books, Compact Discs, and Software," *Organization for Economic Cooperation and Development, OECD, GD* 98 (1998), p. 4; J. Yannis Bakos, "Reducing Buyer Search Costs: Implications for Electronic Marketplaces," *Management Science* 43, no. 12 (1997), pp. 1676–92.

41. Kerry Miller, "eBay Sellers Go Back to School: 10 Tips," *Businessweek*, September 7, 2006.

42. Gillian Ku, Adam D. Galinsky, and J. Keith Murnighan, "Starting Low but Ending High: A Reversal of the Anchoring Effect in Auctions," *Journal of Personality and Social Psychology* 90, no. 6 (2006), pp. 975–86.

43. Patrick Bajari and Ali Hortacsu, "The Winner's Curse, Reserve Prices and Endogenous Entry: Empirical Insights from eBay Auctions," *Journal of Economics* 34, no. 2 (2002), p. 329.

44. Barbara Stern and Maria Royne Stafford, "Individual and Social Determinants of Winning Bids in Online Auctions," *Journal of Consumer Behavior* 5 (July 2006), pp. 43–55.

45. Ku, Galinsky, and Murnighan, "Starting Low but Ending High."

46. Stern and Stafford, "Individual and Social Determinants of Winning Bids in Online Auctions"; Ku, Galinsky, and Murnighan, "Starting Low but Ending High."

47. David Lucking-Reiley, Doug Bryan, Naghi Prasad, and Daniel Reeves, "Pennies from eBay: The Determinants of Price in Online Auctions," *Journal of Industrial Economics*, forthcoming.

48. Uri Simonsohn and Dan Ariely, "eBay's Happy Hour: Non-Rational Herding in Online Auctions," unpublished manuscript.

49. Tanjim Hossain and John Morgan, " ... Plus Shipping and Handling: Revenue (Non) Equivalence in Field Experiments on eBay," *Advances in Economic Analysis and Policy* 6, no. 2 (2006), Article 3; eBay, "Tips for Successful Selling," http://pages.ebay.com/help/sell/seller-tips.html (accessed January 7, 2010).

50. Jeffrey A. Livingston, "How Valuable Is a Good Reputation? A Sample Selection Model of Internet Auctions," *Review of Economics and Statistics* 87, no. 3 (2005), pp. 453–65; Steven T. Anderson, Daniel Friedman, Garrett H. Daniel, and Nirvikar Singh, "Seller Strategies on eBay," April 2004, UC Santa Cruz Economics Working Paper No. 564.

51. This case was written by Elisabeth Nevins Caswell with the textbook authors, Dhruv Grewal and Michael Levy, as a basis for class discussion rather than to illustrate effective or ineffective marketing practices. See Matthew Futterman, "Yankees Slash Prices to Fill Costly Seats at New Park," *The Wall Street Journal*, April 29, 2009; Darren Rovell, "Exclusive: Yankee Ticket Prices Coming Down for the '10 Season,'" *CNBC.com*, September 15, 2009, http://www.cnbc.com/id/32867126 (accessed January 7, 2009); *The Stadium Insider*, "Yankees Sneak In a Price Increase on Bleacher Seats for 2010 Partial Plan Season Tickets," November 28, 2009, http://newstadiuminsider.blogspot.com/2009/11/yankees-sneak-in-price-increase-on.html (accessed January 7, 2010); New York Yankees, "Stadium Seating and Prices," http://newyork.yankees.mlb.com/nyy/ballpark/seating_pricing.jsp (accessed January 7, 2010); New York Yankees, "Spring Training Tickets," http://newyork.yankees.mlb.com/spring_training/tickets.jsp?c_id=nyy (accessed January 7, 2010); StubHub, "Los Angeles Angels at New York Yankee Tickets, April 13, 2010," http://www.stubhub.com/new-york-yankees-tickets/yankees-vs-angels-4-13-2010-898392/?isGen2Event=1 (accessed January 7, 2010).

## Chapter 14

1. Mary Pilon, "Finding Group Discounts Online," *The Wall Street Journal*, August 11, 2009.

2. Jessica Shambora, "Merchants Think Socially, Act Locally," *CNNMoney.com*, December 11, 2009.

3. Based on information from Bespoke Cuisine website, http://www.bespokecuisine.com/cooking-parties/index.php (accessed May 2, 2010).

4. Harald Van Heerde, Els Gijsbrecht, and Koen Pauwels, "Winners and Losers in a Major Price War," *Journal of Marketing Research* 45 (October 2008), pp. 499–518.

5. Thomas T. Nagle and Reed K. Holden, *The Strategy and Tactics of Pricing*, 3rd ed. (Upper Saddle River, NJ: Pearson, 2002).

6. Joe Ferrantegennaro, owner, The Bath & Kitchen Gallery, personal communication, January 20, 2010; Sydney Loney, "Kitchen Trends 2010," *StyleatHome.com*; Sally Beatty, "Avoid These Now-Popular Home Design Trends in 2006," *The Wall Street Journal*, January 3, 2006.

7. Kristina Shampanier, Nina Mazar, and Dan Ariely, "Zero as a Special Price: The True Value of Free Products," *Marketing Science* 26, no. 6 (2007), pp. 742–57; Sucharita Chandran and Vicki G. Morvitz, "The Price of 'Free'-dom: Consumer Sensitivity to Promotions with Negative Contextual Influences," *Journal of Consumer Research* 33, no. 4 (2006), pp. 384–92; E. Shafir and R. H. Thaler, "Invest Now, Drink Later, Spend Never: On the Mental Accounting of Delayed Consumption," *Journal of Economic Psychology* 27 (2006), pp. 694–712; Lisa E. Bolton, Luk Warlop, and Joseph W. Alba, "Consumer Perceptions of Price (Un)Fairness," *Journal of Consumer Research* 29 (March 2003), pp. 474–91; Peter R. Darke and Darren W. Dahl, "Fairness and Discounts: The Subjective Value of a Bargain," *Journal of Consumer Psychology* 13, no. 3 (2003), pp. 328–38; Margaret C. Campbell, "Perceptions of Price Unfairness: Antecedents and Consequences," *Journal of Marketing Research* 36 (May 1999), pp. 187–99; Sarah Maxwell, "What Makes a Price Increase Seem 'Fair'?" *Pricing Strategy & Practice* 3, no. 4 (1995), pp. 21–27.

8. Michael Levy and Barton A. Weitz, *Retailing Management,* 8th ed. (Burr Ridge, IL: Irwin/McGraw-Hill, 2012).

9. John Seabrook, "The Price of the Ticket: What Does It Take to Get to See Your Favorite Band?" *The New Yorker,* August 10, 2009, pp. 34–42.

10. http://www.examiner.com/x-35971-New-Kids-on-the-Block -Examiner~y2010m1d15-American-Express-Contest-and-Pre -sale-details-for-NKOTB-at-Radio-City-Music-Hall (accessed April 9, 2010); Jessica Mador, "Big Acts Make Case for Revisiting Ticket Scalping Rules,"Minnesota Public Radio, November 20, 2009; David Burke, "Tickets to Taylor Swift Concert Sell Out in 10 minutes," *QuadCity Times,* November 6, 2009; Ethan Smith, "Hannah Montana Battles the Bots," *The Wall Street Journal,* October 5, 2007.

11. Dawn C. Chmielewski, Ben Fritz, and Randy Lewis, "Ticketmaster-Live Nation Merger Gets Justice Department's Approval," *LA Times,* January 26, 2010.

12. Geoffrey A. Fowler and Yukari Iwatani Kane, "New Mobile Applications Use Bar-Code Scanners," *The Wall Street Journal,* December 16, 2009; Big In Japan, http://www.biggu.com/.

13. Robert Schindler, "The 99 Price Ending as a Signal of a Low-Price Appeal," *Journal of Retailing* 82, no. 1 (2006).

14. Ibid.

15. Dhruv Grewal, Kent B. Monroe, and R. Krishnan, "The Effects of Price Comparison Advertising on Buyers' Perceptions of Acquisition Value and Transaction Value," *Journal of Marketing* 62 (April 1998), pp. 46–60.

16. Dhruv Grewal and Anne Roggeveen, "Decomposing the Intricate Role of Price, Quality, and Value Relationships," *Legends in Marketing Series: Kent B. Monroe: The Price-Quality-Value Relationship,* Volume 3, Dhruv Grewal and Anne Roggeveen, eds. (New Delhi: Sage, forthcoming).

17. Vanessa O'Connell, "It's 50% Off … Well, Maybe 35%; How Good Are Deals on Members' Only Web Sites?" *The Wall Street Journal,* January 16, 2010; www.hautelook.com (accessed January 20, 2010); www.gilt.com (accessed February 1, 2010).

18. http://www.brooksbrothers.com/IWCatSectionView. process?IWAction=Load&Merchant_Id=1&Section_Id=663 (accessed April 9, 2010).

19. Jyoti Thottam Pune and Niljanjana Bhowmick, "Nano Power," *Time,* April 13, 2009.

20. Eric A. Staub, "As Prices Fall, Blu-Ray Players Are Invited Home," *The New York Times,* December 13, 2009.

21. Amol Sharma, "AT&T's Bet on the iPhone," *The Wall Street Journal,* June 10, 2008.

22. This section draws from Levy and Weitz, *Retailing Management.*

23. Sha Yang and Priya Raghubir, "Can Bottles Speak Volumes? The Effect of Package Shape on How Much to Buy," *Journal of Retailing,* 81, no. 4 (2005), pp. 269–281.

24. This section is adapted from Levy and Weitz, *Retailing Management.*

25. Personal communication with Rob Price, VP of Retail Marketing, CVS, June 16, 2009.

26. http://www.leasingluxurylifestyles.com/category/press/ (accessed January 16, 2010); http://bagborroworsteal.com (accessed January 16, 2010); Alice Park, "The Leasing Life," *Time,* April 1, 2007.

27. Marco Bertini and Luc Wathieu, "Research Note: Attention Arousal through Price Partitioning," *Marketing Science* 27, no. 2 (2008), pp. 236–46; Rebecca W. Hamilton and Joydeep Srivastava, "When 2+2 Is Not the Same as 1+3: Variations in Price Sensitivity across Components of Partitioned Prices," *Journal of Marketing Research* 45, no. 4 (2008), pp. 450–61.

28. Alison Jing Xu and Robert S. Wyer, Jr., "Puffery in Advertisements: The Effects of Media Context, Communication Norms and Consumer Knowledge," *Journal of Consumer Research,* August 2010.

29. "Tesco Rapped Over 'Misleading' Price Claims," *Sky News,* July 29, 2009; www.asa.org.uk/ (accessed April 9, 2010).

30. Joan Lindsey-Mullikin and Ross D. Petty, "Marketing Tactics Discouraging Price Search: Deception and Competition," *Journal of Business Research,* (forthcoming). DOI: 10.1016/ j.jbusres.2009.10.003. Larry Compeau, Joan Lindsey–Mullikin, Dhruv Grewal, and Ross Petty, "An Analysis of Consumers' Interpretations of the Semantic Phrases Found in Comparative Price Advertisements," *Journal of Consumer Affairs* 38 (Summer 2004), pp. 178–87; Larry D. Compeau, Dhruv Grewal, and Diana S. Grewal, "Adjudicating Claims of Deceptive Advertised Reference Prices: The Use of Empirical Evidence," *Journal of Public Policy & Marketing* 14 (Fall 1994), pp. 52–62; Dhruv Grewal and Larry D. Compeau, "Comparative Price Advertising: Informative or Deceptive?" *Journal of Public Policy & Marketing* 11 (Spring 1992), pp. 52–62.

31. Maria Sciullo, "Will Price War Hurt Independent Bookstores," *Pittsburgh Post-Gazette,* October 27, 2009.

32. Uwe E. Reinhardt, "Ending Hospital Price Discrimination against the Uninsured," *The New York Times,* January 8, 2010.

33. Daniel M. Garrett, Michelle Burtis and Vandy Howell, "Economics of Antitrust: An Economic Analysis of Resale Price Maintenance," www.GlobalCompetitionReview.com (2008); Stephen Labaton, "Century-Old Ban Lifted on Minimum Retail Pricing," *The New York Times,* June 29, 2007 (accessed electronically January 25, 2008).

34. "South African Airlines to Be Investigated for Alleged World Cup Price-Fixing," Report DialAFlight, *Business Wire,* February 1, 2010.

35. Garrett, Burtis, and Howell, "Economics of Antitrust"; Labaton, "Century-Old Ban Lifted on Minimum Retail Pricing."

36. This case was written by Kate Woodworth and Britt Hackmann, Babson College in conjunction with the textbook authors (Dhruv Grewal and Michael Levy) as the basis of class discussion rather than to illustrate either effective or ineffective marketing practice. Douglas A. McIntyre, "The Cellular Market in the US Is Saturated," *wallst.com,* April 23, 2010.

37. Verizon website, http://aboutus.vzw.com/aboutusoverview .html (accessed May 2, 2010).

38. AT&T website, "Company Overview," http://www.att.com/gen/ investor-relations?pid=5711, "Key Facts About AT&T," http:// www.att.com/gen/investor-relations?pid=5711, "Corporate History," http://www.att.com/gen/investor-relations?pid=5711 (all accessed May 2, 2010).

39. Sprint Nextel website, "About Sprint Nextel," http://www2 .sprint.com/mr/aboutsprint.do (accessed May 2, 2010).

40. "Price War: Verizon Wireless Cuts Pricing for Unlimited Talk, Text Plans; AT&T Cuts, Too," *About.com,* January 18, 2010.

41. Tim Conneally, "Sprint on the Wireless Price War: We Were Already Cheaper!" *betanews.com,* http://www.betanews.com/ article/Sprint-on-the-wireless-price-war-We-were-already -cheaper/1263944727 (accessed January 19, 2010).

42. "Price War: Following Changes at Verizon Wireless, AT&T, U.S. Cellular Offers Unlimited Calling Plans," http://cellphones.

about.com/b/2010/01/19/price-war-following-changes-at-verizon-wireless-att-u-s-cellular-offers-unlimited-calling-plans.htm (accessed January 19, 2010).

43. Andrew Berg, "U.S. Cellular Joins Price War," *wirelessweek.com*, http://www.wirelessweek.com/News/2010/01/Carriers-Price-War-US-Cellular/ (accessed January 20, 2010).

44. Ellen Goldberg, "Verizon, AT&T Locked in Price War," http://www.nbcdfw.com/news/tech/Verizon-and-ATT-Locked-in-Price-War-81820412.html (accessed January 15, 2010).

45. Olga Kharif, "Verizon Wireless–AT&T 'Price War' May Boost Revenues," *Bloomberg Businessweek*, January 20, 2010.

## Chapter 15

1. Zeynep Ton, Elena Corsi, and Vincent Dessain, "Zara: Managing Stores for Fast Fashion," Harvard Business School, March 2011.

2. Kasra Ferdows, Michael A. Lewis, Jose A. D. Machuca, "Rapid-Fire Fulfillment," *Harvard Business Review*, November 2004.

3. "Combining Art with Science, Zara Competes with 'Fast Fashion,'" *SupplyChainBrain*, February 7, 2008.

4. Ibid.; Ferdows et al., "Rapid-Fire Fulfillment."

5. Felipe Caro, Jérémie Gallien, Miguel Díaz Miranda, Javier García Torralbo, Jose Manuel Corrediora Corras, Marcos Montes Vazques, José Antonio Ramos Calamonte, Juan Correa, "Zara Uses Operations Research to Reengineer Its Global Distribution Process," *Interfaces*, 2010, 40, pp. 71–84.

6. Ibid.; "Combining Art with Science."

7. This chapter draws from Michael Levy and Barton A. Weitz, *Retailing Management*, 8th ed. (Burr Ridge, IL: McGraw-Hill/Irwin, 2012).

8. Based on David Simchi-Levi, Philip Kaminsky, and Edith Simchi-Levi, *Designing and Managing the Supply Chain: Concepts, Strategies and Case Studies*, 2nd ed. (New York: McGraw-Hill Irwin, 2003); and Levy and Weitz, *Retailing Management*. Key components involved in SCM definitions are available in James R. Stock, Stefanie L. Boyer, and Tracy Harmon, "Research Opportunities in Supply Chain Management," *Journal of the Academy of Marketing Science* 38, no. 1 (2010), pp. 32–41. Also see articles in special issue edited by John T. Mentzer and Greg Gundlach, "Exploring the Relationship between Marketing and Supply Chain Management: Introduction to the Special Issue," *Journal of the Academy of Marketing Science* 38, no. 1 (2010), pp. 1–4.

9. http://www.marketingpower.com/_layouts/Dictionary.aspx?dLetter=M (accessed April 12, 2010).

10. http://www.marketingpower.com/_layouts/Dictionary.aspx, accessed August 15, 2010.

11. Terry L. Esper, Alexander Ellinger, Theodore Stank, Daniel Flint, and Mark Moon, "Demand and Supply Integration: a Conceptual Framework of Value Creation through Knowledge Management," *Journal of the Academy of Marketing Science* 38, no. 1 (2010), pp. 5–18.

12. http://www.marketingpower.com/_layouts/Dictionary.aspx.

13. Ibid.

14. Jean Thilmany, "Neiman Marcus Sails through Customs," *Apparel Magazine* 49, no. 2 (2007).

15. Vanessa O'Connell and Peter Latman, "Neiman Enlists Designers in Cost-Cutting Plan," *The Wall Street Journal*, December 10, 2009.

16. Matthew Waller, Brent Williams, Andrea Tangari, and Scot Burton, "Marketing at the Retail Shelf: An Examination of Moderating Effects of Logistics on SKU Market Share," *Journal of the Academy of Marketing Science* 38, no. 1 (2010), pp. 105–17.

17. Anthony Coia, "How Cabela's Is Maximizing Fulfillment Efficiency," *Apparel Magazine* 46, no. 10 (June 2005).

18. http:// http://www.vendormanagedinventory.com/ (accessed April 12, 2010).

19. G. P. Kiesmüller and R. A. C. M. Broekmeulen, "The Benefit of VMI Strategies in a Stochastic Multi-Product Serial Two Echelon System," *Computers and Operations Research* 37, no. 2 (2010), pp. 406–16; Dong-Ping Song and John Dinwoodie, "Quantifying the Effectiveness of VMI and Integrated Inventory Management in a Supply Chain with Uncertain Lead-Times and Uncertain Demands," *Production Planning & Control* 19, no. 6 (2008), pp. 590–600; S. P. Nachiappan, A. Gunasekaran, and N. Jawahar, "Knowledge Management System for Operating Parameters in Two-Echelon VMI Supply Chains," *International Journal of Production Research* 45, no. 11 (2007), pp. 2479–505; Andres Angulo, Heather Nachtmann, and Matthew A. Waller, "Supply Chain Information Sharing in a Vendor Managed Inventory Partnership," *Journal of Business Logistics* 25 (2004), pp. 101–20.

20. R. Glenn Richey, Mert Tokman, and Vivek Dalela, "Examining Collaborative Supply Chain Service Technologies: A Study of Intensity, Relationships, and Resources," *Journal of the Academy of Marketing Science* 38, no. 1 (2010), pp. 77–89; Katerina Pramatari, Theodoros Evgeniou, and Georgios Doukidis, "Implementation of Collaborative E-Supply-Chain Initiatives: An Initial Challenging and Final Success Case from Grocery Retailing," *Journal of Information Technology* 24 (September 2009), pp. 269–81; Kazim Sari, "On the Benefits of CPFR and VMI: A Comparative Simulation Study," *International Journal of Production Economics* 113, no. 2 (2008), pp. 575–86; Mohsen Attaran and Sharmin Attaran, "Collaborative Supply Chain Management: The Most Promising Practice for Building Efficient and Sustainable Supply Chains," *Business Process Management Journal* 13, no. 3 (2007), pp. 390–404; http://www.ediuniversity.com/glossary (accessed January 8, 2008); Mark Barratt, "Positioning the Role of Collaborative Planning in Grocery Supply Chains," *International Journal of Logistics Management* 14 (2003), pp. 53–67.

21. Lingxziu Dong and Kaijie Zhu, "Two-Wholesale-Price Contracts: Push, Pull and Advance-Purchase Discount Contracts," *Manufacturing & Service Operations Management* 9, no. 3 (2007), pp. 291–311; Hyun-Soo Ahn and Philip Kaminsky, "Production and Distribution Policy in a Two-Stage Stochastic Push-Pull Supply Chain," *IIE Transactions* 37, no. 7 (2005), pp. 609–21; W. Masuchun, S. Davis, and J. Patterson, "Comparison of Push and Pull Control Strategies for Supply Network Management in a Make-to-Stock Environment," *International Journal of Production Research* 42, no. 20 (2004), pp. 4401–20.

22. David Maloney, "Home Depot's Supply Chain Remodel," *DCVelocity*, August 1, 2009, http://www.dcvelocity.com/print/article/20090801verticalfocus/.

23. Dan Gilmore, "Aggressive Supply Chain Transformation at Home Depot," *SupplyChainDigest*, June 11, 2009.

24. "Home Depot Nearly Done with Supply Chain Overhaul," *The Journal of Commerce Online*, March 19, 2010.

25. Mary Catherine O'Connor, "American Apparel Makes a Bold Fashion Statement with RFID," *RFID Journal*, April 14, 2008.

26. Claire Swedberg, "American Apparel Adds RFID to Two More Stores, Switches RFID Software," *RFID Journal*, January 12, 2010.

27. Ibid.

28. O'Connor, "American Apparel Makes a Bold Fashion Statement with RFID."

29. http://seekingalpha.com/article/194466-rfid-technology -transforming-food-retailers-like-wal-mart (accessed April 14, 2010).

30. http://www.scdigest.com/assets/On_Target/09-03-10-2.php (accessed April 13, 2010); Gary McWilliams, "Walmart's Radio-Tracked Inventory Hits Static," *The Wall Street Journal,* February 15, 2007, p. B1; Zeynep Ton, Vincent Dessain, and Monika Stachowiak-Joulain, "RFID at the Metro Group," Harvard Business School Publications, 9-606-053, November 9, 2005.

31. Michael Garry, "Supply Chain Systems Seen Boosting Tesco's U.S. Stores," *Supermarket News* 55, no. 43 (2007).

32. André Luís Shiguemoto and Vinícius Amaral Armentano, "A Tabu Search Procedure for Coordinating Production, Inventory and Distribution Routing Problems," *International Transactions in Operational Research* 17, no. 2 (2009), pp. 179–95; Ayse Akbalik, Sekoun Kebe, Bernard Penz, and Najiba Sbihi, "Exact Methods and a Heuristic for the Optimization of an Integrated Replenishment-Storage Planning Problem," *International Transactions in Operational Research* 15, no. 2 (March 2008), pp. 195–214.

33. UPS Supply Chain Solutions Case Study, "Adidas Goes for the Gold in Customer Service" (accessed electronically April 1, 2010).

34. http://www.marketingpower.com/live/mg-dictionary, accessed August 22, 2010.

35. http://www.franchise.org/Franchise-News-Detail.aspx? id=48106 (accessed April 12, 2010); http://www.census.gov/ marts/www/marts_current.pdf (accessed April 12, 2010).

36. 2010 Entrepreneur's Franchise 500 Rankings, http://www .entrepreneur.com/franchises/rankings/franchise500 -115608/2010,.html (accessed April 10, 2010).

37. Ton, Corsi, and Dessain, "Zara: Managing Stores for Fast Fashion."

38. CSRWire, "Gap Inc. Recognized as One of World's Most Ethical Companies for Fourth Year in a Row," *Earthtimes.org*, Press Release, August 2009, posted March 22, 2010.

39. Masha Zager, "Doing Well by Doing Good: Gap Inc.'s Social Responsibility Program," *Apparel Magazine*, August 13, 2009.

40. Lisa Scheer, Fred Miao, and Jason Garrett, "The Effects of Supplier Capabilities on Industrial Customers' Loyalty: The Role of Dependence," *Journal of the Academy of Marketing Science* 38, no. 1 (2010), pp. 90–104; Robert W. Palmatier, Rajiv Dant, and Dhruv Grewal, "A Longitudinal Analysis of Theoretical Perspectives of Interorganizational Relationship Performance," *Journal of Marketing* 71 (October 2007), pp. 172–94; Robert Palmatier, Rajiv Dant, Dhruv Grewal, and Kenneth Evans, "A Meta-Analysis on the Antecedents and Consequences of Relationship Marketing Mediators: Insight into Key Moderators," *Journal of Marketing* 70 (October 2006), pp. 136–53.

41. Donna Davis and Susan Golicic, "Gaining Comparative Advantage in Supply Chain Relationships: The Mediating Role of Market-Oriented IT Competence," *Journal of the Academy of Marketing Science* 38, no. 1 (2010), pp. 56–70; Beth Davis-Sramek, Richard Germain, and Karthik Iyer, "Supply Chain Technology: The Role of Environment in Predicting Performance," *Journal of the Academy of Marketing Science* 38, no. 1 (2010), pp. 42–55; Erin Anderson and Barton Weitz, "The Use of Pledges to Build and Sustain Commitment in Distribution Channels," *Journal of Marketing Research* 29 (February 1992), pp. 18–34.

42. This case was written by Jeanne L. Munger and Kate Woodworth in conjunction with the textbook authors (Dhruv Grewal and Michael Levy) as the basis of class discussion rather than to illustrate either effective or ineffective marketing practice. Jeanne Munger is an associate professor at the University of Southern Maine.

43. Mike Troy, "Wal-Mart's Inventory Equation," *Drugstore News*, September 11, 2006; "Financial Outlook: Restoring the Productivity Loop," *Retailing Today*, June 26, 2006.

44. Sharon Gaudin, "Some Suppliers Gain from Failed Wal-Mart RFID Edict," *Computer World*, April 28, 2008.

45. Stephanie Rosenbloom, "Wal-Mart Unveils Plan to Make Supply Chain Greener," *The New York Times*, February 26, 2010.

46. William B. Cassidy, "Wal-Mart Tightens the Chain," *The Journal of Commerce*, January 18, 2010.

## Chapter 16

1. Janice Bae, "A Chat with the Big Dizzle to the Lizzle," Smart shanghai.com, May 20, 2009, http://www.smartshanghai .com/blog/1290/Interview:_David_Laris.html (accessed March 15, 2010); Gary Bowerman, "Chef David Laris: Is There Anything He's Not Doing?" *CNNGO*, September 13, 2009, http://www .cnngo.com/shanghai/eat/chef-david-laris-there-anything -he-not-doing-272527 (accessed March 15, 2010); Mei Fong, "Revamping the Vamp: Mattel's New Shanghai's Barbie Store and Its Brand Challenge," *ChinaRealtime Report,* http://blogs. wsj.com/chinarealtime/2009/03/06/revamping-the-vamp -mattel%E2%80%99s-new-shanghai-barbie-store-and-its -brand-challenge/tab/article/ (accessed March 15, 2010); Anna Li, "Walking through Barbie Shanghai—The Brand's First Flagship Store Opening March 6, 2009," http://www.barbiemedia .com/admin/uploads/BarbieShanghaiStoreFeatures.pdf (accessed March 15, 2010); Marianne Wilson, "Retail Store of the Year: Barbie's Winning Dreamhouse," *Chain Store Age,* http:// www.chainstoreage.com/story.aspx?id=131829&type=print (accessed March 15, 2010).

2. "2009 Global Powers of Retail," Deloitte, http://public.deloitte. com/media/0460/2009GlobalPowersofRetail_FINAL2.pdf (accessed March 3, 2010).

3. This chapter draws heavily from Michael Levy and Barton A. Weitz, *Retailing Management*, 8th ed. (Burr Ridge, IL: McGraw-Hill/Irwin, 2012).

4. *Industry Outlook: Food Channel* (Columbus, OH: Retail Forward, July 2008); *Industry Outlook: Food Channel* (Columbus, OH: Retail Forward, April 2007).

5. http://supermarketnews.com/profiles/top25-2009/top-25/ (accessed March 3, 2010).

6. *Industry Outlook: Food Channel* (Columbus, OH: Retail Forward, July 2008). p. 23.

7. http://www.fmi.org/glossary/?search=Yes&letter=C (accessed March 3, 2010).

8. http://www.fmi.org/docs/facts_figs/grocerydept.pdf (accessed March 3, 2010).

9. http://www.tmcnet.com/usubmit/2007/10/13/3012485.htm (accessed March 3, 2010).

10. http://www.tmcnet.com/usubmit/2007/10/13/3012485.htm (accessed March 3, 2010).

11. Mary Gustafson, "Trader Joe's Remarkable Journey," *Private Label Buyer,* November 7, 2008, http://www.highbeam.com/doc/1G1-190851257.html (accessed March 15, 2010); Christopher Palmeri, "Trader Joe's Recipe for Success," *BusinessWeek,* February 21, 2008 (accessed electronically March 15, 2010); "Trader Joe's ... The Forgotten Supermarket Giant," *Brand Autopsy,* June 10, 2007 (accessed March 15, 2010); http://www.traderjoes.com (accessed March 14, 2010).

12. *Industry Outlook: Department Stores* (Columbus, OH: Retail Forward, June 2009).

13. *Industry Outlook: Mass Channel* (Columbus, OH: Retail Forward, June 2009).

14. Ibid.

15. http://walmartstores.com/AboutUs/7606.aspx (accessed March 3, 2010); *Industry Outlook: Mass Channel.*

16. *Industry Outlook: Drug Channel* (Columbus, OH: Retail Forward, December 2008).

17. *Industry Outlook: Dollar Stores* (Columbus, OH: Retail Forward, October 2008).

18. http://www.wikinvest.com/industry/Off-price_Retail (accessed March 3, 2010).

19. This section draws from Levy and Weitz, *Retailing Management,* chapter 2.

20. Nancy M. Pucinelli, Dhruv Grewal, Susan Andrzejewski, Ereni Markos, and Tracy Noga, "The Value of Knowing What Customers Really Want: Interpersonal Accuracy as an Environmental Cue," working paper (2010); Sylvie Morin, Laurette Dube, and Jean-Charles Chebat, "The Role of Pleasant Music in Servicescapes: A Test of the Dual Model of Environmental Perception," *Journal of Retailing* 83, no. 1 (2007), pp. 115–30; Liz C. Wang, Julie Baker, Judy A. Wagner, and Kirk Wakefield, "Can a Retail Web Site Be Social?" *Journal of Marketing* 71, no. 3 (July 2007), pp. 143–57; Julie Baker, A. Parasuraman, Dhruv Grewal, and Glenn Voss, "The Influence of Multiple Store Environment Cues on Perceived Merchandise Value and Patronage Intentions," *Journal of Marketing* 66, no. 2 (April 2001), pp. 120–41; Eric R. Spangenberg, Ayn E. Crowley, and Pamela W. Henderson, "Improving the Store Environment: Do Olfactory Cues Affect Evaluations and Behaviors?" *Journal of Marketing* 60, no. 2 (April 1996), pp. 67–80; Michael K. Hui and John E. G. Bateson, "Perceived Control and the Effects of Crowding and Consumer Choice on the Service Experience," *Journal of Consumer Research* 18 (September 1991), pp. 174–84.

21. Kathleen Seiders, Glenn B. Voss, Andrea L. Godfrey, and Dhruv Grewal, "SERVCON: A Multidimensional Scale for Measuring Perceptions of Service Convenience," *Journal of the Academy of Marketing Science* 35, no. 1 (2007), pp. 144–56; Leonard Berry, Kathleen Seiders, and Dhruv Grewal, "Understanding Service Convenience," *Journal of Marketing* 66, no. 3 (July 2002).

22. http://fora.tv/2009/02/13/Weathering_the_Storm_Retail_Solutions_for_All_Seasons#Bag_Borrow_or_Steal_Fashion_Meets_Online_Innovation (accessed October 6, 2009); Paul Demery, "New Capital Wave," *InternetRetailer.com,* September 2008; Sarah Lacy, "The Tech Beat," *BusinessWeek,* March 7, 2006 (accessed electronically October 6, 2009); Kate M. Jackson, "Renting a Handful of Luxury," *Boston Globe,* October 13, 2005 (accessed electronically October 6, 2009); http://www.bagborroworsteal.com (accessed October 6, 2009).

23. Kenneth Hein, "Study: Web Research Nets In-Store Sales," *Brandweek,* May 7, 2007 (accessed electronically December 24, 2007).

24. Douglas MacMillan, "Amazon: Armed to Beat the Recession," *Businessweek.com,* December 9, 2008 (accessed March 15, 2010); Heather Green, "How Amazon Aims to Keep You Clicking," *BusinessWeek,* March 2, 2009 (accessed electronically March 15, 2010).

25. "Sponsored Supplement: Expanding the Reach of Personalization," *Internet Retailer,* March 2010.

26. Scott A. Neslin, Dhruv Grewal, Robert Leghorn, Venkatesh Shankar, Marije L. Teerling, Jacquelyn S. Thomas, and Peter C. Verhoef, "Challenges and Opportunities in Multichannel Customer Management," *Journal of Service Research* 9, no. 2 (2006), pp. 95–112.

27. Randolph E. Bucklin and Catarina Sismeiro, "Click Here for Internet Insight: Advances in Clickstream Data Analysis in Marketing," *Journal of Interactive Marketing* (February 2009), pp. 35–48.

28. Tomas Falk, Jeroen Schepers, Maik Hammerschmidt, and Hans Bauer, "Identifying Cross-Channel Dissynergies for Multichannel Service Providers," *Journal of Service Research* 10, no. 2 (2007), pp. 143–55; David W Wallace, Joan L. Giese, and Jean L. Johnson, "Customer Retailer Loyalty in the Context of Multiple Channel Strategies," *Journal of Retailing* 80, no. 4 (2004), pp. 249–63.

29. Maria Halkias, "Catalogs Make Paper Trails to Retailers," *The Dallas Morning News,* October 9, 2006 (accessed electronically December 24, 2007).

30. Jayne O'Donnell, "Are Retailers Going Too Far Tracking Our Web Habits?" *USA Today,* October 26, 2009.

31. http://www.lsoft.com/resources/optinlaws.asp (accessed March 14, 2010).

32. http://www.ftc.gov/bcp/edu/pubs/business/ecommerce/bus28.shtm (accessed March 14, 2010).

33. Ibid.; Jill Avery, Thomas J. Steenburgh, John Deighton, and Mary Caravella, "Adding Bricks to Clicks: The Contingencies Driving Cannibalization and Complementarity in Multichannel Retailing," *SSRN working paper* (2009), http:\\ssrn.com\abstract=961567.

34. J. C. Williams Group, "Organizing for Cross-Channel Retailing," white paper, Toronto, January 2008; IBM Global Business Services, "Customer Centricity Drives Retail's Multichannel Imperative," white paper, Armonk, NY, 2008.

35. Jie Zhang, Paul Farris, John Irvin, Tarun Kushwaha, Thomas Steenburgh, and Barton Weitz, "Crafting Integrated Multichannel Retailing Strategies," *Journal of Interactive Marketing,* 2010.

36. This case was written by Jeanne L. Munger (University of Southern Maine) and Britt Hackmann (Babson College) in conjunction with the textbook authors Dhruv Grewal and Michael Levy as the basis of class discussion rather than to illustrate either effective or ineffective marketing practice. The authors thank Max Ward, vice president of technology at Staples, who provided valuable input for the development of this case. They also acknowledge that parts of the case are based on information provided by W. Caleb McCann (in collaboration with J. P. Jeannet, Dhruv Grewal, and Martha Lanning), "Staples," in *Fulfillment in E-Business,* eds. Petra Schuber, Ralf Wolfle, and Walter Dettling (Germany: Hanser, 2001), pp. 239–52 (in German).

37. "Office Supply Stores in the US—Industry Report," *IBIS World,* March 23, 2010.

38. http://www.staplescontract.com/stapleslinktour/index.asp (accessed April 6, 2010).

39. 2008 Staples Annual Report (accessed electronically March 23, 2010).

40. Interview with Staples' Vice President of Stores Demos Parneros and Executive Vice President of Merchandising and Marketing Jevin Eagle, June 21, 2009.

## Chapter 17

1. "To Launch Its New Fiery Grilled Wings, KFC Unveils First-Ever Hydrant and Extinguisher Sponsorship Program," January 6, 2010, http://www.kfc.com/about/newsroom/010610.asp (accessed March 20, 2010).

2. "KFC Markets 'Fiery' Wings on Fire Hydrants," *USA Today,* January 6, 2010, http://www.usatoday.com/money/advertising/2010 -01-06-kfc-ads-on-hydrants_N.htm (accessed March 20, 2010).

3. Terence A. Shimp, *Advertising Promotion and Other Aspects of Integrated Marketing Communication,* 8th ed. (Mason, OH: South-Western College Publishers, 2008); T. Duncan and C. Caywood, "The Concept, Process, and Evolution of Integrated Marketing Communication," in *Integrated Communication: Synergy of Persuasive Voices,* eds. E. Thorson and J. Moore (Mahwah, NJ: Lawrence Erlbaum Associates, 1996); see also various issues of the *Journal of Integrated Marketing Communications,* http://jimc.medill.northwestern.edu.

4. Shimp, *Advertising Promotion;* Deborah J. MacInnis, Christine Moorman, and Bernard J. Jaworski, "Enhancing and Measuring Consumers' Motivation, Opportunity," *Journal of Marketing* 55, no. 4 (October 1991), pp. 32–53; Joan Meyers-Levy, "Elaborating on Elaboration: The Distinction between Relational and Item-Specific Elaboration," *Journal of Consumer Research* 18 (December 1991), pp. 358–67.

5. Giselle Tsirulnik, "Macy's Mobilized Print Ad Lets Consumers Tap-to-Buy Merchandise," *Mobilemarketer.com,* May 27, 2010.

6. E. K. Strong, *The Psychology of Selling* (New York: McGraw Hill, 1925).

7. Belinda Luscombe, "How Disney Builds Stars," *Time,* November 2, 2009; http://disney.com.

8. John Philip Jones, "What Makes Advertising Work?" *The Economic Times,* July 24, 2002.

9. http://www.legamedia.net/lx/result/match/0591dfc9787c111 b1b24dde6d61e43c5/index.php, accessed August 23, 2010.

10. Zack Newmark, "Mercedes SLS AMG Integrated Marketing Campaign Outlined," January 28, 2010, http://www.worldcarfans .com/110012824265/mercedes-sls-amg-integrated-marketing -campaign-outlined (accessed March 24, 2010).

11. Chris Barrows, "Unauthorized Verses," *Journal of Integrated Marketing Communication* (Evanston, IL: Northwestern University, 2009).

12. American Marketing Association, *Dictionary of Marketing Terms* (Chicago: American Marketing Association, 2008).

13. American Academy of Child and Adolescent Psychiatry, "Obesity in Children and Teens," http://www.aacap.org/cs/ root/facts_for_families/obesity_in_children_and_teens (accessed March 29, 2010).

14. Bonnie Rochman, "Sweet Spot: How Sugary-Cereal Makers Target Kids," *Time,* November 2, 2009; "The Impact of Food Marketing on Children," http://www.yaleruddcenter.org/ what_we_do.aspx?id=24 (accessed March 29, 2010).

15. http://www.millsberry.com; http://www.jellyneo.net/index .php?go=cocoapuffscross, accessed August 23, 2010.

16. Smart Choices website, http://www.smartchoicesprogram .com/nutrition.html (accessed May 25, 2010).

17. Bonnie Rochman, "The Sugary Brands Doing the Most Kid-Chasing," http://www.time.com/time/specials/packages/ article/0,28804,1931891_1931889_1931865,00.html (October 23, 2009).

18. Marion Nestle, "About Marion Nestle," http://www.foodpolitics .com/about/ (accessed May 25, 2010).

19. Marion Nestle, "General Mills' Big News: Less Sugar," *Food Politics,* December 11, 2009, http://www.foodpolitics.com/tag/ cereals/ (accessed March 29, 2010).

20. http://online.wsj.com/article/SB100014240527487034810045 74646904234860412.html; George E. Belch and Michael A. Belch, *Advertising and Promotion: An Integrated Marketing Communications Perspective* (New York: McGraw-Hill, 2007).

21. Rebecca Lieb, "Q&A: Cindy Krum Cuts through the Mobile Marketing Alphabet Soup of NFC and RFID," http:// econsultancy.com/blog/5608-q-a-cindy-krum-cuts-through -the-mobile-marketing-alphabet-soup-of-nfc-and-rfid (accessed March 16, 2010).

22. Akihisa Fujita, "Mobile Marketing in Japan: The Acceleration of Integrated Marketing Communications," *Journal of Integrated Marketing Communications* (2008), pp. 41–46; Mobile update: http://www.businessinsider.com/henry-blodget-enough- empty-headed-puffery-about-mobile-ads-time-for-ana- lysts-to-stop-jawboning-and-think-2009-10; http://www .informationweek.com/news/security/privacy/showArticle .jhtml?articleID=222300256&subSection=News; http://www .nearbynow.com/info/iphone_platform.html (accessed May 26, 2010).

23. Emily Steel, "How Marketers Hone Their Aim Online," *The Wall Street Journal,* June 19, 2007.

24. Fareena Sulta and Andrew J. Rohm, "How to Market to Generation M(obile)," *MITSloan Management Review,* Summer 2008.

25. Shane Snow, "Inside Foursquare: Checking In before the Party Started (Part 1)," *Wired,* http://www.wired.com/epicenter/ 2010/05/inside-foursquare-checking-in-before-the-party -started-part-i/3/ (accessed May 24, 2010).

26. Foursquare website, http://foursquare.com/ (accessed May 27, 2010).

27. Ludovic Privat, "When Cliché Becomes Reality: Starbucks Coupons for Foursquare Mayors," http://www.gpsbusinessnews .com/When-Cliche-Becomes-Reality-Starbucks-Coupons-for -Foursquare-Mayors_a2265.html (accessed May 26, 2010).

28. Leena Rao, "WeReward's iPhone App Lets You Earn Case for Check-Ins," http://techcrunch.com/2010/05/25/werewards -iphone-app-lets-you-earn-cash-for-check-ins/#ixzz0pAu7dIKz (accessed May 25, 2010).

29. Mobile Outlook 2010, Mobile Marketer, February 4, 2010.

30. "New Trend in Social Networking Could Be Open Invitation to Criminals," http://www.prnewswire.com/news-releases/ geolocation-apps-and-social-networks-can-be-a-dangerous -combo-94918019.html (accessed May 26, 2010).

31. "Number of Cell Phones Worldwide Hits 4.6 Billion," *CBS News,* February 15, 2010, http://www.cbsnews.com/stories/ 2010/02/15/business/main6209772.shtml.

32. Rochman, "Sweet Spot: How Sugary-Cereal Makers Target Kids."

33. www.blogsouthwest.com (accessed June 7, 2010).

34. Chris Lee, "Kevin Smith's Southwest Incident Sets Web All A-Twitter," *Los Angeles Times,* February 16, 2010, http://articles.latimes.com/2010/feb/16/entertainment/la-et-kevin-smith16-2010feb16 (accessed March 29, 2010).

35. Christi Day, "Not So Silent Bob," February 14, 2010, http://www.blogsouthwest.com/blog/not-so-silent-bob (accessed March 29, 2010).

36. Chrysanthos Dellarocas, "Strategic Manipulation of Internet Opinion Forums: Implications for Consumers and Firms," *Management Science* 52 (October 2006), pp. 1577–93; Liyun Jin, "Business Using Twitter, Facebook to Market Goods," *Pittsburgh Post-Gazette,* June 21, 2009.

37. "Brand Channels," YouTube, http://www.gstatic.com/youtube/engagement/platform/autoplay/advertise/downloads/YouTube_BrandChannels.pdf (accessed April 2010).

38. The Home Depot Branded Channel, http://www.youtube.com/user/homedepot?blend=2&ob=4#p/a (accessed April 2010).

39. *Forever 21 Facebook Fan Page,* http://www.facebook.com/#!/Forever21?ref=ts (accessed April 2010).

40. Ibid.

41. Wikipedia, http://en.wikipedia.org/wiki/Home_Shopping_Network (accessed May 26, 2010).

42. Ross Blum, "Where Have All the Customers Gone?" p. 8.

43. "In The Know," YouTube, http://www.gstatic.com/youtube/engagement/platform/autoplay/advertise/downloads/YouTube_InTheKnow.pdf (accessed Fall 2009).

44. "Brand Channels."

45. "YouTube Insight," YouTube, http://www.gstatic.com/youtube/engagement/platform/autoplay/advertise/downloads/YouTube_Insight.pdf (accessed April 2010).

46. Leah Shafer, "Re-Branding the Dynasty: Tori Spelling's HSN Clips on YouTube," http://mediacommons.futureofthebook.org/imr/2010/03/24/re-branding-dynasty-tori-spellings-hsn-clips-youtube (accessed March 25, 2010).

47. This section draws from Michael Levy and Barton A. Weitz, *Retailing Management,* 8th ed. (Burr Ridge, IL: McGraw-Hill/Irwin, 2012).

48. Megan Halscheid, Micheline Sabatté and Sejal Sura, "Beyond the Last Click: Measuring ROI and Consumer Engagement with Clickstream Analysis," *Journal of Integrated Marketing Communications* (2009), pp. 43–50; Vikram Mahidhar and Christine Cutten, "Navigating the Marketing Measurement Maze," *Journal of Integrated Marketing Communications* (2007), pp. 41–46.

49. http://www.riger.com/know_base/media/understanding.html (accessed November 15, 2004).

50. Halscheid et al., "Beyond the Last Click."

51. "Facebook Pages: Insights for Your Facebook Page," http://www.facebook.com/help/?search=insights#!/help/?faq=15221 (accessed April 2010).

52. "Marketing and Advertising Using Google," Google 2007.

53. http://publishing2.com/2008/05/27/google-adwords-a-brief-history-of-online-advertising-innovation/ (accessed June 1, 2008).

54. This case was written by Elisabeth Nevins Caswell in conjunction with the textbook authors, Dhruv Grewal and Michael Levy, as the basis of class discussion rather than to illustrate either effective or ineffective marketing practice. "Red Bull: The Stuff of Beverage Marketing Legends," *SOSE Marketing,* June 24, 2009, http://www.sosemarketing.com/

?p=351 (accessed March 29, 2010); "A Look at a Key Feature of Red Bull's Business," http://www.bized.co.uk/compfact/redbull/redbull7.htm (accessed March 29, 2010); Chris Wilson, "Insider's Look at Red Bull U," February 6, 2009, http://freshpeel.com/2009/02/insiders-look-at-red-bull-u/ (accessed March 29, 2010).

55. "A Look at a Key Feature."

56. "What Does a Student Brand Manager Do?" Red Bull University, http://www.redbullu.com/answer_what.php (accessed March 30, 2010).

# Chapter 18

1. Brittany Hite, "Deciding to Ditch a Successful Ad Campaign," *The Wall Street Journal,* February 23, 2009; http://www.eharmony.com/blog/2009/11/30/eharmony-launches-new-web-chat-advertising-campaign/ (accessed April 6, 2010).

2. Michelle Jeffers, "Behind Dove's 'Real Beauty,'" *Adweek,* September 12, 2005, http://www.allbusiness.com/marketing-advertising/4211506-1.html (accessed March 11, 2010).

3. Dove, http://dove.us/mencare/ (accessed March 11, 2010).

4. Elaine Wong, "Dove's SB Play Builds Buzz among Men," *Brandweek,* February 9, 2010.

5. Kellogg School of Management, "Kellogg Super Bowl Advertising Review 2010 Results," http://kelloggsuperbowlreview.wordpress.com/tag/dove/ (accessed March 11, 2010).

6. George E. Belch and Michael A. Belch, *Advertising and Promotion: An Integrated Marketing Communications Perspective* (New York: McGraw-Hill, 2007); Jef I. Richards and Catherine M. Curran, "Oracles on 'Advertising': Searching for a Definition," *Journal of Advertising* 31, no. 2 (Summer 2002), pp. 63–77.

7. "Global Advertising Downturn Slows Despite Disappointing Q1," http://www.zenithoptimedia.com/gff/pdf/Adspend%20forecasts%20July%202009.pdf (accessed March 11, 2010).

8. Dan Zigmond, Sundar Dorai-Raj, Yannet Interian, and Igor Naverniouk, "Measuring Advertising Quality on Television: Deriving Meaningful Metrics from Audience Retention Data," *Journal of Advertising Research* 49, no. 4 (December 2009), pp. 419–28; Robert G. Heath, Agnes C. Nairn, and Paul A. Bottomley, "How Effective Is Creativity? Emotive Content in TV Advertising Does Not Increase Attention," *Journal of Advertising Research* 49, no. 4 (December 2009), pp. 450–63; Raymond R. Burke and Thomas K. Srull, "Competitive Interference and Consumer Memory for Advertising," *Journal of Consumer Research* 15 (June 1988), pp. 55–68; Kevin Lane Keller, "Memory Factors in Advertising: The Effect of Advertising Retrieval Cues on Brand Evaluation," *Journal of Consumer Research* 14 (December 1987), pp. 316–33.

9. Markus Pfeiffer and Markus Zinnbauer, "Can Old Media Enhance New Media? How Traditional Advertising Pays Off for an Online Social Network," *Journal of Advertising Research* 50, no. 1 (2010), pp. 42–49; Terry Daugherty, Matthew Eastin, and Laura Bright, "Exploring Consumer Motivations for Creating User-Generated Content," *Journal of Interactive Advertising* 8, no. 2 (2008); Anthony Bianco, "The Vanishing Mass Market," *BusinessWeek,* July 12, 2004, pp. 61–68.

10. "Jewelry and Watch Report" (Stevens, PA: Unity Marketing, September 2007).

11. William F. Arens, Michael F. Weigold, and Christian Arens, *Contemporary Advertising,* 12th ed. (New York: McGraw-Hill, 2008).

12. Suzanne Vranica, "Grape Nuts Takes Aim at Men," *The Wall Street Journal,* March 26, 2009; Barry Newman, "No Grape, No Nuts, No Market Share: A Venerable Cereal Faces Crunch Time," *The Wall Street Journal,* June 1, 2009.

13. Tulin Erdem, Michael Keane, and Baohong Sun, "The Impact of Advertising on Consumer Price Sensitivity in Experience Goods Markets," *Quantitative Marketing and Economics* 6 (June 2008), pp. 139–76; Xiaojing Yang and Robert E. Smith, "Beyond Attention Effects: Modeling the Persuasive and Emotional Effects of Advertising Creativity," *Marketing Science* 28 (September/October 2009), pp. 935–49; Matthew Shum, "Does Advertising Overcome Brand Loyalty? Evidence from the Breakfast Cereal Market," *Journal of Economics and Management Strategy* 13, no. 2 (2004), pp. 77–85.

14. "Got Milk?" http://www.gotmilk.com/fun/ads.html (accessed March 11, 2010).

15. Elaine Wong, "Rebecca Romjin Makes Milk Run," *Brandweek,* January 13, 2010.

16. http://www.marketingpower.com/_layouts/Dictionary .aspx?dLetter=P (accessed April 6, 2010).

17. http://blog.cwtv.com/2009/01/23/gossip-girl-chace-crawford -stars-in-psa-campaign-for-teens-for-jeans/ (accessed April 22, 2010).

18. http://www.aad.org/media/psa/index.html (accessed April 22, 2010).

19. The Ad Council, "Historic Campaigns," http://www.adcouncil .org/default.aspx?id=61 (accessed April 5, 2010).

20. World Health Organization, http://www.wpro.who.int/media _centre/fact_sheets/fs_20020528.htm (accessed May 1, 2010).

21. Legacy website, http://www.legacyforhealth.org/PDF/truth _Fact_Sheet.pdf (accessed May 1, 2010).

22. Alina Tugend, "Cigarette Makers Take Anti-Smoking Ads Personally," *The New York Times,* October 27, 2002, Business section.

23. Theodore Leavitt, *The Marketing Imagination* (New York: The Free Press, 1986).

24. Belch and Belch, *Advertising and Promotion: An Integrated Marketing Communications Perspective.*

25. Exxon Mobil, http://www.exxonmobil.com/corporate/news _ad_corpus_clean.aspx (accessed March 14, 2010).

26. Katherine White and John Peloza, "Self-Benefit versus Other-Benefit Marketing Appeals: Their Effectiveness in Generating Charitable Support," *Journal of Marketing* 73 (July 2009), pp. 109–24.

27. Karl Greenberg, "Gillette Is 'Stayin' Alive' with Viral Effort," *Marketing Daily,* April 27, 2009.

28. Darren W. Dahl, Jaideep Sengupta, and Kathleen D. Vohs, "Sex in Advertising: Gender Differences and the Role of Relationship Commitment," *Journal of Consumer Research* 36, no. 2 (2009), pp. 215–31; Jaideep Sengupta and Darren W. Dahl, "Gender-Related Reactions to Gratuitous Sex Appeals in Advertising," *Journal of Consumer Psychology* 18, no. 1 (2008), pp. 62–78.

29. http://wps.prenhall.com/ca_ph_ebert_busess_3/0,6518,224378 –,00.html, accessed August 23, 2010.

30. http://www.adweek.com/aw/content_display/news/digital/ e3i87c96b4228796e1d5aa19258f0fb5703 (accessed April 7, 2010).

31. The following illustrative articles look at the effectiveness of a given media: "Robert Heath, Emotional Engagement: How Television Builds Big Brands at Low Attention," *Journal of Advertising Research* 49, no. 1 (March 2009), pp. 62–73; Lex van Meurs and Mandy Aristoff, "Split-Second Recognition: What Makes Outdoor Advertising Work?" *Journal of Advertising Research* 49, no. 1 (March 2009), pp. 82–92.

32. Arens, Weigold, and Arens, *Contemporary Advertising.*

33. http://adsoftheworld.com/media/print/buenos_aires_zoo _ape, accessed August 23, 2010.

34. Dean M. Krugman, Leonard N. Reid, S. Watson Dunn, and Arnold M. Barban, *Advertising: Its Role in Modern Marketing* (New York: The Dryden Press, 1994), pp. 221–26.

35. Herbert Jack Rotfeld and Charles R. Taylor, "The Need for Interdisciplinary Research of Advertising Regulation: A Roadmap for Avoiding Confusion and Errors," *Journal of Advertising,* Winter 2009.

36. Andrea Thompson, "Misleading Food Labels to Get Makeover," *MSNBC.com,* March 15, 2010, http://www.msnbc.msn.com/ id/35839186/ns/health-diet_and_nutrition/ (accessed March 15, 2010).

37. Debra Harker, Michael Harker, and Robert Burns, "Tackling Obesity: Developing a Research Agenda for Advertising Researchers," *Journal of Current Issues & Research in Advertising* 29, no. 2 (2007), pp. 39–51; N. Kapoor and D. P. S. Verma, "Children's Understanding of TV Advertisements: Influence of Age, Sex and Parents," *Vision* 9, no. 1 (2005), pp. 21–36; Catharine M. Curran and Jef I. Richards, "The Regulation of Children's Advertising in the U.S.," *The International Journal of Advertising and Marketing to Children* 2, no. 2 (2002).

38. http://advertising.utexas.edu/research/terms/index.asp#O (accessed May 12, 2008).

39. Bob Hunt, "Truth in Your Advertising: Avoid Puffery?" *Realty Times,* June 20, 2007.

40. Ashley Heher, "Our Pizza Didn't Taste Good, Domino's Says in New Ads," *Boston Globe,* January 12, 2010.

41. Hunt, "Truth in Your Advertising: Avoid Puffery?"

42. Christina Binkley, "Which Stars Sell Fashion?" *The Wall Street Journal,* February 4, 2010.

43. Diego Rinallo and Suman Basuroy, "Does Advertising Spending Influence Media Coverage of the Advertiser?" *Journal of Marketing* 73 (November 2009), pp. 33–46; Carl Obermiller and Eric R. Spangenberg, "On the Origin and Distinctness of Skepticism toward Advertising," *Marketing Letters* 11, no. 4 (2000), p. 311.

44. Jackie Huba, "A Just Cause Creating Emotional Connections with Customers," 2003, http://www.inc.com/articles/2003/ 05/25537.html.

45. http://www.createapepper.com (accessed March 14, 2010); http://causerelatedmarketing.blogspot.com/2008/03/how -chilis-used-cause-related-marketing.html (accessed March 14, 2010).

46. Personal communication with Rob Price, VP of Retail Marketing, CVS, June 16, 2009; Carol Angrisani, "CVS Moves to Personalization," *SN: Supermarket News* 56, no. 2 (March 24, 2008), p. 29.

47. Stephanie Clifford, "Web Coupons Know Lots about You, and They Tell," *The New York Times,* April 16, 2010.

48. http://sports.espn.go.com/espn/contests/index (accessed April 16, 2010).

49. https://www.stapleseasyrebates.com/img/staples/paperless/ pages/Landing.html (accessed April 7, 2010).

50. Eva A. van Reijmersdal, Peter C. Neijens, and Edith G. Smit, "A New Branch of Advertising: Reviewing Factors That Influence

Reactions to Product Placement," *Journal of Advertising Research* 49, no. 4 (December 2009), pp. 429–49; Pamela Mills Homer, "Product Placement: The Impact of Placement Type and Repetition on Attitude," *Journal of Advertising*, Fall 2009; Elizabeth Cowley and Chris Barron, "When Product Placement Goes Wrong: The Effects of Program Liking and Placement Prominence,"*Journal of Advertising*, Spring 2008.

51. Tom Lowry and Burt Helm, "Blasting Away at Product Placement," *BusinessWeek*, October 15, 2009.

52. www.jcrew.com (accessed April 23, 2010).

53. Hisashi Kurata and Xiaohang Yue, "Trade Promotion Mode Choice and Information Sharing in Fashion Retail Supply Chains," *International Journal of Production Economics* 114 (August 2008), pp. 507–19; Ronald Curhan and Robert Kopp, "Obtaining Retailer Support for Trade Deals: Key Success Factors," *Journal of Advertising Research* 27 (December 1987–January 1988), pp. 51–60.

54. This case was written by Elisabeth Nevins Caswell in conjunction with the textbook authors, Dhruv Grewal and Michael Levy, as the basis of class discussion rather than to illustrate either effective or ineffective marketing practice.

55. Guy Trebay, "She's Famous (and So Can You)," *The New York Times*, October 28, 2007; Lev Grossman, "Tila Tequila," *Time*, December 16, 2006.

56. http://statistics.allfacebook.com/pages (accessed April 15, 2010).

57. Trebay, "She's Famous (and So Can You)"; Grossman, "Tila Tequila."

58. http://www.facebook.com/help/?page=409 (accessed April 7, 2010); Elisabeth A. Sullivan, "Be Sociable," *Marketing News*, January 15, 2008.

59. Andrew LaVallee, "Burger King Cancels Facebook Ad Campaign," *The Wall Street Journal*, January 15, 2009.

## Chapter 19

1. Jessi Hempel, "IBM's All-Star Salesman: As Big Blue's Go-to Guy in Its Fastest-Growing Division in the Fastest-Growing Part of the World, Vivek Gupta Is Out to Sell You on a Very Big Idea," *Fortune Magazine*, September 26, 2008.

2. IBM Case Study, "Bharti Airtel: End-to-End Business Transformation Provides Flexibility for Rapid Growth," http://www-935.ibm.com/services/us/index.wss/casestudy/imc/a1008559?cntxt=a1000414 (accessed April 13, 2010).

3. "The IBM Sales Force: Then and Now," *Fortune Magazine*, September 26, 2008.

4. Joe Wilcox, "IBM Set to Launch New Product Strategy," *CNET News*, February 4, 2000.

5. U.S. Department of Labor, "Occupational Employment and Wages: Sales and Related Occupations," May 2008.

6. This section draws from Mark W. Johnston and Greg W. Marshall, *Relationship Selling*, 3rd ed. (Burr Ridge, IL: Irwin/McGraw-Hill, 2009); and Mark W. Johnston and Greg W. Marshall, *Relationship Selling and Sales Management*, 2nd ed. (Burr Ridge, IL: Irwin/McGraw-Hill, 2007).

7. Geoffrey James, "Selling Gets Complex," *Strategy+Business*, August 27, 2009; Dale Carnegie, *How to Win Friends and Influence People* (New York: Pocket, 1990); Neil Rackham, *SPIN Selling* (New York: McGraw-Hill, 1988).

8. http://www.workz.com/content/view_content.html?section_id=557&content_id=7086 (accessed April 7, 2010).

9. Bill Stinnett, *Think Like Your Customer* (Burr Ridge, IL: McGraw-Hill, 2004).

10. Steve Lohr, "As Travel Costs Rise, More Meetings Go Virtual," *The New York Times*, July 22, 2008.

11. Brad Grimes, "Have Web, Don't Travel," http://pcworld.about.com/magazine/1912p030id65174.htm (accessed April 16, 2010).

12. "Brainstorming Online: Thanks to Web Conferencing, a Chicago Design Firm Wins Clients Overseas and Saves on Travel," *BusinessWeek*, Fall 2005.

13. Joe Sharkey, "On the Road—New Meetings Industry Arises after Boom and Bust," *The New York Times*, February 1, 2010.

14. Pam Baker, "Best Sales Practices: Build Lasting Relationships," *CRM Buyer*, January 27, 2009.

15. Mark W. Johnston and Greg W. Marshall, *Relationship Selling*, 2nd ed. (Burr Ridge, IL: Irwin/McGraw-Hill, 2008).

16. Michael Levy and Barton A. Weitz, *Retailing Management*, 8th ed. (New York: McGraw-Hill/Irwin, 2011); http://www.cesweb.org/exhibitors/default.asp (accessed April 7, 2010).

17. Christine Comaford, "Sales Stuck? Try Sticking to a Script," *BusinessWeek*, April 4, 2008.

18. Christine Comaford-Lynch, "A Bad Lead Is Worse Than No Lead at All," *BusinessWeek*, March 26, 2008.

19. Eric Wilson, "Economy Adjusts Store Relations on Madison Avenue," *The New York Times*, February 18, 2009; Michael Levy, Arun Sharma, and Heiner Evanschitzky, "The Variance in Sales Performance Explained by the Knowledge Structures of Salespeople," *Journal of Personal Selling and Sales Management* 27, no. 2 (Spring 2007), pp. 169–82; Michael Levy and Arun Sharma, "Salespeople's Affect toward Customers: Why Should It Be Important for Retailers?" *Journal of Business Research* 56, no. 7 (July 2003), pp. 523–29; Michael Levy, Arun Sharma, and Ajith Kumar, "Knowledge Structures of Salespeople as Antecedents of Performance: A Comprehensive Test of Key Propositions," *Journal of Retailing* 76, no. 1 (Spring 2000), pp. 53–69.

20. Wilson, "Economy Adjusts Store Relations on Madison Avenue."

21. Eric Wilson, "'Luxury Stores' Personal Touch Is Extended to Holiday Shopper," *NYTimes.com*, December 21, 2009.

22. Barton A. Weitz, Harish Sujan, and Mita Sujan, "Knowledge, Motivation, and Adaptive Behavior: A Framework for Improving Selling Effectiveness," *Journal of Marketing*, October 1986, pp. 174–91.

23. Robert Keller, "Handling Objections in Today's Tough Environment, *SMM*, March 30, 2009.

24. http://www.quotedb.com/quotes/1303 (accessed April 15, 2008).

25. Mark W. Johnston and Greg W. Marshall, *Churchill/Ford/Walker's Sales Force Management*, 9th ed. (Burr Ridge, IL: McGraw-Hill/Irwin, 2009).

26. Jeremy Quittner, "The Art of the Soft Sell," *BWSSmallBiz—Sales*, October 9, 2009.

27. Ibid.; Rachel Emma Silverman, "Selling Girl Scout Cookies at the Office," *Wall Street Journal.com*, February 6, 2009.

28. "B2B Sales Pitching: Why Soft Selling Works," http://bx.businessweek.com/how-to-market-your-small-business/view?url=http%3A%2F%2Fblog.verticalresponse.com%2Fverticalresponse_blog%2F2010%2F04%2Fb2b-sales-pitch-educational-selling-vs-the-hard-sell.html (accessed April 6, 2010).

29. Susan Greco, "Personality Testing for Sales Recruits," *INC.*, March 1, 2009.

30. Johnston and Marshall, *Relationship Selling and Sales Management*, pp. 375–76; Johnston and Marshall, *Churchill/Ford/Walker's Sales Force Management*.

31. Rene Y. Darmon, "Where Do the Best Sales Force Profit Producers Come From?" *Journal of Personal Selling and Sales Management* 13, no. 3 (1993), pp. 17–29.

32. Julie Chang, "Born to Sell?" *Sales and Marketing Management,* July 2003, p. 36.

33. "Mary Kay: Where's the Money?" http://www.marykay.com (accessed September 5, 2006); http://www.Marykay.com/lsoulier; "Mary Kay Museum," www.addisontexas.net (accessed September 5, 2006).

34. Johnston and Marshall, *Relationship Selling and Sales Management*.

35. For a discussion of common measures used to evaluate salespeople, see Johnston and Marshall, *Churchill/Ford/Walker's Sales Force Management*.

36. David H. Holtzman, "Big Business Knows Us Too Well," *BusinessWeek,* June 22, 2007.

37. Johnston and Marshall, *Churchill/Ford/Walker's Sales Force Management*.

38. "Ethical Breach," *Sales & Marketing Management,* July 2004.

39. http://www.thepharmaletter.com/file/370eb820e9e3d7b0 76deb176fe7fca5f/usas-budget-office-reviews-promotional -spending-for-prescription-drugs.html (accessed April 8, 2010); http://www.plosmedicine.org/article/info:doi/10.1371/ journal.pmed.0050001 (accessed April 9, 2010); Erin Stout, "Doctoring Sales," *Salesandmarketing.com,* May 2001; "Pushing Pills, Pharmaceuticals," *The Economist* 366, no. 8311 (February 15, 2003), p. 65; R. Stephen Parker and Charles E. Pettijohn, "Ethical Considerations in the Use of Direct-to-Consumer Advertising and Pharmaceutical Promotions: The Impact on Pharmaceutical Sales and Physicians," *Journal of Business Ethics* 48, no. 3 (December 2, 2003), p. 279; "Pharmaceutical Sales Ethics: New Reforms or Business As Usual?" press release, July 23, 2004, http://www.medzilla.com/press72304.html (accessed September 26, 2006); Kate Moore and Jahi Harvey, "Drug Companies Push Pills to Doctors," *MorningJournal.com,* August 7, 2002.

40. This case was written by Jeanne Munger in conjunction with the textbook authors Dhruv Grewal and Michael Levy as the basis of class discussion rather than to illustrate either effective or ineffective marketing practice. For a discussion of common measures used to evaluate salespeople, see Johnston and Marshall, *Churchill/Ford/Walker's Sales Force Management*.

# credits

## Chapter 1

**Photos/ads**: p. 4, Ryan Anson/AFP Getty Images. p. 6, ©Procter & Gamble. p. 6, ©Guy Cali/Corbis. p. 8, Photo by Theo Wargo/WireImage for Clear Channel Radio New York. p. 8, ©M. Hruby. p. 9, Photo by Julian Finney/Getty Images. p. 9, AP Photo/The Canadian Press, Jacques Boissinot. p. 10, Courtesy The Ritz Carlton Hotel Company, LLC.; Agency: Team One/El Segundo, CA. p. 11, Courtesy The M. Network. p. 12, Photo by Paul Hawthorne/Getty Images. p. 13, Kim White/Bloomberg via Getty Images. p. 14, Courtesy National Fluid Milk Processor Promotion Board; Agency: Lowe Worldwide, Inc. p. 14, Used by Permission of Deutsch Inc. as Agent for National Fluid Milk Processor Promotion Board. p. 15, H.Armstrong Roberts/Retrofile/Getty Images. p. 15, Jamie Grill/Iconica/Getty Images. p. 15, ©Ted Dayton Photography/Beateworks/Corbis. p. 15, Ciaran Griffin/Stockbyte/Getty Images. p. 15, ©Colin Anderson/Blend Images/Corbis. p. 16, Photo by Christopher Peterson/BuzzFoto/FilmMagic/Getty Images. p. 18, Courtesy Starwood Hotels & Resorts; Agency: Deutsch Inc./New York.; Photos: Augustus Butera for Marge Casey & Associates. p. 19, Photo by Tim Boyle/Getty Images. p. 19, Courtesy Southwest Airlines. p. 20, ©Michael Newman/PhotoEdit. p. 20, AP Photo/Gene Blythe. p. 21, Jason Reed/Getty Images. p. 21, ©Edward Rozzo/Corbis. p. 21, Andrew Ward/Life File/Getty Images. p. 21, ©Roy McMahon/Corbis. p. 21, BananaStock/JupiterImages. p. 21, Digital Vision/Getty Images. p. 23, Courtesy BBH-Singapore. p. 24, ©M. Hruby. p. 25, Courtesy The Kaplan Thaler Group, New York, NY. p. 26, ©K. Rousonelos. p. 27, Photo by Thomas Cooper/Getty Images. p. 30, Courtesy of Apple.

## Chapter 2

**Photos/ads**: p. 32-33, ©M. Hruby. p. 34, Courtesy Dunkin Brands, Inc. p. 34, ©Scott Eklund/Red Box Pictures. p. 37, Courtesy TBWA/Hong Kong. p. 38, Roger Tully/Stone/Getty Images. p. 38, Courtesy Netflix Inc. p. 39, Courtesy 3M. p. 42, Used with permission. ©Mother Against Drunk Drivers 2005. p. 43, Photo by Stephen Chernin/Getty Images. p. 44, Richard B. Levine/Newscom. p. 45, *Both images*: Courtesy The Hertz Corporation. p. 46, Courtesy Unilever U.S., Inc. p. 47, Courtesy Amazon.com. p. 48, *Both images*: Courtesy Amazon.com. p. 50, Courtesy ©2008 The Goodyear Tire & Rubber Company. All rights reserved. Agency: McCann Erickson/New York, NY. Creative Director: Craig Markus; Art Director: Tim Dillingham; Copywriter: Mark Ronquillo; Photographer: ©2007 Graham Westmoreland/Friend and Johnson. p. 51, Photo by Chip Somodevilla/Getty Images. p. 55, Photo by Joe Scarnici/WireImage/Getty Images. p. 56, MTV.com website http://www.mtv.com/shows/the_hill/season_6/series.jhtml used with permission by MTV. ©2010 MTV Networks. All Rights Reserved. MTV, all related titles, characters and logos are trademarks owned by MTV Networks, a division of Viacom International Inc. p. 56, Photo by Scott Gries/PictureGroup via AP Images.

## Appendix 2A

**Photos/ads**: p. 68, *No credit*. p. 78, *No credit*.

## Chapter 3

**Photos/ads**: p. 82, AP Photo/Carolyn Kaster. p. 84, AP Photo/CSPS. p. 85, GRANTLANDD®. Copyright Grantland Enterprises; www.grantland.net. p. 86, Dyamic Graphics/JupiterImages. p. 87, AP Photo/Paul Sakuma. p. 87, AP Photo/Pat Sullivan. p. 90, ©Dennis MacDonald/PhotoEdit. p. 90, ©2010 The Dannon Company, Inc., Reprinted with Permission. p. 92, AP Photo/Ali Burafi. p. 93, Ryan McVay/Getty Images. p. 97, ©M. Hruby. p. 98, Courtesy General Mills, Inc. p. 99, *Both images*: ©Newman's Own, Inc. p. 101, ©Wal-mart Stores, Inc. p. 103, GRANTLAND®. Copyright Grantland Enterprises; www.grantland.net. p. 105, GRANTLAND®. Copyright Grantland Enterprises; www.grantland.net. p. 106, GRANTLAND®. Copyright Grantland Enterprises; www.grantland.net. p. 108, Courtesy General Electric Company. p. 113, DynamicGraphics/Jupiter Images.

**Exhibits**: Exhibit 3.2: "American Marketing Association's Code of Ethics, Ethical Norms and Values for Marketers" (www.marketingpower.com). Used by permission of The American marketing Association; Exhibit 3.8: Adapted from Tom Morris, The Art of Achievement: Mastering the 7 Cs of Success in Business and in Life (Kansas City, MO: Andrew McMeel Publishing, 2002); http://edbrenegar.typepad.com/leading_questions/2005/05/real_life_leade.html (accessed January 18, 2010; Exhibit 3.7: Reprinted with permission; Exhibit 3.9: Adapted from C.B. Bhattacharya and Sankar Sen (2004), "Doing Better at Doing Good: When, Why and How Consumers Respond to Corporate Social Responsibilities," California Management Review, 47 (Fall), 9-24.

## Chapter 4

**Photos/ads**: p. 114, Courtesy of iStockphoto with design by Curran & Connors, Inc. p. 118, ©M. Hruby. p. 119, Courtesy Nau, Inc.; p. 121, *Both ads*: Courtesy MINI USA. p. 122, ©Royalty-Free/Corbis. p. 123, Photo by Brian Bahr/Getty Images. p. 124, Getty Images/Stockbyte. p. 124, Courtesy of Hammacher Schlemmer, www.hammacher.com. p. 125, Jochen Sand/Digital Vision/Getty Images. p. 126, *no credit*. p. 126, Comstock/PictureQuest. p. 127, ©2006 Oldemarak, LLC. Reprinted with permission. The Wendy's name, design and logo are registered trademarks of Oldemark, Llc and are licensed to Wendy's International, Inc. p. 127, Courtesy Subway Franchise Advertising Fund Trust. p. 129, AP Photo/Ric Feld. p. 131, Courtesy Domino's Pizza, LLC. p. 132, Kaz Chiba/Digital Vision/Getty Images. p. 137, Photo by Kelly Kline/WireImage for Bragman Nyman Cafarelli/Getty Images.

**Exhibits**: Exhibit 4.6: http://www.infoteachtrends.com (assessed January 7, 2008)

## Chapter 5

**Photos/ads**: p. 140-141, Photo by Astrid Stawlarz/Getty Images. p. 143, Photo by Timothy A. Clary/AFP/Getty Images. p. 143, *No credit*. p. 144, ©M. Hruby. p. 145, ©Newscom. p. 145, Photo by Amy Sussman/Getty Images. p. 146, ©Lou Cypher/Corbis. p. 147, The McGraw-Hill Companies, Inc./Andrew Resek, photographer. p. 147, ©Rachel Epstein/PhotoEdit. p. 149, Courtesy Gilt.com. p. 150, Courtesy Charlotte Russe Holding, Inc. p. 152, AP Photo/Mark Lennihan. p. 154, Courtesy Taco Bell. p. 155, McGruff® and Scruff® are a part of the National Crime Prevention Council's ongoing crime prevention education campaign. p. 155, UPI Photo/John Anderson/Landov. p. 155, The McGraw-Hill Companies, Inc./Andrew Resek, photographer. p. 156, ©Shooting Star. p. 158, Digital Vision/Getty Images. p. 158, Photo by James Devaney/WireImage. p. 159, Courtesy Murphy O'Brien Public Relations/Santa Monica, CA. p. 161, Courtesy Albertson's, Inc. p. 163, The McGraw-Hill Companies, Inc./Emily & David Tietz, photographers. p. 163, ©Digital Vision. p. 163, The McGraw-Hill Companies, Inc./Andrew Resek, photographer. p. 164. Courtesy In-N-Out Restaurant. p. 169, ©M. Hruby.

## Chapter 6

**Photos/ads**: p. 170-171, Courteys Xerox Corporation. p. 173, *Both ads*: Photography and advertisements courtesy of Siemens. p. 174, Car Culture/Getty Images. p. 175, Photo by Eric Ryan/Getty Images. p. 175, AP Photo/Seth Wenig. p. 176, Royalty-Free/CORBIS. p. 177, Times Photo by Toni L. Sandys/Newscom. p. 177, Sylvain Grandadam/The Image Bank/Getty Images. p. 180, ©Custom Medical Stock Photo. p. 183, Courtesy stickK.com. p. 184, ©Eric Espada/CSM/Newscom. p. 190, Press Association via AP Images.

## Chapter 7

**Photos/ads**: p. 192-193, ©Imaginechina Photo Agency p. 195, Courtesy LEGO Company. p. 196, STR/AFP/Getty Images. p. 198, Courtesy Greenpeace USA. p. 200, AP Photo. p. 201, REUTERS/Arko Datta/Corbis. p. 203, Narinder Nanu/AFP/Getty Images. p. 203, REUTERS/Fayza Kabli. p. 204, AP Photo/Greg Baker. p. 208, ©Digital Vision/Getty Images. p. 209, AP Photo/Remy de la Mauviniere. p. 210, Courtesy of Rolex USA. p. 211, Imaginechina via AP Images. p. 211, Imaginechina via AP Images. p. 212, *No credit*. p. 215, Courtesy Ford India Pvt. Ltd. p. 216, Courtesy Campbell Soup Company. p. 216, AP Photo/Jay LaPrete. p. 216, AP Photo/Gurinder Osan. p. 218, Courtesy Zara International, Inc. p. 218, Courtesy Zara International, Inc. p. 220, Photo by Jeff Kravitz/FilmMagic/Getty Images. p. 223, Mark Leong/Redux.

**Exhibits**: Exhibit 7.2: Reprinted with permission, www.nationmaster.com; Exhibit 7.4: From http://www.worldmapper.org. Reprinted with permission; Exhibit 7.7: http://en.wikipedia.org/

# name index

# company index

# index